# CRIMINAL LAW IN CANADA: AN INTRODUCTION TO THE THEORETICAL, SOCIAL AND LEGAL CONTEXTS

## Cases, Notes and Materials

### *Fourth Edition*

*Editor-in-Chief*

**R.P. Saunders**

*Professor of Law, Carleton University*

*Co-editor*

**J.A. McMunagle**

*B.A., LL.B.*

*co-editor of 1st and 2nd editions*

**C.N. Mitchell**

## CARSWELL

A THOMSON COMPANY

The publisher is not engaged in rendering legal, accounting or other professional advice. If legal advice or other expert assistance is required, the services of a competent professional should be sought. The analysis contained herein represents the opinions of the authors and should in no way be construed as being official or unofficial policy of any governmental body.

This work reproduces official English language versions of federal and provincial statutes and regulations. As the federal material, and many of the provincial statutes and regulations also have official French versions, the reader is advised that reference to the official French language material may be warranted in appropriate circumstances.

**National Library of Canada Cataloguing in Publication**

Main entry under title:

Criminal law in Canada: an introduction to the theoretical, social and legal contexts / R.P. Saunders, editor-in-chief; J.A. McMunagle, co-editor — 4th ed.

Previous eds. published under title: An Introduction to criminal law in context.
Includes bibliographical references and index.
ISBN 0-459-27329-9

1. Criminal law–Canada.   2. Criminal law–Canada–Cases.
I. Saunders, Ron P.   II. McMunagle, J.A.

KE8808.2.I58 2002    345.71    C2002-903218-0

The acid-free paper used in this publication meets the minimum requirements of American National Standard for Information Sciences – Permanence of Paper for Printed Library Materials, ANSI Z39.48-1984.

# CARSWELL

A THOMSON COMPANY

One Corporate Plaza, 2075 Kennedy Road, Toronto, Ontario M1T 3V4
Customer Relations
Toronto 416-609-3800
Elsewhere in Canada/U.S. 1-800-387-5164
Fax 1-416-298-5094

*For my son Owen, with love*
*— R.P.S.*


*For my entire family, especially my sister Alison whose courage*
*inspires me on a daily basis, and for the many students I have had*
*the privilege of teaching*
*— J.A.M.*

# EDITOR'S NOTE

The editors gratefully acknowledge the authors, organizations and publishers who have granted permission to reproduce their work in this book. It should be noted that the footnotes and bibliographies of most of the readings have been removed in the interest of space and cost, and readers are directed to the original readings in order to find them.

The editors also acknowledge the valuable contributions of Professor Ross Hastings of the Department of Criminology, University of Ottawa, and Professor Barry Wright of the Department of Law, Carleton University, who wrote original selections for an earlier edition of this book that are included in this edition.

The book also owes a great deal of its direction and structure to one of the original editors of the first two editions, Chet Mitchell, who died in January, 1991, soon after the publication of the second edition. His intellect, warmth, originality and generosity of spirit continue to be missed both at Carleton University where he taught and in the wider academic community.

Finally, I would like to thank the excellent staff at Carswell, and particularly Jilean Bell and Steven Hostetter, for their invaluable support and assistance in the development, design and production of this edition of the book.

R.P. Saunders
July, 2002

# Acknowledgements

The publishers and the authors gratefully acknowledge the authors, publishers and organizations for their permission to reproduce the excerpts contained in this text. Every effort was made to locate the authors and/or publishers of materials contained herein and to obtain permissions, and the Publishers apologize for any errors or omissions.

**A Case for a General Part**
*Don Stuart*
Appearing in Don Stuart, R.J. Delisle and Allan Manson (eds.), *Towards a Clear and Just Criminal Law: A Criminal Reports Forum* (Toronto: Carswell, 1999).

**A Framework for the Correctional Law Review, Working Paper No. 2**
Appearing in *A Framework for the Correctional Law Review, Working Paper No. 2* (Ottawa: Solicitor General of Canada, 1986).

**Adversarial Justice and the Charter of Rights: Stunting the Growth of the "Living Tree"**
*Alan N. Young*
Appearing in (1997), 39 Criminal Law Quarterly 362.

**Ambiguity and Vagueness in the Criminal Law: An Analysis of Types**
*Stephen Kloepfer*
Appearing in (1984-85), 27 Criminal Law Quarterly 94.

**Arrest and Compelling the Appearance of the Accused**
*Heather E. MacKay*
Appearing in Joel E. Pink and David C. Perrier (eds.), *From Crime to Punishment: An Introduction to the Criminal Law System* (Toronto: Carswell, 1999).

**Battered Women: Definition, Models and Prosecutorial Policy**
*A. McGillivray*
Appearing in (1987), 6 Canadian Journal of Family Law 15.

**Canadian Charter of Rights and Freedoms**
*Thomas A. Cromwell*
Appearing in Joel E. Pink and David C. Perrier (eds.), *From Crime to Punishment: An Introduction to the Criminal Law System* (Toronto: Carswell, 1999).

## Commentary
*Christine Boyle*
Appearing in Don Stuart, R.J. Delisle and Allan Manson (eds.), *Towards a Clear and Just Criminal Law: A Criminal Reports Forum* (Toronto: Carswell, 1999).

## Conditional Release from Prison
*Heather E. MacKay*
Appearing in Joel E. Pink and David C. Perrier (eds.), *From Crime to Punishment: An Introduction to the Criminal Law System* (Toronto: Carswell, 1999).

## Controlling the Trial Process: The Judge and the Conduct of Trial
*Stephen A. Cohen*
Appearing in (1977), 36 C.R.N.S. 15.

## Correctional Philosophy, Working Paper No. 1
*Solicitor General of Canada*
Appearing in *Correctional Philosophy, Working Paper No. 1* (Ottawa: Solicitor General of Canada, 1986).

## Criminal Law in Canadian Society
Appearing in *Criminal Law in Canadian Society* (Ottawa: Government of Canada, August 1982).

## Criminal Legislation
*E.G. Ewaschuk, Q.C.*
Appearing in (1983-84), 26 Criminal Law Quarterly 97.

## Courts
*Donald C. Murray*
Appearing in Joel E. Pink and David C. Perrier (eds.), *From Crime to Punishment: An Introduction to the Criminal Law System* (Toronto: Carswell, 1999).

## Doe v. Metropolitan Toronto Board of Commissioners of Police and the Status of Public Oversight of the Police in Canada
*Scott Childs and Paul Ceyssens*
Appearing in (1998), 36 Alberta Law Review 1000.

## Foreword: The Meaning of Gender Equality in Criminal Law
*Dorothy E. Roberts*
Appearing in (1994), 85 Journal of Criminal Law and Criminology 1.

## From Jeremy Bentham to Anne McLellan: Lessons on Criminal Law Codification
*Gerry Ferguson*
Appearing in Don Stuart, R.J. Delisle and Allan Manson (eds.), *Towards a Clear and Just Criminal Law: A Criminal Reports Forum* (Toronto: Carswell, 1999).

**Hadfield to Swain: The Criminal Code Amendments Dealing with the Mentally Disordered Accused**
*A.J. O'Marra*
Appearing in (1993), 36 Criminal Law Quarterly 49.

**Is There a Place for the Victim in the Prosecution Process?**
*Patricia Clarke*
Appearing in (1986), 8 Canadian Criminology Forum 31.

**Judicial Accountability in Canada**
*Ian Greene*
Appearing in Philip Stenning (ed.), Accountability for Criminal Justice: Selected Essays (Toronto: University of Toronto Press, 1995).

**Justice and the Poor**
*National Council of Welfare*
Appearing in National Council of Welfare, *Justice and the Poor* (Ottawa: Minister of Public Works and Government Services Canada, 2000).

**Models of Justice: Portia or Persephone? Some Thoughts on Equality, Fairness and Gender in the Field of Criminal Justice**
*Frances M. Heidensohn*
Appearing in (1986), 14 International Journal of the Sociology of Law 287.

**Penetrating Police Investigative Practice Post-*Morin***
*John A. Epp*
Appearing in (1997), 31 University of British Columbia Law Review 95.

**Postscript — Conditional Sentencing: Recent Developments**
*Julian V. Roberts and Patrick Healy*
Appearing in (2001), 80 Canadian Bar Review 1019.

**Principled Reform of Criminal Procedure**
*Tim Quigley*
Appearing in Don Stuart, R.J. Delisle and Allan Manson (eds.), *Towards a Clear and Just Criminal Law: A Criminal Reports Forum* (Toronto: Carswell, 1999).

**Prosecuting, Plea Bargaining, Control of Advocacy**
*Gavin MacKenzie*
Appearing in *Lawyers and Ethics: Professional Responsibility and Discipline* (Toronto: Carswell, 1999).

**Prosecutorial Accountability in Canada**
*Don Stuart*
Appearing in Philip Stenning (ed.), Accountability for Criminal Justice: Selected Essays (Toronto: University of Toronto Press, 1995).

**Prosecutorial Discretion**
*David Vanek*
Appearing in (1987-88), 30 Criminal Law Quarterly 219.

**Prosecutorial Discretion in a Charter-Dominated Trial Process**
*Wayne Gorman*
Appearing in (2000), 44 Criminal Law Quarterly 15.

**Report of the Canadian Federal-Provincial Task Force on Justice for Victims of Crime**
*Ministry of Supply and Services*
Appearing in *Report of the Canadian Federal-Provincial Task Force on Justice for Victims of Crime* (Ottawa: Supply and Services, 1983).

**Royal Commission on the Donald Marshall, Jr., Prosecution**
*Volume One: Commissioners' Report*
Appearing in the Royal Commission Report (Halifax: Province of Nova Scotia, 1989).

**Sentencing Powers and Principles**
*Kenneth W. Fiske*
Appearing in Joel E. Pink and David C. Perrier (eds.), *From Crime to Punishment: An Introduction to the Criminal Law System* (Toronto: Carswell, 1999).

**Sexual Assault: Substantive Issues Before and After Bill C-49**
*Don Stuart*
Appearing in (1992-93), 35 Criminal Law Quarterly 241.

**Statutory Sentencing Reform: The Purpose and Principles of Sentencing**
*Julian V. Roberts and A. von Hirsch*
Appearing in (1995), 37 Criminal Law Quarterly 220.

**Strategies for Police Accountability and Community Empowerment**
*Ross Hastings and R.P. Saunders*
Appearing in a paper prepared for the CROP-IISL Seminar on *Law, Power and Poverty* held in Onati, Spain, in May 1995.

**The Constitutional Basis of the Criminal Law Power**
*Peter W. Hogg*
Appearing in Peter W. Hogg, *Constitutional Law of Canada*, Fourth Edition (Toronto: Carswell, 1997).

**The General Part in Canada**
*Law Reform Commission of Canada*
Appearing in *Criminal Law. The General Part: Liability and Defences* (Working Paper 29) (Ottawa: Minister of Supply and Services, 1982).

**The Players of a Criminal Trial**
*Frank P. Hoskins*
Appearing in Joel E. Pink and David C. Perrier (eds.), *From Crime to Punishment: An Introduction to the Criminal Law System* (Carswell, 1999).

**The Trial Judge: Pilot, Participant, or Umpire?**
*H. Silverman*
Appearing in (1973), 11 Alberta Law Review 40.

**Three Traditions of Critical Justice Inquiry: Class, Gender, and Discourse**
*D.H. Currie, B.D. MacLean and D. Milovanovic*
Appearing in D.H. Currie and B.D. MacLean (eds.), *Re-Thinking the Administration of Justice* (Halifax: Fernwood Publishing, 1992).

**Toward a Revised Sentencing Structure for Canada**
*Keith Jobson and Gerry Ferguson*
Appearing in (1987), 66 Canadian Bar Review 1.

**Unearthing the Sphinx: The Evolution of Conditional Sentencing**
*Julian V. Roberts*
Appearing in (2001), 80 Canadian Bar Review 1019.

**What is a Conditional Sentence?**
*Department of Justice, Research and Statistics Division*
Appearing in *Conditional Sentences Fact Sheet #1*, Department of Justice, Research and Statistics Division (Ottawa: Department of Justice, 2001).

# Table of Contents

# 1

# CRIMINAL LAW AND GOVERNMENT REGULATION IN PERSPECTIVE

### Crime and The Criminal Law System

*C. Mitchell*

## DEFINING CRIME

### The Legal Definition

Crime can be defined from at least three perspectives: the legal, ethical and contractual. It is natural in a book on criminal law to begin with the legal definition of crime but an informed understanding of crime requires an equal consideration of other definitions.

To lawyers and judges working within the criminal law system, a crime is any act prohibited or punishable by law or, more specifically, is "any form of human behaviour designated by law makers as criminal and subject to penal to penal sanctions." (Parker, 1987). Legalistic definitions of crime are also employed by some criminologists. Michael and Adler (1933:2,5) assert that "the most precise and least ambiguous definition of crime is that which defines it as behaviour which is prohibited by the criminal code" and thus, logically, "if crime is merely an instance of conduct which is proscribed by the criminal code it follows that the criminal law is the formal cause of crime." Quinney (1970) likewise defines "crime" as "a legal category that is assigned to conduct by authorized agents of a politically organized society". The legal definition of crime is simultaneously broad and narrow. It is broad because it means that any form of behaviour can be designated a "crime". Behaviour that is commonplace today, like drinking coffee and smoking tobacco in cafés, was once a serious crime. Centuries ago in some European countries tobacco was declared a dangerous drug and its users were subject to prohibitions and harsh penalties (seldom inflicted) such as flogging, amputation of hands and execution. Similarly, when the coffee drinking habit first developed in Arabia around the 15th century, some municipal governments prohibited both coffee houses and the public sale of the drug. Conversely, behaviour now regarded as criminal was at other times widely accepted. Canadian apothecaries, physicians and pharmaceutical producers in 1900 offered the public a large and varied supply of opiate-based concoctions. Tonics, medicines and "remedies" based on cocaine were also popular. *Vin Mariana*, a mixture of red wine and cocaine, sold especially well, perhaps because it was endorsed by a Roman Catholic Pope and an American President among other celebrities. Anyone selling the exact same products today in Canada faces lengthy imprisonment. Trading in certain chemicals has been designated a "crime". The list of activities that can be designated criminal is endless. For example, before its defeat in 2001, the Taliban government in Afghanistan waged a "war" against most types of music and outlawed the wearing by women of certain types of clothes and adornments. Traditionally, many occupations (money lenders, prostitutes, boxers, gamblers), religions (Jews, Christians, Hugenots) and even ideologies have been designated as crimes. There may a core of "real crimes" that are criminal in every society but there are also behaviours or statuses that are criminalized in one jurisdiction while being ignored, accepted or rated as no more than mild vices in another.

The narrowness of the legal definition of crime stems from the requirement that only behaviour designated by law makers as criminal will count as crime. No matter how harmful or immoral an activity might be, it is not a "crime" unless law makers so designate. If authorized law makers do not exist, a situation prevailing in primitive cultures, then "crime" as we know it will be lacking. McGinley's definition of crime (1981:283) highlights the state's role and the state's interest in crime: "criminal conduct is that conduct which challenges the authority of the state by contravening a categorical imperative wherein the state demands obedience on the basis that the state itself has commanded obedience". The key to the legal definition of crime is therefore the activities of the "law makers". Who are the law makers? The legal answer is those persons authorized by law to make, or create or "designate" law. The most obvious law makers are the municipal, provincial and federal legislators who are authorized by constitutional laws and conventions to create laws within their allotted jurisdiction. Federal legislators have authority to create "criminal" laws and many of these are contained in the Criminal Code. An example of a federally created crime is section 163 of the Code:

> **63.**(1)(b) Everyone commits an offence who makes, prints, publishes, distributes, sells or has in his possession for the purpose of publication, distribution or circulation, a crime comic.

It is not clear why Parliament created this crime. The section has been rarely enforced, and citizens rarely, if ever, bring complaints regarding this crime to the attention of the police. But while there may be no pressing need or popular support for the creation or maintenance of section 163, the behaviour so described is nonetheless a "crime" and remains a crime until amended or removed by legislative or judicial action. McGinnis (1987) found seven cases involving the crime comics sections. The case of *Roher v. The Queen* (1953), 107 C.C.C. 103, is extracted here to provide an example of how legislators, police and judges can, in all earnestness, make the selling of *Dick Tracy* comics a "crime". According to McGinnis, in 1940 a New York psychiatrist, Federic Wertham, launched the first public campaign against crime comics. Wertham claimed these comics caused their readers to become juvenile delinquents and he was particularly critical of *Wonder Woman*. Wertham's war on comics was picked up and promoted by Parent-Teacher Associations (PTA) in Canada and the U.S. British Columbia PTAs recruited E. Davie Fulton, the P.C. member for Kamloops, (and later a federal Minister of Justice and Justice of the B.C. Supreme Court) to champion their cause in Parliament. On the basis of anecdotal horror stories about teenage murders inspired by stacks of crime comics, Fulton and his supporters asserted a direct, indisputable link between comics and real-life crime. In the Parliamentary debates of 1949 no one demanded actual proof that comics caused harm and the Criminal Code was amended solely on the basis of unsubstantiated, unverified and unscientific claims. As the following decision of the Manitoba Court of Appeal illustrates, the issue of actual harm to society is even more remote in the courts than it was in Parliament.

## Roher v. The Queen
### (1953), 107 C.C.C. 103 (Man. C.A.)

Appeal from conviction by Police Magistrate respecting sale of a crime comic. Affirmed.

*F.J. Turner,* Q.C., and *Keith Turner*, for appellant, Roher *C.W. Tupper* Q.C., for the Crown.

McPHERSON C.J.M.: — This is an appeal from a conviction by Maris H. Garton, Esq., Police Magistrate, at the City of Winnipeg, on April 29, 1953, for "that the appellant did unlawfully have in his possession for sale a crime comic contrary to the provisions of section 207, subsections (1)(b) and (3) of the Criminal Code". The appellant was sentenced to pay a fine of $5 and costs or in default thereof to imprisonment for a term of 5 days in common gaol for the Eastern Judicial District. The prosecution was brought as a test case under said section and the appeal is against both conviction and sentence.

The matter is one of considerable importance to the citizens of this country and for the purpose of informing the public of the views of the Court in relation to such prosecution it is advisable to deal with the matter at length and in detail both as to the law and the facts. The difficulty with which administration of the law is faced in prosecuting under said section is that each individual case must necessarily depend entirely upon the publication objected to and its contents.

Section 207 of the *Criminal Code* was amended by 1949 (2nd Sess), c. 13. That amendment consisted of the repeal of the previous s. 207 and enactment of an entirely new section, portions of which, so far as this prosecution is concerned, are as follows:

**207**(1) Every one is guilty of an indictable offence and liable to two years' imprisonment who (b) makes, prints, publishes, distributes, sells or has in possession for any such purpose, any crime comic.

"Crime Comic" is defined in s. 207(3) as follows:

**207**(3) 'Crime Comic' means in this section any magazine, periodical or book which exclusively or substantially comprises matter depicting pictorially the commission of crimes, real or fictitious.

The following provisions of s. 207 are also relevant to a charge of this nature:

**207**(4) No one shall be convicted of any offence in this section mentioned if he proves that the public good was served by the acts alleged to have been done, and that there was no excess in the acts alleged beyond what the public good required.

(6) The motives of the accused shall in all cases be irrelevant.

(7) It shall be no defence to a charge under subsection one that the accused was ignorant of the nature or presence of the matter, picture, model, crime comic or other thing.

The publication upon which the prosecution was based is "No. 62, April, 'Dick Tracey' ", and the appeal is on the ground that the said exhibit "does not exclusively or substantially comprise matter depicting pictorially the commission of crime, real or fictitious". No submission was made that s. 207(4) was a further defence available to the appellant. The exhibit consisted of 34 pages, including the cover, of printed and pictorial contents, of which 10 pages were advertising matter. The appellant admitted that in addition to that on the front cover there were seven pictures in the first story actually depicting the commission of a crime. In answer to a question that I put to appellant's counsel: whether he was submitting that where in any picture there was shown a man firing a revolver and, in the next picture, a man dropping dead from the effects of the shot, that only the second picture would be one depicting crime, he stated that such was his submission. I cannot agree with that interpretation and will briefly describe the first story in the publication:

The book is illustrated by a series of panel pictures — usually 12 to a page — describing the stories. On the first page is shown an "ice-house" set on a pneumatic pontoon, in which an officer of the law has been caught by an electric device set in operation by the would-be murderer, the latter hauling the victim into another room where he applies the "murder mask" in an attempt at murder. The next page shows continuation of the attempted murder: the policeman struggling free and chasing the criminal, who opens a valve in the pontoon for the purpose of sinking it and drowning the policeman inside the building and another on the pontoon outside the building. The following pictures show the policeman struggling to avoid drowning and endeavouring to escape. While they are doing this the criminal goes to another place, commits a murder, then leaves the body and disappears. The pictures then return to the two officers trying to escape from drowning and the next 27 panels depict their struggles and the efforts of other police officers trying to break into the building and rescue them. The illustrations then revert to the previous murder and devote 5 panels to it, showing elimination by the murderer of what might be clues involving him. Returning again to the house on the raft, 7 pictures are allotted to showing the eventual rescue of the two officers from drowning. The next 41 panels depict the criminal's actions in his endeavour to elude police, and their efforts to apprehend him. The ensuing picture shows the criminal arriving to commit a further murder, which he attempts in the third panel on the following page but finds he has mistaken the identity of the would-be victim. For the next 2 pages he proceeds in again attempting to murder the hero of the story but is finally shot by the police in time to rescue the hero. The balance of the story of 15 pictures describes the method in which the murder mask operated and the reasons for the criminal acting as he did.

It is my considered opinion that the whole story as published consists of the depicting of crime in its various phases: namely, preparations for the commission of crime, action taken in accordance with those preparations, and steps taken by the authorities for arrest of the criminal.

The next story is not quite so bloodthirsty. It shows robbery being committed and the knocking down of a child by the robbers' car in their endeavours to escape, the rescue of the child, destruction of clues by the criminals, commission of a second robbery and the get-away of the robbers, and the commission of a further robbery and chase of the criminals by the police. The outcome is unknown, as it is a continued story which at this phase ends in an advertisement to buy the next issue of the paper. The third story depicts the reporting of a murder to the police, the finding of the body, and evidence leading to the arrest of the guilty party.

The fourth story — on a single page — depicts a murder and the arrest of the murderer.

I cannot arrive at any other conclusion than that the whole pictorial part of the exhibit depicts crime in its various phases, and I by no means eliminate those pictures which are explanatory of preparations made to commit the actual crime from being part of the crime itself.

In *R. v. Alberta News Ltd.* (1951), 101 Can. C.C. 219, the publication before the Court was an entirely different style of publication to the one in this case and on the facts stated in the judgment it would appear to have been a proper decision; but I am not commenting on the interpretation of the law in that case although I do agree with the trial Magistrate's adoption of Maxwell on Interpretation of Statutes, 9th ed., p. 280, as follows: 'Among them is the rule that that sense of the words is to be adopted which best harmonises with the context and promotes in the fullest manner the policy and object of the Legislature. The paramount object, in construing penal as well as other statutes, is to ascertain the legislative intent, and the rule of strict construction is not violated by permitting the words to have their full meaning, or the more extensive of two meanings, when best effectuating the intention.' [pp. 221-2]

My interpretation of the section dealing with "crime comics" is that the Legislature wished to enact laws to protect the children of this country from the evil effects of being subjected to publications dealing with crime, and that the word "commission" in the section is not restricted to the actual instantaneous act constituting the crime but includes the preparations for same and all factors which naturally arise in connection with such crime.

The sentence — a fine of $5 or, in default, 5 days' imprisonment — was also appealed against and this Court has the power, if it sees fit, to increase that sentence. In the present case I am not in favour of so doing, because this is a "test" case taken against one of many-hundred vendors of comic books in this city. There have been rumours, and I have been told by people whose statements I would accept, that the system of distribution of these books is such that if a small dealer wishes to procure certain comics which are clean and proper, he can only do so by also purchasing certain additional books designated by the distributors. If this is the existing condition I think it might be worth the attention of the authorities with a view to investigating the facts of the situation which apparently faces the small dealer, whereby he has to buy material he does not require in order to obtain other material he does require for his customers and also to meet business competition in his area.

I might also add what I stated shortly at the end of the hearing in this case: that my personal opinion is that when crimes are committed on a commercial scale for the purpose of making profit a fine is not the proper punishment, as that means only the equivalent of a tax, the severity of which depends upon the profit made by the offender on his whole business. A term in gaol or penitentiary to those who are primarily responsible for commission of the offences would not only be more just and appropriate but also more effective. In the present case the publication is published in St. Louis under management in New York and apparently is imported into Canada, so that original vendors in Canada are the distributors. It is at that point where the most effective restrictive action could be taken.

There is a defence available under s-s. (4), above quoted, if it can be shown that the publication is for the public good. The only defence under this section I have ever heard suggested is that by reading these publications the child acquires a desire to read. To me it is a strange basis upon which to start child education and, logically considered, could be quite easily adapted to other phases of training; for instance, by starting children on "home-brew" they might connoisseurs of fine liquors and whisky and eventually experiment with a drink of milk!

I am aware that in submitting this judgment it is entirely different to those which are usually delivered by this Court, but I do so because in the first place this is a test case in reference to a matter that is definitely harmful to the children of this country; also because many similar cases may arise before Police Magistrates and other Courts and I feel it my responsibility to place clearly before them my views of what constitutes an offence under the section of the Code now before us, not overlooking the basic fact that each publication has to be considered on its own individual merits or demerits.

COYNE J.A.: — I agree with the conclusion of the Chief Justice and his reasons in support. The appeal should be dismissed.

BEAUBIEN J.A.: — I have had the privilege of reading and considering the reasons for judgment of the Chief Justice and I agree with him that the appeal should be dismissed.

*The appeal is dismissed.*

. . .

Within Canada the authority to define criminal law is closely tied to the power to enforce that definition. This power consists of both physical and psychological components. The physical components include the army, police, judges, public prosecutors, prison personnel and government ministries. Armed forces are under direct political control in Canada and are usually assigned the task of dealing with external threats. Under vaguely defined "emergencies", however, Parliament can use the army to put down revolts, rebellions, insurrections and internal security threats. *The War Measures Act*, (since repealed and replaced by the *Emergencies Act*, R.S. 1985, c. 22 (4th Supp.))was employed in 1971 during the FLQ affair to temporarily increase the fire power available to the federal government. Political authority is also backed by more than 55,000 public police in Canada in federal, provincial and municipal agencies. Police authority is supported by the court system comprised of bailiffs, clerks, sheriffs, Justices of the Peace, lawyers, prosecutors and judges. In addition, criminal law matters are overseen by federal agencies such as the departments of Justice, National Revenue, Citizenship & Immigration and the Solicitor General. Finally, wardens, guards, parole officers and forensic psychiatrists are also authorized to exercise coercive state control.

Physical force is not omnipotent and even a modern bureaucratic government constitutes a small elite. Moreover, soldiers and police will not obey every order or enforce every law. Both within and without the government there is significant scope for resistance and revolt. All governments, therefore, attempt to bolster their law creating authority by instilling in citizens a tradition of wilful submission to authority. Legitimation is the process whereby government justifies its coercive apparatus by reference to divine right, historical inevitability or allegedly democratic choice. Legitimation's object is to develop a general sense that political authority is just, good and right. It is important to note here the evident propensity of most people to obey authoritative figures even when ordered to inflict apparently painful penalties on innocent victims (Milgram, 1974). Ironically, this uncritical willingness to obey orders can cause greater social damage than the rebellious acts of a small anti-establishment minority.

One of the standard methods of legitimation is propaganda and the political manipulation of names and titles. Examples include the "Criminal Justice System", "Ministry of Justice" and "Corrections Canada". American police form "Benevolent Associations". Other manipulative titles worth mentioning are "Peace Officers" and honorariums for judges and politicians such as "Your Honour", "Justice Smith", "Right Honourable" and "Your Worship". Calling members of Parliament "Honourable" does not make them so, just as calling a criminal law system a "Justice System" does not make it just. However, the power to define criminal law is held by the same people with the power to bestow propagandistic titles on themselves and their bureaucracies. By calling a certain branch of the state bureaucracy "Justice", the hope is that most people will accept the name at face value.

The legal definition of crime, according to Parker, contains two other elements. One is that the forbidden behaviour be "subject to penal sanctions". As we will suggest below, there are a number of procedural features that distinguish "criminal" law from other varieties of law. The second element mentioned is that criminal law only deals with "human behaviour". In fact, criminal law does not extend to all humans. Many jurisdictions, including Canada, exempt youngsters below a certain age from any criminal liability. This and other exemptions will be discussed below. Suffice it to say now that an exemption from criminal law does not necessarily mean lenient treatment. Dogs are exempt from criminal liability but a dog that bites two people or seriously injures a child will usually be taken into custody and killed by government agents whereas a human who bites two people will not be executed and may not even be incarcerated. In the same way, ten year old children are exempt from criminal law but they are subject to laws forcing school attendance and granting parents or other legal guardians near dictatorial powers.

## Ethical Definition of Crime

The legal definition of crime is a positivist definition; it focuses on describing the law accurately and its critical faculty extends only to questioning whether a given criminal law is properly authorized. In contrast, ethical definitions import a normative aspect and attempt to describe what the criminal law should be. Ethical and legal definitions are readily distinguished: everything that deserves to be declared a crime by some ethical rule is not designated a crime by the legal authorities and all crimes do not deserve to be regarded as unethical. In mapping the intersection of criminal law and morality Wexler (1976:356-9) observes that:

> In modern societies, a great deal of the criminal and quasi-criminal law has nothing to do with moral values; many acts are illegal which are not bad... A great many immoral acts which even [John Stuart] Mill would say that the law could prohibit are not illegal. Our criminal law ignores a great many acts which obviously cause harm to people... Finally, the private morality which the law does embody is often not the morality of the society... [thus] in the face of serious social evil the law seems either to be impotent or to be allied with what is wrong rather than what is right.

A legal definition of crime has unlimited content — "any form of human behaviour" — whereas all ethical definitions limit what should and should not be crimes. The most familiar ethical limit is that only wrongful acts should be made crimes. An ethicist would argue that designating helpful, positive behaviour like charity, working, gift giving and child producing, as criminal will lead to perverse results. The difficulty, of course, is in determining which behaviour is wrongful and which is helpful. When the human population was much smaller and tribal survival depended on a steady production of children, procreation tended to be encouraged and obstacles to procreation, like homosexuality, were often regarded as wrongful. Now, when continued population growth can possibly thwart human survival, some people argue that "excessive" procreation is selfish, shortsighted and unethical.

The key to an ethical definition of crime is the possession of a normative system or set of criteria measuring the degree of wrongness. Most ethicists insist that "crimes" should consist of serious wrongs only. How then can one go about measuring and identifying wrongfulness? There exist three general methods which, for our purposes, we will label the traditional, the intuitional and the consequential.

### Traditional Method

The traditional method of ethical judgment can be usefully compared to the formation of language. Every human language follows certain rules according to which words, letters, sounds or sentences are right or wrong. The sentence — "Sins be after should all crimes all? — is "wrong" because the word order does not follow the rules of the English language (After all, should all sins be crimes?) Language rules develop over a long period and arise through the trial-and-error use of language by many people. There is no centralized rule maker who handed down language laws carved in stone tablets. Similarly, in early cultures the perception of wrongful behaviour was based on custom, taboos and traditions rather than explicit laws. In ancient Greece, circa 1200 BC, the words that come closest to law are "dike" and "tyemis" but they actually mean "custom". Under a purely traditional system of ethical determination, acts like hunting deer in the spring, eating pork or collecting interest on loans are judged wrongful because of the dictates of custom. Wrongfulness is thus determined by consulting tribal elders, reviewing ancient stories and, where written records exist, by reading about earlier customs. One of the earliest recordings of customs is the so-called Code of Hammurabi, carved in 2 metre black basalt columns and erected around 1750 B.C. Hammurabi was perhaps the world's first literate king but his Code does not correspond with modern legislative dictates of a ruler. Instead, the 282 pronouncements on the stele merely recorded practices which by that time were already customary in Babylon. Equivalent social orders are investigated by modern anthropologists who typically find that among customary societies "the use of force is minimal. . .there are leaders rather than rules, and. . .cohesion is achieved by rules rather than by laws and by consensus rather than by dictation". (Uchendu, 1965:46) For the most part, custom provides primitive cultures with a full set of judgments about right and wrong. Interestingly, people who live according to a set of customs will usually be unable to explain the custom in objective or consequential terms. Taboos about hunting will not be explained in terms of sustaining an optimal ratio of prey to predator yet it is likely that the taboo developed precisely to prevent over-hunting. Custom and tradition are still important in contemporary cultures. One example is the traditional judgment that having more than one marriage partner at a time is wrongful behaviour. This judgment is reflected in sections 290 and 293 of the Code which prohibit bigamy and polygamy. While certain cultures in the Islamic and Oriental tradition accepted polygamy, monogamy has long been the custom in the Hellenic and European cultures. Over time matrimonial custom became matrimonial law, church law and finally criminal law when, by an Act of 1603, English law-makers classified bigamy as a capital offence and "felony". When asked to explain why bigamy or polygamy is "wrongful" most Canadians would be hard-pressed to supply a cogent rationale. This by no means suggests that good reasons for condemning polygamy in our social context do not exist, it merely illustrates that traditional judgments about right and wrong are not based on people's awareness of the original or continuing reasons behind the judgment. This process introduces what is probably the greatest weakness of the traditionalist method, namely the incapacity to adapt quickly to altered social conditions. If we do not know the reasons why polygamy was regarded as wrongful it will be difficult to change our customs if the justifying conditions cease to exist. Still, the traditionalist method has its strengths. In a trial-and-error process, customs that did not maintain or improve a people's survival capacity would not tend to be passed on. Certainly, traditional judgments about wrongness should not be dismissed merely because proponents cannot explain their custom. After all, one can use a language quite effectively without conscious awareness of its rules of grammar.

While some custom evolved into or was taken up by law, it is a mistake to regard custom as the natural precursor to law, as a sort of quasi-law. Diamond (1971:45) explains:

"[L]aw is not definite and certain while custom is vague and uncertain. Rather the converse holds. Customary rules must be clearly known; they are not sanctioned by organized political force, hence serious disputes about the nature of custom would destroy the integrity of society' But laws may always be invented, and stand a good chance of being enforced. . . In fascist Germany, customs did not become laws. . . Rather, repressive laws conjured up in the interests of the Nazi Party and its supporters, cannibalized the institutions of German society. . . 'The absolute reign of law' has been synonymous with the absolute reign of lawlessness.

Custom is decentralized, organic and mostly unconscious, and being thus is uniform and egalitarian. Law is centralized, contrived and conscious and for the most part is non-uniform and elitist. State-sponsored efforts by elite French academics to outlaw new words and expressions used by millions of francophones illustrates one of the prime relationships between custom and law. Law is the product of organized, and usually narrow, force. Perhaps the ultimate challenge is to reproduce at a complex legal level the degree of assent and consensus typical of all customary orders.

*Intuitional Method*

The intuitional basis for ethical judgment is personal feeling rather than knowledge of tradition. Intuitionalists determine that a certain practice is right or wrong according to their own response. If they are distressed, disgusted, annoyed, disturbed, dissatisfied or repelled then they will tend to regard the behaviour in question as wrongful. Lord Devlin, a British jurist who favoured linking criminal law with moral judgment, was a traditionalist when he referred to Church of England rules as a basis for judgment but he was an intuitionalist when he appealed to the 'feelings of right-thinking men and women' (Devlin, 1965). For Devlin, using the criminal law to punish homosexual acts was justified, 'If it is the genuine feeling of our society that homosexuality is a vice so abominable that its mere presence is an offence'. One, however, wonders how the judicial members of the House of Lords ascertain what are society's "genuine" feelings or, indeed, how a reified concept like "society" can have feelings.

Feelings or intuitive conclusions may seem a rather unreliable and insubstantial basis for deciding criminal law's content but the method should not be dismissed too hastily. A primary source of feeling is conditioning or inculturation. Conditioning is the process whereby parents train their children to develop a conscience. Guilt and embarrassment probably govern human behaviour far more effectively than do legal penalties. Without conditioning humans will not feel that theft or assault or eating without utensils or defecating in public are "wrong". Since children in a given culture are conditioned to accept a common language and a common set of behaviours, most people's feeling about right and wrong will be in general harmony. This will be most true in stable, insular societies but even among cosmopolitan or ethnically diverse cultures, a broad ethical consensus will exist. This consensus, however, may be overlooked because, psychologically, people's attention is naturally drawn to contrast and change rather than to constant, unvarying norms (Garan, 1982).

Intuitional ethical judgment also includes unconscious assessments. When one stands on a hill top and surveys the surrounding forest, streams and fields, one's judgment of beauty is not based on a conscious, point-by-point deliberation but rather on a more complex and largely automatic assessment. The limited role played by conscious thought in governing human behaviour is discussed at length in *The Origin of Consciousness in the Breakdown of the Bicameral Mind* (Jaynes, 1976). Jaynes' psychological and historical research suggests that self-consciousness is a learned process that evolved only 3,000 years ago and that early civilizations were populated by people with a less evolved, split or "bicameral" consciousness. According to Jaynes, bicameral people were regulated by conditioned and intuitive responses from the brain's right hemisphere which were communicated to the left hemisphere as auditory or visual hallucinations. Furthermore, this guidance was interpreted as directives from "gods", seen initially as the "spirits" of deceased parents and tribal elders. While this system prevailed, laws and police were unnecessary; in ancient Egypt and Sumer there are few if any scenes of brutality or harshness (Wilson, 1984:108). As Jaynes remarks, "Within each bicameral state. . .the people were probably more peaceful and friendly than in any civilization since". This purely intuitive customary system, however, was apparently unable to cope with the larger more complex civilizations coming into existence some 4,000 years ago.

### Consequentialist Method

The final method for judging wrongness can be broadly termed "consequentialist" because the ethical verdict depends on the consequences of the behaviour in question. In simplest terms, an act is wrong if it results in net social harm. The utilitarian version of this method uses happiness or satisfaction as the basis for measuring a harmful result. In the original arguments of Priestly and Bentham, behaviour was right if it contributed to the greatest happiness of the greatest number. Happiness, however, proved to be a problematic criterion by which to measure ethical value. Despite considerable ingenuity, utilitarians could not make happiness a workable guide so, gradually, happiness was replaced by social welfare goals (Mitchell, 1986). Representative of this trend is the economic analysis that judges behaviour good or bad depending on whether it aids or impairs a society's total wealth. Bad behaviour is "diseconomic" and criminal behaviour should, by this theory, be restricted to that which is extremely diseconomic.

Taking things from unconsenting persons, for example, is generally harmful. This harmfulness may not be obvious looking only at the perpetrator and victim because while the victim loses the perpetrator enjoys an offsetting gain. More important, however, are the responses of the millions of potential victims who, in order to avoid being victimized, invest in locks, guns, alarms, guard dogs and security services and who experience anxiety and increased distrust of other people. The key to a consequentialist analysis is a full and thorough accounting of *all* the relevant consequences of a given act. Since a full accounting is difficult, time consuming and expensive, many consequential analysts tend to draw unwarranted conclusions based on insufficient data. It is instructive to compare the three normative systems on this point. A traditionalist has little difficulty identifying theft as wrongful since theft is condemned in ancient texts and even older customs. Theft is also readily judged as wrong intuitionally. Ironically, consequentialists have the most difficulty deciding that theft is wrong because they must actually identify and tabulate the results of theft, a task of immense challenge, so it is not surprising that the consequentialist method is the last to be employed.

## Contractual Definitions of Crime

Contractual definitions of crime are generated along two different strands. One is based on analysis of a hypothetical social contract while the other concerns the practical question of democratic choice.

The social contract is a familiar concept found in the philosophies of Locke, Rosseau, Kant and Rawls. The idea of a social contract is that government and law should be the result of mutual determination between equal contractors. By this measure "crime" will consist only of those behaviours designated as crimes by all the parties to the contract. If all the contractors were artificially rendered equal then Rawls argues that the result must be fair rules (Rawls, 1971:12). The key to a genuine contractual definition of crime is thus mutual forbearance which prevents any contractor exploiting any other. In the "original position" contrived by Rawls, every contractor would in effect be asked: what criminal laws will you impose on yourself in order to protect yourself other people committing the same acts against you? Will you, for example, agree to prohibit theft knowing that by doing so you permit everyone else to punish you if you commit theft? Under these conditions, a crime is essentially a breach of a term of the social contract.

Mutual restraint and agreement is also a central component of Posner's economic theory of criminal law (Posner, 1985). Posner praises the market exchange of goods and services because each party voluntarily gives up their labour to receive something in trade. If this voluntary exchange is rejected by one party who simply takes what she wants at gun point, then the result is crime. Posner, therefore, defines "crime" as "market by-passing". This definition is easy to understand where an explicit market in goods and services exists. But Posner extends the definition beyond acquisitive crimes like theft, fraud, robbery and embezzlement to include the allegedly more personal crimes of violence and passion. This extension is based on the existence of "implicit" markets for fighting, sexual outlet and the like, a point the following fictional examples illustrate.

Arnie and Chris both like fighting. Arnie joins a martial arts club and takes up boxing so he has access to others who will voluntarily fight with him. Chris, on the other hand, attacks unsuspecting people who have not agreed to fight. This is criminal assault because it by-passes an implicit market. The same is true for sexual outlet. Both Bert and Jason seek sexual partners but while Bert dates others and engages in consensual acts only, Jason attacks women and obtains his goal by means of coercion.

It is even possible to conceive of implicit markets for killing other people as a logical extension of duels and war games. In Robert Sheckley's futuristic novel *The 10th Victim* (1965), a few especially adventurous people join in an annual contest whereby participants are alternatively hunter and victim. The object of the game is to kill your opponent (the victims are not told who their hunters are) and the prize is the acquisition of your opponent's property. While this sport obviously results in death, consider in what ways it differs from such dangerous games as mountain climbing, boxing, and All Terrain Vehicle (ATV) riding (which has killed thousands of Canadians and Americans).

The second strand of the contractual definition of crime involves direct democratic choice where "crime" is defined as those acts so designated by some plurality of citizens. On this point Nettler (1982:27) reports that:

> Criminal law is one arm of coercive control. What is at issue in democracies is how the citizenry wishes that force to be used and against which people and which acts. There are no adequate studies addressing this issue. We have no measures of the balance of demands for the manufacture or reduction of criminal law. Surveys have questioned samples of the population about particular questions. . .but we lack comprehensive investigation of public conceptions of wrongs to be pursued as crimes. . . Lacking information about the full roster of wrongs citizens believe should be crimes, attention is advisably limited to the so-called 'classical crimes'. . .(Crimes *mala in se*). . .which have received general condemnation. There seems to be nearly universal agreement in defining as crimes such perennial wrongs as murder, burglary, arson, and a variety of larcenies.

Commentators on criminal law issues frequently make reference to laws which reflect "society's disapproval", which result from "society's demands" or which allegedly flow from the "public's concerns". Two objections must be lodged against such statements. First, one should not personify "society" or "the state" as if there existed some monolithic, animated creature or some collective unconscious that has feelings or opinions. Public opinion, if carefully canvassed, will always be diverse. Second, one should not presume that criminal law reflects a general public or democratic consensus or results from general demands unless one has direct, verifiable and relevant evidence. Politicians creating or supporting a law tend to justify their actions by claiming that the law is in answer to public demand. This appeal to democratic sensibilities should not be accepted on faith since, in fact, there are many instances of criminal law creation that ignore or even contradict broad majoritarian interests.

According to orthodox liberal theory, a free vote in a representative democracy naturally leads to laws that reflect the "will of the people". The concrete formulation of this concept in the U.S. occurs when criminal law prosecutions are entitled *The People v. Smith*. The case title's obvious inference is that all citizens implicitly consent to and benefit from such legal actions. If inappropriate behaviours are made crimes or if serious wrongdoing is ignored then a critical electorate will supposedly vote the offending government out of office and set up a reform regime. Logically, if the Criminal Code is not revised it must mean that no substantial majority wants revision. There are a number of substantial problems or fallacies in the standard liberal theory.

First, voters do not exercise much control over their elected representatives. Voters merely choose between a few party candidates; the preliminary and probably more important competition occurs at the nomination stage. After election, party discipline prevails because party support is the key to promotion, appointments and renomination. Election costs also limit voter control. Few politicians or even parties can afford to finance their own election campaigns so they must seek outside assistance. Such assistance, often from concentrated interest groups like businesses, unions and professions, does not come without conditions and expectations. According to some research, voters' control over elected representatives has declined since the early 1800s. Earlier conditions entailing small governments, part-time legislators, weak political parties, strong political customs and low election expenses have changed. Free elections remain but other political circumstances have altered in ways that permit modern government to be less democratic (Buchanan, 1978, 1984).

The suggestion that criminal laws are selected by the public also presupposes that most people know enough about the *Criminal Code* to have opinions about it. As Downs (1957:255) explains:

> Clearly, the cost of acquiring information and communicating opinions to government determines the structure of political influence. Only those who can afford to bear this cost are in a position to be influential. . . Yet without such knowledge [voters] cannot have policy preferences for the government to pay attention to.

Government agents allege that the modern drug prohibitions are, for example, a response to an initiating and continuing public demand. Historical evidence indicates that the drug laws sparked widespread interest rather than being the result of popular interest (Boyd, 1984; Comack, 1985; Green, 1979; Mitchell, 1986). Contemporary evidence suggests that voters remain ill-informed about the drug laws. Voters do not know how much the laws cost to enforce, what effects the laws have on police or judicial procedures or what social consequences are attributable to the laws. Voters do not know the identity of drug-related lobbyists nor do they know of the links that exist between politicians on one hand and drug producers on the other. The connections between alcohol and tobacco producers and legislators are particularly well-developed but still remain publicly obscure. Arguably, voters are ignorant of these and many other criminal law matters because the cost of informing themselves is greater than any benefit that will follow from being well-informed. In short, voters are "rationally ignorant". This situation is exacerbated either by government making information difficult and expensive to acquire or by government obstructing democratic choice so that even well-informed voters cannot have much impact on legislation.

Democratic input can be increased by a number of means including direct referenda, voter initiatives, special constitutional assemblies, limits on campaign expenses and contributions and, finally, the extension of voting selection to previously appointed positions such as judges, police chiefs, regulatory board members, prison wardens, parole officers, public prosecutors, heads of public corporations and ambassadors. Ensuring maximum democratic input, however, does not in itself guarantee a fair and just result. If voters are unconstrained by constitutional limits, it is probable that the majority will vote for criminal laws that favour themselves even at the expense of persecuted minorities. A country 90% Christian may vote a law prohibiting Islamic practices or a predominantly alcohol-using majority may outlaw a minority practice like cocaine use. The ethical response to this tyranny of the majority is that whether laws are passed by a dictator, a representative body or by direct voter choice, the law makers should be restricted to fair choices.

## THE OBJECTIVE OF GOVERNMENT REGULATION

Criminal law is one method of government regulation. Before considering the methodological characteristics of criminal law in section 3 of this Chapter we begin here with the more substantive question of what activities government should regulate. According to the Canadian Committee on Corrections, the protection of society is not merely the basic purpose, it is "the only justifiable purpose of the criminal process in contemporary Canada". While correct as far as it goes, this statement cannot explain the unique features of criminal law since societal protection is the alleged purpose of almost all government regulation. A genuine need for public safety may justify some government response but that response need not take the form of criminal law. Criminal law is merely one type of legal intervention. In solving a given problem there may be other legal methods that are safer, less expensive, more effective and more respectful of human rights than criminal law. Modern legislators are widely and properly criticized for overusing criminal law, for asking criminal law institutions to solve problems beyond or outside their capabilities. To formulate criminal law policy, it is imperative that one understand both how criminal law works and what criminal law should work at. The following sections consider the type of threats faced by contemporary society.

### Protecting the Environment

One of the gravest long term threats is the modern assault on the earth's biosphere. All facets of the environment are experiencing damage (Howard, 1980). Water supplies are harmed by agricultural by-products, inadequate sewage processing, industrial chemicals and effluent discharges. Polluted water imposes costs on everyone. There are direct physiological costs caused by water-borne diseases like cholera or dysentery or by water-borne toxic chemicals like dioxin. The events of May 2000, in Walkerton, Ontario, are an important reminder of the tragic losses that can result from tainted water. Mercury at a few hundred parts per billion can cause nerve disorders, impaired vision, paralysis and death. There are also financial costs in treating water to eliminate pollutants or in acquiring clean water from more remote sources. The atmosphere is a dumping ground for millions of tons of pollutants. Airborne contaminants including hydrocarbons, sulphur dioxide, oxides of nitrogen, carbon monoxide and lead impose on the public a staggering array of costs (Taylor, *et al.*, 1971). Pollutants eat away at fabrics, metals and the bricks, mortar and stone of buildings causing billions of dollars in damage each year. Acid rain is allegedly defoliating and destroying entire forests of maple, beech, ash and oak. Pollutants also cause direct personal damage ranging from bothersome odours and eye irritation to bronchial disease, premature death and birth defects.

Environmental damage to soil and landscape is another contemporary concern. Pesticides, chemicals, improper land use, and badly designed irrigation can erode, impair or destroy the soil. Soil destruction, in turn, leads to the loss of forests from which the world derives much of its oxygen. Besides deforestation and the advance of deserts, species' habitats are damaged, their migration routes are disrupted and their food sources wiped out. Rare species are hunted, often illegally, for trophies. On the topic of killing animals, livestock can be lawfully killed by human owners and wildlife can be hunted in season. Even where a total ban exists, for example whooping cranes are never in season, wrongful killing of animals is not murder, it is merely a regulatory infraction. This tradition may be changing. Certain species, like giant pandas are so rare that penalties for killing them are likely to escalate. Since the Chinese number a billion and the giant pandas in China only about 600, on the basis of scarcity value some may view pandas as more worthy of protection than humans. Certain other species, like whales, porpoises and apes, are intelligent enough that rare or not, killing them is increasingly seen as seriously wrongful. What, in principle, is the difference between intentionally killing a severely retarded human and killing a chimpanzee with a sign-language vocabulary of 200 words? Should murder be contingent on a species-based test or is such a test chauvinistic and in need of being replaced by an objective test based on intelligence, brain capacity or some other measure of evolutionary development?

Other environmental threats can be briefly noted. Some, like excess radiation, are entirely tasteless, odourless and intangible. Excess radiation may result from atomic fission power plant malfunctions, like the meltdown of a reactor in Chernobyl, in the then USSR, that contaminated crops and animals thousands of kilometres away in Norway and France. Excess radiation may also stem from pollution-related damage to the protective ozone layer that shields life on the planet's surface from ultra-violet radiation. In contrast to radiation, noise is very noticeable pollutant. Excessive noise, mostly from vehicles, construction equipment and amplifiers, now plagues all modern cities. Noise impairs health, lowers the quality of life and devalues real estate. Excessive noise naturally damages hearing but increased noise is also associated with high blood pressure, ulcers, fatigue and anxiety (Turk, *et al.* 1972).

How do wrongs against the environment compare to ordinary crimes such as theft, murder and robbery? Environmental damage is probably more of a threat. Acid rain appears to be stealing more value from property than direct theft, while air and water pollutants likely cause more physical damage than all muggings and assaults. The monetary value of environmental damage is largely unknown, nor are there good estimates of crime-related costs. This paucity of data makes it difficult to rationally order law enforcement resources. Government cannot concentrate preventive efforts on the leading sources of social damage unless some sort of accounting of damages is conducted.

Even where ordinary crimes and environmental assaults cause equal damage they differ in other respects. One difference is the causal complexity typical of environmental damage. Systems and methods must be invented to identify and detect pollutants, trace their sources and learn their effects. This will almost always be difficult. For example, lead poisoning may be due to lead from gasoline, lead from water pipes or lead from smelters. What constitutes a "safe level" of lead in the blood has been periodically lowered over the years. Moreover, lead-related ailments may parallel symptoms from other diseases. Thus it is a daunting task for a lead-poisoning victim to diagnose the condition or to attribute the injury to a specific source of lead. In comparison, the causal issues in ordinary crimes are relatively easy. Victims either witness the crime being committed themselves or witness the immediate consequences when they return, for instance, to discover their apartment ransacked.

A second difference is the scale of harm caused by individual wrongs. With ordinary crimes like assault and robbery, each offence tends to be significantly and acutely damaging. Even at the low end, the average break and either causes over $1000 worth of damage to the victim. Graffiti removal costs the New York City Transit Authority millions of dollars annually. Vandalism can also result in extreme damage such as the case where the removal of a stop sign caused the deaths of four people in a car-truck collision (Francis, 1983). Environmental damage follows quite a different pattern. The damage caused by a specific motorist on a given day is usually very minor. One motorist, like one termite or one army ant, is not a significant threat. However, if we total the effect of millions of motorists aggregated over years, the negative impact is considerable. Prior to 1973, the automobile was the single largest source of air pollution in North America. In addition, the automobile's impact on cities, public safety, economics and culture has been widespread and substantially negative. The different pattern affects people's perception of danger. Acute, easily understood dangers like theft are much more visible than chronic, subtle and aggregated dangers like pollution.

## Regulating the Regulators

Laws are not self-executing. People must be appointed, hired and given power to administer regulations and that power can be abused. Behind the institutional trappings and ceremonies, government is merely an assortment of people paid from the public treasury (McGinley, 1981). A perennial problem with government personnel is who will regulate the regulators. Modern societies have not solved this problem. Government agents from clerks to the highest elected officials routinely break both domestic and international laws (Lieberman, 1972). Government agents may also cause considerable damage by not enforcing laws or by creating laws that abuse citizens. The American Friends Service Committee (1971:10-11) summed up the matter of government wrongdoing:

> Actions that clearly ought to be labelled "criminal" because they bring the greatest harm to the greatest number, are in fact accomplished officially by agencies of government. . . Hundreds of unlawful killings by police go unprosecuted each year. The largest forceful acquisitions of property. . .has been the theft of lands guaranteed by treaty to Indian tribes, thefts sponsored by the government. The largest number of dislocations, tantamount to kidnapping — the evacuation and internment of Japanese-Americans during World War II—was carried out by government with the approval of the courts.

A familiar species of government wrongdoing includes bribe-taking, nepotism, improper use of public property and embezzlement for personal gain. Such acquisitive misbehaviour is often regarded as relatively harmless. Indeed, some Third World regimes pay bureaucrats low salaries with the expectation that income earned from bribery and kickbacks will augment their official remuneration. Bureaucrats may also seek out and promote such entrepreneurial bribery schemes because a bribery-based system gives far greater power and discretion to individual bureaucrats than does a rule-based system. Furthermore, acquisitive corruption is not always a matter of small bribes among minor functionaries. Ferdinand Marcos, when he was President of the Philippines, is reported to have diverted billions of dollars of public funds to his personal use. Similar, if less extensive, theft of public money was evidenced by Argentina's military government in the 1970's and 1980's, by the Duvalier regimes in Haiti, and by a number of other American and African governments. It is not unusual to find that citizens suffer most at the hands of those who are supposedly entrusted to protect public welfare.

A second type of government abuse entails systematic abuses perpetrated not by deviant individuals or personally corrupt leaders but by governing groups establishing wrongful policies. Lieberman cites cases of protectors and police using false evidence to secure convictions, of department heads violating regulations intended to minimize wasteful expenditures and of bureaus engaged in approved but illegal operations. Perhaps most dangerous are abuses accomplished through legitimate channels, policies that are both wrongful and legal. Since some people are prone to regard all lawful edicts as ethically right and all illicit acts as ethically wrong, juxtaposition of the legal with the unethical causes considerable confusion, paralysis and inappropriate response. Examples of legal-unethical policies include the anti-semitic regulations duly passed by the National Socialists in Germany 1933-1945, the racist laws familiar to many regimes and the legal witch hunts against illicit drug users pursued avidly by the Canadian and American governments. The damage done by such policies often far surpasses the damage wrought by ordinary criminals. While the Nazi government proclaimed that Jews were the major threat to German citizens, the actual threat to Germans was the Nazi government (Shirer, 1960).

In the case of the Third Reich, the legitimation of unethical practices was aided and abetted by the German courts. Although opponents of the regime were generally denied a fair trial and although defence lawyers were afraid to raise procedural challenges, judges co-operated with the government. This co-operation extended to collusion between some judges and the Gestapo in the persecution of German jews and to sentencing at least 30,000 people to death between 1942-45 for crimes such as a Jew having sexual intercourse with an "Aryan". Reifner (1986:104) traces the effect of judicial acquiesence:

> In the eyes of the public, the court system — its personnel and structures as well as its traditional habits — had not changed since the regime of the last German Kaiser. The legitimizing effects of the judiciary's involvement in fascist political activity were probably more significant in their impact on the conscience of participants in Nazi terrorism. . .than in their immediate and actual results. If the courts legitimated the system, giving racism a seemingly rational image and making murderous intentions legally realizable, how could ordinary citizens know what was right and wrong, what was criminal and what was patriotic?

A financial example of legal-unethical regulations is the official debasement of currency. At various times in antiquity government treasuries cheated citizens by debasing the official metal coinage. Debasement occurred when the silver and gold content was diluted with brass and copper yet citizens were ordered to accept the new coinage at the original face value. In 100 A.D. a pure silver Roman denarius purchased one bushel of wheat. Two centuries later the denarius was pure copper and it took

3000 of them to buy the same amount of wheat. While spectacular, this rate of inflation pales in comparison with the debasement of paper money which can accomplish the same effect in a single year. When government debases the nation's currency the change affects a transfer of wealth similar to the way that theft transfers wealth from victims to thieves. With currency debasement, the persons most damaged are the elderly on pensions or fixed incomes and the financially unsophisticated. Their wealth is shifted to borrowers, to government and to skilled or lucky speculators. Losing half the value of a pension through currency debasement is equivalent to losing the same amount through fraud or theft. Actually, in some respects, losses through theft are preferable because at least the thief might be apprehended, convicted and ordered to pay restitution or to undergo punishment. The likelihood of government authorities being held responsible for, in effect, counterfeiting their nation's currency is almost nil.

Government-initiated damage reaches its zenith in the waging of war. Casualties in World War I came to about 9 million people. The war squandered Europe's human and material resources to an unprecedented extent. Unfortunately, the amazing amount of war damage in 1914-18 was exceeded in 1939-45. In this second major conflict about 15 million military persons and 35 million civilians perished. The Soviet Union was hardest hit losing 20 million dead and leaving another 25 million homeless. In 1984 Goode estimated that the total number of deaths in legal combat during the 20th century stood at 80 million (Goode, 1984:226). Furthermore, 17 million people had died in wars since 1945, with 25% of the fatalities occurring in just two areas: Korea and Indochina. An optimistic trend to note is the decline in war deaths since the 1950s. Most war deaths now come about through close range killing by machine gun, mortars and small artillery; glamorous and expensive weapons like tanks and airplanes mostly just destroy other tanks and airplanes. There are of course numerous exceptions to this, notably found in the fighting in the former Yugoslavia and in Rwanda.

War killing is usually distinguished from crime or wrongful acts on the grounds that war is authorized and legitimated whereas murder is unauthorized. While the distinction is clear in principle, things are not so straightforward in practice. The U.S. involvement in Vietnam illustrates the point. America's military excursion in Vietnam was implemented by a small number of people in the armed forces and the federal government. The question of war was never put directly to the voters nor was Congress instrumental in the early stages of military escalation. Furthermore, a large portion of the soldiers sent into combat were involuntarily drafted and compelled to kill other people under threat of court martial. Labelling such a war "legitimate" raises grave concerns about the political process and about the objective value of legitimation. This skeptical view does not deny the possibility of a democratically sanctioned war fought by volunteers or draftees raised by universal conscription. But such wars may be the exception, not the rule. Even amongst the supposedly militaristic Germans, a sizeable majority in 1939 would probably have voted against attacking Poland or any other major state. The Nazi regime never put the issue to the voters but then most modern democratic governments do not seek or permit direct voter input on war issues either.

## Regulating the Marketplace

Business abuses involve more than white collar crimes. Certain minor abuses are scarcely regulated. These include legal but irksome practices such as telephone soliciting, junk mailings, distribution of throwaway flyers and advertising on billboards. More problematic is the prevalence of legal but misleading advertising. Such advertising is not false but vital information is left out and false expectations are created. Pharmaceutical promotions of painkillers or analgesics are a prime example. Advertisement for these drugs mention only their initial, short term effects of symptom alleviation. Seldom mentioned are the long term results or the risks of repeated consumption. Tobacco advertising follows the same pattern. The entire focus is on the immediate gratification users can obtain from taking tobacco. Not mentioned is the probability of cancer, addiction, health impairment and death. Tobacco products now bear certain warnings but only because government ordered producers to make the addition. Similar and more extensive warnings are warranted for a large number of drug products.

Businesses may attempt to defraud customers, suppliers and competitors. Business crime in Canada is estimated to cost billions of dollars annually. Such crimes include physicians submitting false claims to medical insurance plans, stock manipulation by inside traders, collusion by firms bidding on government contracts, pyramid sales schemes and a host of other deceitful practices (Croft, 1975). Some cases involve large losses to a few victims. Alberta lawyer Peter Petrasuk stole $2.3 million from his clients, some of whom entrusted him with their life savings. Petrasuk received a 10-year prison term and indirectly spawned a consumer-volunteer organization in 1981 called the Victims of Law Dilemma made up initially of his former clients. A real estate fraud perpetrated by Argosy Financial Group of Canada Ltd. and its president in the 1980's cost a thousand investors about $24 million. Other trust company scams involved Astra Trust Co., Dominion Trust Co., and the Toronto real estate fraud by Greymac Trust Co. and Seaway Trust Co. A recent American example is the collapse of Enron due to the quesionable and fraudulent practices of its senior officers.

In other cases, the losses are spread very thinly over a large group of victims. In the 1980's, the stockbroking firm of E.F. Hutton was fined $2 million (U.S.) for a cheque-kiting operation that ultimately hurt a number of banks and their shareholders. Ivan Boesky was fined the record amount of 138.5 million (U.S.) in 1987 for using insider information to speculate on corporate takeovers. The victims of Boesky's offence were all other buyers and sellers of the affected stock. Boesky, who also received a 3 year jail term, garnered much of his illegal information from Dennis Levine, a New York investment banker who was convicted and fined $362,000. Price fixing is also an excellent example of how businesses can make large illicit gains by stealing small sums from millions of customers. For over forty years General Electric, Westinghouse and two other U.S. corporations conducted a rigged bidding system in order to extract high, non-competitive prices on government products. They also conspired to exclude new competitors, fix the price of products such as lightbulbs and divide the market between them. The result was higher prices for a range of electrical appliances and services and the blockage of new products like lightbulbs that would last longer and use less electricity. Blocking innovation may hurt society more in the long run than fixing prices. In Canada, price-fixing, bid-rigging and other illegal trade practices are regulated federally under various sections of the Competition Act, R.S., 1985, c. C-34.

Businesses or professions that achieve monopolistic market positions gain the power to abuse the public interest. Electric streetcars were the dominant form of urban transit by the 1920s yet they survived in only a few cities thereafter, Toronto being a principal exception. What happened to the trolley car? General Motors joined with Standard Oil and Firestone Tire Company to buy out transit companies in the Depression and replace streetcars with GM buses riding on Firestone tires and fuelled by Standard Oil's diesel fuel. While the three corporations were convicted in 1949 of criminal conspiracy over this matter they received only token penalties (Solomon, 1980). Similar costs are imposed on society by professions. A study by the then Consumer and Corporate Affairs Canada investigated 13 major professions including law, medicine and accounting. The report concluded that mandatory fee schedules, advertising restrictions and barriers to inter-provincial competition cost customers about $700 million per year (Dewees, 1983).

An important avenue of business abuse is the manufacture, sale and distribution of defective products. Some of these defects are the result of inadvertent or accidental mishaps. Michigan Chemical Corporation in 1973 mistakenly mixed livestock feed with PBBs (polybrominated biphenyls) and thereby contaminated thousands of people, pigs and cattle and millions of chickens. Other defects are less accidental. The Ford Pinto, for example, was a poorly engineered car whose defects were known to Ford Motor Company. Indeed, all motor vehicles produced in the 1950s and 1960s suffered from known and correctable defects such as lack of seat belts, unpadded dashboards, poor brakes, obstructed view and high pollution output. These defects were not accidental or the result of ignorance. Finally, some defective products are marketed in direct violation of the law. Pharmaceutical firms have been convicted in a number of cases of doctoring test results and altering data in order to gain approval for new drugs (Mintz, 1965; Silverman & Lee, 1974).

Businesses can also abuse their employees by ignoring safety regulations, by not warning of or alleviating occupational hazards and by deceiving employees about such hazards. Naturally, all activities and all occupations entail some degree of risk. Particularly dangerous occupations include mining, construction, smelting and logging. Interestingly, police work is not a very dangerous occupation. In any case, a risk level above what is reasonably necessary amounts to employee abuse. While this formula is simple in theory, assessing risk levels and attributing causal relationships is difficult in practice, particularly in the case of long term disabilities from dust, pollutants, asbestos, noise and radiation. Connecting this type of disability to employment conditions is daunting partly because other causal agents, like tobacco smoking or viral cancers, may be partly or wholly responsible for an individual's impaired health.

So far we have considered businesses which engage in wrongful practices in the context of conducting a legitimate enterprise. There also exist businesses whose primary activities are illegitimate and which are other referred to as "organized crime". The standard view of organized crime is one in which criminal gangs or mobs, usually of south European extraction, prey on a helpless public. A vicious army of thugs is seen to be at war with decent society. This war involves bribing officials, extorting protection money, murder for hire, kidnapping, car theft rings and the infiltration of unions and legitimate businesses. "Crime fighters" stress the enormous financial impact of organized crime but do not question the legal framework responsible for generating the illegal profits (Government of B.C., 1980). An alternate theory of organized crime adds to or disagrees with the orthodox model. In the alternate view, organized crime centres around illicit marketing opportunities created by government. Here organized crime does not victimize the public, rather it exists to provide popular services like drugs, gambling, risky loans and commercial sex that government has wrongfully prohibited.

A case in point is "loansharking" involving loans at "usurious" rates of interest. Some people cannot acquire legitimate loans because they are poor credit risks or want the money for unapproved or illegal purposes. Such creditors must pay high rates of interest to lenders but the law interferes by making it illegal to make or collect such loans. Specifically, section 347 of the Code makes it an offence to advance anyone credit at an annual interest rate exceeding 60 percent. Legitimate lenders therefore cannot serve the high risk market which, by elimination, falls into the hands of those willing to break the law and to use coercive means to enforce their loan agreements. Police emphasize the assaults and extortion sometimes committed by such lenders but coercive behaviour of that sort is criminal quite apart from special rules about high rate loans. Furthermore, section 347 does not accommodate those situations where through defaults or bonuses an ordinary business deal can exceed the "criminal rate" of interest.

Service crime garners wide support from its customers and from opponents of prohibition. Far from being viewed as "evil", smugglers and purveyors of illicit goods are frequently portrayed as folk heroes engaged in principled opposition to government oppression. Furthermore, organized criminals are not limited to any specific ethnic group. Rather, successive waves of immigrants to North America pursue illicit business partly because established forces block their access to licit businesses and professions. Thus at different periods, historians identify Irish gangs, Jewish gangs, Chinese gangs and, far enough back, even English gangs. This type of organized "crime" is the direct result of law and would disappear immediately with changes in the law. The same is not true for crimes such as robbery or sale of stolen goods. We can see how the "problem" of cigarette smuggling in 1993-4 was largely "solved" by lowering the domestic taxes on these products.

## Regulating Individuals

Human resourcefulness and creativity are not directed solely to beneficial ends. The same talents also appear in the exploitation and harming of other people. Some forms of exploitation are more readily resorted to than others. For example, while wrongdoers stole 108,000 automobiles in Canada in 2000 and there were 174,000 incidents of breaking and entering, only 484 murders took place. This latter statistic represents a 30-year low in the murder rate.

Direct or personal wrongs include much of the substantive content of every jurisdiction's criminal law. They include wrongful killings, unprovoked assault, beating, torture, intimidation, sexual abuse, kidnapping and wrongful detention. While some of these misbehaviours are quite rare, others are relatively common. Murder can be contrasted in this regard with assault or with sexual harassment. Of offences reported by police in Canada, approximately 1 in 10 is a violent crime. Of the 2.5 million crimes reported in 2000, over half were property related.

The exploitation and maltreatment of other people appears throughout recorded history in every complex human society. Such basic continuity should raise some doubts about explanations of violent crimes that focus entirely on the specifics of current political, economic or social conditions. Still, the historically consistent presence of some crime does not deny the possibility of change. Both the rate of wrongdoing and the style of crime may alter dramatically. Since the late 1950s in Canada the official rate of crime has increased significantly over a broad range of fences. While violent crime increased dramatically in the 1970s and 1980s, recent years have seen a drop in the rates of both violent crime and crime in general. Similarly in the U.S., there were large increases in the rate of violent crime in the decades leading up to the 1990s. The U.S. murder rate doubled in the period 1950-1985, and remains four times the Canadian rate.

Besides more crime, the U.S. statistics also record more offences between strangers. But these official figures must be carefully analyzed and hasty conclusions avoided. Official statistics only approximate the real crime rate for a number of reasons including changing definitions of crime, new reporting methods, new police procedures or initiatives and variations in victim reporting. Besides rates of offences, styles of abuse may also change. At one period, murder may be predominantly an acquisitive activity practised by bandits, robbers and highwaymen. At other times, murder may tend to involve sexual motives, religious intolerance, racial tensions or social rebellion. Interestingly, in Canada the greatest risk of being murdered occurs during one's first year of life.

Personal wrongs often inflict physical damage such as injury, maiming, loss of faculties, pain and death. In addition, psychological and emotional harm may accompany the more visible injuries. Damage of this type includes anxiety, sleep disturbance, and loss of self-esteem. Moreover, psychological harm is suffered both by actual victims and by potential victims.

Wrongs directed against others' property comprise over half of officially reported offences. The relative risks of suffering from the traditional wrongs are well documented. If the Canadian rate of theft in 1990 were taken as 1 then other rates are as follows: murder (0.035), robbery (0.14), motor vehicle theft (5) and break and enter (17). Burglary is not only common, it is also costly to the victim in terms of the loss of property and goods; but the cost of property crime must also include the effort, expense and social impact of pursuing property protection measures such as alarm systems, locks, fences, guard dogs, self-defence courses, firearms and private security personnel. Tucker (1985:47) estimated that Americans spent $15 billion on public policing and another $18 billion on all private security employment. Paying 400,000 people to guard old wealth means those human resources cannot be employed in creating new wealth. We should also note the existence of secondary costs. For example, the mere locking of doors is a social cost, one that most people now take for granted but also one that is noticed and resented by people who migrate from remote communities where a locked door is an affront to the integrity of one's neighbours. A society that needs locks everywhere has a higher cost of living than an equal but lock-free society. Economist Gordon Tullock (1981) estimated the consequences of repealing the laws against theft and concluded that such a repeal would cause more theft, more self-defense, a personal arms race and a large decline in productive activity. According to Tucker (1985:181) crime "is a negative-sum game, creating distrust and causing people to cooperate less. It injures the whole society. . .[because] poverty does not cause crime, crime causes poverty". Even minor abuse of private property can be demoralizing; vandalism in particular is a form of social sabotage (Francis, 1983). To function effectively, humans require a certain degree of control over their personal and social environment. Where that personal control is seriously threatened, as is the case now in many decaying urban centres in the U.S., morale suffers. British Telecom's pay phones provide another case study. In 1987 BT recorded 500,000 serious attacks on its 79,000 public telephones with repair costs at $45 million. Poorer areas where people most need the phones suffer the highest rate of vandalism. Revealingly, BT is replacing traditional glassed call boxes because of their vulnerability to vandalism but when such booths were introduced sixty years ago neither theft nor vandalism were problems.

Business-oriented wrongdoings have been mentioned. Businesses themselves, however, are victimized by their employees who, because of their inside knowledge and position of trust, have the opportunity to exploit their employers. Losses through employee theft and pilfering are reported to exceed losses through shoplifting and burglary. Businesses hire security firms to supervise employee behaviour, a task that often entails undercover operations. Particularly vulnerable are financial service business whose employees must handle money and other commercial paper. Brian Molony, an assistant manager of the Toronto branch of the Canadian Imperial Bank of Commerce, was convicted in 1984 of stealing $10.2 million from the bank and served less than half of his 6 year sentence. While the average fraudulent offence in Canada results in the loss of $79,000, the average bank robbery nets only about $3,200.

Employee misbehaviour also includes the violence and vandalism associated with some union activities. Reynolds (1987:135) reports on the incidence and style of union crime in the U.S.:

From 1977 to 1979. . .incidents of labour violence by bombing alone caused $3.8 million in property damage. Between 1975 and 1983, there were 3,157 violent union incidents reported in the popular press. . . . Haggard and Thieblot (1983) analyzed the data on the 2,598 incidents for 1975-81 [and]. . .found 49 deaths attributable to labour violence; $15.2 million in damage to company plant and equipment; 2,732 instances of damage to automobiles; 133 cases of managers' and non-strikers' homes being firebombed, shot at or vandalized; hundreds of cases of sabotage and vandalism; and thousands of shots having been fired. Based on the evidence, the authors' conclusions seemed warranted; labour violence is substantial, systematically applied, and not diminishing, and much of the law enforcement community tacitly allows unions wide latitude to use intimidation and coercive techniques.

Frederic Hayek (1960:267) argues a legal reversal occurred with unions, whereby in the space of a century or so, unions progressed from outlaw status to a privileged place above the general rules of criminal law.

Besides their property and themselves, citizens possess certain rights. Rights, however, are counter-balanced by obligations. A legal right to vote means that government is burdened with a legal obligation to provide the means and opportunity to vote. A legal right to privacy means that others have a legal obligation not to intrude. All rights, legal or moral, have meaning only in light of opposite obligations. These obligations are frequently avoided, which is to say individuals abuse the rights of others. Take the use of public conveniences. People share sidewalks, public transit vehicles, parks and other common areas. Any person's right to use and enjoy these common areas is contingent on the behaviour of others. When individuals behave rudely or obnoxiously in public they infringe on everyone else's rights. The damage may be minor compared to physical assault, yet ill-mannered behaviour has a corrosive effect on the social structure. Such behaviour includes littering, jumping queues, foul language, lack of personal hygiene, excessive noise making, racial or sexual slurs, disrespect for persons with disabilities and unwarranted insults. Citizens also possess certain rights to privacy which are abused through telephone pranks, indecent exposure or high-pressure sales tactics in door-to-door selling.

## METHODS OF GOVERNMENT REGULATION

Many of the threats to public safety described above are counteracted in part by social, cultural and private mechanisms. In his *A Criminal History of Mankind* (1984), Wilson comments that people now have difficulty conceiving of how powerful were the religious and moral codes of a few centuries ago when the "faithful" actually believed that a powerful, vengeful god was always watching them, ready to condemn any transgression (Wilson, 1985:648). Customs are also important non-legal regulators. People generally refrain from appearing in public in a sordid condition not because body odour is illegal but because they are conditioned to be embarrassed by a certain level of uncleanliness. While Europeans of the 14th century viewed bathing with great suspicion, our social standards now require daily personal cleansing. Cultural conditioning is a powerful source of regulation so one might hope that social standards about environmental damage are increasing. A century from now driving an internal combustion vehicle may be viewed with the same distaste which now greets defecating in public. Unfortunately, conditioned conscience, peer pressure and social disincentives do not always provide a satisfactory level of protection. Furthermore, social regulations are primarily preventive. Such regulation lacks the full capacity to compensate victims or to apprehend and punish wrongdoers. Where social regulation fails or is incomplete, some level of government intervention is required.

Some forms of government intervention are less coercive than others. Tax controls and subsidy policies are relatively non-coercive because they merely create incentives to act in certain ways. A tax on alcoholic beverages discourages consumption while a subsidy on pollution-control equipment encourages installation of that equipment. With either the tax or the subsidy, no specific course of action is compelled. Most regulation takes a more coercive form. Standards are set that must be met or certain actions are prohibited. Laws against the use of leaded gasoline or against "underage" alcohol use are examples of direct command-type regulation. All criminal laws are command-type regulations.

Regulation methods vary according to the roles assigned private persons as opposed to the state. Criminal law is primarily a public system. In contrast, tort law is dominated by private initiative. Regulations also vary according to the extent of the coverage. Some regulatory schemes are individualistic, like criminal law, while some involve mass coverage through bureaucratic rather than police controls. In this section, we consider the varieties of public regulation as well as the characteristics of private law schemes.

## Public Law Regulation

### Tax and Subsidy

Punitive or sumptuary taxes such as those levied on tobacco or alcohol products are fault-based and designed to regulate behaviour. As Lon Fuller explained, taxes are "close cousins to the criminal law [when] their principal object is. . .not merely to raise revenue, but to shape human conduct in ways thought desirable by the legislator" (Fuller, 1969:60). The theory behind sumptuary tax regulation is simple. If the use of certain goods or services is generating social harm, that harm can be reduced if use of the offending products is reduced. Economic experiments indicate that as the price of a commercial product increases, purchases of that product decrease. Thus a tax on alcohol should cause a decrease in alcohol consumption and, in fact, such decreases are observed when taxes increase the real price of alcohol (Mitchell, 1983).

Note how a tax control mechanism functions. There is no absolute standard of alcohol-related behaviour established. Citizens are not forced to buy alcohol nor are they compelled to purchase any specific amount. The tax is not individualistic. Instead, the tax regulation is administered impersonally and on a mass scale. No information is gathered about the individual alcohol taxpayer. There is no court, no investigation, no finding of guilt required before the penalty is assessed. The tax penalty is paid merely on the grounds that commercial alcohol is being purchased for consumption. No special allowances need be made or individual cases considered. The cost of the regulatory tax per person affected is extremely low, perhaps pennies per case. This is because the tax is impersonal, because millions of people are penalized and because the regulatory work involved is not labour intensive.

. A sumptuary tax scheme usually imposes a very small penalty. The scale of the penalty is optional, however. In theory, the tax could be set at any level whatsoever. The tax on a litre of rum could be set at $5,000. Two objections are possible to that level of tax. First, such an extreme penalty is not deserved. Second, an excessive tax will have an effect similar to a prohibition on all commercial sales of alcohol. The higher the tax the more incentive is provided to illicit sellers of the taxed product. At a tax rate of $5,000 per litre of liquor there would be almost no taxed sales of the drug. Instead, sales would occur through the blackmarket where the official price would be easily undercut. Insensitivity to tolerable tax levels is apparent in many regimes where government tax or price controls are subverted by underground traders. As noted above, a good example here is the flood of cigarette smuggling into Canada in 1993-4 and the government's response of dramatically reducing domestic taxes in order to curb the activity.

Tax penalties serve as disincentives to discourage certain behaviours. In contrast, subsidies use a carrot approach to reward certain actions. Both approaches focus on preventing wrong doing. Take, for example, the question of vulnerability to crime. Muggers tend to prey on the weakest people — small women, the aged, the intoxicated. Subsidies for women to take self-defense courses, to buy and learn about protective devices (mace, sirens, guns) or to organize mutual protection societies might be a cost effective way to prevent victimization. Defensive measures, as noted, involve investment in human or physical capital. Government subsidies are capable of encouraging such investment or of directing it toward specific goals. Some types of housing arrangements are more conducive to occupant safety than others. If government can identify the superior architectural methods of reducing misbehaviour, then government agencies could subsidize and thus encourage the reproduction of those safer forms of housing or urban design.

To some extent tax and subsidy methods are symmetrical. Unsafe work conditions or defective products could be taxed or subsidies could be awarded to safe work conditions and products. Polluters could be taxed or subsidies given for pollution reduction. But, overall, tax controls are more versatile than the subsidy approach. In many cases a tax limitation could not be reproduced by a positive incentive scheme. A tax on recreational drugs like alcohol cannot be paired against a subsidy scheme achieving the same effect. With tax there will also be fewer administrative decisions needed to identify who qualifies for the penalty.

*Rationing, Zoning and Licensing*

Direct command-type regulations tend to impose universal standards or blanket prohibitions. Section 210 of the Code prohibits the operation of a "bawdy house" anywhere in Canada at any time. Similarly, theft is everywhere prohibited. In contrast, rationing permits some amount of the targeted activity to be conducted while zoning permits the regulated behaviour to occur but only in specified places and usually only at certain times. Rationing is primarily employed in the regulation of minor misbehaviour, the so-called "vices" such as gambling, prostitution and drugs. In 1919 the U.S. government instituted a national prohibition against the sale or manufacture of beverage alcohol while, in contrast, Sweden chose to ration alcohol rather than outlaw it. Men received a more generous ration than women, alcohol offences could result in the loss of one's ration cards and, at one point, married women were not permitted their own ration card. Logan proposes a marijuana rationing scheme for Britain. Under this plan licensed sellers, perhaps pharmacists, would distribute a maximum amount of the drug to each customer per week. Customers would be compelled to restrict their purchases of cannabis to the one supplier with whom they would be registered (Mitchell, 1983).

Like tax controls, rationing systems are a mass-oriented regulatory method. However, unlike taxes, a ration system raises no revenue and tends to be more complicated to administer. The complexity increases as the rationing plan attempts to affect specific individuals. A cannabis tax following the tobacco model would be totally impersonal. In contrast, Logan's cannabis rationing proposal requires a very personal relationship between regulator, seller and customer. The medical prescription of controlled drugs illustrates the level of complexity rationing schemes often attain. An additional problem with rationing is enforcement. Ration cards, like food stamps, are forged, counterfeited or circulated illegally as a form of currency. Large amounts of the rationed product are also diverted from legal to illegal distributors. With popular prescription drugs like the tranquillizers or amphetamine, sometimes most of a legal production run is eventually diverted to illicit sellers. Illicit producers also go into business to supply the artificially restricted demand.

Services as well as products can be rationed. Access to commercial suppliers of sex could be restricted to ration card holders. Such a scheme might also entail a qualification test for those requiring "therapeutic" sex or tourists or members of the armed forces would be permitted sex ration cards by the government. Outside the rationing system, all prostitution would be banned. In some ancient cultures the ritual sale of temple sex by priestesses duplicated many aspects of a rationing system. On a more topical note, countries like the Bahamas ration casino gambling by permitting only tourists, not citizens, to place wagers. A related form of rationing restricts the form of vice available rather than the quantity purchased. Many state and provincial governments now permit citizens to wager unlimited sums through government lotteries and in approved casinos while at the same time prohibiting other forms of gambling.

Zoning controls limits the geographical placement of socially disruptive activities. Under zoning controls, taverns, casinos, bawdy houses, pornography stores, chemical dumps and smelters are not illegal *per se*, they are just restricted to certain locations. Theoretically, there is no limit to what can be permitted in a given zone. A certain zone could be designated an assault centre where people wishing to fight one another would go in search of adventure. In certain respects, such a zone might not differ much from some physical contact sports like martial arts, football or hockey. We will consider below the issue of consent and whether one should be free to consent to assault or homicide.

Licensing controls generally do not restrict quantity or location; rather they affect quality. Licensing arises ostensibly when government is concerned that because the wrong people are dispensing product X the public is endangered. Thus licensing controls exist to ensure that only duly licensed and authorized persons operate taverns, sell lottery tickets, run bawdy houses or prescribe drugs. Again, there is no theoretical limit to what a license holder might be permitted. Ian Fleming's fictional creation James Bond was often referred to as "007", the number on his "license to kill".

Licensing schemes are extremely commonplace in Canada. Most relate to professional or commercial controls whereby only licensed persons can operate taxi cabs, give legal advice, perform surgery, issue warrants or detain certain criminal suspects. Other license schemes are broad based and control activities such as hunting, flying, and driving motor vehicles. Actually, hunting licences are usually just ration cards which control the specific animal population. However, rationing and licensing are readily combined. Drivers in Ontario are licensed under a point program that, in effect, rations traffic infractions. Each offence is worth a specific number of points. Within a two year period drivers that use up their total point allotment lose their license to drive. This scheme may purport to measure a driver's qualifications but it is more readily understood as a ration system. Since the majority of drivers exceed legal speed limits and commit a host of other offences, the loss of points in many cases may be due more to bad luck than to unsafe or especially incompetent driving.

## Direct Command Regulations

This type of regulation establishes certain legal standards and then prohibits any departure from those standards unless specific exemptions are granted. The criminal law prohibition of robbery is an example of this regulatory method but so is the forced schooling of all persons under a specified age (usually 15 or 16 years of age is the statutory standard enforced by the truancy law). While criminal law is probably the most familiar member of the direct command genre of regulation, there are a number of other regulations worth considering.

Three leading examples of mass coverage command regulation are compulsory schooling, compulsory auto insurance and traffic laws. Accepting that mass education is a valuable social objective does not necessarily lead to a legal prohibition against not attending school, which is the offence of truancy. Government could instead pay children directly for attending school or tax them for not attending. Either method might achieve a higher attendance rate than the present method of simply forbidding non-attendance. Truancy rates in some Canadian and U.S. high schools indicate that when a significant portion of students refuse to attend regularly, enforcement resources fail to cope adequately with the challenge. In some New York city schools the truancy rate exceeds 20% of all students and school boards lose permanent track of thousands of students every year. With the present compulsory system there is also the danger of creating harmful incentives. If school is compulsory then students must attend whether or not the school experience is valuable, educational or safe. These dangers may be magnified where the state has a total monopoly on schooling. In that situation, youngsters are forced not only to attend a school but to attend a specific school chosen by the government. Since such schools face little real competition and deal with a captive audience, incentives to deliver a high standard, popularly valued education may well decline over time. From 1966 to 1981 average test scores on the Scholastic Aptitude Test given to American college bound high school seniors declined. Verbal scores fell 11% and math scores fell 7% with the greatest declines occurring at the top of the score distribution (Thurow, 1985).

Most forms of insurance are not compulsory. One is not forced to insure one's life, personal possessions or house. Such was originally the case for automobile users. Individuals could buy auto insurance or not as they wished. Without insurance, however, motorists faced the possibility of having to directly pay for collision damage and for injuries caused to other persons. The first type of damage is of no public concern because it is limited to the motorists themselves. Damage to other people is a different matter. If an uninsured motorist seriously injured some one and was sued in tort law for damages, the likelihood of non-payment was substantial. Wanting to avoid bankruptcy and financial ruin most people willingly purchase insurance to cover claims made against them. Some motorists, though, are judgment proof. They have no significant assets or income hence the threat of liability is of little concern. For this group, insurance must be mandatory. So, as a result of some people's failure to insure against auto-accident liability, all motorists in most jurisdictions are prohibited from driving without such insurance (Ontario has had compulsory insurance since 1979, England since 1930). This rule is coercive but has little impact on the majority of motorists who willingly insure themselves. Interestingly, the same analysis could be applied to criminal law. At present, citizens and foreign guests in Canada are not obliged to carry criminal liability insurance. If someone commits sexual assault their victim can sue them in civil court for money compensation. Unfortunately, many wrongdoers lack the resources to pay such damages. Their victims therefore go uncompensated in tort law while victims of auto-related injuries are guaranteed insured coverage.

Traffic laws, the third example of mass coverage command regulation, constitute the major source of recorded offences. Abolish the automobile and we immediately abolish most criminal or quasi-criminal convictions. According to the Ouimet Report (1969) traffic offences represented almost 90% of the increased crime rate since 1901. Of individuals charged with a legal offence today the great majority are guilty of some driving-related offence. Motor vehicle collisions are clearly a major social threat: between 1945 and 1995 in Canada over 200,000 persons were killed in accidents, a number greater than Canadian fatalities in WW I (60,661) and WW II (42,042). What is not at all clear is whether criminal law regulations help reduce vehicular collisions and mishaps. In seeking to promote auto safety, legislators have relied primarily on prohibitory regulations with an attendant focus on driver error. Other regulatory methods are seldom exploited. For example, some European governments approach speed control much differently than North American regimes. In some residential-pedestrian areas, cars are either excluded or controlled by speed bumps. Called "sleeping policemen" by the British, speed bumps are the most effective device available to reduce vehicular velocity. On major highways in Germany no maximum speed limits are dictated. Both policies reduce the need for direct enforcement. Indirect regulatory schemes of a less coercive nature are also possible. Motor vehicle safety can be promoted by reducing dependence on automobiles, by subsidizing high density habitation and taxing suburbs, by rationing motor car owners, by changing automobile design or by subsidizing public transit. Another preventive strategy would be to raise the initial standard for driver's licences. Originally, no tests were required to obtain a driver's licence; now some standards are set but these are significantly below the level demanded of private pilots. Reward systems are also possible. Good drivers, however defined, could be rewarded with lower insurance costs, free licence renewal, special licence plate stickers, gasoline tax rebates or similar incentives. A few of these methods have been employed by modern legislators but numerous methods that would seriously curtail automobiles have not been used.

Although traffic offence convictions play a central role in the criminal law system, it is not known whether citizens approve of such laws or whether the laws are worth enforcing. Canadian and American studies indicate that from 60-85 percent of all drivers violate the speed limit laws. There is good evidence to suggest that speed contributes little to explaining the death rate of car occupants (Friedland, 1989). Variance in speed between drivers seems a more important factor since accidents increase with the amount of overtaking and passing that occurs and these increase with speed variance. Apparently, it is safest to drive at the 85th percentile speed. At its best, traffic law enforcement is sporadic. At its worst, enforcement is irrational: speed limits are most vigorously enforced on open, uncrowded highways where danger is minimal and least enforced in cities and on congested roads. It is instructive to note that lawmakers decided to rely heavily on criminal law regulation of traffic safety without supporting evidence that their choice was popular or effective.

Another fertile field of command-type regulation relates to business standards and practices. Businesses operate under an array of obligatory commands such as those affecting food product quality, metric measures, packaging, weigh scales, minimum wages, rent control, fire safety requirements and building codes. Despite considerable diversity, these regulatory schemes share important common elements. First, such schemes are the modern product of recent legislation. Second, the behaviour being prohibited is usually not regarded as morally reprehensible. Indeed, in certain cases the forbidden activity is regarded by many citizens as proper and right. Such opinions attach to forced metrification, minimum wage laws and rent controls. Third, the penalties directed against regulatory infractions are usually limited, mild and impersonal. Landlords charging more than rent control regulations permit are not imprisoned or treated "like criminals". Instead, they are subject to financial penalties which, at most, will force them to cease their business operations.

Some offences, particularly traffic violations, follow this pattern. Traditional crimes are a different matter. They are not the product of recent law making but rather are inherited from a long line of historical legal intervention and custom. In part because of their customary foundation, traditional crimes tend to be viewed as repugnant. The penalties inflicted against perpetrators of these wrongs are often severe and highly personal. convicted criminals are not merely put out of business, they are frequently removed altogether from society. Partly because criminal law is older and partly because it usually involves serious offences, it tends to be more formal, individualistic and professionalized than other direct command regulations. Complex rules, often the result of historical circumstances no longer in effect, govern who can arrest criminal offenders, who can prosecute and by what procedures, what evidence is admissible in court and what type of penalty is inflicted. To a greater extent than most other regulatory areas, criminal law is dominated by lawyers, judges and common law developments. To understand criminal law's historic roots it will be helpful to examine its private law forerunner.

## Private Law Regulation

### The Development of Tort Law

Victims who suffer financial or personal loss at the hands of a wrongdoer may seek redress through purely private means. Such self-help may consist of searching for stolen property and taking the property back into possession or of confronting the wrongdoer and through negotiation arranging some form of compensation. This compensation could include return of property, money payment, or personal service by the perpetrator. Finally, victims may retaliate against wrongdoers by doing them counteracting harm. This last form of self-help is still an important feature of international affairs between nation states. Military battles, civil wars, trade embargoes, divestitures and boycotts are examples of methods governments use in response to real or perceived wrongdoings. Why do governments still pursue extra-legal self-help methods of retaliation? The simple answer is the lack of a global government. When Iraq invaded Iran in 1981, the Iranian government could not dial 911 and ask the international police to stop the invasion and arrest the Iraqi leaders.

Without a developed law enforcement apparatus there can be no public law. Since human society evolved from stateless origins, it is natural that community protection began as self-help and then evolved into private law. It was only after the advent of the central state that public law could play an important role. In the early Ionian Greek communities of Ithaca, Pylos and Mycenae (c. 1200 B.C.) the state's only function was defence against foreign invaders. Indeed, even the Trojan "war" was largely a personal vendetta by certain Greeks against the family of Paris over his abduction of Helen. Theft, murder and assault were not public offences. No courts, police or lawyers existed. The tribal or city leader functioned as part-time priest, military commander and judge. There were no organized priesthoods or temples. No large temples appeared in Greece until 800 B.C. By necessity, most people did everything for themselves including farming, hunting, craft making and trade. Odysseus, though king of Ithaca, built his own house. Metal work and prophecy existed as occupational specialties but law did not (Posner, 1981:127-38).

Murder as described in Homer's *Iliad* is a private affair. The murderer faced retaliation by the victim's family who would either kill the murderer or accept a payment in compensation instead. Even the killing of the king Agamemnon was a personal offence against his family or clan, not a crime of treason. At this level of social development, the family dominates. The state was mostly just a loose conglomeration of large families; the kin unit was also the economic, social and judicial unit. Priam, the king of Troy, resided with 50 sons and 12 sons-in-law. Such a family could itself function as a small military unit, and in Homer's saga family loyalties almost always take priority over the common interest. Priam, the father of Paris, champions his son's cause although Paris has offended customs, the other Trojans despise Helen and the entire city of Troy is besieged. Legally, the family was dominant because responsibility and enforcement were collective and they needed to be collective in the absence of public enforcement. Imagine the plight of a single victim of theft. To help themselves they needed to discover the wrongdoer and either retaliate directly or force payment in compensation. They were very unlikely to accomplish those goals without support. A credible threat of retaliation would be needed to prompt the wrongdoer to make amends. Larger families thus provided preventive security and a force capable of retaliating against wrongdoers. Urban street gangs today probably develop for similar reasons.

Like a solitary victim, a single wrongdoer was also in a vulnerable position, given a choice of being killed in retaliation or paying compensation in appeasement. Since single persons would rarely be able to pay sufficient compensation for serious offences like killing, they would need the support of their family. This collective responsibility provided strong incentives for families to police their members very closely. Since everyone would suffer if anyone committed a harmful act, family members endeavoured to prevent wrongdoing. In some cases, families would banish potential troublemakers to avoid retaliation from a victim's clan.

To sum up primitive legal systems, self-help evolves at first into private law where the family, not the state, is the enforcement mechanism. Enforcement begins with direct retaliation, which often leads to feuds, but as wealth increases, retaliation is replaced by compensation. Compensation is socially superior because feuds are minimized and property is merely transferred not destroyed. Compensation schedules in customary law usually set out in fixed detail a schedule of payments where, for example, a killing is worth forty head of cattle or injury to a leg is worth two head. Finally, liability for compensation is strict. Whether one kills another accidentally or intentionally, compensation for the harm is still obligatory. Payment for accidental harms is sometimes less but is not absent altogether.

Since tort law continues today to encompass misbehaviours ("tortious" acts) that also tend to be the most traditional crimes, an obvious puzzle is the existence of two overlapping legal fields. If conversion could be dealt with in civil court why did the state create the mostly equal offence of theft to be prosecuted in a different court? The first part of the answer is the rise of centralized, bureaucratic "states" which are a prerequisite of public law. Various theories explain the state's origin: that it originated from conquest and defence against conquest, or that it arose from large-scale projects (irrigation, bridges), or that it developed through concentrations of wealth permitting specific families to hire retainers (private soldiers) to protect their property. The second part of the answer deals with benefits derived from centralized control and taxation. By reframing a private wrong as a "public" wrong, the compensation is converted into a "fine" payable to the ruler. At the same time, in a centralized state the ruler collectivizes the public loss not covered in a system of private compensation. When a knight was killed, the knight's family suffered a loss but the king was also injured insofar as the knight's military services and other public obligations could not be fulfilled. This analysis suggests that a centralized state expands the scope of public prosecution over time. In the next section the rise of criminal law in England is examined as a test of this hypothesis.

## Private and Public Law in English History

Prior to the Norman conquest of 1066, England had no criminal law, no legislature and no permanent judiciary. Baker explains that the earliest written codes of Anglo-Saxon "law" dealt with custom and focused on fixing the scale of "blood-money" or compensation in lieu of feuding (Baker, 1979:3). Even prior to 1066, however, some police functions had shifted from the kin group to the king's court and the incentives behind this change are worth considering. The traditional justification for developing a centralized, public prosecution system was the king's need to promote peace and discourage outlaws, bandits and rebels. Baker speaks of the "king's peace" and the expansion of "royal justice" as being "necessary to preserve law and order" but he admits that "royal justice" was "beneficial to the king's purse" because the "fiscal profits of punishment fell into the coffers of powerful individuals or of the Crown by right of jurisdiction" (*Ibid.*: 413).

How could the king or other government personnel profit from inventing criminal law? The two primary sources of revenue were confiscation of property and fines. So-called "Pleas of the Crown" first involved wrongs personal to the king. Breaches of the "King's peace" were met by fines and over time kings increased the scope of their "peace" because the fines "were a source of revenue" (Kiralfy, 1965:349). Davidson (1966:78) argues that:

> The fine continued its popularity even after the Norman conquests in 1066, but the real reason behind its popularity now was that it was one of the best ways of financing the Crown and filling the royal coffers. Thus to some extent the fine forestalled and replaced the taxes of later generations. The amercement of minor offences was looked upon as a logical auxiliary to the forfeiture of the estates of convicted felons.

Under the Saxons, all homicide cases were civil actions whereas under the Normans they became crimes for which a "murder fine" was exacted. According to Baker (Id., 15) early Norman legal efforts arose because:

> [T]he pursuit of law and order was profitable. Some pleas of the Crown were purely fiscal, but all criminal justice bore golden fruit in fines and forfeitures. The pipe rolls of the Exchequer testify to the steady revenue from judicature, and in 1301 it was recorded that Edward I 'gained great treasure' to pay his military campaigns by 'causing justice to be done on malefactors'.

Initially, the king's peace was limited to specific public acts, such as neglect of military service, for which no private suit was possible. Special "Peaces" were also applied to specific locations, like highways, and to specific times, like Easter. Eventually, the King's Peace grew to cover all England at all times. Diamond (1971:53) asserts that "every conceivable occasion was utilized for the creation of law in support of bureaucracy and sovereign. We observe no abstract principle, no impartial justice. . .only the spontaneous opportunism of a new class designing the edifice of its power. . . 'it was mainly for the sake of the profits that early justice was administered at all [by the Norman Kings]' ". In Maitland's memorable phrase, 'the king has a peace that devours all others'.

Besides fining wrongdoers, the king's judges were in some instances empowered to confiscate a felon's property. Felonies were "unemendable" wrongs for which one could not simply pay compensation. Originally, these were confined to matters within the king's obvious jurisdiction and included offences such as treason and cowardice in battle, but eventually "treason" came to include private killings and other serious torts. Convicted felons forfeited their lives, their land was returned to their feudal lords and their personal goods or chattels were given over to the king. With lesser wrongs the court ordered both a fine to the king and damages to the victim but no personal compensation was ordered in a felony case.

The law on felonies illustrates the conflict between the traditional, private tort law and the newer, government sponsored criminal law. Since felony victims were not compensated by the king's court, such victims preferred to settle with offenders privately. This became an offence against "royal justice" and was termed "compounding a felony" (Baker 1979:414). Victims then sought other means of avoiding the king's interference. The resulting lack of criminal prosecutions in the 12th and 13th centuries led the king to develop means for compelling subjects to present and prosecute felonies. One means was the creation of the royal office of the "coroner". Coroners, as the king's agents, travelled out to investigate every violent or suspicious death. This was not done out of curiosity but to produce felony convictions. If the coroner suspected foul play then the local community leaders were ordered to identify and produce the guilty parties.

The king also faced internal opposition. The 1352 *Statute of Treason* limited the types of wrongs that could be characterized as "treason" and was passed at the insistence of the barons. Apparently, the barons complained because with every new treason offence created by the king's judges, the king acquired more offenders' property instead of the property going to the barons or their immediate subjects (Kiralfy, 1958:365). There may also have been some concern on the barons' part that a king with unchecked power to create treasons would eventually reclassify their own political opposition, which led to the *Magna Carta*, as treason.

The same social conditions permitting the rise of centralized kingdoms also contributed to the creation of "crime control" problems. Private tort systems depend in primitive cultures or kin group of collective responsibility. By 1066 individualism was beginning to replace the customary notions of collective liability. Combined with greater mobility and cultural diversity, the weakening of kin group policing and compensating meant that more wrongs went uncompensated. "Outlaws" were people unable to pay fines or compensations or who lived as bandits outside towns, villages or feudal manors. These bandits or outlaws were usually gangs centred around a core of brothers or other close relatives and while some outlaw bands were in business for themselves, others operated on behalf of magnates or religious houses (Bellamy, 1973:69-73). Since outlaws were immune from tort restrictions they could only be dealt with by a public group which naturally tended to be organized by the king. Kiralfy, for example, notes that Henry II (1154-1189) took over the job of ridding the community of its worst offenders. Criminal-type or "afflictive" punishments like banishment, execution or maiming arose in connection with the battle against outlaws. In tort law, of course, it made little sense to banish or kill the person from whom you expected compensation.

Still, if satisfactory compensation was not paid the next best solution was pure afflictive punishment and the threat of such penalties must always be in the background for a primitive private law system to be effective. A social dilemma seems to evolve, however, in that a move toward greater flexibility, privacy and personal initiative confounds the conditions necessary for effective tort law enforcement. Fragmented families and independent persons escape the strictures of kin group customs but they render themselves vulnerable to predatory behaviour. In answer to this vulnerability, law enforcement shifts from amateurs to professionals, from private citizens to the king's agents. As to the fundamental cause of criminal law, it may be that kings exploited the opportunities presented by the failure of private law more than they engineered the eclipse of tort law by contrived design. Conquests, kings, soldiers and personal ambition are rather constant factors in any historical equation so the centralizing objectives of the Norman kings cannot, in themselves, explain the rise of public law. Moreover, the same trends are observable in other historical contexts and in other occupations besides government.

Kiralfy observes that the historical distinction between tort and crime "was essentially procedural in its origins" (id., 359). These procedural distinctions remain today and are responsible for the particular features of criminal law. Tort defendants, if found liable, paid damages whereas criminals were fined or subject to afflictive punishments. Tort defendants faced their alleged victims whereas criminal defendants faced the king (the Crown). Naturally since the king controlled the judges and the court, criminal law procedure was stacked against the accused, sometimes to an extreme degree. In tort law, a plaintiff must prove damages and can only extract a monetary penalty proportionate to the harm caused or intended. Since criminal law penalties are fixed by the government and administered by government agents (the judges and prosecutors) there is usually no requirement that damages be proved or that the penalty be justified. A person convicted of possessing LSD in Canada can be fined $5,000 and sentenced to 3 years in prison (under section 6 of the *Controlled Drugs and Substances Act*, S.C. 1996, c. 19) without the prosecutor showing or being able to show any damages at all. Tort law is self-enforcing as victims seek personal compensation whereas criminal law offers very little to individual victims and therefore comes to rely on a professional cadre of law enforcers paid by the king or government. In turn, this professional police force rearranges criminal procedure regarding arrest, search, interrogation and identification of suspects to suit its own bureaucratic interests. Similarly, criminal law transforms the tort plaintiff's independent legal counsel into a bureaucratic Crown Prosecutor. (See Section 4.2)

McGinley (1981:281-2) explains that the state is much more concerned with enforcing criminal rather than civil laws because criminal conduct "challenges the institutional supremacy of the state by questioning its authority". Since obedience is the primary concern, the state prosecutes a law breaker even when the accused's conduct is not morally wrong. Harm to the state occurs, after all, merely through the act of disobedience. Attempted crimes, as attempts at disobedience, leave defendants liable to serious penalties, whereas the concept of attempted tort is sketchy and undeveloped.

## Bibliography

- American Friends Service Committee, *Struggle for Justice* (New York: Hill and Wang, 1971).
- Baker, J.H., *An Introduction to English Legal History* (Toronto: Butterworths, 1979).
- Beauchamp, D.E., *Beyond Alcoholism—Alcohol and Public Health Policy* (Philadelphia: Temple University Press, 1980).
- Bellamy, J., *Crime and Public Order in England in the Later Middle Ages* (Toronto: University of Toronto Press, 1973).
- Boyd, N., "The Origins of Canadian Narcotics Legislation: The Process of Criminalization in Historical Context" (1984), 8 Dalhousie Law Journal 102.
- Buchanan, J., "From Private Preferences to Public Philosophy: The Development of Public Choice", in J. Buchanan, ed.,*The Economics of Politics* (London: Institute of Economic Affairs, 1978).
- Buchanan, J., "The Limits of Taxation", in *Taxation: An International Perspective* (Vancouver: The Fraser Institute, 1984).
- Comack, E., "The Origins of Canadian Drug Legislation: Labelling versus Class Analysis", in T. Fleming, ed., *The New Criminologies in Canada* (Toronto: Oxford University Press, 1985).
- Croft, R., *Swindle—A Decade of Canadian Stock Frauds* (Toronto: Gage Publishers, 1975).
- Davidson, R., "The Promiscuous Fire" (1965), 8 Criminal Law Quarterly 74.
- Devlin, P., *The Enforcement of Morals* (London: Oxford University Press, 1965).
- Dewees, D., ed., *The Regulation of Quality* (Toronto: Butterworths, 1983).
- Diamond, J.S., "The Rule of Law Versus the Order of Custom" (1971), 38 Social Research 42.
- Downs, A., *An Economic Theory of Democracy* (New York: Harper & Row, 1957).
- Ericson, R., *Reproducing Order* (Toronto: University of Toronto Press, 1982).
- Francis, D.B., *Vandalism—The Crime of Immaturity* (New York: Lodestar Books, 1983).
- Friedland, M., *Sanctions and Rewards in the Legal System: A Multidisciplinary Approach* (Toronto: University of Toronto Press, 1989).
- Fuller, Lon, *The Morality of Law* (New Haven: Yale University Press, 1969).
- Garan, D.G., *Against Ourselves: Disorders from Improvements under the Organic Limitedness of Man* (New York: Philosophical Library, 1979).
- Goode, E., *Drugs in American Society*, 2nd ed. (New York: Alfred A. Knopf, 1984).
- Government of British Columbia, The Business of Crime (1980).
- Government of Canada, *The Criminal Law in Canadian Society* (1982).
- Green, M., "The History of Canadian Narcotics Control" (1979), 37 University of Toronto Faculty of Law Review 42.
- Hayek, F., *The Constitution of Liberty* (Chicago: University of Chicago Press, 1960).
- Hills, S.L., *Crime, Power and Morality* (New York: Dodd, Mead & Co., 1971).
- Howard, R., *Poisons in Public—Case Studies of Environmental Pollution in Canada* (Toronto: James Lorimer, 1980).
- Jaynes, J., *The Origins of Consciousness in the Breakdown of the Bicameral Mind* (Boston: Houghton Mifflin, 1976).
- Kiralfy, A.K., *Potter's Historical Introduction to English Law* (London: Sweet & Maxwell, 1958).
- Lieberman, J.K., *How the Government Breaks the Law* (New York: Stein & Day, 1972).

- McGinley, G.P., "An Inquiry into the Nature of the State and its Relation to the Criminal Law" (1981), 19 Osgoode Hall Law Journal 267.
- McGinnis, J., "Bogeman and the Law: Crime, Comics and Pornography" (1988), 20 Ottawa Law Review 3.
- Michael, J. and Adler, M., *Crime, Law and Social Science* (New York: Harcourt Brace, 1933).
- Milgram, S., *Obedience to Authority* (London: Tavistock, 1974).
- Mintz, *The Therapeutic Nightmare* (Boston: Houghton Mifflin, 1965).
- Mitchell, C., "A Comparative Analysis of Cannabis Regulation" (1983), 9 Queen's Law Journal 110.
- Mitchell, C., "The Mispursuit of Happiness: Divorcing Normative Legal Theory from Utilitarianism" (1986), 16 Manitoba Law Journal 123.
- Nettler, G., *Responding to Crime* (Cincinnati: Anderson Publishing, 1982).
- Parker, G., *An Introduction to Criminal Law* (Toronto: Methuen, 1987).
- Posner, R., *The Economics of Justice* (Cambridge: Harvard University Press, 1981).
- Posner, R., "An Economic Theory of the Criminal Law" (1985), 85 Columbia Law Review 1193.
- Quinney, R., *The Problem of Crime* (New York: Dodd, Mead & Co., 1970).
- Rawls, J., *A Theory of Justice* (Cambridge: Harvard University Press, 1971).
- Reifner, U., "The Bar in the Third Reich: Anti-Semitism and the Decline of Liberal Advocacy" (1986), 32 McGill Law Journal 96.
- Reynolds, M.O., *Making America Poorer—The Cost of Labor Law* (Washington: Cato Institute, 1987).
- Sheckley, R., *The 10th Victim* (New York: Ace Books, 1965).
- Silverman, M. & Lee, P., *Pitts, Profits and Politics* (Berkeley: University of California Press, 1974).
- Shirer, W.L., *The Rise and Fall of the Third Reich* (New York: Simon & Schuster, 1960).
- Solicitor General of Canada, "Report of the Canadian Committee on Corrections—Toward Unity: Criminal Justice and Corrections (The Ouimet Report)" (Ottawa: Canada, 1969).
- Solomon, L., *Energy Shock* (Toronto: Pollution Probe Foundation, 1980).
- Taylor, F., Kettle, P., Putnam, R., *Pollution: The Effluence of Affluence* (Toronto: Methuen, 1971).
- Thurow, G., *Rhetoric and American Statesmanship* (Durham: Carolina Academic Press, 1985).
- Tucker, W., *Vigilante—The Backlash Against Crime in America* (New York: Stein & Day, 1985).
- Tullock, G., "The Welfare Costs of Monopolies, Tariffs, and Theft: in Tullock, Buchanan & Tullison, eds., *Towards A Theory of the Rent-Seeking Society* (Texas: A & M University Press, 1981).
- Turk, A., Turk, J., Wittes, J., *Ecology, Pollution, Environment* (Philadelphia: W.B. Saunders, 1972).
- Uchendu, V., *Igbo of Southeast* (London: Holt, Rinehart & Winston, 1965).
- Wexler, S., "The Intersection of Law and Morals" (1976), 54 Canadian Bar Review 351.
- Wilson, C., *A Criminal History of Mankind* (New York: G.P. Putnam's 1984).

## Questions/Discussion

1. What crimes are likely to be dropped in the 21st century? What new crimes will probably be created? As an example of a recently created law, see Bill C-36, the *Anti-Terrorism Act*, which received Royal Assent in December 2001, now S.C. 2001, c. 41. According to the Department of Justice, the Act

   > . . .creates measures to deter, disable, identify, prosecute, convict and punish terrorist groups; provides new investigative tools to law enforcement and national security agencies; and ensures that Canadian values of respect and fairness are preserved and the root causes of hatred are addressed through stronger laws against hate crimes and propaganda. . .

   (http://canada.justice.gc.ca/en/news/nr/2001/doc_28217.html.)

2. Under what social conditions do criminal law controls expand? Conversely, under what imaginable social conditions would criminal law "wither away"?

3. Certain factions want abortion (or prostitution, loan sharking, crime comics, narcotics) to be a criminal offence under almost any circumstances, whereas some others want matters concerning abortion, etc., kept entirely out of the Criminal Code. Using the three different ethical systems described above, analyse the issue of abortion's criminality.

4. If suicide is legal, should competent adults be free to consent to their own death in blood sports like survival games with real ammunition and attractive prizes?

5. Conduct an informal survey to determine what threats to personal and social security most people regard as paramount. As a secondary matter, determine what solutions people favour to meet these threats. What proportion rely on legal solutions?

6. Over the last twenty years, in which countries have governments been more of a threat to society than so-called criminals? In what countries has the reverse been true? In your opinion, what significant features distinguish conditions in these two groups of nations?

7. Should all Canadians over a certain age be compelled to purchase criminal liability insurance in order that all victims of crime would be compensated in civil law, at least where the offender is identified? Would such compulsory criminal insurance be enforceable?

8. Why did tort law precede criminal law and what social factors led to the development of criminal law?

9. Source: D. Koontz, "The Undercity" in R. Elwood, ed., *Future City* (Trident Press, 1973).

   In this short story an old soldier in the former criminal "underworld" talks to his daughter about all the criminal opportunities he once enjoyed:

   > Nearly all forms of gambling were illegal back then. An enterprising young man could step in, buck the law, and clean up a tidy sum with a minimal financial outlay and with almost no personal risk at all. Cops and judges were on the take; clandestine casinos, street games and storefront betting shops thrived. No longer. They legalized it, and they gave us bank clerks for casino managers, CPA's instead of bouncers. They made gambling respectable—and boring.

   > Drugs were illegal then, too. Grass, hash, skag, speed . . . God, an enterprising young kid like yourself could make a fortune in a year. But now grass and hash are traded on the open market, and all the harder drugs are available to all who will sign a health waiver and buy them from the government. Where's the thrill now? Gone. And where's the profit? Gone, too.

> Sex. Oh, kid, the money to be made on sex, back then. It was all illegal: prostitution, dirty movies, picture postcards, erotic dancing, adultery, you name it! Now the government licenses the brothels. . . Hell, kid, even murder was illegal in those days.

Note: This story is predictive and may not be accurate but it did anticipate the rapid rise of legal and government sponsored gambling over the last two decades. How was gambling transformed from a vice to a virtue? Consider also the morality of governments commercially promoting lotteries and casinos when the ads do not mention the remote odds of winning or warn people about the habit forming dangers of gambling.

10. How would people behave if unencumbered by normal legal restrictions? The behaviour of diplomats provides a partial answer to this question because by international law and convention, diplomats (and their families, employees and assistants) are immune from the law of the host nation. In Ottawa for 1983, 4,323 traffic tickets were issued to diplomatic plates. Only 184 were paid, which constitutes 4.2%. The worst offenders were, in order, Nigerians, Algerians, Somalians and the French. The Vatican paid both its tickets. American diplomats paid 31 out of 146 tickets. See C. Ashman & P. Trescott, *Diplomatic Crime* (Washington: Acropolis Books, 1987).

## Further Reading

Some readers may want to learn more about the substantive criminal law in Canada at this stage. A number of texts are available including the following:

* Simon Verdun-Jones, *Criminal Law in Canada: Cases, Questions & The Code; 3d ed.* (Toronto: Harcourt Canada 2002). This text describes many of the basic features of Canadian criminal law, and is written for undergraduates.
* Don Stuart and R. Delisle, *Learning Canadian Criminal Law, 8th ed.* (Toronto: Carswell, 2001). A thorough and detailed statement of the law primarily for law students and practictioners.
* Alison Hatch Cunningham and Curt Griffiths, *Canadian Criminal Justice: A Primer* (Toronto: Harcourt Brace, 1997).
* Kent Roach, *Criminal Law, 2d. ed.* (Toronto: Irwin Law Inc., 2000).

## Useful Websites:

* Access to Justice Network: http://www.acjnet.org/.
* Supreme Court of Canada: http://www.scc-csc.gc.ca/index_e.htm.
* Law Commission of Canada: http://www.lcc.gc.ca/.
* Juristat Canada: http://jurist.law.utoronto.ca/.
* Laws of Canada online: http://laws.justice.gc.ca/en/index.html.
* Department of Justice Canada: http://canada.justice.gc.ca/.
* Criminal Code online: http://laws.justice.gc.ca/en/C-46/index.html.
* Attorney General of Ontario: http://www.attorneygeneral.jus.gov.on.ca/.
* Correctional Service Canada: http://www.csc-scc.gc.ca/.
* Solicitor General of Canada: http://www.sgc.gc.ca/.
* National Crime Prevention Centre: http://www.crime-prevention.org/index_ncpc.html.

- Critical Criminology Justice Association: http://www.critcrim.org/.
- Canadian Criminal Justice Association: http://home.istar.ca/~ccja/angl/index.shtml.
- Uniform Law Conference of Canada: http://www.ulcc.ca/.
- Canadian Judicial Council: http://www.cjc-ccm.gc.ca/.

# 2

# PERSPECTIVES ON CRIMINAL LAW

## Introduction

*R.P. Saunders*

The approaches to and theoretical perspectives on criminal law and criminal justice are many and varied, yet one's approach or perspective çolours the way one sees criminal law in a very fundamental way. It is both ironic and puzzling that legal professionals have for so long been one-dimensional in their orientation and ignored the value of alternative approaches in understanding and formulating criminal law. Criminal law, contrary to what some traditional, legalistic approaches to it might claim, is not a "thing" derived from heaven, from the past, from custom, or from nature; it is a reflection of the views and perspectives of policy-makers on what they want the law, and specifically criminal law, to accomplish. It is also a reflection of their views on human nature and human activity, as well as a statement about the potential of the state to interfere in social conflicts and to control human behaviour in a meaningful and effective manner.

The difficulty is, of course, the definition of what it is one is talking about when the term "law" is used. Are we referring to the actual rules or laws which make up a body we collectively call "law", or are we talking about something wider than this, something that would encompass broader and more ambiguous principles, or rights such as those encompassed in the "Rule of Law" or those found in so-called "natural law" doctrines? We shall see that how writers define law and its institutions is an important factor in determining the scope and method of their inquiry into an understanding of law and reform.

There is also the problem of the use of terminology generally in looking at approaches to law and criminal law. To begin, there are conflicting definitions and terms within law itself, depending upon the particular school of thought one adopts. In addition, there is also the challenge of communicating across disciplines and of understanding the terminology and methodology of other fields of expertise and study. Law as a discipline has done particularly poorly in this regard. For the most part, the mainstream of legal studies has maintained an unhealthy and even anti-intellectual insularity as to other disciplines' approaches to law.

The result has been a lack of rigour and of depth in the work and research which is produced in legal academia, notably when comparisons are made to the body of knowledge and writing in other disciplines. This is especially true in the area of criminal law, where the traditional doctrinal approach of lawyers and legal writers has too often been limited to a narrow analysis of the cases, legislation and processes related to criminal justice. This approach has been criticised as sterile, circular and self-contained, and as having very little to offer in the way of substantive policy choices and effective, meaningful critiques. We shall return to this criticism below and in Chapter 3 in our discussion on the production of criminal law.

In discussing various theories and approaches, there is always the danger of not giving enough credence to one particular perspective versus another. This is not to say that legal writers should strive to be neutral in their presentation, for this is the very criticism one can make of the pretenses of traditional legal theories: they tend toward neutrality and detachment. However, that said, an explanation of other approaches is in order to allow the reader to be exposed to the various perspectives, and thus to become an aware and knowledgeable reader in the area of criminal justice, particularly in understanding the (often undisclosed and unacknowledged) biases and slants others bring to the field. Hopefully, the reader will adopt certain priorities and principles, and ultimately become more fully aware of her or his perspective, the grounds for it, and most importantly, the value of being self-conscious about one's perspective in any examination of criminal law. Such a recognition can only lead to a fuller understanding of the operation of the criminal law and ultimately to better, more progressive and more effective criminal justice policies.

The problem of prioritizing perspectives, of course, need not lead to an exclusionary or insulated approach to criminal law. Depending on how we define our approach, there is usually room to borrow or adapt or subsume other views. The value and worth of different concerns must be emphasized (in some contexts) in a way which gives them more than the perfunctory lip-service often found in traditional legal writings. Each reader should attempt to address the issue of perspective individually and to incorporate and refine what is most valuable and important in the various perspectives.

The remaining sections of this chapter describe and discuss several of the approaches to the analyses of law which are or have been in vogue. In the section immediately following, the traditional orthodox legal view is examined and critiqued. This view is found wanting. The gaps and shortcomings which are discussed have formed part of the impetus behind the development of an alternative or critical perspective; this perspective is described in the third section of this chapter. The second section looks at the contributions of other disciplines to the study and development of criminal law. It describes how disciplines such as sociology, political science, economics and psychology have provided new understandings of criminal law, and have acted as a spur to the development of innovative and challenging perspectives within the discipline of law itself. The third section examines the development and meaning of a critical approach to criminal law. It is important to note that neither this section nor any of the other sections in this chapter attempts to be all-inclusive as to the respective perspectives, but rather each is deliberately selective in its approach to the topic. This is because the purpose of this chapter is not a detailed exposition of the myriad of views which exist. On the contrary, we wish to focus on a selective presentation of the principal themes and directions which have influenced, continue to guide or might in the future contribute to the formulation and implementation of criminal justice policy in Canada. For a good overview of the many and varied issues and schools of thought, see the selection of readings at the end of this chapter.

In the last twenty-five years, feminist writers and researchers have made an enormous contribution to our theoretical understanding of law and to the design and implementation of strategies of resistance and reform. There are many variants of feminism. However, these are linked by the common themes of the inequality of power, and of gender bias, discrimination and injustice in the values and practices of the criminal law. Heidensohn's article is a critique of male-centred approaches and an attempt to set out an alternative feminist model for a criminal justice system, one that would address the real needs and experiences of women. In addition to these articles, there are several attempts throughout the text to highlight feminist perspectives in the context of specific topics, for example in regard to the male-controlled production of criminal law (in Chapter 3), the issue of the battered woman's syndrome both in self defence (in Chapter 7) and in prosecutorial policy (in Chapter 4), and sexual assault (in Chapter 8). In sum, it is important to not only be aware of but also to incorporate the values and concerns of feminism in the development of the theoretical models of and practical strategies for criminal justice.

The final section introduces the reader to historical perspectives on criminal law and their importance in any examination of criminal justice. The law has evolved over a long period of time and has gone through many incarnations in different cultures and eras, yet there is a tendency to ignore the past and the lessons (both positive and negative) we can learn from it. The section also provides a capsule view of the history of criminal law in Canada and prepares the reader for the readings on the production of criminal law (Chapter 3) and on the status of the defence and prosecutor (Chapter 4).

## 2.1 TRADITIONAL LEGAL PERSPECTIVES

*R. P. Saunders*

In looking at traditional orthodox approaches to law in general and criminal law in particular, we can identify several common themes and positions, even though there are many variants and schools within the traditional approaches. Rather than examining and comparing in detail these various schools of thought, it is more useful for our purposes to identify some of these common features and to situate their general approach in the overall range of criminal law perspectives. What then are these common features, and how and why are they important?

The traditional approach within law is one which takes the law as given and fails to explore the social or political dimensions of the institutions, agents, processes and activities of law. It is an approach that concentrates on the written, formal aspects of law and that assumes that the law is a neutral force to be used and manipulated (usually for good) by the state and by individual, legally constituted agents. It is "law-centred" in that law is seen as a good in and of itself to be put to a myriad of uses and purposes which can bring about social change and real progress. While there are differences within the various schools of liberal and conservative thought, the essential approach is one which is formalistic and rule and process-oriented. It assumes a high degree of social consensus and argues that these rules and processes reflect shared values and concerns. It also assumes that law operates primarily for the benefit of the system as opposed to the interests of any of particular individual or group.

Numerous examples of this approach can be found in legal literature and in the policy responses of the state to social problems. These responses of the state are discussed in more detail in Chapter 3, where the book deals with the difficulties inherent in a criminal justice policy formation process which is largely controlled by legal professionals. Too often the response of the state has been limited to a technical "re-formation" or revision of the criminal law to make it better, more efficient and more accommodating. While the criminal law should fulfill these demands, the state must not ignore or avoid other, more social (and often more costly) responses to the problems seen within the criminal justice system. What we see again and again on the part of the state is the use of criminal law to provide a full "answer" to a social problem in a manner which allows the state to silence or manage complaints and to avoid dealing with the root causes of a situation. For example, in the area of sexual assault (discussed in detail in Chapter 8), we have to look beyond changes in the criminal law, and attempt to rid society of sexist and patriarchal structures, relations and attitudes, both within the criminal justice system and in society as a whole. Numerous other examples exist to illustrate this issue, including prostitution (where the legal changes in the law simply tend to make it easier to arrest and convict prostitutes), drunk driving (where the penalties have become more and more harsh in recent years), and victims of crime (where as we shall see in Chapter 4 the state response has often been "cheap" and largely symbolic). The point to remember is that the complex social dimensions of the problems surrounding criminal law must not and cannot be forgotten, yet they often are in a traditional legal approach which focuses almost exclusively on notions of individual guilt and responsibility (see Chapter 6), on the formal aspects of the process and rights which allegedly attach to the individual, and on the rules and regulations that make up the criminal law in its most basic sense, though arguably not its most important.

A term which has been used to describe this orthodox approach is "doctrinal", a term that emphasizes the self-contained and tautological nature of the enterprise. The focus is on what the doctrine and institutions of law are, not the contradictions and debates which are inherent in the formation and implementation of law. This approach ignores the social process of producing and reproducing social structures and social relations. Another term that might be used is "legal fetishism" (Collins, 1982), a term which accurately describes the intellectual orientation of and emotional attachment to the approach. This term, while it has been employed to indicate and delineate Marxist criticisms of law, is used here in a more restricted manner (and only for the purposes of this text) to set out the boundaries of the conventional approach.

The essence of the traditional perspectives is that law is seen as representing a value consensus in society, that law in its formal manifestations, both substantively and in its processes, represents the shared values that society holds collectively. Within this view, the law is seen as fundamental to social order. A legal order is held to be a necessary component of a civilized social order: it serves to mark the acceptable limits of behaviour, to express society's unwillingness to tolerate threats to order, and to mobilize legitimate state institutions in response to these threats. Central to this idea is the belief that "legal rules are at the centre of social life" (Collins, p. 11) and that they satisfy social wants.

Another important feature of the traditional approach is the idea that "law is a unique phenomenon which constitutes a discrete focus of study" (*ibid.*). It reflects the argument that the discipline is "special" due to its unique patterns of institutions and relationships, its possession of a "mode of discourse" used only by lawyers, and the fact that "legal rules also function as normative guides to behaviour" (*ibid.*) and as such are different from other modes of control, such as brute force. Of course, these notions can be, and often are criticized. The idea of law as a necessary is criticized on the grounds that it is much too simplistic and ignores the important role that informal modes of control and non-legal rules can play in shaping and determining the formation and direction of behaviour. The argument is that rather than being law-centred, it is much more valuable to adopt an integrative approach that seeks to study and understand law principally in the context both of the social and political functions that it fulfills, and of the social structures and processes within which it emerges.

The essential criticism of traditional legal approaches is that they are overarchingly oriented toward the formal manifestations of law and the institutions and processes that surround those manifestations. Law school study is still focused on the courts, the cases, and the formal rules, in spite of the calls in the last two decades for more interdisciplinary and socialized approaches to the study of law.[1] It is a technical, professional training which teaches students how to argue, manipulate, and use the rules, and not necessarily to understand the reality and impact of the rules in their social setting. Yet surely this is the most important dimension to legal rules from a policy perspective: such an understanding is a precondition to the development of a criminal justice system which has any potential of meeting the needs of today's society.

This is not to deny that cases, trials and interpretations of the legislation hold a very strong attraction. One need only look to the law schools, or to the entertainment industry with its many lawyers' shows (though most bear little resemblance to the reality of everyday practice). But one has to be careful to resist the seduction of this limited but comforting approach to the criminal justice system: we must look deeper. We have to understand that the dilemmas and contradictions in the law and its stated ideals are very real; that equality is often there in rhetoric but not in practice; that who you are, the colour of your skin, your income, your class background and other social, gender and ethnic factors can all combine to play an important part in the nature and outcome of one's interaction with the criminal justice system. How we incorporate and give meaning and weight to these factors can change our focus and give us new, more progressive insights into criminal law. We will discuss the nature of an alternative to this approach in the third section of this chapter. First, however, we will turn

---

1   See Consultative Group on Research and Education in Law, *Law and Learning: Report to the Social Sciences and Humanities Research Council of Canada* (Ottawa: Social Science and Humanities Research Council of Canada, 1983). For a review of the report, see (1984), 16 Ottawa Law Review 218.

to a brief discussion of the types of questions and issues in the study of law which have been raised by researchers from other social sciences.

## 2.2 LAW IN THE SOCIAL SCIENCES

*Ross Hastings*

The traditional legal perspective is clearly a narrow and one-dimensional approach to the study of the emergence, maintenance and reform of the criminal law. This is unfortunate, given the importance of criminal law to the welfare of society in general and of individuals. It is also surprising, because the criminal law has long been a topic of interest within other disciplines, and is at the centre of some of the most important contemporary debates within the social sciences.

Sociology, psychology, political science and economics have all had something to say about the crucial issues of the origin and the impact of criminal law, and about the orientation and purpose of legal reform. More recently, the inter-disciplinary fields of criminology and of socio-legal studies have become focal points for attempts to formulate an alternative to the traditional legal perspective.

To this point, neither the discipline of criminology nor the field of socio-legal studies has produced a magical answer. For that matter, their biggest contribution to date may lie in the demonstration that the pursuit of a single, all-encompassing theory of criminal law may be the social science equivalent to a child's fantasy of grabbing the pot of gold at the end of a rainbow. Nevertheless, progress has been made. The key lies in the willingness of both criminology and socio-legal studies to accept and value the enormous and bewildering complexity of the criminal law, and to recognize the contributions that other approaches and disciplines have made to our ability to come to grips with this phenomenon.

The purpose of this section is to review briefly the contribution of each of these approaches to the study of criminal law. It will begin with a discussion of what the social sciences of sociology, psychology, political science and economics have made of the law. The focus will be on the different kinds of questions one might ask in attempting to make sense of law, and on the competing approaches one might use in attempting to answer these questions. This will prepare the ground for our discussion on how criminology and socio-legal studies are attempting to formulate an alternative and more critical, analytical perspective.

The issue of the origin and consequences of criminal law has been featured prominently within the field of sociology. The classic sociological authors of the 19th century were concerned with the general issue of how social order was possible in a complex and dynamic society, especially in the light of the dizzying rate of change that marked the transition to so-called modern times, and of the increasing competition and conflict which accompanied the transition to capitalism. Obviously, authors such as Karl Marx, Emile Durkheim and Max Weber developed very different answers to this question, but each focused on the social role of law as a critical dimension of any useful explanatory approach. Marx, for example, emphasized the role of criminal law in smoothing the transition to capitalism by "educating" people to the new idea of the value of private property and by eliminating or restricting the notion of common or collective rights from the criminal law. The legal basis of feudalism, with (for example) its notion of the rights of serfs to have access to common lands was inconsistent with the needs of capitalism, with its notion of private property and individual rights and responsibilities. The transition from one economic system to another required a shift to a legal system which was better adapted to the requirements of the pursuit of profit. Marx also argued that the criminal law, both in terms of content and enforcement served to protect and legitimate the interests of the more politically and economically powerful groups in society.

Durkheim was concerned with the issue of the relationship of law and social change. In his view, social order in modern society was characterized by a transition in the basis of social solidarity. Modern society was too complex, heterogeneous and differentiated to regulate conflicts through the traditional forms of negotiation and separation or restitution which characterized simpler societies. Such procedures reflect an informal and interpersonal world that no longer exists. The impersonal nature of modern social relations means that people deal with each other in a much more limited and specialized way. This requires a legal mechanism that will serve to regulate this process and to assure all participants that their rights and concerns will be protected. The formal criminal law is just such a tool.

Weber focused on law as an aspect of the emerging emphasis on rationality which characterized the modern world. His view was that social order, and the ability of the state to manage society, was based less and less on the direct exercise of power and increasingly on the formal legal authority of the state. People accept the law because they see the state as the legitimate representative of the collective interests. The threat to order, then, is less from invading armies from other countries, and more the inability of the state to generate a consensus on its behalf. The law plays a crucial role in both socializing the law-abiding citizen and controlling those who pose a threat. There are a number of other early sociologists who have made significant contributions to the sociology of law. The common thread to the sociological approach is an insistence on the social character of law. The criminal law does not emerge out of a set of abstract ideals. It reflects a strategic response by some individuals to very real and very situated conflicts, and it has very real consequences for the outcome of these same conflicts. The result is that the analyses of criminal law cannot be disconnected from the social situation within which it emerges and upon which it acts.

This theme is very much a part of those approaches to law which have characterized the fields of political science and economics. However, each has had a different emphasis, and has made a different kind of contribution to our understanding of the causes and consequences of the criminal law. In the case of political science, the emphasis has tended to be on the formal institutional mechanisms where the processes of the creation and reform of the criminal law actually occur. Political scientists begin with the fact that the criminal law is created by the state, and direct their attention to the formal procedures which are involved, and the informal exercise of power and influence that is at the heart of making or changing law. Thus, for example, there is a debate within political science over whether power is legitimately distributed among a plurality of social groups, or is centralized within a relatively small and very powerful elite. This has obvious implications for any understanding of why our society has the law it does. In practical terms, we will want to scrutinize the criminal law to see what its content reflects. For example, our laws on homicide and child abuse probably come as close as any to being a reflection of a consensus over the kinds of protection from violence we all want and expect in a "civilized" society. In such cases, the pluralist approach offers a reasonable explanation of why we have the law we do (though it is less satisfactory as an explanation of the selective application or enforcement of the law among different classes or ethnic groups). On the other hand, the pluralist notion of a neutral state which arbitrates conflicts among relatively equal groups provides a less satisfactory explanation of the content and enforcement of our laws on sexual assault (see Chapter 8 for a full discussion on this issue). It is becoming increasingly clear that the reform of the criminal law may be necessary but far from sufficient in order to improve significantly the protection of women from violence. A number of feminist authors have quite convincingly argued that the criminal law only focuses on individual rights (such as the right to private property), but it is not designed to address collective rights, nor is it able to redress collective inequality or exploitation (cf. Snider, 1988). A more convincing explanation of the situation of women can be found in the critical legal approach to the analysis of the relationship of the state to the legitimation and reproduction of class relations, and in the feminists' contributions to our understanding of the impact of patriarchy and sexism in the production and reform of law. We will return to these themes in the next section.

The field of economics has taken a quite different approach to the law. For the most part, economists interested in the criminal law have been concerned with the issue of efficiency. Their focus is on whether existing laws and practices are effectively serving their presumed roles of deterring criminal acts and preventing recidivism. For example, many of the authors within this approach have focused on the impact of our laws and practices in the area of sentencing. One debate is over the issue of judicial discretion in the sentencing of convicted offenders. On one side, there are those (usually of a more psychological or sociological orientation) who argue that judges must have the leeway to tailor sentences in such a way as to adapt them to the particular situation of the offender. This is necessary to maximize the ability of the criminal justice system to rehabilitate and reintegrate offenders. One might argue, for example, that an upper class corporate criminal does not have to be sent to jail, both because there is less danger to society in letting this person stay free and because this individual is a better prospect for rehabilitation.

However, a number of economists have been very critical of this approach. To begin, there is the obvious problem of discrimination: people guilty of the same act, and who presumably have caused similar degrees of harm to their victims, are treated in very different ways. This is not fair, and it is hard to reconcile this with our society's avowed commitment to the principle of equality before the law. More importantly though, for these economists, there is the very real question of whether this practice may actually contribute to more crime. Economists tend to adopt a classical or utilitarian view of behaviour. This means that they assume individuals rationally assess the potential costs and benefits of behavioural options before proceeding to act. If this is the case, the prevention of crime is largely a matter of making the perceived costs of crime higher than its perceived benefits. Indications are that the most effective way of doing this is by increasing the perceived *certainty* of being caught and punished. On this basis, judicial discretion and the resultant disparity in sentencing is counterproductive, for it reduces people's perception of the likelihood of having to pay for their crimes. In practical terms, this approach provides a fairly convincing explanation of why police roadside checks are a better deterrent to drinking and driving than admonitions by brewers to "drink responsibly" or than the rare (even if severe) sentencing of a convicted impaired driver.

The field of psychology has had relatively little impact on traditional legal approaches. This is somewhat astounding, given the contributions of psychology to our understanding of human perception and social behaviour. For example, the fundamental definitional component of a crime is the notion of individual responsibility (see Chapter 6). Psychologists have made enormous contributions to the explanation of the biological and interactional determinants of social behaviour, yet little of this work has penetrated the traditional approach (or, for that matter, the training of lawyers). Perhaps more importantly, it is psychologists and psychiatrists who are asked to determine those situations when individuals cannot or should not be held responsible for their behaviour. The area of defences and excuses for criminal acts is a major part of the Criminal Code (see Chapter 7). On a more practical level, psychologists have much to tell us about perception and memory which is of enormous relevance to the credibility of victims and witnesses of crime. Yet, it is difficult to detect in the Code, in the cases, or in most traditional legal scholarship, a sophisticated understanding of the debates in psychology over the extent to which individuals are relatively free to control their behaviour or determined by biological or psychological influences which they are relatively powerless to control.

It is clear, then, that the criminal law has been little more that the almost exclusive preserve of lawyers and the courts. It should be equally clear that it is impossible to develop an adequate critical understanding of the creation, application or reform of criminal law without acknowledging and integrating the contributions of other disciplines. More specifically, a critical legal approach must deal with the following issues:

1. How is law created? When do individuals or groups turn to the law to solve their problems or advance their interests?
2. What is the role of the state in this process? Does the state serve as a neutral manager of conflicts in a pluralist society, or does it serve or advance the interests of the more powerful sectors of society?
3. What are the consequences of law? Does the law serve the purposes for which we claim it was intended, or are there hidden agendas buried in the justifications and legitimations which are provided?
4. Where does the law fit in our everyday lives? Does it help to manage relations and resolve conflicts, or does it actually complicate and obfuscate social relations?

The following section provides a brief overview of the development and content of a critical legal studies approach to the criminal law.

## 2.3 THE CRITICAL PERSPECTIVE ON CRIMINAL LAW

*Ross Hastings*

In essence, the critical perspective seeks to overcome the limitations of the traditional legal approaches by providing a fully social perspective on the creation and application of the criminal law and on the process of legal reform. It rejects the limited and exclusionist orientation of the traditional approaches, and the monopoly of legalists in the field of law, in favour of a broader appreciation of the social production and legitimation of law, and of its impact on social relations.

Now, in an ideal world, we would be able to present a fully articulated and universally agreed upon version of the critical perspective. Unfortunately, the development of critical legal approaches has not yet reached this stage, and there are a number of areas and issues over which there is considerable disagreement and debate among individuals who nevertheless consider themselves (and their "opponents") to be critical legal scholars. We will address some of the main points of contention in a moment. For now, suffice it to say that the term "critical approach" is an umbrella concept which groups together a range of conceptual and theoretical options, some of which are very closely related and others which are competing if not contradictory.

There is, however, a general agreement on the goal of a fully social theory of law and reform, and on the necessity of adopting a dialectical approach if we are to be able to construct such a theory. The notion of a dialectical approach is, at one and the same time, one of the most complex and one of the simplest ideas in the social sciences. In its complexity, it harkens back to a complex web of ontological, epistemological and theoretical debates which are well beyond the scope or purpose of this text. In its simplicity, the notion of dialectic warns us against the adoption of any simplistic causal approaches to explanation. It is, in other words, the opposite of what is proposed in the traditional view of law as emerging and existing in a pure state, as some kind of neutral reflection of natural order and social consensus.

Instead, the critical perspective argues that the law must be analyzed and understood dialectically: the law is *both* a social product (it reflects and expresses the outcome of a specific, historically located set of social relations), and *at the same time*, the law has an impact on these same social relations (the law is, in a very real sense, a producer of social relations). The study of law must therefore be situated within the specific time and place, and in the context of specific struggles. This view of the law as both product and producer, as both outcome and active agent, is at the heart of the critical approach.

The remainder of this section will focus on how the critical approach has emerged and developed over the last twenty-five years. It will begin with a discussion of the emergence of the early conflict approaches, and the subsequent rejection of the traditional pluralist/consensus approaches to the creation and enforcement of law. It will then go on to discuss the main conceptual and theoretical options within the critical approach, and attempt to synthesize some of the key points of the critical perspective.

## A.  THE PLURALIST APPROACH TO LAW

The traditional legal approaches to the question of the creation and enforcement of the law are usually grouped under the heading of the pluralist or consensus perspective on social order and the role of the state. In this perspective, it is argued that the law reflects and encodes the consensual values which are most important for the integration and survival of society. Thus, we have laws against homicide because this type of behaviour represents a grave threat to our collective ability to sustain orderly and predictable social relations: such acts go beyond the tolerance limits of our society. On the other hand, we seldom bother to encode less significant social norms, such as the injunction not to eat with one's fingers or not to put one's elbows on the table. The law, then, is reserved for the embodiment and the protection of the most important of our consensually shared social values.

This, however, raises the question as to who decides when a value is important enough to require codification and enforcement. No one is naive enough to believe that this process occurs automatically or spontaneously. The pluralists recognize that it occurs within the social institutions of the state, and reflects the outcomes of the processes that characterize the modern state. To this point, there is little to distinguish this view of the state from most others. The differences are to be found in the pluralist view of how the state works. For the pluralists, the fundamental role of the state is to contribute to the survival of the social system by acting as a site and a mechanism for the resolution, or at least the management and control, of social conflicts. The state is considered to be relatively neutral in this process: its concern is not to take sides, but rather to guarantee that conflicts are managed in such a way that they will not threaten the overall welfare of the system. Pluralists argue it does this by assuring that conflicts are fought out according to consensually agreed upon rules and processes. The state thus functions as a referee or an arbitrator — it does not care who wins, it is only concerned that all parties play by the rules of the game. This approach tends to see the state as relatively open and accessible. This is not to say that power is equally distributed, or that all sectors of society have the same access to or impact on the state. It is rather that the state itself is not seen as having any particular axe of its own to grind. It is there to serve the common good, and to balance competing interests in a manner that will assure and advance the interests of society in general, rather than the interests of any specific group. Moreover, no one argues that the actions of the state always serve an absolute good. There is no doubt that certain laws, or certain patterns of enforcement, have differential impacts on different individuals or groups. The argument is rather that this situation is acceptable, perhaps even necessary, because it represents the best the state can do for the common good given the resources which it has at its disposal and the problems with which it has to cope.

## B.  ALTERNATIVES TO PLURALISM: CONFLICT THEORY

The pluralists thus see the state as operating relatively independently of the competition and conflicts which tend to characterize political and economic relations within a modern capitalist state. The early versions of conflict theory were essentially an attempt to "take on" the pluralists on this point, and to offer an alternative vision of the role of the state and the function of law. The conflict approach argues that society is socially constructed — it is produced and reproduced by individuals and groups engaged in social relations of competition and conflict over the allocation and control of scarce resources. Attention is thus shifted away from the notion of social consensus and towards the analysis of the competing interests of these groups and of their differential access to the kinds of political, economic and ideological power which are necessary if they are to "win" their way.

In this view, the state is an instrument: it serves the interests of the dominant social classes or the elites in our society. The pluralist notion of a neutral state that serves the common good is rejected as a theoretical explanation — the state is rather seen as an agent or tool of the ruling elites and as a legitimating devise that helps them mask their use of the state to advance their economic interests or to control the underclasses in our society. The law is an iron fist hidden within the velvet glove of this appearance of benign neutrality. It serves to patrol and police the borders of social relations in order to maintain the domination of the ruling classes and guarantee the safety of their investments and the advancement of their interests.

This is an attractive approach at a gut level. The problem is that it is as naive and oversimplified as the pluralist view which it is intended to replace. It has the advantage of alerting us to those situations of conflicts of interest and power which the pluralist approaches fail to recognize, much less explain. By the same token, it fails to account for those situations where there may actually be a degree of consensus, or at least where the state cannot be said to be serving the direct interests of the ruling elite. For example, while conflict theory helps us understand our laws on theft or rape, it would be more difficult to argue that our current law on bestiality is an instrument that makes a significant contribution to advancing the economic interests of the ruling elite. More importantly, conflict theory fails to provide a convincing theoretical explanation of the advances which have been made by the underclasses, or of the ability of certain minority groups to use the mechanism of the state to advance their interests, sometimes at the expense of the so-called ruling elite.

The point is that a simplistic conspiracy theory is not an adequate replacement for the pluralists' faith in consensus and the detached neutrality of the state. The conflict approaches did, however, have the enormous benefit of alerting us to the political, economic and ideological realities which underlie and shape social relations. The challenge for critical approaches is to integrate this awareness without falling prey to simple-minded conspiracy theories about the working of the state.

## C. THE EMERGENCE OF THE CRITICAL PERSPECTIVE

The challenge to critical approaches is to come up with a theoretical explanation capable of providing a convincing answer to the following two questions:

1.   How do social structures contextualize and limit social relations and human potential?

A critical approach to the analysis of law and legal reform must be able to appreciate the realities of class relations within modern societies, and to analyze the role of the state in sustaining and reproducing these relations. More specifically, it must address the issue of how the creation and enforcement of the law contribute in a strategic manner to these wider social processes.

2.  What can be done to challenge the existing situation, and to contribute to the reduction and elimination of all forms of inequality?
    The problem with both the pluralist and the instrumentalist approaches is that they provide little guidance for social reform. We need a theory which can be translated into realistic goals and workable strategies for social reform.

In other words, we need a theoretical explanation of law which will provide both an analysis of the creation and impact of the law, and some guidance as to the types of reforms which will contribute to social equality and the welfare of society.

The beginnings of such an explanation are to be found in the structuralist response to the limitations of the instrumentalist approach. The structuralists reject the instrumentalist view of the state. They argue that the idea that the state always acts at the behest of the ruling class is both overly simplistic and historically inaccurate. It fails to recognize that the so-called ruling class is not homogeneous, but rather is characterized by internal conflicts of interests which make it unlikely (to say the least) that it will always and everywhere speak with "one voice". Moreover, it recognizes that social power is not the exclusive property of the ruling classes. There is no doubt that power is not distributed equally in our society, or that the dominant classes are much more likely to possess or control the kinds of economic or ideological resources which will give them a better chance of "getting their way" in most situations of social conflict. Nevertheless, it is also true that the subordinate classes are not without power or influence of their own. The failure to recognize this reality leaves us unable to provide any kind of explanation for social changes which actually do recognize and advance the interests of subordinate or minority groups in our own society.

For the structuralists, the beginning of a more complex and more accurate explanation of these phenomena is a reformulated model of the state. The key to this new model lies in the rejection of the simplistic notion of the state as a mere instrument in the hands of those who have economic power, and in the shift to a view of the state as a site for the production and reproduction of class relations under capitalism. The approach begins with the common sense idea that the groups in power, or at least those groups who benefit from current social arrangements, will obviously wish to preserve and reproduce things much the way they are now — people are not likely to simply give away their power, resources and influence simply because somebody else feels that the current situation is "unfair". This brings us to the strategic question of how change might occur. The argument is that the state is the site where this work is accomplished.

The production and reproduction of social relations are complex and difficult. It involves two tasks, and part of the problem is that these tasks can often be contradictory. The first task or function of the state is to foster the conditions which will facilitate the accumulation of capital. For example, the Free Trade Agreement can be seen as an attempt by the Canadian state to make Canada more attractive to investors; their ability to pursue and increase profits is supposed to result in increased benefits for all. This accumulation task is not a simple one, given the complexity of modern capitalist economies and the internal contradictions in the interests of the dominant economic groups in our society. One need only look to the debates over free trade in Canada, or to the difficulties that Finance Ministers have in proposing budgets which will please all sectors of economic interests to realize that the role of the state is neither simple nor one-dimensional. In most cases, the policies and programmes of the state advance the interests of some at the expense of others. In this sense, the function of the state is not to serve as an instrument of some hypothetical homogeneous capitalist class. Rather, the state is seen as serving the more disembodied and long term interests of the accumulation of capital. This often means that the short run interests of certain groups of capitalists may have to be compromised or sacrificed. To this extent, the structuralists argue that the state in modern capitalism possesses a degree of *relative autonomy* — it is not merely an instrument, but has a sphere of power, influence and interests which set it apart, and sometimes in conflict, with the immediate interests of capitalists.

To this point, we still have a fairly economistic theory of the role of the state: in a sense, all that has been accomplished is to shift the emphasis from the state as an instrument of the ruling elite to the state as an instrument of capitalist accumulation. This is where the structuralists introduce the second role or function of the state. In their view, the state cannot foster accumulation unless it can also assure the role or function of legitimation. On this level, the task of the state is to create and maintain conditions that will foster social cohesion. The logic behind this notion is that capitalist accumulation is impossible unless society is well-ordered. The process of economic production is threatened by labour unrest or social instability; such situations reduce the likelihood that an investor will obtain a profitable return on an investment. In simple terms, investors will be scared off. This not only threatens the profit margins of the economic elite, but it also has consequences for the levels and types of employment in a society, and the quality of life of its citizens. In practical terms, one might try to imagine whether one would be more likely to invest one's money in a stable economy (like Canada, Japan or the United States), or in a society marked by high levels of instability or unrest (like some of the countries in Eastern Europe). Without denying that there are some of us who are altruistic enough to invest our money where it might do other people the most good, the structuralists argue that the capitalists' pursuit of profit will generally result in a tendency to put the money where it is likely to be safest and to extract the greatest return in terms of financial profit.

This legitimation function puts enormous pressure on the state to manufacture public consent to its policies and programmes. One might think, for example, of the massive selling job done on behalf of the free trade agreement in the late 1980s and early 1990s, or of the enormous investments governments now make in what is clearly a selling job on their behalf. The basic strategy of the state to accomplish this legitimation function is to attempt to universalize social interests, to create and foster the impression that the interests of the state in the process of accumulation are identical to the interests of the society as a whole. There are two approaches to accomplishing this task. On the one hand, the state engages in the process of education, where it takes on the ideological work of convincing people of where their real interests lie. On the other hand, the state backs up this educational work with a network of coercive institutions. These are the institutions which patrol the limits of society: their task is to rehabilitate and reintegrate those who have gone wrong, and to control those whose unwillingness or inability to play by the socially constructed rules in force constitute a threat to the processes of accumulation or legitimation. Those who are unable to get along are usually treated through medical or psychiatric institutions, while those who are unwilling to play along usually fall under the purview of the criminal justice system.

The law has a crucial role to play in both the educational and the coercive phases of the legitimation process. The educational phase of the process can only "work" to the extent that people believe that their interests are being served. The state must create the impression that it is neutral, and that its policies and programmes are for the general welfare of all, otherwise its ability to advance the interests of accumulation will be compromised. One component of this attempt to create an appearance of equality is the notion of the rule of law. The idea of the rule of law is that everyone will be treated the same by the state, that we all have the same rights and responsibilities. This democratic principle creates the illusion that the state treats us all the same: we are legal equals, with equivalent rights and responsibilities. However, this apparent legal equality masks the very real social inequalities of resources, power and opportunity which underlie it. We are educated to the belief that this legal equality is all the state can and should provide; the state should not be expected to resolve collective problems. The implication is that social inequalities of class or reward are legitimate, because they are the "fair" (and thus legitimate) result of a competition among individuals who had a relatively equal opportunity to succeed. The results of class competition thus are seen to reflect, for the most part, the ability and hard work of the individuals in question. Social situations of inequality, such as disparities on the basis of gender, race or ethnicity are recognized as problematic, but are usually treated through some relatively minor form of tinkering with the system (such as a public awareness programme or some commitment to a policy of affirmative action on behalf of the minority group in question). The argument is the system may not be perfect, but its blemishes and warts do not require major social surgery. To the extent that the law succeeds in convincing us that rights, responsibilities, and outcomes are individual affairs, the state is able to foster the legitimation of the current realities of inequality and class disparity, and thus to maintain conditions which are propitious for accumulation.

The second, and more obvious, impact of the law is in the sphere of coercion. If the "rule of law" is designed to educate and convince, the enforcement of law is intended to discipline and control. Once again, though, the law can only perform this function efficiently and effectively to the extent that it is generally perceived to be fair, or to treat everyone the same. Thus, the state must convince us that there are no hidden interests being served and that the law works the same for everyone. The typical response to this problem is a legal system which formally excludes certain behaviours for all members of society, but which in practice selectively enforces this formal code in order to serve its primary concern with the tasks of legitimation and accumulation. This is not a simple conspiracy notion of the workings of the law, nor does it assume that all the people who work within the criminal justice system are dupes. One can readily assume good will and good intentions on the part of all involved. This does not change the fact that the operation of the law is selective. Seemingly similar behaviours, such as theft by a poor youth and tax evasion by a rich individual are dealt with quite differently. The inappropriate behaviours of different social classes, such as drug use and abuse among the disadvantaged or among the rich, are not responded to in the same manner or with the same intensity. This is not to say that the rich are immune. For that matter, the appearance of equality is preserved through the occasional ritual sacrifice of some member of the elite who has over-stepped the limits of tolerance (although a cynic might argue that the sin usually lies less in the actual behaviour and more in the incipient threat of a failure of the legal system to respond to the maintenance of the appearance of legal equality).

The point is that the state, in part through the mechanism of the law, tries to organize civil and social life in a manner that sustains and reproduces current social and class arrangements. The law serves the cause by locating rights and responsibilities at the level of the individual rather than at the level of the collectivity (in technical terms, the individual is the juridical object), and in so doing contributes to the legitimating and masking of the real class interests that underlie social relations. The theoretical problem with the model, to this point, is that it tends to overstate the functional relation of law and the state to the abstract requirements of capitalist economies. Law and the state have a tendency to be reduced to structural necessity, and the real struggles which are engaged in by real agents sometimes get lost in the shuffle.

However, this is not a valid criticism of all critical approaches to the analysis of law. The theoretical solution to the problem lies in part in the concept of the rule of law, and in the related requirement for the state to appear neutral if it is to serve the role of fostering accumulation and legitimation within current social arrangements. The very functions which the state must serve, and the necessary tensions and even contradictions in these functions, result in the state possessing a degree of relative autonomy from capital. Its responsibility to manage civil and social life make it a site for social and political conflict. Class conflicts that might have been fought out in purely economic terms in earlier stages of capitalism are now displaced into the "arena" of the state — the state is the place where these conflicts are resolved, but its relative autonomy makes it an active participant (with its own interests and concerns) in the process of constructing resolutions to these conflicts.

The state can only carry on this activity to the extent that it is actually perceived to work, at least to some extent, for most sectors of society (events in the latter part of the last decade and the early part of this one in Eastern Europe provide an illustration of what happens when the state can no longer convince or coerce people into going along). In practical terms, this means that the requirement to appear neutral will sometimes require the state to act in a manner which is inimical to the accumulation of capital (at least for certain groups) or the legitimation of current social arrangements. Examples of such situations in Canada might be found in the institutionalization of medicare in the 1960s, or perhaps, in the ability of French-Canadian Nationalists to exert greater control over the government of Quebec. In both these cases, real changes have occurred from below, so to speak, as the result of the space that the tension in the roles of the state creates for the possibility of social reform.

What does all of this mean for students who wish to make some sense of the law in their everyday lives? The answer is in a series of injunctions about how we should study law. In our view, the law is a reflection and a result of historically situated practices and struggles. To the extent that this is true, it makes little or no sense to approach the law as if it were disconnected from these struggles. In this sense, the traditional approaches to law are clearly unsatisfactory. Their willingness to disconnect the law from social, political and economic realities leaves us with a sterile and dehumanized explanation of law. The critical view is based on the contention that real people make laws under social circumstances which they can influence, though not necessarily control. Any reasonable analysis of law must therefore start with an analysis of the social processes of constructing and applying laws, and of the historically specific social structures and social contexts which limit (but do not determine) the outcomes in question. The law is part of the wider repertoire of social and class struggles. Like any of these struggles, it must be understood as the emergent product of the structures which contextualize its construction, and of the agents who are responsible for the constructive work itself.

In simpler terms, we must see the law as both a product of social relations, and yet as having an impact on these same social relations. This dialectical appreciation of the nature of law means that our theories and explanations must always be specific to the workings of the law in a specific time and a specific place. The critical perspective, with its insistence on the roles and functions of the state, and on the place that the state provides for waging and winning struggles from both above and below, seems to us to hold the greatest promise for constructing the kind of theoretical explanation we have in mind.

What to do in practice with and within the criminal law and its processes continues to present real challenges to those who adhere to a critical perspective. Some attempts have been made to outline the possibilities and potential that particular struggles or programs may hold for leading to meaningful legal and social reform in order to overcome the negativism of earlier approaches and to chart a more positive, progressive course for the future, but much more work remains to be done. In this regard, see an early seminal effort in the Brickey and Comack article under "Further Reading" at the end of this chapter.

## 2.4 FEMINIST PERSPECTIVES ON CRIMINAL LAW

### Foreword: The Meaning of Gender Equality in Criminal Law*

*Dorothy E. Roberts*

* An excerpt from (1994), 85 Journal of Criminal Law and Criminology 1, at 2-5.

Feminist theorizing has grappled with describing the nature of differences between men and women and identifying the relationship of these differences to gender equality. According to this framework, the "difference" approach emphasizes gender disparities and advocates different treatment (sometimes called special protection) for women. The "sameness" approach minimizes the differences between the sexes and advocates the same treatment for men and women based on gender neutrality. Proponents of the "sameness" approach fear that acknowledging gender differences in power or biology perpetuates negative female stereotypes and roles. Feminists who challenge the male bias in criminal law risk similar charges of special treatment of both victims and offenders. Defining gender equality as "similar treatment" causes people to perceive some efforts to protect women from sexual coercion as paternalism. This definition of equality also sees paternalism in efforts to recognize criminal women's distinct situations in determining their culpability or punishment.

Other feminists demonstrated that the very framing of the equality inquiry in terms of sameness and difference ignored an underlying male standard, as well as the systemic subordination of women. they reconceived gender equality as a question of the distribution of power, rather than the differences between the sexes. Thus, the path to gender equality does not lie in either ignoring or glorifying innate differences between men and women. It lies in eradicating society's use of gender differences to keep women in an inferior political status. As Ann Scales observed, "[i]njustice does not flow directly from recognizing differences; injustice results when those differences are transformed into social and economic deprivation. Understanding the mechanisms of injustice requires attention to the operation of the law within the context of particular social circumstances.

Feminists examining criminal law should be concerned with uncovering the ways that the criminal law contributes to women's deprivation by continuing to reflect and protect patriarchal interests. Feminist scholars should use these discoveries to devise ways to transform criminal law into a more egalitarian system that respects all women as self-determining human beings. The ultimate goal is not simply to remove the aspects that disadvantage women, but to describe a feminist vision of criminal justice. Of course, feminists will forever struggle over the best course to take. It is essential, however, to acknowledge the power differences between men and women and then work to eliminate them. As Fran Olsen puts it, it is pointless "to pretend that men and women are similarly situated."

Two additional features are critical to the feminist pursuit of gender equality in criminal law. First, it must recognize that race and class shape women's confrontation with criminal law as much as gender. Race and class help to determine the criminal law's treatment of female victims of crime. For example, the social meaning of rape in America has centered on a mythology that defines Black women as sexual objects. White men's sexual exploitation of Black women during and after slavery was an instrument of white supremacy, as well as male domination. Further, the criminal law has enforced the racial meaning of rape by denying rape's injury to Black women. Angela Harris concluded about the history of rape law, "as a legal matter, the experience of rape did not even exist for black women." Contemporary American juries and law enforcement officials continue to discount the stories of Black victims of sexual assault.

Race and class also influence the criminal law's treatment of female lawbreakers. The punishment of criminal mothers, for example, reflects society's differentiation of mothers based on race and class. Prosecutions of drug use during pregnancy target poor, Black women because these women are subject to greater government supervision and fail to meet the white middle-class ideal of motherhood. Feminist scholars should explore the relationship between racism, class bias, and patriarchy in the criminal law's subordination of women. Achieving gender equality in criminal law requires eliminating racism and class bias from criminal law.

Second, feminists should do more than simply reveal discrimination against or preferential treatment towards women in the government's enforcement of criminal laws. They should also reveal the inequality that is embedded in the very definition of crime — an inequality which reinforces prevailing relationships of power. Laws criminalizing maternal conduct, for example, help to shape the very meaning of motherhood. As noted, the prosecutions of poor, Black crack addicts do more than enforce a neutral law in a discriminatory fashion; they also devalue Black motherhood. I observed elsewhere that "prosecution of these pregnant women serves to degrade women whom society views as undeserving to be mothers and to discourage them from having children. . . . Society is much more willing to condone the punishment of poor women of color who fail to meet the middle class ideal of motherhood. In the same way, laws that punish mothers for failing to protect their children from another's abuse often enforce a subordinating image of mothers as selfless beings. Courts often hold women responsible for harm to their children based on their role as mother, rather than the particular circumstances of the violence. Thus, courts discipline these women even though they are victims of the same violence as their children. These examples show that achieving gender equality in criminal law requires uprooting patriarchal views of women at many levels.

## Feminist Challenges to the Study of Justice*

### D.H. Currie, B.D. MacLean and D. Milovanovic

* An excerpt from "Three Traditions of Critical Justice Inquiry: Class, Gender and Discourse" in D.H. Currie and B.D. MacLean, eds., *Re-Thinking the Administration of Justice* (Halifax: Fernwood Publishing, 1992) at 21-29.

## Feminist Challenges to the Study of Justice

From her observation that every avenue of power in society, including the coercive power of the state, is in male hands, Millett (1970) defined patriarchy as "the rule of the father." Feminists since have disagreed about exactly how this power of men over women operates and is maintained. Although these writers themselves are increasingly dissatisfied with academic categorization of feminist theory, there are predominantly three approaches that systematically explore the nature of patriarchal relations to develop general theories of women's oppression (see Donovan, 1986; Tong, 1989). The first is liberal feminism, which views patriarchy primarily as operating through the unfair rules and practices of gender stereotyping, which perpetuate sex-role dualisms throughout society and disadvantage women. Liberals believe that these rules governing society are based on mistaken or outmoded ways of thinking. Because they view rules themselves as inherently neutral, liberals do not challenge the rules themselves but, rather, emphasize the need for their reform. Radical feminists, on the other hand, associate patriarchal rules directly with the interests of men. This is because they equate patriarchy with the benefits that men derive from the appropriation of women's sexuality and procreative labours. This appropriation occurs through heterosexual relations, especially those within the family. From this perspective patriarchy benefits men both individually and collectively, making it unlikely that they will relinquish privileges embodied by current institutions and the rules of operation of those institutions. Finally, reflecting the influence of Marxist theory and method of inquiry, socialist feminists reject both the liberal emphasis on the cultural sphere of ideas and the radical view of men as sharing a universal interest, arguing instead that we must identify the material basis for the oppression of women within social institutions. Beginning from Engels's recognition that history consists of both the production of daily life and the reproduction of generational life, within socialist feminist debates patriarchy is inextricably linked to class and embraces relations of production and reproduction (as well as the relationship between the two).

## Feminism and the Legislative Branch

Reflecting the emergence of the contemporary women's movement, the past two decades have witnessed feminist legal reform in Canada. Central to this struggle was changing the symbolic representation of women as juridic subjects. The British North America Act of 1867 — as the foundation upon which Canadian society was built — stipulated that only 'persons' could vote, be appointed Senators, or become lawyers and judges. Given that women were legally not 'persons,' they could not exercise these rights. While the status of women as 'persons' was won in the courts by 1929, this blatant example of legal sexism continues to remind feminists today of the important role of law and the necessary for its reform. Beginning in 1970 a growing body of feminist jurisprudence has identified ways in which law and its administration are biased against women, particularly in the areas of employment, the family, the Criminal Code and constitutional rights (see Atcheson, Eberts, and Symes, 1984).

The longest tradition of feminist legal scholarship is grounded in classical liberal theory. While 'enlightenment' philosophers such as Rousseau and Locke excluded women from rights of citizenship on the grounds that women lacked rational and moral thought, during the eighteenth century Mary Wollstonecraft argued that men and women have the same intellectual and moral core: When women do reason differently or incorrectly — as many feminist writers at that time believed they did — it is simply due to their lack of proper training. Following the enlightenment tradition, feminists linked the notion of natural rights with women's emancipation (see Rossi, 1973). Accepting the liberal view that law is inherently neutral, reformers campaigned for the elimination of stereotypical differentiation of women and men and for legislation making it illegal to discriminate against individuals on the basis of their sex. While U.S. struggles crystallized around the latter in the form of the *Equal*

*Rights Amendment,* Canadian feminist struggles focused primarily on the former. Family law in particular has been criticized for perpetuating the legal view of women as subordinate to husbands and primarily responsible for the raising of children (see Boyd and Sheehy, 1989). while the struggle for women to retain earnings and property upon marriage began in the nineteenth century, the increasing divorce rate during the 1960s made apparent the hidden costs of marriage to women. By assuming the unpaid role of mother and wife, women relinquish serious commitment to the labour force, becoming both economically and psychologically dependent upon husbands. With marriage being redefined — both in law and popular culture — as a union *not* binding for life, this dependency translated into a lifetime handicap for divorced women. This is because ownership of matrimonial property was legally interpreted as established through direct financial contribution. As a consequence, women found upon divorce that they were not necessarily entitled to assets acquired during marriage. On this basis women's groups across Canada became involved in a nationwide lobby for reform of family law. This struggle has been effective in eliminating references to traditional views of the 'proper' roles for men and women within marriage and the notion of the unity of the family under the legal identity of the husband. Reflected in the use of gender-neutral language, the terms 'husband' and 'wife' have become replaced with 'spouse,' and the word 'parents' has been substituted for 'mother' or 'father' (see Currie, 1989). Implicit in the outdated language is men's primary responsibility to provide a home and women's destiny as the rearing of children. The general effect of reform has been to redefine marriage as a contractual partnership of equal rather than a sacramental obligation. A similar approach resulted in these types of reforms in employment law and criminal law (see Burt, 1988; Baines, 1988).

As well as removing ideological language and assumptions that perpetuate social differences between the genders, patriation of the Constitution in 1980 provided the opportunity to enshrine the principle of equality in a new *Canadian Charter of Rights and Freedoms* (see Korne, 1983). Although successful, the struggle was not an easy one: Even in the 1980s sexual equality had to be negotiated, fought for, and defended at every stage. While Hosek (1983:295) provides an impressive list of demands that women's groups fought for but did not secure, sections 15(1) and 28 of the *Charter* express commitment to the goal of sexual equality:

> 15(1) Every individual is equal before and under the law and has the right to the equal protection and equal benefit of the law without discrimination and, in particular, without discrimination based on race, national or ethnic origin, colour, religion, sex, age or mental or physical disability . . .

> 28 Notwithstanding anything in this *Charter*, the rights and freedoms referred to in it are guaranteed equally to male and female persons.

With the security of this *Charter*, the efforts of liberal reform appear to have been successful: Most of Canada's laws had been scrutinized for sexist bias and women are guaranteed equal treatment both within and before the law. By the close of the 1980s, legal rights for Canadian women were basically secure. Through a century of struggle women can own property on the same basis as men; they have gained access to professions; they can vote in elections and sit in the Senate; three women now sit in the Supreme Court of Canada; and Canadian women have access to formal redress in the case of alleged discrimination.

## Feminism and the Judiciary

Despite feminist victories, by the 1990s Canadian women were becoming painfully aware of the difference between the symbolic value of law and the material effect of its application. Because the judiciary continues to be dominated by men and patriarchal attitudes about women, the interpretation and application of even gender-neutral laws have been a disappointing experience for Canadian women. A good example of the way in which patriarchal attitudes influence the application of law is provided by the refusal of women into the legal profession in Canada. Annie Macdonald Langstaff, one of the first Canadian women to apply for admission to the bar, was refused in 1915 on the grounds that "to admit a woman, and more particularly a married woman, as a barrister, that is to say, as a *person who pleads cases at the bar before judges or juries in open court and in the presence of the public*, would be nothing short of a direct infringement upon public order and a manifest violation of good morals and public decency (in Baines, 1988:163).

While present-day readers may consider this a 'quaint' reminder of Victorian attitudes towards women, our courts continue to interpret law from a white, middle-class male perspective, thereby discriminating against women. Boyle (1984) shows how sexual assault provisions in the *Criminal Code* have been interpreted and applied in a way that protects 'the falsely accused male.' She documents technical aspects of law that allow judicial discretion as a source of unfair judicial decision-making: the 'chaste/unchaste distinction' as a testament of the credibility of the victim who is reduced to the role of Crown 'witness'; the 'marital immunity' clause which was not removed until 1983; the requirements for corroborating evidence; and the tolerance of questioning the victim on her past sexual conduct and reputation. While these examples point to the clear need to improve the evidentiary and procedural rules in a rape trial, they belie the patriarchal definition of issues that accompanies sexual assault. In contrast to the reality that the majority of rapes are committed by acquaintances or relatives, the dominant view within the courts is that a 'rapist' is a stranger who physically coerces the victim to have intercourse. Cases that do not fit this model are not considered by the court to be rape, or else are subject to less severe penalties, as reasoned by Judge Cross (1975):

> One reason why the maximum punishment for rape is life imprisonment is that the common man considers rapists to be very wicked people. Someone who believes, albeit without reasonable cause, that the woman is consenting may well be stupid and insensitive, but he is not wicked in the sense which the rapist is wicked. . . . Let us consider carefully what the maximum punishment should be, and above all let us not call the crime 'rape' (in Manitoba Association of Women and the Law, 1988)

While this type of law finding has become the impetus for further reform of procedures of criminal law, the contradictory effects of liberal reform in family and constitutional law are only now becoming apparent. Adjudication of family law based upon the assumption of equality has in fact operating to disadvantage women. Removing references to women as economic dependents and notions that children are best cared for by mothers has resulted in diminished financial obligation by husbands for previous wives and children while improving the chances that custody decisions will favour fathers. The problem is that the image of the contemporary family as conveyed by reformed family law stands in direct contradistinction to the reality that many women with children are not employed, that the overall earning potential of women is a fraction of that of men's, and that women still carry the primary burden of responsibility for childcare irrespective of their employment status. As a result of the mere declaration of marriage as an equal partnership, women with or without children became expected to be self-sufficient, so that the administration of reformed family law has had the paradoxical effect of acting against the interests of individual women (see Manitoba Association of Women and the Law, 1988).

Unfortunately, some of the best examples of this contradiction can be found in decisions under the new Charter that blatantly contradict the spirit of equality. In 1986 a District Court judge invoked equality provisions of the Charter to strike down the Criminal Code prohibition against incest on the grounds that it results in a crime for men and not for women. Thus a man who had intercourse with his 11-year-old stepdaughter was acquitted because the Criminal Code did not apply to stepmothers who had intercourse with stepsons. In another similar decision, in 1985, a District Court judge found that statutory rape in the criminal code — sexual intercourse with a female partner under the age of fourteen — was of no force and effect because the prohibition applies only to men (both cases discussed in Mandel, 1989:258-9). Finally, a B.C. Provincial Court judge blocked a paternity suit by a single mother, declaring that all such suits are contrary to the Charter. In this latter case the Court of Appeal did find sex discrimination, but saved the statute in question on the grounds that it "provides a basis for shifting the financial responsibility for the child from the public to the private domain."

While it is possible to talk about victories for women secured by the Charter (see Baines, 1988), there are both empirical and theoretical reasons to predict the Charter decisions on equality will not be any less contradictory than the outcomes of law reform. Given these developments, it is not surprising that Canadian feminist legal scholars are becoming increasingly disenchanted with liberal-democratic notions of the 'rule of law.' Some feminist legal scholars have argued that women should abandon abstractions of law to focus more carefully on the actual results of law finding. Boyd and Sheehy (1989) thus call this school 'result equality feminism.' As an example, Smith (1986) maintains that all proposed legislation should be tested for its effects before its implementation. To ensure equitable results, the benefits and burdens should be measured against the group with the greatest needs as the norm. Radical feminists maintain that it is no mere coincidence that justice currently favours men's interests, rejecting the view that law is inherently neutral or that it can be used as suggested by Smith. Influenced by the works of U.S. psychologist Carol Gilligan and radical feminist lawyer Catherine McKinnon, radicals maintain that law itself is a masculine paradigm and male mode of action that necessarily supports male supremacy (see Greschner, 1986; Lahey, 1984). From this position, writers posit the need for an alternative morality — based upon the feminine principles of care, connection, and community — upon which law should be based. In this way, a bifurcation has appeared between an applied 'feminist legal realism' and a speculative 'feminist legal utopianism.'

In similarly assessing the disappointments of liberal reform, socialist feminists reject a narrow focus on law and law finding themselves. They argue that these processes can only be understood within the broader context of society and social inequality. They point out that the achievement of a formal legal equality does nothing to change the concrete relations between men and women. For example, Fudge argues that: "The success of this litigation demonstrates the courts' willingness to accept arguments advocating formal legal equality when issues of obvious symbolic, though of little material, import are raised. . . . However, the attainment of such formal equality does nothing in itself to further substantive equality for women either within or outside of marriage" (Fudge, 1987:514). From this perspective, socialist feminists argue that the limitations of legal reformism reflect the fundamental contradictions of a 'democratic' society stratified along the lines of class, race, and gender. As Marx noted, individuals can be equalized in law only by abstracting away the differences that distinguish them in real life. In this way, equality in law stands in contradistinction to the reality of the substantive inequalities that groups face in society. While some legal reforms undoubtedly enhance the immediate position of many women, we must not mistake legal reform as the solution to women's secondary position. No matter how extended and democratized, legal rights cannot address fundamental inequalities in society – inequities that can be addressed only through real material transformation.

## Feminism and the Executive Branch

In contrast to the expanding literature on 'women and the law,' relatively little work has bee done on the executive branch of the justice system. This is particularly true for women and prisons, especially within the Canadian context. For the largest part, this neglect reflects the fact that women are a minority of designated 'criminals' in patriarchal cultures. The Royal Commission on the Status of Women (RCSW), for example, reported that in 1967 women made up approximately 12.5 per cent of those convicted of indictable offences in Canada (RCSW, 1970:366). Reflecting the relatively 'minor' nature of their offences, 37.6 of these women received suspended sentences, 46.7 per cent received fines, while only 15.7 per cent were imprisoned. As a consequence, women continue to form only a small fraction of prison populations. Statistics Canada reports that women accounted for just over 17 per cent of adults charged with criminal offences in 1988, up slightly from 15 per cent in 1979 (Statistics Canada, 1990). Not surprisingly, one of the few books on women in the Canadian penal system is aptly titled Too Few to Count (Adelberg and Currie, 1987). Hidden by this focus on numbers, however, is the racist nature of Canadian corrections. The RCSW, for example, found that Indian or Metis women made up anywhere from 46 per cent (Oakalla Prison Farm, BC) to 100 per cent (The Pas Correctional Institution for Women, Manitoba) of women in prisons during 1966.

The relatively small number of women in prisons does not mean that policing is not an issue for Canadian women. A number of writers have documented the way in which women's sexual behaviour within both the private and the public spheres has been more closely scrutinized than that of men (Chesney-Lind, 1985/86, 1974; Geller, 1987). Reflecting this mandate, policing has focused upon, firstly the sexual behaviour of young girls through the 'status offences' of the old Juvenile Delinquency Act and, secondly, the public sexuality of adult women through the regulation of prostitution. Ironically, while the 'common prostitute' may be prosecuted for soliciting men for sexual purposes or even for loitering in order to do so, soliciting or accosting women for sexual purposes by men has only been an offence in Canada since 1985 and then only selectively enforced (Lowman, 1990). As a consequence, sexual harassment is a common experience for women, although it is not legally identified as a limitation upon their equality and freedom (McNeill, 1987; Kelly 1987; Jones, MacLean, and Young, 1986).

Even in cases of criminally defined assault women do not receive the full protection of the law through policing. While the actual number of sexual assaults on women has always been a matter of dispute, Statistics Canada reports rates of 10.2 and 28.5 incidences per 100,000 population for rape and indecent assault on women respectively for the year 1982. At the same time, this report acknowledges that only 39 per cent of sexual assaults on women ever get reported to the police. Even then, rape is showing the greatest increase in all violent crimes. During the decade between 1971 and 1982, the incidence of reported rape increased by 29 per cent. Against common patriarchal wisdom, women are far more likely to be sexually assaulted by someone they know — boyfriends, husbands, fathers, and other family relations — than by the proverbial stranger (see Green, Hebron and Woodward, 1987; Hall, 1985). Added to sexual assault is the recent recognition of the extent of wife battery in Canada. In the first national study of domestic violence, the Canadian Advisory Council on the Status of Women estimated that at least 24,000 Canadian women were battered by husbands or lovers during 1978 (MacLeod, 1980). It is now commonly accepted that one in the women living with men is battered every year (ibid.:16). Criminologists have subsequently expended a great deal of energy exacting the measurement of violence against women, especially by intimates. . . .

At the same time as they documented the widespread frequency of violence against women, feminists and researchers alike have noted that the police response has been one of non-arrest, in the cases of wife battery, and down-criming, in the case of sexual assault. Requests for protection by bettered wives have been dealt with as 'domestic disputes' — temporary and non-serious disagreements between partners, best resolved without police intervention. In the case of rape, researchers (see Clark and Lewis, 1977; Gunn and Minch, 1988) have found that once reported, complaints are more likely to be discounted by police or categorized as less serious offences. As a consequence of this practice, 30 per cent of reported rapes during 1982, for example, were classified by the police as 'unfounded,' compared to 6 per cent of all other violent offences (Manitoba Association of Women and the Law, 1988). Examining the handling of rape cases by police, writers note that victims deemed 'deserving' of patriarchal protection are young, chaste, and white (see Clark and Lewis, 1977). Reflecting developments in other advanced industrialized nations, therefore, women began to complain that policing operates to protect male offenders rather than their female victims.

As a feminist concern, policing highlights the contradictions inherent in the notion that there can be justice for women in a patriarchal culture. At the same time, because it shifts the struggle for justice from the ideological/symbolic realm to the real world of women, the issue of policing highlights the fundamental — and possibly unresolvable — differences between feminists as to the practical agenda. To liberals, police inaction is a clear violation of women's right to equal protection under the law, as guaranteed in the Charter. Accepting the view of law as symbolic of dominant values, liberal feminists have campaigned for the criminalization of domestic violence, arguing that mandatory arrest — as one example of a more positive policing practice — would act as deterrence. They further note that because individual policemen are members of the dominant culture, it is not surprising that they subscribe to sexist, as well as racist, ideologies concerning rape and wife battery. On this basis, liberals have campaigned successfully for programs of police education, the recruitment of female officers to work in particular with female victims of crime, and more sensitive handling of cases during their investigation.

In contrast to the liberal campaigns for reform of policing, radical feminists see violence as the 'normal' component of heterosexual relations. Characterizing violence against women by fathers, husbands, and other patriarchs as fundamental to a patriarchal order, radicals argue that it is therefore inherently contradictory to conceptualize justice in terms of men policing male violence against women. For this reason and as a result of sexist treatment by police, radical feminists working with victims of male violence in Vancouver, for example, refuse to liaise with police. While a radical feminist literature on policing in Canada is virtually non-existent, a number of important books on this theme have appeared in Britain. The writers point out that women are often the targets of policing mandates (Dunhill, 1989) and that because the police themselves benefit from the regulation of women it is unlikely that they will shed their sexist attitudes and behaviours. At the same time, the researchers do not find female policing to be an answer. Female recruits have been described as being as aggressive as their male colleagues if not worse (Mcauley, 1989; Heaven and Mars, 1989), while Radford (1989) argues that because the policing of prostitution and rape benefits the status quo, it is impossible for feminists to work with male authorities on terms that will not compromise women's interests. While it is less clear from a radical perspective how violence against women can be eradicated, most of these writers maintain that the current reality demands tighter surveillance and punishment of masculine aggression. Radical feminists in both Britain and Canada — as well as the United States — have therefore supported liberal campaigns for feminist 'law and order.'" As a feminist struggle for justice, the law and order agenda is defended on a number of grounds: Women only want the same kind of justice that has been given to other victims of crime; feminism is not responsible for problems with the current form of *male* justice, it only asks for the law to be applied consistently, against men; the use of criminal legislation against violence against women establishes the principle of women's dignity as a people by recognition of violence against them as a major crime; and, finally, although law will not diminish crimes and harsher sentencing will not alter the general picture, the use of the justice system can become an occasion for public debates that increase cultural and political awareness of violence against women (see Pitch, 1985:43).

Against this backdrop, socialist feminists have more recently called for a more holistic approach to feminist analyses of police (see Chapters 12 and 13). While not denying that the policing needs of women are real needs, these writers are alarmed at how the current focus upon violence against women can feed into a reactionary law and order lobby. Snider (1991), for example, is critical of how liberal and radical campaigns against violence against women have led to lobbying for new criminal offences, making arrests, charges, and convictions easier, and increasing punishment (1991:239). Elsewhere Currie (1990) explores how expansion of policing as the state's response to wife battery reflects the more general trend in Canada towards the 'institutionalization' of women's issues. Central to feminist critiques of male violence against women is the issue of unequal distribution of societal resources and power. Within a discourse that concerns legal rights, police protection, and criminal justice, this issue is transformed into a technical matter that can be safely met within the current system without any significant changes in relations of power. For this reason, the effect of intervention could well be the strengthening of the very same processes and institutions that give rise to the demand for justice in the first place. A further problem is that this intervention gives an impression that women's needs and their demands for 'justice' have been dealt with, so that in the public's mind feminist demands have been satisfactorily addressed, which makes it more difficult and less acceptable to criticize or lobby for more changes. In this way, while the need for protection from male violence is a real need, satisfying this need through policing or the courts has been conflated with solving the problem.

Feminism has provided us with a powerful set of conceptual tools we can use to gain a critical understanding of the nature of domination and inequality in society and of how these are legitimated within the administration of justice. However, if, as some feminists argue, the administration of justice is an expression of male rationality, then an analysis of the processes by which ideas are themselves the material through which rationality is expressed. When we recognize that ideas are conceptual categories that are discursive, and that these discursive structures are the filters through which reality is comprehended, it becomes necessary to investigate how these discursive structures pertain to structures of domination and their legitimation within the administration of justice. . . .

# Models of Justice: Portia or Persephone?
## Some Thoughts on Equality, Fairness and Gender in the Field of Criminal Justice*

*Frances M. Heidensohn*

*An excerpt from (1986), 14 International Journal of the Sociology of Law 287.

## INTRODUCTION

Questions about gender and justice are firmly on both academic and public agendas at present. What are, however, much less clear, are the basic assumptions which underpin these discussions. When, for example, courts are criticised for being 'unfair' or 'unjust', to women what, in feminist terms, does this mean? Do we have a benchmark against which justice for women can be measured? If not, can we construct one? How is this to be done? These seem to me to be quite fundamental questions which are often skimmed over or ignored. In this paper, I propose to examine what justice for women in the context of criminal justice may mean, what now exists, and what possible alternatives there might be to our present 'system'.

## JUSTICE

Criminal justice can be seen as a series of institutions and systems: (a) as a *moral* or value system where social norms are expressed, supported by penal sanctions and (b) as an *administrative* process, or processes, and also (c) as part of a system of *social control*; which has informal as well as formal structure and sanctions. In practice, of course, all these interact.

When we look at feminist critiques of criminal justice, the importance of stressing these interactions becomes apparent. Most criticisms focus initially on administrative practices: however, these are almost invariably linked to deep-seated assumptions about the roles of men and women and gender-appropriate behaviour. Often, there is a further crucial, socio-economic or other major dimension.

Several writers have criticized the operations of the police and the judiciary in relation to prostitution. McLeod's concept of injustice in the treatment of prostitutes has three levels. First she compares their legal and social status with that of their male clients who are neither charged nor stigmatized (McLeod, 1982, p. 22). She then notes that the unique system of charging and cautioning prostitutes threatens their civil liberties and infringes basic rights (p. 24). Finally, she points to the gender inequalities inherent in our society which make selling sex for gain a relatively attractive occupation for some poor women. (p. 146).

. . .

Similar analyses of criminal injustice to women have been offered in relation to juveniles. Harris suggests that girls receive supervision orders for lesser offences than boys (Harris 1985) and Chesney-Lind that they are punished for sexual misdemeanours which go unpunished in boys (Chelsey-Lind 1973) while Casburn and Parker *et al.* noted that the comparative rarity of girls appearing before juvenile courts led to them being handled as "doubly deviant" and thus waiting longer for decisions, experiencing more invasion of privacy, etc. (Casburn, 1979; Parker *et al.*, 1981).

We can then, I would suggest, summarise modern criticisms of criminal injustice to women as having three main aspects. These are:

(a) that girls or women are not treated *equally* with men and boys — when they are prostitutes, for example, or receive harsher sentences for the same offence;
(b) that females are *unfairly* or unjustly treated in relation to a concept such as 'natural justice' or 'human rights' as in the stigmatising of 'common prostitutes';
(c) that girls or women are *inappropriately* treated in relation to their offence and degree of blame — when their treatment is medicalised, for example.

Now such criticisms seem to me to be located well within the traditional framework of criminal jurisprudence. Indeed the principles they imply correspond closely to those of the 'classical' school.

I suggest calling this model 'Portia' because Shakespeare's heroine in *The Merchant of Venice* neatly encapsulates so many aspects of it. The focus of the 'Portia' model is clearly male and a rational, clear-thinking, procedurally competent male at that. The means of achieving justice are through laws and courts, in the present system, and there is only one world-view which is ultimately valid, that of white middle-class males. The concept of justice is one of legal equity.

Although feminist views on injustice have taken this rational-legal form, I think there are also deeper issues involved, a more profound 'hidden agenda' which we also need to explore. In both academic accounts and even more noticeably, in the views of women defendants and victims in the criminal justice system there is a sense of outrage greater than that which the violation of rational principles would justify (see e.g. Peckham, 1985; Hayes, 1985; Carlen, 1985). Are we then justified in saying that there is a particular female or feminist concept of justice which the criminal justice system of patriarchal society violates? If this is so, what would be special and distinctive about feminist justice: a just treatment of women?

## JUSTICE FOR WOMEN

"Women suffer from systematic social injustice because of their sex. . .that proposition. . .(is) the essence of feminism and. . .anyone who accepts it (is). . .a feminist" argues Radcliffe Richards (1980), p. 14.

Radcliffe Richards following the American philosopher John Rawls (1972), defines justice as fairness and tries in her book to lay down principles of sexual justice and practical rules derived from these. She is almost entirely concerned with *distributive* rather than *retributive* justice, i.e. with how resources are shared out in society, but she observes that: "questions of retributive justice actually reduce to questions of distributive justice" (Radcliffe Richards, 1980, p. 354).

In the course of her discussion of justice, she argues that: "a just society is one in which the least well off groups is as well off as possible" and that 'justice' in "this definition does not entail equality on average between men and women" (pp. 124-125).

As we have noted, much even of the feminist criticism of criminal injustice to women is based on assumptions about equality: women are unfairly treated when they are more harshly punished than comparable men, for the same offence. . . .

Even if the police, the courts and prisons operated with total fairness to women in their own terms (and I do not think that they do) they would still be part of a society which has fundamental injustices based on sex at its core. Three particular aspects are crucial: sexual inequality, the narrow stereotyping of women's behaviour and the distribution of power. Sex should not, in theory, need to be any women's destiny today. In practice, being born a woman is likely to mean being poorer, less well-educated, having a more routine job, carrying a double burden of work in and out of the home; above all having far less autonomy and far fewer real choices in life than being born to manhood.

Within the smaller social space and the lesser share of resources available to them, women are also confined to a narrow range of conventionally acceptable behaviour. 'Wives', 'mothers' and 'typical women' are alleged and supposed to act in certain ways. Some of the key assumptions behind sexual stereotypes are particularly relevant to criminality: thus males are said to be aggressive, females passive; women are thought of as 'naturally' devious and manipulative. Both these features of the social context in which justice is effected depend on a third: the power dimension. Ours is a society in which men are dominant and women subordinate in both private and public spheres — from Parliament to public houses, from the boardroom to the bedroom, power and control are vested in men and largely denied to women.

These features of society cannot be left outside the police station or courtroom when women confront the apparatus of criminal justice. Indeed, it is clear that they are present and pressing in many such situations. Carlen, for example, has pointed out the impossibility of fair and equal treatment for women offenders in her Scottish study because of the poverty, domestic violence and profoundly chauvinistic society they inhabit (Carlen, 1983), while Eaton has shown in London and Kruttschmitt in America that courts may take into account women's 'conventional' feminine behaviour and the informal social control which binds them in considering the sentencing tariff (Eaton, 1985).

Women who have been involved in crime do seem often to react to their experiences in distinctive ways which say a great deal about their perceptions of the 'fairness' of the system. Very few women offenders glory in their misdemeanours in the way some of the male colleagues do by, for example, writing self-justifying accounts of them. When women do recount their experiences, they are much more likely to deny their deviance and stress their virtues and conformity (see Heidensohn, 1985 for an analysis). . . .

I have already suggested that justice for women cannot simply be measured in terms of fair, open and rational treatment for them in the courts (i.e. the Portia model), although these are important dimensions, and our present arrangements do not always do women justice even on these terms. In addition, procedural justice has to be seen in its wider social context and in particular for women, in relation to the disadvantages they experience in society which makes them unequal to men even before they encounter the law. Now it can of course be argued that women are not the only social group to be so disadvantaged. Indeed it is very clear, for instance, that members of ethnic minorities, or unskilled workers or young people can often be in similarly disadvantaged positions. There have been protests and campaigns about injustice and bias, especially as these affect black people. There is however, I believe, a further and very specific way in which women are likely to experience and perceive the criminal justice system as unjust and that is because it is to them a peculiarly alien and unfamiliar world.

Few parts of our social world are quite so notably male than those of crime and its controlling agencies. Crime, according to official records and various other surveys and studies is overwhelmingly a male activity: over 80% of all serious offences are committed by men or boys. Females commit few serious offences and recidivism is far less common. Court appearances by girls and women are even less frequent: 90% of delinquent girls are cautioned even for serious offences. Men, too, predominate in the staffing and manning of the police and the courts. Women also have experience of the police and courts as victims as well as offenders and over several crimes are likely to feel some alienation and ambiguity. Thus in cases of rape and of domestic violence, police responses especially have been highly criticised as being unfair and unfeeling (Toner, 1982).

Women in general are not familiar with the criminal justice system, nor it with them. Indeed criminologists have coined the term "doubly deviant" to describe courts' view of women offenders since they transgress two codes: legal rules about crime and society's approved pattern for proper, conforming womanhood. There is also evidence to suggest that women find their penal treatment unfair for similar reasons (Carlen, 1985), but also too because their lower crime rates do actually lead not to better prisons but to poorer: women are incarcerated further from home, there can be little segregation of offenders, or specialised programmes. . . .

There is considerable support for the view that prison is a harsher and more unusual punishment for women than it is for men (Heidensohn, 1969, 1975; Giallombardo, 1966; Carlen, 1983, 1985; Expenditure Committee, 1978-1970). Among the reasons for this are that women lose more by imprisonment because their family lives are disrupted, their children separated from them and profoundly damaging stigma acquired. Regimes in women's prisons, while sometimes superficially 'softened' with cosmetic coverings of say choice of clothing, are often: "much more rigid than those imposed in the men's prisons" (Carlen, 1985, p.182).

In particular, a form of repressive resocialisation appears to be attempted in some women's prisons, emphasising the need for conformity to good behaviour and conventional femininity, yet in the setting of a corrective institution. Carlen (1985) has pointed out how confusing this is: "Women who have already rejected conventional and (for them) debilitating female roles are constantly enjoined 'to be feminine'".

. . .

Perhaps the reason women are most likely to find the formal machinery of criminal justice harsh and unfair is that most of them, unlike most men, are subject to elaborate and subtle informal social control. I have described elsewhere (Heidensohn, 1985) how pervasively this operates, with women being confined and controlled by their domestic ties, by patriarchal authority, by the division of public and private domains. In addition to this comprehensive and effective network of silken bonds, our society exhorts and prescribes good behaviour and conformity in women through magazines, films and television programmes, as well as the less ephemeral media of folk myth and legend, organised religion and popular culture. Women who confront the abstract system of formal justice are not only treated as 'doubly deviant' as women and offenders, they also experience 'double jeopardy' — they are likely already to have experienced the narrow confines and the informal, but formidable, system of sanctions which penalise deviant women.

Criminal justice is not only a matter of procedural propriety and fairness of tariff (although these are important); it also involves issues of social justice. This is true for all accused persons who may be disadvantaged by adverse social circumstances, but women experience two distinct sorts of disadvantages, which markedly affect their rights and their treatment: they are greatly *over*represented among the poor and the least powerful in our society while at the same time being rarely found to be officially criminal or as crime-control officials. Criminal injustice to women is, then, a compound of legal and administrative inequalities, such as in the treatment of prostitutes and of women who are role-deviant, and of social and sexual injustice. I am still measuring these on the scales derived earlier from traditional philosophical and legal notions, namely equality, fairness and appropriateness, the assumed comparison always being with men. Now I want to look at whether this takes us far enough and answers the questions with which I began.

When men campaign for improvements in their rights whether political, social or economic, their object has always been to achieve parity with other, more privileged *men*. It is rather surprising that arguments about equal treatment with women have hardly ever been used by men seeking redress of grievances. The case made in the 1960s against the criminalizing of private male homosexual activities was based on the concepts of privacy and lack of a victim. Comparisons were made with tolerance to adultery but not in terms of the rights of males and females. A few men have tried to use the Sex Discrimination Act in Britain, to equalise times for leaving work, for example. Women, too, have generally seen the rights of *man* to which they have aspired as being the same rights as *men* have had. This is the first, or 'Portia' model of rights and justice. There are other possibilities. One is to improve women's lot in *relation to their present position* but in a narrow and usually stereotyping fashion.

I suggest calling this the 'essentially feminine', or 'Persephone' approach, because it presupposes that women have certain inherent feminine characteristics different and requiring different treatment from the characteristics of men.

**Table 1**

*Models of Justice*

| Model | Values and Characteristics | System | Concept of Justice | Features |
|---|---|---|---|---|
| Portia | Masculine Rationality Individualism | Civic rights Rule of law | Legal Equality Procedural | Norm is male |
| Persephone | Feminine Caring and personal | Networks Informal | Responsibility Co-operation | Norm is female |

## PORTIA

Almost every feminist movement has sought to achieve the same rights for women as men enjoy. This is only realistic, for two major reasons. Firstly, as it is clear that men are the dominant, powerful group in all known societies, then obviously equality with the strongest is what anyone would seek. Secondly, domestically privatised and isolated as they are, women need access to the public sphere of politics and the market before they can achieve anything and this means access through and alongside men.

Even today, our judicial system is built around males, so that women who encounter it have to measure up to male-based norms and rules which may ignore for instance women's dependency on men or children's dependency on their mothers. Much recent public concern has focused on the sense of injustice felt by men who have to support their former wives, and English law has even been changed in response to this.

Yet many women also have such feelings even if they have not been as fully articulated. Scutt, for example, writing of her study of marriage and divorce in Australia notes:

> "Women have a sense that they are being treated unfairly because they cannot quantify the efforts that they have made, and think at times 'but I did do something that was worthwhile, didn't I?' 'Surely my efforts should be given some recognition in terms of property division?'" (Scutt, pers. comm. and see Scutt & Graham, 1984).

Alternatively, women may be tested against norms about proper female behaviour which are derived from (man-made) stereotypes of femininity. Thus the definition of some forms of murder as infanticide by the mother, or the recent establishment of a defence plea based on premenstrual tension may give some relative leniency to some women, but at considerable cost in paternalism and loss of autonomy to them and many others. Thus *if some women* are impelled to irrational behaviour by their hormonal urges, so the argument goes, then no women can be trusted to be rational and make major decisions. All female deviance can be then regarded as pathological, its source literally within the deviant herself. This was clearly the thinking behind the plans for the new Holloway prison when they were first mooted in 1968 (Faulkner, 1971). Although these plans have long since been overtaken by other ideas about women's criminality, generations of women prisoners have had to suffer their consequences (Heidensohn, 1975; Carlen, 1985).

The alternative for women to the strict rationality of this model is likely to be the use of narrow stereotypes of femininity. Certain actions may be interpreted as explicable because of assumed female characteristics and punishment may be accordingly less (though it will probably be paternalistic and may still be stigmatising).

However, women who fail to conform to expectations of appropriate female behaviours may be treated very much more severely, because of their failure to weep or to show maternal love or even to look 'feminine'. (Such allegations have been made about, for example, the cases of Ruth Ellis (Delaney, 1985), of Christine Villemin (Smyth, 1985), the 'Dingo baby case' and of Karen Tyler (Toynbee, 1986). The 'Portia' model is the most familiar and the most widely accepted model of justice. It is the one that most feminists take for granted in measuring and pointing out deficiencies in present provision and practices. Its flaws are admirably summed up by Scutt:

> "Women confront a legal system that professes to be attuned to the rights of all. It professes the ideals of fairness and equality. Many legal writers, judges and lawyers have concocted a jurisprudence that bolsters that false notion. Yet, as some men have recognised, 'fairness' is accorded only to those (that is, men) having the means to pay, and having the rights deemed worthy of protection. 'Equality' is judged according to the rule that 'some [men] are more equal than others'. It has taken women to press home the place patriarchal notions have in law" (Scutt, 1985).

## PERSEPHONE

If we reject the 'Portia' model and search for alternatives, we come of course into speculative realms. Modern feminist psychologists have proposed important changes in thinking about moral development. Several writers have worked particularly on new psychologies which could offer at least the basis of a new and better moral order. Miller, for example, argues that our present civilisation is built upon the historic subordination of women who become the 'carriers' of all the things: sexuality, emotion, creativity, managing bodily functions which men wished to repress and be dissociated from. In her 'new psychology' women have to recognise these qualities and functions as real strengths and add to them power and self-determination (Miller, 1978, p. 129). What is significant for our purposes in seeking new or alternative models in Miller's work is that she starts from a position of (re)valuing women and their experience and as a base for making moral judgments. As Eisenstein puts it:

> "the goal for women. . . should by no means be to learn to act like, think like and adopt the values of, men and the male-dominant culture. Rather, concepts such as autonomy, power, authenticity, self-determination — all of these should be re-examined and redefined by women. . .(Miller takes) the condition of women as potentially normative for all human beings" (Eisenstein, 1984, pp. 66-68).

Gilligan too seeks to redress the balance in studies of moral development by adding women back in. She describes men and women as having different maturing experiences. Men become detached, autonomous and individualised and take a: "rights conception of morality. . .geared to arriving at an objectively fair or just resolution to moral dilemmas upon which all rational persons could agree" (Gilligan, 1982, p. 21-22)

Women, on the other hand, take part in a different cycle of growth and attachment as soon as they are adult, they become responsible for the care of others and help them in turn to mature, thus perpetuating a cyclical pattern. In consequence, women see moral problems differently (she uses empirical studies to demonstrate this) and thus: "the psychology of women that has consistently been described as distinctive in its greater orientation toward relationships and interdependence implies a *more contextual mode of judgement and a different moral understanding*" (Gilligan, 1982, p. 22).

Gilligan calls this approach Demeter/Persephone after the Homeric myth of mother and daughter whose story exemplifies the cycle of fertility of sowing and reaping, conception and birth. She goes on to stress that men have a 'justice' model of morality, based on rights while women have a 'caring' model. Both, she argues, must be recognised because the:

> "two disparate modes of experience. . .are in the end connected. While an ethic of justice proceeds from the premise of equality — that everyone should be treated the same — an ethic of care rests on the premise of non-violence that no one should be hurt".

How might this translate into a new model of justice?

While women-centered approaches are obviously attractive and one can, on the basis of these writers' work begin to construct notions of justice and even practices, there are difficulties and dangers. The dangers, I think, lie partly in producing a version of justice which is welfare-based and individualised with the problems attendant upon it. However, the central problem is essentially one of *power*: it is possible, just, to envisage a separate, gentler, more sympathetic justice system exclusively reserved for women. That is, after all, what we already have broadly for juveniles: anonymity, informality, an emphasis on familial relationships and emotional maturity rather than strict notions of guilt. But just as adults control the juvenile court so would men still be in charge of female courts. Moreover, it strains credibility to believe that *men* would allow themselves or their peers to be subjected to a new, feminine morality and judgement. Women would thus, I am afraid, be two-fold losers; they might be 'infantilised' and they would also probably see what little influence they can exert over male behaviour through the courts lost. There are interesting avenues still to be explored within this model. It has also to be said that some recent developments in the criminal justice system do have Persephone aspects: community service orders for instance, exemplify an attachment and reparation approach, making the offender literally refurbish the social fabric. Again ideas of conciliation and of victim-offender contact and support schemes are 'outwith' traditional ideas of justice and stress 'caring' rather than 'rights' values.

## CONCLUSION

I have tried in this paper to explore some of the ideas about gender and criminal justice which feminists have increasingly offered us. Most relate to a traditional concept of justice as equality or as fairness, but there was clear evidence of a deep-seated dissatisfaction with such notions, since they ignore huge stretches of women's experiences and their discontent. However, the central problem of alternative, women-centred models lies in patriarchy — the male control of power and resources in our (and every other) society. Nevertheless, they can provide us with heuristic devices to explore and criticise.

There are in everyday practice, many questions faced by professionals, by policy makers, by lawyers and clients which may, I hope be a little illuminated by this discussion. Is it fair for example, for non-delinquent girls to join Intermediate Treatment programmes? Is it fair for them not to? Should rape victim and accused both be anonymous? Should adult female offenders mix with youth custody cases for their own good?

There is also a list of sensible items to be considered when we face the real, sad everyday world:

1.  Even in its own narrow terms, the 'Portia' model can be criticised and evaluated, procedurally and in principle. Courts, for example, have been imprisoning prostitutes for not paying fines. Edwards has criticised defence barristers whose questioning of rape victims is doubtful and seems designed to destroy the victim's character and, in her view, breaks the Bar's code of conduct.
2.  A certain amount can be achieved by education and politics — 'consciousness raising' has clearly helped the introduction of different approaches to rape.
3.  Any new criminal justice or penal measure should, as a matter of routine, be examined for its impact on gender.
4.  While a separate *judicial* system for women is not feasible, and probably not viable, a separate and very different *penal* system is. This might involve small, well-scattered houses or hostels, with good community links and support.

Criminal justice for women involves, as it does for men, social justice too. Whichever model we take needs power and resources to make it work. What an exercise like this reminds us of is that women in our courts, police stations, etc. experience the stigma of 'double deviance' and risk the penalties of double jeopardy. They are fairly helpless before these hazards since they are not of their making or choosing. Little by little, grain of sand by grain of sand things may be changing. Nevertheless, while this is a man's world it will be his concept of justice which will prevail and his will be the one women have to use.

### References
* Baldwin, J. & Bottomley, A.K. (1978) *Criminal Justice*. Martin Robertson: London.
* Carlen, P. (1983) *Women's Imprisonment*. Routledge and Kegan Paul: London.
* Carlen, P. (Ed.), (1985) *Criminal Women*. Polity Press: Oxford.

- Casburn, M. (1979) *Girls Will be Girls*. W.R.R.C.; London.
- Chesney-Lind, M. (1973) Judicial enforcement of the female sex role. *Issues in Criminology 51-69.*
- Delaney, S. (1985) *Observer*, 3 March 1985.
- Eaton, M. (1985) Documenting the defendant: placing women in social inquiry reports. In *Women in Law* (Brophy J. & Smart, C., Eds). Routledge and Kegan Paul: London.
- Edwards, S. (1981) *Women on Trial*. Manchester University Press: Manchester.
- Eisenstein, H. (1984) *Contemporary Feminist Thought*. Unwin: London.
- Expenditure Committee (1978-1979) *Education, Arts and Home Affairs Sub-Committee of the Expenditure Committee; Women and the Penal System.* Evidence in Vols 61-i to 611-xiv.
- Faulkner D.E.R. (1971) The redevelopment of Holloway Prison. *Howard Journal of Penology and Crime Prevention* 13(2).
- Giallombardo, R. (1966) *Society of Women: a study of a Women's Prison.* Wiley: Chichester.
- Gilligan, C. (1982) *In a Different Voice*. Harvard University Press: Cambridge.
- Harris, R. (1985) Towards just welfare. *British Journal of Criminology*, 25.
- Hayes, J. (1985) *My Story*. Brandon: Kerry.
- Heidensohn, F. (1969) Prison for women. Howard Journal.
- Heidensohn, F. (1975) The imprisonment of females. In *The Use of Imprisonment* (McConville, S.: Ed.) Routledge and Kegan Paul: London pp. 43-56.
- Heidensohn, F. (1985) *Women and Crime*. Macmillan: London.
- McLeod, E. (1982) *Women Working: Prostitution Now*. Croom Helm: London.
- Parker, H., Casburn, M. & Turnbull, D. (1981) *Receiving Juvenile Justice*. Blackwell: Oxford.
- Peckham, A. (1985) *A Woman in Custody*. Fontana: London.
- Player, E. (1986) Women's imprisonment: the effects of youth custody. *British Journal of Criminology* (in press).
- Rawls, J. (1972) *A Theory of Justice*. Oxford University Press.
- Radcliffe Richards, J. (1980) *The Sceptical Feminist*. Pelican: Harmondsworth.
- Scutt, J. & Graham, D. (1984) *For Richer, For Poorer: Money, Marriage and Property Rights*. Penguin: Ringwood.
- Scutt, J. (1985) In pursuit of equality: women and legal thought 1788-1984. In *Women, Social Science and Public Policy* (Goodnow, J. & Pateman, C. Eds) Academy of Social Sciences: Australia.
- Smyth, R. (1985) *Observer*, 11 August 1985.
- Toner, B. (1982) *The Facts of Rape*. Arrow Books: London.
- Toynbee, P. (1986) *Guardian*, 17 March 1986.

## 2.5 HISTORICAL PERSPECTIVES ON CRIMINAL LAW

*Barry Wright*

Careful and rigorous historical inquiry tends to confirm many of the suggestions made by scholars doing critical research on modern crime, criminal law and its administration. History, first of all, underlines the relativity of what is defined as crime. The types of behaviour considered criminal, especially when it comes to property offences, have changed considerably over time. The industrial revolution, for instance, transformed property interests, exchange relationships and ways of doing business. New crimes emerged to secure the changing economic realities (Linebaugh, 1985). There has been less change in the definition of violent offences, although there are notable examples such as the ending of the spousal immunity rule in cases of rape in 1983. For all offences there have been important transformations in how they have been administered, reflecting the impact of prevailing cultural, patriarchal and socio-economic influences on power.

History reveals interesting transitions and developments in criminal law institutions. Despite the medieval origins of the public adversarial jury trial, many people are surprised to discover that the basic institutions at the beginning and end of the modern "criminal justice system" — the police and the penitentiary — are relatively recent additions to the system. Law enforcement, including detection, apprehension and prosecution depended largely on private initiative until the early nineteenth century and the controversial establishment of trained "professional" police, which increased the state's surveillance and crime prevention functions enormously (Storch, 1975; Emsley, 1987). Until this period as well, capital punishment governed most serious offences known as felonies, although it was often mitigated by jury verdicts and more importantly, official discretionary pardons made conditional on secondary punishments such as transportation. Minor offences known as misdemeanours were punished by a variety of corporal punishments, fines and occasionally, time in "houses of correction". There were also "gaols" for accused persons awaiting trial but imprisonment was not considered a penal option for convicted serious offenders. In a remarkably short period of time, in the early nineteenth century, capital penalties were repealed and the penitentiary transformed the administration of punishment (Ignatieff, 1985). Discretionary physical punishment and examplary public hangings became less important than the effective disciplinary "processing" of convicted offenders, justified in terms of certain punishment (which for utilitarian reformers was more effective for deterrence than severity of punishment) and the possibilities of rehabilitation.

Transformation, although at a somewhat slower pace, also took place in the criminal trial that lay in between these new disciplinary mechanisms. Prosecutorial authority increasingly became public, as the Crown extended control over the management of routine criminal prosecutions, displacing the private prosecutor by the mid 19th century. Lawyers "colonized" the criminal trial increasingly after the mid 18th century, reducing the victim and the accused to a passive role. The emergence of lawyers as the "motor force" of the trial resulted in the elaboration of procedural and evidentiary rules. Despite the traditional popular assumptions, not to mention those of the legal profession, these innovations did not evolve over centuries through some sort of gradual internal innovation and improvement. Nor did they have much to do with some sort of response to "moral decline." They were tied up with dramatic social change, political crises and ambitious new strategies of power.

These are obviously very broad brush-strokes and those who research the history of crime and criminal law present accounts which are much more complex and detailed. And it should be stressed that there is much contentious historical debate and a variety of interpretations concerning the details of these developments. This reflects the nature of the historical enterprise. It is not an objective science. It is subject to the research limits of the archival records and the interpretative limits of the historian. A variety of interpretations result, some of which are more compelling and rigorous than others. Despite this variety, most serious historians agree that the criminal law and its administration cannot be understood in isolation from social forces and political and economic context. It is not surprising that most of the impetus for the recent proliferation of historical research on criminal law comes not so much from legal scholarship (with its preoccupation with technical doctrine) but from social history, political economy and criminology.

With these *caveats* in mind about over-generalization and related concerns about teleological presentism (judging past events from present day standards rather than those of the period), a brief chronological sketch of developments in criminal law may be set out in terms of the medieval and early modern period, the seventeenth and eighteenth centuries, and finally the nineteenth century when the system as we know it today took shape. It should be noted that the focus is necessarily English criminal law. Canadian provinces "received" English criminal law and English institutional models in the colonial period and our *Criminal Code* which was later developed by the federal government was significantly influenced by Stephen's Draft English Code. The Canadian "content" of our criminal law did not so much arise out of creative innovation but out of necessities of particular Canadian conditions.

After the Norman conquest of 1066 criminal law played an important role in consolidating the power of the new state. Very quickly criminal law came to be regarded as something more than involving the victim or the peace of the local community. Crimes came to be seen as violations of an ambitious new notion, the King's peace. Doctrinally, this led to the separation between torts and those harms seen as breaches of the King's peace — the felony and misdemeanour offences. These criminal offences were tried in royal courts set up in the counties, supervised by the King's local agent — the justice of the peace, who also presided over trials for misdemeanours and organized felony proceedings to be presided over by royal justices on the assize circuits. Trials proceeded adversarially and to deal with the weighing of proof, the jury of local upstanding citizens was devised with the responsibility of delivering the verdict. The political dimensions of these developments are difficult to ignore: the King's peace represented the hegemony of royal power and matters that threatened disorder, the apparatus of the royal courts and the justice of the peace extended administrative presence throughout the countryside, and even the jury may be seen as a way of co-opting local power by involving it in the processes of royal justice.

Arguably, the elaboration of the criminal law system was more important than armed occupation in ensuring long term order and stability. However, over the centuries the formal claims of the law and the personnel in the system sometimes became obstacles, especially as royal rule became more arbitrary. Juries, for instance, would use their power on the verdict to give decisions according to conscience, thereby nullifying the law and indirectly voicing popular protest against oppressive laws or prosecutions. The Court of Star Chamber, originally a mechanism to bring order to common law, was used to by-pass the political inconveniences of regular criminal trials by jury. The political conflicts that led to the English Revolution, the constitutional resolutions of 1689 and later the Act of Settlement had important implications on the administration of criminal law. All citizens had the right to trial by jury, the crown prerogatives on prosecutions were to be exercised circumspectly and judicial tenure was placed on good behaviour rather than royal pleasure.

As a result of these advances the overtly political uses of the criminal law could indeed be increasingly contested using the formal claims derived from constitutional advances which further secured the rule of law. The emergence of a defence bar, notably lawyers such as Thomas Erskine and William Garrow, successfully battled political prosecutions to support political liberties and won important advances for the rights of the accused. Nonetheless, the 18th century saw the criminal law employed in new ways to reinforce the authority of the ruling classes. The administration of criminal law became an important site where ideological functions of the state were developed and refined. Douglas Hay's remarkable synthesis of this period underlines the important role of criminal proceedings in shaping the climate of popular thought. Hay's complex analysis demonstrates how the majesty of the assizes and the claims of justice were balanced with the wide exercise of discretion (mercy through the conditional pardon) in a manner which masked the material interests of the powerful and helped legitimate their authority (Hay, 1975; see also Langbein, 1983 and Linebaugh, 1985). It was an approach which could not survive the pressures created by the industrial revolution. The creation of new property offences and the vast increase in the number of offences punishable by death created huge pressures on the criminal courts. The new definitions of crime were compounded by objective increases in crime caused by the socio-economic dislocations of urbanization, the uncertainties of wage labour and the increased criminal opportunities of city existence. There was an increasing gulf between the terrifying claims of the law (wide ranging capital offences) and its inconsistent application (although felony convictions increased tremendously, not all could be hanged and ever greater numbers of convicts were transported to a penal colony after receiving a conditional pardon.)

As suggested at the outset, the early nineteenth century saw a transformation in criminal law doctrine and its administration. Law enforcement was professionalized, capital offences were radically reduced and punishment became more certain and proportional to the gravity of the offences. Obstensibly utilitarian or humanitarian reforms swept through the system, reaching from the creation of the professional police, changes to prosecutions and trial procedures, through to the creation of the penitentiary for serious offenders. Although in whig accounts the early nineteenth century in England was an era of rational criminal law reform in the name of efficiency and humanitarianism, the progress was not entirely benevolent. The social discipline of criminal law, with new institutions such as police and the penitentiary, reached greater numbers more effectively than was ever possible before (McGowan, 1983).

It is at this point that we can finally shift to Canada. English criminal law and its institutional models were adopted in Canada during the early part of these reforms in England. The British North American colonies obviously had different social problems that an England pre-occupied with urban difficulties and an industrial working class. They nonetheless continued to slavishly follow English developments. When the provinces first developed their own legislatures and courts they formally received English law as the core of their own laws. Thereafter, they could amend or elaborate this core doctrine according to local conditions. This took place in Upper Canada, for instance, in 1792. In 1833 the province adopted forty years' worth of wide-ranging English doctrinal innovations in a single legislative package and construction was commenced on the Kingston penitentiary despite the fact that there was no serious crime problem. The province's ruling elite seemed to embrace the ambitious new criminal law strategies in an attempt to bolster its power (Taylor, 1979). After the Dominion of Canada was established in 1867, consolidation of provincial criminal laws into a national criminal code became part of Sir John A. Macdonald's "national policy" (along with the creation of the North West Mounted Police and an array of economic measures to help secure the vast north west previously governed by the Hudson Bay Company). Canada eventually developed a criminal code in 1892, unlike England, but according to colonial form our code was based on a bill drafted by James Fitzjames Stephen for an English code which failed to get a majority at Westminster (Parker, 1981, Brown, 1989).

There are, of course, important Canadian stories based on a diverse population's particular experiences with the criminal law. The imperial imposition of a system of British law over both the indigenous approaches of native peoples and a pre-existing French legal system, and the resulting uses of criminal law to subjugate diverse groups perceived to stand in the way of national development, is an important theme here (Phillips, Loo and Lewthwaite, 1994). Canadian governments have frequently used the criminal law to deal with perceived national security threats, reflecting loyalist anxieties in the colonial period, anxieties which after confederation were articulated in the form of the Dominion government's powers over "peace, order and good government". The historical record suggests that our governments have apprehended insurrection all too easily, rarely coming under critical scrutiny, perhaps because of Canadians' traditional "deference to authority" (Greenwood and Wright, 1996).

Historical perspectives on the criminal law illustrate the true complexity of the role of criminal law in the exercise of power. History provides us with empirical evidence to support a skepticism which causes us to question assertions that the criminal law comes into being according to consensus and is administered in a democratically accountable manner. It also supports a skepticism towards opposite assertions which reduce the criminal law to an instrument manipulated according to class-interested ends. The uses of criminal law cannot be reduced to the same thing as resorting to state sanctioned violence or military intervention. The state may favour criminal law over brute coercion in order to lend legitimacy to its perceptions and interventions. Such legitimacy is lost if the law is too blatantly manipulated for partisan ends. For this reason criminal proceedings can sometimes be a site of "counter-hegemonic' struggle against authority. History demonstrates both the importance and the complex role of criminal law in the exercise of power.

## Bibliography

- D.H. Brown, The Genesis of the Canadian Criminal Code of 1892 (Toronto, 1989)
- D.O. Carrigan, *Crime and Punishment in Canada: A History* (Toronto, 1991)

- F.M. Greenwood and B. Wright eds., *Canadian State Trials Volume One: Law, Politics and Security Measures, 1607-1837* (Toronto, 1996)
- D. Hay, "Property, Authority and the Criminal Law" in Hay, Linebaugh, Thompson *et al, Albion's Fatal Tree* (New York, 1975)
- M. Ignatieff, "State, Civil Society and Total Institutions: A Critique of Recent Social History of Punishment" in Sugarman ed., *Legality, Ideology and the State* (New York, 1985)
- J. Langbein, "Albion's Fatal Flaws" (1983) 98 *Past and Present*, 96
- P. Linebaugh, "(Marxist) Social History and (Conservative) Legal History: A Reply to Professor Langbein" (1985) 60 *New York L.R.* 242.
- R. McGowan, "The Image of Justice and Reform of the Criminal Law in Early Nineteenth Century England" (1983) 32 *Buffalo Law Review*, 89
- R.C. MacLeod ed., *Lawful Authority: Readings on the History of Criminal Justice in Canada* (Toronto, 1988)
- G. Parker, "The Origins of the Canadian Criminal Code" in D.H. Flaherty ed., *Essays in the History of Canadian Law Volume 1* (Toronto, 1981)
- J. Phillips, T. Loo, and S. Lewthwaite eds, *Essays in the History of Canadian Law Volume V: Crime and Criminal Justice* (Toronto, 1994)
- W. Pue and B. Wright eds., *Canadian Perspectives on Law and Society: Issues in Legal History* (Ottawa, 1988)
- M. Storch, "The Plague of Blue Locusts" (1975) 20 *International Review of Social History*, 61
- C. J. Taylor, "The Kingston Ontario Penitentiary and Moral Architecture" (1979) 12 *Histoire sociale/Social History*, 385

## Questions/Discussion

1. How would a pluralist, a conflict theorist or a critical theorist view the content and enforcement of criminal law? What would be the major points of debate in their respective analyses of the criminal law in the areas of theft, homicide and industrial pollution?
2. How would a pluralist and a critical theorist differ in their approaches to the reform of the laws which regulate behaviours in the area of morality (for example, homosexuality or drugs)?
3. What are the contributions of feminist approaches to the analysis and reform of the criminal law? How do these approaches differ from traditional legal approaches to criminal law?
4. What is the relevance of historical perspectives on criminal law and reform? Is it useful to be informed by the past when we consider changes to the present system?

## Further Reading

- Abella, R., "Equality, Human Rights, Women and the Justice System" (1994), 39 McGill Law Journal 489.
- Bierne, P. and R. Quinney, eds., *Marxism and Law*. (Toronto: Wiley, 1979).
- Brickey, Stephen and Elizabeth Comack, "The Role of Law in Social Transformation: Is a Jurisprudence of Insurgency Possible?" (1987), 2 Canadian Journal of Law and Society 97.
- Brockman, J., " 'Resistance by the Club' to the Feminization of the Legal Profession" (1992), 7 Canadian Journal of Law and Society 47.

- Collins, H. *Marxism and Law* (Toronto: Oxford University Press, 1982).
- Currie, E., "Crime and the Conservatives" (Fall 1985) *Dissent* 427.
- Fitzgerald, M., *et al., Crime and Society: Readings in History and Theory* (London: RKP and Oxford University Press, 1981).
- Mandel, Michael, *The Charter of Rights and the Legalization of Politics in Canada* (Toronto: Thomson Educational Publishing, 1994).
- Nelken, D., "Critical Criminal Law" (1987), 14 Journal of Law and Society 105.
- O'Reilly-Fleming, Thomas, ed., *Post-Critical Criminology* (Toronto: Prentice-Hall Canada, 1996).
- Reiman, J., *The Rich Get Richer and the Poor Get Prison 5th ed.* (Toronto: Allyn and Bacon, 1998).
- Russell, M., "A Feminist Analysis of the Criminal Trial Process" (1989/90), 3 Canadian Journal of Women and the Law 552.
- Russell, Stuart, "The Failure of Postmodern Criminology" (1997), 8 Critical Criminology 61.
- Smart, C., "Feminism and Law: Some Problems of Analysis and Strategy" (1986), 14 International Journal of the Sociology of Law 109.
- Smart, C., *Women, Crime and Criminology: A Feminist Critique* (London: Routledge, 1967).
- Snider, L., "Feminism, Punishment and the Potential of Empowerment" (1994), 9 Canadian Journal of Law and Society 75.
- Snider, L., "The Potential of the Criminal Justice System to Promote Feminist Concerns." Paper presented to the American Society of Criminology (Chicago: November, 1988).

# 3

# THE PRODUCTION OF CRIMINAL LAW

## General Introduction

*R.P. Saunders*

This chapter examines the authoritative sources of criminal law and the problems, issues and concerns associated with both the evolution and the current production of criminal law in Canada. The history of the development of criminal legislation and criminal common law is not a particularly illustrious one in this country and we will examine some of the continuing issues and factors which have led to and continue to create various problems in the area. The focus throughout the chapter is on the processes and the institutions which produce criminal law. In this regard, it should be stressed that we are not exhaustive in our approach to the production of criminal law, for while we focus on two of the principal sources of criminal law — Parliament and the courts — we largely ignore (at least for the moment) another important source in the development of criminal law, that is, administrative law. A fourth source, constitutional law, is examined within the specific context of the role and powers of the courts to make criminal law, and again in Chapter 7 in reference to the developing area of Charter defences.

In regard to administrative law, the effect of the multitude of administrative regulations, internal guidelines, bureaucratic procedures and employee manuals is important and often determining, and should not be forgotten when looking at the more traditional and often more formal aspects of the production of criminal law. This is particularly true in the areas of probation, parole, and prisoners' rights, some of which we examine later in this text. In a similar vein, we must not forget the effects of the exercise of an individual agent's discretion on the operation and enforcement of the law, and we must keep in mind that although the criminal law often appears "neat", self-contained and discrete in its formal manifestations such as legislation and court pronouncements, the reality for the individual involved in the criminal justice system, whether as an accused, a victim, a witness or an agent of the system, can be something very different. Also, such realities can be coloured by the status, gender, class, ethnicity, sexual orientation, language, education and/or past relationship of the individuals involved. We return to many of these issues surrounding the exercise of discretion when the problems associated with police enforcement of the law and the exercise of prosecutorial duties are examined in Chapter 4.

As for the question of why the *process* of producing criminal law is important, it is imperative to be aware that how we proceed with change can be very important as to a reform measure's ultimate worth and success. In this regard, there are various issues that should be kept in mind as we look both at the different ways in which criminal law is produced and at the differing attributes of the responsible institutions. These issues can be used as standards or reference points as the reader proceeds through the chapter in order to evaluate the effectiveness and validity of the various reform mechanisms.

The first issue to keep in mind throughout the chapter is that of "input". Input has several aspects to it which relate to the production of criminal law. "Who" it is who produces the criminal law and their qualifications is a question which was not addressed in traditional legal writings. If the traditional assumptions are that law is representative of society as a whole, that law is merely reflective of widely held and shared values and perspectives, and that the law is neutral in its formulation, the question of "who" the producer is is not especially important. If, however, a more critical or socio-legal stance is taken, then the question takes on an important dimension. In this light, one would want to examine the class, gender, and ethnicity of the state agents as a group and question whether such factors have significant consequences for the criminal law which is produced, enforced and applied. For example, judges as a group are not representative of society as a whole, and women and visible minorities in particular are greatly underrepresented in the judiciary.[1] As a result, can we see any effects of this lack of balance in the criminal law in areas such as sexual assault[2] or domestic violence,[3] or generally in the treatment of native people or visible minorities in the criminal justice system.[4] The same types of questions can also be raised in regard to legislators, police officers and Crown prosecutors.

---

1   According to *Touchstones for Change: Equality, Diversity and Accountability — The Report on Gender Equality in the Legal Profession* prepared by the Task Force on Gender Equality (Ottawa: The Canadian Bar Association, 1993), women represented approximately 12% of federally appointed judges and 13% of provincially appointed judges in 1993. By 1999, these figues had risen to 20% and 22% respectively, according to Justice Claire L'Heureux-Dubé, "Conversations on Equality" (1999), 26 Manitoba Law Journal 273, 283.

2   This issue is dealt with extensively in Chapter 8.

3   See, for example, Tim Quigley, "Battered Women and the Defence of Provocation" (1991), 55(2) Saskatchewan Law Review 223-261, Martha Shaffer, "R. v. Lavallée: A Review Essay" (1990), 22 Ottawa Law Review 607-624, Anne McGillvray, "Battered Women: Definition, Models and Prosecutorial Policy" (1987), 6 Canadian Journal of Family Law 15, excerpted in Chapter 4, Section 2; and D. Brodsky, "Educating Juries: The Battered Woman Defence in Canada" (1987), 25 Alberta Law Review 461; E. Comack, "Justice For Battered Women?" (1988), 22 Canadian Dimension 8; K. White-Mair, "Experts and Ordinary Men: Locating *R. v. Lavallée*, Battered Women Syndrome, and the 'New' Psychiatric Expertise on Women within Canadian Legal History" (2000), 12 Canadian Journal of Women and the Law 406; and *R. v. Lavallée*, excerpted in Chapter 7.

4   See, for example, the *Report of the Commission on Systemic Racism in the Ontario Criminal Justice System* (Toronto: Queen's Printer for Ontario, 1995); the *Report of the Aboriginal Justice Inquiry of Manitoba* (Winnipeg: Aboriginal Justice Inquiry, 1991); The *Report of the Royal Commission on the Donald Marshall, Jr., Prosecution: Findings and Recommendations, Volume One* (Halifax: The Commission, 1989); and Michael Harris, *Justice Denied: The Law versus Donald Marshall* (Toronto: Totem Books, 1986). Excerpts from the Marshall inquiry report are reproduced in Chapter 8, section 2.

In the articles in this chapter it is apparent that the production of criminal law is for the most part controlled by legal professionals. On the one hand, this might seem perfectly natural given the issues, concerns and rights involved and considering what is at stake in the outcome of criminal matters. But if we shift our focus away from traditional legalistic questions, then our response might be different and more critical. If we look at the criminal law as a matter which affects us all in society, as a device which can be seen as only one instrument of social control (albeit an intrusive one) among many, then the argument must be for the widest possible input into its production and enforcement. Choices must be made as to what is to be brought within the ambit of the criminal justice system and alternatives must be examined as to their suitability or superiority, and these decisions must not be left up to any one group of interests, particularly one as narrowly based as the legal profession.[5] But it is not only the lack of participation of a variety of groups in society which creates problems, it is also the type of approach and expertise which legal professionals bring to the job of criminal law reform.

Lawyers are by training and practice process-oriented, concentrating on the rules and procedures by which disputes are taken through the system. The substantive policy issues and choices which lie at the heart of the process, that is, what activities the criminal law is meant to encompass or what it is the criminal law ought to be accomplishing, are not within that area of expertise. Also, by virtue of their common law traditions and reasoning processes — traditions and processes which consistently look backward to precedent and established practice, and which defend the status quo — lawyers tend be quite limited and conservative in their vision.[6] These tendencies are important if we consider the need for forward-looking, flexible and adaptable processes in achieving progressive criminal law reform.

In the work and focus of legal professionals, one also sees a concentration on the formal aspects of the criminal justice system, notably in regard to the centrality which they give to the trial process and the work of judges. The trial process cannot be dismissed as meaningless or unimportant, but the focus must shift to other segments of the system. Not only do the overwhelming number of people charged plead guilty and thereby forgo their right to trial, but such an approach ignores questions of why and how those people arrived in the criminal justice system, as result of whose actions, and just as importantly, who did not make it there, who was weeded out and by what process or according to what criteria. For example, can one see factors such as income status gender or ethnicity at work in the enforcement and prosecution process? These are the types of concerns that are missed if we concentrate on the more formal aspects of the criminal process.

Given the quickly changing nature of society and the consequent nature of the required responses on the part of the criminal law, regressive, formalistic, and legalistic approaches do not serve well the production of criminal law. What *is* needed is

---

5   See Chapter 3 of Olsen's *The State Elite*, under Further Reading, as to the narrowness of the representation (though published in 1980, the book remains a valuable contribution to the literature in this area), as well as various articles given in the reading list of section 2 of this chapter.

6   See generally, E. S. Robinson, *Law and The Lawyers* (Toronto: MacMillan, 1973).

the input of criminal justice and social policy experts, experts both in "society" and in the appropriate policy responses required. Of course, this is an idealized view, for such experts can be wrong or the reforms can be distorted in practice, but recognizing such problems does not deny the potential benefits of opening up the production process to the diversity of views and insights that are too often denied a voice now.

A good example of the closed nature of the process can be found in the former Law Reform Commission of Canada, a federal body which, until 1992, advised the government on, among other things, criminal law reform. The make-up of the LRCC's criminal law project team was almost exclusively legal professionals, and the consultation process was similarly restricted to groups like the defence bar, the chiefs of police, the judiciary, and Crown prosecutors.[7] What could be expected and what did occur was a relatively sterile, legalistic, technocratic approach to criminal law reform, an approach which focused on form over substance. This approach is not exclusive to the work of the Commission, but rather is found generally in the work of the criminal justice bureaucracy itself. How to broaden the input effectively and consistently remains one of the crucial problems facing the criminal justice system. Even with this enhanced input there would be no guarantee that all the resulting policies would be the "right" ones, but at a minimum the increased potential for success would be there along with an increased acceptability of those policies. Interestingly, a new federal Law Commission of Canada was set up in 1996 with, according to the Department of Justice's news release of October, 1995, a promise to adopt "a new approach to law reform, governed by several principles [including] ... responsiveness; innovation; inclusiveness; a multi-displinary approach and openness".

The point of acceptability brings in another and final aspect of the issues surrounding input, that of what we can broadly call "democracy" or accountability. Those who make policy that affects all of society should be accountable and responsible in some manner to those who are affected by the policy. Since the advent of the Canadian Charter of Rights and Freedoms in 1982, we have been faced with the growing intervention by an appointed, tenured judiciary in the production of criminal law. Judicial intervention did occur in the era before the Charter but it was largely restricted to issues surrounding the division of powers, the interpretation of statute law and the control of the process (which affects the content and operation of the law in practice). These issues are addressed in section 2 of this chapter. The point to be kept in mind is the judiciary's lack of accountability to the public which the judiciary allegedly serves (issues of judicial accountability are discussed in more detail in section 3 of Chapter 4). This is particularly important when the lack of representation and the politics and secrecy surrounding the appointment process within the judicial branch are addressed.[8]

---

7  For a discussion of many of these issues surrounding the work of the former Law Reform Commission of Canada, see Ross Hastings and R.P. Saunders, "Social Control, State Autonomy, and Legal Reform: The law Reform Comminssion of Canada" in R.S. Ratner and John L. McMullan, eds., *State Control: Criminal Justice Politics in Canada* (Vancouver: University of British Columbia Press, 1987) at 126-148.

8  See, for example, J. S. Zeigel, "Appointments to the Supreme Court of Canada" (1994), 5 Constitutional Forum 10-15, Peter Russell and J.S. Zeigel, "Federal Judicial Appointments: An

Of course, it is not only the judicial branch where the absence of accountability is evident. Criticisms can be raised about the reality of accountability and responsibility in regard to the federal parliament and the provincial legislatures, but at a minimum there is an argument that the "potential" for accountability exists even though it may not often be attained (for good or for bad[9]). Furthermore, concerns surround the lack of accountability that exists in the exercise of discretion by many criminal justice agents. The exercise of discretion can have a very great impact on the way criminal law in practice is produced and on its real effects on individuals coming in contact with the criminal law. Too often the exercise of discretion is part of a hidden, non-reviewable process over which little or no control is exercised. Good examples of the (often unfettered) exercise of discretion can be found in the work of the Crown Prosecutors and of the police, both of which are discussed in Chapter 4.

Input and its various facets are not the only issues to keep in mind, however, as one proceeds through the readings. Another is that of certainty, the idea that the law should be "knowable" and understandable for all citizens, that the law should be readily accessible. While there is a self-evident sense of fairness in this notion, unfortunately the goal is too often not fulfilled. Criminal law remains the preserve of legal professionals with its arcane language and rituals that allow those professionals to maintain their control. The question to keep in mind is which production process might best accomplish this goal of certainty? Which process is more likely to result in policies accessible to, understood by, and accepted by the greatest number? For example, an argument can be made that statute law is inherently easier to find and to comprehend than case law, which often encompasses a series of cases and requires the ability to distinguish, delineate, and comprehend the various fact situations and rulings. Judicial decisions are largely inaccessible to the layperson because those judgments are written for other lawyers and not the general population that is subject to the rules expounded in the cases. It is not that statute law necessarily or automatically fulfills standards of certainty, but again it is the potential which might exist in one forum versus the other. One of the basic premises of our legal system is that citizens are subject to rules which are set out in advance and therefore, presumably, "knowable". How true is this in practice given the need for lawyers' expertise in criminal cases today, and what is the potential for fulfilling this goal?

Consistency of approach and purpose is another important issue to keep in mind. As we will see in the readings, legislative responses have proven to be haphazard and uneven. In addition, there is a call for the establishment and use of general principles to guide the development of criminal justice policy and to avoid piecemeal reform measures that respond to short term, expedient, political concerns. The present Crim-

---

Appraisal of the First Mulroney Government's Appointments and the New Judicial Advisory Committees" (1991), 41 University of Toronto Law Journal 4-37, J.S. Zeigel, "Federal Judicial Appointments: The Time is Ripe for Change" (1987), 37 University of Toronto Law Review 1-24, and Carl Baar, "Judicial Appointments and the Quality of Adjudication: The American Experience in a Canadian Perspective" (1986), 20 Thémis 1-26.

9   A good example in this regard is the issue of capital punishment which has been abolished as a penalty in the Criminal Code even though surveys of the general population consistently indicate strong support for such a measure.

inal Code has yet to provide these principles, though we can see numerous versions of them proposed in various reports, notably in the government's *Criminal Law in Canadian Society* (which is excerpted below), which stated (p. 38):

> The basic problem confronting criminal law and the criminal justice system ... is not the variety of specific concerns and complaints about particular phenomena — which are mere symptoms — but rather a debilitating confusion at the most basic level, concerning what the criminal law ought to be doing.[10]

The problem of the lack of consistency can be seen not only internally within the individual units of the criminal justice system, but also between different components of the system. The courts often have different goals or principles in mind from those of the legislature, correctional authorities may be attempting to accomplish different goals again, and the same can hold true for the police, Crown prosecutors, parole officers, and probation agencies. The failure to develop a comprehensive set of principles to guide the development and operation of the criminal law both within and between criminal justice institutions is a major problem that continues to cause disharmony and inconsistency.

A final point in this regard is that the process should possess a degree of flexibility so as to allow the criminal law to adapt and adjust readily to changing social conventions and perspectives. The judicial system has often been criticised for the slow development of the law that occurs in the courts. It is a process not particularly well suited to speedy, comprehensive changes in the law, yet under the Charter it is becoming a popular forum for the resolution of criminal justice policy issues. Given the time it takes for a matter to work its way through the court system and the focused and narrow nature of most cases, broad-based policy movement is generally not seen in the courts except over a long period of time.

In sum, the reader should approach an examination of the processes and structures that produce criminal law with a critical and questioning eye. It is important to keep in mind these issues that are germane to the production of criminal law and to be wary of the claims that are made by the producers. The questions of input, certainty, consistency, and flexibility cannot be overlooked in the search for a critical understanding of the origins and substance of criminal law. Criminal law is not a given or a constant from heaven; it expresses real values, and choices have been made by real people who have been influenced by concrete structures and perceptions. To understand the potential, limitations and deficiencies of criminal law, we must understand the dynamics of the relationships and processes which produce it. And such an understanding presupposes that we have in mind certain qualities or standards important in regard to both the processes and the final product.

A final point to make is that the relationship between processes can often be a problematic one in the sense that the failure of one institution or system to adequately deal with a problem can lead to change emanating from another group. One of the arguments about matters such as abortion or many common law defences being dealt

---

10   See also the Law Reform Commission's *Our Criminal Law* (Report 3), 1976, or the report of the Canadian Sentencing Commission, *Sentencing Reform. A Canadian Approach* (1987).

with by the courts is that the legislative authorities have themselves failed to act sufficiently and responsibly. And there is the argument that parliament is sometimes pressured to move on matters such as sexual assault due to the inability and/or insensitivity of the courts in handling the issues involved. The relationship between the processes is, therefore, often an interactive and reflexive one and, though they are presented as compartmentalized subjects, the individual processes are neither isolated nor self-contained.

## 3.1 LEGISLATION AND THE ROLE OF PARLIAMENT

### Introduction

*R.P. Saunders*

The role of parliament in the production of criminal law is an important one: this section addresses the issues and problems that arise in the context of fulfilling that role. There are several dimensions to the role which require examination, including the nature and history of the process, the inherent problems of the current process, the reform mechanisms that attach to the process, the role of the provinces and the constitutional issues surrounding the creation of criminal law. In regard to the latter, this section begins with a basic definition of criminal law from a constitutional perspective, that is, which level of government has the authority under the constitution to make criminal law.

As is obvious from the readings, only the federal parliament has the exclusive power to make acts criminal by virtue of paragraph 27 of section 91 of the Constitution Act, 1867, which gives the federal government authority in regard to "The Criminal Law, except the Constitution of Courts of Criminal Jurisdiction, but including the Procedure in Criminal Matters".[11] This does not mean that the provinces have no role to play, for not only do they enact many laws that carry with them penal sanctions (and are usually referred to as "quasi-criminal laws"),[12] but the provinces also have an important role to play in the implementation and enforcement of the criminal law.[13]

As for the provinces' role in regard to the former, the provinces enact a wide range of laws within their jurisdiction that carry varying types of penalties, including fines and imprisonment. These offenses are generally considered less serious than federal offenses and the penalties that attach are usually less onerous. This perception can be

---

11   See also s. 91(28) Where the federal government is given control over "The Establishment, Maintenance, and Management of Penitentiaries".

12   See s. 92(15) of the Constitution Act, 1867, which gives the provinces authority over "The Imposition of Punishment by Fine, Penalty, or Imprisonment for enforcing any Law of the Province made in relation to any Matter coming within any of the Classes of Subjects enumerated in this Section", that is, within the powers of the provinces as set out in s. 92.

13   See s. 92(14) of the Constitution Act, 1982, which gives the provinces authority in regard to "The Administration of Justice in the Province, including the Constitution, Maintenance, and Organization of Provincial Courts, both of Civil and of Criminal Jurisdiction ... "

deceptive, however, for these provincial offences often serve important regulatory functions and the breaking of them can have serious consequences, if not immediately, then in the long term. For example, individual hunting law violations may not be especially serious and the same is true for the breaking of parking regulations, but if these rules were not there or were continually and uniformly ignored, then wildlife or the free movement of traffic might be endangered. Furthermore, effective environmental regulation is a matter that is increasingly seen as imperative, even though the cumulative damage from pollution is sometimes not seen until years in the future. Also, convictions for these types of offences can have important effects on individuals through the loss of liberty, loss of employment, or the loss of money in the form of fines.

As for the implementation role played by the provinces, how the law is enforced and in what areas (both geographically and topically) have a very real effect on the meaning and experience of the criminal law for all citizens.[14] For example, if police forces are instructed not to lay charges in regard to certain types of crimes, this changes the complexion and substance of the law (see Chapter 4, section 1). Even before the relevant section on abortion in the Criminal Code was ruled invalid and of no effect, the Quebec government had refused to prosecute under the section due to the unwillingness of juries to convict. In the corrections sector, if the provinces do not commit funds to treatment facilities and programmes, the provisions for such in the Criminal Code or the Youth Criminal Justice Act will themselves be of little value to those who were targeted by the drafters of those sections. Therefore, while a great deal of attention may not be focused explicitly on the roles which the provinces play, those roles and responsibilities should be recognized as important and at times determining.

Fortunately, in the last decade, there has been an increasing amount of consultation, co-operation, and co-ordination between the two levels of government. In the area of criminal law reform, this has at times meant in practice the federal government seeking the agreement of the provinces before any reform is designed and implemented. This is often regarded as necessary if the reforms are to be effectively instituted by provincially appointed prosecutors, police and correctional agents. For our limited purposes here, however, we concentrate on the federal power to enact criminal law, although we recognize that this arena represents only one, albeit important, facet of the production process.

The constitutional division of responsibilities between the two levels of government means that the courts are called upon to decide if a government is acting within its sphere of power, and to do that the courts have developed tests when deciding if a particular subject matter properly falls within the criminal power or not. These tests are quite vague and open, and criticisms have been raised that it often comes down to the eye of any particular "beholding" court. In the readings by Hogg and Ewaschuk and in the two cases of *Rio Hotel* and *MacNeil*, note what the tests and important

---

14 The role of municipal authorities can be important in this regard as well in fulfilling their provincially mandated responsibilities, but their role will not be considered separately.

factors are as to determining criminal legislation and subject matter, and ask yourself how certain and helpful these tests really are.

In regard to the historical development of the criminal law in Canada, one of the original problems was the lack of a consistent and comprehensive set of principles, and a consequent lack of direction to guide the evolution of criminal law. At its origin, we can witness this in the adoption of the first Criminal Code in 1892, a code which was not a truly comprehensive code but rather a compilation of the criminal common law and criminal legislation up to that point in time. It was a reflection of not only indigenous case law and legislation, but also (and more importantly) English law in the area. What this means, on the one hand, of course, is that the Criminal Code at the outset was not a break with the past and a new beginning, but rather was a continuation of laws and rules reflecting older conceptions of society, values, and morality, and enshrining "scientific" facts and knowledge from earlier periods. The Code, therefore, in one sense was outdated from its very birth. On the other hand, there was no overarching set of principles and goals with which to not only implement and enforce the code, but also guide the evolution and development of the code.

The problems found with the enactment of the original code can be seen in the course of its development through the years. It was a haphazard and piecemeal development that responded to a series of crises and issues (both real and perceived), political responses that resulted in various add-ons to the code and to criminal legislation in general. The changes were for the most part political and expedient reactions, lacking a commitment to longer term goals of the criminal justice system. The need to remove politics from the process, or at least the need to introduce independent policy advice to the process has been recognized for a long time and was one of the reasons behind the establishment of the now disbanded Law Reform Commission of Canada (LRCC) in 1971 and the Law Commission of Canada in 1996. Many of the same problems remain today, however, in regard to the political, short term nature of the criminal law reform process. While it can be argued that expedient concerns will always be there in some form or another, such concerns should only emphasize the need for independent, principled planning in regard to the long term development of criminal law in Canada. An example of an attempt at the development of a set of guiding principles can be found in the last reading in this section, the excerpt from the 1982 *Criminal Law In Canadian Society* document, which, though dated, remains an example of the type of approach to the issue that agents of the Canadian state have taken in the past. In the last few years, such attempts appear to have been abandoned in favour of the traditional *ad hoc* approach to criminal law reform. On a more operational and practical level, there are also brief readings from the Law Reform Commission of Canada and by Stuart and by Boyle that look at arguments for and against a General Part in the Criminal Code, a section of the Code that, in Stuart's words, would "attempt to state in a comprehensive and coherent fashion those general principles of legal responsibility which apply. . .to any particular offence". The reading by Quigley looks briefly at some of the issues involved in a principled approach to the reform of criminal procedure.

Other problems or issues to keep in mind throughout the readings are those related to input, as noted above in the introduction to this Chapter. Ask yourself who has input into the system and how effective is that input? What type of expertise is being employed in the production of criminal law in this arena and what are the prospects of meaningfully opening up the process to other interests and types of knowledge? The parliamentary process is very often a secretive process with the "real" decisions being made behind closed doors. Many of these concerns are fully addressed only in courses on political decision-making, but they are important to the type of criminal law ultimately produced. Even with its faults, it might be argued that the legislative route is still the most democratic and the one that holds the greatest potential for better and wider input, particularly when we contrast it with the production of criminal law within the judicial process?

## The Constitutional Basis of the Criminal Law Power*

### *P.W. Hogg*

*Excerpt from Hogg, Peter W., *Constitutional Law of Canada*, 4th ed. (Toronto: Carswell, 1997) at 477-480.

### Definition of Criminal Law

The federal Parliament's power to enact "criminal law" has proved very difficult to define. In the *Board of Commerce* case (1922) Viscount Haldane held that the power was applicable only "where the subject matter is one which by its very nature belongs to the domain of criminal jurisprudence". Like Viscount Haldane's definitions of the peace, order, and good government power and the trade and commerce power, this definition of criminal law appeared to be too narrow. Although Viscount Haldane did not spell out what he meant by a "domain of criminal jurisprudence", the phrase could be read as freezing the criminal law into a mould established at some earlier time, presumably 1867.

After Viscount Haldane's death (in 1928), Lord Atkin in the *P.A.T.A.* case (1931) repudiated the domain of criminal jurisprudence theory and made clear that the federal power was "not confined to what was criminal by the law of England or of any Province in 1867", and that "the power may extend to legislation to make new crimes". Lord Atkin in the *P.A.T.A.* case offered a rival definition of criminal law:

> The criminal quality of an act cannot be discerned by intuition; nor can it be discovered by reference to any standard but one: Is the act prohibited with penal consequences?

This definition appeared to be too wide in that it would enable the federal Parliament to expand its jurisdiction indefinitely, simply by framing its legislation in the form of a prohibition coupled with a penalty. Nor was this definition sufficiently qualified when Lord Atkin later said that "the only limitation on the plenary power of the Dominion to determine what shall or shall not be criminal is the condition that Parliament shall not in the guise of enacting criminal legislation in truth and in substance encroach on any of the classes of subjects enumerated in s. 92". This says no more than the trite proposition that a law must be properly classifiable as in relation to the criminal law, and it no doubt contemplates the possibility of a statute in which the prohibition and penalty are unimportant appendages to provisions which really seek to accomplish the legislative goal by other means. Even setting aside this kind of "colourable" statute, which no-one would seriously seek to uphold as criminal, the *P.A.T.A.* definition is still too wide because it would uphold any federal law which employs a prohibition and penalty as its primary mode of operation. If the only characteristics of the criminal law are the formal ones of a prohibition and a penalty, then there is no principled basis for denying to a law with those characteristics the criminal classification.

It is clear that a proper balance in the distribution of legislative powers requires some third ingredient in the definition of criminal law. This was demonstrated in the *Margarine Reference* (1951), where the law in issue simply prohibited the manufacture, importation or sale of margarine. It was common ground that the purpose of this law was to protect the dairy industry. The Privy Council held that, although the law perfectly fitted the criminal form of a prohibition coupled with a penalty, the economic object of protecting an industry from its competitors made the law in pith and substance in relation to property and civil rights in the province.

It follows from the *Margarine Reference* that the elusive third ingredient of a criminal law is typically criminal public purpose. In the Supreme Court of Canada, Rand J., whose reasoning was adopted by the Privy Council, said that a prohibition was not criminal unless it served "a public purpose which can support it as being in relation to the criminal law". And what were the public purposes which would qualify? "Public peace, order, security, health, morality" these are the ordinary though not exclusive ends served by that law ... ". It will be noticed that Rand J. was careful not to give an exhaustive definition of the purpose of the criminal law. It was enough for him to be confident that the protection of the dairy industry was not a qualifying purpose. But while he characterized that purpose as "to benefit one group of persons as against competitors in business", no doubt the proponents of such protective legislation would deny that such a narrow definition was appropriate and would define the purpose in terms of national economic policy of benefit to all Canadians. Rand J.'s tendentious description of the margarine law, and his failure to provide a test for the identification of a typically criminal public purpose, detract from the value of his much-quoted opinion. Indeed, it is fair to say that the requirement of a typically public purpose is really only a slightly more sophisticated formulation of Viscount Haldane's "domain of criminal jurisprudence".

. . .

The *Margarine Reference* should not be read as denying that the criminal law can serve economic ends. A large part of the criminal law is devoted to the protection of private property — a purpose, one might add, which confers a larger benefit on those who own property than on those who do not. But, apart from the traditional crimes of theft and its many variants, various forms of economic regulation have been upheld as criminal law. The *P.A.T.A.* case itself upheld anti-combines (competition) laws under the criminal power, and under this general rubric a variety of federal laws have been upheld, including prohibitions on price discriminations and resale price maintenance and a judicial power to enjoin some of the prohibited practices. The false prospectus provisions of the Criminal Code have been upheld as criminal law, establishing that securities regulation — at least in crude form — is within the criminal law. In short, there is abundant support for Laskin's assertion that "resort to the criminal law power to proscribe undesirable commercial practices is today as characteristic of its exercise as has been resort thereto to curb violence or immoral conduct".

## Re Nova Scotia Board of Censors and MacNeil
### (1978), 44 C.C.C. (2d) 316 at 335 (S.C.C.).

Appeal by the Nova Scotia Board of Censors and the Attorney-General of Nova Scotia from a judgment of the Nova Scotia Supreme Court, Appeal Division, 78 D.L.R. (3d) 46, 36 C.C.C. (2d) 45, declaring certain sections of the *Theatres and Amusements Act*, R.S.N.S. 1967, c. 304, as amended, and certain Regulations made thereunder *ultra vires*.

[Excerpts from the judgment of Ritchie J. are reproduced below.]

RITCHIE J.: — This is an appeal brought with leave of this Court from a judgment of the Appeal Division of the Supreme Court of Nova Scotia rendered pursuant to an application made at the instance of the respondent MacNeil whose standing to initiate the proceedings in a representative capacity on behalf of other Nova Scotians was confirmed by order of this Court (see 55 D.L.R. (3d) 632, [1976] 2 S.C.R. 265, 12 N.S.R. (2d) 85, 5 N.R. 48 [affg 46 D.L.R. (3d) 259, 9 N.S.R. (2d) 506]).

The respondent's application was for a declaration that certain sections of the *Theatres and Amusements Act*, R.S.N.S. 1967 c. 304, as amended, and certain Regulations made thereunder were *ultra vires* and beyond the legislative competence of the Province of Nova Scotia.

The exciting cause of the application appears to have been the exercise by the Nova Scotia Amusements Regulation Board (hereinafter referred to as "the Board") of the authority which the Act purports to confer on it, to prevent a film entitled "Last Tango in Paris" from being exhibited in the theatres of Nova Scotia.

It is the statutory provisions purporting to authorize the Board to regulate and control the film industry within the Province of Nova Scotia according to standards fixed by it, which are challenged by the respondent on the ground that the citizens of Nova Scotia are thereby denied, on moral grounds, their right to exercise their freedom of choice in the viewing of films and theatre performances which might otherwise be available to them, and it is further alleged that the legislation constitutes an invasion of fundamental freedoms.

The questions raised by the application were reserved for the consideration of the Appeal Division by order of Mr. Justice Hart made pursuant to s. 30(3) of the *Judicature Act*, 1972 (NS), c. 2, and that Division having reserved its decision, granted the following order:

It is Hereby Declared that the words 'prohibiting' in sections 2(1)(b) and 2(1)(g) and subsections (2) and (3) of Section 3 of the *Theatres and Amusements Act* are null and void and of no effect being ultra vires the legislature of Nova Scotia.

It is further declared that regulations 4, 5(1), 13, 18 and 32 made pursuant to the *Theatres*

*and Amusements Act* are null and void and of no effect being ultra vires the legislature of
Nova Scotia;

. . .

When the Act and the Regulations are read as a whole, I find that to be primarily
directed to the regulation, supervision and control of the film business within the
Province of Nova Scotia, including the use and exhibition of films in that Province.
To this end the impugned provisions are, in my view, enacted for the purpose of
reinforcing the authority vested in a provincially appointed Board to perform the task
of regulation which includes the authority to prevent the exhibition of films which
the Board, applying its own local standards, has rejected as unsuitable for viewing by
provincial audiences. This legislation is concerned with dealings in and the use of
property (i.e., films) which take place wholly within the Province. . . .

It will be seen that, in my opinion, the impugned legislation constitutes nothing
more than the exercise of provincial authority over transactions taking place wholly
within the Province and it applies to the "regulating, exhibition, sale and exchange of
films" whether those films have been imported from another country or not.

We are concerned, however, in this appeal with a decision of the Appeal Division
of the Supreme Court of Nova Scotia in which the majority quite clearly struck down
the legislation as *ultra vires* on the sole ground that it was concerned with morality
and as such constituted an invasion of the criminal law field reserved to the exclusive
legislative authority of Parliament under s. 91(27) of the *British North America Act,
1867.*

The following passage from the reasons of judgment of the Judges concerned serve
to indicate the narrow basis on which they proceeded:

. . .

Although the Amusements Regulation Board gave no reasons for placing "Last Tango in
Paris" in the so-called rejected classification and thus prohibiting the showing of this film in
theatres in this Province I think it clear from the material before us that this action was taken
because the film was considered by the Board to offend against acceptable standards of
morality.

This leads me to what in my opinion is the sole issue before us in this appeal, namely, has
the Legislature of this Province power to enact legislation under which a board or any other
body or person may, in the interests of public morality, be authorized to prohibit the showing
of a film or is the power to enact such legislation solely reserved for the Parliament of Canada?
The short answer to this question is that the field of public morals is an aspect of criminal
law which falls within the exclusive jurisdiction of the Parliament of Canada under s. 91(27)
of the *British North America Act, 1867* . . .

The same question was answered by Chief Justice MacKeigan in the following in the
following terms [at p. 48 D.L.R., p. 47 C.C.C.]:

Censorship of this type is obviously directed at obscenity and other immoral exhibitions.
Provincial legislation purporting to make such exhibitions offences punishable by prosecution
would indisputably be a direct and invalid invasion of the federal criminal field.

Mr. Justice Coffin expressed himself to the same effect saying [at p. 50 D.L.R., p. 49
C.C.C.]:

I am limiting my conclusions to the jurisdictional point that the legislation is valid criminal law and I am not entering the field of fundamental freedoms.

. . .

Although no reasons were given by the board for the rejection of "Last Tango in Paris", all members of the Appeal Division were satisfied that its exhibition was prohibited on moral grounds and under all the circumstances I think it to be apparent that this was the case. In any event, I am satisfied that the Board is clothed with authority to fix its own local standards of morality in deciding whether a film is to be rejected or not for local viewing.

Simply put, the issued raised by the majority opinion in the Appeal Divisions is whether the Province is clothed with authority under s. 92 of the *British North America Act, 1867* to regulate the exhibition and distribution of films within its own boundaries which are considered unsuitable for local viewing by a local board on grounds of morality or whether this is a matter of criminal law reserved to Parliament under s. 91(27).

In the present context, the question of whether or not the impugned legislation encroaches on the criminal law authority is, in my opinion, best approached in light of the statement made by Kerwin, C.J.C., in the course of his reasons for judgment in *Lord's Day Alliance of Canada v. A.-G. B.C. et al.* (1959), 19 D.L.R. (2d) 97 at p. 102, 123 C.C.C. 81 at p. 87, [1959] S.C.R. 497 at p. 503, where he said:

> In constitutional matters there is no general area of criminal law and in every case the pith and substance of the legislation in question must be looked at.

Under the authority assigned to it by s. 92(27), the Parliament of Canada has enacted the *Criminal Code*, a penal statute the end purpose of which is the definition and punishment of crime when it has been proved to have been committed.

On the other hand, the *Theatres and Amusements Act* is not concerned with creating a criminal offence or providing for its punishment, but rather in so regulating a business within the Province as to prevent the exhibition in its theatres of performances which do not comply with the standards of propriety established by the Board.

The areas of operation of the two statutes are therefore fundamentally different on dual grounds. In the first place, one is directed to regulating a trade or business where the other is concerned with the definition and punishment of crime; and in the second place, one is preventive while the other is penal.

As the decision of the Appeal Division depends upon equating morality with criminality, I think it desirable at this stage to refer to the definitive statement made by Lord Atkin in this regard in the course of his reasons for judgment in *Proprietary Articles Trade Ass'n v. A.-G. Can.,* [1931] 2 D.L.R. 1 at pp. 9-10, 55 C.C.C. 241 at p. 250, [1931] A.C. 310 at p. 324, where he said:

> Morality and criminality are far from co-extensive; nor is the sphere of criminality necessarily part of a more extensive field covered by morality — unless the moral code necessarily disapproves all acts prohibited by the State, in which case the argument moves in a circle. It appears to their Lordships to be of little value to seek to confine crimes to a category of acts which by their very nature belong to the domain of "criminal jurisprudence" . . .

I share the opinion expressed in this passage that morality and criminality are far from co-extensive and it follows in my view that legislation which authorizes the establishment and enforcement of a local standard of morality in the exhibition of films is not necessarily "an invasion of the federal criminal field" as Chief Justice Mackeigan thought it to be in this case.

Even if I accepted the view that the impugned legislation is concerned with criminal morality, it would still have to be noted that it is preventive rather than penal and the authority of the Province to pass legislation directed towards prevention of crime is illustrated by the case of *Bedard v. Dawson et al.*, [1923] 4 D.L.R. 293, 40 C.C.C. 404.

. . .

As I have already said, however, I take the view that the impugned legislation is not concerned with criminality. The rejection of films by the Board is based on a failure to conform to the standards of propriety which it has itself adopted and this failure cannot be said to be "an act prohibited with penal consequences" by the Parliament of Canada either in enacting the *Criminal Code* or otherwise. This is not to say that Parliament is in any way restricted in its authority to pass laws penalizing immoral acts or conduct, but simply that the provincial Government in regulating a local trade may set its own standards which in no sense exclude the operation of the federal law.

There is, in my view, no constitutional barrier preventing the Board from rejecting a film for exhibition in Nova Scotia on the sole ground that it fails to conform to standards of morality which the Board itself has fixed notwithstanding the fact that the film is not offensive to any provision of the *Criminal Code*; and, equally, there is no constitutional reason why a prosecution cannot be brought under s. 163 of the *Criminal Code* in respect of the exhibition of a film which the Board of Censors has approved as conforming to its standards of propriety.

. . .

It will be seen that in my view the impugned legislation "has for its true object, purpose, nature and character" the regulation and control of a local trade and that it is therefore valid provincial legislation.

I now turn to a consideration of the specific section declared to be *ultra vires* by the Appeal Division of Nova Scotia, the validity of which is the subject of the constitutional question directed by order of the Chief Justice. In this regard it is noteworthy that the 1st paragraph of the order of the Appeal Division expressly declares that the word "prohibiting" in s. 2(1)(b) and (g) and s-ss. (2) and (3) of s. 3 are null and void and the use of this word in these sections of the statute forms the basis of the Court's declaration that they are *ultra vires* The Legislature of Nova Scotia. As I find the legislation to have a valid provincial purpose, I take the view that at least the first paragraph of the order made by the Appeal Division is inconsistent with the judgment of this Court in *Quong Wing v. The King* (1914), 18 D.L.R. 121, 23 C.C.C. 113, 49 S.C.R. 440. In that case the legislation prohibited the employment of white women by Chinese and provided a penalty of $100 for its contravention. In the course of his reasons for judgment at pp. 124-5 D.L.R., p. 116 C.C.C., p. 444 S.C.R., Sir Charles Fitzpatrick, C.J., explained the legislation as follows:

> In terms the section purports merely to regulate places of business and resorts owned and managed by Chinese, independent of nationality, in the interest of the morals of women and girls in Saskatchewan.

And in upholding the validity of the legislation he observed that [p. 117 C.C.C.]:

> This legislation may affect the civil rights of Chinamen, but it is primarily directed to the protection of children and girls.
>
> . . .

I conclude from these decisions that if the legislation is found to have been enacted for a valid provincial purpose the prohibition is equally valid. Much the same considerations apply to the Regulations declared to be *ultra vires* by the second paragraph of the order of the Appeal Division. Regulations 4 and 5(1) simply provide that no theatre owner shall permit the use for exhibition in his theatre of any film which has not been authorized under the Regulations.

. . .

. . . Regulation 13 is to the same effect providing as it does that:

> **13.** No person shall advertise any performance unless the permission of the Board has first been obtained.

Regulation 18 is, in my opinion, similarly valid, but I consider it of interest to reproduce s-s. (5) of that Regulation as it appears to me to illustrate the fact that the legislation has been enacted to regulate not only the exhibition of films in theatres, but the whole film business as conducted by film exchanges within the Province. The subsection reads:

> **18**(5) No film exchange shall use, exhibit, sell, lease or exchange any film unless a certificate of the Board has been issued in respect thereof and any film which is used, exhibited, sold, leased or exchanged in violation of this regulation may be confiscated by the Board.

Regulation 32 reads as follows:

> **32**(1) No theatre owner or amusement owner shall permit any indecent or improper performance in his theatre or place of amusement.
>
> (2) No performer shall take part in any indecent or improper performance.
>
> (3) The Board may from time to time define what constitutes an indecent or improper performance within the meaning of these Regulations.

In my view the provisions of this Regulation are in their effect and purpose indistinguishable from s. 159(2) of the *Criminal Code* which provides, in part:

> **159**(2) Every one commits an offence who knowingly, without lawful justification or excuse,
>
> . . .
>
> (b) publicly exhibits . . . an indecent show,

The use of the word "indecent" in both s-ss. (1) and (2) of the Regulation and in the *Criminal Code* is the common factor making the two enactments virtually identical, and the judgment of this Court in *Johnson v. A.G. Alta*, [1954] 2 D.L.R. 625, 108 C.C.C. 1, [1954] S.C.R. 127, constitutes conclusive authority against the validity of such a provincial enactment.

The authority purported to be conferred on the Board by Regulation 32(3) is not an independent enactment and cannot stand alone, nor is it within the legislative authority of the Province to authorize a provincial authority to define what constitutes an offence prescribed by the *Criminal Code*.

Unlike the other provisions of the statute and Regulations to which I have referred, this Regulation is not governed by the decision in *O'Grady v. Sparling, supra; Stephens v. The Queen, supra*, and *Mann v. The Queen, supra*, where the offences created by provincial legislation were of a different character to those enacted by the *Criminal Code*.

In view of the above I find that Regulation 32 is invalid as being indistinguishable from the like provisions of the *Criminal Code*. I am, however, of opinion that this Regulation is clearly severable from the balance of the Regulations and the statute and that it in no way detracts from, varies or curtails the authority vested in the Board under the statute itself.

As I have said, I take the view that the legislation here in question is, in pith and substance, directed to property and civil rights and therefore valid under s. 92(13) of the *British North America Act, 1867* but there is a further and different ground on which its validity might be sustained. In a country as vast and diverse as Canada, where tastes and standards may vary from one area to another, the determination of what is and what is not acceptable for public exhibition on moral grounds may be viewed as a matter of a "local and private nature in the Province" within the meaning of s. 92(1) of the *British North America Act, 1867*, and as it is not a matter coming within any of the classes of subject enumerated in s. 91, this is a field in which the Legislature is free to act.

. . .

As I indicated at the outset, I have taken note of the lengthy judgment of Mr. Justice Macdonald in the Appeal Division in which he finds that the impugned legislation is *ultra vires* as infringing on the fundamental freedoms to which he refers, which include freedom of association; of assembly; of speech; of the press; of other media in the dissemination of news and opinion; of conscience and of religion.

Mr. Justice Macdonald's approach appears to me to be illustrated by the following comment which he makes after referring to censorship legislation relating to morals in other Provinces [at p. 55]:

> The foregoing criteria are of the usual "sex, morals and violence" type that are normally associated with film censorship. In the present case, however, the censorship criterion, being left to the *Board* to determine, *could* be much wider and encompass political, religious and other matters. In my opinion censorship relating to party politics cannot be tolerated in a free society where unfettered debate on political issues is a necessity, subject, of course, to the criminal law, particularly those provisions of the *Criminal Code*, relating to sedition, treason and incitement to crime.

(The emphasis is added.)

It is true that no limitations on the authority of the board are spelled out in the Act and that it might be inferred that it *could* possibly affect some of the rights listed by Macdonald, J.A., but having regard to the presumption of constitutional validity to which I have already referred, it appears to me that this does not afford justifications for concluding that the purpose of the Act was directed to the infringement of one or more of those rights. With the greatest respect, this conclusion appears to me to involve speculation as to the intention of the Legislature and the placing of a construction on the statute which is nowhere made manifest by the language employed in enacting it.

For all these reasons, I would allow this appeal, set aside the judgment of the Appeal Division of Nova Scotia and substitute for the declaration made thereunder a declaration that Regulation 32 made pursuant to the *Theatre and Amusements Act* of Nova Scotia is null and void.

This does not appear to me to be a case in which costs should be awarded.

*Appeal allowed in part.*

## Rio Hotel Ltd. v. Liquor Licensing Board
(1987), 58 C.R. (3d) 387 (S.C.C.).

[Only the judgment of Dickson C.J.C. is reproduced below.]

DICKSON C.J.C.: — The issue in this appeal [from 29 D.L.R. (4th) 662, 69 N.B.R. (2d) 20, 177 A.P.R. 20] is whether a province has legislative authority to prevent "nude entertainment" as one aspect of a legislative scheme regulating the sale of liquor in the province. I have had the benefit of reading the reason for judgment prepared by my colleague Estey J. and, although I am in full accord with his disposition of the appeal, I prefer to reach that conclusion by a different route. I am happy to adopt Estey J.'s recitation of the facts and judicial history of this case.

It has long been settled that under s. 92(13) and (16) or the Constitution Act, 1867, the provinces are vested with legislative authority to regulate the conditions for the sale and consumption of alcohol within the province: see *Ont. (A.G.) v. Can. (A.G.)*, [1986] A.C. 348, 5 Cart. 295 (P.C.) and *Man. (A.G.) v. Man. Licence Holders' Assn.*, [1902] A.C. 73 (P.C.). It is also well settled that in regulating the distribution of alcohol a province may attach conditions to any licence with a view to providing for the "good government" of liquor outlets: see *Hodge v. R.* (1883), 9 App. Cas. 117 at 131 (P.C.). It seems clear therefore that s. 63.01(5) of the Liquor Control Act, R.S.N.B. 1973, c. L-10, which permits the provincial Liquor Licensing Board to attach conditions to a liquor license prohibiting "specified kinds of live entertainment" in licensed premises, is prima facie within the legislative competence of the New Brunswick Legislature.

The difficulty in this case, however, arises because, in granting entertainment license 5199E to Rio Hotel Ltd., the Liquor Licensing Board imposed a condition preventing all "nude entertainment". The appellant contends that this condition relates to public morality and therefore falls within the exclusive jurisdiction of the federal Parliament under the criminal law power of s. 91(27) of the Constitution Act, 1867. Parliament has indeed enacted legislation which relates directly or indirectly to public nudity (ss. 159(2)(b), 163, 169 and 170 of the Criminal Code). It is common ground that these Criminal Code provisions are intra vires the Parliament of Canada. The dispute therefore resolves itself into the following question: Can a provincial prohibition of nude entertainment attached to a liquor licensing scheme operate notwithstanding the more general but related prohibitions contained in the Criminal Code?

The Attorney General of New Brunswick submits that the impugned licence condition is part of a legislative scheme which "has a purpose entirely different from that sought to be served by the criminal law". While the criminal law addresses nudity and obscenity, the license condition is simply directed toward the types of entertainment available as a marketing device for the sale of liquor within the province. This submission clearly calls into play the "aspect doctrine" first articulated by the Privy Council in the late 19th century. The doctrine was summarized neatly by Their Lordships in *Hodge v. R.*, supra, at p. 130: "subjects which in one aspect and for one purpose fall within sect. 92, may in another aspect and for another purpose fall within sect. 91". The inverse proposition is equally true: see also *Russell v. R.* (1982), 7 App. Cas. 829, 2 Cart. 12 (P.C.), and *Citizens Ins. Co. of Can. v. Parsons; Queens Ins. Co. v. Parsons* (1881), 7 App. Cas. 96, 1 Cart. 265 (P.C.).

The operation of the aspect doctrine was discussed fully by this court in *Multiple Access Ltd. v. McCutcheon*, [1982] 2 S.C.R. 161, 18 B.L.R. 138 D.L.R. (3d) 1, 44 N.R. 181 [Ont.], and the relationship between federal legislative paramountcy and the aspect doctrine was explained in some detail. It is unnecessary to here reiterate the analysis. Suffice it to say that when a particular legislative subject matter can be said to have a "double aspect", so that, viewed in one light, the subject falls within the legislative competence of Parliament and, viewed in another light, it falls within the legislative competence of a provincial legislature, federal legislation will be paramount only when there is a direct conflict with the relevant provincial legislation. Mere duplication does not constitute a "direct conflict". Rather, the phrase suggests that, for federal paramountcy to operate, the related federal and provincial legislation must be contradictory. Relying upon the holding of Martland J. in *Smith v. R.*, [1960] S.C.R. 776, 33 C.R. 318, 128 C.C.C. 145, 25 D.L.R. (2d) 225 [Ont.], the majority in *Multiple Access Ltd.* held, at p. 191 [S.C.R.]:

> In principle, there would seem to be no good reasons to speak of paramountcy and preclusion except where there is actual conflict in operation as where one enactment says "yes" and the other says "no" . . .

The double aspect doctrine will apply whenever the contrast between the relative importance of the federal and provincial characteristics of a particular subject matter is not sharp.

Applying these principles to the circumstances of the case at bar, I conclude that the provincial legislation which authorizes the impugned licence condition is intra vires the legislature of New Brunswick. The legislation is, as I have stated, prima facie related to property and civil rights within the province and to matters of a purely local nature. The legislature seeks only to regulate the forms of entertainment that may be used as marketing tools by the owners of licensed premises to boost sales of alcohol. Although there is some overlap between the licence condition precluding nude entertainment and various provisions of the Criminal Code, there is no direct conflict. It is perfectly possible to comply with both the provincial and the federal legislation. Moreover, the sanction for breach of the provincially-imposed licence conditions is suspension or cancellation of the liquor licence. No penal consequences ensue for the nude entertainer or for the holder of the licence. Under the relevant Criminal Code provisions, the primary object is obviously to punish entertainers and proprietors who breach the prohibitions on public nudity. I cannot say that the federal characteristics of this subject matter are palpably more important than the provincial characteristics. The provincial regulatory scheme relating to the sale of liquor in the province can, without difficulty, operate concurrently with the federal Criminal Code provisions.

I should point out that the instant case is distinguishable from the situation discussed in *Westendorp v. R.*, [1983] 1 S.C.R. 43, 32 C.R. (3d) 97, [1983] 2 W.W.R. 385, 23 Alta. L.R. (2d) 289, 20 M.P.L.R. 267, 2 C.C.C. (3d) 330, 144 D.L.R. (3d) 259, 41 A.R. 306, 46 N.R. 30. In that case, the city of Calgary enacted a by-law purportedly in relation to the use of city streets. In fact, one selection of the by-law was a blatant and colourable attempt to punish prostitution. That section was held by this court to be an "intruded provision" that bore no relation, either in subject matter or in the scale of penalties, to the remainder of the by-law. In other words, the prostitution provision could not be said to relate to any head of provincial jurisdiction; it was not truly part of a regulatory scheme authorized under s. 92(13) or 92(16) of the Constitution Act, 1867. The licence conditions in the instant case are only part of a comprehensive scheme regulating the sale of liquor in New Brunswick. There is no colourable intrusion upon a federal head of jurisdiction.

Finally, I agree with Estey J. that this is not an appropriate case in which to deal with freedom of expression as guaranteed by s. 2(*b*) of the Canadian Charter of Rights and Freedoms.

I would dismiss the appeal with costs.

## Criminal Legislation*

### E.G. Ewaschuk, Q.C.

*Excerpts from (1983-84), 26 Criminal Law Quarterly 97.

Criminal legislation covers a broad range of powers, conduct and procedures relating to the general subject-matter of crime. It is legislation which defines which acts or omissions constitute criminal offences, defines who are parties to the offences and prescribes the process by which accused persons may be brought to court, convicted and sentenced or acquitted. It thus involves police powers, court proceedings and corrections. The purpose of this article is to inform the reader of the parameters of criminal legislation in its most general sense. An historical background of criminal legislation in Britain as well as Canada, will be canvassed as will the present system of enacting criminal legislation in Canada.

. . .

## CRIMINAL LEGISLATION IN GENERAL

Under the Constitution Act, 1867, the federal Parliament in Canada has exclusive authority to legislate with respect to criminal law and procedure. Thus, the federal government, since 1867, has enacted various federal criminal Acts, for example: the Criminal Code, the Juvenile Delinquents Act, the Narcotic Control Act, the Food and Drugs Act, the Combines Investigation Act, etc. In so stating, it is clear that not all crimes are found within the Criminal Code, as is commonly believed, and, by definition, provincial governments have no constitutional power to enact criminal legislation. Of course, provincial Legislatures, however, have power to create offences passed in relation to their specific legislative powers. Therefore provincial Legislatures may enact offences in relation to regulation of the highways; *e.g.*, careless driving, speeding, etc.

A threshold question to be determined is: what is the proper legislative subject-matter of criminal law? At one time it was thought that the subject-matter of criminal law was unlimited and that the criminal nature of an act was determined solely by the fact that it was an act "prohibited with penal consequences". That pragmatic definition suffices for a unitary state like Britain but proved unacceptable for a political federation like Canada.

The present acceptable definition of criminal legislation requires the legislation to serve a public purpose and to generally relate to public peace, order, security, health or morality. That criterion was arrived at by the Supreme Court of Canada, and adopted on appeal by the Judicial Committee of the Privy Council, in considering whether federal legislation prohibiting the manufacture, importation or sale of margarine was valid criminal legislation. In striking down this legislation designed to protect the dairy industry, the court decided that the legislation was constitutionally invalid ("colourable") since it could not be justified as the proper subject-matter of criminal law. Consequently, not all types of misconduct may be validly characterized as criminal in nature.

Another important and new factor in considering the validity of criminal legislation is whether the legislation contravenes the Charter of Rights and Freedoms which came into force on April 17, 1982. The Charter displaces the former constitutional doctrine of parliamentary sovereignty by specifically empowering the judiciary to strike down any law inconsistent with a right or freedom guaranteed by the Charter.

A further and most controversial question dealing with criminal law lies in the domain of policy and not legality. It relates to the question of what type of conduct may the state prohibit. In that regard, the philosopher John Stuart Mill, in the 19th century, proffered his criterion which, in effect, held that the state may not prohibit conduct which does not result in substantial harm.

Many agree with him and firmly hold that the state has no business prohibiting moral conduct, especially conduct which is victimless, *e.g.* conduct which involves consenting adults. However, most states do not adhere to that dictum and do in fact prohibit such victimless conduct as gross indecency between consulting adults, gambling and smoking marihuana. The question, as stated, lies in the area of acceptable social policy and values and not pure law.

In the domain of enacted legislation, the Criminal Code, by s. 8, now specifically provides that no person shall be convicted of an offence at common law. That reference is important in so far as the Criminal Code now requires criminal offences to be found in legislative enactments. At common law, crimes were divided into treasons, felonies, misdemeanours and petty offences. A great number of these offences were defined by custom, *i.e.*, by judicial precedent, and not by legislative enactment. For example, under the common law of England, the felonies of murder, manslaughter, mayhem, arson, rape, robbery, burglary, prison breach and rescue of felon were not found in legislative enactments. While some of those offences still remain common law offences in England, no common law offences survive in Canada since the coming into force of s. 8 in 1955. Instead, as stated, the offences must be found in some specific federal enactment.

The Criminal Code is obviously the most important federal enactment relating to criminal legislation. It is roughly composed of three major divisions — that pertaining to the general part, that pertaining to criminal offences and that pertaining to various procedures related to police, courts and corrections. A cursory examination of the Code is important in that it reveals what the Code, with its some 773 sections, does and does not contain. Section 1 relates the title of the enactment while s. 2 is a general interpretation section defining various terms found in several places in the Code itself. Part I contains ss. 3 to 45 and is general in nature. It makes specific reference to various defences which exculpate an accused from a crime. But not all defences are found in the Criminal Code. Some common law defences, unlike common law offences, have escaped being legislated, but continue to afford an accused a justification or excuse not specifically found in the Criminal Code.

. . .

More particularly, the Criminal Code in part defines various crimes and their constitutive elements, *e.g.*, sexual assault. It then specifies the type of offence sexual assault is, *i.e.*, an indictable or summary conviction offence. An indictable offence is more serious and entails maximum punishments of 2, 5, 10 or 14 years' imprisonment or life. A summary conviction offence, on the other hand, entails a maximum of 6 months' imprisonment but in practice usually involves a fine or discharge. The Code then specifies in what circumstances a peace officer or civilian has the power to arrest an accused. It further defines, assuming an arrest for sexual assault, whether or not the accused should be released on bail and under what terms and conditions. It also defines what type of court located in what territorial jurisdiction shall hear the trial of the accused. The Code further defines under what circumstances a preliminary inquiry preceding a trial is required for a charge of sexual assault. However, the Code does not define what evidence is admissible at a preliminary inquiry or trial on a charge of sexual assault. Instead, the common law rules of evidence apply as may the Canada Evidence Act. However, the Criminal Code does define the punishment for the crime of sexual assault, assuming a conviction. It further defines to what court an appeal may be brought by either the accused or the Crown.

It also should be noted that the procedures outline in the Code for processing various types of indictable and summary conviction offences apply as well to criminal offences found in other federal statutes.

. . .

## HISTORICAL BACKGROUND TO THE CRIMINAL CODE

As earlier stated, the common law in England divided crime into three major groups: (1) treason, (2) felony, (3) misdemeanours. As well, there were petty offences tried in local, as opposed to royal, courts. Prior to the invention of the printing press in the 15th century, crime, for the most part, tended to be defined by custom. In other words, judges would refer to past precedents as constituting definitional authority of what conduct was and was not criminal in nature.

However, that is not to say the Parliament did not start to enact criminal legislation at an early date. Indeed as early as 1350, the British Parliament enacted the Statute of Treasons which specified exactly what conduct constituted high treason including, amongst various other matters, demonstrating a manifest intent to kill the King, levying war against the King, adhering to the King's enemy, and giving his enemies aid and comfort. However, for the most part, criminal legislation was minimal until the 19th century.

At the turn of the 19th century, there were over a hundred criminal offences in England punishable by hanging or some more barbaric form of death. Indeed, for most felonies, the only two punishments were death or transportation to the colonies. In fact no power existed to imprison a convicted felon. However, that is not to deny that many convicts were in fact pardoned prior to their scheduled hangings and then shipped from England to do slave labour in the United States or later, in Australia.

With the development of various schools of criminological theory on the European continent, a movement arose demanding widespread reform to criminal punishment and specifically to abolish death as the general punishment for most serious crimes. That movement also took hold in England. Commencing with legislation in the 1830's, mandatory hangings as the fixed punishment for various felonies was progressively abolished.

In the same vein, as the result of eight Royal Commissions' reports on crime, a number of general criminal statutes were enacted in 1861. Although since altered to some degree in name and form, these reform laws have survived in substance until the present. So well received were these criminal statutes that a further Royal Commission was subsequently struck to study the desirability of one Criminal Code for Britain. As a result of many years of study, the Royal Commission in 1879 proposed a self-contained draft Criminal Code. However, due probably to the British love of tradition and history, the proposed Criminal Code was never enacted. Indeed, to this day Britain struggles with more than 200 statutes containing criminal legislation. In many instances, five, six, or even seven statutes creating various criminal offences may apply in respeet of the same conduct.

. . .

The Canadian legal system is divided obviously into the common law and the civil law traditions. Whereas the common law tradition is empirical in nature and tends to evolve on a case by case basis, the civil law tradition is *"a priori"* in nature and favours legislation in respect of all legal subject-matter. Given the blend of the Canadian legal systems, it is little wonder that in 1892 Canada enacted its own Criminal Code without much difficulty, contrary to what took place in Britain.

Prior to 1867, each province enacted its own criminal legislation; however, that legislation generally related to criminal procedure and evidence rather than to criminal offences. Instead, the common law offences, as well as British statutory offences, applied generally to the provinces in Canada. But just two years after Confederation, the federal Parliament enacted several Bills relating to criminal legislation which dealt with offences relating to forgery, larceny, malicious damage to property, offences against the person and coinage, and with respect to criminal procedure, legislation dealing with juvenile offenders, summary conviction, indictable offences and a separate Criminal Procedure Act.

In 1886 those statutes were consolidated although, for the most part, left unchanged. Around this time, work had already reached Canada that Britain was contemplating the need for the passage of one Criminal Code, *i.e.*, one statute containing all criminal law. That need was considered in Canada and response proved generally favourable to the idea of the passage of a self-contained Criminal Code. As a result, the federal Department of Justice began to study the matter.

Finally, in 1892, the federal Parliament enacted the first Criminal Code which came into force on January 1st, 1893, together with a Canada Evidence Act. At that time, Sir John Thompson, the Minister of Justice, stated that the Criminal Code was founded on the draft Code prepared by the British Royal Commission, on Stephen's *Digest of the Criminal Law*, Burbridge's *Digest of the Canadian Criminal Law* of 1889 and various Canadian statutes.

It can be stated fairly that the Criminal Code of Canada was, to a great extent, lifted from the draft Criminal Code proposed by the British Royal Commission. Many of those proposed offences simply duplicated previous English common law or criminal legislation. Indeed, many offences found in the 1892 Criminal Code (Canada) were merely a distillation of offences as defined by judicial precedent. But unlike the uncertainty that continued in Britain, the Criminal Code (Canada) proved invaluable to the judiciary and the legal profession, as well as the police and general public, in readily determining what the elements of various criminal conduct were and the applicable criminal procedures. However, not all common law offences were defined in the Criminal Code and, as earlier stated, it was not until the 1955 Code that common law offences were finally abolished in Canada.

In relation to criminal procedure, very little of the Criminal Code of 1892 duplicated the draft Criminal Code of the Royal Commissioners. Instead, the criminal procedure prescribed by the 1892 Code reflected a hodgepodge of various legislation already passed in Canada as well as a distillation of practice as found in various Canadian texts. The procedure tended to be somewhat uniquely Canadian in flavour. Indeed, the felony-misdemeanour distinction fashioned at common law had already been abolished and replaced by the present classification of indictable and summary conviction offences. All references to the word "malicious" were also deleted from the

Criminal Code. Furthermore, the common law distinction between accessories before the fact and principals in the first degree and principals in the second degree were also abolished and replaced by the concept of "parties" to the offence. In other words, as at present, there were principal parties to criminal offences, as well as secondary parties, but all were guilty in equal degree.

For the most part, the 1892 Code was well received by the Canadian legal profession and gave some semblance of logical order to Canadian criminal law and procedure. Various revisions followed the 1892 Code. Indeed, in 1906 major amendments were enacted to the criminal law. However, the 1927 consolidation was simply that, a consolidation and not a revision of the 1892 and 1906 Codes.

Later it became quite apparent that the Criminal Code contained various anomalies and antiquated terminology requiring excision, rewording and consolidation. Thus in 1947 a Criminal Code Revision Committee was struck to rearrange, simplify and revise the Criminal Code. That Committee reported in 1953 with the result that major amendments came into force on April 1st, 1955, to what has been called the 1955 Code. While the Committee made substantive changes to the Criminal Code, those changes related in many instances to merely form and drafting style and were aimed at putting the Criminal Code into 20th century, as opposed to 19th century, wording.

As a result, many of the offences in the present Code are still based on 19th century morality and value judgments. Indeed, the present Code continues to be a melange of the British Royal Commission's draft Criminal Code, pre-1892 Canadian legislation and indigenous legal treatises, as well as substantive *ad-hoc* amendments passed in more recent times.

Twentieth century amendments have related to such pieces of legislation as those referring to drunk and impaired driving, the breathalyser, therapeutic abortion committees, morality offences by consenting adults, wiretap legislation, dangerous offenders and the firearms acquisition scheme — a regulatory scheme relating to long-arm weapons. Indeed the Criminal Code, with its patchwork of various amendments enacted over the span of nearly 100 years, does not strike even the initiated reader as reflecting a consistent or logical scheme. Instead, it reflects disparate reasoning and drafting styles and does not reflect the values of the 1980s, nor a consistent and intelligible writing style for the present era.

## PRESENT SYSTEM OF ENACTING
## CRIMINAL LEGISLATION

### Sources of Legislation

Sources of government criminal legislation are many. On a daily basis, the Minister of Justice receives dozens of letters from various lawyers, judges, government officials as well as from general members of the public complaining about various provisions of the Criminal Code or some other problems that exists with respect to the criminal justice system. Examining and responding to ministerial correspondence occupies a great deal of Department of Justice officials' time. In the Department, ministerial letters are enclosed in yellow dossiers, affectionately known as "yellow daffodils".

Over the course of the year, many of these letters point out discrepancies in the Criminal Code between various provisions, discrepancies between the English and French versions of criminal statutes, as well as general deficiencies in law. In addition, other Ministers, federal or provincial, and federal or provincial officials correspond with the Minister of Justice asking that various modifications with respect to the criminal justice system be considered.

As a result, many of these complaints are formally considered at a conference termed, "The Uniform Law Conference of Canada" *[Editor's note: The website for this group is www.ulcc.ca.]*, which sits on an annual basis. Members of this conference are called "Commissioners" and come generally from government departments, such as the federal Department of Justice as well as various provincial Attorneys-General Departments. In addition, each province, together with the federal government, generally appoints a member of the private bar to represent the interests of the accused at the criminal side of the conference.

In addition to outside resolutions, each province generally submits its own resolutions for consideration by commissioners on the criminal side.

A resolution will generally state the problem, will relate the background of the problem as well as the current law interpreting the problem, and then set out various alternative solutions to the problem. Finally, the resolution will recommend a solution to the problem. Most resolutions are set forth in a three to four-page format.

During the one-week conference, as many as 50 to 60 resolutions may be considered with a rate of passed resolutions ranging anywhere from 20 to 80%, depending on the nature of the resolution and the nature of the membership in the particular year. Further time may be spent by Commissioners in considering Law Reform Commission reports, as well as federal legislation currently before Parliament.

As a general observation, it is fair to say that the majority of successful resolutions passed at a Uniform Law Conference eventually find their way into enacted federal legislation. For that reason the Conference is perhaps the single most important source of criminal legislation. However, approval of a resolution generally constitutes but the end of a first-stage process which began as a complaint to a particular Minister pointing out some deficiency in the criminal justice system.

Attorneys-General meetings are another important source of criminal legislation. Often Attorneys-General meet at a provincial level in the absence of the federal Minister of Justice. However, when the federal Minister of Justice is invited to meet with his provincial colleagues, then matters of general importance and broad implications to the criminal justice system are often discussed. Sometimes resolutions are considered which deal with policy matters not requiring legislation. However, matters involving broad change to the criminal law are also considered. Where there is general consensus that legislation is required, then obviously the federal Minister of Justice is usually favourably disposed to enact legislation on the recommendation of his provincial counterparts.

The federal Solicitor-General usually attends the Attorneys-General meetings and has an important though secondary voice at these meetings. When, however, police, penitentiary or parole matters are discussed, he discharges the primary federal role in dealing with such matters.

. . .

The Law Reform Commission of Canada is a further source of criminal legislation. The Law Reform Commission was set by the statute in 1972 by the then Minister of Justice, the Honourable John Turner. It was Mr. Turner's wish that the Law Reform Commission, through study papers, working papers and reports, would eventually give the Canadian public a new and modern Criminal Code reflecting present-day values and needs. In fact, in 1970, Mr. Turner had already announced that "the Commission should have a complete rewriting of the Criminal Law as one of its first projects". However, that wish has not as yet come to pass.

Although the Law Reform Commission has published a great number of papers on criminal law, very few of their recommendations have yet found their way into the statute books. But that is not to deny these papers have generated a great deal of study and interest. The papers, in other words, have proved educational and have, to a great extent, changed the way the Canadian legal profession views the criminal justice system.

Little change, as stated, has resulted from the Law Reform Commission recommendations as to how the criminal justice system functions on a technical basis. However, the federal Department of Justice is charged with the responsibility of responding to Law Reform Commission reports with a view to recommending possible legislation. It may therefor be expected that future federal legislation will, in fact, reflect various recommendations of the Law Reform Commission of Canada.

## The Cabinet Process

Criminal legislation is generally enacted through public as opposed to private members' Bills. In other words, criminal legislation is usually proposed by the government of the day and not by private members. To be sponsored by the government, the proposals must go through what is termed a Cabinet process.

The Cabinet process begins with a recommendation from the Minister in charge of the particular legislation. . . .Where a Minister, after receipt of a complaint and examination of the complaint, decides that legislation for which he is responsible requires amendment, he must, then, submit his proposed change to current legislation to his ministerial colleagues.

Thus the federal Minister of Justice will, at certain times, decide that criminal legislation is required. In many instances, he reviews what may be termed a laundry list. An official of the Department of Justice, in charge of criminal legislation, will prepare a background document for the Minister to review, with a view to recommending legislative amendments. That list will detail a particular problem, give a background to the problem with alternative solutions, and a recommendation. A great number of problems may be outlined in that document. A meeting then will follow with the Minister, the Deputy Minister and various other officials to review the proposals. Oftentimes, of course, the document may contain various resolutions already passed by the Uniform Law Conference or at Attorneys-General meetings, or may reflect recommendations of the Law Reform Commission for legislating change.

When the Minister of Justice formally decides that legislative change is required, the commencement of the Cabinet process actually then begins. At this stage, Justice officials will be tasked with the requirement of preparing two documents termed, "A Discussion Paper" and a "Memorandum to Cabinet". The Discussion Paper is the larger of the two documents. It, in fact, will follow what appears to be the general government format outlining the particular program, a background to the problem, and listing various alternative approaches to the problem. However, that document makes no recommendations as to how that problem should be solved. Instead, it is a very neutral document made with the expectation that the document will eventually be made available to the general public. It tends therefore to be a scholarly analysis of theory as well as practice, showing a very detached approach to the problem.

By contrast, the Memorandum to Cabinet is a much shorter document and clearly outlines the particular recommendation of the Minister to his Cabinet colleagues. That document is considered confidential and protected by Crown privilege, and is not to be released to the public. It is a much shorter and tighter document outlining the problem, a brief background to the problem, and making a specific recommendation as to how the problem should be resolved.

Both the Discussion Paper and the Memorandum to Cabinet will be given to Cabinet numbers by Privy Council Office. In many cases, a communications plan is also required. The documents, after being extensively reviewed with the Department of Justice, will then be released on a confidential basis, before being submitted to the Cabinet, for review by various officials in the central agencies *i.e.*, Privy Council Office, the Prime Minister's Office and, in the case of criminal legislation, the Ministry for Social Development. As well, the documents may be sent to officials in the Department of the Solicitor-General, the Ministry of Health and Welfare or the Ministry of Consumer and Corporate Affairs, when those departments have an interest in proposed legislation.

As a result of a review by these officials, further changes may then be made to the documents.

. . .

The next stage of official meetings to discuss the proposed legislation will occur at a standing committee called, "The Committee on Social Development". Again, the same departments are involved but, at this stage, the actual Ministers meet to discuss the implications of the proposed legislation. Of course, the meetings are secret and confidential, though the deliberations and decisions are, in fact, recorded. What occurs at the actual meetings cannot be discussed with outside officials. In fact, officials are permitted within the Cabinet room only when proposals from their department are being discussed.

Eventually, the chairman in charge of this committee will record the vote of his Cabinet colleagues on the proposed legislation. This vote and his recommendation will be forwarded to full Cabinet for further consideration. Justice officials are not permitted to attend the meeting of full Cabinet which tends to be a *"pro forma"* examination of proposed legislation. Only when the subject-matter is controversial or the vote at committee was very close will "full Cabinet" review the proposed legislation in great detail. In those cases, the matter may also be sent to "party caucus" for examination and recommendation by that group as to the political implications involved.

When Cabinet approves the proposed legislation, a record of decision (termed an "RD" in government circles) is sent by Privy Council officials to government drafts-men working for the Department of Justice. These draftsmen are charged with the duty of reflecting the policy decisions reached by Cabinet in legislative form, *i.e.*, with changing the policy decisions into legislative classes. That task is not an easy one.

Oftentimes various meetings will be held between the draftsmen and officials from the Department proposing the legislation to discuss the best means of reflecting the legislative policy in proper legislative language. That is an arduous task, whether conducted in English or French, and oftentimes five, six or seven drafts of the proposed legislation are reviewed before officials are satisfied with the proposed wordings of each clause of the proposed legislation.

. . .

In any event, the agreed legislative form will eventually return to still another committee of Cabinet. That standing committee is called, "The Committee on Leg-islation and House Planning", chaired by the Deputy Prime Minister. Again, that is a partial committee of Cabinet, and various Cabinet members attend those meetings. At those meetings, the proposed Bill is reviewed on a clause-by-clause basis. The sponsoring Minister begins by outlining the general thrust and policy implications of the proposed legislation. The Minister will later respond to broad policy questions whereas Justice officials may explain the details of the proposed Bill, *i.e.*, the wording of the clauses and why the particular wording was chosen. Where Ministers, as they often do, choose to challenge the official as to the proper wording of the clause, a meticulous examination of the Bill results.

Oftentimes the clauses will be redrafted on direction of the chairman to reflect the problems encountered by Ministers with the wording. This is done with a view to simplifying language and to further the intelligibility of the Bill. If the committee then decides that the Bill is to be approved as worded, the chairman prepares a record of decision (RD) which is forwarded to full Cabinet for review.

Eventually the Bill, as yet unnumbered, will be sent to "Priorities and Planning" Committee of Cabinet, the most important sub-committee of Cabinet. That committee is comprised of the Prime Minister and his closest advisors, including the Deputy Prime Minister who advises the Prime Minister and his Cabinet colleagues as to, in the Deputy Prime Minister's view, the importance of the Bill and what priority it should receive in Parliament. After those decisions are made, and only then, will the Bill be tabled in Parliament. At the tabling in Parliament, the Bill ceases to be government property and only then comes within the official domain of Parliament.

### Legislative Process

A Bill receives either a Bill C- or Bill S- number, that is, a Commons or Senate number, on first reading, depending whether the Bill is tabled in the Commons or the Senate. Most criminal legislation originates in the Commons, as it must if financial considerations are involved. Contrary to the expression "first reading" there is in fact no reading. Instead, first reading entails only a formal tabling of a Bill. However, on first reading, a Minister in charge of a government Bill may decide to hold a press conference, where the Bill and a press release are distributed to the media. As well, this may involve a television appearance by the Minister or various officials. This, then, announces to the criminal justice community, as well as to the general public, that Parliament will be considering proposed criminal legislation in the near future.

The first formal statement in Parliament begins the second reading stage. At second reading, the Minister of Justice will make what has been termed a "second reading speech", outlining the general thrust and policy implications of the proposed legislation. In turn, the various Justice critics of the Official Opposition will reply with general statements either supporting or, as is more usual, attacking the Bill in principle. What then follows will be statements by various other members either of the Government or Opposition, and an eventual debate in principle of the Bill. If the Bill survives second reading, as it almost always does with a majority government, the Bill is forwarded to the "Standing Committee on Justice and Legal Affairs of the House of Commons" for consideration as to detail as well as principle.

At committee stage, the members of the committee are divided into approximately the same numbers as their respective parties are represented in the Commons. The Committee is chaired by a non-Cabinet member of the government, with the Justice critics represented at Committee.

The committee process generally begins with another speech by the Minister of Justice, again outlining in principle, but in more detail, the general policy implications of the Bill. This is followed by statements of the Justice critics. Eventually witnesses may be heard. These witnesses, in fact, represent various groups. Often the President of the Canadian Association of Chiefs of Police will attend, as will the President of Civil Liberties Association of Canada, as witnesses at committee stage, to proffer their opinion on the content of the Bill. As well, members of various public-interest groups may testify, as may various law professors, defence and Crown counsel.

It is considered good form for the Minister of Justice not to attend during the testimony of the witnesses so as not to give the impression of possibly intimidating the witnesses as to their testimony. Indeed the Minister of Justice or the sponsoring Minister, as the case may be, attends very few of the meetings other than his speech and the clause-by-clause stage of the Bill, which follows the testimony of witnesses.

The clause-by-clause process consists of a detailed examination of each clause of the Bill starting with clause one. Members of the committee may put questions to the Minister or his officials as to the wording of the particular clause, its implications and consequences, and make objections to the wording. A Minister may reconsider and amend the wording of the clause or in fact, at times, withdraw the actual clause. Eventually the clause will be voted on as worded, and the same process will follow in respect of each clause. Finally, the Bill as a whole will be voted upon and the committee will report back the Bill to the Commons as to the voting on the particular clauses and its general recommendations.

Assuming then that the Bill returns to the Commons for third reading, there is yet another speech by the sponsoring Minister and a further debate on principle, but one generally shorter in length. Then the Bill is voted upon and, if passed, goes to the Senate to begin the same process at the Senate level.

. . .

. . . Eventually, where the Bill is successfully passed at third reading, the Bill will then return to the Senate for formal enactment with the attendance of the Governor-General in the Senate to declare the law enacted.

. . .

However, in most cases, government Bills now do not come into force on the day of enactment, but instead come into force on a day specified in the legislation, or on a day to be proclaimed in the future, by order of Council. This is required to give officials involved in the criminal justice process time to rearrange their affairs to meet the requirements of the proposed legislation, and to educate themselves and others as to the potential impact of the now-enacted legislation.

. . .

### From Jeremy Bentham to Anne McLellan: Lessons on Criminal Law Codification*

*Gerry Ferguson*

*Excerpts from "From Jeremy Bentham to Anne McLellan: Lessons on Criminal Law Codification" by Gerry Ferguson in Don Stuart, R.J. Delisle and Allan Manson, eds., *Towards a Clear and Just Criminal Law: A Criminal Reports Forum* (Toronto: Carswell, 1999) at 193-194, 204-207.

The first Canadian Criminal Code, enacted in1892, was a direct by-product of the codification movement in England which commenced with Jeremy Bentham in the late 18th and early 19th centuries.

### (a)  Jeremy Bentham

Jeremy Bentham is considered by some as the "intellectual father of the codification movement" in English-speaking jurisdictions. Bentham never drafted a complete criminal code, but he did write widely on the merits of codification and prepared detailed plans for codes.

Bentham criticized the unwritten common law as being difficult to ascertain, *ad hoc* rather than comprehensive, and undemocratic in the sense that is was *ex post facto* lawmaking by the judges based on their own preferences but masquerading as the product of legal logic and precedent.

Bentham believed that Parliament should pass all laws, and that judicial discretion should be limited as much as possible.

Bentham saw codification as the enactment by Parliament of a complete and comprehensive statement of the law, done in a rational and scientific manner (*i.e.*, proceeding from general principles to specific principles) and written in clear and comprehensive language which the ordinary citizen could understand.

*(i)  Codification Ideals*

Bentham's objectives of a comprehensible, clear, rational, logical and understandable Criminal Code enacted by Parliament still retain their legitimacy today as the principal codification ideals.

. . .

## (h)  Codification Efforts 1969 to Present

*(i)  Law Reform Commission of Canada*

The enthusiasm in the late 1960s for the pursuit of a "just society" stimulated the notion that law reform on a broad social scale, rather than ad hoc statutory revision, was necessary and appropriate. In 1969, the Report of the Canadian Committee on Corrections (Ouimet Report) recommended that the government establish a Royal Commission to engage in a comprehensive examination of Canada's criminal laws.

Parliament responded by creation of the Law Reform Commission of Canada in 1971. The Commission was intended as a permanent government institution for monitoring the need for Canadian law reform. As such, one of the Commission's first tasks was to undertake a comprehensive review of criminal law, procedure, sentencing and evidence. The Law Reform Commission did much ground-breaking work and was soon publishing many Reports and Working Papers in each of the above areas. Unfortunately, the vast majority of this work did not translate into actual legislation. Indeed, the Law Reform Commission's efforts to effect legislative reform in the first decade of its existence were, by most accounts, a failure.

*(ii)  Government Plan for Review and Accelerated Review of Criminal Law*

By the late 1970s, there was growing dissatisfaction with the pace of Canadian criminal law reform. This dissatisfaction culminated in two pivotal critiques. First, in 1977 the Parliamentary Subcommittee on the Penitentiary System in Canada (chaired by Mark MacGuigan) criticized the government for failing to produce a coherent policy on criminal justice and vigorously urged the government to do so. Second, early that same year the chairman of the Law Reform Commission (Mr. Justice Antonio Lamer) delivered a speech to the Canadian Congress of Criminology and Correction. Lamer endorsed criticisms made by the Parliamentary Subcommittee and advocated a moratorium on all legislative reform of criminal law until the government produced a comprehensive reform policy. Taken together, the two critiques constituted a "ringing condemnation" of the government's *ad hoc* approach to criminal law reform.

By 1979, these critiques—along with a growing backlog of Law Reform Commission reports—spurred the Minister of Justice (Senator Jacques Flynn, in the short-lived Clark government) to announce that a fundamental review of the *Criminal Code* would be undertaken. Later that year, at a conference of federal and provincial ministers of justice, the "Criminal Law Review" was launched. Apparently this was the first time that both federal and provincial governments had committed themselves to a thorough reform of the criminal law in Canada.

The guiding premise of the government's plan for criminal law review was that an "inductive model" of criminal law reform through *ad hoc* amendments to the existing *Code* was inherently flawed. Instead, the Criminal Law Review was premised on a "commitment by the government to systematic reform of the law on the basis of incremental legislation." The plan had three phases. Phase One was the initial research and policy development phase which was to be completed by the Law Reform Commission of Canada. Phase Two was the government policy development stage whereby the government reviewed the work of the Commission and decided what matters would proceed to the legislative stage. Phase Three was introduction of legislation and implementation of it. Under this scheme a fundamental review of all Canadian criminal law was to be completed by 1987 resulting in four large legislative packages—one on crimes, the second on procedure, the third on sentencing and the fourth on evidence.

Between 1979 and 1982, constitutional matters (repatriation of the *Constitution* and enactment of the *Charter*) overshadowed the Criminal Law Review. Very little progress was made during this period. In 1982, in response to a renewed call for an overall policy on criminal justice to guide and facilitate the "Criminal Law Review," the then Minister of Justice, Jean Chretien, published a report entitled *The Criminal Law in Canadian Society* (1982), which clearly set out the aims, purposes and principles of the criminal justice system as well as a number of its current problems.

By 1983 attention was once again focused in an "accelerated" way on the review of the criminal law. Indeed, in 1983 – 1984 an "unprecedented flurry of activity" at the LRCC attracted increasing international attention to the Commission's recodification efforts. Between 1984 and 1987, the Law Reform Commission produced a Code of Substantive Criminal Law (i.e., both the General Part and the Special Part). In 1988, the LRCC published a Report on general principles for recodification of criminal procedure and in 1991, the LRCC published its first instalment of a new Code of Criminal Procedure. Neither the Substantive Criminal Law Code nor the Criminal Procedure Code made it to Phase Three — introduction of new legislation.

. . .

## The General Part in Canada*

*Law Reform Commission of Canada*

*Excerpts from *Criminal Law. The General Part: Liability and Defences* (Working Paper 29) (Ottawa: Minister of Supply and Services, 1982) at 153-160.

. . .Originally in Canada as in England the General Part was basically left to common law. In 1892, however, Parliament enacted a *Criminal Code* based on Stephen's *Digest* and his Draft Code, which the English Parliament had rejected. This first *Criminal Code* recognized the idea of the General Part. At the same time it kept in force such common-law excuses and justifications as were not inconsistent with the *Code* itself. Similarly, the *Criminal Code*, revised in 1955, has a chapter of rules about insanity, duress, criminal participation and other matters. This chapter is, however, incomplete: on the one hand it omits certain items like necessity and drunkenness, and on the other it preserves common-law defences which are not inconsistent with the *Code* or other Acts of Parliament. Our General Part, then, is to be found partly within the *Criminal Code* but partly outside it.

If we turn first to the *Code*, we find, beginning with section 3, a fairly long chapter entitled "Part I—General". In keeping with its title Part I is a general part of the Code rather than of the criminal law. For while a general part of criminal law contains provisions relating to jurisdiction and responsibility, Part I includes numerous additional items (e.g. definitions of terms like "age", "value" and "valuable security") and at the same time omits several matters of relevance to responsibility (e.g. necessity, mistake of act and drunkenness).

In consequence by no means all matters relating to responsibility are dealt with by "Part I—General", which only governs infancy (ss. 12-13), insanity (s. 16), duress (ss. 17-18), ignorance of law (s. 19), participation (ss. 21-23), attempts (s. 24) and various justifications such as legal duty (ss. 25-33), self-defence (ss. 34-37), defence of property (ss. 38-42), exercise of authority (ss. 43-44), performance of surgical operations (s. 45) and consent (s. 14).

Many matters regarding responsibility are dealt with elsewhere in the *Criminal Code*. Causation and provocation are treated in the Part on Homicide. The only definition of recklessness is found in the provisions concerning the offence of mischief. Mistake of act is dealt with only in an ad hoc manner in provisions like those on obscenity, illicit sexual intercourse, and other offences. Lawful excuse, justification and lawful authority are allowed, though not defined, in various offences. General those these rules are in application, we find them scattered throughout the *Code*.

Finally, some matters relating to responsibility are still regulated by common law. The draftsmen of the *Criminal Code*, like those of the English Draft Code of 1876, not wishing to put criminal law into a strait-jacket, laid down in section 7 that common law should plug the gaps left in the *Code*. Accordingly it is to common law that we must turn for the basic concepts of *actus reus* and *mens rea*, the principles underlying the rules on infancy and insanity, the definitions of key terms like "intent", "recklessness" and "negligence" and the rules relating to defences like necessity and drunkenness.

The General Part of Criminal Law in Canada, therefore, is found in these three different areas: in Criminal Code "Part I—General", in the rest of the Criminal Code and in the common law. But wherever it is to be found, any attempt to evaluate its adequacy must rest on an assessment of the purpose and function of a general part.

## Purpose and Function of a General Part

Discussion of the purpose of the General Part can well begin with Jerome Hall. Hall's *General Principles of Criminal Law*, which provides the first comprehensive theoretical treatment in general of the criminal law and in particular of the General Part, divides criminal law into three different constituent elements: (1) rules, (2) secondary principles and (3) basic principles. Rules (e.g. rules defining murder, robbery and other offences) are relatively specific, concern relatively narrow issues and are found mainly in the Special Part. Secondary principles (e.g. principles relating to insanity, mistake and other defences) are wider than rules, concern more general matters and are found mainly in the General Part. Basic principles (e.g. the basic principle of culpability) are widest of all, relate to the most broad and fundamental issues and, in Hall's view, stand strictly outside the law itself.

Each of these three ingredients plays its own particular part. Rules specify what is distinctive about each offence. Secondary principles complete the rules by specifying factors common to all offences, i.e. matters of justification and excuse. Basic principles comprise the fundamental axioms from which the secondary principles are derived. This being so, these three ingredients are to be found unequally distributed in the criminal law. Whereas the Special Part, the part specifying offences, contains merely rules, the General Part, the part specifying defences, may contain rules, secondary principles and basic principles. Hence the General Part's greater depth and increased complexity.

Each of these three ingredients, then, performs a different function. Basic principles illuminate and systematize the criminal law: the principle of responsibility, for example, articulates the moral basis of the criminal law and orients it towards freedom of choice. Secondary principles provide concrete applications of the basic principles: for instance, the principles about mistake, ignorance of fact and various other defences afford specific instances of the principle of responsibility. Finally, there are general rules neither derived from basic or secondary principles nor belonging to evidence or procedure which should find their place within the General Part: e.g. the rules relating to jurisdiction and to limitation of time. Ideally, then, there are three functions for the General Part: to avoid repetition in the criminal law, to facilitate its systematization and to provide it with a theoretical basis.

Avoidance of repetition is primarily the function of general rules. While rules of special application will obviously be located in their own special context, rules of more general application must either be located in a general part or else be re-iterated with reference to each offence. The "year and a day" rule that no one commits culpable homicide unless the death occurs within a year and a day of his wrongful act is a special rules applying only to homicide and therefore rightly located in the sections on homicide. By contrast the infancy rules that no one under seven can be convicted of an offence applies across the board to all offences and would have to be repeated in every offence-creating section unless articulated once and for all in the General Part.

Systematization results from primary and secondary principles. As Hall observes, it was Hale who first brought system and order to the criminal law because he had an eye for "the one in the many". Hale, therefore, and those who followed in his path showed how the various rules and particularly those relating to defences were inter-related and connected by reference to the underlying principles. These principles, then, provide the structure and organization of the criminal law.

Finally, as Hall observes, "theory is concerned with the ultimate ideas which comprise the foundation of a science or a social discipline". As such it can arrange, organize and explain a mass of ordinary data, and so provide a powerful tool for understanding. Just as scientific theory can do this for science, so legal theory can do the same for law, providing it with rationale and coherence, giving practitioners a deeper insight into all the different rules and which make up that law, and enabling courts and lawyers to deal confidently with new unfamiliar problems, with questions arising from social change and with issues surfacing in the field of law reform.

Criminal-law theory, then, to quote Hall once again, provides "a set of ideas by reference to which every penal law can be significantly 'placed', and thus explained". It does so by articulating the basic premises of the criminal law and by deriving from them the various corollaries in terms of defences of infancy, insanity, mistake, igno-rance of fact, necessity, compulsion, duress, automatism, drunkenness and so on. For, roughly speaking, all our criminal law results from the interplay of the two principles that (1) wrongful conduct should be punished and (2) punishment should depend on personal fault. Finding the right balance is the task of the lawmaker and justifying it the task of the theorist.

## Contents of a General Part

Accordingly a General Part needs to be structured on the following lines with propositions at three different levels. It needs to articulate a set of overall objects for the *Criminal Code*. Next it must set out a list of basic principles to guide the operation of the Code towards those objectives. Finally it must contain rules to translate those principles into operational form. Here we briefly discuss each of these three levels.

As Objects section would contain, not the objects of criminal law, but the objects of the *Code*. The difference is this. Whereas the objects of criminal law may be reduction of crime, underlining values, etc., the object of the *Code* will not be only to advance those objects but also to do three other things: to express the basic values of our society in an accessible form, to provide rules for the application of the criminal law and to preserve the side-constraints that limit it.

As well as objects, a Code should set out principles. These are broad guidelines concerning considerations of fairness, justice and morality relating to the achievement of the objects of the *Code* and underlying the application of its operational rules. Whether written into the *Code* or not, such principles exist in fact in criminal law and are to be found as the premises, often unarticulated, of judicial reasoning in the case law. Without them, however, a Code becomes merely a list of rules devoid of structure, rationale or moral underpinning.

Finally, a Code needs rules. While principles are general, abstract and painted in broad terms, rules are particular, concrete and applicable in detail to specific situations.

While principles are the reasons behind the rules, the rules are the operational elements of the *Code*.

In short, a Code needs three types of provisions: objects to provide overall direction, principles to furnish credibility and rules to afford practicality. . . .

## A Case for a General Part*

### *Don Stuart*

*Excerpts from "A Case for a General Part" by Don Stuart in Don Stuart, R.J. Delisle and Allan Manson, eds., *Towards a Clear and Just Criminal Law: A Criminal Reports Forum* (Toronto: Carswell, 1999) at 96, 101-102.

. . .There is broad agreement in Canada and elsewhere that a General Part in a *Criminal Code* is an attempt to state in a comprehensive and coherent fashion those general principles of legal responsibility which apply, in the absence of legislative intent to the contrary, to any particular offence. . . .

A General Part is urgently needed because

1. Basic substantive principles, such as those respecting fault, voluntariness and omissions and the defences of duress and necessity, are missing from the *Criminal Code* which is the document most accessible to Canadians;
2. Although our courts, and the Supreme Court in particular, have tried hard to provide guidance, there is now considerable inconsistency and undue complexity in the law;
3. Our adversary system, which requires cases to be fairly put to impartial judges or juries, and the presumption of innocence, cannot work with legitimacy where there is confusion as to the applicable tests on even basic matters such as the fault requirement or which self-defence rules applies;
4. The law must be capable of being easily understood by counsel and judges of lesser experience and/or competence and not left to esoteric debates;
5. As a matter of efficiency and cost it makes little sense for so many appeals and retrials simply because the law is unclear.

A well-drafted General Part will not miraculously clear up all these deficiencies. It took would require interpretation and *Charter* review. But it should surely go a long way to addressing them.

## Commentary*

### *Christine Boyle*

*Excerpts from "Commentary" by Christine Boyle, in Don Stuart, R.J. Delisle and Allan Manson, eds., *Towards a Clear and Just Criminal Law: A Criminal Reports Forum* (Toronto: Carswell, 1999) at 146-148.

The very concept of a General Part is a troubling one for a feminist criminal lawyer. On the one hand, who can really take issue with the values of clarity, consistency, and accessibility promoted by a codified General Part? The codification project may even be able to include some reform of the criminal law and thus promote justice. On the other hand, there is suspicion that it will either be impossible, or there will not be the political will, to capture differing social realities and complex layers of disadvantage in a statement of abstract principles.

For example, Katherine Bartlett discusses practical reasoning as an aspect of feminist legal method in "Feminist Legal Methods."

> Practical reasoning approaches problems not as dichotomized conflicts, but at dilemmas with multiple perspectives, contradictions, and inconsistencies. These dilemmas, ideally, do not call for the choice of one principle over another, but rather "imaginative integrations and reconciliations," which require attention to particular context. Practical reasoning sees particular details not as annoying inconsistencies or irrelevant nuisances which impede the smooth logical application of fixed rules. Nor does it seem particular facts as the objects of legal analysis, the inert material to which to apply the living law. Instead, new facts present opportunities for improved understandings and "integrations." Situations are unique, not anticipated in their detail, and generalizable in advance. Themselves generative, new situations give rise to "practical" perceptions and inform decision-makers about the desired ends of law.

This suggests that continued judicial evolution, informed by new fact patterns and illuminated by new perspectives on old facts, may hold out more transformative potential than codification, which risks being a conservative exercise.

However Bartlett also points out that "[a]ll major forms of legal reasoning encompass processes of both contextualization and abstraction." Generalizations are useful in focusing on what matters and in making connections. In the criminal context, where so much is at stake for accused and convicted persons, there is general consensus that what matters, matters an awful lot. I would not want my rights to liberty, privacy, or equal status to depend on an ex post facto "imaginative integration." So I find myself in a familiar state of internal conflict.

. . .

## 1.  A CASE AGAINST A CODIFIED GENERAL PART?

From one perspective there has been little feminist attention to the issue of codification, most feminist criminal law reform activity being oriented to specific issues, such as the law of sexual assault. General principles do play a role in feminist analyses but they tend to be equality, cultural, and other forms of diversity, and security of the person, rather than, for instance, fault, causation and excusing conditions. There have thus been two major but parallel pressures for what might be termed relatively progressive criminal law reform (as opposed to the more primitive variety). One is represented by mainstream reform documents. An example is the Canadian Bar Association's *Principles of Criminal Liability: Proposals for a New General Part of the Criminal Law*. One would be hard-pressed to find in it any discussion of the impact of particular proposals on overlapping groups of critics of criminal law such as women and aboriginal peoples. The other is illustrated by extensive feminist writing on criminal law reform and facts in numerous cases. Having said that, however, one might take the view that there has been some convergence in the *Self-Defence Review* and the recent Consultation Paper on *Reforming Criminal Law Defences*.

My main concern about the codification project, to put it bluntly, is that it is much more likely to reflect the mainstream of criminal law reform activity than the feminist critique. It runs the risk of entrenching principles which neglect the interests of groups which have not traditionally had a voice in the framing of criminal law. Ironically, with respect to women, codification at this time would take place when women have just begun to play a significant role in criminal law reform. In this decade Canadians engaged in a public debate about the principles underlying Bill C-49, the reform of the law relating to sexual assault. That debate made it clear that very different visions exist of the fundamental values of the criminal law. Nevertheless Parliament amended the law in a manner supported by very diverse groups of women. In my view this was an historic, but tenuous, breakthrough in terms of women acting as framers, rather than objects, of the criminal law. It is of course theoretically possible that recodification at this point of some optimism about the potential to re-imagine the criminal law could capture a consensus in the interests of women. My concern is that codification is more likely to capture principles developed at a time when women were not in a position to play a significant role in academic, legal, and political debates. Of course, there are other overlapping groups who are even less likely to have a voice in the framing of general principles.

. . .

## Principled Reform of Criminal Procedure*

### Tim Quigley

*Excerpts from "Principles Reform of Criminal Procedure" by Tim Quigley, in Don Stuart, R.J. Delisle and Allan Manson, eds., *Towards a Clear and Just Criminal Law: A Criminal Reports Forum* (Toronto: Carswell, 1999) at 254-257.

. . .

Students, law teachers, practitioners, judges, and police officers all recognize that the procedural aspects of criminal law in the *Criminal Code* are badly in need of reform. Due to piecemeal amendments, prolix legislative drafting and, more recently, the imperatives of the *Canadian Charter of Rights and Freedoms*, determining the law of criminal procedure is frequently a difficult venture. At the same time, the task of reforming criminal procedure is rather daunting. There are constitutional constraints of both the *Charter* and division of powers varieties, comprehensive criminal law reform is not particularly high on any federal government's legislative agenda, and there is considerable controversy over some reform proposals. These various considerations mean that attracting a substantial consensus for reform proposals is a difficult proposition.

In developing these proposals, I have been greatly influenced, although not always persuaded by the work of the Law Reform Commission of Canada, the predecessor of the Canada Law Commission. That body produced many reports and working papers on criminal law and procedure topics. Although sometimes attenuated by decisions interpreting the *Charter* or by more recent *Code* amendments, the recommendations of the Commission are nevertheless very useful as a springboard for discussion.

In particular, it is worth noting that the Law Reform Commission has elaborated certain principles that ought to guide the reform of criminal procedure: fairness, efficiency, clarity, restraint, accountability, participation by the citizenry, and the protection of society. These are sound principles that I have tried to keep in mind. For example, efficiency and clarity would be enhanced through better organization of the *Code* and more simplicity in the language used in legislative drafting. My approach in pursuit of these aims is to recommend an overhaul in the structuring of the *Code* so that, for example, search and seizure provisions are grouped together in one part along with other investigative powers open to the police. At the same time, it is arguable that fairness, accountability, and participation by the public are facilitated through procedures that are coherent and comprehensible. Accountability and participation by the public can also be addressed by more direct legislating by Parliament on issues related to the *Charter*. That is, a possible response to the charge that the courts have usurped the legislative function is for Parliament to take the lead by anticipating *Charter* problems and setting standards in line with *Charter* values, rather than merely reacting to Supreme Court of Canada decisions. Fairness, restraint, and the protection of the public can be, at the least, more adequately assessed if the procedures in question are understandable and accessible. Parliament is usually in a better position than the courts to balance fairness to those accused of crimes and restraint in the use of the criminal process with the need to protect the public. Thus, satisfaction of these principles points in the direction for a greater role for legislation than is presently the case.

Reform of criminal procedure involves more than reorganization and more readable legislative drafting, for there are substantive issues that should also be addressed. For example, there are, at present, few fetters on the exercise of prosecutorial discretion at a number of points in the criminal process. Crown prosecutors may decide, in the case of dual or hybrid offences, whether to proceed summarily or by indictment. They may choose to withdraw or stay charges, take over or halt private prosecutions, refuse to consent to re-election by a defendant, or, under s. 568, require than a defendant be tried by a jury in spite of her or his wish to be tried by a judge sitting alone. In these situations, the only means of controlling improper or capricious decision-making is through the rather restrictive doctrine of abuse of process. Similarly, the police have wide discretion in various contexts during the investigative stage of the process, although there are more often criteria by which those discretionary powers may be exercised. Unlimited or poorly constrained discretion weighs against both accountability and fairness. . . .

For example, the *Criminal Code* presently does not contain any explicit police power to stop motor vehicles. The approach to this issue has been taken through the jurisprudence under the protection accorded by s. 9 of the *Charter* against arbitrary detention, chiefly through the Supreme Court decision in *R. v. Ladouceur*. *Ladouceur* permits unacceptable discriminatory practices in law enforcement. Accordingly, criteria to govern the police power to stop vehicles and other conveyances should be placed in the *Criminal Code*. What the Supreme Court has mandated under the *Charter* establishes minimum constitutional standards only and should not be taken as precluding legislation which exceeds *Charter* standards. . . .

. . .The first recommendation is for a drastic reorganization of the *Code*. As later discussion will show, very often related provisions are contained in quite disparate parts of the *Code*. This is so despite the fact that its various parts on the surface appear to be arranged in a coherent and thematic way. The most outstanding example of this disorganization concerns police investigative powers. These powers are presently scattered throughout the *Code*: arrest powers and the ability to use force are contained in both Parts I and XVI, the major search warrant provisions are contained in Part XV, and the interception of communications is set out in Part VI. Even these are not exhaustive since there are several other police investigative powers provided for specific offences and others are derived from the common law or provincial statutes.

The consolidation of police investigative measures in one part of the Code is strongly recommended. Similarly, wherever possible, related matters should be placed together in one part. Of course, because the steps in the criminal process do not always unfold in the same way in every case, it is impossible to completely achieve this aim. Nevertheless, it is a desirable goal to keep in mind in the reform process.

. . .

## Criminal Law in Canadian Society*

*Excerpts from *Criminal Law in Canadian Society* (Ottawa: Government of Canada, August 1982), at 37-43, 52-54.

## SCOPE, PURPOSE AND PRINCIPLES

### Introduction

It was noted earlier that many thoughtful observers of the recent scene sense a state of crisis about the criminal law: a crisis of legitimacy, of effectiveness, of accountability. Furthermore, many of these same observers ascribe the crisis to a lack of "any clear or acceptable governing conception of what we as a society intend to accomplish under the rubric of criminality . . . " (Parliamentary Subcommittee on Penitentiaries, 1977), to an "absence of any global concept or overall general policy which if woven into the various elements of the criminal justice system, would serve to guide the various services with a uniform philosophy" (Quebec Commission of Enquiry into the Administration of Justice, 1969). The Parliamentary Subcommittee on Penitentiaries, in fact, found a "corrosive ambivalence" concerning the very goals and purposes of criminal justice.

The current debate concerning the proper purpose and scope of criminal law is of comparatively recent vintage, although it entails renewed examination of issues of moral and political philosophy that have been argued since before the Golden Age of ancient Greece.

In addressing this basic issue of the nature of the criminal law — an issue critical to the approach that will be adopted to a host of more specific issues of criminal law and criminal justice policy — it seems useful to distinguish a set of interlinked subsidiary questions:

a) What is and what ought to be the basic purpose of criminal law sanctions: punishment or treatment? And why does criminal law impose sanctions: because it is right to do so or because it works to do so?

b) What conduct should be subject to criminal law sanctions: what is the proper scope of the criminal law?

c) On whom is it justifiable to impose sanctions: only on those who intend harm, or also on those who cause harm without intending it?

d) How far can we go in pursuit of our aims through use of criminal law powers and sanctions?

Answers to these questions will lead to the formulation of a general statement of the appropriate scope, purpose and principles of the criminal law.

*The Nature of Criminal Law*

**Purpose of the Criminal Law**

The basic problem confronting criminal law and the criminal justice system, it is often argued, is not the variety of specific concerns and complaints about particular phenomena — which are mere symptoms — but rather a debilitating confusion at the most basic possible level, concerning what the criminal law ought to be doing.

Part II of this paper traced the swing of the pendulum in the past century away from the so-called retributive orientation of criminal law and toward a utilitarian approach.

In this view, as has been seen, the retributive approach was identified with an anachronistic, backward-looking, punishment-oriented concern with the wrong that had been done. The utilitarian approach, on the other hand, was seen as a modern, forward-looking, non-punishment oriented concern with protecting society by preventing future wrongs — either through changing factors in the environment or the individual offender through rehabilitation, or through the deterrent or simple incapacitative effects of imposing penalties.

This trend in the philosophical justification of criminal law was very strongly felt over the past 100 to 150 years, and it is only in the past decade that the pendulum has reversed itself, in placing more emphasis on criminal law punishment for the sake of justice, to ensure appropriate denunciation for the wrong that has been committed.

In large part, this swing has come about because of growing doubts about and dissatisfaction with the efficacy of the utilitarian approach, as well as perceived loosening of moral bonds in society that has resulted in an allegedly undisciplined and unacceptable lax response to destructive anti-social behaviour.

The call to clarify goals and to resolve an ambiguity in objectives is an understandable one, given the confusion about aims and results, and the growing demand for demonstrated effectiveness in the use of taxpayers' money.

As discussed in the second Part of this paper, the combination of growing crime, growing public concern, and growing criminal justice resources has furthered the swing to control and protection. This trend was accompanied and reinforced by the optimistic belief that we had at hand the tools of individual treatment and social engineering that would permit realization of those goals, allowing us at the same time to lessen our reliance on primitive techniques that came increasingly to be identified with an old-fashioned retributive philosophy.

The recent recession of that optimism, and the recent renewed emphasis on both traditional "justice" and "equity" concerns in general, and on the legitimacy of a retributive justification for punishment, in particular, has defined the terms of the current debate over fundamental criminal law objectives.

Posing the debate in these terms can be a useful means of sharpening understanding of the issues at stake. Many have argued that the utilitarian interest of society in eliminating crime requires that "punishment" and retributive measures (seen as nothing more than vengeance), be replaced with a range of carefully-calibrated tools designed to deter and rehabilitate. Some recent observers argue the opposite case: that the utilitarian efforts of criminal justice have not only failed to protect society and rehabilitate offenders, they have also led us to lose sight of the legitimate interest of society in seeing justice done. On this basis, the justice objectives should not only be revived, they should be given paramount emphasis, with any utilitarian effects on safety or crime reduction being viewed as welcome side effects.

In the face of these apparently irreconcilable perspectives, it is important to clarify several points.

First, the criminal law, for all the efforts and rhetoric expended over the past century, is primarily a punitive institution at root. Certainly the sanctions it metes out — whether justified in the name of treatment, rehabilitation, denunciation, deterrence, incapacitation, or whatever — are and always have been perceived as punitive by almost all of those to whom they are applied. So, whether the question of the purpose of the criminal law is approached from a retributive or a utilitarian direction, it is important to understand that the fundamental nature of criminal law sanctions is punitive.

This should not be particularly surprising since, as Part II discussed, the criminal law and the criminal justice system constitute the end point on a continuum of informal and formal customs, beliefs and institutions of social-control — the end point in terms of the ultimately coercive intervention of the state in the lives of usually non-consenting citizens.

Although it may be agreed that the ultimate characteristic of criminal law sanctions is that they punish, this proposition does not mean that the sanctions awarded under the criminal law are to be harsh, cruel, inhumane, or uninterested in the ultimate effect they have on those subject to them. (Indeed, the concept of justice is seen as imposing limits on the extent to which punishment may be inflicted, in the sense that the traditional doctrine of "an eye for an eye" means that it is unjust to take more than an eye for an eye). Neither does the proposition imply that there is a necessary conflict in imposing punishment for retributive and for utilitarian reasons, although there may be such conflict in particular instances. In many cases, imposing punishment for retributive reasons may well have utilitarian effects in terms of deterrence, denunciation and reaffirmation of social values.

Second, on the basis of the long-term perspective adopted in this paper, it appears necessary to conclude that the debate, cast in "either/or" terms, is unresolvable because it is artificial and unrealistic.

This is so because the criminal law has, and should continue to have, two major purposes:

1.  preservation of the peace, prevention of crime, protection of the public — security goals; and
2.  equity, fairness, guarantees for the rights and liberties of the individual against the powers of the state, and the provision of a fitting response by society to wrongdoing — justice goals.

It must be admitted that there is continuing tension between these two clusters of objectives and that they sometimes come into conflict. Furthermore, while the criminal law is concerned with both sets of purposes, particular components of the criminal justice system place varying emphasis on those purposes.

By recognising the legitimacy of both the utilitarian and the retributive approaches, and by refusing to equate them with security and justice respectively, we may more productively debate the specific point of balance that is to be struck between the two major purposes of the law and the criminal justice system: justice and security. Thus, if the goal is to pursue "justice", utilitarian concerns about security, protection, prevention, treatment and rehabilitation need not be abandoned. Or, if the emphasis is to be on crime control and public protection, arguments appealing to a retributive justification for punishment in the name of "justice" or "just desserts" need not be dismissed as illegitimate. This is an important consideration to bear in mind, since most recent debates on the issue of the major purpose of criminal law are posed in such a way as to suggest there can be only one such legitimate purpose. Acceptance of this assumption of the necessity for a unique purpose may appear more logically or philosophically appealing, but it does not seem to be realistic in terms of the actual uses to which criminal law is put, and the actual effects it has in society.

In the case of the criminal law, most citizens would agree that criminals ought to be punished because they have done wrong, and therefore deserve punishment. But most would also like to see society protected either by the punishment of offenders in order to deter or simply incapacitate, or, perhaps preferably, by the rehabilitation of offenders.

The argument in this section is that no social institution as important or complex as the criminal law can afford the luxury of picking just one purpose — intellectually simple and satisfying though that selection might be. As Henry M. Hart wrote in 1958:

A penal code that reflected only a single basic principle would be a very bad one. Social purposes can never be single or simple, or held unqualifiedly to the exclusion of all other social purposes; and an effort to make them so can result only in the sacrifice of other values which are also important. Thus, to take only one example, the purpose of preventing any particular crime, or crimes generally, is qualified always by the purposes of avoiding the conviction of the innocent and of enhancing that sense of security throughout society which is one of the prime functions of the manifold safeguards of . . . criminal procedure. And the same thing would be true even if the dominant purpose of criminal law were thought to be the rehabilitation of offenders rather than the prevention of offences.

On the basis of this discussion, some important conclusions can be drawn. First, the criminal law and the criminal justice system must pursue two major clusters of objectives — "justice" and "security". Second, criminal sanctions, whether justified in terms of utilitarian or retributive aims, are primarily punitive in nature, and are understood as such by both society and by those on whom they are imposed. Third, acceptance of retributive justifications for punishment implies neither rejection or utilitarian justifications for such punishment, nor the acceptance of harsh, cruel or vindictive forms or levels of punishment. Indeed, the retributive approach that is often expressed in terms of the concept of "justice" acts as a brake in setting a maximum permissible limit on punishment that might otherwise be subject to no such limit in its pursuit of various utilitarian goals such as deterrence, incapacitation, or even rehabilitation. This distinguishes the concept of retribution from that of vengeance. Fourth, recognition of the legitimacy — and necessity — of pursuing two sometimes-conflicting purposes for criminal law directs attention to the need to devise an approach for defining the proper point of balance between these two purposes.

## Proper Scope of the Criminal Law

Part II of the paper touched briefly on the trends in penal legislation over the past century, and Part III raised, as a major perceived problem, the question of the proper scope of the criminal law, as opposed to other forms of response to individual and collective behaviour within society.

Those Parts made the point that the criminal law and the criminal justice system should be conceived of as the ultimate recourse available to society along the continuum of informal and formal conventions, customs and institutions.

It is with this conception in mind that the Law Reform Commission, the Ouimet Committee, and many others have urged the doctrine of restraint in the use of the criminal law and the criminal justice system.

This notion — which has unfortunately and inaccurately been interpreted by some as a call for laxity and leniency — is properly understood as implying the need to examine carefully the appropriateness, the necessity, and the efficacy of employing the criminal law, rather than these other, less intrusive, less coercive means of dealing with particular social problems.

For some forms of conduct, this analysis can be quickly concluded. There is no question that the only adequate and fitting response to such "core" crimes as murder, assault, robbery, and so on is the criminal law. No one seriously suggests otherwise.

For other new, sophisticated and potentially harmful forms of activities — especially those of large-scale organizations — use of the criminal law may also be appropriate in some circumstances, in light of the increased dependence of individuals on such organizations with respect to crucial aspects of everyday existence and, therefore, the increased vulnerability of individuals to harmful actions on the part of such organizations.

But, too often, the response to the emergence of a particular social problem has been almost routine or automatic invocation of the criminal law, or criminal-like sanctions. The discussion above concerning offences of a comparatively trivial or anachronistic nature contained in the Criminal Code, not to mention the huge array of "public welfare" legislation that has grown up in the past century and which relies heavily on criminal sanctions and criminal procedures for its enforcement, bears on this point.

Restraint should be used in employing the criminal law because the basic nature of criminal law sanctions is punitive and coercive, and, since freedom and humanity are valued so highly, the use of other, non-coercive, less formal, and more positive approaches is to be preferred whenever possible and appropriate. It is also necessary because, if the criminal law is used indiscriminately to deal with a vast range of social problems of widely varying seriousness in the eyes of the public, then the authority, credibility and legitimacy of the criminal law is eroded and depreciated. The lumping together off seriously harmful and wrongful conduct with a host of technical, minor, or controversial matters blunts the impact and undermines the effect the criminal law should have as society's institution of ultimate recourse.

The Law Reform Commission and others have argued persuasively for a "pruning" and clarification of the criminal law on the basis of arguments such as these. This process requires consideration of the boundaries that should be drawn to distinguish between criminal law and "public welfare" regulatory and administrative law, criminal law and private morality, and criminal law and civil law.

The Law Reform Commission strongly emphasized the need to distinguish more clearly between "regulatory" offences and "real" crimes. Regulatory processes designed to control certain socially and economically useful enterprises are sometimes viewed as being "too criminal" in nature, because of their inappropriate use of summary conviction criminal procedures to enforce compliance. For the Law Reform Commission, all "real" crimes should appear in the Criminal Code and not in regulatory law, though the Commission also recommends that such distinction be made between crimes and regulatory offences for a number of reasons. These include a need to be parsimonious with the criminal law, in order to preserve the impact of its symbolic and solemn condemnation of violations of "core values". Another reason is the need to observe the principle of equity by ensuring that the most serious transgressions are normally dealt with in a more serious manner and with a more elaborate procedure than other transgressions. In the boundary between criminal law and private morality, various concerns have been expressed about either decriminalizing or diverting from criminal prosecution many acts widely considered crimes of "going to Hell in one's own fashion", such as drug and gambling offences. Some of the offences are considered too minor to be treated with the heavy hand of the criminal law; others are thought to be more effectively dealt with through public education or regulation.

In the boundary between criminal and civil law, there has been considerable interest, in Canada and elsewhere, in diverting from the criminal process certain disputes which are more in the nature of civil wrongs between citizens, or staying criminal prosecutions for the purpose of allowing the offender to make financial or other redress to the victim. In this view, traditional criminal justice emphasis on allocating blame and punishing the blameworthy has not served the interests of the victim, righted the harm done, restored the "social harmony", nor had any positive impact on the offender. Opponents of this "diversion" approach argue that it may have a lesser deterrent effect on wrong-doing, may not serve social needs to denounce criminal behaviour, has not yet shown any success in diverting offenders who would in fact have been handled in criminal court caseloads, and may endanger the legal rights of the accused and the interests of the victim.

## STATEMENT OF PURPOSE AND PRINCIPLES

Recognizing that:

In the Charter of Rights and Freedoms, Canada has guaranteed certain rights and freedoms consonant with the rule of law and with principles of justice fundamental to a free and democratic society;

Canada has, in addition, undertaken international obligations to maintain certain standards with respect to its criminal justice system;

The criminal law is necessary for protection of the public and the establishment and maintenance of social order;

The criminal law potentially involves many of the most serious forms of interference by the state with individual rights and freedoms; and

Criminal law policy should be based on a clear appreciation of the fundamental purpose and principles of criminal law;

It is appropriate to set forth a statement of purpose and principles for the criminal law in Canada.

### *Purpose of the Criminal Law*

The purpose of the criminal law is to contribute to the maintenance of a just, peaceful and safe society through the establishment of a system of prohibitions, sanctions and procedures to deal fairly with culpable conduct that causes or threatens serious harm to individuals or society.

### *Principles to be Applied in Achieving this Purpose*

The purpose of the criminal law should be achieved through means consonant with the rights set forth in the Canadian Charter of Rights and Freedoms, and in accordance with the following principles:

(a) the criminal law should be employed to deal only with that conduct for which other means of social control are inadequate or inappropriate, and in a manner which interferes with individual rights and freedoms only to the extent necessary for the attainment of its purpose;

(b) the criminal law should clearly and accessibly set forth:

    (i) the nature of conduct declared criminal;

    (ii) ithe responsibility required to be proven for a finding of criminal liability;

(c) the criminal law should also clearly and accessibly set forth the rights of persons whose liberty is put directly at risk through the criminal law process;

(d) unless otherwise provided by Parliament, the burden of proving every material element of a crime should be on the prosecution, which burden should not be discharged by anything less than proof beyond a reasonable doubt;

(e) the criminal law should provide and clearly define powers necessary to facilitate the conduct of criminal investigations and the arrest and detention of offenders, without unreasonably or arbitrarily interfering with individual rights and freedoms;

(f) the criminal law should provide sanctions for criminal conduct that are related to the gravity of the offence and the degree of responsibility of the offender, and that reflect the need for protection of the public against further offences by the offender and for adequate deterrence against similar offences by others;

(g) wherever possible and appropriate, the criminal law and the criminal justice system should also provide for:

    (i) opportunities for the reconciliation of the victim, community, and offender;

    (ii) redress or recompense for the harm done to the victim of the offence;

    (iii) opportunities aimed at personal reformation of the offender and his reintegration into the community;

(h) persons found guilty of similar offences should receive similar sentences where relevant circumstances are similar;

(i) in awarding sentences, preference should be given to the least restrictive alternative adequate and appropriate in the circumstances;

(j) in order to ensure equality of treatment and accountability, discretion at critical points of the criminal justice process should be governed by appropriate controls;

(k) any person alleging illegal or improper treatment by an official of the criminal justice system should have ready access to a fair investigative and remedial procedure;

(l) wherever possible and appropriate, opportunities should be provided for lay participation in the criminal justice process and the determination of community interests.

## Questions/Discussion

1. What are the tests used by the courts to determine whether legislation falls within the criminal law power of the federal government? How useful and effective do you think they are? Are they perhaps the best we can hope for given the task which presents itself?

2. Do you think the provinces should be given an explicit, constitutionally empowered role in the formulation of criminal justice policy and legislation? Why or why not? What should be the proper role of the provinces in this area?

3. Describe the process of formulating criminal justice policy and note its weaknesses, strengths and potential? Where and how does it fail, and why? Are the problems in

the process of a fundamental nature (i.e., the process itself is seriously flawed) or are they ones which can be corrected by better practices and better implementation?

4. Describe the development of the Criminal Code in Canada and state what has been wrong with that development. Are political pressures always going to be important in the creation of new criminal laws? Is this good or bad? Why? Do you think truly independent advisory bodies are possible or effective? Why or Why not? What would you do to change the process and do you think such changes would be politically feasible?

5. Do you think that the development of a set of guiding principles is necessary to the ordered evolution of criminal laws in Canada? Can any set of such principles ever be of much value and effect when it comes to actually deciding what will or will not enter the criminal arena? For example, to say that the criminal law should protect society from harm or that it should uphold, defend, and promote important or fundamental values in society does little to tell us what definition of "harm" one is using or what those values are and when the need bolstering in the criminal law.

6. What function or role would a General Part play in a revised Criminal Code of Canada? Is it necessary or desirable?

## Further Reading

• Barnes, J., "The Law Reform Commission of Canada" (1975), 2 Dalhousie Law Journal 62.

• Campbell, Mary E., "Politics and Public Servants: Observations on the Current State of Criminal Law Reform" (2000), 42 Canadian Journal of Criminology 341.

• Goode, M.R. "The Law Reform Commission of Canada, Barnes and Marlin and the Value-Consensus Model" (1977), 4 Dalhousie Law Journal 793.

• Hartt, E.P., "The Limitations of Legislative Reform" (1974), 6 Manitoba Law Journal 1.

• Hastings, Ross and R.P. Saunders, "Social Control, State Autonomy, and Legal Reform: The Law Reform Commission of Canada" in R.S. Ratner and John L. McMullan, eds., *State Control: Criminal Justice Politics in Canada* (Vancouver: University of British Columbia Press, 1987), at 126-148.

• Healy, P., "The Process of Reform in Canadian Criminal Law" (1984), 42 University of Toronto Faculty of Law Review 1.

• Kaiser, A., "New Directions for Canadian Criminal Law Reform: Ensuring an End to Complacency" (1993), 13 Windsor Yearbook of Access to Justice 264-86.

• Letourneau, G., and S. Zimmerman, "Recent Trends in Criminal Law Reform" (1992), 33 Cahiers de Droit 857-84.

• Samek, R., "A Case for Social Law Reform" (1977), 55 Canadian Bar Review 505.

• Steele, Graham, "A Brief History of Canadian Criminal Law" in Joel E. Pink and David C. Perrier, eds., *From Crime to Punishment: An Introduction to the Criminal Law System* (Toronto: Carswell, 1999).

• Stenning, Philip, "Accountability in the Ministry of the Solicitor General of Canada" in Philip Stenning, ed., *Accountability for Criminal Justice: Selected Essays* (Toronto: University of Toronto Press, 1995).

• Stuart, Don, R.J. Delisle and Allan Manson, eds., *Towards a Clear and Just Criminal Law: A Criminal Reports Forum* (Toronto: Carswell, 1999).

• Wood, J., and R. Peck (eds.), 100 Years of the Criminal Code in Canada (Ottawa: Canadian Bar Association, 1993).

## 3.2 THE ROLE OF THE COURTS

### Introduction

*R.P. Saunders*

The roles that the courts play in the development and production of the criminal law can be divided arbitrarily into four categories: i) an interpretive role; ii) a traditional common law role; iii) a Charter role; and iv) a process role. These roles are reflected in the readings which follow. First, the courts are responsible for the interpretation of the existing statute law and thus have a role to play in giving concrete meaning to the words in the statute through the various rules of interpretation that they employ. These rules do not concern us here as they are more useful in a practical sense and are often quite technical. However, the use of these rules may result at times in a distortion of the meaning and intent of the particular statute, or at least a re-interpretation of it.

The first two readings by Hoskins and Murray provide a brief overview of the courts' sources of power and the system of criminal courts in Canada, while the next reading, an excerpt by Kloepfer, gives the reader an introduction to some of the problems inherent in the writing of criminal law and, therefore, in its interpretation. What is to be noted in this area are both the breadth of meanings that are possible even for seemingly simple phrases or terms and also how the courts, in giving meaning to the words of the statute, produce criminal law in a practical sense. This role is not to be undervalued, for not only is it necessary in the specific application of the law, but it is also important in setting out the limits of the law's coverage in the future. The *Paré* case provides an example of the court's fulfilling this role in interpreting the term "while committing" and the consequences of its interpretation on the accused in the case. The question to ask after the case is what guidelines are given for the future for the application of the interpretation of these words to other fact situations?

Another facet of the interpretation role is to give meaning to criminal law by filling out those requirements that are not explicitly set out in the legislation, specifically by addressing the issue of the mental requirement of an offence. This is a very important role and is examined in Chapter 6, for the provisions in the Code usually define only the physical elements of a crime and not the intention or knowledge which is needed for a conviction (see also the readings by the Law Reform Commission of Canada, Stuart, and Boyle on the General Part in the first section of this chapter). As we shall see in Chapter 6, most crimes require some mental element; this is related to some notion of individual blameworthiness that arise *because* the accused did the wrongful acts intentionally or knowingly.

A final and important dimension of the interpretation role (though it could just as properly be classified as a constitutional function) is the court's role as to the constitutional division of powers which was addressed in the previous section. The tests that have been developed and examples of their use were given in that section. This "referee" function of the courts is a necessary one in a federal system such as Canada's and, as noted above, one should focus on the adequacy of the tests developed and their effective use by the courts.

Second, the courts have developed and continue to develop certain common law defences not yet found in statute. This power is explicitly set out in s. 8(3) of the Criminal Code where it is stated that:

> Every rule and principle of the common law that renders any circumstance a justification or excuse for an act or a defence to a charge continues in force and applies in respect of proceedings for an offence under this Act or any other Act of Parliament except in so far as they are altered by or are inconsistent with this Act or any other Act of Parliament.

By way of contrast, s. 9 of the Code expressly disallows common law offences except in the case of contempt of court. Examples of common law offences can be found in the defences of necessity, consent and entrapment, all of which are examined in Chapter 7. The courts will continue to have a free hand in the evolution of these defences until the federal government enacts the relevant provisions in the Code.

What can be said about these first two roles of the courts is that to date the courts have generally not done a particularly good job in the area of criminal law, notably at the highest level, the Supreme Court of Canada. The Supreme Court's interpretation and application of their own guiding principles, such as the need for actual subjective intention, have been at best inconsistent and confusing, and too often guided by what is practical and convenient in the circumstances of the case. In other words, the Supreme Court has not stepped in and filled the vacuum left by the failure of the legislators to articulate first principles.

The third function of the courts in relation to the production of criminal law arises from the constitutional entrenchment of the Charter of Rights and Freedoms in 1982. The Charter is similar to the well known American Bill of Rights, though major differences do exist. The courts derive from the entrenchment of the Charter the power to annul legislation or to intervene in the enforcement of legislation if that legislation or the enforcement procedures violate the rights and freedoms enunciated in the Charter, as interpreted by the courts. For example, in the criminal law sphere, if evidence was improperly obtained and the right to be secure against unreasonable search and seizure was thereby violated, the courts can rule that the evidence is inadmissible if by its admission the administration of justice would be brought into dispute.

Because the Charter is part of the Constitution Act, the "supreme law of Canada", it has given the judiciary much greater power than existed before 1982 in regard to the content and operation of the criminal law. The so-called rights and freedoms as set out in the Charter are not absolutes, but rather only take on the meaning and scope as given to them by the courts. In looking at the Charter's s. 9, the right not to be arbitrarily detained or imprisoned, what standard should we use for the term "arbitrarily" or, for that matter, when is a person "detained"? If the police stop you to ask you some questions, does this amount to being detained, or should something else be required before the right is available? You can look at virtually all the rights in the

Charter in this manner. The Charter sections which most directly concern and impact on the criminal law are sections 7 to 14 ("legal rights") and section 24 (enforcement). Other sections, such as the "fundamental freedoms" in section 2, the qualifying guarantee given in section 1, and the equality provision in section 15 can also be used to intervene (or not to intervene) in the area of criminal law. The reading by Cromwell addresses the important role of the Charter in the production of criminal law, while the excerpt by Young looks at the problems encountered in trying to reform the criminal law through the Charter in the context of an adversarial system.

The final role of the courts is what has been referred to as a "process role", and is the focus of the excerpts from the articles by Hoskins and Cohen. This role has to do with the criminal law that is produced, because if we look at the process which the courts use to structure and control the disputes between the state and the offender in criminal law, we can see that it is up to the parties themselves to take an active role in the proceedings while the judge takes a more passive role. There is a basic assumption that the parties are equal before the court, not only as to the extant parties but also as to the types of defendants which come before the courts. In reality there is a substantial degree of variation in the resources and arguments which the parties can marshall for the courtroom and therefore different levels of access depending upon who you are and how much money you have. Legal aid may be of use in some situations but its availability is far from universal, not only as to the *type* of offence but also as to the income levels of the offender. Cutbacks in funding levels throughout the 1990s further reduced its availability. The point here is not to belabour the lack of equality between parties within the criminal justice system, but rather to illustrate the importance of the type of process that is used in court. In Canada, this process is an adversarial process that puts the burden on the parties to carry the case and that, consequently, gives an unfair advantage to some offenders as opposed to others. What type of lawyer one can hire and what resources one has for pretrial tests or investigations can be important determinants in cases and their results (witness the 1995 murder trial of O. J. Simpson in the United States and the resources he was able to employ in his defence). This is not only important as to the individual results of a case, but it can also be important in the larger sense of what issues get litigated (and therefore what law is produced). For example, who is using the Charter provisions and to what end: one of the first important cases under the Charter was *Hunter v. Southam Inc.* (1984), 11 D.L.R. (4th) 641 (S.C.C.), which was an example of a corporation using the Charter to protect itself from state intervention in the anti-combines area of law, an area where the success rate by the state has traditionally been very poor. Who or what group has the resources and therefore the opportunity to use the courts to develop or manipulate the criminal law in a similar manner?

How the judge conducts the trial and reaches his or her decision can also have an important effect on the results of the trial and therefore the reality of criminal law for individuals or classes of individuals. If there are racist or sexist attitudes, or biases of any kind on the part of the judge that affect the ultimate decision or the legal rule that is expounded, then the results may be unfair. We know that the judiciary is not representative of the diversity of groups and classes found in the general population and that there are many examples of these biases being expressed by various judges, but what can be done? Presumably, there is a need for a better appointment process (see the articles by Baar and by Russell and Ziegel, for example, under Further Reading in section 3 of Chapter 4) to get better judges and a more representative judiciary, but the problem is greater than this. What is also required is a better and more representative "pool" of lawyers from which to select the judges, and this implies a much larger problem of ensuring more diversity on the basis of gender, ethnicity and class origin in our educational institutions, including high school, the university, and ultimately, law school. Of course, this problem of an unrepresentative judiciary is important in all the roles that the courts play in producing criminal law and affects the type of criminal law we have in Canada today. This problem is discussed in the context of feminist concerns in the Canadian Bar Association Task Force Report and in the article by Wilson listed under "Further Reading" in section 3 of Chapter 4.

In conclusion, it is important to note the overall expansion of judicial power and its exercise since 1982, and to realize what this has meant and will mean to the production of criminal law in this country, issues of expertise, democracy, accountability, accessibility and flexibility should be kept in mind as the reader proceeds through the readings below. What are the advantages and disadvantages of producing criminal law in this manner, and what are the ultimate effects of the criminal law that is produced and the crime that actually occurs? Finally, note that we return to several of these issues in Chapter 4 under "Judges" where we look in more detail at the specific roles judges play in the criminal trial, and at the possibilities for establishing greater accountability on the part of the judiciary.

## Powers Generally*

### Frank P. Hoskins

*Excerpts from "The Players of a Criminal Trial" in Joel E. Pink and David C. Perrier, eds., *From Crime to Punishment: An Introduction to the Criminal Law System* (Toronto: Carswell, 1999) at 157-159.

. . .

## Powers Generally

The courts draw their powers from essentially three sources. Obviously the *Criminal Code* gives specific courts certain powers to try offences. Other matters related to the criminal law, but tangential or incidental to the ultimate finding of guilt or acquittal, are also assigned to particular courts by the *Code*. In addition to the *Criminal Code*, all of the courts can look to specific provincial or federal legislation which establishes or continues them. This legislation will indicate how the court is to function, the geographical areas over which it has authority, and the kinds of remedies which it may give. The third main source of power for courts involved in the criminal law in Canada is a common law concept called "inherent jurisdiction." As the phrase indicates, this kind of power to give remedies and deal with matters that arise during the course of criminal proceedings exists because the court exists. Inherent jurisdiction has been used to justify many things, including the right to stop criminal matters from proceeding because they are abusive, and ordering persons to clear the courtroom during a trial. Indeed, some might suggest that inherent jurisdiction is called on as a justification whenever a court wishes to do something that it feels is right, but can point to no legislative authority which says the court may do it. That may be overstating the point a little but it is a broad enough issue that the courts of this country have generally tried to restrict any exercise of inherent jurisdiction to the superior courts of criminal jurisdiction. The justification for this is thought to be that it is the superior courts of justice created in England to dispense the monarch's justice. One shorthand way of describing which courts have "inherent jurisdiction" and which courts do not has been to speak of provincial supreme courts as "superior courts", and all others below these "superior" courts as being "inferior courts." It is now considered more polite to refer to "superior courts" and "statutory courts".

Perhaps the most serious power which the courts have is the power to punish individuals for contempt. Although the matter is a high priority for law reform, at this time contempt is the only except to the rule that no one in Canada can be convicted of a criminal offence unless that offence was enacted in statute at the time of the alleged wrongdoing. Unlike the historical power of the courts of England actually to create offences, Canadian courts have no such power except to the extent that they are reasonably free to determine what constitutes a contempt. There are no minimum or maximum penalties which exist, and there is little guidance in the cases about what will constitute contemptuous behaviour either inside or outside a courtroom.

. . .

## Courts*

### Donald C. Murray

*Excerpts from "Courts" in Joel E. Pink and David C. Perrier, eds., *From Crime to Punishment: An Introduction to the Criminal Law System* (Toronto: Carswell, 1999) at 161-166.

. . .

## THE COURTS

### Justices and Provincial Courts

The first, or entry level, of the court system is the provincial court. Most, if not all, alleged offenders will appear in these courts initially. It is here that summary conviction and "absolute jurisdiction" offences (described in the previous section) are tried. Other indictable offences may be tried in this court if the accused person agrees or elects to be tried there. The *Criminal Code* also gives justices of the peace and provincial court judges other roles to play in the criminal justice system. For example, the *Criminal Code* authorizes justices of the peace and provincial court justices other roles to play in the criminal justice system. For example, the Criminal code authorizes justices of the peace to receive informations (allegations that a criminal offence has been committed by a person), deal with the liberty of an accused person in most circumstances, and also to authorize or overrule the police with respect to the detention of property seized in the course of a criminal investigation. The provincial court may now also grant wiretap authorizations and issue warrants for DNA sample acquisition.

Other than conducting trials themselves, the most important function of the provincial court judges perhaps is to hold preliminary inquiries under Part XVIII of the *Criminal Code*. A preliminary inquiry is held to determine whether there is sufficient evidence to put an accused person on trial for an offence. Sufficient reason exists where the prosecutor leads some evidence with respect to each element of the offence charged against an accused person. While it is not the duty or even the right of a justice conducting a preliminary inquiry to weigh the credibility of witnesses or the strength of the evidence on the whole of the case, which he or she must do on a trial, it is crucial for him or her to be alive to what will required of the Crown in proving the offence charged so that someone is not put on trial and in jeopardy of a criminal punishment unnecessarily. The judicial officer conducing the preliminary inquiry may also commit an accused person to stand trial on one or more offences which were not charged against the accused person but which became apparent from the evidence led against the accused person. The preliminary inquiry, of course, does not determine any issue of guilt or no guilt. The Crown may try again before a second justice if unsuccessful the first time—or the Crown may simply decide to order the accused person to stand trial despite the finding of the preliminary inquiry.

The role of the preliminary inquiry in the criminal process only exists where an accused person chooses, or is required, to be tried in a court higher than the provincial court of a province. The preliminary inquiry may be waived by the defence, but it can serve as a useful process to discover how the Crown will present the evidence at trial and precisely how witnesses react on the witness stand. Defence counsel find it extremely useful to have this dry run to test the admissibility of certain evidence such as statements given to the police and to tie witnesses down to a specific version of events.

The most important quality of the provincial court, particularly where it is conducting a preliminary inquiry, is that it is a statutory court. As such it has only those powers given to it in a statute. Such a court has none of the "inherent jurisdiction" possessed by higher courts, and only a limited power to grant relief to an accused person other than a discharge or acquittal. For example, it is permissible for a provincial court judge to decide that a particular law is unconstitutional and will not be enforced, but when a provincial court judge is conducting a preliminary inquiry he or she cannot grant *Charter of Rights* relief to an accused person.

## Courts of Criminal Jurisdiction

When an accused person elects a trial by a judge alone, his trial is usually held after a preliminary inquiry. The trial court will usually be the supreme court, with the judge sitting without a jury. Historically, the "judge alone" election resulted in a trial before a distinct court part way between the provincial and supreme courts, called a county court. This intermediate level or court has been eliminated. Like the grand jury before it, the institution of a "court of criminal jurisdiction" with more expanded powers than the provincial courts, but fewer powers than the supreme (or equivalent) courts of the province, was an unjustifiable expense in today's world of easier transportation to a more restricted number of judicial matters.

## Superior Courts

The superior courts are the "superior courts of criminal jurisdiction" which are called the supreme, superior or Queen's Bench Court. Very briefly, these courts are superior because they can try any offence under the criminal law of Canada other than a summary conviction offence. These courts can authorize invasions of privacy by wiretap. Judges of these courts will always make themselves available to deal with questions affecting the liberty of any person (whether charged or not), and in fact are the only judicial authorities who may deal with the release of an individual charged with the most serious offences such as murder, treason, and piracy. The supreme courts in each province conduct trials with and without a jury. It is also the court where summary conviction appeals may be taken. The judges who sit on the bench of the supreme court of a province are appointed by the federal government.

In addition to those powers exercised by other courts, the supreme court in each province has authority to "supervise" all courts below it. The supreme court may, by order, halt proceedings in lower courts because of a perceived abuse of procedures, or because of a lack of jurisdiction — such as failures to permit an accused person to make full answer and defence or simply because the lower court has no jurisdiction to proceed any further with respect to the particular criminal matter. These courts may also freely exercise "inherent jurisdiction". Unlike the courts below it, a superior court of criminal jurisdiction is not restricted by any statute from doing what it feels is just and right in the circumstances of any particular case. As a result, this level of court is regarded as the most competent court to determine whether the *Charter* rights of any person have been violated. The court has every ability to give the person applying for a remedy the precise relief which appears to be just and appropriate in the circumstances.

## Provincial Courts of Appeal

The *Criminal Code* recognizes that the superior court of criminal jurisdiction in each province is divided into two parts—a trial division and an appeal division. The appeal bench may be called the Appeal Division or the Court of Appeal, depending upon the province involved. Courts of appeal do not hear trials of any criminal matters. Instead, they hear cases where the Crown or an accused person is aggrieved by a decision in some trial court. These appellate courts consider the correctness in law of the trial court's decision. Such appeals are heard by at least three, and perhaps five, judges. The appeal court justices are appointed by the federal government.

In most circumstances a right to appeal only exists where there is a question of law raised by the decision of the court which first heard the matter. From time to time the Crown or the accused may be upset by a decision for reasons of mixed law and fact, or simply upon an issue of fact. In these cases the party who wishes to appeal must obtain the permission or "leave" of the appeal court.

Appeals based on legal issues will be examined by the court in light of a transcript of trial evidence and any reasons for decision. There is power to hear fresh evidence, but this will not be done if, with reasonable efforts, the evidence could have been adduced at trial. Such new evidence would also have to be relevant to a decisive issue, credible, and such that if it was believed, could have affected the result. Needless to say, new evidence is permitted extremely rarely.

A court of appeal has three broad options before it in disposing of an appeal: it may dismiss the appeal, in which case the lower court decision stands; it may agree that there was a significant error in the lower court and direct a new trial; or, thirdly, is may allow the appeal and substitute the decision made in the lower court with its own decision—so long as this does not involve entering a guilty verdict where a not guilty verdict had been rendered by a jury. Among these three broad alternatives an appeal court has a number of ways of approaching a case.

It is not uncommon for a court of appeal to discover errors in law made at the trial of an accused person. Not every error will constitute a sufficient basis on which to overturn a verdict reached. The error might have been in the accused person's favour, but a conviction resulted anyway. In those circumstances, the court might decide that no substantial wrong or miscarriage of justice had occurred, that the accused person had suffered no prejudice to his position because of the error. Courts of appeal may even find this to be the case where the error was in the Crown's favour, but the evidence of guilt was so overwhelming that no other conclusion would be possible than that the accused person should be found guilty.

While appeal courts will usually strenuously avoid expressing opinions about the strength or weakness of a case, they are entitled to assess the whole of a case and determine whether the result seems unreasonable or unsupported by the evidence. In such situations the court is not considering whether the verdict is unjustified according to its own view of the facts, but whether it is unreasonable, given a rational appreciation of the facts.

Where summary conviction matters are concerned, the *Criminal Code* provides for a shortened appeal process which may be followed directly from the provincial court to the court of appeal. This, however, is only available where the appeal is on a strict question of law or jurisdiction. Unlike the usual appeal process to the county, district or supreme court, factual questions cannot be raised.

The appeal court may also be asked for its opinion on questions by the Minister of Justice for Canada whenever "he desires the assistance of that court". This may be requested where the Minister has a difficult issue to determine in his position as Minister of Justice and wishes to have some judicial assistance with respect to the matter. For example, the Minister may wish to exercise his prerogative of mercy under s. 749 of the *Criminal Code*, or wish to release an imprisoned individual because there are troubling aspects to the case despite a judicial finding of guilt. In this circumstance he may obtain the court's opinion about what to do. Is the case one where an individual should be released unconditionally, or should the accused person be provided with a new trial despite an earlier conviction? Such proceedings are extremely rare.

## Supreme Court of Canada

The Supreme Court of Canada is, like the provincial courts of appeal, strictly an appeals court. Nothing is heard and decided there for the first time in respect of criminal proceedings against an accused person. Instead, only those cases which involve a serious difference of legal opinion are hard, and even then, not all of these. The court is comprised of nine justices appointed by the federal government, with conventional recognition that three are to be from the province of Quebec, one from the Atlantic Provinces, one from Alberta, Saskatchewan and Manitoba, one from British Columbia, and three from Ontario. Subject to constitutional change, this geographical distribution of judicial positions is not legally required, but it has been followed reasonably consistently over the past number of years. The court is extremely busy. Depending upon the importance of the case, five, seven or even nine justices may sit. The court's inclination in recent years has been to emphasize the hearing of constitutional cases, particularly where such cases involve the *Canadian Charter of Rights and Freedoms*.

With respect to criminal matters, there are only two guaranteed rights of appeal to the Supreme Court of Canada. Each of these exist only with respect to indictable offences. A person whose acquittal is overturned by a court of appeal may appeal from that overturned verdict to the Supreme Court of Canada on a question of law. Unlike the ordinary appeal process to the superior court, factual questions cannot be raised.

Otherwise, an appellant (whether the accused person or the Crown) must ask the Supreme Court of Canada for leave to appeal with respect to a question of law. If there is no disagreement in the court of appeal, an appellant must apply for leave to appeal to the Supreme Court of Canada on the ground that the question is one of national importance for the administration of criminal justice in Canada. The Supreme Court of Canada can exercise a degree of control over the cases which it hears, but there are limits to which this can be carried if the court is going to maintain its authority with respect to the development of the criminal law in this country.

In dealing with an appeal, the Supreme Court of Canada may make any order that a court of appeal might have made. Thus, it may set aside a trial verdict on the ground that it is unreasonable or cannot be supported by the evidence, or overturn a decision on the basis that a wrong decision has been made on a question of law. Further, if it feels that there was a miscarriage of justice in any aspect of the case, whether or not the point was even argued before the provincial court of appeal, it may allow the appeal. Similarly, it may dismiss the appeal because there was no substantial wrong or miscarriage of justice toward the Crown or the accused despite a legal error or procedural irregularity.

Historically, a further appeal existed from the Supreme Court of Canada to the Privy Council in England, but, as the country became more independent, so did its judicial institutions and its criminal law. Earlier this century, appeals to the Privy

Council in England were abolished. Since that time, Canadian criminal law has developed independently, but parallel with the criminal law of England and the other Commonwealth jurisdictions. As the court of final resort for criminal matters in Canada, the Supreme Court of Canada has gained increasing respect and done much to foster uniformity in the application of the criminal law to accused persons in this country.

Only a very small percentage of criminal cases ever gets to the Supreme Court of Canada. Except for the broad directions the court can give in the few cases which come before it, much of the substance of Canadian criminal law is determined by the provincial courts of appeal, and manifested in the day to day decisions of the many provincial court judges and justices of the peace. Indeed, for most people who at some time face a criminal charge in this country, it is not the Supreme Court of Canada or even the courts of appeal which have any influence on them. The court system for them is no more than the justices of the peace and provincial court judges who apply and do most of the judging about what is and what is not criminal in this country.

. . .

## Ambiguity and Vagueness in the Criminal Law:
## An Analysis of Types*

*Stephen Kloepfer*

*Excerpt from (1984-85), 27 Criminal Law Quarterly 94.

## INTRODUCTION

A recurrent problem in legal analysis is to distinguish disputes about facts from disputes about *words*. That factual and verbal considerations impinge on one another renders this problem a formidable one. The distinction has, however, much to recommend it. Conceptual clarity can be gained by attempting to distil from a legal controversy the contribution linguistic considerations make to it. Traditional scholarship in the criminal law, for example, has tended to focus more on how the details of an accused's conduct should be differentiated and classified, than on the statutory verbal formulae by which the classification is ultimately effected. Problems of the latter sort have, for the most part, been relegated to the topic of statutory interpretation, and this has resulted in a particular imbalance in criminal law scholarship. The thoughtfulness expended on developing criteria for classifying criminal conduct has far exceeded that devoted to analyzing the technical problems of statutory drafting and interpretation which abound in Canadian criminal law.

The object of this article is to identify more precisely the sorts of semantic problems to which the criminal law recurrently gives rise, and to analyze how contemporary Canadian judges choose among possible statutory meanings and justify their choices. For however much Willis's adumbration of the "literal", "golden", and "mischief" rules was descriptive of judicial approaches to statutes at the time he wrote, it is today in no way descriptive of the complexity of interpretative problems which statutes give rise, of the sophistication with which the ablest of our judges resolve them, or of the various ways in which considerations of context influence the judicial attribution of meaning to statutory words. Indeed, some of the greatest insights into current judicial approaches to statutory interpretation are found in cases which, although presenting a problem of statutory meaning, are disposed of without any consideration of statutory interpretation at all. That received doctrine and current practice appear to have parted company recalls the anecdote about the eminent judge who confessed that "books on spiritualism and statutory interpretation were two types of literary ebullitions he had learned not to read".

The complexity of interpretative problems in the criminal law derives in part from the varieties of "meaning" in communication which insistence on a "literal" or "plain meaning" approach tends to obscure. Professor Dickerson has done much to clarify these distinctions, and he is surely correct in arguing that they constitute vital *matériel* in our continuing "battle against the bewitchment of our intelligence by means of language". Literal meaning is the "meaning carried by language when it is read in its dictionary sense unaffected by considerations of particular context". It must be distinguished from *actual* meaning, which is the meaning of a word or passage when read in a given context, and *true* meaning, which is the meaning disclosed when the word or passage is read in its "proper context".

The problem of what constitutes proper context is an elaborate one, but it may succinctly be described as "the context, shared by the communicant and his audience, that is presupposed by the communication". Although literal meaning may, in a given statutory provision, coincide with actual or true meaning, consideration of proper context typically yields a resultant meaning that differs significantly from literal meaning. Nor, on reflection, is this surprising. The literal meaning of a word or passage in a statute typically has a range of potential reference that is much wider when considered alone that when viewed through the reducing lens of proper context. Accordingly, only when "literal" or "plain meaning" corresponds to true meaning, that is, when it is arrived at by considering proper context, is the doctrine of literalism in statutory interpretation intelligible at all. "Legal meaning" is the meaning assigned to a statutory provision by a court adjudicating a particular legal controversy. The arguable disparity between "legal" meaning and "true" meaning provides the stuff of scholarly criticism and, one hopes, of appellate court emendations.

The necessity of adverting to proper context in order to approximate to true statutory meaning is highlighted by an appreciation of the deficiencies in the vehicle of language itself. Configurations of words have neither the clarity of crystals nor the austere precision of mathematical symbols nor the austere precision of mathematical symbols, and what they *should* be taken to mean in a given context is, in statutes as in other modes of communication, a semantic subset of what they *could* be taken to mean independently of context. Ambiguity and vagueness of language are the primary chronic "disease" which call for contextual therapy, and it is important to distinguish between the different forms of each disease and to identify the various symptoms by which each is recognized.

# AMBIGUITY

Ambiguity, "the condition of admitting of two or more meanings, or being understood in more than one way, or of referring to two or more things at the same time", is perhaps the most serious disease of language in that the intended meaning of an ambiguous word or passage, unlike that of homonymous words which also have multiple layers of reference, is not necessarily resolved by advertence to context. Indeed, legal terminology has exacerbated the problem, by designating additional meanings to words ambiguous in themselves. Examples are such words as "residence", "assignment", "user", "accounting", "process", "information", "tax", "bargain", "traffic", "service" and "fixture".

In a landlord and tenant statute, for example, in the stipulation that "the user of the premises shall be reasonable and all fixtures shall be kept in good repair", it is not clear whether the words "user" and "fixture" are employed in their legal or in their colloquial senses. Legal usage has rendered both terms essentially ambiguous, especially where they are used in a legal or *quasi*-legal context. Accordingly, special care must be taken by lawyers and legislative draftsmen to avoid using ambiguous words where the particular legal context will not render the intended meaning clear. The lawyer or draftsman "should avoid using the ambiguous word (*e.g.*, residence) whenever his intended meaning (*e.g.*, legal home) may be adequately expressed by an unambiguous word (*e.g.*, domicile)". In law, if not in politics, ambiguity is neither desirable nor defensible.

## *Semantic Ambiguity*

The most obvious form of ambiguity found in statutes is semantic ambiguity, where a word's inherent multiplicities of meaning derive from lexicographical usage and exist independently of context. Semantic ambiguity is not confined to single words however; often, whole phrases or passages are semantically ambiguous. For example, s. 237(5) of the Criminal Code provides:

(5)  No certificate shall be received in evidence pursuant to paragraph (2)(d), (e) or (f) unless the party intending to produce it has, before the trial, given to the accused reasonable notice of his intention *together with* a copy of the certificate.

The phrase "together with" in s. 237(5) is semantically ambiguous; it could mean either "at the same time as" or, alternatively, it could mean "in addition to". The admissibility of the certificate of analysis as Crown evidence in a case where a copy of such certificate was not given to the accused at the same time as the Crown notified the accused of its intention to produce the certificate would depend on which connotation of the phrase "together with" is judicially adopted as the legal meaning of that phrase. As it happens, the phrase "together with" in s. 237(5) has been judicially construed to mean "at the same time as", but it is surely better to avoid ambiguous terms at the drafting stage than to give judges yet another opportunity to deny that a term is ambiguous at all.

. . .

## Syntactic Ambiguity

The examples cited above illustrate semantic ambiguity, where the uncertainty of meaning derives from lexicographical usage and does not always yield to suggestive features of context. Another conduit of muddled messages is syntactic ambiguity: a statement is syntactically ambiguous where its grammatical structure gives rise to uncertainties of reference. Syntactic ambiguity is the principal cause of the fallacy of "amphiboly", and expressions in which it occurs are often not without aspects of humour, intended or not. Advertising copy exhibits interesting variations on a theme of syntactic ambiguity, for example: "Safe Driving is No Accident"; "Save Soap and Waste Paper"; "We Dispense With Accuracy"; "Just received! A new stock of sports shirts for men with 15 to 19 necks"; "Siberian Husky, 2 yrs. old, eats anything and especially fond of children". Nor is this form of ambiguity entirely foreign to legal contexts, for example, in the rough-and-tumble of appellate advocacy: "May it please your Lordship to turn it over in what your Lordship is pleased to call your Lordship's mind?" or "Your Lordship is quite right, and I am quite wrong — as your Lordship usually is".

Although syntactic ambiguity often imparts an innocuous humour to poorly-formed sentences, where it finds its way into statutes, especially penal statutes, the consequences can be anything but humorous. An accused's procedural rights, legal culpability, or liability to punishment may depend on how a judge or appellate court construes a statutory provision that is syntactically ambiguous. Indeed, problems of syntactic ambiguity often necessitate the most delicate exercises of judicial judgment. For example, the question may arise, not whether a particular statutory provision applies to the details of an accused's actions, but whether the accused is a member of the class of persons the provision is intended to address.

. . .

## Contextual Ambiguity

Apart from semantic and syntactic ambiguity, statutory provisions may be ambiguous because of competing contextual considerations arising either within the statute or between provisions of two or more statutes. Contextual ambiguities will occur notwithstanding that the meaning and syntax of the provisions in question may be unequivocal. A problem may arise concerning which of two inconsistent statutory directives should be considered controlling, or whether a particular implication should be inferred. For example, where general words in a statute follow a non-exhaustive enumeration of persons, things, or actions that appear to be instances of a single genus, there may arise a question whether the indeterminate "residue" should be restricted to persons, things, or actions of that genus. Although aspects of each of the sorts of contextual ambiguities will converge in a given case, problems of contextual ambiguity may useful be grouped into two broad classes: (i) *internal* contextual ambiguity, where the semantic problem is at least formally localized within the statute; and (ii) *external* contextual ambiguity, where the semantic problem results from the applicability of two or more statutes to the legal controversy. As will become clear below, the judicial resolution of contextual ambiguities typically involves the invocation of general legal principles which provide residual guidance where various forms of statutory uncertainty arise.

### Internal Contextual Ambiguity

Problems of internal contextual ambiguity may take a number of forms, many of which have no counterpart in traditional doctrine on statutory interpretation. Even where the problem is a recurrent feature of statutory language, there is only seldom a rule or principle of interpretation that will reconcile in an acceptable way, and for the right reasons, the different thrusts of meaning occasioned by its occurrence. The uniqueness of proper context from one semantic problem to another usually renders inappropriate the reflexive invocation of alleged rules, canons, presumptions, and so forth. While the result reached in a given case may coincide with the dictates of an established precept of interpretation, such coincidence is often more, as it were, coincidental than casual.

. . .

### External Contextual Ambiguity

Contextual ambiguities are not confined to the interrelationships among provisions in the same statute, for it often happens that more than one statute is pertinent to the legal controversy. Where provisions from two or more enactments are relevant but seemingly irreconcilable, and where a choice has to be made about which provision has, in the circumstances, a greater claim to judicial attention, the problem is one of external contextual ambiguity. The most fertile source of external contextual ambiguity in Canadian criminal law is the often problematic relationship between the Criminal Code and various provisions in the Interpretation Act. For example, in *Re Purdy and The Queen*, the question arose whether s. 27(2) of the Interpretation Act, which makes certain provisions of the Code applicable to offences under all other federal enactments, coupled with the statutory power of a justice to issue search warrants where he is satisfied that there are reasonable grounds to believe that a Criminal Code offence has been committed, could be used to supply the absence of such a power regarding offences against the Broadcasting Act. Section 27(2) or the Interpretation Act and s. 443(1)(b) of the Code are extracted below:

(2) All the provisions of the *Criminal Code* relating to indictable offences apply to indictable offences created by an enactment, and all the provisions of the *Criminal Code* relating to summary conviction offences apply to all other offences created by an enactment, except to the extent that the enactment otherwise provides.

**443**(1) A justice who is satisfied by information upon oath in Form 1, that there is reasonable ground to believe that there is in a building, receptacle or place

. . .

(b) anything that there is reasonable ground to believe will afford evidence with respect to the commission of an offence against this Act . . .

. . .

> may at any time issue a warrant under his hand authorizing a person named therein or a peace officer to search the building, receptacle or place for any such thing, and to seize and carry it before the justice who issued the warrant or some other justice for the same territorial division to be dealt with by him according to law.

In a lucid and libertarian judgment, Mr. Justice Limerick for the New Brunswick Court of Appeal rejected any such implication. He asserted that "there is no right since the *Magna Carta* in any person to invade the home or enter privately occupied lands or buildings in the absence of contractual or statutory provisions", and that legislation derogating from common law rights must be expressed with irresistible clarity where it purports to override them. Since s. 443(1)(*b*) confers this authority only with respect to offences "against this Act", namely, against the Criminal Code, and since s. 27(2) of the Interpretation Act does not incorporate the expression "*mutatis mutandis*", the inexorable conclusion was that the power to issue search warrants under s. 443(1)(*b*) was intended to be restricted to offences under the Criminal Code. Implicit in the court's conclusion was that the power to issue search warrants for offences against the Broadcasting Act must be grounded in a statutory sanction more emphatic than the one contended for by the Crown. On this and other of the issues raised by the appeal, Mr. Justice Limerick's opinion is exemplary of the principle of legality vigorously in play.

The effort required to disentangle the congeries of statutory interrelationships between, for example, the Criminal Code and the Interpretation Act, is highlighted by the Supreme Court of Canada decision in *Colet v. The Queen*. The Crown argued that the power to seize firearms pursuant to a warrant issued under the former s. 105 of the Code included the power to *search* for such firearms, even though s. 105 did not authorize search warrants for that purpose. To bolster this argument, the Crown sought to rely on s. 26(2) of the Interpretation Act, which provides that "where power is given to a person, officer or functionary, to do or enforce the doing of any act or thing, all such powers shall be deemed to be also given as are necessary to enable the person, officer or functionary to do or enforce the doing of the act or thing". It was contended that the power to search was a necessary incident of the power to seize, and therefore that s. 26(2) supplied the deficiency.

The Supreme Court of Canada rejected this contention. Mr. Justice Ritchie put the point forcibly:

> It appears to me to follow that any provision authorizing police officers to search and enter private property must be phrased in express terms and the provisions of the *Interpretation Act* are not to be considered as clothing police officers by implication with authority to search when s. 105(1) and the warrant issued pursuant thereto are limited to seizure. The extensive number of sections of the *Criminal Code* to which reference was made by the trial Judge and which expressly include the dual authority "to search" and "to seize" are enough in themselves to indicate that the deeming provisions of s. 26(2) of the *Interpretation Act* are not applicable to the circumstances.
>
> . . . It is my respectful opinion that if Parliament intended to include the power "to search" in the provisions of s. 105(1), the failure to do so was a clear case of legislative oversight, but that power which has not been expressly conferred cannot be supplied by invoking the provisions of the *Interpretation Act*.

. . .

# VAGUENESS

The discussion thus far has concerned the various forms of ambiguity that occur in penal statutes, and has demonstrated how judges tend to resolve them by invoking principles which pertain, not to the ascertainment of meaning *per se*, but the socio-legal considerations which impel the adoption of one interpretation to the exclusion of another. Vagueness is a qualitatively different form of semantic uncertainty, and it is unfortunate that ambiguity and vagueness have occasionally been treated as though they implied the same contests of meaning.

The salient differences between ambiguity and vagueness have been well articulated by Dickerson:

> Where "ambiguity" in its classical sense refers to equivocation, "vagueness" refers to the degree to which, independently of equivocation, language is uncertain in its respective application to a number of particulars. Whereas the uncertainty of ambiguity is central, with an "either-or" challenge, the uncertainty of vagueness lies in marginal questions of degree. This uncertainty is said to result from the "open texture of concepts".

Statutory language may be ambiguous, vague, or both. For example, the phrase "by that person" in s. 214(5) of the Criminal Code is ambiguous; it is uncertain whether it refers only to the person who causes the death, or to any person who is a party to the murder, notwithstanding that the latter may have taken no part in the actual killing. On the other hand, the phrase "gross indecency" in s. 157 of the Criminal Code is vague: apart from the exceptions set forth in s. 158, whether or not a particular sexual behaviour is "grossly indecent" in law is a question more of putative social tolerance than of probable statutory meaning. That a term may simultaneously be ambiguous and vague is illustrated by the word "residence". For example, where a taxing statute provides a special deduction for taxpayers "having residence in Ontario", it may initially be unclear (a) whether the taxpayer is required to have a place of abode in Ontario, or to be domiciled in Ontario (in the legal sense of "domicile"), and (b) if the context suggest the former meaning, whether a particular place of abode is sufficiently "residential", for example, a yacht that is permanently moored in Toronto Harbour and in which the itinerant taxpayer from time to time resides.

Problems of vagueness in penal statutes may usefully be grouped into two broad categories: (1) internal contextual vagueness, in which vague statutory language is construed in light of its full statutory context and in light of general institutional assumptions such as *stare decisis*: and (2) external contextual vagueness, in which a statute or statutes other than the one directly in issue is relevant, at least formally, to the controversy, but is vague in its prescriptions.

## *Internal Contextual Vagueness*

The most cursory perusal of the Canadian Criminal Code betrays an abundance of vague statutory language. Whether the vagueness inheres in the definition of the offence itself, for example, "act of gross indecency"; "indecent act", and "undue exploitation of sex", "a purpose dangerous to the public peace"; "the course of justice"; "anything that is obscene, indecent, immoral, or scurrilous"; or in the definition of an institutional power, for example, "no substantial wrong or miscarriage of justice", it is obvious that Parliament, by couching its directives in such broad language, has delegated to officials charged with administering them, and ultimately to the courts, the discretionary power to determine whether a particular fact situation should be subsumed within the relevant statutory provision.

Vagueness and generality of statutory language are to some extent unavoidable. As H.L.A. Hart has pertinently observed:

> It is a feature of the human predicament (and so of the legislative one) that we labour under two connected handicaps whenever we seek to regulate, unambiguously and in advance, some sphere of conduct by means of general standards to be used without further official direction on particular occasions. The first handicap is our relative ignorance of fact: the second is our relative indeterminacy of aim.

### External Contextual Vagueness

A recurrent interpretive problem concerning the Criminal Code and other criminal statutes is that of external contextual ambiguity, in that it is grounded in the applicability of more than one statute to the proceedings in question, there are important distinctions between them. Where external contextual ambiguity arises, the "external" statutory provision has at least *some* relevance to the semantic issue presented; the question is not whether the external provision could, if applied, provide guidance, but whether its application is appropriate where the primary statute provides compelling contextual clues which support a different conclusion. Canadian courts have, for example, refused to allow various "all-purpose" sections in the Interpretation Act to be used to enlarge police powers, to lighten the evidentiary obligations of the Crown, or to erode vital distinctions between Criminal Code and juvenile delinquency proceedings.

Where the problem is one of external contextual *vagueness*, however, the external statutory provision offers no assistance on the semantic issue before the court. It is merely a vague exhortation to the judiciary, rather like a pre-game pep talk to a referee who is told that he should follow its dictates regardless of the rules of the game being played. That a conscientious referee will nonetheless adjudicate on the basis of the rules rather than the rhetoric is hardly surprising. Fortunately, this has been the Canadian experience concerning the criminal law and the "remedial" effect of s. 11 of the Interpretation Act thereon.

Section 11 of the Interpretation Act, which applies to all federal enactments, including the Criminal Code, is the primary source of problems of external contextual vagueness in Canadian criminal law. It provides:

> **11.** Every enactment shall be deemed remedial, and shall be given such fair, large and liberal construction and interpretation as best ensures the attainment of its objects.

The judicial controversy to which this section has given rise, especially within the last decade, has been the extent to which it prevails over common law principles of interpretation which lead to conclusions that, on some view at any rate, are not sufficiently "fair, large and liberal". In reference to the interpretation of the criminal law, the controversy has resolved itself into a contest between the arguable dictates of s. 11 and the principle that the accused should receive the benefit of any reasonable ambiguity in a penal statute. Although judicial exchanges on this issue have been lively of late, the principle of strict construction has emerged relatively unscathed.

. . .

## CONCLUSION

The interpretation of modern day criminal legislation is plainly a more sophisticated enterprise than either judges, scholars, or legislative draftsmen have been apt to acknowledge. A better understanding of the different types of semantic problems in the criminal law, and of the range of considerations which judges canvass in attempting to resolve them, confers benefits over and above its intrinsic value to the scholar. The clarification of interpretative problems in the criminal law provides a basis for commentary and criticism where, under the guise of "merely interpreting the statute", important related issues of legality and fairness are not adequately addressed. It also can serve as an aid to legislative draftsmen, whose chosen words become the "fixed verbal form" of legislative policy. While the inherent deficiencies of language ensure that statutes will continue to be attended by an aura of imprecision, a heightened awareness of these deficiencies will, it is hoped, result in statutory texts that speak with greater clarity and structural consistency. This, in turn, would sharpen the criminal policy choices put forward for political assent. For, as Chief Justice Dickson has eloquently declared, "it is unnecessary to emphasize the importance of clarity and certainty where freedom is at stake".

## R. v. Paré
### (1987), 60 C.R. (3d) 346 at 360 (S.C.C.).

Appeal by Crown from judgment of Quebec Court of Appeal setting aside accused's conviction of first degree murder and substituting conviction of second degree murder.

The judgment of the court was delivered by

WILSON, J.: — Section 214(5)(b) of the Criminal Code, R.S.C. 1970, c. C-34, as enacted by S.C. 1974-1975-1976, c. 105, which was in force at the time of the commission of the offence, provided that murder is first degree murder when the death is caused by a person while the person is committing indecent assault. The respondent, Marc-André Paré, indecently assaulted and murdered a 7-year-old boy, Steeve Duranleau. The central issue in this appeal is whether the respondent murdered the child "while committing" the indecent assault.

While ss. 213 and 214 were subsequently amended by "An Act to amend the Criminal Code in relation to sexual offences and other offences against the person and to amend certain other Acts in relation thereto or in consequence thereof". S.C. 1980-81-82-83, c. 125, the amendments are not germane to the issue on this appeal.

## THE FACTS

On 13th July 1982, at about 1:30 in the afternoon, the respondent, Marc-André Paré, then 17 years old, met Steeve Duranleau, a 7-year-old boy. At Paré's suggestion, the two went swimming. After about 15 minutes in the pool Paré offered to take Duranleau to look at some used cars. The offer was only a pretence. Paré's real motive was to get Duranleau alone in order to have sexual relations with him.

After changing, Paré and Duranleau went to a parking lot where they looked at some used cars. Near the parking lot was a bridge that crossed the St. Charles River. Paré lured Duranleau under the bridge. Duranleau wanted to leave, but Paré told him not to and held him by the arm. Paré sat there for the next ten minutes, holding Duranleau by the arm. Then Paré told Duranleau to lie on his back and keep quiet. Paré pulled Duranleau's shorts down and lowered his own pants and underwear. He then lay on top of Duranleau and indecently assaulted him. After ejaculating beside Duranleau's penis, Paré sat up and got dressed.

At this point Duranleau told Paré that he intended to tell his mother about the incident. Paré told him that he did not want him to tell his mother, and that if he did he would kill him. After this exchange of words Paré was certain that the boy would tell his mother as soon as he could. Paré made Duranleau lie on his back. He waited for two minutes with his hand on Duranleau's chest. He then killed Duranleau by strangling him with his hands, hitting him on the head several times with an oil filter, and strangling him with a shoelace.

The accused was charged as follows:

> [TRANSLATION] That in Quebec City, Quebec, on or around 13 July 1982, he illegally and intentionally killed Steeve Duranleau, thereby committing murder in the first degree contrary to ss. 212, 214(5) and 218 of the Criminal Code.

At trial the accused admitted all the facts outlined above. On 7th December 1982 the accused was found guilty of first degree murder. The accused's appeal to the Quebec Court of Appeal was dismissed on 2nd April 1985 (per L'Heureux-Dubé, Beauregard and LeBel JJ.A.), the court substituting a verdict of second degree murder for the jury's verdict of first degree murder: J.E. 85-556. Leave to appeal was granted to the Crown by this court (per Beetz, Lamer and Wilson JJ.) on 27th June 1985 [1985] 1 S.C.R. xii.

## THE COURTS BELOW

### *The Superior Court*

In his charge to the jury Bienvenue J. discussed the meaning of the words "while committing" in s. 214(5) of the Criminal Code. Since this appeal hinges upon the meaning of these words, it is necessary to reproduce the relevant comments of the trial judge:

> Alors l'art. 214(2)(5)(b) [sic-214(5)(b)] nous dit ce qui suit: "Est assimilé au meurtre au premier degré" — je ne pense pas que le mot "assimilé" fasse de difficulté entre vous et moi,

c'est un mot qui veut dire tout simplement *"est* un meurtre au premier degré", ça va, c'est un meurtre au premier degré , ce qui va suivre — "le meurtre concommittant [sic]" — ou, si vous préférez, au lieu de "concommittant" je vais vous suggérer un éventail d'expressions qui veulent dire la même chose, c'est-à-dire "commis a l'occasion de", "commis au moment de", "qui accompagne", etc., ce qui va suivre, "qui c'est produit en même temps que", tous ces mots-là sont des synonymes de "concommittant" — donc "le meurtre concommittant", ou, si vous préférez, "qui a été commis à l'occasion", du crime "prévu a l'art . . . 156" du Code Criminel, "(attentat a la pudeur sur une personne de sexe masculin)" . . .

Vous réalisez, je pense, que c'est même pas nécessaire de le dire, je fais droit à votre intelligence à tous, mais au cas ou on me reprocherait un jour de ne pas l'avoir dit que quant on dit "concommittant", c'est-à-dire "commis en même temps, à la même occasion, au même moment", vous réalisez que le Code ne vas pas jusqu'à exiger qu'au moment où je commets un attentat à la pudeur avec ma main droite je doive commettre mon meurtre avec la main gauche. N'est-ce pas? Le Code est logique dans cela, quant on dit "au même moment, commis dans, à la même occasion", ça veut dire: au cours des mêmes circonstances.

The jury found the accused guilty of first degree murder.

### *The Court of Appeal for Quebec*

Beauregard and LeBel J.A. gave separate reasons; L'Heureux-Dubé J.A. agreed with both. Beauregard J.A. examined the case law and decided that s. 214(5) of the Criminal Code should be restrictively interpreted. He concluded that "while committing" must be contrasted with "after having finished committing". A murder committed after the accused had committed the indecent assault was not a first degree murder. Accordingly, when the trial judge said to the jury that a murder committed "on the occasion of" an indecent assault was a first degree murder, he did not invite the jury to consider the really critical question, namely, whether the murder was committed during the commission of the indecent assault or after the indecent assault was over.

Beauregard J.A. was of the opinion that a properly-directed jury would not have been convinced beyond a reasonable doubt that the accused murdered his victim while committing the indecent assault. Consequently, he dismissed the appeal and substituted a verdict of second degree murder for the verdict of first degree murder.

LeBel J.A. did not agree with Beauregard J.A.'s conclusion that s. 214(5) required the murder and the indecent assault to be absolutely simultaneous. Even if the section were to be construed restrictively, he stated, it must not be deprived of all effect. By reading s. 214(5) in conjunction with s. 213 LeBel J.A. concluded that the words "while committing" demanded a close temporal connection between the indecent assault and the murder. Moreover, he concluded that the murder must be an immediate consequence of the first offence for s. 214(5) to apply. LeBel J.A. found it difficult to conclude that a jury more completely informed of the nuances of the sections in question would have necessarily returned the same verdict. The charge given to the jury, he stated, effectively prevented the jury from directing its attention to the proper meaning of s. 214(5). Therefore, despite his reservations about Beauregard J.A.'s conclusions of law, LeBel J.A. agreed with his disposition of the case.

## THE ISSUE

Counsel for the appellant submit that the Court of Appeal made two errors in law. First, it erred in concluding that s. 214(5) of the Criminal Code created a substantive offence of murder. Second, it erred in its interpretation of the words "while committing" in s. 214(5). I will address both issues, looking first at the general scheme of the murder provisions in the Criminal Code and then turning to the interpretation of the particular wording of s. 214(5).

### The General Scheme

Counsel for the appellant submit that the Court of Appeal viewed s. 214(5) of the Criminal Code as creating a substantive offence of murder. I find nothing in the judgments rendered by the Court of Appeal that suggests that this was the case. In any event, counsel for the respondent acknowledge that such an approach would be improper, and I agree. Section 214 has a completely different function.

The relevant provisions of the Criminal Code are as follows:

**212.** Culpable homicide is murder
(a) where the person who causes the death of a human being
    (i) means to cause his death, or
    (ii) means to cause him bodily harm that he knows is likely to cause his death, and is reckless whether death ensues or not;
(b) where a person, meaning to cause death to a human being or meaning to cause him bodily harm that he knows is likely to cause his death, and being reckless whether death ensues or not, by accident or mistake causes death to another human being, notwithstanding that he does not mean to cause death or bodily harm to that human being; or
(c) where a person, for an unlawful object, does anything that he knows or ought to know is likely to cause death, and thereby causes death to a human being, notwithstanding that he desires to effect his object without causing death or bodily harm to any human being.

**213.** Culpable homicide is murder where a persons causes the death of a human being while committing or attempting to commit high treason or treason or an offence mentioned in section 52 (sabotage), 76 (piratical acts), 76.1 (hijacking an aircraft), 132 or subsection 133(1) or sections 134 to 136 (escape or rescue from prison or lawful custody), 143 to 145 (rape or attempt to commit rape), 149 or 156 (indecent assault), subsection 246(2) (resisting lawful arrest), 247 (kidnapping and forcible confinement) 302 (robbery), 306 (breaking and entering) or 389 or 390 (arson), whether or not the person means to cause death to any human being and whether or not he knows that death is likely to be caused to any human being, if
(a) he means to cause bodily harm for the purpose of
    (i) facilitating the commission of the offence, or
    (ii) facilitating his flight after committing or attempting to commit the offence,
and the death ensues from the bodily harm;
(b) he administers a stupefying or overpowering thing for a purpose mentioned in paragraph (a), and the death ensues therefrom;
(c) he wilfully stops, by any means, the breath of a human being for a purpose mentioned in paragraph (a), and the death ensues therefrom; or
(d) he uses a weapon or has it upon his person
    (i) during or at the time he commits or attempts to commit the offence, or
    (ii) during or at the time of his flight after committing or attempting to commit the offence,

and the death ensues as a consequence.

**214.** — (a)  Murder is first degree or second degree murder . . .
(5) Irrespective of whether a murder is planned and deliberate on the part of any person, murder is first degree murder in respect of a person when the death is caused by that person
(a) while committing or attempting to commit an offence under section 76.1 (hijacking aircraft) or 247 (kidnapping and forcible confinement); or
(b) while committing an offence under section 144 (rape) or 145 (attempt to commit rape) or while committing or attempting to commit an offence under section 149 (indecent assault on female) or 156 (indecent assault on male).

It is clear from a reading of these provisions that s. 214 serves a different function from ss. 212 and 213. Section 212 and 213 create the substantive offence of murder. Section 214 is simply concerned with classifying for sentencing purposes the offences created by ss. 212 and 213. It tell us whether the murder is first degree or second degree. This view of s. 214 was expressly adopted by this court in *R. v. Farrant*, [1983] 1 S.C.R. 124, 32 C.R. (3d) 289, [1983] 3 W.W.R. 171, 4 C.C.C. (3d) 354, 147 D.L.R. (3d) 511, 21 Sask. R. 271, 46 N.R. 337 (per Dickson J. at p. 140), and in *Droste v. R.* [1984] 1 S.C.R. 208, 39 C.R. (3d) 26, 10 C.C.C. (3d) 404, 6 D.L.R. (4th) 607, 3 O.A.C. 179, 52 N.R. 176 (per Dickson J. at p. 218). In this case it is established that the respondent murdered Steeve Duranleau. The issue is whether s. 214(5)(b) makes the murder first degree.

### Section 214(5): "while committing"

#### The Literal Meaning

Did the respondent murder Duranleau while committing an indecent assault? Counsel for the respondent submit that he did not. The argument here is simple. The murder occurred, it is submitted, after the indecent assault was complete. Thus, by a literal reading of s. 214(5) Paré did not murder Duranleau "while committing" an indecent assault.

This argument is a forceful one but by no means decisive. The literal meaning of words could equally be termed their acontextual meaning. As Professor Dworkin points out, the literal or acontextual meaning of words is "the meaning we would assign them if we had no special information about the context of their use or the intentions of their author": see R. Dworkin, Law's Empire (1986), Cambridge, Harvard University Press, at p. 17. Thus the words "while committing" could have one meaning when disembodied from the Criminal Code and another entirely when read in the context of the scheme and purpose of the legislation. It is the latter meaning that we must ascertain.

A preliminary problem in ascertaining the contextual meaning of the phrase "while committing" arises from an inconsistency between the French and English versions of s. 214(5). At the time of the offence the French version of the English words "while committing" was "concomitant". In 1983 the word "concomitant" was replaced by the phrase "en commettant". Is this change in wording in the French version significant to the interpretation of s. 214(5)? I think not. I would agree with Beauregard J.A. of the Quebec Court of Appeal, who said: "Il me semble que la modification n'a rien apporté de nouveau. Le mot 'concommittant' [sic] signifiait 'while committing' ou 'en commettant'."

## The Case Law

I now turn to cases which throw some light on the meaning of the words "while committing". Counsel for the appellant submit that these words in s. 214(5) should not be held to require the murder and the underlying offence to take place simultaneously. They seek to support this contention by reference to the judicial interpretation of the same words in s. 213.

Section 213 transforms culpable homicide into murder where a persons causes the death of a human being "while committing" any one of a number of serious offences, provided that the case falls within one of the four categories listed in ss. 213(a) to 213(d). The cases have consistently construed the words "while committing" in s. 213 to include cases where the homicide is committed during flight after commission of the underlying offence: see *R. v. Vaillancourt* (1974), 31 C.R.N.S. at 82, 16 C.C.C. (2d) 137, affirmed [1976] 1 S.C.R. 13, 31 C.R.N.S. 81, 21 C.C.C. (2d) 65, 54 D.L.R. (3d) 512, 4 N.R. 30 [Ont.]; *R. v. Stevens* (1984), 11 C.C.C (3d) 518, 2 O.A.C. 239 (C.A.). The appellant's argument is that because "while committing" is broadly construed in s. 213 it should also be broadly construed in s. 214(5).

This argument, in my view, is not sound. The particular construction placed on the words "while committing" in s. 213 was mandated by the reference to "flight" in subss. (a)(ii) and (d)(ii) of that section. As Martin J.A. noted in *Stevens* at p. 540: "Any other interpretation [of the words "while committing"] would deprive paras. (a)(ii) and (d)(ii) or s. 213 of any meaning and would render them inoperative . . . ". Section 214(5), however, contains no such references to "flight". Thus no analogy may properly be drawn from judicial interpretation of the words "while committing" in s. 213. The same words appearing in s. 214(5) must be interpreted in the particular context of that section.

In *R. v. Gourgon* (1979), 9 C.R. (3d) 313, affirmed 19 C.R. (3d) 272 (B.C.C.A.), Anderson J. construed the words very narrowly. He stated at p. 319:

> (2) the words "while committing" in s. 214(5) . . . relate to the time of the commission of the offence of "forcibly confining" and to no other time.
>
> I agree that the words "while committing" in s. 214(5) do not apply to "flight", and that unlike s. 213, the words "while committing" do not have to be given an extended meaning to make sense of s. 214(5).
>
> It should be noted, however, that Anderson J.'s comments on the interpretation issue were obiter, since in that case the underlying offence of confinement was continuing at the very instant when the death took place.

. . .

## Strict Construction

Counsel for the respondent argue that the doctrine of strict construction of criminal statutes requires that this court adopt the interpretation most favourable to the accused.

According to this argument the words "while committing" must be narrowly construed so as to elevate murder to first degree only when the death and the underlying offence occur simultaneously. In order to assess the validity of this position we must examine the doctrine of strict construction.

The doctrine is one of ancient lineage. It reached its pinnacle of importance in a former age when the death penalty attached to a vast array of offences. As Stephen Kloepfer points out in his article "The Status of Strict Construction in Canadian Criminal Law" (1983) 15 Ottawa L. Rev. 553, at pp. 556-60, the doctrine was one of many tools employed by the judiciary to soften the impact of the Draconian penal provisions of the time. Over the past two centuries criminal law penalties have become far less severe. Criminal law remains, however the most dramatic and important incursion that the state makes into individual liberty. Thus, while the original justification for the doctrine has been substantially eroded, the seriousness of imposing criminal penalties of any sort demands that reasonable doubts be resolved in favour of the accused.

This point was underlined by Dickson J. in *Marcotte v. Can. (Dep. A.G.)*, [1976] 1 S.C.R. 108 at 115, 19 C.C.C. (2d) 257, 51 L.R. (3d) 259, 3 N.R. 613 [Ont.]:

> It is unnecessary to emphasize the importance of clarity and certainty when freedom is at stake. No authority is needed for the proposition that if real ambiguities are found, or doubts of substance arise, in the construction and application of a statute affecting the liberty of a subject, then that statute should be applied in such a manner as to favour the person against whom it is sought to be enforced. If one is to be incarcerated, one should at least know that some Act of Parliament requires it in express terms, and not, at most, by implication.

. . .

### Applying the Doctrine

As we have noted above, it is clearly grammatically possible to construe the words "while committing" in s. 214(5) as requiring murder to be classified as first degree only if it is exactly coincidental with the underlying offence. This, however, does not end the question. We still have to determine whether the narrow interpretation of "while committing" is a reasonable one, given the scheme and purpose of the legislation.

In my view, the construction that counsel for the respondent would have us place on these words is not one that could reasonably be attributed to Parliament. The first problem with the exactly simultaneous approach flows from the difficulty in defining the beginning and end of an indecent assault. In this case, for example, after ejaculation the respondent sat up and put his pants back on. But for the next two minutes he kept his hand on his victim's chest. Was this continued contact part of the assault? It does not seem to me that the important issues of criminal law should be allowed to hinge upon this kind of distinction. An approach that depends on this kind of distinction should be avoided if possible.

A second difficulty with the exactly simultaneous approach is that it leads to distinctions that are arbitrary and irrational. In the present case, had the respondent strangled his victim two minutes earlier than he did, his guilt of first degree murder would be beyond dispute. The exactly simultaneous approach would have us conclude that the two minutes he spent contemplating his next move had the effect of reducing his offence to one of second degree murder. This would be a strange result. The crime is no less serious in the latter case than in the former; indeed, if anything, the latter crime is more serious, since it involves some element of deliberation. An interpretation of s. 214(5) that runs contrary to common sense is not to be adopted if a reasonable alternative is available.

In my view, such an interpretation has been provided by Martin J.A. in *Stevens*, supra. As noted above, Martin J.A. suggested [at p. 541] that "where the act causing death and the acts constituting the rape, attempted rape, indecent assault or an attempt to commit indecent assault, as the case may be, all form part of one continuous sequence of events forming a single transaction" the death was caused "while committing" an offence for the purposes of s. 214(5). This interpretation eliminates the need to draw artificial lines to separate the commission and the aftermath of an indecent assault. Further, it eliminates the arbitrariness inherent in the exactly simultaneous approach. I would therefore respectfully adopt Martin J.A.'s single transaction analysis as the proper construction of s. 214(5).

This approach, it seems to me, best expresses the policy considerations that underlie the provision. Section 214, as we have seen, classifies murder as either first or second degree. All murders are serious crimes. Some murders, however, are so threatening to the public that Parliament has chosen to impose exceptional penalties on the perpetrators. One such class of murders is that found in s. 214(5), murders done while committing a hijacking, a kidnapping and forcible confinement, a rape, or an indecent assault. An understanding of why this class of murder is elevated to murder in the first degree is a helpful guide to the interpretation of the language.

The Law Reform Commission of Canada addressed this issue in its working paper 33, Homicide (1984). At p. 79 the paper states:

> ... there is a lack of rationale in the law. Subsection 214(5) provides that, whether planned and deliberate or not, murder is first degree murder when committed in the course of certain listed offences. It is curious that the list there given in considerably shorter than that given in section 213 which makes killing murder if done in the commission of certain specified offences. Inspection and comparison of the two lists, however, reveal no organizing principle in either of them and no rationale for the difference between them.

With respect, I disagree. The offences listed in s. 214(5) are all offences involving the unlawful domination of people by other people. Thus an organizing principle for s. 214(5) can be found. This principle is that, where a murder is committed by someone already abusing his power by illegally dominating another, the murder should be treated as an exceptionally serious crime. Parliament has chosen to treat these murders as murders in the first degree.

Refining, then, the concept of the "single transaction" referred to by Martin J.A. in *Stevens*, supra, it is the continuing illegal domination of the victim which gives continuity to the sequence of events culminating in the murder. The murder represents an exploitation of the position of power created by the underlying crime and makes the entire course of conduct a "single transaction". This approach, in my view, best gives effect to the philosophy underlying s. 214(5).

*The Charge to the Jury*

Given this interpretation of s. 214(5), was Bienvenue J.'s charge to the jury acceptable? The trial judge gave of number of definitions of "while committing". I do not think, however, that these definitions would have confused the jury or included events too remote from the underlying offence. The words "while committing" in s. 214(5) include conduct which is part of one continuous sequence of events forming a single transaction to the jury was in line with this interpretation, since it emphasized the need for connection between the two offences, but without demanding that they occur simultaneously.

## CONCLUSION

The respondent murdered Steeve Duranleau two minutes after indecently assaulting him. The killing was motivated by the fear that the boy would tell his mother about the indecent assault. The jury found the respondent guilty of first degree murder. They were entitled to do so. The murder was temporally and causally connected to the underlying offence. It formed part of one continuous sequence of events. It was part of the same transaction.

I would allow the appeal and restore the conviction of first degree murder.

*Appeal allowed; conviction restored.*

## The Players of a Criminal Trial*

### *Frank P. Hoskins*

*Excerpts from "The Players of a Criminal Trial" in Joel E. Pink and David C. Perrier, eds., *From Crime to Punishment: An Introduction to the Criminal Law System* (Toronto: Carswell, 1999) at 169, 170-172.

. . .

## THE ADVERSARIAL SYSTEM OF CRIMINAL JUSTICE

The criminal trial process in Canada is based in the accusatorial or adversarial criminal justice system, which functions on the premise that every person is innocent until proven guilty, on relevant evidence, beyond a reasonable doubt. The fact that a person has been charged with a particular offence means only that he has been accused of a crime. Such a person is presumed innocent until his or her guilt is established on relevant evidence beyond a reasonable doubt, before an independent justice, with or without a jury. It is a principle of fundamental justice in our system that accused persons are not called upon to demonstrate their innocence or justify their conduct. However, once the Crown establishes a *prima facie* case against the accused, it is up to the accused to call evidence or face conviction.

The adversarial nature of the trial process has been recognized as a principle of fundamental justice.

. . .

The adversarial or accusatorial system of criminal justice has been justified over the years by many judges, lawyers and legal commentators as capable of promoting the finest approximation of the truth.

Unlike our adversarial system of criminal justice, countries in Europe employ the inquisitorial system of criminal justice, which places the obligation on the judiciary to ferret out the facts and thus ascertain the truth. Judges do not wait for the truth to emerge from the contentions of the opposing parties. In the inquisitorial system of criminal justice, the judge is expected to make the thorough investigations necessary to bring out the truth and prepare the case for trial. It is the responsibility of the trial judge to bring out the relevant facts, not the prosecution and defence.

The accused is brought before an examining judicial officer who makes an exhaustive preliminary inquiry. If the inquiry judge finds reasons to believe that the accused committed a crime, then an indictment is prepared by the prosecuting officers assigned to a particular court. After the preparation of the indictment, the accused is brought to trial. The court usually consists of three or more judges assisted by a jury. The judges take a very active part in the trial process, conducting most of the direct and cross-examinations of the witness.

The principal distinguishing characteristic between the adversarial (accusatorial) and inquisitorial systems of criminal justice resides in the relative passivity of the judge in the adversarial system. In the adversarial or accusatorial system of criminal justice, judges do not themselves conduct investigations into criminal cases independent of both Crown and defence, nor do they usually delegate others to do so.

. . .

It is a well-established tenet in our Canadian legal system that the advocates (both Crown and defence) are expected to act as strong advocates within the adversarial process. In that regard, it is both permissible and desirable that the advocates vigorously pursue a legitimate result to the best of their ability. In the pursuit of justice, rules of just conduct that govern court practice and procedure will govern the conduct of litigation. Rules of evidence also control the court process; insofar as they control the presentation of facts before the court. This vigorous pursuit of justice is a critical element of our criminal justice system; as the essential purpose and feature of our adversarial system of criminal justice is the attainment of the truth. It should be noted, however, that judges, lawyers and legal scholars recognize the inherent weakness of using the adversarial system of criminal justice in the search for the truth.

In the authoritative textbook entitled "The Law of Evidence in Canada," the esteemed authors note that:

> . . . because our system is an adversarial one where fact presentation is controlled by the litigants and their counsel, this goal can be elusive in many cases. Apart from this deficiency in the framework in which the evidence is presented, the evidence itself may be inherently weak due, for example, to the imperfect recollection or perception of witnesses. In an attempt to limit these frailties, many of the rules of evidence are concerned with ensuring the reliability of accuracy of the evidence the court receives.

Obviously, our adversarial system of criminal justice places a heavy burden on the players of a criminal trial. The Judge, Crown and defence must strenuously strive for perfection in performing their respective roles in the trial process.

It is a well-established principle that the adversarial system of criminal justice owes a duty of fairness to the players of a criminal trial within the constructs of the trial process.

It is trite to say that in order to maintain the public confidence and respect in the effectiveness of the Canadian criminal justice system, the courts must ensure that trials are fair and that they appear to be fair to the informed and reasonable observer. This is the fundamental goal of the justice system in a free and democratic society. The principles of fundamental justice require that the criminal trial process be a fair one. Accordingly, each player in the trial process must ensure that there is a fair hearing.

. . .

## Controlling the Trial Process: The Judge and The Conduct of Trial*

*Stanley A. Cohen*

*(1977), 36 C.R.N.S. 15.

## INTRODUCTION

The role of the judge in the conduct of a criminal trial is one calling for great sensitivity. If often requires the delicate balancing of important societal values. The actual manner in which a judge conducts a criminal trial will either enhance respect for the administration of justice or it will detract from it.

The purpose of this portion of this study is to place in high relief the nature and complexity of many of the vexing questions which must be confronted and adequately answered by our judiciary if the judicial system is to retain its credibility with the Canadian people.

The adversary system — the basic procedural structure of the criminal trial — merits and receives consideration in the pages which follow. The role and the response of the trial judge to counsel, and to the accused, is analyzed — both in terms of ideal types and of present shortcomings. In this regard, attention is focused upon the various forms of judicial intervention into the trial process which are presently manifest, and an attempt is made to discern the limitations upon such conduct.

Obviously the analysis offered infra cannot aspire to the final resolution of such highly complex and contentious issues. Nevertheless, the just resolution of them is absolutely crucial to the criminal justice system and to the administration of justice generally.

# PASSIVE AND ACTIVE MODELS OF JUDICIAL DEMEANOUR IN THE CONDUCT OF TRIAL

## *The Adversary Process and the Search for Truth*

"Truth, like all other good things, may be loved unwisely — may be pursued too keenly — may cost too much."

An eminent commentator and jurist reflecting on our legal system poses this question: "Is the quest for justice synonymous with the search for truth?" His answer is qualified: "In most cases, yes. Truth and justice will emerge in a happy coincidence. But not always. Nor should it be thought that the judicial process has necessarily failed if justice and truth do not end up in perfect harmony. Such a result may follow from the law's deliberate policy."

It cannot be denied that the criminal trial process is intimately concerned with the discovery of truth. But, over and above this, its concern is to do justice between man and man. Prejudice, innuendo, opinion and speculation are viewed as poor hand maidens in the cause of justice. Hence the criminal trial is not held "at large" and not "every piece of damning prejudice" will there be received into evidence. The truth is one thing. The law has regard for other values as well, as Freedman C.J.M. (the commentator above referred to) has advised us. A whole network of procedural and evidentiary rules exist to regulate and modulate Canadian trials and thus secure the end of fundamental justice.

The criminal trial process is therefore best regarded as a *qualified* search for truth.

This well-tempered inquiry is pursued in an unusual setting. The citizen and the state confront each other as opponents, or adversaries, and conduct a battle or "fight" according to age-hardened and time-tested rules and procedures.

The criminal trial is the paradigm of this adversary process. It has its detractors as well as its proponents. There are many who proclaim that it is well-suited to the task of discovering truth:

> Many lawyers maintain that the 'fight' theory and the 'truth' theory coincide. They think that the best way for a court to discover the facts in a suit is to have each side strive as hard as it can, in a keenly partisan spirit, to bring to the court's attention the evidence favorable to that side. Macaulay said that we obtain the fairest decision 'when two men argue, as unfairly as possible, on opposite sides', for 'then it is certain that no important consideration will altogether escape notice'.

In the adversarial setting of the criminal trial this partisan battle involves a clash between the public interest in the suppression of crime and the protection of the public, and the countervailing public interest in the protection of individual rights and liberties.

Because the state is possessed of enormous manpower and economic resources to aid in the process of fact-finding and research, and because the individual does not have similar resources at his disposal, an attempt is made, through the formulation of evidentiary and procedural rules, to "right the balance". This is done in order that the battle of adversaries (which follows the laying of criminal charges) be perceived by the citizenry of the state as an essentially "fair" contest.

As mentioned, in purely objective terms this attempt to strike a balance between the competing claims of the individual and the state must on occasion work in such a way as to actually suppress some of the truth: A wife's evidence is not available in order to condemn her husband, the accused person is generally not obliged to criminate herself, and where the accused does not testify, evidence of his prior misdeeds is generally not available to the prosecution in its efforts to prove its case.

The adversary process as carried on in the criminal courts has (in complimentary terms) been described as an attempt to secure "justice between man and man". Truth is pursued, but not over-zealously and always with an eye toward relevancy and the avoidance of undue prejudice.

To continental lawyers the notion of fabled British justice is something of a puzzle:

> The continental courts claim to have only one aim — the discovery of the truth. The English adversary system claims to settle an issue between the prosecution and the defendant and it is a commonplace remark that this emphasises the sporting element in an English trial. This sporting element is a psychological factor of the greatest importance, for it is out of it that there arises the notion of 'fair play' for the accused. It has recently been argued that with the steady growth of professionalism in crime and the increase (as alleged) in the number of acquittals of those guilty of crime, this notion of a sporting element should be abandoned.

Abandoning the "sporting element" of Anglo-Canadian justice is an extreme suggestion. Freedman C.J.M. indicates that our law "makes its choice between competing values and declares that it is better to close the case without all the available evidence being put on the record. We place a ceiling price on truth".

Nevertheless, there are many who feel that we have fixed the price badly; that there has been "too much tenderness toward prisoners" and that in pursuing "justice" too avidly we have weakened the social fabric.

Jerome Frank is undoubtedly correct when he states that "frequently the partisanship of the opposing lawyers blocks the uncovering of vital evidence or leads to a presentation of vital testimony in a way that distorts it." At the same time, however, it must be remembered that "in the system of trial which we have evolved in this country the judge sits to hear and determine the issues raised by the parties, *not to conduct an investigation or examination on behalf of society at large*". Consequently the criminal trial, as we have noted, is not held "at large". Its terms of reference are circumscribed by many restraints. The requirement of "relevence" is as much an efficiency device designed to avoid needless tangential forays as it is a construct aimed at insuring fundamental fairness in the conduct of the inquiry.

But is there "too much tenderness towards prisoners in these matters"? Is "truth" being sacrificed at the mantle of "justice"? Jerome Frank, himself once a judge of the United States Court of Appeal for the Second Circuit, found many deficiencies to exist in the adversary trial — deficiencies which not only worked to deny truthful facts to the court, but which also worked to frustrate the cause of justice. Judge Frank felt that certain elements inherent in the nature of an adversarial contest operated so as to frustrate even the *qualified* search for truth which our courts presently conduct. He asserted that:

1.  The whole atmosphere of the courtroom bewilders witnesses.
2.  Lawyers, before trial, "coach" the witnesses who will appear for their clients, not

only with regard to the story they will tell, but also the demeanour they should assume in testifying so as to give the most favourable personal impression.

3.   Dishonest lawyers use this accepted practice to encourage perjury.
4.   Lawyers attempt to discredit witnesses through exercise of the art of cross-examination, regardless of the truth of what these witnesses may be saying.
5.   Lawyers refuse to concede facts harmful to their clients if they think the adversary cannot prove them, and they will not help to correct inaccurate statements of witnesses favourable to their clients.
6.   Lawyers rely, wherever possible upon surprise as a tactic to keep the adversary from preparing to rebut particular testimony favourable to their clients.
7.   The adversary process is deficient because a party may not have the funds to pay for an investigation, before trial, to assemble evidence on his behalf and to rebut evidence on which the other party may rely.

In fairness to Judge Frank much of the above commentary is directed at the adversary system in the context of a civil, rather than a criminal, trial. But the above remarks have much relevance to criminal trials as well.

Those criticisms of the adversary system are not insubstantial. Basically they imply that one of two serious options ought to be implemented:

1.   The adversary system ought to be drastically altered in terms of its evidentiary and procedural structure. Irrationality ought to be weeded out and imbalances should be rectified.
2.   The adversary system ought to be done away with altogether and should be replaced by an inquisitorial system.

Option (1) above is already in a protean state of existence. The drift of law reform in Canada is towards a whittling away of the historic rights and privileges which have been accorded to accused persons. The process has been slow, but it is inexorable. *Trial by jury* is not a commonplace of our criminal justice system; it is a rarity. Indications are that it will become rarer still. Our rules of evidence, their absurdities notwithstanding, are more honoured in the breach than in practice: see N. Brooks, book review on McWilliams, Canadian Criminal Evidence, and Sopinka and Lederman, "The Law of Evidence in Civil Cases" (1976), 54 Can Bar Rev. 179 at 182. Suggestions for criminal law reform emanating from the Law Reform Commission of Canada include the removal of the accused's right to silence. The present Canadian position with respect to the use of illegally obtained evidence (see *Regina v. Wray*, 11 C.R.N.S. 235, [1971] S.C.R. 272, [1970] 4 C.C.C. 1, 11 D.L.R. (3d) 673) renders much of our rhetoric about "fundamental fairness" a sham and an "embarrassment". Notwithstanding the protestations of some that "the Criminal is living in a Golden Age", the record does not support the charge.

Despite the benefit of reasonable doubt which is accorded to an accused; despite the burden of proof under which the prosecution must labour; and despite the prisoner's right to silence — despite all of these "heavily-weighted advantages" — "the scales of criminal justice are not balanced".

As mentioned, serious resource imbalances exist as between prosecution and accused. In many cases (and here the field is ever-expanding) the onus of proof has been shifted by legislation to the accused.

Against this backdrop our two adversaries are asked to join arms in regulated battle. While, indeed, we still have two adversaries left to fight this battle, the ground under foot is continually shifting. Many hands are "tinkering with the works". Coherency of vision, and unity of purpose, is absent from most of this process.

Its defects notwithstanding, it appears unlikely that there is substantial support in the Canadian legal community for the proposition that the adversary system ought to be *completely* dismantled. Proponents of such change favour the adoption of an inquisitorial system based upon the experience of continental Europe.

The adversary system possesses the "justifications" which (its proponents argue) cannot be compensated for by an inquisitorial process:

1. Truth is more likely to emerge if the parties themselves, motivated by their own self-interest, have control of investigating and presenting the facts to the tribunal; and
2. The tribunal's decision will be morally acceptable to the parties since it was made by one not involved in the presentation of evidence and therefore by one not committed to the particular cause of any single party.

Proponents of the inquisitorial system are more likely to take issue with the first of the propositions, than the second. In their view the continental-style inquiry is unparalleled as a truth-seeking device.

There is, of course, not simply one inquisitorial system utilized by all judicial systems not founded on the Anglo-Saxon. Great differences of approach are apparent from country to country. If a single distillation of the core elements of *the* inquisitorial system is possible, this admiring portrait offered by Edson Haines (Haines, J. of the Ontario Supreme Court) would represent its best qualities as well as any:

> . . . the task of the judge in most foreign systems of law is akin to that of the scientist in the laboratory, to ascertain the real truth by all proper means. Essentially the enquiry into the circumstances devolves upon the court and the investigating judge or officer may take considerable time in developing the evidence both for and in favour of the accused. Frequently those injured in the incident giving rise to the charge are also represented, and it is not unusual for the verdict to deal not only with guilt or innocence but also with civil responsibility, so that all matters may be concluded in the one proceeding. Complicated rules of evidence are unknown. The tendency is to admit all testimony on the theory that the court gives to all evidence the weight it deserves. The accused is questioned as the facts are developed during the investigation and his explanations are checked out by the court which also searches out and examines witnesses for the accused. Serious trials often commence with the examination of the accused which has the advantage at the outset of discovering those areas in dispute and those about which there is no controversy. They really try the man as well as the facts. Consequently the record of the accused, good or bad, is before the court. A feature emphasized in many jurisdictions is that the acquittal of the guilty is a threat to the security of society.

A discourse on the superiority of one system or another in this context is not a particularly useful or fruitful exercise. Our history, societal values and political institutions have quite naturally enclosed us in a cocoon of biases and predilections.

However, certain features of the utopian paradigm sketched by Haines, J. do invite obvious responses from the common lawyer.

First among these is the grave risk of prejudice which is assumed in the portrait above mentioned. Innuendo, speculation, opinion and irrelevancies can present a damning trap for any accused person. To assert that judges will offset this danger by weighting evidence in relation to its perceived reliability is to saddle ordinary humans with a very unordinary burden.

"Judging the man as well as the facts" certainly carries with it the risk of convicting *the man* in absence of truly probative facts.

It may well be true that "the acquittal of the guilty is a threat to the security of society", but to the common law lawyer the graver risk to the *viability* of society is posed by the conviction of the innocent.

Not mentioned in the summary provided by Haines, J. is the standard to be utilized for the assessment of guilt. What contrast is there to the common law's presumption of innocence and the necessity for unanimity among our jurymen? In a French assize court, for example, there are three professional magistrates (a president and two assessors) and nine jurymen (selected from 25 drawn by lot for each assize). The whole tribunal deals with both law and fact. If the accused is unable to secure a majority in the vote as to his guilt he will be convicted — a far cry from our jury trials where one man's conscience may ultimately hold sway over jury's deliberations.

The inquisitorial system has been attacked on the basis that its paternalistic character "unavoidably raises suspicions of bias and tastes of despotism." The sufficiency of the inquiry conducted in terms of its fact-gathering mechanism, the ability of the party to bring his views and questions to the attention of the inquisition at the investigative phase, and the inability of the tribunal to contemplate all of the positions which a defendant might wish to advance are pointed to as serious, general defects of such a system.

### The Role of the Trial Judge in the Adversary Process

The greater part of this analysis will be devoted to exploring the specific limitations under which trial judges labour in handling various aspects of the trial process. How far a judge can or should proceed to enter into the trial arena is to a certain extent governed by the nature of the problem with which he is presented.

Obviously the role of the trial judge in dealing with an accused who is unrepresented by counsel will be far different from the considerations guiding his conduct when both parties are represented.

The proper response of the court to incompetency in counsel also may prompt the trial judge to deviate from otherwise normal standards of judicial conduct.

Other matters, such as the judicial examination or cross-examination of witnesses or judicial determinations to call witnesses to assist the court in its fact-finding enterprise or expressions of personal opinion by the trial judge, are not generally situation-inspired, but rather are usually expressions of a particular conception of the role of the trial judge in the entire trial process.

Is the trial judge to be an *active* force in the adversarial contest which he characteristically oversees and regulates? Or is his role more properly conceived as a *passive* one, with his interventions for the most part confined to clarifying obscurities and keeping the course of the trial within the orderly channels provided for by rules of evidence and procedure? Is the role of the trial judge essentially an active or a passive one? Does he play the role of pilot, participant or umpire?

In traditional terms, the role of the trial judge conducting a criminal trial has unquestionably been viewed as a passive one.

Denning L.J. in *Jones v. National Coal Bd.*, [1957] 2 Q.B. 55 at 64, [1957] 2 All E.R. 155, details the passive conception of the judicial role as well as it can be sketched:

> ... it is for the advocates, each in his turn, to examine the witnesses, and not for the judge to take it on himself lest by so doing he appear to favour one side or the other ... The judge's part in all this is to harken to the evidence, only himself asking questions when it is necessary to clear up any point that has been overlooked or left obscure; to see that the advocates behave themselves seemly and keep to the rules laid down by law; to exclude irrelevancies and discourage repetition; to make sure by wise intervention that he follows the points that the advocates are making and can assess their worth; and at the end to make up his mind where the truth lies. If he goes beyond this, he drops the mantle of a judge and assumes the role of an advocate; and the change does not become him well.

Sir Edmund Fry on the occasion of being named a Lord Justice of appeal in England summarized his view of the duty of a judge in *any* court:

> Give a benign and receptive listening to each side, so as to feel the full force of the argument on each side, and then judge between them.

It has been said that if a trial judge opts for a more active role — if he, so to speak, "descends into the arena" — he then is "liable to have his vision clouded by the dust of conflict': per Lord Greene M.R. in *Yuill v. Yuill*, [1945] P. 15, [1945] 1 All E.R. 183 at 189. To this it may be added that it then becomes difficult for him to avoid the appearance of bias or prejudice.

> Whatever the variations, a central core of agreed standards defines the trial judge as the neutral, impartial, calm, non-contentious umpire standing between the adversary parties seeing that they observe the rules of the adversary game. The bedrock premise is that the adversary contest is the ideal way to achieve truth and a just result rested upon the truth.

The author of the above-quoted statement acknowledges that even in the passive conception of the judicial role, the idea of the judge solely, or even primarily as "umpire", is not universally accepted. Denning L.J., to whom we have previously referred, also says as much [p. 63]:

> Even in England, however, a judge is not a mere umpire to answer the question 'How's that?' His object, above all, is to find out the truth, and to do justice according to law.

An American jurist commenting on the conception of the trial judge as purely playing an "umpireal" role claims that this view suffers from an inadequate appreciation of the true relationship between judges and lawyers in the trial process:

> Unfortunately, true understanding of the judicial process is not shared by all lawyers or judges. Instead of regarding themselves as occupying a reciprocal relationship in a common

purpose, they are apt to think of themselves as representing opposite poles and exercising divergent functions. The lawyer is active, the judge passive. The lawyer partisan, the judge neutral. The lawyer imaginative, the judge reflective.

There is a grain of truth in this critique. The qualities of activism and imagination and, to a degree, even partisanship (where abuse and obstruction of the court's process is involved) are not foreign to the judicial demeanour, even within the parameters of the so-called "passive" conception of the judicial role. The fact is that our system does provide considerable latitude for effective or just intervention by the trial judge in the adversary fight about the facts. (These latitudes are explored more fully in the body of this work.)

However, a major limiting factor circumscribing both the role and aspirations of *any* trial judge is the fact that the trial judge is quintessentially (in criminal matters) unprepared in terms of both advance exposure to, and investigation of, the facts. (In civil cases he will at least have the benefit of the pleadings, affidavits and other supporting material including, on occasion, extensive factual admissions.) Unlike his counterpart in civil law countries he does not have the dossier of the investigating magistrate before him.

Without an investigative file, the . . . trial judge is a blind and blundering intruder, acting in spasms as sudden flashes of seeming light may lead or mislead him at odd times.

Its banality notwithstanding, what goes without saying in discussions centering on the nature of the judicial role is the sentiment that "the essence of the judicial role, active or passive, is impartiality and detachment, both felt and exhibited."

There is an activist conception of the judicial role, different in *kind* from the passive one. The activist ideal (if it can be so described) seeks to eschew the vision of a trial judge powerless to enter the fray in instances where he perceives an overt and patent thwarting of the pursuit of justice through the artful but unfair (not illegal) manipulation of rules and procedures. To such a trial judge the triumph of "justice" may appear as a different thing from the advocate's notion of victory.

The activist trial judge must basically, and most truthfully, be seen to be at odds with the adversary process. In order to be effective in his role he must constantly be straining and testing the very limits of the role which he has been asked to play. His efforts undoubtedly will on occasion meet with rebuke in the higher courts. But ultimately the disagreements between these two judicial levels must be perceived to be disagreements over basic philosophy.

The activist judge is a foe of the adversary system. He is most accurately described as an "adversary judge". Since his aim generally is to reform the system, in ideal terms he should do open battle with it. Characteristically such a judge is both "outspoken" and "creative", although his more traditional critics might employ less enthusiastic adjectives in describing his activity.

Jerome Frank and Marvin Frankel are two American jurists who admirably live up to this portrait. In Canada, Edson Haines (Haines J. of the Ontario Supreme Court) has played a similar role. By their learned commentary, their irascible and uncompromising courtroom demeanour, they vividly present without artifice or deceit — the alternative, full-blown. Basically, these and other "activist" judges do not favour the outright abolition of the adversary process but rather they operate under "the hypothesis that the tensions and contradictions in the trial judge's role may reflect remediable imperfections in the system he administers".

For the present, the activist model of judicial demeanour is out of the mainstream of normative judicial behaviour. However, as we have noted, many hands are at work tinkering with the mechanisms of the adversary process. As these mechanisms are altered the role of the trial judge will, in degree, be affected. If pre-trial discovery (even partial discovery) of the accused becomes a reality and this information becomes available to the court, the adequacy of the pre-trial preparation on the trial judge will be greatly enhanced. If pre-trial conferences between counsel for all parties and the trial judge become a common-place of the system this also will alter the role of the trial judge. If the right to silence of the accused is forfeited the adversary system will be immeasurably affected.

Not all, or indeed any, of these changes should be viewed as salutary. As suggestions for reform, however, they have been kicked about for a long time. And as we enter into yet another era of "law and order" (or, as we choose to call it in Canada, "peace and security") there is no predicting the mood of our legislators.

Yesterday's (or today's) judicial iconoclast may well become tomorrow's archetype. For the moment, however, this picture (which is really a description of the ideal-passive type) is the one which prevails:

> An overtly active judge may give the appearance of a meddler; but equally, a passive and quiescent trial judge may give the appearance of indifference. The public may have a legitimate complaint about the appearance and doing of justice — not just against counsel — but against a Bench which renders judgments based on technical evidentiary deficiencies or errors ... A trial judge who endeavours to assist counsel, parties, and witnesses in the proper, complete and logical development of all aspects of a case within the confines of the rules of evidence and the adversary system, neither favouring one side or the other, nor expressing any bias, but still remaining dispassionate and neutral (but not disinterested or indifferent) will gain the respect of all concerned with the administration of a viable system of justice.

## Canadian Charter of Rights and Freedoms*

### *Thomas A. Cromwell*

*Excerpts from "The Players of a Criminal Trial" in Joel E. Pink and David C. Perrier, eds., *From Crime to Punishment: An Introduction to the Criminal Law System* (Toronto: Carswell, 1999) at 381-385.

I

The Constitution is a set of rules that governs the ways our laws are made and, to a degree, administered. It is the "supreme law of Canada", Parliament and the Legislatures are bound by its provisions. Any law inconsistent with it is invalid and of no force and effect. Ultimately, however, it is up to the courts to decide whether laws are inconsistent with the Constitution. In making this determination, they must interpret the Constitution and decide how its provisions apply in particular circumstances.

The courts in Canada have been doing this from the time of Confederation in 1867. The Constitution, at that time called the *British North American Act* (*B.N.A. Act*), set limits on the powers of Parliament and the Legislatures and laid down many other requirements concerning the governing of the new country. The courts were called on frequently to decide whether these limits and requirements were being met, and their decisions, although often not popular, were obeyed by all concerned. The main point is that the courts in Canada have, for a long time, interpreted and applied the provisions of the Constitution.

In April, 1982, a new dimension was added to the Constitution. The *Canadian Charter of Rights and Freedoms* (hereinafter the *Charter*) became Part I of the newly patriated *Constitution Act*. For the first time in Canada, the supreme law included guarantees of certain rights and freedoms which, subject to certain limitations, must be observed by all who make or administer the law. The courts were no longer required simply to decide whether the various limits and requirements as set out in the old *B.N.A. Act* are being observed; they were required to decide whether legislation or actions by officials offend any of the rights and freedoms guaranteed in the *Charter*.

In one sense, the addition of the *Charter* to the Constitution changed a great deal; but in another, it changed very little. For the first time, the courts in Canada are required to measure government action against a broadly phased code of rights and freedoms. But in doing so, they continue to do what they have done for over one hundred years: interpret and apply the Constitution to particular situations.

II

. . .

The *Charter* begins with a guarantee and also a limitation. Section 1 of the *Charter* guarantees the rights and freedoms set out later in the text, subject to "such reasonable limitations prescribed by law as can be demonstrably justified in a free and democratic society." This underlines the important point that the rights set out in the *Charter* are *fundamental* but not *absolute*. Rights may be limited by laws which serve, in reasonable ways, other important objectives in a free and democratic society.

The *Charter* guarantees fundamental rights such as freedom of conscience and religion (s. 2); democratic rights, such as the right to vote (ss. 3-5); mobility rights, such as the right to enter and leave Canada (s. 6); legal rights, which we will discuss in more detail in a moment (ss. 7-14); and equality rights (s. 15). The *Charter* also contains protection of the official languages of Canada (ss. 18-22) and minority language educational rights (s. 23). In addition, the *Charter* also gives the courts power to grant "appropriate and just" remedies to anyone whose rights and freedoms have been infringed (s. 24). In summary, the *Charter* guarantees certain rights, subject to reasonable limitations which may be imposed by law. The courts have the responsibility of interpreting these provisions, applying them to specific situations and awarding remedies where the guaranteed rights have been infringed.

It is important to note that, because of s. 32, the *Charter* applies only to what is often loosely called "state action."

III

The *Charter* has had and will continue to have considerable impact on the criminal justice system. As you will see as you read the legal rights sections of the *Charter* (ss. 7-14), most of the rights listed relate most directly to some aspect of the criminal process. Consider some examples. With respect to the investigation of crime, there is protection against unreasonable search and seizure and from arbitrary detention (ss. 8 and 9). Upon arrest, there are requirements that the arrested person be told the reasons for the arrest and be informed of and accorded the right to retain and instruct counsel (s. 10). When charges have been laid, the accused person has the right to be tried within a reasonable time and to be presumed innocent until proven guilty (s. 11). And there is a right not to be subjected to any cruel and unusual treatment or punishment (s. 12). The *Charter*, as you can see, has implications for every phase of the criminal process.

It is no surprise that the *Charter* speaks so significantly to the way in which the criminal law is administered. The criminal process brings the power of the state to bear upon individuals. It may well result in the deprivation of liberty and bring the stigma of a criminal conviction. The verdict of guilty in a criminal case is a formal and public denunciation of an accused's unlawful conduct and is usually accompanied by punishment which is to deter the offender and others from future criminal acts. The seriousness of the process and the individual's relative weakness, when compared to the power of the state, have long combined to suggest the need for safeguards for those suspected or accused of crimes: most of the rights mentioned in the legal rights section of the *Charter* are far from new ideas. Security against unreasonable search and seizure, freedom from arbitrary detention and imprisonment and the right to be presumed innocent until proven guilty have long been part of our Anglo-Canadian heritage. What the *Charter* has done is not so much create new rights, but rather strengthen rights long recognized by requiring that those creating legislation and those acting under it observe these rights at all times.

The *Charter* may come into play in the criminal process in several ways. It may be used as the basis of a challenge to the legislation under which an accused is charged. For an example, a law requiring a business to remain closed on Sundays may be challenged on the basis that it offends the right to freedom of conscience and religion guaranteed under s. 29(a) of the *Charter*. The argument is not that the police have acted improperly in any way in charging the business with the offence of being open for business when the legislation prohibits it, but simply that the legislature has violated the *Charter* by creating the offence. The *Charter* may also be used to attack legislation that confers power on the police. For example, statutes that authorize a search may be attacked as infringing the right to be free of unreasonable search and seizure. In such a case, the conduct of the police may be challenged even though such conduct may have been carried out in exact compliance with the relevant legislation. The challenge is to the legislation itself which authorized the police conduct, not the conduct itself.

Quite apart from being used to challenge legislation which creates offences or gives the police certain powers, the *Charter* may also be used to challenge the manner in which the police have used their powers. For example, upon arrest or detention, everyone has the right to be informed promptly of the reasons and to be informed of the right to retain and instruct counsel without delay. And once a person is charged with an offence, he or she has the right to be informed of the specific offence. It will usually be the responsibility of the police to see that these rights are observed because they will be doing the detaining, arresting or charging.

The *Charter* also directly affects criminal procedure at trial. The accused has a right to be tried within a reasonable time, not to be compelled to be a witness in the proceedings, to be presumed innocent until proven guilty and so forth (see ss. 11, 13 and 14). All of these rights affect the manner in which proceedings before the court must be conducted and the courts must govern their proceedings accordingly.

So far we have mentioned a number of quite specific legal rights which are guaranteed by the *Charter* and how they may affect the criminal process. There is, however, one other legal right that is very broadly phrased and may be the most important of all the legal rights. It is the right to "life, liberty and security of the person" and "not to be deprived thereof except in accordance with the principles of fundamental justice" (s. 7). This provision cuts across the whole of the criminal process, from the legislation creating the offence to the way in which a charge under the legislation is tried. The courts are still struggling with the meaning of "life, liberty and security of the person" as well as with the phrase "the principles of fundamental justice," but this section of the *Charter* has already had enormous impact in several areas, including criminal justice.

## IV

What may the court do if a *Charter* right has been limited? First, it must consider whether the limitation is one which is permitted under s. 1 of the *Charter* as being prescribed by law and demonstrably justified in a free and democratic society. If it concludes that the infringement is not saved in this way, then the court may take either or both of two courses of action. It may simply declare that the challenged legislation or action is inconsistent with the *Charter* or it may also (or instead) use its powers under s. 24 to award an "appropriate and just" remedy—that is, to order some corrective action in favour of the person whose rights have been infringed. For example, if a person has been charged under a statute which the court finds offends the *Charter*, in addition to declaring the statute to be of no force and effect, it may also quash (*i.e.*, set aside) the information of indictment charging the person. Alternatively, the court might "stay" (*i.e.*, halt) the proceedings against the person or perhaps even award damages (*i.e.*, require payment of a sum of money) to the person. All of these options may be open to the court in its efforts to award a remedy which is appropriate and just.

Section 24(2) gives the courts a very specific remedial power which is both new and controversial. It requires the court to exclude evidence obtained in a manner that infringed or denied any rights and freedoms guaranteed by the *Charter*, but only if its admission into evidence "would bring the administration of justice into disrepute."

This is a major change from the law in force before the *Charter* and, as well, is a remedy that is and will continue to be sought frequently in criminal cases. . . .

# Adversarial Justice and the Charter of Rights: Stunting the Growth of the "Living Tree"*

*Alan N. Young*

*Excerpts from (1997), 39 Criminal Law Quarterly 362 at 362-367, 406-408.

## Introduction

In February, 1991, Bishop Hubert O'Connor was charged with various sexual offences arising out of incidents which took place while he was a principal of a residential school in the 1960s. On June 4, 1992, defence counsel applied for, and obtained, a court order requiring disclosure of the complainants' medical, counseling, and school records. Despite repeated warnings from various judges, the Crown failed to comply with this order, and on December 7, 1992, judicial patience ran out and a stay of proceedings was entered. After appeals to the British Columbia Court of Appeal and the Supreme Court of Canada, a new trial was ordered, and on July 25, 1996, Bishop O'Connor was convicted and was sentenced to two and a half years' imprisonment.

Even if one assumes that justice has been served and an accused person has been justly punished for his crimes, one has to wonder how it is possible in the era of the *Canadian Charter of Rights and Freedoms* for a trial to drag on for five years and for a Crown attorney to obstruct compliance with a court order with relative impunity. Although the Supreme Court of Canada characterized the actions of the Crown as "shoddy and inappropriate" and as "extremely high-handed and thoroughly reprehensible", the court determined that this was not the "clearest of cases" to attract the remedy of a stay of proceedings for abuse of process or for violation of s. 7 of the Charter. The question remains how it is possible in an era of constitutional review for "shoddy" and "reprehensible" Crown conduct to attract censure but not to attract any meaningful remedy.

Similarly, on November 7, 1996, the Ontario Court of Appeal dismissed an appeal in which the accused claimed that his rights to a trial within a reasonable time had been violated because a trial that should have taken four days lasted nearly two years. Twenty hours of court time took place on 20 separate days over some 20 months; however, the court concluded that the accused suffered no demonstrable prejudice. Nevertheless, the court recognized that this piecemeal and scattered approach to a criminal trial was problematic and it stated:

> The manner in which the trial proceeded was most unsatisfactory. The twenty hours of court time required for evidence and argument leading to the conviction of the appellant took place on twenty days over some twenty months. In our view this is a most unsatisfactory manner for a criminal trial to proceed, particularly when the matter involves allegations of sexual assault involving young child. We would hope that those responsible for scheduling in the

provincial courts will review their procedures in order that similar situations may be avoided in the future.

Reasonable people might disagree with the response of the courts to the claims of constitutional impropriety raised in these cases; however, it is hard to gainsay the conclusion that these two trials do not serve as models of fair process. The very fact that these two trials could proceed in such a chaotic fashion raises the question of whether the enactment of the Charter of Rights has effected any positive change in our criminal process. Without doubt there have been monumental decisions and effective remedying of official misconduct in isolated cases, yet, after 15 years of charter litigation, there has not been any documented and significant structural reform of our criminal process.

It may be unfair to condemn the Charter for failing to achieve a goal which was never intended. The courts have candidly stated on many occasions that the "Charter does not intend a transformation of our legal system" or that the "Charter was not intended to turn the Canadian legal system upside down". None the less, Chief Justice Lamer has recognized that "we cannot shrink from our task of interpreting the Charter in a full and fair manner, even when, and perhaps especially when, we are confronted with the possibility of resulting *significant institutional reform*" (emphasis added). Although the Charter may not have been intended to reinvent the wheel, it is clear that some of the legal rights protected by the Charter cannot be comfortably accommodated within the existing structure of our criminal process. It should not be surprising that the criminal justice system, whose structure evolved over hundreds of years in the absence of constitutionally entrenched rights, might have difficulty adapting to the demands of constitutional imperatives.

In this article, I will briefly examine how one fundamental component of our criminal process has stymied the full development and implementation of legal rights. In a nutshell, it is my contention that the logic of adversarial justice has skewed the implementation of legal rights. Although adversarial justice has many components, the defining characteristic of adversarial justice is the notion that control of the process should be left in the hands of the litigants. That is to say, primary responsibility for the collection and presentation of evidence is left in the hands of the Crown and defence, with the trier of fact occupying the role of passive umpire. This defining feature of adversarial justice can undercut the foundation for the implementation of constitutional rights because so much will depend upon the good faith exercise of discretion of Crown counsel and the competence of defence counsel.

In assessing the impact of the Charter, most commentators explore the issue of whether constitutional rights serve to paralyze law enforcement or unduly burden prosecutors. This article will not explore this tiresome issue, but will examine the impact of the Charter from a different angle. It will be argued that the failure of the Charter to effect meaningful structural reform can be partially attributed to the adversarial logic of leaving the impetus for constitutional scrutiny in the hands of defence counsel. As "champion" of the interests of the accused, defence lawyers bears the burden of ensuring that their client's constitutional rights have been respected by police, prosecutors and judges. Therefore, in the absence of some institutional mechanism for supervisory, quality control over the process, the implementation of constitutional rights is contingent upon the competency of counsel. We may operate upon an assumption that counsel for the defence is always competent and diligent; however, this is merely an idealized conception of the logic of adversarial justice. In the real world, there are good lawyers, bad lawyers, diligent lawyers and lazy lawyers, and it may be naïve to believe that effective implementation of legal rights can be secured by leaving responsibility for the enforcement of these rights in the hands of the defence bar.

This article will be divided into two parts. In Part I, the article will outline instances in which constitutional doctrine is structured in a manner so as to leave primary responsibility for the enforcement of legal rights in the hands of defence counsel. In Part II, the article will explore two leading cases in which it will be demonstrated that even judicial decisions, with a strong due process perspective, can become unraveled and ineffective due to implicit reliance upon the competency of defence counsel. In the end, it is hoped that the reader will reach the position that clear, comprehensive and self-executing rules and procedures are the best safeguard for the implementation of constitutional rights, rather than leaving enforcement of the rights to the good faith discretion of the Crown and the tenacity of defence counsel. Although it undercuts the logic of adversarial justice, it is submitted that the only effective way of ensuring institutional respect for constitutional rights is to ensure that all the players (*e.g.*, police, Crown, defence counsel and judge) share equally the burden of being vigilant in preventing constitutional violations.

## PART I

## The Operation of the Charter of Rights within an Adversarial Framework

Adversarial criminal justice contemplates a stylized battle between an individual and a state representative. Accordingly, one of the purposes served by a system of rights is to correct the balance of advantages to ensure that the adversaries are similarly empowered. A fair fight requires that the parties are not grossly mismatched in terms of power and resources. On the one hand the enactment of the legal rights provisions of the Charter serves to level the playing field between prosecutor and accused; on the other hand, the developing jurisprudence under the Charter has the potential to undercut the noble aspirations of correcting the balance of advantage.

An abstract set of legal rights is of little value unless the rights-holder has the resources to assert his/her rights in an effective manner. We mistakenly assume that counsel for the defence, as champion of the accused, always has the ability and resources to advance constitutional claims successfully on behalf of his/her client. If the jurisprudence under the Charter consistently places the burden of assertion and proof upon the accused and his/her counsel, we run the risk of leaving the protection of the Charter in the hands of lawyers of varying degrees of competence. It must be recognized that the legal process rights are not designed to benefit designated individuals. They are designed to structure and constrain governmental power, and in their ordering of state/citizen relations they insure to the benefit of all residents.

Accordingly, one would expect that state officials would share the responsibility for ensuring that legal rights are given full effect. None the less, when one begins to chronicle the first 15 years of Charter jurisprudence, it becomes readily apparent that defence counsel, with their limited resources, bear the burden of ensuring that state officials act in accordance with the constitutional imperatives. . . .

*[Editor's note: After discussing several examples of cases involving legal rights under the Charter, the author continues:]*

## PART II

## The Myth of Procedural Rights

In Part I, it was argued that excessive reliance upon competent defence counsel to uncover and present Charter claims may not be a simple affirmation of the basic values of our cherished adversarial system, but rather may actually be a major short-coming of the Charter. Regardless of whether this may or may not be true, there is something dangerous in leaving enforcement of rights entirely to defence counsel. There is a risk that leading precedents which appear to celebrate and protect procedural rights will contain the seeds of their own demise. Hidden within the rhetoric of celebrating rights, there exists an underlying premise which undercuts the practical value of the right. Building upon the theme in Part I of this article, it is my submission that some, if not many, of the leading cases can only provide mere symbolic protection of a right because the cases do not provide defence counsel with adequate tools to pursue the rights claim. It is simply assumed that counsel for the defence has some form of magical powers which will allow the lawyer to perfect his or her Charter claim within the limiting framework of an adversarial system of justice.

Some commentators contend that constitutional rights are mythical in that they merely provide an appearance of justice while in substance they are woefully deficient. These critical scholars see the entrenchment of rights as serving a legitimation function, i.e., making the system appear more civilized while really doing nothing to combat and reduce repression. As David Rudovsky has commented,

> The most significant social impact of the constitutional principles of due process and equal protection is not their effect on crime, which is minimal or nonexistent, or even the basic fairness they can and do provide in some circumstances. Rather, it is the appearance of fairness they lend the criminal justice system, as well as their legitimation of a class and race-biased judicial process. Indeed a critical view of each aspect of the criminal justice system, including the criminalization of conduct, police investigation, arrest, prosecution and incarceration, reveals the very significant degree to which these protections are unrealized promises.

Although these legitimation theories rely upon an overstated and false notion of conspiracy amongst judges, lawyers, police and politicians, there is a kernel of truth in their perspective. Procedural rights are often viewed as obstacles to achieving justice. They thwart the truth-seeking function of a criminal trial and clutter the process with ceremonial rituals having little to do with guilt or innocence. More often than not, courts will conceal their disdain for procedural rights (or more accurately, providing remedies for violations of procedural rights), but on occasion, the truth emerges. In 1987, the Alberta Court of Appeal dismissed a s. 9 arbitrary detention claim by an impaired driver who had been detained for hours longer than necessary. After expressing concern that "trials will bloat" if Charter rights become the focal point of a criminal trial, the court indicated that the "answer is to discourage the redress of Charter infringements within the trial unless they are clearly relevant to the offence". Accordingly, the court concluded that:

> An adversarial criminal trial should retain its traditional function. Leaving aside clear and defined heads of exclusion such as involuntary confessions, unauthorized interceptions of private communications and the objects of s. 24(2) of the Charter, a criminal trial remains an inquiry, under all relevant evidence, to determine whether the accused, in truth, is guilty of a criminal offence.

Assuming that there is an unspoken judicial reluctance to provide concrete remedies for violations of procedural rights which have nothing to do with guilt or innocence, it would not be surprising to find courts imposing obstacles in the path of a successful invocation of s. 24(1) of (2) with respect to a violation of procedural rights. Sometimes these obstacles are hidden within the text of a judgment which appears to be responsive to due process considerations. . . .

## Questions/Discussion

1. Discuss the ways in which the courts produce criminal law in Canada, and assess the value and effectiveness of those roles. What do you see as the principal problems with the courts' roles in producing criminal law and why? Can these problems be corrected and, if so, how?
2. How can the problems of interpretation of the criminal law be overcome or perhaps minimized? Will problems of this type always be with us to some degree given the vagaries of the fact situations which can arise?
3. Do you agree that the Charter of Rights and Freedoms has advanced or enhanced the production of a more progressive criminal law in Canada? Why or why not? What role would you like the courts to play in the production of criminal law in Canada?
4. What is your position on the adversarial system of justice in this country relative to the courts' role in producing criminal law? Do you believe that it results in better criminal law? Why or why not?

## Further Reading

- Abella, R.S., "The Judicial Role in a Democratic State" (2001), 26 Queen's Law Journal 573.
- Beatty, D., "Constitutional Conceits: The Coercive Authority of Courts" (1987), 37 University of Toronto Law Journal 183.
- Campbell, C., "The Canadian Left and the Charter of Rights" (1984), 2 Socialist Studies 30.
- Cohen, S., "The Role of the Forensic Expert in a Criminal Trial" (1978), 1 C.R. (3d) 289.
- Delisle, R.J., "The Admissibility of Expert Evidence: A New Caution Based on General Principles" (1994), 29 C.R. (4th) 267-273.
- Friedland, M., "Legal Rights Under the Charter" (1984), 24 Criminal Law Quarterly 430.

- Glasbeek, H. and M. Mandel, "The Legalisation of Politics" (1984), 2 Socialist Studies 84.
- Gold, M., "The Mask of Objectivity: Politics and Rhetoric in the SCC" (1985), 7 Supreme Court Law Review 455.
- Hovius, B. and R. Martin, "The CCRF and the Supreme Court of Canada" (1983), 61 Canadian Bar Review 354.
- Laforest, G., The CCRF — An Overview" (1983), 61 Canadian Bar Review 19.
- Mandel, Michael, *The Charter of Rights and the Legalization of Politics in Canada* (Toronto: Thomson Educational Publishing, 1994).
- Martin, R., "The Judges and the Charter" (1984), 2 Socialist Studies 66.
- McDonald, D.C., "Opinion Evidence" (1978), 16 Osgoode Hall Law Journal 321.
- McLachlin, B., "The Role of the Court in the Post-Charter Era: Policy-Maker or Adjudicator?" (1990), 39 University of New Brunswick Law Journal 43.
- Olsen, D., *The State Elite* (Toronto: McClelland and Stewart Ltd., 1980).
- Russell, P., The Judiciary in Canada: Third Branch of Government (Toronto: McGraw-Hill Ryerson, 1987).
- Russell, P., "The Political Purposes of the CCRF" (1983), 61 Canadian Bar Review 30.
- Sugunas, Shalin M., "Contextualism: The Supreme Court's New Standard of Judicial Analysis and Accountability" (1999), 22 Dalhousie Law Journal 126.
- Volpe, P., "Psychiatric Testimony in the Criminal Prosecution Process" (1989), 10 Canadian Criminology Forum 26-39.
- Weiler, K., "Of Courts and Constitutional Review" (1988-89), 31 Criminal Law Quarterly 121.

# 4

# CRIMINAL LAW — PERSONNEL, PARTICIPANTS, AND POWERS

## General Introduction

This chapter examines the various agents and participants in the criminal law system and the powers and rights that they exercise. In addition to looking at the roles they play in the production of criminal law at its operational level — and therefore keeping in mind the issues raised in Chapter Three relating to input, consistency, certainty, and flexibility — it is particularly important to address the issue of how accountable are the agents of the state to the citizens they supposedly serve. What mechanisms exist or might be established in order to achieve an accountable criminal law system at the level of its enforcement, the level that has the greatest impact on those who come in contact with it. This issue arises particularly in regard to the roles played and powers exercised by the police, the prosecution, and the judiciary. We shall see in the readings that the level of accountability is generally not high in regard to these agents, in spite of the important roles they play. The reader should address the question of what might be done to enhance accountability and transparency within the system while maintaining the capacities of the agents to do their jobs properly and effectively.

A final point to note is that this chapter does not purport to cover all the participants in the criminal law system. For example, the role played by juries is not looked at here, and the important duties and obligations of correctional workers, whether they are prison guards, probation workers or parole officers, are not examined in this chapter. Issues related to the latter are, however, looked at in the next chapter.

## 4.1 POLICE

### Introduction

The matter of accountability is particularly important in the context of the police as can be seen in a number of recent issues and events that have faced the various police forces in this country. They range from the conduct of the RCMP at the APEC summit in Vancouver in November 1997, to concerns over unnecessary and intrusive strip searches, to criticisms of police conduct in relation to several wrongful convictions in recent years. As well, there has been controversy surrounding the Department of Justice's *White Paper on Law Enforcement and Criminal Liability*, introduced in June 2000, which proposed limited protection from criminal liability for police officers and others carrying out law enforcement duties. The issue of accountability is therefore an important focus of the readings that follow.

This section begins with a brief reading by Mitchell looking at the historical development of the police and their evolution into the modern, professional forces we see today. In this regard, keep in mind the Canadian context whereby today there are various types of forces at the federal, provincial, and municipal levels enforcing various types of laws enacted at each of these jurisdictional levels. The MacKay reading that follows introduces the reader to the arrest powers of the police in this country, as well as some of the constraints on these powers. The last three readings, by Epp, Hastings and Saunders, and Childs and Ceyssens address issues of control and accountability in relation to the police, and look at the various ways in which the police might be held answerable for their actions.

## Historical Development

*Chet Mitchell [edited by R.P. Saunders]*

Police history is largely a story of the eclipse of private prosecution and the rise of a professional law enforcement body capable of action against both individual tortfeasors (criminals) and rebellious groups (rioters, rebels, insurrectionists, and terrorists).

Law enforcement is a task requiring incentives. If enforcement is left in private hands, which is by far the cheapest method, the incentives can take four general forms. First, victims can be legally empowered to prosecute alleged wrongdoers in hope of receiving compensation. Second, citizens can be compelled by law to serve as volunteer police. Third, citizens may be rewarded on a bounty system for apprehending offenders and; finally, citizens can be hired by others to enforce the law as part of general private security services. In agricultural, non-commercial societies, such as England in 1285, the first two incentive schemes are employed because they require the least outlay or specialization. As Stenning (1981) comments "without some notable exceptions . . . if the private victim or complainant in Medieval England did not initiate and conduct the prosecution of an alleged offender there would normally be no prosecution".

The private, self-policing of English towns and villages was based on custom and compulsion. All adult men served on the "watch" on a roster basis under the direction of a constable (Cooper, 1981). The constable was elected for each parish or shire from among the male citizens. Those who refused to serve as constables and those who failed to assist the watchmen in making an arrest were subject to penalties. But police service, while an imposition, was also a source of pride for small property holders elevated above the labouring poor by holding a minor parochial office such as constable. Evidently, this system is economical and effective in a stable, low population society because law enforcement in such a context is not a high-skilled, full-time, or specialized task. Government ranked military and tax matters a much higher priority than criminal law. Tort law was also economical because the aggrieved party acted as detective, prosecutor and witness without state subsidy or bounty. Historians generally agree that England from 1290-1485 experienced ineffective public policing. Part of the problem was official corruption. According to Bellamy (1973:12-14):

> Almost as productive of lawlessness as the king's absence on his military campaigns was the corruption of officials. In all but the most sophisticated societies the holding of office allows suitable opportunity for illegal gain since the relative paucity of officials per head of population does not permit a comprehensive system of surveillance of one by another . . . [The] public order office which offered the greatest opportunity for dishonest behaviour and on which contemporaries cast the gravest aspersions was that of sheriff.

We noted earlier that the Crown weakened tort law incentives by creating "felonies" which individuals had to prosecute but for which they received no recompense. By the 1820s private prosecutors often wanted no part of a conviction for a new reason: because of the severe penalties inflicted on convicts. Police constables were also deterred by the expense of prosecution, which they incurred by having to jail the accused. Eventually, the *Criminal Justice Act* of 1826 in England made it possible for parish constables to recover the cost of detaining suspects in jail. The same Act also empowered courts to award payment to a private prosecutor of misdemeanours and by 1837 the death penalty was repealed for all property offences. Rude (1985) reports that while these reforms increased prosecutions somewhat, incentives remained inadequate. Tort incentives also decreased with greater social mobility, complexity and individuality since these changes meant that many wrongdoers could not or would not pay damages. When wrongdoers are "judgement-proof", one logical recourse is to substitute afflictive punishment for compensation. Another tactic is to enforce a period of personal service on the defendant in lieu of a money payment and this strategy was also employed in England. Writing about the 1700s in England, Douglas Hay (1975:40) explains:

> Almost all prosecutions were initiated by private persons, at their discretion, and conducted in accordance with their views. Accustomed to organized state police and rigorous state prosecution, French visitors were inclined to marvel at this peculiar English institution . . . The victim of the crime could decide himself upon the severity of the prosecution, either enforcing the letter of the law, or reducing the charge. He could even pardon the offence completely by not going to court. The reformers' objections to this system are well known. Private prosecution was capricious and uncertain and too often rogues escaped due to the distaste, compassion or fear of the victims . . . In a rural parish with a relatively settled population there were many alternatives to a rigorous prosecution. The accused man could be made to post a bond not to offend again, or be given the choice of leaving the neighbourhood . . . He might also be allowed to escape the law by making compensation for his crime . . .

Perhaps more importantly, as social complexity increases private plaintiffs are less likely to know or be able to discover the tortfeasor's identity. Detective services, such as those provided for fictional Victorian clients by Sherlock Holmes, could be purchased, but for the bulk of petty torts, which included the wrongful appropriation of firewood, tools, food and livestock, the cost of finding and suing tortfeasors would be greater than the damages recoverable. One's resources were better spent on preventive security measures.

Under the same modern conditions, the volunteer police force also became problematic.

An unpaid citizen's police force requires compulsory service, otherwise "free riders" attempt to enjoy the benefits of policing without contributing their share. Since urban development is based on specialization and commercialization, both of which discourage citizen policing, the usual solution to free rider problems is to collect compulsory taxes and use the revenue to hire full time professional police. Commercial development increases taxable capacity while impeding the close, communal network necessary for volunteer forces.

The Royal Irish Constabulary, a model for the later Northwest Mounted Police in Canada, was established in 1786 and with the Metropolitan Police Act of 1829, the foundations of a professional police force were laid in London. Since the new police broke with a long tradition of citizen enforcement it was natural that they departed little from former procedures. Unlike soldiers, the new police were unarmed, under local civilian control and exercised no more powers of enforcement than ordinary citizens. Sir Robert Peel's principles of law enforcement of 1829 reflected the close legal connection between police and citizens. According to the 7th principle:

> The police at all times should maintain a relationship with the public that gives reality to the historic tradition that the police are the public and that the public are the police; the police are the only members of the public who are paid to give full-time attention to duties which are incumbent on every citizen in the interests of community welfare.

Since their foundation, however, the police have rapidly diverged from this ideal of "professional" citizen by acquiring special legal authority, by effectively usurping the role of private prosecutor and by serving a government mandated social control function.

In Canada the NWMP illustrate the government's need for replacing local and/or private police with a quasimilitary police force under direct federal command. Founded in 1873 the NWMP ostensibly existed to police the western plains, shelter Indians from abusive American traders and keep the peace between settlers and Indians. Actually, there was scant evidence that local authorities, including Indian and Metis leaders, were unable to resolve their own problems. But what local interests would not do is loyally promote federal government policies favouring multinational railway, land development and trading corporations, nor would native leaders cooperate in programs designed to weaken, ignore or destroy their own land claims. Up to the present day the RCMP's deliberate policy includes minimizing the degree to which their officers identify with or become attached to their assigned community. The advantages of central command from Ottawa are lessened by local sympathies.

From a low cost, unprofessional police system still largely motivated by personal compensation, Western governments have moved towards a high cost, professional police system where little if any funds flow into victim compensation. In Canada, one police officer served on average over 700 people in 1962 while in 1999 this figure was reduced to 550; this is reflected in the rise in the per capita cost of policing from $137 in 1985 to $206 in 1999 (Statistics Canada, 1999). It is important to note as well that approximately two-thirds of the budget allocated for the criminal law system is devoted to police services (most of which comprised police salaries), while a very small amount goes to items such as legal aid and victim compensation.

**Bibliography**

- Bayley, D., "Ironies of American Law Enforcement" (1980), The Public Interest 45.
- Bellamy, J., *Crime and Public Order in England in the Later Middle Ages* (Toronto: University of Toronto Press, 1973).
- Goode, W., "The Protection of the Inept" (1967), 32 American Sociological Review 1.
- Griffiths, C., *et al.*, *Criminal Justice in Canada: An Introductory Text* (Markham: Butterworths, 1980).
- Hay, Douglas, "Property, Authority and the Original Law", in Hay, F., P. Linebaugh, E.P. Thompson, eds., *Albion's Fatal Tree* (London: Allen Lane, 1975).
- Rude, G., *Criminal and Victim: Crime and Society in Early Nineteenth Century England* (Oxford: Clarendon Press, 1985).
- Statistics Canada, *Police Resources in Canada, 1999* (Ottawa: Minister of Industry, 1999).
- Stenning, P., "The Legal Status of Police in Canada: A Study Paper Prepared for the Law Reform Commission of Canada" (1981).

## Arrest and Compelling the Appearance of the Accused*

### *Heather E. MacKay*

*Excerpts from "Arrest and Compelling the Appearance of the Accused" in Joel E. Pink and David C. Perrier, eds., *From Crime to Punishment: An Introduction to the Criminal Law System* (Toronto: Carswell, 1999) at 50-51, 53-57, 59-63.

## HISTORICAL BACKGROUND

The powers of arrest and compelling a person's appearance before the courts are as old as the law itself. The deprivation of liberty has usually marked the beginning of a person's contact with the criminal justice system. Traditionally, police could arrest, without a warrant, any person whom they had reasonable and probable grounds to believe had committed a felony. For example, if an officer saw a masked person running away from a bank and someone at the bank's door was saying, "Stop that thief!", the officer could arrest that person without a warrant. Similarly, persons involved in a misdemeanour breaching the peace (such as a drunken brawl on a street) could be arrested without a warrant. However, under common law, the police had no power to arrest without a warrant for less serious statutory offences, such as violations of the *Liquor Control Act*.

Where an arrest without a warrant could not be made, common law required a summons or warrant be issued by a justice of the peace. If no summons or warrant could be obtained and no arrest power existed, the person would remain free. There would be no way to get that person before the courts.

Arrest powers were part of the common law, that is law created by court cases. In 1892, the Parliament of Canada decided to consolidate all the common law principles relating to criminal justice into The *Canadian Criminal Code* of 1892. Initially, the Code contained a long list of offences where a person could be arrested and compelled to appear without a warrant. However, there were a large number of minor offences which required a summons or warrant to be issued by a justice of the peace before a person could be compelled to appear in court. This made law enforcement and crime prevention difficult and time-consuming. It was not until the 1950s that the *Code* was reformed to expand the power to arrest without a warrant where a police officer has caught the person "red-handed." Given the broad powers of arrest without a warrant and issuing summons or warrant, the legal system can compel a person to appear in court in virtually all meritorious cases.

## THE ACT OF ARREST

"Arrest" is not defined in the *Code*; it has been interpreted by the courts. There are two ways that an arrest can be effected:

(1) actual physical seizure or touching of the person's body with the idea of detaining him or her [custodial arrest]; or

(2) use of words of arrest, so long as the person submits to the arrest and goes with the person making the arrest [symbolic arrest].

By including symbolic arrest in the concept of what constitutes an arrest, courts have recognized a policy to avoid unnecessary violence in the detention of persons. This policy is also indicated in ss. 25, 26 and 27, which provide justification of the use of force during the arrests of persons, but only as much as is necessary. If excessive force is used by either a citizen or an officer when making an arrest, the justification is lost and the person making the arrest may be subject to assault or related charges.

. . .

## POWERS OF ARREST — PRIVATE CITIZENS

### Authority for Arrest without Warrant

Section 494 of the Code limits a private citizen's power of arrest to three situations. The words of s. 494 permits arrest in the following cases:

(a) a person found "committing an indictable offence";

(b) a person who, "on reasonable grounds", the citizen "believes has committed a criminal offence and is escaping from and freshly pursued by persons who have lawful authority to arrest that person"; or

(c) a person found committing a criminal offence in respect of property where the person making the arrest is the property's owner or possessor or acting with their authorization.

These arrest powers apply to "anyone". Although they are generally referred to as "citizen's" powers of arrest, they are equally applicable to police and other peace officers. The usual form that a "citizen's" arrest takes involves private security guards and the like. Real citizens' arrests are relatively few. This is understandable for two reasons. First, people usually do not want to get involved in potentially dangerous situations (contrary to what TV would have you believe). Second, few people know and understand the powers of arrest in a way that would make them comfortable enough to intervene in situations where these powers arise. Understanding the extent of arrest powers of citizens is crucial to avoid being sued for false arrest if one intervenes in a crime situation.

. . .

## POWERS OF ARREST — PEACE OFFICERS

### Authority for Arrest without Warrant

The powers of arrest of peace officers are broader than those conferred upon citizens. Peace officers can compel suspects to attend court through their traditional powers of arrest without warrant or by use of an appearance notice, which became available for use under the *Bail Reform Act* and through provisions of the *Code*.

A peace officer's powers of arrest without a warrant are determined in s. 495 of the *Code*. An officer is empowered to make a warrantless arrest where:

(a) a person has committed or, the officer believes on reasonable grounds, has committed or is about to commit an indictable offence [s. 495(1)(*a*)];
(b) a person found [apparently] committing a criminal offence [s. 49(1)(*b*)];
(c) an officer has reasonable grounds to believe that a warrant of arrest or committal is outstanding in that jurisdiction (s. 495(1)(c).

. . .

#### *"Has committed or about to commit"—past and future offences*

This arrest power overlaps with its private citizen complement — the "hot pursuit" arrest. Like the private citizen, an officer must have either personal knowledge the offence was committed on reasonable grounds to believe the person has committed an offence. The "offence" must be an indictable one not a summary conviction offence, as those terms were previously explained. Officers have a broader power than citizens because they can also arrest where a person is "about to commit" an indictable offence.

. . .

#### *"Caught in the act"—present offence*

This arrest power is much broader than the citizen's equivalent because an officer can arrest any person found *apparently* committing a *criminal* offence. There are two additional aspects that confer this expanded power — "apparently" and "criminal" offence. While a citizen has to be certain that an offence is occurring, an officer only has to be satisfied the offence seems to be in progress. When a court assesses whether an arrest is lawful or not under this power, it considers the situation as it was "apparentlqc. However, the test of what is apparent is based on what a reasonable person in the officer's shoes would believe, not the officer's view.

. . .

*"Outstanding warrant"*.

It may seem contradictory to allow an arrest without a warrant where there is a valid outstanding warrant. However, this provision is a concession to the practicalities of law enforcement. Say a person named in a warrant has evaded the authorities and is located by police officers. They know a warrant is outstanding but do not have time to obtain the warrant itself without risking the escape of the accused. The officers can make the arrest based on their knowledge of the outstanding warrant. This power is particularly effective in light of the "Canada-wide" warrant which allows police in another province in Canada to make an arrest for an offence which took place outside their own jurisdiction. However, if it can be shown that is was clearly feasible for an officer to obtain the warrant prior to arrest, the failure to do so will make the arrest unlawful.

## Limits placed upon Police Arrest Powers

Subsection 495(2) places considerable restraint on police powers of arrest without a warrant. It states that peace officers *shall not arrest* without a warrant in the following cases:

(1) an indictable offence which is in the absolute jurisdiction of a provincial court judge, as set out in s. 553 of the *Criminal Code* (includes theft under $5,000; possession of stolen goods under $5,000; keeping a gaming, betting or bawdy-house, etc.);
(2) an offence by which a person may be prosecuted via indictment or summarily, *i.e.*, a "hybrid" offence; or
(3) an offence punishable on summary conviction.

An arrest can only be made in these situations where the officer reasonably believes it is necessary to establish the identity of the person, to preserve evidence, to prevent continuation of the offence or that the person will fail to attend court. It should, however, be noted that a person arrest by an officer who fails to comply with s. 495(2) cannot rely on this subsection to argue the officer was not in execution or his or her duty in making an arrest. It is these limits on arrest powers that create the need for other mechanisms to compel the court appearance of a person. Section 496 authorizes an officer to issue an appearance notice where he or she decides not to arrest a person under s. 495(2). . . .

Although an officer is entitled to question any person in order to obtain information with respect to a suspected offence, he or she has no lawful authority to compel that person to answer. Nor can an officer detain a person for questioning or further investigation unless or she makes an arrest on a specific charge or has reasonable grounds to believe that the person is about to commit an indictable offence, *i.e.*, the arrest power under s. 495(1)(*a*).

. . .

## Rights and Duties upon Arrest

*Reasons for arrest*

Regardless of whether an arrest is made with or without a warrant, s. 29 of the *Code* imposes a duty on the person making the arrest to inform the arrestee of the basis of arrest. In a case where a warrant or process is outstanding, the arrestee must be notified as to the document under which the arrest is made. While before the *Charter* it was unnecessary in such a case to inform the person of the reasons for arrest s. 10(a) of the *Charter* now requires an arrestee be promptly informed of the substance of the offence. Also, once the warrant or process exists arising out of a formal charge, that is, an information, s. 11(a) of the *Charter* is triggered and failure by a police officer to give reasons for arrest would justify resisting arrest.

. . .

*Right to a lawyer*

Section 10(b) of the Charter imposes a duty on anyone making an arrest to inform the person of the right to obtain and instruct counsel "without delay". Police officers have other duties in regards to this section:

(1) the person must be informed of the availability of free legal assistance through Legal Aid or duty counsel;
(2) a reasonable opportunity to contact counsel must be provided. The duty to facilitate contact with counsel includes the duty to offer use of the telephone. That use must be in private without officers present;
(3) the duty to cease questioning or otherwise attempting to obtain evidence from the arrestee until the right is exercised must be observed; and
(4) the person must be told that the right includes a right of choice of counsel and only if that lawyer is unavailable within a reasonable time, depending on the circumstances, will the person have to make another choice.

The arrestee must be reasonably diligent in the exercise of the right to counsel in order for these correlative duties to arise; if not, they are suspended and not a bar to police continuing their investigation. Also, if the arrestee clearly and unequivocally waives the right (*e.g.*, "no, I don't want a lawyer"), then the police can proceed.

*Right to enter premises to make arrest*

The Supreme Court has held that warrantless arrest in a dwelling is in general prohibited under the *Charter*. Exceptions to the prohibition recognized by the Court include circumstances of hot pursuit.

. . .

*Search incident to arrest*

Under the old common law of arrest, police were permitted to search the person under arrest and seize anything in his or her possession or immediate surroundings. This search power was used to guarantee the safety of police and the accused, to prevent the accused from escape or to provide evidence against the accused. Section 8 of the Charter protects persons from unreasonable search and seizure. Thus, a search incident to arrest must be for a valid objective related to the proper administration of justice; if not, anything found in the search may be excluded from evidence.

Further, a search must not be conducted in an abusive manner and the constraint used should be proportionate to the circumstances. . . .

Where a person is detained for a search incident to arrest, he or she has the right to be informed of the right to counsel. . . .

*Power to require fingerprinting*

Whether an arrest is made with or without a warrant, if the officer in charge of the case decides to release the accused on an appearance notice, promise to appear or recognizance, fingerprinting may be ordered. This power is governed by subs. 501(3) of the *Code*. Fingerprints can only be required where the alleged charge is an indictable offence. The officer will set out the time when and the place where the accused will be required to appear for this purpose. Fingerprinting is authorized under the *Identification of Criminals Act*.

*Duty to take arrestee before a justice*

Section 503 of the *Code* places a duty upon a peace officer, who makes an arrest with or without a warrant, to take the arrested person before a justice within 24 hours of arrest (s. 503(1)(a)) or, if a justice is not available in that time, as soon as possible thereafter (s. 503(1)(*b*)). . . .

## Penetrating Police Investigative Practice Post-Morin*

*John A. Epp*

*Excerpts from (1997), 31 University of British Columbia Law Review 95 at 95-99; 101-109; 116-117.

## I. INTRODUCTION

The wrongful convictions of Donald Marshall Jr., David Milgaard, William Nepoose, and Guy Paul Morin, for murder are just a few reminders of the frailties of the administration of justice in Canada. Exposure of these miscarriages of justice has led to the close scrutiny of those who have sworn to uphold the law as police officers. Yet little of practical significance has been done as a result. . . .

"Who will watch the watchman?" is a most vexing question. Warren E. Burger, who would later serve as Chief Justice of the United States Supreme Court, once stated:

> After the passage of many years, and more than thirty years as a lawyer and a judge, I cannot tell you who, under our existing law and institutions, will watch the watchman—the police-man—in the sense of holding him individually accountable when he breaks one law in his effort to enforce another.

. . .

Arguably the solution may be even more generic and yet more difficult to realize. It appears that revision of basic police methodology and attitude will be the only effective solution in the Canadian context. . . .

## II.  THE WATCHMAN, "COP CULTURE" AND INVESTIGATIONS

Police share a bond, or culture, which greatly influences their point of view and actions. The "cop culture" is characterized by an extreme sense of mission in police work, and solidarity amongst closely grouped colleagues. The culture is shaped by training and management methods and the nature of police duties. Many who partic-ipate to the extreme in the "cop culture" may be described as having the police "working personality." Such police adhere to a self-revised version of the law where the end, to a certain degree, is used to justify the means.

Danger and authority are prominent factors in shaping the "cop culture." The danger involved in the confrontation with disorderly groups and the apprehension of suspects requires members to adhere to a reciprocal commitment to assist one another without hesitation. From this mutual commitment in the face of potential physical danger has grown a requirement of unfailing loyalty in all matters where a line can be drawn on the basis of "us versus them." Police may become isolated from the public, and police working groups may become isolated from superiors. Where the latter has occurred police primarily adhere to the expectations of the working group, regardless of service policy. Within the group, there may exist an ingrained aversion to challenging colleagues' judgments, or to complaining openly about malpractice. Unfailing loyalty is reinforced by the implied threat of withdrawal of collegial support in the face of actual physical danger or exposed indiscretions. Loyalty among the working group is further reinforced by general indoctrination by the organization itself regardless the importance of team play and loyalty to the service. Tangible actions by the service reinforce these principles. Superiors tend not to reward those who seek to implement change or report improper conduct. Indiscretions are over-looked generally as a reward for good service. Further, overlooking indiscretions facilitates "a kind of implied blackmail" to ensure loyalty.

. . .

The police are trained to secure the conviction of criminals. Some police adopt the mentality — a "working personality" — that they are masters of their trade and are, therefore, the best equipped to determine the guilt or innocence of suspects. Consequently some police hold the view that the law can be ignored while they are pursuing convictions. . . .

## III. AN OVERVIEW OF SUGGESTED SOLUTIONS

### A. INTRODUCING SUGGESTED SOLUTIONS

> The police are, in effect, the first and main keepers of the integrity and fairness of the criminal justice system. . . . [T]he police have a profound and taxing responsibility to balance individual rights with society's need for security.

Since some sectors in the police have not fulfilled this responsibility, it becomes necessary to determine how this situation can be corrected. Many proposed solutions have been put forward in the literature. Some proposals focus on the period post-investigation, and suggest behaviour modification primarily through the exclusion of improperly obtained evidence; increased use of criminal prosecutions or civil actions against offending police; or more stringent complaint and disciplinary procedures. Other proposed solutions focus on the period during investigation. Among the proposals for behaviour modification are a legislated code of investigation, and judicial or prosecutorial supervision of investigations. Finally, other proposed solutions seek to avoid malpractice before an investigation begins through improved recruitment, training and management within the service.

. . .

### B. POST-INVESTIGATION BEHAVIOUR MODIFICATION

### 1. EXCLUSION

For decades American courts have attempted to deter police illegality through the systematic exclusion of evidence obtained through illegal means. No discretion to admit otherwise inadmissible evidence is available to the court where the impugned evidence is apparently probative and reliable, thereby greatly hampering the truth seeking function of the court. Currently the Supreme Court of Canada is of the view that the discretionary exclusion remedy in s. 24(2) of the *Canadian Charter of Rights and Freedoms* is not designed to act as a remedy for police misconduct. In *R. v. Collins*, Lamer C.J. stated "[i]t is not open to the courts in Canada to exclude evidence to discipline the police, but only to avoid having the administration of justice brought into disrepute." It is possible, however, that a level of frustration could be reached so as to motivate the court to take on a disciplinary role.

Regardless of whether one would agree that the Supreme Court should move in this direction, the question still remains as to whether the exclusion of illegally obtained evidence is an effective way to control police investigative misconduct. Warren E. Burger, later Chief Justice of the United States Supreme Court, concluded that the exclusion of evidence was ineffective as a deterrent to improper law enforcement methods. The lack of effectiveness of this approach is exposed in five ways. First, in most cases the investigator is not informed that the lack of success in the prosecution hinged on his illegal acts, or if he is so informed, the time lapse nullifies any notable impact. Second, where an offending investigator does receive notice in a timely fashion through either being present at judgment or reading a newspaper account, an investigator's lack of formal legal training tends to allow him or her to justify the acquittal on the basis that the prosecution was the victim of some indefensible "technicality." Third, police are rarely disciplined by the force for steps taken which later are declared illegal by a court and lead to exclusion of evidence. Without some proximate chance of punishment for illegal actions there can be no realistic deterrent effect. Fourth, the extent to which many civilians sympathize with police efforts in crime detection, and thereby misunderstand the importance of the goal of the court, allows the offending investigator a measure of public sympathy. Finally, the potential exclusion of evidence might be irrelevant in the context, for example, of a short-term goal of removing contraband from circulation.

The Royal Commission on Criminal Procedure and the Task Force on the Uniform Rules of Evidence in Canada both concurred in the inescapable conclusion that the exclusion of evidence was not an effective method of controlling police malpractice.

## 2. CRIMINAL PROSECUTION

Certainly criminal prosecutions will remain one route by which some illegal police activities will be discouraged. Perhaps criminal proceedings should be used more frequently in attempting to control police investigatory activities. It would be eccentric, however, to claim that the possibility of criminal sanction presently serves as a serious constraint on police misconduct. A number of points support this conclusion and they can be conveniently raised in three non-exclusive groups—practical, legal and core issues.

Practically speaking, the civilian complainant might be afraid of retaliatory action by members of the working group of the accused investigator. Secondly, the complainant in practice must attract the cooperation of the Crown in bringing the prosecution. Simply stated, the cost of marshalling a private prosecution is prohibitive. Furthermore, the Crown could intervene and stay the matter. And finally, the Crown has the resources to arrange for the investigation of the complaint. However, attracting the sympathy of the Crown is not automatic. Police enjoy a certain status in the community, and the greater the status of the wrongdoer the less likely criminal laws will be applied against him. Also the close working relationship between some investigators and prosecutors reduces the likelihood of complainant sympathy. . . .

Even though criminal sanctions have a role to play in controlling some police, the core issue still remains. Prosecutions of an individual officer's crimes in the line of duty do not affect the entire "cop culture," especially among those who share the "working personality." Therefore increased use of criminal sanctions will not provide the desired behaviour modification in day-to-day police investigations.

## 3. CIVIL LAW SUITS

Police misconduct during the investigation stage can be addressed in civil suits. Causes of action include assault, battery, false imprisonment, intimidation, intentionally causing nervous shock and harassment, trespass to land, trespass to goods and conversion, malicious prosecution or arrest, conspiracy, misfeasance in a public office, and *Charter* breach. The civil suit has the advantage of the lower standard of proof. Studies have demonstrated that civil actions against the police produce tangible results in a vastly greater number of cases than those complaints pursued through the citizen complaint process.

However, a civil suit is not effective in exercising day-to-day control over police misconduct. It is too blunt and imperfect. Problems in pursuing this remedy include, first, the manner in which police powers are framed. "Reasonable suspicion" is a standard which is readily satisfied. Further many actions are taken under the command of a warrant. Thus it is difficult to make individual officers accountable. Secondly, the common law has defined the elements of the torts of Charter breach, malicious prosecution and false imprisonment in such a manner as to make it difficult for the plaintiff to succeed. At the other extreme, the defences of consent and prosecutorial immunity are given the widest application. Thirdly, bloated court calendars effectively ensure that civil actions against the police do not give a speedy or accessible remedy. Finally, the cost of pursuing a civil action is high and it can be extremely difficult to obtain legal aid for this purpose.

Even if a civil action is successful it has minimal impact on police practice. This is due to a series of factors. First and foremost, damages are paid out of public funds and not by the offending police officer. Further, it is unusual for disciplinary proceedings to be taken against policemen where civil actions have been taken. Finally, the judgment is directed against the individual and does not seek to address the deeper issues. The defendant's environment — "cop culture," management and training — which fostered the misconduct is beyond the scope of the judgment. A California study revealed that less than fifty percent of police found liable in civil suits consequently altered their behaviour in any way. Therefore, civil actions cannot be used an effective device to discipline the police.

## 4. INTERNAL DISCIPLINE AND CITIZEN COMPLAINTS

Professions, including the police, are expected to keep their own house in order by careful selection, training, goals, and supervision. The execution of duties is governed through self-control by individual police, combined with defined supervisory layers, and international disciplinary systems. It has been argued that the disciplinary system should be the primary method by which investigative malpractice is addressed. Certainly a well-managed and well-disciplined service would be made up of open-minded, efficient investigators and, failing that, administrative remedies would be expedient and effective.

Internal discipline, as a check against investigative malpractice, suffers from the inherent bias of the "cop culture." Among those who intercept and enforce discipline rules are those who understand and sympathize with the subjective police view of a proper investigation. Where the police are of the view that they are not required to search for exculpatory evidence or pass such information on to the prosecutor, it is unrealistic to expect a police officer to report such behaviour by a colleague. Even where the breach of discipline is obvious, informing on a police colleague requires "sheer moral courage," observed a former policeman. . . .

. . . Complaint systems have been justly criticized over the years as lacking in thorough investigation, and being unduly secretive, slow and biased. Complaints are viewed by some police as malicious interference with legitimate police work, and worthy of retaliation. Some chiefs of police have taken the view that the officer, not the complainant, is rightly seen as the victim. Even though some jurisdictions have taken steps to address these criticisms through the implementation of revised schemes, the basic distrust generated through the past experience will continue to hamper efforts to gain confidence in the system. Thus it is clear that the complaint and disciplinary systems do not provide the solution to police malpractice in investigations.

5. CONCLUSION REGARDING POST-INVESTIGATION SOLUTIONS

Attempts to eliminate or significantly reduce police malpractice in the investigation of crime through solutions centered on measures such as the exclusion of evidence, criminal or civil proceedings, and internal discipline or citizen complaints are likely to be ineffective. The problems with each measure vary, except for one common denominator. Each proposed solution suffers from the inability to impact the "cop culture" and "working personality" in investigation. Post-investigative solutions suffer from a more general problem as well. Self-interest in defending allegations of malpractice divert energy away from the search for the actual perpetrator. Each proposed solution involves a lapse of time which tends to make it more difficult to detect the convict the actual perpetrator of the original crime once the proceedings against the wrongfully accused, or errant police officer, are finally concluded.

. . .

D. RECRUITMENT AND TRAINING PRIOR TO INVESTIGATION

In addition to inadequate supervision, *RC Marshall*, *RCCJ* and Warren Burger share the view that many of the problems in police investigations are attributable to inadequate training. Certainly this was a significant factor in the Morin case. Undoubtedly the recruitment of good candidates and better training would assist in reducing investigative malpractice.

Police training in a formal setting is brief, typically lasting less than six months. Primary emphasis is placed on statutes, and operational skills including tactics, such as shooting, movement and cover, surveillance and explosives. Only modest instruction is given in investigative skills. Formal training fails to address the very practical conflicts between the realities and pressures of the job and legal and ethical requirements. And inevitably, instruction is saturated with the "cop culture."

Incomplete training retards the ability of a constable to perform at an acceptable level. Inadequate supervision and management techniques impair appropriate development and maturity. Further, the new constable is left more susceptible to the undesirable influences within the service. Researchers for the *RCCJ* noted the ease with which young police officers in the CID were pulled into the "working personality," almost without realizing it.

A commitment to principled training is important and must be the starting point for all reform. However, the concepts of an ethical investigation must also be fully integrated into the policies and practices of the police organization. Therefore, one must return to the question of how the current "cop culture" and "working personality" are to be restructured to safeguard and reinforce a revised training regime. Continuing professional education is one avenue, but the few hours available for classroom instruction can have no more than a limited impact. The RC Marshall suggested that the police should adopt a code of ethics. However, enforcement questions render this suggestion hollow.

Unfortunately, changes in recruitment, training and codes alone will not bring about the desired level of change. It is submitted that meaningful internal and public scrutiny are fundamental requirements of any reform process. . . .

*[Editor's note:*

*The oversight provisions for the police in Ontario are found in* An Act to Renew the Partnership between the Province, the Municipalities and the Police and to Enhance Community Safety, *which came into force in 1997 (S.O. 1997, c. 8). It resulted in a major overhaul of the system then in place which had been hailed a model for civilian oversight and which had been in place since 1990. The highlights of the Act are as follows:*

- *the oversight responsibilities which had been vested in an independent Office of the Police Complaints Commissioner passed to the appointed local police services boards;*
- *there was a move to treat public complaints more in the manner of internal discipline infractions, with the locus of initial investigation moving from an internal bureau of complaints (which would no longer be mandated as it had been prior to the Act) to the local chief of police. The system of independent Boards of inquiry was abolished;*
- *greater control over citizen complaints was to be exercised by the local chief of police;*
- *generally, the review provisions were weakened (e.g., no independent investigation resources are provided for); and*
- *there was a greater stress on the adversarial, individualistic nature of the complaint process. We see this in section 57, which restricts eligible complainants to those who have been "directly affected by the policy, service, or conduct that is the subject of the complaint".]*

# Strategies for Police Accountability and Community Empowerment*

## Ross Hastings and R.P. Saunders

*Excerpts from: "Strategies for Police Accountability and Community Empowerment", a paper prepared for the CROP-IISL Seminar on *Law, Power and Poverty* held in Onati, Spain, in May 1995.

. . .

The message which emerges from the experience of civilian review of police misconduct in Ontario is similar to findings from most other North American jurisdictions: there is little in either current legislation or practices which broadens the notion of police accountability beyond the assessment of the performance of individual officers and its fit with either the criminal law or other policy and procedural regulations.

There is little indication that the popular notion of police service and accountability to client communities has been translated into operational structures and processes which give these same communities a partnership role in decisions relating to the definition of problems and priorities within a community, nor in the design, implementation or evaluation of the programs or initiatives which constitute the service to these clients. This point is even more salient when one considers that many of the communities in which the police operate are characterized by high levels of disorder, tension and conflict. The performance of the police in such contexts can have a significant impact on the way a community evolves and develops.

At its heart, the problem begins at the conceptual level with the failure to distinguish adequately between the different potential operational meanings of the general notion of involving the community (as either a client or a partner) in policing, and of the more specific concern with the relation of police accountability mechanisms to this process. The concept of accountability should be conceived of as a continuum involving a number of different options and approaches. The continuum runs the gamut of possibilities between the two extremes of complete police autonomy and complete community control. Obviously, neither of these is desirable or realistic; they serve to provide end points for the debates over where exactly to locate a workable approach to accountability.

The first possibility is to involve the public as **complainants** in accountability processes. This has been the most popular position to date. It reflects the consensus that individual officers must work within the confines and constraints of the criminal law and other relevant regulations. In operational terms, the result is a tendency to involve the public as victims or witnesses of police abuse who may bring complaints to the attention of the relevant police authority (usually, at least initially, the police service in which the officer is employed). The key point here is that neither the complainant nor the general public exercise any control over the process beyond the point of the complaint, and many of these processes also fail the test of transparency. Even if it were possible to develop a perfect system for identifying and sanctioning individual officers, this approach does little or nothing to address problems at the corporate level of a police service. In addition, it neglects the broader structural factors responsible for current trends in crime and disorder, and in the maintenance of the legitimacy of the police among client groups and communities.

The second possibility is to include the public as either an **advisor** to the police or as a **participant** in the delivery of policing services. The benefit of this approach is that it goes part of the way towards opening up a police service to public input. Moreover, the participation of the public seems to have a beneficial impact on the quality of the contacts and relations between the police and the public. The problem is that it is still the relatively autonomous police professionals who retain control over what to do with the public's input, and over the nature of the activities in which the public is allowed to participate. At this level, we really have little more than a new approach to the *delivery* of traditional types of police services, with little or no real increase in community power or control.

The third possibility is to involve the community as a **partner** in the design and delivery of policing services. The focus of accountability here shifts from the individual officer to the police service. The concern is to develop structures and processes for addressing and redefining the problem of the redistribution of power and control in what are supposed to be partnerships between the police and the community in the co-production of social order. At this level, accountability involves giving mobilized community groups and their representatives a real and significant role within these partnerships. It also places a responsibility on either the police or other levels of government to assist in the mobilization of disadvantaged groups. Current accountability mechanisms fail this test: they not only are unable to address the larger notions of police accountability and responsiveness but, more importantly, in appropriating the discourses of accountability they mask the real challenge which remains to be faced in the next few years.

### Doe v. Metropolitan Toronto Board of Commissioners of Police and the Status of Public Oversight of the Police in Canada*

*Scott Childs and Paul Ceyssens*

*Excerpts from (1998), 36 Alberta Law Review 1000 at 1000-1004.

. . .

*Doe* raises several prominent issues in police oversight, most notably the availability of damages under the *Charter of Rights and Freedoms* and a potentially onerous new duty on the police to warn potential victims of crime. . . .

## II.  THE FACTS AND THE FINDINGS

The facts of the *Doe* case are not complex. In 1986, Jane Doe was attacked by a serial rapist. She sued, alleging that the two police investigators were responsible for her injuries. She also sued the chief of police, the governing body of the police force, and the Board of Commissioners of Police. Since the serial rapist confined his attacks to a small geographic area and an easily identifiable class of victims, Doe argued that she has become "part of a narrow and distinct group of potential victims," (the victims were all single, white women who resided in second or third floor apartments with accessible balconies that had been used to gain access).

Doe claimed damages on two grounds. First, she maintained that the police were negligent in that they failed to warn her of a danger that they knew (or ought to have known) existed or, absent such a warning, that they failed to protect her adequately against the danger. Secondly, she alleged the police breached her rights guaranteed under ss. 7 and 15(1) of the *Charter of Rights and Freedoms*, which provide as follows:

> 7. (1) Everyone has the right to life, liberty and security of the person and the right not to be deprived thereof except in accordance with the principles of fundamental justice.
> 15. (1) Every individual is equal before and under the law and has the right to the equal protection and equal benefit of the law without discrimination and, in particular, without discrimination based on race, national or ethnic origin, colour, religion, sex, age or mental or physical disability.

The defendants made unsuccessful preliminary attempts to dismiss the civil action. An eight-week trial occurred in late 1997, and the Ontario Court (General Division) awarded judgment in favour of Jane Doe in July 3, 1998.

The Court rejected the evidence of the police that they did not warn women they knew to be at risk on the basis that the attacker would relocate and continue to offend. Rather, the Court concluded that "the real reason a warning was not given in the circumstances of this case was because [the investigators] believed that women living in the area would become hysterical and panic, and their investigation would thereby be jeopardized." In a parallel investigation into similar (though more violent) attacks elsewhere in the city, different investigators in the same police force issued a series of effective public warnings to alert potential victims.

The Court found the police negligent in the circumstances of this case. The Court ruled that police could have and should have provided a "meaningful" warning to the women who were at particular risk:

> That warning could have been by way of canvass of their apartments, by a media blitz, by holding widely publicized public meetings or any one or a combination of these methods. Such warning should have alerted the particular women at risk, and advised them of suggested precautions they might take to protect themselves.

The Court noted that the police owe a duty to prevent crime as well as a duty to protect life and property and made the following observation:

> [T]he police failed utterly in their duty to protect these women and [Jane Doe] in particular from the serial rapist the police knew to be in their midst by failing to warn so that they may have had the opportunity to take steps to protect themselves.

> It is no answer for the police to say women are always at risk and as an urban adult living in downtown Toronto they have an obligation to look out for themselves. Women generally do, everyday of their lives, conduct themselves and their lives in such a way as to avoid the general pervasive threat of male violence which exists in our society. Here police were aware of a specific threat or risk to a specific group of women and they did nothing to warn those women of the danger they were in, nor did they take any measures to protect them.

The Court then went on to find that the police had breached Doe's Charter rights. In particular, the Court held that:

> [Police] deprived [Jane Doe] of her right to security of the person by subjecting her to the very real risk of attack by a serial rapist — a risk of which they were aware but about which they quite deliberately failed to inform the plaintiff [or other women] and where in the face of that knowledge and their belief that the rapist would certainly attack again, they additionally failed to take any steps to protect the plaintiff or other women like her.

Likewise, on the issue of equality rights as guaranteed by s.15(1) of the Charter, the Court concluded as follows:

> [T]he conduct of this investigation and the failure to warn in particular, was motivated and informed by the adherence to rape myths as well as sexist stereotypical reasoning about rape, about women and about women who are raped. [Jane Doe] therefore has been discriminated against by reason of her gender and as the result [her] rights to equal protection and equal benefit of the law were compromised.

The Court made one award of general damages—$175,000—for both the negligence and the violation of Jane Doe's *Charter* rights, as well as other smaller awards of damages.

## III. DOE AND RECENT TRENDS IN POLICE CIVIL LIABILITY

The past ten to fifteen years have seen dramatic change in the legal landscape of policing in Canada. This change is evident in nearly every facet of the legal regulation of the police—in some cases the legal developments have been both sudden and very profound. Some of this change has occurred through the civil law process.

Despite the extensive publicity afforded the Doe case, however, it should not be seen as the dawn of a new age of police accountability through the civil law process. Although Doe does set important new ground in two particular areas, the significance of the case should not be overstated, and it is more properly viewed as one in a large number of recent cases where the civil courts have examined an important aspect of police conduct in detail and found it wanting.

Indeed, the trends in police civil liability can be summarized in five statements:

1. civil actions against the police have significantly increased in number in the past ten years;
2. many of these cases are unprecedented—they involve novel causes of action that have no previously been the subject of civil claims against the police;
3. courts of law are awarding judgment against the police in many important cases;
4. courts of law are making large awards of damages and costs against the police;
5. other similar cases often follow on the heels of a successful plaintiff.

*Doe*, then, is one example of this trend, albeit a conspicuous example. It occurred in the past ten years, it involved a cause of action that had not previously been ruled upon by a court of law in Canada, the court awarded judgment against the police, and significant damages resulted. However, the civil courts have scrutinized many other areas of police activity in recent years.

One such emerging area is negligent investigation. In a number of cases, persons who have been charged by the police have sued in negligence after criminal proceedings have been disposed of in their favour. The leading judgment in this area is *Beckstead v. Ottawa (City)*. There, police charged Beckstead with two criminal offences relating to the use of an acquaintance's bank card. The investigation was deficient in a number of respects: the security photo of the suspect showed a person who did not resemble Beckstead, police did not interview the victim, and the police officer who charged Beckstead decided to charge her even before he interviewed her. Beckstead attended court on eight occasions over a period of six months before the Crown withdrew the charges. In its judgment, the trial court allowed the claim of negligence, stating that police owed a duty to "perform a careful investigation of the complaint" before laying a charge. The Ontario Court of Appeal, in a very brief judgment, dismissed the Board's appeal. It agreed with the trial judge, concluding that "[t]he police officer acted with indifference to the consequences of laying the charge and fell short of even the rudimentary steps which might have been taken to establish reasonable and probable grounds." The Court also dismissed an appeal against the award of general damages, concluding that the award of $20,000 was "modest." The ultimate cost of this judgement, of course, is significantly higher, including as it does other damages, interest and costs. *Beckstead* represents a further illustration of contemporary trends: the case is recent, the cause of action is unprecedented, the plaintiff obtained judgment against the police, the court-awarded significant damages to the plaintiff, and other similar decisions have since resulted.

. . .

## Questions/Discussion

1. Why should anyone bother to enforce the law? Describe the different incentive schemes by which people are motivated to involve themselves in law enforcement. Which systems do you think would work best for the following crimes: shoplifting, assault, illegal gambling, environmental offences, murder.
2. Despite the lack of effective public policing in Britain in the period 1770-1830, many citizens were reluctant to support the formation of such a police force. Explain their reluctance.
3. Argue the case for and against the police having special authority to carry handguns.
4. Investigate the complaints procedure in your local police force. What is the most effective way to make the police accountable to the public? What are the dangers of a police force which is not accountable?
5. How can you determine whether a given police force is performing adequately and behaving appropriately? What sort of information would you like to have to make this determination? Is such information available anywhere?
6. "The pursuit of a professionalized, politically neutral police force — narrowly focused on 'serious crime' and relying on new technologies — eventually weakened the bonds between private citizens and the police, and shifted the burdens of enforcement to a public agency that could not succeed by itself." Excerpt from M. Moore & G. Kelling, "'To Serve and Protect': Learning from Police History" (1982-3), 69-72 *The Public Interest* 49-65.
7. The deaths of Helene Betty Osborne in The Pas, J.J. Harper in Winnipeg, and the Nova Scotia case of Donald Marshall, Jr. suggest very strongly that Canadian police are often racist regarding native persons. Besides assigning blame in individual cases,

what might be done to better protect Inuit, Metis and other aboriginal peoples from police discrimination?

**Further Reading**

- Bayley, David, "Getting Serious About Police Brutality" in Philip Stenning, ed., *Accountability for Criminal Justice* (Toronto: University of Toronto Press, 1996).
- Cryderman, B. and A. Fleras, *Police, Race and Ethnicity. 2nd ed..* (Toronto: Butterworths, 1992).
- de Lint, Willem, "Regulating Autonomy: Police Discretion as a Problem for Training" (1998), 40 Canadian Journal of Criminology 277-304.
- Delisle, R.J., "Judicial Creation of Police Powers" (1993), 20 C.R. (4th) 29-33.
- Goldsmith, Andrew and Colleen Lewis, eds., *Civilian Oversight of Policing: Governance, Democracy, and Human Rights* (Oxford: Hart Publishing, 2000).
- Hastings, Ross and R.P. Saunders, "Strategies for Police Accountability and Community Empowerment" in Asbjorn Kjonstad and Peter Robson, eds., *Poverty and the Law* (Oxford: Hart Publishing, 2001).
- Landau, Tammy, "When Police Investigate Police: A View from Complainants" (1996), 38 Canadian Journal of Criminology 291-315.
- Hogan, M., D. Brown & R. Hogg, *Death in the Hands of the State* (Australia: Redfern Legal Centre, 1988).
- Law Reform Commission of Canada, *Arrest. Working Paper 41* (Ottawa: Law Reform Commission of Canada, 1985).
- Macleod, R.C. and D. Schneiderman, *Police Powers in Canada: The Evolution and Practice of Authority* (Toronto: University of Toronto Press, 1994).
- MacMillan, Craig, "The Legal Advice Gap in Policing" (1997), 55 Advocate (Van.) 845-854.
- Moore, K., "Police Implementation of Supreme Court of Canada Charter Decisions: An Empirical Study" (1992), 30 Osgoode Hall Law Journal 547-577.
- Ontario Race Relations and Policing Task Force, *Report of the Race Relations and Policing Task Force* (Toronto: Race Relations and Policing Task Force, 1989).
- Randall, Melanie, "Sex Discrimination, Accountability of Public Authorities and the Public/Private Divide in Tort Law; An Analysis of *Doe v. Metropolitan Toronto (Municipality) Commissioners of Police*" (2001), 26 Queen's Law Journal 451-495.

# 4.2 PROSECUTOR/DEFENCE

## Introduction

This section introduces the reader to some of the issues surrounding the roles played by the prosecutor and by the defence counsel in the criminal law system. Given that the prosecutor is the state official charged with enforcing the criminal law in the courts, it is particularly important to look at the control or accountability mechanisms that exist to limit the exercise of his or her discretion. As we shall see, the exercise of discretion on the part of the prosecutor in Canada is largely unfettered. As for the defence counsel, the issues relating to accountability are obviously different, although there are several control mechanisms in place that can affect their actions. However, these mechanisms ultimately have little effect on the actions of the defence.

# Prosecutorial Arrangements and Powers in Canada*

## *Don Stuart*

*Excerpts from "Prosecutorial Accountability in Canada" in Philip Stenning, ed., *Accountability for Criminal Justice: Selected Essays* (Toronto: University of Toronto Press, 1995) at 330-332.

. . .

## Prosecutorial Arrangements and Powers in Canada

The historical origins and establishment of the Canadian system of Crown prosecutors has been well described elsewhere (Grosman, 1969: ch. 2; Stenning, 1986: Part 1).

Although Canada, since 1892, has had a Criminal Code that applies across the country, there is a complex division of prosecutorial authority between federal and provincial jurisdictions. Although Canada still has in principle a system of private prosecution in which any individual can prosecute, in practice the vast majority of criminal prosecutions are conducted by salaried Crown attorneys under the authority of provincial attorneys general. The attorneys general are elected politicians who also serve in Cabinet.

The authority for prosecution of criminal offences is but one of the responsibilities of the attorney general (see for example, Section 5 of the Minister of the Ontario attorney General Act) [RSO 1990]. On a day-to-day basis, the vast bulk of criminal prosecutions are conducted by individual Crown prosecutors who act as agents for the attorney general. Unlike district attorneys in the United States, Crown prosecutors in Canada are appointed, not elected. Unlike district attorneys, they have no separate investigatory arm and are thus forced to rely exclusively on investigation by police forces.

The Canadian tradition is that prosecutors play a quasi judicial role in a special relation to the court. The role of prosecuting counsel is that of 'ministers of justice' rather than partisan advocates. . . .

Most Canadian prosecutors would reject the view of one United States prosecutor that 'your true purpose is to convict the guilty man who sits at the defence table, and to go for the jugular as viciously and as rapidly as possible . . . You must never forget that your goal is total annihilation' (Lathan, 1988:59, 17).

Canadian legislatures and Parliament have repeatedly attempted over the years to declare criteria on which police discretion is to be exercised in a wide variety of contexts such as powers to search, arrest, and release prior to trial. In stunning contrast, Crown attorneys have virtually unfettered discretion as to when to charge, what to charge, and when the charge should be reduced or dropped (see generally Morgan, 1986; Stenning, 1986:199-329). Common law powers such as the right to withdraw a charge, give discovery to defence counsel, and accept a plea bargain have been largely unlimited by the courts. So too, statutory powers such as the right to take over a private prosecution, to enter a stay of proceedings, or to decide in the case of dual offences to proceed by way of indictment or by way of summary conviction (which has important implications for the accused, such as the right to choose a jury trial and as to the maximum penalty) are simply given to the attorney general or the agents without any statutory guidelines. The Law Reform Commission of Canada (Canada, LRC, 1990) has recently recommended that guidelines be published, although their recommendation is that they not be imposed by legislatures.

All Crown attorneys have this panoply of powers. The few special prosecutorial powers which can only be exercised at the discretion of the attorney general are also unlimited. Such powers include the power to directly indict to avoid a preliminary inquiry or where there has been a discharge at a preliminary inquiry, consent to prosecute in the case of some offences such as willful promotion of hatred, and nudity in a public place, and also permission to make an application to have an accused declared a dangerous offender, leading to indeterminate detention.

. . .

## Prosecuting*

### Gavin MacKenzie

*Excerpts from *Lawyers and Ethics: Professional Responsibility and Discipline* (Toronto: Carswell, 1999) at 6-1 – 6-7; 6-9; 6-14 – 6-17.

. . .

The ethical principles that govern prosecutors are all variations of the same rule of professional conduct: the prosecutor's duty is not to seek a conviction, but to see that justice is done. As Rumpole realizes, it is not a role with which lawyers trained in the adversary system's sporting theory of justice feel entirely comfortable.

Norman Schwartz, a former prosecutor, describes the tension that prosecutors must try to resolve:

> The advocate in you says you should do everything you can to convict someone you believe is guilty. Yet you have a duty to do justice, to help the other side, even to year down your own case. The potential is there for terrible conflict.

Not all prosecutors succeed in resolving the conflict. "This 'innocent until proven guilty' business doesn't hold with a prosecutor," says an American assistant district attorney featured in James Mills's book *The Prosecutor*. "In court it's an adversary system—for me he's guilty and I'm out to make twelve other people agree with me."

Examples of such unreconstructed adversarial spirit abound. In a 1987 Illinois case, a prosecutor in closing argument called the accused person a "mutant from hell." In a 1991 case, a prosecutor was censured publicly by the Supreme Court of Kansas for failing to personally confirm the truth of a statement that she had made to a jury in a rape trial. The prosecutor had said to the jury that the accused person had transmitted gonorrhea to the victim. In fact there was no evidence that the victim was either contracted or was treated for gonorrhoea.

Such cases demonstrate that Professor Alan M. Dershowitz was right when he wrote that many prosecutors reverse the motto on the wall of the United States Justice Department. The motto proclaims that the government "wins its point whenever justice is done." Many prosecutors believe, wrote Dershowitz, that justice is done whenever the government wins its point.

The prosecutor's duty has been expressed in many different ways, The best known Canadian statement is that of Justice Rand in a 1955 decision of the Supreme Court of Canada:

> The role of prosecutor excludes any notion of winning or losing; his function is a matter of public duty than which in civil life there can be none charged with greater personal responsibility. It is to be performed with an ingrained sense of the dignity, the seriousness and the justness of the judicial proceedings.

In the same case, Justice Taschereau added that the prosecutor's role is quasi-judicial.

These two themes have been repeated continually. Prosecutors who keep them in mind are unlikely to violate their responsibilities: prosecutors must not allow themselves to be betrayed by feelings of rivalry or competitiveness, and should approach their responsibilities with the even-handedness of a judge rather than with the partisan spirit of an advocate. The duty of fairness applies even in cases in which the prosecutor believes in good faith that the accused person is guilty.

Thus in a 1934 decision of the Ontario Court of Appeal, Justice Riddell said as follows:

> . . . a criminal prosecution is not a contest between the State and the accused in which the State seeks a victory, but being an investigation, it is the duty of prosecuting counsel . . . to lay all the facts before the jury, those favourable to the accused as those unfavourable to him.

One of the reasons for this significant modification of the adversary system is that prosecutors play a dual role. Prosecutors are not just advocates who are responsible for obtaining convictions of guilty accused persons; they are also administrators of justice who are responsible for seeing that innocent persons are not prosecuted, convicted, or punished. Their role is one of considerable power. Studies have shown that the outcome of more cases is determined by prosecutors' decisions than by the decisions of any other component of the criminal justice system. . . .

It does not follow from the prosecutor's duty to see that justice is done that the prosecutor must avoid advocacy. Chief Justice Kerwin of the Supreme Court of Canada wrote in the leading Canadian case that counsel for the Crown is entitled to examine all the evidence and ask the jury to come to the conclusion that the accused is guilty as charged. the prosecutor may present the government's position "in forcible and direct language", so long as the language is not inflammatory. . . .

## WHO IS THE CLIENT?

Prosecutors often make decisions that, in civil litigation, would be made by clients rather than lawyers. Their duty is to serve the public interest. They do not have clients in the conventional sense.

Prosecutors do, however, have constituencies. These include, most importantly, the police, victims of crime, other government officials, and the judiciary. Each of these constituencies attempts to influence prosecutorial decisions in much the same way clients attempt to influence the decisions that must be made in any litigation. None, however, can accurately be described as the prosecutor's client.

. . .

## THE CHARGING DECISION

In three Canadian jurisdictions, namely British Columbia, Quebec, and New Brunswick, Crown Attorneys decide whether criminal prosecutions should be initiated. In all other Canadian jurisdictions, this decision is made by the police. In all jurisdictions, the decision whether to continue a prosecution or ask that charges by stayed, withdrawn, or dismissed, is made by prosecutors.

Each of these decisions has important consequences. Because the process becomes public when a charge is laid, the charging decision is particularly crucial. A public announcement that a person has been charged with an offence often causes as much damage to that person as does a conviction. The expense of defending a criminal case can be considerable, but in most cases, considerations of cost pale in significant in comparison to the personal trauma and damage to reputation sustained by the accused person.

In British Columbia, the sole function of some Crown Attorneys is to review investigative reports to decide whether charges recommended by the police should be approved. The Crown Attorneys who perform this function have been directed as a matter of policy to approve charges only if they are satisfied on the evidence available (including evidence reflecting the likely defence, if available) that (i) there is a substantial likelihood of conviction and (ii) it is in the public interest that a prosecution should be undertaken.

The Ministry of the Attorney General policy in which this two-pronged test is articulated makes it clear that the substantial likelihood of conviction standard is significantly stricter than either the *Criminal Code's* reasonable and probable grounds test or a *prime facie* case test. Factors that the policy requires the Crown Attorney to weigh in considering the second prong of the test include the nature and seriousness and the allegations, the personal circumstances if the accused (including his or her personal record), the likelihood of achieving the desired result by means other than a criminal prosecution (such as an established diversion process), the harm suffered by the victim, and the cost of the prosecution compared to the social benefit to be gained by it.

Proponents of the traditional system, which remains in place in most other provinces, content that the British Columbia charge approval system erodes the independence of the police. Proponents of the British Columbia system argue that the damage caused by publication of a charge can be sufficiently harsh that the process should not become public unless and until it is clear that there is a likelihood of conviction. The British Columbia system is thus fairer to accused persons. It is also more objective—police officers who have expended considerable time and energy investigating a possible offence may feel that their efforts have been wasted if charges are not laid.

Finally, though perhaps least importantly, the British Columbia system is more efficient than the traditional system.

In 1987, Justice Thomas G. Zuber, in his capacity as author of the Report of the Ontario Court Inquiry, recommended that Crown prosecutors should be involved in the determination of what charge should be laid to a far greater degree than has been the case in the past.

In a 1990 working paper, the Law Reform Commission of Canada emphasized the necessity of contingency and fairness in the determination of both which prosecutions should be commenced and which should be discontinued. The Commission recommended: that the advice of a public prosecutor be sought by the police before a charge is laid; that guidelines be issued by Attorneys-General so that the basis of charging decisions is less obscure than was formerly the case; that the guidelines require prosecutors to weigh the available evidence rather than merely decide whether there is a prima facie case; that the guidelines require prosecutors to conclude that a prosecution is justified in the public interest before advising that a charge be laid; and that the standard for commencing a prosecution should not be so strict as to discourage prosecutions that are in the public interest though the likelihood of conviction may be somewhat less than "substantial."

. . .

It is likely, and, for the reasons expressed above, it is desirable, that Canadian prosecutors in the future will play an increasingly direct and important role in deciding whether charges should be laid and, if so, what those charges should be. At present, rules of professional conduct do not specifically address the prosecutor's professional responsibility in laying charges or discontinuing proceedings. The rules say simply that "the prosecutor exercises a public function involving much discretion and power, and must act fairly and dispassionately.

In the United States, prosecutors frequently become involved not only in deciding what charges should be laid, but in deciding what or who should be investigated. The power to make such decisions, like the power to decide who should be charged, is a dangerous one, raising questions of selective and arbitrary enforcement and favouritism.

. . .

. . . The approval of a charge, and the continuance of a prosecution, should require the prosecution to be satisfied after reviewing the admissible evidence of each of the following:

(1)  that there is a reasonable likelihood of conviction;
(2)  that a fair-minded person would be satisfied beyond a reasonable doubt of the suspect's guilt; and
(3)  that it is in the public interest that the prosecution be brought or continued.

. . .

## IMPERMISSIBLE TACTICS

As a result of their duty to approach their responsibilities with quasi-judicial fairness rather than in a partisan spirit, prosecutors' advocacy must be much more restrained than that of lawyers representing either persons accused of criminal offences or parties to civil proceedings. Limitations imposed on all advocates in the interest of discouraging forensic excesses apply a fortiori to prosecutors, and prosecutors are subject to limitations that do not apply to advocates for private parties who are discharging their duty of resolute partisanship. Thus it is particularly important that prosecutors do not express personal opinions concerning the guilt of an accused person or the credibility of witnesses, or make other prejudicial or inflammatory remarks to the court. It is also important that prosecutors refrain from speaking to witnesses called by them who are being cross-examined.

The prosecutor's duty to ensure that an accused person receives a fair trial heightens the prosecutor's duty of care. Prosecutors must take reasonable steps to assess the truth or falsity, and not just the plausibility, of evidence that they lead; they must not lead evidence that they know, or ought to know, is false. They must personally confirm the truth of statements that they make to the court. Prosecutors who are reckless as to the truth of such statements violate their duty to do justice.

It should be no answer to allegations of prosecutorial misconduct for prosecutors to say that they are merely "fighting fire with fire", or responding to provocation in the form of impermissible tactics on the part of the defence. The same rules do not apply to prosecution and defence counsel, who play dramatically different roles in the process. The impediment to a fair trial is the same whether or not the prosecutor is provoked. The proper course for a prosecutor to follow if defence counsel exceed the limits of acceptable advocacy is to object and ask the trial judge to intervene. They should not respond in kind.

Like all lawyers, prosecutors have a duty not to communicate directly with persons who are represented by counsel except with counsel's consent. Prosecutors also have a duty, as, again, do all lawyers, to deal in good faith with lay persons who are lawfully representing others or themselves. Both duties must be observed particularly scrupulously by prosecutors. It would be highly improper for a prosecutor to attempt to obtain directly from an accused person a waiver of such rights as the right to remain silent, the right to counsel, and the right to a preliminary inquiry.

Although, again, the practices are not explicitly prohibited by current Canadian rules of professional conduct, prosecutors should ensure that arrangements that they make with witnesses do not risk influencing the witnesses' testimony. Arrangements whereby accomplices' sentences are deferred until after they testify at the trials of other alleged parties to their offences enable prosecutors to maintain strong and coercive holds over witnesses, and may well risk influencing the witnesses to testify falsely in the hope that they will be rewarded with more lenient sentences.

Other tactics that, at least in some circumstances, may violate the prosecutor's duty to act fairly and dispassionately include: issuing subpoenas to defence counsel; using accused persons' criminal records to impeach credibility in situations in which the prejudicial effect of doing so outweighs the asserted justification of casting doubt on credibility; unnecessarily interrupting defence counsel's examination of witnesses; adopting a belligerent attitude toward accused persons, defence counsel, or defence witnesses; and pursuing lines of questioning or argument that are clearly irrelevant or otherwise impermissible, such as cross-examination of an accused person that suggests that he or she has previously been suspected of another crime.

. . .

## THE MAGISTERIAL PROSECUTOR

Prosecutors come in two models: the adversarial model and the magisterial model.

The adversarial model of prosecutor promotes law enforcement values to the exclusion of all others. Accused persons are consistently overcharged, as aggressive and indiscriminate charging is one of many legitimate weapons in the prosecutor's arsenal in a legal contest with the defence.

The adversarial prosecutor will exploit the laxity, inexperience, or incompetence of defence counsel because to do so is consistent with the prosecutor's combative approach. Game-like bargaining and the pursuit of maximum sentences are also characteristic of the adversarial model's approach, which can be summarized in a word as "zealous."

The magisterial model of prosecutor (the adjective is derived from the noun "magistrate") exemplifies a professional ethic that rejects lawyerly partisanship and rivalry. The claims of both law enforcement and fundamental justice are considered objectively. The magisterial model's approach is quasi-judicial and moderated. Ensuring the fairness of accused persons' trials is as important a goal as the protection of the public.

A less aggressive formulation of charges reflects not a policy of leniency but a careful evaluation of the practical likelihood of proving the charges, and of what result is truly warranted on the available, and admissible, evidence.

Other distinguishing qualities of the magisterial model of prosecutor include a willingness to make full and prompt disclosure and a repudiation of questionable trial tactics, in combination with appropriate firmness.

The adversarial model of prosecutor has no place in our process. The line should be discontinued. Prosecutors should come only in the magisterial model.

### Accountability of the Crown Attorney to the Attorney General*

#### *Don Stuart*

*Excerpts from "Prosecutorial Accountability in Canada" in Philip Stenning, ed., *Accountability for Criminal Justice: Selected Essays* (Toronto: University of Toronto Press, 1995) at 336; 337-340; 341-343; 345-348.

. . .

### Accountability of the Crown Attorney to the Attorney General

All Crown attorneys, whether full- or part-time, are employed by the attorney general and are clearly administratively responsible to him or her, given that the attorney general has the power to terminate their employment.

. . .

Most attorneys general content themselves with issuing policy guidelines on specific matters. Just how general and non-binding they are can be gauged by considering two Ontario examples.

As of 1 January, 1988, the Ministry of the Attorney General issued ten principles applicable to plea discussions. One of these principles related to expediency: 'Expediency in reducing workload is not acceptable as a reason for accepting a plea to a lesser offence or to a lesser number of offences. Expediency in this sense does not include weaknesses in the Crown's case on the major charge or charges, which may be a valid reason for accepting a plea to a lesser offence or to a lesser number of offences' (Ontario, Ministry of the Attorney General, 1988: Policy No. P-1, par. 2). However, the guideline ended with the following paragraph designed not to fetter discretion: 'These principles are not rules to be applied rigidly or to be considered binding in every situation. However, although a Crown Attorney must have a free and unfettered discretion as to how to apply these principles, the Crown Attorney also has a continuing responsibility to conduct all plea discussions in accordance with their spirit' (ibid.).

A 20 March 1984 direction as to the prosecution of cases of domestic violence encourages Crown attorneys to proceed with a prosecution against the wishes of the complainant: 'The Crown Attorney should accede to a request by the complainant not to proceed only after giving the request careful and serious consideration. This is clearly in line with the view that domestic violence is in the realm of the other criminal offences and must be treated as equally serious, and not regarded as solely a private family matter' (Ontario, Ministry of the Attorney General, 1984: 2). However, the director of crown attorneys was quick to add that a Crown attorney continues to have the jurisdiction to withdraw the charge 'when circumstances warrant.' . . .

### Prosecutor's Liability against Civil Suits

Can an accused aggrieved by the conduct of the attorney general or the Crown prosecutor recover monetary damages in a civil suit?

Until the recent landmark ruling of the Supreme Court of Canada in *Nelles v Ontario* [1989], the weight of judicial authority, particularly in Ontario, was that prosecutors had an absolute immunity against such actions. . . .

Since *Nelles* [1989], an accused can therefore hold the attorney general and/or the prosecutors personally legally accountable by a civil suit if there is proof on a balance of probabilities of a malicious prosecution. Apart from the considerable hurdles to such actions mentioned by the Supreme Court, other considerations suggest that the remedy will likely be largely ineffective (Stenning, 1986:347; Hogg, 1989:511).

Actions for malicious prosecution cannot be brought where there was a conviction. They require a plaintiff prepared to undertake the notoriously high costs of such litigation. Furthermore, experience throughout the common law world indicates that actions for malicious prosecution rarely succeed. They are no remedy against the incompetent or negligent Crown attorney. There is thus still a contrast with the civil liability of police officers who, in addition to liability for malicious prosecution, face potential liability for breaches of duties of care or statutory duty.

It is still too early to verify the claims of some Crown prosecutors in Ontario that *Nelles* [1989] has indeed resulted in a number of vexatious law suits, especially from those defence counsel who conduct their practice as street fighters and are now prepared to add the threat of a civil suit to their arsenal of intimidation tactics in their fight against the Crown attorneys. One suspects, however, for the reasons already given, that such concerns will turn out to be largely groundless. The Supreme Court itself noted that the province of Quebec has allowed suits against the attorney general and Crown prosecutors since 1986, and there has been no evidence of a flood of claims.

## Judicial Review

In the case of the vast bulk of prosecutorial conduct in trial courts, the above picture is one of most limited accountability in any of the senses of legal, political, or administrative accountability. It seems clear that the most important form of accountability of Crown attorneys lies in the discretion and power of trial judges to control the criminal process over which they preside.

Trial judges have always been prepared to exercise an overriding discretion to control the trial process itself in various rulings on matters of fair procedure and the application of the rules of evidence. However, prior to the enactment of the Charter of Rights and Freedoms [1982], courts showed extreme reluctance to review the exercise of the unlimited powers of discretion given to Crown attorneys. The reluctance has been based on a notion of separation of powers. There are also concerns that the administration of criminal justice would be jeopardized by endless applications for review and would transfer too much discretion to judges.

. . .

Now, under the entrenched Charter, which is the supreme law, review of the exercise of discretion of prosecutors or an attorney general can no longer be resisted on the basis of a doctrine of separation of powers. In *Operation Dismantle* [1985], the Supreme Court confirmed that decisions of the executive branch of government, including Cabinet decisions, are subject to review by the courts under the Charter. Courts have, however, continued to resist frontal attacks, based on the Charter, on discretionary powers of prosecutors (and police), although they have accepted that the exercise of power in particular, exceptional case may require judicial intervention.

. . .

Unfortunately, the most recent ruling from the Supreme Court of Canada also points to non-intervention. In *Scott* [1991] a Crown attorney entered a stay in a drugs case to avoid an unfavourable evidentiary ruling that would have revealed an informer's identity and immediately recommenced the same proceedings in another court. The Supreme Court ruled six to three that the conduct should not result in a stay as an abuse of process. On the evidence, the minority view is compelling. This was surely the type of undue manipulation of the judicial process that the power to stay is designed to control. The Crown had the option of calling no evidence and appealing the resulting acquittal.

The practical effect of *Scott* [1980] may be that applications to stay as an abuse of process will now hardly ever succeed. This would be disappointing, as the stay as an abuse is the major vehicle for holding trial prosecutors to account. It also seems clear that the principles upon which the doctrine rests are highly contentious and confused (*Stuart*, 1991:100-3).

## Discriminatory Law Enforcement Contrary to Section 15 of the Charter

. . .

Thus far, courts have resisted attempts to use the equality guarantee in Section 15 to protect against discriminatory law enforcement by the police or prosecutors in a particular case. An argument that enforcement was discretionary will not do. There will have to be clear evidence of discrimination. The lack of success of such claims thus far suggests that criminal courts will continue to be an inadequate forum for consideration of such serious, but difficult-to-substantiate charges as racism. The charter is not a panacea and will be no substitute for such special inquiries as the Manitoba Aboriginal justice inquiry (1991a, b), which substantiated systemic racism in the Manitoba justice inquiry (1991a, b), which substantiated systemic racism in the Manitoba justice system. That inquiry took three years and cost three million dollars.

## The Right to Be Tried Within a Reasonable time under Section 11(b) of the Charter

Prior to the enactment of Section 11(b), there were few statutory limitation periods in criminal prosecutions in Canada. Since Section 11(b), anyone charged with an offence has the right 'to be tried within a reasonable time.' There have been literally thousands of cases regarding this right since 1982. The Section 11(b) challenge may also be the most politically charged, because the court's constitutional duty to assess delay necessarily involves the judiciary in direct assessment of administrative and political decisions as to the deployment of scarce public resources. In this determination, the conduct of the prosecutor is front and centre.

In the Supreme Court's leading decision in *Askov* [1990], the court determined that there were four groups of factors to be considered: the length of the delay, explanation for the delay, waiver, and prejudice to the accused (for a detailed consideration, see Stuart, 1991:230-46). Under the group of factors entitled 'explanation for the delay,' the court directs consideration of delays attributable to the Crown, which will weigh in favour of an accused, and also systemic or institutional delays—delay caused by lack of resources such as courtrooms, judges, and Crown counsel—which will also weigh against the Crown. In the case of institutional delay, the court fashioned a test of comparing jurisdictions across Canada under which it is necessary to have in mind a rough comparison with the best districts of comparable geography, population, and resources. In *Askov* [1990] itself, the court stayed charges of conspiracy to extort and weapons charges on the basis of a delay of almost two years between the preliminary hearing and the trial caused by a lack of facilities in the Brampton court district, which, from the point of view of delay, said the court, was the worst district not only in Canada but, so far as studies indicated, 'anywhere north of the Rio Grande.' The court indicated that the period of delay in such a case should have been in the range of some six to eight months.

After *Askov* [1990l], some 100,000 criminal charges were permanently stayed in Ontario alone, including thousands of impaired driving charges, and a substantial number of assaults, fraud, sexual assault, and drug-related charges. In *Bennett* [1991] the Ontario Court of Appeal called for restraint in the exercise of the Section 11(b) discretion by trial judges, holding that the six- to eight-month period mentioned in *Askov* [1990] had been wrongly interpreted as a mechanical limitation. Trial judges were expected to exercise judgment in the remedy of stay and to do their best to apply each of the factors mentioned in *Askov* [1990].

. . .

. . . Since *Morin* [1992] the deluge of cases being stayed for unreasonable delay has become a trickle. The court may have got cold feet too quickly. Despite the change in direction, *Askov* [1990] is still important for its major effect on the chronic problem of court delay, especially in Ontario. When the judges began throwing out thousands of valid charges because of delay, politicians were forced to react. New resources were quickly directed at courts and new management strategies employed. The Charter had been used to force a major reassessment of a long-festering problem.

. . .

## Prosecutorial Discretion in a Charter-Dominated Trial Process*

### Wayne Gorman

*Excerpts from (2000), 44 Criminal Law Quarterly 15 at 18-20; 21-23; 25; 27-30.

. . .

Since the proclamation of the *Canadian Charter of Rights and Freedoms*, Crown prosecutors have been subjected to continuous allegations of abuse of process. Every decision is subject to criticism and allegations of improper motives are readily and easily made.

One area that has been subject to a substantial amount of litigation is the use of prosecutorial discretion. Accused persons have attempted to challenge everything from decisions on whether to proceed by summary conviction or indictment to what witnesses will or will not be called at trial. Though the Charter *has* provided an avenue for such arguments that did not exist before, and though it has legitimized abuse of process as a defence, a review of the judicial considerations of such attacks on the use of Crown discretion illustrates that they have generally been spectacularly unsuccessful. This discretion remains alive and vibrant; examples of this will follow. The test to be applied when a prosecutor's motives are questioned has been set very high. The comments of the Alberta Court of Appeal in *Kostuch* are reflective of that standard:

> Assuming that the court has power to review prosecutorial discretion, that power will be exercised only in cases where there has been flagrant impropriety in the exercise of the prosecutorial discretion. This rule has been clearly established by the Court, and we accept it as correct. In R. v. Balderstone et al. (1983) 8 C.C.C. (3d) 532 at 539 (Man.C.A.), (leave to appeal refused, [1983] 2 S.C.R. V) Monnin C.J.M. stated as follows:
>
> > The judicial and executive must not mix. These are two separate and distinct functions. The accusatorial officers lay informations or in some cases prefer indictments. Courts or the curia listen to cases brought to their attention and decide them on their merits or on meritorious preliminary matters. If a judge should attempt to review the actions of conduct of the Attorney General—barring flagrant impropriety—he could be falling into a field which is not his and interfering with the administrative and accusatorial function of the Attorney General or his officers. That a judge must not do.

In *R. v. D. (R.C.)*, the accused was convicted of murder. A new trial was ordered and the accused sought to be tried, pursuant to s. 686(5.1) of the *Criminal Code*, by a judge without a jury. This requires the Crown's consent. The Crown refused to give it. The accused applied to the Supreme Court of Newfoundland for an order allowing him to be tried by a judge without a jury, alleging an abuse of process. In rejecting this argument Halley J. stated:

> The Attorney General is charged with the proper administration of justice in this Province. In discharging that responsibility the Attorney General and his Crown prosecutors are called upon to exercise prosecutorial discretion many times each day. It is not appropriate for the judiciary to review the Crown's use of its discretionary powers unless there is some "flagrant" impropriety.
>
> In order to prevent accused persons from going on "fishing expeditions" the Courts require that the accused meet a threshold test. Unless that threshold test is met, the actions of the Crown will not be investigated or examined by the Court. In *addition, the Crown will not be required to give an explanation of its decision.*
>
> In this case the Accused made allegations in relation to the Crown's decision which amounted to mere speculation and conjecture. There was no evidence of "flagrant" impropriety in the exercise of the crown's prosecutorial discretion. Having failed to meet the "threshold" test this Court does not have the power to enter upon a review of the exercise of the Crown's discretion to refuse to consent to a judge alone trial for the Accused.
>
> Where there is no evidence of improper conduct or impropriety by the Crown there can be no breach of the Accused's section 7 or section 11 Charter rights. In addition, there is no constitutional right to a non-jury trial in a murder case.

As was stated earlier, the exercise of prosecutorial discretion has been challenged on a regular basis. However, these challenges have failed. . . .

## The Decision to Proceed: Selection of Appropriate Charges

In *R. v. V. (K.S.)*, the Crown decided to charge a 13-year-old accused with sexual assault contrary to s. 271 of the Code. The Crown could have charged the accused under s. 151 of the Code (touching for a sexual purpose); however, if it had done so, s. 150.1(3) (position of trust or authority required if accused is 12 or 13 years of age), which does *not* apply to s. 271, would have afford a defence. The trial judge concluded that this exercise of discretion violated s. 7 of the Charter. The Crown appealed. The Newfoundland Court of Appeal, in very succinct terms, stressed the principle that these are decisions for the Crown to make. In the court's view it is for the Crown "to bring whatever charge against the alleged offender that it deems fit in the circumstances". The court also held that:

> As to prosecutorial discretion, the law is established that where there is conduct which might constitute an offence under more than one section of the Criminal Code, the Crown has a discretion with respect to the offence or offences for which the accused person is to be prosecuted.

. . .

## Intervening in Private Prosecutions

Though a private citizen can initiate a private prosecution, the Attorney General has an overriding authority to intervene and take over the prosecution. Private informants have been less than pleased with such action and have attacked (unsuccessfully) the Attorney General's authority to do so.

In *R. v. Osiowy* the Saskatchewan Court of Appeal stated that it is settled that:

> . . . an individual has the right to initiate a private prosecution. It is also settled that the Attorney-General has the right to intervene and take control of a private prosecution. Included in the right to intervene and take control is the power to direct a stay pursuant to s. 508. It follows, then, that a private informant has the right to initiate proceedings, but that right does not give him the liberty to continue the proceedings should the Attorney-General decide to intervene and invoke s. 508(1) and direct the entry of a stay of proceedings. Once the Attorney-General or counsel on his behalf intervenes and assumes control of the prosecution, that counsel's rights are paramount to the private person's or his counsel's rights. The discretion of the Attorney-General to enter a stay is not reviewable in the absence of some flagrant impropriety on the part of the Crown officers. No such impropriety has been suggested here.

## Electing to Proceed by Summary Conviction or by Indictment

The Crown has the discretion to proceed by indictment or by summary conviction in "hybrid offences". With the increased number of such offences in the *Criminal Code* this is a discretion that provides the Crown with significant power.

In *R. v. Smythe* the Supreme Court of Canada concluded that the exercise of such a discretion did *not* violate the "Canadian Bill of Rights".

In a post-Charter decision the Ontario Court of Appeal stressed that the *lack* of such a discretion might violate the Charter. . . .

## Direct Indictments

Section 577 of the Code allows the Crown to proceed directly to trial by the preferring of a direct indictment. This use of discretion has received considerable challenge, including the argument that the Charter protects an accused's right to have a preliminary inquiry. However, this purported right has been held not to exist and the Crown's discretion to proceed by direct indictment has been consistently upheld.

. . .

## Requiring that the Accused Be Tried by a Judge and Jury

Section 568 of the Code provides the Attorney General with the discretion to override an accused's election as regards the mode of trial and to require that he or she be tried by a judge and jury.

In *R. v. Hanneson* the accused elected to be tried by a judge sitting alone. The Attorney General exercised his discretion under s. 568 of the Code, requiring that the trial be held by a judge sitting with a jury. The accused applied to have s. 568 declared to be unconstitutional.

O'Driscoll J. held that "There is nothing in the Charter which guarantees an accused a Charter right to elect to be tried by a court other than a court composed of a judge and jury." The court concluded:

> It follows, therefore, that since the only Charter or constitutional right an accused has regarding mode of trial is the one set out in s. 11(f) of the Charter, there could not possibly be a Charter infraction under s. 7 and/or s. 15 in this case because the Attorney-General for Ontario, by utilizing s. 498 of the *Code*, has directed that the accused will proceed to "an impartial trial by jury"—the very thing that the Constitution guarantees him. . . .

## Deciding what Witnesses to Call

As stated earlier, the Crown prosecutor in Canada has a "quasi-judicial" function. However, Crown prosecutors also have an adversarial role to play in the trial process and can do so forcefully when required:

> . . . while it is without question that the Crown performs a special function in ensuring that justice is served and cannot adopt a purely adversarial role towards the defence (*Boucher v. the Queen*, [1955] S.C.R. 16; *Power, supra*, at p. 616), it is well recognized that the adversarial process is an important part of our judicial system and an accepted tool in our search for the truth: see, for example, *R. v. Gruenke*, [1991] 3 S.C.R. 263, at p. 295, per L'Heureux-Dubé J. Nor should it be assumed that the Crown cannot act as a strong advocate within this adversarial process. In that regard, it is both permissible and desirable that it vigorously pursue a legitimate result to the best of its ability. Indeed, this is a critical element of this country's criminal law mechanism: *R. v. Bain*, [1992] 1 S.C.R. 91; *R. v. Jones*, [1994] 2 S.C.R. 229; *Boucher, supra*. In this sense, within the boundaries outlined above, the Crown must be allowed to perform the function with which it has been entrusted, discretion in pursuing justice remains an important part of that function.

Therefore, the Crown prosecutors have the discretion to conduct their case in the manner they deem appropriate, including deciding what witnesses to call or not to call: . . .

## The Entering of a Stay of Proceedings

Section 579 of the Criminal Code provides the Crown prosecutor with a broad discretion to "pause" a prosecution by entering a stay of proceedings. In *R. v. Light*, Mr. Justice Wood concluded that it "will be a rare case in which a stay of proceedings would be likely to give rise to a legitimate complaint on the part of an accused who benefits from the exercise of such discretion". However, it has given rise to numerous applications, which have consistently been found to be illegitimate. In *R. v. Scott*, a Crown prosecutor entered a stay of proceedings after the trial judge ruled that an informer's identity could be revealed. The Crown subsequently lifted the stay and commenced the trial before a new trial judge. The accused was convicted. He complained bitterly that the Crown's actions were abusive and an affront to judicial authority. However, a majority of the Supreme Court of Canada disagreed. Mr. Justice Cory concluded that "The actions of the Crown were not abusive. They were aimed solely at protecting the identity of the police informer, a value which has long been recognized as important to society." This is an important judgment because it illustrates the importance of the Crown being able to consider important societal interests even when those interests conflict with those of an accused. It illustrates that the interests of the accused cannot be viewed in splendid isolation as if other competing interests have no competing value.

. . .

## Battered Women: Definition, Models and Prosecutorial Policy*

*A. McGillivray*

\* Excerpts from (1987), 6 Canadian Journal of Family Law 15.

## INTRODUCTION

Perhaps, the last bastion of unregulated individualism and closed to public scrutiny, the family may shield acts of violence equal to any atrocity committed by stranger upon stranger, or by an act of war or terrorism. The family is not considered a legal entity by the state, nor has the issue of state responsibility for family order been widely addressed in light of broader goals of peace and social order. Ours is a violent society divided in its pursuit of peace. The family — autonomous, hierarchical in structure and separated into discrete arenas of authority — is a microcosm reflecting and influencing the structure and attitudes of the larger sphere. Despite the mutuality of social and family reform, there remains tremendous reluctance to involve the blunt processes of the state in the delicate and sacrosanct web of family relationships.

Wife battering appears to be an anomaly in a liberal democracy overtly committed to social order, but is in fact a deviance so widespread it is almost a social norm. Violence toward women by their husbands has at the least been tolerated and, in many societies, institutionalized. Throughout the world, both historically and presently, it is a phenomenon so large that its existence has become accepted as part of the social milieu. "Only rarely is the objective condition interpreted as worthy of attention." The legal right of the *pater familias* to punish his wife, children and slaves found support in church doctrine and in the common law, and this doctrine continues to influence legal judgments in this century.

Historically, the state's interest has been the control, rather than the denunciation, of wife battering, as evidenced by a regulation limiting the size of the stick used by a husband to discipline his wife to the size of a man's thumb — hence, the rule of thumb.

. . .

In sheer numerical terms, wife battering is a major social problem. One in ten Canadian women in an intimate marital-type situation will be assaulted by her partner this year. The assault will be repeated for one in twenty and those who bring criminal charges will have been assaulted an average of thirty-five times. The rate is much higher for native women, who comprise fifty percent of battered women in Saskatchewan. The Law Reform Commission of Canada calls the wife battering problem "serious" and the Canadian Association of Social Work Administrators identifies it as the "current most pressing concern within the spectrum of domestic violence".

In 1983, in response to this major problem, Saskatchewan's Minister of Justice announced the implementation of a range of policies directed at reducing spousal violence including expanded shelter and counselling programs, batterer therapy, public education, statistical monitoring and reduction of discretion in the criminal prosecution of batterers. In the following discussion, Saskatchewan's new prosecutorial policy is examined within the context of the various definitions and the etiology of wife battering; the abuse models that have been formulated and the implications of criminal sanctions in wife battering cases; and also on the discretionary power exercised by the battered woman witness. Regrettably, the results of the Saskatchewan Department of Justice two-year study of this new policy were unavailable at the time of publication of this paper.

. . .

## THE CRIMINAL LAW
### *Prosecutorial Policy*

Efforts to ground policy in models are most difficult where the area is new, the data incomplete and the proposed policy heavily value-laden. In the final analysis, a policy choice is made in hopes that implementation will itself generate needed data and new models. Such a policy choice was the decision of Saskatchewan's Minister of Justice, announced in December 1983, to limit discretion in the prosecution of wife batterers.

Discretion — investigative, prosecutorial and judicial — is as much a hallmark of the Canadian legal system as is the right of the accused to make full answer and defence. Criminal acts are not equally prosecuted, nor are judges bound to dispose of cases in any rigidly controlled fashion to achieve absolutely uniform sentencing. The decision to control prosecutorial discretion in wife battering cases is properly a policy determination. It was made on the urging of feminist groups, who have historically been in the forefront of family law reform, in the belief that public attitudes toward family violence can be changed through enforcement of criminal sanctions.

### The Saskatchewan No-Drop Policy

The Director of Public Prosecutions for Saskatchewan, Kenneth McKay, described the policy and its rationale as follows:

> [T]he Minister of Justice instructed that the Crown press for more serious sentences in cases of spousal violence. In addition, the department instituted measures to ensure that the law was properly enforced in this area . . . .The efforts of the department were aimed at changing attitudes to family violence so that they were treated as any other offence — public, not private issues. Police were instructed not to put the onus on the complainant, but to lay charges as they would in any other case, that is, where the evidence supported charges; prosecutors were instructed not to discontinue cases if the only reason for doing so was the reluctance of the complainant; and courts were pressed for firmer sentences.

A Saskatoon Crown prosecutor described the policy as "get the charges into Court" by doing everything possible at all costs to ensure that prosecutions of batterers go ahead, particularly where there has been a serious assault. Individual prosecutors now have no discretion to drop charges in wife-battering cases, but if circumstances warrant — the assault is minor, the victim vindictive — charges may be dropped upon approval by the Director of Public Prosecutions in Regina. This ensures province-wide consistency in policy application.

Prior to the institution of the policy, discretion was exercised primarily on the basis of the victim's choice. Implicit was an individual-level model of wife abuse, a model inappropriate to a situational-level judgment. The relationship between victim and offender and the repetitive nature of abuse led to an assumption by prosecutors that the victim in at least some cases had consented to the act. In any event, the domestic setting was a screen of privacy to be respected if the victim so desired. Police also took into account the factor of danger in interfering in domestic disputes: approximately seventy-five percent of all police injuries (including deaths) incurred on duty happened while responding to domestic calls. Also since women frequently wanted charges withdrawn, police and prosecutors tended to avoid the matter at the outset. The D.P.P. summed [up] the situation prior to the new policy:

> Because of the relationship of the persons involved in spousal violence cases, there was a tendency to consider them as personal matters — private disputes limited to parties involved. Thus, the police were reluctant to lay charges unless the complainant personally swore the information; where charges were laid, the prosecutor was reluctant to proceed if the victim was unwilling to continue; and where a conviction was registered the court appeared reluctant to sentence in any meaningful way.

The criminal law is less concerned with the interests of a particular victim than with deterrence of crime in general and the interest of society at large. Prosecuting the abuser not only requires the victim to testify against someone with whom she has had a close relationship; she must also undergo cross-examination ("isn't it true that you bruise easily?"), and she may be subjected to the offender's increased resentment and violence as a result. Criminal prosecution cannot prevent future violence by the batterer or assist his family in reorganizing their lives. It is not surprising, then, that a majority of theorists, therapists and family lawyers have ascribed only a minor role to criminal sanctions in wife abuse.

However, visible problems require visible solutions if the state is to be seen as responsive to social needs. Allocation of funding for research, education and therapy, as provided for in Saskatchewan, is an important step but lacks the firm disapproval expressed by criminal sanctions. The prosecution of abusers sends the clear message that society will not tolerate their acts. This didactic power of criminal justice is increasingly viewed by reformers as a vital component of programs aimed at the reformation of social attitudes. The no-drop prosecutorial policy is evidence of the consensus between reformers and the state that social interests are to take precedence over the immediate interests of the victim. Still, the policy is beneficial to a victim who wants the prosecution to proceed. As the D.P.P. noted:

> Some of the results of the new efforts are obvious. By treating these cases as public issues, pressure was taken off the victim who is often locked in a cycle of violence. Since the matter is no longer her personal action, she is better able to resist pressure or intimidation from the offender, and in many cases psychological and emotional pressures she is subject to are lessened. It also appears to be better for the offender since it brings home the serious criminal nature of his activities.

On the other hand, based on preliminary data on the no-drop policy issued in 1985 by the Policy, Planning and Evaluation Branch of the Saskatchewan Department of Justice, a significant number of victims do not want the prosecution pursued. In thirty-five percent of the two hundred thirty-two reported cases during an eight-month period, the victim requested that charges be dropped. In twenty-five percent of cases the victim "actively hindered" prosecution.

. . .

### Social Workers and Police

While statistics for the years preceding the introduction of the policy are unavailable, interviews with social workers, police, prosecutors and family court judges indicate the policy has resulted in perceptible changes.

. . .

Workers recommend to their clients that they lay charges but contacting the police remains the victim's responsibility. The policy has changed the situation in that the laying of charges will now be followed up by police and prosecutors.

. . .

Attitudes, however, have yet to change. The attitude of the legal profession and the police [still] is, "Why go back? If she's stupid enough to go back the first time, why should we get involved again, especially the third or fourth time?" Because of those attitudes a crisis worker recently wondered whether the no-drop policy had been revoked.

. . .

Pressure to establish wife battering crisis services has steadily increased over the past three years. One worker estimated that two to three requests per day for intervention or information are made to the Saskatoon Crisis Unit, and approximately twenty-five percent of calls come from the police. In an abusive situation the priority is to find a safe place for the victim so that counselling and legal services can begin.

. . .

When a victim changes her mind, police are irritated and if the violence has ended by the time police arrive, no charges can be laid if she is the sole witness. However, a conscientious officer can lay charges based on reasonable suspicion for breach of the peace, one of the most valuable tools for dealing with family violence.

The dual role police are expected to fulfil further complicates intervention. Trained to deal with violence through complex role-plays with actors using weapons, police respond to all calls fully prepared for violence. Instead, they may end up as unwilling arbitrators.

. . .

The Director of Interval House, Saskatoon's shelter, preferred that police refrain from counselling. Offhand statements by police may lead a victim to think she is responsible for provoking the violence. Often the offender's apologetic charm can fool the police into thinking the situation has been resolved; but when they leave, the victim may be beaten for calling them. Police are not trained to counsel.

. . .

The director further observed that the criminal process is useful, though, because it shows the victim she is not to blame. Criminal charges also show the abuser that society views his acts as a crime. But in order for there to be any possibility of effective deterrence, the abuser must believe he will be caught. Secondly, sentencing must be appropriate. Neither circumstance is yet the case. . . .

### Prosecutors and the Court

According to one crown prosecutor, more people have been convicted subsequent to the policy than in the same time period preceding it. The estimate is one case per week for each of eleven Saskatoon prosecutors, twice the number before the policy. This prosecutor, like the police officers interviewed, would prefer to retain the discretion to drop cases involving very minor assaults or changed circumstances where proceeding is not the public interest. The policy does simplify dealing with victims, who can now be told, "Sorry, we have no choice but to go ahead with the charges." The frustration of dealing with reluctant witnesses, however, continues.

The police share this view. They may have put a lot of work into a case, and are often sympathetic to the woman and appalled by her injury. Without her full co-operation the best they can hope for in sentencing is probation instead of discharges. One officer took photographs of a terribly beaten woman and showed them to the judge when the victim was reluctant to testify, but it made no difference; the officer had not witnessed the beating itself and the man was acquitted. In most cases there is no witness except the victim herself. Photographs and circumstantial evidence are not sufficient for a conviction. The police are called only to corroborate. Any other witnesses, including children, will be subpoenaed but usually there are none.

Related to the problem of reluctant witnesses and another major source of frustration is sentencing. Despite the emphasis in the policy on pressing for stiffer sentences, sentencing continues to be lenient.

. . .

In the opinion of police officers, rules of evidence and procedure governing assault cases are at their discriminatory worst in spousal violence cases. Consent is an issue only where there is assault without physical injury; yet police corroboration may be required even where there is other evidence of injury. Evidence of injury is no substitute for the witness's own testimony as it is, for example, when the victim cannot testify in a murder trial. The co-operation of the victim is vital to conviction and meaningful sentencing and therefore to fulfilment of the overall policy goals.

There are two common scenarios. In the first, the victim testifies about the beating but claims that she and the accused have reconciled. . . .

The second scenario involves the witness who "can't remember". She may recognize her husband and remember her own name, but nothing else, even if she laid the charge. Nothing further can be done and the case is dismissed. The prosecutor may be told that there is no point in proceeding if the woman is not going to give evidence, particularly where the police have laid charges against the woman's wishes.

The Justice Department policy has removed discretion from the hands of the victim, the police and the prosecutor, but cannot remove it from the court. Whether it is fear of reprisal, mistaken belief in reconciliation, or the value for the victim in preserving the relationship, the court is reluctant to exacerbate her situation by removing the offender from the family against her wishes. The court, in dismissing the case for want of prosecution or in handing down lenient sentences, is in effect returning discretionary power to the victim. Women who want to withdraw from prosecution or are coerced into withdrawal have a number of options: they can avoid calling the police in the first place and thereby lose that source of protection; they can fail to appear in court; they can claim reconciliation, conveniently lose their memory or refuse to testify on the witness stand. In the final analysis, the victim controls every stage of the criminal process.

. . .

## CONCLUSION

Wife battering has been and remains endemic to our society. Only recently has battering been brought out of the family unit into the open and been recognized as a serious social problem requiring attention and action. Deeply rooted in the patriarchal, male-dominated social and legal systems to which we belong, violence against women is a major problem requiring major system and social reform.

> [The ideology of violence against wives] remains imbricated in the legal system .... The ideology itself must be dismantled. The legal system has been committed to a patriarchal ideology. It is this that must be challenged if violence against women is to diminish and ultimately to cease.

Minor social reform measures do not directly address the need for major system and social reform. Advocacy and counselling programs, the unwritten policy against prosecuting victims who fail to testify and the no-drop policy all contradict, rather than further, gender equality ideals and it may argued that special treatment of battered women by a patriarchal male-dominated criminal justice system merely extends chauvinist protectionism into yet another arena. Short-term measures carry the message that the system is basically good and merely shore up a system which should be razed and rebuilt or left to crumble under the weight of its inadequacies.

Of the several models available, if the patriarchal one is chosen and social revolution along feminist lines is the selected remedy, then short-term measures will be rejected. Many supporters of this model bypass the criminal justice system and concentrate instead on service provision and public education to reduce society's glorification of violence and improve the social condition of women. But this extreme position denies both the immediate feminist interest in establishing wife-battering as a criminal concern and the interests of women caught up in the process. The position further pretends to a prescience of the means of revolution when, in reality, we lack both the tools and the shared vision required to engineer drastic social change. Moreover, reforms do not always appear to have the desired effects.

> Legal reforms have ambiguous and contradictory effects. Yet the only way to bring about major changes may be to begin with minor ones. We must make political decisions and act, even though our efforts may sometimes backfire. The more completely and accurately we analyze reforms, the greater the possibility we have to promote reforms that ? sometime in the future ? we will recognize to have been the beginnings of a revolution.

Any reform measure which promises a modicum of relief requires, along with careful analysis, acceptance of some degree of contradiction.

In the search for a new model of human relations it becomes practical to theorize about utopianism on a meta-societal level. World and social conditions have progressed well beyond the point where this can be dismissed as mere idealism. To solve the problem of wife battering, family violence must be viewed as a reflection of society which in turn reflects an outmoded ideology — which is detrimental to human civilization. While definition, model-building and police derivation for the curtailment of spousal violence are prerequisite to effective action, however refined and empirically accurate this process may become, policy-makers and court and agency personnel need to be reminded that the state of things as they are cannot dictate how things should be. A normative leap is required. The state's decision to intervene, and the formulation and implementation its intervention policy, remain in the realm of values and ethics.

## Plea Bargaining*

### David Vanek

*Excerpts from "Prosecutorial Discretion" (1987-88), 30 Criminal Law Quarterly 219 at 235-237.

. . .

There is nothing wrongful or improper about the Crown and defence counsel engaging in discussions concerning a case fixed for trial. Indeed, discussions are fully justified that relate to the disclosure of the evidence with respect to the strength or weakness of the case for the Crown or the defence. On the other hand, a Crown prosecutor should be expected to decide upon a course of action based upon his own independent assessment and judgment and not on the basis of a bargain or deal with defence counsel involving a trade-off. What is objectionable is the administration of justice in accordance with an agreement between counsel reached outside the purview of the court whereby, in consideration of a plea of guilty to one charge, the Crown agrees to withdraw other and often much more serious charges. Dispositions effected by plea bargaining rather than normal court procedures are fostered by an underfunded justice system, lack of Crown counsel and judges, and heavy case loads. Faced with the apparent impossibility of disposing of a huge docket of cases fixed for trial on a single day, understandably, Crown counsel tend to carry out their assignment by avoiding the necessity of conducting trials or other lengthy hearings and disposing of the case list by plea bargaining their way through the docket. The consequences may sometimes be nothing short of disastrous.

The disposition of criminal charges on the basis of a "deal" made between the Crown prosecutor and defence counsel constitutes plea bargaining. The various vehicles for the exercise of Crown discretion above-discussed, particularly the alleged absolute right to withdraw charges, are the devices by which the criminal law is administered, in large measure, not by decisions of judges in open court, but by Crown prosecutors through settlements made out of court and in secret that the judges are invited to endorse and which they may often stamp with approval as a valid exercise of prosecutorial discretion. Two cases are set out below as hypothetical but illustrative of what may often occur in practice:

An accused is charged with counts of assaulting a police officer, common assault, and assault when resisting arrest. He is arraigned on the charge of assaulting a police officer and pleads guilty to the lesser and included offence of common assault. Crown counsel reads into the record the facts indicating that the assault alleged was simply the pushing of a police officer who sought to arrest the accused. The plea to the lesser offence is accepted and the accused is convicted of that offence accordingly. It then appears that the pushing was only part of an entire episode in which the accused after the pushing ran off, was apprehended by other officers, a scuffle followed and blows were exchanged between him and another police officer who ultimately effected an arrest. In submissions on sentence defence counsel states that the Crown has agreed to join with him in a joint submission for a sentence of a conditional discharge. He also lets fall (perhaps inadvertently) that a part of the consideration for the plea and sentence is the agreement of his client to withdraw a charge before the Police Complaints Bureau laid by his client against, not the complainant, but the officer who ultimately effected the arrest.

In another case, the accused was originally charged with robbery. After a preliminary inquiry he was committed for trial on that charge. When he appeared for trial in another court, the accused pleaded not guilty to the charge of robbery, but guilty to the lesser and included offence of attempted theft under—a plea that may have been rejected by the judge on his original attendance for trial. He was found guilty of this lesser offence and granted a conditional discharge upon terms of an order of probation requiring him to perform 150 hours of community service. It is apparent that he did not perform any hours of community service. Accordingly, he was charged with failing to comply with the terms of the order of probation. On this charge, the accused comes for trial before the Provincial Court where the trial is conducted by Crown counsel appointed *pro tem* (commonly referred to as a "rent-a-crown"). Although witnesses are in attendance and testify for the Crown, it turns out that the only evidence to prove the most critical feature of the case, namely, that the accused refused or failed to do any work, is purely hearsay and hence not admissible. When the charge is dismissed, the shout of triumph of the accused as he exits the courtroom resounds hollowly throughout the court. He has beaten the system!

. . .

## Plea Bargaining*

*Gavin MacKenzie*

*Excerpts from *Lawyers and Ethics: Professional Responsibility and Discipline* (Toronto: Carswell, 1999) at 6-11 – 6-13.

. . .

## PLEA BARGAINING

Canadian rules of professional conduct that address the responsibility of lawyers in plea bargaining consider the issue primarily from the perspective of the defence counsel. The C.B.A. Code makes it clear, however, that the public interest must not be compromised by agreeing to a guilty plea, an admonition that would appear to be directed at least equally to prosecutors. Ontario's rules provide, somewhat more specifically, that "the public interest must not . . . be sacrificed in pursuit of an apparently expedient means of disposing of doubtful cases."

For overworked prosecutors a plea bargain means less work, more time to devote to other cases, and perhaps fewer nights and weekends at the office. Most prosecutors are paid not by the hour, but by the year. When working for a fixed fee, defence counsel also may have a financial incentive to negotiate a plea bargain: it takes far less time to bargain most cases than to try them.

Negotiated pleas can and usually do result in just dispositions of cases, and can contribute also to the efficient use of scarce prosecutorial and judicial resources. It is important that pleas not be negotiated for reasons of expedience where such dispositions are not in the public interest and, particularly, where it is not clear that the accused is in fact guilty.

A trial judge has jurisdiction to refuse to accept a plea to a lesser offence, despite the concurrence of the prosecutor, where on the agreed facts the accused is guilty of the offence charged. Thus in a 1990 decision, the Ontario Court of Appeal held that a trial judge did not err in refusing to accept a plea bargain whereby the accused pleaded guilty to common assault where the facts as stated by the Crown Attorney supported a finding of assault with a weapon. The court observed that trial judges in most cases do, and should, give great weight to the decision of counsel for the prosecution, as a representative of the public interest, to accept a plea of guilty to an included or lesser offence. The court added that its decision should not be taken as a holding that a trial judge would be wrong in accepting a plea to an included or lesser offence. The court added that its decision should not be taken as a holding that a trial judge would be wrong in accepting a plea to an included or lesser offence even through the facts might indicate that the full offence was committed where a case is made out that the result reflects a reasonable exercise of prosecutorial discretion having regard to the public interest in the effective administration of justice.

If a plea bargain is made, the Crown has a duty to uphold it. In a 1980 decision Justice Krever, who was then a member of the Ontario High Court of Justice, had occasion to consider whether the court should allow a prosecutor to repudiate an agreement entered into by a prosecutor who formerly had carriage of the case on the ground that the agreement was not in the public interest. One of three co-accused had entered into an agreement with the prosecution whereby she agreed to give a statement to the police and to testify against one of her co-accused in exchange for immunity from prosecution. She had fulfilled the first of the two obligations that she had undertaken—by providing an inculpatory statement to the police—when a second prosecutor who had been assigned responsibility for the case repudiated the agreement.

Justice Krever granted a motion for an order staying the proceedings against the accused person who had entered into the agreement, holding that there was considerable merit in her submission that the Crown's repudiation of the plea bargain "undermines the administration of justice and brings the entire system of the administration of justice into disrepute." Moreover, Justice Krever added, if permitted to withdraw from the agreement, the Crown would have caused serious prejudice to the applicant in her defence.

. . .

## THE ROLE OF DEFENCE COUNSEL

### Historical Development

*Chet Mitchell*

Until the 18th century, the accused did not have the right to be represented by legal counsel except in treason prosecutions mounted by the Crown. In the vast majority of cases, the accused defended himself or herself against a private prosecutor who was usually the victim. Often the accused did not even have an advance look at the prosecutor's evidence. The court was primarily concerned with the nature of the accused person's spontaneous responses to the prosecutor's case. The judge was thought to owe a limited responsibility to the accused in terms of explaining what had to be disproved in the prosecutor's case. All this started to change in the 1730s and 1740s and lawyers soon became the main "motor force" of the criminal trial. Much historical work on this transition remains to be done but it appears that the emergence of lawyers was due to two factors. One involved the increasing resort to lawyers acting on behalf of victims as agents in private prosecutions. The costs of legal counsel for the prosecutor were easier to bear with the rapidly increasing popularity of prosecution associations; property owners tended to subscribe to these to collectively deal with "crime problems". Another factor involved structural changes to the profession and the emergence of barristers who had the clear right to appear in all courts of law. With prosecutors increasingly resorting to skilled legal representation the accused's position in the trial was substantially disadvantaged and judges started to admit defence counsel on a discretionary basis when requested (Beattie, 1986:340-62). The clear legal right to defence counsel was only recognized in 1836 in Canada (at about the same time it was recognized in England). Of course the practical right to defence counsel has only emerged within the past fifty years with the emergence of legal aid.

Traditional descriptions of the role of defence counsel read very much like descriptions of the role of professional prosecutor. Both were said to have a duty to the court to see that justice was done. This meant that defence counsel was not to suppress or distort the truth on behalf of a client. Counsel owed a duty to their clients to represent their interests, of course, but this did not make counsel a mere agent of their clients (Savage, 1959). In formal terms, defence lawyers are "officers of the court". Historically, lawyers on either side of criminal trials in Canada were expected to owe their primary allegiance to the state and their profession (Maloney and Cassels, 1989).

## The Role of Defence Counsel*

### Frank P. Hoskins

*Excerpts from "The Players of a Criminal Trial" in Joel E. Pink and David C. Perrier, eds., *From Crime to Punishment: An Introduction to the Criminal Law System* (Toronto: Carswell, 1999) at 177-179.

## THE ROLE OF THE DEFENCE COUNSEL

The theoretical motion of the role of defence counsel in the adversarial criminal trial process is to "represent his/her client resolutely, honourably and within the limits of the law." A defence counsel must also "ask every question, raise every issue and advance every argument, however distasteful, that the advocate reasonably thinks will help the client's case. Or, to phrase it another way, the role of defence counsel is to protect the interests of his or her client. There are, nonetheless, several limits on the extent to which her or she may do so.

It should be noted that the defence counsel is not the alter ego of his or her client. The function of defence counsel is to provide professional assistance and advice. Defence counsel must, accordingly, exercise his or her professional skill and judgement in the conduct of the case and not allow him- or herself to be a mere mouthpiece for the client. It is, of course, fundamental to his or her role that defence counsel should, while acting with proper courtesy to the court, fearlessly uphold the interest of his or her client without regard to any unpleasant consequence to him- or herself or any other person.

. . .

It is trite to say that defence counsels are necessary for the proper functioning of the adversary process. As previously mentioned, the adversarial trial process is an attempt by two contestants with differing views to persuade a trial judge. Without the presence of defence counsel, there would be no adversary for the Crown. Hence, it is the function of the defence counsel to fearlessly raise every question and advance every argument that they believe will advance their client's case. Defence counsel, however, in executing their professional duties on behalf on their client, cannot or should not become judgmental of the client's alleged misconduct. Defence counsel must not usurp the function of the judge and/or jury.

It is the defence counsel's responsibility, not the client's, to decide what witnesses to call, whether a witness should be cross-examined, and if so how it should be done. There is at least one decision that only the client can make and that is the decision as to whether to plead guilty or not guilty.

It should also be noted that even if the client admits his or her guilt to defence counsel, it does not preclude defence counsel from forcing the Crown to prove each and every essential element of the offence charged. There is, however, an ethical restriction on defence counsel with respect to the manner in which he or she is entitled to conduct the defence for the client. Notwithstanding the right of an accused to require the Crown to prove his or her guilt beyond a reasonable doubt, defence counsel is under a duty, after making a thorough and exhaustive investigation of the facts and the relevant law. Defence counsel must be satisfied that the Crown has sufficient evidence on each and every essential element of the charge and thus there is a *prima facie* case against his or her client. Further, defence counsel must be satisfied that the client possessed the requisite *mens rea* and completed the actus reas of the offence (charge) before advising the client how to plead to the charge. Although defence counsel is free to advise his or her client in strong terms as to the plea that should be entered, the ultimate choice is that of the client's and it must be a free and informed choice.

Defence counsel must take their instructions from the client. However, defence counsel is not bound to follow instructions that are unreasonable and, in proper cases, is entitled to refuse to act for a client who rejects their advice or where there is a breach of trust in the client-solicitor relationship.

Furthermore, defence counsel cannot promote their client's interests by introducing false evidence or making misleading statements, as that would pervert justice. This does not mean, however, that defence counsel has any duty to assist the Crown in discovering or presenting evidence that could incriminate the client. Thus, the defence counsel role is not to assist in the search for the truth, but to verify the results of the search conducted by the Crown. In essence, the role of defence counsel could be likened to making mathematics examines—he or she checks the calculations to make sure that they are correct. Defence counsel then points out to the trier of fact (judge or jury) any computations that do not add up and mentions any factors that were left out of the math by the Crown.

As well, the defence counsel must refrain from asserting their own personal views on the merits of the case. They are to be involved in the case only professionally, not personally. It is defence counsel's job to present the evidence of others to the court and to argue about the legal significance of that evidence, but they themselves cannot give evidence.

The defence counsel is constrained by a duty of honesty. As previously mentioned, the defence counsel cannot knowingly present false or misleading evidence. If the client admits elements of the offence (charge) to his or her defence counsel, then defence counsel is precluded from settling up an affirmative defence that is inconsistent with those admissions. Defence counsel, however, can still test the strength of the Crown's case and raise any technical or procedural deficiencies as a defence. Hence, the role of the defence counsel can be seen as a shepherd of the criminal trial process itself. They are there to ensure that if the accused is convicted, that it was done according to the proper procedure and as a result of sufficient, convincing and admissible evidence. They are there only to force the Crown to play by the rules. He/she is not there to cheat in order to obtain an acquittal for the client.

. . .

## Control of Advocacy*

*Gavin MacKenzie*

*Excerpts from *Lawyers and Ethics: Professional Responsibility and Discipline* (Toronto: Carswell, 1999) at 4-53 – 4-54; 4-58 – 4-59.

## CONTROL OF ADVOCACY

Excesses in advocacy are subject to formal control in three ways: first, by direct judicial intervention in the form of contempt citations and orders requiring lawyers personally to pay costs; second, by indirect judicial intervention in the form of procedural and evidentiary rulings and orders requiring parties to pay costs, all of which may influence advocacy by influencing the outcome of litigation; and, third, by disciplinary sanctions imposed by law societies.

The second means of control is by far the most significant. Most competent judges go through an entire judicial career without imposing a contempt sanction on a lawyer, and though orders requiring lawyers to pay costs personally have become more common in recent years, such sanctions are generally imposed only in egregious cases. Disciplinary sanctions, except in cases involving the falsification of evidence or attempts to obstruct justice, have been exceedingly rare.

The rarity of direct intervention to control excesses, either by courts or law societies, reflects tolerance for lapses that are inevitable in the emotionally heated atmosphere of adversarial trials, and recognition of the fact that more subtle means of control are available. Courts and law societies appreciate, too, that contempt citations and disciplinary sanctions may have the effect of inhibiting the vigorous partisan advocacy that is required in an adversary system.

. . .

## Contempt of Court

The *Criminal Code* preserves the authority of courts to impose punishment for contempt of court, but does not define the offence. In a 1984 case, the Ontario Court of Appeal defined the term "contempt of court" in such a way as to include words or acts "which are intended or likely to interfere with or obstruct the fair administration of justice." The Law Reform Commission of Canada in its report on contempt of court identified four types of contempts:

(1) Disruption of judicial proceedings, including conduct in the courtroom that is offence or disorderly, as well as disobedience to orders made concerning the conduct of judicial proceedings.
(2) Defiance of judicial authority, including disobedience to court orders amounting to outright defiance, and public challenges to judicial authority.
(3) Affronts to judicial authority, including conduct calculated to insult a court, and attacks on the independence, impartiality, or integrity of a court or of the judiciary.
(4) Interference with pending judicial proceedings, including the publication of information that the publisher knows or ought to know may interfere with the proceedings.

Convictions of lawyers for contempt of court, as mentioned above, are rare. . . .

## Law Society Disciplinary Sanctions

Rules of professional conduct provide that lawyers' professional obligations to be courteous and civil to the court and to those engaged on the other side are not co-extensive with the obligations the breach of which are punishable as contempt of court. A consistent pattern of rude, provocative or disruptive conduct by a lawyer, the rules provide, even though unpunished as contempt, might well merit discipline.

Discourtesy in litigation has nevertheless been visited with disciplinary sanctions only rarely. In a 1984 case, the Law Society of Upper Canada reprimanded publicly a lawyer who had interfered with the orderly administration of justice by repeatedly making offensive remarks to opposing counsel and deliberately spilling coffee on opposing counsel's notes during a cross-examination on an affidavit in an official examiner's office. Two years later, the same lawyer was suspended from practice for three months as a result of his repeated refusal to stand when addressing the court in a criminal case.

Attempts to mislead courts or tribunals, or to obstruct justice, are somewhat more frequently the basis of disciplinary proceedings. In another 1984 Ontario case, a lawyer was suspended for one month for making false submissions in speaking to sentence on behalf of a client charged with being an inmate in a common bawdy-house. The lawyer told the court that the accused was a divorced single parent who was supporting two young children, and who had resorted to prostitution because she was in desperate financial trouble. In fact, the accused had never been married, was not supporting any children, had given up her only child for adoption ten years earlier, and had no serious financial difficulties at the relevant time.

. . .

## Plea Bargaining*

### *Gavin MacKenzie*

*Excerpts from *Lawyers and Ethics: Professional Responsibility and Discipline* (Toronto: Carswell, 1999) at 7-20.1.

. . .

Criminal defence lawyers will often realize a more favourable result for clients by plea bargaining than by trying cases. Indeed, because of the potential for more favourable outcomes, defence lawyers have a duty to attempt to negotiate a plea bargain in appropriate cases. In a 1983 case, the United States Court of Appeals for the Sixth Circuit allowed no appeal from conviction on the ground of ineffective assistance of counsel where the accused person's lawyer at trial had made no effort to negotiate a plea bargain. The court regarded attempts to negotiate plea bargains to be reflective of basic competence.

Criminal defence lawyers must nevertheless be vigilant to ensure that their clients' right to put the Crown to the proof of its case is not sacrificed for the sake of expediency. Professor Alan Dershowitz has pointed out that in many cases both prosecutors and defence counsel have incentives to negotiate plea agreements—incentives that many tempt them to breach their duties to the public and their clients respectively if they are not conscientious. Defence counsel who receive flat fees for cases may be tempted to bargain as many cases as possible. Thus if a lawyer receives $5,000 for a case, and is able to negotiate a plea bargain in ten hours, the lawyer will earn $500 an hour. If it takes the lawyer 100 hours to try the case, the lawyer will earn $50 an hour—which may not be enough to pay the overhead.

. . .

## LEGAL AID

Another issue is that of legal aid and its effect on the role played by defence counsel. Unlike prosecutors, in the past defence counsel were paid by their private clients; this has changed dramatically with the rise of legal aid in most jurisdictions. Now both sides are often paid by the state.

Like most welfare schemes, legal aid is a complex, rule-laden program that was not designed with significant input from the people (criminal defendants) it is supposed to serve. While in the U.S. accused have a constitutional right to counsel, in Canada this right is qualified (except with young offenders) to cases where the judge determines that a fair trial demands counsel and where the accused lacks the means to employ a lawyer (see *R. v. Rowbotham* (1988), 41 C.C.C. (3d) 1 (Ont. C.A.). Provincial legal aid plans vary. Ontario's plan generally only covers criminal cases where there is a threat of imprisonment or loss of livelihood, and with drastic cuts in the funding of legal aid in 1996, it appears likely that only those facing imprisonment will receive legal assistance in the future. Applicants must pass a means test based on disposable income, assets and family composition. The focus of assistance is on the trial, but criminal defendants often need the most legal assistance at the time of arrest and questioning. Worse, the fee structures and incentives of legal aid may result in lawyers merely going through the motions of providing a defence, of making only "the noises of a defence" (Ericson & Baranek, 1982:201). The following case considers a number of issues central to the operation, adequacy and fairness of provincial legal aid plans:

## Regina v. Rockwood
### (1989), 49 C.C.C. (3d) 129 (N.S. C.A.).

Chipman J.A.: — This is an appeal from a decision of MacDonald J. denying the appellant's motion that the Attorney-General or the Nova Scotia Legal Aid Commission be compelled to fund competent counsel of his choice for the defence of charges against him, and until such funding and counsel were obtained, for a stay of proceedings.

The appellant describes himself in his affidavit as a self-employed real estate syndicator. On September 19, 1987, an information was sworn charging him with 20 counts of theft, breach of trust, and fraud. He appeared in court in answer to the charges on October 19, 1987. At that time he was represented by Lance Scaravelli who he was advised had expertise in criminal defence work. The preliminary hearing commenced on May 16, 1988. Saying that it was because of a shortage of funds, the appellant instructed Mr. Scaravelli to waive the preliminary hearing. Shortly thereafter the appellant was committed for trial on the charges and, as well, Mr. Scaravelli withdrew because the appellant was unable to pay for his services.

The date fixed for trial was April 3, 1989, and on being assigned to the case in the fall of 1988, MacDonald J. sought out the names of counsel and learned the appellant had none. He thereupon set a pre-trial conference for December 15, 1988, and arranged to have the R.C.M.P. notify the appellant thereof. As MacDonald J. said in his decision, the early pre-trial conference was chiefly to impress upon the appellant his need to obtain legal representation without further delay. At this pre-trial conference the appellant advised MacDonald J. that he had seen Nova Scotia Legal Aid regarding counsel the previous day. He was advised that there would be a further pre-trial conference at a later date and that it was "quite imperative" that he have counsel at that time to represent him.

In mid-February, 1989, a further pre-trial conference was called for March 1st. The appellant was unable to attend and it was rescheduled for March 7th. At this pre-trial conference the Crown prosecutor raised a summary of the facts which the Crown hoped to establish in support of the charges. At this time the appellant advised that his preliminary application for legal aid was turned down, but that he had appealed this decision and expected a ruling at the end of that week. The court then advised the appellant of his responsibilities in the matter and that the case would proceed to trial on April 3, 1989, with or without counsel.

On March 13, 1989, MacDonald J. was advised that the Nova Scotia Legal Aid Commission had issued a certificate to fund counsel on behalf of the name of counsel retained by Legal Aid on his behalf. A further pre-trial conference was held on March 23rd with the applicant's counsel and the Crown prosecutor present. Yet another pre-trial conference was held on March 28th at which time it appeared that the charges were ready for trial on April 3rd.

On Sunday afternoon, April 2nd, Victor Goldberg, a barrister, contacted MacDonald J. advising that the appellant had discharged his counsel and that he would be appearing on the appellant's behalf the following day to make a motion. On April 3rd, the schedule day of trial, the matter was adjourned to April 6th and the jury panel dismissed with instructions to return again on April 10th. After hearing both counsel, MacDonald J. considered that it would be unfair both to the appellant and to the prosecution to hold the trial on April 10th.

On April 6, 1989, Mr. Goldberg presented his motion to MacDonald J.

. . .

MacDonald J. . . . dismissed the motion and ordered the appellant to return on May 9, 1989, to answer to the charges and have a new trial date set. We are advised that this date has been set for November, 1989.

The appellant bases his claim to entitlement to "competent counsel of his choice" on both the common law and the Charter.

It has been said that legal aid, in its broadest sense, has existed as long as the law itself. There is a long-standing tradition in the Bar of service given either without charge or for less than it is worth to those unable to pay or pay adequately for a criminal defence. In particular, members of the Bar have responded, when called on by the court in the exercise of its inherent jurisdiction to do so, to defend indigents appearing without counsel. Such people have, over the years, been defended and defended well, often by inexperienced counsel. As the volume and complexity of criminal litigation increased, this system was inadequate to deal with the need. As was said by the Ontario Court of Appeal in *R. v. Rowbotham* (1988), 41 C.C.C. (3d) 1 at p 69, 63 C.R. (3d) 113, 35 C.R.R. 207 (Ont. C.A.):

> In former times, counsel (sometimes eminent counsel) were appointed by the trial judge to defend an indigent accused charged with a capital offence. Counsel appointed by the trial judge in those circumstances frequently acted without remuneration. Members of the defence Bar also defended many other kinds of criminal charges on a purely voluntary basis. Having regard to the increase in the length and complexity of modern trials and the increased overhead costs, the appointment of counsel to act without remuneration is no longer feasible and, indeed, in many cases, would be unfair to counsel.

In response to this inadequacy, legal aid programmes were established throughout Canada. In Nova Scotia, a formal legal aid system was constituted in 1972, and the service is now provided pursuant to the *Legal Aid Act*, S.N.S. 1977, c. 11. Such a programme has done much to respond to the ever increasing need, but no realist would argue that this system is perfect. As in other areas of service, provided by the government, budgetary constraints are a fact of life.

Under neither the legal aid system now in force nor under its predecessor of *ad hoc pro bono* service by individual members of the Bar does one think in terms of wide latitude of choice of counsel on the part of the recipients. Counsel for the appellant was unable to point to any authority showing that a choice outside of those counsel willing to serve within the system was a matter of entitlement.

. . .

The position under the Charter is, I think, succinctly stated by the Ontario Court of Appeal in *R. v. Rowbotham, supra*, at pp. 65-6:

> The right to retain counsel, constitutionally secured by s. 10(b) of the Charter, and the right to have counsel provided at the expense of the state are not the same thing. The Charter does not *in terms* constitutionalize the right of an indigent accused to be provided with funded counsel. At the advent of the Charter, legal aid systems were in force in the provinces, possessing the administrative machinery and trained personnel for determining whether an applicant for legal assistance lacked the means to pay counsel. In our opinion, those who framed the Charter did not expressly constitutionalize the right of an indigent accused to be provided with counsel, because they considered that, generally speaking, the provincial legal aid systems were adequate to provide counsel for persons charged with serious crimes who lacked the means to employ counsel. However, *in cases not falling within provincial legal aid plans*, ss. 7 and 11(d) of the Charter, which guarantee an accused a fair trial in accordance with the principles of fundamental justice, require funded counsel to be provided if the accused wishes counsel, but cannot pay a lawyer, and representation of the accused by counsel is essential to a fair trial.

It is submitted that this Charter guarantee contains three elements: (a) funded counsel; (b) competent counsel, and (c) counsel of choice. While it is not suggested that every indigent must be automatically provided with funded legal counsel, implicit in these guarantees is such funded counsel when the indigent faces a complex and serious charge. In *Panacui v. Legal Aid Society of Alberta* (1987), 40 C.C.C. (3d) 459, [1988] 1 W.W.R. 60, 54 Alta. L.R. (2d) 342 (Alta. Q.B.), McDonald J. said at p. 466:

> In my view, the foregoing statement of the purposes and interests which ss. 7, 10(b) and 11(d) are meant to protect when the issue is the scope and extent of the right to counsel, lead me irresistibly to the conclusion that a person charged with an offence that is serious and complex, when he cannot afford to retain counsel, is constitutionally entitled to have counsel provided to assist him at the expense of the state.

In making reference to funded counsel, nothing is said in these authorities about the degree of expertise of counsel an indigent accused is entitled to expect. In order to render the Charter rights meaningful, I believe counsel provided must be sufficiently qualified to deal with the matter at issue with a reasonable degree of skill.

Again, however, the case-law on the Charter aspect of this appeal does not go so far as to give the indigent a right of choice beyond those counsel willing to serve within the constraints of the Legal Aid programme. During the course of argument, counsel for the appellant conceded that the authorities did not establish that "choice" extended to any counsel, but only to those reasonably competent to handle the matter at hand. As MacDonald J. recognized in his decision, to extend the Charter right to the point contended for by the appellant could introduce chaos into the administration of justice.

*Appeal dismissed*

. . .

Aside from the issue of fee-for-service, defence counsels' incentives must be examined to see where their primary interests lay. To begin with, criminal defendants are often from low income groups and unlike wealthier clients they do not tend to build a long term relationship with their lawyers. This may weaken the criminal lawyer's incentives to provide the level of service necessary to build repeat business. Second, defence counsel deal repeatedly with the same judges, prosecutors and court officers. In many ways, these people are all part of the same "team", a team that does not include the accused (Ericson & Baranek, 1982). Plea bargaining exaggerates this exclusionary effect, because bargaining does not take place in court where the accused can witness it and make some assessment of defence counsel's ability. Rather, bargaining occurs in secret between familiar "adversaries" away from the accused's view. Third, defence counsel are members of a monopoly profession and owe their livelihood to their profession's capacity to lobby government for laws that successfully exclude competitors, like former police officers or paraprofessionals, from courtroom advocacy. This protection is probably vital in the case of defence counsel because most of their work is routine and unsophisticated, and thus many could be readily replaced by low-cost competitors without law degrees, if such people were free to compete. Criminal lawyers, therefore, strive to maintain professional solidarity and to support a criminal law system that elevates them over their clients and over potential competitors. This reasoning does not suggest, however, that defence lawyers do not make spirited and sometimes personally risky efforts to protect their client's interests.

## Questions/Discussion
1.   Describe the powers and duties of public prosecutors in Canada today.
2.   In what way are Crown Prosecutors politically independent? Should they be? Why or why not?
3.   Why have both prosecutors and defence counsel largely abandoned the trial process? Does plea bargaining serve the interests of justice?
4.   What are the duties of the defence counsel to the client and to the court? How has advent of legal aid schemes affected the performance of these duties?

## Further Reading
* Beattie, J.M., *Crime and the Courts in England, 1660-1800* (Princeton: Princeton University Press, 1986).
* Burns, Peter, "Private Prosecutions in Canada: The Law and a Proposal for Change" (1975), 21 McGill Law Journal 269.
* Code, Michael, "Crown Counsel's Responsibilities When Advising the Police at the Pre-Charge Stage" (1998), 40 Criminal Law Quarterly 326.

- Colarco, Paul, "The Ontario Court of Appeal Gives the Green Light to Re-litigate Criminal Convictions by Suing Your Lawyer" (2000), 31 C.R. (5th) 129.
- Colarco, Paul, "*S. (F.)*: When Crowns Go Bad (Again!)" (2000), 31 C.R. (5th) 173.
- Davis, Kenneth, *Discretionary Justice* (Champaign: University of Illinois Press, 1971).
- Edwards, John LL. J., "The Office of the Attorney General—New Levels of Public Expectations and Accountability" in Philip Stenning, ed., *Accountability for Criminal Justice: Selected Essays* (Toronto: University of Toronto Press, 1995).
- Ericson, R. & Baranek, P., *The Ordering of Justice* (Toronto: University of Toronto Press, 1982).
- Gourlie, William, "Role of the Prosecutor: Fair Minister of Justice with Firm Convictions" (1982), 12 Manitoba Law Journal 31.
- Grosman, Brian, "The Role of the Prosecutor: New Adaptations in the Adversarial Concept of Criminal Justice" (1969), 11 Canadian Bar Review 580.
- Harper, J. and McWhinnie, A., *The Glasgow Rape Case* (London: Hutchinson, 1984).
- Hay, Douglas, "Controlling the English Prosecutor" (1983), 21 Osgoode Hall Law Journal 165.
- Law Reform Commission of Canada, *Private Prosecutions*, Working Paper 52 (1986) (P. Burns, Principal Consultant).
- Maloney, M. and Cassels, J., "Critical Legal Education: Paralysis with a Purpose" (1989), 4 Canadian Journal of Law and Society 99.
- Moody, S.R. and J. Toombs, *Prosecution in the Public Interest* (Edinburgh: Scottish Academic Press, 1982).
- Orkin, M.M., "Defence of One Known to be Guilty: An Extract from 'Legal Ethics'" (1958-59), 1 Criminal Law Quarterly 170.
- Savage, C.C., "The Duties and Conduct of Crown and Defence Counsel in a Criminal Trial" (1958-59) 1 Criminal Law Quarterly 164.
- Stenning, P.C., *Appearing for the Crown: A Legal and Historical Review of Prosecutorial Authority in Canada* (Brown Legal Publications, 1986).
- Stuesser, Lee, "Abuse of Process: The Need to Reconsider" (1994), 29 C.R. (4th) 92.
- Turner, K., "The Role of Crown Counsel in Canadian Prosecutions" (1962), 40 Canadian Bar Review 439.

## 4.3 JUDGES

### Introduction

Many of the issues which arise in the context of the personnel of the courts were addressed in Chapter 3. This section delineates the actual role which the judges play in directing the criminal trial process, but in looking at that role the problems which were witnessed previously should not be forgotten. As we saw in Chapter 3, it is evident that those who staff the courts can play a determining role in the formulation of criminal law, and these same agents can also have an important effect in the evolution of and on the consequences of particular trials. The technical role which judges play in the trial process and how they play it are discussed in the Silverman and Hoskins articles below, while the issue of the accountability of the judiciary is addressed in the ready by Greene.

# The Trial Judge: Pilot, Participant, or Umpire?*

*H. Silverman*

*Excerpts from (1973), 11 Alberta Law Review 40.

. . .

Canadian courts dealing with the role of the trial judge emphasize that while there is an appropriate place and time for his intervention in the trial, and while he has the right to summarize and comment upon the evidence in a jury trial so long as he makes it clear that the jury are the sole judges of the facts, the prime prerequisite is that there must be a fair trial for the accused wherein the trial judge is not an umpire; nor should he assume the role of counsel for the defence or the prosecution (although when the accused is not represented his function is more all-embracing than that) or make remarks before the jury prejudicial to the accused such as indicating his conviction or the accused's guilt.

. . .

In a criminal case the trial judge can call witnesses. The position has been explained in this way in *Rex v. Skelly*:

> As McDermott's name was endorsed on the indictment, the prisoner's counsel had the right to place him in the witness-box for examination. The prosecutor is not bound to call witnesses merely because their names are on the back of the indictment, but the prosecutor ought to have all such witnesses in court, so that they may be called by the defence if wanted. If, however, they are called by the defendant he makes them his own witnesses: per Alderson B., in *Regina v. Woodhead* (1847) 2 C.&K. 520.

The trial judge also, in the exercise of his discretion, might have called any witness whose name was on the indictment, as was done by Littledale J. in *Rex v. Beezley* (1830) 4 C.&P. 220, and by Patteson J. in *Regina v. Holden* (1838) 8 C.&P. 606 at 610.

The trial judge cannot interfere with the Crown's right to determine which material witness to call, even where his name appears on the back of an indictment, especially where the Crown decides not to call such witness deeming him to be unreliable.

While the trial judge (and the Crown) need not provide witnesses for the accused, he should see to it that the Crown informs the accused so that the accused has "knowledge of the witnesses who are to be called against him and the general character of the evidence they are to give". A trial judge need not inform an indigent accused who requests assistance that the Crown will assist him in obtaining required witnesses. A trial judge can ask how an accused pleads, and "if the reply is not a clear admission of all the elements of the crime" he "must proceed to inquire into the charge without further questioning". Once the Crown closes its case, it is within the trial judge's discretion whether he will permit the Crown to re-open its case, as, for example, where the defence does not call evidence and the Crown motion to re-open is not based upon "any charge of position on the part of the defendant, nor of the discovery of fresh evidence by the Crown."

A trial judge should not be in a hurry to complete the proceedings. The limits of his intervention and his duties were delineated by Ferguson J.A. in *Rex. v. West*, where he said:

> We do not doubt that, objectionable as it may be, the trial judge has a right to ask leading questions, also to endeavour to speed the trial, and even to tell counsel that he is wasting time, and that he also has the right to suggest . . . that counsel waive their rights to address the jury. These . . . are matters of discretion and good judgement, not entitling us to interfere unless we are of opinion that they resulted in a manifest injustice being done to the accused.

. . .

A compendium of a trial judge's functions would read as follows: he should not intervene inordinately during the trial; he should keep control of the proceedings, and should not, for example, permit the jury to examine and cross-examine witnesses; he should not usurp the function of counsel; within the bounds of proper advocacy he should allow counsel to proceed with the continuity of examination and cross-examination; and should give the fullest opportunity of cross-examination, so long as the right is not abused by prolix, irrelevant, insulting questions; and should not stop a trial without hearing all the available evidence, nor prejudge the outcome of the trial; nor should he indicate that he favours the prosecution or the accused or take the initiative by acting as counsel for the prosecution.

. . .

During a trial (civil or criminal) the presiding judge need not be mute; but this does not give him a licence to make offensive and prejudicial remarks with respect to the accused or his case.

When he sums up for the jury he should not merely repeat or summarize the evidence, "nor should [he] place his own constriction upon the evidence or otherwise usurp the function of the jury . . . [but] the judge ought to make clear to the jury, in a way they cannot fail to understand, what are the determinative factual issues in dispute, upon which proof of guilt must stand or fall."

In this summing-up he must set out the accused's position and the evidence in support of it; he should present to the jury any defence that may arise from the evidence, whether or not it is raised by defence counsel, and tell the jury that they are the sole judges of the facts which does not preclude him from expressing his personal view as to the character of police witnesses, or from commenting upon the credibility of witnesses (but he must not do so during the testimony of the witness); and he need not spend the same amount of time, in his summing-up, for the defence and prosecution.

The trial judge is in a special position when the accused is not represented by counsel, and it has been said that the court "in effect acts as counsel for him and is vigilant to see that nothing is done that would prejudice him"; and "the court shall extend its helping hand to guide him throughout the trial in such a way that his defence, or any defence the proceedings may disclose, is brought out to the jury with its full force and effect".

## ASSESSORS AND EXPERTS

In *Phillips*, Evans J.A. says that an expert, under Rule 267, is appointed "solely to assist the judge in understanding the evidence" and the "drawing of inferences, the deciding of issues, the interpretation of the so-called phenomenon and the reaching of conclusion are all matters within the exclusive jurisdiction of the trial judge and cannot be delegated". He continues:

> I do not think that a court can say, in effect, 'I believe that this accident resulted from some unusual circumstance and I propose to call in an expert to assist me in discovering the cause.' Such a procedure is inquisitional rather than judicial.
>
> The expert is not a judicial officer charged with the responsibility of determining matters in issue, nor is he a Court-appointed investigator empowered to advance possible theories and state, as conclusions of fact, opinions based on matters not advanced in evidence.

The expert, he explains, should not examine, nor cross-examine; he is not a partisan advocate; a Court-appointed expert explains the evidence, as adduced in his special field, so that the trial judge may better comprehend complex factual matters, and he concludes that he doubts that a person appointed under Rule 267 is an assessor; more properly he should be called an expert.

. . .

If Rule 267 is properly used, where there is extensive, complex evidence, the trial judge can profit from the assistance of an expert; however, even before the restrictions suggested in *Phillips* there was a reluctance by trial judges to avail themselves of the utility of this procedure, which has been attributed to the "mystique and sanctity of the adversary procedure."

## AN EVALUATION

The foregoing discussion has dealt with the civil and criminal trial process separately; and this is partly due to ease of organization of the material; and partly because this is an obvious division. It is trite to say that basically the rules of evidence in criminal and civil trials are the same. This is subject to obvious differences, *e.g.* the standards of proof required, and statutory requirements.

. . .

In civil cases the claims of competing private persons are set out in pre-trial proceedings (pleadings, discovery, interlocutory motions, particulars, and so on) which define the issues; in criminal trials it is the government (it would offend the Harold Laski concept of sovereignty to use the word "state" here) which claims that the citizen has transgressed against community rules; and in civil trials pecuniary damages result, whereas in the criminal trial the result is a fine and/or gaol.

By their nature, although each is a trial, the civil and criminal trials are different, and the role of the trial judge in each must necessarily differ.

. . .

There are differences concerning the calling of witnesses in civil and criminal cases. In the former, of course, the stakes are different; but in any event it is a difference of proceeding — in the civil case counsel for the plaintiff develops the case as he wants, but in a criminal trial the prosecution has a duty to call all witnesses it considers fit for the prosecution, subject only to the limitations that

(a) it should make the defence aware of all of its witnesses, and
(b) that need not call witnesses it considers unreliable.

In civil cases the trial judge with the consent of counsel may call witnesses; but in criminal cases, in the situations discussed, we have seen that a trial judge may of his own motion call witnesses.

. . .

In criminal cases too, where the defence fails to put to the jury a defence which could arise upon the evidence adduced, the trial judge, as pilot, should put that defence to the jury. Should he go so far as to suggest to defence counsel where there is an obvious gap or deficiency in the defence evidence that that should or could or may be developed?

So long as he does not usurp the function of counsel and refrains from entering into the dust of the arena, the trial judge should be able to act in all of the aforesaid matters as suggested. If there is some substantial area which a trial judge feels should be explored to fully expose the issues, then he should invite counsel to deal with the matters which appear critical to the Bench, and if counsel refuse, then the matter will probably end there. Moreover, as Wyzanski says, "a court . . . cannot rely on knowledge gained dehors the record, except in so far as it comes within the narrow ambit of the doctrine of judicial notice" but a judge, in certain cases, "has a duty to elicit facts in addition to those that are offered by the parties."

Wigmore wrote that the English judge "has never ceased to perform an active and virile part as a director of the proceedings and as an administrator of justice;" and he felt that the judge's right to interrogate should be left to his discretion. This viewpoint is obviously too broad a statement of the judge's role, in light of the jurisprudence we have surveyed; but, perhaps, it is the best overall test to apply in all actions, be they civil or criminal.

. . .

## CONCLUSION

A trial is a trial, whether civil or criminal; but the objectives, standards of proof, and applicable statutory materials vary greatly in these two arenas. The trial judge's functions in a civil and criminal trial are substantially similar. A trial judge is not a machine-formed computer and "often perceives the facts according to his idiosyncratic biases", nevertheless, in the absence of a clearer understanding of the actual functioning of the judicial mind in the decision-making process, and for the moment accepting the fact that the adversary-trial system, as we know it, operates reasonable well, we should be able to accept the following:

(1) A trial should not be a laboratory, but it should embark upon the ascertaining of all relevant and material facts concerning the issues of the case.

(2) When the evidence indicates that the issues have not been adequately defined in the pre-trial proceedings, counsel should be permitted to expand, re-define and if necessary use other and wider and broader grounds of claim, subject to adjournment and full rights of amendment and examinations, and costs; and, of course, bearing in mind the need for finality to all proceedings.

(3) Where scientific or other experiments may shed light on the fact-finding process, subject to the rights of counsel to define the limits of same, the trial should embrace such possibilities.

(4) With the consent of counsel, the trial judge should be able to call and re-call witnesses; and in exceptional circumstances (*e.g.*, a custody and/or access application) he should be allowed leeway to call witnesses to clarify and expand upon areas he feels have not been adequately or properly developed.

(5) A trial judge should be able to make use of an expert where there is extensive and complex evidence so that he may better comprehend the same.

(6) A trial judge may intervene to assist the clarification of evidence, and to prevent prolix and lengthy proceedings; but his intervention should be infrequent, and should not interfere with the conduct of the trial by counsel as they want to present their cases.

(7) During the course of a trial a trial judge should never express any bias or favour for any side.

(8) In summing-up before a jury, the trial judge should deal adequately with the evidence, and while he can comment upon the credibility of witnesses, unless there are patent cases of gross manipulation of evidence by witnesses, he should leave the issue of credibility to the jury.

(9) In criminal cases, the trial judge should never of his own motion call any witness to which the defence objects; but he may call a witness in unusual circumstances (*Tregear*). In the summing-up he must deal fully with the defence theory and the evidence in support and indicate to the jury and defences which, although not presented, are available upon the adduced evidence; and he should never favour the prosecution or the accused in his comments during the trial or in the summing-up.

The trial judge can be a pilot who guides the trial along sedate, orderly lines within the confines of the rules of evidence and the applicable law. He is certainly more than an umpire, watching the sporting-theory of litigation in action; and he is less than a participant in that he should not enter into the fray of combat nor take on the mantle of counsel.

. . .

## The Role of the Judge*

*Frank P. Hoskins*

*Excerpts from "The Players of a Criminal Trial" in Joel E. Pink and David C. Perrier, eds., *From Crime to Punishment: An Introduction to the Criminal Law System* (Toronto: Carswell, 1999) at 172-175.

. . .

## THE ROLE OF THE JUDGE

The judiciary is perceived by some legal commentators as a third arm of government, separate from and independent of the political parties, the legislative, and the executive. Their role is to maintain the rule of law, to uphold the Constitution, and to administer justice, impartially, according to law.

The judiciary in Canada exercise wide powers. They enjoy judicial independence, security of tenure, and financial security. Most importantly, they enjoy the respect, and embrace the confidence of the vast majority of Canadians. Judicial independence is reinforced, not only by tenure, but also by the legal immunity from reprisals for decisions that are unpopular with the public and/or the government. To protect their impartiality, the law gives them substantial immunities from actions based on their exercise of judicial powers. Judicial independence is an element of the constitutional systems of judicial impartiality.

The government cannot direct judges on how to decide cases, or how to exercise judicial discretion. Judges are not bound by policies created and employed by the government. Judges are only bound by the laws that Parliament and/or the legislative enact.

The trust reposed in the public has been earned by the judge's ability to conduct trials fairly and impartially. Impartiality is the cornerstone of our criminal justice system and thus the judiciary vigorously preserves it. Judges must be sensitive to the need not only to be fair, but also to appear to all reasonable observers to be fair to all Canadians of every race, religion, nationality and ethnic origin. The courts must be held to the highest standards of impartiality. A trial will be rendered unfair if the words or actions of the presiding judge give rise to a reasonable apprehension of bias to the informed and reasonable observer.

The public rightfully expects judges to undertake an open-minded, carefully considered and dispassionately deliberate investigation of the complicated reality of each case before them.

Impartiality can be described as a state of mind in which the judge is disinterested in the outcome of the trial and is open to persuasion by the evidence and submissions of counsel. Hence there is, and must be, a presumption of impartiality of the judiciary in order to maintain the public confidence in the effectiveness of the criminal trial process.

Judges are expected to conduct themselves with integrity, impartiality, diligence and equality. Adherence to these fundamental principles promotes public confidence in an effective criminal justice system.

The traditional view of the role of the trial judge has been that of a passive participant. Lord Denning, a famous English jurist, had occasion to comment on the role of a trial judge:

> ... it is for the advocates, each in his turn, to examine the witnesses, and not for the judge to take it on himself lest by so doing he appear to favour one side or the other: ... The judge's part in all this is to hearken to the evidence, only himself asking questions of witnesses when it is necessary to clear up any point that has been overlooked or left obscure; to see that the advocates behave themselves seemly and keep to the rules laid down by law; to exclude irrelevancies and discourage repetition; to make sure by wise intervention that he follows the points that the advocates are making and can assess their worth; and at the end to make up his mind where the truth lies. If he goes beyond this, he drops the matter of a judge and assumes the robe of an advocate; and the change does not become him well.

Lord Denning further stated:

> Even in England, however, a judge is not a mere umpire to answer the question "How's that?" His object, above all, is to find out the truth, and to do justice according to law.

A trial judge will rarely descend into the arena with counsel and take an active role, because he or she risks the possibility of having his or her vision clouded with the dust of the conflict.

The trial judge has a wide discretion in the conduct of the trial, and although she or he is always at liberty to question a witness to clarify a point or to explore an issue further, extensive interventions by a trial judge in the unfolding of the evidence are not the norm in our adversarial system. Extensive questioning by the trial judge risks producing an impression that the judge is pursuing a preconceived view of the facts.

Commenting on the right of the trial judge to question witnesses, Martin J.A., an experienced and learned jurist, stated:

> A criminal trial is, in the main, an adversarial process, not an investigation by the judge of the charge against the accused, and, accordingly, the examination and cross-examination of witnesses are primarily the responsibility of counsel. The judge, however, is not required to remain silent. He may question witnesses to clear up ambiguities, explores some matter which the answers of a witness have left vague or, indeed, he may put questions which should have been put to bring out some relevant matter, but which have been omitted. Generally speaking, the authorities recommend that questions by the judge should be put after counsel has completed his examination, and the witnesses should not be cross-examined by the judge during their examination-in-chief.

It should be noted that a trial judge who endeavors to assist counsel and witnesses in the proper, complete and logical developments of all aspects of a case within the confines of the rules of evidence and the adversarial system, while maintaining complete impartiality, will advance the respect and confidence of all concerned with the effectiveness of the criminal trial process.

It is the duty of the trial judge to decide all questions of law, both substantive and procedural, which arise during the course of the proceedings. During the course of a trial, the judge may be called upon to make many significant rulings that could affect the outcome of the case. For example, trial judges must rule on issues concerning the admissibility of evidence such as: confession, hearsay, opinion evidence, relevance and materiality of evidence, documentary evidence, and weighing the effect of the evidence-weighing its probative value against its prejudicial effect. There are too many potential legal and evidentiary issues to mention that could arise during the course of a trial. However, it is suffice to say that the trial judge must be prepared to be called upon at any time during the trial to make a legal ruling regarding a legal and/or factual issue.

As one noted author aptly stated:

> On any average day in court a judge is routinely called on to exhibit the face of a diplomat, the wisdom of Solomon, the patience of a peace negotiator. A judge under our system doesn't have to be perfect but he or she had better come awfully close.

In jury trials, the trial judge does not determine issues of act. The "trier of fact" in jury trials is the jury. The jury's function is to determine from the evidence the facts to make a proper application of the law relating to those facts as explained by the trial judge. It is the exclusive responsibility of the trial judge to interpret the law and state to the jury what principles of law are applicable to the facts of the case, and such statement and exposition of the law are binding on the jury. In other words, the jury must apply the law to the facts as they find them. The jury is the "trier of fact," and the trial judge is the only expert on the law with the responsibility of instructing the jury on the law.

In jury trials, the jury is entitled to accept all of the testimony of a witness, part of the testimony of a witness, or none of the testimony of a witness. If the jury accepts part of the testimony of a witness, it is not then bound to accept all of the witness testimony. If the jury rejects part of the testimony of a witness, it is not then required to reject all of the testimony of a witness. In other words, a jury, as the "trier of fact" is free to accept or reject all, part, or none of the testimony of a witness.

The jury's verdict must be unanimous and all jury members must be present in court when the verdict is given, and either Crown or defence has the right to have the jury polled.

If a verdict is "guilty," then the trial judge must impose the appropriate punishment.

. . .

## Judicial Accountability in Canada*

### *Ian Greene*

* Excerpts from "Judicial Accountability in Canada" in Philip Stenning, ed., *Accountability for Criminal Justice: Selected Essays* (Toronto: University of Toronto Press, 1995) at 355-356; 362-367; 369-372.

Typically, when a judge is asked who he or she is accountable to, the answer will be 'to God,' 'to my conscience' or 'to the public.'

Judges do think of themselves as accountable, but not according to the usual standards of line accountability. One of the best descriptions of the lack of line accountability regarding judges has been drafted by R. MacGregor Dawson and Norman Ward:

> The unique functions which the judiciary perform in the government make it imperative that judges should be given a different position from that of the great majority of government

officials . . . Judicial independence . . . involves the removal of most of the punitive influences which surround ordinary officials, particularly for the enforcement of political responsibility, which usually imply the power of a super to remonstrate, reprimand, and even remove from office . . . To this political irresponsibility is added a civil and criminal irresponsibility as well. Under the common law a judge is not liable to civil or criminal action for acts committed within his jurisdiction while performing his judicial duties. (Dawson and Ward, 1970:395-6)

Dawson and Ward explain how this absence of line accountability is for the greater public good of ensuring that judges can make decisions independently and impartially, without fear of a superior looking over their shoulder and without fear of the possibility of an angry litigant, upon losing a case, harassing them . . . making judges' 'politically irresponsible for the greater good for the polity is more extensively developed in Dawson's doctoral dissertation, *The Principle of Official Independence* (1922:28ff). Here, Dawson explains how removing the fetters of political responsibility not only encourages independence of thought, but stimulates the highest standards of performance among professionals who are used to self-discipline and who resent imposed discipline.

Some of the less-positive sides of the independence theme are explored by Don K. Price in *The Scientific Estate* (1965). Price analyses the independence given by governments over the centuries first to the clergy in government employ, then to lawyers and judges, and most recently to scientists. This independence, according to Price, is required as much because it is demanded by these experts as it is given for the good of society. Experts insist on a fair degree of autonomy as a condition of working for government. Therefore, Price claims, experts in government employ often have a fair amount of scope to set their own agendas, and their agendas are not necessarily in the best interests of society as a whole.

In this essay it will be argued that judges are accountable in a number of ways that are often overlooked, but that the whole issue of judicial accountability needs far more careful consideration by the judges themselves. The essay begins with a reconsideration of the concept of accountability, then moves to an analysis of judicial independence before the various actual mechanisms of accountability are appraised.

## An Approach to Accountability

Accountability in the public sector is too often thought of purely in terms of line accountability. Line accountability means having to answer for one's actions to a supervisor who is in turn answerable to a senior supervisor and so on right up to the minister who is answerable to Parliament, which is answerable to the people at election time. At each point along this bureaucratic structure of command supervisors may enforce their authority by taking disciplinary action against disobedient or ineffective subordinates. Subordinates, however, may not be held to account for anything not contained in their job descriptions or required of them by law; the superior-inferior relationship is a legal one.

. . .

## Mechanisms of Accountability for Judges

There are a number of other mechanisms of accountability — actual and potential — that may be more appropriate for Canadian judges than line accountability or budget accountability; each of them may be more or less effective depending on the circumstances. They are analysed below according to whether they are formal, self-imposed, or potential.

FORMAL MECHANISMS OF ACCOUNTABILITY

. . .

### Appointment and Promotion

Judicial appointment procedures can be thought of as a front-end mechanism of accountability. In our system, once judges are appointed there is nothing that can be done to remove them as long as they attend court, hear and decide the cases on their lists, are polite to litigants, and do not get convicted of a serious offence, get involved in politics, or behave in such a way that their moral principles are called into question (Russell, 1987:176). An apportionment procedure that results in the selection of the best possible candidates for judgeships in the first place is therefore necessary to promote optimum judicial performance.

Until recently judicial appointments were determined primarily by political patronage. Fortunately, there were enough good lawyers who were owed favours by the parties controlling the federal and provincial governments in Canada that a number of good judicial appointments were made, along with some very inappropriate ones (ibid:113ff). The main problem was that the pool of available talent was often limited to supporters of the party in power.

. . .

Patronage remains a factor in many federal judicial appointments, although some improvements have been made over the past three decades. Changes to the old patronage system began in the 1970s when the federal minister of justice established a system of nation-wide contacts with prominent lawyers and judges to recruit outstanding candidates. As well, the names of potential appointees were given to a committee of the Canadian Bar Association for comment. In 1988 the justice minister established a system of provincial and territorial assessment committees; the committees were set up to advise the minister whether potential federal appointees are qualified for the job. These five-member committees represent the judiciary, the legal profession, the provincial or territorial attorney general, and the federal minister of justice. Their major weakness is that they are limited to commenting on names put forward by the minister of justice, who tends to put forward the names of the party faithful. A recent study has shown that the Conservative government of the 1980s tended to appoint judges who were known supporters of the Progressive Conservative party to all courts with federal judges except the Supreme Court of Canada (Russell and Ziegel, 1989). Unlike the procedures in Ontario and Quebec, the federal assessment committees cannot advertise for applications.

The new selection procedure in Ontario, which was established by the Liberal attorney general in 1989, and continued under the New Democratic party administration, is arguably the best in the country in terms of recruiting the most able candidates for the bench. The judicial appointments advisory committee is composed of fourteen persons from across Ontario; although it includes representatives of the legal profession and the judiciary, half of its members are non-lawyers and half are women. The chair is a university professor who has been a leading advocate of court reform in Canada. When vacancies in the provincial bench occur, the committee advertises extensively for applicants and has found no shortage of would-be judges among lawyers of ten years' standing or more. Applicants must fill out detailed application forms, and those who are short-listed are interviewed. The committee looks not only for candidates who have high academic and professional qualifications, but also for candidates who demonstrate compassion and who have a demonstrated record of community service.

The committee has endeavoured to recommend to the Ontario Judicial Council and the attorney general candidates who would create a more representative judiciary — a bench that more closely resembles the ethnic and gender diversification of Ontario society (McCormick and Greene, 1990:253 – 4). Until now, the federal and provincial judiciaries have tended to over-represent those of English and French ethnicities and those from the middle and upper socioeconomic brackets, and 93 per cent of Canadian judges in 1990 were men (ibid.:59 ff). A judiciary is more likely to be accountable in the sense of demonstrating optimum performance if the selection procedure is designed both to select the most qualified candidates for judicial office, and candidates who more broadly represent the entire community. A degree of representativeness is important because when the law is unclear, judges fill in the gaps and, in effect, make policy. They are more likely to make policy that is acceptable to the political community the more they are representative of that community (Strayer, 2983:297 ff).

## The Role of the Chief Judge or Chief Justice

. . .

Chief judges and justices are typically described by the *puisne* (regular) judges and justices as 'first among equals.' Because of judicial independence, it is not proper for the chief to try to influence *puisne* judges regarding their decisions about particular cases (except if the chief is a member of an appeal panel, in which case each member of the panel may try to persuade other panel members). Regarding case-flow duties other than assigning cases and setting schedules, the regular judges think of the chief judge or justice as someone who can make suggestions but who cannot give orders. . . .

In spite of these limitations on the authority of the chief judges and justices, they can often serve to promote accountability simply by having informal chats with *puisne* judges about whom some criticism has been received. If a chief receives a complaint about a judge's behaviour, having a word with the judge in question might resolve the problem. The chief has no formal authority to discipline or suspend, depending on the personality of the chief and the openness of the *puisne* judge to the chief's counsel. This approach to accountability may be an example of what Marshall (1978) refers to as a 'explanatory and cooperative' style of accountability.

. . .

*Judicial councils:*

. . .

The Canadian Judicial Council, consisting of all federally appointed chief justices and judges and associate chief judges and justices, was established by Parliament in 1971, both to promote judicial education and to deal with complaints about federally appointed judges. In 1994 this body consisted of thirty-five judges. It is chaired by the Chief Justice of the Supreme Court of Canada. If the council receives a complaint for which there is enough evidence to warrant an inquiry, it has the power to conduct the inquiry and if necessary, to recommend removal of a judge. Prior to the creation of the council, complaints about federally appointed judges were dealt with by the minister of justice, who would establish a judicial inquiry into the conduct of a judge if the evidence warranted such a procedure. Since 1867 no Canadian superior court judge has ever been removed, although the joint-address procedure was initiated for the removal of Mr Justice Leo Landreville in 1966; Landreville, however, resigned before he was removed. . . .

During the 1992-3 fiscal year, the council received 127 complaints, but only one produced enough evidence to warrant an inquiry. The matter concerned a complaint from a chief justice that a judge in his court had become unable to carry out his duties because of 'age or infirmity.' . . .

Prior to 1993 only two inquiries had been conducted by the council. The first, in 1982, was a result of remarks made by Mr Justice Thomas Berger of the British Columbia Supreme Court at a university convocation in late 1981. Berger criticized the 5 November, 1981 constitutional accord, and his remarks also appeared in the Globe and Mail. The council reprimanded Berger for his foray into politics, but concluded that his behaviour had not constituted an offence serious enough to warrant removal. Berger eventually resigned in any case (McCormick and Greene, 1990:51).

The second inquiry, in 1990, was in the aftermath of the Donald Marshall, Jr, affair. In 1983 the Nova Scotia Court of Appeal acquitted Marshall of murder after he had been wrongly convicted and had spent eleven years in jail, but in 1988 a royal commission found that the court had wrongly blamed Marshall for being partly responsible for the miscarriage of justice (Nova Scotia, Royal Commission on the Donald Marshall, Jr, Prosecution, 1989: vol. 1, p. 125). As a result, the attorney general of Nova Scotia requested an inquiry by the Canadian Judicial Council. The council concluded that there had been no judicial misconduct on the part of three continuing members of the Nova Scotia Court of Appeal. However, the inquiry committee which the council had established concluded that the judges had been guilty both of legal error and inappropriate comments. 'But neither legal error nor inappropriate language are grounds for removal of a judge from office' (Canadian Judicial Council, 1991:14).

The provinces have all established provincial judicial councils since the early 1970s. Typically, they are composed of all the federally and provincially appointed chief justices and chief judges, as well as the associate chiefs, in each province, sometimes with the addition of representation from the bar as well as from non-lawyers. . .

## Courts Advisory Committees

. . .

To tackle problems of coordination and to provide a vehicle for public input into the improvement of the provincial courts system, the report of Mr Justice Thomas Zuber in 1987 recommended the establishment of courts management advisory committees at the provincial and regional levels in Ontario (Zuber, 1987). Such committees were actually established in 1991, and they have representation from the groups mentioned above as well as from the lay public. If these committees are given a clear and practical mandate, and if the potentially explosive problems relating to interpersonal relations on these committees are approached with tact, they could have a tremendous potential not only to promote better coordination among the various personnel involved in court activities, but to promote accountability. . . .

## Continuing Education

During the past two decades, several associations have been involved in organizing conferences and educational seminars for judges. The Canadian Judicial Council has organized educational seminars for federally appointed judges, and there are national and provincial associations for provincially appointed judges that have established impressive educational programs. . . .

## Annual Reports

It has become a tradition over the past decade or so for the chief justice of Ontario to present a report at the annual ceremonial opening of the courts in January of each year. The statement constitutes an annual report of the achievements of Ontario's judiciary, and it has become an important vehicle for demonstrating the accountability of the Ontario judiciary to the people of Ontario. The adoption of a similar tradition in other jurisdictions may help to promote judicial accountability. . . .

## Self-Accountability

Most judges consider that self-accountability is a more important factor in encouraging quality judicial performance than the formal mechanisms of accountability discussed above (Paterson, 1983:195 ff). Judges generally value the making of fair judgments and the writing of quality opinions not because of the possibility of reprimand from the chief justice or a judicial council, but because their self-esteem depends on their own assessments of themselves regarding how they measure up as judges.

EFFECT OF YEARS IN PRIVATE PRACTICE

On average, provincially appointed judges come to the bench with fifteen years' experience in the practice of law, while federally appointed judges average about twenty years' experience. . . .

What this background experience indicates is that most judges are used to self-discipline rather than discipline imposed from above.

PUBLIC OPINION AND MEDIA REPORTS

Judges tend to be sensitive to criticism of their judgments in newspapers and other media, and they value a public reputation as being fair, even if somewhat conservative (Griffith, 1977:202 – 16). If a judge's decision or behaviour is criticized in the media, it is not considered appropriate for the judge to respond; a response could be considered as entering into the political fray in violation of judicial independence. However, media criticism of judges is rare, partly because until 1986, those criticizing the judiciary in the media might have been charged with contempt of court. The principle behind the contempt offence was that criticism of the judiciary (even if accurate) might cause the public to lose respect for the courts, and this loss of respect could have serious consequences for social order.

In 1986 a radical Toronto lawyer was charged by the Crown with 'scandalizing the court,' a form of statutory contempt. He had complained that the courts and the police stick together like 'Krazy Glue,' and his remarks were picked up by a reporter. He was acquitted in the Ontario Court of Appeal, which found that the Charter rights to freedom of expression took precedence over the law of contempt (R v Kopyto [1988]). With the relaxation of the law of contempt, the media may not act somewhat more freely in terms of publishing criticism of judicial decisions or behaviour. Such critiques may help to promote judicial accountability by providing consequences, in terms of a negative public image, for lapses in judicial performance.

THE ACADEMIC PRESS

Judges, and especially appeal court judges, generally try to keep abreast of the articles in the major law journals and to read books that comment on the judiciary. . . .

OPINIONS OF OTHER JUDGES

It is important for most judges to be respected by their colleagues on the bench. In a survey of the attitudes of Alberta judges at all levels, the judges were asked what the qualities are that cause a judge to gain the respect of his or her fellow judges. It was found that the judges valued 'the qualities of diligence and industry, of humaneness, of patience and courtesy, of a knowledge of the law and intelligence, of a sense of fair play and decisiveness [in that order]. . . .

*Editor's note: Greene goes on to discuss several other potential mechanisms of accountability, including evaluations by lawyers of individual judges (similar to student evaluations of professors, program evaluations to decide if the judiciary is fulfilling its goals, and surveys of those who have been involved with the system. Ultimately, he concludes that "[p]robably the most important accountability mechanism for the promotion of fairness is the self-discipline that judges have learned through their years in the practice of law prior to becoming judges" and that "[f]ront-end accountability for fairness can be promoted through non-partisan procedures to select the most capable candidates . . . . " (at 374).*

## Questions/Discussion

1. What is the proper role of the judge in controlling the trial process? Should the role be redefined in order to give the judge a more active part to play in the conduct of the proceedings? Why or why not?

2. Identify the various ways in which judges can be held to account. What do you regard as the most effective way to hold judges accountable for the criminal law they produce? Why? Should a wrongfully convicted person be entitled to sue the judges for negligence where the judge has made errors in the course of the trial? Why or why not?

## Further Reading

- Baar, C., "Judicial Appointments and the Quality of Adjudication: The American Experience in a Canadian Perspective" (1986), 20 Thémis 1.
- Brooks, N., "The Judge and the Adversary System" in Allen Linden, ed., *The Canadian Judiciary* (Toronto: York University, 1976), p.89.
- Brooks, N., "Evidence" (1975), 7 Ottawa Law Review 600.
- Canadian Bar Association Task Force on Gender Equality. *Touchstones for Change: Equality, Diversity and Accountability — The Report on Gender Equality in the Legal Profession* (Ottawa: The Canadian Bar Association, 1993).
- Dickson, B., "The Rule of Law: Judicial Independence and the Separation of Powers" (1985), 9 Provincial Judges 4.
- Gibson, D., "Judges as Legislators: Not Whether but How: (1986), 25 Alberta Law Review 249.
- Laskin, B., "A Judge and His Constituencies" (1976), 7 Manitoba Law Journal 1.
- McLachlin, B., "The Role of Judges in Modern Commonwealth Society" (1995), 53 Advocate 681-687.
- Nemetz, N., "The Concept of an Independent Judiciary" (1986), 20 University of British Columbia Law Review 285.
- Ontario Law Reform Commission. *Appointing Judges: Philosophy, Politics and Practice* (Toronto: Ontario Law Reform Commission, 1991).
- Russell, P. and J.S. Ziegel, "Federal Judicial Appointments: An Appraisal of the First Mulroney Government's Appointments and the New Judicial Advisory Committees" (1991), 41 University of Toronto Law Journal 4-37.
- Tanovich, David, "Testing the Presumption That Trial Judges Know the Law: The Case of *W. (D.)*" (2001), 43 C.R. (5th) 298-307.
- Tollefson, E.A., "The Quality of Judicial Appointments: A Collateral Issue" (1971), 21 University of Toronto Law Journal 162.
- Wilson, B., "Will Women Judges Really Make a Difference?" (1990), 24 Gazette 261.

- Ziegel, J.S., "Appointments to the Supreme Court of Canada" (1994), 5 Constitutional Form 10-15.

## 4.4 VICTIMS

### Introduction

*Ross Hastings*

The rise of interest during the last twenty years in the plight of victims of crime and their proper role is an interesting one in the light of the developments which have actually occurred in the Canadian criminal justice system. The rhetoric on the part of the state in support of the victim of crime has not been matched by real initiatives and real funding and, moreover, it has not been translated into a more humane and more effective criminal justice system for any of the participants. However, the Canadian criminal justice system has come some way in its recognition of the problems experienced by victims of crime, and in its willingness to recognize that it bears some of the responsibility for responding to these problems in an effective and humane manner. The question to be asked is whether this new consciousness has been (or can be) translated into new policies and practices within the criminal justice system, and whether any of this can make a significant impact on the situation of victims of crime.

The so-called "costs" of criminal injuries, and the subsequent requirements of victims of crime, involve a broad range of physical, financial and emotional injuries which are discussed in more detail in the excerpt from the *Justice for Victims of Crime* report below. There is general agreement, however, that they can be summarized into three general types of concerns (Normandeau, 1983; Waller, 1981):

1.  Access to the information and programmes necessary to prevent crime, or at last reduce the vulnerability to criminal injury;
2.  Recovery of the physical, financial and emotional well-being which was experienced by the victim before the criminal act; and
3.  Treatment by the criminal justice system which is just and humane, and which is responsive to the desire of victims to be fully informed and protected during their experience within the system.

There has been some optimism generated within both the criminal justice system and the victims' movement by the changes which have been made to date. There is also a degree of optimism that the rhetoric on the part of the state might actually be translated into policies and real support for victims of crime.

There are, however, a number of reasons to be guarded in assessing both the progress that the movement on behalf of victims has made, and its potential for further advances. The future may be less promising than it seems. The victim has acquired a presence in the public consciousness and within the policies and programmes of the criminal justice system; it can be said that victims are better treated than before, though perhaps not universally or uniformly, depending on the type of victim you are and the type of crime you have been subject to. It can also be argued that supporters and advocates within the victims' movement have been somewhat seduced by the appearance of a consensus around the definition of the problems experienced by victims of crime and the solutions to this situation, and as a result have neglected the ideological and political conflicts which are part of the attempt by the criminal justice system to respond to any new initiative. It is often assumed that the movement on behalf of victims has such a sound and legitimate moral base that progress is simply a question of raising people's consciousness about what needs to be done, and applying a little political pressure to the most responsive points of the state and its criminal justice system.

This is naive. It ignores the real debates over just exactly what victims need, who should provide for these needs, and who should pay the costs of this response. The fact of the matter is that there are very real options to choose on each of these questions. For the most part, the objectives of the victims' movement have been translated and operationalized on the basis of traditional or conservative approaches to social organization and the role of the criminal justice system. The practical result has been a tendency to favour programmes either based on the responsibility of the offender to repair the damage done to an innocent victim of crime, or which attempt to facilitate and encourage the participation of victims and witnesses of crimes in the criminal justice system in order to improve the efficiency and success of the system. At this point in time, there is little indication of any meaningful support for programmes which are based on the recognition of a collective responsibility for the kind of society we live in, and consequently for the types and rates of crime which we experience. In practice, this means the state is much more willing merely to "recognize" victims than it is to respond to their needs in an effective manner.

Compared to earlier times, victims have won recognition; it is difficult to imagine a criminal justice policy in today's society which would not at least acknowledge their existence and the responsibility of the criminal justice system or the state generally to do *something* for them. The real question remains as to who will be responsible for creating, financing, and delivering these new initiatives. It is here that the differences between the traditional and the critical perspectives are the most evident and the most important. The critical orientation will generally emphasize the collective responsibility for the consequences of the organization of the social system. The argument is that crime is in large part a function of our social and cultural arrangements, and thus the state (through the mechanism of the taxation system) should be responsible for taking care of the victims created by this situation. In this sense, victims of crime are just one category of people who suffer the consequences of our social arrangements. It is argued that they should be treated much the same way as unemployed people who receive state sponsored medical care.

On the other hand, the traditional orientation places the burden of responsibility to repair the damage done to an innocent victim of a criminal act on the offender who caused that damage. This reflects the tendency of these more conservative approaches to see the criminal act as an indicator of an unwillingness or a refusal on the part of the offender to accept the responsibilities which go along with citizenship. According to this point of view, the permissiveness and moral pluralism which characterize contemporary society require a concentration on strategies of deterrence (usually through more punishment) and control (usually through target hardening and increased surveillance). Within this perspective, social renewal has a moral rather than an economic meaning. This, in part, is how government cutbacks in social services and the expansion of the criminal justice system have been justified in recent years.

In an examination of the Canadian state's responses to date, it is evident that the policies and programmes on behalf of victims of crime have been much more characterized by the latter type of traditional or conservative approaches to criminal justice policy. An overview of initiatives in this field suggests that:

1.  Relatively few new resources have been allocated to victims; public recognition and the expressed commitment of the criminal justice system have not been translated into a massive infusion of new programmes, services or resources.

2.  A large part of the new resources which have been directed to victims have been invested in programmes designed to inform and support victims and witnesses of crime who participate in the criminal justice process. There is little doubt of the benefit of such programmes to these individuals, but it is also true that their basic justification lies in their potential to reduce the costs and increase the efficiency of the criminal justice system. In this sense, victims are a *means* to promote the organizational goals of the system ? this does not represent a fundamental rethinking of the system.

3.  There has been an indication of some increase in the use of reparative sanctions in sentencing. However, the primary motivation of this shift lies in the conviction that this represents a cheaper (but at least as effective) manner of denouncing and punishing criminal behaviour, and reintegrating the offender into society. The motivation, in other words, is not necessarily to help the victim; this is a worthwhile but secondary consequence of this development. There is also little indication that these measures constitute a significant means of repairing the damage done to victims of crime, given both the lack of funds on the part of the offender and the reluctance of judges to engage in this type of sentencing exercise. One should also not ignore that such measures are a means of reducing the number of new "clients" which the prisons must house, and thus can save the state some money on this level also. Finally, it can be asked whether these measures may not have the unanticipated consequence of increasing the number of people who come under the control of the criminal justice system, without really improving the lot of the victim. Because the system appears more humane, it is often the case that more people are brought within the ambit of the system who might otherwise not have been.

4.  There is a tendency to look to the offender to find the new revenues which are necessary to fund victims' programmes, for example, through fine surcharges or other such measures. This reflects the conservative tendency primarily to blame offenders and hold them responsible for the consequences of their behaviour. However, it is a limited approach, in light of the inability of the system to identify, arrest and convict a significant proportion of those who are guilty of offences.

5.  The very notion of "victims of criminal acts" is restricted to the traditional categories of crimes against the person or property (the so-called predatory or

street crimes). There has been almost no attention given to victims of corporate or white-collar crime, nor to victims of offences which fall under other types of regulatory legislation.

6. For the most part, only "innocent" victims of crime are likely to receive the state's sympathy or help. Those who have contributed to their own victimization, either through their "negligence" or "unworthiness", or by allegedly precipitating the act in question, are usually judged to be less worthy of consideration. In discussing the criminal injuries compensation schemes adopted in most of the provinces, Murphy (1982:544-55) states:

> The applicant is also required to "co-operate fully with the Board" and will probably be expected to undergo a medical examination and testify under oath at the hearing.
>
> The victim's behaviour at the time of the commission of the offence and subsequent to it, is a decisive factor in determining the amount, if any, to be awarded. The Board "shall consider and take into account any behaviour of the victim that directly or indirectly contributed to his injury or death." This broad wording gives the Boards considerable latitude in rendering a decision. The Ontario Reports supply an adequate number of examples as to what constitutes an unworthy victim. There are numerous instances where claimants have had their awards reduced or denied because of: failing to report to the police within a reasonable time, participation in criminal conduct, membership with the underworld, homosexuality, drunkenness, family disputes, immoral conduct, imprudent behaviour, as defined by the board members themselves.

The argument is, therefore, that the state, while quite vocal in its support of victims of crime, has been quite conservative in its approach to policies and programmes on behalf of these victims. For the most part these initiatives have reflected a humanitarian willingness to be charitable to worthy (blameless) victims. There is little indication of any large scale political movement towards funding the kinds of crime prevention and victim assistance programmes which would be necessary to insure victims against the damages caused by crime or the fear of crime. On the contrary, the creation and implementation of initiatives on behalf of victims have been dominated more by a concern to reduce the social and fiscal obligations of the state and to place the responsibility for the consequences of crime on individual offenders. And it seems unlikely that this political situation will change much in the near future. The result is that the victims' movement is likely to have to continue to content itself with fiscal crumbs, and to have to depend on the kindness and good will of volunteers who are willing to invest their own time and energy to come to the aid of victims of criminal acts.[1] What has been witnessed in the first half of the 1990's is a rise in the number and vigour of victims' groups that lobby for harsher criminal penalties for offenders as part of a broader package of victims' rights.

The final issue is the proper role of the victim in the criminal justice system. Once the state recognizes the needs of victims, then how should these needs be met? There is an argument that while the needs are real, the place to address them is *not* the criminal justice system. Better treatment of the victim in the system is required but

---

1　This is especially true for victims of sexual assault and domestic violence, where the victims of such crimes have always relied on the crisis centres and shelters which are set up, staffed and supported by women volunteers.

the full-fledged participation of the victim in the criminal process would add little while at the same time creating an imbalance in a process which is already slanted against the offenders and the fulfilment of their rights in practice; the role of the victim in the prosecution process is discussed in the Clarke article below. What is required is an effective, well-advertised, and well-funded delivery system for the necessary counselling, compensation, and crime prevention services.

## Report of the Canadian Federal-Provincial Task Force on Justice for Victims of Crime*

*Ministry of Supply and Services*

*Excerpts from *Report of the Canadian Federal-Provincial Task Force on Justice for Victims of Crime* (Ottawa: Supply and Services, 1983).

### ISSUES — OVERVIEW

The victim and the victim's place in the criminal justice system have been the focus of increasing attention in several countries over the past twenty years. In some jurisdictions this interest has resulted in significant changes or additions being made to legislation. Starting with New Zealand in 1964, many countries have established various forms of state compensation to victims of crime. Some jurisdictions have delineated certain rights for victims of crime and encompassed these in legislation; some have enacted statutes which ensure that wherever possible restitution shall be made to the victim; others have passed legislation which legitimizes the victim's interest as an active participant in the criminal justice process.

Sometimes changes in administrative methods or in operational programmes have accompanied changes in legislation, or have occurred where the latter were seen to be unnecessary or untimely. Services have been developed to meet what are considered to be the legitimate needs of victims, particularly in the case of those perceived to be the most vulnerable such as women and young children.

. . .

Increasing concern for the victim has arisen partly from humanitarian reasons such as having regard for the victim's loss or suffering, partly because it would seem to be only just or equitable that the state owes an obligation to the victim beyond that owed to citizens in general, and partly because the success of any criminal justice system is dependent upon the co-operation of victims and witnesses of crime. It should be a matter of grave concern that research and victimization surveys indicate that some victims are reluctant to report certain crimes and witnesses are often reluctant to cooperate with the agents of the system in their attempts to apprehend and prosecute the offender.

One of the reasons for this is that the victims themselves felt that the incident was too minor to report. In addition, however, research reveals an undercurrent of disillusionment. Indeed, many victims appear to feel that the system would only fail them or ignore them if they invoked it. These feelings may have resulted from a previous unsatisfactory experience with the system or from lack of information as to what it can and cannot be expected to accomplish.

The sense of disillusion takes many forms. If people no longer feel confident in the ability of society's institutions to protect them, then they look to their own protection. It is not by chance that private security forces have expanded remarkably in the past ten years, that the burglar alarm business is a growth industry or that self-defence classes flourish. Nor is it by chance that we have witnessed an emergence of groups who believe either that the law is not functioning or is not functioning as they want it to, and who attempt to provide their own response to what they perceive to be an absence of law and order; a growth in the number of commercial enterprises which deal privately with the fraudulent activities of their employees rather than report them; a number of witnesses who do not come forward because they know they will not be compensated adequately for the loss of wages incurred by adjournments and delays.

When society fails to protect its members from criminal activity, they may suffer physically, emotionally, or financially. These are the costs of victimization — but are not the only costs. Others are incurred by the manner in which our system of justice operates, and arise from the discomfort, the inconvenience, and sometimes — it must be said — the discourtesy and humiliation the victim faces as the process unfolds. Even though the very survival of the system rests upon the willing co-operation of victims to report crimes and of witnesses to testify, the manner in which they are dealt with often does little to inspire or encourage that co-operation. The victim is often given little assistance to overcome the effects of his victimization and provided with little, if any, information about the progress of the case; he may receive little or no compensation for his losses and it is unlikely that he will be consulted with regard to any decisions which are made. It is often the case that the victim is twice victimized: once by the offence and once more by the process.

It is understandable that victims contrast their neglect with the attention given to offenders. Their rights are made known to them, different agencies are prepared to assist them to obtain bail; the case against them must be disclosed to their legal representatives but the latter are under no similar obligation to make any disclosure to the prosecutor; probation officers, correctional workers and parole officers are prepared to give offenders all the assistance they can; alternatives to incarceration such as community resource centres, and measures such as temporary absence, day passes, etc., which are designed to reduce the negative effects of incarceration all work to the offenders' benefit.

While some generally view the sentences currently imposed by courts as being inadequate to properly protect society and the victims, others view any form of incarceration as being counter-productive. The Task Force believes that in appropriate cases there are many alternatives which are now available to the court to increase the offenders' chances of rehabilitation and decrease the damaging effects of prison life. In focussing more concern on the plight of the victim one must not lose sight of the need to safeguard the accused. The interests of the criminal justice system can only be served in securing criminal justice, not in seeking revenge. Consequently, it is with misgiving that we view legislation enacted or proposed in foreign jurisdictions which would appear to have that intention.

Focussing concern solely upon offenders can be a disservice to victims in many ways. For example, restitution as a sentence has been justified on the basis that it contributes to the rehabilitation of the offender. Rarely is it considered in light of its benefit to the victim. Bearing in mind that wherever possible victims should be restored to the position they enjoyed prior to the victimization, then restitution becomes a very important component of a sentence. The Report indicates that we believe restitution should be considered in all appropriate cases. Although this will present some difficulties, we believe that these will be outweighed by the benefits.

It is commonplace today to hear that the victim is the 'forgotten' actor in the criminal justice system. The Task Force does not believe that victims are forgotten — or even, as some would have it, ignored — but we do believe that victims have been neglected. We do not find it difficult to understand how easily this can occur within a system where it is the responsibility of the state, not the victim, to identify, prosecute and punish the offender; where the principal parties involved are the offender and the state — each being represented by others who speak for them — and where the victim's involvement is almost entirely limited to that of giving testimony. Ours is an adversarial system where the victim is not one of the adversaries.

. . .

In their first experience with the process of criminal justice many victims are bewildered and confused. They find it difficult to understand why their stolen property cannot be returned to them promptly when it has been recovered; why they are not informed of the existence of a Criminal Injuries Compensation Board; why they are not informed well in advance of court hearings; why a case was delayed, then adjourned and again adjourned — and again; why a charge was reduced; why the true impact of the crime upon them and their family was not brought to light during the hearing; why the case was remanded for sentence and they were not informed of the date; why the offender was not ordered to make restitution. In many instances it is, unfortunately, the case that very few services are provided to victims and they receive little information about the process.

. . .

Although it may appear to be sensible, appropriate and just to encourage the participation of the victim in the process, to achieve this in the context of our present system poses some problems. It has been argued that to do so would cause further delay in the courts, would increase the cost burden on the system, would result in more severe punishments for the offenders, would compromise the procedural safeguards which have been established to ensure civil rights of the offender, and so on.

It is the contention of this Report that the arguments advanced against any change in this regard are by no means convincing. Nor, can it be said, have other jurisdictions been persuaded by them. In France, in the U.S.A., and in Australia, we find examples of recent legislation which give the victim an expanded role in the criminal justice system. In our opinion the question to be addressed is no longer whether the victim should participate in the process or not. The question is rather the extent of this participation.

Few would quarrel with the decision, which has been reached in countries which have addressed the issue, that victims be provided the opportunity to inform the court of the impact of the crime upon them. Nor would many disagree that the Court should be required to give thought to the victim's concerns in the determination of a sentence since, in fact, attorneys and judges often take into consideration the effect upon the victim before arriving at a sentencing decision.

More disagreement is apparent, however, when the method of the victim's participation is considered at the time of sentencing and when victim participation is considered at other stages of the criminal process, e.g., at the determination of the charge, at bail hearings and at the time of parole decisions. We believe that the victim should most certainly be informed of these various decisions. We do not believe that the victim should be, or need be, involved at each of the critical points in the process.

. . .

## THE NEEDS OF VICTIMS OF CRIME IN CANADA

As mentioned earlier the needs of victims of crime refer to those consequences of victimization which are not being dealt with through the practices of the justice or social services systems. The benefit of this approach is that it allows us to identify what remains to be done to satisfy the goals of the justice for victims of crime initiative. The purpose of this section is to attempt to present a more precise definition of the actual needs of victims of crime in Canada at this point in time.

Overall there would seem to be four broad types of needs. A discussion of these needs is summarized in the diagram below which attempts to specify the major responses to the consequences of victimization, and to identify the subsequent needs of victims. Obviously some of the responses can deal with more than one specific type of consequence or injury, but the diagram deals with each response terms of its *primary* impact.

*Report of the Canadian Federal-Provincial Task Force on Justice*
*for Victims of Crime*

| Consequences of Victimization | Current Primary Responses | Gaps or Beneficiaries in Response (Needs) |
|---|---|---|
| 1. Physical Injury | state medical insurance | — limits or exclusions may discriminate against victims<br>— inconsistent service to rape victims |
| 2. Financial Injury or Property Damage | a) private insurance<br>b) civil justice system<br>c) criminal justice system | coverage not universal little actual reparation is obtained reparative sentencing does not result in a significant degree of reparation |
|  | d) criminal injuries compensation | little impact due to low funding and public awareness |
| 3. Emotional Injury | services to victims of crime | lack of resources results in limited access to these services |
| 4. Secondary Injury | police and court services to victims and witnesses | such services are only beginning to emerge, and few are fully established |

## Needs Resulting from Physical Injury

The Canadian health care system adequately insures victims against most of the physical costs of victimization. Nevertheless, there are certain limits and exclusions built into every plan which may have the unintended consequence of discriminating against victims of crime. For example, some provinces are considering the adoption of user fees for hospital patients, or allowing doctors to engage in extra billing of patients for the services they provide. In either case, such practices can potentially affect many victims, and will obviously have their greatest impact on the most vulnerable economically.

Victims can attempt to recover these costs by civil suits, reparative criminal sentences, or criminal injuries compensation schemes. However, these options provide only limited remedies for the physical injury to the victim.

Certain medical practices can also be problematic. For instance, many victims of sexual assault find it difficult to receive the kinds of physical and legal treatment they require when they present themselves to hospital emergency wards. While there have been improvements in this area, there is reluctance on the part of some medical staff to become involved in the legal technicalities of the evidentiary requirements of sexual assault. Overall, then, it would seem that there are certain physical costs of crime which are not currently being remedied.

## Needs Resulting from Financial Loss or Property Damage

The Canadian justice system is much less able to deal successfully with the financial losses to victims of crime. Those victims who do obtain satisfaction generally do so through participation in private insurance schemes. However, not everyone can afford such coverage. Moreover, there are many forms of property which have an emotional or sentimental significance and which cannot be replaced for any amount of money. Victims of crime can also make use of the civil law process to obtain reparation for their losses. However, this is of limited value for most victims because it is difficult to identify and bring to justice the offender in question. Even assuming this can be done, there is still no guarantee that the accused will be found legally responsible, or will be willing and able to make reparation for the harm done.

Nor does the victim generally find satisfaction within the criminal law process. Little use is made of reparative sanctions; the focus of sentencing is on the needs of society, and the sanction chosen usually reflects the court's assessment of the fairest and most effective way to make the offender bend to those needs. The sentencing process is not designed to give priority to the wishes or desires of victims.

Finally, some financial reparation can be obtained through criminal injuries compensation schemes. However, these programmes are limited mostly to victims of violent crime. Moreover, they are underfunded by the jurisdictions which operate them, and almost unknown to the vast majority of the Canadian public. Overall, then, a number of changes are required in both the legal system and in government policy and practice before any significant improvements can be expected in this area.

### Needs Arising from Emotional Injury

One of the more promising trends in recent years is the emergence of a network of social services designed to meet the emotional needs of victims. The prototype of such service groups was the sexual assault centre which emerged over the last two decades. These centres provide information, guidance and support to victims of sexual assault. Similarly service groups are available for assaulted women and for a few other types of victims. The long-term benefits to victims of crime of immediate crisis counselling and support have been well documented and the value of such service cannot be overstated. It is, of course, important to recognize that when services of this kind are provided they must be delivered in such a way that the integrity of the victim's evidence will not be adversely affected.

The major problem faced by service groups of this kind is the difficulty of guaranteeing an adequate level of financial support. They are too often forced to go from one budgetary crisis to the next. This situation is demoralizing, and leaves these groups vulnerable to the vagaries of public opinion (as reflected in donations) and the cost-cutting realities of an era of fiscal restraint. Until there is some formal recognition of the value of such services, and a corollary decision to guarantee a higher level of priority to the support of these services, there is little reason to expect much improvement in this area. Obviously, the impact of this will be proportionately greater for the most vulnerable victims of crime.

### Needs Resulting from Secondary Victimization

The willingness of the criminal justice system to acknowledge the impact of their current practices is very promising. A great many police forces have already initiated programmes which are aimed at improving the quality of their service to victims and witnesses and others are planning to do so. The rate of development of services at the prosecutorial and court level has been slower, perhaps in part because of an expressed concern that services must be delivered in a manner which guards against interference with the evidence of potential witnesses.

Another problem is that there is so much to be done that the very enormity of the task can be intimidating. Moreover, the extra costs and labour required for such programmes, at least at the implementation stage, can be a disincentive, and it would appear that victims and witnesses are likely to be required to carry certain costs as a result of their participation in the criminal system.

## INFORMATION NEEDS

Almost every study made of victims of crime highlights the fact that victims place the need for information as their highest priority. What happens now? Who will tell me what to do? Will I have to go to court? What will happen at the court and what do I have to say? When will I get my property back? — these and many other questions are common to those working in the system. They should be dealt with patiently and thoroughly, given the emotional experience accompanying victimization, the complexities of the legal system and the desire to see that justice is done.

The system itself has information needs and these are dealt with later in the report but it would be logical to assume, in the light of what we have learned, that if the victims' needs are better satisfied, then the system will be perceived by them to be relevant and purposeful and its efficiency may thereby be improved. Victims will have a better understanding of what is expected of them and the reasons for those expectations.

. . .

## EXISTING SERVICES

What the Report has said so far on the consequences of victimization is not intended to imply that nothing is being done for the victims of crime. We have already established that the Canadian system of medical insurance provides protection against the direct physical consequences of a criminal injury. Moreover, victims have at least a limited potential for recovering their financial losses through civil suits, reparative criminal sentences or criminal injuries compensation schemes. The shortcomings of each of these options are significant. Nevertheless, these programmes and policies are in place and can be improved.

There has also been a recent trend towards providing services to victims of crime to assist them in overcoming the emotional and secondary consequences of victimization. The first such services were generally directed to dealing with the needs of special groups of victims, and focussed primarily on victims of sexual assault or child abuse. More recently, police forces, court systems and private agencies have become involved in this area, largely by attempting to provide information, assistance and support to victims or witnesses of crime.

. . .

## The Objectives of Services to Victims

Every needs-assessment study has illustrated the confusion and bewilderment of victims in the face of their involvement with the criminal justice system, and has detailed their lack of awareness of some of the programmes and services which are available to help them deal with the consequences of victimization. When available these different services to victims are a response to this expressed desire for information and support. There are differences in the specific goals or emphases of individual programmes. However, there seems to be a consensus that services to the victims or witnesses of crime have five major objectives.

- To provide victims and witnesses with information on the case in which they are involved, and on their rights and responsibilities within the criminal justice process.

. . .

- To assist victims in dealing with the consequences of victimization, and in coping with the aftermath of crime.

. . .

- To provide crisis intervention services.

. . .

- To sensitize workers within the criminal justice system to the situation of victims, and to train those workers to recognize and respond to the needs of victims and witnesses.

. . .

- To co-ordinate victim-based efforts, and to assure that victims are aware of the services which are available to them.

. . .

Unfortunately, the consensus over objectives has not resulted in a widespread expansion of these services.

. . .

## The Responsibility for Providing Services

The CCSD survey indicates that there is a great deal of controversy over which components of the justice system should provide services to victims, and over the range of services which should be provided. In large part, this reflects considerable differences of opinion as to the appropriate role of criminal justice agencies in relation to victims. While sensitive to the situation of victims, many practitioners are concerned that victim assistance may compromise the ability of the system to satisfy the needs of society and to guarantee the rights of the accused. The practical result of such concerns is a debate over the most appropriate manner for allocating the responsibility for such services. Some argue that the criminal justice system should fulfil this responsibility, while others insist that such work is better done by private social service agencies such as the Salvation Army, the John Howard Society, etc.

. . .

## *The Organization and Delivery of Services*

The CSSD Survey found that there is a great deal of support for providing services to victims and witnesses within the framework of existing programmes and services, or by redeploying existing resources to deal with new responsibilities. This is accompanied by an increasing reluctance to adopt the 'special project' approach, largely because of a resistance to sharing the costs of these programmes or a reluctance to becoming involved in programmes which require major or sustained injections of new resources.

In practical terms, this has meant that services are either provided directly by agencies within the justice system, or indirectly by contracting the task out to the private social service network. In the former case, the services can be based in police departments, in the court system, in correctional agencies or in some combination of the three.

There are three approaches to a police-based system of providing services. The first is to create a specialized services unit within the police force to deal with the requirements of victims. This approach has been adopted by the police forces in Edmonton, Calgary and Kitchener-Waterloo. The second approach is to blend the victim services unit within an existing service or division of the police force. St. John and Regina are developing proposals based on this strategy. The third approach is to attempt to reorganize existing resources so that a police department can maximize the return on current resources. The city of Vancouver and the R.C.M.P. are perhaps the best examples of proposals for operationalizing such an initiative. As an illustration, the CCSD survey indicates a high level of recognition on the part of most R.C.M.P. detachments of the importance of victims' services as an inherent element of a police officer's responsibilities.

Moreover, the majority of detachments indicate that they provide services to victims and witnesses, especially in the area of linking the victim or witness to the legal system. Unfortunately, this commitment does not seem to be accompanied by a plan to develop services or by a participation in community-based planning or inter-agency co-ordination.

Court-based services are generally concerned primarily with the welfare and requirements of witnesses, and with the objective of improving the court process. This could involve an improved case management system such as the one being developed in British Columbia, or the provision of improved services to witnesses (e.g., transportation, babysitting). In either case, the product generally springs from the belief that such services will result in faster and more efficient justice by assuring the participation of more co-operative witnesses.

The final strategy is the combined victims/witnesses services approach, which directs the police to an emphasis on victims and the court-based unit to assisting witnesses. The only fully operational unit of this type is based in Winnipeg, where the victim and witness components were developed concurrently under a single advisory committee. It is too early to assess conclusively the potential advantages of this two-tiered approach, but it does seem to maximize the potential for rationalizing scarce resources in this area.

. . .

## Is There a Place for the Victim in the Prosecution Process?*

*Patricia Clarke*

*Excerpts from (1986), 8 Canadian Criminology Forum 31.

Victims of crime once were the central actors in bringing offenders to justice. Today they are neglected outsiders in a system which could not function without them, yet is not accountable to them, provides no role for them and does not necessarily serve them, for ours is "an adversary system in which the victim is not one of the adversaries" (Federal-Provincial Task Force, 1983:5).

. . .

## EVOLUTION OF THE PROSECUTION PROCESS

Before there was a formal legal system, all wrongs were private wrongs. Victims and their families exacted the penalties. To temper and regulate such private justice, in Anglo-Saxon law there gradually grew a system of restitution with fixed payments for various wrongs. At the same time there grew the notion that while some incidents were private disputes, which in the development of law became torts to be dealt with in civil courts, other acts threatened the fabric of society and destroyed "the King's peace". For such acts the offender made payment not only to the victim but also to the lord or the king. Holdsworth (1909:38) claims this was "the germ of the idea that wrong is not simply the affair of the injured individual — an idea which is the condition precedent to the growth of a criminal law".

Gradually as this idea developed, the victim lost control of the conflict and it became the property of the state. The focus shifted from a dispute between the offender and the victim, in which the offender was bound to make reparation to the person he had injured, to the relationship between the offender and society, in which the offender had injured society and must be punished by society. Common law developed to prevent victims from receiving reparations until they did all they could to bring the offender to justice and forbid victims to agree not to prosecute in order to get back their property. Individuals could not condone a crime against the state (Hudson & Galway, 1975:24).

The key to a criminal proceeding thus became, in essence, the exclusion of the victim as one of the parties. Full participation by the victim, Christie says (1977:3), presupposes elements of civil law.

Just as the state came to replace the victim as the injured party, so it gradually replaced the victim as the prosecuting party. Until the late 18th century, trials normally were conducted by the victim-prosecutor and the defendant (Beattie, 1986:313). By the 19th century Blackstone was able to state categorically that the sovereign "is therefore the proper person to prosecute for all public offences and breaches of the peace, being the person injured in the eye of the law" (Hagan, 1983:268).

In the evolution of the prosecution process, then, two important things have happened, according to Christie (1977:3) one, that both parties are being represented; and second, that the one represented by the state, the victim, "is so thoroughly represented that for the most part he has been pushed completely out of the arena". The victim is a double loser: his property may have been stolen by the offender, but "his conflict has been stolen by the state" (Christie, 1982:93). When the private conflicts become state property, they are made to serve "the ideological interests of state-subject authority relations and the organizational interests of the individual citizens" (Ericson & Baranek, 1982:4).

## ROLE OF THE VICTIM IN THE PROSECUTION PROCESS

This transfer of the dispute between two persons into a dispute between one of them and the Crown means, according to Shearing and Stenning (1983:9), that victim neglect is not a "minor deficiency" in the justice system but arises from a "fundamental feature". The state owns the conflict and the roles left to victims are; (1) to supply the system with raw material; (2) to give the evidence the system requires; and (3) to serve as a "ceremonial" or "symbolic presence" (Hagan, 1983:7) which legitimizes the mobilization of the law against the accused.

The fundamental policy objectives of the criminal justice system are based on a classical concept of society as a contract between a neutral arbitrating state and rational individuals. The state provides society and its members with a reasonable degree of security, and ensures just treatment for the accused (Griffiths et al., 1980:6). Punishments must be established if the sovereign is to "defend the public liberty, entrusted to his care, from the usurpation of individuals" (Vold, 1979:24), and they must be fixed, known and in relation to the crime. These policy objectives ignore the victim as such, other than as a member of society. The second objective implies, far from participation by the victim, a moderation and rationality in the punishment the accused might otherwise receive from those who believe themselves wronged. The resulting court process may be seen as a sort of morality play where certain values are publicly affirmed, certain conduct publicly denounced, and certain persons identified, blamed and rejected as "criminals". "The process uses accused persons to help define the relationship between the individual and the state" (Ericson & Baranek, 1982:215). Victims and their needs simply are not part of the script.

As the process has evolved, the chief power left to victims is the power not to surrender their conflict to the state — not to report the victimization. More than half of victims appear to exercise this right (Task Force, 1983:14). Once the state takes over, they lose virtually all other power. They have no right to testify, although they may do so if they are called by the Crown and if theirs is the uncommon case which goes to trial. Approximately up to 70% of cases are settled by a guilty plea. They have no right to express their views on bail or sentencing, though a judge or prosecutor is free to ask for them. They have no right to receive restitution, although they may in certain circumstances have a right to apply for it.

In the prosecution, the Crown represents the interests of the community, which may or may not coincide with the interest of the victims. The Crown must consider, for example, priorities on police time and court time for investigating and prosecuting, availability of evidence, chances of a conviction, public attitudes toward the offence, desirability of plea negotiations, the protection of the community and the rehabilitation of the offender. The victim has no way to challenge these Crown decisions.

Not only does the Crown have to consider wider concerns than those of the victim, but it can be argued that to seem to represent the victim, or to press the victims' claim, might prejudice the Crown's function as an impartial presenter of all the evidence. Indeed, for the Crown to give any assistance or status to the alleged victim, which would not be given to any witness, might compromise the rights of the accused. Even to equate the complainant with a victim could prejudge facts to be proved, for instance in a sexual assault case where consent is an issue.

## THE VICTIM MOVEMENT

Having been detached over the centuries from the prosecution process, some victims have organized to attempt to get back in. In the last few years such groups have mushroomed across North America. In Canada 28 groups claim 150 chapters in every province and 250,000 to 400,000 members (Toronto Star, 1984:1). Their numbers comprise an effective lobby, but are only a fraction of those eligible. Individual victims in Canada number at least 1.6 million a year. Organizational victims may be even more numerous: in a study by Hagan (1983:35) they made up two-thirds of a random sample.

A number of factors appear to be involved in the birth and growth of victim groups. First, is "a widespread and apparently increasing fear of crime" of which Taylor (1983:93) says "countless research studies" have provided evidence. The fear, partly justified and partly promoted by the media, is expressed in purchases of burglar alarms and double-locks, in self-defence classes, in private security patrols and programmes such as Neighbourhood Watch, and in victim groups.

Second, is the law and order movement, which argues that the criminal justice system is "soft on criminals", thereby turning them loose to create more victims. It supports more "rights" for victims to balance what it claims are too many rights for "criminals".

Third, is the women's movement, which began with advocacy and assistance for rape victims and in some jurisdictions achieved changes in statues and rules of evidence which provided more rights for victim-witnesses.

Fourth, is the self-help movement, growing out of the protest movements of the 1960's, which leads people who don't trust big government or bureaucracy to form their own groups to represent themselves.

Fifth, is the general humanitarian impulse to help people in trouble (and earn political points) which in other fields has led to worker compensation programmes or the motorists' unsatisfied judgement fund.

Victim advocacy groups differ in their concerns and their goals. Some complain most about neglect, carelessness and insensitivity from police and the courts. They can't find out what is happening in their case, they can't understand what goes on in court and they are not notified when their case is coming up or when it is settled. These groups want more information, more support services, more "sensitivity".

Others complain that victims cannot get restitution for their losses, or even get back their stolen property promptly. According to a 1976 survey in Alameda County, California (Karmen, 1984:148), 30% of victims never got back the stolen property used as evidence, 42% never learned the outcome of their case, and 61% of those eligible for the state's crime compensation fund were not informed of its existence. These victims want more effective compensation schemes and help in applying to them.

Still others such as Mothers Against Drunk Driving want stiffer laws for specific offences. And some want an active role in the prosecution process. They want to be acknowledged as a party to the proceedings, to be given access to the crown case, to be supplied with reasons for every decision, even given a veto on plea negotiations and sentence submissions. Donald Sullivan, spokesman for a Canadian conference of victims groups, says they want laws to give victims "a place in the courtroom" and rights in court "equal to those of the offender" (Toronto Star, 1985:2).

. . .

## PROPOSALS FOR CHANGE

It appears then that victims have almost no enforceable rights in the prosecution process. It also appears that they are excluded from any real rights in the process by its very nature as a conflict between the state and accused. Within those limits, several ways have been suggested to recognize and recompense the victim.

One is financial reparation. Three of the 79 recommendations of the Task Force deal with this. A second is a "victim impact" statement, to be requested before sentencing, the subject of another Task Force recommendation. A third is a "victims' advocate" who attempts to influence the prosecution process. Two such experiments have been tried in the United States (McDonald, 1976:153). In one a lawyer was employed as a "victim advocate" to attempt to influence the process through out-of-court negotiations. In the other, a volunteer group of victim advocates attended court hearings en masse for a time, until they tired of it, and claimed fewer charges were dismissed or remanded when they were present. The second programme raises questions about fairness to the accused. As Griffiths says (1980:32), "The prototype of community involvement . . . is the lynch mob". The first raises questions about who pays the advocate. If the victims pay, they may feel twice victimized. If the state pays, that may compromise its stance that the community, not the victim, is the injured party. In any case, such advocates have no standing in court since the victim is not one of the adversaries.

## RESTITUTION AND COMPENSATION

The Task Force proposals on reparation would; (1) amend s. 653 of the Criminal Code to require judges to consider restitution "in all appropriate cases" and to provide an opportunity for victims to make representation about their ascertainable losses; (2) empower the court to impose a jail term for wilful default on a restitution order; (3) amend s. 388 to raise its present limit on restitution for property damage from $50 to $500. Restitution as part of a probation order under s. 663 would continue unchanged.

"Whenever possible," the Task Force explains, "victims should be restored to the position they enjoyed prior to the victimization" (Task Force, 1983:35). The Law Reform Commission of Canada in its paper on Restitution and Compensation describes restitution as a "natural and just response" to the victim's plight which should be a "central consideration" in sentencing (Working Paper 5, 1974:6,8).

Yet such remedies for the victim already exist. Several sections of the Criminal Code make it possible for the court to order restitution. These remedies appear to be seldom used. While Canadian data are lacking (Burns, 1980:29), the Task Force thinks judges are "reluctant" to use them (Task Force, 1983:54). It does not explain why judges would be reluctant to use its new proposals.

Outside the criminal process, victims may apply to provincial crime injury compensation boards in all provinces except Prince Edward Island, or collect for property losses from private insurance, or file a civil suit both for property loss and for suffering and get judgement not only against the offender but, where negligence can be proved, against third parties.

. . .

The compensation schemes outside the criminal process are not well used either. They are usually limited to victims of violent crime but are available regardless of whether an offender has been identified or convicted. In Ontario, one in 55 eligible victims actually seeks compensation (Globe & Mail, 1984:2). A study of the New York and New Jersey schemes showed that fewer than 1% of all victims of violent crime even applied to the boards, and only 35% of those who applied were compensated (Elias, 1983:219).

As for the possibility of civil suit, Allen Linden reported that 1.5% of victims surveyed collected anything by suit, although 74.2% of those studied suffered some economic loss (Linden, 1968:29).

Whether or not restitution is a "natural response", there appear to be a number of reasons why judges are reluctant to use the existing provisions and legislators are reluctant to impose more effective ones ? reasons involving the criminal process, the objectives of sentencing, constitutional division of powers, and sometimes no doubt a combination of ignorance and inertia. Judge Cartwright of York County, in *Regina v. Kalloo* (Unreported; quoted in Moskoff, 1983:11), commented:

> "those few Crown counsel who are even aware of the existence of this section (653) which allows the victim of an indictable offence to apply for an order to satisfy loss or damage to property caused in the commission of a crime are equally indifferent to its application."

He went on to suggest that if the Attorney General were paid by commission on completed restitution orders, "blood would be flowing from stones" all over Ontario (Moskoff, 1983:11).

The difficulty of getting blood from stones, however, is one reason restitution orders are seldom made, and civil suit is often useless as well. In making restitution a condition of probation under s. 663(2)(e), a judge is bound to consider an offender's ability to pay. (He is not so bound under 2.653.) Observation of the courts indicates that many offenders, particularly against property, have neither jobs nor assets.

A further reason for caution is the Supreme Court of Canada ruling in *R. v. Zelensky* (1978; 2 C.R. (3d) 107 (S. C.C.)) that proceedings for restitution under s. 653 must not take on any character of a civil suit, and therefore the criminal court must not determine issues regarding the amount to be awarded. Restitution can be imposed, then, only when the amount is not in dispute, which Moskoff comments makes the section a "toothless tiger" (Moskoff, 1983:11). Burns comments that judges hesitate to order restitution under s. 663 as well, first because they fear using criminal law to enforce civil obligations, and second because they see it as suitable only for simple cases in which there is no dispute either over the amount involved or the offender's ability to pay (Burns, 1980:25).

In addition, a restitution order once made is hard to enforce. Those made under s. 653 must be enforced by the victim as a civil judgement, if the offender has assets and can be located. Those made under s. 663(2)(e) are intended to be monitored by probation officers. If the probation officers notice that payments have not been made, and if they decide to charge the offender with failure to comply with probation, and if the offender can be located, they must prove the offender "wilfully" defaulted. If they succeed, the maximum penalty is a $500 fine and/or six months in jail. Note that the victim is not the complainant in the enforcement procedure.

The most serious problem with restitution involves the nature of the criminal process. Civil wrongs have grown in law to be those for which injured persons seek their own monetary compensation. Criminal wrongs have become a public relationship between offenders and the state with a public response applied through penal sanctions. The historical tie between the two remains in the Criminal Code provisions for restitution (s. 653 and s. 663) which the Law Reform Commission describes as carry-overs "grudgingly grafted onto penal law to save the victim the expense of a civil suit" (Working Paper 5, 1974:9). They enable the victim to circumvent civil procedure by obtaining a criminal judgement, enforceable as if were civil, by a more expeditious and less expensive process. An example of the civil nature of s. 653 is that it comes into operation "on application" of the victim, not on the initiative of the court.

The British North America Act gives jurisdiction over criminal law and procedure to the federal parliament (1867:sect. 91(27)) but authority over property and civil rights to the provinces. This division, says Burns, means "an almost insurmountable obstacle to the establishment of efficient restitution systems in Canada" (1980:29).

Further, criminal courts are constituted to determine a persons's criminal responsibility, not his/her civil liability. The two have different standards of proof and different rules of evidence. For example, examination for discovery is a civil procedure not available in the criminal court. An accused person would not have the same safeguards around challenging a victim's claim for damages in criminal court than would be available in civil court. For the criminal court to try and make such a determination raises the danger of infringing on the powers reserved to the civil court. Widespread use of restitution orders might encourage use of the criminal courts as a collection agency, and lead to threatening prosecution to collect a debt.

A further set of problems arises because the focus in sentencing is not on what is pleasing to the victim but on what is good for the offender and for society. Though the Law Reform Commission say restitution as a "rational sanction" and the *Zelensky* decision accepted its "valid character" as part of the sentencing process, restitution cannot be argued in the criminal court on the basis that it would return the victim to wholeness or compensate for suffering. The only constitutional way to make the civil liability to the victim a valid part of the criminal sentence is to actively locate it within criminal law. The purpose which has been alleged is that it will deprive the offender of the fruits of crime, deter those who might hope to profit illegally, and facilitate the rehabilitation of the accused.

. . .

And finally, there are difficulties in implementing effective and just restitution schemes.

Crown attorneys will have discretion whether to recommend restitution, and judges will have discretion whether to order it. Can justice then be equal for offenders, or victims? The victims cannot "shop" for a judge who is known to make restitution orders.

Would the law fall unevenly on the person who steals $10 million and cannot possibly make restitution, and the person who steals $100 and can? If restitution is a correctional measure, imposed for the good of the offender, should it not then be imposed regardless of whether the victim has been paid for the loss by insurance?

Defence counsel often tell the court, in a bid for a more lenient sentence, that full or partial restitution has been made. If this does in fact result in leniency, does that mean that if a rich man and a poor man both break a window, and the rich man can afford to replace it, then he receives a less severe sentence than the poor man for the same offence?

What happens if there are several offenders? If one has no ability to pay, or reneges on payment, do the others pay more to make up the victim's total loss? Suppose there are multiple victims, and as part of plea negotiations some charges are dropped. Which victims are then to receive restitution?

Finally, if victims of crime are entitled to be restored to their original status, why not every victim? Why limit the recompense to those cases of property loss in which an offender can not only be identified, charged, convicted, and sentenced to make restitution but can actually pay damages?

Yet with all their flaws, restitution programmes (inside the criminal process) and compensation schemes (outside of it) have been legislated in many jurisdictions in the last 20 years. Though often underfunded, unadvertised and underused, obviously they have merits for lawmakers. For one, they enable governments faced with rising crime rates and rising public concern over crime to say, "Look what we're doing for the victims." Roger Meiners points out that large numbers of compensation pro-grammes were established at least in part as a palliative for increasing crime and relatively inefficient restitution (Meiners, 1978:9-44). Voters are told that something will be done for them when and if they are victimized and few will find out otherwise. Elias claims compensation has:

"justified strengthened police forces, provided political advantages to its supporters, facilitated social control of the population and yet substantially failed in providing most victims with assistance" (1983:213).

A second purpose is to keep the victim from demanding a real role in the prosecution process. As Hagan says, such programmes open the possibility of bringing the victim back into the system without actually doing it, symbolically conveying a sense of concern while doing little to alter the actual origin of the concern (1983:160).

## VICTIM IMPACT STATEMENTS

The other proposal of the Task Force, aside from restitution, to bring the victim back into the prosecution process was to amend the Criminal Code to "permit" the introduction of a victim impact statement "to be considered" at the time of sentencing (Task Force, 1983:157). Such a statement would presumably enable victims to tell the judge of their suffering and of any monetary loss as a result of the crime. Presumably they would then feel that somebody was paying attention to what happened to them.

At present nothing, except pressure of time, prevents a judge from asking to hear from a victim, or when ordering a pre-sentence report from asking that the victim be consulted. The intent of the Task Force proposal is to require the judge to request such a statement.

That proposal raises serious questions. To the degree that the statement dealt with monetary loss, it could be considered in assessing restitution as part of a sentence, subject to concerns already discussed about the purposes of sentencing and conflict with civil courts, particularly if the amount of the loss were in dispute. Questions arise whether the determination of loss would have to be based on receipts of appraisals, which might be difficult for some victims to produce; whether the statement would have to be sworn; whether it would be subject to contest by the accused, and if contested, whether the whole question would not then have to be referred to a civil court for adjudication.

To the degree that the statement dealt with pain or suffering, its usefulness would be questionable as long as the focus in sentencing is on the protection of society and the rehabilitation of the accused. A shut-in widow whose television set is stolen may suffer more from its loss than the wealthy bachelor who is seldom home, but that should weigh less with the judge than the characteristics of the offence, the previous record of the offender and the perceived need to deter such behaviour in the community. If the purpose of the sentence is to rehabilitate the offender, then its nature should be determined by presumed experts. If its purpose is deterrence, then it should be certain and predictable, not subject to modification by the victim. If the purpose is retribution, then the punishment must fit the crime rather than the victim (Karmen, 1984:155).

Then there is the problem of how the statement will be submitted. Ninety-eight percent of cases are concluded in the provincial courts (Griffiths et al., 1980:146) and about 70% of these without a trial (Griffiths et al., 1980:147). Dockets are crowded, hearings are rushed and pre-sentence reports are rare. If the victim is not present when the accused pleads guilty, how often will judges be willing to delay sentence to hear from the victim?

Perhaps too, it is only an assumption that many victims really want this input, or any input, into their cases. A Philadelphia judge, Lois Porer, who routinely offers victims a chance to speak on sentence, says they seldom do (Karmen, 1984:230). Since victim impact statements were legislated in Connecticut in 1981, only 3% of victims appear at sentence hearings (Karmen, 1984:231). When as an experiment victims were invited to take part in plea-bargaining sessions on their cases in Dade County, Florida, only a third attended. Those who were present generally spoke only in answer to questions, approved what the professionals suggested and were "passive and docile" (Heinz & Kerstetter, 1980:172).

## RESISTANCE TO CHANGE

Having looked at the "rights" of the victim in the prosecution process and at proposals to give victims a larger role, it remains to ask: would these proposals, or any proposals, make any real difference in the conduct of the courts?

As we have seen, restitution is seldom ordered. Compensation schemes are seldom used. The majority of victims do not accept the limited opportunities to participate which are offered to them. It is not clear whether the last is because they don't care, or because they don't think it will make any difference, or because as the Dade County study suggests the system is not diligent in notifying them of opportunities (Heinz & Kerstetter, 1980:173).

One of the reasons advanced for helping victims is to encourage them to cooperate with the system in reporting more victimizations. In the United States, the percentage of incidents of violence which were reported to police went from 46% in 1973 to 47% in 1981, and of household burglaries from 47% in 1973 to 51% in 1981, despite the launching of numerous victim-assistance programmes during that period (Karmen, 1984:168).

After reviewing a decade of action and advocacy on behalf of victims in the United States, Weigend concluded it had generated "much rhetoric, more knowledge . . . but little change" (1983:91).

Criminal justice systems are like any bureaucracy. They operate in their own interests. They are subject to what Karmen calls "goal displacement" (1984:169), which means that they substitute for the official goals of doing justice and serving the public, the unofficial goals of getting through the workload expeditiously, covering up mistakes and making themselves look as essential as possible so funding won't be cut. As King points out:

"Imagine for example the approach of the victim of a serious crime. He wishes to see the offender punished and deterred from further offences. Now compare that approach with that of a court administrator, whose major concern is the efficient running of the system, clearing the workload for the day and avoiding any unnecessary delays ... The one looks to the magistrate to revenge his loss ... and to compensate him, the victim, while the other looks at his watch and wonders how long the case is going to last and whether the morning list will be completed by one o'clock" (1981:13-14).

A place for victims in the prosecution process is limited to one that does not interfere with the smooth working of the system or the privileges and convenience of its principles.

Most reforms, as we have seen, seem to be intended to inform or assist or conciliate the victim, and these are worthy goals, but they involve no real rights or participation.

. . .

## CONCLUSION

. . .

What would we do if we were really serious about helping victims of crime? We would fund adequately and advertise widely a government-supported compensation fund. It would not be funded, as is often suggested, by convicted offenders, for that would imply that offenders are a distinct group and would hold all in that group, who happened to be caught, liable for the damage inflicted by some. Rather it might be funded like medical insurance (one might contribute to OHIP and to VICE — Victims Insurance (against) Criminal Enterprises), recognizing first, that there are more offenders than ever that are caught; second, that the definition of which acts are crimes and therefore which persons are offenders is made by society and changes from time to time; and third, that society has an obligation to those who suffer from one of its inevitable features. We would allow compensation both for material loss and for pain and suffering, and whether or not an offender has been identified. Yes, there would be cheating, just as people cheat now on claims for private insurance. But if private insurers live with that risk, surely a public scheme can.

## References
* Beattie, J., 1986 "Administering Justice Without Police; Criminal Trial Procedure in Eighteenth Century England", in R. Donelan (Ed.), The Maintenance of Order in Society: A Symposium. Ottawa: Canadian Police College (forthcoming).
* Burns, P., 1980 Criminal Injuries Compensation. Vancouver: Butterworths.
* Christie, N., 1977 "Conflicts as Property", British Journal of Criminology, Vol. 1.
* Christie, N., 1982 Limits to Pain. Oxford: Martin Robertson.
* Elias, R., 1983 "Symbolic Politics of Victim Compensation", Victimology, Vol 18.
* Ericson, R.V. & Baranek, P.M., 1982 The Ordering of Justice: A Study of Accused Persons as Dependents in the Criminal Process. Toronto: Butterworths.
* Federal-Provincial Task Force, 1983 Justice for Victims of Crime. Ottawa: Ministry of Supply and Services.
* Globe & Mail, 1985 "Subway Vigilante Describes Shooting in New York". Toronto, Jan 3.
* Globe & Mail, 1984 "Justice Secretary Proposes Fund Finances by Convicted Offenders". Toronto, April 10.
* Griffiths, C.T. et al., 1980 Criminal Justice in Canada. Toronto: Butterworths.

- Hagan, J., 1983 Victims Before the Law: The Organizational Domination of Criminal Law. Toronto: Butterworths.
- Heinz, A.M. & Kerstetter, W.A., 1980 "Victim Participation in Plea Bargaining: A Field Experiment", in W.F. McDonald and J.A. Cramer (Eds.) Plea Bargaining. Lexington, Mass. : D.C. Heath.
- Holdsworth, J., 1909 A History of English Law. Vol. II, Part II, Section II. London: Methuen.
- Hudson, J. & Galway, B., 1975 Considering the Victim: Readings in Restitution and Victim Compensation. Springfield Ill.: Charles Thomas.
- Karmen, A., 1984 Crime Victims: An Introduction to Victimology. Monterey: Brooks/ Cole.
- King, M., 1981 The Framework of Criminal Justice. London: Croom Helm.
- Klein, J., 1978 "Revitalizing Restitution: Flogging a Horse that May Have Been Killed for a Just Cause:", Criminal Law Quarterly, Vol. 20.
- Law Reform Commission of Canada, 1974 Working Paper 5: Restitution and Compensation. Ottawa: Information Canada.
- Linden, A.M., 1968 Report of Osgoode Hall Study on Compensation for Victims of Crime. Toronto: Osgoode Hall Law School.
- McDonald, W.F., 1976 Criminal Justice and the Victim. Beverly Hills: Sage.
- Meiners, F., 1978 Victims Compensation: Economic, Legal, and Political Aspects. Toronto: D.C. Heath.
- Moskoff, F., 1983 "Compensation and Restitution as Part of the Criminal Process", Advocates Society Journal, Vol. 10.
- Shearing, C.D. & Stenning, P.C., 1983 Private Security and Public Justice: The Challenge of the 80's. Montreal: Institute for Research on Public Policy.
- Taylor, I., 1983 Crime, Capitalism, and Community. Toronto: Butterworths.
- Toronto Star, 1985 "Crime Victims — Conference Approves Organization of National Lobby Groups", Feb. 11.
- Toronto Star, 1984 "Victims of Violence: Too Many to Ignore", Nov 11.
- Vold, G.B., 1979 Theoretical Criminology. New York: Oxford.
- Weigend, T., 1983 "Problems of Victim-Witness Assistance Programs", Victimology, Vol. 3.
- Weiler, D. & Desgagne, J.D., 1984 Victims and Witnesses of Crime in Canada: Ottawa: Ministry of Supply and Services.
- Zelensky, R.V. et al., 1978 2 C.R. (3rd) 197 (S. C.C.).

## HIGHLIGHTS OF BILL C-79

Highlights of Bill C-79, the *Victims of Crime Act*, passed June 1999, by the federal government, and excerpted from the *Backgrounder* to the bill, published by the Department of Justice in April 1999:

### Preamble

The preamble to the *Act to amend the Criminal Code (Victims of Crime)* gives concrete expression to Parliament's commitment to respond to the concerns of victims of crime. It highlights the need to reconcile the rights of victims and witnesses with the rights of the accused and to ensure that victims and witnesses are treated with courtesy, compassion and respect. The preamble also underscores that the views and concerns of victims of crime should be taken into account, particularly with respect to decisions that have an impact on their safety, security and privacy.

## Victim Surcharge on Offenders

A victim surcharge is an additional penalty imposed on offenders at the time of sentencing. It is collected by the provincial and territorial governments, and used to provide programs, services and assistance to victims of crime within their jurisdiction.

Proposed amendments would:

- make the victim surcharge automatic to ensure it is applied consistently to all offenders, except where the offender demonstrates undue hardship;
- change the amounts of the surcharge to provide mandatory, minimum amounts. Currently, the surcharge is an amount up to 15% of a fine, where a fine is imposed, and up to $35 for other dispositions. Under the proposed legislation, the surcharge amounts will be:
  - 15% of any fine imposed on the offender;
  - if no fine is imposed, $50 in the case of an offence punishable by summary conviction and $100 in the case of an offence punishable by indictment; or
  - an increased surcharge, at the discretion of the judge, in appropriate circumstances.

The victim surcharge revenue will continue to remain in the jurisdiction within which it is collected and will continue to be used for victim services, programs and assistance provided by provincial and territorial governments.

## Victim Impact Statements

A victim impact statement is a written statement prepared by the victim and considered by the court at the time of sentencing of an offender. It allows victims to participate in the proceedings by describing the impact of the crime on them and their families. Proposed amendments would:

- ensure that the victim is permitted to read an impact statement at the time of sentencing if he or she wishes to do so. At present, a judge is required to consider the written statement but allowing the victim to read it is discretionary;
- require the judge to ask, before imposing sentence, whether the victim has been informed of the opportunity to prepare a victim impact statement;
- authorize adjournments to permit a victim to prepare a statement or to submit other evidence to the court about the impact of the crime;
- require that victim impact statements be considered by courts and Review Boards following a verdict of not criminally responsible on account of mental disorder; and
- clarify that at proceedings to determine whether an offender sentenced to life in prison should have his or her parole eligibility reduced (s. 745.6 hearings), the information provided by the victim may be oral or written. At present, the *Criminal Code* provides

that any information provided by the victim will be considered; however, in practice, some victims have been discouraged from making an oral statement.

## Consideration of Victim's Safety in Bail Decisions

Proposed amendments would:

- ensure that the responsible judicial officer (officer in charge, justice of the peace or judge) considers the safety and security of the victim in any decision about an accused's bail;
- where an accused is released pending trial, require the judge to consider including as a condition to bail that the accused abstain from any direct or indirect communication with the victim and any other condition necessary to ensure the safety and security of the victim; and
- ensure that the particular concerns of the victim are considered and highlighted in decisions on the imposition of special bail conditions, including in firearms prohibitions and in criminal harassment offences.

## Facilitating Testimony

Proposed amendments would:

- extend to victims of sexual or violent crime up to 18 years of age protections which restrict personal cross . . . examination by self . . . represented accused persons by providing for the appointment of counsel to conduct the cross . . . examination;
- permit a victim or witness with a mental or physical disability to have a support person present while giving testimony;
- clarify that s. 486(3), which provides for a publication ban on the identity of sexual offence complainants, will protect their identity as victims of sexual offences as well as any other offences perpetrated on them by the accused; and
- permit a judge to restrict publication of the identity of a wider range of victims or witnesses where the victim has established a need for such an amendment and where the judge considers it necessary for the proper administration of justice.

## Information About Life Sentences

Proposed amendments would:

- require a judge to state for the record and for the benefit of surviving victims that an offender convicted of murder who has received a life sentence may apply for a reduction in the number of years before he or she is eligible to apply to a court for parole after serving at least 15 years of the sentence; and
- clarify that at proceedings to determine whether an offender should have his or her parole eligibility reduced (s. 745.6 hearings), the information provided by the victim may be oral or written, at the option of the victim. At present, the *Criminal Codep* provides that any information provided by the victim will be considered; however, in practice, some victims have been discouraged from making an oral statement.

## Questions/Discussion
1. What are the needs of the victims of crime and how should they be met? Which of

these needs have been met to date and how? What "gaps" remain in the provision of services?

2.   What is the proper role of victims of crime in the criminal justice system? What roles do victims currently play in the system and how would you change those roles?

3.   What is the role of the state in responding to the needs of the victims of crime? Should the state be fully responsible for preventing crime and repairing the damages caused by crime or should the state limit itself to the role of arresting and convicting offenders and extracting compensation from them for their crimes? What is the philosophical basis of your position?

### Further Reading

* Berthiaume, Michelle, *The Influence of Victims' Advocacy on Criminal Justice Policy: The Case of CAVEAT* (M.A. Thesis, Carleton University, Ottawa, Canada, 2001).
* Burns, P., *Criminal Injuries Compensation* 2nd Edition (Toronto: Butterworths, 1992).
* Canadian Resource Centre for Victims of Crime, *Balancing the Scales: The State of Victims' Rights in Canada* (Ottawa: Canadian Resource Centre for Victims of Crime, 1998).
* Cohen, Shaughnessy, *Victims' Rights: A Voice, Not a Veto: Report of the Standing Committee on Justice and Human Rights* (Ottawa: House of Commons, 1998).
* Cooley, D., "Criminal Victimization in Male Federal Prisons" (1993), 35 Canadian Journal of Criminology 479-495.
* Langer, R., "Battered Women and the Criminal Injuries Compensation Board: Re A.L." (1991), 55 Saskatchewan Law Review 453-465.
* Murphy, R., "Compensation for Victims of Crime: Trends and Outlooks" (1982), 8 Dalhousie Law Journal 530.
* Normandeau, A., "Pour une Charte des Droits des Victimes d'Actes Criminels" (1983), 2 Revue de Science Criminel et de Droit Pénal Comparé 209.
* Roach, Kent, *Due Process and Victims' Rights: The New Law and Politics of Criminal Justice* (Toronto: University of Toronto Press, 1999).
* Roach, Kent, "Crime Victims and Substantive Criminal Law" in Don Stuart, R.J. Delisle and Allan Manson, eds., *Towards a Clear and Just Criminal Law: A Criminal Reports Forum* (Toronto: Carswell, 1999).
* Skurka, S., "Two Scales of Justice: The Victim as Adversary" (1993), 35 Criminal Law Quarterly 334-354.
* Victims Symposium, "Perspectives on Proposals for a Constitutional Amendment Providing Victim Participation in the Criminal Justice System" (1987), 34 The Wayne Law Review 1.
* Young, A., "Two Scales of Justice: A Reply" (1993), 35 Criminal Law Quarterly 355-375.

## 4.5  THE ACCUSED

### Introduction

In this section we look at several issues in regard to the ways in which an accused is "selected" for involvement in the criminal process. Obviously, not everyone who commits an offence as defined by the *Criminal Code* or other legislation is processed through the system—many are never reported or caught, many are ignored by the authorities, and many are diverted either informally (*e.g.*, when a young offender is let off with a warning by the police officer) or formally (through various state-sanctioned diversion schemes). What is important is why some offenders are processed through the system while others are not. Why are some people labelled criminals while others have no record whatsoever attached to their name? Such questions speak to the fairness, effectiveness and equality of the system. While we will never have and do not want 100 per cent enforcement and prosecution, we want to ensure that all offenders are treated the same according to reasons based on considerations of law and policy, and not, for example, on the individual biases of a state agent, the social status or race of the offender, or the systemic biases of the system as a whole.

The two readings below examine these issues in different ways. The Mitchell reading looks at the variety of ways in which individuals become offenders and enter the criminal process, while the subsequent excerpt from the "Justice and the Poor" report specifically examines the ways in which the socio-economic status of the individual affects the likelihood of becoming an accused.

## Selecting Accused: Characteristics of the Offender

*Chet Mitchell*

Accused are selected primarily by the nature of the criminal offence created and the social context in which offenders operate. We will compare in this regard three different types of offences: acquisitive crime, violent crime and vice crimes.

Rude's study (1985) of criminals and victims in early nineteenth century England provides some examples of the first type of offence: from 1805-1850 in England up to 80 percent of all crimes involved larceny. During a period when London police took 71,000 people into custody only six were tried for murder and less for rape or robbery. Crimes of violence were rare. Instead, common larcenists stole very common items — mostly food, clothing and household goods (Id.:10). In London, the typical larceny was an "inside job" by a servant or an employee. Not surprisingly in these conditions most offenders were classified by the court records as "labourers", with "gentlemen" comprising a mere 0.2% of convicted criminals. Gentlemen obviously did not need to take food or firewood from each other or steal their servants' meagre belongings. This does not imply that gentlemen refrained from criminal activities, merely that they did not commonly commit the sort of offences which resulted in police action. Assaults and other offences against servants may have been common but these would tend to be compensated, hushed up or left unreported for fear of reprisal and job loss.

Cesare Lombroso (1835-1909) made detailed anatomical measurements of Italian convicts searching for the physical and mental characteristics indicative of the "born criminal". Lombroso made two major errors: he failed to employ control groups which would have demonstrated that even paragons of official virtue had retreating foreheads and highly developed frontal sinuses or other criminal "traits", and he failed to account for those "criminals" not in prison because their social status or type of offence precluded criminal prosecution. Later, Goring in England and Hooton in the U.S. noted that "criminals" tended to be biologically inferior, shorter in stature and lighter in weight than average but again their work ignored the legal process by which offenders are "selected" by legislators, police, prosecutors, judges and juries. In modern acquisitive crimes such as tax evasion some studies indicate a greater or lesser propensity to offend depending on personal factors such as age and gender but it is generally recognized that opportunity is the major determinant. Self-employed persons such as farmers, waiters, plumbers, investors or artists evade tax far more often than employed persons whose tax is withheld at source by their employers (Mitchell, 1985). Since tax evasion is common and widespread and since the offenders' motives are so well-understood, forensic psychologists do not usually seek out personal flaws to explain the behaviour of tax evaders.

A different picture emerges when we turn to the violent and full-time offender who transgresses against norms common to every society, norms that prohibit theft, murder, assault, fraud and robbery. To begin with, serious crimes are perpetrated primarily by young men. Most apprehended property offenders are teenagers; the age peak for violent offences is the early twenties. Few serious crimes involve persons over forty years of age. Serious crimes are extreme examples of unethical or diseconomic behaviours and they are unethical, as noted, because they by-pass voluntary exchange mechanisms and thus take the shortest possible route to satisfaction. Logically, it should then follow that committed criminals in the conventional sense should exhibit an exaggerated degree of self-centredness. Wilson and Herrnstein (1985) found that the two personality traits most clearly associated with delinquency and crime are impulsiveness and contempt for others. These authors argue that foreshortened time horizons and relative lack of concern about approval render some people insensitive to social incentives (such as employment rewards and legal penalties) and unwilling to defer gratification. Samenow (1984) made a lengthy and detailed study of habitual and violent criminals for whom serious crime was a way of life, not an occasional aberration, and he concluded that such persons thought and behaved in similar ways. They demanded loyalty from family but were themselves completely disloyal; they felt contempt for their parents' advice and authority regardless of parental social status; they felt entitled to whatever they could grab or steal; they were profoundly anti-work and consistently irresponsible in almost every aspect of their lives. According to Samenow, if one counted every arrestable act committed by a typical forty year old career criminal "the toll would climb into the tens of thousands of crimes" (Id.:114).

Samenow's work is primarily descriptive and is noteworthy because of its accuracy and perception. It does not explain why one child in a family of four siblings happens to possess a "criminal personality" while the other children do not. Nor does it employ a control group in the sense of searching among people earning a legitimate living to find cases of the same extreme self-centredness unaccompanied by violence and crime. Wilson and Herrnstein (1985) do sketch out a tentative theory of crime causation noteworthy in part because it opposes conventional criminological wisdom which attributes crime to the social environment. In contrast, Wilson and Herrstein argue that once the influence of personality traits, family socialization and early school experiences are taken into account there is not much left to explain about serious offenders. Absent from their list are later influences such as employment rates, neighbourhoods, income level and peer influence.

Finally, theorizing a "criminal personality" does not foreclose a sociological analysis of crime. According to Beauchamp (1980) deviation from behavioral norms tends to follow a common pattern whether one examines alcohol intake, driving or serious crime. For example, with alcohol most people are abstainers or light users. Deviating from this norm are a smaller group who drink regularly and a much smaller group who consume very large quantities of the drug. As a result of this pattern, 10 percent of alcohol users consume more than 50 percent of all alcohol. Rule or law deviation appears to follow a similar distribution and again the small minority of extreme rule breakers commit the majority of all offences. Following Allports' work on conforming behaviour Beauchamp (Id.:109) argues that the distribution of conformity with a law or norm is unimodal and heavily weighted toward compliance:

> [T]he great majority of individuals conformed rather closely to the rule; a smaller group broke the rule noticeably and barely conformed; and, finally, a very small group flagrantly ignored the rule. Allport noted that when compliance was monitored (such as when a policeman is stationed at the intersection where the stop sign was located) the rate of conformity increased, with the rate of non-conformity and violation declining.

While alcohol users' physiology, age, sex and training play a part in their becoming heavy users a critical sociological factor is the per capita rate of intake of the entire population. If the total amount of alcohol consumption declines there is a concurrent decrease in the alcoholic intake of extreme users, a change that obviously occurs apart from any individualistic determinants. In other words, personal characteristics and circumstances affect who will be an extreme criminal or an alcohol abuser but general or sociological factors affect the quantity and the type of crime committed, as well as its style and severity. Wilson (1984:472) for example, traces the appearance of the grudge-against-society murderer back to Pierre Francois Lancenaire in 1834. Influenced by Rousseau, Lancenaire became a minor celebrity composing his *Memoirs* in prison and blaming "Society" for his murders and robberies. While the intelligent, articulate murderer is a familiar contemporary figure both in fact and in fiction (starting perhaps with Dostoevsky's *Crime and Punishment* in 1866) such crimes and criminals would probably have been impossible or incomprehensible to feudal societies.

Biased offender selection is most pronounced in the area of vice offences usually because the offence is designed legislatively or interpreted by police to regulate certain class, gender, or occupational subgroups. Two examples will illustrate the process from opposite sexual biases: prostitution and narcotics.

England's *Street Offences Act* of 1959 in subsection 1(1) prohibits a woman loitering or soliciting publicly for the purpose of sexual prostitution. In 1984 there were 8,836 prosecutions under this subsection (Edwards, 1987:43). Imprisonment for this offence was abolished in 1983 but a significant number of women offenders under this and other Acts, are still imprisoned for defaulting on fines. In England, as elsewhere, Parliament and police are preoccupied with the streetwalker whereas male customers and managers ("pimps") are either outside the law or rarely prosecuted.

This bias is exaggerated in England because males are not liable to prosecution under subsection 1(1), only women are affected. The *Sexual Offences Act* provided, for the first time in 1985, a measure that criminalized "persistent soliciting" by customers (always men) seeking prostitutes. Canada followed Britain's lead in outlawing brothels, thereby forcing prostitutes into street soliciting in the first place and putting female-operated houses out of business. The stage was thus set for male managers and organized crime to exploit prostitutes and for the women to suffer from increased vulnerability from customers, managers and policemen. Comparing the police dynamics of chasing organized crime or street solicitors Edwards (Id.:56) notes that "evidence sufficient to convict a streetwalker is comparatively easy to obtain, being merely the word of two police officers "whereas convicting the manager of a club or massage parlour for procuring requires several days police observation" so higher, cheaper conviction rates are achieved by focussing on prostitutes.

In their study of Canadian cannabis convictions under the *Narcotic Control Act,* Boyd, Lowman and Mosher (1987) discovered inequalities between offenders by jurisdiction, sex and age. Between 1976 and 1981 when the average conviction rate per 100,000 population was 103, the rate in Quebec was 69 and in Alberta was 350. More striking was the discrimination correlated with gender. Between 1956-65 about 33 percent of persons convicted under the NCA were female, whereas by 1970 this proportion had fallen to seven percent. Now, the ratio of males to females convicted pursuant to the NCA is about twelve to one with a specific emphasis on young men: "it is male youth without access to private space who are disproportionately subject to the control of the criminal law . . . It is the [cannabis] user and the context of that use that are controlled, not use or possession per se" (Id.:27).

## Bibliography

- Beauchamp, D.E., *Beyond Alcoholism — Alcohol and Public Health Policy* (Philadelphia: Temple University Press, 1980.
- Blumberg, A. "The Practice of Law as a Confidence Game: Organizational Cooperation of a Profession" (1967), 1 Law Society Review 15.
- Boyd, N., *et al.*, "Case Law and Drug Convictions: Testing the Rhetoric of Equality Rights" (1987), Criminal Law Quarterly 487.
- Edwards, S. M., "Prostitutes: Victims of Law, Social Policy and Organized Crime", in P. Carlen and A. Worral, eds., *Gender, Crime and Justice* (London: Open University Press, 1987).
- Mitchell, C.N., "Willingness to Pay: Taxation and Taxation Compliance" (1985), 15 Memphis State University Law Review 127.
- Rude, G., *Criminal and Victim: Crime and Society in Early Nineteenth Century England* (Oxford: Clarendon Press, 1985).
- Samenow, S., *Inside the Criminal Mind* (New York: Times Books, 1984).
- Wilson, C., *A Criminal History of Mankind* (New York: G.P. Putnam's, 1984).
- Wilson, J.Q., and Herrnstein, R.J., *Crime and Human Nature* (New York: Simon and Schuster, 1985).

## Justice and the Poor*

### The National Council of Welfare

*Excerpts from The National Council of Welfare, *Justice and the Poor* (Ottawa: Minister of Public Works and Government Services Canada, 2000) at 4-7; 8-16; 19-20; 23; 24-25; 26-27; 52-53; 54-56.

## THE POLICE AND THE POOR

*Crime and delinquency are "found" among the poor because that is where they are sought.*

W.K. Greenaway

Police services are the most important element of the criminal justice system. In financial terms, they account for 60 percent of all government spending on justice, while expenses on correctional services account for 25 percent, followed by courts at 9 percent, and legal aid at 6 percent. The police are the most crucial component of the system because they are the gatekeepers, the ones whose decisions to arrest and to lay charges draw people into the criminal justice process. When police decisions are biassed in ways that bring too many low-income people before the courts, it is inevitable that those who are tried and convicted and sentenced are also disproportionately poor.

. . .

To determine whether law enforcement discriminates against low-income people, Canadian criminologist Thomas Gabor suggests we start by asking who breaks the law.

### Who Commits Crimes?

Until the 1960s, it was widely assumed that poverty bred crime and that most crimes were committed by young men with lower-class backgrounds. This assumption was based on statistics showing that the majority of those who were arrested, convicted, and imprisoned were then, as they are now, males under the age of 25 from families in which the parents had little education and low incomes and held inferior jobs or no jobs at all. To account for this, criminologists developed many explanations. One was the social disorganization theory, which said that specific neighbourhood conditions, such as poverty, high mobility and multi-ethnicity, caused a breakdown of traditional values which led to crime. Another was the opportunity theory, according to which lower-class people were more likely to engage in crime because they were blocked from achieving financial success by legal means.

Everyone was therefore surprised in the 1960s when U.S. researchers discovered that criminal behaviour was not linked exclusively to lower-status people and poor neighbourhoods. Using self-report studies, which asked (mostly young) participants to reveal, in total confidence and without fear of punishment, what illegal actions they had committed, researchers made two shocking discoveries.

First of all, the vast majority of all male adolescent participants reported having committed illegal acts that could have landed them before youth courts. Girls were much less likely to engage in illegal behaviour. When Canadian criminologist Marc LeBlanc questioned 3,000 young Montrealers, he found that more than 90 percent had committed delinquent acts in the previous year, and that more than 80 percent had contravened the Criminal Code. The most common offences were shoplifting, vandalism, driving a car under the influence of alcohol or taking mild drugs, especially marijuana. Nine percent had committed more serious crimes such as robbery.

The second surprise was that the children of parents with professional jobs were as likely to report having committed illegal acts as the children of poorer parents with low-status jobs. Contrary to the strong link between crime and social class of origin that had been taken for granted until then, it seemed that they were not related at all.

. . .

Most experts now agree that the social status and income of the parents have little or no direct effect on the likelihood that children will turn to delinquency, although they may in some cases have indirect effects by amplifying life problems that can lead to crime. For example, children with learning difficulties whose parents have little education and whose inner-city schools offer inadequate remedial programs may get less help with their problems than similar children with better-educated parents in more affluent neighbourhoods with better schools. This can result in more children from poor backgrounds doing badly at school, and it has been established that there is a strong association between school failure and the likelihood of becoming a repeat offender, to the point where school performance in adolescence is one of the best predictors of both juvenile delinquency and adult criminality.

Research has found that the children most at risk of becoming delinquents and criminals face the following circumstances:

> (1) they receive little love, affection, or warmth, and are physically or emotionally rejected and/or abandoned by their parents; (2) they are inadequately supervised by parents who fail to teach them right and wrong, who do not monitor their whereabouts, friends, or activities, and who discipline them erratically and harshly; and (3) they grow up in homes with considerable conflict, marital discord, and perhaps even violence . . . Families at greatest risk of delinquency are those suffering from limited coping resources, social isolation, and (among parents) poor parenting skills.

Given the lack of resources and greater vulnerability of young people from disadvantaged backgrounds, it is a tribute to their parents that the differences in criminal behaviour between youths from lowincome and more affluent families are not evident. Two Ontario studies which looked at the family characteristics of incarcerated adolescents found that money worries played a minor role. Most prominent were physical abuse between the parents and toward the children, family breakdown with estranged fathers, and excessive drinking by the parents and the children.

Following the inconclusive findings of self-report studies on the relationship between crime and socioeconomic background, academic interest in this subject greatly diminished. By the early 1990s, criminologists were concentrating instead on other theories, such as the psychological or biological factors that are or may be associated with criminal personalities, the bad influence of delinquent friends, or the effects of policing methods on criminal behaviour.

While this research has been useful, criminologist John Hagan of the University of Toronto thinks it would be a serious mistake to assume that socioeconomic status makes no difference and to give up the search for the link between social characteristics and crime. Hagan points out that although the relationship between the social status of the parents and crime is very weak, it has been demonstrated that the personal status of older youths and adults, particularly their own job situation, is clearly related to criminal behaviour. Unemployed men, whatever their family backgrounds, are more likely to be involved in crimes against property, such as theft and breaking and entering. What has not been established is whether unemployment leads to crime or the other way around.

Most likely, crime and unemployment form a vicious circle. A Quebec survey of employers found that having a criminal record can drastically reduce one's chances of finding a job: 58 percent would not hire someone who had just been released from a penitentiary, even if the applicant had all the qualifications for the position. Larger employers were even less likely than small ones to want to hire people with criminal records. Most important, the consequences of past dealings with the criminal justice system are much more severe for people from lower-class backgrounds than for those whose families are better off. This is because lower-class ex-offenders are more stigmatized and are less likely to have family connections to find them jobs that enable them to forget the past and start a new life.

. . .

Do these studies of street youth confirm the old theory that poverty breeds crimes? Yes, in the sense that immediate and extreme poverty leads people to do anything to meet their basic needs. On the other hand, the Toronto studies found no evidence that most young street criminals come from low-income families. There was some over-representation of street youths from families with unemployed heads: seven percent of the homeless kids, compared to two percent of school kids, had at least one unemployed parent. But the other 93 percent of street youths had parents whose occupations were similar to those of the parents of children still at school.

In the Prairie provinces, the studies showed that many Aboriginal people live in conditions of extreme poverty. They make up a large majority of adult skid row residents (including many released ex-offenders) and a majority of the runaways and street youth. However, Aboriginal street youths were arrested mostly for small thefts and for trivial or technical offences, such as failure to report to their probation officers. This is consistent with reports that in spite of their extremely high arrest rates, Aboriginal people show little criminal intent and commit mostly petty offences while under the influence of alcohol or to obtain alcohol.

. . .

Far away from life on the street, there has been an increasing awareness in the last few decades that official crime statistics immensely underestimate white-collar and corporate crimes. These include a huge range of offences, including tax fraud and bank embezzlement at the simpler end, and enormously complex corporate stock and securities fraud and antitrust violations at the other end, as well as numerous types of criminal negligence causing occupational injury or death. In her book about corporate crime in Canada, Laureen Snider writes that:

> Although corporate crime receives much less publicity than the assaults, thefts, and rapes most people think of when they hear the word "crime," it actually does more harm, costs more money, and ruins more lives than any of these. Corporate crime is a major killer, causing more deaths in a month than all the mass murderers combined do in a decade. Canadians are killed on the job by unsafe (and illegal) working conditions; injured by dangerous products offered for sale before their safety is demonstrated; incapacitated by industrial wastes released into the air or dumped into lakes and rivers; and robbed by illegal conspiracies that raise prices and eliminate consumer choice . . . Canadians are twenty-eight times more likely to be injured at work than by assault . . . People are 10 times more likely to be killed by conditions at their workplace than to be victims of homicide . . .
>
> Corporate crime . . . also causes staggering losses in financial terms . . . While the average robber in the United States nets $338, the average federally convicted white-collar criminal takes $300,000 . . . In a reverse Robin Hood process, antitrust offences and tax evasion transfer billions of dollars from the poor to the rich . . . All the street crime in a given year in the United States costs an estimated $4 billion, less than 5 percent of the average yield of corporate criminals.

Who commits these crimes? Certainly not the poor, or extremely few of them. The most common motive is not need, but greed. The more complex the crime, the more powerful and socially prominent the perpetrators tend to be. As they say, "The best way to rob a bank is to own one."

. . .

What are we to conclude from all this about the people who commit crimes in Canada? The answer appears to be that almost all Canadians break the law at some point in their lives, but that most of these illegal acts are not serious and are usually committed in adolescence. Among older youths and adults, those who commit most criminal offences are men who are at the extremes of the social spectrum. At one end are criminals who were not necessarily from poor families, but who are now without legitimate employment and sometimes destitute. They are most feared by the public and are responsible for a large share of common or street crimes. At the other end are higher-class, white-collar criminals, who are responsible for more deaths and steal much more money than the poor, but are seldom called criminals and are seldom condemned by a society in which many people believe that "greed is good."

## Who Do the Police Arrest and Charge for Crimes?

If it is so doubtful that most juvenile delinquents come from low-income families, why is it that studies throughout the world find that young people from poor families are massively overrepresented among those who are arrested, convicted or imprisoned for breaking criminal laws? And if higher-class criminals do considerably more harm to our society than poor criminals, why is it that prisons are so full of poor people that they could be called—to borrow an appropriate expression from a U.S. critic—our national poorhouses?

Part of the answer is that the illegal acts of more affluent youths and adults are much less likely to come to the attention of the authorities. In the relatively rare instances when well-off people are caught and charged, they are dealt with less harshly than poorer people who commit similar acts. These problems are aggravated by public attitudes and law enforcement policies and practices that directly or indirectly discriminate against the poor.

According to criminologist Maurice Cusson, the main reason delinquent boys from well-off families are much less likely to be arrested and found guilty of criminal acts is that affluent families can draw on many more resources than their poor counterparts. Cusson cites the example of Jean-Sébastien, the son of a rich businessman, who showed serious behaviour problems from birth. Sent to an exclusive school where he did badly, he stole money from classmates and was expelled with no charges laid. Back home, he stole large sums from both parents. In another private school for difficult children, he set fire to the building, which was totally destroyed. His parents reimbursed the school for the damages and no charges were laid, and they paid again when he stole the cashbox at his next school. And so on for many years until, as a last resort, Jean-Sébastien was finally sent to work on a cattle ranch owned by his uncle in South America, where he settled down and did all right.

The most striking aspect of this abbreviated story is that in spite of having committed dozens of illegal acts, including a very serious one—arson—Jean-Sébastien did not once appear before a judge. His family was always able to solve the problems by paying the victims and dissuading them from laying charges and by finding other private solutions for their son. If Jean-Sébastien had been born to poor parents in a poor neighbourhood, there is little doubt that he would have faced many judges and seen the inside of many detention houses.

. . .

When surveys of satisfaction with police services are done in poor neighbourhoods, they often find that residents feel both underpoliced and overpoliced. Complaints of too little policing are made by fearful citizens and victims of crime who feel that the police do not do enough, or react quickly enough to protect them from criminal acts. Witnesses who appeared before the Canadian Panel on Violence Against Women felt that calls for help about domestic violence which originate in public housing complexes are answered much more slowly than those originating from middle-class neighbourhoods. Women, and especially low-income older women, are most fearful about the possibility of becoming victims of crime and therefore most likely to want greater protection by the police.

One result of the greater dependence of poor people on the police is that low-income neighbourhoods produce a much greater volume of calls to the police than more affluent areas. Because of this, and because low-income neighbourhoods also produce higher arrest rates and higher official crime rates, it was assumed until quite recently that most crime victims were poor and that most crimes take place in urban, low-income, densely populated areas with transient populations and many single-parent families. Police authorities use these figures to make decisions about the deployment of police officers and resources to different parts of towns and cities, with the result that a disproportionate number of police patrols are assigned to poor areas.

Starting in the 1980s, these long-standing assumptions about poor neighbourhoods and crime were challenged by research findings demonstrating that calls to the police and official crime rates show only a tip of the crime iceberg. Victimization surveys done by Statistics Canada in 1982, 1988 and 1993 revealed that 24 percent of all Canadians over the age of 15 had been victims of at least one crime in the year before the surveys. The 1993 survey found that "90 percent of sexual assaults, 68 percent of assaults, 53 percent of robberies, 54 percent of vandalism, 48 percent of motor vehicle theft or attempted theft, and 32 percent of break-and-enters were not reported to the police." For wife assaults, it was estimated that less than seven percent were ever brought to the attention of the justice system. These rates of reporting crimes to the police are similar to those found in international surveys that included several European countries along with Canada and the United States.

. . .

According to Daniel Koenig, a sociologist at the University of Victoria, increasing the number of police officers can have the perverse effect of increasing the official crime rate. He points out that in Canada between 1962 and 1988, the rates of reported offences in many categories rose much faster than the increases in real offences as reported by victims, and that these increases in reported crimes followed increases in per-capita police strength. This suggests that increases in official crime rates mostly reflect changes in police activity, with additional police officers doing more investigations and generating more arrests for less serious offences.

Similarly, it was argued that the higher per-capita number of police officers in the North and in Saskatchewan is one of the causes of the disproportionate incarceration of Aboriginal people. This was demonstrated when some Aboriginal people who felt underpoliced requested that police detachments be established in their communities. The result was an almost instant "crime wave," with the police making arrests and laying charges for problems that were until then dealt with in other ways. This experience led analysts to conclude that the original problem was not so much underpolicing as under-servicing, and that what these communities really needed were alcohol and family violence workers, traditional healers, mental health workers, sexual abuse counsellors and the like instead of more police and more residents being sent to jail.

The equivalent happened to adolescents in the cities when police forces, reacting to public fears about youth crime, established youth gang units to concentrate even more on young people's activities:

> It does not stretch the imagination too far to deduce that the creation of special gang units will increase the amount of youth crime detected, and hence recorded, in the official statistics. Similarly, in a climate of concern about youth crime, the police will be more inclined to arrest than discharge the juveniles that they encounter on the street.

. . .

The most frequent targets of these "stop and frisk" operations are people who are considered menacing by local merchants and residents. This includes young people who look different or low-class (for example, with shaved heads or Mohawk hairdos, tattoos, torn jeans, eyebrow rings, leather and chains) or who visibly belong to groups that are perceived to be poor and to have higher official crime rates, such as Blacks and Aboriginal people. Given such intense police scrutiny, it is inevitable that the risk of being caught with a "joint" is considerably greater for an unemployed young "punk" from a low-income neighbourhood or for a Black or Aboriginal youth than for a white middle-class student who uses the same drug in the basement or backyard of his suburban home. Police officers admit that they harass young people who hang out without doing anything wrong because "We get calls to go break it up."

The problem was well illustrated in a large study which looked at the probability that marijuana users aged 18 and older would be arrested in three metropolitan areas of the United States. When participants were asked if they used the drug, students were far and away the most likely to say yes, followed by white-collar workers and then, very far behind, by blue-collar workers. Comparing this against arrest records in which possession of marijuana was the only charge, the researchers found that blue-collar users had by far the highest arrest rates, followed by student users and, far behind, by white-collar users. In addition, within each of the three categories, young users, Black users of all ages, and users with a prior arrest record were greatly overrepresented.

. . .

Social class and race can also make a difference in the treatment of female suspects by the police. Studies revealed that some police officers gave women the "chivalrous treatment," meaning that they were more lenient with women than men in similar circumstances. The main problem is that this benefited some female suspects more than others, in particular those who were middle- or upper-class, White, well groomed and apparently submissive, and who reacted by "crying, pleading for release for the sake of their children, claiming men have led them astray. " Women who did not fit this stereotype, who were not White, or who were drunk, unkempt, hostile or selling sex, were treated as harshly as men.

Attitude also affects police decisions on whether to arrest male suspects and charge them. Numerous studies in the U.S. and Canada found that in situations involving similar illegal acts and similar criminal records, disrespectful suspects were more likely to be arrested and charged than suspects with good social skills who showed deference toward police officers and contrition for their actions. When the police assess suspects' attitudes and manners, they are assessing them in a way that is prejudicial toward lower-class, immigrant and minority groups. The result is that White middle-class suspects, who are better educated and better informed, who are more likely to hire a lawyer and to initiate false arrest cases and libel suits against the police, are treated with greater care and tolerance and are almost never subjected to police violence. It was no coincidence that 52 of the 85 people who were bitten by unleashed police patrol dogs in Regina in 1981-82 turned out to be Aboriginal.

Police officers are notoriously intolerant of insolence and lack of respect, especially by young people. For them, disrespect means:

... not only physical aggression and other overtly hostile acts that threaten officers' safety, but also resistance in the form of actions or statements that merely challenge officers' authority or legitimacy (e.g., denying an officer's accusation or questioning an officer's judgment) and even passive acts of noncompliance (e.g., failing to respond to an officer's questions or requests) that imply that officers are "not taken seriously."

In a 1997 national survey, Canadian police officers deplored what they felt was an overall decline in the respect young people have for authority. As an example, they mentioned their frustration that "many of the young people they had come into contact with were aware of their rights and willing to flaunt this fact in the face of the police." Police experts write that some working-class people also have learned hostile or suspicious attitudes toward the police, which can lead to violent encounters when the police label them and treat them as "troublemakers" or "assholes" or "scum" In such situations, the underlying factor seems to be an expectation of trouble on both sides that turns into a self-fulfilling prophecy.

When such intolerant police attitudes are combined with racial or other stereotyping or anti-immigrant feelings—which are as common among police officers as among the working-class and lower-middle-class population from which most of them are drawn—the results can be explosive. This problem is most severe for Blacks and Aboriginal people, who combine being members of visible minorities, being among Canada's poorest groups, and having suffered centuries of injustice by authorities that have left them with feelings of fear, suspicion and hostility toward the police ("Black" refers to Canadians of African ancestry, 42 percent of whom were born in Canada.) . . .

The location of an illegal act also makes a difference in the police decision to charge, with a greater likelihood of charges being laid for the same offences when they are committed in low-income urban areas and, probably, on Aboriginal reserves.

. . .

Police expectations can provoke problems, according to Ottawa sociologist Dennis Forcese. "For example, in subsidized housing communities, with their concentration of . . . working-class tenants, the police generally expect trouble to occur, and often precipitate difficulties in a self-fulfilling way by a heavy-handed presence." Police attitudes can lead to very different exercises of police discretion. Depending on a police officer's expectations, a group of young people shouting in the street in the middle of the night can appear to be either normal kids on a night out who should indulgently be told to hush up, or dangerous members of an adolescent gang who should be taken to the station and charged with disturbing the peace.

One of the most crucial factors in the police decision on whether to charge suspects is whether they have police or court records. In research on juveniles in Ontario, this factor was even more important than the seriousness of the illegal acts committed, so that young people with a record who had committed a trivial offence were more likely to be charged than youths without a record who had committed a more serious act.

. . .

Finally, in addition to these police practices, there are at least two questionable government policies that increase the criminalization of the poor. The first is in the area of domestic abuse and concerns "mandatory charge" rules requiring police officers to make an arrest when there is some physical evidence that an assault has taken place, even if the victim does not want them to do so. These rules were adopted following research findings which suggested that arrest was the most effective way of deterring violence in these situations. Much discussion has taken place on many aspects of this policy, including criticisms that mandatory charges reduce women's options and increase their danger by driving family abuse underground because wives no longer dare to call the police.

. . .

The most recent research on the subject supports the view that for poor women at least, mandatory charging rules may do more harm than good. When all the studies are put together, the consensus among researchers is now as follows:

1.  Arrest reduces domestic violence in some cities, but increases it in others;
2.  Arrest reduces domestic violence among employed people, but increases it among the unemployed;
3.  Arrest reduces domestic violence in the short run, but can increase it in the longer run.

. . .

The other government policy that contributes in a major way to the criminalization of the poor is the U.S-inspired "war on drugs," in which intensive street-level police operations and vigorous prosecutions aim at imprisoning offenders no matter how small the amount of drugs involved. These campaigns have been condemned as "cynical fear-mongering" orchestrated by governments in order to gain public support with promises of restoring law and order, and to distract people from economic problems by scapegoating unpopular groups. The fears this produces in the population are further exploited by police forces seeking bigger budgets and by mass media that thrive on sensational stories about drugs and crime.

Since the mid-1980s, Canada has imitated the United States in making law enforcement its main strategy to control drug use. Experts agree that this "war on drugs" is futile in controlling drug use, as shown by the fact that the price of cocaine, the war's signature drug, which should have risen if dealing was becoming riskier and drugs less available, has instead continued to drop. In Canada, because marijuana is no longer imported but is now grown locally, its price has not changed in 20 years, leading some to note that a cannabis "high" now costs half the price of its equivalent in beer or wine. The only real impact of the drug war has been to imprison large numbers of low-income small suppliers and users, a disproportionate number of whom are Black.

. . .

Compared to all the law enforcement policies and practices for common crimes we have just seen, the law enforcement efforts directed toward uncovering and punishing white-collar and corporate offences are minuscule. Laureen Snider reports that in the 1980s, when government regulation was seen as an onerous burden which crippled free enterprise, agencies entrusted with controlling businesses were savaged in the United Kingdom, the United States and Canada. The result was a virtually risk-free atmosphere in which white-collar criminals thrived and business ethics plummeted.

. . .

The other enforcement difference is that white-collar and corporate offences are much less likely to be reported to the authorities than common crimes such as thefts, burglaries and assaults. Common crimes are usually reported to the police by victims, witnesses, neighbours and businesses, while others are discovered in routine police patrols. Many, if not most white-collar crimes never come to light at all because many of their victims, including the general public, consumers and the corporation's employees, often do not know they were victimized, do not have the resources to unravel complex conspiracies, or blame themselves for having been taken in by clever scams.

When corporate crimes are uncovered, they are most likely to be hushed up and handled internally. Employers are often reluctant to lay charges against employees who embezzled their funds or defrauded them. They are afraid it will make them look bad, or think it is not worth the time and expense involved in testifying and participating in criminal investigations. For obvious reasons, corporate crimes that benefit companies are seldom reported. On the contrary, in the last few decades an increasing number of managers "complained of superiors' pressure to support incorrect viewpoints, sign false documents, overlook superiors' wrongdoing, and do business with superiors' friends." While increasing the pressure from the top, company executives also learn to look the other way so that when a long-standing consumer fraud is uncovered or an unsafe mine finally collapses and kills workers, they can avoid criminal responsibility by truthfully saying they did not know what was going on.

In the very small proportion of cases where white-collar crimes are detected, authorities often have the choice of proceeding under the Criminal Code or through "quasi-criminal" administrative procedures under statutes such as provincial securities legislation, occupational safety regulations, the Income Tax Act, or laws that prohibit the sale of dangerous products or the dumping of poisonous residues into the water or air. The choice is almost always to proceed administratively, which has the effect of whitewashing the behaviours involved so that they are not clearly and officially defined as crimes. Most, if not all administrative enforcement agencies also have policies favouring informal settlements in which offenders are let off in exchange for paying a fine and promising to mend their ways. For example, federal tax authorities have a long-standing policy of not prosecuting tax evaders if they pay up when they are caught. (Note: tax avoidance is legal, tax evasion is not.) As a result, "only impecunious or recalcitrant tax evaders show up in the statistics."

This gentle treatment is totally different from the treatment common criminals receive at the hands of the justice system. No policy exists to say that pickpockets will not be charged if they hand over the wallets they stole and promise to reform. And although executives who foster life-threatening working conditions are not so different from bank robbers who panic and kill someone, and rich men who cheat on their income tax are just as dishonest (or more) as poor mothers who cheat the welfare department, we all know which ones are going to be exposed as criminals in the front pages of indignant tabloids.

The enormous class biases of our laws and law enforcement methods were best summed up by Roland Penner, former Attorney General of Manitoba:

> Let's suppose I became philosopher-king and I could make any changes I wanted. Suppose I decided that minor social control offences and crimes without victims were to be eliminated from the Criminal Code. Also suppose that minor property offenders were to be dealt with in the community rather than in jails. At the same time suppose that I made tax evasion, knowingly polluting the environment, false advertising, fraudulent bankruptcy, and price-fixing crimes which carried automatic jail terms. Now, let's introduce the proverbial "man from Mars" who always gets into stories like this one. He arrives and I take him on a tour of (the provincial jail near Winnipeg). What would he say? "You sure have a problem with your middle-class White people, don't you?"

. . .

## Diversion

The most modern use of the Crown's power to suspend or withdraw charges is through diversion, which removes from the formal criminal justice process people charged with minor offences who do not have serious criminal records. At first, this could only be done for young accused aged 12 to 17, but since 1996 it can be done for people of all ages. To be eligible for diversion, the accused must admit responsibility for their offences and agree to participate in alternative measures programs. This usually entails having to perform acts of contrition or redress, such as writing an essay, writing a letter of apology to the victim, performing community service work, providing restitution or compensation, or making a charitable donation. Except in Ontario, those who complete the programs successfully do not have to go to court, although they acquire an RCMP or police record. In Ontario, diversion can happen only following a court appearance.

Diversion saves court time, which is very attractive to clogged courts. It also recognizes that bringing inexperienced offenders into the criminal justice system can do more harm than good. Although diversion is increasingly used in Canada, we are still far behind many other countries in that regard.... [Diversion rates are as follows:]... in Canada (25 percent), the United States (53 percent), Great Britain (57 percent) and New Zealand (61 percent). Canada's record would be even worse if it were not for Quebec, where nearly 50 percent of young offender cases were diverted to alternative measures in 1993.

. . .

Diversion decisions are also very uneven because of differences in the availability of alternative programs—few or none exist in remote and Aboriginal communities, for example—and the offences covered. People who committed drug offences are only eligible for diversion in the provinces where these charges are prosecuted by provincial Crown attorneys, that is in Newfoundland, Quebec and Alberta. This has serious consequences for Black men, who are massively overrepresented among those charged with drug offences in Ontario. Most worrisome, considering the proportion of poor accused who are denied bail, is that people who are detained in custody until their trials are generally considered ineligible for diversion.

Another type of diversion is used to remove from the justice system people who are mentally ill. An elderly man who had been arrested for minor theft was visibly confused when he made his first appearance in a Toronto court in 1996 to face the charge. Because a new Mental Health Court Support Program had recently been set up, experts were on hand to conduct a quick mental health assessment. When the tests indicated that the man was probably suffering from dementia, the mental health workers recommended diversion and found him a bed in a nursing home.

Mental health court programs are rare, however, and many mentally ill people who appear before Canadian courts end up in jail. A 1990 study of remand prisoners in Vancouver found that 18 percent were severely mentally disordered.

. . .

The most frequent cause of criminal charges being withdrawn is that victims and witnesses are unwilling to co-operate. Some of these are sexual assault cases in which the victims are reluctant to appear in court or are afraid of revenge. Others involve situations in which the offenders and victims come to an agreement to settle out of court. Quebec critics cite the Belmoral Mine case as a classic example. After ten years of drawn-out procedures, criminal complaints against the company officers whose actions had allegedly caused the death of employees were withdrawn in 1990 after the company committed itself to paying $25,000 to each of the victims' families.

Needless to say, poor offenders are not in a position to make generous offers to their victims. This can be a severe handicap, because "When victims receive restitution, their desire to punish the offender is greatly reduced." Victims who were not compensated for their losses are more likely to insist that charges be proceeded with and taken to trial, even when the offences are relatively small. The wishes of complainants or victims are an important factor in Crown decisions to proceed or not with a case.

Finally, prosecutors' decisions concerning the type of charge can make an important difference. Criminal Code offences are classified into three types: summary conviction offences, which are the least serious; indictable offences, which are the most serious; and mixed offences, which are in the middle and include most offences. In the case of mixed offences, the Crown can choose to proceed as if the offence were either a summary conviction offence or an indictable offence. This choice can have serious consequences for sentencing. For example, a person convicted of the indictable offence of common assault can be sentenced to a maximum of five years in prison and receive an unlimited fine. The same person convicted on summary conviction for the same common assault faces a maximum of six months in prison and a $2,000 fine. (Another difference is that accused people who are charged with indictable offences can choose to be tried by a jury, instead of a judge alone.)

What criteria do Crown prosecutors use to make these decisions? As well as the seriousness of the harm done, the accused's previous record, and the length of time since the offence was committed (because there is a six-month limit on summary conviction), they also consider other, more discretionary factors. The Ontario Commission on Racism found that for charges involving drug offences and assaulting a police officer, Toronto Crown prosecutors were more likely to proceed by indictment when the accused were Blacks. The Commission cautioned that in the absence of details on the incidents, it was not possible to conclude that the differences were due to discrimination. Still, these and many other Crown decisions to proceed by indictment rather than by summary conviction raise concerns because they are heavily based on information contained in police reports.

## Questions/Discussion
1. List the infractions of provincial and federal laws that you know you have committed in the last five years. Of the total, what portion resulted in: some police response, arrest, trial, and conviction.
2. As a group, attempt to estimate the laws or types of laws that are: least enforced, most frequently broken, and broken by the greatest proportion of Canadians. What elements, if any, do these laws have in common? Then determine, what laws are: most vigorously enforced, least frequently broken, and broken by the smallest proportion of the population?
3. Considering the relatively minor penalties for impaired driving infractions, speculate about why a disproportionate number of criminal trial and appeal court decisions involve "breathalyser" cases? Is it the nature of the penalties, the offence or perhaps the offenders?

## Further Reading
- Burchfiel, K., "The Economic Organizations of Crime: A Study of the Development of Criminal Enterprise" (1977-78), 20 Criminal Law Quarterly 478.
- Cornish, D., & R. Clarke, eds., *The Reasoning Criminal: Rational Choice Perspectives on Offending* (New York: Springer-Verlag, 1986).
- Irwin, J., *The Felon* (Englewood Cliffs: Prentice-Hall, 1970)
- Linden, Rick, ed., *Criminology: A Canadian Perspective — 4th edition* (Toronto: Harcourt Brace Canada, 2000).
- Mann, W.E., ed., *Social Deviance in Canada* (Toronto: Copp Clark, 1971).
- Reiman, Jeffrey, *The Rich Get Richer and The Poor Get Prison: Ideology, Class, and Criminal Justice — 6th edition* (Boston: Allyn and Bacon, 2001).

# 5

# SENTENCING AND PUNISHMENT

## 5.1 SENTENCING

### Introduction

There is little consensus on solutions to problems in the sentencing process; what is agreed upon is that there are a great many problems in the area and that few solutions have been successful to date. One of the principal problems is usually stated as being one of disparity, the fact that there may be a great deal of difference between the sentences that are given to two separate individuals who commit the same crime and in the same circumstances. It is not that all types of disparity are wrong. For example, when cases are not alike, there might be very good reasons to attach different sentences to the convictions; it is only when the cases are virtually the same that the question of unfairness arises. This is not to say that all factors determine the "sameness" of a case. The fact that the offender's eyes may be different colours would not be a relevant difference, while the previous criminal records of the individuals may be. The questions, therefore, are what are the causes of the unwarranted and unfair disparity that does occur in this country and how can it be reduced (the other aspect of disparity, disparity in actual time served, is dealt with in section 2, below). These questions, among others, are addressed in the excerpts from the article by Jobson and Ferguson and from the *Justice and the Poor* report, while Fiske discusses the range of possible sentences. The article by Roberts and Von Hirsch addresses the matter of statutory sentencing principles and Bill C-41, which was passed by Parliament in June 1995. The legislating of principles was part of an attempt to, among other goals, reduce disparity in sentencing. The case of *Hollinsky* that follows examines the application of sentencing principles to a particular fact situation with unusual results.

The other principal issue in regard to sentencing is the overuse of incarceration as a means of punishment and this is looked at in section 2 under "Punishment". Other current issues in sentencing that receive less attention here are those of the use of sentencing circles, the mandate under section 718.2(e) of the *Criminal Code* regarding the sentencing of Aboriginal offenders, the selection of dangerous offenders, the sentencing of female offenders, and conditional sentences (readings on all these issues can be found under "Further Reading"), and conditional sentences are examined in Chapter 8).

## Toward a Revised Sentencing Structure for Canada*

*Keith Jobson and Gerry Ferguson*

*Excerpts from (1987), 66 Canadian Bar Review 1.

. . .

### *Origins*

Our current sentencing scheme was not originally derived from the realities of modern life in Canadian society. It was adapted, with little alteration or discussion, from an English model during the colonial period: Stephen's English Draft Code of 1879. Following that model, every offence, no matter how minor, may be dealt with by imprisonment. The maximum terms of life, fourteen, ten, five, two years and six months in prison, in the Criminal Code, can be traced to nineteenth century legislation and penal practices in England. There, during the first half of the last century, the death penalty was prescribed for a wide range of offences including some which were relatively trivial, such as theft of a sheep. The harshness of this regime was mitigated to some extent through administrative action. For example, in England in 1717, and later, in the Canadian colonies, officials could arrange the commutation of death sentences, on condition that the person consent to be transported for fourteen years, or such other term as specified, to penal work in various English colonies. Over time the most common terms to which the offender could be transported to work in penal servitude were life, twenty-one, fourteen or seven years. This administrative practice was later reflected in legislation permitting judicial sentences of transportation. Still later, in England in the 1840s, after transportation was abolished, sentences of imprisonment (penal servitude) were introduced with terms of fourteen or seven years. Preference for penal terms of life, fourteen, ten and seven years was reflected in colonial legislation and in the current Code.

The Canadian colonies also retained the English distinction of imprisonment for less than two years in a local prison and sentences of more than two years in "penal servitude" in a penitentiary. The reason for the distinction was that conditions in local prisons, in England, as documented by John Howard, were thought to be so bad that it was considered inhumane to keep people in them for longer than two years. As a result, those serving longer sentences were sent to a "penitentiary", where it was believed that conditions were more humane. By the 1830s, English legislation authorizing penal servitude (imprisonment in excess of three years) was being copied into Canadian colonial statute books. With Confederation, in 1867, criminal law became a federal matter, along with penitentiaries, but terms of less than two years were to be served in provincially controlled prisons.

The first real break from English legislation, but not English values and ideas, came in 1892, when Sir John Thompson presented the Canadian Parliament with a Code of Criminal Law. This Code was based closely on the English Draft Code of 1879 which drew heavily on the existing statutory law of England at the time. Stephen's Draft Code, however, abolished the common law classification of offences as felonies and misdemeanours and replaced it with a classification of indictable and summary conviction offences. The terms of imprisonment in Sir John Thompson's Code of 1892 drew on English and pre-Confederation Canadian colonial statutes. The sentencing provisions of the Code were adopted by the Canadian Parliament with little discussion or debate. Over the years sentencing provisions have been amended to provide for probation and conditional discharges; parole was added on. Still, the 1892 Code remains basically unchanged today in its classification and sentencing structure.

. . .

## CURRENT PROBLEMS

Given that there is no clear statement of policy and a want of accessible guidelines and precedents in Canadian sentencing law, that the judiciary and prosecution are obliged to exercise the broad discretion which that law confers on them in the absence of a coherent philosophical basis, and that we still rely for the most part on a system of crime classification that dates back to Colonial days, it is not surprising that a number of serious problems plague the present Canadian sentencing process. With the adoption of the Charter as part of the supreme law of the land, Canada has entered an era where charges of arbitrariness, disparity, inequity and vagueness will receive strict scrutiny. The various aspects of this nation's sentencing law which contribute to its present unsatisfactory state have been analyzed by us extensively elsewhere. Hence, these problems will here by given only such brief mention as is required to lay the foundations for the central focus of this paper: our discussion of reform proposals.

### Mandatory Punishment

A number of statutory provisions in Canadian law compel our courts to impose a prescribed minimum punishment in the event of conviction of certain offences.

. . .

### Excessive Punishment

Several factors contribute to the problem of excessive punishment. First, many of the maximum penalties set by statute are historically high. In various offences, in practice, the actual punishments imposed are so far from these maximum penalties that the latter are rendered useless as guidelines. Second, the present system of ranking punishments in terms of such maxima contributes to the problem. The need for review is apparent in many provisions. For example, do we agree that forgery of passports (punishable by up to fourteen years) is a more serious crime than assault causing bodily harm (punishable by no more than 10 years)? Related to these issues is the matter of uneven offence descriptions. A number of offences are described in very broad terms. Take, for example, robbery. Is it realistic to leave open the possibility of a life sentence in all cases of robbery? A better approach would be to categorize that crime into, perhaps, three offences, simple robbery, armed robbery and aggravated armed robbery, with different terms for each.

Finally, excessive punishment results from the judicial tendency to impose prison terms in many cases where imprisonment is inappropriate. Until such time as statutory guidance is provided to assist the judiciary in determining what types of cases warrant imprisonment as opposed to probation, fines and other less intrusive penalties, the unnecessary over-crowding of Canadian jails will no doubt continue.

. . .

### Disparity

Quite apart from ethical concerns relating to the justice of individualized sentencing, sections 7 and 15 of the Charter call into question the constitutionality of excessive disparity. Although it may be argued that no two cases are alike, wide disparity in the sentences given to offenders who commit virtually the same offence cannot be supported solely on the basis of "individualized" justice. Indeed, the typical factors taken into account in "individualizing the sentence", namely, the personality of the offender, the likelihood of recidivism and the circumstances of the offence, may have little to do with the harshness of the sentence. Instead, the skill of the defence counsel in negotiating a plea bargain or in representing an accused in a sentencing hearing, or whether counsel are involved at all, are believed to be far more weighty factors in obtaining lenient sentences.

### Lack of Fair Notice

In *R. v. Robson* the British Columbia Court of Appeal proposed the following test of what constitutes fair notice: does the law serve to give a person of ordinary intelligence fair notice of what is forbidden? It is suggested here that fair notice extends even further; that it should include notice not only of the conduct that is forbidden, but also the consequences of conviction for such conduct. The wide discretion and high statutory maximum terms which prevail in present offence provisions do not fulfil this latter requirement. In light of the wide disparity of sanctions which are imposed for many crimes, can it be said that the law is accessible and capable of being understood by ordinary persons in the criminal courts; or are the law and the outcome too frequently inaccessible to them — another institutional mystery?

### Parole

It is our conclusion that parole and remission laws are complex, inaccessible and unknowable. In fact, since parole and remission laws do not set firm standards for release, revocation or suspension, it might even be said that parole is not governed by law at all in many cases.

. . .

### Role of the Victim

Another problematic aspect of the Canadian sentencing process is its failure to address the role of the victim. Historically, victims played a large part in the system. They brought a charge and reparation orders were a common sentencing feature. Today, however, criminal charges are generally a prosecutorial concern, and punishments are comprised primarily of imprisonment, fines and probation orders. Some movement has been made toward giving victims some recognition in pilot projects where victim impact statements are heard at the time of sentencing as well as in the conditions judges attach to probation orders. Still, the majority of victims remain a peripheral concern of the system. The extant sentencing structure does little to address the injury suffered by those against whose person and property crimes are committed. It is an inherent feature of our proposed "just deserts" model for punishment that attempts be made through sentencing to repair the harm done by offenders.

. . .

### Sentencing Powers and Principles*

*Kenneth W. Fiske*

*Excerpts from "Sentencing Powers and Principles" in Joel E. Pink and David C. Perrier, eds., *From Crime to Punishment: An Introduction to the Criminal Law System* (Toronto: Carswell, 1999) at 281-284; 277; 280.

. . .

## TYPES OF SENTENCES

When the subject of punishment for criminal offences is raised, people tend to think of it in terms of imprisonment. However, imprisonment is but one form of punishment that may be ordered as a consequence of a conviction for a criminal offence.

Imprisonment is, of course, physical confinements and restraint of an offender within a penal institution for the duration of the term of the sentence, subject to early release on parole. A term of imprisonment of two years or more must be served in a federal penitentiary (*Criminal Code*, s. 743.1). On the other hand, an offender sentenced to imprisonment for less than two years serves it in a provincial correctional facility. The maximum term of imprisonment that can be served in a provincial institution is two years less one day.

Generally speaking, a sentence commences when it is imposed (s. 719). An exception is the intermittent sentence (s. 732). This type of sentence permits the offender to serve his sentence of imprisonment at intermittent times (for example, on weekends). A sentence of imprisonment can be made intermittent only if it does not exceed 90 days in length. The offender is subject to a probation order at all times when he is not in actual confinement in jail. Part of a day served in an institution counts as one full day in reduction of the intermittent sentence. For example, an individual ordered to serve a sentence intermittently on weekends from Friday evening to Monday morning is deemed to have served four days in jail each weekend.

The *Code* provides (s. 731) that, upon conditions set out in a probation order, a judge may choose to suspend the passing of sentence altogether and order the offender released from custody. A suspended sentence is not available in respect of offences committed for which a minimum punishment is prescribed. Should the offender breach any of the conditions of the probation order during its term, he is liable to be returned to court to be sentenced for the offence for which sentence was originally suspended. He is also subject to additional penalties for breaching the probation order.

Probation cannot be ordered as a sentence by itself. It must be combined with either a fine or a term of imprisonment not exceeding two years (s. 731). Note that probation cannot be ordered in addition to both a fine and imprisonment. The term of any probation order cannot exceed three years (s. 732.2). A court cannot order one probation order to be served consecutive to another (that is, one after the other).

Section 732.1 provides for the form and content of a probation order. Certain conditions are mandatory in every probation order. The *Code* lists a number of optional conditions and grants to the court making the order the power to impose other reasonable conditions.

A probation order comes into force on the date it is made, except in the case where the offender is sentenced to imprisonment, in which case the order becomes effective upon the expiration of that part of the sentence. The conditions and term of a probation order may be subsequently changed by the court (s. 732.2). In addition, a probation order made in one province may be transferred to another (s. 733). Although the subject of some debate, it appears a judge may order that an offender serve a period of probation following the expiration of an intermittent sentence.

Another familiar type of sentence is the fine (s. 734). The word "fine" is defined (s. 716) to include "a pecuniary penalty or other sum of money, but does not include restitution." In the case of an indictable offence for which the maximum punishment does not exceed five years, the offender may be either fined in lieu of any other prescribed punishment or he may be fined in addition to that punishment. However, if the offence is one for which a minimum term of imprisonment is provided, the offender cannot be fined in lieu of the term of imprisonment. An individual convicted of an indictable offence punishable by imprisonment for more than five years may be fined in addition to, but not in lieu of, the other punishment prescribed. In the case of a summary conviction offence, and unless otherwise provided, an individual is liable to a fine in addition to or in lieu of any other punishment that may be imposed.

In sentencing an offender to payment of a fine following conviction for a criminal offence, a judge may direct that a term of imprisonment in default of payment of the fine be imposed. A corporation convicted of either an indictable or summary conviction offence is subject, of course, to a fine only (s. 735).

A novel form of sentencing is the absolute and conditional discharge (s. 730). A discharge is not available to a corporation. To qualify for a discharge, an offender cannot have committed an offence for which a minimum punishment is prescribed, or an offence the maximum penalty for which is imprisonment for 14 years or more. The judge must be satisfied that a discharge order is in the best interests of the accused and not contrary to the public interest. If an accused is discharged either absolutely or conditionally, he does not stand convicted of the offence in respect of which the order is made. However, the accused may appeal against the finding of guilt as if it were a conviction, and the Crown may appeal against the decision not to convict the accused as if it were an acquittal. A number of cases have set out the criteria which a court should consider when determining whether to discharge an accused.

If an accused who has been discharged on conditions prescribed in a probation order and, while bound by the probation order, commits an offence, including the offence of breach of probation (s. 734), the court that ordered the conditional discharge may revoke the discharge, convict the accused of the offence to which the discharge relates and impose the appropriate sentence as if a conviction had been entered at the time of the discharge. The court may also exercise the powers granted by s. 732.2(5).

A special form of punishment is the indeterminate sentence which may be imposed upon an accused who has been found by the court to be a dangerous offender under Part XXIV of the *Code*. An accused must be convicted of a "serious personal injury offence" as defined by s. 752 in order to be sentenced as a dangerous offender. Other mandatory criteria to support the finding of an accused as a dangerous offender are set out in s. 753. Although an accused has been declared a dangerous offender, it does not mean that an indeterminate sentence must then be imposed. The judge may either sentence him to a federal penitentiary for an indeterminate period of time in place of any other sentence that may be imposed for the offence, or the judge may, having declared the accused a dangerous offender, sentence him to a definite term of imprisonment within the limits prescribed for the particular offence of which he was convicted.

A person declared a dangerous offender under Part XXIV of the Code and sentenced to an indeterminate period of imprisonment is eligible for parole after serving three years of the sentence. The Parole Board must consider the dangerous offender for parole at this time, and every two years thereafter if parole is not granted (s. 761).

Another special form of sentence concerns the eligibility for parole of an individual who has been convicted of second degree murder under s. 235(1). An offender convicted of this offence must be sentenced to imprisonment for life. Section 745.4 provides that the trial judge, in imposing sentence, must determine the period of imprisonment the offender will serve before being eligible for parole, which cannot be less than 10 years. Having regard to certain factors enumerated in s. 745.4, the judge may, in his discretion, substitute for the 10-year minimum a term of imprisonment greater than 10 but not more than 25 years which the offender will serve before being eligible for parole.

In cases where a jury has convicted the accused of second degree murder, the presiding judge must ask them for a recommendation respecting the number of years the accused will serve before being eligible for parole (s. 745.2). The jury need not make a recommendation and the presiding judge, although required to consider it, is not bound by the jury's recommendation if one is made.

For the purposes of appeals against sentence in proceedings by indictment, a number of declarations and orders made under the *Code* are deemed to be part and parcel of the sentencing process. One such order is that relating to parole eligibility following conviction for second degree murder.

A trial judge who convicts a person of impaired driving (s. 253(a)), driving with an excessive blood/alcohol concentration (s. 253(b)), or refusing or failing to comply with an A.L.E.R.T. or breathalyzer demand (s. 254), must make an order against the offender under s. 259 prohibiting that person from operating a motor vehicle for a period of time, the limits of which are set out in the subsection and depend upon whether it is a first, second or subsequent offence.

Other dispositions include mandatory and discretionary prohibition orders respecting the possession of firearms, ammunition and explosive substances (s. 100(1) and (2); discretionary prohibition orders respecting the operation of a motor vehicle (s. 259); orders for punitive damages resulting from the unlawful use of wiretaps (s. 194(1)); forfeiture orders respecting things seized under valid search warrants (s. 199(3)); restitution or forfeiture orders dealing with property obtained by the commission of criminal offences (s. 491.1); and orders for compensation for loss of property as a result of criminal offences (ss. 738, 739). At first glance, such dispositions may not be considered elements of the range of sentences open to a court in exacting punishment for criminal behaviour. However, they are as much a part of the process of sentencing as imprisonment, fines, and probation. As noted, some of the orders described fall within the discretion of the judge to impose, while others are mandatory and must be made in addition to the other punishment prescribed for the offence.

. . .

The *Criminal Code* gives the trial judge a discretion to not impose a jail sentence. If the sentence is not a minimum term of imprisonment and is less than two years and the trial judge is satisfied that the accused is not a danger to the safety of the community, he or she may order that the term of imprisonment be served in the community rather than in a jail. Section 742.1 states:

Where a person is convicted of an offence, except an offence that is punishable by a minimum term of imprisonment, and the court

(a) imposes a sentence of imprisonment of less than two years, and
(b) is satisfied that serving the sentence in the community would not endanger the safety of the community and would be consistent with the fundamental purpose and principles of sentencing set out in sections 718 to 718.2,

the court may, for the purposes of supervising the offender's behaviour in the community, order that the offender serve the sentence in the community, subject to the offender's complying with the conditions of a conditional sentence order made under section 742.3

. . .

If a trial judge orders this, he is then obliged to have the accused enter into a conditional sentence order (s. 742.3) which requires the accused to do the following:

(a) keep the peace and be of good behaviour;
(b) appear before the court when required to do so by the court;
(c) report to a supervisor;

(d) remain within the jurisdiction of the court unless written permission to go outside the jurisdiction is obtained from the court or the supervisor;

(e) notify the court or the supervisor in advance of any change of name or address, and promptly notify the court or the supervisor of any change of employment occupation;

(f) to abstain from the consumption of alcohol or intoxicating substances;

(g) abstain from owning or possessing or carrying a weapon;

(h) provide for the support or care of dependants;

(i) perform up to 240 hours of community service over a period not exceeding 18 months;

(j) attend treatment programs provided by the province; and

(k) comply with any other reasonable condition.

If an accused person who is on a conditional sentence order violates it, another hearing will be held and, if satisfied on the balance of probabilities that the offender has without reasonable excuse breached a condition of a conditional sentence order, the court may:

(a) take no action;

(b) change the optional conditions;

(c) suspend the conditional sentence and direct the offender serve in custody a portion of the unexpired sentence; or

(d) terminate the conditional sentence altogether and direct the offender be committees to custody until expiration of his sentence (s. 742.6(9)).

. . .

## Justice and the Poor*

### *National Council of Welfare*

*Excerpts from National Council of Welfare, *Justice and the Poor* (Ottawa: Minister of Public Works and Government Services Canada, 2000) at 60-2; 63; 64; 65-8; 70; 72-4.

## Imprisoning the Most Disadvantaged

Following decades of complaints that the sentences imposed by Canadian judges were wildly inconsistent and simply reflected their individual prejudices, the Criminal Code was amended in 1996 to specify that sentencing should have the following objectives: 1) to denounce unlawful conduct; 2) to deter the offender and others from committing offences; 3) to separate offenders from society where necessary; 4) to rehabilitate offenders; 5) to provide reparations to victims or the community; and 6) to promote a sense a sense of responsibility in offenders and acknowledge the harm they did. According to some experts, these objectives are almost useless in bringing about more consistency in sentencing, since judges remain free to pick and choose the objectives in the Code that suit their own views.

More promising are other 1996 amendments that introduced sentencing principles. The most important are: 1) that a sentence must be proportional to the gravity of the offence and the responsibility of the offender; and 2) that all reasonable available sanctions other than imprisonment should be considered for all offenders, especially if they are Aboriginal. The reason for the special mention of Aboriginal people was the recognition, following the findings from several task forces and commissions of inquiry, that "racism and discrimination have played a major role in the difficulties that Aboriginal people have experienced with the criminal justice system."

In a judgment issued in April 1999, the Supreme Court unequivocally ruled that this new provision concerning Aboriginal offenders was not simply a restatement of existing practices, but new law that requires judges to approach the sentencing of Aboriginal people "individually, but also differently, because the circumstances of aboriginal people are unique." Part of this uniqueness, according to the Supreme Court, is that there is widespread bias against Aboriginal people within Canada, and "evidence that this widespread racism has translated into systemic discrimination in the criminal justice system." The concrete result has been a massive overrepresentation of Aboriginal Canadians in penal institutions:

> By 1997, aboriginal peoples constituted close to 3 percent of the population of Canada and amounted to 12 percent of all federal inmates. The situation continues to be particularly worrisome in Manitoba, where in 1995-96 they made up 55 percent of admissions to provincial correctional facilities, and in Saskatchewan, where they made up 72 percent of admissions. A similar, albeit less drastic situation prevails in Alberta and British Columbia.

The purpose of the new Criminal Code provision concerning the sentencing of Aboriginal people, according to the Supreme Court, is to force courts to take special steps to remedy this discrimination. From now on, sentencing judges are obliged to proceed with sensitivity and understanding of the difficulties Aboriginal people face within the criminal justice system and society at large and to take into account "all of the surrounding circumstances regarding the offence, the offender, the victims, and the community, including the unique circumstances of the offender as an Aboriginal person." If the offender has no legal representation, judges must now do whatever can be done to obtain the necessary information. The Supreme Court expects this fairer process to produce fewer prison sentences for minor offences, but sentences similar to those of non-Aboriginals when the crimes committed are very serious and violent ones

Commenting more broadly on the new Criminal Code provisions, the Supreme Court wrote that they were meant to respond to the general problem of overincarceration in Canada, and should therefore reduce prison sentences for all ethnic groups.

. . .

Children and adults continue to be imprisoned in droves in spite of the fact that the majority of the experts in the field, as well as every inquiry and commission on the justice system in the past 150 years, have condemned imprisonment as being harsh and ineffective in reducing crime. On the contrary, what they found was that

> Most of those in prison are not dangerous. However, cruel lock-ups, isolation [and] the injustices and harassment deliberately inflicted on prisoners unable to fight back, make non-violent inmates violent, and those already dangerous more dangerous. . .

The recommendations of these reports reveal constant themes, which are that imprisonment does not educe crime, that it should be avoided if possible, and that it should be reserved for the most serious offences, particularly those involving violence.

. . .

Unfortunately, the April 1999 decision of the Supreme Court did not go on to specify when sentences of imprisonment should and should not be used. Many observers of our criminal courts believe that prison populations will not diminish until judges are given no option. It is therefore unclear what effect, if any, the new Criminal Code principles will have on the sentencing of people from non-Aboriginal groups, and especially for Blacks. The Ontario Commission on Racism found that Blacks were more likely to be sentenced to prison than Aboriginal people. In 1992-93, Black men were imprisoned at five times the rate for Whites, while the rate for Aboriginal men was three times the rate for Whites.

The greatest prison overrepresentation the Commission on Racism found in Ontario was for Black and Aboriginal women. The likelihood of being sent to an Ontario prison was five times higher for Aboriginal women and seven times higher for Black women than for women who were White. Studies suggest that judges' reactions to women offenders are similar to those of the police. They tend to be lenient and "chivalrous" with women who fit the traditional female stereotype, who live in "normal" two-parent families and are "dependent, gentle and compliant," and to treat the women who do not conform to this White cultural model the same as men.

Discrimination in sentencing is particularly common with young girls. They are more likely than young men to be brought to youth court and to be detained "for their own protection" on the basis of non-criminal administrative offences such as "breach of bail conditions" and "failure to appear in court."

. . .

Even if judges treated men and women equally in handing out sentences, the impact would be harsher on women. Because more women have incomes below the poverty line than men, they cannot afford to pay the same fines. Most imprisoned women are poor mothers, and the worst offence many of them committed is shoplifting.

. . .

There is also evidence that imprisonment may be psychologically harder for women than men. Part of it is that there are fewer women's prisons, making the distances longer between the women's home communities and the institutions. The impact of confinement may also be more severe for women because a greater proportion were victims of physical and emotional abuse. At least 80 percent of federally sentenced women were abused, and an even greater proportion of Aboriginal women. Self-injurious behaviour, including suicide, attempted suicide and self-mutilation (slashing) is more common in women's prisons than in men's. In 1991-2, six Aboriginal women committed suicide at the Prison for Women in Kingston, Ontario, which housed only about 110 women.

Most painful for women inmates, perhaps, is the separation from their children. The cost of incarcerating female offenders includes child care and also the immense human cost of separating mothers from their children. It is not unusual for inmate mothers to be declared "unfit" parents whose children are taken away by child welfare authorities. Women's prison conditions are also harsher than men's. Because there are so few of them compared to male inmates, minor and serious female offenders are often housed together in maximum-security institutions, and female prisoners have access to a much smaller range of programs, treatment facilities and resources.

. . .

## Disparities in Sentencing

Apart from ordering harsher punishments to members of disadvantaged groups, how consistent have Canadian judges been in handing out sentences? To find out, researchers gave a group of judges the same hypothetical cases, asking them what sentences they would hand down in such situations. The answers varied tremendously, with the greatest differences showing up for a case of assault causing bodily harm (the loss of sight in one eye). The judges' sentences ranged from a $500 fine with six months' probation to five years in a penitentiary. Given such huge disparities, it is not surprising that stories circulate about lawyers who advise their clients to do anything, including breaking a leg if necessary, to avoid appearing before some notorious "hanging judges."

Huge disparities in sentencing exist both within and between Canadian jurisdictions. One survey concluded that there were wide differences in the sentences of offenders charged with possession of marijuana in five locations in Ontario. Disparities in sentencing between the provinces and territories are also huge. One indication is different rates of imprisonment. In 1994, the number of adult sentenced inmates actually in prison on a given day per 1,000 residents was: 1.43 in Newfoundland, 1.27 in Prince Edward Island, 1.52 in Nova Scotia, 1.22 in New Brunswick, 0.88 in Quebec, 0.76 in Ontario, 1.43 in Manitoba, 1.93 in Saskatchewan, 1.29 in Alberta, 0.81 in British Columbia, 2.56 in Yukon, and 7.08 in the Northwest Territories. The average for Canada was 0.98.

Among the provinces, Ontario had the lowest rate and Saskatchewan the highest. Both territories had much higher rates than the provinces. The Northwest Territories, the only Canadian jurisdiction in 1994 where the majority of residents were Aboriginal people, had a phenomenally high rate of 7.08 people in prison per 1,000 inhabitants.

. . .

Apart from differences in the severity of judges, the other possible explanation for the disparities in incarceration rates between the jurisdictions is differences in the number of criminal charges. The rationale behind this explanation is that perhaps judges from some jurisdictions send more people to jail because they hear proportionally more cases and issue proportionally more sentences than their colleagues in other provinces and territories. [But]. . . higher official crime rates and higher rates of criminal charges do not necessarily reflect more real offences but may be the result of stricter enforcement policies, or of stronger police forces that launch more investigations and lay more charges for minor offences.

Crime rates do not explain disparities between the jurisdictions, however, because when researchers looked at the number of prison inmates per 1,000 people charged with crimes, instead of per 1,000 people in the population, the results still showed huge differences in the rates of imprisonment. The rank order of the jurisdictions was changed, though, indicating that charging more people with crimes has some effect on imprisonment. This relationship seems clearest for the jurisdictions with the highest rates of criminal charges, which are the Northwest Territories (rate of 89.6 charges per 1,000 residents in 1994), Yukon (67.0), Saskatchewan (40.2), Manitoba (33.7) and Alberta (33.1). These jurisdictions also had the highest or near-highest rates of imprisonment.

But outside these jurisdictions, there seems to be little relationship between rates of criminal charges and rates of imprisonment. Newfoundland, Prince Edward Island, and Quebec, for example, had very different rates of imprisonment but shared the same lowest rate of criminal charges (21.8 per 1,000 residents).

. . .

Another, more direct source of information on disparities in prison sentences in different parts of Canada is the sentences judges issue for specific offences.

. . .

. . .Ontario judges handed out more prison sentences than judges from the other provinces for practically all the offences listed. This is surprising because we just saw that Ontario has the lowest rate of imprisonment in Canada. Next in severity were judges from Prince Edward Island, who were less consistent in sending offenders to jail than their Ontario colleagues, but who had the highest overall rate of imprisonment for these offences at 42 percent. Territorial judges also seem to have been very severe for cases involving Level 2 assaults, which are assaults with a weapon or causing physical harm.

At the other end of the spectrum are judges from Quebec and Nova Scotia, who consistently sent the smallest proportion of offenders to prison for all the offences listed. Judges from Saskatchewan and Alberta also sent relatively few offenders to jail, which again seems surprising because we saw above that these provinces have the highest provincial rates of imprisonment.

. . .

[Also, there is] an inverse relationship between the percentage of offenders judges sent to prison and the length of the prison sentences they ordered. Judges from Ontario and Prince Edward Island, who sent more people to jail than their provincial colleagues, imposed the shortest sentences, presumably because the offenders they sent to jail were less deserving of severe punishment. For Ontario, the combined effect of jailing more minor offenders for shorter periods of time produces a relatively low rate of imprisonment in provincial prisons.

Judges from Quebec, Nova Scotia, Saskatchewan and Alberta, on the other hand, sent a much smaller percentage of convicted offenders to jail but issued the longest sentences. The overall result for Quebec and Nova Scotia is a relatively low rate of imprisonment in provincial prisons. Things are different for Saskatchewan and Alberta, which have the highest rates of imprisonment in provincial prisons, perhaps because of their very high rates of criminal charges.

· · ·

[Also,] most of the people judges send to prison did not commit violent offences. According to a 1990 report by the federal Justice Department,

> In federal institutions, the percentage of offenders admitted for violent crimes has risen in recent years, although a significant percentage are still admitted for property crimes. Minor property or alcohol-related driving offences have accounted for the highest percentage of admissions to provincial institutions for the last several years. The offences of theft, possession of stolen goods and break and enter [burglary] are the next highest offences on admission. The statistics consistently show that three out of every ten admissions are for fine default.

> Concern has been expressed about the appropriateness of using incarceration for property and non-violent offenders. Crowded prisons are not schools of citizenship.

· · ·

## Sentences and Factors Used in Sentencing

If Canadian judges are too severe and send too many poor offenders to prisons, why do opinion polls regularly indicate that most Canadians believe sentences to be too lenient? When the public was asked more specific questions, the answers revealed that most people have very little idea of actual sentencing practices and draw their information from sensational media stories that denounce exceptionally lenient sentences. When the Canadian Sentencing Commission, which was appointed by the federal government to do a major study on the subject in the late 1980s, asked a representative group what proportion of crimes they thought involved violent acts, three-quarters estimated that 30 to 100 percent of crimes were violent, while the reality was close to 6 percent. They also believed that about 50 percent of ex-offenders committed other offences while they were still on parole (supervised release), while the actual figure is around 5 percent.

Canadian studies carried out in the past decade found that the gap between the public's and judges' perceptions of sentences is exaggerated. When members of the public and judges were asked what sentences they would hand out in identical cases, the vast majority of both groups agreed on which offenders should be sent to jail. And when ordinary people were given more information about the types of sentences judges can choose from, they actually became less punitive than the judges and recommended fewer sentences of imprisonment for some types of offences. The Canadian Sentencing Commission concluded that the public wants more severe sentences for violent offenders, but that it favours limitations on imprisonment for the non-violent offences that make up the bulk of criminal and prison caseloads.

How do judges make decisions on sentences? One influential factor is previous sentences issued by other judges, especially by higher courts. These past decisions suggest a range of punishments for each type of offence, from very severe to very lenient depending on a large number of possible mitigating and aggravating circumstances, such as a supportive family background (mitigating) or a previous criminal record (aggravating). Within such loose upper and lower limits, which are not necessarily binding, sentences are very individual decisions based on judges' personal views, life experiences and cultural values. Almost always, they are the views, life experiences and values of White upper-middle-class men who have at best a vague understanding of the life conditions of the mostly poor offenders on whom they pass judgment.

Sentences for relatively minor offences are usually made in minutes, with almost no information about the offenders' backgrounds and the circumstances that led to their offences. This maximizes the risk that these decisions will be influenced by stereotypes, which are preconceived expectations about certain groups of people. Experts who know how judges make decisions advise people who are about to be sentenced: "You need to make a good impression on the judge. When you go to court, be clean and neatly dressed. . .be polite. . .show respect for the court. . .call the judge 'Your Honour,' speak clearly. . .don't eat or chew gum." People who work with women offenders say that "Many women cannot afford to dress 'respectfully'."

For more serious cases and for young offenders, judges often order pre-sentence reports that are usually prepared by probation officers, most of whom are White middle-class men. Victims also sometimes make "impact statements" to the court if they wish. Pre-sentence reports are very influential, with studies showing that judges follow their recommendations in 80 to 85 percent of cases. Comments about the harm done by the insensitivity of some of these reports reveal very narrow conventional standards of behaviour for offenders. Aboriginal offenders often receive negative assessments because they are perceived as being withdrawn, unresponsive and showing little remorse. Black offenders often receive negative assessments because probation officers perceive them as being aggressive, troublesome and uncooperative. White middle-class offenders, who share the judges' values, instinctively know they will receive more lenient sentences if they are, or pretend to be, humble and remorseful.

In the rare cases where the person being sentenced is rich, the sentencing scene becomes an elaborate stage. As sometimes seen on television, rich offenders stride into the courtroom surrounded by teams of sad but supportive family members and high-powered lawyers, all of them looking wonderful with expensive haircuts and designer suits. Psychiatrists are brought in to describe obscure syndromes that supposedly caused the defendants to lose control. (The most imaginative was the "Twinkie defence" used in a California trial, where a killer was found to have diminished responsibility as a result of eating too much junk food.) Even if the offence was heinous, such as murder, rape, or defrauding people of millions of dollars, pillars of the community come forward to testify with tears in their eyes that the offence was a tragic exception to a life of virtue, and that the offenders are the kindest and most generous persons they have ever known.

Strange as it may seem, the severity of the harm caused is often the least important factor judges and juries take into account in sentencing. A textbook on criminal justice illustrates this with the following example:

On the same day in June 1985, Robert Rowbotham, 35, of Toronto, and Michael Waite, 22, of Drayton, Ontario, were sentenced in different Ontario courtrooms for the crimes of drug trafficking and criminal negligence causing death. Both charges carried a maximum sentence of life imprisonment. . .Rowbotham was sentenced to 20 years in a federal prison for his part in a large marijuana importing drug operation . . . Waite received a sentence of two years less a day in a provincial jail after killing four teenagers on a hayride. He was driving down the wrong side of a road with only his foglights on in the dark, after drinking seven bottles of beer.

. . .

## Purpose and Principles of Sentencing — Section 718 of the *Criminal Code*

## Purpose

718. The fundamental purpose of sentencing is to contribute, along with crime prevention initiatives, to respect for the law and the maintenance of a just, peaceful and safe society by imposing just sanctions that have one or more of the following objectives:

(a)  to denounce unlawful conduct;

(b)  to deter the offender and other persons from committing offences;

(c)  to separate offenders from society, where necessary;

(d)  to assist in rehabilitating offenders;

(e)  to provide reparations for harm done to victims or to the community; and

(f)  to promote a sense of responsibility in offenders, and acknowledgment of the harm done to victims and to the community.

## Fundamental principle

718.1 A sentence must be proportionate to the gravity of the offence and the degree of responsibility of the offender.

## Other sentencing principles

718.2 A court that imposes a sentence shall also take into consideration the following principles:

(a)  a sentence should be increased or reduced to account for any relevant aggravating or mitigating circumstances relating to the offence or the offender, and, without limiting the generality of the foregoing,

  (i)   evidence that the offence was motivated by bias, prejudice or hate based on race, national or ethnic origin, language, colour, religion, sex, age, mental or physical disability, sexual orientation, or any other similar factor,

  (ii)  evidence that the offender, in committing the offence, abused the offender's spouse or common-law partner or child,

  (iii) evidence that the offender, in committing the offence, abused a position of trust or authority in relation to the victim, or

(iv) evidence that the offence was committed for the benefit of, at the direction of or in association with a criminal organization, or

(v)  evidence that the offence was a terrorism offence;

shall be deemed to be aggravating circumstances;

(b)  a sentence should be similar to sentences imposed on similar offenders for similar offences committed in similar circumstances;

(c)  where consecutive sentences are imposed, the combined sentence should not be unduly long or harsh;

(d)  an offender should not be deprived of liberty, if less restrictive sanctions may be appropriate in the circumstances; and

(e)  all available sanctions other than imprisonment that are reasonable in the circumstances should be considered for all offenders, with particular attention to the circumstances of aboriginal offenders.

## Statutory Sentencing Reform: The Purpose and Principles of Sentencing*

*Julian Roberts and A. von Hirsch*

*Excerpts from (1995), 37 *Criminal Law Quarterly* 220.

## 1. INTRODUCTION

Sentencing reform has been advocated for many years now, by academics, criminal justice practitioners, advocacy groups, members of the public and the news media.[1] One of the reasons for this continued interest in sentencing has been the succession of commissions of inquiry and government reports that have examined the topic and recommended reform.[2] Sentencing reform now seems at hand: in June, 1994, the federal government introduced Bill C-41, "An Act to amend the Criminal Code (sentencing) and other Acts in consequence thereof", which is likely to pass into law in 1995. [*Editor's note: Bill C-41 was passed in June 1995.*] This bill is the successor to Bill C-90, which represented the federal government's rather belated response to two landmark reports, one by the Canadian Sentencing Commission[3] (released in 1987) and the other by the House of Commons Standing Committee on Justice and Solicitor General (the Daubney Committee) in 1988.[4] The process of parliamentary review of Bill C-90 was brought to a premature conclusion within a month and the mandate of the government expired shortly thereafter. The new Bill (Bill C-41) received 2nd Reading on October 18, 1994, and was referred to the Standing Committee on Justice and Legal Affairs. At the time of publication hearings are expected to be held in the near future. In light of the widespread interest in sentencing reform and the fact that the government is just beginning its mandate, Bill C-41 stands a very good chance of receiving passage in the spring of 1995. If a sentencing bill is passed it will constitute the first major statutory revisions to sentencing in many years.[5]

Bill C-41 would introduce several changes to the sentencing process. The bill provides the courts with more options to distinguish between serious violent offenders and less serious property offenders. As well, there are provisions to assist the victims of crime and proposals to ensure that offenders motivated by hate or who take advantage of a position of trust are dealt with more severely. The bill also creates a new disposition known as a conditional sentence. In this article we critically examine the most important component in Bill C-41: a statement regarding the purposes and principles of sentencing that would become part of the *Criminal Code*[6] of Canada. The reason for focusing upon the statement of purpose is that it could have far-reaching symbolic and practical effects upon the sentencing system. This is particularly true for this bill, since the government's sentencing reform initiative no longer contains a sentencing guideline scheme. Although federal government policy documents and ministerial statements have always included some form of guideline scheme (whether presumptive or merely advisory in nature), formal sentencing guidelines no longer appear to be part of the current sentencing reform initiative in Canada.

## 2. STATEMENT OF THE PURPOSE AND PRINCIPLES OF SENTENCING

The potential benefits of a statutory statement of the purpose(s) of sentencing are clear. At the present, in the absence of such a statement, judges are free to follow their own individual sentencing philosophies, which can vary greatly from case to case, and from judge to judge. And since sentencing means many things to different people, the result is a great deal of variation in both the choice and application of the various sentencing purposes. This alone must be responsible for a substantial amount of variation in sentencing practices across the country.[7] What is needed is a clear pronouncement from Parliament which would guide judges at the trial court level, and also the appellate courts across the country. It is a professed aim of Bill C-41 to provide such guidance.

. . .

The challenge to drafters of a statement of sentencing purpose and principle is to reconcile diverse and frequently conflicting sentencing aims. The task is not impossible, and nor does it necessarily mean promoting a single sentencing purpose at the expense of all others. Multi-purpose statements can still offer guidance and affect sentencing practices at the trial court level but they must specify the conditions under which certain aims are favoured over others. This section of the article will also necessitate some discussion of the utility of sentencing guidelines, for guidelines are the means by which a statement of purpose effects changes in sentencing practices. The statement of purpose is the compass and guidelines the road map. Without the guidelines, judges know roughly where they are going but not necessarily how to get there. Without the statement, judges would be following instructions in the absence of a clear sense of over-all direction.

### (1) Bill C-41

The statement of purpose and principle contained in Bill C-41 is a hybrid containing elements of several previous proposals, notably those advanced by the Canadian Sentencing Commission and the Daubney Committee. This latest incarnation of a statement of the purposes of sentencing was the culmination of widespread consultation by the federal Department of Justice. It is unlikely then that a radically different statement of purpose will appear in the near future. In our view, while it is important to have a statutory statement, the proposal contained in Bill C-41 can be significantly improved.

. . .

The statement of purpose proposed by Bill C-41[11] contains four elements: (i) A fundamental purpose of sentencing, which might be termed the *raison d'etre* of the whole process; (ii) a series of fully 10[12] objectives or goals, the fulfilment of which would promote the fundamental purpose of sentencing; (iii) a fundamental principle to limit, presumably, the influence of the objectives; and finally (iv) a series of five subordinate sentencing principles that interact with the fundamental principle. We shall discuss each element in turn (see Appendix A for the full text of the statement).

### (a) The Fundamental Purpose of Sentencing

According to Bill C-41, the fundamental purpose of sentencing is to "contribute, along with crime prevention initiatives, to respect for the law and the maintenance of a just, peaceful and safe society by imposing just sanctions that have one or more of the following objectives".[13] We shall not dwell at length upon the fundamental purpose,[14] except to note that it draws upon, but is not the same as, the Canadian Sentencing Commission's proposed statement.[15] It is worth noting also that the language of the fundamental purpose reflects the dual nature of the whole statement, which incorporates elements of both the utilitarian and the retributivist traditions. By talking of "crime prevention initiatives" the statement raises the notion that a particular sentencing policy can have an important impact upon crime rates. At the same time, the phrase "just sanctions" clearly anticipates the principle of proportionality and sentencing according to a desert-based philosophy.

### (b) The Objectives of Sentencing

According to the statement in Bill C-41, no matter what kind of sanction is selected by the judge, it must have at least one of the sentencing objectives specified in the bill. The statement enunciates 10 objectives that the "just sanctions" are designed to fulfil. These are the usual candidates that have been advanced over the years, namely: denunciation; individual deterrence; general deterrence; incapacitation; reparation to the individual; restitution to the community; the promotion of a sense of responsibility in offenders; acknowledgement of the harm done to victims; acknowledgement of the harm to communities, and the creation of opportunities to assist in the offender's rehabilitation. Since the judge may pick and choose from among this menu of sentencing purposes, the result is little more than a legislated statement of the status quo.

Whatever one's reaction to the fundamental purpose ascribed to the sentencing process by Bill C-41, there can be little disagreement that its role will be largely symbolic. It conveys a message that will have little *practical* impact in terms of sentencing practices. In contrast, the list of sentencing objectives is more instrumental than symbolic: it provides judges with a number of alternatives which may all lead to different dispositions. What it does not do, however is inform judges as to the conditions under which one objective should be privileged over the rest. No indication is provided to the sentencing judge as to when deterrence is appropriate, or when denunciation might take precedence of restitution or reparation.

An hypothetical example illustrates the difficulties. Consider a case of domestic violence in which a judge is about to impose sentence upon an offender convicted of assaulting his wife. The fundamental purpose of sentencing advocated by Bill C-41 prompts the judge to seek a just sentence, and then points him or her towards the specific objectives. Which of the 10 sentencing objectives is relevant in this particular case? Should the judge choose objective (a) ("to denounce unlawful conduct") and send the man to prison in order to convey a message that Canadian society will not tolerate spousal assault? Or should the offender be allowed to remain at liberty (and at home), provided he attends some form of counselling programme for husbands who assault their wives? If the latter objective is more appropriate, their objective (d) "to assist in rehabilitating offenders" is the relevant aim to be pursued. The choice provides judges with a dilemma that they are likely to resolve in their own individual way, as they have done in the past. The Bill C-41 formulation will not prove of much *practical* assistance to judges, for it fails to inform them of the conditions under which different sentencing purposes are appropriate. The likely consequence is that judges will continue to sentence as before and sentencing practices at the trial court level will not be affected.

## (c) The Fundamental Principle of Sentencing

The next section of the statement makes a sentencing judge's task still more complex. It contains a list of principles, in accordance with which the sentencing decision is to be taken. These principles include a fundamental principle — that of proportionality — and subordinate principles relating to the use of mitigating and aggravating factors, consistency in sentencing, totality, restraint and the use of incarceration. The fundamental principle states that: "A sentence must be proportionate to the gravity of the offence and the degree of responsibility of the offender."[16]

This straightforward expression of proportionality in sentencing is important and represents a clear departure from the current vacuum in the *Criminal Code*. By endorsing a fundamental principle of this nature, the drafters of Bill C-41 took a step towards making sentencing more consistent and philosophically coherent. In theory at least, this desert-based principle should limit the influence of the utilitarian sentencing objectives that precede it. Thus, a judge wishing to impose a severe, exemplary sentence to "send a message to others" will be restricted to the limits of a proportionate disposition. The imposition of disproportionately harsh or lenient sentences imposed in pursuit of some utilitarian goal (usually deterrence or rehabilitation) will be discouraged by this fundamental principle. In our view, the fundamental principle is the best part of the bill's proposed statement.

The weakness of this section of the proposed statement is that the fundamental principle is embedded within a lengthy statement and confined on two sides: first by the preceding 10 objectives, and second by the five subsequent principles. This gives rise to two problems. First, the influence of the principle of proportionality could be undermined by all these objectives. Second, there is no guidance provided for sentencing judges as to exactly how the objectives and principles affect the principle of proportionality, or how they relate to each other. Some articulation of the interrelationships between all these components is necessary; none is, in fact, provided.

### (d) Secondary Sentencing Principles

Three of the five principles are simply old bromides with which judges are already familiar. The first principle, for example, states that: "a sentence should[17] be increased or reduced to account for any relevant aggravating or mitigating circumstances relating to the offence or the offender...."[18] Since an important part of the process of determining the nature and quantum of punishment consists of evaluating relevant mitigating and aggravating factors, this principle is an enunciation of the obvious[19] and will come as little surprise to judges in Canada. The same can be said for principle (b) that "a sentence should be similar to sentences imposed on similar offenders for similar offences committed in similar circumstances".[20] This principle modestly strengthens the bill's statement on proportionality, by stating that there should be parity between the penalties assigned to offenders whose crimes are equally serious. Thus it has some degree of usefulness, in contrast to its predecessor, principle (a), which has little or no practical significance.[21]

The third principle (c) states that "where consecutive sentences are imposed, the combined sentence should not be unduly long or harsh".[22] This is a statutory enunciation of the totality principle, which the sentencing process has for some time articulated to prevent the imposition of excessively long sentences upon offenders convicted of multiple offences. Canadian Courts of Appeal have long provided guidance to trial court judges in this regard. Accordingly, few judges are unaware of the problem, or the solution that has evolved in Canada as well as England and Wales.[23] It is not clear why the principle needs to be enshrined in the *Criminal Code*.[24] The remaining two principles are more interesting, and in their final incarnation (as with other provisions of this bill) differ significantly from earlier formulations. They both relate to the issue of the over-use of incarceration in Canada.

### (i) Restricting the Use of Incarceration in Canada

The emphasis on incarceration as a sanction in Canada has been noted by many groups and individuals. Statistics have long demonstrated the high rates of imprisonment in this country. Comparison of international incarceration rates reveals that Canada ranked third in the West (after the United States and Switzerland) with an incarceration rate of 92 per 100,000 population.[25] Accordingly, a fundamental policy goal supported by a wide constituency of experts has been effecting a reduction in

Canada's reliance on incarceration as a sentencing option. Any sentencing bill should attempt to reduce, to the extent possible, the number and duration of sentences of imprisonment, particularly for non-violent offenders. In fact, this has been a stated aim of federal government policy for some time.[26] Bill C-41 attempts to restrict the use of imprisonment by means of principles (d) and (e).

### (ii) Principle of Restraint

Principle (d) declares that "an offender should not be deprived of liberty, if less restrictive alternatives may be appropriate in the circumstances".[27] This is the principle of restraint, which has a long tradition in this country. As the Canadian Sentencing Commission noted in its report, restraint in the application of the criminal law is consistent with the position taken by every commission of inquiry in Canada from the Brown Commission[28] in the mid-19th century to the Nielsen Task Force that reported in 1986.[29] The notion of restraint is most closely associated with the work of the Law Reform Commission of Canada. However, earlier versions were far more general than the wording adopted in Bill C-41.

As formulated by the Law Reform Commission of Canada, the principle of restraint encompasses many aspects of the criminal law and is not restricted to the issue of sentencing. With relation to sentencing in particular, both the Law Reform Commission[30] and the Sentencing Commission argued that restraint should encompass *all* kinds of dispositions. Thus in the latter's proposed statement of sentencing purpose, the principle of restraint followed the paramount principle (that the sentence be proportionate to the gravity of the offence and the degree of responsibility of the offender) and was expressed in the following way: "a sentence should be the least onerous sanction appropriate in the circumstances"[31] Bill C-41 restricts the application of restraint to sentences of imprisonment. While it is important to affirm this principle in statutory form, in our view, the application used here is too narrow. Judges need to constantly question whether a less intrusive sanction would be appropriate if the law is to be truly faithful to the spirit of parsimony in sentencing. This means that if a discharge is appropriate, a fine should not be imposed, and so forth. The more restrictive wording contained in Bill C-41 is also a change from the Department of Justice policy document of 1990, which endorsed the exact wording of the Sentencing Commission's statement.[32]

### (iii) Alternatives to Incarceration

Continuing the spirit of the preceding principle, the last principle (e) argues that "all available alternatives to imprisonment that are reasonable in the circumstances should be considered for all offenders, with particular attention to the circumstances of aboriginal offenders".[33]

*(iv)  Imprisonment and Offenders from Visible Minorities*

It has long been known that Canada's penal institutions contain a disproportionate number of aboriginal offenders. The most recent statistics from provincial correctional systems across the country show that almost one inmate in four is aboriginal. Over half of all admissions in some provinces such as Saskatchewan and Manitoba, are aboriginals.[34] It might seem churlish to criticize any attempt to redress this problem, but the issue of over-incarceration touches all kinds of offenders, not simply aboriginals.

Aboriginal Canadians are not the only visible minority that is over-represented in penal institutions. In fact, data from the province of Ontario show that the racial disproportion of blacks in the province's jails is far greater than that associated with aboriginals. Thus custodial admissions data for 1992-93 reveal that 16% of inmates admitted were black, compared to 6% for aboriginals.[35] Research is now accumulating that shows a sustained pattern of discrimination against blacks in the province's criminal justice system. It seems clear that Black inmates in the Province of Ontario are subject to negative treatment that is not accorded other categories of inmate.[36] Imprisonment also poses special problems for female offenders. The Daubney Committee reported a survey which found that over 80% of female inmates were mothers and over half of these were single parents. Incarceration clearly creates conditions of exceptional hardship for these categories of offenders, but Bill C-41 focuses exclusively on aboriginal offenders.

Will Bill C-41 accomplish its stated goal of curbing the use of incarceration as a sanction in Canada? Simply *suggesting* that judges consider other sentencing options is unlikely to have much impact upon sentencing practices across the country. In all probability, judges already consider alternatives to incarceration before they imprison offenders.[37] Bill C-41 should restrict judges from imposing imprisonment *unless specific conditions are met*. This would be the first step towards effective guidance. The second would consist of specific guidelines which would specify the kinds of cases and conditions that should give rise to different dispositions.[38]

The wording of Bill C-41's principle regarding incarceration represents a significant dilution of the original formulation. The discussion document published by the Department of Justice in 1990 followed a much stronger tack. It laid down specific conditions that *had* to be fulfilled *before* a sentence of imprisonment could be imposed.

The exclusionary nature of this 1988 document is modeled upon the Sentencing Commission's statement, but is to be found in formulations in other jurisdictions as well. For example, s. 1(2) of the English *Criminal Justice Act 1991* states:[39] the court shall not pass a custodial sentence on the offender unless it is of the opinion —

(a) that the offence, or the combination of the offence and one other offence associated with it, was so serious that only such a sentence can be justified for the offence; or

(b) where the offence is a violent or sexual offence, that only such a sentence would be adequate to protect the public from serious harm from him.

In contrast to both these formulations, Bill C-41 would permit judges considerably greater latitude in terms of imposing sentences of incarceration. In short, the diluting of the principle of restraint is a clear weakness of the statement. The imposition of sentences of imprisonment needs to be constrained to a substantially greater degree if any consequential impact upon incarceration rates to be achieved. This is particularly true since sentencing guidelines are no longer a part of the government's reform package. In the absence of guidelines, all hope of changing sentencing practices resides with the statement of purpose, which accordingly must be expressed in language that is both unequivocal and forceful.

### (v) Summary

Would the statement of purpose proposed in Bill C-41 (in the words of the Minister's press release) provide "clear direction from Parliament on the purpose and principles of sentencing"? In our view, the answer is that with one exception, the proposed statement merely codifies themes that have evolved about the sentencing process and would not provide direction in the sense of giving judges a tool to promote consistency. The only practical advice for judges contained in the statement is to be found in the fundamental principle, which, it will be recalled, states that a sentence "must be proportionate to the gravity of the offence and the degree of responsibility of the offender". This may well constrain judicial behaviour. It will, in theory at least, discourage judges from imposing disproportionately harsh sentences to achieve deterrence, of disproportionately lenient sentences in order to promote the rehabilitation of the offender. The major hope of success for Bill C-41 lies with this fundamental principle.

The weakness of the over-all bill is that a rather confusing statement of purpose is all that is offered to effect changes in sentencing practices. This statement is the only means of giving life to the acknowledged policy goals of limiting unwarranted disparity and reducing the use of imprisonment as a sanction. It is unlikely to prove sufficient. If the statutory statement is the sole means of effecting change, then it should clearly specify the conditions under which certain sentencing options such as custody should be imposed. The statute contained in Bill C-41 closes off few options for the sentencing judge, and accordingly offers little *practical* guidance.

. . .

[After formulating and discussing an alternate statute, the authors continued:]

### 3. CONCLUSIONS

The importance of a statutory statement of sentencing purpose and principle cannot be over-stated. Judges, criminal justice professionals and indeed all those with an interest in sentencing will look to such a document as a statement from Parliament about sentencing policy. The importance of the statement is enhanced in the Canadian context, because unlike other jurisdictions (such as the United States) sentencing reform in this country does not involve a formal guideline system. Thus the goals of reducing the use of incarceration, promoting proportionality in sentencing and reducing the amount of sentencing disparity must all be accomplished, in larger degree, by the statement of purpose. Finally, after so much time coming, a statement of sentencing purpose passed in 1995 is unlikely to be changed in the near future. Once legislation is passed, sentencing will disappear from the criminal justice radar screen for years to come. The attention of the criminal justice system will turn elsewhere and the opportunity for further reform will not arise again for some time. The statement of purpose that enters the *Criminal Code* as a result of this sentencing reform initiative is likely to remain with us for years. It is important that the best possible statement be drafted.

. . .

1  See, for example, editorial commentary on the previous sentencing reform bill (Bill C-90) in *The Globe and Mail*, Toronto, July 2, 1992, at p. A18.

2  For a summary of recent events in the area of sentencing, see J. Roberts and A. von Hirsch, "Sentencing Reform in Canada: Recent Developments" (1992), 23 Revue Générale de Droit 491.

3  *Report of The Canadian Sentencing Commission: Sentencing Reform: A Canadian Approach* (Ottawa: Ministry of Supply & Services Canada, 1987). Chair O. Archambault (hereafter the commission), pp. 1-592.

4  House of Commons Standing Committee on Justice and Solicitor General, *Report of the Standing Committee on its Review of Sentencing, Conditional Release and Related Aspects of Corrections* (Ottawa: Ministry of Supply & Services Canada, 1988), pp. 1-300.

5  The closest Canada has come to significant sentencing reform was the *Criminal Law Reform Act of 1984*, Bill C-19, which died on the order paper when Parliament was dissolved in 1984.

6  R.S.C. 1985, c. C-46, as amended.

7  For recent data on variation in sentencing practices, see Canadian Centre for Justice Statistics, *Sentencing in Adult Criminal Provincial Courtsp* (Ottawa: Statistics Canada, 1993). As well, a great deal of empirical research has demonstrated the importance of the sentencing objective in determining the nature and quantum of the sentence: see, for example R. McFatter, "Sentencing Strategies and Justice: Effects of Punishment Philosophy on Sentencing Decisions" (1978), 36 Journal of Personality and Social Psychology 1490.

. . .

11  Bill C-41, s. 718.

12  There are only six actual subsections in the bill but some contain more than one objective. For example, s. 718(*b*) includes both general and special deterrence. For the purposes of clarity, we discuss the objectives independently here.

13  Bill C-41, s. 718. This statement of purpose is derived from the report of the Canadian Sentencing Commission. The commission attributed this purpose to the criminal law rather than sentencing *per se*. For further information on this issue, see J. Roberts and A. von Hirsch, "Sentencing Reform in Canada: Recent Developments" (1992), 23 Revue Générale de Droit 319.

14  See J. Roberts and A. von Hirsch, "Sentencing Reform in Canada", *supra*, footnote 2.

15  The commission proposal had two purposes, one for the criminal law and a related one for the sentencing process: see *Commission, supra*, footnote 3, at pp. 125-56.

16  Bill C-41, s. 718.1.

17  Bill C-41 contains a subtle shift in language from its predecessor, Bill C-90. The earlier bill simply suggested that a sentence "may" be changed to account for aggravating and mitigating circumstances.

18  Bill C-41, s. 718.2(*a*).

19  It is the conceptual equivalent of saying to professors that the grade assigned to a student's paper should reflect both the good and the bad points.

20  Bill C-41, s. 718.2(*b*).

21  In between principles (a) and (b), Bill C-41 introduces a statutory aggravating factor. It states that evidence that the offence was motivated by hate, or that the offender abused a position of trust, shall be deemed an aggravating circumstance. This clause — not present in the preceding Bill C-90 — raises its own set of problems. However, restrictions on space prevent us exploring the issue further in this article.

22  Bill C-41, s. 718.2(*c*).

23  See A. Ashworth, *Sentencing and Penal Policy* (London: Weidenfeld & Nicolson, 1983), pp. 259-68; D.A. Thomas, *Principles of Sentencing* (London: Heinemann, 1979), pp. 56-61.

24  A statement of purpose and principle need not, and in fact cannot, include all relevant sentencing principles. For example, a great deal has been written about the principle that has evolved whereby defendants who plead guilty are accorded a more lenient sentence than accused who are found guilty. Should this "discount" be enshrined in the guiding statute as well?

25  See S. Mihorean and S. Lipinski, "International Incarceration Patterns, 1980-1990" (1992), 12 Juristat Service Bulletin 12.

26  See for example, the report on sentencing published by the Government of Canada in 1982: "Sentencing" (Ottawa: Department of Justice Canada, 1982) at p. 34, and also the discussion documents released by the federal government in 1990.

27  Bill C-41, s. 718.2(*d*).

28  Brown Commission, *Second Report of the Commissioners of the Penitentiary Inquiry* (Ottawa, 1849).

29  Nielsen Task Force Report on the Justice System, *The Justice System — A Study Team Report to the Task Force Program Review* (Ottawa, Minister of Supply & Services, 1986).

30  See Brief submitted to the Canadian Sentencing Commission by the Law Reform Commission of Canada (Ottawa: Law Reform Commission of Canada, March, 1985).

31  See *Commission, supra*, footnote 3, at p. 154.

32  See Government of Canada, *Directions for Reform: A Framework for Sentencing, Corrections and Conditional Release* (Ottawa: Ministry of Supply & Services Canada, 1990).

33  Bill C-41, s. 718.2(*e*).

34  Canadian Centre for Justice Statistics, *Adult Correctional Services in Canada, 1992-1990* (Ottawa, Statistics Canada, 1993).

35  Data supplied to the authors by the Ontario Ministry of the Solicitor General and Correctional Services, August 15, 1994.

36  See Commission on Systemic Racism in the Ontario Criminal Justice System, *Racism Behind Bars: Interim Report* (Toronto, Queen's Printer for Ontario, 1994).

37  See C. Laprairie "The role of sentencing in the over-representation of aboriginal people in correctional institutions" (1990), 32 Can. J. Crim. at pp. 429-40 for a thoughtful discussion of this issue.

38  For further discussion of this issue, see A. Doob, "Community Sanctions and Imprisonment" (1990), 32 Can. J. Crim. at pp. 415-28.

39  See *Criminal Justice Act* (U.K.), . . . The Act has subsequently been revised.

## Regina v. Hollinsky
### (1995), 103 C.C.C. (3d) 472 (Ont. C.A.)

Appeal by the Crown from a sentence imposed by Nosanchuk Prov. Div. J., *infra*, following the accused's conviction on two counts of dangerous driving causing death. The judgment appealed from is as follows:

*March 9, 1995.*

NOSANCHUK PROV. DIV. J. (orally): — On July 30, 1994, at 1:45 a.m. an automobile accident with very tragic consequences occurred. A 1985 Pontiac Sunbird, driven by Kevin Hollinsky, age 19, in an easterly direction on Wyandotte St. E. near St. Luke Rd. in Windsor, went out of control. It struck two hydro poles and ended up on a lawn next to a house. Two passengers, Joseph Camlis and Andrew Thompson died as a result of the injuries sustained in the accident. Todd Giles, another passenger, suffered injuries to his mouth and a punctured lung. These injuries had no lasting effect and were not life-threatening. The driver, Kevin Hollinsky, escaped uninjured.

The Sunbird was observed driving at a speed in excess of the speed limit about two blocks before the accident occurred. It overtook and cut in front of one auto; it then drove close behind a second auto, and, in the process of overtaking the second auto, the auto driven by Kevin Hollinsky skidded out of control and a single car accident with the tragic consequences indicated earlier occurred.

On February 2, 1995, Kevin Hollinsky pleaded guilty to a count in an information alleging that on July 30, 1994, he drove a motor vehicle in a manner that was dangerous to the public, thereby causing the death of Joseph Camlis, contrary to s. 249 of the *Criminal Code* [s. 249 [rep. & sub. R.S.C. 1985, c. 27 (1st Supp.), s. 36; *am idem*, c. 32 (4th Supp.), s. 57; 1994, c. 44, s. 11] and to a further count alleging an identical offence causing the death of Andrew Thompson.

The prosecution in this case has submitted that the court ought to impose a prison term of from eight to 12 months in an Ontario reformatory to deter other potential dangerous drivers from committing similar offences. The prosecutor concedes that in this case there is no real issue as to specific deterrence of Kevin Hollinsky. The victims were his very best friends and the enormity of the loss will unquestionably deter him from committing a similar offence in the future. The prosecutor argues, however, that a message must be sent out to any prospective offenders that the penalty of a prison term in at least the range indicated must follow for similar criminal conduct.

Defence counsel has urged the court to impose a non-custodial term on the accused. He has argued that a non-custodial sentence in cases of dangerous driving causing death are not entirely unprecedented. He has contended that this is a unique case, submitting that, "No punishment could possibly make up for the loss of the lives that occurred".

In the support of his submission in this case, defence counsel has the overwhelming and unqualified support of the families of both deceased victims, Andrew Thompson and Joseph Camlis. This court was exceedingly impressed and moved by the out-pouring of compassion on the part of these families for Kevin Hollinsky, and their collective determination to respond to their own terrible losses in a constructive manner.

There was a recognition by them of the obvious guilt that would be suffered by Kevin Hollinsky for many years, if not for the rest of his life, as the result of the commission of the offence. There was a recognition of the torment that he has gone through and will continue to go through. There was an absence of bitterness and a desire to take positive and healing steps. There was a determination to participate in a program of public education to prevent such a tragedy from reoccurring as a tribute to the memories of Joseph Camlis and Andrew Thompson.

To accomplish that purpose, the families have already contacted the Windsor Police Services, and have volunteered their personal participation in attending schools throughout the area on a program of public education. They propose to have Kevin Hollinsky join them, which he is willing to do. They propose to use by way of demonstration the debris of the automobile in which their sons perished. They have committed themselves to going out and telling young students, in their own words, about the horrible and devastating tragedy of July 30, 1994, in the company of Kevin

Hollinsky, in order to educate the young students about the need for responsible driving.

The conduct and attitude of the parents of the victims in this case is, indeed, a tribute to the capacity of the human spirit to respond affirmatively and with profound compassion to an awful tragedy.

The families of the victims have pleaded with the court, both in correspondence and in oral testimony, not to impose a custodial term on Kevin Hollinsky. "What useful purpose could be served", they have contended, "by sending Kevin Hollinsky to prison? Has he not suffered enough? Surely, the loss of his two very best friends is ample punishment".

Counsel for the accused has also reminded the court of the deep psychological wounds that could well be suffered by Kevin as a result of the offence. These pleas that were made on behalf of Kevin Hollinsky by the families of the victims were very powerful, very sincere, and have made the task of sentencing in this case incredibly difficult.

The sworn duty of this court is to uphold the law and to impose a just sentence according to the law. The court is obliged to balance the interests of the accused and the state. The fact that a criminal prosecution has been launched makes this case a matter of public concern. The commission of a criminal offence can never be simply a private matter between the accused and the family of the victim.

In determining the appropriate sentence in this case, the court must bear in mind that the overriding consideration in sentencing is the protection of the community and society. The sentencing court has the duty of imposing a fit and just sentence according to well-established sentencing principles of specific deterrence, general deterrence rehabilitation and denunciation. Any sentence that is imposed on an accused person ought to involve a wise blending of all of the above elements.

The court has been referred to numerous trial and appellate decisions delivered by courts across the country. As counsel for the accused has pointed out, sentences for the commission of the offence of dangerous driving causing death range from a suspended sentence to a penitentiary term. . . .

While alcohol may have been a factor in the case before the court, it must be observed that the prosecutor withdrew the charges of operating a motor vehicle while impaired by alcohol and causing death, stating that in his opinion, it could not be established that the death was related to operating a motor vehicle while impaired by alcohol. In addition, the prosecutor withdrew a charge alleging that the accused operated a motor vehicle with a concentration of alcohol in his blood that exceeded 80 mg of alcohol in 100 ml of blood. . . .

At the time of the commission of the offence, Kevin Hollinsky was a young man of 19 years of age. He has an unblemished past with no criminal record or record of traffic offences. He comes from a caring, devoted, and loving family. He was described as a kind, gentle, and loving young man by the families of both of the deceased victims, and by a former teacher.

His employer indicated that he has proven to be a trustworthy and loyal employee, that he has a good sense of values, and shows a great amount of loyalty to the company and to fellow workers. His employer describes him as always friendly and professional in dealing with customers and suppliers. He has always shown a willingness to learn new tasks and carries out work assigned to its full completion. His punctuality, neatness, and enthusiasm make him a person one can trust and respect.

The relationship of Kevin Hollinsky to his two deceased friends was unique. The devotion and loyalty of one to the other was remarkable. The impact of the deaths upon Kevin Hollinsky has been devastating. Joseph Camlis and Andrew Thompson were like brothers to him. The court has no doubt that Kevin Hollinsky would gladly serve any amount of time in prison in exchange for the return of his deceased friends.

Kevin Hollinsky has demonstrated great remorse and feels enormous guilt. He is currently receiving psychotherapy from a family physician who has indicated that he has, to quote the doctor, "undergone a great deal of anxiety and a depressive reaction that has changed his life tremendously". The doctor was impressed that Kevin Hollinsky was, to quote the doctor, "a decent young man who made a mistake and suffered a tremendous loss". The doctor is of the opinion that Kevin can learn from his mistake and be helpful to others.

Kevin Hollinsky has accepted responsibility for the offences and pleaded guilty before the commencement of the preliminary inquiry. The public has been saved the considerable expense of a preliminary inquiry and a trial. He is prepared to perform extensive community service to atone for the offence. As part of this service, he would attend on a regular basis to speak to students at local schools, and to openly explain the circumstances of the tragic event of July 30, 1994, with a view to impressing them with the immense risks involved in driving an automobile, particularly in driving it in a dangerous manner.

In this endeavour, the accused is fully supported by the parents of the victims and members of their families. The message delivered would undoubtedly leave an indelible and lasting impression on the students to whom it is delivered.

In addition, Kevin Hollinsky has been found suitable to perform community service work under the special work assignment program set up by Reaching Out in this community. This program involves a specified number of hours of labour-intensive work, doing litter pick-up and other heavy labour with non-profit organizations in a community, that need assistance with special projects. The program is designed for offenders who would otherwise serve a period of custody in prison were it not for the availability of the program. It can serve as a concrete alternative to imprisonment in this case.

Kevin Hollinsky has also been found suitable to do further community service that would be required of him over the balance of any probationary period to which he is sentenced. That service would involve working with youth groups in his community and doing other community service work that would benefit the community.

The court has no doubt that the accused is highly motivated and will perform all of the community service that has been outlined previously in an exemplary fashion. This court is convinced that there are, indeed, extraordinary circumstances in this case that lead the court to conclude that a term of imprisonment is not necessary in order to achieve the objective of general deterrence. The arrest of the accused, his public prosecution in court, the fact that he now has a record of conviction for two serious offences under the *Criminal Code* of Canada, the fact that he will lose his licence to drive a motor vehicle for an extended period of time, the fact that as an alternative to imprisonment he will be performing worthwhile and extensive community service, personally attending as required to repeatedly send a message of public education to other young persons, serves the need for general deterrence in this community in relation to the offences before this court.

The court has decided to seize the opportunity presented by this unique set of circumstances to make available the voices of the accused and the families of the victim through public education in this community. What more compelling message in the service of deterrence could be sent than the knowledge of the crushing devastation caused by the loss of the young person's two best friends as a result of the commission of the offences that are before the court? The elaborate community service program that has been arranged in the unique circumstances of this case as an alternative to imprisonment will serve the principle of general deterrence more effectively than simply the knowledge that a reformatory term of eight to 12 months was imposed. . . .

In conclusion, this court emphasizes that this is a unique and exceptional case. No member of the public ought to conclude that the fact that you have not gone to prison is a precedent for other cases of dangerous driving. The exceptional support and the affirmative action taken by the families of the victims, and your own family, have convinced this court that in this unique case as an alternative to imprisonment, the kind of community service that you will undertake will serve the ends of justice and will, in the long run, serve protection of the community far more effectively than would the imposition of any prison term. . . .

The following judgment was endorsed on the appeal record.

BY THE COURT: — Although an offence of this nature would usually require a custodial sentence, we have reviewed the carefully considered reasons of the trial judge and having regard to the exceptional circumstances of this case, we are in general agreement with these reasons. The Crown concedes that there is no concern on its part in this case with respect to the specific deterrence or rehabilitation of the appellant. It is only concerned with the matter of general deterrence. We have had the benefit of viewing the results of the performance by the respondent of the community service required from him as part of his sentence and in particular his participation in appearing before more than 8,300 students on 14 occasions emphasizing the terrible consequences of dangerous driving while drinking. This fresh evidence filed on behalf of the respondent is indicative of the powerful deterrent effect of this type of program as projected by the trial judge.

Moreover, the fresh evidence indicates that the respondent has successfully performed all but 75 hours of the 750 hours of community service required of him and it would be considerably more harsh to impose a custodial sentence at this time than it would have been in the first instance. For these reasons, although leave to appeal is granted, the appeal is dismissed.

*Appeal dismissed.*

## 5.2 PUNISHMENT

### Introduction

*R.P. Saunders and C. Mitchell*

Another problem in sentencing is the type and severity of punishment that is given out. Canada has one of the highest incarceration rates in the world, and yet it is a self-evident fact that prisons do little but brutalize and harden those who have been put into them. The rates of homicide, sexual assault, assault, and suicide within prisons are very high, but there is little concern or interest on the part of the general population. There is an attitude that those who are imprisoned deserve everything they get, in spite of the argument that most of those imprisoned are not convicted of violent offences. For example, the profile of those in federal prisons — that is, those institutions that presumably house those convicted of the most serious offences — indicates that only 35 percent of the inmates have been convicted for violent offences. In fact, the public overestimates the amount of violent crime generally, as documented in the *Report of the Sentencing Commission* (see Further Reading). The simple fact is that prisons do not work and yet the courts and legislators continue to turn to them as a solution.

Next to the police, the most numerous and expensive public servants engaged in the criminal legal system are those employed in penalizing convicted criminals. In 1979, there were approximately 8,000 staff to handle the 9,500 federal prison inmates incarcerated in Canada at a cost of well over a billion dollars. By 1985, 12,000 federal inmates cost $1.5 billion to imprison, while by the year 2001 there were approximately 12,800 federal inmates and 18,600 provincial inmates at a cost of $2.5 billion. The average annual cost for a federal male prisoner was $66,381 in 2000-2001, while the figure for a female inmate was $110,473. In addition, there is the National Parole Board staff that supervises paroled inmates and an army of court clerks and sheriffs administering and collecting fines from the majority of convicted persons. Attention usually focuses on prison and post-prison supervision because these penalties are labour-intensive, expensive, and extremely intrusive compared to the levying of fines. Unfortunately, as noted above, Canadian judges, more than many of their counterparts elsewhere, rely on incarceration so the sentencing process as well as the administration of jails and prisons is of particular concern in Canada. On the positive side, the numbers of those serving time in federal prisons has dropped slightly since 1997 and remains well below those of the United States:

**Number of inmates per 100,000 population (2000):**

| | |
|---|---|
| United States | 699 |
| New Zealand | 149 |
| England & Wales | 124 |
| **Canada** | **118** |
| Scotland | 115 |
| Australia | 108 |

| Germany | 97 |
| Italy | 94 |
| France | 89 |
| Austria | 84 |
| Switzerland | 79 |
| Sweden | 64 |
| Denmark | 61 |
| Finland | 52 |

Generally, both the provincial and federal governments administer prison services. Convicts are allotted to one level or the other according to the length of their prison sentence: two years or longer (not including consecutive sentences) and the prisoner goes into a federal penitentiary. Half of the admissions to provincial jails served sentences under one month with only about 5 percent sentenced to more than a year. At the federal level, the Canadian Penitentiary Service and the National Parole Service merged in 1979 into the Correctional Service of Canada (CSC). The CSC operates about 60 institutions including maximum, medium and minimum security prisons, camps, farms, community centers, and psychiatric facilities. The more secure prisons average less than 500 inmates and are considerably smaller than the largest American prisons. At the provincial level, a variety of institutions exist that differ from federal prisons in two important respects. First, as noted, all the convicted inmates at provincial facilities are serving short sentences, usually under a month, and many are locked up only on weekends. Second, in many cases the convicted share space with the non-convicted, usually persons on remand awaiting trial. At the provincial level, therefore, there is no stable, long-term population of convict inmates and little emphasis on "correctional" programs. In Ontario, there is also the controversial issue of privatizing prison facilities, which has begun to some degree in the last few years and has been widely criticized by those in the field.

The *Constitution Act, 1867*, in subsection 91(2), provides that the 'establishment, maintenance and management of Penitentiaries' is a matter of exclusive federal jurisdiction, but also grants the provinces power over 'public and reformatory prisons' in subsection 92(6). *Criminal Code* section 743.1 sets out the 'two year rule' by which the two levels of government divide prisoners. The rationale for this division is not clear. The distinction may be historical: in pre-1867, a "penitentiary" meant a place of confinement for convicts sentenced to two or more years of incarceration. Another possibility is that the federal government's exclusive power to make criminal law is consistent with authority over prisons containing "real criminals" whereas the provincial prisons contain those convicted of regulatory offences to which little moral condemnation attaches. In this latter case perhaps the provincial 'reformatory prison' parallels a school or a hospital, both of which fall under exclusive provincial jurisdiction. Regardless of the reason for the jurisdictional split, the division of prisoners creates certain difficulties among which are an impediment to national standards and national record keeping. Another concern is that a lengthy prison term can mean a transfer to a distant federal prison out of the home province. On a minor note, jurisdiction over offenders depends on the type and length of sentence, not on the jurisdiction that enacted the relevant statutory offence. Persons convicted under federal or provincial laws may be sent to ether provincial or federal jails. In practice, few provincial offences lead to penitentiary because such offences rarely authorize lengthy confinement and, if they do, judges will rarely impose such penalties under provincial law (Hogg, 1985).

Modern prisons generate numerous administrative problems because they interfere massively with normal legal rights and personal autonomy. Voting rights, privacy rights, freedom of association, right to counsel and numerous other indices of normal citizenship have been denied by authorities and by prison conditions. These denials and social deprivations flow logically the guiding principles espoused by the inventors of prisons, though of these deprivations have been challenged (at times successfully) and are being challenged in the courts under the *Charter*.

The primary thesis behind the creation of prisons was that criminals required the rehabilitating influences only the carefully controlled prison environment could deliver. Writing about the Auburn and Pennsylvania prison systems of the early to mid 1800s, Rothman explains their common assumptions:

> Convinced that deviancy was primarily the result of the corruptions pervading the community. . .they believed that a setting which removed the offender from all temptations and substituted a steady and regular regimen would reform him. . .The penitentiary, free of corruptions and dedicated to the proper training of the inmate, would inculcate the discipline that negligent parents, evil companions, taverns, houses of prostitution, theatres, and gambling halls had destroyed. Just as the criminal's environment had led him into crime, the institutional environment would lead him out of it. The duty of the penitentiary was to separate the offender from all contact with corruption. . .There was obviously no sense to removing a criminal from the depravity of his surroundings only to have him mix freely with other convicts within the prison.

Supporters of the Pennsylvania system could boast that their inmates were 'perfectly secluded' from the world and 'hopelessly separated' from family and friends. The exclusion ideal led prison wardens to prohibit letters, visits, and even news from outside the prison walls. Later, New York officials relented somewhat, allowing prisoners to receive one visit in the course of their sentence and to send one letter (written by the chaplain and censored by the warden) every four months. Wardens of that period also considered the whip, the iron gag, the ball and chain, and other corporal punishments indispensable for maintaining the strict order necessary to achieve their rehabilitative ends.

The appropriateness of prison as either a retributive or rehabilitative instrument is one that is subject to much debate, and prisons are generally viewed as breeding grounds of criminal activity and violence. The first two readings look at some of the issues and goals surrounding the corrections sector, while the third reading from the *Justice and Poor* report addresses the unrepresentativeness of those who serve time in federal and provincial jails.

To reduce the severity of the imprisonment, there is also the possibility of parole, which allows for the inmate to be released under supervision into the community before the expiration of his or her sentence. Given the discretionary nature of the process, this obviously creates another layer of potential disparity in that offenders who have committed the same wrongful act and have been sentenced to same quantum of time in jail end up serving very different amounts of time. How the parole authorities exercise their discretion can have a very great effect on the actual time spent in custody. The reading by MacKay looks at the variety of conditional releases available.

## Correctional Philosophy, Working Paper No. 1*

### *Solicitor General of Canada*

*Excerpts from *Correctional Philosophy, Working Paper No. 1* (Ottawa: Solicitor General of Canada, 1986).

. . .

## Part II:
## THE PURPOSE AND PRINCIPLES OF THE CRIMINAL LAW AND IMPLICATIONS FOR CORRECTIONS

### *Rehabilitation*

Although rehabilitation has generally been discredited as a legitimate justification for *sentencing* an offender to imprisonment, no major report has ever recommended an end to rehabilitation as a goal of *corrections*. Even in 1977 Parliamentary Sub-committee, which rejected the use of imprisonment in order to rehabilitate offenders, said that "once a decision to imprison has been taken. . ., the correctional techniques employed should be aimed at encouraging and assisting personal reformation by wrongdoers". Thus, imprisonment (and corrections generally) contribute to the pro-tection of society, in the Sub-committee's view, in two ways:

> "Protection of society" as a purpose of imprisonment includes not only protection during a term of imprisonment by the physical removal of a person who is dangerous or who has failed to respect values that are protected by the criminal law, but also the protection of society after his release by means of a prison system designed to assist him towards personal reformation.

Corrections is the only segment of the criminal justice system which is supposed to assist and encourage the offender to overcome the factors which contribute to his criminality. Other stages in the criminal justice system may occasionally or acciden-tally have this effect, but it is only after sentencing that any government agency is authorized to try to "treat" an offender. Even in an era of financial restraint, most corrections professionals, academics, and even members of the public still support the principle of rehabilitation, perhaps simply on the grounds that it would be irre-sponsible and cynical to give up so soon.

Despite the foregoing, it is nonetheless true that during the 1970's in Canada, rehabilitation fell into disfavour as a correctional ideal. The disfavour was on two fronts: first, that rehabilitation had been costly and ineffective, and second, that it had caused more cruelty and longer punishment than the intentionally "punitive" model which had preceded it.

In fact most of the allegations that treatment is "tyrannical" stem from the study of a few jurisdictions, primarily California and Maryland, and the concerns arose from the use of extremely lengthy or indeterminate prison sentences combined with a highly interventionist treatment philosophy. Nonetheless, there is probably some truth to the notion that offenders see an element of unfairness in almost any attempt to rehabilitate them. After all, virtually any type of personal change is in some respects painful. For offenders, "personal information" (as the 1977 Parliamentary Sub-committee on the Penitentiary System put it) can entail a painful and difficult struggle to give up alcohol or drugs, working at a low-paying and unsatisfying job instead of pursuing the risk and excitement of less legitimate earnings, or a protracted process of acquiring new methods of recognizing and dealing with anger and frustration.

Despite this painful element to rehabilitation, however, it is probably fair to say that most people would support rehabilitation if it were proven to be effective and if it did not create excessive additional punishment, costs and risks. How strong is the case, then, that rehabilitation is proven to be ineffective?

Some criminologists have in fact characterized this as one of the greatest overgeneralizations in criminal justice. They argue that most evaluated programs in corrections could, in the word of one official, be characterized (as was one particularly well-documented one) as "a poorly conceptualized program that was inadequately delivered by unqualified personnel to individuals who might have been appropriately assigned to it".

Has "rehabilitation", even in the form just described, been "proven" ineffective, however? Is the evaluative research on programs definitive? Here again, the bulk of expert opinion has it that the quality of evaluative research has, in the main, approached that of the programs themselves. Probably the most authoritative review of the literature, by the U.S. National Academy of Science Panel on Research and Rehabilitation Techniques, concludes that most of the research in the area has been inconclusive if not meaningless, because of poor methodology and a tendency to "evaluate" a multifaceted correctional experience (such as probation) as if it were a single phenomenon. Very little correctional research to date has been sophisticated enough to differentiate which offenders are helped — and which are made worse — by which techniques under which conditions. Most programs, with good and bad results, thus are felt to have, overall, "no effect."

We are of the view then, that it cannot be concluded that rehabilitation is ineffective. The evidence is too sparse, and the actual attempts to design, fund, and carry out a rehabilitative model for corrections have, to date, been inconsistent and incomplete. Should corrections therefore continue to try to correct offenders?

The best protection for society is widely acknowledged to be the re-integration of offenders into the community as law-abiding citizens. Actively pursuing the goal of encouraging and assisting the personal reformation of offenders, rather than relying on punishment and deterrence to achieve the same goal, is thought by the Working Group to be more appropriate for three reasons.

First, it treats individual offenders as responsible individuals capable of change and taking charge of their lives.

Second, it gives a role to correctional authorities which is positive, humane and which actively supports the long term criminal justice objectives. This role, rather than one which emphasizes the containment of inmates and maintenance of order, is far more rewarding for staff who assume responsibility for assisting and encouraging offenders to take advantage of rehabilitation opportunities.

Finally, the rehabilitative approach holds more potential than a simple punishment/ deterrence approach, simply because it recognizes the inevitable reality that there are causal factors which contribute to criminality which no amount of punishment will remedy. By this we means such things as unemployment, poor impulse control, lack of job skills, low frustration tolerance, functional illiteracy, poor social and problem-solving skills, inability to cope with emotional stress. Many of these problems can be effectively dealt with through teaching offenders cognitive and behavioral skills. Offenders are extremely unlikely to learn the necessary skills themselves, and punishment through deterrence or simple incapacitation will not teach them. Experience also suggest that offenders are unlikely to take advantage of program opportunities unless they are actively encouraged to do so, and one of the most effective incentives to program participation is a high-quality program.

### *Reconciliation*

Reconciliation — of the offender with society, or the offender with the individual victim — has gained greater legitimacy in recent years. Long considered more appropriate to the civil courts which resolve disputes between individuals, restitution to victims as a sentence in criminal matters has grown with the increased recognition of victims' rights in the past decade. In addition, sentences which involve service to the community generally, such as community service orders, have become more common. All these reflect a greater recognition of the need to make reconciliation more prominent as a criminal justice goal.

### *The Influence of Public Attitudes on the Delineation of a Correctional Philosophy*

What the public has a right to reasonably expect from corrections should and will affect how corrections views its mandate. First and foremost, the public expects protection from crime, especially violent crime. For corrections, this means carrying out the requirements of the sentence, including the maintenance of a sufficient degree of security to prevent escapes from correctional institutions. It means always having regard for the potential risk to the public interest in all decisions about the treatment and handling of offenders. The public also has a right to expect that the punitive and deterrent aspects of the sentence will be respected by correctional authorities, and that any conditional release from imprisonment following the service of the punitive portion of a sentence will be made in accordance with the overall criminal justice goals of justice and security.

Once a decision has been made by the court to use imprisonment in an individual case, the public also has a right to expect that what goes on inside institutions will be optimally directed towards reducing the offender's chances of coming back. The 1977 Parliamentary Sub-committee on the Penitentiary System said that "society has spent millions of dollars over the years to create and maintain the proven failure of prisons.

Incarceration has failed in its two essential purposes — correcting the offender and providing permanent protection to society". The Sub-committee went on to recommend both the availability of more community based alternatives to incarceration, and the wiser use of the time which imprisoned offenders spend incarcerated. In the Sub-committee's view, imprisonment too often becomes just a very expensive warehousing operation. "Personal information" instead was what the Sub-committee felt should be the goal of prisons. The public too has a right to expect more for its imprisonment dollars than a revolving-door warehouse.

The public also reasonably expects that its tax monies will be spent in the most effective possible way. Public attitude surveys suggest that it is violent crime which most concerns Canadians, and that the public is more willing to accept non-carceral handling of nonviolent offenders than many criminal justice professionals assume. This is a reasonable approach, especially in view of the high costs of imprisonment. As competition among social programs for increasingly scarce tax dollars increases, it makes sense to reserve the most costly correctional intervention for those who most deserve or require it.

## A Framework for the Correctional Law Review, Working Paper No. 2*

### Solicitor General of Canada

*Excerpts from *A Framework for the Correctional Law Review, Working Paper No. 2* (Ottawa: Solicitor General of Canada, 1986).

. . .

### Judicial Attitudes and Decisions

Case law relating to corrections has generally been dependent upon the attitude of the courts to the prospect of going behind prison walls to scrutinize correctional practices and to review the internal decision-making procedures of prison officials.

Until relatively recently, Canadian courts exhibited a marked reluctance to assume an active role in reviewing the activities and decisions of prison administrators. This judicial reticence, known as the "hands-off" approach, had the effect of immunizing prisons and the actions of prison officials from public scrutiny.

One justification for the courts' approach was the belief that, having regard to the difficulties inherent in running a prison and safe-guiding prison security, the job should be left to those best equipped to handle the situation — the prison administrators themselves. A second reason for the "hands-off" approach was the suggestion that confrontations between inmates and prison administrators would escalate, and would in fact be fuelled by the courts' open reception to suits brought to challenge conditions in Canadian prisons. Furthermore, the enormity of the task of rectifying conditions was regarded as a cogent factor militating against judicial interference. In this regard, the *Parliamentary Sub-Committee on the Penitentiary In Canada* stated:

> The gross irregularities, lack of standards and arbitrariness that exist in our penitentiaries, by their very quantity, make and always have made, the possibility of judicial intervention into prison mattes a rather impracticable, time consuming and dismaying prospect. . .The sheer immensity of the task of straightening it out is enough to discourage even the most committed members of the judiciary.

One of the strongest reasons offered in explanation of the courts "hands-off" attitude was the once-popular notion that, once convicted and sentenced to a term of incarceration, a prisoner became automatically stripped of all rights.

Although the concept of civil death, whereby a person lost all rights upon conviction, was abolished in Canada in 1892, the traditional view of courts, that review of prison administration was something beyond their jurisdiction, lingered.

Further factors involved two vitally important administrative law principles: first, that the only decisions which could be characterized as judicial or quasi-judicial were those which affected a person's rights; and second, that only decisions which could be characterized as judicial or quasi-judicial were subject to judicial review. Since prisoners were regarded as having few "rights", most of the decisions made by prison officials were regarded as being purely administrative in nature and were therefore immune from review by the courts. As a consequence, "inmates who had few rights, also had few remedies and were left essentially defenceless against the wide-ranging administrative decision-making power of the prison authorities".

Only as recently as the 1970's did changes begin to take place. A series of decisions which relied, essentially, on the argument that an individual in prison does not lose "the right to have rights" served to strengthen the position of those in favour of offender rights. In *R. v. Solosky* the Supreme Court of Canada expressly endorsed the proposition that a person confined to prison retains all civil rights, except for those necessarily limited by the nature of incarceration or expressly or impliedly taken away by law. Moreover, the Supreme Court endorsed the "least restrictive means" approach which recognized that the courts have a balancing role to play to ensure that any interference with inmates' rights by institutional authorities is for a valid correctional goal and must be the least restrictive means available.

In other cases, the Federal Court applied the cruel and unusual punishment clause of the *Canadian Bill of Rights* to administrative segregation, and the courts began to develop the common law duty to act fairly in decisions affecting both inmates and parolees.

It is not entirely clear why the courts gradually began to assume a more active role in reviewing prison officials' decision-making procedures and to intervene to recognize and protect offender rights. It has been suggested from a sociological perspective that the increased awareness of inmates' rights paralleled a growing movement, which was particularly strong in the United States, for the extension of legal rights to a broad spectrum of groups in society such as racial minorities, children, women and the handicapped. It came to be recognized that prisons operated as autonomous systems insulated from public scrutiny and external review and that this lack of public visibility make it impossible for prisoners to assert their claims on their own behalf. Strong and persistent activist groups were formed to challenge the status quo. reminiscent of John Howard's model of outside inspection, pubic scrutiny and judicial intervention came to be regarded as effective ways of controlling abuses of power behind prison walls.

It has also been suggested that the gradual acceptance of the rehabilitative ideal within corrections as a primary goal of correctional institutions was one of the most important factors which set the stage for the growth of judicial scrutiny of penitentiary operations. Despite the drawbacks of the rehabilitative model, it was reasoned that since most inmates are expected to be eventually released into society, they should learn to respect authority and to participate in the democratic control of that authority of being able to challenge what may appear to be unfair or arbitrary exercises of power by prison officials.

Apart from these explanations, the shift in judicial attitudes may be looked upon as a practical consequence of the significant and radical developments which occurred in the sphere of administrative law generally. The recognition in England of a duty of procedural fairness in administrative matters opened the door to permit judicial review of decisions which could not be properly characterized as either judicial or quasi-judicial.

The notion was transported to Canada and first appeared in a dissenting judgment of Dickson J. in *Howarth v. National Parole Board*. In that case, Dickson J. stated, *inter alia*, that an administrative decision must be made "judicially" where the decision has a serious impact on the person involved.

> "It is not necessary that a body should be a court of law . . . before it falls under a duty to act judicially.
>
> . . .
>
> Generally speaking if 'rights' are affected by the order or decision. . .the function will be classified as judicial or quasi-judicial and this is particularly so when the exercise of administrative power seriously encroaches on property rights or the enjoyment of personal liberty."

. . .

The role of the courts in requiring that certain restrictions be placed on the penitentiaries' ultimate carceral power was reflected in the simultaneous treatment of three cases by the Supreme Court of Canada in December, 1985: *Morin v., National Special Handling Unit Review Committee et al.; R. v. Miller; and Cardinal et al. v. Director of Kent Institution.* The court dealt with largely procedural questions relating to inmates' access to the *habeas corpus* remedy in a manner which reaffirms recognition of inmate rights, in this case of rights to "residual liberty" in regard to placing inmates in administrative segregation and special handling units. Characterizing such practices as creating "a prison within a prison", the Court held that even though inmates have a limited right to liberty, they must be treated fairly in regard to any limitations on the liberty they retain as members of the general prison population.

Emerging from this examination of the impact of the courts on corrections is the fact that the courts now seem willing to scrutinize the administration and practices of penitentiaries. Even prior to the Charter, the courts played an important role in recognizing and legitimizing the rights of inmates. At this stage, it appears that the power of the courts has been strengthened under the Charter and that their efforts to provide procedural protections and substantive content to the rights of offenders continue.

. . .

## Justice and the Poor*

### National Council of Welfare

*Excerpts from National Council of Welfare, *Justice and the Poor* (Ottawa: Minister of Public Works and Government Services Canada, 2000) at 91-2; 93-5; 96.

## Imprisonment

Canada does not publish good statistics on its court sentences for adults. This contributes to disparity in sentencing, since judges cannot be expected to hand down sentences that are consistent with those of their colleagues when they do not know what they are. Court statistics for young offenders are better kept.

For adults, the most recent available statistics on sentences for federal criminal offences only cover provincial courts in nine jurisdictions in 1993-94. They indicate that the ten offences that sent the largest numbers of offenders to prison were, in order, failure to appear before the court (20,588 people); break and enter/burglary (19,733); failure to comply with a court order (15,755); being unlawfully at large (13,695); driving while disqualified (7,814); drug trafficking (7,245); impaired driving — over 80 mg of alcohol (5,402); minor assault (4,730); robbery (4,704); and theft under $1,000 (4,284). By comparison, only 85 people were sent to prison for manslaughter, 126 for aggravated sexual assaults and 486 for aggravated non-sexual assaults.

For young people under age 18, the ten offences which produced the largest numbers being sent to secure custody in all Canadian courts in 1997-98 were failure to comply with a court disposition (2,378); break and enter/burglary (1,794); failure to appear before the court (1,152); theft under $1,000 (937); possession of stolen property (840); minor assault (717); escaping custody (692); robbery (525); assault with a weapon (423); and being unlawfully at large (414).

Except for robbers, youths convicted of assaults with a weapon, and perhaps escapees, there is no indication that the offenders in the top ten categories that fill our prisons have committed violent acts. The little we know about offenders who fail to appear for their court hearings, or who fail to comply with court conditions, suggests that many of them are alcoholics or drug addicts, street kids or other homeless people, or members of other marginal groups who are incapable of keeping track of things like when and where they are due to appear in court (or to go back to prison after an authorized absence, for those who are unlawfully at large).

The huge numbers sent to jail for failing to appear and other technical violations also demonstrate how easily people with irregular lifestyles, or people who are fully occupied by basic survival, such as many Aboriginal people, can be captured by the criminal justice system for trivial offences and then never let go. Between 1987 and 1997, the number of charges against young people for failure to appear increased by 129 percent. Since criminal law provides that a person should not be found guilty unless he or she intended to commit an offence, and such intention is missing when people simply forget to appear, or are too disorganized to remember what day it is, or suffer from mental illnesses that make intentions impossible, the large number of convictions for technical violations raises serious doubts about the quality of these people's legal representation, assuming they had some.

. . .

Although no Canada-wide study has been done to confirm it, mental health experts believe that the proportion of mentally ill who end up in our prisons has increased as deinstitutionalization continues to push more people into the community who would formerly have been kept in psychiatric facilities. Many of them are on the street, with estimates that between 20 and 30 percent of homeless people in Canada are mentally ill. U.S. studies indicate that many people fall through the cracks of the system by being considered too "dangerous" to be accepted for treatment but not disturbed enough to be committed.

As a result, "the criminal justice system may have become the institution that cannot say no. . .the default option for disposition of persons who are not able to be treated within the mental health system." After finding that the probability of being arrested was 20 percent greater for the same offence when the suspects showed signs of mental disorder, U.S. experts commented that "Clearly, the way we treat our mentally ill is criminal." According to Judge David Cole, the situation is not better in Canada:

> What most of us [judges] are doing is a lot of routine processing of petty offenders — most of whom are mentally ill. We are getting tired of watching the parade.

Two other offences among the top ten for adults, impaired driving and driving while disqualified, are also related to alcohol. For impaired driving, judges may have been obliged to order a prison sentence because minimum sentences of imprisonment are specified in the law for second offences (minimum of 14 days in prison) and subsequent offences (minimum of 90 days). A British Attorney General called mandatory minimum punishments "a great evil" that "tends to corrupt the administration of justice by creating a will to circumvent it." The rumour in Canadian legal circles is that when Crown prosecutors encounter situations where a prison sentence would have devastating effects on "respectable" people, they "forget" to inform the court that the accused have previous impaired-driving convictions. These lapses of memory are not likely to happen when the accused are unemployed low-income people.

The Canadian Sentencing Commission reported that almost all the submissions it received on this issue argued for the abolition of mandatory minimum penalties. One of the reasons was that "an accused person facing a mandatory term of incarceration has nothing to gain by pleading guilty and may take full advantage of procedural tactics and appeal mechanisms that he or she may otherwise have eschewed." Sophisticated legal tactics of this kind are beyond the reach of low-income defendants represented by lawyers from tight-fisted legal aid administrations.

If their legal manoeuvres fail, "respectable" people who are found guilty of impaired driving for a second or subsequent time can still avoid going to jail by asking the judge to give them another type of non-prison prison sentence (the first one we saw was a conditional sentence). This is an "intermittent sentence," which can be served on weekends, for example. This type of sentence is given to people of good character and "is often imposed to permit the offender to continue employment."

. . .

The top ten offences that send the largest numbers of people to prison also include two small offences, minor assault and theft under $1,000. Why were such small offenders sent to prison? There are many reasons, and all of them work to the disadvantage of the poor. The first reason is that people who have no money have no bargaining power in court. When an Ottawa duty counsel was asked whether poor and affluent defendants received equal treatment in the court where she worked, she indignantly denied any possibility of discrimination. On second thought, however, she admitted that poor defendants had less negotiating power in her bargaining sessions with prosecutors over "less time for more fine." Because poor people have no money for "more fine," they routinely end up doing more time for the same offences.

. . .

Poor offenders are also sentenced to prison more often than others because they are more likely to have criminal records and to have already been to prison. At first glance, a criminal record seems to be a reasonably objective factor to use in determining whether an offender is basically a good person who should be given another chance, or a hardened criminal who should be locked up to protect society. As we saw throughout this report, however, the criminal justice system is so biased against low-income people that previous convictions may reveal less about poor offenders' criminal dispositions than about the extent to which they were discriminated against.

This is most obvious in the treatment of Aboriginal people and Blacks, but it is also true of other poor people caught in the cycle of interminable arrests and convictions for minor offenses. Clayton Ruby writes that one of the most common errors committed by judges consists of handing out very long prison sentences for minor offences to people who have extensive criminal records. A typical example of this was described earlier, in which a homeless Montreal man was sentenced to a year in jail for stealing a bottle of wine. Ruby cites many appeal courts that reversed such decisions on the principle that "Breaking and entering a town dump and stealing a small quantity of scrap metal consisting of copper wire and a coil for a car heater, probably worth less than $1" must be treated as a trivial crime regardless of the length of the offender's record. Unfortunately for poor people with long records who receive such abusive sentences, the chance of their cases reaching an appeal court quickly enough to do them any good is less than a thousand to one.

## Conditional Release from Prison

### Heather E. MacKay

*Excerpts from "Conditional Release from Prison" in Joel E. Pink and David C. Perrier, eds., *From Crime to Punishment: An Introduction to the Criminal Law System* (Toronto: Carswell, 1999) at 405; 406-407; 409-10; 412-13; 415; 416-17; 420-21.

. . .

"Parole", as it is known to lay persons, includes several forms of conditional release: unescorted temporary absences ("quotas"), day parole and full parole. Statutory release is what lay people would know as "time off for good behaviour". Both types of release are governed by the *Corrections and Conditional Release Act* ("the

*CCRA*"), which replaced the *Parole Act* and the *Penitentiary Act* (collectively referred to here as "the old Acts"). Parole and statutory release decisions are made either by the National Parole Board ("the Board") or similar provincial boards. . . .

The purpose of conditional release is, as stated in s. 100 of the *CCRA*, "to contribute to the maintenance of a just, peaceful and safe society by means of decisions on the timing and conditions of release that will best facilitate the rehabilitation of offenders and their reintegration into the community as law-abiding citizens". This section in effect reaffirms the concept of incarceration followed by gradually less restrictive confinement of an individual as the correct method to achieve "reform" of the offender. Whether that still admirable goal is achieved in the harsh realities of the Canadian penitentiary system remains hotly debated. The other debate on this stated purpose centers around the question of whether the public is really interested in such lofty principles such as rehabilitation. Certainly in more recent years, public opinion, or at least a vocal minority within the public, has moved towards a more retributive stance in respect of criminal offenders. However, those debates are for another time. The purpose of this chapter is to create some familiarity with the framework in place to deal with conditional release in Canada.

Section 101 of the *CCRA* sets out the mandatory principles that must be followed by the Board and provincial boards. These principles can be summarized as follows:

(a) that the protection of society is the paramount principle governing conditional release;
(b) that all information available that is relevant must be considered, including the information from the trial, the sentencing, corrections officials, the victim(s) and the offender;
(c) that parole boards must be more open and communicate more effectively with offenders, victims and the public as well as other parts of the justice system;
(d) that the least restrictive decision be made which satisfies the paramount principle;
(e) that boards adopt policies and that members are properly trained; and
(f) that offenders be provided with the relevant information, reasons for decisions and access to review of decisions to ensure fair process.

While one might comment that some of these principles would seem to be stating the obvious, apparently they were deemed important enough, or perhaps history had demonstrated the need, for their statement in writing. It may be that by stating these principles clearly, the public is one of the key target audiences and that the *CCRA* in itself is a tool which partly achieves the "open communications" principle (see (c) above).

All decisions to grant parole can only be made when in the opinion of the Board or provincial board the following criteria have been satisfied:

(a) the offender will not, by reoffending, be an undue risk to society before his or her sentence expires;
(b) release of the offender will contribute to the protection of society by facilitating re-integration of the offender into society as a law-abiding citizen.

These two criteria in fact put into legislation the primary considerations that have been used regularly by parole boards since their creation.

. . .

## TYPES OF CONDITIONAL RELEASE

### Unescorted Temporary Absences (UTAs)

Generally recognized as the first type of conditional release for which an inmate can become eligible, the UTA is the most limited form of release in both duration and the purposes for which it can be permitted. Eligibility for a UTA depends on the nature of the sentence being served, the security classification of the offender and the reason presented for requesting the absence. Maximum security offenders are not permitted any UTAs; medium security offenders are entitled to fewer ad shorter absences than those classified as minimum security offenders. Special provisions apply to offenders serving life or indeterminate sentences:

(1)  An inmate serving a **life sentence**:

(a)  as other than a *minimum punishment* must serve four years before becoming eligible for a UTA;

(b)  as a *minimum punishment* must serve:

- seven years, if his or her parole ineligibility period is the "minimum" 10 years (as would be the case for a straightforward second degree murder conviction);
- more than seven and less than 22 years where the parole ineligibility period has been set between 10 and 25 years (where the offender is convicted of second degree murder in circumstances that warrant the extension of the ineligibility period);
- 22 years, where the inmate has been convicted of first degree murder and is ineligible for parole until 25 years of the sentence has been served.

(2)  An inmate serving an indeterminate sentence must serve three years before becoming eligible for UTAs.

In all other cases, an inmate must serve one-sixth of his or her sentence, or six months, whichever is greater. The only time these minimum ineligibility periods can be overridden is if an offender's life or health is in danger and a UTA is needed to permit emergency medical treatment. The health exception does not apply to inmates serving life as a minimum punishment; those inmates will only be granted an **escorted** temporary absence in order that medical treatment can be administered. . . .

### Day Parole

Section 119 of the *CCRA* has changed the eligibility dates for day parole from ts predecessor, the *Parole Act*. While inmates serving less than two years can still be granted parole after one-sixth of their sentence is served, those serving two years or more must serve the greater of six months or one-third of their sentence minus six months, *i.e.*, six months before the eligibility date for full parole. Where an offender was sentenced to preventive detention (before October 15, 1977), he or she must have served one year before being eligible for day parole. An inmate who is designated a dangerous offender, and has therefore been sentenced to an indeterminate period of detention, must have served three years of his or her sentence before day parole can be considered. Offenders who are serving a life sentence as a minimum punishment are only eligible for day parole three years prior to the expiration of the parole ineligibility period imposed by s. 746.1(2) of the *Criminal Code*. Thus, the ineligibility period for UTAs and day parole are identical for these offenders. . . .

## Full Parole

Eligibility for full parole under the *CCRA* is subject to provisions in the *Criminal Code*. Generally speaking, an inmate must serve the lesser of one-third of his or her sentence or seven years. For offenders, serving a life-sentence (other than as a minimum punishment), seven years, including any time served between arrest and conviction, must be served before being eligible for full parole. These ineligibility periods can be lengthened under s. 743.6 of the *Criminal Code* in the case of designated violent, sexual and drug offences, where the court orders one-half of the sentence to be served before being eligible for full parole. However, to make such an order, the court must be satisfied, based upon the evidence, that the offender cannot be rehabilitated in the usual one-third of his or her sentence

Full parole eligibility dates for inmates serving life sentences for murder and treason are set out in s. 742 of the *Criminal Code* as follows:

(a) first degree murder: 25 years;
(b) second degree murder with prior murder conviction: 25 years;
(c) second degree murder: 10 years or a longer period of up to 25 years, if that time has been substituted by the judge or jury.

. . .

## Accelerated Parole

An inmate may be entitled to an accelerated parole review where it is his or her first time in federal penitentiary. Inmates are ineligible for accelerated parole review when they:

(a) have been sentenced for murder, any of the violent or sexual offences in Schedule or drug offences in Schedule II, where the court has ordered one-half of the sentence to be served before full parole eligibility;
(b) are serving a life sentence (other than as minimum punishment); or
(c) have had their day parole revoked.

Further, an inmate who following the first sentence receives an additional sentences disqualified from the accelerated process upon the imposition of the second sentence. . . .

## Parole by Exception

Prior to 1977, the National Parole Board had broad powers to grant parole before statutory eligibility dates. Public criticism led to a narrowing of this discretion. From a public viewpoint, the important inmate groups excluded from consideration for parole by exception are: dangerous offenders (both violent and sexual) and those serving a life sentence as minimum punishment or as a commuted death sentence. In order to be eligible for parole by exception, an inmate must show that he or she falls into one of the following categories:

(a)   terminally ill;
(b)   physical or mental health likely to suffer serious damage if incarceration continues;
(c)   the penalty is an excessive hardship not foreseen at the time of sentencing; or
(d)   the inmate is subject to any kind of deportation or extradition order.

. . .

## Statutory Release

The final type of conditional release is statutory release, formerly known as mandatory supervision. Prior to the new CCRA, inmates were entitled to a certain minimum amount of remission days which reduced the amount of time to be served in custody. Remission could also be earned based upon the inmate's behaviour during his or her incarceration (*e.g.* ,if an inmate was industrious, he or she could earn up to one-third of the sentence "off"). However, the *CCRA* simplified this remission system: all inmates are entitled to statutory release after having served two-thirds of their sentences for any and all offences. For inmates sentenced before the CCRA went into effect (November 1, 1992), the old remission system still applies unless they reopened, in which case their statutory release date is the later of the two-thirds mark and their credited remission date under the old system. Statutory release is an entitlement of an offender granted upon meeting all requirements, unlike parole which is a privilege. Once the release date is determined, penal officials must release the inmate who then can remain "at large" until the expiration of his or her sentence.

While statutory release is an entitlement, like other forms of release, it can be revoked. This is the main difference from the previous remission system, which resulted in a real time reduction of the sentence served. Statutory release entitles the inmate to be at large while still serving the full term of his or her sentence. As long as the inmate abides by the conditions of his or her statutory release, he or she is not liable to return to custody unless the release is suspended, cancelled, terminated, or revoked. Thus, if statutory release is revoked, unless otherwise ordered by the Board, the inmate is entitled to a "second chance". The second release date is calculated as two-thirds of the remainder of the unserved portion of the sentence. This date applies regardless of the inmate having earned remission from the previously applicable *Penitentiary Act.*

. . .

## CONDITIONS OF RELEASE

All types of release as discussed in the previous section are permitted only upon conditions. Sections 133 and 134 of the *CCRA* and ss. 161 and 162 of the Regulations set out what conditions are imposed and how they can be varied to meet the reintegration needs of the offender while ensuring protection of the public. As previously discussed, conditional releases can be authorized by the Board, the Commissioner or the head of the penal institution, with the Board dealing with the complex cases and serious offenders while penal institution heads deal mainly with more routine cases and non-violent offenders. Every offender released on UTA, parole, or statutory release are subject to the following conditions:

(a)  on release, travel directly to the designated place of residence and report to parole supervisor immediately;
(b)  remain within Canada and the boundaries set by the parole supervisor;
(c)  obey the law and keep the peace;
(d)  inform the parole supervisor immediately upon arrest or police questioning;
(e)  always carry the release certificate and ID card, and produce them upon request by a police officer or the inmate's parole supervisor;
(e)  report to police as instructed by the parole supervisor; and
(f)  not own, possess, or have control of any weapon.

Additional condition for offenders on day parole and UTA:

(a)  return to the penitentiary at the time provided provided for in the release certificate.

Additional condition for parole (day and full) statutory release:

(a)  advise parole supervisor of initial address and then report immediately:

   (1)  any change of residence;
   (2)  any change in employment, training or volunteer work;
   (3)  any change in domestic or financial situation and on the parole supervisor's requirement, any change in family situation; or
   (4)  any change which could reasonably affect the offender's ability to comply with conditions of parole or statutory release.

Other conditions can be imposed by whoever releases the offender, as long as they are reasonable and necessary for the dual purpose of protecting society and facilitating the reintegration of the offender. In addition to any conditions imposed, an offender must comply with any instructions given by a Board member, a person designated by the Chair, the institutional head or the offender's parole supervisor. Such instructions must relate to the conditions imposed. . . .

### Questions/Discussion
1.  Describe and explain the historical background of Canada's sentencing regime.
2.  What are the causes of disparity in the Canadian criminal justice system? How can

disparity be reduced in the system? What factors should be important in distinguishing similar cases and giving different sentences?

3.   How would a judge determine the usual or normal sentence for a given crime? What guidance about maximum and minimum penalties is available in the *Criminal Code*?

4.   According to the Correctional Law Review, the public has a right to expect that its taxes are being spent effectively to provide criminal justice and protection. What evidence can you find in the prison system that this goal is being met?

5.   Should it matter when sentencing a bank robber whether $5,000 or $50,000 was stolen, or whether bank robberies are increasing or decreasing in the jurisdiction?

6.   Do you agree with the "idea" of parole? Why or why not? If you agree, what functions should it serve and what goals should it have? If you disagree, what alternative do you see to parole and what would you gain by abolishing parole? In this regard, see the readings by Brodeur and Doob under "Further Reading".

7.   To what extent and in what ways might some Canadian prisoners be said to be "political prisoners"?

## Further Reading

*   Baum, D.J., *Discount Justice* (Toronto: Burns & MacEachern Ltd., 1979), ch. 5.
*   Benzvy-Miller, S., "Integrating Sentence and Parole" (1990), 32 Canadian Journal of Criminology 493-502.
*   Brodeur, J.-P., "The Attrition of Parole" (1990), 32 Canadian Journal of Criminology 530-510.
*   Canada, *Sentencing Reform: A Canadian Approach: Report of the Canadian Sentencing Commission* (Ottawa: Supply & Services, 1987).
*   Correctional Service of Canada, *Contributing to the Protection of Society Through Assistance and Control: An Overview of Canada's Correctional Service* (Ottawa: Correctional Service of Canada, 1993).
*   "Criminal Sentencing Symposium" (1982), 4 Loyola University of Chicago Law Journal.
*   Doob, Anthony, N., "Should Canada Maintain Its System of Discretionary Release from Prison?" in Don Stuart, R.J. Delisle and Allan Manson, eds., *Towards a Clear and Just Criminal Law: A Criminal Reports Forum* (Toronto: Carswell, 1999).
*   Hatt, Ken, "Strategies of Governance and Canadian Sentencing Legislation, 1984-1997" (1999), 14 Canadian Journal of Law and Society 101-129.
*   Healy, Patrick, "Questions and Answers on Conditional Sentencing in The Supreme Court of Canada" (1999), 42 Criminal Law Quarterly 12-37.
*   Irving, Joy, *Implications of "Dangerousness": Implications of Indeterminacy in Canada's Dangerous Offender Provisions* (M.A. Thesis, Carleton University, Ottawa, Canada, 2001).
*   Jull, Kenneth, "Reserving Rooms in Jail: A Principled Approach" (1999), 42 Criminal Law Quarterly 67-115.
*   Jull, K., "Sentencing, Corrections and Conditional Release: Principles or a Penitentiary by Any Other Name?" (1992), 34 Criminal Law Quarterly 443-468
*   Landreville, P., "Prison Overpopulation and Strategies for Decarceration" (1995), 37 Canadian Journal of Criminology 39-60.
*   LaPrairie, C., "The Role of Sentencing in the Over-representation of Aboriginal People in Correctional Institutions" (1990), 32 Canadian Journal of Criminology 429-440.
*   Lowman, J. and B. MacLean, "Prisons and Protest in Canada" (1991), 18 Social Justice 130.

- Manson, Allan, "Accountability and the National Parole Board" in Philip Stenning, ed., *Accountability for Criminal Justice: Selected Essays* (Toronto: University of Toronto Press, 1995).
- Manson, Allan, "The Conditional Sentence: A Canadian Approach to Sentencing Reform, or Doing the Time Warp Again" (2001), 44 Criminal Law Quarterly 375-398.
- Manson, Allan, "The Reform of Sentencing" in Don Stuart, R.J. Delisle and Allan Manson, eds., *Towards a Clear and Just Criminal Law: A Criminal Reports Forum* (Toronto: Carswell, 1999).
- Moffatt, K., "Creating Choices or Repeating History: Canadian Female Offenders and Correctional Reform" (1991), 18 Social Justice 184-203.
- Nadin-Davis, P., *Sentencing in Canada* (Toronto: Carswell, 1982).
- National Parole Board, *Balancing Public Safety and Personal Responsibility* (Ottawa: National Parole Board, 1994).
- Ouimet, M. and E. Coyle, "Fear of Crime and Sentencing Punitiveness: Comparing the General Public and Court Practitioners" (1991), 33 Canadian Journal of Criminology 149-162.
- Palys, T. and S. Divorski, "Explaining Sentence Disparity" (1986), 28 Canadian Journal of Criminology and Corrections 347.
- Petrunik, M., *The Makings of Dangerous Offenders: The Origins, Diffusion and Use of Legislation for Dangerous Offenders* (Ottawa: Solicitor General of Canada, 1984).
- Pink, J. and D. Perrier (eds.), *From Crime to Punishment* (Toronto: Carswell, 1989)
- Report of the Task Force on Federally Sentenced Women, *Creating Choices* (Ottawa: Solicitor General of Canada: 1990).
- Roach, Kent, "Crime Victims and Sentencing" in Don Stuart, R.J. Delisle and Allan Manson, eds., *Towards a Clear and Just Criminal Law: A Criminal Reports Forum* (Toronto: Carswell, 1999).
- Roberts, Julian V., and David P. Cole, eds., *Making Sense of Sentencing* (Toronto: University of Toronto Press, 1999).
- Roberts, Julian V., "The Hunt for the Paper Tiger: Conditional Sentencing After Brady" (1999), 42 Criminal Law Quarterly 38-66.
- Roberts, Julian V. and Carol LaPrairie, "Sentencing Circles: Some Unanswered Questions" (1996), 39 Criminal Law Quarterly 69-83.
- Ruby, C., *Sentencing* (Toronto, Butterworths, 1994).
- Schiffer, M., "The Sentencing of Mentally Disordered Offenders" (1976), 14 Osgoode Hall Law Journal 307.
- "Sentencing Symposium" (1989), 7 Behavioural Sciences and the Law.
- Statistics Canada (Canadian Centre for Justice Statistics), *Adult Correctional Services in Canada 1994-95* (Ottawa: Minister of Industry, 1996).
- Stenning, Philip and Julian V. Roberts, "Empty Promises: Parliament, The Supreme Court, and the Sentencing of Aboriginal Offenders" (2001), 64 Saskatchewan Law Review 137-168.
- Watson, J. et al., *Principles of Sentencing in Canada* (Scarborough Ontario: Carswell, 1993).

# 6

# CRIMINAL LAW LIABILITY

## General Introduction

This chapter examines the issues surrounding the definition and attachment of criminal law liability. The first section, 6.1 provides an introduction to the elements of criminal liability, looking at what are the definition and requirements of a crime in (general) legal terms and what are the problems in practice which are encountered when applying these elements to real fact situations? The two elements of a crime usually required are the actus reus (see subsection 6.1.1) and the mens rea (see subsection 6.1.2), the physical and the mental elements of a crime.[1] We will see that while the physical elements are delineated in the legislation, the mental elements are often left unspecified. In these situations it is up to the court to specify the requirements as to the intention, knowledge, or mental state needed. Furthermore, there are crimes and quasi-crimes which do not require any mental element; the crime is complete on the completion of the actus reus. Such offences are called strict and absolute liability offences, and are dealt with in subsection 6.1.3 of this chapter.

The second section of this chapter is entitled "Incomplete Offences" and at first sight this term might appear to be contradictory, in that if the offence is not complete, then there is no offence. However, the term refers to a class of offences where the intended purpose is, with the possible exception of conspiracy, not fully carried out, offences that present special problems in regard to their rationale, formulation and application. Subsection 6.2.1 addresses the subject of "attempts" in criminal law and deals with those situations where the offence which was planned has not been completed for some reason, yet the law still attaches criminal liability for the attempt which was made. At what stage the law intervenes and according to what rationale will concern us in this subsection.

Subsections 6.2.2 and 6.2.3 concern two crimes, neither of which requires the full completion of the planned offence. Counselling involves those situations where one party counsels another to commit a crime and the crime which has been counselled is never committed; but criminal liability will attach to the person who did the counselling in the first place, even though the person's goal was never achieved. The final part of the second section deals with "conspiracy", an offence where an agreement to carry out another crime results in criminal liability to those who enter the agreement, whether or not the agreement is put into action. How close this comes to

---

1   The terms have been criticized because they derive from the common law and are not used in criminal legislation. For the purposes of our analysis, however, the terms will suffice to provide a framework for the examination of some of the important issues which present themselves in the area of criminal law liability

punishing people for their bad thoughts or intentions — something the criminal law does not do if only one person is involved — is one question to keep in mind, particularly when examining the rationale behind the offence.

The last section in this chapter examines the attachment of criminal liability to individuals for their acts. For example, how and for what acts does the law attach blame to certain people who may not have physically done the required acts, but who did assist in or encourage the offence in some way? While this section on "parties to the offence" does not deal with crimes per se or the elements of a crime, it is important because it sets out the circumstances under which criminal liability will be attached to individuals for their actions.

A final question to keep in mind throughout the chapter is to what extent is there a convergence of theory and practice: what do the courts say are the theoretical requirements for finding criminal liability and what do they do in practice in the actual application of the legal rules to the fact situations? Serious discrepancies in this regard might tell us that the theoretical underpinnings of the courts' approaches might need to be rethought or, on the other hand, might suggest that the practice of the courts must be reoriented to put it in line with criminal law principles and ideals.

## 6.1   ELEMENTS OF AN OFFENCE

### 6.1.1   Actus Reus

**Introduction**

Traditionally, each criminal offence is made up of two distinct elements. The first element is referred to as the "actus reus", or guilty act. The second element is referred to as the "mens rea", or guilty mind, and will be discussed in detail in subsection 2 of this chapter. In order for Crown Prosecutors to secure a conviction, they have the legal or persuasive burden of proving both of these elements beyond a reasonable doubt.

The words "actus reus" and "mens rea" are derived from the legal maxim, *actus non facit reum nisi mens sit rea*, which when translated means there is no guilty act without a guilty mind. Interestingly, however, the Criminal Code and other criminal legislation does not make use of these terms expressly. Rather, these terms are merely the traditional language used by the courts when analyzing a particular criminal offence. Some legal scholars, have argued that the use of these expressions is confusing and should be abandoned.[1]

These issues surrounding actus reus are few and not complex, and for the most part are well highlighted in the cases which follow. In practice, what is at issue is the proof being adduced to prove that the accused actually committed the physical elements of the crime as outlined in the relevant legislation. As a rule, such questions of fact concerning actus reus do not concern us too much since they relate to evidentiary questions such as the cause of death of the victim in murder cases, the cause of fire in arson cases, or the source of pollution in environmental offences. What is of interest is the way in which the courts view the actus reus as a question of law; that is, how do they deal with the causal factors within the confines of the legislation and particularly, how do they deal with the situation where a person omits to do something (rather than does a criminal act) which results in harm being done?

Actus reus can refer to just the prohibited conduct or act of omission of the accused, or it can refer to the prohibited conduct and/or the consequences of the prohibited conduct or omission. An example of the former would be found in perjury in section 131 of the Criminal Code, where the wrongful conduct is the giving of a false statement under oath knowing that the statement is false (and with the intent to mislead the Court). An example of the latter would be one of the classes of murder (see sections 229-232 of the Criminal Code), where the death of a human being must have occurred as a consequence of the accused's actions; the question is "Did the accused cause the death of the victim?" In this regard, the issue of causation is an important one in connecting the acts of the accused to the death. Obviously there is a need for some causal relationship between the act done and the consequences which are required for the crime, as well as a common law voluntariness requirement. In the case of murder, death may have resulted from a number of different factors, and three of the cases (*Jordan, Smith and Beardsley*) which follow set out the test and guidelines that the courts use in making a determination as to whether or not the accused can be held liable for his or her actions. Essentially, such tests are applied to determine whether a valid legal causal connection has been made between the act and the consequences. In addition, the Code contains several provisions which relate to the issue of causation; for example, sections 225 ("death from treatment of injury") and 226 ("acceleration of death due to injury").[2]

The final four cases deal with the issue of omissions in the criminal law, the principal point being that a legal duty generally must be found in the criminal law in order to hold the person liable for omitting to do something, i.e., for a failure to fulfil the duty. *Lavin* is an example where there was no legal duty to do anything and therefore no offence for omitting to do something. In regard to omissions, ask yourself what is the content of the duty and how well is it set out; is the nature and extent of the duty understandable to the ordinary citizen? What does it take to breach a particular duty? These duties are often set out in only the most general terms; see, for example section 215 of the Code where a duty to provide the "necessaries of life" is created in respect of certain relationships, including those of parent/child and husband/wife. Even when a duty is not explicitly set out in the legislation, courts can sometimes find that an omission to do something amounts to a criminal act. This was the situation in the *Thornton* case where the donation of blood which Mr. Thornton knew contained H.I.V. antibodies constituted a common nuisance and thereby endangered the life, safety and health of the public.

The *Fagan* case highlights not only a situation where there was no duty to act, but also illustrates a further requirement in regard to actus reus and mens rea. The usual requirement is that the two elements occur simultaneously. In *Fagan*, the court, faced with the fact that there was no duty to act on the part of the accused when he failed to act, effectively "stretched out" the actus reus so that in the majority's interpretation of the events there was a coincidence of the actus reus and mens rea. Such "continuing acts" may be valid in some circumstances,[3] but in this case the construction appears to be a rather artificial device which the courts can use to achieve the coincidence of actus reus and mens rea. Compare *Fagan* with the Supreme Court of Canada's decision in *Cooper*, where the court held that in the context of a death caused by manual strangulation it was sufficient that the intent and the act of strangulation coincided at some point. Which analysis do you prefer and why?

**Footnotes**

1. See, for example, Stuart, D. and R. Delisle, Learning Canadian Criminal Law. 8th ed. (Toronto: Carswell, 2001).
2. See also sections 223, 224, 227 and 228.
3. See *Meli v. The Queen*, (1954), 1 W.L.R. 228 (P.C.) and referred to in *Cooper*, below, where the accused struck the victim and, thinking him dead, threw the body over a cliff. But the victim was not dead and only died from the fall. The defence argument was that when the actus reus of killing was done there was no mens rea to kill, only to dispose of the body, and when there was the mens rea to kill, there was not the actus reus of murder because the victim had not died.

### Regina v. Jordan
### (1956), 40 A.C. 152

Only the judgment of Hallet J. is reproduced below.

HALLET J.: — This is an exceedingly unusual case, and it might from one point of view be described as a difficult case, but we think that it can be dealt with with comparative brevity. We have considered the points that arise and have no doubt about any of them and it is the desire of the court that I should deliver judgement at once.

The facts of the case, so far as I need refer to them, are as follows. The appellant, together with three other men, all serving airmen of the United States Forces, were charged with the murder of a man named Beaumont as the result of a disturbance which arose in a cafe at Hull. Beaumont was stabbed with a knife. There was no evidence that any one of the other three used a knife on Beaumont or was acting in concert with the man who did use the knife, and accordingly Byrne J., who tried the case, directed the acquittal of those three men. With regard to the appellant it was ultimately conceded by Mr. Veale, who appeared for him in the court below and in this court, that he did use the knife and stab Beaumont. Beaumont was admitted to hospital very promptly and the wound was stitched up, but none the less he died not many days after. In those circumstances the appellant was tried for murder. Various defences were raised, accident, self-defence, provocation and stabbing in the course of a quarrel. On all of those defences the direction of the learned judge is not in any way challenged and the jury rejected them.

Mr. Veale told us, with his usual frankness, that the original intention of the defence was not to lodge an appeal, but certain information reached the United States authorities and the defence became in a position to put forward further evidence, and in particular the evidence of two doctors, Dr. Keith Simpson and Mr. Blackburn, whose standing is beyond question.

Application was made to the court for leave to call this additional evidence. It is only in the most exceptional circumstances, and subject to what may be described as exceptional conditions, that the court is ever willing to listen to additional evidence. There are most obvious reasons, which I need not restate, because they have been stated with authority on more than one occasion before, why such applications should be granted only with great restraint.

. . .

[After referring to the summing-up and the medical evidence at the trial, his Lordship continued.] The further evidence is said to show that death was not, to use the words of Byrne J., "consequent upon the wound inflicted". On the contrary, both the doctors called are of opinion that, from the medical point of view, it cannot be described as caused by the wound at all. Whether from the legal point of view it could be described as caused by the wound is a more doubtful question. There are a number of cases in which the judges have discussed in what circumstances a death can be regarded as the result of a wound where something other than the inflicting of the wound has been the immediate cause of death. The circumstances vary very much. The judges in each case have ruled in the light of the circumstances with which they had to deal, and out of four cases the jury acquitted in two and convicted in two. First, as to the requirements allowing fresh evidence to be called; in the present case it seems clear to us that the fresh evidence was not in any true sense available at the trial. It did not occur to the prosecution, the defence, the judge, or the jury that there could be any doubt but that the stab caused death. The trial proceeded upon that basis. In those circumstances we thought it right to take the view that this was the case where the evidence sought to be given had not been in any true sense available at the trial.

. . .

I have not yet referred to what is perhaps the most important case from the present point of view, *Harding* (1936) 25 Cr. App. R. 190. The headnote is short: "Conviction of murder quashed after the court had heard fresh medical evidence as to the cause of death, the court emphasizing the fact that such reception of fresh evidence was to be regarded as wholly exceptional". I hope I have made it plain that this court has well in mind that such reception must be wholly exceptional.

As to the second requisite, namely, that the evidence proposed to be tendered is such that, if the jury had heard that evidence, they might very likely, and indeed probably would, have come to a different verdict, we feel that, if the jury had heard two doctors of the standing of Dr. Keith Simpson and Mr. Blackburn give evidence that in their judgement death was not due to the stab wound but to something else, the jury might certainly have hesitated very long before saying that they were satisfied that death was due to the stab wound. The jury, of course, would not be bound by medical opinion, but flying in the face of it, particularly in a capital case, is a thing any jury would hesitate to do. When Mr. Stanley-Price was trying to assist the court by cross-examining those doctors with a view to showing that they were mistaken in their opinions, and when he told us that he was prepared to tender the evidence of doctors who would, according to his instructions, probably express other opinions, we felt bound to say that the question is not whether we, if we were a jury, would have accepted and acted on the opinions those gentlemen expressed, but whether the jury in all probability would have allowed their verdict to be affected by them.

There is one further aspect that it is important I should emphasize lest this case is cited in some other case. There were two things other than the wound which were stated by these two medical witnesses to have brought about death. The stab wound had penetrated the intestine in two places, but it was mainly healed at the time of death. With a view to preventing infection it was thought right to administer an antibiotic, terramycin.

It was agreed by the two additional witnesses that that was the proper course to take, and a proper dose was administered. Some people, however, are intolerant to terramycin, and Beaumont was one of those people. After the initial doses he developed diarrhoea, which was only properly attributable, in the opinion of those doctors, to the fact that the patient was intolerant to terramycin. Thereupon the administration of terramycin was stopped, but unfortunately the very next day the resumption of such administration was ordered by another doctor and it was recommended for the following day. The two doctors both take the same view about it. Dr. Simpson said that to introduce a poisonous substance after the intolerance of a patient was shown was palpably wrong. Mr. Blackburn agreed.

Other steps were taken which were also regarded by the doctors as wrong — namely, the intravenous introduction of wholly abnormal quantities of liquid far exceeding the output. As a result the lungs became waterlogged and pulmonary oedema was discovered. Mr. Blackburn said that he was not surprised to see that condition after the introduction of so much liquid, and that pulmonary oedema leads to broncho-pneumonia as an inevitable sequel, and it was from broncho-pneumonia that Beaumont died.

We are disposed to accept it as the law that death resulting from any normal treatment employed to deal with a felonious injury may be regarded as caused by the felonious injury, but we do not think it necessary to examine the cases in detail or to formulate for the assistance of those who have to deal with such matters in the future the correct test which ought to be laid down with regard to what is necessary to be proved in order to establish causal connection between the death and the felonious injury. It is sufficient to point out here that this was not normal treatment. Not only one feature, but two separate and independent features, of treatment were, in the opinion of the doctors, palpably wrong and these produced the symptoms discovered at the post-mortem examination which were the direct and immediate cause of death, namely, the pneumonia resulting from the condition of oedema which was found.

The question then is whether it can be said that, if that evidence had been before the jury, it ought not to have, and in all probability would not have, affected their decision. We recognize that the learned judge, if this matter had been before him, would have had to direct the jury correctly on how far such supervening matters could be regarded as interrupting the chain of causation; but we feel that in the end it would have been a question of fact for the jury depending on what evidence they accepted as correct and the view they took on that evidence. We feel not uncertainty at all that, whatever direction had been given to the jury and however correct it had been, the jury would have felt precluded from saying that they were satisfied that death was caused by the stab wound.

For these reasons we come to the conclusion that the appeal must be allowed and the conviction set aside.

*Conviction quashed.*

## Regina v. Smith
### (1959), 47 A.C. 121

[Only the judgment of The Lord Chief Justice is reproduced below.]

The appellant was convicted by a general court-martial at Verden, Germany, on July 2, 1958, of the murder of Pte. William Creed and was sentenced to imprisonment for life.

The appellant was a private soldier in the King's Regiment. On April 13, 1958, a company of that regiment was sharing a barracks with a company of the Gloucestershire Regiment. On that night a fight developed in which three men of the Gloucestershire Regiment were stabbed and one of them, Pte. Creed subsequently died. Immediately after the fight the regimental sergeant-major of D Company of the King's Regiment paraded a number of soldiers, including the appellant, and said: "I am going to get to the bottom of this fighting and whoever did it must step forward". No one then stepped forward and the regimental sergeant-major questioned each man about his movements at the material time. The appellant said that he was in bed. The regimental sergeant-major then said: "I am not leaving; I am staying here until you give me an answer about this fight". The appellant then stepped forward and said that he had done the stabbing with a bayonet. He was then taken into custody. About 7.30 on the following morning he was interviewed by a sergeant of the Special Investigations Branch who, after administering the usual caution, referred to what had happened the night before and the appellant's admission at that time. The appellant replied: "Yes, I am not denying it. I stabbed three of them all right," and then made a written statement under caution to the same effect.

The deceased man had received two bayonet wounds, one in the arm and one in the back, the latter of which, unknown to anybody, had pierced the lung and caused haemorrhage. A fellow-member of his company, who was trying to carry him to the medical reception station, twice tripped and let the deceased man fall on the ground. When he ultimately was brought to the reception station, a transfusion of saline solution was attempted and failed. When his breathing seemed impaired he was given oxygen and artificial respiration was applied. He died after he had been in the station about an hour and about two hours after the original stabbing. There were no facilities whatsoever for blood transfusion. A medical witness who gave evidence for the defence said that had those facilities been available and blood transfusion been administered, the chances of the recovery of the deceased man would have been 75 per cent.

The Lord Chief Justice: In this court a number of points have been taken, and quite properly taken, by Mr. Bowen on his behalf, but there are, in the view of the court, only two which merit consideration. The first one is the question whether two alleged confessions given by the appellant were wrongly admitted in evidence . . . . [After finding the confessions were admissible, the Chief Justice continued:]

The second ground concerns a question of causation. The deceased man in fact received two bayonet wounds, one in the arm and one in the back. The one in the back, unknown to anybody, had pierced the lung and caused haemorrhage. There followed a series of unfortunate occurrences. A fellow member of his company tried to carry him to the medical reception station. On the way he tripped over a wire and dropped the deceased man. He picked him up again, went a little further, and fell apparently a second time causing the deceased man to be dropped on to the ground. Thereafter he did not try a third time, but went for help and ultimately the deceased man was brought into the reception station. There, the medical officer, Captain Millward, and his orderly were trying to cope with a number of other cases, two serious stabbings and some minor injuries, and it is clear that they did not appreciate the seriousness of the deceased man's condition or exactly what had happened. A transfusion of saline solution was attempted and failed. When his breathing seemed impaired, he was given oxygen and artificial respiration was applied, and in fact he died after he had been in the station about an hour, which was about two hours after the original stabbing. It is now known that, having regard to the injuries which the man had in fact suffered, his lung being pierced, the treatment that he was given was thoroughly bad and might well have affected his chances of recovery. There was evidence that there is a tendency for a wound of this sort to heal and for the haemorrhage to stop. No doubt his being dropped on the ground and having artificial respiration applied would halt or at any rate impede the chances of healing. Further, there were no facilities whatsoever for blood transfusion, which would have been the best possible treatment. There was evidence that, if he had received immediate and different treatment, he might not have died. Indeed, had the facilities for blood transfusion been available and been administered, Dr. Camps, who gave evidence for the defence, said that his chances of recovery were as high as 75 per cent.

In these circumstances Mr. Bowen urges that not only was a careful summing-up required, but that a correct direction to the court would have been that they must be satisfied that the death of Private Creed was a natural consequence and the sole consequence of the wound sustained by him and flowed directly from it. If there was, says Mr. Bowen, any other cause whether resulting from negligence or not, or if, as he contends here, something happened which impeded the chance of the deceased recovering, then the death did not result from the wound. The court is quite unable to accept that contention. It seems to the court that if at the time of death the original wound is still an operating cause and a substantial cause, then the death can properly be said to be the result of the wound, albeit that some other cause of death is also operating. Only if it can be said that the original wounding is merely the setting in which another cause operates can it be said that the death does not result from the wound. Putting it another way, only if the second cause is so over-whelming as to make the original wound merely part of the history can it be said that the death does not flow from the wound.

There are a number of cases in the law of contract and tort on these matters of causation, and it is always difficult to find a form of words when directing a jury or, as here, a court, which will convey in simple language the principle of causation. It seems to the court enough for this purpose to refer to one passage in the judgement of Lord Wright in The Oropesa, reported in [1943] p. 32, where he says (at p. 39): "To break the chain of causation it must be shown that there is something which I will call ultroneous, something unwarrantable, a new cause which disturbs the consequence of events, something which can be described as either unreasonable or exraneous or extrinsic." To much the same effect was a judgement on the question of causation given by Denning J., as he then was, in *Minister of Pensions v. Chennel* in [1947] K.B. 250.

Mr. Bowen placed great reliance on a case decided in this court, Jordan (1956) 40 Cr. App. R. 152, and in particular on a passage in the headnote which says "*Semble*, that death resulting from any normal treatment employed to deal with a felonious injury may be regarded as caused by that felonious injury, but that the same principle does not apply where the treatment employed is abnormal." Reading those words into the present case, Mr. Bowen says that the treatment that this unfortunate man received from the moment that he was struck to the time of his death was abnormal. The court is satisfied that Jordan (*supra*) was a very particular case depending upon its exact facts. It incidentally arose in this court on the grant of an application to call further evidence, and leave having been obtained, two well-known medical experts gave evidence that in their opinion death had not been caused by the stabbing, but by the introduction of terramycin after the deceased had shown that he was intolerant to it and by the intravenous introduction of abnormal quantities of liquid. It also appears that at the time when that was done the stab wound which had penetrated the intestine in two places had mainly healed. In those circumstances the court felt bound to quash the conviction, because they could not say that a reasonable jury, properly directed, would not have been able on that to say that there had been a break in the chain of causation; the court could only uphold the conviction in that case if they were satisfied that no reasonable jury could have come to that conclusion.

In the present case it is true that the Judge-Advocate did not, in his summing-up, go into the refinements of causation. Indeed, in the opinion of this court, he was probably wise to refrain from doing so. He did leave the broad question to the court whether they were satisfied that the wound had caused the death in the sense that the death flowed from the wound, albeit that the treatment he received was in the light of after-knowledge a bad thing. In the opinion of this court, that was on the facts of the case a perfectly adequate summing-up on causation: I say "on the facts of the case", because in the opinion of the court they can only lead to one conclusion. A man is stabbed in the back, his lung is pierced and haemorrhage results; two hours later he dies of haemorrhage from that wound; in the interval there is no time for a careful examination and the treatment given turns out in the light of subsequent knowledge to have been inappropriate and, indeed, harmful. In those circumstances no reasonable jury or court could, properly directed, in our view possibly come to any other conclusion than that the death resulted from the original wound. Accordingly, the court dismisses this appeal.

*Appeal dismissed.*

## People v. Beardsley
### (1907), 113 N.W. 1128 (Michigan Sup. Ct.)

McALVAY, C.J. Respondent was convicted of manslaughter before the circuit court for Oakland county, and was sentenced to the state prison at Jackson for a minimum term of one year and a maximum term not to exceed five years.

He was a married man living at Pontiac, and at the time the facts herein narrated occurred he was working as a bartender and clerk at the Columbia Hotel. He lived with his wife in Pontiac, occupying two rooms on the ground floor of a house. Other rooms were rented to tenants, as was also one living room in the basement. His wife being temporarily absent from the city, respondent arranged with a woman named Blanche Burns, who at the time was working at another hotel, to go to his apartments with him. He had been acquainted with her for some time. They knew each other's habits and character. They had drunk liquor together, and had on two occasions been in Detroit and spent the night together in houses of assignation. On the evening of Saturday, March 18, 1905, he met her at the place where she worked, and they went together to his place of residence. They at once began to drink, and continued to drink steadily, and remained together, day and night from that time until the afternoon of the Monday following, except when the respondent went to his work on Sunday afternoon. There was liquor at these rooms, and when it was all used they were served with bottles of whisky and beer by a young man who worked at the Columbia Hotel, and who also attended respondent's fires at the house. He was the only person who saw them in the house during the time they were there together. Respondent gave orders for liquor by telephone. On Monday afternoon, about 1 o'clock, the young man went to the house to see if anything was wanted. At this time he heard respondent say they must fix up the rooms, and the woman must not be found there by his wife, who was likely to return at any time. During this visit to the house the woman sent the young man to a drug store to purchase, with money she gave him, camphor and morphine tablets. He procured both articles. There were six grains of morphine in quarter-grain tablets. She concealed the morphine from respondent's notice, and was discovered putting something into her mouth by him and the young man as they were returning from the other room after taking a drink of beer. She in fact was taking morphine. Respondent struck the box from her hand. Some of the tablets fell on the floor, and of these respondent crushed several with his foot. She picked up and swallowed two of them, and the young man put two of them in the spittoon. Altogether it is probable she took from three to four grains of morphine. The young man went away soon after this. Respondent called him by telephone about an hour later, and after he came to the house requested him to take the woman into the room in basement which was occupied by a Mr. Skoba. She was in a stupor, and did not rouse when spoken to. Respondent was too intoxicated to be of any assistance, and the young man proceeded to take her downstairs. While doing this, Skoba arrived, and together they put her in his room on the bed. Respondent requested Skoba to look after her, and let her out the back way when she waked up. Between 9 and 10 o'clock in the evening, Skoba became alarmed at her condition. He at once called the city marshal and a doctor. An examination by them disclosed that she was dead.

Many errors are assigned by respondent, who asks to have his conviction set aside. The principal assignments of error are based upon the charge of the court and refusal to give certain requests to charge, and are upon the theory that under the undisputed evidence in the case, as claimed by the people and detailed by the people's witnesses, the respondent should have been acquitted and discharged. In the brief of the prosecutor, his position is stated as follows: "It is the theory of the prosecution that the facts and circumstances attending the death of Blanche Burns in the house of the respondent were such as to lay upon him a duty to care for her, and the duty to take steps for her protection, and failure to take which was sufficient to constitute such an omission as would render him legally responsible for her death. . . .

There is no claim on the part of the people that the respondent was in any way an active agent in bringing about the death of Blanche Burns, but simply that he owed her a duty which he failed to perform, and that in consequence of such failure on his part she came to her death." Upon this theory a conviction was asked and secured.

The law recognizes that under some circumstances the omission of a duty owed by one individual to another, where such omission results in the death of the one to whom the duty is owing, will make the other chargeable with manslaughter. . . . This rule of law is always based upon the proposition that the duty neglected must be a legal duty, and not a mere moral obligation. It must be a duty imposed by law or by contract, and the omission to perform the duty must be the immediate and direct cause of death. . . . Although the literature upon the subject is quite meager and the cases few, nevertheless the authorities are in harmony as to the relationship which must exist between the parties to create the duty, the omission of which establishes legal responsibility. One authority has briefly and correctly stated the rule, which the prosecution claims should be applied to the case at bar, as follows: "If a person who sustains to another the legal relation of protector, as husband to wife, parent to child, master to seaman, etc. knowing such person to be in peril, wilfully and negligently fails to make such reasonable and proper efforts to rescue him as he might have done, without jeapordizing his own life, or the lives of others, he is guilty of manslaughter at least, if by reason of his omission of duty the dependent person dies." "So one who from domestic relationship, public duty, voluntary choice, or otherwise, has the custody and care of a human being, helpless either from imprisonment, infancy, sickness, age, imbecility, or other incapacity of mind or body is bound to execute the charge with proper diligence, and will be held guilty of manslaughter, if by culpable negligence he lets the helpless creature die." 21 Am. & Eng. Enc. of Law (2d Ed.) p. 192, notes and cases cited.

The following brief digest of cases gives the result of our examination of American and English authorities, where the doctrine of criminal liability was involved when death resulted from an omission to perform a claimed duty. We discuss no cases where statutory provisions are involved. In Territory v. Manton, 8 Mont. 95, 19 Pac. 387, a husband was convicted of manslaughter for leaving his intoxicated wife one winter's night lying in the snow, from which exposure she died. The conviction was sustained on the ground that a legal duty rested upon him to care for and protect his wife, and that for his neglect to perform that duty, resulting in her death, he was properly convicted. State v. Smith, 65 Me. 257, is a similar case. A husband neglected to provide clothing and shelter for his insane wife. He left her in a bare room without fire during severe winter weather. Her death resulted. The charge in the indictment is predicated upon a known legal duty of the husband to furnish his wife with suitable protection. In State v. Behm, 72 Iowa, 533, 34 N.W. 319, the conviction of a mother of manslaughter for exposing her infant child without protection was affirmed upon the same ground. . . . In a federal case tried in California before Mr. Justice Field, of the United States Supreme Court, where the master of a vessel was charged with murder in omitting any effort to rescue a sailor who had fallen overboard, the learned justice, in charging the jury, said: "There may be in the omission to do a particular act under some circumstances, as well as in the commission of an act, such a degree of criminality as to render the offender liable to indictment for manslaughter. . . .

In the first place, the duty omitted must be a plain duty. . . . In the second place, it must be one which the party is bound to perform by law, or by contract, and not one the performance of which depends simply upon his humanity, or his sense of justice and propriety. United States v. Knowles, 4 Sawy. (U.S.) 517, Fed. Cas. No. 15,540. . . . The case of Reg. v. Nicholls, 13 Cox. Crim. Cases, 75, was a prosecution of a penniless old woman, a grandmother, for neglecting to supply an infant grandchild left in her charge with sufficient food and proper care. The case was tried at Assizes in Stafford, before Brett J., who said to the jury: "If a grown up person chooses to undertake the charge of a human creature, helpless either from infancy, simplicity, lunacy, or other infirmity, he is bound to execute that charge without, at all events, wicked negligence, and if a person who has chosen to take charge of a helpless creature lets it die by wicked negligence, that person is guilty of manslaughter." The vital question was whether there had been any such negligence in the case designated by the trial judge as wicked negligence. The trial resulted in an acquittal. The charge of this nisi prius judge recognizes the principle that a person may voluntarily assume the care of a helpless human being and, having assumed it, will be held to be under an implied legal duty to care for and protect such person; the duty assumed being that of caretaker and protector to the exclusion of all others. . . .

These adjudicated cases and all others examined in this investigation we find are in entire harmony with the proposition first stated in this opinion. Seeking for a proper determination of the case at bar by the application of the legal principles involved, we must eliminate from the case all consideration of mere moral obligation, and discover whether respondent was under a legal duty towards Blanche Burns at the time of her death, knowing her to be in peril of her life, which required him to make all reasonable and proper effort to save her, the omission to perform which duty would make him responsible for her death. This is the important and determining question in this case. If we hold that such legal duty rested upon respondent, it must arise by implication from the facts and circumstances already recited. The record of this case discloses that the deceased was a woman past 30 years of age. She had been twice married. She was accustomed to visiting saloons and to the use of intoxicants. She previously had made assignations with this man in Detroit at least twice. There is no evidence or claim from this record that any duress, fraud or deceit had been practiced upon her. On the contrary, it appears that she went upon this carouse with respondent voluntarily, and so continued to remain with him. Her entire conduct indicates that she had ample experience in such affairs.

It is urged by the prosecutor that the respondent "stood towards this woman for the time being in the place of her natural guardian and protector, and as such owed her a clear legal duty which he completely failed to perform." The cases cited and digested establish that no such legal duty is created based upon a mere moral obligation. The fact that this woman was in his house created no such legal duty as exists in law and is due from a husband towards his wife, as seems to be intimated by the prosecutor's brief. Such an inference would be very repugnant to our moral sense. Respondent had assumed either in fact or by implication no care or control over his companion. Had this been a case where two men under like circumstances had voluntarily gone on a debauch together and one had attempted suicide, no one would claim that this doctrine of legal duty could be invoked to hold the other criminally responsible for omitting to make effort to rescue his companion. How can the fact that in this case one of the parties was a woman change the principle of law applicable to it? Deriving and applying the law in this case from the principle of decided cases, we do not find that such legal duty as is contended for existed in fact or by implication on the part of respondent towards the deceased, the omission of which involved criminal liability. We find no more apt words to apply to this case than those used by Mr. Justice Field, in United States v. Knowles, supra: "In the absence of such obligations, it is undoubtedly the moral duty of every person to extend to others assistance when in danger . . . and, if such efforts should be omitted by any one when they could be made without imperilling his own life, he would by his conduct draw upon himself the just censure and reproach of good men; but this is the only punishment to which he would be subjected by society."

Other questions discussed in the briefs need not be considered.

The conviction is set aside, and respondent is ordered discharged.

### Regina v. Lavin
(1992), 76 C.C.C. (3d) 279 (Que. C.A.)

Appeal by the accused from a judgment of Boilard J., 23 M.V.R. (2d) 273, dismissing his appeal from conviction on a charge of obstructing a peace officer. VALLERAND J.A. concurs with TYNDALE J.A.

TYNDALE J.A.: — The details of this case are summarized in the opinion of Madam Justice Tourigny; with respect, I come to a different conclusion.

As a preliminary, I wish to bring up a point of fact. My colleague writes, in the fourth paragraph [translation]: "For the second time, Lavin replied that he had no radar warning device . . ." That is from the version of Officer Lépine, but it is not the version accepted by the trial judge.

Appellant testified as follows [translation]:

Q. Now then, during the time you heard, you heard the second constable who testified, who was Mister Lépine . . .

R. Hum, hum.

Q.. . . say that when he asked you about the radar detector, that you denied having one, is that a fact?

R. No, I never denied having a radar detector.

Q. Was there any discussion between you and he about whether — and the fact you had one or not?

R. No, the discussion was whether or not he could search me and get it from me. He knew I had it, and I knew that he knew I had it, there was no discussion about that.

The trial judge said [translation]: ". . . I cast no doubt on Mr. Lavin's testimony; he is an honest man — who in fact decided to do only what the law obliged him to do, in his opinion . . .". And so I take it as a fact that appellant did not deny possession of the detector.

Appellant was charged with wilfully obstructing a peace officer in the execution of his duty. He was found guilty, not of unlawful possession of a detector, not because he put the detector in his pocket, but because he refused to hand it over. I am not aware of any provision of law by which he was obliged to agree with the officer's request to give him the detector. If he was under no obligation, surely he had the right to refuse and did not thereby obstruct the officer.

On appellant's refusal, he was arrested; knowing that the arrest gave the officer the right to search him, he immediately handed over the offending apparatus.

The officer's knowledge, and not mere suspicion, of appellant's unlawful possession makes this case distinguishable from the precedents cited by Tourigny J.A.

. . .

*Moore v. The Queen* (1978), 43 C.C.C. (2d) 83, 90 D.L.R. (3d) 112, [1979] 1 S.C.R. 195 (not cited), was a case of refusal to identify himself; the majority held that, in the circumstances, there was a duty to answer; in our case, I see no duty to deliver. The minority, denying the duty to answer (and I suppose the majority would have agreed if there were no duty), held that a person is not guilty of obstruction merely by him doing nothing, unless there is a legal duty to act; that *omission to act* in a particular way will entail criminal liability only where a *duty to act* arises at common law or by statute. The constable had the right to arrest if necessary to establish identity, but it did not follow that refusal amounted to obstruction; as in our case, the constable had the right to arrest if necessary to search, but refusal did not amount to obstruction.

It seems to me that wilful obstruction requires either some positive act, such as concealment of evidence, or an omission to do something which one is legally obliged to do, and that neither requirement is fulfilled in this case.

I would allow the appeal with costs.

TOURIGNY J.A. (dissenting) (translation): — The appellant (Lavin) appeals from a decision of the Superior Court [23 M.V.R. (2d) 273] affirming his conviction by a judge of the Quebec Court on a charge of obstructing a peace officer in the execution of his duty, pursuant to s. 129 of the *Criminal Code*.

The facts are of some importance in this case. Lavin was driving toward Montreal over a bridge when he saw a police car approaching from behind. He thought the vehicle was pursuing someone in front of him, but put in his pocket "just in case", the radar warning device attached to his car's sun visor. It turned out that it was Lavin whom the police officer wished to stop, because he had seen the wire of the device hanging from the sun visor and had subsequently seen Lavin concealing the object on his person.

After the vehicles were stopped, Lavin, informed of the situation by the officer, telephoned his lawyer and refused to hand over the warning device as the officer requested; the officer also telephoned for instructions and a second police officer arrived on the scene.

The officer who had followed Lavin in his car repeated to Lavin that he had seen the warning device and that he had also seen him performing the act of concealing it, and again requested that he hand it over. For the second time, Lavin replied that he had no radar warning device and suggested that the police officer search his car.

After the second refusal to hand over the device, the officer informed Lavin that he could be charged with obstructing a peace officer.

Later, after informing Lavin of his rights, the second officer who had arrived on the scene arrested him. Lavin then offered to hand over the device.

He was accused of obstructing an officer in the execution of his duty.

In this court, Lavin submitted that the refusal to hand over the device did not constitute an obstruction. "It is a non-action", he argues, in contrast to situations in which a person has performed the act of putting his hand in his pocket or of grabbing at his coat, for example.

Lavin argues that he did nothing to prevent the search, and that, in fact, the police officer did not attempt to search him. He submits as well that the factual evidence does not demonstrate any intention on his part to inhibit the work of the police officers.

The deputy prosecutor, for his part, argues that, once informed by the police officer that he had observed the presence of the warning device and the action to conceal it, his refusal to hand over the object was a voluntary act of obstruction that must be seen in the context of all the actions taken by Lavin. These actions, says the deputy prosecutor, demonstrate that Lavin knew he was committing an offence, that at a minimum he did not want the police officer to notice the device in passing, even if he initially thought the officer's attention was directed at someone else and that, in this context, the refusal to hand over the device cannot be anything but a voluntary act.

. . .

Even on the assumption that Lavin did not conceal the warning device *for the purpose* of concealing it from the police but only "just in case" they were to see it in passing, it is true none the less that, after being accosted by the police and informed by them of what they had seen, he continued to deny the facts and to conceal the offending object. In my opinion, this is sufficient intention to satisfy the requirements of the law — not to mention the invitation to search the vehicle when he knew the police would find nothing there. The need for the police in such circumstances to ensure that the evidence will be preserved justifies their attempt, in the performance of their duties, to get their hands on relevant objects, particularly when they have seen them and observed the action taken to conceal them.

It is, therefore, my opinion that we should reach the same conclusion as this court did in *Lajoie*, and dismiss the appeal.

*Appeal allowed.*

## Regina v. Thornton
### (1991), 1 O.R. (3d) 480 (Ont. C.A.)

Appeal by the accused from his conviction on a charge of committing a common nuisance and from sentence

The judgment of the court was delivered by

GALLIGAN J.A.: — The presence in a person's blood of antibodies to Human Immunodeficiency Virus (HIV) indicates that the person is probably infected with Acquired Immune Deficiency Syndrome (AIDS). AIDS is a grave illness which is usually fatal. It is infectious and particularly contagious through the blood.

All of this is now well known. The appellant knew it in November 1987. In fact, he was well informed about AIDS and its means of transmission. He knew as well that he was a member of a group which was highly at risk of contracting AIDS. Moreover, he knew that he had twice tested positive for HIV antibodies and that he was therefore infectious. He knew that the Canadian Red Cross collected blood for transfusion to persons in need of it and that AIDS is transmitted by blood. He also knew that the Red Cross would not knowingly accept donations of blood from persons who had tested positive to HIV antibodies or who were members of his high risk group. Nevertheless, on November 16, 1987, he donated blood to the Red Cross at a clinic in Ottawa. Fortunately, the Red Cross's screening process detected the contaminated blood and it was put aside.

The appellant was charged with an offence contrary to s. 176(1)(*a*) of the *Criminal Code*, R.S.C. 1970, c. C-34. That provision is now s. 180 of the *Criminal Code*, R.S.C. 1985, c. C-46, and in these reasons for judgment reference will be made to the present provision. He was charged that he:

> . . . on or about the 16th day of November, 1987, at the City of Ottawa in the said Judicial District did commit a common nuisance endangering the lives or health of the public by donating to the Canadian Red Cross Society a quantity of his blood knowing that his blood had previously been found to contain antibodies to Human Immunodeficiency Virus and intentionally withholding the information for the Canadian Red Cross Society, contrary to Section 176(a) [*sic*] of the Criminal Code of Canada.

He was convicted of the charge by Flanigan J., sitting without a jury, and sentenced to a term of 15 months' imprisonment. He appeals both his conviction and his sentence.

Counsel for the appellant attacked the conviction on three grounds:

1. that, reprehensible as the appellant's conduct may have been, it did not amount to an offence known to the law;

2.   that it was not proved that his conduct endangered the lives or health of the public or any member of it;

3.   that the appellant did not have the necessary *mens rea*.

The provisions of s. 180 of the *Code* are:

180.(1) Every one who commits a common nuisance and thereby

(*a*) endangers the lives, safety or health of the public, or

(*b*) causes physical injury to any person,

is guilty of an indictable offence and liable to imprisonment for a term not exceeding two years.

(2) For the purposes of this section, every one commits a common nuisance who does an unlawful act or fails to discharge a legal duty and thereby

(*a*) endangers the lives, safety or health, property or comfort of the public; or

(*b*) obstructs the public in the exercise or enjoyment of any right that is common to all the subjects of Her Majesty in Canada.

I will deal first with the argument that the appellant's conduct did not amount to an offence known to law. If, in the circumstances, the appellant's act of donating blood which he knew was HIV-contaminated to the Red Cross was neither an unlawful act nor a failure to discharge a legal duty, then the indictment does not allege an offence known to law.

Section 180(2)(*a*) provides that a common nuisance is committed by either the doing of an unlawful act or the failure to discharge a legal duty which endangers the lives or health of the public. For the purposes of this appeal, I am prepared to assume the correctness of Mr. Greenspon's cogent argument that the words "unlawful act" must be taken to mean conduct which is specifically proscribed by legislation. The *Code* does not make it an offence to donate contaminated blood. Counsel were unable to refer the court to any other statutory provision, federal or provincial, which does so. On the assumption, therefore, that the appellant's conduct could not constitute an "unlawful act" I will examine whether it amounted to a failure to discharge a "legal duty".

I am unable to find any provision in the *Code* or any other statute which I can read as specifically imposing a legal duty upon a person to refrain from donating contaminated blood. The immediate issues therefore is twofold. Can a "legal duty" within the meaning of s. 180(2) be one which arises at common law or must it be one found in a statute? Is there a "legal duty" arising from a common law the breach of which, assuming the other essential elements of the offence were proved, could be the basis of an offence under s. 180?

There are no cases deciding whether the "legal duty" in s. 180(2) must be a duty imposed by statute or whether it can be a duty according to common law. However, the "duty imposed by law" which forms part of the definition of criminal negligence set out in s. 219 of the *Code* has been held to be either a duty imposed by statute or a duty arising at common law. The provisions of s. 219 are as follows:

219. (1) Every one is criminally negligent who

(*a*) in doing anything, or

(*b*) in omitting to do anything that it is his duty to do, shows wanton or reckless disregard for the lives or safety of other persons.

(2) For the purposes of this section, "duty" means a duty imposed by law.

In *R. v. Coyne* (1958), 124 C.C.C. 176, 31 C.R. 335, the New Brunswick Supreme Court Appeal Division considered the criminal negligence provision of the *Code* in relation to a hunting accident. Speaking for that court, Ritchie J.A. held at pp. 179-80 C.C.C.:

> The "duty imposed by law" may be a duty arising by virtue of either the common law or by statute. Use of a firearm, in the absence of proper caution, may readily endanger the lives or safety of others. Under the common law anyone carrying such a dangerous weapon as a rifle is under the duty to take such precaution in its use as, in the circumstances, would be observed by a reasonably careful man. If he fails in that duty and his behaviour is of such as character as to show or display a wanton or reckless disregard for the lives or safety of other persons, then, by virtue of s. 191, his conduct amounts to criminal negligence . . .

In *R. v. Popen* (1981), 60 C.C.C. (2d) 232, this court also had occasion to consider the nature of the "duty imposed by law" contained in the definition of criminal negligence. It was a child abuse case. In giving the judgment of the court, Martin J.A. said at p. 240 C.C.C.:

> . . . a parent is under a legal duty at common law to take reasonable steps to protect his or her child from illegal violence used by the other parent or by a third person towards the child which the parent foresees or ought to foresee.

The effect of that judgment is to hold that the common law duty, which was there described, was a "duty imposed by law" within the meaning of s. 219 because the court held that its breach could amount to criminal negligence.

These decisions lead me to the opinion that it is well settled that, for the purpose of defining criminal negligence, a "duty imposed by law" includes a duty which arises at common law.

While the words "legal duty" in s. 180(2) are not the same as a "duty imposed by law" used in s. 219, they have exactly the same meaning. It follows, therefore, that the meaning given to a "duty imposed by law" in s. 219 should also be given to the "legal duty" contained in s. 180(2). Thus, I am of the opinion that the legal duty referred to in s. 180(2) is a duty which is imposed by statute or which arises at common law. It becomes necessary, then, to decide whether at common law there is a duty which would prohibit the donating of blood known to be HIV-contaminated to the Red Cross.

While this is not a civil case and the principles of tort law are not directly applicable to it, the jurisprudence on that subject is replete with discussions about the legal duties of one person to another which arise at common law. The jurisprudence is constant that those duties are legal ones, that is, they are ones which are imposed by law. Throughout this century and indeed since much earlier times, the common law has recognized a very fundamental duty, which while it has many qualifications, can be summed up as being a duty to refrain from conduct which could cause injury to another person.

. . .

The editors [William James Byrne and Andrew Dewar Gibb] of the 4th edition of Thomas Bevin, *Negligence in Law* (London: Sweet & Maxwell, 1928), vol. 1 at p. 8, have described the fundamental common law duty of one person toward another and the rationale for it:

> Before the law every man is entitled to the enjoyment of unfettered freedom so long as his conduct does not interfere with the equal liberty of all others. Where one man's sphere of activity impinges on another man's, a conflict of interests arises. The debateable land where these collisions may occur is taken possession of by the law, which lays down the rules of mutual intercourse. A liberty of action which is allowed therein is called a right, the obligation of restraint a duty, and these terms are purely relative, each implying the other. Duty, then, as a legal term indicates the obligation to limit freedom of action and to conform to a prescribed course of conduct. *The widest generalisation of duty is that each citizen "must do no act to injure another".*

(Emphasis added)

. . .

That brief reference to jurisprudence in civil matters shows that there is deeply embedded in the common law a broad fundamental duty which, although subject to many qualifications, requires everyone to refrain from conduct which could injure another. It is not necessary to decide in this case how far that duty extends. At the very least, however, it requires everyone to refrain from conduct which it is reasonably foreseeable could cause serious harm to other persons. Accepting, as I have said, that a "legal duty" within the meaning of that term in s. 180(2) includes a duty arising at common law, I think that the common law duty to refrain from conduct which it is reasonably foreseeable could cause serious harm to other persons is a "legal duty" within the meaning of that term in s. 180(2).

Donating blood which one knows to be HIV-contaminated to an organization whose purpose is to make the blood available for transfusion to other persons clearly constitutes a breach of the common law duty to refrain from conduct which one foresees could cause serious harm to another person. It is thus a failure to discharge a "legal duty" within the contemplation of s. 180(2). It is therefore my conclusion that the indictment which alleges the commission of a nuisance by the donation of blood which the appellant knew to be HIV-contaminated does allege an offence known to law. The first argument made by counsel for the appellant cannot be accepted.

Counsel for the Crown referred to a number of cases where, at common law, the courts held that the exposing of others to the risk of becoming infected by a contagious disease constituted a common nuisance. Those cases are: *R. v. Vantandillo* (1815), 4 M. & S. 73, 105 E.R. 762, *R. v. Burnett* (1815), 4 M. & S. 272, 105 E.R. 835, and *R. v. Henson* (1852), Dears. C.C. 24, 20 L.T.O.S. 63, 16 J.P. 711. I have not cited them as authority in this case because s. 9(*a*) [rep. & sub. R.S.C. 1985, c. 27 (1st Supp.), s. 6] of the *Code* abolishes common law offences. They are, however, very helpful for two reasons. The first is they seem to be based upon the fundamental duty recognized by the common law to refrain from conduct which one can foresee could cause injury to others. The second reason is perhaps a stronger one. It has been said by the editor of the 6th edition of *Tremeearr's Annotated Criminal Code* (Toronto: Carswell, 1964) at p. 241 that the statutory definition of a common nuisance contained in the *Code* "does not differ from a criminal common nuisance at common law". Those cases show that the conduct of donating blood known to be HIV-contaminated, if it exposed others to the risk of infection, is conduct very similar to that which the law has recognized to be a criminal common nuisance for almost 200 years. Finding that conduct to constitute a common nuisance under s. 180 is consistent with the common law position and does not extend it.

. . .

In the light of the findings of the trial judge on the issue of credibility and in the light of all of the other evidence, there can be no doubt that this appellant had personal knowledge that he should not donate his blood, that it was possible for it to get through the testing screen and that it could cause serious damage to the life and health of members of the public. It follows that he knew that, by giving his blood to the Red Cross, he was endangering the lives and health of other members of the public. It therefore becomes necessary to decide whether some lesser form of *mens rea* could satisfy the requirements of s. 180. This appellant knew personally the danger to which the public was subjected by his donation of blood. He clearly had *mens rea*. Mr. Greenspon's third argument fails.

It is my opinion that the appellant was properly convicted of the offence under s. 180. Accordingly, I would dismiss the appeal from conviction.

With respect to sentence, the trial judge did not impose the maximum sentence prescribed by law. The maximum sentence must be reserved for the worst offender committing the worst category of the offence. The sentence imposed took into account that, because of his prior good record, the appellant would not fall into the category of the worst offender. The offence, however, can certainly be categorized as among the worst offences. The appellant's conduct verges on the unspeakable. It cried out for a sentence which would act as a deterrent to others and which would express society's repudiation of what he did. One must have great compassion for this man. He faces a terrible future. Nevertheless, the sentence demonstrates no error in principle and is one that is eminently fit.

While I would allow the application for leave to appeal sentence, I would dismiss the appeal from sentence.

*Appeal dismissed.*

[Note: An appeal to the Supreme Court of Canada was dismissed in June, 1993.]

*Editor's note: In the case of R. v. Cuerrier (1998), 127 C.C.C. (3d) 1, the accused had been charged with two counts of aggravated assault under section 268 of the* Criminal Code *after having unprotected sex with two women. He knew at the time he was HIV-positive and did not tell the women, who testified that, had they had known, would not have had unprotected sex with him. On appeal from his acquittal on both counts, the Supreme Court allowed the appeal by the prosecution and ordered a new trial. Below are excerpts from two of the judgments:*

According to Cory J. (Major, Bastarache and Binnie JJ. concurring):
> . . .Section 265(3)(c) simply states that no consent is obtained where the complainant submits or does not resist by reason of "fraud". . . .

> The first requirement of fraud is proof of dishonesty [which can include nondisclosure of important facts]. In light of the provisions of s. 265, the dishonest action or behaviour must be related to the obtaining of consent to engage in sexual intercourse, in this case unprotected intercourse. The actions of the accused must be assessed objectively to determine whether a reasonable person would find them to be dishonest. . . .

> The extent of the duty to disclose will increase with the risks attendant upon the act of intercourse. The failure to disclose HIVpositive status can lead to a devastating illness with fatal consequences. In those circumstances, there exists a positive duty to disclose.

> The second requirement of fraud is that the dishonesty result in deprivation, which may consist of actual harm or simply a risk of harm. Yet it cannot be any trivial harm or risk of harm that will satisfy this requirement in sexual assault cases where the activity would have been consensual if the consent had not been obtained by fraud. . . .

> At the outset it can be accepted that fraud pertaining to the nature and quality of the act or the identity of the partner will still constitute fraud which can be found to vitiate consent. What other acts of dishonesty which give rise to the risk of deprivation can have the same effect?

> As early as 1917 courts in the United States accepted that a woman's consent to sexual intercourse is vitiated by the man's fraudulent concealment of the risk of infection from venereal disease. . . .

> Persons knowing that they are HIVpositive who engage in sexual intercourse without advising their partner of the disease may be found to fulfil the traditional requirements for fraud namely dishonesty and deprivation. That fraud may vitiate a partner's consent to engage in sexual intercourse. . . .

> The existence of fraud should not vitiate consent unless there is a significant risk of serious harm. . . .

> It was also contended that criminalization would further stigmatize all persons with HIV/ AIDS. However it cannot be forgotten that the further stigmatization arises as a result of a sexual assault and not because of the disease. Just as an HIV-positive individual convicted of armed robbery will be further stigmatized but it will not be related to the status of his health. To proceed by way of a criminal charge for assault is not to "criminalize" the respondent's activities. Rather, it is simply to apply the provisions of the Code to conduct which could constitute the crime of assault and thereby infringe s. 265. . . .

According to McLachlin J. (Gonthier J. concurring):
> . . .[A]n explanation may be suggested for why deceit as to venereal disease may vitiate consent while deceit as to other inducements, like promises of marriage or fur coats, does not. Consent to unprotected sexual intercourse is consent to sexual congress with a certain person and to the transmission of bodily fluids from that person. Where the person represents that he or she is diseasefree, and consent is given on that basis, deception on that matter goes to the very act of assault. The complainant does not consent to the transmission of diseased fluid into his or her body. This deception in a very real sense goes to the nature of the sexual act, changing it from an act that has certain natural consequences (whether pleasure, pain or pregnancy), to a potential sentence of disease or death. It differs fundamentally from deception as to the consideration that will be given for consent, like marriage, money or a fur coat, in that it relates to the physical act itself. It differs, moreover, in a profoundly serious way that merits the criminal sanction.

## Fagan v. Commissioner of Metropolitan Police
### [1969] 1 Q.B. 439.

[Only the judgments of James J. and Bridge J. are reproduced below.]

On October 25, 1967, the appellant, Vincent Martel Fagan, appealed to Middlesex Quarter Sessions against his conviction at Willesden magistrates' court upon a charge preferred by David Morris, a constable of the Metropolitan Police Force, for and on behalf of the respondents. He had been convicted of assaulting David Morris when in the execution of his duty on August 31, 1967, contrary to section 51 of the Police Act, 1964. The appellant's appeal was dismissed.

. . .

*Cur. adv. vult.*

. . .

JAMES J.: — The appellant, Vincent Martel Fagan, was convicted by the Willesden magistrates of assaulting David Morris, a police constable, in the execution of his duty on August 31, 1967. He appealed to quarter sessions. On October 25, 1967, his appeal was heard by Middlesex Quarter Sessions and was dismissed. This matter now comes before the court on appeal by way of case stated from that decision of quarter sessions.

The sole question is whether the prosecution proved facts which in law amounted to an assault.

On August 31, 1967, the appellant was reversing a motor car in Fortunegate Road, London, N.W. 10, when Police Constable Morris directed him to drive the car forwards to the kerbside and standing in front of the car pointed out a suitable place in which to park. At first the appellant stopped the car too far from the kerb for the officer's liking. Morris asked him to park closer and indicated a precise spot. The appellant drove forward towards him and stopped it with the offside wheel on Morris's left foot. "Get off, you are on my foot," said the officer. "Fuck you, you can wait," said the appellant. The engine of the car stopped running. Morris repeated several times "Get off my foot." The appellant said reluctantly "Okay, man, okay." and then slowly turned on the ignition of the vehicle and reversed it off the officer's foot. The appellant had either turned the ignition off to stop the engine or turned it off after the engine had stopped running.

The justices at quarter sessions on those facts were left in doubt as to whether the mounting of the wheel on to the officer's foot was deliberate or accidental. They were satisfied, however, beyond all reasonable doubt that the appellant "knowingly, provocatively and unnecessarily allowed the wheel to remain on the foot after the officer said "'Get off, you are on my foot.'" They found that on those facts an assault was proved.

Mr. Abbas for the appellant relied upon the passage in Stone's Justices' Manual (1968), Vol. 1, p. 651, where assault is defined. He contends that on the finding of the justices the initial mounting of the wheel could not be an assault and that the act of the wheel mounting the foot came to an end without there being any mens rea. It is argued that thereafter there was no act on the part of the appellant which could constitute an actus reus but only the omission or failure to remove the wheel as soon as he was asked. That failure, it is said, could not in law be an assault, nor could it in law provide the necessary mens rea to convert the original act of mounting the foot into an assault.

Mr. Rant for the respondent argues that the first mounting of the foot was an actus reus which act continued until the moment of time at which the wheel was removed. During that continuing act, it is said, the appellant formed the necessary intention to constitute the element of mens rea and once that element was added to the continuing act, an assault took place. In the alternative, Mr. Rant argues that there can be situations in which there is a duty to act and that in such situations an omission to act in breach of duty would in law amount to an assault. It is unnecessary to formulate any concluded views on this alternative.

In our judgement the question arising, which has been argued on general principles, falls to be decided on the facts of the particular case. An assault is an act which intentionally — or possibly recklessly — causes another person to apprehend immediate and unlawful personal violence. Although "assault" is an independent crime and is to be treated as such, for practical purposes today "assault" is generally synonymous with the term "battery" and is a term used to mean the actual intended use of unlawful force to another person without his consent. On the facts of the present case the "assault" alleged involved a "battery". Where an assault involves a battery, it matters not, in our judgement, whether the battery is inflicted directly by the body of the offender or through the medium of some weapon or instrument controlled by the action of the offender. An assault may be committed by the laying of a hand upon another, and the action does not cease to be an assault if it is a stick held in the hand and not the hand itself which is laid on the person of the victim. So for our part we see no difference in principle between the action of stepping on to a person's toe and maintaining that position and the action of driving a car on to a person's foot and sitting in the car whilst its position on the foot is maintained.

To constitute the offence of assault some intentional act must have been performed: a mere omission to act cannot amount to an assault. Without going into the question whether words alone can constitute an assault, it is clear that the words spoken by the appellant could not alone amount to an assault: they can only shed a light on the appellant's action. For our part we think the crucial question is whether in this case the act of the appellant can be said to be complete and spent at the moment of time when the car wheel came to rest on the foot or whether his act is to be regarded as a continuing act operating until the wheel was removed. In our judgement a distinction is to be drawn between acts which are complete — though results may continue to flow — and those acts which are continuing. Once the act is complete it cannot thereafter be said to be a threat to inflict unlawful force upon the victim. If the act, as distinct from the results thereof, is a continuing act there is a continuing threat to inflict unlawful force upon the victim. If the act, as distinct from the results thereof, is a continuing act there is a continuing threat to inflict unlawful force. If the assault involves a battery and that battery continues there is a continuing act of assault.

For an assault to be committed both the elements of actus reus and mens rea must be present at the same time. The "actus reus" is the action causing the effect on the victim's mind (see the observations of Park B. in *Regina v. St. George*). The "mens rea" is the intention to cause that effect. It is not necessary that mens rea should be present at the inception of the actus reus; it can be superimposed upon an existing act. On the other hand the subsequent inception of mens rea cannot convert an act which has been completed without mens rea into an assault.

In our judgement the Willesden magistrates and quarter sessions were right in law. On the facts found the action of the appellant may have been initially unintentional, but the time came when knowing that the wheel was on the officer's foot the appellant (1) remained seated in the car so that his body through the medium of the car was in contact with the officer, (2) switched off the ignition of the car, (3) maintained the wheel of the car on the foot and (4) used words indicating the intention of keeping the wheel in that position. For our part we cannot regard such conduct as mere omission or inactivity.

There was an act constituting a battery which at its inception was not criminal because there was no element of intention but which became criminal from the moment the intention was formed to produce the apprehension which was flowing from the continuing act. The fallacy of the appellant's argument is that it seeks to equate the facts of this case with such a case as where a motorist has accidentally run over a person and, that action having been completed, fails to assist the victim with the intent that the victim should suffer.

We would dismiss this appeal.

BRIDGE J. (dissenting): — I fully agree with my Lords as to the relevant principles to be applied. No mere omission to act can amount to an assault. Both the elements of actus reus and mens rea must be present at the same time, but the one may be superimposed on the other. It is in the application of these principles to the highly unusual facts of this case that I have, with regret, reached a different conclusion from the majority of the court. I have no sympathy at all for the appellant, who behaved disgracefully. But I have been unable to find any way of regarding the facts which satisfies me that they amounted to the crime of assault. This has not been for want of trying. But at every attempt I have encountered the inescapable question: after the wheel of the appellant's car had accidentally come to rest on the constable's foot, what was it that the appellant did which constituted the act of assault? However, the question is approached, the answer I feel obliged to give is: precisely nothing. The car rested on the foot by its own weight and remained stationary by its own inertia. The appellant's fault was that he omitted to manipulate the controls to set it in motion again.

Neither the fact that the appellant remained in the driver's seat nor that he switched off the ignition seem to me to be of any relevance. The constable's plight would have been no better, but might well have been worse, if the appellant had alighted from the car leaving the ignition switched on. Similarly I can get no help from the suggested analogies. If one man accidentally treads on another's toe or touches him with a stick, but deliberately maintains pressure with foot or stick after the victim protests, there is clearly an assault. But there is no true parallel between such cases and the present case. It is not, to my mind, a legitimate use of language to speak of the appellant "holding" or "maintaining" the car wheel on the constable's foot. The expression which corresponds to the reality is that used by the justices in the case stated. They say, quite rightly, that he "allowed" the wheel to remain.

With a reluctantly dissenting voice I would allow this appeal and quash the appellant's conviction.

*Appeal dismissed.*

## Regina v. Cooper
### (1993), 78 C.C.C. (3d) 289 (S.C.C.)

Appeal by the Crown from a judgment of the Newfoundland Court of Appeal, 89 Nfld. & P.E.I.R. 1, 12 W.C.B. (2d) 424, allowing an appeal by the accused from his conviction for second degree murder.

LAMER C.J.C. (dissenting): — I have read the reasons of my colleague, Justice Cory, and adopt his exposition of the facts, the law and, save what is hereinafter said, his comments with respect to s. 212(*a*)(ii) of the *Criminal Code*, R.S.C. 1970, c. C-34 (now R.S.C. 1985, c. C-46, s 229 (*a*)(ii).

It is crucial to a correct charge under s. 212(*a*)(ii) that the jury understand that there must be intention to cause bodily harm which the accused knows is likely to cause death. Intention to cause bodily harm, without knowledge that such is likely to cause death, is not sufficient. Given the position of the defence in this case, a clear understanding of this aspect was essential to a fair trial.

Intentionally and consciously choking someone for only a few seconds might or might not constitute the infliction of "bodily harm" is not defined in that section, there is a statutory definition in s. 245.1 (now s. 267) which also applies to ss. 245.3 (now s. 269) and s. 246.2 (now s. 272):

> 245.1(2) .   .   . "bodily harm" means any hurt or injury to the complainant that interferes with his or her health or comfort and that is more than merely transient or trifling in nature.

This definition provides some general guidance about the interpretation of the term "bodily harm" in s. 212(*a*)(ii) and makes the point that bodily harm includes a broad spectrum of hurts and injuries.

I do not raise this point to question whether the accused here intended to cause bodily harm. That was conceded in the argument before us. I raise it rather to emphasize that the intention to cause bodily harm by no means leads inexorably to the conclusion that the accused knew that the bodily harm was likely to cause death. It is, of course, this second aspect which is essential to a finding of guilt of murder under s. 212(*a*)(ii). Particularly with respect to an action such as grabbing by the neck, there may be a point at the outset when there is no intention to cause death and no knowledge that the action is likely to cause death. But there comes a point in time when the wrongful conduct becomes likely to cause death. It is, in my view, at that moment or thereafter, that the accused must have a conscious awareness of the likelihood of death. This awareness need not, however, continue until death ensues.

Cooper intended to choke the deceased and cause her bodily harm. Under s. 212(*a*)(i), it was open to the jury to infer from his conduct and on all of the evidence that in doing so he intended to kill her. To be found guilty under s. 212(*a*)(ii), however, he must have been aware of the fact that he persisted in choking her long enough for it to become likely that death would ensue.

This instruction, given the particular facts of this case and the nature of the defence presented by the accused, had to be given. Additionally, the jury should have been instructed to consider the evidence of drunkenness in relation to this awareness. In my respectful view, upon a reading of the whole charge, this was not done adequately.

I would dismiss the appeal.

L'HEUREUX-DUBÉ, SOPINKA AND GONTHIER JJ. concur with Cory J.

CORY J.: — At issue, on this appeal, is the nature of the intent required to found a conviction for murder pursuant to s. 212(a)(ii) of the *Criminal Code*, R.S.C. 1970, c. C-34 (now R.S.C. 1985, c. C-46, s. 229(a)(ii).

## Factual background

The respondent Lyndon Cooper and the deceased Deborah Careen lived in Labrador City, Newfoundland. At one time, they had been friends and lovers. On January 30, 1988, they met at a gathering place known as the K-Bar in Labrador City. Although by this time the respondent was living with somebody else, they spent the evening together at the bar. There is no doubt that they consumed a considerable amount of alcohol. Eventually, Cooper, the deceased and a mutual friend left the bar in a taxi. After they dropped off the friend they continued in the cab to the residence of another of Cooper's friends where he borrowed a Jeep. Cooper then drove the deceased to the secluded parking-lot of a power station.

At the parking-lot the respondent testified that he and the deceased engaged in some form of consensual sexual activity. He said that they began to argue at one point and that the deceased struck him. At this he became angry. He hit the deceased and grabbed her by the throat with both hands and shook her. He stated that this occurred in the front seat of the Jeep. He then said that he could recall nothing else until he woke in the back seat and found the body of the deceased beside him. He had no recollection of causing her death. He pushed her body out of the Jeep and drove away. Later during the drive to his home he found one of her shoes in the vehicle and threw it out into the snow.

The expert evidence established that the deceased had in fact been struck twice. However, these blows could not have killed her. Rather death was caused by "a classic pattern of one-handed manual strangulation". That same evidence confirmed that death by strangulation can occur as quickly as 30 seconds after contact with the throat and that a drunken victim is likely to die from asphyxiation more quickly than a sober one. None the less, the presence of *petechial haemorrhages* on the neck of the deceased and the finding that the hyoid bone in her throat was not fractured suggested to the expert that death occurred rather more slowly, probably after two minutes of pressure. The position of the defence was that the respondent was so drunk that he blacked out shortly after he started shaking her with both hands. Thus, it was said that the respondent did not have, (i) the required intent to commit murder, or (ii) alternatively, did not foresee that holding someone by the neck was likely to cause death. . . .

*Analysis*

*The nature of the intent required to secure a conviction under s. 212(a)(ii).*

Section 212(a)(ii) provides:

212. Culpable homicide is murder

(*a*) where the person who causes the death of a human being

. . .

(ii) means to cause him bodily harm that he knows is likely to cause his death, and is reckless whether death ensues or not;

This section was considered in *R. v. Nygaard, supra*. On the issue of the requisite intent the court was unanimous. At p. 435, it was said: The essential element is that of intending to cause bodily harm of such a grave and serious nature that the accused knew that it was likely to result in the death of the victim. The aspect of recklessness is almost an afterthought

. . .

The aspect of recklessness can be considered an afterthought since to secure a conviction under this section it must be established that the accused had the intent to cause such grievous bodily harm that he knew it was likely to cause death. One who causes bodily harm that he knows is likely to cause death must, in those circumstances, have a deliberate disregard for the fatal consequences which are known to be likely to occur. That is to say he must, of necessity, be reckless whether death ensues or not.

The concept of recklessness was considered by this court in *R. v. Sansregret* (1985), 18 C.C.C. (3d) 223, 17 D.L.R. (4th) 577, [1985] 1 S.C.R. 570. At p. 233 it was said:

[Recklessness] is found in the attitude of one who, aware that there is danger that his conduct could bring about the result prohibited by the criminal law, nevertheless persists, despite the risk. It is, in other words, the conduct of one who sees the risk and who takes the chance.

The same words can apply to s. 212(*a*)(ii) with this important addition: it is not sufficient that the accused foresee simply a *danger of death: the accused must foresee a likelihood* of death flowing from the bodily harm that he is occasioning the victim.

It is for this reason that it was said in *Nygaard* that there is only a "slight relaxation" in the *mens rea* required for a conviction for murder under s. 212(*a*)(ii) as compared to s. 212(*a*)(i). The position was put in this way at p. 436:

. . .[where] two accused form the intent to repeatedly and viciously strike a person in the head with a baseball bat realizing full well that the victim will probably die as a result. None the less they continue with the bone-splintering, skull-shattering assault. The accused . . . must have committed as grave a crime as the accused who specifically intends to kill . . . I would conclude that the crime defined in s. 212(*a*)(ii) [now s. 229(*a*)(ii)] can properly be described as murder and on a "culpability scale" it varies so little from s. 212(*a*)(i) as to be indistinguishable.

The intent that must be demonstrated in order to convict under s. 212(*a*)(ii) has two aspects. There must be (a) subjective intent to cause bodily harm; (b) subjective knowledge that the bodily harm is of such a nature that it is likely to result in death.

It is only when those two elements of intent are established that a conviction can properly follow.

*What degree of concurrency is required between the wrongful act and the requisite mens rea?*

There can be no doubt that under the classical approach to criminal law it is the intent of the accused that makes the wrongful act illegal. It is that intent which brings the accused within the sphere of blameworthiness and justifies the penalty or punishment which is imposed upon him for the infraction of the criminal law. The essential aspect of *mens rea* and the absolute necessity that it be present in the case of murder was emphasized by Lamer J. (as he then was) in *R. v. Vaillancourt* (1987), 39 C.C.C. (3d) 118, 47 D.L.R. (4th) 399, [1987] 2 S.C.R. 636. At p. 133, he stated: " It may well be that, as a general rule, the principles of fundamental justice require proof of a subjective *mens rea* with respect to the prohibited act, in order to avoid punishing the 'morally innocent'."

. . .

However, not only must the guilty mind, intent or *mens rea* be present, it must also be concurrent with the impugned act. Professor D. Stuart has referred to this as "the simultaneous principle": see *Canadian Criminal Law*, 2nd ed. (1987), p. 305. The principle has been stressed in a number of cases. For example in *R. v. Droste* (1979), 49 C.C.C. (2d) 52, 18 C.R. (3d) 64 (Ont. C.A.), the accused had intended to murder his wife by pouring gasoline over the interior of the car and setting fire to it while she was within it. Before he could light the gasoline the car crashed into a bridge and ignited prematurely. As a result both his children were killed rather than his wife. He was charged with their murder and convicted. On appeal Arnup J.A., speaking for the Court of Appeal in directing a new trial, stated at pp. 53-4:

> . . . the trial Judge did not instruct the jury of the necessity of the Crown showing that at the time of the occurrence at the bridge, the appellant, intending to kill his wife, had done an act with that intention, and in the course of doing so his children were killed. *In short, he did not tell them that the mens rea and the actus reus must be concurrent . . .*

(Emphasis added).

Yet, it is not always necessary for the guilty act and the intent to be completely concurrent: see, for example, *Fagan v. Metropolitan Police Commissioner*, [1983] 3 All. E.R. 442 (Q.B.)

There is, then, the classic rule that at some point the *actus reus* and the *mens reas* or intent must coincide. Further, I would agree . . . that an act (*actus reus*) which may be innocent or no more than careless at the outset can become criminal at a later stage when the accused acquires knowledge of the nature of the act and still refuses to change his course of action.

The determination of whether the guilty mind or *mens rea* coincides with the wrongful act will depend to a large extent upon the nature of the act. For example, if the accused shot the victim in the head or stabbed the victim in the chest with death ensuing a few minutes after the shooting or stabbing, then it would be relatively easy to infer that the requisite intent or *mens rea* coincided with the wrongful act (*actus reus*) of shooting or stabbing. As well, a series of acts may form part of the same transaction. For example the repeated blows of the baseball bat continuing over several minutes are all part of the same transaction. In those circumstances if the requisite intent coincides at any time with the sequence of blows then that could be sufficient to found a conviction.

An example of a series of acts that might be termed a continuous transaction appears in *Meli v. The Queen*, [1954] 1 W.L.R. 228 (P.C.). There the accused intended to kill the deceased, and to this end struck a number of blows. The effect of the blows was such that the accused thought the victim was dead and threw the body over a cliff. However, it was not the blows but rather the exposure suffered by the victim while he lay at the base of the cliff that resulted in the death. It was argued on behalf of the accused that when there was the requisite *mens rea* (during the beating) death did not ensue and when death did ensue there was no longer any intention to kill. The judicial committee of the Privy Council concluded that the entire episode was one continuing transaction that could not be subdivided in any way. At some point, the requisite mens rea coincided with the continuing series of wrongful acts that constituted the transaction. As a result, the conviction for murder was sustained. I agree with that conclusion.

*Application of the "contemporaneous" principles to this case*

Gushue J.A. indicated that persisting or continuing knowledge by the accused that the act he was performing was likely to cause death was required in order to obtain a conviction. He wrote at p. 5:

> A simple reading of what the Supreme Court said in this regard in *Nygaard* makes it very clear that an extremely high degree of knowledge by an accused of what he is doing and *persisting* in must be demonstrated before the requisite intent may be found to exist.

(Emphasis added.)

Yet, with respect, I do not think that it is always necessary that the requisite *mens rea* (the guilty mind, intent or awareness) should continue throughout the commission of the wrongful act. There is no question that in order to obtain a conviction the Crown must demonstrate that the accused intended to cause bodily harm that he knew was ultimately so dangerous and serious that it was likely to result in the death of the victim. But that intent need not persist throughout the entire act of strangulation. When Cooper testified that he seized the victim by the neck, it was open to the jury to infer that by those actions he intended to cause her bodily harm that he knew that was likely to cause her death. Since breathing is essential to life, it would be reasonable to infer the accused knew that strangulation was likely to result in death. I would stress that the jury was, of course, not required to make such an inference but, on the evidence presented, it was open to them to do so.

Did the accused possess such a mental state after he started strangling the victim? Here death occurred between 30 seconds and two minutes after he grabbed her by the neck. It could be reasonably inferred by the jury, that when the accused grabbed the victim by the neck and shook her that there was, at that moment, the necessary coincidence of the wrongful act of strangulation and the requisite intent to do bodily harm that the accused knew was likely to cause her death. Cooper was aware of these acts before he "blacked out". Thus although the jury was under no compulsion to do so, it was none the less open to them to infer that he knew that he was causing bodily harm and knew that it was so dangerous to the victim that it was likely to cause her death. It was sufficient that the intent and the act of strangulation coincided at some point. It was not necessary that the requisite intent continue throughout the entire two minutes required to cause the death of the victim.

Gushue J.A. in his reasons relied upon and stressed the following quotation from *R. v. Nygaard, supra*, at p. 435:

> Thus the section requires the accused to intend to cause the gravest of bodily harm that is so dangerous and serious that he knows it is likely to result in death and to *persist in that conduct* despite the knowledge of the risk.

(Emphasis added.)

The emphasized words refer to the *conduct* of an accused. Those words should not be taken as requiring a persistent or continued *awareness* of a likelihood of death right up to the moment of death or until the precise moment when it is established that death was likely to occur. Once it is demonstrated beyond a reasonable doubt that an accused has knowingly caused bodily harm that he knew was likely to cause the death of the victim and the victim dies as a result of the injuries inflicted, then he may be found guilty of murder under s. 212(*a*)(ii).

The Court of Appeal asked whether "continuing awareness on his part was what he was doing and its probable result [was] established". The accused argued that in using this expression the Court of Appeal was not going so far as to require the presence of a continuous intent up to the moment of death. Rather, he contended that the court was merely stating that in order for there to be a conviction under this section the *mens rea* must be present at or after the point at which it becomes likely the death will ensue. It was his position that if the intent to cause bodily harm that the accused knew was likely to cause death should disappear before the point was reached at which death became likely then the accused could not be found guilty. He stated that it was only at this point that the *mens rea* and *actus reus* could coalesce into the crime described in s. 212(*a*)(ii).

This argument should not be accepted. It would require the Crown to provide expert evidence as to the moment at which death physiologically became a likelihood. It would be impossible to fix the time of the "likelihood" of death and difficult to provide evidence as to the duration of the requisite intent of the accused. That cannot be the meaning of this section. Neither the plain wording of this section nor any concept of fairness require the Crown to demonstrate such a complex chronological sequence. In order to obtain a conviction under s. 212(*a*)(ii), the Crown must prove that the accused caused and intended to cause bodily harm that he knew was likely to cause the death of the victim. If death results from a series of wrongful acts that are part of a single transaction then it must be established that the requisite intent coincided at some point with the wrongful acts.

On this issue the trial judge correctly instructed the jury when he stated:

When he grabbed her by the neck and shook her, did he intend to cause her bodily harm, which he knew was likely to cause her death and was reckless whether death ensued or not. In other words, he wouldn't have to be there until she died . . . He could formulate all of that intent at that point in time, even though he doesn't remember the final outcome.

It was on this ground that the Court of Appeal directed the new trial. Although it can never be determinative of the issue, it is significant that defence counsel at trial took no objection to this or any other aspect of the charge. In any event for the reasons set out earlier, I must disagree with the Court of Appeal's conclusion on this issue. A new trial should not have been granted on this ground.

### The knowledge of the likelihood of death

The appellant seeks to uphold the order directing a new trial on two other grounds. The first, and the more important of these, is the issue raised before the Court of Appeal that the trial judge did not adequately instruct the jury that the Crown must establish that Cooper *knew* that the bodily injury that he was inflicting was likely to cause the death of the victim. I cannot agree with that contention.

It is true that from one or two excerpts from the charge the jury could have inferred that an intent to cause bodily harm was all that was required in order to convict. Yet on numerous occasions the trial judge stated and repeated that the jurors had to be satisfied beyond a reasonable doubt that Cooper meant to cause bodily harm that he *knew* was likely to cause death and was reckless whether death ensued or not . . .

Upon a careful reading and review of the charge as a whole, I am satisfied that there were no errors committed by the trial judge that would justify a new trial.

In the result, I would set aside the order of the Court of Appeal directing a new trial and restore the conviction.

McLachlin and Iacobucci JJ. concur with Cory J.

*Appeal allowed; conviction restored.*

### Questions/Discussion

1. Do you think the results in the cases of *Jordan* and *Smith* can be reconciled? Why or why not?
2. What is your liability in the situation where you shoot A but just before A dies, B comes along and shoots A through the head, effectively killing A? What if after being shot by you, A in agony finishes himself off by cutting his own throat? If in both of these situations, the original wound is one of the causes of death, then attaching liability is no problem, for your actions need not be the only cause of death, just one of the causes. For example, in an American case, *People v. Lewis* (1899), 57 Pac. 470, the defendant mortally wounded the victim, but before dying of the wound, the victim slits his own throat. In the case, the court said that both wounds were operative at the time of death and both contributed to the death. In *Bradley v. The Queen*, [1956] S.C.R. 723, the victim was in a fight with the defendant which left the victim with a fractured skull; the defendant then removed the victim's coat and left him unconscious in the cold. The victim died partly as a result of exposure. The Supreme Court of Canada said that the exposure was caused by the abandoning of the victim in these circumstances and therefore the defendant was liable.

3. If A goes to kill B by shooting him, but misses and B escapes from the building only to be hit and killed by a bus a hundred metres down the street, should A be held liable for "causing" the death of B? What breaks the chain of causation in such situations? Would your answer be the same if B were killed two hours later by a bus or if B were killed by a bus the next day on the way to the police station to report the attempted killing?

4. Under the current law, if I watch a blind person walk into traffic or toward a cliff there is no duty on my part to do anything, assuming there is no special relationship between the two of us. Should there be such a duty created in the Criminal Code? Why or why not? The former Law Reform Commission of Canada proposed the following provision for a new code:

> Failure to Rescue.
> (a) General Rule. Everyone commits a crime who, perceiving another in immediate danger of death or serious harm, does not take reasonable steps to assist him [or her].
> (b) Exception Clause . . . (a) does not apply where the person cannot take reasonable steps to assist without risk of death to himself [or herself] or another person or where he [or she] has some other valid reason for not doing so.

Do you agree with such a provision? What problems do you see in actually applying such a rule? For example, how does one define the content of such a duty in any particular circumstances. Should the law incorporate such a moral duty to assist or should we continue to rely on other social or moral pressures to accomplish the same ends?

5. If I drop poison in my soup by mistake and then say nothing when V comes along by chance and starts to eat it, should I be held liable for the death which is caused? I did nothing intentionally or knowingly, and when it could be argued I had formed an evil intent (when I knowingly watched V eat my poisoned soup), I merely omitted to do or say anything.

6. What are the nature and the significance of "continuing acts" in criminal law as expressed in *Fagan*? Does the concept pose any danger to traditional principles of criminal liability? Why (or why not)? What is your opinion of decision of the dissenting judge in the case?

## Further Reading

- Mewett, A. and M. Manning, *Mewett and Manning on Criminal Law, 3rd ed.* (Markham: Butterworths, 1994).
- Roach, Kent, *Criminal Law, 2d edition* (Toronto: Irwin Law, 2000) at 65-95.
- Samek, R. "The Concepts of Act and Intention and Their Treatment in Jurisprudence" (1963), 41 Australasian Journal of Philosophy 198.
- Stuart, D., and R. Delisle, *Learning Canadian Criminal Law, 8th ed.* (Toronto: Carswell, 2001).

## 6.1.2   Mens Rea

### Introduction

Theoretically, the notion of individual intention and/or knowledge in the criminal law (and therefore individual "fault" or blameworthiness) is central to a finding of guilt or criminal liability. As stated by the Law Reform Commission of Canada,

The basic thrust of the responsibility principle is clear and simple but its detailed analysis and application have become confusing. Its basic thrust is *no liability without fault* — a proposition enjoying general acceptance.[1]

In practice, it can be argued that the requirement of a guilty mind is at times ignored in the interests of protecting society. This tension between the requirement of individual moral fault and the desire to protect society is a very real one both in the literature and in the day-to-day work of the courts. A difficulty is that while lip service is often paid to this traditional subjectivist approach, it is not unusual for the courts in practice to either ignore the requirement or *assume* that it is present; this is particularly true, as we shall see, in cases of criminal negligence.

This section of the chapter examines the meanings of mens rea, the difficulties of applying those meanings to real life fact situations, and what the courts do in response to those problems. A general criticism in this area of criminal law is that there is too often an inconsistency between what the courts say they are doing in applying a so-called fundamental principle of criminal liability (i.e., the requirement of actual and subjective intent of knowledge) and what they actually do. Keep this criticism in mind as you read through the cases, and assess the validity and value of the principle.

One of the first difficulties we find in this area is in regard to the meaning of guilty intention and its operation within the criminal justice system. The problem of defining what is meant by intention or individual responsibility is a vexing one — how we explain notions of responsibility on the part of an individual is coloured by one's own particular perspective on or approach to the role of individual agency and free will in human conduct. Are individual actions to be interpreted in light of the social structures in which they operate? Should we see human actions strictly as the reflection of biological urges or needs? And what of the problems of the differing attributes and developmental environments of individuals — should these factors be reflected in our concept of individual blameworthiness and the determination of guilt?

The criminal justice system in theory assumes that all people are alike when determining guilt or innocence, yet in reality this assumption is far from the truth. People are vastly different in their backgrounds, abilities, opportunities, and resources: should these differences be pertinent to the issue of individual responsibility in the criminal law? As is obvious from the cases which follow, the courts adopt a relatively unproblematic view of mens rea in this regard. *Beaver* and *King* discuss the requirement for mens rea while *Ladue* deals (not satisfactorily) with the situation where the intent of the individual does "match" the physical acts of the accused.[2] *Droste* is a case where the intended victim and the actual victims differed, and involves a discussion of the type of liability which will attach in such situations.

Another problem with the meaning of mens rea is raised in the area of recklessness where less than a full intention or less that full knowledge is sometimes found sufficient to satisfy the requirement of mens rea. There is, as with full intention, the notion of individual blameworthiness to the extent that there is some degree of fault which can be attributed to the accused, for example in a situation where the accused has knowingly run a risk and harm has resulted. The accused does not have full intention or knowledge in regard to his or her actions and its consequences, but there is a sense of wrongfulness nonetheless. This mental state is still required to be subjective, however, and the question is what mental state is sufficient to satisfy the mens rea requirement and what are the problems which are involved.

While in theory mens rea is a necessary element to be present in order to be convicted of a crime, there are many exceptions to this very general rule. For example, as we shall see in the final subsection (6.1.3.), there are criminal laws where no mens rea element need be proven at all. This is perhaps less of a problem than those situations where the courts, though seemingly requiring mens rea, in practice ignore the traditional call for actual, subjective intent. As noted above, this is particularly true in the area of criminal negligence where the courts seem to punish for actions or for conduct which on their face demonstrate a wanton disregard for the safety of others, even though the accused may not actually have addressed his or her mind to the dangerousness of the conduct (whether of stupidity, thoughtlessness, or just lack of intent). The courts, rightly or wrongly, are balancing the requirement of subjective intent and the protection needs of the public. When the choice is exercised in favour of the latter, the test becomes more of an objective one: that is, did the conduct of the accused breach standards of reasonableness in the conduct to be expected by the general public. The test then is *not* one of what was the intent or knowledge of the accused at the time of the act (for example, did she actually foresee the danger and run the risk anyway?) These issues are looked at in the last three cases in this section.

**Footnotes**

1   Law Reform Commission of Canada, *Working Paper 29: The General Part —* Liability and Defences (Ottawa: Ministry of Supply and Services, 1982), p. 172.
2   The issues raised in *Ladue* are more fully explored in Chapter 7, section 2.1, in regard to the *Kundeus* case.

## Beaver v. The Queen
### (1957), 118 C.C.C. 129 (S.C.C.)

Appeal by accused from a decision of the Ontario Court of Appeal, 116 Can. C.C. 231, affirming a conviction for possession and sale of a drug and from another decision of the same Court finding the accused an habitual criminal. Reversed in part.

[Only excerpts from the judgment of Cartwright is reproduced below.] CARTWRIGHT J.: — The appellant was tried jointly with one Max Beaver before His Honour Judge Forsyth and a jury in the Court of General Sessions of the Peace for the County of York on an indictment reading as follows:

"The jurors for our Lady the Queen present that

"LOUIS BEAVER and MAX BEAVER, at the City of Toronto, in the County of York, on or about the 12th day of March, in the year 1954, unlawfully did sell a drug, to wit, diacetyl-morphine, without the authority or a licence from the Minister of National Health and Welfare or other lawful authority, contrary to Section 4(1)(f) of the Opium and Narcotic Drug Act, Revised Statutes of Canada, 1952, Chapter 201 and amendments thereto.

"The said jurors further present that the said Louis Beaver and Max Beaver, at the City of Toronto, in the County of York, on or about the 12th day of March, in the year 1954, unlawfully did have in their possession a drug, to wit, diacetylmorphine, without the authority of a licence from the Minister of National Health and Welfare or other lawful authority, contrary to Section 4(1)(d) of the Opium and Narcotic Drug Act, Revised Statutes of Canada 1952, Chapter 201, and amendments thereto;

AND FURTHER that the said Louis Beaver is an habitual criminal;

"AND FURTHER that the said Max Beaver is an habitual criminal."

On September 19, 1955, the accused were found guilty on both counts and on the same day the learned trial judge found them to be habitual criminals. On October 17, 1955, the learned Judge sentenced them to 7 years' imprisonment on each count, the sentences to run concurrently, and also imposed sentences of preventive detention.

Max Beaver has since died and we are concerned only with the case of the appellant.

The appellant appealed to the Court of Appeal for Ontario against both convictions and against the finding that he was an habitual criminal. These appeals were dismissed.

On February 19, 1957, the appellant was given leave to appeal to this Court [117 Can. C.C. 340, [1957] S.C.R. 119] from the convictions on the two counts on the following grounds:

1. The learned trial Judge erred in failing to instruct the jury that, if they accepted the evidence of Louis Beaver or were in doubt as a result of it, he was not guilty of the offence.

2. The learned trial Judge erred in holding that the accused Louis Beaver was guilty of the offence charged whether he knew the package handed by the accused Max Beaver to the Police were drugs or not.

3. The learned trial Judge erred in instructing the jury that the only point that they had to decide was whether in fact the package handed the police by the accused Max Beaver was diacetylmorphine.

4. The charge to the jury by the learned trial judge and the Court of Appeal is in error in holding that the accused Louis Beaver could be convicted of the offence charged in the absence of knowledge on his part that the substance in question was a drug.

By the same order, leave to appeal from the finding that the appellant was an habitual criminal was granted, conditionally upon the appeals from the convictions being successful.

It is not necessary to set out the facts in detail. There was evidence on which it was open to the jury to find (i) that Max Beaver sold to a police officer, who was working under cover, a package which in fact contained diacetylmorphine, (ii) that the appellant was a party to the sale of the package, (iii) that while the appellant did not have the package on his person or in his physical possession he and Max Beaver were acting jointly in such circumstances that the possession which the latter had of the package was the possession of both of the accused, and (iv) that the appellant had no knowledge that the substance contained in the package was diacetylmorphine and believed it to be sugar or milk.

I do not mean to suggest that the jury would necessarily have made the fourth finding but there was evidence on which they might have done so, or which might have left them in a state of doubt as to whether or not the appellant knew that the package contained anything other than sugar or milk.

The learned trial Judge, against the protest of the appellant, charged the jury, in effect, that if they were satisfied that the appellant had in his possession a package and sold it, then, if in fact the substance contained in the package was diacetylmorphine, the appellant was guilty on both counts, and that the questions (i) whether he had any knowledge of what the substance was, or (ii) whether he entertained the honest but mistaken belief that it was a harmless substance were irrelevant and must not be considered. Laidlaw J.A. who delivered the unanimous judgment of the Court of Appeal, [116 Can. C.C. 231], was of opinion that this charge was right in law and that the learned trial Judge was bound by the decision in *R. v. Lawrence*, 102 Can. C.C. 121, [1952] O.R. 149, to direct the jury as he did. The main question on this appeal is whether this view of the law is correct.

The problem is one of construction of the *Opium and Narcotic Drug Act*, R.S.C. 1952, c. 201, and particularly the following sections, which at the date of the offences charged read as follows:

"**4**(1) Every person who . . .

"(d) has in his possession any drug save and except under the authority of a licence from the Minister first had and obtained, or other lawful authority; . . . .

(f) manufactures, sells, gives away, delivers or distributes or makes any offer in respect of any drug, or any substance represented or held out by such person to be a drug, to any person without first obtaining a licence from the Minister, or without other lawful authority; . . .

is guilty of an offence, and is liable

"(i) upon indictment, to imprisonment for any term not exceeding seven years and not less than six months, and to a fine not exceeding one thousand dollars and not less than two hundred dollars, and, in addition, at the discretion of the judge, to be whipped; or

"(ii) upon summary conviction, to imprisonment with or without hard labour for any term not exceeding eighteen months and not less than six months, and to a fine not exceeding one thousand dollars and not less than two hundred dollars.

"(2) Notwithstanding the provision of the *Criminal Code*, or of any other statute or law, the court has no power to impose less than the minimum penalties herein prescribed, and shall, in all cases of conviction, impose both fine and imprisonment."

"**11**(1) No person shall, without lawful authority or without a permit signed by the Minister or some person authorized by him in that behalf, import or have in his possession any opium pipe, opium lamp, or other device or apparatus designed or generally used for the purpose of preparing opium for smoking, or smoking or inhaling opium, or any article capable of being used or as part of any such pipe, lamp or other device or apparatus.

"(2) Any person violating the provisions of this section is liable, upon summary conviction, to a fine not exceeding one hundred dollars, and not less than fifty dollars, or to imprisonment for a term not exceeding three months, or to both fine and imprisonment."

"**15.** Where any person is charged with an offence under paragraph (a), (d), (f), or (g) of subsection (1) of section 4, it is not necessary for the prosecuting authority to establish that the accused had not a licence from the Minister or was not otherwise authorized to commit the act complained of, and if the accused pleads or alleges that he had such licence or other authority the burden of proof thereof shall be upon the person so charged."

"**17.** Without limiting the generality of paragraph (d) of sub-section (1) of section 4, any person who occupies, controls, or is in possession of any building, room, vessel, vehicle, enclosure or place, in or upon which any drug or any article mentioned in section 11 is found, shall, if charged with having such drug or article in possession without lawful authority, be deemed to have been so in possession unless he prove that the drug or article was there without his authority, knowledge or consent, or that he was lawfully entitled to the possession thereof."

In the course of the argument counsel also referred to the following provisions of other statutes of Canada:

The *Interpretation Act*, R.S.C. 1952, c. 158, s. 28(1):

"**28**(1) Every act shall be read and construed as if any offence for which the offender may be

"(a) prosecuted by indictment, howsoever such offence may be therein described or referred to, were described or referred to as an indictable offence;

"(b) punishable on summary conviction, were described or referred to as an offence; and all provisions of the *Criminal Code* relating to indictable offences, or offences, as the case may be, shall apply to every such offence."

The *Criminal Code*, R.S.C. 1927, c. 36, s. 5:

"**5**(1) In this Act, unless the context otherwise requires, . . .

"(b) having in one's possession includes not only having in one's own personal possession, but also knowingly,

"(i) having in the actual possession or custody of any other person, and

"(ii) having in any place, whether belonging to or occupied by one's self or not, for the use or benefit of one's self or of any other person.

(2) If there are two or more persons, and any one or more of them, with the knowledge and consent of the rest, has or have anything in his or their custody or possession, it shall be deemed and taken to be in the custody and possession of each and all of them."

The judgment in appeal is supported by earlier decisions of Appellate Courts in Ontario, Quebec and Nova Scotia, but a directly contrary view has been expressed by the Court of Appeal for British Columbia. While this conflict has existed since 1948, this is the first occasion on which the question has been brought before this Court.

It may be of assistance in examining the problem to use a simple illustration. Suppose X goes to the shop of Y, a druggist, and asks Y to sell him some baking soda. Y hands him a sealed packet which he tells him contains baking soda and charges him a few cents. X honestly believes that the packet contains baking soda but in fact it contains heroin. X puts the package in his pocket, takes it home and later puts it in a cupboard in his bathroom. There would seem to be no doubt that X has had actual manual and physical possession of the package and that he continues to have possession of the package while it is in his cupboard. The main question raised on this appeal is whether, in the supposed circumstances, X would be guilty of the crime of having heroin in his possession?

It will be observed at once that we are not concerned with the incidence of the burden of proof or of the obligation of adducing evidence. The judgment of the Court of Appeal states the law to be that X must be convicted although he proves to the point of demonstration that he honestly believed the package to contain baking soda.

I have examined all the cases referred to by counsel in the course of their full and helpful arguments but do not propose to refer to them in detail as the differences of opinion which they disclose are not so much as to the principles by which the Court should be guided in construing a statute which creates a crime as to the result of applying those principles to the Act with which we are concerned.

The rule of construction has often been stated.

. . .

In *R. v. Tolson* (1889), 23 Q.B.D. 168 at p. 188, Stephen J. says: "I think it may be laid down as a general rule than an alleged offender is deemed to have acted under that state of facts which he in good faith and on reasonable grounds believed to exist when he did the act alleged to be an offence. I am unable to suggest any real exception to this rule, nor has one ever been suggested to me." And adds at p. 189: "Of course, it would be competent to the legislature to define a crime in such a way as to make the existence of any state of mind immaterial. The question is solely whether it has actually done so in this case."

I adhere to the opinion which, with the concurrence of my brother Nolan, I expressed in *R. v. Rees*, 115 Can. C.C. 1 at p. 11, 4 D.L.R. (2d) 406 at p. 415, [1956] S.C.R. 640 at p. 651 that the first of the statements of Stephen J. quoted above should now be read in the light of the judgment of Lord Goddard C.J., concurred in by Lynskey and Devlin JJ. in *Wilson v. Inyang*, [1951] 2 All E.R. 237, which, in my opinion, rightly decides that the essential question is whether the belief entertained by the accused is an honest one and that the existence or non-existence of reasonable grounds for such belief is merely relevant evidence to be weighed by the tribunal of fact in determining that essential question.

. . .

When the decisions as to the construction of the *Opium and Narcotic Drug Act* on which the respondent relies are examined it appears that two main reasons are assigned for holding that *mens rea* is not an essential ingredient of the offence created by s. 4(1)(d), these being (i) the assumption that the subject-matter with which the Act deals is of the kind dealt with in the cases of which *Hobbs v. Winchester Corp.*, [1910] 2 K.B. 471, is typical and which are sometimes referred to as "public welfare offence cases", and (ii) by implication from the wording of s. 17 of the Act.

As to the first of these reasons, I can discern little similarity between a statute designed, by forbidding the sale of unsound meat, to ensure that the supply available to the public shall be wholesome, and a statute making it a serious crime to possess or deal in narcotics; the one is to ensure that a lawful and necessary trade shall be carried on in a manner not to endanger the public health, the other to forbid altogether conduct regarded as harmful in itself. As a necessary feature of his trade, the butcher holds himself out as selling meat fit for consumption; he warrants that quality; and it is part of his duty as trader to see that the merchandise is wholesome. The statute simply converts that civil personal duty into a public duty.

. . .

As to the second reason, the argument is put as follows. Using again the illustration I have taken above, it is said (i) that the words of s. 17 would require the conviction of X if the package was found in his bathroom cupboard "unless he prove that [it] was there without his authority, knowledge or consent", that is, he is *prima facie* presumed to be guilty but can exculpate himself by proving lack of knowledge, and (ii) that since no such words as "unless he prove that the drug was in his possession without his knowledge" are found in s. 4(1)(d) it must be held that Parliament intended that lack of knowledge should be no defence.

In my view all that s. 17 accomplishes, still using the same illustration, is, on proof that the package was in his cupboard, to shift to X the onus of proving that he did not have possession of the package. To this X would answer: "Of course I had possession of the package, I bought it, paid for it, carried it home and put it in my cupboard. My defence is that I thought it contained baking soda. I had no idea it contained heroin." If it be suggested that X could not usefully make this reply if what was found in his house was not a sealed package but an article of the sort described in s. 11 the answer would appear to be that any person might not recognize an opium lamp or an article capable of being used as part of such a lamp. The wording of s. 17 does not appear to me to compel the Court to construe s. 4 as the Court of Appeal has done. It still leaves unanswered the question: Has X possession of heroin when he has in his hand or in his pocket or in his cupboard a package which in fact contains heroin but which he honestly believes contains only baking soda? In my opinion that question must be answered in the negative. The essence of the crime is the possession of the forbidden substance and in a criminal case there is in law no possession without knowledge of the character of the forbidden substance.

. . .

In my view the law is correctly stated in the following passage in the judgment of O'Halloran J.A., with whom Robertson J.A. concurred, in *R. v. Hess* (1948) 94 Can. C.C. 48 at pp. 50-1: "To constitute 'possession' within the meaning of the criminal law it is my judgment, that where as here there is manual handling of a thing, it must be co-existent with knowledge of what the thing is, and both these elements must be coexistent with some act of control (outside public duty). When those three elements exist together, I think it must be conceded that under s. 4(1)(d) it does not then matter if the thing is retained for an innocent purpose."

If the matter were otherwise doubtful I would be drawn to the conclusion that Parliament did not intend to enact that *mens rea* should not be an essential ingredient of the offence created by s. 4(1)(d) by the circumstance that on conviction a minimum sentence of 6 months' imprisonment plus a fine of $200 be imposed.

. . .

The conclusion which I have reached on the main question as to the proper construction of the word possession makes it unnecessary for me to consider the other points raised by Mr. Dubin in his argument as to the construction of s. 4(1)(d). For the above reasons I would quash the conviction on the charge of having possession of a drug.

As to the charge of selling, as is pointed out by my brother Fauteux, the appellant's version of the facts brings his actions within the provisions of s. 4(1)(f) since he and his brother jointly sold a substance represented or held out by them to be heroin; and I agree with the conclusion of my brother Fauteux that the conviction on the charge of selling must be affirmed.

For the above reasons, I would dismiss the appeal as to the first count (that is, of selling) but would direct that the time during which the appellant has been confined pending the determination of the appeal shall count as part of the term of imprisonment imposed pursuant to that conviction. As to the second count (that is, of having possession) I would allow the appeal.

*Appeal from conviction for possession of drug allowed; appeals from conviction for sale of a drug and finding of being an habitual criminal dismissed.*

# Regina v. King
## (1962), 133 C.C.C. 1 (S.C.C.)

Appeal from a decision of the Ontario Court of Appeal, 129 Can. C.C. 391 [1961] O.W.N. 37, quashing a conviction for impaired driving. Affirmed.

Only the judgment of Ritchie is reproduced below.

Ritchie, J.: — This is an appeal by Crown at the instance of the Attorney-General for Ontario from a judgment rendered by the majority of the Court of Appeal of that Province (MacKay, J.A., dissenting) which allowed the respondent's appeal from a conviction entered against him after a trial *de novo* held before Judge Timmins of the County Court of the County of York for the offence of driving a motor vehicle while his ability to do so was impaired by a drug contrary to s. 223 of the *Cr. Code.*

The circumstances giving rise to this appeal are that on October 8, 1959 the respondent went to his dentist's office, by appointment, for the purpose of having two teeth extracted, and that he was there injected with a drug known as sodium pentothal, a quick-acting anaesthetic which produces unconsciousness, removes pain and gives a certain amount of relaxation during the period of an operation, and before using which the dentist stated that it was the practice of his office to have patients sign a printed form containing the following warning: "Patients are cautioned not to drive after anaesthetic until head clears." After he had regained consciousness, the respondent paid his bill by cheque to a nurse who was in attendance and who stated that at this time he appeared "perfectly normal" and that she warned him not to drive his car until his head was "perfectly clear" to which he replied that he intended to walk. The respondent says that he heard no such warning and remembers signing no form containing any warning, but he does remember getting into his car which he had parked about a block away and proceeding across an intersection, after which he became unconscious, and his car ran into the left rear portion of a parked vehicle, whereafter the police appeared to find that he was staggering and that his physical co-ordination was poor. This was later verified by a sergeant at the police station where the respondent was submitted to certain tests. Medical evidence was given to the effect that this mental and physical condition was consistent with the after-effects of being injected with sodium pentothal and that this drug may induce a state of amnesia accompanied by a period during which the subject may feel perfectly competent to get in a car and drive and in the next second or so be in a condition in which he would not know what was happening. The respondent stated that he did not know anything about the drug which was administered to him.

The learned County Court judge convicted the respondent on the ground that "he knew that he had a drug and he was given a warning with respect to driving a motor car" and also that "he took the responsibility of going to the car, he took the responsibility of driving his car knowing that he had had a drug".

The respondent's sole defence was that he had no knowledge of the effect of the drug which resulted in his being unaware of any warning and unaware of the fact that he was impaired when he took the responsibility to drive and did drive his car.

. . .

The question of law so determined was made a ground of appeal and for leave to appeal to the Court of Appeal of Ontario, and Mr. Justice MacKay, in the course of his dissenting opinion, stated the issue before the Court in the clearest terms, saying [at p. 396 Can. C.C.]: "I think all of these grounds of appeal raise only one issue, that is, to what extent, if at all, does the doctrine of *mens rea* apply to this offence?"

. . .

The provisions of s. 223 of the *Code* are as follows:

"**223.** Every one who, while his ability to drive a motor vehicle is impaired by alcohol or a drug, drives a motor vehicle or has the care or control of a motor vehicle, whether it is in motion or not, is guilty of an indictable offence or an offence punishable on summary conviction and is liable

(a) for a first offence, to a fine of not more than five hundred dollars and not less than fifty dollars or to imprisonment for three months or both,

(b) for a second offence, to imprisonment for not more than three months and not less than fourteen days, and

(c) for each subsequent offence, to imprisonment for not more than one year and not less than three months."

. . .

As there is no express language in s. 223 of the *Cr. Code* disclosing the intention of Parliament to rule out *mens rea* as an essential ingredient of the crime therein described, it becomes necessary to determine whether it can be said that such an intention is disclosed by necessary implication.

In classifying the types of statute in which such an intention has been implied, the learned authors, writing under the title "Criminal Law and Procedure" in 10 Hals., 3rd ed., p. 275, adopt the three exceptions to the general rule which are suggested by Wright, J., in *Sherras v. DeRutzen, supra*, at p. 921 and state:

"Most statutes creating a strict liability fall under three heads. First, where the acts are not criminal in any real sense, but are prohibited under a penalty in the public interest. Secondly, where the acts are public nuisances; thus, an employer has been held liable on indictment for a nuisance caused by workmen without his knowledge and contrary to his orders. Thirdly, where, although the proceeding is criminal in form, it is really only a summary mode of enforcing a civil right."

Mr. Justice MacKay concluded that s. 223 of the *Cr. Code* comes within the first exception to the general rule in that it is "an act perhaps not criminal in any real sense but which is in the public interest prohibited". He finds that [at p. 403 Can. C.C., p. 52 O.W.N.]:

"A person whose ability to drive is impaired by alcohol or drugs, driving on the highway, is a danger to the general public and in my view the offence falls within the first classification referred to by Wright J. in the *Sherras* case. It is an act perhaps not criminal in any real sense but which is in the public interest prohibited."

. . .

In my view the enactment of s. 223 of the *Cr. Code* added a new crime to the general criminal law, and neither the language in which it was enacted nor the evil which it was intended to prevent are such as to give rise to a necessary implication that Parliament intended to impose absolute liability unless the impaired condition which the section prohibits was brought about by some conscious act of the will or intention.

Consideration of this phase of the question should not be concluded without noting the decision in *Armstrong v. Clark*, [1957] 1 All E.R. 433, in which the Queen's Bench Division had to consider the question of "whether the taking of insulin by the respondent was, in the circumstances which occurred, to be regarded as taking a drug which would make him liable to be found guilty of an offence under s. 15(1)" of the *Road Traffic Act*, and in which Lord Goddard said [at pp. 435-6]:

"This case must go back with a direction that the justices may take into account a great many things, but they must remember, and everyone must remember, that this section was designed for the protection of the public, and if people happen to be in a condition of health that renders them subject to going into a coma, or forces them to take remedies which may send them into a coma, the answer is that they must not drive because they are a danger to the rest of Her Majesty's subjects.

I do not think that anything that was said by Lord Goddard in that case can be taken as changing the Law with respect to *mens rea* in statutory offences as it was stated by the same learned Judge and adopted by this Court in the cases hereinbefore referred to. It is noteworthy, however, that in the course of this decision, Lord Goddard does make the observation [at p. 435] with respect to the statutory offence with which he was dealing: "The penalty, I need hardly say, is entirely at the discretion of the bench."

The existence of *mens rea* as an essential ingredient of an offence and the method of proving the existence of that ingredient are two different things, and I am of opinion that when it has been proved that a driver was driving a motor vehicle while his ability to do so was impaired by alcohol or a drug, then a rebuttable presumption arises that his condition was voluntarily induced and that he is guilty of the offence created by s. 223 and must be convicted unless other evidence is adduced which raises a reasonable doubt as to whether he was, through no fault of his own, disabled when he undertook to drive and drove, from being able to appreciate and know that he was or might become impaired.

If the driver's lack of appreciation when he undertook to drive was induced by voluntary consumption of alcohol or of a drug which he knew or had any reasonable ground for believing might cause him to be impaired, then he cannot, of course, avoid the consequences of the impairment which results by saying that he did not intend to get into such a condition, but if the impairment has been brought about without any act of his own will, then, in my view, the offence created by s. 223 cannot be said to have been committed.

The existence of a rebuttable presumption that a man intends the natural consequences of his own conduct is a part of our law, but its application to any particular situation involves a consideration of what consequences a man might be reasonably expected to foresee under the circumstances.

In the course of the lecture on "The Criminal Law" which is contained in the well-known work by O.W. Holmes, Jr. on *The Common Law* that learned author says [at p. 57]:

> "As the purpose is to compel men to abstain from dangerous conduct, and not merely to restrain them from evil inclinations, the law requires them at their peril to know the teachings of common experience, just as it requires them to know the law."

It seems to me that it can be taken as a matter of "common experience" that the consumption of alcohol may produce intoxication and, therefore, "impairment" in the sense in which that word is used in s. 223, and I think it is also to be similarly taken to be known that the use of narcotics may have the same effect, but if it appears that the impairment was produced as a result of using a drug in the form of medicine on a doctor's order or recommendation and that its effect was unknown to the patient, then the presumption is, in my view, rebutted.

For all the above reasons, I do not think that the Court of Appeal erred in holding that *mens rea* was an essential element of the offence of driving while impaired contrary to s. 223 of the *Cr. Code*, but I am of opinion that that element need not necessarily be present in relation both to the act of driving and to the state of being impaired in order to make the offence complete. That is to say, that a man who becomes impaired as the result of taking a drug on medical advice without knowing its effect cannot escape liability if he became aware of his impaired condition before he started to drive his car just as a man who did not appreciate his impaired condition when he started to drive cannot escape liability on the ground that his lack of appreciation was brought about by voluntary consumption of liquor or drug. The defence in the present case was that the respondent became impaired through no act of his own will and could not reasonably be expected to have known that his ability was impaired or might thereafter become impaired when he undertook to drive and drove his motor vehicle.

I would dismiss this appeal.

*Appeal dismissed.*

## Regina v. Ladue
### [1965] 4 C.C.C. 264 (Y.T. C.A.)

Appeal by accused from a conviction for indecently interfering with a dead human body contrary to s. 167(b) of the *Cr. Code.*

The judgment of the Court was delivered by

DAVEY, J.A.: — Ladue either copulated or attempted to copulate with a dead woman and was convicted under s. 167(b) of the *Criminal Code* of indecency interfering with a dead human body. The material part of the section reads as follows:

"**167.** Every one who

(b) improperly or indecently interferes with or offers any indignity to a dead human body or human remains, whether buried or not,

is guilty of an indictable offence and is liable to imprisonment for five years."

The only point of substance in Ladue's appeal against his conviction is whether the learned trial Judge was right in holding that it was not open to the appellant to contend that he was not guilty because he did not know the woman was dead. There was considerable evidence upon which the learned Judge might have held, if he had not considered the defence untenable in law, that while Ladue knew what he was doing physically, he was so intoxicated that he did not realize the woman was dead. Subject to what I have to say later that would have been a good defence.

In his oral reasons the learned trial Judge, in dealing with the effect of intoxication upon the appellant's understanding, said this:

"What does the argument amount to? The only way you can make it, the only way in which you could make this argument — certainly I don't know. She was dead. He thought she was unconscious. Because she was dead? No. That is about it. At the time of the incident can a person be heard to say 'that it didn't occur to me she was dead, and I am therefore innocent.' I will tell you, I will not listen to such an argument. That would be an admission he was having intercourse with a person . . ."

It is a fundamental principle of criminal law that, unless excluded by statute, *mens rea,* that is guilty intention, is necessary to constitute a crime, and that a person doing an act is not guilty of a crime if his mind be innocent: *R. v. Prince* (1875), L.R. 2 C.C.R. 154: *R. v. Tolson* (1889), 23 Q.B.D. 168, *per* Willis, J., at pp. 171-2. I see nothing in s. 167(b) to exclude that principle. Accordingly it was open to the appellant to attempt to rebut the inference of *mens rea* flowing from what he deliberately did to the body by proving that he did not know the woman was dead.

But in attempting to defend himself in that way the appellant runs into the insuperable difficulty alluded to by the learned trial Judge. The appellant could not have failed even in his drunken state, to perceive that the woman was unconscious, and incapable of giving her consent to copulation. Indeed the appellant does not suggest that he thought he had her consent to the act. So if the woman was alive he was raping her. Therefore it is impossible for him to argue that, not knowing her to be dead, he was acting innocently. An intention to commit a crime, although not the precise crime charged, will provide the necessary *mens rea* under a statute in the form of s. 167(b):

. . .

It follows that in my respectful opinion the learned trial Judge was right in the particular circumstances of this case in saying that he would not entertain an argument that appellant was innocent because he did not know the woman was dead.

It becomes necessary at this point to notice our decision in *R. v. McLeod* (1954), 111 C.C.C. 106, 20 C.R. 281, 14 W.W.R. 97, in which we dismissed a Crown appeal against an accused's acquittal on a charge of assaulting a peace officer engaged in the execution of this duty on the ground that knowledge that the victim was a peace officer and was engaged in the execution of his duty was an essential ingredient of the crime, and that the accused did not know those essential facts. Of the three Judges who sat on that appeal I alone held that the accused had committed a common assault; consequently it became essential for me to consider the submission of Crown counsel that on the authority of *R. v. Prince*, the fact that the accused had in any event committed a common assault supplied the necessary *mens rea* and made him guilty of the aggravated offence even though he did not know the victim was a Peace Officer. In the course of my reasons I considered *R. v. Prince* and *R. v. Tolson*, I adhere to the views I expressed there, and it is unnecessary to repeat them. The neat distinction between *R. v. McLeod*, and the case at bar is that in the former we held as a matter of interpretation that knowledge that the victim was a peace officer and was engaged in the execution of his duty was a specific ingredient of the crime charged in that case, and that the charge had not been established in the absence of proof of that specific knowledge. But as a matter of interpretation I do not consider knowledge that the body is dead to be a specific ingredient of an offence against s. 167(b). All that is required is *mens rea* in the widest sense.

*Mens rea* is an uncertain term, and what it means varies with the different crimes and the statutes defining them . . . .

The nature of the offence under s. 167(b) and the language of that section would not seem to require knowledge that the body is dead as a specific ingredient of an offence under that section, because in most cases that fact would be clear, and proof of a deliberate act improperly or indecently interfering with a body that was in fact dead would be sufficient proof of a criminal intention or *mens rea*. It would be only in the most exceptional case where the offender might have any doubt whether a body was quick or dead, and in such a case he might defend himself by showing that he did not know the body was dead and that according to his understanding he was acting lawfully and innocently. That is what the appellant cannot show in this case, because if the woman was alive he was raping her.

I would dismiss the appeal.

*Appeal dismissed.*

## Regina v. Droste
(1982), 34 O.R. (2d) 588 (C.A.)

Appeal by accused against his conviction on two counts of first degree murder. The judgement of the Court was delivered orally by

MARTIN J.A.: — The appellant was convicted on two counts of first degree murder and now appeals from those convictions. Count 1 charged the appellant with having on February 27, 1977, committed first degree murder on the person of Rolf Maurice Droste; count 2 charged the appellant with having on the same day committed first degree murder on the person of Monique Jean Droste. Rolf Maurice Droste and Monique Jean Droste are the children of the appellant.

The case for the Crown was that the appellant formed a plan to kill his wife. The plan involved saturating his car with gasoline, simulating an accident by running the car into the abutment of a bridge, rendering his wife unconscious by hitting her on the head with an instrument, setting fire to the car and escaping therefrom himself. The Crown alleges that in carrying out the plan, the appellant by accident or mistake caused the death of his two children.

A fellow employee of the appellant, one Holdsworth, testified that the appellant disclosed to him a number of plans to kill his wife. Holdsworth testified to the following effect. He said that the appellant's final plan to kill his wife, as disclosed to him, was that the appellant intended to crash his car into a bridge near St. Mary's, after soaking the interior of the car with gasoline, filling the gasoline tank and placing a five-gallon can of gasoline in the trunk of the car. The occupants would be wearing seat belts. The appellant had made a pipe at work inside of which he had poured molten zinc, and which the appellant said he would use to render his wife unconscious. Holdsworth said that the appellant told him he would ignite the fire by placing fuel-soaked rags under his seat, and told him on the Wednesday prior to Sunday, February 27th, that he was going to carry out the plan the following Sunday. Holdsworth said that he did not inform the police about what the appellant had told him because he did not take the appellant seriously. However, when he read the newspaper account of the accident on Monday, February 28th, he contacted the police.

Brenda Lee Lukings, also a co-worker at the plant where the appellant was employed, testified that the appellant told her that he was going to kill his wife by doing something to the automobile, such as fixing the brakes so that his wife would die in a car crash.

Linda May Sears, another co-worker testified that the appellant told her that he wished to kill his wife so he could live with his girl-friend down the street.

The appellant was sexually involved with a married woman at the time of the occurrence in question, although both the appellant and the woman denied that it was a serious relationship. The Crown, however, alleged that the relationship constituted a motive for the appellant's intention to kill his wife.

The appellant and his wife had been invited to attend a birthday party at the home of a friend on February 27, 1977. The friend lived a distance of 2.5 miles away by the most direct route or 4.8 miles by the route which the appellant, in fact, took. On the morning of February 27th the appellant went to a gas station where he had the tank of the car filled with gasoline. He also had a five-gallon container filled with gasoline which was placed in the trunk. There was also evidence that the appellant had used gasoline that day to clean the interior of the car. The appellant said that he had used, perhaps, a pint from the container which was used to soak rags which were applied to the car to remove grease from the interior. The appellant that morning also re-activated the seat belts of the car which had not been in use; he said that he re-activated the seat belts because there had been a number of accidents which had occurred in his own family and accidents involving close friends.

In the early afternoon of February 27, 1977, the appellant, his wife and the two children left in the car to attend the birthday party. The appellant's wife complained that the car smelled of gasoline fumes.

The appellant's wife testified that as they approached a bridge over the Otter Creek she noticed flames shooting up into the vehicle between the two seats by the gear shift. She testified that the appellant began to put out the flames with his right hand. She said that at this point the appellant reached down in the seat and took a screwdriver with an orange handle on it and proceeded to hit her on the left side of the back of the head with the handle part of the screwdriver. He continued to yell at her and told her to let go of the steering wheel. The car then crashed into the abutment. The appellant denied that he had hit wife on the head with a screwdriver or with any other instrument and said that the collision with the bridge was caused by the car pulling sharply and unexpectedly to the right. No screwdriver was found at the scene but a pipe to which adhered melted metal, composed principally of zinc, was found under the springs of the front seat.

Among the other injuries sustained by the wife was a laceration of the scalp. The medical evidence indicated that the injury was more consistent with having been caused by a blow on the head with an instrument than by striking her head on the front of the car.

The appellant's wife was able to extricate herself from the car through the driver's door and she then helped the appellant out of the vehicle. They then endeavoured to get the children from the back seat, but were unable to do so. At this point a Mr. Arnott arrived at the scene and he observed that the fire at this time was in the front of the vehicle. When Mr. Arnott opened the door to remove the children from the vehicle he said that he was met by flames which shot over his head and made a roaring sound. The appellant's wife sat in Mr. Arnott's car and the appellant ran up a laneway and began knocking on the door of a farmhouse seeking to get assistance. The children unfortunately were not able to be removed from the car and they both died of asphyxia as a result of the fire.

Samples taken from the interior of the car contained gasoline. There was also a plastic container found in the trunk of the car and evidence was given of the results of tests, from which an inference might be drawn, that some four gallons had been removed from the five-gallon can. Expert evidence was called by the Crown, the effect of which was, that the fire did not emanate in the engine, but was caused by an accelerant applied to the interior of the car. Professor Sandler was called by the defence and, he concluded, on the basis of the observations of persons at the scene and the quantity of gasoline found in the samples removed from the car, that the fire originated in the engine and travelled to the back of the car. He was also of the view that the fire burned naturally and was not due to an accelerant. He was of the opinion that the quantity of gasoline found in the interior of the car got there after the fire had started as a result of the burning and possibly by gasoline flowing from the container in the trunk into the interior of the car.

The appellant testified in his own defence, denied that he had planned to kill his wife and said that the collision with the bridge was an accident. He also denied that he had told Holdsworth that he planned to kill his wife.

On that evidence the jury found the appellant guilty of first degree murder on both counts. It was not, and in our view, it could not successfully be contended that the verdict of the jury was unreasonable or unsupported by the evidence.

The first ground of appeal is that the trial judge erred in instructing the jury that, if they found that the appellant's intention to kill his wife was the result of planning and deliberation, it was open to the jury to convict him of first degree murder in respect of the death of the children. Mr. Kluwak's submission was that a conviction for first degree murder cannot be supported on the basis that the accused planned and deliberated the killing of his wife and by accident or mistake caused the death of his children; that ss. 212(b) and 214(2) of the *Criminal Code*, R.C.S. 1970, c. C-34 cannot be combined to found a conviction for first degree murder and the trial judge erred in failing to so instruct the jury. He contended that the death of the victim must be planned and deliberate. Section 212(b) reads:

**212.** Culpable homicide is murder

. . .

(b) where a person, meaning to cause death to a human being or meaning to cause him bodily harm that he knows is likely to cause his death, and being reckless whether death ensues or not, by accident or mistake causes death to another human being, notwithstanding that he does not mean to cause death or bodily harm to that human being . . .

Section 214(2) [rep. & sub. 1974-75, c. 105, s. 4] reads:

214(2) Murder is first degree when it is planned and deliberate.

The trial judge instructed the jury with respect to s. 212(b) and directed them that if the Crown had satisfied them beyond a reasonable doubt that the appellant caused the death of the children by asphyxia resulting from the fire, and at the time he caused their death he intended to kill Mrs. Droste, then the prosecution had proved second degree murder. The trial judge did not put to the jury that part of s. 212(b) which provides that it is murder if a person meaning to cause bodily harm that he knows is likely to cause death and being reckless whether death ensues to one human being by accident or mistake causes death to another human being. He further instructed the jury that it was only if they were satisfied beyond a reasonable doubt that the appellant had committed second degree murder that they could then consider whether the appellant was guilty of first degree murder. He then accurately instructed the jury with respect to the elements of planning and deliberation.

We think that the trial judge correctly instructed the jury that if they were satisfied beyond a reasonable doubt that the appellant's intention to kill his wife was planned and deliberate and that in the course of carrying out that intention he caused the death of the children by accident or mistake, that the resulting murder constituted first degree murder.

Section 214(2) provides that "murder" is first degree murder when "it" is planned and deliberate. Where murder as defined by s. 212(b) is committed and that murder is planned and deliberate the murder is first degree murder even though the planned and deliberate intention to kill took effect on a person other than the intended victim.

As we have indicated, we are satisfied that a conviction for first degree murder may be supported on the basis of a combination of ss. 212(b) and 214(2) and we are unable to accept the submission of Mr. Kluwak that in order to constitute first degree murder under s. 214(2) the planning and deliberation must be with respect to the person actually killed.

. . .

We are also of the view that the transference of a planned and deliberate intention to kill one person to the actual victim is in accord with the general principles of the criminal law. Clearly, the moral culpability of one who intends to kill one person, preceded by planning and deliberation, but who by accident or mistake kills another person, is the same as if he had succeeded in killing his intended victim.

. . .

It is well established that if an accused acting under such provocation as would reduce murder to manslaughter, shoots at one person with the intention of killing him, but accidently kills a third person the intention extenuated by provocation is transferred from the intended victim to the actual victim and the accused in those circumstances is guilty of manslaughter only. See *R. v. Gross* (1913), 23 Cox C.C. 455. By parity of reasoning the transferrence of an intention which is aggravated by the fact that it is planned and deliberate is transferred from the intended victim to the actual victim.

. . .

*Appeal dismissed.*

## Regina v. Tutton
### [1989] 1 S.C.R. 1392

Appeal from a judgment of the Ontario Court of Appeal (1985), 18 C.C.C. (3d) 328, setting aside convictions by Salhany Co. Ct. J. sitting with jury and ordering a new trial. Appeal dismissed.

The judgment of DICKSON C.J. and WILSON and LaFOREST JJ. was delivered by

WILSON J.: — I have had the benefit of the reasons of my colleagues Justices McIntyre and Lamer and I agree with them that the appeal should be dismissed and a new trial ordered because the trial judge's charge failed to make clear to the jury that the Crown had the burden to prove all the elements of the offence of manslaughter by criminal negligence. I do not, however, agree with my colleagues' conclusion that criminal negligence under s. 202 of the *Criminal Code*, R.S.C. 1970, c. C-34, consists only of conduct in breach of an objective standard and does not require the Crown to prove that the accused had any degree of guilty knowledge. I also have reservations concerning the approach my colleagues suggest is available in order to relieve against the harshness of the objective standard of liability which they find in s. 202 and to ensure that the morally innocent are not punished for the commission of serious criminal offences committed through criminal negligence.

The facts and the judgments below are fully set out in the judgment of my colleague McIntyre J. I wish only to emphasize two points. The respondent's defence in this case centred around their claim of honest but mistaken belief as to the nature of their son's condition. Although the respondents were aware that their son was a diabetic who needed regular insulin injections, they claimed that because of their religious convictions they sincerely believed that he had been cured by divine intervention and were unaware of the serious nature of his illness following the withdrawal of insulin. For example, in a statement provided to the police shortly after her son's death from the complications of diabetic hyperglycemia the respondent Carol Anne Tutton stated:

> Complete faith in Jesus and obedience to the word of God is the reason for our decision to cease giving Chris insulin. Since I have accepted Jesus as my personal Saviour and Lord, He has revealed himself to me in vision and spoke in words of his own that Christopher is healed and further that complete faith in Him not man's doctrine or shall I say the world's teachings will bring forth the manifestation of this healing. Standing on the promises of God and His holy Word 100%, Wednesday, October 14, 1981 I did not administer Christopher insulin. Thursday and Wednesday Christopher ate, played normally although Thursday evening he became sick to his stomach. Friday I kept him home from school and he kept liquids in his stomach. Saturday morning until approximately 1:00 PM he was resting comfortably. I left him to make myself a sandwich about five perhaps ten minutes, rechecked him and found he was not breathing. My husband administered mouth to mouth resuscitation until the police department arrived about five minutes later.

The second point which I wish to emphasize is that the Ontario Court of Appeal (1985), 18 C.C.C. (3d) 328 would not have applied an objective standard of liability in this case. Dubin J.A. stated at p. 345:

> I do not think, however, that a loving and caring parent who omits to seek medical assistance because of the honest but mistaken belief that his or her child was not in need of such assistance should be found to have shown a wanton or reckless disregard for its life or safety merely because it can be said that reasonable parents would have responded otherwise, or even that in omitting to seek medical assistance, there was a marked and substantial departure from the standard of care of reasonable parents. In such a case, I think a distinction should be made between acts of commission and acts of omission and, in the latter case, a subjective test should be used.

The Court of Appeal concluded that the trial judge erred in instructing the jury that no *mens rea* was required for the crime of manslaughter by means of criminal negligence.

. . .

For convenience, I reproduce here the relevant sections of the *Criminal Code*:

**197**(1) Every one is under a legal duty

(a) as a parent, foster parent, guardian or head of a family, to provide necessaries of life for a child under the age of sixteen years;

. . .

(2) Every one commits an offence who, being under a legal duty within the meaning of

subsection (1), fails without lawful excuse, the proof of which lies upon him, to perform that duty, if

(a) with respect to a duty imposed by paragraph (1)(a) or (b),

   (i) the person to whom the duty is owned is in destitute or necessitous circumstances, or

   (ii) the failure to perform the duty endangers the life of the person to whom the duty is owed, or causes or is likely to cause the health of that person to be endangered permanently; or

. . .

**202**(1) Every one is criminally negligent who

(a) in doing anything, or

(b) in omitting to do anything that it is his duty to do,

shows wanton or reckless disregard for the lives or safety of other persons.

**205**(1) A person commits homicide when, directly or indirectly, by any means, he causes the death of a human being.

(2) Homicide is culpable or not culpable.

(3) Homicide that is not culpable is not an offence.

(4) Culpable homicide is murder or manslaughter or infanticide.

(5) A person commits culpable homicide when he causes the death of a human being,

(a) by means of an unlawful act,

(b) by criminal negligence,

(c) by causing that human being, by threats or fear of violence or by deception, to do anything that causes his death, or

(d) by wilfully frightening that human being, in the case of a child or sick person.

**219.** Every one who commits manslaughter is guilty of an indictable offence and is liable to imprisonment for life.

I wish to deal first with the implications of my colleagues' approach in this case. By concluding that s. 202 of the *Criminal Code* prohibits conduct and the consequences of mindless action absent any blameworthy state of mind, they have, in effect, held that the crime of criminal negligence is an absolute liability offence. Conviction follows upon proof of conduct which reveals a marked and substantial departure from the standard expected of a reasonably prudent person in the circumstances regardless of what was actually in the accused's mind at the time the act was committed.

. . .

My colleague Mcintyre J. has concluded that upon the wording of s. 202 it is an inescapable conclusion that Parliament intended liability to follow upon proof of the act or conduct described in the section. In particular, he stresses the reference to conduct which *shows* wanton or reckless disregard for the lives and safety of others and the fact that what is prohibited is criminal *negligence*.

. . .

Section 202 of the *Code* is, in my view, notorious in its ambiguity. Since its enactment in its present form in the 1955 Amendments to the *Criminal Code* it has bedeviled both courts and commentators who have sought out its meaning. The interpretation put upon it usually depends upon which words are emphasized. On the one hand, my colleague's judgment demonstrates that emphasizing the use of the words "shows" and "negligence" can lead to the conclusion that an objective standard of liability was intended and the proof of unreasonable conduct alone will suffice. On the other hand, if the words "wanton or reckless disregard for the lives or safety of other persons" are stressed along with the fact that what is prohibited is not negligence *simpliciter* but "criminal" negligence, one might conclude that Parliament intended some degree of advertence to the risk to the lives or safety of others to be an essential element of the offence. When faced with such fundamental ambiguity, it would be my view that the court should give the provision the interpretation most consonant, not only with the test and purpose of the provision, but also, where possible, with the broader concepts and principles of the law: see also *R. v. Paré*, [1987] 2 S.C.R. 618.

It is obviously important to give meaning and effect to each word employed in s. 202. Under that section every one is criminally negligent who in doing or in omitting to do anything that it is his duty to do shows wanton or reckless disregard for the lives or safety of other persons. As I have stated, the presumption when we are dealing with a serious criminal offence should be in favour of a requirement of some degree of mental blameworthiness if the text and purpose of the section are susceptible of such an interpretation. This Court, in its previous consideration of s. 202, concluded that it was intended to prohibit advertent negligence in the sense that the accused must be fixed with an awareness of the risk that is being prohibited.

. . .

It is my view that the jurisprudence of this Court to date establishes that the criminal negligence prohibited under s. 202 is advertent negligence. I would not hesitate to depart from these precedents for solid reasons but I cannot, with due respect to those who think otherwise, agree that the case for the adoption of an objective standard of liability has been made out to the extent required to justify a departure from this Court's previous decisions.

. . .

As I have suggested above, the words of the section can reasonably bear an interpretation which leaves room for the mental element of awareness of advertence to a risk to the lives or safety of others or wilful blindness to such risk. Conduct which shows a wanton or reckless disregard for the lives and safety of others will by its nature constitute *prima facie* evidence of the mental element, and in the absence of some evidence that casts doubt on the normal degree of mental awareness, proof of the act and reference to what a reasonable person in the circumstances must have realized will lead to a conclusion that the accused was aware of the risk or wilfully blind to the risk.

Professor Glanville Williams in his work *Criminal Law: the General Part* (2nd ed. 1961) explained the minimal nature of the mental element for advertent negligence and the important evidentiary use of objective standards in determining the subjective state of mind of what he terms advertent negligence. He defined the requirements of recklessness in advertent negligence as follows at pp. 53-55:

> If the actor foresaw the probability of the consequences he is regarded as reckless, even though he fervently desired and hoped for the exact opposite of the consequence, and even though he did his best (short of abandoning his main project) to avoid it . . . Recklessness is any determination to pursue conduct with knowledge of the risk involved though without a desire that they should eventuate.

> . . .

> . . . recklessness may be a mere passing realization, instantly dismissed, which leaves no mark upon conduct.

> . . .

The minimal nature of the requirement of a blameworthy state of mind and the relevance of the objective standard as a rebuttable mode of proof suggests to me that a holding that s. 202 requires proof of the mental element of advertence to the risk or wilful blindness to the risk will not undermine the policy objectives of the provision. The loss in terms of deterrence and social protection would seem to be negligible when the retention of a subject standard would at most offer protection for those who due to some peculiarity or unexpected accident commit conduct which, although it shows a reckless or wanton disregard for the lives or safety of others, can be explained as inconsistent with any degree of awareness of or wilful blindness to such a risk. Should social protection require the adoption of an objective standard it is open to Parliament to enact a law which clearly adopts such a standard. In my respectful view this Court should not do it for them.

. . .

To sum up, although I agree with my colleagues as to the proper disposition of this appeal, I am unable to agree with their conclusion that the offence of manslaughter by criminal negligence consists of conduct in breach of an objective standard.

The reasons of McINTYRE and L'HEUREUX-DUBÉ JJ. were delivered by

McINTYRE J.: — This appeal raises again the question of criminal negligence, as defined in s. 202 of the *Criminal Code*, R.S.C. 1970, c. C-34, and the test to be applied by a jury in its application to a given case.

The respondents, Carol Anne Tutton and Arthur Thomas Tutton, were the parents of a five-year-old child, Christopher Tutton, who died on October 17, 1981. After a trial before judge and jury, the Tuttons were convicted of manslaughter because of his death. They appealed the conviction. The Court of Appeal (Dubin, Goodman, Tarnopolsky JJ.A.) in a judgment written for the court by Dubin J.A. (as he then was) allowed the appeals, set aside the convictions, and directed new trials. This appeal is taken by the Crown, by leave granted May 23, 1985.

The Tuttons, according to the evidence, which was unquestioned on this point, had a good reputation in their community for honesty and integrity and, as well, they were loving and responsible parents. They were also deeply religious and they belonged to a religious sect which believes in faith healing. Their religious convictions did not prevent them from seeking and acting on medical advice nor from taking medicines, but they believed that Divine intervention could miraculously effect cures for illnesses and ailments beyond the power of modern medical science.

In April of 1979, their family physician, a general practitioner named Love, diagnosed the child, Christopher, as a diabetic and admitted him to hospital where he remained for some weeks. While the child was in hospital, his mother attended classes at a diabetic education centre where she received instruction regarding insulin injections and the impact of diet and exercise on diabetes and diabetics. She also attended in July of 1979 a full week of seminars at a juvenile diabetic clinic to gain an understanding of her son's condition and to learn how to deal with it. There was then evidence upon which the jury could conclude that Mrs. Tutton has made herself competent to deal with her child's illness under general supervision from the family physician.

Throughout the son's illness, the Tuttons main concern was to find a cure for the boy. They both believed that there would be a spiritual cure. They discussed the possibility with Dr. Love who considered that there was no possibility of a miraculous cure, and in November of 1979 a diabetic specialist from the Sick Children's Hospital in Toronto advised the respondents that their son would never be able to discontinue his insulin injections. He told the respondents not to discontinue the insulin treatments. However, on October 2, 1980, Mrs. Tutton stopped giving the child insulin in the belief that he was being healed by the power of the Holy Spirit. In two days, the child became quite ill and was taken to a hospital emergency unit. The physician who attended the child said that on admission to hospital the child was dangerously ill, suffering from diabetic acidosis, a potentially fatal disorder which was due to the absence of insulin. The doctor admonished the parents when he learned that they had consciously withheld the insulin. He told the parents that insulin would be required by their son for life, and after this incident Mr. Tutton assured the family physician that insulin would not be withheld in future without consulting a doctor. A year later, however, insulin was again stopped. Mrs. Tutton believed that she had a vision of God in which she was told that Christopher was cured, that no more insulin was needed, and that God would take care of her son. The insulin injections were stopped on October 14, 1981. Mr. Tutton did not know of the withdrawal of insulin until October 15 but on learning of it he approved. The child sickened quickly. On October 17, he was taken to the hospital where he was pronounced dead on arrival. The forensic pathologist who conducted a postmortem examination gave his opinion that death was caused by complications of diabetic hyperglycemia. The respondents were jointly charged with manslaughter in an indictment which provided:

ARTHUR TUTTON and CAROL TUTTON stand charged that between the period of the 14th day of October, 1981, and the 17th day of October, 1981, both dates inclusive, at the Township of Wilmot, in the Judicial District of Waterloo, being the parents of Christopher Tutton, they did cause the death of Christopher Tutton, age five years, by criminal negligence, to wit, they did, without lawful excuse, omit to provide necessaries of life to Christopher Tutton, which was their duty to provide, thereby showing wanton and reckless disregard for the life or safety of the said Christopher Tutton, and did thereby commit manslaughter contrary to the Criminal Code.

Particulars were given in these terms:

It is further particularized that the said Arthur Tutton and Carol Tutton failed, without lawful excuse, while their said son, Christopher, was in necessitous circumstances,
(1) to provide insulin to him
(2) to obtain timely medical assistance for him.

. . .

At trial, the defence was that as far as the Crown's case rested on the failure to provide insulin the Tuttons honestly believed that Christopher had been cured by Divine intervention and, therefore, no further insulin was necessary. This would raise the defence of an honest though mistaken belief in the existence of a circumstance or circumstances which, if present, would render their conduct non-culpable. It was also argued that as far as the Crown's case depended upon a failure to provide timely medical assistance for their son, the parents were unaware of the fact that he was seriously ill as a result of the withdrawal of the insulin and, accordingly, their conduct in this regard could not be said to exhibit a wanton or reckless disregard for the life or safety of their son.

. . .

In reaching a conclusion as to whether the conduct of an accused person has shown, within the meaning of s. 202 of the *Criminal Code*, wanton or reckless disregard for the lives or safety of other persons, the authorities dictate an objective test: see the review of the authorities on this subject by Cory J.A. for the Court of Appeal in *R. v. Waite* (1986), 28 C.C.C. (3d) 326, approved in this court, [1989] 1 S.C.R. 1436. Indeed, in the Court of Appeal, Dubin J.A. accepted the objective test as one of general application, but made an exception in cases where the conduct complained of consisted of an act or acts of omission, as opposed to those of commission. In such cases, it was his view that occasions would arise where a subjective test would be required where acts of omission were under consideration. He considered this was such a case. It is my view, however, that no such distinction as Dubin J.A. would adopt may be made. I am wholly unable to see any difference in principle between cases arising from an omission to act and those involving acts of commission. Indeed, the words of s. 202 of the *Code* make it clear that one is criminally negligent who, in doing anything or in omitting to do anything that it is duty to do, shows wanton or reckless disregard for the lives or safety of other persons. The objective test must, therefore, be employed where criminal negligence is considered for it is the conduct of the accused, as opposed to his intention or mental state, which is examined in this inquiry.

Our concept of criminal culpability relies primarily upon a consideration of the mental state which accompanies or initiates the wrongful act, and the attribution of criminal liability without proof of such a blameworthy mental state raises serious concerns. Nonetheless, negligence has become accepted as a factor which may lead to criminal liability and strong arguments can be raised in its favour. Section 202 of the *Criminal Code* affords an example of its adoption. In choosing the test to be applied in assessing conduct under s. 202 of the *Code*, it must be observed at once that what is made criminal is negligence. Negligence connotes the opposite of thought-directed action. In other words, its existence precludes the element of positive intent to achieve a given result. This leads to the conclusion that what is sought to be restrained by punishment under s. 202 of the *Code* is conduct, and its results. What is punished, in other words, is not the state of mind but the consequence of mindless action. This is apparent, I suggest, from the words of the section, which make criminal, conduct which *shows* wanton or reckless disregard. It may be observed as well that the words "wanton or reckless" support this construction, denying as they do the existence of a directing mental state. Nor can it be said that criminal negligence, as defined in s. 202, imports in its terms some element of malice or intention. This point was made in the Crown's factum in paragraph 41, which provided, in part:

> The plain and ordinary meaning of the terms "wanton" and "reckless" when used in connection with the concept of negligence would seem to include a state of being heedless of apparent danger. Section 202(1) does not use the term "reckless" as an extended definition of intention or malice, but rather employs the terms as part of a definition of conduct which amounts to "negligence" in a criminal context.

In my view, then, an objective standard must be applied in determining this question because of the difference between the ordinary criminal offence, which requires proof of a subjective state of mind, and that of criminal negligence. In criminal cases, generally, the act coupled with the mental state or intent is punished. In criminal negligence, the act which exhibits the requisite degree of negligence is punished. If this distinction is not kept clear, the dividing line between the traditional *mens rea* offence and the offence of criminal negligence becomes blurred. The difference, for example, between murder and manslaughter, both unlawful killings, is merely one of intent. If the question of an accused's intent had to be considered and separately proved in offences under s. 202 of the *Code*, the purpose of the section would be defeated because intentional conduct would perforce be considered under other sections of the *Code* and s. 202, aimed at mindless but socially dangerous conduct, would have no function. For these reasons, the objective test should be employed and, in my view, the Court of Appeal was in error in concluding in this case that a subjective test would be required. The test is that of reasonableness, and proof of conduct which reveals a marked and significant departure from the standard which could be expected of a reasonably prudent person in the circumstances will justify a conviction of criminal negligence.

. . .

The application of an objective test under s. 202 of the *Code*, however, may not be made in a vacuum. Events occur within the framework of other events and actions and when deciding on the nature of the questioned conduct surrounding circumstances must be considered. The decision must be made on a consideration of the facts existing at the time and in relation to the accused's perception of those facts. Since the test is objective, the accused's perception of the facts is not to be considered for the purpose of assessing malice or intention on the accused's part but only form a basis for a conclusion as to whether or not the accused's conduct, in view of his perception of the facts, was reasonable. This is particularly true where, as here, the accused have raised the defence of mistake of fact. If an accused under s. 202 has an honest and reasonably held belief in the existence of certain facts, it may be a relevant consideration in assessing the reasonableness of his conduct. For example, a welder, who is engaged to work in a confined space believing on the assurance of the owner of the premises that not combustible or explosive material is stored nearby, should be entitled to have his perception, as to the presence or absence of dangerous material, before the jury on a charge of manslaughter when his welding torch causes an explosion and a consequent death.

As noted earlier, the Tuttons raised the defence of mistake of fact at trial. They argued that the failure to supply insulin was based on the belief that the child had been cured by Divine intervention and that the failure to provide medical care in timely fashion was based upon the belief that the child was not seriously ill, so medical assistance was not necessary. The trial judge, it was argued, was in error in telling the jury that for any such belief to be effective as a defence it must have been reasonably held. It was held in this Court in *Pappajohn v. The Queen*, [1980] 2 S.C.R. 120, that an honest, though mistaken, belief in the existence of circumstances which, if present, would make the questioned conduct non-culpable would entitle an accused to an acquittal. It was also held in *Pappajohn v. The Queen* that the honest belief need not be reasonable, because its effect would be to deny the existence of the requisite *mens rea*. The situation would be different, however, where the offence charged rests upon the concept of negligence, as opposed to that of the guilty mind or blameworthy mental state. In such case, an unreasonable though honest belief on the part of the accused would be negligently held. The holding of such a belief could not afford a defence when culpability is based on negligent conduct. I would therefore conclude that the trial judge made no error in charging the jury to the effect that any mistaken belief which could afford a defence in a charge of criminal negligence would have to be reasonable.

. . .

I would dismiss the appeal and confirm the direction for a new trial.

*Appeal dismissed.*

## Regina v. Hundal
### (1993), 79 C.C.C. (3d) 97 (S.C.C.)

Appeal by the accused from a judgment of the British Columbia Court of Appeal, 63 C.C.C. (3d) 214, 6 C.R. (4th) 215, 29 M.V.R. (2d) 108, 12 W.C.B. (2d) 475, dismissing his appeal from conviction on a charge of dangerous driving causing death.

[Only the judgement of Cory is excerpted below.]

CORY J.: — At issue on this appeal is whether there is a subjective element in the requisite *mens rea* which must be established by the Crown in order to prove the offence of dangerous driving described in s. 233 of the *Criminal Code*, R.S.C 1970, c. C-3, as amended by 1985, c. 19, s. 36 (now R.S.C. 1985, c. C-46, s. 249).

*Factual background*

The accident occurred at about 3:40 in the afternoon in downtown Vancouver. The streets were wet at the time, a situation not uncommon to that city. The downtown traffic was heavy. The appellant was driving his dump truck eastbound on Nelson Street, a four-lane road, approaching its intersection with Cambie Street. At the time, his truck was overloaded. It exceeded by 1160 kilograms the maximum gross weight permitted for the vehicle. He was travelling in the passing lane for eastbound traffic. The deceased was travelling southbound on Cambie Street. He had stopped for a red light at the intersection with Nelson Street. When the light turned green, the deceased proceeded into the intersection through a crosswalk, continued south across the two lanes for westbound traffic on Nelson Street and reached the passing lane for east-bound traffic. At that moment, his car was struck on the right side by the dump truck killing him instantly.

The appellant stated that when he approached the intersection of Nelson and Cambie Streets he observed that the light had turned amber. He thought that he could not stop in time so he simply honked his horn and continued through the intersection when the impact occurred. Several witnesses observed the collision. They testified that the appellant's truck entered the intersection after the Nelson Street traffic light had turned red. It was estimated that at least one second had passed between the end of the amber light and the time when the dump truck first entered the intersection. A Vancouver police officer gave evidence that the red light for Nelson at this intersection is preceded by a three-second amber light and there is a further one-half-second delay before the Cambie light turned green. One witness observed that the deceased's vehicle had travelled almost the entire width of the intersection before it was struck by the truck. Another witness, Mr. Mumford, had been travelling close to the appellant's truck through some 12 intersections. He testified that on an earlier occasion, the appellant went through an intersection as the light turned red. He estimated the speed of the truck at the time of the collision was between 50 and 60 km/h. . . .

*Analysis*

The relevant portion of s. 233 read as follows:

233(1) Every one commits an offence who operates

   (*a*)  a motor vehicle on a street, road, highway or other public place in a manner that is dangerous to the public, having regard to all the circumstances, including the nature, condition and use of such place and the amount of traffic that at the time is or might reasonably be expected to be on such place;

                                        . . .

(4) Everyone who commits an offence under subsection (1) and thereby causes the death of any other person is guilty of an indictable offence and is liable to imprisonment for a term not exceeding fourteen years.

At the outset it must be admitted that the cases dealing with driving offences are not models of clarity. Professor Stuart in his book *Canadian Criminal Law*, 2nd ed. (1987), p. 202, states quite frankly that the law with regard to driving offences is a mess. He writes:

   As a matter of theory the law of driving offences has long been in a mess. The offence of careless driving may require simple or gross negligence, the more serious offence of dangerous driving involves simple negligence although sometimes the courts talk about an "advertence" requirement; and the most serious offence of negligent driving required on one view, advertent recklessness and, on another gross inadvertent negligence. The law has been so confused that it has almost certainly been ignored. There is a fairyland quality to the esoteric analysis involved. Statistics indicate that most prosecutors have been content to rely on the provincial careless driving offence.

Professor Peter Burns aptly described the search for the appropriate *mens rea* for dangerous driving as being as "elusive as the legendary Minotaur": Burns, "An Aspect of Criminal Negligence or How the Minotaur Survived Theseus Who Became Lost in the Labyrinth", 48 Can. Bar Rev. 47 (1970), at p. 60.

*Earlier cases dealing with this section . . .*

These cases unfortunately support the contention of academic writers that decisions relating to dangerous driving are somewhat confusing if not contradictory and provide little in the way of guidance. For their part, lower courts have increasingly tended to fix an objective standard for the offence.

. . .

*The constitutional requirement of mens rea*

The appellant contends that the prison sentence which may be imposed for a breach of s. 233 (now s. 249) makes it evident that an accused cannot be convicted without proof beyond a reasonable doubt of a subjective mental element of an intention to drive dangerously. Certainly every crime requires proof of an act or failure to act, coupled with an element of fault which is termed the *mens rea*. This court has made it clear that s. 7 of the *Canadian Charter of Rights and Freedoms* prohibits the imposition of imprisonment in the absence of proof that the element of fault: see *Reference re: s. 94(2) of Motor Vehicle Act* (1985), 23 C.C.C. (3d) 289, 24 D.L.R. (4th) 536, [1985] 2 S.C.R. 486, and *R. v. Vaillancourt* (1987), 39 C.C.C. (3d) 118, 47 D.L.R. (4th) 399, [1987] 2 S.C.R. 636.

Depending on the provisions of the particular section and the context in which it appears, the constitutional rquirement of *mens rea* may be satisfied in different ways. The offence can require proof of a positive state of mind such as intent, recklessness or wilful blindness. Alternatively, the *mens rea* or element of fault can be satisfied by proof of negligence whereby the conduct of the accused is measured on the basis of an objective standard without establishing the subjective mental state of the particular accused. In the appropriate context, negligence can be an acceptable basis of liability which meets the fault requirement of s. 7 of the Charter: see *R. v. Wholesale Travel Group Inc.* (1991), 67 C.C.C. (3d) 193, 84 D.L.R. (4th) 161, [1991] 3 S.C.R. 154. Thus, the intent required for a particular offence may be either subjective or objective.

A truly subjective test seeks to determine what was actually in the mind of the particular accused at the moment the offence is alleged to have been committed. In his very useful text, Professor Stuart puts it this way in *Canadian Criminal Law, ibid.*, at pp. 123-4, and p. 125:

What is vital is that *this accused* given his personality, situation and circumstances, actually intended, knew or foresaw the consequence and/or circumstance as the case may be. Whether he "could", "ought", or "should" have foreseen or whether a reasonable person would have foreseen is not the relevant criterion of liability.

. . .

In trying to ascertain what was going on in the accused's mind, as the subjective approach demands, the trier of fact may draw reasonable inferences from the accused's actions or words at the time of his act or in the witness box. The accused may or may not be believed. To conclude that, considering all the evidence, the Crown has proved beyond a reasonable doubt that the accused "must" have thought in the penalized way is no departure from the subjective substantive standard. Resort to an objective substantive standard would only occur if the reasoning became that the accused "must have realized it if he had thought about it".

(Emphasis in original.)

On the other hand, the test for negligence is an objective one requiring a marked departure from the standard of care of a reasonable person. There is no need to establish the intention of the particular accused. The question to be answered under the objective test concerns what the accused "should" have known. The potential harshness of the objective standard may be lessened by the consideration of certain personal factors as well as the consideration of a defence of mistake of fact: see McIntyre J., and Lamer J. as he then was, in *R. v. Tutton* (1989), 48 C.C.C. (3d) 129, [1989] 1 S.C.R. 1392, 69 C.R. (3d) 289, and *R. v. Waite* (1989), 48 C.C.C. (3d) 1, [1989] 1 S.C.R. 1436, 69 C.R. (3d) 323. Nevertheless, there should be a clear distinction in the law between one who was aware (pure subjective intent) and one who should have taken care irrespective of awareness (pure objective intent).

## What is the mens rea required to prove the offence of dangerous driving?

The nature of driving offences suggests than an objective test, or more specifically a modified objective test, is particularly appropriate to apply to dangerous driving. I say that for a number of reasons.

### (a) The licensing requirement

First, driving can only be undertaken by those who have a licence. The effect of the licensing requirement is to demonstrate that those who drive are mentally capable of doing so. Moreover, it serves to confirm that those who drive are familiar with the standard of care which must be maintained by all drivers. There is a further aspect that must be taken into consideration in light of the licensing requirement for drivers. Licensed drivers choose to engage in the regulated activity of driving. They place themselves in a position of responsibility to other members of the public who use the roads.

As a result, it is unnecessary for a court to establish that the particular accused intended or was aware of the consequences of his or her driving. The minimum standard of physical and mental well-being coupled with the basic knowledge of the standard of care required of licensed drivers obviate that requirement. As a determining subjective intent, is simply not necessary in light of the fixed standards that must be met by licensed drivers.

### (b) *The automatic and reflexive nature of driving*

Secondly, the nature of driving itself is often so routine, so automatic that it is almost impossible to determine a particular state of mind of a driver at any given moment. Driving motor vehicles is something that is familiar to most adult Canadians. It cannot be denied that a great deal of driving is done with little conscious thought. It is an activity that is primarily reactive and not contemplative. It is every bit as routine and familiar as taking a shower or going to work. Often it is impossible for a driver to say what his or her specific intent was at any moment during a drive other than the desire to go from A to B.

It would be a denial of common sense for a driver, whose conduct was objectively dangerous, to be acquitted on the ground that he was not thinking of his manner of driving at the time of the accident.

### (c) *The wording of s. 233 (now s. 249)*

Thirdly, the wording of the section itself which refers to the operation of a motor vehicle "in a manner that is dangerous to the public, having regard to all the circumstances" suggests that an objective standard is required. The "manner of driving" can only be compared to a standard of reasonable conduct. That standard can be readily judged and assessed by all who would be members of juries.

Thus, it is clear that the basis of liability for dangerous driving is negligence. The question to be asked is not what the accused subjectively intended but rather whether, viewed objectively, the accused exercised the appropriate standard of care. It is not overly difficult to determine when a driver has fallen markedly below the acceptable standard of care. There can be not doubt that the concept of negligence is well understood and readily recognized by most Canadians. Negligent driving can be thought of as a continuum that progresses, or regresses, from momentary lack of attention giving rise to civil responsibility through careless driving under a provincial Highway Traffic Act to dangerous driving under the *Criminal Code*.

### (d) *Statistics*

Fourthly, the statistics which demonstrate that all too many tragic deaths and disabling injuries flow from the operation of motor vehicles indicate the need to control the conduct of drivers. The need is obvious and urgent. Section 233 (now s. 249) seeks to curb conduct which is exceedingly dangerous to the public. The statistics on car accidents in Canada indicate with chilling clarity the extent of the problem. The number of people killed and injured each year in traffic accidents is staggering. Data from Transport Canada shows that, in 1991, the number of deaths related to traffic accidents in Canada was 3,654. In 1990, there were 178,423 personal injury traffic accidents, 630,000 property-damage accidents and 3,442 fatal accidents. These figures highlight the tragic social cost which can and does arise from the operation of motor vehicles. There is therefore a compelling need for effective legislation which strives to regulate the manner of driving vehicles and thereby lessen the carnage on our highways. It is not only appropriate but essential in the control of dangerous driving that an objective standard be applied.

In my view, to insist on a subjective mental element in connection with driving offences would be to deny reality. It cannot be forgotten that the operation of a motor vehicle is, as I have said so very often, automatic and with little conscious thought. It is simply inappropriate to apply a subjective test in determining whether an accused is guilty of dangerous driving.

### (e) *Modified objective test*

Although an objective test must be applied to the offence of dangerous driving, it will remain open to the accused to raise a reasonable doubt that a reasonable person would have been aware of the risks in the accused's conduct. The test must be applied with some measure of flexibility. That is to say the objective test should not be applied in a vacuum but rather in the context of the events surrounding the incident.

There will be occasions when the manner of driving viewed objectively will clearly be dangerous, yet the accused should not be convicted. Take, for example, a driver who, without prior warning, suffers a totally unexpected heart attack, epileptic seizure or detached retina. As a result of the sudden onset of a disease or physical disability the manner of driving would be dangerous, yet those circumstances could provide a complete defence despite the objective demonstration of dangerous driving. Similarly, a driver who, in the absence of any warning or knowledge of its possible effects, takes a prescribed medication which suddenly and unexpectedly affects the driver in such a way that the manner of driving was dangerous to the public, could still establish a good defence to the charge although it had been objectively established. These examples, and there may well be others, serve to illustrate the aim and purpose of the modified objective test. It is to enable a court to take into account the sudden and unexpected onset of disease and similar human frailties as well as the objective demonstration of dangerous driving.

A modified objective test was aptly described by McIntyre J. in *R. v. Tutton, supra*, at pp. 140-1. Although he was dealing with criminal negligence, his words, at p. 140, are apt in considering the dangerous driving section which is essentially concerned with negligent driving that constitutes a marked departure from the norm:

> The application of an objective test under s. 202 of the *Criminal Code*, however, may not be made in a vacuum. Events occur within the framework of other events and actions and when deciding on the nature of the questioned conduct, surrounding circumstances must be considered. The decision must be made on a consideration of the facts existing at the time and in relation to the accused's perception of those facts. Since the test is objective, the accused's perception of the facts is not to be considered for the purpose of assessing malice or intention on the accused's part but only to form a basis for a conclusion as to whether or not the accused's conduct, in view of his perception of the facts, was reasonable . . . If an accused under s. 202 has an honest and reasonably held belief in the existence of certain facts, it may be a relevant consideration in assessing the reasonableness of his conduct. For example, a welder, who is engaged to work in a confined space believing on the assurance of the owner of the premises that no combustible or explosive material is stored nearby, should be entitled

to have his perception, as to the presence or absence of dangerous materials, before the jury on a charge of manslaughter when his welding torch causes an explosion and a consequent death.

In summary, the *mens rea* for the offence of dangerous driving should be assessed objectively but in the context of all the events surrounding the incident. That approach will satisfy the dictates both of common sense and fairness. As a general rule, personal factors need not be taken into account. This flows from the licensing requirement for driving which assures that all who drive have a reasonable standard of physical health and capability, mental health and a knowledge of the reasonable standard required for all drivers.

In light of the licensing requirement and the nature of driving offences, a modified objective test satisfies the constitutional minimum fault requirement for s. 233 (now s. 249) of the *Criminal Code* and is eminently well suited to that offence.

It follows then that a trier of fact may convict if satisfied beyond a reasonable doubt that, viewed objectively, the accused was, in the words of the section, driving in a manner that was "dangerous to the public, having regard to all the circumstances, including the nature, condition and use of such place and the amount of traffic that at the time is or might reasonably be expected to be on such place." In making the assessment, the trier of fact should be satisfied that the conduct amounted to a marked departure from the standard of care that a reasonable person would observe in the accused's situation.

Next, if an explanation is offered by the accused, such as a sudden and unexpected onset of illness, then in order to convict, the trier of fact must be satisfied that a reasonable person in similar circumstances ought to have been aware of the risk and of the danger involved in the conduct manifested by the accused. If a jury is determining the facts, they may be instructed with regard to dangerous driving along the lines set out above. There is no necessity for a long or complex charge. Neither the section nor the offence requires it. Certainly the instructions should not be unnecessarily confused by any references to advertent or inadvertent negligence. The offence can be readily assessed by jurors who can arrive at a conclusion based on common sense and their own everyday experiences.

### Application of these principles to the facts

Let us now consider whether the modified objective test was properly applied in this case. The trial judge carefully examined the circumstances of the accident. He took into account the busy downtown traffic, the weather conditions, and the mechanical conditions of the accused vehicle. He concluded, in my view very properly, that the appellant's manner of driving represented a gross departure from the standard of a reasonably prudent driver. No explanation was offered by the accused that could excuse his conduct. There is no reason for interfering with the trial judge's finding of fact and application of the law.

In the result the appeal must be dismissed.

*Appeal dismissed.*

## Regina v. Creighton
### (1993), 83 C.C.C. (3d) 246 (S.C.C.)

[Only the judgement of McLachlin is excerpted below.]

McLACHLIN J.: — This appeal considers the constitutional status of s. 222(5)(*a*) of the *Criminal Code*, R.S.C. 1985, c. C-46. In particular, the constitutional question stated by the Chief Justice asks: "Does the common law definition of unlawful act manslaughter violate s. 7 of the *Canadian Charter of Rights and Freedoms*?" The facts and judgments below have been set out by the Chief Justice. In brief, Mr. Creighton was convicted of manslaughter, arising from the death of Kimberly Ann Martin, who died as a result of an injection of cocaine given by Mr. Creighton. The trial judge found that the death constituted manslaughter either on the ground that it was caused by an unlawful act, or on the ground that it was caused by criminal negligence.

I respectfully disagree with the Chief Justice on two points. The first is his conclusion that the common law offence of manslaughter in unconstitutional because it does not require foreseeability of death. The Chief Justice concludes that the offence of manslaughter must be "read up" to include this requirement in order to bring it into line with the principles of fundamental justice enshrined in s. 7 of the *Canadian Charter of Rights and Freedoms*, and in particular with the principle that the moral fault required for conviction be commensurate with the gravity and the stigma of the offence. In my view, the offence of unlawful act manslaughter as defined by our courts and those in other jurisdictions for many centuries, is entirely consistent with the principles of fundamental justice. There is no need to read up its requirements; as it stands, it conforms to the Charter.

The second point on which I respectfully diverge is the Chief Justice's conclusion that the standard of care on the objective test in manslaughter and in crimes of negligence varies with the degree of experience, education, and other personal characteristics of the accused. This leads the Chief Justice to hold Mr. Creighton to a higher standard of care than that of the reasonable person in determining if he would have foreseen the risk in question, because of Creighton's long experience as a drug user (at p. 20, reasons of Chief Justice) [*ante*, p. 360]. For the reasons set out below I believe the appropriate standard to be that of the reasonable person in all the circumstances of the case. The criminal law is concerned with setting minimum standards of conduct; the standards are not to be altered because the accused possesses more or less experience than the hypothetical average reasonable person.

I will turn first to the common law test for manslaughter, and address the constitutional question as stated by the Chief Justice.

A. *Constitutionality of the requirement of foreseeability of bodily injury in manslaughter*

   1. *The mens rea of manslaughter*

The *Criminal Code* defines three general types of culpable homicide. There is murder, the intentional killing of another human being. There is infanticide, the intentional killing of a child. All other culpable homicides fall into the residual category of manslaughter (s. 234).

Manslaughter is a crime of venerable lineage. It covers a wide variety of circumstances. Two requirements are constant: (1) conduct causing the death of another person, and (2) fault short of intention to kill. That fault may consist either in committing another unlawful act which causes the death, or in criminal negligence. The common law classification of manslaughter is reflected in the definition of culpable homicide in s. 222(5) of the *Criminal Code*:

222(5) A person commits culpable homicide when he causes the death of a human being,

(*a*) by means of an unlawful act;

(*b*) by criminal negligence;

The structure of the offence of manslaughter depends on a predicate offence of an unlawful act or criminal negligence, coupled with a homicide. It is now settled that the fact that an offence depends upon a predicate offence does not render it unconstitutional provided that the predicate offence involves a dangerous act, is not an offence of absolute liability, and is not unconstitutional: *R. v. DeSousa* (1992), 76 C.C.C. (3d) 124, 95 D.L.R. (4th) 595, [1992] 2 S.C.R. 944. But a further objection is raised in this case. It is said that the offence of manslaughter is unconstitutional because it requires only foreseeability of the risk of bodily harm and not foreseeability of death, and that the trial judge erred in requiring only foreseeability of bodily harm.

The cases establish that in addition to the *actus reus* and *mens rea* associated with the underlying act, all that is required to support a manslaughter conviction is reasonable foreseeability of the risk of bodily harm. While s. 222(5)(*a*) does not expressly require foreseeable bodily harm, it has been so interpreted: see *R. v. DeSousa, supra*. The unlawful act must be objectively dangerous, that is, likely to injure another person. The law of unlawful act manslaughter has not, however, gone so far as to require foreseeability of death. The same is true for manslaughter predicated on criminal negligence; while criminal negligence, *infra*, requires a marked departure from the standards of a reasonable person in all the circumstances, it does not require foreseeability of death.

Certain early authorities suggest that foreseeability of the risk of bodily harm is not required for manslaughter. . .

In more recent times, the prevailing view has been that foreseeability of bodily harm is required for manslaughter. . .

This court in *R. v. DeSousa, supra*, confirmed that a conviction for manslaughter requires that the risk of bodily harm have been foreseeable. . .

So the test for the *mens rea* of unlawful act manslaughter in Canada, as in the United Kingdom, is (in addition to the *mens rea* of the underlying offence) objective foreseeability of the risk of bodily harm which is neither trivial nor transitory, in the context of a dangerous act. Foreseeability of the risk of death is not required. The question is whether this test violates the principle of fundamental justice under s. 7 of the Charter.

## 2. *Constitutionality of the "foresight of bodily harm" test for manslaughter*

Before venturing on analysis, I think it appropriate to introduce a note of caution. We are here concerned with a common law offence virtually as old as our system of criminal law. It has been applied in innumerable cases around the world. And it has been honed and refined over the centuries. Because of its residual nature, it may lack the logical symmetry of more modern statutory offences, but it has stood the practical test of time. Could all this be the case, one asks, if the law violates our fundamental notions of justice, themselves grounded in the history of the common law? Perhaps. Nevertheless, it must be with considerable caution that a twentieth century court approaches the invitation which has been put before us: to strike out, or alternatively, rewrite, the offence of manslaughter on the ground that this is necessary to bring the law into conformity with the principles of fundamental justice.

As I read the reasons of the Chief Justice, his conclusion that the offence of manslaughter as it stands is unconstitutional, rests on two main concerns. First, it is his view that the gravity or seriousness of the offence of manslaughter, and in particular the stigma that attaches to it, requires a minimum *mens rea* or foreseeability of death. Secondly, considerations of symmetry between the element of mental fault and the consequences of the offence mandate this conclusion. I will deal with each concern in turn.

### (a) *Gravity of the offence*

A number of concepts fall under this head. Three of them figure among the four factors relevant to determining the constitutionality of a *mens rea* requirement, as set out by this court in *R. v. Martineau* (1990), 58 C.C.C. (3d) 353, [1990] 2 S.C.R. 633, 79 C.R. (3d) 129:

1. the stigma attached to the offence, and the available penalties requiring a *mens rea* reflecting the particular nature of the crime;
2. whether the punishment is proportionate to the moral blameworthiness of the offender, and
3. the idea that those causing harm intentionally must be punished more severely than those causing harm unintentionally.

The Chief Justice in his reasons places considerable emphasis on the first factor of stigma. He argues that "there may well be no difference between the *actus reus* of manslaughter and that of murder; arguably both give rise to the stigma of being labelled by the state and community as responsible for the wrongful death of another" (at p. 11) [*ante*, p. 355]. But later in his reasons he concedes that "the stigma which attaches to a conviction for unlawful act manslaughter", while "significant . . . does not approach the opprobrium reserved in our society for those who *knowingly* or *intentionally* take the life of another" (emphasis is original). The Chief Justice goes on to observe that "[i]t is for this reason that manslaughter developed as a separate offence from murder at common law." Nevertheless, in the end the Chief Justice concludes that the "constitutional imperative", taken with other factors, requires a minimum *mens rea* of foreseeability of the risk of death, suggesting that stigma may remain an important factor in his reasoning.

To the extent that stigma is relied on as requiring foreseeability of the risk of death in the offence of manslaughter, I find it unconvincing. The most important feature of the stigma of manslaughter is the stigma which is *not* attached to it. The *Criminal Code* confines manslaughter to non-intentional homicide. A person convicted of manslaughter is *not* a murderer. He or she did *not* intend to kill someone. A person has been killed through the fault of another, and that is always serious. But by the very act of calling the killing *manslaughter* the law indicates that the killing is less blameworthy than murder. It may arise from negligence, or it may arise as the unintended result of a lesser unlawful act. The conduct is blameworthy and must be punished, but its stigma does not approach that of murder.

To put it another way, the stigma attached to manslaughter is an appropriate stigma. Manslaughter is not like constructive murder, where one could say that a person who did not in fact commit murder might be inappropriately branded with the stigma of murder. The stigma associated with manslaughter is arguably exactly what it should be for an unintentional killing in circumstances where the risk of bodily harm was foreseeable. There is much common sense in the following observation:

> The offender has killed, and it does not seem wrong in principle that, when he is far from blameless, he should be convicted of an offence of homicide. To some extent it must be an intuitive conclusion, but it does not seem too difficult to argue that those who kill, and who are going to be convicted of something, should be convicted of homicide. That, after all, is what they have done.

(Adrian Briggs, "In Defence of Manslaughter", [1983] Crim. L.R. 764 at p. 765.)

It would shock the public's conscience to think that a person could be convicted of manslaughter absent any moral fault based on foreseeability of harm. Conversely, it might well shock the public's conscience to convict a person who has killed another only of aggravated assault — the result of requiring foreseeability of death — on the sole basis that the risk of death was not reasonably foreseeable. The terrible consequence of death demands more. In short, the *mens rea* requirement which the common law has adopted — foreseeability of harm — is entirely appropriate to the stigma associated with the offence of manslaughter. To change the *mens rea* requirement would be to risk the very disparity between *mens rea* and stigma of which the appellant complains.

I come then to the second factor mentioned in *Martineau*, the relationship between the punishment for the offence and the *mens rea* requirement. Here again, the offence of manslaughter stands in sharp contrast to the offence of murder. Murder entails a mandatory life sentence; manslaughter carries with it no minimum sentence. This is appropriate. Because manslaughter can occur in a wide variety of circumstances, the penalties must be flexible. An unintentional killing while committing a minor offence, for example, properly attracts a much lighter sentence than an unintentional killing where the circumstances indicate an awareness of risk of death just short of what would be required to infer the intent required for murder. The point is, the sentence can be and is tailored to suit the degree of moral fault of the offender. This court acknowledged this in *Martineau*, at p. 362: "The more flexible sentencing scheme under a conviction for manslaughter is in accord with the principle that punishment be meted out with regard to the level of moral blameworthiness of the offender." It follows that the sentence attached to manslaughter does not require elevation of the degree of *mens rea* for the offence.

This brings me to the third factor relating to the gravity of the offence set out in *Martineau*, the principle that those causing harm intentionally must be punished more severely than those causing harm unintentionally. As noted, this principle is strictly observed in the case of manslaughter. It is by definition an unintentional crime. Accordingly, the penalties imposed are typically less than for its intentional counter-part, murder.

I conclude that the standard of *mens rea* required for manslaughter is appropriately tailored to the seriousness of the offence.

(b)  *Symmetry between the element of fault and the consequences of the offence*

The Chief Justice correctly observes that the criminal law has traditionally aimed at symmetry between the *mens rea* and the prohibited consequences of the offence. The *actus reus* generally consists of an act bringing about a prohibited consequence, *e.g.*, death. Criminal law theory suggests that the accompanying *mens rea* must go to the prohibited consequence. The moral fault of the accused lies in the act of bringing about that consequence. The Chief Justice reasons from this proposition that since manslaughter is an offence involving the prohibited act of killing another, a *mens rea* of foreseeability of harm is insufficient; what is required is foreseeability of death.

The conclusion that the offence of manslaughter is unconstitutional because it does not require appreciation of the consequential risk of death rests on two propositions: (1) that risk of bodily harm is appreciably different from risk of death in the context of manslaughter, and (2) that the principle of absolute symmetry between *mens rea* and each consequence of a criminal offence is not only a general rule of criminal law, but a principle of fundamental justice which sets a constitutional minimum. In my view, neither of these propositions is free from doubt.

I turn first to the distinction between appreciation of the risk of bodily harm and the risk of death in the context of manslaughter. In my view, when the risk of bodily harm is combined with the established rule that a wrongdoer must take his victim as he finds him and the fact that death did in fact occur, the distinction disappears. The accused who asserts that the risk of death was not foreseeable is in effect asserting that a normal person would not have died in these circumstances, and that he could not foresee the peculiar vulnerability of the victim. Therefore, he says, he should be convicted only of assault causing bodily harm or some lesser offence. This is to abrogate the thin-skull rule that requires that the wrongdoer take his victim as he finds him. Conversely, to combine the test of reasonable foreseeability of bodily harm with the thin-skull rule is to mandate that in some cases, foreseeability of the risk of bodily harm alone will properly result in a conviction for manslaughter.

What the appellant asks us to do, then, is to abandon the "thin-skull" rule. It is this rule which, on analysis, is alleged to be unjust. Such a conclusion I cannot accept. The law has consistently set its face against such a policy. It decrees that the aggressor must take his victim as he finds him. . . .

The principle that if one engages in criminal behaviour, one is responsible for any unforeseen actions stemming from the unlawful act, has been a well-established tenet for most of this century in Canada, the U.S. and U.K. . . .

The thin-skull rule is a good and useful principle. It requires aggressors, once embarked on their dangerous course of conduct which may foreseeably injure others, to take responsibility for all the consequences that ensue, even to death. That is not, in my view, contrary to fundamental justice. Yet the consequence of adopting the amendment proposed by the Chief Justice would be to abrogate this principle in cases of manslaughter.

In fact, when manslaughter is viewed in the context of the thin skull principle, the disparity diminishes between the *mens rea* of the offence and its consequence. The law does not posit the average victim. It says the aggressor must take the victim as he finds him. Wherever there is a risk of harm, there is also a practical risk that some victims may die as a result of the harm. At this point, the test of harm and death merge.

The second assumption inherent in the argument based on symmetry between *mens rea* and each consequence of the offence is that this is not only a general rule of criminal law, but a principle of fundamental justice — a basic constitutional requirement. I agree that as a general rule the *mens rea* of an offence relates to the consequences prohibited by the offence. As I stated in *R. v. Theroux* (1993), 79 C.C.C. (3d) 449 at p. 458, 100 D.L.R. (4th) 624, [1993] 2 S.C.R. 5: Typically, *mens rea* is concerned with the consequences of the prohibited *actus reus*." Yet our criminal law contains important exceptions to this ideal of perfect symmetry. The presence of these exceptions suggests that the rule of symmetry is just that — a rule — to which there are no exceptions. If this is so, then the rule cannot be elevated to the status of a principle of fundamental justice which must, by definition, have universal application.

It is important to distinguish between criminal law theory, which seeks the ideal of absolute symmetry between *actus reus* and *mens rea*, and the constitutional requirements of the Charter. As the Chief Justice has stated several times, "the Constitution does not always guarantee the 'ideal'": *R. v. Lippé* (1991), 64 C.C.C. (3d) 513 at p. 532. . . .

I know of no authority for the proposition that the *mens rea* of an offence must always attach to the precise consequence which is prohibited as a matter of constitutional necessity. The relevant constitutional principles have been cast more broadly. No person can be sent to prison without *mens rea*, or a guilty mind, and the seriousness of the offence must not be disproportionate to the degree of moral fault. provided an element of mental fault or moral culpability is present, and provided that it is proportionate to the seriousness and consequences of the offence charged, the principles of fundamental justice are satisfied.

The principles of fundamental justice, viewed thus, empower Parliament to recognize that, notwithstanding the same level of moral fault, some offences may be more or less serious, depending on the consequences of the culpable act. . . .

Thus it cannot be said that the law in all circumstances insists on absolute symmetry between the *mens rea* and the consequences of the offence. Sometimes it does not insist on the consequences at all, as in crimes of attempts. Sometimes, as in unlawful act manslaughter, it elevates the crime by reason of its serious consequences while leaving the mental element the same.

Just as it would offend fundamental justice to punish a person who did not intend to kill for murder, so it would equally offend common notions of justice to acquit a person who has killed another of manslaughter and find him guilty instead of aggravated assault on the ground that death, as opposed to harm was foreseeable. Consequences can be important. . . .

Thus when considering the constitutionality of the requirement of foreseeability of bodily harm, the question is not whether the general rule of symmetry between *mens rea* and the consequences prohibited by the offence is met, but rather whether the fundamental principle of justice is satisfied that the gravity and blameworthiness of an offence must be commensurate with the moral fault engaged by that offence. Fundamental justice does not require absolute symmetry between moral fault and the prohibited consequences. Consequences, or the absence of consequences, can properly affect the seriousness with which Parliament treats specified conduct.

### 3. *Policy considerations*

I have suggested that jurisprudential and historic considerations confirm a test for the *mens rea* of manslaughter based on foreseeability of the risk of bodily injury, rather than death. I have also argued that the considerations of the gravity of the offence and symmetry between the *mens rea* of the offence and its consequences do not entail the conclusion that the offence of manslaughter as it has been historically defined in terms of foreseeability of the risk of bodily harm is unconstitutional. It is my view that policy considerations support the same conclusion. In looking at whether a long-standing offence violates the principles of fundamental justice, it is not amiss, in my view, to look at such considerations.

First, the need to deter dangerous conduct which may injure others and in fact may kill the peculiarly vulnerable supports the view that death need not be objectively foreseeable, only bodily injury. To tell people that if they embark on dangerous conduct which foreseeably may cause bodily harm which is neither trivial nor transient, and which in fact results in death, that they will not be held responsible for the death but only for aggravated assault, is less likely to deter such conduct than a message that they will be held responsible for the death, albeit under manslaughter not murder. Given the finality of death and the absolute unacceptability of killing another human being, it is not amiss to preserve the test which promises the greatest measure of deterrence, provided the penal consequences of the offence are not disproportionate. This is achieved by retaining the test of foreseeability of bodily harm in the offence of manslaughter.

Secondly, retention of the test based on foreseeability of bodily harm accords best with our sense of justice. I have earlier alluded to the view, attested to by the history of the offence of manslaughter, that causing the death of another through negligence or a dangerous unlawful act should be met by a special sanction reflecting the fact that a death occurred, even though death was not objectively foreseeable. This is supported by the sentiment that a person who engages in dangerous conduct that breaches the bodily integrity of another and puts that person at risk may properly be held responsible for an unforeseen death attributable to that person's peculiar vulnerability; the aggressor takes the victim as he finds him. The criminal law must reflect not only the concerns of the accused, but the concerns of the victim, and where the victim is killed, the concerns of society for the victim's fate. Both go into the equation of justice.

Finally, the traditional test founded on foreseeability of the risk of bodily harm provides, in my belief, a workable test which avoids troubling judges and juries about the fine distinction between foreseeability of the risk of bodily injury and foreseeability of the risk of death — a distinction which, as argued earlier, reduces to a formalistic technicality when put in the context of the thin-skull rule and the fact that death has in fact been inflicted by the accused's dangerous act. The traditional common law test permits a principled approach to the offence which meets the concerns of society, provides fairness to the accused, and facilitates a just and workable trial process.

### 4. *Summary on the constitutionality of the test of foresight of bodily harm for manslaughter*

The foregoing considerations lead me to conclude that the fact that the *mens rea* of manslaughter requires foreseeable risk of harm rather than foreseeable risk of death does not violate the principles of fundamental justice. In the final analysis, the moral fault required for manslaughter is commensurate with the gravity of the offence and the penalties which it entails, and offends no principle of fundamental justice. The next issue is the nature of the objective test establishing foresight of bodily harm, to which I now turn.

### B. *The nature of the objective test*

I respectfully differ from the Chief Justice on the nature of the objective test used to determine the *mens rea* for crimes of negligence. In my view, the approach advocated by the Chief Justice personalizes the objective test to the point where it devolves into a subjective test, thus eroding the minimum standard of care which Parliament has laid down by the enactment of offences of manslaughter and penal negligence.

By way of background, it may be useful to restate what I understand the jurisprudence to date to have established regarding crimes of negligence and the objective test. The *mens rea* of a criminal offence may be either subjective or objective, subject to the principle of fundamental justice that the moral fault of the offence must be proportionate to its gravity and penalty. Subjective *mens rea* requires that the accused have intended the consequences of his or her acts, or that, knowing of the probable consequences of those acts, the accused have proceeded recklessly in the face of the risk. The requisite intent or knowledge may be inferred directly from what the accused said or says about his or her mental state, or indirectly from the act and its circumstances. Even in the latter case, however, it is concerned with " 'what was actually going on in the mind of this particular accused at the time in question' ": L'Heureux-Dubé J. in *R. v. Martineau, supra*, at p. 367, quoting Stuart, *Canadian Criminal Law*, 2nd ed. (1987), p. 121.

Objective *mens rea*, on the other hand, is not concerned with what the accused intended or knew. Rather, the mental fault lies in the failure to direct the mind to a risk which the reasonable person would have appreciated. Objective *mens rea* is not concerned with what was actually in the accused's mind, but with what should have been there, had the accused proceeded reasonably.

It is now established that a person may be held criminally responsible for negligent conduct on the objective test, and that this alone does not violate the principle of fundamental justice that the moral fault of the accused must be commensurate with the gravity of the offence and its penalty: *R. v. Hundal* (1993), 79 C.C.C. (3d) 97, [1993] 1 S.C.R. 867, 19 C.R. (4th) 169.

However, as stated in *Martineau*, it is appropriate that those who cause harm intentionally should be punished more severely than those who cause harm inadvertently. Moreover, the constitutionality of crimes of negligence is also subject to the caveat that acts of ordinary negligence may not suffice to justify imprisonment. . . . To put it in the terms used in *Hundal*: The negligence must constitute a "marked departure" from the standard of the reasonable person. . . .

It follows from this requirement, affirmed in Hundal, that in an offence based on unlawful conduct, a predicate offence involving carelessness or negligence must also be read as requiring a "marked departure" from the standard of the reasonable person.

. . .

To this point, the Chief Justice and I are not, as I perceive it, in disagreement. The difference between our approaches turns on the extent to which personal characteristics of the accused may affect liability under the objective test. Here we enter territory in large part uncharted. To date, debate has focused on whether an objective test for *mens rea* is ever available in the criminal law; little has been said about how, assuming it is applicable, it is to be applied. In *R. v. Hundal, supra*, it was said that the *mens rea* of dangerous driving should be assessed objectively in the context of all the events surrounding the incident. But the extent to which those circumstances include personal mental or psychological frailties of the accused was not explored in depth. In these circumstances, we must begin with the fundamental principles of criminal law.

*Underlying principles*

The debate about the degree to which personal characteristics should be reflected in the objective test for fault in offences of penal negligence engages two fundamental concepts of criminal law.

The first concept is the notion that the criminal law may properly hold people who engage in risky activities to a minimum standard of care, judged by what a reasonable person in all the circumstances would have done. This notion posits a uniform standard for all persons engaging in the activity, regardless of their background, education or psychological disposition.

The second concept is the principle that the morally innocent not be punished. . . . This principle is the foundation of the requirement of criminal law that the accused must have a guilty mind, or *mens rea*.

I agree with the Chief Justice that the rule that the morally innocent not be punished in the context of the objective test requires that the law refrain from holding a person criminally responsible if he or she is not capable of appreciating the risk. Where I differ from the Chief Justice is in his designation of the sort of educational, experiential and so-called "habitual" factors personal to the accused which can be taken into account. The Chief Justice, while in principle advocating a uniform standard of care for all, in the result seems to contemplate a standard of care which varies with the background and predisposition of each accused. Thus an inexperienced, uneducated, young person, like the accused in *R. v. Naglik*, S.C.C. Nos. 22490 and 22636, September 9, 1993, could be acquitted, even though she does not meet the standard of the reasonable person. . . . On the other hand, a person with special experience, like Mr. Creighton in this case, or the appellant police officer in *R. v. Gosset, supra*, will be held to a higher standard than the ordinary reasonable person.

I must respectfully dissent from this extension of the objective test for criminal fault. In my view, considerations of principle and policy dictate the maintenance of a single, uniform legal standard of care for such offences, subject to one exception: incapacity to appreciate the nature of the risk which the activity in question entails.

This principle that the criminal law will not convict the morally innocent does not, in my view, require consideration of personal factors short of incapacity. The criminal law, while requiring mental fault as an element of a conviction, has steadfastly rejected the idea that a person's personal characteristics can (short of incapacity) excuse the person from meeting the standard of conduct imposed by the law. . . .

In summary, I can find no support in criminal theory for the conclusion that protection of the morally innocent requires a general consideration of individual excusing conditions. The principle comes into play only at the point where the person is shown to lack the capacity to appreciate the nature and quality or the consequences of his or her acts. Apart from this, we are all, rich and poor, wise and naive, held to the minimum standards of conduct prescribed by the criminal law. This conclusion is dictated by a fundamental proposition of social organization. As Justice Oliver Wendell Holmes wrote in *The Common Law* (1881), p. 108: ". . . when men live in society, a certain average of conduct, a sacrifice of individual peculiarities going beyond a certain point, is necessary to the general welfare".

The ambit of the principle that the morally innocent shall not be convicted has developed in large part in the context of crimes of subjective fault — crimes where the accused must be shown to have actually intended or foreseen the consequences of his or her conduct. In crimes of this type, personal characteristics of the accused have been held to be relevant only to the extent that they tend to prove or disprove an element of such offences, personal factors can come into play. But beyond this, personal characteristics going to lack of capacity are considered under the introductory sections of the *Code* defining the conditions of criminal responsibility and have generally been regarded as irrelevant.

What then is the situation for crimes of inadvertence? Here actual intention or knowledge is not a factor; hence personal characteristics are not admissible on that ground. Nor, in my view, can a case be made for considering them on any other basis, except in so far as they may show that the accused lacked the capacity to appreciate the risk. This appears to be the settled policy of the law, applied for centuries to offences involving manslaughter or penal negligence based on objectively assessed fault. Here, as in crimes of subjective intent, the courts have rejected the contention that the standard prescribed by the law should take into account the individual peculiarities of the accused, short of incapacity. . . .

To the principle of a uniform minimum standard for crimes having an objective test there is but one exception — incapacity to appreciate the risk. . . .

Consistent with these principles, this court has rejected experiential, educational and psychological defences falling short of incapacity. Thus it has excluded personal characteristics short of incapacity in considering the characteristics of the "ordinary person" for the defence of provocation for the offence of murder. . . .

To summarize, the fundamental premises upon which our criminal law rests mandate that personal characteristics not directly relevant to an element of the offence serve as excuses only at the point where they establish incapacity, whether the incapacity be the ability to appreciate the nature and quality of one's conduct in the context of intentional crimes, or the incapacity to appreciate the risk involved in one's conduct in the context of crimes of manslaughter or penal negligence. The principle that we eschew conviction of the morally innocent requires no more.

This test I believe to flow from the fundamental premises of our system of criminal justice. But drawing the line of criminal responsibility for negligent conduct at incapacity is also socially justifiable. In a society which licenses people, expressly or impliedly, to engage in a wide range of dangerous activities posing risk to the safety of others, it is reasonable to require that those choosing to undertake such activities and possessing the basic capacity to understand their danger take the trouble to exercise that capacity: see *R. v. Hundal, supra.* Not only does the absence of such care connote moral fault, but the sanction of the criminal law is justifiably invoked to deter others who choose to undertake such activities from proceeding without the requisite caution. Even those who lack the advantages of age, experience and education may properly be held to this standard as a condition of choosing to engage in activities which may maim or kill other innocent people.

The criminal law, as noted, is concerned with setting minimum standards of behaviour in defined circumstances. If this goal is to be achieved, the minimum cannot be lowered because of the frailties or inexperience of the accused, short of incapacity.

. . .

But the social justification for a uniform standard of care stops at the point of incapacity. Convicting and punishing a person who lacks the capacity to do what the law says he or she should have done serves no useful purpose. . . .

These considerations suggest that the practical as well as the theoretical concerns of the criminal law in the field of penal negligence are best served by insisting on a uniform standard of conduct for everyone, subject to cases where the accused was not capable of recognizing and avoiding the risk attendant on the activity in question. Beyond this, the standard should not be individualized by reason of the peculiar personal characteristics of the accused. . . .

As I see it, the recognition that those lacking the capacity to perceive the risk should be exempted from criminal conviction and punishment does not entail the conclusion that the standard of care must be adjusted to take into account the accused's experience and education. The only actor-oriented question apposite to *mens rea* in these cases is whether the accused was capable of appreciating the risk, had he or she put her mind to it. If the answer is yes . . . that is an end of the matter.

It may be that in some cases educational deficiencies, such as illiteracy on the part of a person handling a marked bottle of nitroglycerine in the Chief Justice's example, may preclude a person from being able to appreciate the risk entailed by his or conduct. Problems of perception may have the same effect; regardless of the care taken, the person would have been incapable of assessing the risk, and hence been acquitted. But, in practice, such cases will arise only exceptionally. The question of *mens rea* will arise only where it has been shown that the accused's conduct (the *actus reus* constitutes a dangerous and unlawful act (as in unlawful act manslaughter), or a marked departure from the standard care of a reasonably prudent person (as in manslaughter by criminal negligence, or penal negligence offences). This established, conflict with the prohibition against punishing the morally innocent will arise only rarely. . . .

Mental disabilities short of incapacity generally do not suffice to negative criminal liability for criminal negligence. The explanations for why a persons fails to advert to the risk inherent in the activity he or she is undertaking are legion. They range from simple absent-mindedness to attributes related to age, education and culture. . . .

This is not to say that the question of guilt is determined in a factual vacuum. While the legal duty of the accused is not particularized by his or her personal characteristics short of incapacity, it is particularized in application by the nature of the activity and the circumstances surrounding the accused's failure to take the requisite care. . . . The question is what the reasonably prudent person would have done in all the circumstances. Thus a welder who lights a torch causing an explosion may be excused if he has made an inquiry and been given advice upon which he was reasonably entitled to rely, that there was no explosive gas in the area. . . .

The matter may be looked at in this way. The legal standard of care is always the same — what a reasonable person would have done in all the circumstances. The *de facto* or applied standard of care, however, may vary with the activity in question and the circumstances in the particular case. . . .

A person may fail to meet an elevated *de facto* standard of care in either of two ways. First, the person may undertake an activity requiring special care when he or she is not qualified to give that care. Absent special excuses like necessity, this may constitute culpable negligence. An untrained person undertaking brain surgery might violate the standard in this way. Secondly, a person who is qualified may negligently fail to exercise the special care required by the activity. A brain surgeon performing surgery in a grossly negligent way might violate the standard in this second way. The standard is the same, although the means by which it is breached may differ.

Just as the adoption of a uniform standard of care which is blind to personal characteristics of the accused short of incapacity precludes lowering the standard for deficiencies of experience and temperament, so it precludes raising the standard for special experience or training. Since the criminal law is concerned with setting minimum standards for human conduct, it would be inappropriate to hold accused persons to a higher standard of care by reason of the fact that they may be better informed or better qualified that the person of reasonable prudence. Some activities may impose a higher *de facto* standard than others; brain surgery requires more care than applying an antiseptic. But as discussed earlier, this flows from the circumstances of the activity, not from the expertise of the actor.

The foregoing analysis suggests the following line of inquiry in cases of penal negligence. The first question is whether *actus reus* is established. This requires that the negligence constitute a marked departure from the standards of the reasonable person in all the circumstances of the case. This may consist in carrying out the activity in a dangerous fashion, or in embarking on the activity when in all the circumstances it is dangerous to do so.

The next question is whether the *mens rea* is established. As is the case with crimes of subjective *mens rea*, the *mens rea* for objective foresight and risking harm is normally inferred from the facts. The standard is that of the reasonable person in the circumstances of the accused. If a person has committed a manifestly dangerous act, it is reasonable, absent indications to the contrary, to infer that he or she failed to direct his or her mind to the risk and the need to take care. However, the normal inference may be negated by evidence raising a reasonable doubt as to lack of capacity to appreciate the risk. Thus, if a *prima facie* case for *actus reus* and *mens rea* is made out, it is necessary to ask a further question: did the accused possess the requisite capacity to appreciate the risk flowing from his conduct? If this further question is answered in the affirmative, the necessary moral fault is established and the accused is properly convicted. If not, the accused must be acquitted. . . .

I conclude that the legal standard of care for all crimes of negligence is that of the reasonable person. Personal factors are not relevant, except on the question of whether the accused possessed the necessary capacity to appreciate the risk.

## C. *Application of the law to this appeal*

The trial judge properly found that Mr. Creighton committed the unlawful act of trafficking in cocaine. He also found that he was guilty of the criminal negligence, using the standard which I view as correct, the standard of the reasonable person. The only remaining question, on the view I take of the law, was whether the reasonable person in all the circumstances would have foreseen the risk of bodily harm. I am satisfied that the answer to this question must be affirmative. At the very least, a person administering a dangerous drug like cocaine to another has a duty to inform himself as to the precise risk the injection entails and to refrain from administering it unless reasonably satisfied that there is no risk of harm. That was not the case here, as the trial judge found.

The conviction was properly entered and should not be disturbed. Like the Chief Justice, I find it necessary to consider the alternative ground of manslaughter by criminal negligence.

I would answer the constitutional question in the negative and dismiss the appeal.

*Appeal dismissed.*

*Editor's note: One of the latest cases decided in the Supreme Court of Canada that deals with criminal negligence causing death is* R. v. Morrisey *(2000), 148 C.C.C. (3d) 1, where the Court looked at section 220 of the Code. This section states: "Every person who by criminal negligence causes death to another person is guilty of an indictable offence and liable (a) where a firearm is used in the commission of the offence, to imprisonment for life and to a minimum punishment of imprisonment for a term of four years; and (b) in any other case, to imprisonment for life." In the case, Gonthier J. states in part:*

> Generally speaking, Parliament prescribes penalties in the Criminal Code to punish individuals who not only commit a wrongful act, but who also commit that wrongful act intentionally. However, even in the absence of any intent to bring about a given result, Parliament has also created criminal liability under s. 219 for people whose conduct evinces a wanton or reckless disregard for the lives or safety of other people. To be convicted of an offence under s. 220, that wanton or reckless disregard must have caused the death of another person. To receive fouryear minimum sentence, a firearm must have been used in the commission of this offence.

> The standard that must be met for a conviction under s. 220(a) is therefore higher than a negligence standard in the civil context. To be convicted under this provision, one must have acted in a manner that represents a marked departure from the norm. . . . Where the risk of harm is very great, as is the case in criminal negligence in the use of firearms causing death cases, it is often easy to conclude that the accused must have foreseen the consequences. . . . Nonetheless, in all cases, the Crown must prove more than the simple fact that a gun discharged, causing death. Section 220(a) is not an absolute liability offence. It requires proof of conduct which is such a marked departure from the behaviour of a reasonably prudent person as to show a wanton or reckless disregard for the life or safety of others.

## Questions/Discussion

1.  Why does the law continue to use terms like actus reus and mens rea when such terms could be put into everyday language which would be better understood by all? The use of Latin terms is found throughout the law and it can be argued that the purpose best served is that of denying access to the law to the greatest number of citizens, as well as that of increasing the mystique of the law (whether deserved or not).
2.  What is the meaning of mens rea for you? Should it continue to be regarded, at least in theory, from a subjectivist point of view, or would you favour an explicitly objectivist approach to the doctrine? Why or why not?
3.  If A is given a package in Columbia to take into Canada and is arrested by customs on entering the country because it turns out the package contains cocaine, under what circumstances should A be held liable for importing cocaine? For example, if A did not address her mind as to what might be in the package because a good, trusted

friend had given it to her and told her it was a gift for his mother? What if the package was given to her by a stranger on the street but A never bothered to check the package or make any inquiries because she is an exceptionally trusting individual who thinks well of everyone? Should such naivety or blindness to the possible consequences relieve A of criminal liability on the grounds she did not have the intent to import the drugs? What role should the protection of the public play in these determinations (assuming for the moment that the public requires protection) as opposed to considerations of individual responsibility or blameworthiness?

4.  What are the problems in theory and practice posed by laws involving criminal negligence and recklessness for traditional concepts of individual responsibility and blameworthiness?

5.  Should Parliament attempt to specify a definition and test for the requisite mens rea for criminal negligence rather than leaving such to the courts? What type of mens rea do you think would be sufficient for criminal negligence? Should the test be subjective or objective? What is your rationale for the definition and test which you would adopt?

### Further Reading

*   Buxton, R., "Some Simple Thoughts on Intention", [1988] Criminal Law Review 484.
*   Fruchtman, Earl, "Recklessness and the Limits of Mens Rea: Beyond Orthodox Subjectivism" (1987), 29 Criminal Law Quarterly 315.
*   Galloway, D., "Why the Criminal Law is Irrational" (1985), 35 University of Toronto Law Journal 25.
*   Mewett, A. and M. Manning, *Mewett and Manning on Criminal Law, 3rd ed.* (Markham: Butterworths, 1994.
*   Roach, Kent, *Criminal Law, 2nd ed.* (Toronto: Irwin Law, 2000) at 124-163.
*   Stuart, Don, and R. Delisle, *Learning Canadian Criminal Law, 8th ed.* (Toronto: Carswell, 2001).
*   Verdun-Jones, S., *Criminal Law in Canada: Cases, Questions and the Code, 3rd ed.* (Toronto: Harcourt Canada, 2002) at 83-150.

## 6.1.3    Strict and Absolute Liability

### Introduction

This area of criminal law creates an exception to the general rule that crimes consist of an actus reus and mens rea. For a variety of reasons which are detailed in the *Sault Ste. Marie* case below, there a large number of crimes and quasi-crimes which do not require a mens rea to be present for criminal liability to attach. Before *Sault Ste. Marie*, these types of offences were referred to as either strict or absolute liability offences (or, generally public welfare offences), as opposed to so-called "true crimes" which required a mens rea. Subsequent to the case, public welfare offences were divided into two categories: strict liability offences, which allowed for a defence of due diligence or reasonable care, and absolute liability offences, for which no defences were available once the actus reus was proven. The old category of true crimes remained the same. The rationale for this new categorization of strict versus absolute liability offences is detailed quite clearly in the *Sault Ste. Marie* case. The situation as it existed before 1978 and the unfairness which such gave rise to are illustrated in the judgment of the first case, *Rex v. Ping Yuen*. Finally, the important effect of the Charter in this area is seen in the *Burt* and *Wholesale* cases. In addition to the legal questions and the rationales and problems presented by these types of offences, this area of the law is a very good example of the courts explicitly creating new criminal law rather than waiting for Parliament to act.

## Rex v. Ping Yuen
### (1921), 36 C.C.C. 269 (Sask. C.A.)

Appeal by defendant from the judgment of Brown C.J.K.B, refusing defendant's application to quash the summary conviction made by the Magistrate under the Sask. Temperance Act, 1917, ch. 23, see 35 (*Cf.*Sask. Temperance Act R.S.S. 1920, ch. 194, sec. 522) The appeal was dismissed, Lamount, J.A. dissenting.

Only the judgment of Turgeon, J.A. is reproduced below.

TURGEON, J.A.: — The appellant is a vendor of soft drinks at Moosomin. On December 6th, 1920, a police officer, acting under a search warrant, found upon his premises three bottles of beer which were shown under analysis to contain more than 1.13% of alcohol per weight. This beer was, therefore, an "intoxicating liquor" within the definition of the Saskatchewan Temperance Act, and an information was laid against the appellant under sec. 35 of that Act (then c. 23 of the Statutes of 1917), which is, in part, as follows:

> **35.**(1) In case any person engaged in the business of selling soft drinks or non-intoxicating liquors keeps or has with his stock of such drinks or liquors or on his business premises any liquor as defined by this Act, such person shall be guilty of an offence, etc.

The magistrate found the accused guilty and his memorandum of conviction reads as follows:

> The accused is found guilty. In my opinion the accused did not know that the contents of the bottles contained more than 1.13% absolute alcohol by weight and the fine and cost were paid under protest. Judgment, fine $50.00 and costs $4.50, and in default of payment of the said sums to imprisonment in the common gaol at Regina for a period of 15 days.

It was admitted by the Director of Prosecutions, on the hearing of this appeal, that the accused was innocent of any guilty intention. He bought the bottles from a firm of wholesale grocers and they purported to contain, and he believed that they contained, a beverage not prohibited by the act; that is, beer of less than the prohibited strength.

He could not have ascertained the fact that they contained liquor in excess of the alcoholic strength allowed by law without having each bottle opened and its contents analyzed, a proceeding which, of course, nobody suggests he should have followed. Under these circumstances the question to be decided is: Was the appellant really guilty of an infraction of the Act, in view of the total absence on his part of any wrongful knowledge or intention, of that usual but not invariable element of guilt known as *mens rea*?

A great number of authorities were cited to us by counsel on both sides. The older cases have been reviewed in recent years in decisions given in the various provinces of Canada, and the result is certainly very confusing. I think, however, that it can be said that the well-known rule of *mens rea* applies to infractions of all penal statutes (whether the subject matter of the Statute lies, in Canada, within the jurisdiction of the Dominion Parliament or of the Provincial Legislatures), unless the Statute itself expressly or by necessary implication excludes its application, and provides that the mere doing of the act shall call forth the penalty, regardless of the state of mind of the accused. If I am right in this, it remains to be determined whether the appellant in this case can be said to be guilty of the offence charged against him, when it is admitted that no knowledge, or intention, or neglect to take feasible precautions against mistakes, can be imputed to him.

. . .

I am of the opinion that the case at Bar is governed by the authority of *Reg. v. Woodrow.* . . . the same considerations apply, I think, as in that case, and for the same reasons I am forced to the conclusion that the real intent of the section of the Temperance Act, 1917 (Sask.), under which the charge was laid, is to penalise the mere "keeping" or "having" of intoxicating liquors in a stock of soft drinks which are offered for sale to the public. "Soft drinks" or "non-intoxicating liquors" as referred to in the statute are liquors of various sorts, some alcoholic and some non-alcoholic, but containing in the case of the former such a small proportion of alcohol as not to render them intoxicating. Among this variety is beer, which is the specific article dealt with in this case. When the proportion of alcohol in this beer is greater than that allowed by the Act the beer is deemed to be intoxicating, and the merchant who keeps it in stock is guilty of a breach of the Act. Therefore in the case of beer in this Province, it seems to me to be the true intent of the Act that persons who deal in the article are made responsible for its being of a certain quality, namely, not more than 1.13% of alcoholic content, and when they have a too strong alcoholic article in their possession they are liable to the penalty just as the tobacco dealer is liable under the English Tobacco Act when his tobacco is adulterated. It is true that the accused in *Reg. v. Woodrow* could have avoided trouble by having his tobacco analyzed, and that this precaution was not feasible in this case where the beer was purchased and left in bottles, but I do not think that this provided a sufficient distinction to affect the result.

. . .

I think, therefore, that the order of the Chief Justice of the King's Bench should be affirmed, and the appeal dismissed with costs.

*Appeal dismissed.*

### Regina v. Sault Ste. Marie
### (1978), 3 C.R. (3d) 30 (S.C.C.)

The judgment of the court was delivered by

DICKSON J.: — In the present appeal the court is concerned with offences variously referred to as "statutory", "public welfare", "regulatory", "absolute liability", or "strict responsibility", which are not criminal in any real sense but are prohibited in the public interest: *Sherras v. De Rutzen*, [1985] 1 Q.B. 918 (D.C.) Although enforced as penal laws through the utilization of the machinery of the criminal law, the offences are in substance of a civil nature and might well be regarded as a branch of administrative law to which traditional principles of criminal law have but limited application. They relate to such everyday matters as traffic infractions, sales of impure food, violations of liquor laws, and the like. In this appeal we are concerned with pollution.

The doctrine of the guilty mind expressed in terms of intention or recklessness, but not of negligence, is at the foundation of the law of crimes. In the case of true crimes there is a presumption that a person should not be held liable for the wrongfulness of his act if that act is without mens rea: *R. v. Prince* (1875), L.R. 2 C.C.C. 154 (C.C.R.); *R. v. Tolson* (1989), 23 Q.B.D. 168 (C.C.R.); *R. v. Rees*, [1956] S.C.R. 640, 24 C.R. 1, 115 C.C.C. 1, 4 D.L.R. (2d) 406; *Beaver v. R.*, [1957] S.C.R. 531, 26 C.R. 193, 118 C.C.C. 129; *R. v. King*, [1962] S.C.R. 746, 38 C.R. 52, 133 C.C.C. 1, 35 D.L.R. (2d) 386. Blackstone made the point over 200 years ago in words still apt: "to constitute a crime against human law, there must be first a vicious will, and secondly, an unlawful act consequent upon such vicious will": Blackstone's Commentaries, vol 4, p. 21. I would emphasize at the outset that nothing in the discussion which follows is intended to dilute or erode that basic principle.

The appeal raises a preliminary issue as to whether the charge, as laid, is duplicitous and, if so, whether ss. 732(1) and 755(4) [re-en. 1974-75-76, c. 93, s. 94] of the Criminal Code, R.S.C. 1970, c. C-34, preclude the accused city of Sault Ste. Marie from raising the duplicity claim for the first time on appeal. It will be convenient to deal first with the preliminary point and then consider the concept of liability in relation to public welfare offences.

The city of Sault Ste. Marie was charged that it did discharge or cause to be discharged or permitted to be discharged or deposited, materials into Cannon Creek and Root River, or on the shore or bank thereof, or in such place along the side that might impair the quality of the water in Cannon Creek and Root River, between 13th March and 11th September 1972. The charge was laid under s. 32(1) of the Ontario Water Resources Act, R.S.O. 1970, c. 332 [title am. 1972, c. 1, s. 70(1)], which provides so far as relevant, that every municipality or person that discharges or deposits or causes or permits the discharge or deposit of any material of any kind into any water course or on any shore or bank thereof or in any place that may impair the quality of water, is guilty of an offence and, on summary conviction, is liable on first conviction to a fine of not more than $5,000 and on each subsequent conviction of a fine of not more than $10,000 or to imprisonment for a term of not more than one year or to both fine and imprisonment.

Although the facts do not rise above the routine, the proceedings have to date had the anxious consideration of five courts. The city was acquitted in Provincial Court (Criminal Division) but was convicted following a trial de novo on a Crown appeal. A further appeal by the City to the Divisional Court was allowed and the conviction was quashed [30 C.C.C. (2d) at 260]. The Court of Appeal for Ontario on yet another appeal directed a new trial [30 C.C.C. (2d) 257 at 283]. Because of the importance of the legal issues, this court granted leave to the Crown to appeal and leave to the city to cross appeal.

To relate briefly the facts, the city on 18th November 1970 entered into an agreement with Cherokee Disposal and Construction Co. Ltd. for the disposal of all refuse originating in the city. Under the terms of the agreement, Cherokee became obligated to furnish a site and adequate labour, material and equipment. The site selected bordered Cannon Creek which, it would appear, runs into the Root River. The method of disposal adopted is known as the "area" or "continuous slope" method of sanitary land fill, whereby garbage is compacted in layers which are covered each day by natural sand or gravel.

Prior to 1970, the site had been covered with a number of fresh-water springs that flowed into Cannon Creek. Cherokee dumped material to cover and submerge these springs and then placed garbage and wastes over such material. The garbage and wastes in due course formed a high mound sloping steeply toward, and within 20 feet of, the creek. Pollution resulted. Cherokee was convicted of a breach of s. 32(1) of the Ontario Water Resources Act, the section under which the city has been charged. The question now before the court is whether the city is also guilty of an offence under that section.

In dismissing the charge at first instance, the judge found that the city had had nothing to do with the actual disposal operations, that Cherokee was an independent contractor and that its employees were not employees of the city. On the appeal de novo Judge Vannini found the offence to be one of strict liability and he convicted. The Division Court in setting aside the judgment found that the charge was duplicitous. As a secondary point, the Divisional Court also held that the charge required mens rea with respect to causing or permitting a discharge. When the case reached the Court of Appeal that court held that the conviction could not be quashed on the ground of duplicity because there had been no challenge to the information at trial. The Court of Appeal agreed, however, that the charge was one requiring proof of mens rea. A majority of the court (Brooke and Howland JJ.A.) held there was not sufficient evidence to establish mens rea and ordered a new trial. In the view of Lacourciere J.A., dissenting, the inescapable inference to be drawn from the findings of fact of Judge Vannini was the city had known of the potential impairment of waters of Cannon Creek and Root River and had failed to exercise its clear powers of control.

The divers, and diverse, judicial opinions to date on the points under consideration reflect the dubiety in these branches of the law.

. . .

## THE MENS REA POINT

The distinction between the true criminal offence and the public welfare offence is one of prime importance. Where the offence is criminal, the Crown must establish a mental element, namely, that the accused who committed the prohibited act did so intentionally or recklessly, with knowledge of the facts constituting the offence, or with wilful blindness toward them. Mere negligence is excluded from the concept of the mental element required for conviction. Within the context of a criminal prosecution a person who fails to make such inquiries as a reasonable and prudent person would make, or who fails to know facts he should have known, is innocent in the eyes of the law.

In sharp contrast, "absolute liability" entails conviction on proof merely that the defendant committed the prohibited act constituting the actus reus of the offence. There is no relevant mental element. It is no defence that the accused was entirely without fault. He may be morally innocent in every sense yet be branded as a malefactor and punished as such.

Public welfare offences obviously lie in a field of conflicting values. It is essential for society to maintain, through effective enforcement, high standards of public health and safety. Potential victims of those who carry on latently pernicious activities have a strong claim to consideration. On the other hand, there is a generally held revulsion against punishment of the morally innocent.

Public welfare offences evolved in mid-19th century Britain (*R. v. Woodrow* (1846), 15 M. & W. 404, 153 E.R. 907, and *R. v. Stephens* (1986), L.R. 1 Q.B. 702) as a means of doing away with the requirement of mens rea for petty police offences. The concept was a judicial creation, founded on expediency. That concept is now firmly embedded in the concrete of Anglo-American and Canadian jurisprudence, its importance heightened by the ever-increasing complexities of modern society.

Various arguments are advanced in justification of absolute liability in public welfare offences. Two predominate. Firstly, it is argued that the protection of social interests requires a high standard of care and attention on the part of those who follow certain pursuits and such persons are more likely to be stimulated to maintain those standards if they know that ignorance or mistake will not excuse them. The removal of any possible loophole acts, it is said, as an incentive to take precautionary measures beyond what would otherwise be taken in order that mistakes and mishaps be avoided. The second main argument is one based on administrative efficiency. Having regard to both the difficulty of proving mental culpability and the number of petty cases which daily come before the courts, proof of fault is just too great a burden in time and money to place upon the prosecution. To require proof of each person's individual intent would allow almost every violator to escape. This, together with the glut of work entailed in proving mens rea in every case, would clutter the docket and impede adequate enforcement as virtually to nullify the regulatory statutes. In short, absolute liability, it is contended, is the most efficient and effective way of ensuring compliance with minor regulatory legislation and the social ends to be achieved are of such importance as to override the unfortunate by-product of punishing those who may be free of moral turpitude. In further justification, it is urged that slight penalties are usually imposed and that conviction for breach of a public welfare offence does not carry the stigma associated with conviction for a criminal offence.

Arguments of greater force are advanced against absolute liability. The most telling is that it violates fundamental principles of penal liability. It also rests upon assumptions which have not been, and cannot be, empirically established. There is no evidence that a higher standard of care results from absolute liability. If a person is already taking every reasonable precautionary measure, is he likely to take additional measures, knowing that however much care he takes it will not serve as a defence in the event of a breach? If he has exercised care and skill, will conviction have a deterrent effect upon him or others? Will the injustice of conviction lead to cynicism and disrespect for the law, on his part and on the part of others? These are among the questions asked. The argument that no stigma attaches does not withstand analysis, for the accused will have suffered loss of time, legal costs, exposure to the processes of the criminal law at trial and, however one may downplay it, the opprobrium of conviction. It is not sufficient to say that the public interest is engaged and, therefore, liability may be imposed without fault. In serious crimes, the public interest is involved and mens rea must be proven. The administrative argument has little force. In sentencing, evidence of due diligence is admissible and therefore the evidence might just as well be heard when considering guilt. Additionally, it may be noted that s. 198 of the Highway Traffic Act of Alberta, R.S.A. 1970, c. 169, provides that upon a person being charged with an offence under this Act, if the judge trying the case is of the opinion that the offence (a) was committed wholly by accident or misadventure and without negligence and (b) could not by the exercise of reasonable care or precaution have been avoided, the judge may dismiss the case. See also s. 230(2) [am. 1976, c. 62, s. 48] of the Manitoba Highway Traffic Act, R.S.M. 1970, c. H60, which has a similar effect. In these instances at least, the legislature has indicated that administrative efficiency does not foreclose inquiry as to fault. It is also worthy of note that historically the penalty for breach of statutes enacted for the regulation of individual conduct in the interests of health and safety was minor — $20 or $25; today, it may amount to thousands of dollars and entail the possibility of imprisonment for a second conviction. The present case is an example.

Public welfare offences involve a shift of emphasis from the protection of individual interests to the protection of public and social interests: see Sayre, "Public Welfare Offences" (1933), 33 Colum, L. Rev. 55; Hall, "Principles of Criminal Law", [1947] Ch. 13; Perkins, "The Civil Offence" 91952), 100 U. of Pa. L. Rev. 832; Jobson, "Far From Clear" (1975-76), 18 Cr. L.Q. 294. The unfortunate tendency in many past cases has been to see the choice as between two stark alternatives: (i) full mens rea; or (ii) absolute liability. In respect of public welfare offences (within which category pollution offences fall) where full mens rea is not required, absolute liability has often been imposed. English jurisprudence has consistently maintained this dichotomy: see 2 Hals. (4th), para. 18, Criminal Law, Evidence and Procedure. There has, however, been an attempt in Australia, in many Canadian courts, and indeed in England to seek a middle position, fulfilling the goals of public welfare offences while still not punishing the entirely blameless. There is an increasing and impressive stream of authority which holds that where an offence does not require full mens rea, it is nevertheless a good defence for the defendant to prove that he was not negligent.

Dr. Glanville Williams has written: "There is a half-way house between *mens rea* and strict responsibility which has not yet been properly utilized, and that is responsibility for negligence": Criminal Law, The General Part, 2nd ed., p. 262. Morris and Howard in Studies in Criminal Law (1964), p. 200, suggest that strick responsibility might with advantage be replaced by a doctrine of responsibility for negligence strengthened by a shift in the burden of proof. The defendant would be allowed to exculpate himself by proving affirmatively that he was not negligent.

. . .

There have been several cases in Ontario which open the way to acceptance of a defence of due diligence. In *R. v. McIver*, [1965] 2 O.R. 475, 45 C.R. 401, [1965] 4 C.C.C. 182, the Court of Appeal held that the offence charged, namely, careless driving, was one of strict liability but that it was open to an accused to show that he had a reasonable belief in facts which, if true, would have rendered the act innocent. MacKay J.A., who wrote for the court, relied upon *Sherras v. De Rutzen*, supra, *Proudman v. Dayman*, supra, *Maher v. Musson* (1934) 52 C.L.R. 100, and *R. v. Patterson*, [1962] 2 Q.B. 429, 46 Cr. App. R. 106, [1962] 1 All E.R. 340 (C.C.A.), in availing an accused the opportunity of explanation in the case of statutory offences that do not by their terms require proof of intent.

. . .

We have the situation therefore in which many courts of this country, at all levels, dealing with public welfare offences favour: (1) *not* requiring the Crown to prove mens rea; (2) rejecting the notion that liability inexorably follows upon mere proof of the actus reus, excluding any possible defence. The courts are following the lead set in Australia many years ago and tentatively broached by several English courts in recent years.

It may be suggested that the introduction of a defence based on due diligence and the shifting of the burden of proof might better be implemented by legislative act. In answer, it should be recalled that both the concept of absolute liability and the creation of a jural category of public welfare offences are the product of the judiciary and not of the legislature. The development to date of this defence, in the numerous decisions I have referred to of courts in this country as well as in Australia and New Zealand, has also been the work of judges. The present case offers the opportunity of consolidating and clarifying the doctrine.

The correct approach, in my opinion, is to relieve the Crown of the burden of proving mens rea, having regard to *Pierce Fisheries* and to the virtual impossibility in most regulatory cases of proving wrongful intention. In a normal case, the accused alone will have knowledge of what he has done to avoid the breach and it is not improper to expect him to come forward with the evidence of due diligence. This is particularly so when it is alleged, for example, that pollution was caused by the activities of a large and complex corporation. Equally, there is nothing wrong with rejecting absolute liability and admitting the defence of reasonable care.

In this doctrine it is not up to the prosecution to prove negligence. Instead, it is open to the defendant to prove that all due care has been taken. This burden falls upon the defendant as he is the only one who will generally have the means of proof. This would not seem unfair as the alternative is absolute liability which denies an accused any defence whatsoever. While the prosecution must prove beyond a reasonable doubt that the defendant committed the prohibited act, the defendant must only establish on the balance of probabilities that he has a defence of reasonable care.

I conclude, for the reasons which I have sought to express, that there are compelling grounds for the recognition of three categories of offences rather than the traditional two:

1.  Offences in which mens rea, consisting of some positive state of mind such as intent, knowledge, or recklessness, must be proved by the prosecution either as an inference from the nature of the act committed or by additional evidence.
2.  Offences in which there is no necessity for the prosecution to prove the existence of mens rea; the doing of the prohibited act prima facie imports the offence, leaving it open to the accused to avoid liability by proving that he took all reasonable care. This involves consideration of what a reasonable man would have done in the circumstances. The defence will be available if the accused reasonably believed in a mistaken set of facts which, if true, would render the act or omission innocent, or if he took all reasonable steps to avoid the particular event. These offences may properly be called offences of strict liability. Estey C.J.H.C. so referred to them in *Hickey's* case.
3.  Offences of absolute liability where it is not open to the accused to exculpate himself by showing that he was free of fault.

Offences which are criminal in the true sense fall in the first category. Public welfare offences would prima facie be in the second category. They are not subject to the presumption of full mens rea. An offence of this type would fall in the first category only if such words as "wilfully", "with intent", "knowingly" or "intentionally" are contained in the statutory provision creating the offence. On the other hand, the principle that punishment should in general not be inflicted on those without fault applies. Offences of absolute liability would be those in respect of which the legislature had made it clear that guilt would follow proof merely of the proscribed act. The overall regulatory pattern adopted by the legislature, the subject matter of the legislation, the importance of the penalty and the precision of the language used will be primary considerations in determining whether the offence falls into the third category.

## ONTARIO WATER RESOURCES ACT, s. 32(1)

Turning to the subject matter of s. 32(1) — the prevention of pollution of lakes, rivers and streams — it is patent that this is of great public concern. Pollution has always been unlawful and, in itself, a nuisance: *Groat v. Edmonton*, [1928] S.C.R. 522, [1928] 3 D.L.R. 725. A riparian owner has an inherent right to have a stream of water "come to him in its natural state, in flow, quantity and quality": *Chasemore v. Richards* (1859), 7 H.L. Cas. 349 at 382, 11 E.R. 140. Natural streams which formerly afforded "pure and healthy" water for drinking or swimming purposes become little more than cesspools when riparian factory owners and municipal corporations discharge into them filth of all descriptions. Pollution offences are undoubtedly public welfare offences enacted in the interests of public health. There is thus no presumption of a full mens rea.

There is another reason, however, why this offence is not subject to a presumption of mens rea. The presumption applies only to offences which are "criminal in the true sense", as Ritchie J. said in *R. v. Pierce Fisheries*, supra, at p. 278. The Ontario Water Resources Act is a provincial statute. If it is valid provincial legislation (and no suggestions was made to the contrary), then it cannot possibly create an offence which is criminal in the true sense.

. . .

The Divisional Court of Ontario relied on these latter authorities in concluding that s. 32(1) created a mens rea offence.

. . .

One comment on the defence of reasonable care in this context should be added. Since the issue is whether the defendant is guilty of an offence, the doctrine of respondeat superior has no application. The due diligence which must be established is that of the accused alone. Where an employer is charged in respect of an act committed by an employee acting in the course of employment, the question will be whether the act took place without the accused's direction or approval, thus negating wilful involvement of the accused, and whether the accused exercised all reasonable care by establishing a proper system to prevent commission of the offence and by taking reasonable steps to ensure the effective operation of the system. The availability of the defence to a corporation will depend on whether such due diligence was taken by those who are the directing mind and will of the corporation, whose acts are therefore in law the acts of the corporation itself. For a useful discussion of this matter in the context of a statutory defence of due diligence see *Tesco Supermarkets v. Nattrass*, [1972] A.C. 153, [1971] 2 All E.R. 127 (H.L.).

The majority of the Ontario Court of Appeal directed a new trial as, in the opinion of that court, the findings of the trial judge were not sufficient to establish actual knowledge on the part of the city. I share the view that there should be a new trial, but for a different reason. The city did not lead evidence directed to a defence of due diligence, nor did the trial judge address himself to the availability of such a defence. In these circumstances, it would not be fair for this court to determine upon findings of fact directed toward other ends, whether the city was without fault.

I would dismiss the appeal and direct a new trial. I would dismiss the cross-appeal. There should be no costs.

*Appeal and cross-appeal dismissed.*

## Regina v. Burt
### (1988), 38 C.C.C. (3d) 299 (Sask. C.A.)

Appeal by the Crown from the dismissal of its appeal by Gerein J., 21 C.C.C. (3d) 138, 47 C.R. (3d) 49, [1985] 5 W.W.R. 545, 40 Sask. R. 214, 35 M.V.R. 244, from the accused's acquittal on a charge contrary to ss. 141 and 253 of the *Vehicles Act (Sask.)*.

Only the judgment of Wakeling is reproduced below.

WAKELING J.A.: — This appeal places in question whether s. 253 of the *Vehicles Act*, R.S.S. 1978, c. V-3 (the Act), offends s. 7 of the *Canadian Charter of Rights and*

*Freedoms* when it seeks to hold an owner of a vehicle responsible for the actions of the driver of that vehicle.

The facts indicated the respondent is the owner of a vehicle which was being driven, with his permission, by another in such a manner as to create an excessive noise which prompted the laying of a charge under s. 141 of the Act. The identity of the driver was not known, so the charge was laid against the respondent as the owner of the vehicle by virtue of the application of s. 253 of the Act which makes an owner liable for the action of the driver when such actions are in violation of the Act. Section 253 reads:

> **253.** The owner of a motor vehicle, tractor or trailer, other than a public service vehicle, is liable for violation of any provision of this Act in connection with the operation of the motor vehicle, tractor or trailer, unless he proves to the satisfaction of the provincial magistrate or justice of the peace trying the case that at the time of the offence the vehicle, tractor or trailer was not being operated by him, nor by any other person with his consent, express or implied.

The trial judge dismissed the charge on the bass that s. 253 offends s. 7 of the Charter. On appeal, Gerein J. upheld the decision of the trial judge and dismissed the appeal [21 C.C.C. (3d) 138, 47 C.R. (3d) 49, [1985] 5 W.W.R. 545].

The sections of the Charter in question are

> **1.** The *Canadian Charter of Rights and Freedoms* guarantees the rights and freedoms set out in it subject only to such reasonable limits prescribed by law as can be demonstrably justified in a free and democratic society.

> **7.** Everyone has the right to life, liberty and security of the person and the right not to be deprived thereof, except in accordance with the principles of fundamental justice.

It is obvious that s. 253 has created a situation where a person can be convicted of a driving offence under the Act without having anything to do with the driving of the vehicle. The appellant's position is that the establishment of such an offence by mere ownership has the effect of eliminating the need for *mens rea* which is so fundamental a concept in law that its absence constitutes a breach of the principles of fundamental justice.

There have been several cases dealing with the interpretation and application of s. 7 of the Charter with somewhat varied views expressed and results obtained. However, since the argument presented on this appeal, the Supreme Court decision in Reference re s. 94(2) of Motor Vehicle Act (the *B.C. Motor Reference* Case) (1985), 23 C.C.C. (3d) 289, 24 D.L.R. (4th) 536, [1985] 2 S.C.R. 486, has become available, and it has gone far to provide guidance on the interpretation to be given s. 7 of the Charter.

The *B.C. Motor Reference* case dealt with a law which provided that a person who drove a motor vehicle while prohibited from driving or where his licence had been suspended, was guilty of an offence and required to go to prison even though he might not have known he had been prohibited from driving or that his licence had been suspended. It was an absolute liability offence involving a mandatory sentence of imprisonment.

The basic concepts which can be distilled from the Supreme Court judgment include:

1.   That s. 7 enshrines substantive and not merely procedural rights.

2. That the "principles of fundamental justice" referred to in the section do not constitute a protected right, but a qualifier to the protected right not to be deprived of "life, liberty and security of the person"; their function is to set the parameters of that right.

3. That it is not only permissible but appropriate to review the legislation which is being challenged in order to determine whether the legislation offends against the rights established by s. 7.

4. The phrase, "principles of fundamental justice", does not have the same meaning as natural justice. It has a broader meaning that includes an element of substantive right in addition to the concept of procedural fairness which is contemplated in the application of the words "natural justice".

5. That absolute liability in the penal law is contrary to principles of fundamental justice and an absolute liability offence violates s. 7 only if and to the extent it has the potential of depriving one of life, liberty or security of the person (*i.e.*, the penalty of imprisonment is an option open to the trial judge).

6. Administrative expediency will seldom serve as reason for the application of s. 1 of the Charter to save a violation of s. 7.

The question raised by this appeal requires a determination of the application of the above concepts to the facts in this case.

The legislation under review clearly intends that a person may be convicted of an offence even though that person has done nothing wrong. There is no reason to distinguish the situation here where the owner does not know how his vehicle is being operated, yet is responsible for the violations of the driver, from one where an owner is unaware that he has been prohibited from driving or that his licence has been cancelled, yet is guilty of operating the vehicle against the law.

In the *B.C. Motor Reference* case, the point was clearly made that the concept of imprisonment for an absolute liability offence was unacceptable as being contrary to the long-held view against imprisonment of the morally innocent. It then goes further to say that not every absolute liability offence is objectionable but it is if it violates the right to liberty given by s. 7 and that right is violated if the trial judge has the option of imposing imprisonment as a penalty for the offence. Lamer J., dealing with the above, had the following to say at p. 311 C.C.C., p. 515 S.C.R.:

> In my view it is because absolute liability offends the principles of fundamental justice that this Court created presumptions against Legislatures having intended to enact offences of a regulatory nature falling within that category. This is not say, however, and to that extent I am in agreement with the Court of Appeal, that, as a result, absolute liability *per se* offends s. 7 of the Charter. A law enacting an absolute liability offence will violate s. 7 of the Charter only if and to the extent that it has the potential of depriving of life, liberty, or security of the person. Obviously imprisonment (including probation orders) deprives persons of their liberty. An offence has that potential as of the moment it is open to the judge to impose imprisonment. There is no need that imprisonment, as in s. 94(2), be made mandatory.

All of this tends to narrow down the issue in this case rather considerably. If the trial judge was required to impose a sentence of imprisonment or had the option for such a sentence, it seems clear this appeal cannot succeed. The question then remaining is whether in this case, where imprisonment could only occur as the result of the non-payment of a fine, the appeal must likewise fail.

With reference to the application of s. 7, is there a basis to distinguish a sentence which is restricted to payment of a fine, with imprisonment for non-payment, from one where the sentence is for imprisonment in the first instance? To the person in prison, it is of little consequence to have it said the original sentence only required payment of a fine and he is in jail because of his failure to do so. The prisoner will surely be convinced he is in jail because he was found guilty of the original offence and will be inclined to accuse judges and lawyers who say otherwise of exercising their legal skills to distinguish where no real difference exists.

If the penalty of imprisonment or the prospect of imprisonment for the commission of an absolute liability offence is offensive to the principles of fundamental justice referred to in s. 7, it seems logical to conclude that imprisonment for failure to pay a fine for the same offence is also offensive. To conclude otherwise is to draw rather narrow distinctions which the Supreme Court has so far been careful not to do, no doubt for the reason that it prefers to take a broader more purposive approach to the interpretation of the Charter than it has done to other instruments.

An interesting and useful article has recently been published entitled "Imprisonment in Default and Fundamental Justice", 28 Crim. L.Q. p. 251 (1985-86), in which the question of fines and resultant imprisonment for non-payment is discussed. The author seems to generally agree with the views already expressed as the following extract would indicate [p. 264]:

> The courts have already ruled that it is contrary to fundamental justice for the legislature to impose mandatory imprisonment in connection with an offence of absolute liability with no opportunity to explain. It is no less offensive to settled notions of decency to tolerate an administrative practice of imprisonment, not upon proof of some positive act such as driving while licence suspended, but merely upon the happenstance of financial incapacity, a condition that goes to status, not to wilful act or omission.

Having reached the conclusion that this case involves an absolute liability offence and that the prospect for imprisonment for non-payment of a fine brings it within the ambit of the principles drawn from the recent *B.C. Motor Reference* case, it follows that s. 7 of the Charter has been violated.

It is then necessary to consider the possible application of s. 1 of the Charter to determine if the violation of the right might be acceptable by reason that the legislation constitutes "a reasonable limit(s) prescribed by law as can be demonstrably justified in a free and democratic society".

One can readily conclude that the Crown perceives a social benefit in being able to hold a registered owner responsible for the actions of the driver of his vehicle in certain instances such as where identity of the driver is otherwise unavailable. It makes it possible to assess liability for an offence where society's interests are perceived to require some sanction, and makes vehicle owners more aware of the need to be sure their vehicle is in the hands of a responsible driver. If this benefit is categorized as an administrative expediency, then it is useful to consider the following comment of Lamer J. from the *B.C. Motor Reference* case at p. 313 C.C.C., p. 518 S.C.R.:

Administrative expediency, absolute liability's main supportive argument, will undoubtedly under s. 1 be invoked and occasionally succeed. Indeed, administrative expediency certainly has its place in administrative law. But when administrative law chooses to call in aid imprisonment through penal law, indeed sometimes criminal law and the added stigma attached to a conviction, exceptional, in my view, will be the case where the liberty or even the security of the person guaranteed under s. 7 should be sacrificed to administrative expediency, successfully come to the rescue of an otherwise violation of s. 7 but only in cases arising out of exceptional conditions, such as natural disasters, the outbreak of war, epidemics, and the like.

The recent decision of *R. v. Oakes* (1986), 24 C.C.C. (3d) 321, 26 D.L.R. (4th) 200, 65 N.R. 87, has given further guidance on the approach to be taken to the application of s. 1 of the Charter. It has indicated [at p. 348 C.C.C., paraphrase] that the party who alleges its application has the obligation to establish:

(a) the measures responsible for a limit in a Charter right must be of "sufficient importance to warrant overriding a constitutionally protected right or freedom": *R. v. Big M Drug Mart Ltd., supra*, at p. 430 C.C.C., p 366 D.L.R., p. 352 S.C.R.;

(b) and where (a) above has been established, the means chosen are reasonably and demonstrably justified.

The Crown was prepared to stand on the justification for this legislation being self-evident given the object and purpose of the Act and the existence of legislation of a similar nature in other provinces. While there is perhaps more than administrative expediency here, the Crown falls short of meeting the burden which is upon it to justify the violation of the Charter right involved in this case as a result of the application of either of the above-mentioned tests.

For the reasons mentioned, the appeal is dismissed.

*Appeal dismissed.*

## Wholesale Travel Group Inc. v. The Queen
### (1991), 67 C.C.C. (3d) 193 (S.C.C.)

[Excerpts from the judgement of Cory are reproduced below.]

CORY J.: — The fundamental issue raised on this appeal is whether regulatory statutes which impose a regime of strict liability for breach of their provisions infringe ss. 7 and 11(*d*) of the *Canadian Charter of Rights and Freedoms*.

*Factual background and pertinent legislation*

The Wholesale Travel Group Inc. ("Wholesale Travel") was charged with five counts of false or misleading advertising contrary to s. 36(1)(*a*) of the *Competition Act*, R.S.C. 1970, c. C-23. The charges were laid after Wholesale Travel advertised vacation packages at "wholesale prices" while at the same time charging consumers a price higher than the cost incurred by the company in supplying those vacation packages. The matter proceeded to trial in Provincial Court. Before any evidence was heard, Wholesale Travel brought a motion challenging the validity of ss. 36(1) and 37.3(2) of the *Competition Act* on the basis that those sections violate ss. 7 and 11(*d*) of the *Canadian Charter of Rights and Freedoms* and are, therefore, of no force and effect.

The offence of misleading advertising is described in s. 36(1)(*a*) of the *Competition Act*. Although the Act has since been amended, the applicable provisions remain unchanged. I shall, therefore, refer to the old section numbers under which the appellant was charged. Section 36(1)(*a*) (now s. 52(1)(*a*)) reads as follows:

> 36(1) No person shall, for the purpose of promoting, directly or indirectly, the supply or use of a product or for the purpose of promoting, directly or indirectly, any business interest, by any means whatever,
>
> > (*a*) make a representation to the public that is false or misleading in a material respect;

Subsection (5) prescribes the penalties available upon conviction. It states:

> 36(5) Any person who violates subsection (1) is guilty of an offence and is liable
>
> > (*a*) on conviction on indictment, to a fine in the discretion of the court or to imprisonment for five years or to both; or
> > (*b*) on summary conviction, to a fine of twenty-five thousand dollars or to imprisonment for one year or to both.

The Act sets forth a statutory defence to the charge. Section 37.3(2) (now s. 60(2)) provides:

> 37.3(2) No person shall be convicted of an offence under section 36 or 36.1, if he establishes that
>
> > (*a*) the act or omission giving rise to the offence with which he is charged was the result of error;
> > (*b*) he took reasonable precautions and exercised due diligence to prevent the occurrence of such error:
> > (*c*) he, or another person, took reasonable measures to bring the error to the attention of the class of persons likely to have been reached by the representation or testimonial; and
> > (*d*) the measures referred to in paragraph (*c*), except where the representation or testimonial related to a security, were taken forthwith after the representation was made or the testimonial published.

It is important to note that all four conditions must be met before the statutory defence can prevail.

Wholesale Travel contends that the statutory scheme and, in particular, the combined operation of the offence prescribed in s. 36(1)(*a*) and the statutory defence set forth in s. 37.3(2), infringes ss. 7 and 11(*d*) of the Charter. . . .

## Issues

On July 26, 1990, the Chief Justice stated the following constitutional questions:

1. Does s. 37.3(2) of the *Competition Act*, R.S.C. 1970, c. C-23, as amended, in whole or in part violate ss. 7 or 11(*d*) of the *Canadian Charter of Rights and Freedoms*?
2. Does s. 36(1)(*a*) of the *Competition Act*, in and of itself or when read in combination with s. 37.3(2) of the *Competition Act*, violate ss. 7 or 11(*d*) of the *Charter*?

3.   If either question 1 or 2 is answered in the affirmative, is (are) the impugned provision(s) saved by s. 1 of the *Charter*?

## I.  *Regulatory offences and strict liability*

### A.  *The distinction between crimes and regulatory offences*

The common law has long acknowledged a distinction between truly criminal conduct and conduct, otherwise lawful, which is prohibited in the public interest. Earlier, the designations *mala in se* and *mala prohibita* were utilized; today prohibited acts are generally classified as either crimes or regulatory offences.

While some regulatory legislation such as that pertaining to the content of food and drink dates back to the Middle Ages, the number and significance of regulatory offences increased greatly with the onset of the Industrial Revolution. Unfettered industrialization had led to abuses. Regulations were, therefore, enacted to protect the vulnerable — particularly the children, men and women who laboured long hours in dangerous and unhealthy surroundings. Without these regulations many would have died. It later became necessary to regulate the manufactured products themselves and, still later, the discharge of effluent resulting from the manufacturing process. There is no doubt that regulatory offences were originally and still are designed to protect those who are unable to protect themselves. . . .

The distinction between true crimes and regulatory offences was recognized in Canadian law prior to the adoption of the Charter. . . .

The *Sault Ste. Marie* case recognized strict liability as a middle ground between full *mens rea* and absolute liability. Where the offence is one of strict liability, the Crown is required to prove neither *mens rea* nor negligence; conviction may follow merely upon proof beyond a reasonable doubt of the proscribed act. However, it is open to the defendant to avoid liability by proving on a balance of probabilities that all due care was taken. This is the hallmark of the strict liability offence: the defence of due diligence.

Thus, *Sault Ste. Marie* not only affirmed the distinction between regulatory and criminal offences, but also subdivided regulatory offences into categories of strict and absolute liability. The new category of strict liability represented a compromise which acknowledged the importance and essential objectives of regulatory offences but at the same time sought to mitigate the harshness of absolute liability which was found, at p. 363 C.C.C., p. 171 D.L.R., to "violate" "fundamental principles of penal liability".

## *The rationale for the distinction*

It has always been taught that there is a rational basis for distinguishing between crimes and regulatory offences. Acts or actions are criminal when they constitute conduct that is, in itself, so abhorrent to the basic values of human society that it ought to be prohibited completely. Murder, sexual assault, fraud, robbery and theft are all so repugnant to society that they are universally recognized as crimes. At the same time, some conduct is prohibited, not because it is inherently wrongful, but because unregulated activity would result in dangerous conditions being imposed upon members of society, especially those who are particularly vulnerable.

The objective of regulatory legislation is to protect the public or broad segments of the public (such as employees, consumers and motorists, to name but a few) from the potentially adverse effects of otherwise lawful activity. Regulatory legislation involves a shift of emphasis from the protection of individual interests and the deterrence and punishment of acts involving moral fault to the protection of public and societal interests. While criminal offences are usually designed to condemn and punish past, inherently wrongful conduct, regulatory measures are generally directed to the prevention of future harm through the enforcement of minimum standards of conduct and care.

It follows that regulatory offences and crimes embody different concepts of fault. Since regulatory offences are directed primarily not to conduct itself but to the consequences of conduct, conviction of a regulatory offence may be thought to import a significantly lesser degree of culpability than conviction of a true crime. The concept of fault in regulatory offences is based upon a reasonable care standard and, as such, does not imply moral blameworthiness in the same manner as criminal fault. Conviction for breach of a regulatory offence suggests nothing more than that the defendant has failed to meet a prescribed standard of care.

That is the theory but, like all theories, its application is difficult. For example, is the single mother who steals a loaf of bread to sustain her family more blameworthy than the employer who, through negligence, breaches regulations and thereby exposes his employees to dangerous working conditions, or the manufacturer who, as a result of negligence, sells dangerous products or pollutes the air and waters by its plant? At this stage it is sufficient to bear in mind that those who breach regulations may inflict serious harm on large segments of society. Therefore, the characterization of an offence as regulatory should not be thought to make light of either the potential harm to the vulnerable or the responsibility of those subject to regulation to ensure that the proscribed harm does not occur. It should also be remembered that, as social values change, the degree of moral blameworthiness attaching to certain conduct may change as well.

Nevertheless there remains, in my view, a sound basis for distinguishing between regulatory and criminal offences. The distinction has concrete theoretical and practical underpinnings and has proven to be a necessary and workable concept in our law. . . .

B. *The fundamental importance of regulatory offences in Canadian society*

Regulatory measures are the primary mechanisms employed by governments in Canada to implement public policy objectives. What is ultimately at stake in this appeal is the ability of federal and provincial governments to pursue social ends through the enactment and enforcement of public welfare legislation.

Some indication of the prevalence of regulatory offences in Canada is provided by a 1974 estimate by the Law Reform Commission of Canada. The commission estimated that there were, at that time, approximately 20,000 regulatory offences in an average province, plus an additional 20,000 regulatory offences at the federal level.

By 1983, the commission's estimate of the federal total had reached 97,000. There is every reason to believe that the number of public welfare offences at both levels of government has continued to increase.

Statistics such as these make it obvious that the government policy in Canada is pursued principally through regulation. It is through regulatory legislation that the community seeks to implement its larger objectives and to govern itself and the conduct of its members. The ability of the government effectively to regulate potentially harmful conduct must be maintained.

It is difficult to think of an aspect of our lives that is not regulated for our benefit and for the protection of society as a whole. From cradle to grave, we are protected by regulations; they apply to the doctors attending our entry into this world and to the morticians present at our departure. Every day, from waking to sleeping, we profit from regulatory measures which we often take for granted. On rising, we use various forms of energy whose safe distribution and use are governed by regulation. The trains, buses and other vehicles that get us to work are regulated for our safety. The food we eat and the beverages we drink are subject to regulation for the protection of our health. In short, regulation is absolutely essential for our protection and wellbeing as individuals, and for the effective functioning of society. It is properly present throughout our lives. The more complex the activity, the greater the need for and the greater our reliance upon regulation and its enforcement. For example, most people would have no idea what regulations are required for air transport or how they should be enforced. Of necessity, society relies on government regulation for its safety.

## II.  *The offence in the present case*

### *Competition legislation generally*

The offence of misleading advertising with which Wholesale Travel is charged is found in the *Competition Act* (the "Act"). This Act, like its predecessor, the *Combines Investigation Act* is aimed at regulating unacceptable business activity. . .

The nature and purpose of the Act was considered in greater detail in *Thomson Newspapers, supra*. LaForest J. pointed out that the Act is aimed at regulating the economy and business with a view to preserving competitive conditions which are crucial to the operation of a free market economy. . . .

### *The offence of false or misleading advertising*

Is the offence of false or misleading advertising regulatory in nature? It seems to me that the fact that the provision is located within a comprehensive regulatory framework would ordinarily be sufficient to demonstrate its regulatory nature. Several other considerations point to the same conclusion.

The offence of misleading advertising has existed in Canada since 1914. It is not without significance that it was, in 1969, transferred from the *Criminal Code* to the *Combines Investigation Act*, a step which confirms the regulatory nature of the offence. The provision was amended in 1975 to provide for a defence of due diligence, converting the offence from absolute to strict liability.

It is true that the availability of imprisonment as a sanction for breach of a statute might be taken to indicate that the provision is criminal in nature. However, this fact is not itself dispositive of the character of an offence. Rather, one must consider the conduct addressed by the legislation and the purposes for which such conduct is regulated. . . .

The appellant has argued that conviction for the offence of false advertising carries a stigma of dishonesty, with the inference that the accused falsely advertised for the purposes of obtaining economic advantage. It is said that nothing could be more damaging to a business that the implication that it has made dishonest representations. In my view, however, the offence does not focus on dishonesty but rather on the harmful consequences of otherwise lawful conduct. Conviction suggests only that the defendant has made a representation to the public which was in fact misleading and that the defendant was unable to establish the exercise of due diligence in preventing the error. This connotes a fault element of negligence rather than one involving moral turpitude. Thus, any stigma that might flow from a conviction is very considerably diminished.

In summary, the offence of false advertising possesses the essential characteristics which distinguish regulatory offences from those which are truly criminal. Accordingly, it should be considered to be a regulatory offence rather than a crime in the ordinary sense.

### III.  *A contextual approach to Charter interpretation*

#### A.  *The importance of considering Charter rights in context*

. . .

It is now clear that the Charter is to be interpreted in light of the context in which the claim arises. Context is relevant both with respect to the delineation of the meaning and scope of Charter rights, as well as to the determination of the balance to be struck between individual rights and the interests of society.

A contextual approach is particularly appropriate in the present case to take account of the regulatory nature of the offence and its place within a larger scheme of public welfare legislation. This approach requires that the rights asserted by the appellant be considered in light of the regulatory context in which the claim is situated, acknowledging that a Charter right may have different scope and implications in a regulatory context than in a truly criminal one.

Under the contextual approach, constitutional standards developed in the criminal context cannot be applied automatically to regulatory offences. Rather, the content of the Charter right must be determined only after an examination of all relevant factors and in light of the essential differences between the two classes of prohibited activity.

. . .

The contextual approach first requires that the appellant's claim be considered and weighed in light of the realities of a modern industrial society, where the regulation of innumerable activities is essential for the benefit of all. It is vital that the fundamentally important role of regulatory legislation in the protection of individuals and groups in Canadian society today be recognized and accepted. Canadians rely on and expect their governments to regulate and control activities which may be dangerous to others.

. . .

The scale and importance of public welfare legislation in Canada is such that a contextual approach must be taken to the issues raised in this appeal.

### B. *The basis for the differential treatment of regulatory offences*

In the present case, the contextual approach requires that regulatory and criminal offences be treated differently for the purposes of Charter review. Before proceeding to the substantive analysis, however, it is necessary to consider the justifications for differential treatment. They are two-fold: the first relates to the distinctive nature of regulatory activity, while the second acknowledges the fundamental need to protect the vulnerable through regulatory legislation.

### 1. *The licensing justification*

Those who argue against differential treatment for regulatory offences assert that there is no valid reason to distinguish between the criminal and regulatory accused. Each, it is said, is entitled in law to the same procedural and substantive protections. This view assumes equality of position between criminal and regulatory defendants; that is to say, it assumes that each starts out from a position of equal knowledge, volition and "innocence". The argument against differential treatment further suggests that differentiating between the regulatory and criminal defendants implies the subordination and sacrifice of the regulatory accused to the interests of the community at large. Such a position, it is argued, contravenes our basic concern for individual dignity and our fundamental belief in the importance of the individual. It is these assumptions which the licensing justification challenges.

Criminal law is rooted in the concepts of individual autonomy and free will and the corallary that each individual is responsible for his or her conduct. It assumes that all persons are free actors, at liberty to choose how to regulate their own actions in relation to others. The criminal law fixes the outer limits of acceptable conduct, constraining individual freedom to a limited degree in order to preserve the freedom of others. Thus, the basis of criminal responsibility is that the accused person has made a deliberate and conscious choice to engage in activity prohibited by the *Criminal Code*. The accused person who is convicted of an offence will be held responsible for his or her actions, with the result that the opprobrium of society will attach to those acts and any punishment imposed will be considered to be deserved.

The licensing argument is directed to this question of choice. Thus, while in the criminal context, the essential question to be determined is whether the accused has made the choice to act in the manner alleged in the indictment, the regulated defendant is, by virtue of the licensing argument, assumed to have made the choice to engage in the regulated activity. The question then becomes not whether the defendant chose to enter the regulated sphere but whether, having done so, the defendant has fulfilled the responsibilities attending that decision. . . .

The licensing concept rests on the view that those who choose to participate in regulated activities have, in doing so, placed themselves in a responsible relationship to the public generally and must accept the consequences of that responsibility. Therefore, it is said, those who engage in regulated activity should, as part of the burden of responsible conduct attending participation in the regulated field, be deemed to have accepted certain terms and conditions applicable to those who act within the regulated sphere. Foremost among these implied terms is an undertaking that the conduct of the regulated actor will comply with and maintain a certain minimum standard of care.

The licensing justification is based not only on the idea of a conscious choice being made to enter a regulated field but also on the concept of control. The concept is that those persons who enter a regulated field are in the best position to control the harm which may result, and that they should, therefore, be held responsible for it.. . .

The licensing justification may not apply in all circumstances to all offenders. That is, there are some cases in which the licensing argument may not apply so as to permit the imputation to an accused of choice, knowledge and implied acceptance of regulatory terms and conditions. This may occur, for instance, where the nature of the regulated conduct is so innocuous that it would not trigger in the mind of a reasonable person the possibility that the conduct was regulated.

The nature of the regulated conduct will itself go far to determining whether the licensing argument applies. It is useful to distinguish between conduct which, by virtue of its inherent danger or the risk it engenders for others, would generally alert a reasonable person to the probability that the conduct would be regulated, from that conduct which is so mundane and apparently harmless that no thought would ordinarily be given to its potentially regulated nature. In the latter circumstances, the licensing argument would not apply. . . .

By virtue of the decision to enter the regulated field, the regulated person (here the appellant) can be taken to have accepted certain terms and conditions of entry. To paraphrase LaForest J., the procedural and substantive protections a person can reasonably expect may vary depending upon the activity that brings that person into contact with the state. Thus, the extent of Charter protection may differ depending upon whether the activity in question is regulatory or criminal in nature.

In this way, the licensing argument provides a link between the distinction between criminal and regulatory offences and the differential treatment of those two categories for the purposes of Charter review. There is, as well, a second justification for differential treatment.

## 2. *The vulnerability justification*

The realities and complexities of a modern industrial society couples with the very real need to protect all of society and particularly its vulnerable members, emphasize the critical importance of regulatory offences in Canada today. Our country simply could not function without extensive regulatory legislation. The protection provided by such measures constitutes a second justification for the differential treatment, for Charter purposes, of regulatory and criminal offences. . . .

Regulatory legislation is essential to the operation of our complex industrial society; it plays a legitimate and vital role in protecting those who are most vulnerable and least able to protect themselves. The extent and importance of that role has increased continuously since the onset of the Industrial Revolution. Before effective workplace legislation was enacted, labourers — including children — worked unconscionably long hours in dangerous and unhealthy surroundings that evoke visions of Dante's *Inferno*. It was regulatory legislation with its enforcement provisions which brought to an end the shameful situation that existed in mines, factories and workshops in the nineteenth century. The differential treatment of regulatory offences is justified by their common goal of protecting the vulnerable. . . .

It follows that a contextual approach is required in the present case in order that the distinctive nature of regulatory offences and their fundamental importance in Canadian society may be considered. Both licensing and the vulnerability considerations justify differential treatment, for the purposes of Charter interpretation, of crimes and regulatory offences. This, then, is the basis upon which the present case must be approached.

### IV. *The constitutionality of strict liability*

The appellant argues that strict liability violates the Charter on two bases. First, it is said that, at least where imprisonment is available as a sanction, s. 7 of the Charter requires a minimum fault element of guilty intent or wilful blindness to be proven; it is argued that, under s. 7, negligence is an insufficient degree of fault to justify a conviction. Secondly, the appellant alleges that the traditional requirement in strict liability offences that the defendant establish due diligence on a balance of probabilities violates the presumption of innocence guaranteed by s. 11(*d*) of the Charter. Let us consider these submissions.

### A. *Section 7: the mens rea issue*

Wholesale Travel contends that wherever imprisonment is available as a penalty for breach of a regulatory statute, the failure to require the Crown to prove guilty intent as an essential element of the offence violates s. 7 of the Charter. It is constitutionally impermissible, it is argued, to impose liability on the basis of lack of reasonable care. Thus, it is the appellant's position that strict liability as defined in *Sault Ste. Marie* has been superseded and rendered invalid by the Charter. The appellant's argument, if accepted, would eliminate any distinction between criminal and regulatory offences.

The question to be determined at this stage is what level of *mens rea* is required by s. 7 of the Charter. . . .

What emerges from *Reference re: s. 94(2) of Motor Vehicle Act* and *Vaillancourt* is that the principles of fundamental justice referred to in s. 7 of the Charter prohibit the imposition of penal liability and punishment without proof of fault. Fault was, thus, elevated from a presumed element of an offence in *Sault Ste. Marie* to a constitutionally required element under the Charter. These cases did not, however, decide what level of fault is constitutionally required for every type of offence; rather, they make it clear that the degree of fault required will vary with the nature of the offence and the penalties available upon conviction. *Reference re: s. 94(2) of Motor Vehicle Act* does establish, however, that where imprisonment is available as a penalty, absolute liability cannot be imposed since it removes the fault element entirely and, in so doing, permits the punishment of the morally innocent.

The question which must now be determined is as follows: in situations where imprisonment is available as a penalty, does s. 7 require proof of a degree of fault greater than negligence? That is to say, must a positive mental state be established in order to justify a conviction? . . .

Does s. 7 require in all cases that the Crown prove *mens rea* as an essential element of the offence? The resolution of this question requires that a contextual approach be taken to the meaning and scope of the s. 7 right. Certainly, there can be no doubt that s. 7 requires proof of some degree of fault. That fault may be demonstrated by proof of intent, whether subjective or objective, or by proof of negligent conduct, depending on the nature of the offence. While it is not necessary in this case to determine the requisite degree of fault necessary to prove the commission of particular crimes, I am of the view that with respect to regulatory offences, proof of negligence satisfies the requirement of fault demanded by s. 7. Although the element of fault may not be removed completely, the demands of s. 7 will be met in the regulatory context where liability is imposed for conduct which breaches the standard of reasonable care required of those operating in the regulated field.

It should not be forgotten that *mens rea* and negligence are both fault elements which provide a basis for the imposition of liability. *Mens rea* focuses on the mental state of the accused and requires proof of a positive mental state of mind such as intent, recklessness or wilful blindness. Negligence, on the other hand, measures the conduct of the accused on the basis of an objective standard, irrespective of the accused's subjective mental state. Where negligence is the basis of liability, the question is not what the accused intended but rather whether the accused exercised reasonable care. The application of the contextual approach suggests that negligence is an acceptable basis of liability in the regulatory context which fully meets the fault requirement in s. 7 of the Charter.

It is argued, however, that to place regulatory offences in a separate category from criminal offences, with a lower fault standard, puts the accused charged with the breach of a regulatory provision in a fundamentally unfair position. It is a violation of the principles of fundamental justice under s. 7, it is said to allow the defendant to go to jail without having had the protection available in criminal prosecutions — that is, proof of *mens rea* by the Crown.

I cannot accept this contention. Regulatory offences provide for the protection of the public. The societal interests which they safeguard are of fundamental importance. It is absolutely essential that governments have the ability to enforce a standard of reasonable care in activities affecting public welfare. The laudable objectives served by regulatory legislation should not be thwarted by the application of principles developed in another context.

It must be remembered that regulatory offences were historically developed and recognized as a distinct category precisely for the purpose of relieving the Crown of the burden of proving *mens rea*. This is their hallmark. The tremendous importance of regulatory legislation in modern Canadian industrial society requires that courts be wary of interfering unduly with the regulatory role of government through the application of inflexible standards. Under the contextual approach, negligence is properly acceptable as the minimum fault standard required of the regulatory legislation by s. 7.

What some writers have referred to as "licensing" considerations lead to the same conclusion. The regulated actor is allowed to engage in activity which potentially may cause harm to the public. That permission is granted on the understanding that the actor accept, as a condition of entering the regulated field, the responsibility to exercise reasonable care to ensure that the proscribed harm does not come about. As a result of choosing to enter a field of activity known to be regulated, the regulated actor is taken to be aware of and to have accepted the imposition of a certain objective standard of conduct as a pre-condition of being allowed to engage in the regulated activity. In these circumstances, it misses the mark to speak in terms of the "unfairness" of an attenuated fault requirement because the standard of reasonable care has been accepted by the regulated actor upon entering the regulated sphere.

Further, from a practical point of view, it is simply impossible for the government to monitor adequately every industry so as to be able to prove actual intent or *mens rea* in each case. In order to do so, governments would have to employ armies of experts in every conceivable field. For example, it would be necessary to continuously monitor a myriad of complex activities that are potentially dangerous to members of society. Such activities include manufacturing and mining procedures, food and drug manufacturing, processing and packaging.

In our complex society, the government can, as a practical matter, do no more than to demonstrate that it has set reasonable standards to be met by persons in the regulated sphere and to prove beyond a reasonable doubt that there has been a breach of those standards by the regulated defendant. . . .

For these reasons, I conclude that the appellant's claim that strict liability offences violate s. 7 of the Charter cannot succeed. The requirements of s. 7 are met in the regulatory context by the imposition of liability based on a negligence standard. Therefore, no violation of s. 7 results from the imposition of strict liability.

B. *Section 11(d): onus and the due diligence defence*

Wholesale Travel argues that the placing of a persuasive burden on the accused to establish due diligence on a balance of probability violates the presumption of innocence as guaranteed by s. 11(*d*) of the Charter. As the due diligence defence is the essential characteristic of strict liability offences as defined in *Sault Ste. Marie*, the appellant's s. 11(*d*) claim represents a fundamental challenge to the entire regime of regulatory offences in Canada. . . .

This court has recently considered the meaning of the presumption of innocence in the criminal context, particularly as applied to reverse onus provisions. It is now clear that it is the net effect of a reverse onus provision on the determination of the guilt or innocence of an accused rather than the precise nature of the provision that must be examined under s. 11(*d*). . . .

What must now be determined is whether the s. 11(*d*) standard which has been developed and applied in the criminal context should be applied to regulatory offences.

## The content of the presumption in the regulatory context

Much of what has been said in regard to the validity of strict liability under s. 7 of the Charter is applicable as well to the s. 11(*d*) question of onus. The importance of regulatory legislation and its enforcement strongly support the use of a contextual approach in the interpretation of the s. 11(*d*) right as applied to regulatory offences. . . .

The reasons for ascribing a different content to the presumption of innocence in the regulatory context are persuasive and compelling. As with the *mens rea* issue, if regulatory mechanisms are to operate effectively, the Crown cannot be required to disprove due diligence beyond a reasonable doubt. Such a requirement would make it virtually impossible for the Crown to prove regulatory offences and would effectively prevent governments from seeking to implement public policy through regulatory means.

It has been suggested that requiring the Crown to prove negligence beyond a reasonable doubt, either as part of its case or after the accused adduces some evidence raising a reasonable doubt as to due diligence, would represent an acceptable compromise: it would, it is said, lessen the burden on the accused while still allowing for the effective pursuit of the regulatory objective. I cannot accept this contention. While such an approach would undoubtedly be beneficial to the accused, it would effectively eviscerate the regulatory power of government by rendering the enforcement of regulatory offences impossible in practical terms. Under this approach, the Crown would be forced to prove lack of reasonable care where the accused raises a reasonable doubt as to the possibility of due diligence.

It is difficult to conceive of a situation in which a regulated accused would not be able to adduce *some* evidence giving rise to the possibility that due diligence was exercised. For instance, an environmental polluter would often be able to point to *some* measures it had adopted in order to prevent the type of harm which ultimately resulted. This might raise a reasonable doubt that it had acted with due diligence no matter how inadequate those measures were for the control of a dangerous situation. . . .

Thus, the question is not whether the accused has exercised *some* care, but whether the degree of care exercised was sufficient to meet the standard imposed. If the false advertiser, the corporate polluter and the manufacturer of noxious goods are to be effectively controlled, it is necessary to require them to show on a balance of probabilities that they took reasonable precautions to avoid the harm which actually resulted. In the regulatory context, there is nothing unfair about imposing that onus: indeed, it is essential for the protection of our vulnerable society. . . .

Nor can I accept the contention that there is little practical difference between requiring the accused to prove due diligence on a balance of probabilities and requiring only that the accused raise a reasonable doubt as to the exercise of due diligence. Professor Webb, in his article, *ibid.*, deals with this argument in the following terms, at p. 467:

> Some might argue that in practice there is no workable distinction between an offence which requires the accused to prove due diligence on the balance of probabilities to avoid conviction, and one that permits the accused to raise a reasonable doubt as to the existence of due diligence. Trial judges will find a way to convict those whom they feel are guilty of negligence, the argument would go, regardless of   burdens of proof. This type of reasoning certainly contradicts the statement of the trial judge in *Whyte, [supra]*, who contended that in the absence of a balance of probability presumption, he would have found reasonable doubt as to whether the accused had "care and control" of a motor vehicle.

Webb then goes on, at p. 467, to identify the deleterious effects on prosecution of regulatory offences which would result from requiring the Crown to prove negligence:

> The "there is no difference in practice anyway" argument also fails to recognize the different quantity and quality of evidence which administrators would be forced to provide to prosecutors in preparation for a case. If an evidential rather than a persuasive burden is adopted, merely raising a reasonable doubt as to the existence of due diligence would then shift the burden of proof to the prosecutors to *prove negligence*. Prior to any case reaching the prosecution stage, administrators would be under an obligation to collect all the evidence necessary to prove negligence. In effect, prosecutors would be more likely to turn down a request from administrators for a prosecution unless proof of negligence could be established. Given the difficulty in accumulating such information, it is not unlikely that there would be a chilling effect on use of the prosecution mechanism. Once it became noticeable that less cases were reaching the courts, it is possible that regulatees would receive the signal that, in most·circumstances, the offence of negligence was not enforceable.

(Emphasis in original.)

I agree with these conclusions of Professor Webb. To reduce the onus on the accused would, from a practical point of view, raise insurmountable barriers for the Crown seeking to enforce a regulatory scheme.

In these circumstances, it cannot be contended that requiring the prosecution to prove negligence beyond a reasonable doubt would still allow for the effective achievement of regulatory objectives. To the contrary, its effect would be, in practical terms, to render the regulatory power of governments ineffectual.

Nor can it be argued that other solutions would be satisfactory; there is simply no other practical solution. Both with respect to the consumption of government resources and the intrusiveness of regulatory measures, the consequences of a finding that the due diligence defence violates s. 11(*d*) of the Charter would be extremely severe. Governments would be forced to devote tremendous expenditure, in terms of monetary and human resources, to regulatory enforcement mechanisms. Armies of investigators and experts would be required in order to garner sufficient evidence to establish negligence or disprove due diligence beyond a reasonable doubt.

Further, a marked expansion in enforcement mechanisms by definition implies an escalation in the intrusiveness of regulatory measures. The greater the burden of proof on the Crown, the greater the likelihood that those charged with the enforcement of regulatory measures would have to resort to legislation authorizing search and surveillance in order to gather sufficient evidence to discharge that onus.

As with the s. 7 challenge, licensing considerations support the conclusion that strict liability does not violate s. 11(*d*) of the Charter. The licensing argument attributes to the regulated actor knowledge and acceptance, not only of the standard of reasonable care itself, but also of the responsibility to establish on a balance of probabilities the exercise of reasonable care. Acceptance of this burden is an implied term and a precondition of being allowed to engage in activity falling within the regulated sphere. Regulated actors are taken to understand that, should they be unable to discharge this burden, an inference of negligence will be drawn from the fact that the proscribed result has occurred.

I wish to emphasize, however, that the difference in the scope and meaning of s. 11(*d*) in the regulatory context does not imply that the presumption of innocence is meaningless for a regulated accused. The Crown must still prove the *actus reus* of regulatory offences beyond a reasonable doubt. Thus, the Crown must prove that the accused polluted the river, sold adulterated food, or published a false advertisement. However, once having established this beyond a reasonable doubt, the Crown is presumptively relieved of having to prove anything further. Fault is presumed from the bringing about of the proscribed result, and the onus shifts to the defendant to establish reasonable care on a balance of probabilities.

For these reasons, I conclude that the presumption of innocence as guaranteed in s. 11(*d*) of the Charter is not violated by strict liability offences as defined in *Sault Ste. Marie*. The imposition of a reverse persuasive onus on the accused to establish due diligence on a balance of probabilities does not run counter to the presumption of innocence, notwithstanding the fact that the same reversal of onus would violate s. 11(*d*) in the criminal context.

## C. *The imprisonment concern*

Much has been made in this appeal of the potential use of imprisonment as a sanction for breach of strict liability offences. The Chief Justice considers the use of imprisonment to be determinative of the Charter analysis. With respect, I am unable to agree. The availability of imprisonment in no way alters my conclusion that strict liability does not violate either ss. 7 or 11(*d*) of the Charter.

The Charter does not guarantee an absolute right to liberty: rather, it guarantees the right not to be deprived of liberty except in accordance with the principles of fundamental justice. Thus, while the availability of imprisonment undoubtedly triggers Charter review, it does not resolve the ultimate question. What must be determined is whether, in a given case, the possibility of a sentence of imprisonment comports with the principles of fundamental justice. It is whether the principles of fundamental justice have been violated, not the availability of imprisonment, which is the determinative consideration. . . .

The ultimate question is whether the imposition of imprisonment on the basis of strict liability comports with the principles of fundamental justice. For the reasons set out earlier concerning the underlying rationale of regulatory offences, I am of the opinion that it does.

Regulatory schemes can only be effective if they provide for significant penalties in the event of their breach. Indeed, although it may be rare that imprisonment is sought, it must be available as a sanction if there is to be effective enforcement of the regulatory measure. Nor is the imposition of imprisonment unreasonable in light of the danger than can accrue to the public from breaches of regulatory statutes.

. . .

### E. *Section 1*

In light of my conclusion regarding the appellant's ss. 7 and 11(*d*) claims, there is no need to proceed to s. 1. However, had it been necessary to consider the matter, the same reasons I have set forth in finding that neither ss. 7 nor 11(*d*) are necessarily infringed by strict liability offences would have led me to conclude that strict liability offences can be justified under s. 1 of the Charter.

### V. *Application to s. 36(1)(a) and s. 37.3(2)*

Section 36(1)(*a*) of the *Competition Act* creates the offence of false or misleading advertising. Section 37.3(2) provides a statutory defence to that charge. The defence will only lie where all four conditions set out in paras. (*a*) through (*d*) are met. While paras. (*a*) and (*b*) in essence describe the common law defence of due diligence, paras, (*c*) and (*d*) create additional conditions which must be met before the defence will lie.

### *The validity of paras. (c) and (d) of s. 37.3(2)*

Paragraph (*c*) of s. 37.3(2) requires an accused who has made a misleading representation to take positive steps to bring the error to the attention of those to be likely affected by it. Paragraph (*d*) requires this to be done promptly. The effect of these provisions is to impose an obligation on the accused to make a prompt retraction as a precondition to relying on the defence of due diligence.

The Court of Appeal unanimously held that paras. (*c*) and (*d*) of s. 37.3(2) may in some circumstances require conviction where there is no fault on the part of the accused. I agree with this conclusion. Even where an accused can establish the absence of negligence in the making of misleading representations, paras. (*c*) and (*d*) none the less require conviction if the accused has failed to make a prompt correction or retraction. In these circumstances, the accused would be deprived of the defence of due diligence and the offence would be tantamount to absolute liability, since liability could be imposed in the absence of fault on the part of the accused.

Such a result clearly violates s. 7 of the Charter. As Lamer J. stated in *Reference re" ss: 94(2) of Motor Vehicle Act, supra*, at p. 293 C.C.C., p. 541 D.L.R.:

> A law that has the potential to convict a person who has not really done anything wrong offends the principles of fundamental justice and, if imprisonment is available as a penalty, such a law then violates a person's right to liberty under s. 7 of the *Canadian Charter of Rights and Freedoms*.

Nor do I think that paras. (*c*) and (*d*) can be justified under s. 1 of the Charter. The Crown has filed little evidence to support its position that paras. (*c*) and (*d*) can be saved by s. 1. Perhaps this is itself a sufficient basis for finding that those paragraphs are not justifiable.

There are, however, additional grounds for reaching this conclusion. Assuming that there is a rational connection between the requirement of corrective advertising and the legislative objective of seeking to prevent the harm resulting from misleading representations, it cannot be said that the impugned provisions constitute a minimal impairment of the rights of the accused. Further, the availability of imprisonment as a sanction far outweighs the importance of the regulatory objective in correcting false advertising after the fact. In short, there is no proportionality between means and ends. Paragraphs (c) and (d) cannot then be justified under s. 1 of the Charter.

## The validity of paras. (a) and (b)

These paragraphs in essence put forward the common law defence of due diligence. Where imprisonment is available as a penalty for breach of a statute, s. 7 of the Charter requires proof of fault before liability can be imposed. I have concluded, however, that the fault requirement is different for regulatory than for criminal offences. In the regulatory context, it is appropriate that fault should be imposed on the basis of negligence. There is, therefore, no violation of s. 7 resulting from the removal of the *mens rea* requirement in strict liability offences. It follows that paras. (a) and (b) of s. 37.3(2 do not violate s. 7 of the Charter.

It has been noted earlier that the s. 11(d) presumption of innocence has a different scope and meaning in relation to regulatory as opposed to criminal offences. In my view, the imposition in strict liability offences of a reverse persuasive onus on the accused to establish due diligence is proper and permissible and does not constitute a violation of the s. 11(d) and presumption of innocence. I, therefore, conclude that paras. (a) and (b) of s. 37.3(2) do not violate s. 11(d) of the Charter.

## VI. *Conclusion*

Strict liability offences, as exemplified in this case by the combination of s. 36(1)(a) and s. 37.3(2)(a) and (b) of the *Competition Act*, do not violate either ss. 7 or 11(d) of the Charter. Neither the absence of a *mens rea* requirement nor the imposition of an onus on the accused to establish due diligence on a balance of probabilities offends the Charter of rights of those accused of regulatory offences.

Regulatory legislation is essential to the functioning of our society and to the protection of the public. It responds to the compelling need to protect the health and safety of the members of our society and to preserve our fragile environment. The imposition of strict liability is both reasonable and essential to the operation of regulatory schemes.

## VII. *Disposition*

Since paras. (c) and (d) of s. 37.3(2) of the *Competition Act* violate s. 7 of the Charter and cannot be justified under s. 1, they must be struck down and declared to be of no force or effect. What remains in s. 36(1)(a) and s. 37.3(2)(a) and (b) is a strict liability regulatory offence. These provisions are valid and enforceable. In the result I would dismiss the appeal and allow the Crown's Appeal to the extent required to reflect this disposition.

*Appeal by accused dismissed; appeal by Crown allowed in part.*

## Questions/Discussion

1. What is the distinction between strict and absolute liability offences, and do you think the distinction is a valid one? What are the policy reasons given in *Sault Ste. Marie* to justify the categories? Do you agree with them? What problems remain after the case? For example, if public welfare offences are not "true crimes", then why do we continue to treat them as such and process offenders within the criminal justice system? Now that a defence is possible, might the courts be more likely to require less than a full mens rea?

2. Do you think that the possibility of a defence of due diligence will give companies an incentive to take preventive measures? Also, should the "reasonableness" of the steps taken be judged differently for corporations versus individuals, or for those who are engaged in profit-making versus others? Is there an argument that those who profit should have a higher standard of due diligence to meet that those who do not profit from the activity?

3. There has been a concern raised that the new categorization will make it more difficult to prosecute polluters successfully; see the Jeffery article listed below. The concern is that standards of care or due diligence will be set by the polluters themselves because they have knowledge of, and expertise in, the industry's practices — advantages which the courts and prosecutors lack.

4. What is the effect of the Charter in this area as seen in the *Burt* and *Wholesale* cases. Do you agree with the way the Charter is being used in this area of criminal law? Why or why not?

## Further Reading

- Hutchinson, A., "*Sault Ste. Marie, Mens Rea* and The Halfway House: Public Welfare Offences Get a Home of Their Own" (1979), 17 Osgoode Hall Law Journal 415.
- Jeffrey, M., "Environmental Enforcement and Regulation in the 1980's: *Regina v. Sault Ste. Marie* Revisited" (1984), 10 Queen's Law Journal 43.
- Mewett, A. and M. Manning, *Mewett and Manning on Criminal Law, 3rd ed.* (Markham: Butterworths, 1994).
- Richardson, G. "Strict Liability for Regulatory Crime: the Empirical Research", [1987] Criminal Law Review 295.
- Roach, Kent, *Criminal Law, 2d ed.* (Toronto: Irwin Law, 2000) at 164-182.
- Ruby, C. and K. Jull, "The Charter and Regulatory Offences: A Wholesale Revision" (1992) 14 Criminal Reports (4th) 226-44.
- Stuart, Don, and R. Delisle, *Learning Canadian Criminal Law, 8th ed.* (Toronto: Carswell, 2001).
- Verdun-Jones, S., *Criminal Law in Canada: Cases, Questions and the Code, 3d ed.* (Toronto: Harcourt Canada, 2002).

## 6.2   INCOMPLETE OFFENCES

### 6.2.1   Attempts

**Introduction**

The issues surrounding attempts in the criminal law arise due to the fact that the intended object of the person's criminal intent was not completed, yet one tends to think in terms of a fully completed act. Conceptually, it is problematic because ordinarily in the criminal law the state is attaching liability for the action *and* the wrongful intent; in attempts, that action has been halted or thwarted at some stage before the completion of the act for a variety of possible reasons. For example, D may plan to rob a bank, may buy the gun she intends to use and map out her getaway route. However, on the chosen day, D may decide to abort the plan for any number of reasons. She may decide to give up a life of crime and pursue another career, or she may merely decide to try out her plan on another day. In the alternative, D may arrive at the scene of the planned crime and discover that the bank is closed due to a holiday, that police are present in the area of the bank, or perhaps that the target bank has closed permanently. In which of these situations should D be guilty of attempted robbery? In any one of them? In all of them? Or do we have enough information? For example, was D on her way into the bank when she changed her mind or was she merely getting up on the morning of the planned robbery when she had a change of heart or of plan? Was she headed into the bank when she saw the police in the vicinity and decided to abort her plan?

This type of information is often crucial because an attempt takes place before the completion of the intended crime. Therefore, the courts have to decide at what point in time the attempt is complete and liability will attach for an attempted crime; in other words, they decide what constitutes a valid actus reus in attempts. Obviously, the courts will not wait until the full crime has been completed before saying the police can intervene, for that approach would destroy the preventative ideal behind the concept of attempts. But at what point does liability occur? The courts in Canada, following the wording in section 24 of the Criminal Code, the principal "attempts" provision, say that an attempt is complete if the accused's acts have gone beyond "mere preparation". As for what is "mere preparation" and therefore attracting no penal consequences versus what is beyond preparation and consequently an attempt which is subject to sanction, the answer depends upon the facts of each case. The cases of *Sorrell* and *Bondett* and *Deutsch* provide examples of where (and why) the courts will find a valid attempt in differing fact situations.

Another issue in this area is that of "impossibility", the situation where the actus reus of the completed offence is impossible to complete under the circumstances. Examples here include the case of *Scott* below where the pickpocket attempted to steal from an empty pocket; they also include the situation where D tries to kill someone who is already dead but D does not know it, or the situation where D tries to kill someone by sticking pins in a model of that person. Should the law excuse impossible attempts and if so why? Section 24 states that a criminal attempt is made "whether or not it was possible under the circumstances to commit the offence", and this has been taken to mean that all types of impossible attempts are criminal regardless of the reason for the impossibility. Some jurisdictions have tried to distinguish between types of impossible attempts (legally versus physically impossible) and the *Smith* case below is an example of that sort of reasoning. Brown's article presents a full discussion of the issues in this area. Do you think such distinctions are valid or useful, particularly if one purpose of attempts is to discourage the individual from trying again and considering that the accused is being convicted for his or her wrongful intent to do the crime coupled with overt actions towards completing it? Should we reward the incompetent or the stupid when they attempt impossible criminal ends or when they use impossible means to accomplish their goals? Of course, if we look at the penalty provisions for attempts in section 463 it might be argued that those who fail in their criminal purpose are indeed being rewarded with lower maximum penalties in most cases. If liability attaches essentially for the evil purpose, then why are the maximum penalties not the same as if the accused was successful?

Another issue is raised in the situation where the accused has abandoned the criminal purpose for "good", altruistic reasons (for example, where the accused has realized the wrongfulness of his or her ways and decides to reject the criminal purpose). What is the argument for punishment in such cases? Under the current law, once an attempt has been made, it cannot be abandoned in the legal sense and liability will still attach, though the sentence will likely be more lenient. The rationale is that once a crime of any type has been committed, it cannot be "disowned" by the perpetrator, and that this is as true for attempts as for any other crime.

A final point about the actus reus of attempts is that in regard to certain offences, it is difficult to envisage attempts of them being made. We see this in criminal negligence (sections 219-221), for example, where it is difficult to comprehend situations where someone attempts to be negligent, or in offences involving being a found-in in a common gaming house (section 201) or a found-in in a common bawdy-house (section 210). Also, in strict and absolute liability offences it is difficult to see liability attaching for an attempt, if not because such fact situations are hard to conceive, then because the courts would be reluctant on policy grounds to extend liability for these types of offences too far. And attempts are just that, extensions of criminal liability to include acts which have yet to culminate in a full offence.

In general, the mens rea of an attempt is the intent to commit the full offence, but in certain crimes this may not be appropriate. The *Ancio* case is an example of this problem where the court attached a narrow mens rea to the crime of attempted murder, specifically an intent to kill. This intent is narrower than the intention which is sometimes sufficient in certain types of the full murder offences. Given the murder provisions in the Code, and the fact that attempts are one step removed from the full offence, the courts are perhaps justly concerned about extending liability too far. In a similar vein, there is a reluctance to put two incomplete crimes "together", for example in "attempted counselling" or "counselling conspiracy", due to a fear that this would result in extending criminal liability too far from the completed offence.[1]

## Regina v. Deutsch
### (1986), 52 C.R. (3d) 305 (S.C.C.)

Appeal by accused from judgment of Ontario Court of Appeal, 5 C.C.C. (3d) 41, reversing accused's acquittal of attempting to procure females for illicit intercourse with other persons, and ordering new trial.

[Only the judgment of LeDain is reproduced below. Also, this is a case where the appellant represented himself before the Supreme Court, a situation which rarely happens.]

LEDAIN J. (BEETZ, McINTYRE and WILSON JJ. concurring): — This appeal [from 5 C.C.C (3d) 41], which involves a charge of attempting to procure a person to have illicit sexual intercourse with another person contrary to s. 195(1)(a) of the Criminal Code, raises two issues: the distinction between attempt and mere preparation, and the meaning of "illicit sexual intercourse".

The appeal is from the judgment of the Ontario Court of Appeal on 17th March 1983 setting aside the acquittal of the appellant by Graburn Co. Ct. J. on 13th August 1982 of the charge of attempting to procure a person to have illicit sexual intercourse with another person and ordering a new trial of the appellant on that charge.

. . .

During the period covered by the indictment, which is the three months ending on or about 3rd September 1981, the appellant was carrying on a business known as "Global Franchises Marketing", which was engaged in selling franchises of various kinds. During this period the appellant placed an advertisement in newspapers in Ottawa, Hamilton and Toronto inviting applications for the position of secretary/sales assistant and conducted interviews with three women who responded to the advertisement and with a police officer who posed as an applicant for the position and recorded the interview on a tape-recorder. The advertisement read as follows:

---

ENJOY TRAVEL

Secretary-Sales Assistant to Sales Executive, $600-$800 per month to start plus commission, bonuses, company benefits and expenses. Must be free to travel extensively. Call 746-2440 ask for Mel.

---

In the interviews the appellant indicated that a secretary/sales assistant would be expected to have sexual intercourse with clients or potential clients of the company where that appeared to be necessary to conclude a contract. The appellant also indicated that a successful secretary/sales assistant could earn as much as $100,000 per

---

1   See, under "Further Reading", references to "Attempts" in Mewett and Manning or Stuart and Delisle.

year through commission or bonus on the sale of franchises. The appellant did not make an offer of employment to the three applicants who testified at his trial. After hearing what the position required they said they were not interested and the interviews were terminated. Nor did he make an offer of employment to the police officer who posed as an applicant, but when she told him she was interested in the position despite its requirements he told her to think it over and let him know.

The appellant was tried upon an indictment containing two counts: attempting to procure female persons to become common prostitutes, and attempting to procure female persons to have illicit intercourse with another person. Graburn Co. Ct. J. acquitted the appellant on both counts. He found that the appellant intended that a person hired for the position should have sexual relations with clients or potential clients, but he held, as a matter of law, that the acts of statements of the appellant did not, in the absence of an offer of employment, constitute the actus reus of an attempt to procure. In his opinion they were mere preparation. He accordingly did not find it necessary to decide whether the sexual intercourse contemplated by the appellant would be illicit sexual intercourse within s. 195(1)(a) or make those who engaged in it common prostitutes within s. 195(1)(d), as it then read.

The Ontario Court of Appeal (Martin, Houlden and Robins JJ.A.) dismissed the appeal from the acquittal on the charge of attempting to procure female persons to become common prostitutes, but allowed the appeal from the acquittal on the charge of attempting to procure female persons to have illicit sexual intercourse with another person and directed a new trial of the appellant on that count of the indictment. The court held that the trial judge erred in concluding that the acts or statements of the appellant could not, in the absence of an offer of employment, constitute an attempt to procure rather than mere preparation. It held that there was evidence from which the trial judge could have concluded that there was both the mens rea and the actus reus required for an attempt to procure. The court also held that the sexual intercourse contemplated by the appellant would be illicit sexual intercourse within s. 195(1)(a). The appellant appeals from the judgment of the Court of Appeal with respect to the second count of the indictment.

The appellant, who appeared in person on the appeal, expressed his grounds of appeal in several different ways, but in my opinion there are only two issues that require consideration by the court:

(1) whether the Court of Appeal erred in holding that the acts or statements of the appellant could, as a matter of law, constitute an attempt to procure rather than mere preparation; and

(2) whether the Court of Appeal erred in holding that the sexual intercourse contemplated by the appellant would be illicit sexual intercourse within s. 195(1)(a) of the Code.

I propose to begin with the consideration of what is meant by "illicit sexual intercourse" in s. 195(1)(a) of the Criminal Code, which, at the relevant time, provided:

**195.**(1) Every one who

(a) procures, attempts to procure or solicits a female person to have illicit sexual intercourse with another person, whether in or out of Canada.

. . .

is guilty of an indictable offence and is liable to imprisonment for ten years.

Martin J.A., delivering the unanimous judgment of the Court of Appeal, said with reference to the meaning of "illicit sexual intercourse" at p. 52:

"Illicit sexual intercourse" in s. 195(1)(a) merely connotes sexual intercourse with another not authorized by law and it is not necessary for the sexual intercourse procured with another to be in itself criminal: see *R. v. Robinson* (1946), 92 C.C.C. 223, [1948] O.R. 857, [1949] 2 D.L.R. 531.

. . .

I am of the respectful opinion that the Court of Appeal did not err in holding that the sexual intercourse contemplated by the appellant would be "illicit sexual intercourse" within s. 195(1)(a) of the Code.

I turn now to the question whether the acts or statements of the appellant could, as a matter of law, constitute the actus reus of an attempt to procure a person to have illicit sexual intercourse with another person, contrary to s. 195(1)(a) of the Code. The general provision of the Code defining the constituent elements of an attempt to commit an offence is s. 24, which provides:

**24.**(1) Every one who, having an intent to commit an offence, does or omits to do anything for the purpose of carrying out his intention is guilty of an attempt to commit the offence whether or not it was possible under the circumstances to commit the offence. (2) The question whether an act or omission by a person who has an intent to commit an offence is or is not mere preparation to commit the offence, and too remote to constitute an attempt to commit the offence, is a question of law.

The issue is whether, if there was the necessary intent, the acts of the appellant were mere preparation to commit the offence of procuring a person to have illicit sexual intercourse with another person or whether any of them was a step in the commission of the offence, and the extent to which that distinction is to turn on the relative remoteness of the act in question from what would have been the completion of the offence. This issue, as s. 24 indicates, is a question of law. The appellant contends that the Court of Appeal erred in holding that one of the acts of the appellant could, if there was the necessary intent, constitute the actus reus of an attempt to procure.

. . .

The Court of Appeal held that the trial judge had not made a finding as to whether the appellant had the requisite mens rea of intent to commit the offence of procuring, but that the holding out of large financial rewards in the course of the interviews could, as a matter of law, constitute the actus reus of an attempt to procure. Martin J.A. said at p. 50:

The trial judge, as previously mentioned, found that the respondent intended that "the women in question" should have sexual intercourse with clients or potential clients if necessary to obtain a contract. I interpret that finding in its context as a finding that the respondent in the interviews with the three young women who answered the advertisement and with Constable Barkey did state and meant to state that the position required them to have sexual intercourse with clients or potential clients, and further that he contemplated that such sexual intercourse would take place as incidental to the employment. The trial judge made no finding that the respondent endeavoured to persuade the applicants to take the job and it is, I think, clear on the evidence that the respondent did not expressly attempt to persuade them to take such employment and indeed the trial judge found that the respondent had never offered the position to any of them. The holding out of large financial rewards in the context of the interviews was capable, however, of not only providing evidence of an intention to induce the applicants to become so employed, but was also capable of constituting the *actus reus* of an attempt to procure the applicants to have illicit sexual intercourse contrary to s. 195.

. . .

Several different tests for determining whether there is the actus reus of attempt, as distinct from mere preparation to commit an offence, have been identified as reflected at one time or another in judicial decisions and legislation. All of them have been pronounced by academic commentators to be unsatisfactory in some degree. For a thorough analysis of the various tests, with suggestions for an improved test, see Meehan, The Law of Criminal Attempt: A Treatise (1984), c. 5, pp. 79-146, and Stuart, Canadian Criminal Law: A Treatise (1982), p. 529 et seq.

. . .

In my opinion the distinction between preparation and attempt is essentially a qualitative one, involving the relationship between the nature and quality of the act in question and the nature of the complete offence, although consideration must necessarily be given, in making that qualitative distinction, to the relative proximity of the act in question to what would have been the completed offence, in terms of time, location and acts under the control of the accused remaining to be accomplished. I find that view to be compatible with what has been said about the actus reus of attempt in this court and in other Canadian decisions that should be treated as authoritative on this question.

. . .

In my opinion, relative proximity may give an act which might otherwise appear to be mere preparation the quality of attempt. That is reflected, I think, in the conclusion of the majority in *Henderson* and in the conclusion of the Ontario Court of Appeal with respect to actus reus in *R. v. Sorrell* (1978), 41 C.C.C. (2d) 9. But an act which on its face is an act of commission does not lose its quality as the actus reus of attempt because further acts were required or because a significant period of time may have elapsed before the completion of the offence.

In the case at bar the Court of Appeal agreed with the trial judge on the applicable meaning of "procure". The meaning selected by the trial judge and approved by the Court of Appeal was "to cause, or to induce, or to have a persuasive effect upon the conduct that is alleged". Martin, J.A. expressed his agreement at p. 49 with the following statement of the issue by the trial judge:

> The question for decision is did Mr. Deutsch attempt to cause or attempt to induce or attempt to have a persuasive effect upon the woman in question to have illicit sexual intercourse with another person . .

I agree that the sources referred to by the trial judge and Martin J.A. support the meaning given by them to the word "procure".

The Court of Appeal differed with the trial judge as to what would have constituted the completed offence of procuring a person to have illicit sexual intercourse with another person. The trial judge held that the offence of procuring would have been completed, in the particular context of this case, by the acceptance of an offer of employment. The Court of Appeal held, citing *R. v. Johnson*, [1964] 2 Q.B. 404, [1963] 3 W.L.R. 1031, 48 Cr. App. R. 25, [1961] 3 All E.R. 969, and *R. v. Gruba*, 66 W.W.R 190, [1969] 2 C.C.C. 365 (B.C.C.A.), that the offence of procuring a person to have illicit sexual intercourse with another person is not committed unless sexual intercourse actually takes place. In the appeal to this court the respondent accepted this statement of the law as to what is required for the complete offence of procuring a person to have illicit sexual intercourse with another person. It was not challenged, and I accept it for the purposes of deciding whether the acts of the appellant could, as a matter of law, constitute the actus reus of an attempt to procure.

I agree with the Court of Appeal that if the appellant had the necessary intent to induce or persuade the woman to seek employment that would require them to have sexual intercourse with prospective clients then the holding out of the large financial rewards in the course of the interviews in which the necessity of having sexual intercourse with prospective clients was disclosed could constitute the actus reus of an attempt to procure. It would clearly be a step, and an important step, in the commission of the offence. Before an offer of employment could be made in such circumstances an applicant would have to seek the position despite its special requirement. Thus such inducement or persuasion would be the decisive act in the procuring. There would be little else that the appellant would be required to do towards the completion of the offence other than to make the formal offer of employment. I am further of the opinion that the holding out of the large financial rewards in the course of the interviews would not lose its quality as a step in the commission of the offence, and thus as an actus reus of attempt, because a considerable period of time might elapse before a person engaged for the position had sexual intercourse with prospective clients or because of the otherwise contingent nature of such sexual intercourse.

For these reasons I would dismiss the appeal. I agree with the Court of Appeal that because the trial judge did not make a finding as to whether or not there was the necessary intent to procure there must be a new trial.

*Appeal allowed; new trial ordered.*

## Regina v. Sorrell and Bondett
### (1978), 41 C.C.C. (2d) 9 (Ont. C.A.)

Appeal by the Crown from the accused's acquittal on a charge of attempted robbery.

BY THE COURT: — The Attorney-General of Ontario appeals against the acquittal of the respondents on a charge of attempted robbery.

The respondents were tried at Kingston before His Honour Judge Campbell, sitting without a jury, on an indictment containing three counts.

Count 1 charged the respondents jointly with, on or about March 3, 1977, attempting to rob Peter Mason of Aunt Lucy's Fried Chicken store at 240 Montreal St. in Kingston. Count 2 charged the respondent Sorrell with carrying, at the time and place aforesaid, a concealed weapon, to wit: a Smith and Wesson revolver. Count 3 charged the respondent Sorrell with having in his possession, at the time and place aforesaid, a Smith and Wesson revolver, knowing the same was obtained by an offence committed in Canada punishable on indictment. The respondent Sorrell, on arraignment, pleaded guilty to the charge of carrying a concealed weapon contained in count 2; his plea of guilty was accepted by the trial Judge after the evidence was completed, and he was sentenced to imprisonment for 18 months. The trial Judge acquitted the respondent Sorrell on count 3, on the ground that the Crown had failed to prove the necessary element of guilty knowledge. The Crown does not appeal the acquittal of Sorrell on count 3, and we are not further concerned with it.

On the evening of Thursday, March 3, 1977, Miss Dawn Arbuckle was the cashier at Aunt Lucy's Fried Chicken store at 240 Montreal St. in Kingston. The store is located at the corner of Montreal and Markland Sts., the customer entrances being on Montreal St. Mr. Peter Mason was the manager of the store. The regular closing time for the store was 11:00 p.m., but, on the evening in question, since almost all the chicken had been sold, the manager decided to close the store earlier, and locked the customer entrances at approximately 10:45 p.m. Around 10 minutes to 11:00 Miss Arbuckle noticed two men, wearing balaclavas, on the Markland St. side of the store; they then came to one of the customer entrances on Montreal St. The area outside the store was illuminated, and the lights normally on in the store, when open, were still on.

One of the men was wearing a blue ski jacket and the other was wearing a brown coat. The balaclavas worn by the two men were pulled down completely over their heads, and one man was also wearing sunglasses. Miss Arbuckle said that the balaclava worn by one man was blue and white in colour, and that worn by the other man was brown and white.

One of the men rapped on the door and on the window. The manager, who had been mopping the floor, turned around and said, "Sorry we are closed", and returned to his mopping. The two men turned toward each other, and made a gesture of surprise. At this time Miss Arbuckle noticed that one of the men had a silver-coloured gun in his hand. The two men then walked away on Montreal Street in the direction of Princess St.; whereupon Mr. Mason, the manager, telephoned the police. Two officers in a cruiser responded to the call, drove to the area and saw the two men, whose clothing corresponded to the description that the officers had been given, walking on

Montreal St. The officers drove past the two men, then made a U-turn and drove back towards them.

As the officers passed the two men, before making the U-turn, they saw one of the men throw "an article of material" towards a snow bank on the side of the street. The two men, who proved to be the respondents, were then arrested. The respondent Sorrell had a loaded .357 Magnum revolver concealed in his waistband. The gun was loaded with six Dominion .38 shells, and another five Dominion .38 shells were removed from the respondent Sorrell's pants' pocket.

An officer conducted a search of the immediate area where the respondents had been arrested, and found a brown balaclava on a snowbank on the side of Montreal St. The point on Montreal St. where the respondents were arrested was some 411 yards from the Aunt Lucy's store, where the attempted robbery is alleged to have occurred. The officer proceeded along Montreal St. in the direction of the Aunt Lucy's store, and found a blue balaclava in the middle of the sidewalk on Montreal St. at the intersection of Raglan St.

Neither of the respondents testified in his defence.

The Crown appeals against the acquittal of the respondents on the charge of attempted robbery on the ground that the trial Judge erred in law in holding that the acts of the respondents did not go beyond mere preparation, and hence did not constitute an attempt.

Section 24 of the *Code* defines an attempt as follows:

> **24**(1) Every one who, having an intent to commit an offence, does or omits to do anything for the purpose of carrying out his intention is guilty of an attempt to commit the offence whether or not it was possible under the circumstances to commit the offence.
>
> (2) The question whether an act or omission by a person *who has an intent to commit an offence* is or is not mere preparation to commit the offence, and too remote to constitute an attempt to commit the offence, is a question of law.

(Emphasis supplied.)

In order to establish the commission of the offence of attempted robbery charged, it was necessary for the Crown to prove that the respondents:

(i) Intended to do that which would in law amount to the robbery specified in the indictment (*mens rea*), and

(ii) took steps in carrying out that intent which amounted to more than mere preparation (*actus reus*).

By virtue of s. 24(2) of the *Code*, the existence of element (i) is a question of fact, but whether the steps taken are sufficient to satisfy element (ii) is a question of law.

. . .

In the present case, there was no evidence of the intent to rob other than that furnished by the acts relied on as constituting the *actus reus*. There was no extrinsic evidence in the form of statements of intention, or admissions by the respondents showing what their intention was.

The prosecution in this case was forced to rely exclusively upon the acts of the accused, not only to constitute the *actus reus*, but to supply the evidence of the necessary *mens rea*. This Court in *R. v. Cline, supra*, rejected the so-called "unequivocal act" test for determining when the stage of attempt has been reached. That test excludes resort to evidence *aliunde*, such as admissions, and holds that the stage of attempt has been reached only when the acts of the accused show unequivocally on their face the criminal intent with which the acts were performed. We are of the view that where the accused's intention is otherwise proved, acts which on their face are equivocal, may none the less, be sufficiently proximate to constitute an attempt. Where, however, there is no extrinsic evidence of the intent with which accused's acts were done with the intent to commit the crime that the accused is alleged to have attempted to commit, and hence insufficient to establish the offence of attempt.

Counsel for the respondents while conceding that the trial Judge's reasons are not free of ambiguity, submitted that they are reasonably open to the interpretation that he was searching for evidence that satisfied him beyond a reasonable doubt that the accused intended to rob the store in question, and at the end of his quest was not satisfied beyond a reasonable doubt, that the acts done by the accused supplied the necessary proof of intent.

We think that this submission accurately states the basis upon which the trial Judge acquitted the respondents, and the Crown has not satisfied us that but for the self-misdirection with respect to which complaint is made, that the verdict of the trial Judge would not necessarily have been the same. It is not to the point that, on the evidence, we would have reached a different conclusion with respect to the respondent's intentions.

Because of the view which we have taken, it is unnecessary to consider the difficult question whether, in the circumstances, the conviction of the respondent Sorrell on the charge of carrying a concealed weapon "at the time and place aforesaid" would preclude his conviction of the charge of attempted robbery, by virtue of the principle enunciated in *Kienapple v. The Queen* (1974), 15 C.C.C (2d) 524, 44 DL.R. (3d) 351, [1975] 1 S.C.R. 729.

For the reasons given the appeal must be dismissed.

*Appeal dismissed.*

## Regina v. Scott
[1964] 2 C.C.C. 257 (Alta. C.A.)

MacDONALD, J.A.: — This is an appeal from a conviction made by Magistrate Read whereby the appellant Kenneth Scott was convicted upon a charge that he,

"on the 13th day of July A.D. 1963, at Calgary in the said province, did, unlawfully attempt to commit an indictable offence, to wit: did unlawfully attempt to steal cash valued at less than $50.00, the property of Leonard Dodd, contrary to Section 406(c) of the Criminal Code."

The case was tried under Part XVI of the *Criminal Code*. Section 467(b) states:

"**467.** The jurisdiction of a magistrate to try an accused is absolute and does not depend upon the consent of the accused where the accused is charged in an information

. . .

"(b) with attempted theft."

During Stampede week in Calgary, the complainant Dodd, shortly after midnight on July 13, 1963, was attending a street dance. He felt something in his right-hand back pocket, and on reaching back he found a hand in his pocket. While the hand was still in his pocket, Dodd grabbed the wrist above the hand and managed to hold the person whose wrist he had grabbed until the police arrived. The accused was the person whose hand was in Dodd's pocket.

There was a wallet in Dodd's pocket containing a credit card, driver's licence, birth certificate, and other valuable papers, but there was no money in the wallet. There is no evidence that Dodd had any money in that pocket.

There can be no doubt about the appellant's attempt to steal from the pocket of Dodd. The difficulty arises from the fact that he was charged with attempting to steal money, while there is nothing in the evidence to show that Dodd had any money in his pocket.

. . .

In the present case, the appellant pickpocket could not know what was in the pocket of Dodd. I think, however, it is a self-evident fact that a pickpocket is desirous of stealing money. A pickpocket could not be convicted of stealing money unless the money was there, but it does seem that an attempt to steal money stands on an entirely different footing.

It seems to be that the proper and reasonable inference to be made under the circumstance that existed was that the appellant had the intent to steal money from the pocket of Dodd. The evidence established that the appellant did an act towards the accomplishment of that objective.

. . .

The fact that the Crown failed to prove that there was money in Dodd's pocket cannot, in my view, make the charge bad in law.

It follows that the conviction must be affirmed.

The appellant also appeals against the sentence of one year imposed by the Magistrate. The maximum sentence for stealing when the value of what is stolen is less than $50, is two years: see *Code*, s. 280(b). For an attempt to steal less that $50, the maximum sentence would be one year: see *Code*, s. 406(b).

In the case at bar, the learned Magistrate imposed the maximum sentence, undoubtedly taking into consideration the fact that the accused had two previous convictions for breaking and entry since March of 1960. I do not think this is a case where the maximum sentence should have been imposed. I would accordingly reduce the sentence to six months.

JOHNSON, J.A. (dissenting): — The complainant was attending a street dance in the early hours of the morning of July 13, 1963, at the City of Calgary. He was standing in a crowd watching the dancing when he felt a hand in his pocket. He grabbed the wrist of the appellant while the hand was still in the pocket, and, after grappling with him, was able to hold the appellant until the police arrived. The pocket contained a wallet; it contained no money but did contain a credit card, driver's licence, birth certificate, and "other valuable papers" not enumerated or otherwise described. The appellant was charged that he did,

> "unlawfully attempt to commit an indictable offence, to wit: did unlawfully attempt to steal cash valued at less than $50.00, the property of Leonard Dodd, contrary to Section 406(c) of the Criminal Code."

. . .

The neat point for consideration in this appeal is whether a charge is good that attempts to particularize what the Crown believes the accused was attempting to steal when the Crown fails to prove the intent to steal that particular object, either by direct evidence or by a reasonable inference.

When a pickpocket puts his hand in a person's pocket, very likely he does not know what he will get. He is, of course, after some property of the victim. If it is a purse or a billfold that he is seeking, as appears to have been the case with this appellant, it was in the past possible to draw the inference that cash in some form was all that the thief was after. It is not so easy to draw such an inference at the present time when wallets and billfolds contain other items which may be at least as valuable, such as credit cards, letters of credit, cheques, and other documents which can be used to obtain money or for identification by which money can be obtained. The information in the present case has the additional objection that it mentions "cash valued at less than $50.00". No doubt this sum was inserted to give the Magistrate absolute jurisdiction, but the inference that the appellant's expectation was so limited when he put his hand in the complainant's pocket is difficult to draw.

. . .

It would appear that an information or indictment simply charging the appellant with an attempt to commit theft from the person of the complainant would have been good in this case: *R. v. Ring, supra*. Certainly one which charged him with an attempt to steal a wallet would have been good. A charge of an attempt to steal "the property of the complainant" would also appear to be good, and the Court in such case would not require that such property" be particularized: *R. v. Johnson et al.* (1864), 34 L.J.M.C. 24.

Though I do so with some hesitation, I have concluded that a conviction based upon the information in this case, having regard to the evidence, is not justified. The appeal is allowed and the conviction quashed.

KANE, J.A., concurs with MacDONALD, J.A.

*Appeal from conviction dismissed; appeal from sentence allowed.*

## Regina v. Smith
### [1973] 2 W.L.R. 942

LORD WIDGERY C.J. gave the judgment of the court. On September 28, 1972, at the Liverpool Crown Court this defendant was convicted of attempted handling of stolen goods. It is perhaps as well to read the terms of the count in the indictment. The particulars of the offence were:

"On or about September 28, 1971, in the County of Hertford, dishonestly attempted to assist in the disposal by or for the benefit of Alan Christopher Dixon, George James Mooney, Paul John Maeder and other persons unknown of 890 cartons of corned beef, the property of Arbuckle Smith & Co. Ltd., knowing or believing the same to have been stolen."

The essence of it was dishonestly attempting to assist in the disposal of those goods. He was convicted on that count and sentenced to 12 months' imprisonment. There was another count in the indictment charging conspiracy, arising out of the same circumstances, but the jury were directed to return a verdict of not guilty on that count.

What had happened was this. On September 18, 1971, there was a burglary at a warehouse in Liverpool, and a very large quantity of corned beef in cartons was stolen. Ten days later on September 28 two police officers on duty at night saw a large van proceeding down a main road near Sutton Coldfield, and their attention was directed to it because it was obviously overloaded, or had a load which had shifted, in other words it was all down on one side. They stopped the vehicle, the driver was a man called Dixon; he had a man named Nicholson with him. The van was loaded with cartons of corned beef, and for the purposes of this judgment I shall state the facts as the jury must have found them to be, and the jury clearly accepted that the cartons of corned beef in this van were part of the proceeds of the theft in Liverpool 10 days before.

The van and the two men in it were taken by the police officers to Sutton Coldfield police station. There was a brief conference between the police officers and members of the regional crime squad. The upshot of it was that it was decided to let this van go on its way to London with the police keeping an eye on it with a view to catching some of the other people who were concerned in the theft and disposal of these goods. So after what was really quite a brief interval, the van set off for London; it had two police officers on board and was trailed by other police officers in a car. They got to the London end of the M1 motorway at about seven o'clock at the Scratchwood Service Area, as it is called, because this was the place where Dixon, the driver of the vehicle, told the police that he was to rendezvous with those who were to take the corned beef on. At the Scratchwood Service Area there were a number of people, including the defendant, who were obviously there to receive this vehicle, and who were responsible for the transfer of the goods to other vehicles and the ultimate distribution of the goods to the ultimate receivers. I take the matter quite briefly, and I do not consider further the fact that many of these facts were disputed in the trial. It suffices for present purposes to say that in view of the jury's verdict, one can regard the defendant as being one, if not, the leader, of a party waiting at the Scratchwood Service Area for this van with a view to disposing of the contents.

It is clear that not only were they there for that purpose, but that when the van arrived the defendant took a leading part in making arrangements for the future disposal of the goods. There were such troubles as a burst tyre and things of that kind, and he evidently was taking a leading part in seeing that the goods were made mobile again and went on to their ultimate destination. In the end the police officers made their identity known, and the defendant was eventually arrested.

The reason why he was not charged with handling stolen goods was a perfectly simple one, namely, that by the time the vehicle got to Scratchwood Service Area and the defendant began to take an active part in the affair, the corned beef was, as a matter of law, no longer stolen goods. The reason is that by section 24(3) of the Theft Act 1968, which deals with certain offences relating to stolen goods, there is this provision:

> "But no goods shall be regarded as having continued to be stolen goods after they have been restored to the person from whom they were stolen or to other lawful possessions or custody, or after that person and any other person claiming through him have otherwise ceased as regards those goods to have any right to restitution in respect of the theft."

So in brief, as a matter of law, although the goods were undoubtedly stolen goods when they left the Liverpool warehouse, they ceased to be stolen goods as soon as the police got hold of them at Sutton Coldfield, and they were then restored to lawful custody. Consequently when the defendant began to perform his functions at the Scratchwood Service Area, the goods with which he was dealing, totally unknown to him, were not stolen goods at all. Accordingly there could be no question of charging him with handling stolen goods. Instead he was charged with attempting to handle stolen goods. And this is another case in which the court has to consider whether a person can be said to commit the offence of attempting to commit a criminal offence, if the offence is not capable of being committed by reason of circumstances unknown to the accused. The fact that an attempt is charged means, of course, that the prosecution are not able or minded to try and prove the full offence. It goes without saying that a man is not to be charged with or convicted of an attempt except on the basis that he had not gone the whole distance and actually committed the full offence itself.

Attempts arising out of a failure on the part of the accused to complete the full offence usually fall into two main classes. The first class is the type of case where the accused has embarked on a course of conduct which, if completed, will result in an offence but for some reason breaks off that course of conduct and never completes the action required to amount to the offence. There are dozens of examples of which one can think of attempts which come into that class: the pickpocket who puts his hand in a man's pocket only to find it empty; the burglar who is disturbed by the police when he is in the process of trying to break open the window; the safebreaker who finds when he gets to the safe, it is too difficult for him and he cannot open it. these are all people who have set out on a course of conduct which if completed in accordance with their intention would have amounted to a criminal offence, but who have desisted for one reason or another before the full course of criminality has been pursued. In general, and I emphasise that this court is only concerned to deal with those cases in generality, a charge of attempt can properly be laid in that type of case. It matters not that the accused might never have completed the major offence in any event.

But the second class is the one into which the present facts fall. The second class of case where attempt is sought to be charged is where the accused has meticulously and in detail followed every step of his intended course believing throughout that he was committing a criminal offence and when in the end it is found he has not committed a criminal offence because in law that which he planned and carried out does not amount to a criminal offence at all. That is this case, and the question whether in such circumstances the accused can properly be charged with an attempt is on the authorities a very much more difficult one, and indeed the questions raised are question which have been canvassed in New Zealand and the United States of America as well as in the courts of this country.

I think one can conveniently start with the modern cases and not take too long going through the earlier authorities of which counsel's industry has reminded us this morning. I approach this question first of all by looking at *Rex v. Percy Dalton (London) Ltd.* (1949) 33 Cr. App. R. 102. This is an immediate post-war case when there were still controlled prices or maximum permitted prices for the sale of various commodities. The accused in *Rex v. Percy Dalton (London) Ltd.* were charged with having sold pears at a price in excess of the current permitted price for pears. It seems fairly clear that the accused thought that they were breaking the law, in their words, that they knew the maximum price and thought that they were charging a price in excess; but when the case was heard out to its end and the details were examined, it was found that in fact they had not exceeded the maximum price and that therefore an offence of breach of the appropriate regulation had not been made out. The question then arose as to whether it was possible to charge them with attempting to commit the offence of selling in excess of the maximum price. The court held that it was not, and there is a passage which this court finds of particular value, and which indeed has been approved on other occasions in this court also. It appears in the judgment of the court given by Birkett J., at p. 110:

> "All the acts of the company" — the defendant in that case —"have been considered by the jury in coming to that conclusion; and we feel it impossible to say on the same facts that the company can be convicted of the attempt to sell above the maximum price when the completed transaction was no offence. Steps on the way to the commission of what would be a crime, if the acts were completed, may amount to attempts to commit that crime, to which, unless interrupted, they would have led; but steps on the way to the doing of something, which is thereafter done, and which is no crime, cannot be regarded as attempts to commit a crime."

That principle, as I say, has been adopted with approval in *Reg. v. McDonough* (1962) 47 Cr. App. R. 37; it is a principle which this court regards as being laid down by *Rex v. Percy Dalton London Ltd.*, 33 Cr. App. R. 102 and one which prima facie we ought to follow, and of course if we follow that principle it means that the defendant in this case must succeed, because in the end when he had carried out the full course of conduct which he had in mind, he had not committed the offence of having stolen goods because the goods were no longer stolen.

. . .

One comes therefore finally to the most recent case on this topic, which is *Reg. v. Curbishley* (1970) 55 Cr. App. R. 310, decided in this court. This was a case in which the appellants as parties to a plan concerned with the movement of stolen goods had been assigned as their part in the plan to take a vehicle to a certain place, there to pick up the stolen goods now before us. They knew that the goods were going to be stolen goods; they knew that they were going to handle stolen goods in the technical sense. They went there in accordance with the plan, but when they got there the goods were not there and they therefore had to turn round and come home again. The convictions which had been recorded at the Buckinghamshire quarter session of dishonestly attempting to assist in the removal or disposal of stolen goods were upheld. We do not think that *Reg. v. Curbishley* is really in any way inconsistent with Birkett J.'s dictum in *Rex v. Percy Dalton (London) Ltd.*, 33 Cr. App. R. 102, nor do we think that it really carries weight against the defendant in the present appeal, because on the brief facts which I have outlined you have on the face of it a clear example of a man who sets out to commit a criminal offence, and who is unable to complete the full course of action which would amount to the commission of that offence by reason of some intervention on the part of others. The only reason why they did not commit the full offence was because the goods were not there when they went to pick them up. That seems to me to fall into the first of the two classes of attempt cases to which I earlier referred, and not to be in any way inconsistent with the argument put forward by Mr. Hytner today. Mr. Morgan picks up a sentence on p. 315 and seeks to put a somewhat different complexion on the case, because it is to be observed on p. 315 that the goods had not only been removed when the appellant arrived to collect them, but had been removed by the police. Of course if they had been removed by the police they might well have go back into lawful custody as a result of that, and *Reg. v. Curbishley* might then become on all fours with the case we are deciding.

We are not impressed by that argument because there is not a word in the report to suggest that anyone regarded removal by the police as significant or that the point we have to decide was argued at all. On its face it seems to be a straightforward example of class one attempts where the only reason why the full offence was not committed was that the accused broke off the course of events at some stage before the full details of the crime had been worked out. We do not therefore regard *Reg. v. Curbishley* as being any significant obstacle in the path of the appellant in this case.

In the end we have come to the conclusion that we ought to follow the principle in *Rex v. Dalton (London) Ltd.*, 33 Cr. App. R. 102 enunciated by Birkett J. supported by *Reg. v. Donnely* [1970] N.Z.L.R. 980 and against which, as far as English authority is concerned, we only have to set the authority of *Reg. v. Miller*, 49 Cr. App. R. 241 which, for the reasons I have already given, does not seem to us to be a compelling one. Accordingly, we think the conviction was wrong in this case, that the appeal should be allowed and the conviction should be quashed.

*Appeal allowed.*
*Conviction quashed.*
*Prosecution costs to be paid out of central funds.*

. . .

## Regina v. Ancio
### (1984), 10 C.C.C (3d) 385 (S.C.C.)

Appeal by the Crown from a judgment of the Ontario Court of Appeal, 63 C.C.C. (2d) 309, 34 O.R. (2d) 437, allowing an appeal by the accused from his conviction for attempted murder.

[Only the judgment of McIntyre J. is reproduced below.]

McINTYRE J.: — This appeal involves consideration of the mental element required for proof of the crime of attempted murder, the subject of this Court's earlier judgment in *Lajoie v. The Queen* (1973), 10 C.C.C (2d) 313, 22 D.L.R. (3d) 618, [1974] S.C.R. 399.

At the date of the events which give rise to this appeal the respondent had been married some 25 years. His wife had left the matrimonial home and was living with one Kurely. The respondent was depressed and had been drinking to excess on the date in question. He telephoned his wife at Kurely's residence and told her he was afraid that their 23-year-old son was about to commit suicide and asked her to meet him. She refused to co-operate. Later the same evening the respondent broke into a friend's home while its owners were absent and took away three shot-guns. He sawed off the barrel of one, loaded it, and taking some extra ammunition with him went to Kurely's apartment building and gained entry by breaking the glass in the front door. On hearing the noise caused by the breaking glass, Kurely came from his bedroom to investigate, carrying a chair with a jacket hanging on it. He saw the respondent, carrying the shot-gun, ascending the stairs to the second floor. He threw the chair and jacket, hitting the respondent. The gun went off. The blast missed Kurely by some three feet but put a hole in the jacket which had been on the chair. A struggle followed in which Kurely appears to have wrested the gun from the respondent. When the police arrived, having been called during the course of the fight between the two men, Kurley was on the floor with his head partly under a bed and with the respondent upon him striking him weakly.

Shortly after his arrest the respondent stated to the police:

> I just went over to see my wife. I had phoned her earlier. I broke the window and went in. Then I heard what sounded like a gun go off. You are lucky you got here when you did. I had him by the throat and I would have killed him.

According to the respondent's account of events, the gun was discharged accidentally, although under tests conducted by the police the weapon was not found to be prone to accidental discharge.

The respondent was charged with a number of offences arising out of this affair but only one, that of attempted murder, is involved in the appeal. It was contained in the first count of the information and was in these terms:

> . . . did attempt to murder Michael Kurely by discharging a sawed off shotgun at him contrary to s. 222 of the *Criminal Code* of Canada.

He elected trial by judge alone and was convicted. The conviction was quashed in the Court of Appeal and a new trial directed [63 C.C.C. (2d) 309, 34 O.R. (2d) 437]. This appeal is taken by leave of this Court.

The trial judge disposed of the other charges against the respondent and made a finding that he had broken into Kurley's apartment building with intent to use the shot-gun to force his wife to leave. He said:

> I turn now to the very real point of the charge of attempted murder, and having made the finding I have of the break and enter at the house at 108 6th Street, with intent to commit an

indictable offence, wither [sic] forceable confinement or worse. Forceable confinement if you accept the evidence of the accused, I feel probably worse than that.

He then referred to s. 213(d) of the *Criminal Code* which is in these terms:

**213.** Culpable homicide is murder where a person causes the death of a human being while committing or attempting to commit ... (kidnapping an forcible confinement). . .(breaking and entering) ... whether or not the person means to cause death to any human being and whether he knows that death is likely to be caused to any human being, if

. . .

(d) he uses a weapon or has it upon his person

    (i) during or at the time he commits or attempts to commit the offence, or
    (ii) during or at the time of his fight after committing or attempting to commit the offence, and the death ensues as a consequence.

Noting that breaking and entering with intent to commit an indictable offence is one of the offences named in the section, he convicted the respondent of attempted murder on the basis that the respondent had carried and used a weapon int the course of a breaking an entry with intent to effect forceable confinement of his wife.

The judgment of the Court of Appeal (MacKinnon A.C.J.O., Dubin and Lacourciere JJ.A.) was written by MacKinnon A.C.J.O. He accepted the submission by counsel for Ancio that the finding of fact which formed the basis of the conviction were that the respondent committed the offence of breaking and entering Kurely's [residence and that he had in his possession a weapon during the commission of the offence. He then considered whether these findings of fact in the absence of any finding of an intent to kill or cause bodily harm were sufficient to support a conviction for attempted murder by the interaction of ss. 24(1) and 213(d) of the *Criminal Code*, and said [at p. 319]:

There is no question in the instant appeal that the trial Judge was satisfied beyond a reasonable doubt that the appellant intended to break and enter the Kurrelli [sic] premises and intended to have in his possession the sawed-off shot-gun. The appellant was charged with the offence of attempted murder and the "offence" referred to in s. 24(1) is the offence of "attempted murder" and not the offence of break and enter while carrying a weapon on his person. If death had ensued in the instant case it would have been constructive murder, but from the standpoint of an attempt, can there be an intention to attempt an unintentional act without more?

and further [at p. 320]:

In the law of attempts it is the *mens rea* which is fundamental and in the circumstances of this case there must be the intention either to mean to cause death or in the case of attempted murder, as now established by *R. v. Lajoie* (1973), 10 C.C.C. (2d) 313, 33 D.L.R. (3d) 168, [1974] S.C.R. 399, meaning to cause the victim bodily harm knowing it is likely to cause his death, and reckless whether death ensues or not. The trial Judge, accordingly in this case, had to be satisfied beyond a reasonable doubt (or a jury if one is present) that the Crown has established the required intent under s. 212(a)(i) or 212(a)(ii).

He then went on to hold that while there was evidence before the trial judge from which he could have drawn the necessary inferences regarding the intent to kill or cause bodily harm likely to cause death, he had not done so, and as a result had not made the finding necessary to support the conviction. Accordingly, the conviction was quashed and a new trial was ordered.

The Crown contended in this Court that the Court of Appeal was in error in holding that the *mens rea* in attempted murder was limited to an intention to cause death (s. 212(a)(i)), or an intention to cause bodily harm knowing it to be likely to cause death and being reckless whether death ensues (s. 212(a)(ii)). The Crown's position was stated in its factum in these words:

> . . .the intention for attempted murder is not restricted to an actual intention to kill or an intention to cause grievous bodily harm that one knows is likely to cause death and is reckless whether death ensues or not, but *extends to an intention to do that which constitutes the commission of the offence of murder as defined in ss. 212 and 213 of the Criminal Code. It is the Crown's position that s. 24 and s. 213(d) in combination can for the basis for a conviction of attempted murder.*

(Emphasis added.)

                               . . .

The common law recognition of the fundamental importance of intent in the crime of attempt is carried forward into the *Criminal Code*. A reading of s. 24 of the *Code* and all its predecessors since the enactment of the first *Code* in 1892 confirms that the intent to commit the desired offence is a basic element of the offence of attempt. Indeed, because the crime of attempt may be complete without the actual commission of any other offence and even without the performance of any act unlawful in itself, it is abundantly clear that the criminal element of the offence of attempt may lie solely in the intent. As noted by Glanville Williams, *Criminal Law: The General Part*, 2nd ed. (1961), para. 207, p. 642, in discussing attempts: "An *actus reus* . . . need not be a crime apart from the state of mind. It need not even be a tort, or a moral wrong, or a social mischief." The question now arises: What is the intent required for an attempt to commit murder? As has been indicated earlier, the Crown's position is that the intent required for a conviction on a charge of attempt to murder is the intent to do that which will, if death is caused, constitute the commission of murder as defined in ss. 212 and 213 of the *Code*, so that a combination of ss. 24 and 213(d) can form the basis for a conviction of attempted murder. The respondent, on the other hand, argues that although the authorities presently limit the intent to that which would constitute murder as defined in s. 212 of the *Code*, logic and principle dictate that the intent should be limited to the specific intent to kill described in s. 212(a)(i).

While it is clear from ss. 212 and 213 of the *Criminal Code* that an unintentional killing can be murder, it is equally clear that whatever mental elements may be involved and whatever means may be employed there cannot be a murder without a killing. Section 24 of the *Code* defines, in part, the offence of attempt as "having an intent to commit an offence". As Estey J. observed in *R. v. Quinton* (1947), 88 C.C.C. 231 at pp. 236-7, [1948] D.L.R. 625 at p. 630, [1947] S.C.R. 234 at pp. 235-6, in referring to the then s. 72(now s. 24):

> This section requires that one to be guilty of an attempt but intend to commit the completed offence and to have done some act toward the accomplishment of that objective.

The completed offence of murder involves a killing. The intention to commit the complete offence of murder must therefore include an intention to kill. I find it impossible to conclude that a person may intend to commit the unintentional killings described in ss 212 and 213 of the *Code*. I am then of the view that the *mens rea* for an attempted murder cannot be less than the specific intent to kill.

As I have said earlier, there is a division of opinion upon this point and strong arguments have been raised in favour of the Crown's position that a "lesser intent" such as that provided in s. 212(a)(ii) or even no intent at all relating to the causing of death as provided in s. 213(d), may suffice to found a conviction for attempted murder. This view is supported in *Lajoie*. In my view, with the utmost respect for those who differ, the sections of the *Criminal Code* relied on in that case to not support that position.

. . .

It was argued, and it has been suggested in some of the cases and academic writings on the question, that it is illogical to insist upon a higher degree of *mens rea* for attempted murder, while accepting a lower degree amounting to recklessness for murder. I see no merit in this argument. The intent to kill is the highest intent in murder and there is no reason in logic why an attempt to murder, aimed at the completion of the full crime of murder, should have any lesser intent. If there is any illogic in this matter, it is in the statutory characterization of unintentional killing as murder. The *mens rea* for attempted murder is, in my view, the specific intent to kill. A mental state falling short of that level may well lead to conviction for other offences, for example, one or other of the various aggravated assaults, but not a conviction for an attempt at murder. For these reasons, it is my view that *Lajoie* should no longer be followed.

I would accordingly dismiss the Crown's appeal and confirm the Court of Appeal's order for a new trial.

*Appeal dismissed.*

### Questions/Discussion
1. What is the rationale behind "attempts" in criminal law? What should we be punishing for in regard to attempts?
2. What is the test for deciding when the actus reus of a criminal attempt has occurred? Do you think this is a "real" test or is it so vague as to amount to "I know an attempt when I see one"? Are you in favour of a test which would give greater or less freedom of action to an individual who is thinking of committing a crime?
3. Should individuals who voluntarily abandon their criminal purpose for altruistic reasons be completely relieved of criminal liability? What is the purpose of punishing such people?
4. Explain the differences between "legal impossibility" and "physical impossibility" as they relate to attempts in criminal law. Are the differences of any relevance in Canadian criminal law today? Do you think that they should or should not be relevant in attaching criminal liability for attempts? Why or why not?
5. Do you agree with the decision in *Ancio*? Why or why not?

**Further Reading**

- Galloway, D., "Patterns of Trying: A Critique of Fletcher on Criminal Attempts" (1982), 7 Queen's Law Journal 232.
- MacKinnon, P., "Making Sense of Attempts" (1982), 7 Queen's Law Journal 254.
- Meehan, E., *The Law of Criminal Attempt: A Treatise* (Toronto: Carswell, 1984).
- Mewett, A. and M. Manning, *Mewett and Manning on Criminal Law, 3rd ed.* (Markham: Butterworths, 1994).
- Roach, Kent, *Criminal Law, 2d ed.* (Toronto: Irwin Law, 2000) at 96-104.
- Stuart, Don, and R. Delisle, *Learning Canadian Criminal Law, 8th ed.* (Toronto: Carswell, 2001).
- Verdun-Jones, S., *Criminal Law in Canada: Cases, Questions and the Code, 3d ed.* (Toronto, Harcourt Canada, 2002).

## 6.2.2   Counselling

**Introduction**

Counselling is an offence under section 464 of the Criminal Code which states that it is a crime when someone counsels another person to commit an offence *and* that person does not commit the counselled offence. In situations where the person *does* commit the offence, the provisions relating to "parties to the offence" in section 21 or section 22 are then applicable; these provisions are looked at in section 6.3 below. As for the requirements of the offence in section 464, first, something must be done which amounts to counselling, and this may be words, actions, or gestures. There must also be, as is evident it *McLeod*, a recipient for the counselling though the recipient need not be influenced by the counselling. Finally, what is counselled must be either an indictable offence or an offence punishable on summary conviction.

Problems which are raised in regard to counselling relate to issues surrounding the actus reus and mens rea of the offence. As for the actus reus, there is no clear meaning of the term "counselling" and what amounts to such activity. There is thus a need to rely heavily on the cases for its meaning, rather than having it clearly set out in the Code. Second, it is unclear what the mens rea requirements are for the offence. Is a full wrongful intent needed or is recklessness sufficient? Both of these issues are important, particularly in the area of legitimate dissent and its boundaries. For example, is a writer breaking the law on counselling by advocating withholding of the payment of income taxes as one method of protesting Canada's participation in the *war on terrorism* or by suggesting the blocking of roads to protest hazardous waste dumping in that area? What is the meaning of counselling and is the running of the risk that an offence may be encouraged as a result of one's actions enough (that is, recklessness versus a full intention to have an offence carried out)? The code provision does not distinguish between these examples of dissent and the hiring of someone to kill your spouse. Obviously, differences in motive are important at the penalty stage, but perhaps we need clearer distinctions and boundaries set out in the legislation itself, rather than leaving it to the vagaries of prosecutors' policies or personalities. The case which follows is in fact a very good example of the dangers of an open-ended provision such as counselling in that the case against the counter-culture newspaper was arguably borderline at best.

## Regina v. McLeod
### (1970), 1 C.C.C. (2d) (B.C. C.A.)

Appeal by the accused from their conviction on a charge of counselling another person to commit an indictable offence contrary to s. 407(a) of the *Criminal Code*.

The judgment of the Court was delivered by

MacLEAN, J.A.: — This is an appeal by Georgia Straight Publishing Ltd. and its Editor-in-Chief Dan McLeod, against convictions of the company and McLeod for that:

> between the 27th day of March, A.D. 1969 and the 4th day of April, A.D. 1969 unlawfully did counsel another person, to wit, Penelope Ann York, to commit an indictable offence, which was not committed, to wit, to cultivate marihuana, contrary to the provisions of Sec. 6 of the Narcotic Control Act, S.C. 1960-1961 Chapter 35.

Section 407(a) of the *Criminal Code* under which the charge is laid provides that:

> (a) every one who counsels, procures or incites another person to commit an indictable offence is, if the offence is not committed, guilty of an indictable offence and is liable to the same punishment to which a person who attempts to commit that offence is liable; . . .

Then s. 6(1) and (2) of the *Narcotic Control Act*, 1960-61 (Can.), c. 35, provides that:

> 6(1) No person shall cultivate opium poppy or marihuana except under authority of and in accordance with a licence issued to him under the regulations.
>
> (2) Every person who violates subsection (1) is guilty of an indictable offence and is liable to imprisonment for seven years.

The prosecution arose from an article which appeared in the issue of the weekly newspaper Georgia Straight of March 28th-April 3, 1969, in the centre two pages of the publication. The left-hand page is occupied by a picture of the plant *cannabis sativa*.

The article starts with a paragraph reading as follows:

> THIS IS A CHAIN LETTER. WITHIN THE NEXT FIFTY-FIVE DAYS YOU WILL RE-CEIVE THIRTY-ELEVEN-HUNDRED POUNDS OF CHAINS.
>
> In the meantime, plant your seeds.

Then follows in large capital letters the legend "PLANT YOUR SEEDS". This is followed again by a number of paragraphs reading as follows under the heading "Growing and Cultivating Pot":

> This should help you grow better quality plants in less time.
>
> The first thing in growing a better plant, naturally, would be to start with seeds of good quality. If you or some of your friends have had access to good grass, use those seeds. After all, not all the grass we smoke does the same thing for us.

Select the largest seeds and place them between two napkins, blotting paper, etc. and add enough water to cover the napkins. The cover the top or put them in a dark closet for two or three days, until the seeds have sprouted at least a half inch or longer.

These paragraphs are followed by detailed instructions for planting, fertilizing, cultivating and harvesting of the plant.

The article concludes with the exhortation "Plant Your Seeds".

The evidence discloses that a copy of the allegedly offending issue was purchased by the witness, Miss York, at the corner of Georgia and Granville Streets in Vancouver. On April 2, 1970, Miss York admitted that she was not influenced by the counselling contained in the newspaper. She said that she was amused by that part of the article which referred to the chain letter.

The learned Provincial Judge has held, and I think correctly, that:

... if the person bought the paper and the only fair inference is that it was on public sale at the corner of Georgia and Granville Street and if the person bought the paper and read it, they were in fact being counselled to grow marijuana.

Defence counsel has suggested that "counselling" is not complete unless the person to whom the communication is directed has been influenced by the communication. I cannot accept this submission as it is in my view there is no justification for such a limited meaning to the word "counselling".

In *Brousseau v. The King* (1917), 29 C.C.C. 207, 39 DL.R. 114, 56 S.C.R. 22, Sir Charles Fitzpatrick C.J. said at p. 208:

I construe "counsel" used in collocation with "procure" to mean "advise" or "recommend" and the demand made in the admitted circumstances means at least that.

In *Rex v. Higgins*, 2 East 5 at 17, Lord Kenyon said: —

"It is argued that a mere intent to commit evil is not indictable, without an act done; but is there not an act done when it is charged that the defendant solicited another to commit a felony? The solicitation is an act."

At p. 209 of the report Davies, J. said:

I think s. 69 of the Criminal Code clearly makes a person who counsels or procures another to commit an offence, guilty of a specific offence, whether the person so counselled actually commits the offence he is counselled to commit or not.

In my view the purchaser of this newspaper was counselled to cultivate marijuana.

It is submitted that if this conviction were to be upheld that the "freedom of the press" (as that expression is used in s.1(f) of the *Canadian Bill of Rights*, 1960 (can.), c. 44) would be interfered with.

In the case of *Koss v. Konn* (1961), 40 D.L.R. (2d) 242, 36 W.W.R. 100, this Court dealt with an allegation that a section of the *Trade-Unions Act* infringed "freedom of speech", as that expression is used in s. 1(d) of the *Canadian Bill of Rights*. The majority judgment was given by Tysoe, J.A., and he quoted [p. 264 D.L.R.] the following words of Lord Wright in *James v. Commonwealth of Australia*, [1936] A.C. 578:

"Free' in itself is vague and indeterminate . . . Free speech does not mean free speech; it means speech hedged in by all the laws against defamation, blasphemy, sedition and so forth; it means freedom governed by law."

The same principle applicable to freedom of speech must in my opinion apply to "freedom of the press". In my view s. 407 of the *Criminal Code* as it applies to the appellant does not interfere with "freedom of the press". The freedom which the appellant enjoys is as Lord Wright expressed it a freedom "hedged in by all the laws against defamation, blasphemy, sedition and so forth".

The offence committed by the appellant has been part of the criminal law of Canada for many years and is also an offence in many of the common law countries.

Lastly the appellant submits that there was no evidence of criminal intent. Counsel does not suggest that the offence was other than deliberate but he suggests that the offending article was a "spoof", or was written in a humorous vein "with tongue in cheek".

I have read the article and in fact the whole paper and I can find nothing which even suggests that the appellant was doing anything other than deliberately counselling readers of the paper to cultivate marijuana. I would dismiss the appeal of the company.

However, I think that the evidence falls short of being sufficient to convict the appellant Dan McLeod, and according I would allow his appeal and set aside his conviction.

*Appeal as to Georgia Straight Publishing Ltd. dismissed;*
*appeal as to McLeod allowed.*

## Questions/Discussion

1. Do you agree with the decision in *McLeod*? Why or why not? Do you think the decision poses any danger to the free communication of dissemination of ideas in society? Can you think of similar situations where information is provided which might be interpreted as counselling an offence? For you, what amounts to or should amount to the actus reus and the mens rea of counselling?

2. As noted in the introduction above, the Code does not distinguish between activities many people consider legitimate dissent and protest and the hiring of someone to kill your spouse. Should it? Why or why not? If you did want to make such a distinction, how would you do it in the Code?

## Further Reading

- Fitzgerald, O., and L. Douglas, "Counselling and Conspiracy" (1984), 16 Ottawa Law Review 331.
- Mewett, A. and M. Manning, *Mewett and Manning on Criminal Law, 3rd ed.* (Markham: Butterworths, 1984).
- Roach, Kent, *Criminal Law, 2d ed.* (Toronto: Irwin Law, 2000) at 107-111.
- Stuart, Don, and R. Delisle, *Learning Canadian Criminal Law, 8th ed.* (Toronto: Carswell, 2001).
- Verdun-Jones, S., *Criminal Law in Canada: Cases, Questions and the Code, 3d ed.* (Toronto: Harcourt Canada, 2002).

## 6.2.3 Conspiracy

### Introduction

Conspiracy is a separate offence as set out in section 465 of the Criminal Code whereby it is an offence to conspire to commit murder, to commit an indictable offence other than murder, and to commit an offence punishable on summary conviction, and also to conspire to falsely prosecute someone. What is missing from the section is a definition of conspiracy" and for this definition it is necessary to go to the common law requirements for a conspiracy. The *O'Brien* case which follows sets out well the provisions of conspiracy as it has been interpreted by the courts. Central to the offence is the presence of an agreement to carry out an offence; the required nature of this agreement is set out in the case.

The rationale behind the offence is one of prevention, the idea that when several people have a shared criminal purpose, there is a greater risk to society, and the state has the right to step in before the attainment of the purpose. The criticism is that the state is sometimes punishing people for the thoughts which they hold in common, when those who hold such thoughts individually would not be sanctioned unless or until they act upon them. Yet individuals may hold those goals more strongly than those who share them and present more of an actual risk or danger than a group.

Another criticism of the provision has to do with the uncertainty that arises over what offences are to be included in the term "offences punishable of summary conviction".[1] Does it include provincial offences and if so, should it? The criticism is that provincial offences are not as serious as most of those in the Code, and therefore that criminal conspiracy should not encompass such minor offences. There is also the argument that only Parliament should be responsible for the production of criminal sanctions and "for the sake of certainty and comprehensiveness, the Criminal Code should be self-contained".[2]

### The Queen v. O'Brien
#### [1954] S.C.R. 666

[Only the judgments of Taschereau J. and Rand J. are reproduced below.]

TASCHEREAU, J.: — The Attorney General of British Columbia appeals from a judgment of the Court of Appeal which ordered a new trial. It held that there had been misdirection.

The charge for which the respondent was convicted was that, in the City of Vancouver, British Columbia, between the 30th day of November, 1952, and the 14th day of January, 1953, the respondent unlawfully conspired with one Walter John Tulley and others, to commit a certain indictable offence, namely, kidnapping.

---

1 See generally, O. Fitzgerald and L. Douglas, "Counselling and Conspiracy" (1984), 16 Ottawa Law Review 331 at 337.

2 *Ibid.*, p. 340.

Tulley, the alleged co-conspirator, was not charged, but at the trial, being called as a Crown witness, he gave an account of various meetings he had with the respondent, and explained that both had agreed, at the request of the latter, to kidnap one Joan Margaret Pritchard. He said in his evidence that he never had any intention of going through with this plan, but was just fooling the respondent, or hoaxing him. He also explained that he denounced the whole scheme to the police authorities, and the respondent was arrested.

The learned trial Judge in his charge said: —

Counsel for the accused has suggested that the offence is not complete, because Tulley, in his own evidence, said that he had had at no time any intention of carrying out that agreement. I tell you as a matter of law, gentlemen, *that the offence was complete*, if, in point of fact, the accused and Tulley did make the agreement which is charged against him, *even though Tulley never at any time had any intention of carrying the agreement into effect.*

The Court of Appeal, Mr. Justice Robertson dissenting, held that this constituted misdirection, and therefore, ordered a new trial.

The contention of the respondent which was accepted by the majority of the Court of Appeal, is that Tulley, not having any intention to carry through the common design, could not be a party to the conspiracy, and that therefore, O'Brien the respondent, could not alone be found guilty of the crime. It is common ground that no others were involved in the conspiracy. The mere agreement, without any intention to carry into effect the common design would, according to the submission of the appellant, be sufficient.

I think there has been some confusion as to the element of intention which is necessary to constitute the offence. It is, of course, essential that the conspirators have the *intention to agree*, and this agreement must be complete. There must also be a common design to do something unlawful, or something lawful by illegal means. Although it is not necessary that there should be an overt act in furtherance of the conspiracy, to complete the crime, I have no doubt that there must exist *an intention to put the common design into effect*. A common design necessarily involves an intention. Both are synonymous. The intention cannot be anything else but the will to attain the object of the agreement. I cannot imagine several conspirators agreeing to defraud, to restrain trade, or to commit any indictable offence, without having the intention to reach the common goal.

I fully agree with some of the statements that have been made by the Court of Appeal of Quebec in *Rex v. Kotyszyn*. The head note reads: —

There was no common design between the accused and the policewoman, and there was no agreement between them *since the policewoman had no intention of undergoing the operation.* Consequently there *was neither a conspiracy* nor an *attempt to conspire.*

In the same case, at page 269, Mr. Justice MacKinnon said:

There can be no conspiracy when one wants to do a thing and the other does not want to do it.

Stephen (Commentaries on the laws of England, 21st Ed., Vol. 4) says at page 166:—

The object of the agreement may be the accomplishment of an unlawful act, or of a lawful act by unlawful means. In other words it must be unlawful either in *its aims or in its methods.*

The two elements of agreement and of *common design* are specifically stated to be essential ingredients of the crime of conspiracy. Willes, J. in *Mulcahy v. The Queen:*

A conspiracy consists not merely in the intention of two or more, but in the agreement of two or more to do an unlawful act, or to do a lawful act by unlawful means. So long as such a design rests in intention only, it is not indictable. When two agree to carry it into effect, the very plot is an act in itself, and the act of each of the parties . . . punishable if for a criminal object . . .

This is not the case of the conspirator, who after having completed the crime, withdraws from the conspiracy. If a person, with one or several others, agrees to commit an unlawful act, and later, after having had the intention to carry it through, refuses to put the plan into effect, that person is nevertheless guilty, because all the ingredients of conspiracy can be found in the accused's conduct. But, when the conspiracy has never existed, there can be no withdrawal.

The definition of conspiracy itself supposes an aim. People do not conspire unless they have an object in view. The law punishes conspiracy so that the unlawful object is not attained. It considers that several persons who agree together to commit an unlawful act, are a menace to society, and even if they do nothing in furtherance of their common design, the state intervenes to exercise a repressive action, so that the intention is not materialized, and does not become harmful to any one. The intention must necessarily be present because it is the unlawful act necessarily flowing from the intention, that the state wishes to prevent.

In the case at bar, there is evidence that although he made an agreement with the respondent, Tulley never intended to carry the plan through and kidnap Mrs. Pritchard. On the other hand, there is also evidence that may indicate that he intended to attain the object of the agreement. Did Tulley have this intention or not? This is a question for the jury, and I would invade a domain which is not mine, if I attempted to answer it.

It has been said that if the submission of the respondent were the law, it would be impossible to obtain a conviction on a charge of conspiracy, because the mental state of the accused very often remains in the sphere of uncertainty. All crimes where intention is an essential element would then become impossible to prove. Various factors have come into play, and with their help it is then possible to determine what the intention was. There is a presumption for instance, that a person who does an act intends to do it. As well, numerous circumstances will indicate if an alleged thief intended to rob, or if a killer intended to murder. Conspiracy is not in a different class. It is within the exclusive province of the jury, to weigh all the evidence and to determine all these questions of fact, and to say whether the intentional element is revealed by the evidence.

But I do think that the jury were not properly instructed when they were told that, even without the intention to commit the kidnapping, which was necessarily the common design, the conspiracy was complete by the agreement. The jury were not free to weigh the evidence because, being improperly instructed, they had to disregard what is in my view one of the most important elements of the crime for which the accused was charged.

I agree with the Court of Appeal that there was misdirection, and that consequently there must be a new trial. It has been suggested that the Court of Appeal should have dismissed the appeal, on the ground that although there was misdirection, a properly instructed jury would have necessarily come to the same conclusion. (Cr. Code 1014). With this proposition, I entirely disagree. There is evidence that would justify a properly instructed jury to acquit or to convict, and I do not think in either alternative, that the verdict would be set aside as unreasonable.

I would dismiss the appeal.

RAND J.: — I agree that a conspiracy requires an actual intention in both parties at the moment of exchanging the words of agreement to participate in the act proposed; mere words purporting agreement without an assenting mind to the act proposed are not sufficient. The point of difference between the judgments below is the meaning to be given the word "agreement". In the opinion of Robertson J.A. there was an agreement when Tulley in effect said "I will" even though at that moment his mind was "I won't". The mens rea here appears to lie in the intent to utter the words "I will"; but this severance of the intention to speak the words from that of carrying out the action they signify is a refinement that seems to me to be out of place in a common law crime. Modern statutes have introduced offences in which the objective or physical acts themselves are struck at but they are irrelevant to the unwritten offences. Bishop's Criminal Law, 9th Ed. Vol. II, p. 131 puts it thus: —

> Obviously there must be, between the conspirators, a concert of will and endeavour, not a mere knowledge, acquiescence or approval or a mere several attempt to accomplish the particular wrong . . . Where there are only two, and one simply joins in appearance to draw the other on, neither is a conspirator.

and at p. 132: —

> As soon as this union of will is perfected, the offence of conspiracy is complete, — no act beyond is required . . . It is sufficient if the minds of the parties meet understandingly so as to bring about an intelligent and deliberate agreement to do the acts an commit the offence charged, although such agreement be not manifested by any formal words.

The question raised is, in my opinion, concluded by the judgment of the House of Lords in *Mulcahy v. The Queen*. In that case a prosecution had been brought under *The Crown and Government Security Act*, 11 Vict., c. 12. The indictment following the language of the statute alleged that the accused with five other persons "did feloniously and wickedly compass, imagine, invent, devise, and intend to deprive and depose Our Lady the Queen from the style, honour, and royal name of the Imperial Crown of the United Kingdom of Great Britain and Ireland" and proceeded to declare that the accused did "express, utter, and declare by divers overt acts and deeds hereinafter mentioned, that is to say". The overt acts were then alleged: —

> In order to fulfill, perfect and bring to effect his felonious compassing, imagination, invention, devise and intention aforesaid, they . . . feloniously and wickedly did combine, conspire, confederate, and agree with (19 other persons all named) and with divers other evilly disposed

persons, to the jurors aforesaid unknown to raise, make, and levy insurrection and rebellion against Our said Lady the Queen within this realm.

The statute required the expression of compassing and intending by overt acts and it was necessary, therefore, to allege them. The question raised was whether a conspiracy was such an act.

The House held that it was. This means that the act of conspiracy was sufficient to establish both the compassing and the intention to do the forbidden act, or to put it in another form, that in conspiracy there is not only agreement to do the act proposed signified by words or other means of communication, but also the coexistent intent in each to do it. If that were not so, conspiracy would not have evidenced the *intention* of those charged "to deprive and depose, etc." The language of Willes J. at p. 317 of the report bears out that view. In the course of considering the argument that conspiracy rests in intention only and that an overt act must consist in some external manifestation or deed, he says: —

> A conspiracy consists not merely in the intention of two or more, but in the agreement of two or more to do an unlawful act, or to do a lawful act by unlawful means. So long as such a design rests in intention only, it is not indictable. When two agree to carry it into effect, the very plot is an act in itself, and the act of each of the parties, promise against promise, actus contra actum, capable of being enforced, if lawful, punishable if for a criminal object or for use of criminal means.

In that language he distinguishes between the intention of each person severally and the communicated assent between them to carry out the intention. In stressing the necessity for agreement he assumes the existence of intent.

. . .

On the contrary view, even if both parties had been without the intent to carry out the scheme, each seeking to incriminate the other, they would have drawn guilt upon themselves.

Assuming, then, the truth of the evidence of Tulley that at no time did he ever intend to go along with the proposal made to him, there was no conspiracy.

I would therefore dismiss the appeal.

*Appeal dismissed.*

## Questions/Discussion

1. What are the elements of criminal conspiracy in Canada today? What problems exist in the definition of and the rationale for the law on conspiracy?
2. Do you agree with the test for agreement in *O'Brien* that it should be essentially a subjective and not an objective one? Is the public less protected by the use of such a test? Why didn't the court focus on the subjective belief of O'Brien rather than the intention of Tulley?
3. Do you think that people who agree in common to commit a crime are necessarily more dangerous than a lone individual who holds a strong criminal intent? Is there a danger with this offence of punishing people for the ideas they hold rather than the criminal acts they do? How could the offence be more narrowly defined to protect against such dangers?

**Further Reading**
- Mewett, A., and M. Manning, *Mewett and Manning on Criminal Law, 3rd ed.* (Markham: Butterworths, 1994).
- Roach, Kent, *Criminal Law, 2d ed.* (Toronto: Irwin Law, 2000) at 104-107.
- Stuart, Don, and R. Delisle, *Learning Canadian Criminal Law, 8th ed.* (Toronto: Carswell, 2001).
- Verdun-Jones, S., *Criminal Law in Canada: Cases, Questions and the Code, 3d ed.* (Toronto: Harcourt Canada, 2002).

# 6.3   ATTACHING LIABILITY: THE LIMITS OF LIABILITY

## Introduction

This section focuses on "parties to the offence" and examines the ways in which and the degree to which the criminal law will attach liability for the actions of individuals. Specifically, it focuses on the operation of section 21 of the Code, a device by which criminal liability is attached. Section 21 is examined through the cases in regard to its two subsections.[1] Subsection (1) of section 21 states that a person becomes a party to an offence in one of three ways: by actually committing it, by doing or omitting to do anything for the purpose of aiding someone to commit it, or by abetting someone to commit it.

The first method is not problematic, for it concerns the person who actually shoots someone and is liable for murder or who actually robs the bank and is liable for armed robbery. Problems of proof may present themselves in individual cases as to who did or caused what, but these issues do not concern us. It is the latter two methods that raise more difficult issues, particularly if we keep in mind that the liability that attaches for an offence is equal in all three cases (though the extent of participation may be a factor at sentencing). A person is equally (legally) guilty for murder whether that person pulls the trigger or sells the gun knowing what it is to be used for.

If one is held liable for an offence by virtue of acts or omissions which assist in or encourage the doing of that offence by another person, then what acts or omissions do the courts find amount to aiding or abetting? Such questions can be answered only in the context of individual fact situations, but generally speaking, the courts have said that "mere presence" is not enough to constitute sufficient assistance or encouragement. But what types of activities or relationships make presence more than mere presence? We see in *Kulbacki* a situation where the car owner's presence and failure to do or say something was transformed into encouragement of the crime, even though he did nothing explicitly or overtly to encourage the offence. What other situations or relationships might be found sufficient to satisfy the attachment of criminal liability where one party *fails* to do something to *discourage* another party from committing a crime? Also, what would Kulbacki have to have done to satisfy the court: protest,

---

1   Section 22 contains analogous provision to those in s. 21 in the matter of counselling where the offence has been committed, as opposed to s. 464, which was looked at in section 6.2.2., above.

protest strongly or threaten? We are left with a great deal of uncertainty after this case as to what is expected in such situations or, for that matter, when such situations occur and under what circumstances. The *Salajko* case gives us an example of mere presence, where the accused was seen with his pants down during a gang rape but did nothing else. Can you envisage scenarios where for the very same actions the defendant would be found liable? For example, what if the accused had been the gang's leader?

Subsection (2) of section 21 is a provision which enlarges the liability of an accused to include offences which the individual did not necessarily knowingly aid or encourage. The classic situation is where two or more persons agree to rob a bank and in the course of the robbery one of the gang members kills or injures an innocent third party. To what extent should other members of the gang be liable for the death or injuries? This provision sets out the requirements for attaching liability to the other gang members for such actions and consequences. The subsection states that when two or more persons have formed a common intention to carry out an unlawful purpose and to assist each other therein, each is liable for the actions of the other if in the carrying out of the common purpose the other gang member commits an offence which each knew or ought to have known would be a probable consequence of carrying out the plan.

It is important, then, to determine what that common design is, as the case of *Henderson* demonstrates. A criticism here is that the term "unlawful purpose" is too vague and all-encompassing, and that it should be restricted to truly criminal or serious purposes. For example, illegal parking is an unlawful purpose, yet it would not seem to be the type of planned criminal activity envisaged by the drafters of the Code. Finally, it is important to note that an objective test is used for attaching liability in this subsection. Even if the accused did not subjectively foresee the type of offence which a fellow gang member would commit in the course of the planned crime, that accused will still be guilty of the other member's crime if a reasonable person would have foreseen it as a probable consequence of carrying out the plan.

## Regina v. Kulbacki
### [1966] 1 C.C.C. 1676 (Man. C.A.)

The judgment of the Court was delivered by

MILLER, C.J.M.: — This is an appeal by way of stated case from B.P. McDonald, P.M., under the provisions of s. 734 of the *Criminal Code*.

The accused was charged with driving a motor vehicle in a manner dangerous to the public contrary to s. 221(4) [enacted 1960-61, c. 43, s. 3] of the *Criminal Code*, and the learned Magistrate, after hearing the evidence, convicted the accused.

The accused, a young man 20 years of age, was not actually driving the motor vehicle himself but was the owner of it and had permitted a female infant, 16 years of age, although duly licensed to drive, to take the wheel of the car and drive the motor vehicle over an unimproved municipal highway in excess of 90 m.p.h. The accused, who was sitting in the front seat beside the driver, was charged with the substantive offence. According to the stated case, the accused did or said nothing to stop, prevent, or attempt to stop or prevent the driver of the car from driving in the manner in which she did.

The Crown contended that the conviction was proper in that the accused had aided and abetted the commission of the offence and, as such, under s. 21(1) of the *Code*, was liable to the same extent as if he had been driving the vehicle.

The defence was strictly one of law that the accused, although present, did nothing to encourage the commission of the offence and did not omit to do anything that [would have] contributed to its commission. The defence maintained that, although the accused was present, he did not participate in the commission of the crime but was merely a passive observer, and, at the most, guilty of mere passive acquiescence. Accused argued that he did not have any duty and was not under any liability to do anything as long as he did not in some way encourage the commission of the offence . . .

Each of the above-cited cases was decided on its own special facts and the only principles of application to the instant case are that the accused, in order to have been convicted, must have done something to encourage the commission of the offence or omitted to do something which assisted in its commission. It appears to me that when the accused, the owner of car, sat in the front seat on the passenger's side and permitted this young lady to increase the speed to such a dangerous rate, he did, by his lack of action, encourage her to violate the law. Certainly it would not have been wise for him to have grabbed the wheel at this dangerous speed, not at any time when the car was being driven in excess of 60 m.p.h., as to do so would probably have been catastrophic. To turn off the ignition, as was suggested to us by the Crown, might not have been the best course either. In no uncertain terms he should have told this young lady, the minute she started to speed on this municipal road, to desist and slow down. In my opinion, the failure to even protest is equivalent to encouragement and is fatal to his defence.

The Crown cited to us two very pertinent cases with which I will deal briefly:

The first was *Du Cros v. Lambourne*, [1907] 1 K.B. 40, 21 Cox C.C. 311. The facts of that case are very similar to the facts in the instant case. There, the accused, who had permitted a young lady to drive his car, was charged with the substantive offence when she drove it in an improper manner, and was convicted on the ground that he was an aider and abettor. In 21 Cox C.C. at p. 315, Lord Alverstone, C.J., said:

> "'If Miss Godwin was then driving, she was doing so with consent and approval of the appellant, who was the owner and in control of the car, and was sitting by her side, and he could and ought to have prevented her driving at such excessive and dangerous speed, but instead thereof he allowed her to do so, and did not interfere in any way.'"

The Court of Appeal held that on that finding of fact it was justified in convicting the accused as if he were the driver, as he was an aider, abettor, etc.

The other case in *R. v. Halmo*, 76 C.C.C. 116, [1941] 3 D.L.R. 6, [1941] O.R. 99, a decision of the Ontario Court of Appeal. In that case the owner of the vehicle was found guilty o the offence of reckless driving committed by his chauffeur.

It is true that in the *Halmo* case, *supra*, the accused, owner of the car, had full knowledge that his chauffeur was intoxicated; in fact, they became intoxicated together. Perhaps in the *Halmo* case circumstances are stronger than in the instant case but, nevertheless, it is an authority in support of the Crown's position. The *Halmo* and the *Du Cros* cases were discussed with apparent approval by the Manitoba Court of Appeal in *R. v. Harder*, 88 C.C.C. 21, 3 C.R. 49, [1947] 2 D.L.R. 593. The *Halmo* case was referred to by the Supreme Court of Canada in another *R. v. Harder* case reported (1956), 114 C.C.C. 129, 23 C.R. 295, 4 D.L.R. (2d) 150, and apparently approved. The following quotation from the *Halmo* case has some application to the instant case (At p. 127 [C.C.C.]):

> "The facts combine to make the accused a person who had in his charge and under his control the motor vehicle in question: (a) He was the owner of the motor vehicle; (b) He was the master of Mayville, his hired servant, who was driving the car; (c) He was personally present at all material times both before and at the time when the motor vehicle was being driven in a manner dangerous to the public.

> "Being personally present and having in his charge and under his control the motor vehicle, he is a principal party to the offence of a breach of s. 285(60(a) of the *Code, Reg. v. Brown* (1878), 14 Cox C.C. 144. He was guilty of negligence in that being so in charge and control of a dangerous machine, he failed and omitted to control his drunken chauffeur and to prevent him from driving the car to the danger of the public."

Every passenger is an unlawfully driven motor vehicle is not necessarily subject to conviction as an aider and abettor, as it is conceivable that a passenger might not have any authority over the car or any right to control the driver, but that is not the situation in the instant case. As above stated, he failed to make any effort to stop or prevent the commission of the offence when he was in a position to do so and when he had the authority to do so.

Therefore, as intimated, I am of the opinion that the learned Magistrate was right in convicting the accused of the substantive offence on the ground that he was an aider and abettor and liable to conviction by virtue of s. 21(1) of the *Criminal Code*. The learned Magistrate's question ought to be answered in the affirmative. The appeal should be dismissed and the conviction affirmed.

*Appeal dismissed.*

## Regina v. Salajko
### [1970] 1 C.C.C. 352 (Ont. C.A.)

The judgment of the Court was delivered orally by

GALE, C.J.O.: — This particular appellant was present when some 15 young men, if one can dignify them by that term, raped a girl in a lonely field near New Dundee in this province. Because of the frightful circumstances the girl was able to identify only three of those who were present. They were charged with rape and all were found guilty. Two of the appellant's co-accused, Francis and White, were identified as having had intercourse with the girl. She admitted, however, that this appellant did not have intercourse with her. The Crown placed its case against him on the basis of s. 21(1)(b) and (c) of the *Criminal Code*.

At the conclusion of the Crown's case, counsel for Salajko moved for a directed verdict of acquittal but it was denied. Eventually, after a recharge by the learned Judge on aiding and abetting and after the jury had come back for further instructions in that regard, the jury found the appellant guilty.

In our view there was no evidence upon which a jury, properly charged, could reasonably come to the conclusion beyond any reasonable doubt that this man had aided or abetted the outrages performed by the others. When this proposition was put to Mr. Hachborn for the Crown he candidly admitted that the evidence was very weak and relied solely on the fact that at one stage the accused was seen to be near the girl with his pants down while she was being raped by others. The accused gave an explanation as to the incident but quite apart from it we do not think that the evidence can be translated into a conclusion that the accused was aiding or abetting the others when they were ravaging the girl. Passive acquiescence is not sufficient to induce such a finding and Mr. Hachborn can point to no other evidence to suggest anything in the way of aiding or counselling or encouragement on the part of the accused with respect to that which was being done by the others. Accordingly, there simply was no evidence upon which a jury could properly arrive at a verdict of guilty against this particular accused.

We are also of the view that the learned Judge's direction with respect to abetting was in error. In this respect, and in answer to a question put to him by the jury, he seemed to indicate that a person could abet another in the commission of an offence and so be guilty of the offence if knowingly he stands by while the offence is being committed. I have in mind the following which appears at p. 401 of the transcript:

> HIS LORDSHIP: To my mind in the context of the word "abet" it would involve the understanding of what was going on in a particular situation and without active encouragement, because the word "encourage" is used, to stand by and, I suppose, in the sense, adopt and approve . . . it is a rather negative word . . . what is taking place.

> "Encourage" and "uphold" to my mind import something that is an active thing. "Countenance" is the passive encouragement. That is the way I would understand it.

We do not think that passive encouragement, if there be such a thing, can render a person guilty of an offence and refer to the following taken from Jowitt, Dictionary of English Law, p. 9, where abet is defined "to encourage or set on" and an abettor is "an instigator or setter on, one who promotes or procures a crime to be committed".

The evidence indicates clearly that this accused did not either aid or instigate or promote or procure the commission of the crime of the others, and accordingly the appeal will be allowed, the conviction quashed and a verdict of acquittal entered with respect to this accused.

*Appeal allowed; accused acquitted.*

## Henderson v. The King
[1948] S.C.R. 226

[Only the judgment of Taschereau, J. is reproduced below.]

TASCHEREAU, J.: — The appellant Henderson and one Harry Medos were jointly indicted at Vancouver B.C. for the murder of Charles Boyes, a police officer. The two accused were given separate trials, as a result of which Medos was found guilty and executed, and Henderson who was tried before Manson, J. was also convicted.

It appears from the evidence that the appellant, Medos, and one Cartier conspired together to commit a holdup at the premises of the Royal Bank of Canada, on the east side of Renfrew Street, directly opposite the Java Inn at Vancouver. The next day, the three men were seen in a maroon Mercury car, coming west, on 2nd Avenue. It was observed that the car turned into the first lane facing south, and backed out to 2nd Avenue again, and then went east, from whence it had come, and proceeded to the stop sign at Renfrew Street, and turned north on Renfrew Street in the direction of the bank, but proceeded only about two car lengths when it swerved to the right, making a U turn and proceeded at a fast rate of speed east on 2nd Avenue. The bandits who were on their way to the bank to commit the intended hold-up, had obviously detected a police car that was parked in front of the Java Inn facing south, and found that the occasion was not favourable to carry out their plot. After having made this U turn, they proceeded in their car for about a mile and a half, and then abandoned it on Kitchener Street, and walked west toward the Great Northern Railway yards.

They had admittedly been under close observation by the police, for when they arrived in the yards, Officers Boyes and Ledingham drove their car into the yards near the roundhouse, and accosted them on the railway track where all five crossed the line of tracks they were on, to another set of tracks. A few seconds later, Detective Sergeant Hoare arrived, and standing directly opposite the appellant, he said: "Who are you fellows anyway?" and coming nearer the appellant, Hoare said: "What is your name?" The two questions remained unanswered, and looking at the appellant, Hoare saw a gun tucked in the top of his overalls which he pulled out. He had just taken this gun, when the whole line of men broke up and the appellant, Medos and Carter sprang in different directions. Medos who was the first to move was pursued by Officer Boyes, Ledingham going after Carter. Medos had hardly ran six or seven steps when he turned and shot Boyes, and Carter fired at Ledingham. Medos then aimed at Hoare. Unfamiliar with the appellant's revolver, and therefore unable to use it, Hoare moved rapidly towards a pile of steel plates, trying to reach for his gun, but a bullet struck him in the left thigh and he fell to the ground. He however tried to get his gun out of the holster, but was at that moment struck by another bullet in the upper part of his right arm, and another shot passed by the left side of his face. He succeeded in sitting up, and he saw Boyes lying dead on the ground, and Medos still running. He then raised his gun to his right knee, and aimed at Medos, but seeing Carter running in an north-westerly direction, he transferred his aim to Carter and shot him to the ground. He then aimed at Medos who fell. He fired another shot which killed Carter, and a second shot at Medos.

As a result of the shooting, Officer Boyes and Ledingham and Carter were killed. Medos succeeded in escaping with the appellant, but both were discovered soon after in the basement of a house on 5th Avenue where they were arrested. In the interval, appellant had changed his outer clothing, and later Medos' gun was found in the basement containing one live shell. The gun taken from Henderson by Detective Sergeant Hoare was fully loaded with live shells, and in the appellant's pocket were found five other live shells which fitted his gun.

It is the contention of the Crown that Henderson, together with Medos and Carter, formed a common intention to commit a crime by violence, viz. to hold up and rob the Royal Bank of Canada on Renfrew Street, and to assist each other therein, and that it was a part of the common intention to overcome all resistance by force of arms, either in the bank or outside the bank, and to resist lawful apprehension by the police, and if pursued to shoot if necessary. The Crown further states that such common intention *was at no time abandoned* by appellant, that the common design was frustrated by the police and that it was only the presence of a Police car immediately across the street form the bank, which caused the bandits to change their mind, so that instead of continuing their unlawful purpose, they then directed their attention to resisting lawful apprehension.

The Crown further submits that in view of section 69(2) of the *Criminal Code*, which reads as follows: —

> **2.** If several persons form a common intention to prosecute any unlawful purpose, and to assist each other therein, each of them is a party to every offence committed by anyone of them in the prosecution of such common purpose, the commission of which offence was, or ought to have been known to be a probable consequence of the prosecution of such common purpose.

The jury, being properly instructed by the learned trial judge, could find that such a common intention was formed, and that in the *prosecution* of such common purpose one or more of the trio shot and killed Officer Boyes, and that the commission of that offence was or ought to have been known to be a probable consequence of the *prosecution* of such common purpose.

The Crown also submits that it was put to the jury by Crown counsel, that even if the jury could not find that the common purpose was as comprehensive as was put to them, there was another view which could be taken, namely, that when the trio abandoned the motor car on Kitchener Street, they had already committed a crime, that is to say, they had *attempted* to hold up and rob the bank, within the meaning of section 72 of the *Code* which is in the following words: —

> **72.** Every one who, having an intent to commit an offence, does or omits an act for the purpose of accomplishing his object is guilty of an attempt to commit the offence intended whether under the circumstances it was possible to commit such offence or not.
>
> . . .
>
> **2.** The question whether an act done or omitted with intent to commit an offence is or is not only preparation for the commission of that offence and too remote to constitute an attempt to commit it, is a question of law.

It is said that these three men, when their attempt to hold up the bank was frustrated, formed a common intention to resist lawful apprehension, which is in itself an unlawful purpose within the meaning of section 69, and that during the *prosecution* of such common purpose, murder was committed by one of their number.

. . .

I would first like to deal with the contention that the three conspirators while on their way to the bank, were guilty of *an attempt* to commit a hold-up and rob the

Royal Bank of Canada. With deference with other views expressed, I cannot agree with this submission. Of course, the conspiracy to rob the bank was complete and this in itself was a crime, but I do not believe that the subsequent facts revealed by the evidence show the essential ingredients of an attempt, within the meaning of section 72 of the *Criminal Code*.

An intent, an act of preparation, and an attempt must not be confused. A mere intent is not punishable in criminal law, even if coupled with an act of preparation. As it was said in *Regina v. Eagleton* at p. 538: —

> The mere intention to commit a misdemeanour is not criminal. Some act is required, and we do not think that all acts towards committing a misdemeanour are indictable. Acts remotely leading towards the commission of the offence are not to be considered as attempts to commit it, but acts immediately connected with it are . . .

. . .

I entirely agree with what Mr. Justice O'Halloran says in his dissenting judgment:

> For an act to be an attempt, it must take place between the attemptor and the attemptee and be proximate to the crime about to be committed.

Here, the trio were seen in an automobile in the direction of the bank; but the plot was frustrated by the presence of the police. There was nothing done by the trio, no overt act *immediately connected* with the offence of hold-up and robbing. Although it may be said that no one could doubt the express purpose of the bandits, I do not believe that it can be held that the mere fact of going to the place where the contemplated crime is to be committed, constitutes an attempt. There must be a closer relation between the victim and the author of the crime; there must be an act done which displays not only a preparation for an attempt, but a commencement of execution, a step in the commission of the actual crime itself.

. . .

Section 72, para. 2 of the *Criminal Code* says that the question whether an act done or omitted with intent to commit an offence, is or is not only preparation for the commission of that offence, and too remote to constitute an attempt to commit it, is a question of law.

The jury were told by the learned trial judge that:

> the (trio) could not be prosecuted for robbing a bank, but they could be prosecuted for attempting to rob a bank . . . the attempt is complete when they take any steps in connection with it.

This statement of law, is, I think, erroneous. The jury might have thought that it was while trying to escape, after having committed an act, which they were told was *a crime*, that the bandits started the shooting as a result of which the killing ensued. this obviously confused the issue and was prejudicial to the accused.

I further believe, however, that the question whether or not the bandits were guilty of an attempt, is entirely foreign to the case.

There is no possible doubt that the three accused in view of the evidence produced, were guilty of conspiracy. The common unlawful purpose was to hold up and rob the

Royal Bank of Canada, and it is also common ground that they intended to assist each other in the prosecution of that purpose. But, their common purpose having been frustrated, was obviously not pursued, and it was not therefore in the *prosecution* of such common purpose that Officer Boyes was killed.

To my mind the real issues are the following: —

Was there at any moment a concerted plot formed by Medos, Carter and Henderson to resist legal apprehension with violence? It may well be that this plot if it did exist, was made originally when it was agreed to rob the bank, or it may be that it was formed after the bandits were frustrated in the prosecution of the hold-up. If such a plot did exist, the shooting being the result of a conspiracy, the two of course might be guilty of murder. The common intention would then be to resist legal apprehension; that would be the unlawful purpose. Each one of the trio wold be a party to any other offence, committed by any one of them, in the prosecution of the common purpose, if he had known, or ought to have known, that it was a probable consequence of the original common purpose. It may happen, however, and this was for the jury to determine, that Henderson had ceased to be a party to the conspiracy, and that the shooting which started after he had been disarmed and under virtual arrest, was the spontaneous act of Medos. Then, the act of one, would not have been the act of all.

In order that section 69(2) may find its application, the co-conspirators must form not only a common intention to prosecute an unlawful purpose, but they must agree also "to assist each other therein", and therefore, if a man is disarmed and made incapable of furnishing the promised assistance, the situation is obviously changed. It is settled law that a person who has been a party to prosecute a common illegal purpose, may disassociate himself with his original co-conspirators. As early as in 1828, in *Rex v. Edmeads*, Baron Vaughan said at the Berkshire Assizes (Carrington & Paynes Reports, Vol. 3): —

> If it could be shown that either of them separated himself from the rest, and showed distinctly that he would have no hand in what they were doing, the objection would have much weight in it.

. . .

In *Rex v. Croft* it was held that the agreement may be expressly determined and that if it comes to an end before the crime is committed, the party who has put an end to the agreement is not guilty. The question whether the agreement has been put to an end, must be judged in view of all the circumstances revealed by the evidence, and I have no doubt that it is a question for the jury. It was for them to say, if in view of the evidence the appellant had been a party to the conspiracy, if such a conspiracy was ever formed, and it was also within their exclusive province to find, after have been properly instructed, that he had detached himself from any further association with the other conspirators.

Unfortunately, all these aspects of the case were not dealt with, and these omissions were, I believe, highly prejudicial to the accused. The defence was not presented so as to give it all its force and effect. It is true that no witnesses were called on behalf of the appellant, but it is nevertheless the duty of the trial judge, in his charge to the jury, to explain the exculpatory effect of the evidence, whether it is given by the witnesses for the Crown or for the accused. *Wu v. The King*. It was the fundamental right of the appellant, who has been charged of murder, purely by construction of the law, which in this particular case creates a presumptive guilt, to have all the features of his defence adequately put to the jury.

I have come to the conclusion that this has not been done, and that the Crown has not established to my satisfaction that the verdict would have been the same, if the proper direction had been given.

The appeal should be allowed, the conviction quashed and a new trial directed.

*Appeal allowed and new trial directed.*

### Questions/Discussion

1.  Describe and discuss the nature and operation of section 21(1) of the Criminal Code. Do you think that it has been fairly interpreted in the cases which you have read? For example, do you agree with the decisions in *Kulbacki* and *Salajko*? Why or why not? What types of relationships do you think might give rise to the results which are seen in *Kulbacki*? Is this case a dangerous precedent in that we are left with a great deal of uncertainty after the decision as to what relationship will transform mere presence into something more and also as to what was "required" of the accused?

2.  Do you think that there should be a separate provision in the Code to distinguish the nature and degree of criminal liability of those who actually do the crime from the liability of those who aid or abet? In situations of offences with minimum penalties, leniency in sentencing is not possible in order to take account of the varying degrees of blameworthiness.

3.  Describe and discuss the nature and operation of section 21(2) of the Criminal Code. Do you think that the subsection is fair in light of traditional principles of individual blameworthiness? Should an objective test be used to determine what might take place in the course of carrying out a planned offence? What are the problems with using a subjective test in such situations?

4.  Do you agree with the court's decision in *Henderson* as to its interpretation of what was the planned offence? Note that unlike criminal attempts and conspiracy, there is the possibility of "withdrawal" from the plan and therefore being relieved of liability for other offences which may occur in its carrying out; depending on the circumstances, however, liability may still attach for an attempt of conspiracy in regard to the planned offence.

### Further Reading

*   Mewett, A., and M. Manning, *Mewett and Manning on Criminal Law 3rd ed.* (Markham: Butterworths, 1994).
*   Roach, Kent, *Criminal Law, 2d ed.* (Toronto: Irwin Law, 2000) at 111-119.
*   Rose, V.G., *Parties to an Offence* (Toronto: Carswell, 1982).
*   Sornarajah, M., "Common Intention and Murder Under the Criminal Codes" (1981), 59 Canadian Bar Review 727.
*   Stuart, Don, and R. Delisle, *Learning Canadian Criminal Law, 8th ed.* (Toronto: Carswell, 2001).
*   Verdun-Jones, S., *Criminal Law in Canada: Cases, Questions and the Code, 3d ed.* (Toronto: Harcourt Canada, 2002).

# 7

# DEFENCES

## General Introduction

This chapter outlines defences to and denials of criminal liability, both complete and limited. Complete defences result in the acquittal of the accused whereas limited or partial defences can result in a conviction on a less serious charge, for example in the defences of provocation and intoxication. The four sections which follow are divided according to four arbitrary categories of defences: justifications and excuses, absence of intent or knowledge, policy defences, and mental or emotional impairment.

Justifications and excuses for our purposes are those types of defences which essentially admit that the offence was done, but offer an excuse for the defendant's actions. The defendant may argue that there were threats or force involved in the doing of the crime and for that reason he or she ought to be excused under section 17 of the Code. On the other hand, the argument of self defence may be raised by virtue of section 34 or the common law defence of consent may be used. These latter two defences raise particular concerns in the area of women and the criminal justice system. For example, there is the issue of the "battered women's defence" and its acceptance in and use by the courts. In the case of consent, we return to this defence in the final chapter in the section on sexual assault and the concerns raised by women's groups and others over the treatment of consent and the related issues in mistake of fact (see 7.2.1, below, and particularly the *Pappajohn* case).

Section 2 focuses on an absence of intent or knowledge, and is in essence an argument that the mens rea element of the offence has not been satisfied. At issue in this section is the type of mistaken belief or knowledge which is necessary to obviate guilt. Mistakes of fact are valid legal mistakes and the first subsection deals with the requirements of such mistakes. The second subsection examines mistakes (or ignorance) of law, mistakes which are not usually valid in relieving liability. The important question is how to determine what is a mistake of fact and what is a mistake of law because so many issues involve mixed questions of fact and law; for example, matters such as divorce and ownership involve legal relationships yet also encompass assertions as to fact in the everyday sense of the terms.

Section 3 highlights the increasing role played by the courts in the formulation of criminal justice policy, notably due to the advent of the Canadian Charter of Rights and Freedoms. The first subsection introduces us to the common law defence of entrapment where some of the problems associated with traditional judge-made law — uncertainty and lack of expertise — can be seen. The second topic on Charter protections deals only very briefly with the impact of the Charter on criminal law. Given the breadth of the area, a deeper examination must be left to other sources, notably those concerned either with the procedural aspects of the criminal law or with the Charter alone.

The fourth and final section deals with certain pleas which are all based on some type of mental or emotional impairment. The impairment may be caused by mental illness, drug use, disease, a blow to the head, or anger. The source of impairment determines whether the impaired accused falls within the scope of the defences of mental disorder, intoxication, provocation or automatism. Controversy surrounds all of these pleas. One concern with provocation is the application of the "ordinary person" test in determining whether the accused's loss of control is acceptable. This question is addressed in *Hill*. Another issue has been the impact of the anger exhibited by the accused on the *mens rea* required for murder and this issue is addressed in *Parent*.

A glance at the legal literature on the defence of mental disorder will confirm that this plea remains highly contentious. Dozens of articles call for the complete abolition of the plea and just as many argue for its retention. Some psychiatric experts argue that mental illness, the cornerstone of this defence, is a myth. Critics also suggest that while the mentally ill are sent away for treatment to be released when they are cured or at least not dangerous, the treatment given is not effective and mental health experts cannot predict accurately. Sorting the mad from the bad may be impossible, and even if theoretically possible, may be confounded by opposing institutional interests. The 1992 changes to the law in Canada are discussed in the excerpts from the O'Marra article.

The intoxication doctrine is controversial both legally and scientifically. Scientifically, the intoxication plea is questioned because there is considerable doubt that alcoholic or other drug impairments have the effects assumed by the courts. In particular, while the entire plea is premised on intoxicated offenders acting without intention, researchers report that drug impairment rarely, if ever, negates intent. With this background in mind, note the Supreme Court's most recent pronouncement in *Daviault* and Parliament's response in enacting section 33.1(1) of the Criminal Code. This section effectively takes away the defence of extreme intoxication for general intent crimes of violence, and thus far has withstood Charter scrutiny by the courts. In regard to this latter issue, see *R. v. Vickberg* (1998), 16 C.R. (5th) 164 (B.C. S.C.).

With automatism, a major difficulty is drawing the line between mental disorder and automatism, a problem illustrated by the *Rabey* case. Automatism cases often deal with physical or functional causes for the alleged involuntary behaviour. Such causes include epilepsy, brain tumour and blows to the head. Much more problematic are the cases involving so-called "psychological blows" which psychiatrists claim can be equivalent to physical blows. It is questionable whether any such "dissociative" states are valid excuses. Indeed, it is not clear how a psychological blow leading to violence differs in fact from provocation.

## 7.1   JUSTIFICATIONS AND EXCUSES

### 7.1.1   Duress

**Introduction**

One of the first questions that arises in regard to duress is why is it necessary to have a separate defence for duress or compulsion; if a person has been forced through threats to commit a crime, then it might be argued that the mens rea for the crime is not present. However, it must be kept in mind that "why" a person commits a crime is usually not important and many crimes merely require that an accused has knowingly or intentionally done the acts which make up the actus reus of the crime. People who do criminal acts under duress do so knowingly or intentionally, but there is an understandable excuse for their doing the acts. It is this excuse which the defence of compulsion in section 17 of the Code is permitting, though in a strictly limited way. Other types of excuses or reasons for doing the acts, such as "I needed the money to buy food so I robbed the bank" or "I killed him because I was mad at him" do not work, because they are either not viewed as socially valid excuses or might excuse too many people for their harmful acts.

We can see in section 17 that the law is allowing for people who have been subject to physical threats (though not necessarily *against* themselves) to be relieved of criminal liability for their actions. But this is not a blanket relief; it is one which is strictly circumscribed. First, it can be used only for threats of immediate death or grievous bodily harm, which has been interpreted in *Carker* below to mean that the threat must be one which is to be carried out immediately. The facts in the case show how unfair and unrealistic that interpretation can be, particularly in a prison environment like Carker's. Second, the person making the threat must be present when the offence is committed; again, the situation in *Carker* shows how narrow an interpretation the courts had taken. As for either of these requirements, the person threatened may realistically be motivated to commit the offence out of fear, even though the harm may be in the future or the person threatening may not be present when the offence is committed. Surely it would be more just and also more true to the rationale of the excuse to forgive those who subjectively believe that the threat will be carried out and who act as a direct result of that threat whether or not these first two requirements are met.[1]

Two major exceptions are given in section 17 as to who can make use of the defence. First, the defence is not available to a person who is "a party to a conspiracy or association whereby the person is subject to compulsion". In other words, the section is saying that such people have put themselves at risk in the first place and should not now be able to take advantage of the defence; they are not blameless in the circumstances. The second exception is that duress is not available as a defence in regard to certain crimes listed in section 17, crimes such as murder, sexual assault,

---

1   See also the Supreme Court of Canada decision in this regard in *R. v. Hebert* (1989), 49 C.C.C. (3d) 59 (S.C.C.).

robbery, and arson. The Code in effect is making a policy choice for the individual in such threatening situations, that if you go ahead and do one of the listed crimes, the excuse of duress can never be used.

It is this second exception which formed the basis of the *Paquette* case. The accused had been charged with murder and therefore, presumably, could not avail himself of the defence of duress. Yet he was successful in being able to use the common law defence of duress which is effective against murder charges. In such a situation the accused attempts to argue that the defence in section 17 does not apply to his or her case for the purpose of using the wider common law defence. The *Paquette* case outlines the situations under which the accused can escape the restrictions of the statutory defence. The *Hibbert* case follows the same line of reasoning as in *Paquette* and also discusses the situation where a "safe avenue of escape" exists for the accused. The final case, *Ruzic*, provides the most recent and most exhaustive treatment of the defence of duress by the Supreme Court. The question that arises after this case is whether *Carker* would be decided the same way today.

## The Queen v. Carker (No. 2)
### [1967] 2 C.C.C. 190 (S.C.C.)

Appeal by the Attorney-General of British Columbia from the judgment of the British Columbia Court of Appeal, [1966] 4 C.C.C. 212, 48 C.R. 313, 56 W.W.R. 65, quashing the accused's conviction on a charge of committing mischief and directing a new trial.

The judgment of the Court was delivered by

RITCHIE, J.: — This is an appeal by the Attorney-General of British Columbia from a judgment of the Court of Appeal of that Province, from which MacLean, J., dissented, and by which it was ordered that the respondent's conviction, for unlawfully and wilfully damaging public property and thereby committing mischief, should be set aside and that a new trial should be had.

At the trial the respondent admitted having damaged the plumbing fixtures in the cell where he was incarcerated at Oakalla Prison Farm in British Columbia but, through his counsel, he sought to introduce evidence to show that he had committed this offence under the compulsion of threats and was therefore entitled to be excused for committing it by virtue of the provisions of s. 17 of the *Criminal Code* and that he was also entitled to avail himself of the common law defence of "duress" having regard to the provisions of s. 7(2) of the *Criminal Code*.

Under the latter section it is provided that:

"7(2) Every rule and principle of the common law that render any circumstance a justification or excuse for an act or a defence to a charge continues in force and applies in respect of proceedings for an offence under this Act.. *except in so far as they are altered by or are inconsistent with this Act or any other Act of the Parliament of Canada*" (The italics are my own.)

I agree with the learned trial Judge and with MacLean, J.A., that in respect of proceedings for an offence under the *Criminal Code* the common law rules and principles respecting "duress" as an excuse or defence have been codified and exhaustively defined in s. 17 which reads as follows"

> "17. A person who commits an offence under compulsion by threats of immediate death or grievous bodily harm from a person who is present when the offence is committed is excused for committing the offence if he believes that the threats will be carried out and if he is not a party to a conspiracy or association whereby he is subject to compulsion, but this section does not apply where the offence that is committed is treason, murder, piracy, attempted murder, assisting in rape, forcible abduction, robbery, causing bodily harm or arson."

At the outset of the proceedings at the trial in the present case and in the absence of the jury, Mr. Greenfield, who acted on behalf of the accused, informed the Court that he intended to call evidence of compulsion and duress and he elected to outline the nature of this evidence which was that the offence had been committed during a disturbance, apparently organized by way of protest, to damage property at the Prison Farm in the course of which a substantial body of prisoners, shouting in unison from their separate cells, threatened the respondent who was not joining in the disturbance that if he did not break the plumbing fixtures in his cell he would be kicked in the head, his arm would be broken and he would get a knife in the back at the first opportunity.

The question which the learned trial Judge was required to determine on Mr. Greenfield's application was whether the proposed evidence which had been outlined to him indicated a defence or excuse available at law; he decided that it did not and the majority of the Court of Appeal having taken a different view, the Attorney-General now appeals to this Court.

There can be little doubt that the evidence outlined by Mr. Greenfield, which was subsequently confirmed by the evidence given by the ringleaders of the disturbance in mitigation of sentence, disclosed that the respondent committed the offence under the compulsion of threats of death and grievous bodily harm, but although these threats were "immediate" in the sense that they were continuous until the time that the offence was committed, they were not threats of "immediate death" or "immediate grievous bodily harm" and none of the persons who delivered them was present in the cell with the respondent when the offence was committed. I am accordingly of opinion that the learned trial Judge was right in deciding that the proposed evidence did not afford an excuse within the meaning of s. 17 of the *Criminal Code*.

In the course of his most thoughtful judgment in the Court of Appeal, [[1966] 4 C.C.C. 212 at p. 224, 48 C.R. 313, 56 W.W.R. 65], Norris J., had occasion to say:

> "The question as to whether or not the person threatening was present goes to the question of the grounds for the fear which the appellant might have. In my opinion a person could be present making a threat although separated by the bars of the cell. These are all matters which should have gone to the jury, as was the question of whether or not the threat of death or grievous bodily harm was an immediate one — a question of degree. They might well consider that the threat was immediate as being continuous, as it was in this case, that it would be all the more frightening because of the uncertainty as to when it actually might happen, and therefore force him to act as he did."

With the greatest respect it appears to me that the question of whether immediate threats of future death or grievous bodily harm constitute an excuse for committing a crime within the meaning of s. 17 and the question of whether a person can be "present" within the meaning of that section when he is locked in a separate cell from the place where the offence is committed are both questions which depend upon the construction to be placed on the section and they are therefore questions of law and not questions of fact for the jury. (See *Vail v. The Queen, ex rel. Dickson*, 129 C.C.C. 145, at p. 150, 26 D.L.R. (2d) 419, [1960] S.C.R. 913, 33 W.W.R. 325; *Sikyea v. The Queen*, [1965] 2 C.C.C. 129 at p. 131, 44 C.R. 266, [1964] S.C.R. 642.

In support of the suggestion that the threat in the present case was "immediate and continuous" Norris J., relied on the case of *Subramaniam v. Public Prosecutor*, [1956] 1 W.L.R. 965, in which the Privy Council decided that the trial Judge was wrong in excluding evidence of threats to which the appellant was subjected by Chinese terrorists in Malaya. In that case it was found that the threats were a continuous menace up to the moment when the appellant was captured because the terrorists might have come back at any time and carried them into effect. Section 94 of the *Penal Code* of the Federated Malay States, which the appellant sought to invoke in that case provided [see p. 968]:

"**94.** Except murder and offences included in Chapter VI punishable by death, nothing is an offence which is done by a person who is compelled to do it by threats, which, at the time of doing it, reasonably cause the apprehension that instant death to that person will otherwise be the consequence: . . . "

The distinctions between the *Subramaniam* Case and the present one lie in the fact that Subramaniam might well have had reasonable cause for apprehension that instant death would result from his disobeying the terrorists who might have come back at any moment, whereas it is virtually inconceivable that "immediate death" or "grievous bodily harm" could have come to Carker from those who were uttering the threat against him as they were locked up in separate cells, and it is also to be noted that the provisions of s. 17 of the *Criminal Code* are by no means the same as those of s. 94 of the *Penal Code* of the Federated Malay States; amongst other distinctions the latter section contains no provision that the person who utters threats must be present when the offence is committed in order to afford an excuse for committing it.

Both Norris, J., and Branca, J., in delivering their separate reasons for judgment in the Court of Appeal, expressed the view that the evidence which was tendered should have been admitted on the issue of whether the respondent acted wilfully in damaging the prison plumbing or whether he was so affected by the threats uttered against him as to be incapable of adopting any other course than the one which he did.

The relevant provisions of the *Criminal Code* read as follows:

"**372**(1) Every one commits mischief who wilfully
(a) destroys or damages property . . . .

"(3) Every one who commits mischief in relation to public property is guilty of an indictable offence and is liable to imprisonment for fourteen years."

On this phase of the matter, Norris, J., had this to say [pp. 225-6]:

"In making the ruling which he did, the learned trial Judge deprived the appellant of what could be a substantial defence to the charge or an excuse under s. 17. Without hearing the evidence, the jury could not decide whether the act was in fact wilful. This was not a matter on which the Judge might rule. The lengths to which the evidence might go to disprove the essentials of the charge or to prove the requirements of s. 17 could never, in the absence of the evidence of witnesses, be apparent either to the learned Judge or to the jury."

With the greatest respect, this portion of Mr. Justice Norris' reasons for judgment appears to overlook the fact that "the length to which the evidence might go . . . " was fully outlined to the learned Judge by counsel for the respondent when he was making the application.

In this regard it is important to bear in mind the fact that "wilful" as it is used in Part IX of the *Criminal Code* is defined in s. 371(1) which reads, in part, as follows:

"**371**(1) Every one who causes the occurrence of an event by doing an act or by omitting to do an act that it is his duty to do, knowing that the act or omission will probably cause the occurrence of the event and being reckless whether the event occurs or not, shall be deemed, for the purposes of this Part, wilfully to have caused the occurrence of the event."

The evidence outlined to the learned trial Judge discloses that the criminal act was committed to preserve the respondent from future harm coming to him, but there is no suggestion in the evidence tendered for the defence that the accused did not know that what he was doing would "probably cause" damage. Accepting the outline made by defence counsel as being an accurate account of the evidence which was available, there was in my view nothing in it to support the defence that the act was not done "wilfully" within the meaning of s. 371(1) and 372(1) of the *Criminal Code* and there was accordingly no ground to justify the learned trial Judge in permitting the proposed evidence to be called in support of such a defence.

In view of all the above, I would allow this appeal, set aside the judgement of the Court of Appeal and restore the conviction.

*Appeal allowed; conviction restored.*

## Paquette v. The Queen
[1977] 2 S.C.R. 189

The judgment of the Court was delivered by

MARTLAND, J.: — The facts which give rise to this appeal are as follows:

During the course of a robbery at the Pop Shoppe, in the City of Ottawa, on March 18, 1973, an innocent bystander was killed by a bullet from a rifle fired by one Simard. The robbery was committed by Simard and one Clermont, both of whom, together with the appellant, were jointly charged with non-capital murder. Simard and Clermont pleaded guilty to this charge.

The appellant was not present when the robbery was committed or when the shooting occurred. The charge against him was founded upon s. 21(2) of the *Criminal Code*. Section 21 provides as follows:

**21.**(1) Every one is a party to an offence who
(a) actually commits it,
(b) does or omits to do anything for the purpose of aiding any person to commit it, or
(c) abets any person in committing it.

(2) Where two or more persons form an intention in common to carry out an unlawful purpose and to assist each other therein and any one of them, in carrying out the common purpose, commits an offence, each of them who knew or ought to have known that the commission of the offence would be a probable consequence of carrying out the common purpose is a party to that offence.

The appellant made a statement to the police, which was admitted in evidence at the trial and which described his involvement in the matter as follows: On the day of the robbery Clermont telephoned the appellant for a ride as his own car was broken. Clermont asked the appellant where he used to work and was told at the Pop Shoppe. Clermont told him to drive to the Pop Shoppe because Clermont wanted to rob it, and when the appellant refused, Clermont pulled his gun and threatened to kill him. Simard was picked up later and also a rifle. The appellant drove them to the Pop Shoppe. The appellant had been threatened with revenge if he did not wait for Clermont and Simard. The appellant, in his statement, stated he was afraid and drove around the block. After the robbery and homicide Clermont and Simard attempted twice, unsuccessfully, to get into the appellant's car. Three of the Crown's witnesses supported this latter statement. The appellant did not testify at trial but relied on the above statement and two other statements also introduced at the trial by the Crown to support his argument that he had no intention in common with Simard and Clermont to carry out the robbery; i.e.:

(1) An oral statement to a police officer on his arrest that he had been threatened with death "if he squealed".
(2) The written statement to the police outlined above in which he stated that he had only participated in the robbery by driving because he was threatened with death;
(3) A statement to his girl friend the day after the robbery that he was forced to do it.

The trial judge charged the jury as follows:

Now, the defence are asserting that Paquette participated in this robbery because he was compelled to do so, and in that connection I charge you that if Paquette joined in the common plot to rob the Pop Shoppe under threats of death or grievous bodily harm, that would negative his having a common intention with Simard to rob the Pop Shoppe, and you must find Paquette not guilty.

The appellant was acquitted. The Crown appealed to the Court of Appeal for Ontario. The reasons delivered by that Court make it clear that the appeal would have been dismissed had it not been for the decision of this Court in *Dunbar v. The King*.

. . .

Counsel for the Crown submits that the principles of law applicable to the excuse or defence of duress or compulsion are exhaustively codified in s. 17 of the *Criminal Code*, and that the appellant is precluded from relying upon this provision because of the exception contained at the end of it. Section 17 provides:

17. A person who commits an offence under compulsion by threats of immediate death or grievous bodily harm from a person who is present when the offence is committed is excused

for committing the offence if he believes that the threats will be carried out and if he is not a party to a conspiracy or association whereby he is subject to compulsion, but this section does not apply where the offence that is committed is treason, murder, piracy, attempted murder, assisting in rape, forcible abduction, robbery, causing bodily harm or arson.

In my opinion the application of s. 17 is limited to cases in which the person seeking to rely upon it has himself committed an offence. If a person who actually commits the offence does so in the presence of another party who has compelled him to do the act by threats of immediate death or grievous bodily harm, then, if he believes the threats would be carried out, and is not a party to a conspiracy whereby he is subject to such compulsion, he is excused for committing the offence. The protection afforded by this section is not given in respect of the offences listed at the end of the section, which include murder and robbery.

The section uses the specific words "a person who commits an offence". It does not use the words "a person who is a party to an offence." This is significant in the light of the wording of s. 21(1) which, in para. (a), makes a person a party to an offence who "actually commits it". Paragraphs (b) and (c) deal with a person who aids or abets a person committing the offence. In my opinion s. 17 codifies the law as to duress as an excuse for the actual commission of a crime, but it does not, by its terms, go beyond that. *R. v. Carker*, in which reference was made to s. 17 having codified the defence or excuse of duress, dealt with a situation in which the accused had actually committed the offence.

The appellant, in the present case, did not himself commit the offence of robbery or of murder. He was not present when the murder occurred, as was the case in *R. v. Farduto*, and *R. v. Warren*, to which counsel for the Crown referred. In the former case the accused provided the razor with which the murderer cut the throat of the victim in his presence. The Court was of the view that the trial judge could conclude that there was no case of such compulsion as would constitute an excuse. In the latter case the accused, the brother of the actual murderer was present with him over a period of time after the robbery occurred and before the deceased was killed in his presence. The report does not indicate the nature of the compulsion alleged. The emphasis appears to have been on the subnormal intelligence of the accused making him willing to go along with what was suggested to him.

The appellant could only be considered to be a party to the murder on the basis of the application of s. 21(2). Section 21(1) is not applicable because the offence to which he is alleged to be a party is murder, and it is clear that he did not commit murder, nor did he aid or abet in its commission.

Subsection (2) is only applicable if it is established that the appellant, in common with Simard and Clermont, formed an intention to commit robbery. The question in issue is as to whether the trial judge erred in law in telling the jury that if the appellant joined in the plot to rob under threats of death or of grievous bodily harm, this would negative such common intention.

I have already stated my reasons for considering s. 17 to be inapplicable. That being so, the appellant is entitled, by virtue of s. 7(3) of the *Code*, to rely upon any excuse or defence available to him at common law. The defence of duress to a charge of murder against a person who did not commit the murder, but who has alleged to have aided and abetted, was recently considered by the House of Lords in *Director of Public Prosecutions for Northern Ireland v. Lynch*, in which the decided cases were fully reviewed.

. . .

I am in agreement with the conclusion reached by the majority that it was open to Lynch, in the circumstances of that case, to rely on the defence of duress, which had not been put to the jury. If the defence of duress can be available to a person who has aided and abetted in the commission of murder, then clearly it should be available to a person who is sought to be made a party to the offence by virtue of s. 21(2). A person whose actions have been dictated by fear of death or of grievous bodily injury cannot be said to have formed a genuine common intention to carry out an unlawful purpose with the person who has threatened him with those consequences if he fails to co-operate.

. . .

I would allow the appeal, set aside the judgment of the Court of Appeal, and restore the verdict of acquittal.

*Appeal allowed.*

## Hibbert v. The Queen
### (1995), 99 C.C.C (3d) 193 (S.C.C.)

Appeal by the accused from a judgment of the Ontario Court of Appeal dismissing his appeal from conviction for aggravated assault.

The judgment of the court was delivered by

[1] LAMER, C.J.C.: — This appeal presents a number of important questions, each having to do with the role of duress as a defence to criminal charges. In order to resolve these issues, we must first examine the theoretical basis underlying the rule that criminal liability does not attach to a person who commits the *actus reus* of an offence as a result of threats of death or bodily harm from a third party. In particular, this court must decide whether it is open to a person charged as a party to an offence to argue that, because his or her actions were coerced, he or she did not possess the *mens rea* necessary for party liability. This argument must be weighed against the alternative position — namely, that duress does not "negate" the *mens rea* for party liability, but that persons who commit certain criminal acts under duress may none the less be excused from criminal liability under the common law "defence of duress". It is also necessary for the court to address certain questions having to do with limitations on this defence's availability. Specifically, we are asked to determine whether accused persons are foreclosed from recourse to the defence if they failed to avail themselves of a "safe avenue of escape" from the situation of coercion when such a safe avenue was available. If this is indeed the case, we must go on to consider whether the existence of such a "safe avenue" is to be determined on an objective basis, or from the subjective viewpoint of the accused.

I
## FACTUAL BACKGROUND

[2] On November 25, 1991, shortly before 1:00 a.m. Fitzroy Cohen was shot four times with a semi-automatic handgun as he stood in the lobby of the apartment building he lived in. The shots were fired by Mark Bailey, an acquaintance of Cohen whom Cohen knew by his street names, "Quasi" or "Dogheart". At the time of the shooting, Bailey was accompanied by the appellant, Lawrence Hibbert, who was a close friend of Cohen. Cohen had descended from his apartment to the lobby at the appellant's request, unaware that Bailey was waiting below with gun in hand.

[3] Cohen survived the shooting. At the appellant's trial, Cohen testified that for some time prior to the shooting he had been aware that Bailey was seeking a confrontation with him. Bailey, Cohen believed, was seeking revenge for an incident that had taken place the previous year, in which Bailey had been robbed by a rival drug dealer named Andrew Reid while Cohen and several others stood by, watching and laughing. Cohen testified that he had been told that Bailey had subsequently attacked one of the men involved in the robbery on a busy street, firing several shots at him (but missing). He also knew that Andrew Reid had been murdered. Cohen said that he had told the appellant, whom he described as his "best friend", about the robbery of Bailey.

[4] The appellant, who testified at trial, stated that at the time of the shooting he owed Bailey $100 as payment for drugs he had purchased from him some months earlier. He testified that he had been attempting to avoid Bailey, but that on the evening of November 24, 1991, he had accidently run into him in the lobby of an apartment building in Etobicoke where he had gone to visit friends. Bailey had approached the appellant and indicated that he was armed with a handgun. The appellant testified that Bailey ordered him to take him to Cohen's apartment. When he refused, the appellant stated, Bailey had led him to the basement and punched him in the face several times. The appellant testified that he feared for his life, and that he believed that Bailey would shoot him if he continued to refuse to assist him. He stated that it was this fear that led him to agree to lead Bailey to Cohen's apartment.

[5] Bailey and the appellant went out to Bailey's car, where Bailey's girlfriend and another young woman were waiting. The appellant got into the back seat, while Bailey drove. The women testified that the appellant was quiet during the drive, but that his mood was neither noticeably happy or unhappy. At trial, one of the young women recalled that the appellant had made a remark to the effect that "this might be the last time I'm going to see you".

[6] Bailey dropped the two women off at their apartment, and told the appellant to get into the front seat. The appellant testified that they stopped at a telephone booth, and that Bailey ordered him to call Cohen and ask him to meet him downstairs in 20 minutes. The appellant did so, telling Cohen that he "had something for him". According to the appellant, Bailey stood by the phone booth during his conversation with Cohen, and could hear what the appellant said to Cohen. Cohen and his girlfriend, Beverley St. Hillaire, confirmed that they had received a telephone call from the

appellant, essentially as the appellant described. They testified that the appellant had sounded "normal", but that he had been more abrupt than he usually was.

[7] Bailey and Hibbert arrived at Cohen's apartment building approximately half an hour after making the phone call. The appellant testified that Bailey drew his gun and pointed it at him as they got out of the car. They went to the front door of the building where, following Bailey's orders, the appellant called Cohen's apartment on the building intercom, while Bailey kept his gun trained on him. The appellant's testimony, which was confirmed by Cohen, was that ordinarily when visiting Cohen he would not use the building's front door, but would instead enter the building through a side door that could be opened from the outside using a technique Cohen had taught him. Cohen also confirmed the appellant's testimony that he had asked Cohen to "come down" to the lobby, but that he had not asked Cohen to "buzz him in" (*i.e.*, press a button on the intercom that would unlock the building's outer door). The appellant testified that he had hoped that Cohen would not unlock the building's front door, so that when he came downstairs he would see Bailey through the locked glass outer door and have a chance to retreat to safety. However, Cohen buzzed the outer door open without being asked to do so, and Bailey and the appellant went into the lobby.

[8] According to the testimony of both Cohen and Hibbert, Cohen took the stairs from his second-floor apartment to the lobby. When he emerged into the lobby, he was met by Bailey, who grabbed him and pointed the gun at his chest, saying "You're dead now, pussy." Bailey led Cohen into the ground-floor hallway, where (according to both Cohen and the appellant's testimony) he turned to Hibbert and told him to "stay some place where I [can] see you." After a brief exchange of words with Cohen, Bailey pushed Cohen away and fired four shots at him, striking him in the groin, legs and buttocks. Saying "Come, Pigeon" (the appellant's nickname), Bailey and the appellant left the building by the side door. Cohen testified that during the incident the appellant said nothing, and made no effort to intervene. He described the appellant as "all sweating", and said that the appellant was unable to look at him. The appellant, however, testified that he had repeatedly pleaded with Bailey, "Quasi, don't kill him."

[9] The appellant testified that from the moment he first encountered Bailey that evening he had believed Bailey would shoot him if he refused to co-operate, and stated that he had been "terrified" throughout his time in Bailey's company. Under cross-examination, he declared that he believed that he had had no opportunity to run away or warn Cohen without being shot.

[10] After leaving the building, Bailey drove the appellant back to Etobicoke. The appellant testified that Bailey threatened to kill him if he went to the police. Upon his return to Etobicoke, the appellant spoke to Cohen's brother about what had happened, and called Cohen's mother and Cohen's apartment. He subsequently called his own mother, before going to sleep. The next morning, he turned himself in to the police. Bailey, however, was never apprehended.

[11] The appellant was charged with attempted murder. On March 19, 1992, following a trial by jury in the Ontario Court of Justice (General Division) presided over by Webber J., he was acquitted of this charge, but was convicted of the included offence of aggravated assault and sentenced to four years' imprisonment. On July 15,

1993, his appeal of his conviction to the Court of Appeal for Ontario was dismissed, although the court allowed his appeal from sentence, reducing his sentence from four years to time served (some 15 months).

## II
## RELEVANT STATUTORY PROVISIONS

*Criminal Code*, R.S.C. 1985, c. C-46

8(3) Every rule and principle of the common law that renders any circumstance a justification or excuse for an act or a defence to a charge continues in force and applies in respect of proceedings for an offence under this Act or any other Act of Parliament except in so far as they are altered by or are inconsistent with this Act or any other Act of Parliament.

. . .

17. A person who commits an offence under compulsion by threats of immediate death or bodily harm from a person who is present when the offence is committed is excused for committing the offence if the person believes that the threats will be carried out and if the person is not a party to a conspiracy or association whereby the person is subject to compulsion, but this section does not apply where the offence that is committed is high treason or treason, murder, piracy, attempted murder, sexual assault, sexual assault with a weapon, threats to a third party or causing bodily harm, aggravated sexual assault, forcible abduction, hostage taking, robbery, assault with a weapon or causing bodily harm, aggravated assault, unlawfully causing bodily harm, arson or an offence under sections 280 to 283 (abduction and detention of young persons).

. . .

21(1) Every one is a party to an offence who

(*a*)  actually commits it,
(*b*)  does or omits to do anything for the purpose of aiding any person to commit it; or
(*c*)  abets any person in committing it.

(2) Where two or more persons form an intention in common to carry out an unlawful purpose and to assist each other therein and any one of them, in carrying out the common purpose, commits an offence, each of them who knew or ought to have known that the commission of the offence would be a probable consequence of carrying out the common purpose is a party to that offence.

. . .

## IV
## GROUNDS FOR APPEAL

[16] Lawrence Hibbert appeals his conviction to this court on the grounds that the trial judge's charge to the jury on the issue of duress contained several errors. First, he argues, the trial judge erred by instructing the jury that the defence of duress operated by "negativing common intention". The appellant objects further to the trial judge's statement that the defence of duress was unavailable to an accused who failed to avail himself or herself of a "safe avenue of escape". As an alternative to the latter argument, the appellant submits that even if the "safe avenue of escape" rule exists,

the trial judge erred by not advising the jury that the existence or non-existence of such an avenue was to be determined by reference to the appellant's subjective belief.

V

ANALYSIS

A. *Introduction*

[17] The issues raised in this appeal must be analyzed in several stages. First, it is necessary to consider the fundamental question of why it is that a person who performs an act that would otherwise constitute the *actus reus* of a criminal offence will not be held criminally liable at common law if he or she did so as a result of threats of death or bodily harm. That is, we must examine the theoretical nature of the common law defence of duress, and determine its relationship to basic *mens rea* principles. We must also consider the question of whether the availability of the defence of duress is limited by a "safe avenue of escape" rule. Once these questions have been addressed, it will then be possible to assess the learned trial judge's charge to the jury on duress, and to determine whether the jurors were correctly advised of the principles they were to apply to their deliberations.

B. *The relationship between mens rea and the defence of duress*

(1) *The common law defence of duress in Canada*

[18] The defence of "duress *per minas*" ("duress by threat") has a long history at common law. References to the defence can be found in the writings of such venerable commentators as Hale and Blackstone (see J. Ll. J. Edwards, "Compulsion, Coercion and Criminal Responsibility (1951), 14 Mod. L. Rev. 297 at pp. 298-9; and P. Rosenthal, "Duress in the Criminal Law" (1989-90), 32 C.L.Q. 199 at pp. 200*ff*). In spite of the defence's antiquity, however, many important aspects of its nature and its details have remained unresolved, or have been shrouded with uncertainty. As Professor Edwards, *supra*, observed in 1951 (at p. 297):

> Judged by the absence of any satisfactory modern authority, it must be very rare for the accused to set up as a defence that he committed the alleged crime under the compulsion of another person. Indeed, the whole field of learning on this defence to criminal liability is both meagre and unsatisfactory.

[19] In Canada, a defence of duress was included in the first *Criminal Code*, enacted in 1892 (S.C. 1892, c. 29). Section 12 of the original *Code* (the predecessor of the current *Code*'s s. 17) provided that "compulsion by threats of immediate death or grievous bodily harm from a person actually present at the commission of the offence shall be an excuse for [its] commission" (subject to certain specified conditions being met). For many years, it seems to have been generally assumed (although never conclusively established) that the existence of a codified version of the defence of duress left no room for further development of the common law defence in Canada.

As Ritchie J. remarked, *obiter*, in *R. v. Carker*, [1967] 2 C.C.C. 190 at p. 191, [1967] S.C.R. 114, 2 C.R. (N.S.) 16: "[I]n respect of proceedings for an offence under the *Criminal Code* the common law rules and principles respecting "duress" as an excuse or defence have been codified and exhaustively defined in s. 17". In *R. v. Paquette* (1976), 30 C.C.C. (2d) 417, 70 D.L.R. (3d) 129, [1977] 2 S.C.R. 189, however, this court determined that s. 17 of the *Code* does not constitute an exhaustive codification of the law of duress. Rather, the court held, s. 17 applies only to persons who commit offences as *principals*. Accordingly it remains open to persons who are liable as *parties* to offences to invoke the common law defence of duress, which remains in existence by virtue of s. 8(3) of the *Code* (which preserves those common law defences not expressly altered or eliminated by Parliament). The common law rules governing situations of duress thus remain an important aspect of Canadian criminal law.

[20] The holding in *Paquette* that the common law defence of duress is available to persons liable as parties is clear and unambiguous, and has stood as law in Canada for almost 20 years. The case has a second aspect, however, that is less firmly established, having given rise to differing interpretations, and having been the subject of considerable debate in the legal community. The controversy stems from certain comments made by Martland J. on the issue of the relationship between duress and the *mens rea* for party liability under s. 21(2) of the *Code*. The facts in *Paquette* were as follows. The accused had been charged as a party to non-capital murder. He had driven two acquaintances, Clermont and Simard, to a store. After Paquette had dropped them off, Clermont and Simard robbed the store, and during the course of the robbery an innocent bystander was shot and killed. Paquette was not present at the shooting, having driven away from the store once Clermont and Simard had entered. Although he circled the block and returned to the store, there was evidence that he had refused to let Clermont and Simard get back into the car. In a statement made to the police, Paquette indicated that he had driven Clermont and Simard to the scene of the crime only after Clermont had pointed a gun at him and threatened to kill him if he refused. At trial, the issue of duress had been left to the jury, which acquitted the accused. On appeal, the Ontario Court of Appeal ordered a new trial, on the grounds that the statutory defence of duress contained in s. 17 of the *Code* could not, by the express terms of the section, be invoked as a defence to a charge of murder or robbery.

[21] As noted above, the main holding of the court was that s. 17 applied only to principals and not to parties, from which it followed that Paquette could rely on the common law defence of duress, to which the restrictions set out in s. 17 did not apply. Martland J. went on, however, to make an observation regarding duress and the mental element of party liability under s. 21(2) of the *Code*, stating (at p. 423):

> A person whose actions have been dictated by fear of death or of grievous bodily injury cannot be said to have formed a *genuine* common intention to carry out an unlawful purpose with the person who has threatened him with those consequences if he fails to co-operate.

(Emphasis added). The significance of this comment in terms of the judgment as a whole is rather difficult to determine. Martland J. had earlier endorsed the decision of the House of Lords in *Director of Public Prosecutions for Northern Ireland v*

*Lynch*, [1975] A.C. 653, in which a majority of the House of Lords had clearly taken the view that the common law defence of duress provided an *excuse*, rather than operating by negating *mens rea*. Thus, Martland J. evidently did not intend to suggest that duress provides a defence at common law *only* when the accused's culpable mental state can be said to have been "negated". Instead, he appears to have been holding out an alternative route by which a person charged as a party under s. 21(2) could escape criminal liability, distinct from the "defence of duress" *per se* — that is, a "defence" founded not on concepts of excuse or justification, but based instead on the absence of an essential element of the offence.

[22] Seen in this way, *Paquette* stands for the proposition that duress can provide a "defence" in either of two distinct ways — as an excuse, or by "negating' *mens rea*. In the present case, the appellant argues that this is a correct view of the law, and submits that the trial judge erred by not placing both alternatives before the jury. What falls to be considered, therefore, is the validity of the proposition that the *mens rea* for party liability under the *Criminal Code* can be "negated" by threats of death or bodily harm. That is, the court is called upon to reconsider whether the second aspect of our judgment in *Paquette* reflects a correct understanding of the law of duress in Canada.

### (2) *Duress and mens rea*

[23] That threats of death or serious bodily harm can have an effect on a person's state of mind is indisputable. However, it is also readily apparent that a person who carries out the *actus reus* of a criminal offence in response to such threats will not necessarily lack the *mens rea* for that offence. Whether he or she does or not will depend both on what the mental element of the offence in question happens to be, and on the facts of the particular case. As a practical matter, though, situations where duress will operate to "negate" *mens rea* will be exceptional, for the simple reason that the types of mental states that are capable of being "negated" by duress are not often found in the definitions of criminal offences.

[24] In general, a person who performs an action in response to a threat will *know* what he or she is doing, and will be aware of the probable consequences of his or her actions. Whether or not he or she *desires* the occurrence of these consequences will depend on the particular circumstances. For example, a person who is forced at gunpoint to drive a group of armed ruffians to a bank will usually know that the likely result of his or her actions will be that an attempt will be made to rob the bank, but he or she may not desire this result — indeed, he or she may strongly wish that the robbers' plans are ultimately foiled, if this could occur without risk to his or her own safety. In contrast, a person who is told that his or her child is being held hostage at another location and will be killed unless the robbery is successful will almost certainly have an active subjective desire that the robbery succeed. While the existence of threats clearly has a bearing on the *motive* underlying each actor's respective decision to assist in the robbery, only the first actor can be said not to *desire* that the robbery take place, and neither actor can be said not to have knowledge of the consequences of their actions. To determine whether *mens rea* is "negated" in a particular case,

therefore, the first question that must be asked is whether the mental element of the offence in question is defined in such a way that either an actor's motives or his or her immediate desires have any direct relevance. As A.W. Mewett and M. Manning explain:

> *Mens rea* . . . has more than one meaning. It can entail a purpose, a desire to achieve an objective; it can entail merely knowledge that consequences will follow or that circumstances exist; it can entail only recklessness, that is, some advertent or perhaps inadvertent disregard of the consequences or circumstances. What suffices for liability depends upon the particular offence with which we are dealing. If a person is compelled to do an act which he does not wish to do, and therefore does it "against his will", why, it may be asked, does he have a defence not of compulsion but simply of lack of *mens rea* The answer is that this is quite true, but only if the *mens rea* required for the particular offence in question is of the sort that is negatived by a person being compelled to do something against his will.

(*Mewett and Manning on Criminal Law*, 3rd ed. (Toronto: Butterworths, 1994), at p. 520.)

[25] As Dickson J. (as he then was) observed in *Lewis v. The Queen* (1979), 47 C.C.C. (2d) 24 at p. 33, 98 D.L.R. (3d) 111, [1979] 2 S.C.R. 82, "[t]he mental element of a crime ordinarily involves no reference to motive". Instead, he noted, "[i]n most criminal trials the mental element, the *mens rea* with which the Court is concerned, relates to "intent". Intention, however, is distinct from desire or subjective wish. As Lord Simon of Glaisdale stated in *Lynch, supra* (dissenting, but on another issue), at p. 690:

> [A]n *intention* to bring about a consequence of an act can co-exist with a *desire* that such consequences should not ensue . . . [A] *wish* is a particular instance of *desire* . . . . [T]herefore, an *intention* to perform an act with foreseen consequences can co-exist with a *wish* not to perform the act or that its consequences should not ensue (this is crucial in considering the juridical effect of duress).

(Emphasis in original.) Parliament is, of course, entitled to define the mental element of criminal offences in whatever manner it sees fit (subject, of course, to the requirements of s. 7 of the *Canadian Charter of Rights and Freedoms*: see, for instance *Reference re: Section 94(2) of the Motor Vehicle Act* (1985), 23 C.C.C. (3d) 289, 24 D.L.R. (4th) 536, [1985] 2 S.C.R. 486; *R. v. Vaillancourt* (1987), 39 C.C.C. (3d) 118, 47 D.L.R. (4th) 399, [1987] 2 S.C.R. 636; *R. v. Martineau* (1990), 58 C.C.C. (3d) 353, [1990] 2 S.C.R. 633, 79 C.R. (3d) 129; and *R. v. Logan* (1990), 58 C.C.C. (3d) 391, 73 D.L.R. (4th) 40, [1990] 2 S.C.R. 731). Thus, Parliament could choose to make it an element of a given offence that the perpetrator have some particular *desire* at the time of the commission of the *actus reus*, or even make it a precondition for liability that an actor have a particular *motive* for performing a prohibited act. In the present appeal, of course, we are not called upon to conduct an exhaustive review of the *Criminal Code* for the purposes of identifying any or all offences with mental elements that might be capable of being negated by duress. Rather, the present case, like *Paquette*, involves the special situation of liability under s. 21 of the *Code*. Thus, our analysis can be restricted to the question of whether the *mens rea* requirements for party liability contained in s. 21 are of the sort that can, in some circumstances, be "negated" by coercion. Since the sole aspect of s. 21 left with the jury in the appellant's trial was s. 21(1)(*b*), the analysis could, strictly speaking, be restricted to that subsection. It is difficult, however, to embark upon an examination of the mental element of s. 21(1)(*b*) without being seen as inferentially commenting on s. 21(2), thereby calling into question the court's holding in *Paquette, supra*. In my view, in order to avoid creating undue confusion and uncertainty in the law, it is appropriate that we address the issue of the continued validity of *Paquette's* statements on the relation between duress and *mens rea* under s. 21(2), head on. I will thus extend my analysis beyond what is strictly necessary for the resolution of the present appeal by considering s. 21(2) in addition to s. 21(*b*).

### (3) *The mens rea requirements for party liability under s. 21*

#### (a) *Section 21(1)(b)*

[26] As noted earlier, s. 21(1)(*b*) imposes criminal liability as a party on anyone who "does or omits to do anything for the purpose of aiding any person to commit" an offence. Although a person who is a party to an offence is guilty of committing *that* offence, rather than a separate crime (as in the case for accessories after the fact), s. 21(1)(*b*) contains its own *mens rea* requirement, distinct from that applicable to the principal who actually commits the underlying offence. As the subsection states, party liability as an "aider" requires acts or omissions "for the purpose" of aiding the commission of the offence. In order to understand what effect, if any, duress might have on the *mens rea* of an aider, it is thus necessary to determine what "for the purpose" means in this context.

[27] It is impossible to ascribe a single fixed meaning to the term "purpose". In ordinary usage, the word is employed in two distinct senses. One can speak of an actor doing something "on purpose" (as opposed to by accident), thereby equating purpose with "immediate intention". The term is also used, however, to indicate the ultimate ends an actor seeks to achieve, which imports the idea of "desire" into the definition. This dual sense is apparent in the word's dictionary definition. For instance, the Oxford English Dictionary, 2nd ed. (1989), defines "purpose" alternatively as "[t]hat which one sets before oneself as a thing to be done or attained; the object which one has in view" and as "[t]he action or fact of intending or meaning to do something; intention, resolution, determination". The first of these definitions reflects the notion of one's "purpose" as relating to one's ultimate object or desire, while the latter conveys the notion of "purpose" as being synonymous with "intention".

. . .

My conclusions in the present case on the proper interpretation of the word "purpose" as it is employed in s. 21(1)(*b*) of the *Code* are thus restricted to this particular subsection. It may well be that in the context of some other statutory provision a different interpretation of the term will prove to be the most appropriate.

[31] As I said, when Parliament drafts a statute in language that, on its face, supports more than one meaning, it is appropriate for a court to consider which of the alternative interpretations that are available best accords with Parliament's intention (see my

remarks in *R. v. McIntosh* (1995), 95 C.C.C. (3d) 481 at pp. 489*ff.*, [1995] 1 S.C.R. 686, 36 C.R. (4th) 171). As I will explain, I am of the view that in the context of s. 21(1)(*b*) of the *Code*, the second of the two meanings of "purpose" discussed above — that is, the interpretation that equates "purpose" with "intention" — best reflects the legislative intent underlying the subsection.

. . .

[38] Finally, I am satisfied that the interpretation of the *mens rea* for liability under s. 21(1)(*b*) that I am proposing will not result in unjust convictions in cases involving coercion by threats of death or bodily harm, since in these cases the common law defence of duress will remain available to the accused. As I will explain shortly, this defence, properly understood, provides an excuse to persons who assist in the commission of offences as a result of threats of serious violence. On the other hand, interpreting "purpose" as equivalent to "desire" in s. 21(1)(*b*) would result in the introduction of unnecessary complication into the law. Under such an interpretation, juries in duress cases would have to be provided with extremely complex instruction that would, in the end, have very little, if any, impact on the final determination of guilt or innocence. As a matter of logic, the issue of whether an accused can invoke an excuse or justification arises only *after* the Crown has proven the existence of all the elements of the offence, including *mens rea*. Thus, if "purpose" were understood as incorporating "desire", and hence as being susceptible to "negation" by duress, trial judges would have to instruct juries accordingly. This would require judges, and juries, to delve into the arcane issue of whether a person who intentionally commits an offence in order to save his or her own skin commits the offence "on purpose" — a question of some philosophical significance, perhaps, but no easy matter for a judge to explain succinctly, or for a jury to comprehend readily. At the same time, trial judges would *also* have to provide juries with alternative instructions on the excuse-based common law defence of duress. While in many cases an aider who actively desires the commission of the offence he or she aids will not be able to legitimately claim that he or she acted under duress, this will not inevitably be so (consider, for instance, the hypothetical example, discussed earlier, of the parent whose child is held hostage by confederates of robbers, who is told that the child will be released unharmed only if he or she assists in the *successful* commission of a robbery). Consequently, in at least some cases juries would be forced to consider two alternate legal routes leading to an acquittal by reason of duress. This complication would, however, have little or no practical effect, since there will be few, if any, cases involving parties in which a "defence" of "negation of *mens rea* by duress" would succeed where recourse to the excuse-based common law defence of duress would not also lead to an acquittal. As Professor Stuart observes (D. Stuart: *Canadian Criminal Law: a Treatise*, 3rd ed. (Scarborough, Ont: Carswell, 1995)), introducing the notion of duress "negating" *mens rea* into the analysis serves only to muddy the conceptual waters. As he points out (at p. 420):

> The advantages [of viewing the operation of duress solely in terms of an excuse] are more than linguistic. If the defence of duress is viewed like any other justification or excuse as based squarely on policy considerations allowing one who has committed an *actus reus* with

*mens rea* to escape in certain circumstances, the policy issues are focused without confusing the matter as one of *mens rea*.

[39] For these reasons, I conclude that the expression "for the purpose of aiding" in s. 21(1)(*b*), properly understood, does not require that the accused actively view the commission of the offence he or she is aiding as desirable in and of itself. As a result the *mens rea* for aiding under s. 21(1)(*b*) is not susceptible of being "negated" by duress. The trial judge's charge to the jury in the present case was thus incorrect in two respects. First, the reference to the relevant mental state in the present case as being a "common intention to carry out an unlawful purpose" was erroneous since, unlike *Paquette*, what was at issue in the present case was s. 21(1)(*b*), as opposed to s. 21(2). Second, in light of the mental element for commission of an offence under s. 21(1)(*b*), the suggestion that duress might "negate" the accused's *mens rea* was also incorrect.

### (b) *Section 21(2) and the decision in Paquette*

[40] The preceding discussion suffices to resolve the question of the relation between duress and *mens rea* that directly arises in the present case. As I indicated earlier, however, I believe that in the interests of avoiding undue confusion in the law that applies to duress cases I should proceed further, and look expressly at the question of whether the interpretation of s. 21(2)'s mental element that was adopted by the court in *Paquette, supra*, remains correct in light of the interpretation of s. 21(1)(*b*) I am now adopting. To be sure, the respective *mens rea* requirements of the two subsections are defined differently — while s. 21(1)(*b*) imposes party liability on persons who "do or omit to do anything *for the purpose* of aiding any person to commit [an offence]", s. 21(2) establishes that "persons [who] form *an intention in common* to carry out an unlawful purpose and to assist each other therein" are liable for criminal offences committed by the principal that are foreseeable and probable consequences of carrying out the "common purpose". There is, however, a close connection between the two subsections, arising from the evident similarities that exist between certain aspects of s. 21(2)'s requirements and the terms of s. 21(1)(*b*). As I have explained in the previous section, a person who does something "for the purpose of aiding" another to commit a criminal offence (and who is thus liable under s. 21(1)(*b*)) invariably "intends" to assist the principal to carry out "an unlawful purpose" — an "intention" that its not susceptible of being "negated" by the fact that it arises as the result of threats of death or bodily harm. Furthermore, the terms "aid" and "assist" are virtually synonymous. Section 21(2), however, contains two further qualifications — the accused's intention must be "an intention in common" with the principal, and the intention to assist must be reciprocal (that is, two or more persons must have "an intention in common . . . to *assist each other* therein"). The question that must be addressed, therefore, is whether these additional qualifications on the requisite "intention" raise the prospect of an accused's *mens rea* being "negated" by duress. In particular, we must consider whether the requirement that the accused have an "intention *in common*" with another person has this effect.

. . .

[44] For these reasons, I am of the view that the comments of Martland J. in *Paquette, supra*, on the relation between duress and *mens rea* in the context of s. 21(2) can no longer be considered the law in Canada. I hasten to point out, however, that overturning this holding in *Paquette* does not affect the validity of that case's first aspect, namely, that the common law defence of duress continues to apply in cases involving party liability under s. 21 of the *Code*. Furthermore, it can be noted in passing that, on the facts of *Paquette*, the accused's acquittal could well have been supported on the basis of the excuse provided by the common law defence of duress rather than on the notion that his intention to assist in the commission of the robbery was "negated" by duress.

### (4) *Conclusions on duress and mens rea*

[45] The conclusions that can be extracted for the discussion in the previous sections may be summarized as follows:

1. The fact that a person who commits a criminal act does so as a result of threats of death or bodily harm can in some instances be relevant to the question of whether he or she possessed the *mens rea* necessary to commit an offence. Whether or not this is so will depend, among other things, on the structure of the particular offence in question — that is, on whether or not the mental state specified by Parliament in its definition of the offence is such that the presence of coercion can, as a matter of logic, have a bearing on the existence of *mens rea*. If the offence is one where the presence of duress is of potential relevance to the existence of *mens rea*, the accused is entitled to point to the presence of threats when arguing that the Crown has not proven beyond a reasonable doubt that he or she possessed the mental state required for liability.
2. A person who commits a criminal act under threats of death or bodily harm may also be able to invoke an excuse-based defence (either the statutory defence set out in s. 17 or the common law defence of duress, depending on whether the accused is charged as a principal or as a party). This is so regardless of whether or not the offence at issue is one where the presence of coercion also has a bearing on the existence of *mens rea*.
3. The mental states specified in s. 21(1)(*b*) and (2) of the *Criminal Code* are not susceptible to being "negated" by duress. Consequently, it is not open to persons charged under these sections to argue that because their acts were coerced by threats they lacked the requisite *mens rea*. Such persons may however, seek to have their conduct *excused* through the operation of the common law defence of duress.

It should be reiterated, however, that the holding in the present case is based on an interpretation of the particular terms of two specific offence-creating statutory provisions, s. 21(1)(*b*) and (2) of the *Criminal Code*. The question of whether other offences can be found either in the *Code* or in some other statute, that are defined in such a way that the presence of coercion *is* relevant to the existence of *mens rea*, remains open.

## C. *The "safe avenue of escape" requirement in the common law of duress*

[46] The second and third issues raised by the appellant have to do with the so-called "safe avenue of escape" rule. The court must decide whether such a rule in fact exists, and, if it does, whether the availability of a "safe avenue" is to be determined on an objective or subjective basis. In my opinion, it is best to start the analysis by examining the juristic nature of the defence of duress and its relationship to other common law defences, since I am of the view that by so doing the answers to the questions posed in the present appeal will become clear.

. . .

*Is the existence of a safe avenue of escape to be determined subjectively or objectively?*

[56] The remaining question on this appeal raises a potentially more difficult issue, namely, the question of whether the existence of a "safe avenue of escape" is to be determined objectively or on the basis of the accused's own subjective knowledge and awareness at the time. How this question is answered depends, in my view, on how one conceives of the notion of "normative involuntariness" upon which the defence of duress is based. That is, is an action "normatively involuntary" when the actor *believes* that he has no real choice, or is this the case only when there is *in fact* no reasonable alternative course of action available?

. . .

*Conclusions on duress and "safe avenue of escape" requirement*

[62] My conclusions on the second and third issues raised by the appellant can thus be summarized as follows. An accused person cannot rely on the common law defence of duress if he or she had an opportunity to safely extricate himself or herself from the situation of duress. The rationale for this rule is simply that in such circumstances the condition of "normative involuntariness" that provides the theoretical basis for both the defences of duress and necessity is absent — if the accused had the chance to take action that would have allowed him or her to avoid committing an offence, it cannot be said that he or she had no real choice when deciding whether or not to break the law. Furthermore, I believe that the internal logic of the excuse-based defence, which has theoretical underpinnings directly analogous to those that support the defence of necessity (as set out in *Perka, supra*), suggests that the question of whether or not a safe avenue of escape existed is to be determined according to an objective standard. When considering the perceptions of a "reasonable person", however, the personal circumstances of the accused are relevant and important, and should be taken into account.

. . .

[67] Although the errors identified above are in themselves sufficient, in my

opinion, to entitle the appellant to a new trial, I will briefly address the other points raised by the appellant. As I have explained, I am of the view that the trial judge did not err in instructing the jury that the appellant could not rely on the defence of duress if the Crown established that he had failed to avail himself of a safe avenue of escape. Furthermore, while I believe the trial judge should have instructed the jury that the existence of such an avenue was to be determined objectively, taking into account the personal circumstances of the appellant, on the particular facts of this case, I am not persuaded that his failure to do so affected the jury's decision, since there was no indication, on the facts, that any of the appellant's personal attributes or frailties rendered him unable to identify any safe avenues of escape that would have been apparent to a reasonable person of ordinary capacities and abilities.

## VI
## CONCLUSION

[68] With respect, I am of the view that the trial judge erred in his instructions to the jury on the law of duress. Since I do not believe that it can be said that this error necessarily had no impact on the jury's verdict, I believe that there should be a new trial. According, the appeal is allowed, the appellant's conviction is set aside, and a new trial is ordered.

*Appeal allowed; new trial ordered.*

## Regina v. Ruzic
## (2001), 153 C.C.C. (3d) 1 (S.C.C.)

Appeal by the Crown from a judgment of the Ontario Court of Appeal (reported (1998), 55 C.R.R. (2d) 85, 41 O.R. (3d) 1) dismissing a Crown appeal from a conviction on a charge of importing narcotics.

The judgment of the court was delivered by

LeBEL J.: — On April 29, 1994 Marijana Ruzic, a Yugoslav citizen, landed at Pearson Airport in Toronto carrying two kilograms of heroin strapped to her body and a false Austrian passport. When the heroin was found on her, she was arrested, charged and tried for possession and use of a false passport and unlawful importation of narcotics. At trial, Ruzic successfully challenged the constitutionality of s. 17 of the Criminal Code, R.S.C. 1985, c. C-46, raised the common law defence of duress and was acquitted by a jury. The Crown appealed the acquittal without success to the Ontario Court of Appeal. This appeal now raises, as a core issue, the constitutional validity, under s. 7 of the Canadian Charter of Rights and Freedoms, of s. 17 of the Criminal Code and more precisely of some of the conditions restricting the admissibility of the defence of duress. For reasons differing in part from those of the Court of Appeal, I will suggest that s. 17 of the Criminal Code be declared unconstitutional in part, that the acquittal of the respondent Ruzic be upheld and that the appeal be dismissed.

# I. FACTS

The respondent Marijana Ruzic was born in Belgrade in the former Yugoslavia. She was 21 years old when she entered Canada. When heroin was discovered on her, she was charged with three offences, two of which proceeded to trial: possession and use of a false passport contrary to s. 368 of the Criminal Code, and unlawful importation of a narcotic contrary to s. 5(1) of the Narcotic Control Act, R.S.C. 1985, c. N-1.

Ms. Ruzic admitted having committed both offences but claimed that she was then acting under duress and should thus be relieved from any criminal liability. She testified that, two months before her arrival in Canada, a man named Mirko Mirkovic approached her while she was walking her dog in the streets of Belgrade, where she lived in an apartment with her mother. She described him as a warrior and believed he was paid to kill people in the war. An expert witness testified at trial that, in 1994, large paramilitary groups roamed Belgrade and engaged in criminal and Mafia-like activities. The same expert maintained that people living in Belgrade during that period did not feel safe. They believed the police could not be trusted. There was a real sense that the rule of law had broken down.

From there began a series of encounters between Mirkovic and the respondent while she was walking her dog. Each time he approached her, he knew more about her, although she had shared no details of her life with him. He phoned her at home. He told her he knew her every move. Ms. Ruzic alleged that his behaviour became more and more intimidating, escalating to threats and acts of physical violence. On one occasion, he burned her arm with a lighter. On another, he stuck a syringe into her arm and injected her with a substance that smelled like heroin and made her nauseous. She indicated that these physical assaults were coupled with sexual harassment and finally threats against her mother.

On April 25, 1994, Mirkovic phoned the respondent and instructed her to pack a bag and meet him at a hotel in central Belgrade. Once there, he allegedly strapped three packages of heroin to her body and indicated that she was to take them to a restaurant in Toronto. He gave her the false passport, a bus ticket from Belgrade to Budapest and some money. He told her to fly from Budapest to Athens, and then from Athens to Toronto. When she protested, he warned her that, if she failed to comply, he would harm her mother.

Ms. Ruzic arrived in Budapest on April 26. Late that evening, she boarded a plane to Athens, where she arrived early the next day. She then purchased a ticket to Toronto. She missed that flight, exchanged her ticket for the next available flight, and left for Toronto two days later, on April 29.

During the two months prior to her journey to Canada, Ms. Ruzic testified that she did not tell her mother or anyone else about Mirkovic. She was afraid he would harm whoever she told. She did not seek police protection because she believed the police in Belgrade were corrupt and would do nothing to assist her. She maintained that she followed Mirkovic's instructions out of fear for her mother's safety. She made no attempt while in Budapest or Athens to seek the assistance of police or other government officials. Similarly, before her arrest, she did not ask any Canadian authorities for help. She asserted that she believed the only way she could protect her mother was to obey Mirkovic's orders.

## II. CONSTITUTIONAL AND STATUTORY PROVISIONS

### Canadian Charter of Rights and Freedoms:

1. The Canadian Charter of Rights and Freedoms guarantees the rights and freedoms set out in it subject only to such reasonable limits prescribed by law as can be demonstrably justified in a free and democratic society.

. . .

7. Everyone has the right to life, liberty and security of the person and the right not to be deprived hereof except in accordance with the principles of fundamental justice.

### Criminal Code, R.S.C. 1985, c. C-46:

8. (3) Every rule and principle of the common law that renders any circumstance a justification or excuse for an act or a defence to a charge continues in force and applies in respect of proceedings for an offence under this Act or any other Act of Parliament except in so far as they are altered by or are inconsistent with this Act or any other Act of Parliament.

. . .

Ms. Ruzic was tried before Herold J. and a jury. Her main line of defence was that she acted under duress. She conceded that her claim of duress did not meet the immediacy and presence requirements of s. 17 of the Criminal Code. Mirkovic's threats were not of immediate death or bodily harm and he was not present when she committed the offence. Furthermore, the threats were directed at her mother. She accordingly challenged the constitutionality of s. 17 under s. 7 of the Charter, in order to raise the common law defence of duress that, in her mind, did not incorporate the requirements of immediacy and presence.

. . .

Lamer C.J.C. stated the following constitutional questions:

1. Do the requirements in s. 17 of the Criminal Code, R.S.C. 1985, c. C-46, that a threat must be of immediate death or bodily harm and from a person who is present when the offence is committed infringe the rights of an accused person as guaranteed by s. 7 of the Canadian Charter of Rights and Freedoms?
2. If the answer to Question 1 is yes, is the said infringement of the s. 7 rights a reasonable limit that can be demonstrably justified under s. 1 of the Canadian Charter of Rights and Freedoms?
3. Does s. 17 of the Criminal Code, R.S.C. 1985, c. C-46, infringe the rights of an accused person as guaranteed by s. 7 of the Canadian Charter of Rights and Freedoms by precluding access to the defence of duress where the threat is to a third party?
4. If the answer to Question 3 is yes, is the said infringement of the s. 7 rights a reasonable limit that can be demonstrably justified under s. 1 of the Canadian Charter of Rights and Freedoms?

The first and central question before us is thus framed in the same way that it was in the courts below: do the immediacy and presence requirements in s. 17 of the

Criminal Code infringe s. 7 of the Charter, and, if so, can they be justified under s. 1? This question raises several subsidiary matters:

- Are statutory defences owed special deference by reviewing courts?
- Is it a principle of fundamental justice that only morally voluntary conduct can attract criminal liability?
- Do the immediacy and presence requirements in s. 17 infringe this principle? Is a broader interpretation of s. 17 possible as argued by the appellant, in order to avoid a declaration of unconstitutionality?
- What can the common law tell us on the defence of duress?
- If there is a violation of s. 7, can it be justified under s. 1?
- As an alternative question, do the immediacy and presence requirements in s. 17 infringe the principle that constitutional rights should not be restricted in a manner that is arbitrary or unfair?

At issue also is whether s. 17 of the Criminal Code infringes s. 7 of the Charter by precluding access to the defence of duress where the threatened harm is directed not at the accused, but at a third party.

. . .

# V. ANALYSIS

A. Are statutory defences owed special deference by reviewing courts?
*[Ed.: After answering this question in the negative, Lebel J. continued:]*

B. Is it a principle of fundamental justice that only morally voluntary conduct can attract criminal liability?

Whether it is a principle of fundamental justice under s. 7 of the Charter that morally involuntary conduct should not be punished is a novel question before this court. We are thus called upon to canvass once more the contents of the principles of fundamental justice, this time in the context of the defence of duress as framed by s. 17 of the Criminal Code.

The court has on numerous occasions confirmed that the principles of fundamental justice are to be found in the basic tenets of our legal system. . .

The notion of moral voluntariness was first introduced in *R. v. Perka*. . .for the purpose of explaining the defence of necessity and classifying it as an excuse. . . .

Extending its reasoning in *Perka* to the defence of duress, the court found in *R. v. Hibbert*. . .that it too rests on the notion of moral voluntariness. . . .

Thus duress, like necessity, involves the concern that morally involuntary conduct not be subject to criminal liability. Can this notion of moral voluntariness be recognized as a principle of fundamental justice under s. 7 of the Charter? . . .

1. Moral voluntariness and moral blameworthiness

As we will see below, this court has recognized on a number of occasions that moral blameworthiness is an essential component of criminal liability which is protected under s. 7 as a principle of fundamental justice. . . .

This controversy about the concepts of moral blamelessness and moral involuntariness brings us back to the foundations of criminal responsibility. In the analysis of duress and of its relationship with the tenets of the criminal justice system, is it appropriate to equate moral blamelessness with moral involuntariness?

Even before the advent of the Charter, it became a basic concern of the criminal law that criminal responsibility be ascribed only to acts that resulted from the choice of a conscious mind and an autonomous will. In other words, only those persons acting in the knowledge of what they were doing, with the freedom to choose, would bear the burden and stigma of criminal responsibility. Although the element of voluntariness may sometimes overlap both actus reus and mens rea. . ., the importance of mens rea and of the quality of voluntariness in it underscores the fact that criminal liability is founded on the premise that it will be borne only by those persons who knew what they were doing and willed it. . . .

To equate moral involuntariness with moral innocence would amount to a significant departure from the reasoning in Perka and Hibbert. It would be contrary to the court's conceptualization of duress as an excuse. Morally involuntary conduct is not always inherently blameless. Once the elements of the offence have been established, the accused can no longer be considered blameless. This court has never taken the concept of blamelessness any further than this initial finding of guilt, nor should it in this case. The undefinable and potentially far-reaching nature of the concept of moral blamelessness prevents us from recognizing its relevance beyond an initial finding of guilt in the context of s. 7 of the Charter. Holding otherwise would inject an unacceptable degree of uncertainty into the law. It would not be consistent with our duty to consider as principles of fundamental justice only those concepts which are constrained and capable of being defined with reasonable precision. I would therefore reject this basis for finding that it is a principle of fundamental justice that morally involuntary acts should not be punished.

2. Moral voluntariness and voluntariness in the physical sense

The respondent's second approach, which relates moral voluntariness back to voluntariness in the physical sense, rests on firmer ground. It draws upon the fundamental principle of criminal law that, in order to attract criminal liability, an act must be voluntary. Voluntariness in this sense has ordinarily referred to the actus reus element of an offence. It queries whether the actor had control over the movement of her body or whether the wrongful act was the product of a conscious will. Although duress does not negate ordinarily actus reus per se (just as it does not ordinarily negate mens rea as we have just seen), the principle of voluntariness, unlike that of moral blamelessness, can remain relevant in the context of s. 7 even after the basic elements of the offence have been established. Unlike the concept of moral blamelessness, duress in its voluntariness perspective can more easily be constrained and can therefore more justifiably fall within the principles of fundamental justice, even after the basic elements of the offence have been established.

. . .

Punishing a person whose actions are involuntary in the physical sense is unjust because it conflicts with the assumption in criminal law that individuals are autonomous and freely choosing agents. . . . It is similarly unjust to penalize an individual who acted in a morally involuntary fashion. This is so because his acts cannot realistically be attributed to him, as his will was constrained by some external force. . . .

Although moral involuntariness does not negate the actus reus or mens rea of an offence, it is a principle which, similarly to physical involuntariness, deserves protection under s. 7 of the Charter. It is a principle of fundamental justice that only voluntary conduct — behaviour that is the product of a free will and controlled body, unhindered by external constraints — should attract the penalty and stigma of criminal liability. Depriving a person of liberty and branding her with the stigma of criminal liability would infringe the principles of fundamental justice if the accused did not have any realistic choice. The ensuing deprivation of liberty and stigma would have been imposed in violation of the tenets of fundamental justice and would thus infringe s. 7 of the Charter.

C. Do the immediacy and presence requirements in s. 17 infringe the principle of involuntariness in the attribution of criminal responsibility?

It remains to be seen whether s. 17 respects this guiding principle of criminal justice that demands that society refrain from punishing morally involuntary action. The respondent argues that s. 17 of the Criminal Code does indeed infringe s. 7 of the Charter by reason of its underinclusiveness. The strictness of the immediacy and presence requirements in s. 17 means that individuals could be found guilty of involuntary actions.

Section 17 limits the defence of duress to a person who is compelled to commit an offence under threats of immediate death or bodily harm from a person who is present when the offence is committed. To counter the respondent's arguments, the appellant's key submission was that s. 17 is capable of being read down in a way that would make it less restrictive and more consistent with the Charter. The appellant argues that the immediacy and presence requirements do not dictate that the threatener be physically present at the scene of the crime. Rather, they require a temporal connection between the commission of the offence and the threatener's presence, in the sense that the threatener must be able to execute the threat immediately should the accused fail to comply. The respondent replies that the appellant's proposed interpretation would stretch the language of s. 17 beyond recognition. As counsel for one of the interveners put it during the hearing of this appeal, it would amount to construing presence as absence and immediate as some time later.

The plain meaning of s. 17 is quite restrictive in scope. Indeed, the section seems tailor-made for the situation in which a person is compelled to commit an offence at gun point. The phrase present when the offence is committed, coupled with the immediacy criterion, indicates that the person issuing the threat must be either at the scene of the crime or at whatever other location is necessary to make good on the threat without delay should the accused resist. Practically speaking, a threat of harm will seldom qualify as immediate if the threatener is not physically present at the scene of the crime.

. . .

*Carker* and *Paquette* state clearly that s. 17 means the threatener must be physically present at the scene of the offence, at the time it takes place, otherwise the defence of duress is not available to the accused. I agree with the respondent that a threat will seldom meet the immediacy criterion if the threatener is not physically present at or near the scene of the offence. The immediacy and presence requirements, taken together, clearly preclude threats of future harm.

Neither the words of s. 17 nor the court's reasons in *Carker* and *Paquette* dictate that the target of the threatened harm must be the accused. They simply require that the threat must be made to the accused. Section 17 may thus include threats against third parties. However, as discussed above, the language of s. 17 does not appear capable of supporting a more flexible interpretation of the immediacy and presence requirements. Even if the threatened person, for example, is a family member, and not the accused person, the threatener or his accomplice must be at or near the scene of the crime in order to effect the harm immediately if the accused resists. Thus, while s. 17 may capture threats against third parties, the immediacy and presence criteria continue to impose considerable obstacles to relying on the defence in hostage or other third party situations.

Thus, by the strictness of its conditions, s. 17 breaches s. 7 of the Charter because it allows individuals who acted involuntarily to be declared criminally liable. Having said that, it will be interesting to see how the common law addresses the problem of duress, especially with respect to the immediacy component. . . .

D. The common law of duress

1. The Canadian common law of duress

In Canada, the common law defence of duress has freed itself from the constraints of immediacy and presence and thus appears more consonant with the values of the Charter. It was never completely superseded by the provision of the Criminal Code. . . .

The analysis in *Hibbert* remains focused on the concept of a safe avenue of escape. Although the common law defence traditionally covers situations of threats susceptible of immediate execution by the person present and uttering threats, this immediacy requirement has been interpreted in a flexible manner by Canadian jurisprudence. . . .

> Notably, at common law, there is no requirement that the threats be made by a person who is present at the scene of the crime. It has been said that the threat must be immediate or imminent and that persons threatened must resort to the protection of the law if they can do so. While the defence is not available to those who have an obvious safe avenue of escape , I agree with Martin J.A. that the operative test is whether the accused failed to avail himself or herself of some opportunity to escape or render the threat ineffective (references omitted).

. . .

*[After discussing the approaches in other jurisdictions, Lebel J. continued:]*

5. Summary: Rejection of the immediacy requirement at common law

This review of the common law defence of duress confirms that, although the common law is not unanimous in the United States, a substantial consensus has grown in Canada, England and Australia to the effect that the strict criterion of immediacy is no longer a generally accepted component of the defence. A requirement that the threat be imminent has been interpreted and applied in a more flexible manner. . . .

E. The breach of s. 7 of the Charter: Conclusion in the case at bar
. . .The underinclusiveness of s. 17 infringes s. 7 of the Charter, because the immediacy and presence requirements exclude threats of future harm to the accused or to third parties. It risks jeopardizing the liberty and security interests protected by the Charter, in violation of the basic principles of fundamental justice. It has the potential of convicting persons who have not acted voluntarily.

. . .

IV. Disposition

The appellant's submissions cannot be accepted. The immediacy and presence requirement of s. 17 of the Criminal Code infringe s. 7 of the Charter. As the infringement has not been justified under s. 1, the requirements of immediacy and presence must be struck down as unconstitutional. The Court of Appeal and the trial judge were right in allowing the common law defence of duress to go to the jury, and the trial judge adequately instructed the jury on the defence.
I would dismiss the appeal and confirm the acquittal of the respondent.

. . .

*Appeal dismissed*

**Questions/Discussion**
1. Do you think the reasoning in the court in *Carker* was correct? Do you think the decision was fair? If not, then how would you interpret section 17? Do you think that the court had a real choice in light of the wording of the section? Should the section be as restrictively worded as it is now? Do you think that *Carker* has been overruled by *Ruzic*?
2. Why do we not allow the defences in certain types of offences? Do you agree with such exclusions? Why or why not? If a person is effectively forced to do a crime, then why shouldn't the defence be available in the interests of fairness?
3. Do you agree with the provision excepting those who have been involved in an association whereby they have been subject to the duress? If the defence is in effect withdrawn, can it be argued that they are being punished for the wrong reasons, i.e., that they were a member of a criminal group, and not for the crime which they were forced to commit?
4. Do you agree with the decision in *Paquette*? Why or why not? Are your reasons based on the legal reasoning in the decision or ultimately on the "fair" result which was achieved? Do you think that in fact it was the result which the court decided on first and then found a purely technical means to reach it? Would the court have been

more "honest" to admit that in situations such as Paquette's, an exception should be made on policy grounds, that it was an obvious oversight on the part of the legislators when they passed the law?

5. Do you agree with the reasoning and the decision in *Hibbert*? Why or why not?

**Further Reading**
- Borins, Stephen, "The Defence of Duress" (1981-82), 24 Criminal Law Quarterly 191.
- Elliott, D.W., "Necessity, Duress and Self-Defence", [1989] Criminal Law Review 611.
- Mewett, A. and M. Manning, *Mewett and Manning on Criminal Law*, 3rd ed. (Markham: Butterworths, 1994).
- Roach, Kent, *Criminal Law, 2d ed.* (Toronto: Irwin Law, 2000) at 279-292.
- Rosenthal, P., "Duress in the Criminal Law" (1990), 32 Criminal Law Quarterly 199-226.
- Schaffer, M., "Coerced into Crime: Battered Women and the Defence of Duress" (1999), 4 Canadian Criminal Law Review 272.
- Stuart, Don, and R. Delisle, *Learning Canadian Criminal Law, 8th ed.* (Toronto: Carswell, 2001).
- Verdun-Jones, S., *Criminal Law in Canada: Cases, Questions and the Code*, (Toronto: Harcourt Brace Jovanovich Canada, 1989), pp. 265-275.

## 7.1.2  Necessity

**Introduction**

In using the common law defence of necessity, the accused is making the argument that "I had to commit the crime, I had no realistic choice in the matter". In the two cases which follow, the decisions outline the circumstances when this argument will be successful and excuse the accused from being held liable for the offence. In particular, *Perka* outlines the factors which a court will look for in assessing whether the defence is available. Furthermore, this case also presents an interesting debate on the proper rationale or foundation for the defence. The majority in *Perka* argues for the restricted basis of "excuse" (i.e., it is right to excuse people for acts which are "normatively involuntary", acts which ordinary people would feel compelled to do), while Wilson in her dissenting opinion states that the defence's basis rests in the broader and more inclusive conception of "justification" (i.e., the idea that it is wrong to punish those who do wrongful acts when those acts are "morally justified", though as the reader will see Wilson takes a rather narrow view of what is morally justified in linking such moral obligations to legal duties). The second case, *Roberts*, presents an application of the tests laid out in *Perka* to a much more common fact situation. Finally, there is a short excerpt relating to duress from the well known *R. v. Latimer* case in which Robert Latimer was convicted of second degree murder for killing his disabled daughter.

One limitation which is suggested as to the use of the defence is that in situations where the accused has been negligent to some extent in creating the emergency in the first place, then perhaps the defence should not be available. In such cases defendants would be taking advantage of situations which they brought about. This is an argument which is raised in the *Breau* case in the "Self Defence" section below (see 7.1.3).

## Perka v. The Queen
### (1984), 14 C.C.C. (3d) 385 (S.C.C.)

[Only the judgments of Dickson J. and Wilson J. are reproduced below.]

DICKSON J.: — In this case we consider (i) a recurring legal problem, the "necessity" defence; (ii) what is commonly known as the "botanical" or "*cannabis* species" defence.

## FACTS

The appellants are drug smugglers. At trial, they led evidence that in early 1979 three of the appellants were employed, with 16 crew members, to deliver, by ship, (the "Samarkanda") a load of *cannabis* (marijuana) worth $6,000,000 or $7,000,000 from a point in international waters off the coast of Colombia, South America to a drop-point in international waters 200 miles off the coast of Alaska. The ship left Tumaco, Colombia, empty with a port-clearance document stating the destination to be Juneau, Alaska. For three weeks the ship remained in international waters off the coast of Colombia. While there, a DC-6 aircraft made four trips, dropping into the water shrimp-nets with a total of 634 bales of *cannabis* which were retrieved by the ship's long-boats.

A "communications" package was also dropped from a light aircraft, giving instructions for a rendezvous with another vessel, the "Julia B", which was to pick up the cargo of *cannabis* from the "Samarkanda" in international waters off the coast of Alaska. *En route*, according to the defence evidence, the vessel began to encounter a series of problems; engine breakdowns, overheating generators and malfunctioning navigation devices, aggravated by deteriorating weather. In the meantime, the fourth appellant, Nelson, part-owner of the illicit cargo, and three other persons left Seattle in a small boat, the "Whitecap", intending to rendezvous with the "Samarkanda" at the drop-point in Alaska. The problems of the "Samarkanda" intensified as fuel was consumed. The vessel became lighter, the intakes in the hull for sea-water, used as a coolant, lost suction and took in air instead, causing the generators to overheat. At this point the vessel was 180 miles from the Canadian coastline. The weather worsened. There were eight-to-ten-foot swells and a rising wind. It was finally decided for the safety of ship and crew to seek refuge on the Canadian shoreline for the purpose of making temporary repairs. The "Whitecap" found a sheltered cover on the west coast of Vancouver Island, "No Name Bay". The "Samarkanda" followed the "Whitecap" into the bay but later grounded amidships on a rock because the depth sounder was not working. The tide ran out. The vessel listed severely to starboard, to the extent that the captain, fearing the vessel was going to capsize, ordered the men to off-load the cargo. That is a brief summary of the defence evidence.

Early on the morning of May 22, 1979, police officers entered No Name Bay in a marked police boat with siren sounding. The "Samarkanda" and the "Whitecap" were arrested, as were all the appellants except Perka and Nelson, the same morning. The vessels and 33.49 tons of *cannabis* marijuana were seized by the police officers.

Charged with importing *cannabis* into Canada and with possession for the purpose of trafficking, the appellants claimed they did not plan to import to Canada or to leave their cargo of *cannabis* in Canada. They had planned to make repairs and leave. Expert witnesses on marine matters called by the defence testified that the decision to come ashore was, in the opinion of one witness, expedient and prudent and in the opinion of another, essential. At trial, counsel for the Crown alleged that the evidence of the ship's distress was a recent fabrication. Crown counsel relied on the circumstances under which the appellants were arrested to belie the "necessity" defence; when the police arrived on the scene most of the marijuana was already onshore, along with plastic ground sheets, battery-operated lights, liquor, food, clothing, camp stoves and sleeping-bags. Nevertheless, the jury believed the appellants and acquitted them.

The acquittal was reversed on appeal.

. . .

## THE NECESSITY DEFENCE

### *History and Background*

From earliest times it has been maintained that in some situations the force of circumstances makes it unrealistic and unjust to attach criminal liability to actions which, on their face, violate the law. Aristotle, *Ethics* (Book III, 1110 a), discusses the jettisoning of cargo from a ship in distress and remarks that "any sensible man does so" to secure the safety of himself and his crew.

. . .

To much the same purpose Kant, in *The Metaphysical Elements of Justice* (translator Ladd, 1965), discussing the actions of a person who, to save his own life sacrifices that of another, says at p. 41:

> A penal law applying to such a situation could never have the effect intended, for the threat of an evil that is still uncertain (being condemned to death by a judge) cannot outweigh the fear of an evil that is certain (being drowned). Hence, we must judge that, although an act of self-preservation through violence is not inculpable, it still is unpunishable.

In those jurisdictions in which such a general principle has been recognized or codified it is most often referred to by the term "necessity". Classic and harrowing instances which have been cited to illustrate the arguments both for and against the principle include the mother who steals food for her starving child, the shipwrecked mariners who resort to cannibalism (*R. v. Dudley and Stephens* (1884), 14 Q.B.D. 273), or throw passengers overboard to lighten a sinking lifeboat (*United States v. Holmes* (1842), 26 Fed. Cas. 360), and the more mundane case of the motorist who exceeds the speed-limit taking an injured person to the hospital.

. . .

In Canada the existence and the extent of a general defence of necessity was discussed by this Court in *Morgentaler v. The Queen* (1975), 20 C.C.C. (2d) 449, 53 D.L.R. (3d) 161, [1976] 1 S.C.R. 616. As to whether or not the defence exists at all I had occasion to say, at p. 497 C.C.C., p. 209 D.L.R., p. 678 S.C.R.:

> On the authorities it is manifestly difficult to be categorical and state that there is a law of necessity, paramount over other laws, relieving obedience from the letter of the law. If it does exist it can go no further than to justify non-compliance in urgent situations of clear and imminent peril when compliance with the law is demonstrably impossible.

Subsequent to *Morgentaler*, the courts appear to have assumed that a defence of necessity does exist in Canada. On the later trial of Dr. Morgentaler, the defence of necessity was again raised on a charge of procuring a miscarriage. Some admissible evidence was made in support of the plea and the case went to the jury, which rendered a verdict of not guilty.

. . .

In the present appeal the Crown does not challenge the appellants' claim that necessity is a common law defence preserved by *Criminal Code* s. 7(3). Rather the Crown claims the trial judge erred in (1) instructing the jury on the defence in light of the facts, and (2) imposing the burden of disproof of the defence upon the Crown, rather than imposing the burden of proof on the appellants.

### The Conceptual Foundation of the Defence

In *Morgentaler, supra*, I characterized necessity as an "ill-defined and elusive concept". Despite the apparently growing consensus as to the defence of necessity that statement is equally true today.

. . .

Working Paper 29 of the Law Reform Commission of Canada, *Criminal Law The General Part: Liability and defences* (1982), p. 93, makes this same point in somewhat more detail:

> The rationale of necessity, however, is clear. Essentially it involves two factors. One is the avoidance of greater harm or the pursuit of some greater good, the other is the difficulty of compliance with law in emergencies. From these two factors emerge two different but related principles. The first is a utilitarian principle to the effect that, within certain limits, it is justifiable in an emergency to break the letter of the law if breaking the law will avoid a greater harm than obeying it. The second is a humanitarian principle to the effect that, again within limits, it is excusable in an emergency to break the law if compliance would impose an intolerable burden on the accused.

Despite any superficial similarities, these two principles are in fact quite distinct and many of the confusions and the difficulties in the cases (and, with respect, in academic discussions) arise from a failure to distinguish between them.

Criminal theory recognizes a distinction between "justifications" and "excuses". A "justification" challenges the wrongfulness of an action which technically constitutes a crime. The police officer who shoots the hostage-taker, the innocent object of an assault who uses force to defend himself against his assailant, the good Samaritan who commandeers a car and breaks the speed laws to rush an accident victim to the hospital, these are all actors whose actions we consider *rightful*, not wrongful. For such actions people are often praised, as motivated by some great or noble object. The concept of punishment often seems incompatible with the social approval bestowed on the doer.

In contrast, an "excuse" concedes the wrongfulness of the action but asserts that the circumstances under which it was done are such that it ought not to be attributed to the actor. The perpetrator who is incapable, owing to a disease of the mind, of appreciating the nature and consequences of his acts, the person who labours under a mistake of fact, the drunkard, the sleepwalker: these are all actors of whose "criminal" actions we disapprove intensely, but whom, in appropriate circumstances, our law will not punish.

. . .

As a "justification" this residual defence can be related to Blackstone's concept of a "choice of evils". It would exculpate actors whose conduct could reasonably have been viewed as "necessary" in order to prevent a greater evil than that resulting from the violation of the law. As articulated, especially in some of the American cases, it involves a utilitarian balancing of the benefits of obeying the law as opposed to disobeying it, and when the balance is clearly in favour of disobeying, exculpates an actor who contravenes a criminal statute. This is the "greater good" formulation of the necessity defence: in some circumstances, it is alleged, the values of society, indeed of the criminal law itself, are better promoted by disobeying a given statute than by observing it.

With regard to this conceptualization of a residual defence of necessity, I retain the scepticism I expressed in *Morgentaler, supra*, at p. 497 C.C.C., p. 209 D.L.R., p. 678 S.C.R. It is still my opinion that, "[n]o system of positive law can recognize any principle which would entitle a person to violate the law because in his view the law conflicted with some higher social value". The *Criminal Code* has specified a number of identifiable situations in which an actor is justified in committing what would otherwise be a criminal offence. To go beyond that and hold that ostensibly illegal acts can be validated on the basis of their expediency, would import an undue subjectivity into the criminal law. It would invite the courts to second-guess the Legislature and to assess the relative merits of social policies underlying criminal prohibitions. Neither is a role which fits well with the judicial function. Such a doctrine could well become the last resort of scoundrels and, in the words of Edmund Davies L.J. in *Southwark London Borough Council v. Williams et al.*, [1971] Ch. 734 [ at p. 746], it could "very easily become simply a mask for anarchy".

Conceptualized as an "excuse", however, the residual defence of necessity is, in my view, much less open to criticism. It rests on a realistic assessment of human weakness, recognizing that a liberal and humane criminal law cannot hold people to the strict obedience of laws in emergency situations where normal human instincts, whether self-preservation or of altruism, overwhelmingly impel disobedience. The objectivity of the criminal law is preserved; such acts are still wrongful, but in the circumstances they are excusable. Praise is indeed not bestowed, but pardon is, when one does a wrongful act under pressure which, in the words of Aristotle in *The Nicomachean Ethics* (translator Ress, p. 49), "overstrains human nature and which no one could withstand".

. . .

At the heart of this defence is the perceived injustice of punishing violations of the law in circumstances in which the person had no other viable or reasonable choice available; the act was wrong but it is excused because it was realistically unavoidable.

Punishment of such acts, as Fletcher notes at p. 813, can be seen as purposeless as well as unjust:

> . . . involuntary conduct cannot be deterred and therefore it is pointless and wasteful to punish involuntary actors. This theory . . . of pointless punishment, carries considerable weight in current Anglo-American legal thought.

Relating necessity to the principle that the law ought not to punish involuntary acts leads to a conceptualization of the defence that integrates it into the normal rules for criminal liability rather than constituting it as a *sui generis* exception and threatening to engulf large portions of the criminal law. Such a conceptualization accords with our traditional legal, moral and philosophic views as accords with our traditional legal, moral and philosophic views as to what sorts of acts and what sorts of actors ought to be punished. In this formulation it is a defence which I do not hesitate to acknowledge and would not hesitate to apply to relevant facts capable of satisfying its necessary prerequisites.

. . .

## Preliminary Conclusions as to the Defence of Necessity

It is now possible to summarize a number of conclusions as to the defence of necessity in terms of its nature, basis and limitations:

(1) the defence of necessity could be conceptualized as either a justification or an excuse;

(2) it should be recognized in Canada as an excuse, operating by virtue of s. 7(3) of the *Criminal Code*

(3) necessity as an excuse implies no vindication of the deeds of the actor;

(4) the criterion is the moral involuntariness of the wrongful action;

(5) this involuntariness is measured on the basis of society's expectation of appropriate and normal resistance to pressure;

(6) negligence or involvement in criminal or immoral activity does not disentitle the actor to the excuse of necessity;

(7) actions or circumstances which indicate that the wrongful deed was not truly involuntary do disentitle;

(8) the existence of a reasonable legal alternative similarly disentitles; to be involuntary the act must be inevitable, unavoidable and afford no reasonable opportunity for an alternative course of action that does not involve a breach of the law;

(9) the defence only applies in circumstances of imminent risk where the action was taken to avoid a direct and immediate peril;

(10) where the accused places before the court sufficient evidence to raise the issue, the onus in on the Crown to meet it beyond a reasonable doubt.

## The Judge's Charge

The trial judge concluded that there was before him an adequate body of evidence to raise the issue of necessity and proceeded to direct the jury with respect to the defence. As I have earlier indicated, the Crown disputes whether the defence was open to the accused in the circumstances of the case and submits further that if it was in fact available, the trial judge erred in his direction.

In my view, the trial judge was correct in concluding that on the evidence before him he should instruct the jury with regard to necessity. There was evidence before him from which a jury might conclude that the accuseds' actions in coming ashore with their cargo of *cannabis* were aimed at self-preservation in response to an overwhelming emergency.

. . .

In the course of his charge on the issue of necessity the trial judge instructed the jury, using the specific words that appear in *Morgentaler v. The Queen* (1975), 20 C.C.C. (2d) 449, 53 D.L.R. (3d) 161, [1976] 1 S.C.R. 616, to the effect that they must find facts which amount to "an urgent situation of clear and imminent peril when compliance with the law is demonstrably impossible" in order for the appellants' noncompliance with the law against importation and possession of *cannabis* to be excused. That is the correct test. It is, with respect, however, my view that in explaining the meaning and application of this test, the trial judge fell into error.

The trial judge was obliged, in my opinion, to direct the jury's attention to a number of issues pertinent to the test for necessity.

. . .

In my view, this was a serious error and omission going to the heart of the defence of necessity. The error justifies a new trial.

I would dismiss the appeals.

. . .

WILSON J.: — The factual background of this case, the history of the litigation in the courts below and the grounds on which the appeal was taken in this Court are very fully set out in the reasons for judgment of the Chief Justice (Dickson J. at the date of the hearing) and it is not necessary for me to repeat them. Indeed, inasmuch as the Chief Justice's conclusion as to the defence of necessity seems clearly correct on the facts of this case and his disposition of the appeal manifestly just in the circumstances, I am dealing in these reasons only with the proposition very forcefully advanced by the Chief Justice in his reasons that the appropriate jurisprudential basis on which to premise the defence of necessity is exclusively that of excuse. My concern is that the learned Chief Justice appears to be closing the door on justification as an appropriate jurisprudential basis in some cases and I am firmly of the view that this is a door which should be left open by the court.

As the Chief Justice points out, criminal law theory recognizes a distinction between justification and excuse. In the case of justification the wrongfulness of the alleged offensive act is challenged; in the case of excuse the wrongfulness is acknowledged but a ground for the exercise of judicial compassion for the actor is asserted. By way of illustration, an act may be said to be justified when an essential element of the offence is absent, so that the defence effectively converts the accused's act from wrongful to rightful. Accordingly those defences which serve to establish a lack of culpable intent on the part of the accused, or which demonstrate that, although the accused intended to commit the act, the act was one which the accused was within his rights to commit may be labelled justification in so far as they elucidate the innocent nature of the act giving rise to the charge. Such doctrines as mistake of fact, automatism, etc., which, in the words of Lord Hailsham of St. Marylebone in *Director of Public Prosecutions v. Morgan*, [1975] 2 All E.R. 347 (H.L.), are raised in order to "negative" *mens rea*, may be appropriately placed in this category as they are invoked in order to undermine the very ingredient of culpability. Similarly, the accused who claims to have acted out of self-defence or provocation is utilizing aggressive force against another individual raises a justificatory defence in that he asserts the essential rightfulness of his aggressive act.

On the other hand, an excuse requires the court to evaluate the presence or absence of the accused's will. In contemporary jurisprudence the most forceful champion of excuse in criminal law has been Professor George Fletcher who has advocated a trend toward individualizing the conceptual basis for culpability so that all circumstances subjectively relevant to the accused be considered by the court. As such, the jury is requested to exercise compassion for the accused's predicament in its evaluation of his claim: "I couldn't help myself": Fletcher, "The Individualization of Excusing Conditions", 47 So. Cal. L.R. 1264 at p. 1269 (1974).

. . .

Thus, the nature of an excuse is to personalize the plea so that, while justification looks to the rightness of the act, excuse speaks to the compassion of the court for the actor.

As Chief Justice Dickson points out, although the necessity defence has engendered a significant amount of judicial and scholarly debate, it remains a somewhat elusive concept. It is, however, clear that justification and excuse are conceptually quite distinct and that any elucidation of a principled basis for the defence of necessity must be grounded in one or the other.

Turning first to the category of excuse, the concept of "normative involuntariness" stressed in the reasons of the Chief Justice may, on one reading, be said to fit squarely within the framework of an individualized plea which Professor Fletcher indicates characterizes all claims of excusability. The notional involuntariness of the action is assessed in the context of the accused's particular situation. The court must ask not only whether the offensive act accompanied by the requisite culpable mental state (i.e., intention, recklessness, etc.) has been established by the prosecution, but whether or not the accused acted so as to attract society's moral outrage.

. . .

On the other hand, the necessity of an act may be said to exempt an actor from *punishment*, since the person who acts in a state of what the Chief Justice calls "normative involuntariness" may be viewed as having been moved to act by the instinct for self-preservation. If so, the defence does not invoke the court's compassion but rather embodies an implicit statement that the sanction threatened by the law (i.e., future punishment in one form or another) could never overcome the fear of immediate death which the accused faced. Accordingly, in such a case the law is incapable of controlling the accused's conduct and responding to it with any punishment at all. Although such an act dictated by the necessity of self-preservation is a voluntary one (in the normal sense of the word), its "normative involuntariness" (in the sense that the actor faced no realistic choice) may form the basis of a defence if this is conceived as based on the pointlessness of punishment rather than on a view of the act itself as one of the accused was entitled to commit.

. . .

Returning to the defence of necessity as a justification, it may generally be said than an act is justified on grounds of necessity if the court can say that not only was the act a necessary one but it was rightful rather than wrongful. When grounded on the fundamental principle that a successful defence must characterize an act as one which the accused was within his rights to commit, it becomes immediately apparent that the defence does not depend on the immediacy or "normative involuntariness" of the accused's act unless, of course, the involuntariness is such as to be pertinent to the ordinary analysis of *mens rea*. The fact that one act is done out of a sense of immediacy or urgency and another after some contemplation cannot, in my view, serve to distinguish the quality of the act in terms of right or wrong. Rather, the justification must be premised on the need to fulfil a duty conflicting with the one which the accused is charged with having breached.

. . .

Similarly, the Chief Justice in his reasons for judgment in the present case correctly underlines the fact that a utilitarian balancing of the benefits of obeying the law as opposed to disobeying it cannot possibly represent a legitimate principle against which to measure the legality of an action since any violation of right permitted to be justified on such a utilitarian calculus does not, in the Chief Justice's words "fit[s] well with the judicial function". The maximization of social utility may well be a goal of legislative policy but it is not part of the judicial task of delineating right and wrong.

. . .

Accordingly, not only can the system of positive law not tolerate an individual opting to act in accordance with the dictates of his conscience in the event of conflict with legal duties, but in cannot permit acts in violation of legal obligations to be justified on the grounds that the social utility is thereby increased. In both situations the conflicting "duty" to which the defence arguments point is one which the court cannot take into account as it invokes considerations external to a judicial analysis of the rightness or wrongness of the impugned act. As Lord Coleridge C.J. succinctly put it in *Dudley and Stephens, supra,* at p. 287: "Who is to be the judge of this sort of necessity?"

On the other hand, in some circumstances defence counsel may be able to point to a conflicting duty which courts can and do recognize. For example, one may break the law in circumstances where it is necessary to rescue someone to whom one owes a positive duty of rescue (see *R. v. Walker* (1979), 48 C.C.C. (2d) 126, 5 M.V.R. 114 (Ont. Co Ct.)), since failure to act in such a situation may itself constitute a culpable act or omission: see *R. v. Instan,* [1893] 1 Q.B. 450. Similarly, if one subscribes to the viewpoint articulated by Laskin C.J.C. in *Morgentaler, supra* and perceives a doctor's defence to an abortion charge as his legal obligation to treat the mother rather than his alleged ethical duty to perform an unauthorized abortion, then the defence may be invoked without violating the prohibition enunciated by Dickson J. in *Morgentaler* against choosing a non-legal duty over a legal one.

It must be acknowledged, however, that on the existing state of the law the defence of necessity as justification would not be available to the person who rescues a stranger since the absence of a legal duty to rescue strangers reduces such a case to a conflict of a legal with a purely ethical duty. Such an act of rescue may be deserving of no punishment and, indeed, deserving of praise, but it is nevertheless a culpable act if the law is violated in the process of the rescue.

. . .

In similar fashion the ethical considerations of the "charitable and the good" must be kept analytically distinct from duties imposed by law. Accordingly, where necessity is invoked as a justification for violation of the law, the justification must, in my view, be restricted to situations where the accused's act constitutes the discharge of a duty recognized by law. The justification is not, however, established simply by showing a conflict of legal duties. The rule of proportionality is central to the evaluation of a justification premised on two conflicting duties since the defence rests on the rightfulness of the accused's choice of one over the other.

As the facts before the court in the present case do not involve a conflict of legal duties it is unnecessary to discuss in detail how a court should go about assessing the relative extent of two evils. Suffice it to say that any such assessment must respect the notion of right upon which justification is based. The assessment cannot entail a mere utilitarian calculation of, for example, lives saved and deaths avoided in the aggregate but must somehow attempt to come to grips with the nature of the rights and duties being assessed. This would seem to be consistent with Lord Coleridge's conclusion that necessity can provide no justification for the taking of a life, such an act representing the most extreme form of rights violation. As discussed above, if any defence for such a homicidal act is to succeed, it would have to be framed as an excuse grounded on self-preservation. It could not possibly be declared by the court to be rightful. By contrast, the justification analysis would seem to support those cases in which fulfilment of the legal duty to save persons entrusted to one's care is preferred over the lesser offences of trespass or petty theft: see *Mouse's Case* (1608), 12 Co. Rep. 63, 77 E.R. 1341; *Amiens, Ch. corr. April 22, 1898*, S. 1899.2.1 (*Menard's Case*). The crucial question for the justification defence is whether the accused's act can be said to represent a furtherance of or a detraction from the principle of the universality of rights.

In summary, it seem to me that the category of "normative involuntariness" into which an act done in the interests of self-preservation falls is characterized not by the literal voluntariness of the act but by its unpunishable nature. As such, the act may be exempted from culpability if it arose in a life-threatening situation of necessity. Where, however, a defence by way of excuse is premised on compassion for the accused or on a perceived failure to achieve a desired instrumental end of punishment, the judicial response must be to fashion an appropriate sentence but to reject the defence as such. The only conceptual premise on which necessity as an excuse could rest is the inherent impossibility of a court's responding in any way to an act which, although wrongful, was the one act which any rational person would commit.

Where the defence of necessity is invoked as a justification the issue is simply whether the accused was right in pursuing the course of behaviour giving rise to the charge. Thus, where the act otherwise constitutes a criminal offence (i.e., it embodies both *mens rea* and the *actus reus*) the accused must show that he operated under a conflicting legal duty which made his seemingly wrongful act right. But such justification must be premised on a right or duty recognized by law. This excludes conduct attempted to be justified on the ground of an ethical duty internal to the conscience of the accused as well as conduct sought to be justified on the basis of a perceived maximization of social utility resulting from it. Rather, the conduct must stem from the accused's duty to satisfy his legal obligations and to respect the principles of the universality of rights.

I would dismiss the appeals.

*Appeals dismissed.*

## Regina v. Roberts
(1987), 65 Nfld. & P.E.I.R. 343 (P.E.I. C.A.)

[Only the judgment of Carruthers, C.J. is reproduced below.]

[1] CARRUTHERS, C.J.: — This is an appeal from a conviction of an offence of impaired driving contrary to s. 237(a) of the Criminal Code.

[2] The notice of appeal sets forth two grounds of appeal, namely:

"1. That the learned trial judge erred in finding that the appellant was in fact impaired.

"2. That the learned trial judge erred in law by misinterpreting the defence of necessity and by not leaving the defence of necessity open to the appellant."

[3] The facts giving rise to the charge occurred sometime around 1 a.m. on March 24, 1986, at Charlottetown. The appellant's mother, who had not been well for two or three weeks previous to this incident, developed "an awful pain below the heart" and asked the appellant to drive her to the hospital. The appellant testified:

"Well, Mum had come downstairs, she wasn't fully dressed and I had to get her dressed. She wanted to go to the hospital because she had an awful pain below the heart. So we got her dressed and I said 'do you want to take the ambulance?' and she said 'no, I am not going in the ambulance, you will drive me.' So I knew I had a bottle of beer in me or two bottles and I said 'well, probably get a taxi' and 'no' she said, 'you drive me right now.' So on the way out . . . "

[4] The appellant left with her mother for the hospital and on the way to the hospital she was stopped by Cpl. Walker who testified that he had observed the vehicle driven by the appellant swerve onto the sidewalk area, strike a snowbank, and return to the center of the street. As a result he stopped the vehicle and later charged the appellant with impaired driving.

. . .

[12] It is clear from the transcript that the trial judge was satisfied beyond a reasonable doubt as to the guilt of the appellant.

. . .

[14] I dismiss the appellant's first ground of appeal as I cannot say that the conclusions reached by the trial judge are either unreasonable or that they are unsupported by the evidence.

[15] The second ground of appeal raises the defence of necessity. The appellant submits that the trial judge did not give proper consideration to the defence of necessity and erred by not applying the defence.

[16] It is clear from the transcript that the trial judge did deal with the defence of necessity. He states:

"Defence of necessity, again the law is quite clear and I don't think there is any argument on the law, it's on the facts. Was there a necessity for the accused to drive her mother? I hold there was not. Indeed (she) herself could have called the taxi, could have called the ambulance. The only reason she wanted to drive her mother was because her mother was insisting to save $3. She was not 50 kilometers away as that case was. She didn't call a taxi and get no answer. Anybody could have driven her mother that night. There was no urgency so as that she had to drive her herself."

[17] The leading decision in Canada on the defence of necessity is *Perka et al. v. The Queen*, [1984] 2 S.C.R. 232; 55 N.R. 1; 13 D.L.R. (4th) 1; 42 C.R. (3d) 113; [1984] 6 W.W.R. 289; 14 C.C.C. (3d) 385 (S.C.C.) in which Dickson, C.J.C., made a very thorough analysis of the matter.

. . .

[18] Counsel for the appellant submits that the trial judge erred as he did not consider all of the conclusions enumerated by Dickson, C.J.C. It may well be that he did not consider each and every one of these conclusions. In my opinion it was not necessary for him to do so in this case. He has dealt with what Dickson, C.J.C., said would almost certainly be the most important consideration in most cases when the defence is raised; was there any reasonable legal alternative to the legal response open to the accused?

[19] He held that there was a reasonable legal alternative open to the accused. I am satisfied that he did not make any error of law in dealing with the defence of necessity. I dismiss the appellant's second ground of appeal.

[20] I cannot say that the conclusions reached by the trial judge are either unreasonable or that they are unsupported by the evidence.

[21] The appeal is dismissed.

*Appeal dismissed.*

*Editor's note: The Supreme Court of Canada also looked at the requirements of the defence of necessity in the well known case of* R. v. Latimer *(2001), 39 C.R. (5th) 1 (S.C.C.) in which Robert Latimer was convicted of second degree murder for killing of disabled daughter. He had testified that he had killed his daughter out of love due to his concern for her ongoing pain and suffering. The trial judge had not allowed the jury to consider the defence of necessity. The Supreme Court, in upholding his conviction and his sentence to life in prison with no chance of parole for at least ten years, had the following to say about the defence:*

The Availability of the Defence of Necessity
(a) The Three Requirements for the Defence of Necessity

*Perka* outlined three elements that must be present for the defence of necessity. First, there is the requirement of imminent peril or danger. Second, the accused must have had no reasonable legal alternative to the course of action he or she undertook. Third, there must be proportionality between the harm inflicted and the harm avoided.

. . .

Before applying the three requirements of the necessity defence to the facts of this case, we need to determine what test governs necessity. Is the standard objective or subjective? A subjective test would be met if the person believed he or she was in imminent peril with no reasonable legal alternative to committing the offence. Conversely, an objective test would not assess what the accused believed; it would consider whether in fact the person was in peril with no reasonable legal alternative. A modified objective test falls somewhere between the two. It involves an objective evaluation, but one that takes into account the situation and characteristics of the particular accused person. We conclude that, for two of the three requirements for the necessity defence, the test should be the modified objective test.

The first and second requirements — imminent peril and no reasonable legal alternative — must be evaluated on the modified objective standard described above. As expressed in *Perka*, necessity is rooted in an objective standard: "involuntariness is measured on the basis of society's expectation of appropriate and normal resistance to pressure" (p. 259). We would add that it is appropriate, in evaluating the accused's conduct, to take into account personal characteristics that legitimately affect what may be expected of that person. . . .

While an accused's perceptions of the surrounding facts may be highly relevant in determining whether his conduct should be excused, those perceptions remain relevant only so long as they are reasonable. The accused person must, at the time of the act, honestly believe, on reasonable grounds, that he faces a situation of imminent peril that leaves no reasonable legal alternative open. There must be a reasonable basis for the accused's beliefs and actions, but it would be proper to take into account circumstances that legitimately affect the accused person's ability to evaluate his situation. The test cannot be a subjective one, and the accused who argues that he perceived imminent peril without an alternative would only succeed with the defence of necessity if his belief was reasonable given his circumstances and attributes. We leave aside for a case in which it arises the possibility that an honestly held but mistaken belief could ground a "mistake of fact" argument on the separate inquiry into mens rea.

The third requirement for the defence of necessity, proportionality, must be measured on an objective standard, as it would violate fundamental principles of the criminal law to do otherwise. Evaluating the nature of an act is fundamentally a determination reflecting society's values as to what is appropriate and what represents a transgression.

The evaluation of the seriousness of the harms must be objective. A subjective evaluation of the competing harms would, by definition, look at the matter from the perspective of the accused person who seeks to avoid harm, usually to himself. The proper perspective, however, is an objective one, since evaluating the gravity of the act is a matter of community standards infused with constitutional considerations (such as, in this case, the s. 15(1) equality rights of the disabled). We conclude that the proportionality requirement must be determined on a purely objective standard.

## Questions/Discussion

1. Which rationale for the defence of necessity do you agree with in *Perka*? Why? Would you allow for an even wider defence in this area based upon a wider meaning of "justification" than Wilson in her judgment is willing to give?

2. Should people who steal to eat be free of liability, especially in an era of social service cutbacks and lack of real choice for the destitute in such situations?

3. Is the defence of necessity too restrictive as to the situations in which the court will accept it? Should the courts be the ones who make the law in this area or do we need legislation for greater clarity and certainty? In this regard, the Law Reform Commission of Canada (Report 31) has recommended the following:

   (a) General Rule. No one is liable if: (i) he [or she] acted to avoid immediate harm to the person or immediate serious damage to property; (ii) such harm or damage substantially outweighed the harm or damage resulting from that crime; and (iii) such harm or damage could not effectively have been avoided by any lesser means.

   (b) Exception. This clause does not apply to anyone who himself [or herself] purposely causes the death of, or seriously harms, another person.

   What changes would result from the addition of such a clause to the Code? How helpful do you think this provision would be?

4. Do you think the decision in *Roberts* is fair given the circumstances the accused found herself in? To what extent should the courts try to "second-guess" the choices made by individuals in extreme situations?

5. Do you agree with the decision in *Latimer*? Why or why not? Should the defence of necessity have been left to the jury for its determination as to its availability in the fact situation?

## Further Reading

- Elliott, D.W., "Necessity, Duress and Self-Defence" [1989] Criminal Law Review 611.
- Galloway, D., "Necessity as a Justification: A Critique of *Perka*" (1986), 10 Dalhousie Law Journal 158.
- Mewett, A. and M. Manning, *Mewett and Manning on Criminal Law*, 3rd ed. (Markham: Butterworths, 1994).
- Morgan, E., "The Defence of Necessity: Justification or Excuse?" (1984), 42 University of Toronto Faculty of Law Review 165.
- Roach, Kent, *Criminal Law, 2d ed.* (Toronto: Irwin Law, 2000) at 273-279.
- Stuart, D., *Canadian Criminal Law: A Treatise*, 2nd ed. (Toronto: Carswell, 1987), pp. 432-448.

- Stuart, Don, and R. Delisle, *Learning Canadian Criminal Law, 8th ed.* (Toronto: Carswell, 2001).
- Verdun-Jones, S., *Criminal Law in Canada: Cases, Questions and the Code,* (Toronto: Harcourt Brace Jovanovich Canada, 1989) at 255-265.

## 7.1.3   Self Defence

### Introduction

Self defence is a codified defence found in sections 34-37 of the Code (with the exception of a situation as in *Breau*) and is, for the most part, well explained in the case of *Cadwallader* which follows. The defence applies principally to charges of murder, manslaughter and assault. The principal section that concerns us is section 34, which deals with unprovoked attacks on the accused, and which is itself divided into two areas of applicability.[1] The first subsection of section 34 deals with those situations where the force used by the accused was not intended to cause death or grievous bodily harm. The test for the amount of force that is allowed in such circumstances in an objective one of no more force than is necessary. If the accused does not come within subsection (1), the subsection (2) might be applicable where the accused causes death or grievous bodily harm. The tests for the permissable use and amount of force in this case are found in paragraphs (a) and (b) of the subsection.

First, there must be a "reasonable apprehension of death or grievous bodily harm from the violence with which the assault was originally made or with which the assailant pursues his [or her] purposes". Second, as to the degree of force, the test is essentially a subjective one, that is, that the accused believes on reasonable grounds that she or he could not otherwise be preserved from death or grievous bodily harm. It is important, therefore, at the outset to determine which subsection of section 34 applies as the tests are very different. Note as well that as to the amount of force which is permitted the test is not an exact one and the courts are willing to give some leeway in the degree of force applied, whichever test is employed.[2] Finally, note that when the accused passes the preliminary test yet misjudges and uses too much force, there is no reduction in the liability found.

The section of the Code dealing with situations where the accused has provoked the assault, section 35, is not dealt with here because its availability and usefulness are so restricted. Read the section and note its rather onerous and some might say unrealistic requirements. The other section which is dealt with in the cases, section 37, involves the prevention of an attack. The *Lavallée* case that follows it highlights a particular problem in the area of self defence relating to domestic violence. The various restrictions in the self defence provisions, coupled with regressive, mistaken and stereotypical attitudes towards the victims of domestic violence, have often made it difficult to effectively mount a defence in situations where the battered woman

---

1   See section 36 for the meaning of "provocation" in this area.
2   See *R. v. Ogal* (1928), 50 C.C.C. 71 (Alta C.A.) where the court said the accused need not "measure with nicety" the amount of force used.

strikes back. Self defence is more readily available in situations where the death occurs in the course of a fight precipitated by the deceased and thus fits within the traditional mould. Many cases involving battered women, however, arise after a prolonged period of battering but not in the course of a contemporaneous attack; rather, the assault by the woman often occurs when the man is asleep or unconscious. It is ironic that the criminal law has been so slow to intervene in cases of domestic violence, yet has usually been unable or unwilling to deal effectively with cases where the woman ultimately protects herself or her children. The recognition in *Lavallée* of the complex issues surrounding the problems of battered women in Canada is a hopeful sign that the legal framework may be changing to meet their needs and circumstances.

A final section to note is section 43 which deals, not with self defence, but with statutory protection for parents and teachers who use force to correct a child's behaviour. In such cases there is not criminal liability if the person in authority uses no more force than is reasonable under the circumstances. Analogous protections are provided to masters of ships in section 44 and to surgeons in section 45.

## Regina v. Cadwallader
### [1966] 1 C.C.C. 380 (Sask. Q.B.)

SIROIS, J.: — John Kenneth Marcella Cadwallader of Kyle, Saskatchewan, a 14-year-old boy, was charged that he was on or about October 24, 1964, at the White Bear District, in the Province of Saskatchewan, a juvenile, and that he did unlawfully kill and slay one John Cadwallader, thereby committing manslaughter and thus violating the *Criminal Code* of Canada, and did thereby commit a delinquency contrary to the provisions of the *Juvenile Delinquents Act*, R.S.C. 1952, c. 160.

The trial was held at Swift Current, Saskatchewan, before His Honour Judge J.H. Sunstrum, Judge of the Juvenile Court for Saskatchewan, commencing on January 27th, and ending on February 1, 1965. At the close of the hearing the learned Juvenile Court Judge gave an oral judgment as follows:

"Now you can just stand up, Mr. Cadwallader. You are charged on the 24th day of October, 1964, at the White Bear district, a juvenile, did unlawfully kill and slay one, John Cadwallader, thereby committing manslaughter, and thus violating a provision of the Criminal Code of Canada, and thereby commit a delinquency, contrary to the provisions of the Juvenile Delinquents Act.

"Now we have heard evidence over the last few days as to the circumstances under which the body of your father was found, and the explanation you gave this morning. The explanation is that your father was coming up the stairs with a loaded 30-30 and apparently with the intention of carrying out a threat to kill you. Now your evidence is that you took your .22 and put a loaded magazine in it and then swung around and, without aiming, shot at your father, who then apparently fell down the stairs, and a total of five wounds were found in the body of your father. Now I feel that the last shot, particularly the one that was fired from a very close distance to the body of your father, and possibly any that were fired after the first one or two. You stated that the third one you were on the stairs at the time you fired the third shot, the fourth shot that you were possibly three-quarters of the way up the stairs, and then the fifth shot fired when the gun was only a few inches away. Now I feel that the extent of force used here was far more than was reasonable under the circumstances. I don't feel that you had any concern at that time that your father was in any condition to — able to carry out any threat to kill you, and therefore I find you guilty of the charge, and you will be found guilty of committing a delinquency contrary to the provisions of the Juvenile Delinquents Act."

The delinquent was committed to the Director of Child Welfare for the Province of Saskatchewan and a condition was imposed that he not be allowed to have or use firearms until he reaches the age of 21 years.

The special grounds for appeal against the judgment set out above as stated in the notice of appeal as amended are as follows:

"(a) The learned Juvenile Court Judge erred in law in that he completely misconstrued the law and the evidence relating to self-evidence;
(b) The learned Juvenile Court Judge erred in law in that he misconstrued the law and evidence relating to the amount of force used;
(c) The learned Juvenile Court Judge should have dismissed the charge before him, in that the evidence clearly showed self-defence on the part of the applicant;
(d) The learned Juvenile Court Judge erred in that there was no evidence whatsoever to support the finding that the applicant was guilty of committing a juvenile delinquency."

It may be of assistance to review the salient facts of the incident as well as some of the antecedent so as to better understand what took place and why it took place.

The appellant, an only child reached his 14th birthday a few months before the tragedy. His mother had passed away on July 19, 1956, before the boy was six years of age. The child was cared for by an uncle and aunt for approximately one school year after his mother died. Thereafter the father hired a housekeeper who reared the child in a fashion until the end of 1963, and from that time on the appellant and his father lived alone together. From the evidence it would seem that the father was reserved and quiet; his social contacts were very limited; he had a strange sense of humour and was inclined to be moody. While the father and son relationship seemed normal and healthy to outsiders, it in fact according to the boy's evidence left much to be desired. They lived in the father's house in Kyle during the week so the boy could attend school. But on weekends and during the summer holidays they would go to the farm and indulge in their favorite pastime — firing guns of various descriptions. The appellant in his evidence related over twenty incidents prior to the tragedy — these occurring with increasing frequency in the years 1962 to 1964 — wherein the father seemed to want to do away with him or to kill him. The appellant, who is possessed of above average intelligence and who had always done well in school previously, began to slip badly academically in June and again in September and October of 1964. Something obviously was worrying and troubling him but he refused to tell anyone about his personal problems. During the week of October 18, 1964, remains of a mammoth were located in the Kyle district and specialists from the University came down to unearth the discovery. The appellant and his father drove down from Kyle, as did many others, to see the men at work on Wednesday, October 21st. The appellant found out that they would be busy on the project until the coming Saturday or Monday of the following week. The appellant and his father talked about the discovery on their return to Kyle, at which time the father told the boy, "You will be in the ground before the mammoth is out of the ground." The father was serious when he spoke these words and the boy's apprehension increased.

On Friday, October 23rd, the boy and his father went to the mammoth site again and continued on to the farm for the week-end as was the custom. On Saturday morning, the 25th, the father and son had breakfast together but the boy did not go out to work as he had just recovered from a cold and was not feeling his normal self. About 1:30 p.m. the father and son had a light dinner together, after which the father went outside to repair the fence. The boy went upstairs to lay down on his bed again as he was not feeling well. About 3:30 p.m. the boy heard his father make a lot of noise on the doorstep, he mumbled as he entered the house, slammed the door, and he was heard to say: "I'm going to kill that God Damned little bastard." The father walked noisily to his room (situated roughly beneath the boy's room), started loading a 30-30, pumped a shell into the barrel, and walked noisily again across the kitchen towards the stairway. The boy arose from his bed and peeked over the edge of the stairway; he saw his angry and determined father start up the stairs with the 30-30 rifle in his hand. The boy figured this was it — that his father was coming up to get him. The boy returned to his bed, quickly grabbed the magazine on the nail keg as well as his semi-automatic Cooey rifle leaning against the east wall, and slipped the magazine into the gun. The boy swung around and saw his father up the steps aiming at him with his 30-30 rifle. The boy took a quick shot without aiming; there followed four other shots, according to the evidence, but the accused at the time did not remember. He was "a little scared and excited" and "it all happened so quickly." The evidence of the pathologist as well as the photographs and the boy's recollection of the rapid series of events at the crucial moment seem to indicate that two shots followed quickly after the first one before or as the father and his gun started to fall back down the stairs. The fourth shot was fired with the boy standing near the top or about three quarters up the stairs, the father was still partly on the stairs and the bullet struck him in the back. The father was still moving around and the boy says he was still scared of his ability to shoot. The accused followed down the stairs and fired the fifth and last shot in the neck of the deceased from a distance of about three inches. Either the fourth or fifth shot could have been fatal whereas the first three shots were not.

The boy, under rigorous cross-examination, staunchly maintained that he did not want to kill his father but that up until the final or fifth shot he figured his father was still able to shoot him. The boy's feelings and reactions at the tragic moment were, I believe, adequately summarized in his answers to the following questions:

"Q.4616. Well why did you hold the gun up to his head and shoot three inches away? Why did you do that?
A. Well there is so much strain and everything . . . "

And again later on:

"Q.4813. Why did you move the 30-30 rifle at all?
A. I apparently didn't — I hadn't had sleep for a long time — and I didn't think at the time."

. . .

The teachers who taught the boy all agreed he was a good boy, that he caused no problem in school and that he was of above average intelligence. But they all agreed that from June, 1964, onward, when his marks mysteriously plummeted down, that the boy had a problem although he refused to communicate with them on the subject.

. . .

The appellant's defence was self-defence. The Crown agrees with this but submits that the force used by the appellant was excessive and that the conviction for manslaughter should be upheld.

The evidence establishes that the events immediately prior to the actual shooting constituted an unprovoked assault by the deceased upon the appellant.

. . .

While a person is not justified in killing another because of fear, there are many cases where killing in self-defence has been condoned on the ground of the necessity to preserve life.

. . .

Self-defence proceeds from necessity and each case must therefore be determined upon its own facts. The force used can only be justified when it is necessary for the avoidance or prevention of an offered injury, and again it must be no more than is necessary under the circumstances. To use an extreme example, you could not use a tank against a chariot. But if one believes he is in danger of life or limb he is entitled to use such force as would effectually put his assailant out of action. Where the means of defence used is not disproportionate to the severity of the assault, the plea is valid although the defender fails to measure with nicety the degree of force necessary to ward off the attack and inflicts serious injury. The test as to the extent of justification is whether the accused used more force *than he on reasonable grounds believed necessary*. It is not an objective test; the determination must be made according to the accused's state of mind at the time. The question is: Did he use more force than he on reasonable grounds believed to be necessary?

To establish the defence there should be evidence — (a) that the facts amount to self-defence, and (b) that the mode of defence used was justifiable under the circumstances.

When the defence of self-defence is raised it does not affect the burden upon the Crown of establishing its case — that is of proving all accused guilty of the offence beyond a reasonable doubt. All that the accused has to do to establish this defence is introduce evidence raising at least a reasonable doubt as to his guilt; the burden rests on the prosecution of negativing that defence. If, on consideration of the whole of the evidence, the jury are either convinced of the innocence of the prisoner or are left, in doubt whether he was acting in necessary self-defence they should acquit.

The appellant in this instance is a 14-year-old boy, who barely remembers his mother — he was five years old when she died. For most of the time thereafter he lived a closed life with a father who was a strange man in many ways. Incidents punctured this boy's life with his father, especially in the two years prior to the tragedy and particularly in the summer and fall of 1964 which worried and frightened this boy. Such an incident, previously referred to, occurred in the course of a conversation with his father a few days only before the tragedy. On the afternoon of the fateful day the boy was lying on his bed, he was not well and was worried. His angry father was coming up the stairs with a 30-30 to kill him. The boy was trapped and he reacted in the only way it seems to me that an ordinary person would under the circumstances. Can one adequately visualize the fear, terror and confusion which would grip any man, let alone a 14-year-old boy in a situation such as this.

It is clear that he acted in self-defence. On his uncontradicted evidence he used only sufficient force as he reasonably thought necessary under the circumstances to put his assailant out of action. You cannot put a higher test on a 14-year-old boy than that known to our law.

In my respectful opinion the case against the appellant was not proved with that certainty, in the light of all the evidence, which is necessary in order to justify a verdict of guilty. Therefore upon that ground the appeal is allowed and it is directed that this conviction be quashed.

*Appeal allowed; conviction quashed.*

## Regina v. Breau
### (1959), 125 C.C.C. 84 (N.B. S.C)

WEST J.: — The accused was convicted by Magistrate Morrissey of Northumberland County for that he "did kill a bull moose contrary to section 22(a) of the Game Act of New Brunswick". The case is before me on review under s. 46 of the *Summary Convictions Act*, R.S.N.B. 1952, c. 220. Under s. 115 of the *Game Act*, R.S.N.B. 1952, c. 95 it is my duty to hear and determine the review upon the merits of the case only.

The accused admits he killed the moose at the time and place charged, but contends he did so in self defence. He says he was hunting with two companions near Renous, Northumberland County on October 25, 1958. He separated from his companions and when alone met a bull moose on a woods road. The moose charged him and in self defence he shot it. Shortly after, his companions rejoined him and helped dress it. The moose had been shot in the breast. The three men then went out to the main highway where they met a truck driver who happened to be passing and told him they had shot a moose and asked where they might find a game warden. They were informed if they waited around one would probably be along. Shortly afterwards a game warden arrived and the accused told him he had shot a moose in self defence and went with the warden to show him the carcass. The story of the accused was corroborated in many important details by the evidence of the game warden and the truck driver.

The relevant sections of the *Game Act* are 22(a) and 106(1) which read as follows:

"**22.** Any one is guilty of an offence who hunts, takes, hurts, injures, shoots, wounds, kills or destroys, "(a) a cow moose, calf moose, bull moose, cow caribou or calf caribou, at any time or season."

"**106**(1) Where on the prosecution of an offence under this Act it is proven that the person charged with such offence had in his possession the game or fur bearing animal or any part thereof in respect to which he is charged, the onus shall be on the person charged to prove that he did not commit the offence charged."

The submission of the accused is that the finding of the Magistrate is contrary to the evidence, and that he was justified in shooting the moose in self defence.

. . .

I have come to the conclusion that the account given by the accused as to the shooting must be accepted as true. The only question remaining is whether under the *Game Act* self defence is available as a justification or excuse for shooting a moose. In the recent case of *R. v. Vickers* [unreported] which was before the Chief Justice of the Queen's Bench Division on review the learned Judge states "self defence is not open as an excuse or as a defence" to anyone who violates the provisions of s. 22(a) of the Act. Such was the view of an able Judge whose opinions are entitled to great respect. However, it must be considered as *obiter* as the case was decided on other grounds.

Apart from the *Vickers* case I have been unable to find any authority directly in point. It becomes necessary therefore to rely on certain fundamental legal doctrines. It has long been a principle of the common law that a person may with impunity kill another in self defence. It is recognized that in certain circumstances an individual may through necessity employ self help for his protection and preservation rather than wait for the protection of the law, which may come too late.

. . .

These principles of the common law are given express statutory recognition in ss. 34 and 35 of the *Criminal Code*. See Crankshaw's Criminal Code, 7th ed., s. 17 and pp. 83 *et seq.* Such is in keeping with the statement of Blackstone, *supra*: "Self-defence, therefore, as it is justly called the primary law of nature, so it is not, neither can it be in fact, taken away by the law of society."

The same rule applies when a person is attacked by an animal.

. . .

The Crown argues the accused voluntarily went into the woods and placed himself in a position where he might be attacked by a moose and therefore must accept the consequences. I cannot accept such a submission. The accused was lawfully in the woods and engaged on a lawful mission. Through no fault of his own he found himself in a situation of dire peril from which he could only extricate himself by taking the action he did. In my view his acts were warranted under the principles of the common law above noted.

To alter a clearly established principle of the common law a distinct and positive legislative enactment is necessary. Statutes are not presumed to make any alteration in the common law further or otherwise than the Act expressly declares. See Craies on Statute Law, 5th ed., p. 114. There is no specific language in the *Game Act* taking away the right of self defence nor is there any language which by necessary implication does so. Hence the defence remains open to the accused.

The finding of the Magistrate will be set aside and the conviction quashed. There will be no order for costs.

*Appeal allowed.*

# Regina v. Lavallée
## (1990), 55 C.C.C (3d) 97 (S.C.C.)

[Excerpts from the judgment of Wilson J. are reproduced below.]

WILSON J.: — The narrow issue raised on this appeal is the adequacy of a trial judge's instructions to the jury regarding expert evidence. The broader issue concerns the utility of expert evidence in assisting a jury confronted by a plea of self-defence to a murder charge by a common law wife who had been battered by the deceased.

## THE FACTS

The appellant, who was 22 years old at the time, had been living with Kevin Rust for some three to four years. Their residence was the scene of a boisterous party on August 30, 1986. In the early hours of August 31 after most of the guests had departed the appellant and Rust had an argument in the upstairs bedroom which was used by the appellant. Rust was killed by a single shot in the back of the head from a .303 calibre rifle fired by the appellant as he was leaving the room.

The appellant did not testify but her statement made to police on the night of the shooting was put in evidence. Portions of it read as follows:

> Me and Wendy argued as usual and I ran in the house after Kevin pushed me. I was scared, I was really scared. I locked the door. Herb was downstairs with Joanne and I called for Herb but I was crying when I called him. I said, "Herb come up here please." Herb came up to the top of the stairs and I told him that Kevin was going to hit me actually beat on me again. Herb said he knew and that if I was his old lady things would be different, he gave me a hug. OK, we're friends, there's nothing between us. He said "Yeah, I know" and he went outside to talk to Kevin leaving the door unlocked. I went upstairs and hid in my closet from Kevin. I was so scared . . . My window was open and I could hear Kevin asking questions about what I was doing and what I was saying. Next thing I know he was coming up the stairs for me. He came into my bedroom and said "Wench, where are you?" And he turned on my light and he said "Your purse is on the floor" and he kicked it. OK then he turned and he saw me in the closet. He wanted me to come out but I didn't want to come out because I was scared. I was so scared. [The officer who took the statement then testified that the appellant started to cry at this point and stopped after a minute or two.] He grabbed me by the arm right there. There's a bruise on my face also where he slapped me. He didn't slap me right then, first he yelled at me then he pushed me and I pushed him back and he hit me twice on the right hand side of my head. I was scared. All I though about was all the other times he used to beat me, I was scared, I was shaking as usual. The rest is a blank, all I remember is he gave me the gun and a shot was fired through my screen. This is all so fast. And then the guns were in another room and he loaded it the second shot and gave it to me. And I was going to shoot myself. I pointed it to myself, I was so upset. OK and then he went and I was sitting on the bed and he started going like this with his finger [the appellant made a shaking motion with an index finger] and said something like "You're my old lady and you do as you're told" or something like that. He said "wait till everybody leaves, you'll get it then" and he said something to the effect of "either you kill me or I'll get you" and that was what it was. He kind of smiled and then turned around. I shot him but I aimed out. I though I aimed above him and a piece of his head went that way.

The relationship between the appellant and Rust was volatile and punctuated by frequent arguments and violence. They would apparently fight for two or three days at a time or several times a week. Considerable evidence was led at trial indicating that the appellant was frequently a victim of physical abuse at the hands of Rust. Between 1983 and 1986 the appellant made several trips to hospital for injuries including severe bruises, a fractured nose, multiple contusions and a black eye . . .

A friend of the deceased, Robert Ezako, testified that he had witnessed several fights between the appellant and the deceased and that he had seen the appellant point a gun at the deceased twice and threaten to kill him if he ever touched her again. Under cross-examination Ezako admitted to seeing or hearing the deceased beat up the appellant on several occasions and, during the preliminary inquiry, described her screaming during one such incident like "a pig being butchered" . . .

At one point on the night of his death Rust chased the appellant outside the house and a mutual friend, Norman Kolish, testified that the appellant pleaded with Rust to "leave me alone" and sought Kolish's protection by trying to hide behind him. A neighbour overheard Rust and the appellant arguing and described the tone of the former as "argumentative" and the latter as "scared" . . .

Three witnesses who attended the party testified to hearing sounds of yelling, pushing, shoving and thumping coming from upstairs prior to the gunshots. It is not disputed that two shots were fired by the appellant. The first one went through a window screen. It is not clear where Rust was at the time. The appellant in her statement says that he was upstairs, while another witness places him in the basement. The second shot was the fatal one . . .

The police officer who took the appellant's statement testified to seeing a red mark on her arm where she said the deceased had grabbed her. When the coroner who performed an autopsy on the deceased was shown pictures of the appellant (who had various bruises), he testified that it was "entirely possible" that bruises on the deceased's left hand were occasioned by an assault on the appellant. Another doctor noted an injury to the appellant's pinkie finger consistent with those sustained by the adoption of a defensive stance.

The expert evidence which forms the subject matter of the appeal came from Dr. Fred Shane, a psychiatrist with extensive professional experience in the treatment of battered wives. At the request of defence counsel Dr. Shane prepared a psychiatric assessment of the appellant. The substance of Dr. Shane's opinion was that the appellant had been terrorized by Rust to the point of feeling trapped, vulnerable, worthless and unable to escape the relationship despite the violence. At the same time, the continuing pattern of abuse put her life in danger. In Dr. Shane's opinion the appellant's shooting of the deceased was a final desperate act by a woman who sincerely believed that she would be killed that night:

> . . . I think she felt, she felt in the final tragic moment that her life was on the line, that unless she defended herself, unless she reacted in a violent way that she would die. I mean he made it very explicit to her, from what she told me and from the information I have from the material that you forwarded to me, that she had, I think to defend herself against his violence.

Dr. Shane stated that his opinion was based on four hours of formal interviews with the appellant, a police report of the incident (including the appellant's statement), hospital reports documenting eight of her visits to emergency departments between 1983 and 1985, and an interview with the appellant's mother. In the course of his testimony Dr. Shane related many things told to him by the appellant for which there was no admissible evidence. They were not in the appellant's statement to the police and she did not testify at trial. For example, Dr. Shane mentioned several episodes of abuse described by the appellant for which there were no hospital reports. He also related the appellant's disclosure to him that she had lied to doctors about the cause of her injuries. Dr. Shane testified that such fabrication was typical of battered women. The appellant also recounted to Dr. Shane occasions on which Rust would allegedly beat her, then beg her forgiveness and ply her with flowers and temporary displays of kindness. Dr. Shane was aware of the incidents described by Ezako about the appellant's pointing a gun at Rust on two occasions and explained it as "an issue for trying to defend herself. She was afraid that she would be assaulted". The appellant denied to Dr. Shane that she had homicidal fantasies about Rust and mentioned that she had smoked some marijuana on the night in question. These facts were related by Dr. Shane in the course of his testimony.

The appellant was acquitted by a jury but the verdict was overturned by a majority of the Manitoba Court of Appeal and the case sent back for retrial.

. . .

## ISSUES ON APPEAL

It should be noted that two bases for ordering a new trial are implicit in the reasons of the majority of the Court of Appeal. In finding that "absent the evidence of Dr. Shane, it is unlikely that the jury, properly instructed, would have accepted the accused's plea of self-defence" the Court of Appeal suggests that the evidence of Dr. Shane ought to have been excluded entirely. The alternative ground for allowing the Crown's appeal was that Dr. Shane's testimony was properly admitted but the trial judge's instructions with respect to it were deficient. Thus, the issues before this Court are as follows:

1. Did the majority of the Manitoba Court of Appeal err in concluding that the jury should have considered the plea of self-defence absent the expert evidence of Dr. Shane?
2. Did the majority of the Manitoba Court of Appeal err in holding that the trial judge's charge to the jury with respect to Dr. Shane's expert evidence did not meet the requirements set out by this Court in *Abbey*, thus warranting a new trial?

## ANALYSIS

### Admissibility of Expert Evidence

In *Kellier (Village of) v. Smith*, [1931] S.C.R. 672, at p. 684, this Court adopted the principle that in order for expert evidence to be admissible " the subject-matter of the inquiry must be such that ordinary people are unlikely to form a correct judgment about it, if unassisted by persons with special knowledge". More recently, this Court addressed the admissibility of expert psychiatric evidence in criminal cases in *R. v. Abbey, supra*. At p. 42 of the unanimous judgment Dickson J. (as he then was) stated the rule as follows:

> With respect to matters calling for special knowledge, an expert in the field may draw inferences and state his opinion.An expert's function is precisely this: to provide the judge and jury with a ready-made inference which the judge and jury, due to the technical nature of the facts, are unable to formulate. "An expert's opinion is admissible to furnish the Court with scientific information which is likely to be outside the experience and knowledge of judge or jury. If on the proven facts a judge or jury can form their own conclusions without help, then the opinion of the expert is unnecessary" (*turner* (1974), 60 Crim. App. R. 80, at p. 83, *per* Lawton L.J.).

. . .

The need for expert evidence in these areas can, however, be obfuscated by the belief that judges and juries are thoroughly knowledgeable about "human nature" and that no more is needed. They are, so to speak, their own experts on human behaviour. This, in effect, was the primary submission of the Crown to this Court.

The bare facts of this case, which I think are amply supported by the evidence, are that the appellant was repeatedly abused by the deceased but did not leave him (although she twice pointed a gun at him), and ultimately shot him in the back of the head as he was leaving her room. The Crown submits that these facts disclose all the information a jury needs in order to decide whether or not the appellant acted in self-defence. I have no hesitation in rejecting the Crown's submission.

Expert evidence on the psychological effect of battering on wives and common law partners must, it seems to me, be both relevant and necessary in the context of the present case. How can the mental state of the appellant be appreciated without it? The average member of the public (or of the jury) can be forgiven for asking: Why would a woman put up with this kind of treatment? Why should she continue to live with such a man? How could she love a partner who beat her to the point of requiring hospitalization? We would expect the woman to pack her bags and go. Where is her self-respect? Why does she not cut loose and make a new life for herself? Such is the reaction of the average person confronted with the so-called "battered wife syndrome". We need help to understand it and help is available from trained professionals.

The gravity, indeed, the tragedy of domestic violence can hardly be overstated. Greater media attention to this phenomenon in recent years has revealed both its prevalence and its horrific impact on women from all walks of life. Far from protecting women from it the law historically sanctioned the abuse of women within marriage as an aspect of the husband's ownership of his wife and his "right" to chastise her. One need only recall the centuries old law that a man is entitled to beat his wife with a stick "no thicker than his thumb".

Laws do not spring out of a social vacuum. The notion that a man has a right to "discipline" his wife is deeply rooted in the history of our society. The woman's duty was to serve her husband and to stay in the marriage at all costs "till death do us part" and to accept as her due any "punishment" that was meted out for failing to please her husband. One consequence of this attitude was that "wife battering" was rarely spoken of, rarely reported, rarely prosecutive, and even more rarely punished. Long after society abandoned its formal approval of spousal abuse tolerance of it continued and continues in some circles to this day.

Fortunately, there has been a growing awareness in recent years that no man has a right to abuse any woman under any circumstances. Legislative initiatives designed to educate police, judicial officers and the public, as well as more aggressive investigation and charging policies all signal a concerted effort by the criminal justice system to take spousal abuse seriously. However, a woman who comes before a judge or jury with the claim that she has been battered and suggests that this may be a relevant factor in evaluating her subsequent actions still faces the prospect of being condemned by popular mythology about domestic violence. Either she was not as badly beaten as she claims or she would have left the man long ago. Or, if she was battered that severely, she must have stayed out of some masochistic enjoyment of it.

. . .

## THE RELEVANCE OF EXPERT TESTIMONY TO THE ELEMENTS OF SELF-DEFENCE

In my view, there are two elements of the defence under s. 34(2) of the *Code* which merit scrutiny for present purposes. The first is the temporal connection in s. 34(2)(a) between the apprehension of death or grievous bodily harm and the act allegedly taken in self-defence. Was the appellant "under reasonable apprehension of death or grievous bodily harm" from Rust as he was walking out of the room? The second is the assessment in s. 34(2)(b) of the magnitude of the force used by the accused. Was the accused's belief that she could not "otherwise preserve herself from death or grievous bodily harm" except by shooting the deceased based "on reasonable grounds"?

The feature common to both 34(2)(a) and 34(2)(b) is the imposition of an objective standard of reasonableness on the apprehension of death and the need to repel the assault with deadly force.

. . .

If it strains credulity to imagine what the "ordinary man" would do in the position of a battered spouse, it is probably because men do not typically find themselves in that situation. Some women do, however. The definition of what is reasonable must be adapted to circumstances which are, by and large, foreign to the world inhabited by the hypothetical "reasonable man".

I find the case of *State v. Wanrow*, 559 P.2d 548 (1977), helpful in illustrating how the factor of gender can be germane to the assessment of what is reasonable. In *Wanrow* the Washington Supreme Court addressed the standard by which a jury ought to assess the reasonableness of the female appellant's use of a gun against an unarmed intruder. The Court pointed out that the appellant had reason to believe that the intruder had molested her daughter in the past and was coming back for her son. The appellant was a 5'4" woman with a broken leg. The assailant was 6'2" and intoxicated. The Court first observed, at p. 558, that "in our society women suffer from a conspicuous lack of access to training in and the means of developing those skills necessary to effectively repel a male assailant without resorting to the use of deadly weapons." Later it found that the trial judge erred in his instructions to the jury by creating the impression that the objective standard of reasonableness to be applied to the accused was that of an altercation between two men. At p. 559, the Court makes the following remarks which I find apposite to the case before us:

> The respondent was entitled to have the jury consider her actions in the light of her own perceptions of the situation, including those perceptions which were the product of our nation's "long and unfortunate history of sex discrimination." Until such time as the effects of that history are eradicated, care must be taken to assure that our self-defence instructions afford women the right to have their conduct judged in the light of the individual physical handicaps which are the product of sex discrimination. To fail to do so is to deny the right of the individual woman involved to trial by the same rules which are applicable to male defendants.

I turn now to a consideration of the specific components of self-defence under s. 34(3) of the *Criminal Code*.

### Reasonable Apprehension of Death

Section 34(2)(a) requires than an accused who intentionally causes death or grievous bodily harm in repelling an assault is justified if he or she does so "under reasonable apprehension of death or grievous bodily harm". In the present case, the assault precipitating the appellant's alleged defensive act was Rust's threat to kill her when everyone else had gone.

It will be observed that subsection 34(2)(a) does not actually stipulate that the accused apprehend *imminent* danger when he or she acts. Case law has, however, read that requirement into the defence: see *Reilly v. The Queen, supra; R. v. Baxter* (1975), 33 C.R.N.S. 22 (Ont. C.A. ): *R. v. Bogue* (1976), 30 C.C.C. (2d) 403 (Ont. C.A.). The sense in which "imminent" is used conjures up the image of "an uplifted knife" or a pointed gun. The rationale for the imminence rules seems obvious. The law of self-defence is designed to ensure that the use of defensive force is really necessary. It justifies the act because the defender reasonably believed that he or she had no alternative but to take the attacker's life. If there is a significant time interval between the original unlawful assault and the accused's response, one tends to suspect that the accused was motivated by revenge rather than self-defence. In the paradigmatic case of a one-time bar room brawl between two men of equal size and strength, this inference makes sense. How can one feel endangered to the point of firing a gun at an unarmed man who utters a death threat, then turns his back and walks out of the room? One cannot be certain of the gravity of the threat or his capacity to carry it out. Besides, one can always take the opportunity to flee or to call the police. If he comes back and raises his fist, one can respond in kind if need be. These are the tacit assumptions that underlie the imminence rule.

All of these assumptions were brought to bear on the respondent in *R. v. Whynot*, (1983) 9 C.C.C. 449 (N.S.C.A.) . . . . The Court stated at p. 464:

I do not believe that the trial judge was justified in placing s. 37 of the *Code* before the jury anymore than he would have been justified in giving them s. 34. Under s. 34 the assault must have been underway and unprovoked, and under s. 37 the assault must be such that it is necessary to defend the person assaulted by the use of force. No more force may be used than necessary to prevent the assault or the repetition of it. In my opinion, no person has the right in anticipation of an assault that may or may not happen, to apply force to prevent the imaginary assault.

The implications of the Court's reasoning is that it is inherently unreasonable to apprehend death or grievous bodily harm unless and until the physical assault is actually in progress, at which point the victim can presumably gauge the requisite amount of force needed to repel the attack and act accordingly. In my view, expert testimony can cast doubt on these assumptions as they are applied in the context of a battered wife's efforts to repel an assault.

The situation of the appellant was not unlike that of Jane Stafford in the sense that she too was routinely beaten over the course of her relationship with the man she ultimately killed. According to the testimony of Dr. Shane these assaults were not entirely random in their occurrence. The following exchange during direct examination elicited a discernible pattern to the abuse:

> Q. How did they react during the tension that preceded the beatings? How would her . . .
> A. Well, typically before a beating there's usually some verbal interchange and there are threats and typically she would feel, you know, very threatened by him and for various reasons.

> He didn't like the way she dressed or if she — didn't like the way she handled money or she wasn't paying him enough attention or she was looking at other men, all sorts of reasons, and she would be defending herself, trying to placate him, which was typical, saying, you know, trying to calm him down, trying to soothe him, you know, so nothing violent would happen and sometimes it would work. You know, as people's experiences indicated or as people who write about this process, if you will, have indicated. But often, as reflected by what she has told me, and the information I have from other people, such as her mother, often it would fail and she would end up being beaten and assaulted.

> Q. And that would be followed by this forgiveness state?
> A. It typically would be followed by, you know, this make-up period.

Earlier in his testimony Dr. Shane explained how this "make-up" period would be characterized by contrite and affectionate behaviour by Rust:

> In this particular case she documented many times, after he would beat her, he would send her flowers and he would beg her for forgiveness and he would love her and then the relationship would come back to a sense of equilibrium, if you will . . . But then, because of the nature of the personalities, it would occur again.

The cycle described by Dr. Shane conforms to the Walker Cycle Theory of Violence named for clinical psychologist Dr. Lenore Walker, the pioneer research in the field of the battered wife syndrome.

. . .

Dr. Walker defines a battered woman as a woman who has gone through the battering cycle at least twice. As she explains in her introduction to *The Battered*

*Woman* at p.. xv, "Any woman may find herself in an abusive relationship with a man once. If it occurs a second time, and she remains in the situation, she is defined as a battered woman".

Given the relational context in which the violence occurs, the mental state of an accused at the critical moment she pulls the trigger cannot be understood except in terms of the cumulative effect of months or years of brutality. As Dr. Shane explained in his testimony, the deterioration of the relationship between the appellant and Rust in the period immediately preceding the killing led to feelings of escalating terror on the part of the appellant:

> But their relationship some weeks to months before was definitely escalating in terms of tension and in terms of the discordant quality about it. They were sleeping in separate bedrooms. Their intimate relationship was lacking and things were building and building to a point where she couldn't — she felt so threatened and so overwhelmed that she had to — that she reacted in a violent way because of her fear of survival and also because, I think because of her, I guess, final sense that she was — that she had to defend herself and her own sense of violence toward this man who had really desecrated her and damaged her for so long.

Another aspect of the cyclical nature of the abuse is that it begets a degree of predictability to the violence that is absent in an isolated violent encounter between two strangers. This also means that it may in fact be possible for a battered spouse to accurately predict the onset of violence before the first blow is struck even if an outsider to the relationship cannot. Indeed, it has been suggested that a battered woman's knowledge of her partner's violence is so heightened that she is able to anticipate the nature and extent (though not the onset) of the violence by his conduct beforehand.

. . .

Where evidence exists than an accused is in a battered relationship, expert testimony can assist the jury in determining whether the accused had a "reasonable" apprehension of death when she acted by explaining the heightened sensitivity of a battered woman to her partner's acts. Without such testimony I am skeptical that the average fact-finder would be capable of appreciating why her subjective fear may have been reasonable in the context of the relationship. After all, the hypothetical "reasonable man" observing only the final incident may have been unlikely to recognize the batterer's threat as potentially lethal. Using the case at bar as an example the "reasonable man" might have thought, as the majority of the Court of Appeal seemed to, that it was unlikely that Rust would make good on his threat to kill the appellant that night because they had guests staying overnight.

The issue is not, however, what an outsider would have reasonably perceived but what the accused reasonably perceived, given her situation and her experience.

Even accepting that a battered woman may be uniquely sensitized to danger from her batterer, it may yet be contended that the law ought to require her to wait until the knife is uplifted, the gun pointed or the fist clenched before her apprehension is deemed reasonable. This would allegedly reduce the risk that the woman is mistaken in her fear, although the law does not require her fear to be correct, only reasonable.

In response to this contention, I need only point to the observation made by Huband J.A. that the evidence showed that when the appellant and Rust physically fought the appellant "invariably got the worst of it". I do not think it is an unwarranted generalization to say that due to their size, strength, socialization and lack of training, women are typically no match for men in hand-to-hand combat. The requirement imposed in *Whynot* that a battered woman wait until the physical assault is "underway" before her apprehensions can be validated in law would, in the words of an American court, be tantamount to sentencing her to 'murder by installment'; *State v. Gellegos*, 719 P.2d 1268 (N.M. 1986), at p. 1271) . . .

### *Lack of Alternatives to Self-Help*

Subsection 34(2) requires an accused who pleads self-defence to believe "on reasonable grounds" that it is not possible to otherwise preserve him or herself from death or grievous bodily harm. The obvious question is if the violence was so intolerable, why did the appellant not leave her abuser long ago? This question does not really go to whether she had an alternative to killing the deceased at the critical moment. Rather, it plays on the popular myth already referred to that a woman who says she was battered yet stayed with her batterer was either not so badly beaten as she claimed or else she liked it. Nevertheless, to the extent that her failure to leave the abusive relationship earlier may be used in support of the proposition that she was free to leave at the final moment, expert testimony can provide useful insights. Dr. Shane attempted to explain in his testimony how and why, in the case at bar, the appellant remained with Rust.

. . .

One is that the spouse gets beaten so badly — so badly —that he or she loses the motivation to react and becomes helpless and becomes powerless. And it's also been shown sometimes, you known, in — not that you can compare animals to human beings, but in laboratories, what you do if you shock an animal, after a while it can't respond to a threat on its life. It becomes just helpless and lies there in an amotivational state, if you will, where it feels there's no power and there's no energy to do anything.

So in a sense it happens in human beings as well. It's almost like a concentration camp, if you will. You get paralyzed with fear.

The other thing that happens often in these types of relationships with human beings is that the person who beats or assaults, who batters, often tries — he makes up and begs for forgiveness. And this individual, who basically has a very disturbed or damaged self-esteem, all of a sudden feels that he or she — we'll use women in this case because it's so much more common — the spouse feels that she again can do the spouse a favour and it can make her feel needed and boost her self-esteem for a while and make her feel worthwhile and the spouse says he'll forgive her and whatnot.

Apparently, another manifestation of this victimization is a reluctance to disclose to others the fact or extent of the beatings. For example, the hospital records indicate that on each occasion the appellant attended the emergency department to be treated for various injuries she explained the cause of those injuries as accidental. Both in its address to the jury and in its written submissions before this Court the Crown insisted that the appellant's injuries were as consistent with her explanations as with being battered and, therefore, in the words of Crown counsel at trial, "the myth is, in this particular case, that Miss Lavallee was a battered spouse". In his testimony Dr. Shane testified that the appellant admitted to him that she lied to hospital staff and others about the cause of her injuries. In Dr. Shane's opinion this was consistent with her overall feeling of being trapped and helpless:

> . . . she would never say that she'd been abused by the man with whom she was living and that usually happened because of this whole process. He would beg her. I mean she would tell me that on occasions he would beat her and then the police would be called by, I think, on one occasion a neighbour and he got down on his knees and he begged forgiveness and he loved her and he felt so terrible about it. And so this would be a typical scenario. Whenever she would go to the hospital, that he would attempt to, I think, attempt to have her forgive him and he would love her so much more.

. . .

The account given by Dr. Shane comports with that documented in the literature. Reference is often made to it as a condition of "learned helplessness", a phrase coined by Dr. Charles Seligman, the psychologist who first developed the theory by experimenting on animals in the manner described by Dr. Shane in his testimony. A related theory used to explain the failure of women to leave battering relationships is described by psychologist and lawyer Charles Patrick Ewing in his book *Battered Women Who Kill* (1987). Ewing describes a phenomenon labelled "traumatic bonding" that has been observed between hostages and captors, battered children and their parents, concentration camp prisoners and guards, and batterers and their spouses. According to the research cited by Ewing there are two features common to the social structure in each of these apparently diverse relationships. At pp. 19-20, he states:

> The first of these common features is an imbalance of power "wherein the maltreated person perceives himself or herself to be subjugated or dominated by the other". The less powerful person in the relationship — whether battered women, hostage, abused child, cult follower, or prisoner — becomes extremely dependent upon, and may even come to identify with, the more powerful person. In many cases, the result of such dependency and identification is that the less powerful, subjugated persons become "more negative in their self-appraisal, more incapable of fending for themselves, and thus more in need of the high power person." As this "cycle of dependency and lowered self-esteem" is repeated over time, the less powerful person develops a "strong affective bond" to the more powerful person in the abusive relationship.

> The second feature common to the relationships between battered woman and batterer, hostage and captor, battered child and abusive parent, cult follower and leader, and prisoner and guard is the periodic nature of the abuse. In each relationship, the less powerful person is subjected to intermittent periods of abuse, which alternate with periods during which the more powerful, abusive person treats the less powerful person in a "more normal and acceptable fashion."

. . .

This strong "affective bond" may be helpful in explaining not only why some battered women remain with their abusers but why they even profess to love them. Of course, as Dr. Ewing adds, environmental factors may also impair the woman's ability to leave — lack of job skills, the presence of children to care for, fear of retaliation by the man, etc. may each have a role to play in some cases.

This is not to say that in the course of a battering relationship a woman may never attempt to leave her partner or try to defend herself from assault. In *The Battered Woman Syndrome* Dr. Walker notes at p. 30 that women sometimes "react to men's violence against them by striking back, but their actions are generally ineffective at hurting or stopping the men. They may be effective in controlling the level of the man's violence against them."

. . .

The same psychological factors that account for a woman's inability to leave a battering relationship may also help to explain why she did not attempt to escape at the moment she perceived her life to be in danger.

. . .

I emphasize at this juncture that it is not for the jury to pass judgment on the fact than an accused battered woman stayed in the relationship. Still less is it entitled to conclude that she forfeited the right to self-defence for having done so. I would also point out that traditional self-defence doctrine does not require a person to retreat from her home instead of defending herself. *R. v. Antley* (1963), 42 C.R. 384 (Ont. C.A.). A man's home may be his castle but it is also the woman's home even if it seems to her more like a prison in the circumstances.

If, after hearing the evidence (including the expert testimony), the jury is satisfied that the accused had a reasonable apprehension of death or grievous bodily harm and felt incapable of escape, it must ask itself what the "reasonable person" would do in such a situation. The situation of the battered woman as described by Dr. Shane strikes me as somewhat analogous to that of a hostage. If the captor tells her that he will her in three days time, is it potentially reasonable for her to seize an opportunity presented on the first day to kill the captor or must she wait until he makes the attempt on the third day? I think the question the jury must ask itself is whether, given the history, circumstances and perception of the appellant, her belief that she could not preserve herself from being killed by Rust that night except by killing him first was reasonable. To the extent that expert evidence can assist the jury in making that determination, I would find such testimony to be both relevant and necessary.

In light of the foregoing discussion I would summarize as follows the principles upon which expert testimony is properly admitted in cases such as this:

1. Expert testimony is admissible to assist the fact-finder in drawing inferences in areas where the expert has relevant knowledge or experience beyond that of the lay person.
2. It is difficult for the lay person to comprehend the battered wife syndrome. It is commonly thought that battered women are not really beaten as badly as they claim, otherwise they would have left the relationship. Alternatively, some believe that women enjoy being beaten, that they have a masochist strain in them. Each of these stereotypes may adversely affect consideration of a battered woman's claim to have acted in self-defence in killing her mate.
3. Expert evidence can assist the jury in dispelling these myths.

4. Expert testimony relating to the ability of an accused to perceive danger from her mate may go to the issue of whether she "reasonably apprehended" death or grievous bodily harm on a particular occasion.
5. Expert testimony pertaining to why an accused remained in the battering relationship may be relevant in assessing the nature and extent of the alleged abuse.
6. By providing an explanation as to why an accused did not flee when she perceived her life to be in danger, expert testimony may also assist the jury in assessing the reasonableness of her belief that killing her batterer was the only way to save her own life.

Quite apart from Dr. Shane's testimony there was ample evidence on which the trial judge could conclude that the appellant was battered repeatedly and brutally by Kevin Rust over the course of their relationship. The fact that she may have exhibited aggressive behaviour on occasion or tried (unsuccessfully) to leave does not detract from a finding of systematic and relentless abuse. In my view, the trial judge did not err in admitting Dr. Shane's expert testimony in order to assist the jury in determining whether the appellant had a reasonable apprehension of death or grievous bodily harm and believed on reasonable grounds that she had no alternative but to shoot Kevin Rust on the night in question.

Obviously the fact that the appellant was a battered woman does not entitle her to an acquittal. Battered women may well kill their partners other than in self-defence. The focus is not on who the woman is, but on what she did.

. . .

Ultimately, it is up to the jury to decide whether, *in fact*, the accused's perceptions and actions were reasonable. Expert evidence does not and cannot usurp that function of the jury. The jury is not compelled to accept the opinions proffered by the expert about the effects of battering on the mental state of victims generally or on the mental state of the accused in particular. But fairness and the integrity of the trial process demand that the jury have the opportunity to hear them.

. . .

I would accordingly allow the appeal, set aside the order of the Court of Appeal, and restore the acquittal.

*Appeal allowed; acquittal restored.*

**Note:** In October, 1995, the government announced a federal review of murder cases involving women convicted of killing their abusive partners. spouses or guardians in self defence. Judge Lynn Ratushny has been appointed to undertake the review. The "Terms of Reference" of the task force are as follows (Excerpt from Department of Justice News Release, October 4, 1995):

In recent years, there have been developments in our understanding of the law of self-defence as it relates to battered women who have been involved in abusive relationships. There are concerns that women convicted of homicide in these circumstances may not have received the benefit of the defence of self-defence when it may have been available to them.

We also now have an increased understanding of abusive relationships and their impact upon those who have been battered, and how this might support the use of the defence. Questions have also been raised about the circumstances under which these types of offences occurred and about whether our criminal law sentencing processes and sentencing tools are adequate to deal with these circumstances.

Accordingly, the Honorable Lynn Ratushny, a judge of the Ontario Court of Justice (Provincial Division) is appointed:

i) to review the cases of women under sentence in federal and provincial institutions who apply for a remedy and who are serving a sentence for homicide in circumstances in which the killing allegedly took place to prevent the deceased from inflicting serious bodily harm or death;

ii) to make recommendations in appropriate cases to the Government of Canada for individual women whose circumstances merit consideration for the granting of the royal prerogative of mercy;

iii) to clarify the availability and the scope of the defences available to women accused of homicide in the circumstances set out above; and

iv) to make recommendations as considered appropriate with respect to possible law reform initiatives stemming from the review.

In July 1997, Judge Ratushny delivered her final report. She had reviewed 98 cases but made recommendations in relation to only seven women. Specifically, the report recommended that three women be pardoned, three women receive remission of their sentence, and one woman receive a review of her case by a Court of Appeal. The Minister of Justice responded by invoking the royal prerogative of mercy in four of the cases, and she exercised her authority under section 690 of the Criminal Code for a fifth case and referred the case to a Court of Appeal for review. In the two remaining cases, the Minister was not prepared to grant a remedy due to the particular facts of the cases.

## Questions/Discussion

1. Do you agree with the differing test in section 34? Why or why not? What do you think is the rationale for an objective test versus a subjective test in regard to the amount of force in subsections (1) and (2)?

2. There is an argument in some decisions in other jurisdictions that if the accused satisfies all the tests in section 34(2), except the last as to the amount of force, then some consideration should be given to this in attaching liability. The defence is sometimes referred to as "excessive self defence" and results in a conviction on a lesser and included offence (for example, murder might be reduced to manslaughter). Do you agree with this type of approach that has been rejected in Canada to date? For a reference to the defence, see *R. v. Brisson* (1982), 69 C.C.C. (2d) 97 (S.C.C.), and O'Brien under Further Reading.

3. Do you agree with the approach taken in the *Lavallée* decision? Why or why not? What problems do you foresee in the application of this decision in other cases? See also the recent case of *R. v. Pétal* (1994), 87 C.C.C. (3d) 97 (S.C.C). For a feminist critique of the use of the "Battered Women Syndrome", see Comack under Further Reading.

4. The then Law Reform Commission of Canada proposed in its Report 31, *Recodifying Criminal Law*, that there be one general rule relative to defence of the person: no one would be liable " . . . if he [or she] acted as he [or she] did to protect himself [or

herself] or another person against unlawful force by using such force as was reasonably necessary to avoid the harm or hurt apprehended". Do you agree with such a formulation? Do you think that such a section would change what the courts do in practice? Should it include a special provision for battered women who strike back to protect themselves or their children?

## Further Reading

- Bailey, M., "The Fall of the Half-Way House: The Supreme Court of Canada in *Gee, Brisson and Faid*" (1984), 22 Alberta Law Review 473.
- Brodsky, D., "Educating Juries: the Battered Women Defence in Canada" (1987), 25 Alberta Law Review 461.
- Burt, L., "The Battered Woman Syndrome and the Plea of Self-Defence: Can the Victim and the Accused be Strangers" (1993), 27 University of British Columbia Law Review 93-98.
- Comack, E., "Justice for Battered Women?" (1988), vol. 22, no. 3, of Canadian Dimension 8.
- Ferguson, Gerry, "Self Defence: Selecting the Applicable Provisions" (2000), 5 Canadian Criminal Law Review 179-219.
- Mewett, A., and M. Manning, *Mewett and Manning on Criminal Law*, 3rd ed. (Markham: Butterworths, 1994).
- O'Brien, N.C., "Excessive Self-Defence: A Need for Legislation" (1982-83), 25 Criminal Law Quarterly 441.
- Roach, Kent, *Criminal Law, 2d ed.* (Toronto: Irwin Law, 2000) at 273-279.
- Stalker, A., "Self Defence and Consent: The Use of Common Law Developments in Canadian Criminal Code Analysis" (1994), 32 Alberta Law Review 484-510.
- Stuart, Don, and R. Delisle, *Learning Canadian Criminal Law, 8th ed.* (Toronto: Carswell, 2001).
- Trotter, Gary T., "*R. v. Pawliuk*: Further Efforts to Clarify the Self-Defence" (2001), 40 C.R. (5th) 56-65.
- White-Mair, Kimberley, "Experts and Ordinary Men: Locating *R. v. Lavallée*, Battered Women Syndrome, and the 'New' Psychiatric Expertise on Women in Canadian Legal History" (2000), 12 Canadian Journal of Women and the Law 406-438.

## 7.1.4 Defence of Property

### Introduction

There is little to say about the defence of defence of property outside the case below. The main distinctions made in this area relate to the type of property being protected; is it real or movable (personal) property? If it is personal property (section 38) then you have the right to prevent someone from taking it or to take it back, if you do not strike or cause bodily harm to the trespasser. If the trespasser persists in trying to keep it or in trying to take it, then the trespasser is deemed to commit an unprovoked assault and your actions are then protected by the self defence provisions in section 34. If someone is trying to break into your home, then you have the right to use as much force as necessary to prevent that person from entering, or to remove the trespasser (sections 40-41). If the trespasser resists attempts at blocking or removing her or him, then it is deemed that an unprovoked assault has been committed by the trespasser and your actions are protected again by the provisions of section 34.[1]

## Regina v. Born With a Tooth
### (1992), 76 C.C.C. (3d) 169 (Alta. C.A.)

Appeal by the accused from his conviction on charges of possession of a weapon for purpose dangerous to the public peace, pointing a firearm, obstruction of police, assault police and use of a firearm while committing an offence.

BY THE COURT: — This is an appeal from conviction by a jury on seven of eight counts relating to an incident on September 7, 1990. The accused was found guilty of possession of a rifle for a purpose dangerous to the public peace, pointing a rifle at Constable Raymond Gaultier, obstruction of Constable Gaultier in the execution of his duty, obstruction of Constable Brian McKenna in the execution of his duty, assault of Constable Gaultier, use of a rifle while committing an assault, and use of a rifle while obstructing a peace officer.

The grounds of appeal alleged include the failure of the trial judge to put the defence theory fairly to the jury; refusal by the trial judge to admit evidence relevant to the defence theory; abuse or intimidation of defence counsel and defence witnesses, and failure to order a stay on at least some counts on invocation of the rule in *R. v. Kienapple* (1974), 15 C.C.C (2d) 524, 44 D.L.R. (3d) 351, [1975] 1 S.C.R. 729.

We shall, for the reasons now offered, order a new trial for failure to admit relevant evidence. In the result, it is not necessary to comment on all the grounds, although, as counsel observed during argument, there is considerable overlap among them.

Because of our decision, we shall avoid unnecessary discussion of the evidence of the case. Some factual background, however, is needed to explain the relevancy issues. What follows is, as far as it goes, not in dispute.

The incident occurred on the banks of the Oldman river where it flows through the Peigan Indian reserve, which the band members call the Peigan nation. The Peigan long ago surrendered a narrow strip of land alongside the river, and Alberta now has title to it under the *Land Titles Act*, R.S.A. 1980, c. L-5. This parcel, with other parcels, has been referred to as the "right of way". Many years ago, the river-bank included in the right of way was built up to form a dyke, or berm, and a weir and diversion canal were built, all as part of the irrigation system in that area. The Peigan later challenged the validity of the original surrender in a suit, which apparently the parties settled on June 11, 1981. The true meaning of the settlement agreement has, more recently, become a new matter of dispute between the Peigan (or perhaps more accurately some Peigan) and Alberta.

One term of the settlement agreement commits the Peigan to do what is needed to gain for Alberta a ministerial permit under the *Indian Act*, R.S.C. 1985, c. I-5, to enter

---

1   For examples of cases where these deemed assault provisions have been used in the context of offences rather than in the creation of defences, see *R. v. Kellington* (1972), 7 C.C.C. (2d) 564 (B.C. S.C.) and *R. v. Spencer* (1977), 38 C.C.C. (2d) 303 (B.C. S.C.).

the right of way to make dykes and other works, and to maintain and repair these works. On April 20, 1981, and again on June 2, 1981, the band council had resolved to request such a permit, and, also on June 11, the Minister of Indian Affairs issued a permit that authorized Alberta to ". . . enter upon and use . . ." the right of way (A.B., p. 708).

Sometime in 1990, at least by August 2nd, the accused and other Peigan, together with some well-wishers, made camp on Peigan lands about 200 feet from the dyke and not on the right of way. Save for the camp and the irrigation works, the area was not otherwise habited or developed. On August 7th, officers from Alberta Environment noted a hole in the dyke. The effect of that was to divert the water into an old river channel instead of a diversion canal. On August 29th, Alberta sought and received an injunction in Queen's Bench against interference, among other things, with

> . . . access to the . . . Right-of-Way by Her Majesty, her servants, employees . . . for the purpose of restoring . . . damage . . . and . . . operating and maintaining the Headworks System . . .

On August 29th, an officer of the R.C.M.P. attended at the Peigan camp to serve the injunction. The accused was not present, but others were served. The Assistant Deputy Minister for the Environment testified that he overflew the site regularly and that, between August 30th and September 7th, he saw the hole in the dyke grow larger. That witness then resolved to take workers to the site to make repairs, and requested the assistance of the R.C.M.P.

On September 7th, at 9:00 a.m., some of these workers, accompanied by police officers, moved across the reserve toward the right of way. About 10 people, including the accused, awaited them on the dyke. They called the new arrivals trespassers, and threw rocks. When they closed to a short distance, the accused raised his rifle and shot it into the air at least twice. (Some witnesses also said that the accused pointed the rifle at officers. This was challenged. The jury convicted on the charge of pointing it at one officer, and acquitted on the charge of pointing it at the other).

Just before her opening statement, counsel for the accused told the presiding judge (A.B., p. 372) that she relied upon the defence offered by s. 41(1) of the *Criminal Code*, which provides

> 41(1) Every one who is in peaceable possession of a dwelling-house or real property . . . is justified in using force to prevent any person from trespassing on the dwelling-house or real property, or to remove a trespasser therefrom, if he uses no more force than is necessary.

The theory of the defence, as finally explained to us at the oral hearing of this appeal, was the following:

— The Peigan, including the accused, had been in actual possession of the right of way for some time prior to September 7th. Moreover, this occupation was peaceable because it had in fact not been challenged by Alberta.

— Alberta's failure to give reasonable notice made it a trespasser. It had *no* right of exclusive possession. Under the settlement agreement, it held only a licence to work the right of way. Even that right must be exercised reasonably, and in the circumstances of this case that meant, notwithstanding the injunction, on notice to the occupants.

— In any event, the R.C.M.P. did not enter the right of way merely to keep the peace or enforce the injunction; their real purpose was to attack and eject the occupants. This illegal purpose they demonstrated before entry by a huge show of force. They were thus trespassers.

— In all these circumstances,the action of the accused was reasonable force to prevent a trespass or eject a trespasser. The accused did not obstruct Alberta in a lawful entry to effect repairs, and did not act in breach of the injunction.

In our view, this defence should have been put to the jury if any support for it existed in the evidence, and if it is sound in law. It is probably correct to say that, at the close of the trial, the essential evidentiary base was absent. But we are bound to say that this may have been because of some exclusionary rulings.

The learned trial judge excluded evidence from the defence about what the Peigan were doing at the right of way prior to September 7th. Evidence of their activity could be relevant because it would be evidence of use and occupation, and might also be evidence of peaceable possession. It seems that at least some of this activity was religious and ceremonial in nature, and Ms. Gainer began by attempting to lead evidence about Peigan tradition generally. She explained to us, if not the learned trial judge, that she had sought to introduce this evidence so that the jury could better understand the significance of the activity of the campers, including the accused. For this reason, it was admissible as relevant to the defence theory.

The learned trial judge gained the impression that the sole purpose of the evidence was to lay a foundation for a claim to a right, based upon Peigan laws and traditions not Canadian law, to repel Alberta if it came on the right of way. This would be tantamount to a claim of right, based on higher law, to defy the injunction. That is not a defence known to Canadian law, and a jury must be so instructed. But that does not warrant keeping the evidence out if it is admissible for other reasons.

The evidence about activity and evidence explaining the cultural significance of activity, might also have been relevant to show the state of mind of the accused.

The learned trial judge also rejected this ground. Assuming that the state of mind of the accused is relevant, the defence can show evidence of surrounding circumstances from which the jury might draw an inference about the state of mind of the accused, even if the accused shall not testify: see *Lampard v. The Queen*, [1969] 3 C.C.C. 249 at pp. 255-6, 4 D.L.R. (3d) 98, [1969] S.C.R. 373. See also *R.v. Nealy* (1986), 30 C.C.C. (3d) 460 at pp. 468-9, 54 C.R. (3d) 158, 17 O.A.C. 164 (Ont. C.A.)., and the cases discussed there.

The learned trial judge also curtailed cross-examination designed to raise a doubt with the jury about the true intentions of the police. Moreover, in his charge he instructed the jury that the police had behaved reasonably. He may express his views to the jury, but he must leave relevant issues of fact for them to decide.

In general terms, the learned trial judge forbad any evidence tending to show peaceable possession by the Peigan on the ground that the title to the lands held by

Alberta conclusively decided all questions of that sort. His views were later repeated to the jury. . . .

In short, he had concluded that, as a matter of law, the accused was himself a trespasser and could not possibly invoke the defence.

With respect, and even assuming these statements of law are correct, they would curtail but not eliminate the defence theory. One question posed for the jury by the defence theory was whether Alberta by its conduct had in fact granted or suffered peaceable possession of the right of way to the Peigan. That question is not foreclosed by production of title. Nor does the title necessarily answer a second question raised by the defence theory: whether the R.C.M.P. had come on the lands for an unlawful reason, one, for example, not sanctioned by Alberta. The Crown theory was that Alberta had a right to enter to work the dyke, and to invite the police to enter to keep the peace, and both did only that. The defence theory was that at least the police entered with another and illegal intent, that their conduct as they arrived evidenced that contrary intent, and that they were trespassers. That is a question of fact that survives resolution of the title dispute.

Moreover, it is not beyond argument that the settlement agreement did not "abrogate in any way" the title of Alberta. We make no definitive ruling because not enough material is before us and because it is neither necessary nor appropriate to do so. But, assuming the agreement applies to the titled lands, it contains terms that seem to derogate title, as, for example, this term in clause 4 (A.B., p. 718):

> Both parties recognize that the Band retains control and ownership of all mines, minerals and natural resources, including wildlife under their protection upon the subject lands.

In any event, the title and title disputes do not necessarily resolve a s. 41 defence. Here, the accused admitted, at least before us, that Alberta had a right to go on the right of way to repair and maintain the dyke. It is not clear to us that the Crown position was that the Peigan, and the accused, had *no* right to be on the right of way. The Crown position, as we understand it, was that they had no peaceable possession if their claim to possession extended to any control of the access by Alberta to the irrigation works. And that limit on a claim to possession was conceded before us by the accused, as indeed he must concede in the light of the injunction order and in the light of the terms of the settlement agreement and the permit, even if they receive the interpretation most generous to him. And the jury must be so instructed. But other aspects of the title dispute can await another day.

We agree, however, with the learned trial judge that the jury must be told, as a matter of law, that no notice need have been given by Alberta to the accused about its proposed exercise of its right of entry other than the notice required by the injunction, which is, simply, actual knowledge of it. To say otherwise would be to suggest that the injunction was itself illegal, a position not available to the accused as a matter of law. If he thought the injunction was illegal, he, like other Canadians, was none the less bound to obey it until he succeeded in having it vacated. Again, however, this circumscribes but does not eliminate the defence. Indeed the defence might be available if the entry by Alberta was lawful and by the R.C.M.P. was unlawful.

It would be extremely unfair to the trial judge to speak of these or any other errors at the trial without some explanatory comment. Simply put, the defence theory we heard and here expressed was never put to him, at least not in comprehensible terms. It became quite clear early in the trial that the learned trial judge found it difficult to comprehend how the defence could be available in this case. That difficulty, and the failure of the defence counsel to articulate compelling answers to his questions, largely account for almost all grounds of appeal. Counsel was at once argumentative and vague. She asserted positions but said almost nothing to explain them. This led to repeated clashes during the remainder of the trial, to the impugned admissibility rulings, to the sharp comments by the judge, and to the complaint about disparagement of the defence in the charge. Worse, counsel defied the rulings by repeatedly leading evidence like that already excluded. By the end of the trial, the trial judge was limiting himself to the occasional protesting interjection. . . .

To avoid a repeat of the confusion at the next trial, we conclude with some general comments about the rule in s. 41. while they express our understanding of the law, we caution that not all points were fully argued before us.

The defence contains four elements. This means that, before an accused can benefit from it, the jury must have at least a doubt about all four. If a jury is convinced beyond any reasonable doubt that any one element is missing, the defence must fail. The four elements are these: the accused must be in possession of land; his possession must be *peaceable*; the victim of the assault must be a trespasser, and the force used to eject the trespasser must be reasonable in the circumstances.

As to the first, the word "possession" has here its usual meaning in criminal law: see *Beaver v. The Queen* (1957), 118 C.C.C. 129, [1957] S.C.R. 531, 26 C.R. 193. The defence will fail if the accused, in fact, has no control over the land in question: see *R. v. Spencer* (1977), 38 C.C.C. (2d) 303, 3 R.P.R. 61, [1978] 1 W.W.R. 250 (B.C.S.C.). But for possession, control need not be exclusive: see *R. v. Dillabough* (1975), 28 C.C.C. (2d) 482 (Ont. C.A.), and *Re British American Oil Co. Ltd. and Halpert* (1959), 21 D.L.R. (2d) 110, [1960] O.R. 71 (Ont. C.A). Because control is largely a matter of fact, this element includes a question of fact to be decided by the jury.

The demand that the possession be "peaceable" greatly limits the defence. That word is *not* synonymous with peaceful. It is not enough for the accused to show he kept the peace while on the land. Historically, it meant a possession that did not provoke a breach of the peace: see Stephen, *A History of the Criminal Law of England*, vol. III, pp. 13-4 (London: MacMillan and Co., 1883).

. . .

For the purpose of the *Code*, the term must mean a possession not seriously challenged by others. If it were otherwise, then every property dispute could be resolved legitimately by force. The evident object of the law is the exact opposite: the defence should be available only to those whose possession has not been seriously questioned by somebody before the incident in question. It is not necessary for us to make a definitive statement how serious and immediate must the challenge be before the defence is lost. That is a question to be decided on the precise facts of each case. We but aside, as not necessary for decision, the question whether one can invoke the defence against a trespasser totally unaware that one's possession is under challenge from some third party.

Whether a previous serious challenge existed is a question of fact for decision by the jury. But the judge often will be required to inform the jury about questions of law to assist them in that determination. The strength in law of a claim to a *right* of possession, for example, will often be determinative. But the seriousness of the challenge will turn more on the likelihood of a breach of the peace than on the strength of a legal title. This is because, as the Law Reform Commission has suggested, the key to peaceable possession is whether the possession is such, and the challenge to it is such, the situation is "unlikely to lead to violence": see Law Reform Commission of Canada, report No. 30 (1987), p. 38. . . .

The third element is that the victim of the ejectment must be a trespasser. If that person has a right to be on the land, even if the accused also has a right to be on the land, the defence is not available. This element often will require a judge to direct the jury about matters of law, because the right to be on the land is a legal consequence. But that consequence always arises as a result also of matters of fact, and they must be left to the jury.

A nice question arises if the victim has the right to go on the land for one purpose, but goes on in fact for another, unlawful, purpose. A water meter inspector has a right of entry for one limited purpose. If she in fact enters to steal the refrigerator, and an irate home owner who knows her true purpose ejects her, can the accused owner invoke s. 41 and say that the inspector was a trespasser? Some authorities seem to suggest an affirmative answer: see *R. v. Collins*, [1973] 1 Q.B. 100 (C.A.), and *R. v. Jones*, [1976] 3 All E.R. 54 [1976] 1 W.L.R. 673 (C.A.) and *R. v. Walkington*, [1979] 2 All E.R. 716. . . . But see the criticism by Glanville Williams, *Textbook of Criminal Law*, 2nd ed, pp. 847-50 (London: Stevens & Son, 1983), albeit in the context of what amounts to proof of an element of the offence of breaking and entering. This court, in *R. v. Farbridge* (1984), 15 C.C.C. (3d) 521, 42 C.R. (3d) 385, [1985] 2 W.W.R. 56, 34 Alta. L.R. (2d) 394, accepted the criticism, and took a narrower view. We held that a person who enters lawfully does not become a trespasser unless and until he does something in furtherance of his unlawful purpose. Thus, in the example given, the homeowner might not be able to eject the meter inspector until she reaches for the refrigerator, or turns away from the path to the meter. But that contradictory activity might well arise before actual entry, as when the inspector is seen coming up the front walk pushing a large refrigerator dolly.

The last requirement is that only necessary force be used. Of course, all the other facts will also bear on that. But the issue can be quite separate.

In sum, the defence is available to an accused when the jury has at least a doubt whether the accused has a measure of control over the land, whether that assertion of control has been seriously challenged, whether the challenger has a right to come on the land, and whether, objectively speaking, the force used was reasonable in the circumstances.

As regards the first two elements, and the factual content of the third element, the defence of mistake is also available. . . . An accused might, honestly but mistakenly, believe that he has a measure of control over the lands, or that his supposed control is unchallenged, or he might believe in a set of facts which, if true, makes the victim a trespasser. But honest mistake of fact appears not to be enough for the last element, because that requires that the reasonableness of the force meet an objective, not just a subjective, test: see *R. v. Scopelliti* (1981), 63 C.C.C. (2d) 481, 34 O.R. (2d) 524 (C.A.).

Nor does honest but mistaken belief about entitlement trigger a defence. The general criminal rule, stated in s. 19 of the *Criminal Code*, R.S.C. 1985, c. C-34, is that all citizens of Canada have a duty to inform themselves correctly about the law, and failure to do so is no defence to a charge. A defence based on an error of law is not available on any of the charges before the court because none require, as a necessary element of the *mens rea*, that the accused be aware that he is interfering with the legal rights of others. In the result, the opinion of the accused about the merit of his title claim, or that of his victim, is not directly relevant to the defence.

Nor of course, does an honest opinion about the rightness of one's cause offer any justification, under Canadian criminal law, for violent acts. No doubt many criminals persuade themselves that their crime is somehow justified. But the principles of civil disobedience dissociate civil protest from other crime, and from revolution, by ready acceptance of the legal consequences of action forbidden by the state.

We allow the appeal and order a new trial. The accused shall appear at the next Queen's Bench arraignment at Fort Macleod for determination of the time and place of trial.

*Appeal allowed; new trial ordered.*

## Questions/Discussion

1. Should there be a separate defence of property defence which is not related to a defence of person provision? The then Law Reform Commission of Canada in its Report 31, *Recodifying Criminal Law*, proposed the following:

   **3(11)** Protection of Movable Property. No one in peaceable possession of movable property is liable for using such force, not amounting to purposely causing the death of, or seriously harming, as is reasonably necessary to prevent another person from unlawfully taking it or to recover it from another person who has just unlawfully taken it.

   **3(12)** Protection of Immovable Property. . . . General Rule. No one in peaceable possession of immovable property is liable for using such force, not amounting to purposely causing the death of, or seriously harming, as is reasonably necessary to prevent trespass, to remove a trespasser or to defend the property against another person taking possession of it.

   Do you think that such clauses are better than the existing law. Why or why not?

## Further Reading

- Kathol, T., "Defence of Property in the Criminal Code" (1993), 35 Criminal Law Quarterly, 453-479.
- Mewett, A., and M. Manning, *Mewett and Manning on Criminal Law*, 3rd ed. (Markham: Butterworths, 1994).
- Stuart, Don, and R. Delisle, *Learning Canadian Criminal Law, 8th ed.* (Toronto: Carswell, 2001).

## 7.1.5 Consent

### Introduction

Certain offences, such as assault, sexual assault, or theft, incorporate lack of consent into their very definition. Given stereotypical attitudes toward victims of sexual assault, the issue of consent or the lack of consent has been particularly important in such cases; these issues are examined in the next chapter. Generally, though, the argument as to the lack of consent in such cases is quite simply a defence that the actus reus of the crime has not been fulfilled. What becomes important in this defence, then, is what exactly has been consented to. We see this in the *Maki* case, in which one hockey player was charged for assaulting another. Technically, many sports allow for contact between players (and thus assaults) to occur; but legally the question is what is the limit of that consent? Normally, we agree to the usual types of assaults which may take place in the course of a game. When someone steps outside the usual rules, then it can be deemed that consent to such conduct is not present. A case in the Alberta Court of Appeal highlights this idea. In the course of a fist fight, one party bit off the left ear of the other party; the court said:

> We are all of the view that whatever consent was given did not extend to the infliction of injuries with the teeth.
> The two parties may have agreed to engage in a fist fight but the consent of neither of them went to the point where either of them consented to have the other apply his teeth in the manner which the appellant did in this contest.
> In our view, at the point where the complainant was attacked by the appellant using his teeth to bite the various appendages of the complainant's body, the consent ceased to be operative.[1]

The *Jobidon* decision below would further limit the notion of consenting to the normal rules within the context of so-called consensual fist fights. It quotes with approval the following passage from *Attorney-General's Reference (No. 6 of 1980)*, [1981] 2 All E.R. 1057 (C.A.):

> Where two persons fight (otherwise than in the course of sport) in a public place can it be a defence for one of those persons to a charge of assault arising out of the fight that the other consented to fight? ...
>
> The answer to this question, in our judgment, is that it is not in the public interest that people should try to cause or should cause each other actual bodily harm for no good reason. Minor struggles are another matter. So, in our judgment, it is immaterial whether the act occurs in private or in public; it is an assault if actual bodily harm is intended and/or caused. This means that most fights will be unlawful regardless of consent.

### Regina v. Maki
#### (1970), 1 C.C.C. (2d) 333 (Ont. Prov. Ct.)

CARTER, PROV. CT. J.: — Mr. Maki is charged under s. 231(2) of the *Criminal Code*: assault causing bodily harm. The case is basically a simple one factually but

---

1   *R. v. Loonskin*, quoted in *the Lawyers Weekly,* February 9, 1990.

complicated to some extent in that the alleged assault occurred during the playing of a National Hockey League exhibition game and that there has not been such a prosecution in the past. The game was between the St. Louis Blues and the Boston Bruins, played at the Ottawa Civic Centre in the City of Ottawa on September 21, 1969.

I have considered the facts carefully and, although, as would be expected in such a fast moving situation, there are some inconsistencies in the evidence, the occurrence appears to have taken place in the following manner.

I might say in reviewing the facts I have [given] a great deal of weight to the evidence of the referee Mr. Bodenistel and of course to the evidence of Mr. Maki himself. I found both to be credible witnesses, as in fact were all the witnesses in the case.

At about the 11-minute mark of the first period St. Louis had shot the puck into the Boston zone and behind and to the left of the Boston net. Mr. Maki and Mr. Green followed the puck into the area and collided at this point. Mr. Green pushed or punched Mr. Maki in the face with his glove and, it would appear, caused some injury to his mouth. At this point the referee signalled a delayed penalty for an infraction by raising his arm and play continued. The two players, it would appear, broke apart at this juncture with Mr. Maki skating to the area in front of the Boston net and the puck was moved into the centre ice area. There is some evidence of spearing by Maki against Green, but this fact is in some considerable doubt. There is evidence that Mr. Maki was somewhat dazed as a result of the incident behind the net. This is borne out by evidence given by Mr. Maki and by Mr. Larkin.

At this point the two players came together again at some point in front of the Boston net, sticks swinging, and as a result Mr. Green's unfortunate injury occurred at this time. There is no doubt that Mr. Green swung at Mr. Maki first and struck him on the neck or shoulders. Mr. Maki states that Mr. Green then made another move or motion towards him with his stick and that Mr. Green's stick was above his shoulders and held by both hands. Mr. Maki then swung at Mr. Green and his stick hit Mr. Green's stick and glanced from there to the side of Mr. Green's head causing the injuries in question. It seems clear from the photographs filed that this was the case and that if Mr. Green's stick had not been raised as it was, the blow would probably have landed on Green's shoulder. Most witnesses testified that the blow struck was not, as one witness testified, a baseball-type swing. These are the main facts as I find them. There were other motions or movements by the players during this period, but these are the main point that the fact that Mr. Green indicated that he wanted no prosecution of Mr. Maki is of little or no interest in this case. The fact that he did not testify either for the Crown or defence is somewhat unusual, but I place no weight on that fact as well.

I will deal first with the law upon which I have based my decision — that is, self-defence, as put forward by defence counsel.

This whole affair took place in a matter of two to five seconds in a game noted for its speed and bodily contact. We have evidence to indicate that Mr. Green is a very aggressive, hard-hitting player, and Maki of course is fully aware of this. Section 34 of the *Criminal Code* reads as follows:

**34**(1) Every one who is unlawfully assaulted without having provoked the assault is justified in repelling force by force if the force he uses is no more than is necessary to enable him to defend himself.

(2) Every one who is unlawfully assaulted and who causes death or grievous bodily harm in repelling the assault is justified if

(a) he causes it under reasonable apprehension of death or grievous bodily harm from the violence with which the assault was originally made or with which the assailant pursues his purposes, and

(b) he believes, on reasonable and probable grounds, that he cannot otherwise preserve himself from death or grievous bodily harm.

The law in this regard briefly stated therefore is that on a charge of this sort there must be an acquittal if the Court is left in any doubt as to whether the accused was acting in self-defence, that is where self-defence is raised as a defence. The Court must also consider the reasonableness of the force used under the circumstances and the state of mind of the accused at the time in question.

Mr. Maki in his evidence states, and I am paraphrasing to some extent: "I was trying to protect myself"; "I didn't aim at any particular part of his body"; "I swung in desperation to protect myself". And in cross-examination he stated again that he was protecting himself: "trying to ward off Green"; "I was not angry at Green I was just protecting myself"; "I expected he would still come after me if I turned away"; "swung in desperation"; "I didn't know I would cause him serious injury", and so on. A number of witnesses including the referee could not assess clearly the severity of the blow. The referee also indicated in his evidence that Maki did not seem angry or to have lost his temper. He was the man who was watching the whole affair much more closely than anybody else. Mr. Finn, one of the linesmen, stated that he had no problem separating Maki from the fight area and that Maki did not appear to want to get back at Mr. Green.

It is to be emphasized that the paramount obligation is upon the Crown to have proved the guilt of the accused beyond all reasonable doubt. It is also important to note as in *R. v. Ogal*, 50 C.C.C. 71, [1928] 3 D.L.R. 676, 23 Alta. L.R. 511, cited by defence counsel, that where the means of defence used is not disproportionate to the severity of the assault a plea of self-defence is valid, although the defender, in this case Maki, fails to measure with nicety the degree of force necessary to ward off the attack and inflicts serious injury thereby. Green was the aggressor up to the point of Maki's blow to Green.

Can I, considering the fact situation as I have found it to be, find beyond any reasonable doubt that Maki intended to injure Green; that Maki should not have been under any reasonable apprehension of bodily harm, and that Maki used excessive force under the circumstances? I think not — I must have a doubt in my mind on all three points and the charge is dismissed.

I feel, however, that although it does not form part of my reasons for acquittal, I must comment on the merit of some of the Crown Attorney's submissions as to the defence of consent put forward by defence counsel. If the fact situation in this case had been such that no doubt was raised in my mind regarding self-defence, I would not have hesitated to convict the accused. The defence of consent would in my opinion have failed. Although no criminal charges have been laid in the past pertaining to athletic events in this country, I can see no reason why they could not be in the future where the circumstances warrant and the relevant authorities deem it advisable to do so. No sports league, no matter how well organized or self-policed it may be, should thereby render the players in that league immune from criminal prosecution. I agree with Mr. Cassells when he states that consent to bodily injury as a defence to criminal prosecution has its limitations. I refer to the words of Stephen J., in *R. v. Coney et al.* (1882), 8 Q.B.D. 534 at p. 549, when he states:

> In cases where life and limb are exposed to no serious danger in the common course of things, I think that consent is a defence to a charge of assault, even when considerable force is used, as, for instance, in cases of wrestling, single-stick, sparring with gloves, football, and the like; but in all cases the question whether consent does or does not take from the application or force to another, its illegal character, is a question of degree depending upon circumstances.

Thus all players, when they step onto a playing field or ice surface, assume certain risk and hazards of the sport, and in most cases the defence of consent as set out in s. 230 of the *Criminal Code* would be applicable. But as stated above there is a question of degree involved, and no athlete should be presumed to accept malicious, unprovoked or overly violent attack. Bastin, J., states it this way in *Agar v. Canning* (1965), 54 W.W.R. 302 at p. 304; affirmed 55 W.W.R. 384:

> But a little reflection will establish that some limit must be placed on a player's immunity from liability. Each case must be decided on its own facts so it is difficult, if not impossible, to decide how the line is to be drawn in every circumstance. But injuries inflicted in circumstances which show a definite resolve to cause serious injury to another, even when there is provocation and in the heat of the game, should not fall within the scope of the implied consent.

The adoption of such principals in the future world, I feel certain, be a benefit to the players, of course, to the general public peace and, in particular, to young aspiring athletes who look to the professionals for guidance and example.

I would like at this point to thank counsel for the excellent manner in which the case was presented. Their arguments were extremely helpful to me and may form guide-lines in the future.

*Charge dismissed.*

For a recent example of the prosecution of a professional athlete, see *R. v. McSorley*, [2000] B.C.J. No. 1993.

## Jobidon v. The Queen
### (1991), 66 C.C.C. (3d) 454 (S.C.C.)

On appeal by the accused to the Supreme Court of Canada, held, the appeal should be dismissed.

Excerpts from the judgment of Gonthier, J. are reproduced below:

GONTHIER J.: At issue in the present appeal is the role of consent in the criminal offence of assault. More particularly, the issue is whether the absence of consent is an essential element of this offence when it relates to a fist fight where bodily harm is intentionally caused.

## I—STATEMENT OF FACTS

The appellant, Jules Jobidon, was charged with manslaughter for the unlawful act of killing Rodney Haggart — through the offence of assault (alternatively, through an act of criminal negligence). The incident leading to the charge was a fist fight between the two men, in a parking lot outside a hotel near Sudbury, Ontario, on September 19, 1986. At the date of the killing, Rodney Haggart was 25 years old. He had consumed some beer. His blood alcohol level, measured a few hours after the incident, was 160 mg. of alcohol per 100 ml. of blood, but the trial judge found that Haggart appeared "perfectly fine" and "perfectly normal". Jobidon, a young, fit and powerful man, had also been drinking beer prior to the fight, but in the opinion of the trial judge was not inebriated.

The two men initiated their aggression in the bar of the hotel. With his brother and a few friends, Haggart was celebrating his impending marriage. He approached Jobidon, who was also in the hotel with friends, and started a fight with him. Haggart was larger than the appellant, and had previous training as a boxer. In this first encounter, Haggart was prevailing when the owner of the hotel separated the combatants and told Jobidon and his brother to leave the hotel. Jobidon and Haggart exchanged angry words in the lobby, and the trial judge found that the two men agreed the fight was not over.

Jobidon and his brother waited outside in the parking-lot. When the Haggart party exited the hotel their respective older brothers began fighting at the far end of the lot. Jobidon and Haggart argued. A crowd of people, many of whom had come outside to see the fight, gathered around them.

While Haggart and Jobidon stood facing each other, Jobidon struck Haggart with his fist, hitting him with great force on the head and face. Haggart was knocked backward onto the hood of a car. The trial judge determined that Haggart was rendered unconscious by this initial punch and that he appeared to be "out cold". He was not moving and offered no resistance to the appellant. Immediately after throwing that first punch, Jobidon continued forward. In a brief flurry lasting no more than a few seconds he struck the unconscious victim a further four to six times on the head. The trial judge found that there was no interval between Haggart's fall and the continued punching. The punches were part of "one single continuing transaction. . .one fluid event, punctuated by specific blows". The judge noted that the most reliable witness testified that it all happened so quickly he thought Haggart would bounce off the hood and resume the fight.

Instead, Haggart rolled off the hood and lay limp. He was taken to the hospital in a coma, where he died of severe contusions to the head. Medical evidence showed that he had sustained extensive bruising and abrasions to the head and neck. It was determined that the cause of death was one or more of the punches he had received at the hand of the appellant in the parking-lot.

The trial judge found that Jobidon did not intend to kill Haggart, nor did he intend to cause the deceased serious bodily harm. However, the possibility of injury more serious than a bruise or bloody nose, such as a broken nose, was contemplated. Jobidon intentionally hit Haggart as hard as he could, but believed he was fighting fair. He did not depart intentionally from the kind of fight that Haggart had consented to. Jobidon believed that Haggart had consented to a fair fight, the object of which was to hit the other man as hard as physically possible until that person gave up or retreated. The trial judge also found that, although mistaken, and not supported by objective facts, Jobidon honestly believed that after Haggart had been struck onto the hood of the car he was merely stunned, but still capable of fighting back, and still trying to fight.

Jobidon was tried before a judge of the Supreme Court of Ontario, and was found not guilty of manslaughter: The judge held that Haggart's consent negated assault, and held further that Jobidon had not been criminally negligent. The respondent appealed the judge's holding of assault to the Ontario Court of Appeal, which allowed the appeal, set aside the acquittal, and substituted a guilty verdict on the charge of manslaughter:

. . .

## Issues on appeal

There is one principal issue raised in this appeal; and one ancillary issue. The principal issue is whether absence of consent is a material element which must be proved by the Crown in all cases of assault or whether there are common law limitations which restrict or negate the legal effectiveness of consent in certain types of cases. A secondary issue is whether Jobidon could be convicted of manslaughter on a basis other than that of an unlawful act of assault.

. . .

265 (1) A person commits an assault when
    (a) without the consent of another person, he applies force intentionally to that other person, directly or indirectly; . . .
(2) This section applies to all forms of assault, including sexual assault, sexual assault with a weapon, threats to a third party or causing bodily harm and aggravated sexual assault.
(3) For the purposes of this section, no consent is obtained where the complainant submits or does not resist by reason of
    (a) the application of force to the complainant or to a person other than the complainant;
    (b) threats or fear of the application of force to the complainant or to a person other than the complainant;
    (c) fraud; or
    (d) the exercise of authority.
(4) Where an accused alleges that he believed that the complainant consented to the conduct that is the subject-matter of the charge, a judge, if satisfied that there is sufficient evidence and that, if believed by the jury, the evidence would constitute a defence, shall instruct the jury, when reviewing all the evidence relating to the determination of the honesty of the accused's belief, to consider the presence or absence of reasonable grounds for that belief.

. . .

The connection between the two offences of assault and manslaughter is found in s. 222 (formerly s. 205) of the Code. That section provides a definition of manslaughter which is contingent on an unlawful act causing death:

222(4) Culpable homicide is murder or manslaughter or infanticide.
(5) A person commits culpable homicide when he causes the death of a human being,
    (a) by means of an unlawful act; . . .

The offence of assault is a foundation offence upon which other offences against the person are constructed. Of course assault is also unlawful. It therefore follows from s. 222 that when an assault is committed and causes the death of a person, the assailant is thereby criminally liable for manslaughter. It also follows that if consent acts as a defence to assault, it will indirectly act as a defence to a charge of manslaughter based on assault.

. . .

The appellant argued that the 1983 amendments to s. 265 reflected Parliament's intent to replace any common law doctrines that might have negated the legal effectiveness of consent to an act which would otherwise constitute assault. In particular, reference was made to s. 265(3), which sets out four factors that may vitiate consent: application of force, threats of force, fraud, or the exercise of authority. It was argued that because Parliament explicitly specified these factors, any others, even though they may have applied prior to 1983, could no longer be drawn from the common law. Since the trial judge found that Haggart had consented to the fight and did not hold that such consent was invalidated on any of the four grounds, it should be effective, and should serve as a defence to assault as the plain words of ss. 265(1) and 265(2) appear to require.

While at first glance the appellant's argument may seem cogent, it is ultimately unpersuasive. Parliament did not set foot into new territory when listing the four vitiating factors in s. 265(3). On the contrary it will be seen that, for the most part, that list merely concretized, and made more explicit, basic limits on the legal effectiveness of consent which had for centuries formed part of the criminal law in England and in Canada. Their expression in the Code did not reflect an intent to remove the existing body of common law which Already described those limitations and their respective scope. The Code just spelled them out more clearly, in a general form.

That common law is rich and extensive, with roots reaching back well into the decades preceding Canada's adoption of the Code of 1892.

. . .

The appellant argues that the interpretation favouring limits on consent being advanced here would render s. 265(1)(a) ("without the consent of another") otiose and meaningless, in so far as s. 265(2) specifies that s. 265(1)(a) is to apply to all forms of assault, including assault causing bodily harm. However, this objection is not sustainable.

By specifying in s. 265(2) that s. 265 is to apply to all forms of assault, Parliament undoubtedly sought to ensure that the basic elements of the offence of assault in ss. 265(1)(a) to (c), the circumstances listed in s. 265(3) for vitiating consent due to a coerced or misinformed volition, and the required state of mind for raising a defence in s. 265(4), would be applied without exception, irrespective of the peculiar form of assault. That is plain. Yet it does not follow from that expression that Parliament intended to eliminate the common law prescription of objects or forms of conduct to which legally effective consent may not be given. Section 265 was deliberately left open in that regard, for the above reasons.

. . .

Limits on consent to assault have long been recognized by English and Canadian courts. We have already seen the earliest antecedents of them in the English jurisprudence, in fist fights and otherwise; here we are concerned only with the former situation. In present times as well, the English courts have on the whole been very consistent when confronted by assaults arising from fist fights and brawls. Since the English cases have set the over-all direction for the Canadian common law in the assault context, and apparently continues to do so, it is of particular relevance in the circumstances of this case. The Canadian authorities also favour limits on consent. However, in recent years there has evolved a mixed record across provincial courts of appeal. This appeal therefore presents a timely opportunity for clarification.

. . .

**Policy considerations**

Foremost among the policy considerations supporting the Crown is the social uselessness of fist fights. As the English Court of Appeal noted in the Attorney-General's Reference, it is not in the public interest that adults should willingly cause harm to one another without a good reason. There is precious little utility in fist fights or street brawls. These events are motivated by unchecked passion. They so often result in serious injury to the participants. Here, it resulted in a tragic death to a young man on his wedding day.

There was a time when pugilism was sheltered by the notion of "chivalry". Duelling was an activity not only condoned, but required by honour. Those days are fortunately long past. Our social norms no longer correlate strength of character with prowess at fisticuffs. Indeed, when we pride ourselves for making positive ethical and social strides, it tends to be on the basis of our developing reason. This is particularly true of the law, where reason is cast in a privileged light. Erasing longstanding limits on consent to assault would be a regressive step, one which would retard the advance of civilized norms of conduct.

Quite apart from the valueless nature of fist fights from the combatants' perspective, it should also be recognized that consensual fights may sometimes lead to larger brawls and to serious breaches of the public peace. In the instant case, this tendency was openly observable. . . .

Related to a deterrence rationale is the possibility that, by permitting a person to consent to force inflicted by the hand of another, in rare cases the latter may find he derives some form of pleasure from the activity, especially if he is doing so on a regular basis. It is perhaps not inconceivable that this kind of perversion could arise in a domestic or marital setting where one or more of the family members are of frail or unstable mental health.

. . .

Of course this appeal does not concern sadism or intentional killing. But it comes close to mutilation. In any event, the weight of the argument could hold true for fights. If aggressive individuals are legally permitted to get into consensual fist fights and they take advantage of that license from time to time, it may come to pass that they eventually lose all understanding that that activity is the subject of a powerful social taboo. They may too readily find their fists raised against a person whose consent they forgot to ascertain with full certitude. It is preferable that these sorts of omissions be strongly discouraged.

Wholly apart from deterrence, it is most unseemly from a moral point of view that the law would countenance, much less provide a backhanded sanction to the sort of interaction displayed by the facts of this appeal. The sanctity of the human body should militate against the validity of consent to bodily harm inflicted in a fight.

Some would say the offence of assault should not be concerned with these considerations. They might argue that in respect of street fights, deterrence and express disapprobation of the law is already contained in other provisions of the Criminal Code. For instance, Parliament has seen fit to prohibit "prize-fighting", on penalty of criminal sanction, in s. 83.

However, while it is true that s. 83 prohibits prize-fighting, it is unlikely that section would apply to the situation giving rise to this appeal, nor to the wide range of cases which arise in like fashion. . . .

The policy preference that people not be able to consent to intentionally inflicted harms is heard not only in the register of our common law. The Criminal Code also contains many examples of this propensity. As noted above, s. 14 of the Code vitiates the legal effectiveness of a person's consent to have death inflicted on him under any circumstances. The same policy appears to underlie ss. 150.1, 159 and 286 in respect of younger people, in the contexts of sexual offences, anal intercourse, and abduction, respectively.

Some may see limiting the freedom of an adult to consent to applications of force in a fist fight as unduly paternalistic; a violation of individual self-rule. Yet while that view may commend itself to some, those persons cannot reasonably claim that the law does not know such limitations. All criminal law is "paternalistic" to some degree — top-down guidance is inherent in any prohibitive rule. That the common law has developed a strong resistance to recognizing the validity of consent to intentional applications of force in fist fights and brawls is merely one instance of the criminal law's concern that Canadian citizens treat each other humanely and with respect.

Finally, it must not be thought that by giving the green light to the common law, and a red light to consent to fights, this court is thereby negating the role of consent in all situations or activities in which people willingly expose themselves to intentionally applied force. No such sweeping conclusion is entailed. The determination being made is much narrower in scope.

## Conclusion

How, and to what extent is consent limited?

The law's willingness to vitiate consent on policy grounds is significantly limited. Common law cases restrict the extent to which consent may be nullified; as do the relevant policy considerations. The unique situation under examination in this case, a weaponless fist fight between two adults, provides another important boundary.

The limitation demanded by s. 265 as it applies to the circumstances of this appeal is one which vitiates consent between adults intentionally to apply force causing serious hurt or non-trivial bodily harm to each other in the course of a fist fight or brawl. (This test entails that a minor's apparent consent to an adult's intentional application of force in a fight would also be negated.) This is the extent of the limit which the common law requires in the factual circumstances of this appeal. It may be that further limitations will be found to apply in other circumstances. But such limits, if any, are better developed on a case-by-case basis, so that the unique features of the situation may exert a rational influence on the extent of the limit and on the justification for it.

Stated in this way, the policy of the common law will not affect the validity or effectiveness of freely given consent to participate in rough sporting activities, so long as the intentional applications of force to which one consents are within the customary norms and rules of the game. Unlike fist fights, sporting activities and games usually have a significant social value; they are worthwhile. . . .

There is also nothing in the preceding formulation which would prevent a person from consenting to medical treatment or appropriate surgical interventions. Nor, for example, would it necessarily nullify consent between stuntmen who agree in advance to perform risky sparring or daredevil activities in the creation of a socially valuable cultural product. A charge of assault would be barred if the Crown failed to prove absence of consent in these situations, in so far as the activities have a positive social value and the intent of the actors is to produce a social benefit for the good of the people involved, and often for a wider group of people as well. This is a far cry from the situation presented in this appeal, where Jobidon's sole objective was to strike the deceased as hard as he physically could, until his opponent either gave up or retreated. Fist fights are worlds apart from these other forms of conduct.

Finally, the preceding formulation avoids nullification of consent to intentional applications of force which cause only minor hurt or trivial bodily harm. The bodily harm contemplated by the test is essentially equivalent to that contemplated by the definition found in s. 267(2) of the Code, dealing with the offence of assault causing bodily harm. The section defines bodily harm as "any hurt or injury to the complainant that interferes with the health or comfort of the complainant and that is more than merely transient or trifling in nature".

On this definition, combined with the fact that the test is restricted to cases involving adults, the phenomenon of the "ordinary" schoolyard scuffle, where boys or girls immaturely seek to resolve differences with their hands, will not come within the scope of the limitation. That has never been the policy of the law and I do not intend to disrupt the status quo. However, I would leave open the question as to whether boys or girls under the age of 18 who truly intend to harm one another, and ultimately cause more than trivial bodily harm, would be afforded the protection of a defence of consent. . . . The appropriate result will undoubtedly depend on the peculiar circumstances of each case.

. . .

I would uphold the decision of the Court of Appeal. The appeal is dismissed.

## Questions/Discussion
1. Do you agree with the results in *Jobidon*? Why shouldn't people be able to agree to fight each other? What is special about hockey or other types of contact sports where assaults within the rules of the game are permitted? Is the court in *Jobidon* trying to accomplish another purpose (of stopping street fights) by subverting the defence of consent; in other words if we agree that lack of consent is an element of assault, then why *should* the courts ignore the existence of consent in many non-sports fights while deeming it available in sports?
2. If we allow the defence in fist fights, then what are the limits to "normal" fist fights? Does it depend upon who you are and your experience in such situations? Does it depend upon the location of the fight (for example, the sidewalk versus a private dwelling, or perhaps even "good" versus "bad" parts of town?
3. In the situation of domestic violence, stereotypical attitudes give rise to questions such as "why didn't the woman leave" and thus implicitly support the notion that she consented to some extent. Such attitudes ignore, of course, the lack of real choices in the woman's life. Obviously, such a defence could not be used explicitly by the violent husband or boyfriend in court, but such an attitude can contribute to the reluctance on the part of police agents, prosecutors, and the courts to get involved and to treat such assaults as real crimes.

## Further Reading
- Bryant, A., "Consent and Constructive Manslaughter" (1989), 67 C.R. (3d) 193.
- Doherty, D. and D. Stuart, "Jobidon: Consensual Combat and the Crime of Manslaughter — Two Views" (1987), 59 C.R. (3d) 216.
- Stuart Don, and R. Delisle, *Learning Canadian Criminal Law, 8th ed.* (Toronto: Carswell, 2001).
- Usprich, S.J., "Annotation" (1992), 7 C.R. (4th) 235 [discusses *Jobidon* decision].

## 7.2  ABSENCE OF INTENT OR KNOWLEDGE

### 7.2.1  Mistake of Fact

**Introduction**

The common law defence of mistake of fact is available in those cases where the requisite mens rea of the crime has not been fulfilled. For example, if you take an umbrella believing it to be yours, then you lack the requisite intent to steal. In cases such as this, criminal liability will not attach given that you believed in a set of circumstances which, if true, would have made your acts innocent. The problem is what type of mistake of fact will relieve you of criminal responsibility? While the first case, *Williams*, gives an example of the successful use of the defence, the problem presented in *Kundeus* is that although the belief or knowledge of the accused was not entirely innocent, his intent was *not* the intent to do the offence with which he was charged. In the case, the court seems to say that any wrongful intent will suffice, but this "transfer of intent", particularly involving the transfer of intent to do a less serious crime to the actus reus of a more serious crime, seems problematic and is given no limitations. Ordinarily, offences are legally defined as the actus reus plus the mens rea, and our common sense understanding is that both relate to the *same* crime. *Kundeus* challenges this conception and allows for the combining of the actus reus for crime "x" and the mens rea for crime "y" to find liability for crime "x". Ask yourself what limits should be placed on such transfers or if they should be allowed at all.

The last case, *Pappajohn*, deals with both the quality of the mistaken belief, a belief which we can see need not be reasonable but only "honest", and the conditions of its availability. This correlates well with the ideal of the mens rea as actual and subjective, yet presents certain problems in the area of sexual assault (or rape as the offence was known before 1983). In a society which promotes sexist stereotypes of women, which encourages attitudes suggesting that women do not really know what they want, and which teaches men to see women as essentially sexual objects, is it safe to rely solely on the accused's belief as to the existence of consent on the part of the woman? Parliament was of the view that it was not and responded by enacting section 273.2 of the *Criminal Code* which restricts the availability of apprehended consent as a defence to charges of sexual assault. The issues surrounding this matter are more fully explored in the next chapter.

Finally, note that certain types of mistakes of fact are obviously irrelevant to attaching liability. For example, it is no defence to say as a thief you only meant to steal $100 but by mistake you took $150, or that you mistakenly stole a car from A rather than your intended victim B. In addition, certain statutory provisions makes some types of mistakes irrelevant in criminal law. A good example can be found in section 150.1(4) of the Criminal Code where it is no defence in regard to some sexual offences against minors under 14 years of age that the accused believed that the minor was older (unless the accused took all reasonable steps to ascertain the complainant's age).

## Regina v. Williams
(1987), 80 N.S.R. (2d) 220 (Prov. Ct.)

[1] CURRAN, P.C.J.: — I want to thank counsel for the way this matter was dealt with. I am satisfied that the facts were fully put before me at the time of the hearing in May and that the issues and arguments have been thoroughly canvassed in the extensive briefs that were filed.

[2] These three matters were heard separately, in accordance with proper criminal procedure. However, there were agreed statements of fact in all three cases that were in large part identical. Besides that, some of the Crown evidence heard in one trial was adopted as part of the other trials. Consequently, most of the issues in the three cases are the same. I will render one decision on the common issues and deal separately with any issue that is peculiar to any one case.

[3] For several years Mr. Williams has been Clerk of the Provincial Court in Yarmouth and Justice of the Peace for the Province of Nova Scotia. In the early 1980's he was asked by the local detachment of the R.C.M.P. to take pleas from persons, usually American tourists, charged with narcotics and drug offences upon their arrival aboard the ferries from Maine.

[4] Most of the charges were laid when court was not in session in Yarmouth. No Provincial Court judge resided in Yarmouth at that time. Apparently both the R.C.M.P. and Mr. Williams wanted to cause as little inconvenience as possible to the persons charged.

[5] From 1981 to 1984 Mr. Williams attempted to obtain some instructions from the Attorney-General's Department about whether he ought to handle such charges. Mr. Williams was aware of a statement on page 4 of the *Handbook for Justices of the Peace* issued by the Department of Attorney-General that:

> "A justice shall not accept a plea of guilty except for charges arising from provincial legislation."

Nevertheless, he felt obliged to do what he could to assist with the problem brought to his attention by the R.C.M.P. Consequently, he took pleas on those charges.

[6] In 1984 Mrs. Crosby and Mrs. MacConnell were hired to work in the Provincial Court office in Yarmouth. Mrs. MacConnell was appointed a Justice of the Peace. Mrs. Crosby, who had been made a J.P. in 1978 during a previous stint with the Provincial Court, was declared to be "designated" as were the others.

[7] None of the accused ever received any instructions about their powers and duties as Justices. They were merely given the Handbook for Justices of the Peace and sent off on their own. Their knowledge about the position was very limited.

[8] By 1985 Mr. Williams had become annoyed with the R.C.M.P. because of the large number of drug charges laid against tourists. He thought that most of the matters should have been left in the hands of Customs authorities to seize the substances and levy administrative penalties. Consequently, Mr. Williams and the other accused began to grant absolute discharges in all but the more serious drug cases. The number of charges did not decrease.

[9] By the end of 1985, the R.C.M.P. had complained about the amount of paper work they had to do in relation to the charges. They convinced Mr. Williams that discharges

were not always appropriate. Mr. Williams and the other accused then met and decided to grant discharges only when Customs had collected an administrative penalty. In cases where there was no Customs penalty they would impose fines. They agreed on fines of $50.00 for most circumstances. That was notwithstanding the fact that the typical Yarmouth Provincial Court fine against landlubbers was $300.00. It seems that the accused were attempting to do their bit for Nova Scotia tourism.

[10] Each of the accused dealt with several drug charges in 1986, particularly during the time covered by the information. More often than not they imposed absolute discharges. On just a few occasions they remanded persons for later appearance in Provincial Court. In all other cases they imposed fines, usually of $50.00. Almost all the charges were laid against American citizens.

[11] On one occasion when imposing sentence, Mrs. MacConnell said that the fine was $50.00 American or $65.00 Canadian. It is alleged that on three occasions Mr. Williams imposed such a two-tier fine. On all other occasions the three accused merely said there would be a fine of a certain number of dollars, usually $50.00, and would not state the currency. I am satisfied that they intended the fines in those cases to be in Canadian funds of the stated amount.

[12] On the two occasions when the face amount of the fine was paid in Canadian funds, Mrs. MacConnell turned those funds in full over to the Provincial Court in Yarmouth. The nominal amounts of all other fines imposed by the three accused were paid in American funds. None of the persons who paid such a fine testified. There is no way of knowing whether or not they had any interest in what happened to the exchange on their American funds.

[13] As mentioned previously, there was one occasion on which Mrs. MacConnell assessed a fine of $50.00 American or $65.00 Canadian. She testified that as soon as she said those words, she knew something was wrong because, in her words, "the fine was fifty dollars." Whether or not she said so was not clear. In any event, I am satisfied that she did not explain to the person involved, Norman C. Schneider, that $50.00 Canadian would be sufficient. It seems clear to me that Mr. Schneider would have been left with the impression that the fine was $50.00 U.S.

. . .

[17] Few, if any, of the transactions involving any of the accused took place during regular working hours or at the courthouse. Most, if not all, took place during odd hours at the R.C.M.P. detachment. There was no one available to collect fine payment other than the justices themselves. Each of them merely accepted payment of the nominal amount in the funds offered, usually American. Exchange was neither requested nor given. On the next work day, the justice took the U.S. funds to the bank, exchanged them for Canadian, paid the nominal amount of the fine in Canadian funds to the Provincial Court office and kept the difference.

[18] The entire amount so kept by the three accused amounted only to a few hundred dollars. None of the accused ever made any attempt to disguise what he or she was doing. In fact, the practice was obviously well known, at least by the R.C.M.P. Until the charges were laid, no one ever suggested to any of the accused that what they were doing was improper.

[19] It was not until March 2, 1987 that the Attorney-General's Department formulated a policy for Provincial Court offices in relation to the receipt of U.S. funds. The instructions direct that the first $5.00 of any exchange above the nominal amount outstanding be kept by the court office as a processing fee. The balance was to be returned to the person who made the payment.

. . .

[36] I am satisfied that if there were any thefts they were from the persons who paid the American funds and not the federal Crown. On that basis, the prosecution has not made out its case, . . .

[37] In the alternative, I would say the following. Ownership or interest in the property, including U.S. currency, is clearly a matter of law. However, there have been countless disputes over property where more than one party incorrectly believed that it had a property interest or a right to the property without even having a property interest. It is clear that mistakes about the right to property are no mistakes of law, but mistakes of fact. Persons who make such mistakes because of honest beliefs may be civilly liable, but they are not guilty of crimes.

. . .

[39] In order for there to be a theft, the taking must be done fraudulently, that is, with a dishonest intention: *R. v. Dalzell* (1983), 57 N.S.R. (2d) 148; 120 A.P.R. 148; 6 C.C.C. (3d) 112 (C.A.). Proof only that something was taken without lawful right does not establish a crime. Moral wrongdoing must be shown.

[40] I attach considerable significance to the fact that the accused did nothing whatever to disguise their actions. I recognize that just because something is done openly does not necessarily mean it is done honestly. Some particularly brazen thieves use openness as a way of, in effect, disguising their thievery. However, I am convinced that these three accused persons did everything in the open because the thought never even crossed their minds that they were doing something wrong.

[41] There is another significant point. If the accused had concocted a scheme to fleece unsuspecting tourists, one would have expected them to impose fines on every occasion possible and to make those fines as large as possible. Instead, they ordered more discharges than fines, and the fines they did impose were very small.

[42] If the accused were wrong about their right to the exchange, they were honestly wrong.

. . .

[46] I am troubled as well by the way in which this investigation was carried out. Apparently by June of 1986 someone was aware of a problem in the handling of American funds used to pay drug fines. The authorities must have known the accused were basically honest people. For the life of me, I do not understand why they did not confront the accused about what was taking place. Instead, things were allowed to proceed with the full knowledge of at least some members of the R.C.M.P. Those members of the R.C.M.P. who were present when the fines were imposed and paid were put in the position of almost being accomplices. I doubt that any of the American

tourists who overpaid their fines would be grateful to the R.C.M.P. for saying nothing and letting this happen. Application of a little common sense might have prevented any of these charges from arising.

[47] I find the three accused not guilty.

*Accused acquitted.*

## The Queen v. Kundeus
### [1976] 2 S.C.R. 272

[Only the judgments of Laskin C.J.C. and De Grandpre J. are reproduced below.]

LASKIN C.J.C. (dissenting): — The issue in this appeal, brought by the Crown with leave of this Court, is whether the British Columbia Court of Appeal was right in concluding that the prosecution had failed to establish the necessary *mens rea* on a charge of trafficking in a restricted drug, namely lysergic acid dythalamide (LSD), contrary to the *Food and Drugs Act*, R.S.C. 1970, c. F-27. I take the factual considerations to be those narrated and found by the trial judge (who had convicted the accused) and which were accepted by the British Columbia Court of Appeal.

Briefly, they are as follows, based on the evidence of the undercover policeman who was involved in the transaction with the accused. The latter was at a table in a beer parlour calling out "speed, acid, MDA or hash" to passers-by. The policeman asked for hash or acid, to which the accused replied that he was all sold out. He then offered to sell mescaline at two dollars. The policeman accepted the offer and paid the accused four dollars for two "hits". The accused left, returned in five minutes, and handed the policeman two capsules. In fact, these capsules contained LSD. The British Columbia Court of Appeal took the reasons of the trial judge as involving a finding that although the accused in fact sold LSD he intended to sell and thought he was selling mescaline and the policeman thought he was buying mescaline. The record in this Court does not admit of any other view.

It was not contended by the Crown, and, indeed, could not be under the applicable legislation, that proof of the *actus reus* involved in the charge was alone enough to support the conviction; proof of *mens rea* also rested upon the Crown: see *Beaver v. The Queen*. The conviction can, of course, be easily supported if it be enough to establish that the accused intended to traffic in drugs and that is immaterial, save as a matter of description in the charge, what particular drug or class of drug was the subject of the trafficking. Such a view overlooks the legislative scheme governing various drugs and the applicable penal provisions. On that view, the accused would have to risk the range of penalties applicable to the trafficking in the drug which was in fact sold, albeit he thought that he was selling one with respect to which a much lighter scale of penalties was prescribed.

The scheme of the *Food and Drugs Act* is of considerable relevance in this case. Sections 40 and 42, on which the prosecution was based, are in Part IV of the Act dealing with "restricted drugs", which are those included in Schedule H, and LSD is one of those mentioned. Part III of the Act deals with "controlled drugs" which are those included in Schedule G, and among them are amphetamine and methamphetamine. Sections 33 and 34 are provisions in Part III (relating to controlled drugs) which are to the same effect as ss. 40 and 42 relating to restricted drugs under Part IV. Sections 40 and 42 read as follows:

**40**. In this Part,

"possession" means possession as defined in the *Criminal Code*;

"regulations" mean regulations made as provided for by or under section 45;

"restricted drug" means any drug or other substance included in Schedule H;

"traffic" means to manufacture, sell, export from or import to Canada, transport or deliver, otherwise than under the authority of this Part or the regulations.

**42**.(1) No person shall traffic in a restricted drug or any substance represented or held out by him to be a restricted drug.

(2) No person shall have in his possession any restricted drug for the purpose of trafficking.

(3) Every person who violates subsection (1) or (2) is guilty of an offence and is liable
(a) upon summary conviction, to imprisonment for eighteen months; or
(b) upon conviction on indictment, to imprisonment for ten years.

Mescaline is neither a controlled drug nor a restricted drug, but is a drug within Schedule F, included thereunder by virtue of s. 15 of the Act ("no person shall sell any drug described in Schedule F") and governed by regulations made pursuant to s. 25 of the Act. Section 15 of the Act is in Part I which deals with adulterated food, drugs and cosmetics, with deceptive advertising and labelling, with control of standards of manufacturing and with the sanitary condition of premises. Part II of the Act deals with administration and enforcement of the Act by inspectors and includes very wide regulation-making powers set out in s. 25. Penalties for violation of the Act or of the regulations are prescribed by s. 26 which reads as follows:

**26.** Every person who violates any of the provisions of this Act or the regulations is guilty of an offence and is liable
(a) on summary conviction for a first offence to a fine not exceeding five hundred dollars or to imprisonment for a term not exceeding three months, or to both, and for a subsequent offence to a fine not exceeding one thousand dollars or to imprisonment for a term not exceeding six months, or to both; and
(b) on conviction upon indictment to a fine not exceeding five thousand dollars or to imprisonment for a term not exceeding three years, or to both.

It is common ground that any offence under the Act or regulations relating to the sale of mescaline would be punishable under s. 26. On the other hand, this provision would have no application to controlled or restricted drugs in the face of the penalty provisions of ss. 34 and 42 which alone govern illegal dealing in them. A comparison of the respective penalty provisions governing mescaline and LSD shows how much heavier the penalty is in respect of illegal dealing in the latter than in the former, both where the prosecution is on summary conviction and on indictment.

The regulation respecting mescaline is Regulation C.01.041 which prohibits the sale of any substance containing a drug listed or described in Schedule F unless on written or verbal prescription, and the regulation goes on to elaborate on these types of prescriptions. I may observe here that it is not an offence to possess mescaline but it is an offence to possess a controlled or a restricted drug for the purpose of "trafficking", defined (as already noted) to include, *inter alia*, selling transporting and delivering.

. . .

It was the contention of the appellant Crown that the required proof of *mens rea* was furnished by evidence showing what Crown counsel called a general intention to traffic in drugs; and, this being shown, it was immaterial that the accused did not intend to traffic in the specific drug which was named in the charge but thought (as did his purchaser) that he was trafficking in another drug. Crown counsel thus takes the position to which I referred earlier in these reasons, and he stated in this connection that the accused could meet the case against him only by relying on mistake of fact which must be an honest mistake on reasonable grounds that the facts believed by him to be true would not attract culpability of any drug offence. That, according to Crown counsel, was not this case.

. . .

The third issue, which is tied in with the first, is whether mistake of fact is shown on proof that, on the facts as the accused honestly believed them to be, he was innocent of the offence charged, albeit guilty of another offence, or whether he must show that he was innocent of any offence.

. . .

Even if it be proper to describe trafficking in controlled drugs, whatever be the drug, or trafficking in restricted drugs, whatever be the drug as being, in each case, a description of the same crime. I think it is impossible to bring mescaline within either category when it stands entirely outside the group of controlled or restricted drugs and is governed by other statutory provisions than those governing controlled or restricted drugs. I am unable to agree that where *mens rea* is an element of an offence, as it is here, it can be satisfied by proof of its existence in relation to another offence unless, of course, the situation involves an included offence of which the accused may be found guilty on his trial of the offence charged.

Is any general principle deductible . . . ? Certainly, it cannot be said that, in general, where *mens rea* is an ingredient of an offence and the *actus reus* is proved it is enough if an intent is shown that would support a conviction of another crime, whether more or less serious than the offence actually committed. Coming to the particular, to the case before this Court, where proof is made of an *actus reus* that, in a general sense, is common to a range or variety of offences which require *mens rea* but those offences differ as to gravity by reason of different classifications and different penalties, is a charge of a more serious offence established by proof only that the accused intended to commit and could have been found guilty of a less serious, a lesser offence? The matter, in terms of principle, depends on how strict an observance there should be of the requirement of *mens rea*. If there is to be a relaxation of the requirement, should it not come from Parliament, which could provide for the substitution of a conviction of the lesser offence, in the same way as provision now exists in our criminal law for entering a conviction on an included offence?

This position is the one taken by the Model Penal Code of the American Law Institute (1962) which provides as follows in s. 2.04(2):

> Although ignorance or mistake would otherwise afford a defense to the offence charged, the defence is not available if the defendant would be guilty of another offense had the situation been as he supposed. In such case, however, the ignorance or mistake of the defendant shall reduce the grade and degree of the offense of which he may be convicted to those of the offense of which he would be guilty had the situation been as he supposed.

In the present case, and under present Canadian law, this sensible solution to a difficult problem is not open to this Court.

There may be some regret on the part of a court to free a person who appears to be guilty of an offence with which he has not been charged. That regret, if any there be, cannot be a vehicle for making a particular charge which cannot be proved serve as a foundation for imposing culpability of another, which is not an included offence. If there is to be a modification of principle in a situation like the present one, it must come from Parliament.

. . .

There is another consideration which should be brought into account in this case. The Crown's case was built on evidence of an undercover policeman which must have been as well known to the prosecuting authorities before the trial. I can appreciate that there could have been some difficulty in determining what charge should be laid on the facts disclosed by the chief Crown witness. Although the Crown may have felt that it could support the charge actually laid, it could also, as a matter of precaution, have laid a charge of attempting to traffic in mescaline. Such a charge is supportable under s. 24 of the *Criminal Code* which makes it immaterial whether it was possible or not to commit the intended offence: see 10 Halsbury, 3rd ed., p. 306; *R. v. Scott.* I have already indicated the view of the facts that the record compels. If there should be any doubt on the evidence whether the accused offered and intended to sell mescaline, that doubt cannot be translated into an affirmative finding, certainly not in this Court, that he offered and intended to sell LSD. At the worst, it would require a new trial.

I see no such doubt and, on the considerations I have canvassed, I would dismiss the appeal.

The judgment of MARTLAND, JUDSON, RITCHIE, PIGEON, DICKSON, BEETZ and De GRANDPRE JJ. was delivered by

De GRANDPRE J.: — With leave of this Court, the Crown appeals the unanimous judgment of the British Columbia Court of Appeal setting aside the conviction of the respondent.

. . .

The Court of Appeal disagreed with the conclusion reached by the trial judge and specifically refused to follow *R. v. Custeau.* The conviction was consequently set aside.

*Mens rea* cannot, of course, be examined without reference to *Beaver v. The Queen*. In that case, there was evidence on which the jury might have found that Beaver had no knowledge that the substance was a drug but believed it to be sugar of milk. It is in that context that the following excerpt from the reasons of Cartwright J., as he then was, must be read (p. 538):

> . . . the essential question is whether the belief entertained by the accused is an honest one and that the existence or non-existence of reasonable grounds for such belief is merely relevant evidence to be weighed by the tribunal of fact in determining that essential question.

The question to which Cartwright, J. was directing his attention is made very clear in the illustration he uses at p. 536:

> It may be of assistance in examining the problem to use a simple illustration. Suppose X goes to the shop of Y, a druggist, and asks Y to sell him some baking soda. Y hands him a sealed packet which he tells him contains baking-soda and charges him a few cents. X honestly believes that the packet contains baking-soda but in fact it contains heroin. X puts the package in his pocket, takes it home and later put it in a cupboard in his bathroom. There would seem to be no doubt that X has had actual manual and physical possession of the package and that he continues to have possession of the package while it is in his cupboard. The main question raised on this appeal is whether, in the supposed circumstances, X would be guilty of the crime of having heroin in his possession.
>
> It will be observed at once that we are not concerned with the incidence of the burden of proof or of the obligation of adducing evidence. The judgment of the Court of Appeal states the law to be that X must be convicted although he proves to the point of demonstration that he honestly believed the package to contain baking-soda.

Our facts are different. They are very simple and not contradicted. One reading of them is that Kundeus was offering LSD for sale, actually sold LSD and received payment therefor. On that reading, it is obvious that the conviction should have been affirmed.

Another reading is that adopted by the Court of Appeal and expressed by McFarlane J.A., speaking for the Court (p. 345):

> The evidence disclosed, and the trial Judge found, that the appellant offered to sell mescaline at two dollars to a police constable acting undercover. The constable accepted the offer and paid the appellant four dollars for two "hits". The appellant left, returned in about five minutes and handed the constable two capsules which were found, on analyses, to contain LSD.
>
> I think I must interpret the reasons for judgment of the trial Judge as a finding that although the appellant did in fact sell LSD he thought he was selling, and intended to sell, mescaline and that the constable also thought he was purchasing Mescaline.

Assuming that this reading of the trial judgment is the proper one, was the Court of Appeal right in holding that the necessary *mens rea* had not been proved? I do not believe so.

. . .

No evidence having been tendered by the accused, it is not possible to find that he had an honest belief amounting to a non-existence of *mens rea* and the Court of Appeal was in error in its conclusion.

The quality of respondent's conduct is not to be determined by the existence or non-existence of a binding civil agreement as to the purchase of LSD between him and the constable.

. . .

I would allow the appeal, set aside the Order of the Court of Appeal of British Columbia and restore the judgment at trial together with the sentence imposed thereat.

*Appeal allowed.*

## Pappajohn v. The Queen
### (1980), 52 C.C.C. (2d) 481 (S.C.C.)

[Only the judgment of McIntyre J. is reproduced below.]

MCINTYRE, J.: — The appellant appeals his rape conviction, which was affirmed in the Court of Appeal for British Columbia with one dissent [45 C.C.C. (2d) 67, 5 C.R. (3d) 1983, [1979] 1 W.W.R. 562], upon the ground that the trial Judge failed to put to the jury the defence of mistake of fact. That ground is expressed in the appellant's factum in these words:

Did the learned trial judge err in failing to instruct the jury on the question of honest belief by the accused that the Complainant consented to intercourse and thus on the facts of this case, failed to put properly before the jury a defence, such failure being a non-direction amounting to mis-direction?

A consideration of the facts of the case is vital to a resolution of the problem it poses. The complainant was a real estate sales-woman employed by a well-known and well-established real estate firm in Vancouver. She was successful in her work. The appellant is a businessman who was anxious to sell his home in Vancouver and he had listed it for sale with the real estate firm with which the complainant was associated. She was to be responsible for the matter on her firm's behalf. On August 4, 1976, at about 1:00 p.m., she met the appellant by appointment at a downtown restaurant for lunch. The purpose of the meeting was to discuss the house sale. The lunch lasted until about 4:00 or 4:30 p.m. During this time, a good deal of liquor was consumed by both parties. The occasion became convivial, the proprietor of the restaurant and his wife joined the party, and estimates of the amount of alcohol consumed varied in retrospect, as one would expect. It does seem clear, however, that while each of the parties concerned had a substantial amount to drink, each seemed capable of functioning normally.

At about 4:00 p.m. or shortly thereafter, they left the restaurant. The appellant drove the complainant's car while she sat in the front passenger seat. They went to the appellant's house, the one which was listed for sale, to further consider questions arising in that connection. Up to the time of arrival at the home, at about 4:30 or 5:00 p.m., there is no significant variation in their accounts of events. From the moment of arrival, however, there is a complete divergence. She related a story of rape completely against her will and her protests and struggles. He spoke of an amorous interlude involving not more than a bit of coy objection on her part and several acts of intercourse with her consent. Whatever occurred in the house, there is no doubt that at about 7:30 p.m. the complainant ran out of the house naked with a man's bow tie around her neck and her hands tied behind her back with a bathrobe sash. She arrived at the door of a house nearby and demanded entry and protection. The occupant of the house, a priest, admitted her. She was in an upset state and exhibited great fear and emotional stress. The police were called and these proceedings followed. More detailed reference to the facts will be made later.

When the defence closed its case and before the trial Judge commenced his charge, the jury was excluded while counsel for the appellant argued that on the facts of the case as it appeared from the evidence, the trial Judge should put the defence of mistake of fact to the jury. He contended that the appellant was entitled to have the Judge tell the jury that if the appellant entertained an honest but mistaken belief that the complainant was consenting to the acts of intercourse as they occurred, the necessary *mens rea* would not be present, and the appellant would be entitled to an acquittal. Reliance for this proposition was placed upon *Director or Public Prosecutions v. Morgan,* [1975] All E. R. 347 (H.L.), and *R. v. Plummer and Brown* (1975), 24 C.C.C. (2d) 497, 31 C.R.N.S. 220 (Ont. C.A.). The trial Judge refused to accede to the defence counsel's request.

. . .

In the Court of Appeal, this ruling found support in the majority judgment of Farris, C.J.B.C., with whom Craig, J.A., agreed. The majority adopted the view that the issue emerging from the evidence was a simple one of consent or no consent. In a dissenting judgment, Lambert, J.A., was of the opinion that there was sufficient evidence to put the defence to the jury. He would have directed the jury that the accused was entitled to an acquittal if the jury found that he entertained an honest and *reasonably held* mistaken belief in the existence of consent. This is a view which I cannot share in view of the pronouncement in this Court in *Beaver v. The Queen* (1957), 118 C.C.C. 129 at pp. 136-7, [1057] S.C.R. 531 at p. 538, 26 C.R. 193.

. . .

In relating the law to the facts of any case, we must keep in mind what it is that the trial Judge must look for in the evidence in deciding whether there is, in the words of Fauteux, J., "some evidence or matter apt to convey a sense of reality in the argument, and in the grievance". In this case, to convey such a sense of reality, there must be some evidence which if believed would support the existence of a mistaken but honest belief that the complainant was in fact consenting to the acts of intercourse which admittedly occurred. This requires a more detailed recital of the evidence than would ordinarily be necessary.

The complainant, after describing the events of the early afternoon in the restaurant, said that upon entering into the house where discussions were to take place regarding its sale, the appellant seized her and pushed her down the hallway to the bedroom. She resisted his pushing and tried to reason with him. He said that he was going to break her and began, as soon as the bedroom was reached, to remove her blouse. She said she protested and screamed and grew hysterical and tried to reason with him but was not fighting him in a physical way. When he continued to remove her blouse, she realized he was going to rape her. She tried to escape but he threw her onto the bed and she became totally hysterical. She just lay on the bed and screamed. She then said she tried to rise from the bed but he held out his arm and told her to remove his cuff-links, she refused and then she tried to escape. He pushed her back onto the bed, removed her skirt, nylons and panties, but not her brassiere or slip. She remained on the bed screaming, then she observed that he was undressed, although did not actually recall him undressing. She described various conversations in which she told him she was not able to take birth control pills and was without any contraceptive protection. She said that she and the man she lived with were attempting to have a baby and she was at that time ovulating. This information came, she said, from her lover who was a gynaecologist and he later gave evidence confirming these matters. She tried to persuade the appellant to desist but he would not be put off and finally had intercourse with her against her will. She said that the appellant had told her he would not ejaculate in her and she described three short acts of intercourse all against her will in which no ejaculation occurred. After some time the appellant left the bed and got a bow tie from a drawer and a sashcord from a dressing gown. Again, against her will, he tied the bow tie over her mouth as a gag and tied her hands behind her back. She struggled against this and threw herself from the bed onto the floor. He put her back on the bed and while her hands remained tied had intercourse again from the rear. During all this time she said she was at times pleading and reasoning with him, at times hysterical and screaming, and at times endeavouring to avoid and escape him. She said at one stage when she saw him get the tie and cord that she decided that he was going to kill her. Shortly after the incident of falling off the bed, and by this time some three hours had elapsed, she said he left the room. She seized the opportunity to escape and fled from the house naked with her hands still tied behind her back. She ran down an alley and pounded at the door of a nearby house. She was admitted and the police were called. During all this period, she insisted that she did not consent to any of the acts of intercourse. She insisted that she was hysterical, fearful and helpless in his hands and she escaped as soon as she could.

The appellant, in giving evidence on his own behalf, said that upon arrival at the house, he entered and went immediately to the bathroom. On this return to the front of the house, he led the complainant into the living room. They sat on the couch and began to kiss. During this episode, she removed her necklace and left her car keys on a table in the living room. They then moved into the bedroom where she consented to the removal of her clothes. He hung her blouse in the closet and put her other garments, after folding them, at the foot of the bed. He agreed that she refused to undo his cufflinks but he undressed and they then had intercourse with her consent. He admitted to three occasions and admitted that he had had no ejaculations. The whole performance, while with her consent, was not very successful. He admitting getting the tie to gag her and the cord to bind her, saying that it was done as an act of bondage to stimulate sexual activity. He said that when bound she suddenly threw herself from the bed and was hysterical and screaming. He said that he put her back on the bed. He left to find a cigarette and on his return she had gone. He did not know where. He waited for some time then put some clothes on and had a look around the house and the yard but could not find her. He insisted that everything was done with her consent. She made no serious resistance to his advances beyond making such coy inquiries as "George, what are you doing?" He says he would not have forced her if she had resisted, that she made no objection to his advances, and, that when she threw herself from the bed he desisted from any further efforts at intercourse and did not have intercourse after that event.

It will be seen at once that there is a fundamental conflict between the two stories. Her version excludes consent and any possible mistaken belief in consent. His version speaks of actual consent and no suggestion of any mistaken belief could arise. To find support for the defence asserted by the appellant, the other evidence must be considered.

When the complainant gained admission to the house where she sought help, she was observed to be in a distraught and emotional condition. She complained that she had been assaulted or raped or that someone was attempting to rape her. She was evidently fearful.

She wanted to have her gentleman friend called and the call was made. The police were called as well. The priest, who had admitted her to the house, removed the cords from her wrists and found that they had been tightly tied. He gave evidence that he had some difficulty in untying her.

After the complainant had spoken to the police, they went to the appellant's house. Some 40 minutes had elapsed since she had left it. The appellant asked if they came about the girl. He denied he had raped her. He said she was willing, that he didn't resist much and that she had suddenly become hysterical and had run away. He did not follow her because he did not know what to do and when he first discovered her absence he was naked himself. In the house, the police found the necklace in the living-room with the car keys. They found the complainant's blouse hanging in the closet in the bedroom, the complainant herself had seen it there before her escape. They found her underclothes folded at the foot of the bed with the exception of her slip which was in the bed sheets. Further examination revealed that the clothing of the complainant was undamaged, that is, untorn, though the complainant said that she did observe a torn shoulder strap in her slip the next day. Medical evidence found the following physical marking or injuries upon the body of the complainant. There were three scratches, two on her chest and one on her back, a red mark on the inside of her upper right arm, reddened areas on the front of both wrists. There was no bruising or redness on her mouth, throat, neck, the inside of her thighs or legs, and no injury or any kind of redness was observed about the vagina area.

In summary then, this was the state of evidence when the trial Judge was called upon to make his ruling. It became his task to apply the rule enunciated above. In assessing his resolution of the matter, we must consider the situation as it presented itself to him at the time. Speculation as to what the jury did, or would have done after being charged, is not relevant here.

With that thought in mind and, bearing in mind that the object of the judicial search must be evidence of a mistaken but honest belief in the consent of the complainant, one must first ask the question "Where is this evidence to be found?" It cannot be found in the evidence of the complainant. She denies actual consent and her evidence cannot provide any support for a mistaken belief in consent. Her conduct, according to her description, is that of a terrified, hysterical, non-consenting woman who resisted the appellant's advances, albeit unsuccessfully, and when able fled from his house in search of assistance. Turning then to the evidence of the appellant, it immediately becomes apparent that his evidence speaks of actual consent, even co-operation, and leaves little if any room for the suggestion that she may not have been consenting but he thought she was. The two stories are, as has been noted before, diametrically opposed on this vital issue. It is not for the trial Judge to weigh them and prefer one to the other. It is for him in this situation, however, to recognize the issue which arises on the evidence for the purpose of deciding what defences are open. In this situation the only realistic issue which can arise is the simple issue of consent or no consent. In my opinion, the trial Judge was correct in concluding that there simply was not sufficient evidence to justify the putting of the defence of mistake of fact to the jury.He left the issue of consent and that was the only one arising on the evidence.

In reaching this conclusion, I am not unmindful of the evidence of surrounding circumstance which were said to support the appellant's contention. I refer to the absence of serious injury suffered by the complainant and the absence of damage to clothing, as well as to the long period of time during which the parties remained in the bedroom. These matters may indeed be cogent on the issue of actual consent but, in my view, they cannot by themselves advance a suggestion of mistaken belief. The finding of the clothes at the foot of the bed, the necklace and the keys in the living-room, are equally relevant on the issue of actual consent and, in my view, cannot affect the issue which was clearly framed by the opposing assertions of consent and non-consent.

It would seem to me that if it is considered necessary in this case to charge the jury on the defence of mistake of fact, it would be necessary to do so in all cases where the complainant denies consent and an accused asserts it. To require the putting of the alternative defence of mistaken belief in consent, there must be, in my opinion, some evidence beyond the mere assertion of belief in consent by counsel for the appellant. This evidence must appear from or be supported by sources other than the appellant in order to give it any air of reality. In *R. v. Plummer and Brown, supra*, Evans, J.A. (as he then was), speaking for the Ontario Court of Appeal, considered that there was such evidence as far as Brown was concerned and directed a new trial because the defence had not been put. In that case, the complainant had gone to Plummer's "pad" where she had been raped by Plummer. Brown entered the room where the rape occurred after Plummer had gone. Apparently, he had arrived at the house separately from Plummer. It was open on the evidence to find that he was unaware then that Plummer had threatened the complainant and terrorized her into submission. He had intercourse with her and she said that because of continuing fear from Plummer's threats, she submitted without protest. In these special circumstances, the defence was required. The facts clearly established at least an air of reality to Brown's defence. In *Morgan*, there was evidence of an invitation by the complainant's husband to have intercourse with his wife and his assurance that her show of resistance would be a sham. In other words, there was evidence explaining, however preposterous the explanation might be, a basis for the mistaken belief. In the case at bar, there is no such evidence.

Where the complainant says rape and the accused says consent, and where on the whole of the evidence, including that of the complainant, the accused, and the surrounding circumstances, there is a clear issue on this point, and where as here the accused makes no assertion of a belief in consent as opposed to an actual consent, it is unrealistic in the absence of some other circumstance or circumstances, such as are found in the *Plummer and Brown* and *Morgan* cases, to consider the Judge bound to put the mistake of fact defence. In my opinion, the trial Judge was correct in refusing to put the defence on the evidence before him.

I might add that I have had the advantage of reading the reasons of my brother Dickson, J., and while it is apparent that I am unable to accept his view on the evidentiary question, I am in agreement with that part of his judgment dealing with the availability as a defence to a charge of rape in Canada of what is generally termed the defence of mistake of fact.

I would dismiss the appeal.

*Appeal dismissed.*

## Questions/Discussion

1. Do you agree with the results and the reasoning of the majority in *Kundeus*? Do you think the decision is theoretically correct as to what we are punishing or should be punishing for in criminal law? Should intent be "transferred" at all, even to an actus reus which turns out to be less serious than the intended criminal conduct? Is the intent or mens rea to be considered that of the specific intent involved in the doing of an actus reus or is it a more general notion of some wrongful or blameworthy intent? Which should it be? For a full discussion of competing conceptions of mens rea, see Weiler's article in "Further Reading", below.

2. Is the requirement that the mistake need only be honest and not reasonable satisfactory? Should we include a reasonableness test to protect society from stupid or unreasonable people or should the focus be on individual moral culpability continue? If reasonableness is not generally included in the test, then should the law make special requirements in the case of sexual assault and claims of mistaken belief as to consent in light of the attitudes and stereotypes which surround women victims and the issues of consent (see section 273.2 of the Code)? What types of justifications can be advanced to require special criteria in one particular area of the criminal law to alter a general defence of mistake of fact?

## Further Reading

- Mewett, A., and M. Manning, *Mewett and Manning on Criminal Law*, 3rd ed. (Markham: Butterworths, 1994).
- Pickard, T., "Culpable Mistakes and Rape: Relating Mens Rea to the Crime" (1980), 30 University of Toronto Law Journal 75.
- Roach, Kent, *Criminal Law, 2d ed.* (Toronto: Irwin Law, 2000) at 151-163.
- Stuart, Don, and R. Delisle, *Learning Canadian Criminal Law, 8th ed.* (Toronto: Carswell, 2001).
- Weiler, J., "*R. v. Kundeus*: the Saga of Two Ships Passing in the Night" (1976), 14 Osgoode Hall Law Journal 457.

- Williams, J., "Mistake of Fact: The Legacy of *Pappajohn v. The Queen* (1985), 63 Canadian Bar Review 597.

## 7.2.2   Ignorance of the Law

### Introduction

"Ignorance of the law is no excuse" is a well known phrase and one which is essentially true. The inability to use mistake of law as a defence is codified in section 19 of the Criminal Code. The difficulty in this area of law comes in trying to label mistakes as either those of fact or of law. As noted in the introduction to this chapter, many mistakes relate to combined matters of law and fact, yet how the mistake is categorized is vitally important as to its potential as a defence. The following cases give examples of how the courts treat various types of mistakes. We can see as well that in situations where the mistake of law has been genuine and has been relied upon, then it can be used as a mitigating factor at the time of sentencing.

There is an argument that certain types of mistake of law known as "officially induced errors" should be accepted as valid defences. The situation where such would arise is where a person has been directly misled by a government official; for example, you are told by a government official you do not need a licence to hunt and then you are arrested for hunting without a licence. The argument is that you have relied upon the advice of an official who should have known the applicable law, and that you should not be held liable for reasonably relying on the official's incorrect advice. The defence has been used successfully in some lower courts and an example is given in *Cancoil Thermal Corporation* and *Parkinson* below.

### Regina v. Shymkowich
#### (1954), 110 C.C.C. 97 (S.C.C.)

Only the judgment of Rand J. is reproduced below.

RAND J.: — The external facts in this appeal are few and simple. The accused removed from a booming ground, within which a lumber company, the prosecutor, had exclusive privileges for the putting down of mooring dolphins, the ancorage of booms, a line of piles and a log haul-up, two logs belonging to the company which at the time of removal had become lodged against the easterly end of a line of booms. He did that by entering the water area over a boundary line of single logs a distance of approximately 40 ft. and towing the two logs out and down the Fraser River where on the following day he sold them, along with 23 others, for $80 or so.

He was believed in saying that he did not intend to do anything wrong and that he thought he had the right to do what he did. This both the County Court Judge who tried him and the Court of Appeal [108 Can. C.C. 194] have found to be an answer to the charge laid.

. . .

What, then, he believed was that by a general law he had a right to collect them as he did, to dispose of them, and in effect to require the owners to pay him or the person to whom he transferred them remuneration for his salvage work. Is that admissible as a defence? I have no doubt that it is not. As Kenny in his Outlines of Criminal Law, 1952 ed. at pp. 48-9 says: "The final condition is, that the mistake, however reasonable, must not relate to matters of law but to matters of 'fact'. For a mistake of law, even though inevitable, is not allowed in England to afford any excuse for crime. *Ignorantia juris neminem excusat.* The utmost effect it can ever have is that it may occasionally, like drunkenness, rebut the existence of the peculiar form of *mens rea* which some particular kind of crime may require."

This principle is embodied in s. 22 of the *Cr. Code*: "The fact that an offender is ignorant of the law is not an excuse for any offence committed by him."

A claim to ownership of a chattel, although it may depend on matter of law, is, in most cases, a question of fact, or its legal basis may, in the ordinary sense of the word, be subsumed in "fact". This enhances the difficulty of separating legal from factual elements in any relation to property and in any case it may resolve itself into a refined conceptual distinction. But a distinction between justifying an act as authorized by law and as a *bona fide* belief in a property interest does seem to correspond with an instinctive discrimination between the two concepts.

This idea is given its best expression by Lord Westbury in *Cooper v. Phibbs* (1867), L.R. 2 H.L. 149 at p. 170 in the following language: "It is said, '*ignorantia juris haud excusat*' but in that maxim the word '*jus*' is used in the sense of denoting general law, the ordinary law of the country. But when the word '*jus*' is used in the sense of denoting a private right, the maxim has no application. Private right of ownership is a matter of fact; it may be the result also of a matter of law; but if parties contract under a mutual mistake and misapprehension as to their relative and respective rights, the result is, that that agreement is liable to be set aside as having proceeded upon a common mistake."

This language was used in a civil proceeding but it furnishes a most helpful distinction for the application of the maxim in criminal law of which it has always been taken to be a basic principle.

The taking into possession and the conversion of the logs obviously was intended to deprive the owner temporarily at least of its property and this comes within the express language of the definition of theft given by the Criminal Code.

I would therefore allow the appeal and direct a judgment of conviction upon the second count, with a fine of $25 imposed on the accused.

[ESTEY J., with whom FAUTEUX J. concurred, held that the "respondent, in taking these logs out of the possession of the company, could not be said to have an honest and reasonable belief in the existence of facts which, if true, would have constituted a defence and, therefore . . . he possessed mens rea."]

[LOCKE J. dissented on the basis that "to constitute the offence, the act must be done fraudulently and without colour of right. In Stephen's History of the Criminal Law, vol. 3, p. 124, the learned author says " . . . A man who takes possession of property which he really believes to be his own does not take it fraudulently, however unfounded his claim may be. This, if not the only, is nearly the only case in which ignorance of the law affects the legal character of acts done under its influence."]

*Appeal allowed.*

## Regina v. Campbell and Mlynarchuk
### (1972), 10 C.C.C. (2d) 26 (Alta. Dist. Ct.)

KERANS, D.C.J. (orally): — This is an appeal by Darlene Agatha Campbell from conviction and sentence.

. . .

On a charge before the summary conviction Court that she did, between February 9, 1972, and February 21, 1972, at the City of Edmonton, in the Province of Alberta, unlawfully take part as a performer in an immoral performance at Chez Pierre's situated at 10615- Jasper Ave., Edmonton, contrary to s. 163(2) of the *Criminal Code*.

This matter, therefore, comes before me by way of a trial *de novo*. That section provides, in s-s. (2):

> (2) Everyone commits an offence who takes part or appears as an actor, performer, or assistant in any capacity, in an immoral, indecent or obscene performance, entertainment or representation in a theatre.

The facts before me are relatively straightforward. On the dates in question, at the place in question, the appellant danced on stage, before an audience. At the start of her performance, she was wearing some clothes. By the end of her performance, she was not wearing any clothes. The dance was described to me as a "go-go dance" which, I understand, is a violent movement of almost all parts of the body, more or less in time to strongly rhythmic music.

I have no doubt in coming to the conclusion that this is a performance within the meaning of the section, and that, in doing what she did, the appellant took part as a performer in that performance. On the question of whether or not the performance was immoral, both counsel have agreed that I am bound to follow the recent decision of the Appellate Division of the Supreme Court of Alberta in *R. v. Johnson (No. 1)* (1972), 8 C.C.C. (2d) 1, [1972] 5 W.W.R. 638. This was a stated case before the learned Riley, J. [6 C.C.C. (2d) 462, [1972] 3 W.W.R. 226], and appealed from him to the Appellate Division.

In that case, McDermid, J.A., speaking for the Court, said, after drawing attention to the fact that s. 170 of the *Criminal Code* makes it a crime for anyone to appear nude in a public place, that he understood the enactment of that offence, by the Parliament of Canada, and, I quote, "declared that it is a breach of a moral standard in Canada". And he goes on, "We know of no better way of establishing a moral standard than a declaration by the Parliament of Canada, so the Provincial Judge was justified in accepting this as his standard in finding that the dance by the respondent in the nude was an immoral performance." I understand, therefore, that since, to be nude in a public place is itself an offence; to perform in the nude, therefore, is an immoral performance within the meaning of the charging section. Therefore, I must conclude that the performance here was immoral within the meaning of that section.

I have been told that the decision of the Appellate Division has been appealed to the Supreme Court of Canada [8 C.C.C. (2d) 279]. In some cases it is considered appropriate to adjourn or reserve, pending the outcome of an appeal. In my view, this rule should not be followed in the case of appeals from the Appellate Division to the Supreme Court of Canada, for various reasons. One is the delay of time involved. Therefore, on this point, the position of the parties would have to be that, should the Appellate Division decision not be upheld, my decision must also be appealed.

. . .

The next argument raised on behalf of the appellant is that the appellant lacked the necessary *mens rea* for this offence. The facts in this respect were these: she engaged to do this performance, where, earlier, she had refused to engage to do this performance, because she relied upon the statement made to her, by Pierre Couchard,that he, in turn, had been informed that a Supreme Court Judge had, to use his words because he also gave evidence, "Ruled that we could go ahead with bottomless dancing." That decision arose out of a charge in the City of Calgary, of a business acquaintance of Couchard, who was the manager of the place where this performance took place. Ironically, the decision to which Couchard and the appellant referred is the decision at the Trial Division level in *R. v. Johnson (No. 1)*, to which I earlier referred, and which, the witnesses tell me, obtained some newspaper publicity. It was a decision then, that subsequently was reversed on appeal.

Mistake of fact is a defence to a criminal charge, where it can be said that the facts believed by the accused, if true, would have afforded him a defence. It is also said that a mistake of mixed fact and law is a defence. I understand that proposition to be correct, simply because, if there is a mistake of mixed fact and law, then there is a mistake of fact. In my view, there was no mistake of fact by the appellant here. What she was told had happened, in fact, did happen.

. . .

This is not a situation like others, where a mistake of law can be a defence, not because a mistake of law is a defence, but because a mistake of law can negative a malicious intent required for that crime. Thus, for example, where the law requires that a person wilfully, or maliciously, or knowingly, does something wrong, it could conceivably be a defence as negativing intention, to show that, because of the mistake in the understanding of the law, there was no wilful intent or malice. This is not one of those situations, as no such special intention is required for this offence. The only *mens rea* required here is that the appellant intended to do that which she did. And there is no suggestion, for a moment, that she lacked that *mens rea*.

This statement, that mistake of law is no defence, is contained in the *Criminal Code*, in s. 19, under the old numbering, which says:

> **19.** Ignorance of the law by a person who commits an offence is not an excuse for committing that offence.

Excuse, or legal justification, is a defence at law, and I understand that defence to mean that it is a defence to a criminal charge to show that the act complained of was authorized by some other law. Section 19 says that defence is not available, in effect, when a person has made a mistake as to whether or not this act is excused by another law or authorized by another law.

Properly understood, in my view, the section removing ignorance of the law as a defence, in criminal matters, is not a matter of justice, but a matter of policy. There will always be cases, not so complicated as this, where honest and reasonable mistakes as to the state of the law will be the explanation of the conduct of an accused. In such a circumstance, one cannot help but have sympathy for the accused. But that situation, traditionally, is not a defence. It is not a defence, I think, because the first requirement of any system of justice, is that it work efficiently and effectively. If the state of understanding of the law of an accused person is ever to be relevant in criminal proceedings, we would have an absurd proceeding. The issue in a criminal trial would then not be what the accused did, but whether or not the accused had a sufficiently sophisticated understanding of the law to appreciate that what he did offended against the law. There would be a premium, therefore, placed upon ignorance of the law.

. . .

I have given some consideration as to whether or not this position varies at all, because of the unique circumstances here, where the appellant relied upon a specific judgment of a Court very immediate in terms of time and place, as opposed to a solicitor's opinion or some understanding as to the law. There is not question that there is something of an anomaly here. Reliance on a specific order, of a specific Judge, granted at a specific time and place, seems, at first sight, not to be ignorance of the law, but knowledge of the law. If it turns out that that Judge is mistaken, then, of course, the reliance on that Judge's judgment is mistaken. The irony of this: people in society are expected to have a more profound knowledge of the law than are the Judges. I am not the first person to have made that comment about the law, and while it is all very amusing, it is really to no point.

The principle that ignorance of the law should not be a defence in criminal matters is not justified because it is fair, it is justified because it is necessary, even though it will sometimes produce an anomalous result.

When this appellant relied on the decision of the learned trial Judge, she relied on his authority for the law. As it turns out, that reliance was misplaced, as misplaced as reliance on any statement as to the law I might make. Less so, I am sure.

. . .

I, therefore, conclude that the mistake of law of the appellant affords no defence to her on this charge. There being no other defences, and the facts necessary having been made out, the conviction of the Court below, in my opinion, was correct. The appeal as to conviction is dismissed.

. . .

I should have been more careful in my language a moment ago, when I said the appeal as to conviction was dismissed. Under the new law, I should have more properly said that I find the appellant guilty of the charge, and will hear argument as to whether or not to allow or dismiss the appeal as to conviction.

. . .

Well, I have already indicated, in a quotation from Kenny, that, in this awkward situation, the matter does not afford a defence, but should certainly be considered in mitigation of sentence. Indeed, there are several cases, not as awkward as this, in the law reports, involving a person who had an honest and reasonable mistake in belief as to the law, and for whom the Courts expressed sympathy, and, in respect of whom, sentence was mitigated.

It is at this stage where the scales of justice are balanced. Clothed with very recent power to refuse to enter a conviction I can now balance the scales of justice even more delicately.

. . .

I have no power to give a pardon, but I do have power to give an absolute discharge. In my view, this is the proper case.

. . .

I am not aware, perhaps I am naive, but I am not aware that these tawdry nude night-club acts, of this sort, have become a prevalent problem in our community. Therefore, I think, out of the sense of justice, and certainly not out of any sense of approval for what this lady did, it would be appropriate for me to grant her an absolute discharge, and that is what I do.

*Accused discharged absolutely.*

### Regina v. Cancoil Thermal Corporation and Parkinson
(1986), 27 C.C.C. (3d) 295 (Ont. C.A.)

Appeal by the Crown from the accused's acquittal on charges contrary to ss. 14 and 16 of the *Occupational Health and Safety Act* (Ont.).

The judgment of the court was delivered by

LACOURCIERE J.A.: — The Crown appeals by leave, on a pure question of law, against the order of the Honourable Judge Alan R. Campbell in the District Court of Ontario at Kingston dismissing two appeals from the judgment of His Honour Judge Baker acquitting the respondents. On January 10, 1985, the respondents had pleaded not guilty to the following charges:

> . . . Cancoil Thermal Corporation . . . as Employer on or about the 20th day of March, 1984 at the Township of Pittsburg in the County of Frontenac and Province of Ontario, did commit the offence of failing to ensure that the measures and procedures prescribed by section 28 of Revised Regulations of Ontario, 1980, Regulation 692 were carried out in the work place in an industrial establishment, to wit, a factory located at Kingston Mills Road East, Contrary to section 14(1)(c), the Occupational Health and Safety Act, R.S.O. 1980, c. 321.

*Particulars:* A machine having an exposed moving part that endangered the safety of a worker was not equipped with and guarded by a guard or other device which prevented access to the moving part. Stewart Pare was injured as a result.

(2) and further that Cancoil Thermal Corporation, Part Lot 41, Conc. 4, Pittsburg Township, as Employer, on or about the 20th day of March, 1984, at the Township of Pittsburg in the County of Frontenac and the Province of Ontario, did commit the offence of failing to ensure that the equipment, materials and protective devices prescribed by Section 28 of Revised Regulations of Ontario, 1980, Regulation 692 were provided in an industrial establishment, to wit, a factory located at Kingston Mills Road East. Contrary to section 14(1)(a), the Occupational Health and Safety Act, R.S.O. 1980, c. 321.

*Particulars:* [same as above]

... Terence Parkinson — on or about the 20th day of March, 1984 at the Township of Pittsburg in the County of Frontenac and Province of Ontario, did commit the offence of failing to ensure that a worker worked in the manner and with the protective devices, measures and procedures required by section 28 of Revised Regulations of Ontario, 1980, Regulation 692 in an industrial establishment, to wit, a factory located at Kingston Mills Road East. Contrary to section 16(1)(a), the Occupational Health and Safety Act, R.S.O. 1980, c. 321.

*Particulars*: [same as above]

## The Facts

The respondent corporation is in the business of manufacturing heat transfer coils at a factory located outside of Kingston. In December, 1983, the company took delivery of a large metal shearing machine, known as a "Newton Shear", which was needed to cut the metal used in the production of the casings for the coils. The blade of this "Newton Shear" was operated by means of a "foot pedal" located seven and one-half inches from the floor. When this foot pedal was depressed,the clutch would engage, the "hold down" mechanism would clamp the inserted piece of metal in place, and the blade would come down and cut the metal. When the foot pedal was not depressed, the blade was in the up position and was not in motion. Needless to say, when the shearing mechanism was engaged by the depression of the foot pedal, the blade of the machine became dangerous to its operator.

When the respondent corporation took delivery of the Newton Shear, the machine was equipped with a "guard" which had been installed by its manufacturer to prevent access to the blade area of the machine by the operator during its operation. However, the respondent Parkinson, who was the supervisor and foreman of the factory, and Mr. Datta, its general manager, felt that the guard created a hazard in that its presence made it more difficult for the operator to clear away pieces of scrap metal. Accordingly, they decided to remove the guard from the machine. No other guard or similar safety device was installed on the machine as a replacement. It was felt that the hold down device provided sufficient safety to the operator of the machine. However, there were openings in the hold down mechanism which permitted physical access to the blade area of the machine. With the guard removed, there was nothing on the machine to prevent physical access to the blade.

On March 20, 1984, a 26-year-old employee, Stuart Bradford Pare, while engaged in the operation of the metal shearing machine, accidently cut off the tips of six of his fingers (three fingers on each had) down to approximately the first joint. After cutting large pieces of metal into smaller pieces of a specified size, Mr. Pare, following what he described as the accepted procedure, had used his fingers to push a small piece of scrap metal through the machine and onto the floor. In the process of doing this he accidentally depressed the foot pedal on the machine, activating the blade mechanism.

There can be no doubt that the guard which came installed on the machine would have prevented this accident, acting as a barrier to prevent the operator's hands or fingers from going into the area of the cutting blade. Mr. Pare had been employed by the respondent as a machine operator for seven or eight months. Before March 20, 1986, he had operated the machine on one occasion and only for a short period; there was a conflict of evidence at trial as to the specific instructions given to him on safety precaution in the operation of the machine. Mr. Pare had helped Mr. Parkinson to modify the machine by removing the guard.

It will be more convenient to detail later the inspection of this machine made by an inspector of the Ministry of Labour before the accident, in January, 1984, and on the day after the accident when he made an order that the machine could not be used until the guard was replaced.

### The Statutory Provisions

Generally, the *Occupational Health and Safety Act,* R.S.O. 1980, c. 321, is designed to protect the health and safety of workers in Ontario and is administered and enforced by the Ministry of Labour. Part VIII of the Act deals with enforcement. Inspectors are given broad powers to inspect the work place and to make orders, without the requirement of a hearing, where they find that a contravention of the Act or regulation creates a danger or hazard to the health or safety of a worker. Part IX deals with offences and penalties. The general penalty section is s. 37(1) which provides as follows:

37(1) Every person who contravenes or fails to comply with,
(a) a provision of this Act or the regulations;
(b) an order or requirement of an inspector or a Director; or
(c) an order of the Minister,
is guilty of an offence and on conviction is liable to a fine of not more that $25,000 or to imprisonment for a term of not more than twelve months, or to both.

The information alleged that the respondent corporation had breached s. 14(1)(a) and (c) which provide:

14(1) An employer shall ensure that,
(a) the equipment, materials, and protective devices as prescribed are provided;

. . .

(c) the measures and procedures prescribed are carried out in the workplace;

It was alleged that the respondent was in breach of s. 28 of the regulations, R.R.O. 1980, Reg. 692, which provides:

28. Where a machine or prime mover or transmission equipment has an exposed moving part that may endanger the safety of any worker, the machine or prime mover or transmission equipment shall be equipped with and guarded by a guard or other device that prevents access to the moving part.

The information against the respondent Parkinson was based on s. 16(1)(a) which states:

16(1) A supervisor shall ensure that a worker,
(a) works in the manner and with the protective devices, measures and procedures required by this Act and the regulations;

I should note at this time that the Act provides a statutory equivalent of the defence of due diligence. This provision does not apply to the offence charged against the respondent corporation under s. 14(1)(a). Section 37(2) of the Act provides as follows:

37(2) On a prosecution for a failure to comply with,
(a) subsection 13(1);
(b) clause 14(1)(b), (c) or (d); or
(c) subsection 16(1),
it shall be a defence for the accused to prove that every precaution reasonable in the circumstances was taken.

The specific exclusion of this statutory defence in the case of offences under s. 14(1)(a) would suggest that the Legislature, as a matter of policy, had determined that the subsection creates an offence of absolute liability as defined in *R. v. City of Sault Ste. Marie* (1978), 40 C.C.C. (2d) 353, 85 D.L.R. (3d) 161, [1978] 2 S.C.R. 1299. However, if s. 14(1)(a) were treated as creating an absolute liability offence, it would offend s. 7 of the *Canadian Charter of Rights and Freedoms,* the right to life, liberty and security of the person and the right not to be deprived thereof except in accordance with the principles of fundamental justice. Under s. 37(1), a violation of s. 14(1)(a) may attract a term of imprisonment. In *Reference re. s. 94(2) of Motor Vehicle Act* (1985), 23 C.C.C. (3d) 289, 24 D.L.R. (4th) 536, [1985] 2 S.C.R. 486, the Supreme Court of Canada held that the combination of absolute liability and the potential penalty of imprisonment was a violation of s. 7 of the Charter. In the words of Lamer J. at p. 311 C.C.C., p. 515 S.C.R.:

A law enacting an absolute liability offence will violate s. 7 of the Charter only if and to the extent that it has the potential of depriving of life, liberty or security of the person.
Obviously, imprisonment (including probation orders) deprives persons of their liberty. An offence has that potential as of the moment it is open to the judge to impose imprisonment. There is no need that imprisonment, as in s. 94(2), be made mandatory.
I am therefore of the view that the combination of imprisonment and of absolute liability violates s. 7 of the Charter. . .

To avoid a violation of s. 7 of the Charter, s. 14(1)(a) must be treated as creating a strict liability offence. The defence of due diligence was available to the respondents.

. . .

### The Defence of Estoppel or Officially Induced Error

The difficult question is whether there exists on this record any room for the defence of estoppel or of "officially induced error" of law.

The inspector from the Ministry of Labour (Occupational Health and Safety Division), Mr. J.J. Ogoniek, had inspected the factory on January 16, 1984, more than two months before the accident. At the time of the inspection, the guard installed by the manufacturers had been removed. Although the machine had not been put into production, it was run while the inspector was present so that he could observe the cycle of operation. The absence of the manufacturer's guard was pointed out by the respondent Parkinson. According to the evidence of the respondent Parkinson, the inspector commented that it was "safe to remove the particular piece of metal in question and that with the machine being operated according to instructions that it was safe to do so." Mr. Pare who had not then operated the machine, stated that he had "no unresolved health and safety concerns". In any event, the inspector was satisfied apparently that no provision of the Act or regulations was being contravened and he made no order pursuant to his powers under s. 29 of the Act. However, on March 21st, the day after the accident, the inspector issued an order that the metal shear was not to be used until access to the blade area had been blocked. This order was complied with on the following day "by welding 1/4 inch x 1 inch steel bars across the openings in the hold down".

On the record, it is clear that the inspector was an official of the Occupational Health and Safety Division of the Ministry of Labour, appointed for the purpose of inspection and examination of the work place and that he was clothed with wide powers to enforce compliance with the Act and its regulations.

The defence of "officially induced error", exists where the accused, having adverted to the possibility of illegality, is led to believe, by the erroneous advice of an official, that he is not acting illegally. In *R. v. Walker and Somma* (1980), 51 C.C.C. (2d) 423, Martin J.A., in an *obiter dictum*, left open the possibility of this defence, and stated at p. 429:

> I would not wish to be taken to assent to the proposition that if a public official charged with responsibility in the matter led a defendant to believe that the act intended to be done was lawful, the defendant would not have a defence if he were subsequently charged under a regulatory statute with unlawfully doing that act: see "Excusable Mistake of Law", [1974] Crim. L.R. 652 at p. 660, by A.J. Ashworth. I leave aside that difficult question until it is necessary to decide it. Suffice it to say that no suggestion arises in this case that the respondents were misled by Customs officials.

An article by Professor P.G. Barton, "Officially Induced Error as a Criminal Defence: A Preliminary Look", 22 C.L.Q. 314 (1979-80), contains a helpful consideration of this defence.

In *R. v. MacDougall* (1981), 60 C.C.C. (2d) 137 at p. 160, 46 N.S.R. (2d) 47, 10 M.V.R. 236, the Nova Scotia Court of Appeal, *per* Macdonald J.A., recognized the defence in the following words:

> The defence of officially induced error has not been sanctioned, to my knowledge, by any appellate Court in this country. The law, however, is ever-changing and ideally adapts to meet the changing mores and needs of society. In this day of intense involvement in a complex society by all levels of Government with a corresponding reliance by people on officials of such Government, there is, in my opinion, a place and need for the defence of officially induced error, at least so long as a mistake of law, regardless how reasonable, cannot be raised as a defence to a criminal charge.

On a further appeal to the Supreme Court of Canada, Ritchie J. appeared to give approval to the defence [1 C.C.C. (3d) 65 at p. 71, 142 D.L.R. (3d) 216, [1982] 2 S.C.R. 605]:

> It is not difficult to envisage a situation in which an offence could be committed under mistake of law arising because of, and therefore induced by, "officially induced error" and if there was evidence in the present case to support such a situation existing it might well be an appropriate vehicle for applying the reasoning adopted by Mr. Justice Macdonald. In the present case, however, there is no evidence that the accused was misled by an error on the part of the registrar.

The defence of "officially induced error" is available as a defence to an alleged violation of a regulatory statute where an accused has reasonably relied upon the erroneous legal opinion or advice of an official who is responsible for the administration or enforcement of the particular law. In order for the accused to successfully raise this defence, he must show that he relied on the erroneous legal opinion of the official and that his reliance was reasonable. The reasonableness will depend upon several factors including the efforts he made to ascertain the proper law, the complexity or obscurity of the law, the position of the official who gave the advice, and the clarity, definitiveness and reasonableness of the advice given.

I agree with the following statement made by Professor Barton in the article referred to *op. cit.* at p. 331:

> Where the advice is given by an official who has the job of administering the particular statute, and where the actor relies on this advice and commits what is in fact an offence, even if the agency cannot be estopped does it follow that the actor should be excused? To do so is not to condone an illegality or say that the agency is estopped into a position of illegality, but to recognize that the advice was illegal but excuse the actor because he acted reasonably and does not deserve punishment.

It may well be that the individual respondent and the respondent corporation in the s. 14(1)(c) count (either count against the corporation would probably fall under the *Kienapple* principle [see *Kienapple v. The Queen* (1974), 15 C.C.C. (2d) 524, 44 D.L.R. (3d) 351, [1975] 1 S.C.R. 729], if a conviction were entered against it under the other count) need not rely on this novel defence if they can satisfy the trier of fact that they acted with due diligence. But, although it may at times overlap with the defence of due diligence, the defence of "officially induced error of law" is separate and distinct and can be asserted, in the same way as other defences.

In the present case, it will be for the trier of fact to decide whether the accused has proved, by a preponderance of evidence, that he was misled by the inspector into thinking that the removal of the manufacturer's guard would not be in contravention of the law. The record makes it clear that the inspector was an official involved in the administration of the relevant law, presumably familiar with the Act and regulations and having the expertise to determine whether a machine was equipped with the prescribed safety devices. Ordinarily, mistake of law cannot be successfully raised as a defence to a criminal or *quasi*-criminal charge or regulatory offence, but an officially induced error of law may, in some circumstances, constitute a valid defence. This will, of course, depend on whether the opinion of the official was reasonable in the circumstances and whether it was reasonable for the accused to follow it.

The evidence in the present case is too sparse and inconsistent to allow an appellate court to determine the availability of the defence. Officially induced error was not relied on at trial and was only raised by the court, *proprio motu* during the argument of the appeal. However, I should, in fairness, point out that the respondent relied on the defence of estoppel which would encompass the other defence. If a new trial is directed, the prosecution as well as the defence may adduce further evidence. I note that the inspector of the Ministry, J.J. Ogoniek, was present at the trial but was not called by either party although his reports were filed.

### Conclusion

For these reasons, I would allow the appeal, set aside the acquittals of both respondents and direct a new trial.

*Appeal allowed; new trial ordered.*

### Questions/Discussion

1. Do you agree that ignorance of the law should be no excuse or can you think of situations where it should affect criminal liability? Do you think that the result in *Campbell* and *Mylnarchuk* is fair or that an exception should have been made in the circumstances of the case?
2. Should the defence of officially induced error be accepted in Canada? If yes, then what rationale would you use to support its acceptance and what limitations would you place on it? If no, then why not?
3. Do you think that mistakes of law versus fact can be neatly categorized as one or the other? What tests can be used to delineate the two types of mistakes? Do we in the end have to rely solely on arbitrary distinctions made by the courts in previous cases?

### Further Reading

- Kastner, N., "Mistake of Law and the Defence of Officially Induced Error" (1985-86) 28 Criminal Law Quarterly 308.
- Mewett, A., and M. Manning, *Mewett and Manning on Criminal Law*, 3rd ed. (Markham: Butterworths, 1994).
- Stuart, Don, and R. Delisle, *Learning Canadian Criminal Law, 8th ed.* (Toronto: Carswell, 2001).
- Ward, R., "Officially Induced Error of Law" (1988/89), 52 Saskatchewan Law Review 88-114.

## 7.3  POLICY DEFENCES

## 7.3.1  Entrapment

### Introduction

Entrapment generally occurs when police go beyond the use of decoys, spies and informers, and instead encourage or even pressure a person into committing an offence for the purpose of securing an arrest. English courts reject a defence of entrapment, while U.S. courts have long accepted entrapment as a substantive defence. In Canada, there has been a great deal of uncertainty about the nature of the common law defence of entrapment in the past. Should it result in an acquittal, like self-defence, or should it merely allow the court to exclude certain evidence? Alternatively, should judges leave the issue to consideration at sentencing or should a successful plea of entrapment result in a stay of proceedings? Judicial views on the nature of entrapment depend in large part on whether they see it as a matter of abusive police practice, or as an issue affecting the blameworthiness of the accused.

In the landmark decision of *Mack* in 1988, the Supreme Court of Canada finally decided many of the issues surrounding the rationale and the availability of the defence. As you will see in the case, the focus of inquiry of the courts is now on assessing the actions of the police rather than examining the accused's state of mind. Such an approach illustrates the policy basis of the defence, that the courts do not want to be a party to abusive or coercive behaviour by the police. Because of this "abuse of process" approach, the remedy adopted is not an outright acquittal but rather a "stay of proceedings" by the judge which effectively ends the proceedings against the accused. The decision put an end to a great deal of uncertainty which had surrounded the defence for a long while. *Barnes* is an example of a case decided soon after *Mack* but in which the defence of entrapment fails on the facts.

## Mack v. R.
### (1989), 67 C.R. (3d) 1 (S.C.C.)

APPEAL by accused from judgment of British Columbia Court of Appeal, 49 C.R. (3d) 169, 23 C.C.C. (3d) 421, affirming accused's conviction of possession of narcotic for the purpose of trafficking, 34 C.R. (3d) 228, and refusing stay of proceedings. December 15, 1988. The judgment of the court was delivered by
LAMER J.: —

## INTRODUCTION

The central issue in this appeal concerns the doctrine of entrapment. The parties, in essence, ask this court to outline its position on the conceptual basis for the application of the doctrine and the manner in which an entrapment claim should be dealt with by the courts. Given the length of these reasons due to the complexity of the subject, I have summarized my findings on pp. 68-71 [pp. 449-450] of these reasons.

## THE FACTS

The appellant was charged with unlawful possession of a narcotic for the purpose of trafficking. He testified at trial and, at the close of the case for the defence, brought an application for a stay of proceedings on the basis of entrapment. The application was refused and a conviction entered by Wetmore Co. Ct. J., sitting without a jury, in written reasons reported 34 C.R. (3d) 228. A notice of appeal from that decision was filed with the British Columbia Court of Appeal but the appeal books were not filed within the time prescribed. Counsel for the appellant sought and obtained, with the consent of Crown counsel, an order dispensing with the requirement that transcripts of evidence be filed and permitting counsel to base their arguments solely on the reasons for judgment of Wetmore Co. Ct. J. The Chief Justice of British Columbia directed that a panel of five judges hear the appeal. For the reasons given by Craig J.A., on behalf of the court, the appeal was dismissed. This decision is now reported at 49 C.R. (3d) 169, 23 C.C.C. (3d) 421. Leave to appeal was granted by this court.

It is necessary to describe in some detail the relevant facts. In view of the particular procedural history of this appeal, I think it is appropriate to reproduce in its entirety the summary of the evidence provided in the reasons for judgment of Wetmore Co. Ct. J. (at pp. 234-37).

> Through information obtained from an officer of the Ontario Provincial Police, one Momotiuk was brought to British Columbia. This man had apparently been dealing in narcotics in Kenora, Ontario. He was placed under police "handlers" in Vancouver, he visited the accused on a number of occasions, and eventually a transaction was set up whereby the accused would deliver cocaine to Momotiuk.
>
> The accused testified. He first met Momotiuk in 1979 in Montreal where the accused was visiting one Franks. The accused understood Franks and Momotiuk to be associated in some clothing franchise.
>
> The accused at this time was attempting to develop some property for sale near De Roche, British Columbia, and told Franks and Momotiuk of this and both expressed some interest in buying. Both arrived in British Columbia in October 1979. In the course of this visit the accused says that Momotiuk told him he was a drug trafficker in Kenora and wanted some "Thai pot". The accused says he had no interest.
>
> Momotiuk, according to the accused, called later still wanting to make drug deals, and the accused told him he was interested only in real estate deals.
>
> The accused again went to a yoga retreat near Montreal in December 1979. Franks and Momotiuk visited him there. Momotiuk produced some cocaine, which he and Franks used, and again asked the accused to become a supplier. A few days later they met again. At this time conversation was directed to show Momotiuk as an importer of drugs on a large scale, and again the accused was invited to join in and refused.
>
> In January and February there were approximately seven telephone calls from Momotiuk to the accused soliciting his involvement. The accused says he refused.
>
> In mid-February 1980 Momotiuk visited the accused again, asking him to supply drugs. The accused says he told Momotiuk he was not interested and asked to be left alone. Momotiuk continued to visit two or three times and telephoned.
>
> In March the accused says Momotiuk arrived again. They went for a walk in the woods. Momotiuk produced a pistol and was going to show the accused his markmanship. He was dissuaded because of the probability of startling the horses nearby. The accused says that at this remote area Momotiuk said, "A person could get lost." This the accused says was a threat. He says the matter of drugs was again raised and the accused says he was adamant that he had no knowledge of drug sources.
>
> The accused was asked to phone him twice and did not. One Matheson attended at the accused's residence on 13th March with a message that Momotiuk was very excited and wanted to see him at the Biltmore Hotel. The accused says he wanted nothing to do with Momotiuk but was terrified of him and agreed to go into town to the Biltmore. He also says that Matheson told him Momotiuk had some friends with him. This the accused took to be other members of this illegal syndicate.

While en route to the city he twice noted a car which seemed to be following him. This was probably so, because undercover police officers were doing a surveillance at the time.

On arrival at the hotel he met Momotiuk. Again he was informed of the syndicate. He was asked then if he wished to see the buying power. The accused agreed. He was directed to a car outside the hotel. In this car was an open briefcase with $50,000 exposed. The custodian, unknown to the accused, was an undercover policeman.

The accused returned to the hotel, Momotiuk asked him to get a sample and gave him $50 for this purpose.

The accused left and went to a supplier he had known of from years back. This supplier, one Goldsmith, now dead, heard the accused's story and agreed to supply "in order to get Doug (Momotiuk) off me". He obtained the sample and delivered it to Momotiuk, who tested it and said to get a much as he could. He returned to the supplier and offered $35,000 to $40,000 for a pound.

At the meeting the following day the accused had still not acquired the drugs and he says that at this point he was told to get his act together, in a threatening way.

I need not detail the accused's evidence of the following two days. He obtained 12 ounces of cocaine, and was to pay $27,000 for it. This credit, he says, was extended to him by Goldsmith on the basis of payment when delivered to Momotiuk. It was in the course of this delivery that he was arrested.

It is on the basis of this testimony that the accused says he was entrapped. Momotiuk, Matheson and Franks did not testify. Neither did "Bonnie", the accused's former wife, who was apparently present at one of the Montreal meetings, where cocaine was produced and some discussion took place.

The accused has drug convictions in 1972 and 1976, two in 1978 and one in 1979. Those in 1976, one in 1978 and one in 1979 involved cocaine. He says his former use of drugs arose to relieve back pain, but in 1978 he discovered relief from yoga and gave up the use of narcotics. The offence in 1979 was a fall from grace when he met up with old friends.

. . .

## POSITION OF THE PARTIES

. . .

### Appellant

The appellant asserts that there are two types of entrapment. The first is objective and involves an evaluation of police conduct in order to determine whether prosecution of the accused would amount to an abuse of the court's process. It is submitted that this analysis is a question of law to be addressed by the trial judge. If objective entrapment is found, the proper remedy is a stay of proceedings. This is purely a question of police misconduct and as such is determined wholly independently of the accused's state of mind.

The second type of entrapment is subjective and the focus is on the accused's state of mind. The test is whether the accused possesses the necessary predisposition to commit the crime; if he or she does not, then the element of mens rea is missing. This can exist, in the appellant's submission, even when the police are "blameless" in terms of the character of their conduct toward the accused.

The appellant draws an analogy to other excusing defences, such as necessity, which focus on the accused's response to a given set of facts. The appellant asserts that in subjective entrapment where the inquiry is on the accused's state of mind, like other mens rea issues, the question is one of fact to be decided by the jury. The onus would lie on the Crown to prove beyond a reasonable doubt that the accused was predisposed to commit the offence. In the result, the appellant submits, his conviction should be quashed as the trial judge stated he had a reasonable doubt as to whether the appellant was entrapped.

### Respondents

The respondent asserts that there is only one conception of entrapment and it is rooted in the doctrine of abuse of process. Entrapment is not a defence since the necessary mens rea will be present and the conduct of the accused will be neither excused nor justified. The respondent submits, however, that the test for determining whether or not there has been unlawful entrapment is an amalgam of subjective and objective tests: the defence is limited to situations where the conduct of the police has gone beyond permissible limits *and* the crime would not have been committed but for such activity. The police conduct must be, to use the respondent's phrase, the causa sine qua non of the offence.

With respect to procedural issues, the respondent asserts, the question of entrapment is one of law to be decided by the trial judge. The onus would be on the accused to establish on a balance of probabilities that the proceedings amounted to an abuse of the court's processes.

## ANALYSIS

### The Context

One need not be referred to evidence to acknowledge the ubiquitous nature of criminal activity in our society. If the struggle against crime is to be won, the ingenuity of criminals must be matched by that of the police; as crimes become more sophisticated so too must be the methods employed to detect their commission. In addition, some crimes are more difficult to detect.

. . .

I would note that in addition to so-called "victimless" or "consensual" crimes, active law enforcement techniques may be used to combat crimes where there are victims, but those victims are reluctant to go to the police because of intimidation or blackmail, as may be the case with the offence of extortion. Further, some criminal conduct may go unobserved for a long time if the victims are not immediately aware of the fact that they have been the subject of criminal activity, in the case, for example, of commercial fraud and also bribery of public officials. In general it may be said that many crimes are committed in secret and it is difficult to obtain evidence of their commission after the fact.

Obviously the police must be given considerable latitude in the effort to enforce the standards of behaviour established in the criminal law.

. . .

*There is a crucial distinction, one which is not easy to draw, however, between the police or their agents — acting on reasonable suspicion or in the course of a bona fide inquiry — providing an opportunity to a person to commit a crime, and the state actually creating a crime for the purpose of prosecution.* The former is completely acceptable, as is police conduct that is directed only at obtaining evidence of an offence when committed: see *Amato*, per Estey J. at p. 446. *The concern is rather with law enforcement techniques that involve conduct that the citizenry cannot tolerate.* In many cases the particular facts may constitute a classic example of what may be referred to as "entrapment", which has been described by an American judge as *"the conception and planning of an offense by an officer, and his procurement of its commission by one who would not have perpetrated it except for the trickery, persuasion, or fraud of the officer"*: *Sorrells v. U.S.*, 287 U.S. 435 at 454, 77 L. Ed. 413, 53 S. Ct. 210 (1932) per Roberts J., cited by Dickson C.J.C. in *Jewitt*, at p. 145.

. . .

[After a discussion of Canadian and American cases, he continues:]

### The Rationale

*The Regulation of the Administration of Justice*

It is critical in an analysis of the doctrine of entrapment to be very clear on the rationale for its recognition in Canadian criminal law. Much of what is contained in the opinion of Justice Estey in *Amato* provides this rationale. As was explained by Estey J., central to our judicial system is the belief that the integrity of the court must be attained. This is a basic principle upon which many other principles and rules depend. If the court is unable to preserve its own dignity by upholding values that our society views as essential, we will not long have a legal system which can pride itself on its commitment to justice and truth and which commands the respect of the community it serves. It is a deeply ingrained value in our democratic system that the ends do not justify the means. In particular, evidence or convictions may, at times, be obtained at too high a price. This proposition explains why as a society we insist on respect for individual rights and procedural guarantees in the criminal justice system. All of these values are reflected in specific provisions of the Charter, such as the right to counsel, the right to remain silent, the presumption of innocence and in the global concept of fundamental justice. Obviously, many of the rights in ss. 7 to 14 of the Charter relate to norms for the proper conduct of criminal investigations and trials, and the courts are called on to ensure that these standards are observed.

The principles expressed in the Charter obviously do not emerge in a legal, social or philosophical vacuum. With respect to criminal law in particular, the courts have, throughout the development of the common law and in the interpretation of statutes, consistently sought to ensure that the balance of power between the individual accused and the state was such that the interests and legitimate expectations of both would be recognized and protected. Lord Devlin, in *Connelly v. D.D.P.*, [1964] A.C. 1254, [1964] 2 W.L.R. 1145, 48 Cr. App. R. 183, [1964] 2 All E.R. 401 at 438 (H.L.), made the following apposite observation in this regard:

> ... nearly the whole of the English criminal law of procedure and evidence has been made by the exercise of the judges of their power to see that what was fair and just was done between prosecutors and accused. The doctrine of autrefois was itself doubtless evolved in that way.

It is my view that in criminal law the doctrine of abuse of process draws on the notion that the state is limited in the way it may deal with its citizens. The same may be said of the Charter, which set out particular limitations on state action and, as noted, in the criminal law context ss. 7 to 14 are especially significant.

. . .

It is the belief that the administration of justice must be kept free from disrepute that compels recognition of the doctrine of entrapment. In the context of the Charter, this court has stated that disrepute may arise from "judicial condonation of unacceptable conduct by the investigatory and prosecutional agencies": *R. v. Collins*, [1987] 1 S.C.R. 265 at 281, [1987] 3 W.W.R. 699, 13 B.C.L.R. (2d) 1, 56 C.R. (3d) 193, 33 C.C.C. (3d) 1, 38 D.L.R. (4th) 508, 28 C.R.R. 122, 74 N.R. 276. The same principle applies with respect to the common law doctrine of abuse of process. Conduct which is unacceptable is, in essence, that which violates our notions of "fair play" and "decency" and which shows blatant disregard for the qualities of humanness which all of us share.

The power of a court to enter a stay of proceedings to prevent an abuse of its process was, as noted earlier, confirmed by this court in *Jewitt, supra*. The appropriateness of the court's exercise of the power, as well as the circumstances in which it may be used, is discussed in the following passage (at pp. 136-37, per Dickson C.J.C.):

> I would adopt the conclusion of the Ontario Court of Appeal in *R. v. Young, supra* [(1984), 40 C.R. (3d) 289], and affirm that "there is a residual discretion in a trial court judge to stay proceedings where compelling an accused to stand trial would violate those fundamental principles of justice which underlie the community's sense of fair play and decency and to prevent the abuse of a court's process through oppressive or vexatious proceedings". I would also adopt the caveat added by the Court in *Young* that this is a power which can be exercised only in the "clearest of cases".

It is essential to identify why we do not accept police strategy that amounts to entrapment. There could be any number of reasons underlying what is perhaps an intuitive reaction against such law enforcement techniques but the following are, in my view, predominant. One reason is that the state does not have unlimited power to intrude into our personal lives or to randomly test the virtue of individuals. Another is the concern that entrapment techniques may result in the commission of crimes by people who would not otherwise have become involved in criminal conduct. There is perhaps a sense that the police should not themselves commit crimes or engage in unlawful activity solely for the purpose of entrapping others, as this seems to militate against the principle of the rule of law. We may feel that the manufacture of crime is not an appropriate use of the police power. It can be argued as well that people are already subjected to sufficient pressure to turn away from temptation and conduct themselves in a manner that conforms to ideals of morality; little is to be gained by adding to these existing burdens. Ultimately, we may be saying that there are inherent limits on the power of the state to manipulate people and events for the purpose of attaining the specific objective of obtaining convictions. These reasons and others support the view that there is a societal interest in limiting the use of entrapment techniques by the state.

The competing social interest is in the repression of criminal activity. Further, our dependence on the police to actively protect us from the immense social and personal cost of crime must be acknowledged. There will be differing views as to the appropriate balance between the concepts of fairness and justice and the need for protection from crime, but it is my opinion that it is universally recognized that some balance is absolutely essential to our conception of civilized society. In deciding where the balance lies in any given case it is necessary to recall the key elements of our model of fairness and justice, as this is the only manner in which we can judge the legitimacy of a particular law enforcement technique.

It must be stressed, however, that the central issue is not the power of a court to *discipline* police or prosecutorial conduct but, as stated by Estey J. in *Amato* (at p. 461), "the avoidance of the improper invocation by the state of the judicial process and its powers". In the entrapment context, the court's sense of justice is offended by the spectacle of an accused being convicted of an offence which is the work of the state (*Amato*, at p. 447). The court is, in effect, saying it cannot condone or be seen to lend a stamp of approval to behaviour which transcends what our society perceives to be acceptable on the part of the state. The stay of the prosecution of the accused is the manifestation of the court's disapproval of the state's conduct. The issuance of the stay obviously benefits the accused but the court is primarily concerned with a larger issue: the maintenance of public confidence in the legal and judicial process. In this way, the benefit to the accused is really a derivative one. We should affirm the decision of Estey J. in *Amato*, that *the basis upon which entrapment is recognized lies in the need to preserve the purity of administration of justice.*

### The Guilt of the Accused

Both the appellant and respondent agree that the rationale for recognition of the entrapment doctrine lies in the inherent jurisdiction of the court to prevent an abuse of it own processes. The respondent asserts that this is the exclusive rationale; the appellant submits that it is open to the court to view entrapment as also bearing on the accused's culpability and as such it would operated as a substantive defence.

It is not fruitful, in my view , to deal with impermissible police conduct through the vehicle of substantive criminal law doctrine. There are three problems with the appellant's proposition. Firstly, the conduct of the police or their agents in most cases will not have the effect of negativing mens rea or, for that matter, actus reus. (There may be exceptional cases, however: see, for example, the decision of this court in *Lemieux v. R.*, [1967] S.C.R. 492, 2 C.R.N.S. 1, [1968] 1 C.C.C. 187, 63 D.L.R. (2d) 75 [Ont.].) The physical act of the accused is a voluntary one and the accused will have an aware state of mind. The prohibited act will have been committed intentionally and with knowledge of the facts which constitute the offence and the consequences which flow from them.

However they may be defined, the essential elements of the offence in issue will have been met in most cases, and it is from this general position that the doctrine of entrapment should develop.

. . .

Secondly, while the argument that the accused is not culpable because his or her conduct may be excused is more plausible, it is ultimately not compelling. For entrapment to be recognized as an excusing defence, it is clear that the focus must be directed at the effect of the external or internal circumstances on the accused.

. . .

There is a third and perhaps more fundamental problem with the notion that entrapment relates to the blameworthiness or culpability of the accused: if this is the proper theoretical foundation for allowing the claim of entrapment, then on what principled basis can we justify limiting the defence to situations where it is the state, and not a private citizen, who is the entrapping party? Professor Colvin makes this point in the following passage (at p. 232):

> Considering entrapment from the standpoint of the theory of criminal culpability, the better arguments are for recognizing the defence in a procedural rather than an exculpatory form. This is not to deny that circumstances of entrapment can sometimes provide an excuse which might merit recognition by way of a special defence. But, if the argument for an excusing defence is accepted, it demands much more than the entrapment defence as it has been hitherto conceived. The arguments for an entrapment defence have been made with respect to entrapment by the police or their agents. Yet in almost all cases, the accused would not have known who was entrapping him. It is therefore immaterial to his culpability whether it happened to be the police or someone else. The argument for an excusing defence can only be sustained as an argument for a defence of wider application, available wherever someone has been pressured into committing an offence by another person. The defence of duress represents a limited concession to the view that exculpation can be appropriate in this kind of situation. There has, however, been little support for extending its rationale to cases of persistent solicitation. In addition, the arguments for making entrapment an excusing defence have generally been confined to entrapment by the police or their agents. If the defence is to be subject to this limitation, it is best conceived as an aspect of abuse of process. [citations omitted]

. . .

I remain firmly of the view that the true basis for allowing an accused the defence of entrapment is *not* culpability. I will summarize the main reasons. Firstly, in most cases the essential elements of the offence will have been met. Secondly, the circumstances in which an accused is placed in an entrapment situation are not agonizing in the sense acknowledged by the defences of duress or necessity. Where the police conduct does amount to duress, that defence can be pleaded in conjunction with an abuse of process allegation. I would not, however, that any "threats" by the police, even if insufficient to support the defence of duress, will be highly relevant in the assessment of police conduct for the purpose of an abuse of process claim. The third reason why I am unwilling to view entrapment as relating to culpability is that if it did, there would not be a valid basis on which to limit the defence to entrapment by the state. The lack of support for an extension of the defence to provide against entrapment by private citizens demonstrates that the real problem is with the propriety of the state employing such law enforcement techniques for the purpose of obtaining convictions. If this is accepted, then it follows that the focus must be on the police conduct.

### The Proper Approach

. . .

To summarize then, the police must not, and it is entrapment to do so, offer people opportunities to commit crime unless they have a reasonable suspicion that such people are already engaged in criminal activity or unless such an offer is made in the course of a bona fide investigation. In addition, the mere existence of a prior record is not usually sufficient to ground a "reasonable suspicion". These situations will be rare, in my opinion. If the accused is not alleging this form of entrapment, the central question in a particular case will be: Have the police gone further than providing an opportunity and instead employed tactics designed to induce someone into the commission of an offence?

There is, therefore, entrapment when (a) the authorities provide an opportunity to persons to commit an offence without reasonable suspicion or acting mala fides, as explained earlier, or (b) having a reasoning suspicion or acting in the course of a bona fide inquiry, they go beyond providing an opportunity and induce the commission of an offence. As I have already mentioned, the first form of entrapment is not likely to occur. The police of this country are generally resorting to the type of investigatory technique of providing opportunities only in relation to targeted people or locations clearly, and therefore reasonably, suspected of being involved in or associated with criminal activity, or again are already engaged in a bona fide investigation justifying the provision of such opportunities.

As regards the latter form of entrapment, to determine whether police conduct gives rise to this concern, it is useful to consider whether the conduct of the police would have induced the average person in the position of the accused, i.e., a person with both strengths and weaknesses, into committing the crime. I believe such a test is useful not only as an analytical mechanism that is consistent with objective analysis, but also because it corresponds to one of the reasons why the defence is thought desirable. In other words, it may be inevitable that when apprised of the factual context of an entrapment case, members of the community will put themselves in the position of the accused; if a common response would be that anyone could have been induced by such conduct, this is a valuable sign that the police have exceeded the bounds of propriety. The reasoning does not go so far as to imply that the accused is therefore less blameworthy; rather, it suggests that the state is involved in the *manufacture* as opposed to the detection of crime.

An objective approach which uses the hypothetical person test only is subject to some criticism. For example, Professor Park argues (at pp. 270-71):

> The defence creates a risk that dangerous chronic offenders will be acquitted because they were offered inducements that might have tempted a hypothetical law abiding person. More subtly, it creates a danger that persons will be convicted who do not deserve punishment. This danger stems from its attempts to evaluate the quality of government conduct without considering the defendant's culpability. The notion that sauce for the wolf is sauce for the lamb leads to unhappy consequences, since the sauce will be brewed with wolves in mind. Because many targets are professional criminals, judges will be reluctant to rule that entrapment has occurred simply because an agent found it necessary to appeal to friendship, make multiple requests, or offer a substantial profit. Yet approval of such conduct would lead to unfair results in cases where the target was law-abiding but ductile. For example, conviction of someone who has been solicited by a friend may be fair enough in the general run of cases, but unfair if the target was a nonpredisposed person who would not have committed the type of crime charged but for a request from that particular friend.

The response to this is twofold. Firstly, I agree that there is a danger of convicting "lambs" or people who have a particular vulnerability such as a mental handicap or who are suffering from an addiction. In those situations, it is desirable for the purposes of analysis to consider whether the conduct was likely to induce criminal conduct in those people who share the characteristic which appears to have been exploited by the police. I am not, however, in agreement with the assertion that it is fair for the police in the general run of cases to abuse a close relationship between friends or family members, as compared to that between acquaintances, contacts or associates, for the purpose of inducing someone into the commission of an offence, and thus I do not consider this a valid criticism of the hypothetical person test. The nature of the relationship at issue is relevant and in certain cases it may be that the police have exploited confidence and trust between people in such a manner as to offend the value society places on maintaining the dignity and privacy of interpersonal relationships.

Secondly, I do not find the danger of acquitting wolves particularly troublesome. It assumes that it cannot be said that chance exists that a predisposed person would not have committed the particular offence were it not for the use of inducement that would have caused a nonpredisposed person to commit the offence. More fundamentally, this perspective is part of a larger view-point that in certain cases it would be better for society to send someone to jail for committing a crime, even if fundamental rights and procedural guarantees normally provided to an accused have been disregarded. The familiar refrain is that the end justifies the means. This view is, however, entirely inconsistent with the model of fairness which exists both within and alongside substantive criminal law doctrine. Could not the same comment of "acquitting wolves" be made where an accused's right to counsel or to remain silent have been flagrantly violated and the evidence of his or her confession to the crime is excluded? In the short term, it may well be "better" for society to convict such persons, but it has always been held that in the long term it would undermine the system itself. If the rule of law is to have any meaning and provide the security which all in society desire, it is axiomatic that it be extended to every individual.

I am not of the view that the hypothetical or average person model is the *only* relevant method of analysis. There may be situations where it cannot be concluded that a hypothetical person would likely have committed the offence under the same circumstances, and yet the presence of other factors supports the conclusion that the police involvement in the instigation of crime has exceeded the bounds of propriety.

. . .

## SUMMARY

In conclusion, and to summarize, the proper approach to the doctrine of entrapment is that which was articulated by Estey J. in *Amato,* and elaborated upon in these reasons. As mentioned and explained earlier, there is entrapment when:

(a) the authorities provide a person with a opportunity to commit an offence without acting on a reasonable suspicion that this person is already engaged in criminal activity or pursuant to a bona fide inquiry; or

(b) although having such a reasonable suspicion or acting in the course of a bona fide inquiry, they go beyond providing an opportunity and induce the commission of an offence.

It is neither useful nor wise to state in the abstract what elements are necessary to prove an entrapment allegation. It is, however, essential that the factors relied on by a court relate to the underlying reasons for the recognition of the doctrine in the first place.

Since I am of the view that the doctrine of entrapment is not dependent upon culpability, the focus should not be on the effect of the police conduct on the accused's state of mind. Instead, it is my opinion that as far as possible an objective assessment of the conduct of the police and their agents is required. The predisposition, or the past, present or suspective criminal activity, of the accused is relevant only as a part of the determination of whether the provision of an opportunity by the authorities to the accused to commit the offence was justifiable. Further, there must be sufficient connection between the past conduct of the accused and the provision of an opportunity, since otherwise the police suspicion will not be reasonable. While disposition of the accused is, though not conclusive, of some relevance in assessing the initial approach by the police of a person with the offer of an opportunity to commit an offence, *it is never relevant* as regards whether they went beyond an offer, since that is to be assessed with regard to what the average non-predisposed person would have done.

The absence of a reasonable suspicion or a bona fide inquiry is significant in assessing the police conduct because of the risk that the police will attract people who would not otherwise have any involvement in a crime and because it is not a proper use of the police powers to simply go out and test the virtue of people on a random basis. The presence of reasonable suspicion or the mere existence of a bona fide inquiry will, however, never justify entrapment techniques: the police may not go beyond providing an opportunity, regardless of their perception of the accused's character and regardless of the existence of an hones inquiry. To determine whether the police have employed means which go further than providing an opportunity it is useful to consider any or all of the following factors:

— the type of crime being investigated and the availability of other techniques for the police detection of its commission;

— whether an average person, with both strengths and weaknesses, in the position of the accused would be induced into the commission of a crime;

— the persistence and number of attempts made by the police before the accused agreed to committing the offence;

— the type of inducement used by the police, including deceit, fraud, trickery or reward;

— the timing of the police conduct, in particular whether the police have instigated the offence or became involved in ongoing criminal activity;

— whether the police conduct involves an exploitation of human characteristics such as emotions of compassion, sympathy and friendship;

— whether the police appear to have exploited a particular vulnerability of a person such as a mental handicap or a substance addiction;

— the proportionality between the police involvement, as compared to the accused, including an assessment of the degree of harm caused or risked by the police, as compared to the accused, and the commission of any illegal acts by the police themselves;

— the existence of any threats, implied or express, made to the accused by the police or their agents; and

— whether the police conduct is directed at undermining other constitutional values.

This list is not exhaustive, but I hope it contributes to the elaboration of a structure for the application of the entrapment doctrine. Thus far, I have not referred to the requirement in *Amato*, per Estey J., that the conduct must, in all the circumstances, be shocking or outrageous. I am of the view that this is a factor which is best considered under procedural issues to which I will now turn.

## PROCEDURAL ISSUES

The resolution of the issues surrounding the manner in which an entrapment claim should be considered at trial is, in my view, entirely dependent upon the conceptual basis for the defence, outlined earlier. If I were of the opinion that there was a substantive or culpability-based defence of entrapment, I would readily come to the conclusion that the defence raised a question of fact, which should be decided by a jury when there is a sufficient evidentiary basis on which to raise the defence, and I would hold that the onus would rest on the crown to disprove the existence of entrapment beyond a reasonable doubt. Having come to the opposite view-point on the rationale for recognizing the doctrine of entrapment. I am not persuaded that the adoption of rules which historically, and by virtue of the Charter, conform to most substantive defences is either necessary or correct. It seems to me, however, that this court must be clear on how an entrapment claim is to be handled, as a brief review of some lower court decisions suggests that there is, at present, and understandably so, a great deal of confusion on the matter.

### *Who Decides: Judge or Jury?*

Both the appellant and the respondent agree that objective entrapment, involving police misconduct and not the accused's state of mind, is a question to be decided by the trial judge and that the proper remedy is a stay of proceedings. I too am of this view. The question of unlawful involvement by the state in the instigation of criminal conduct is one of law, or mixed law and fact. In *Jewitt*, in a passage cited previously, Dickson C.J.C. expressed this opinion (at p. 145): "Staying proceedings on the basis of abuse of process, and in particular, on the basis of the defence of entrapment, in my view, amounts to a decision on a complex question of law and fact."

. . .

### *Who Bears the Burden of Proof and on What Standard?*

In my opinion the best way to achieve a balance between the interests of the court as guardian of the administration of justice and the interests of society in the prevention and detection of crime is to require an accused to demonstrate by a preponderance of evidence that the prosecution is an abuse of process because of entrapment. I would also note that this is consistent with the rules governing s. 24(2) applications (*Collins*, supra, at p. 277), where the general issue is similar to that raised in entrapment cases: Would the administration of justice be brought into disrepute?

. . .

In conclusion, the onus lies on the accused to demonstrate that the police conduct has gone beyond permissible limits to the extent that allowing the prosecution or the entry of a conviction would amount to an abuse of the judicial process by the state. The question is one of mixed law and fact and should be resolved by the trial judge. A stay should be entered in the "clearest of cases" only.

## DISPOSITION

In determining whether the doctrine of entrapment applies to the present appeal, this court is restricted to the summary of evidence provided by Westmore Co. Ct J. in his reasons. I am of the view that a stay of proceedings should be entered in this case. While the trial judge had the advantage of hearing the testimony of the appellant, and normally findings on entrapment cases should not be disturbed because of this, I am concerned that in this case too much emphasis was placed on the appellant's state of mind. Earlier in my summary of the decisions below I cited a passage from the trial judge's reasons wherein he stated that the fundamental issue was the appellant's state of mind and his predisposition to crime. This, perhaps, explains why in his conclusion the trial judge stated the appellant was not entrapped because he acted out of a desire to profit from the transaction. If the trial judge had been permitted only to evaluate the conduct of the police objectively, I think he might well have and, in any event, ought to have come to the conclusion that the police conduct amounted to entrapment.

From the facts it appears that the police had reasonable suspicion that the appellant was involved in criminal conduct. The issue is whether the police went too far in their efforts to attract the appellant into the commission of the offence.

Returning to the list of factors I outlined earlier, this crime is obviously one for which the state must be given substantial leeway. The drug trafficking business is not one which lends itself to the traditional devices of police investigation. It is absolutely essential, therefore, for police or their agents to get involved and gain the trust and confidence of the people who did the trafficking or who supply the drugs. It is also a crime of enormous social consequence which causes a great deal of harm in society generally. This factor alone is very critical and makes this case somewhat difficult.

The police do not appear, however, to have been interrupting an ongoing criminal enterprise, and the offence was clearly brought about by their conduct and would not have occurred absent their involvement. The police do not appear to have exploited a narcotics addiction of the appellant, since he testified that he had already given up his use of narcotics. Therefore he was not, at the time, trying to recover from an addiction. Nonetheless, he also testified that he was no longer involved in drugs and, if this is true, it suggests that the police were indeed trying to make the appellant take up his former lifestyle. The persistence of the police requests, as a result of the equally persistent refusals by the appellant, supports the appellant's version of events on this point. The length of time, approximately six months, and the repetition of requests it took before the appellant agreed to commit the offence also demonstrate that the police had to go further than merely providing the appellant with the opportunity once it became evident that he was unwilling to join the alleged drug syndicate.

Perhaps the most important and determinative factor in my opinion is the appellant's testimony that the informer acted in a threatening manner when they went for a walk in the woods, and the further testimony that he was told to get his act together after he did not provide the supply of drugs he was asked for. I believe this conduct was unacceptable. If the police must go this far, they have gone beyond providing the appellant with an opportunity. I do not, therefore, place much significance on the fact that the appellant eventually committed the offence when shown the money. Obviously the appellant knew much earlier that he could make a profit by getting involved in the drug enterprise and he still refused. I have come to the conclusion that the average person in the position of the appellant might also have committed the offence, if only to finally satisfy this threatening informer and end all further contact. As a result I would, on the evidence, have to find that the police conduct in this case was unacceptable. Thus, the doctrine of entrapment applies to preclude the prosecution of the appellant. In my opinion the appellant has met the buren of proof and the trial judge should have entered a stay of proceedings for abuse of process.

I would accordingly allow the appeal, set aside the conviction of the appellant, order a new trial and enter a stay of proceedings.

*Appeal allowed.*

# Barnes v. R.
## (1991), 3 C.R. (4th) 1 (S.C.C.)

February 28, 1991. LAMER C.J.C. (WILSON, LA FOREST, SOPINKA, GON-THIER, CORY and STEVENSON JJ. concurring): —

This case involved a consideration of the defence of entrapment as set out by this Court in *R. v. Mack*, [1988] 2 S.C.R. 903, 67 C.R. (3d) 1, [1989] 1 W.W.R. 577, 90 N.R. 173, 44 C.C.C. (3d) 513, 37 C.R.R. 277. In particular, this Court is asked whether the accused was subjected to random virtue-testing by an undercover police officer in the city of Vancouver. This case also raises the question of whether this Court, at the request of the Crown, has jurisdiction to modify the decision of a court of appeal which has allowed an appeal by the Crown from a judicial stay of proceedings entered at trial.

### Facts

On January 12, 1989, the appellant sold one gram of hashish to an undercover police officer near the Granville Mall area of Vancouver. The parties do not dispute the facts surrounding the sale which are as follow:

The undercover officer was involved in a "buy-and-bust" operation conducted by the Vancouver Police Department. In a buy-and-bust operation, undercover police officers attempt to buy illicit drugs from individuals who appear, in the opinion of the officers, to be inclined to sell such drugs. If an officer is successful, the individual is immediately arrested for trafficking.

This particular operation was undertaken by the Department with respect to the Granville Mall area in the city of Vancouver, which covers a six-block section of Granville Street. On the day of the arrest, the undercover officer approached the accused, Philip Barnes, and his friend, as they were walking towards Granville Street. The officer testified at trial that she approached the accused and his friend because she had "a hunch, a feeling that they'd — possibly might be in possession." She believed that he and his friend fit the description of persons who possibly had drugs in their possession, and who would be willing to sell to her. "I had a feeling. They fit my general criteria. I look for males hanging around, dressed scruffy and in jeans, wearing a jean jacket or leather jacket, runners or black boots, that tend to look at people a lot."

The officer indicated that there was nothing else that aroused her suspicions. The officer approached the accused and asked him if he had any "weed". He said "no", but his friend repeated to him: "She wants some weed." The accused again responded negatively. The officer persisted and the accused then agreed to sell a small amount of cannabis resin to the officer for $15.00. Shortly afterwards, the accused was arrested by another officer and small amounts of cannabis resin and marijuana were seized from his person.

The accused was tried in the Country Court of Vancouver before Leggatt Co. Ct. J., and was found guilty of trafficking in cannabis resin, of the included offence of possession of cannabis resin for the purpose of trafficking, and of possession of marijuana. The accused conceded that he sold illicit drugs to the officer, but argued that a judicial stay for entrapment should be directed. He claimed that he had no intention of selling drugs on the day in question, but felt sorry for the undercover officer; he agreed to sell only because he believed that his friend wanted to meet a woman and that this was a way of gaining an introduction. The trial Judge held that the police officer had engaged in "random virtue testing", which was unacceptable according to the judgment of this Court in *Mack*, supra, and therefore ordered a judicial stay of the proceedings.

The British Columbia Court of Appeal allowed the Crown's appeal and ordered a new trial. . . .

## Analysis

### Did the Police Officer Engage in Random Virtue-Testing?

To resolve this appeal, this Court must consider whether the conduct of the undercover police officer was acceptable in light of the guidelines set out in *Mack*. In *Mack*, I attempted to define the circumstances in which police conduct in the course of investigating and uncovering criminal activity ceases to be acceptable and, instead, amounts to the unacceptable entrapment of individuals. The defence of entrapment is based on the notion that limits should be imposed on the ability of the police to participate in the commission of an offence. As a general rule, it is expected in our society that the police will direct their attention towards uncovering criminal activity that occurs without their involvement. . . .

It is apparent that the police officer involved in this case did not have a "reasonable suspicion" that the accused was already engaged in unlawful drug-related activity. The factors that drew the officer's attention to this particular accused — his manner of dress, the length of his hair — were not sufficient to give rise to a reasonable suspicion that criminal acts were being committed. Furthermore, the subjectiveness of the officer's decision to approach the accused, based on a "hunch" or "feeling" rather than extrinsic evidence, also indicates that the accused did not, as an individual, arouse a reasonable suspicion.

Consequently, the police conduct in this case will amount to entrapment *unless* the office presented the accused with the opportunity to sell drugs *in the course of a bona fide inquiry*. In my opinion, the police officer involved in this case was engaged in such a *bona fide* investigation. First, there is no question that the officer's conduct was motivated by the genuine purpose of investigating and repressing criminal activity. The police department had reasonable grounds for believing that drug-related crimes were occurring throughout the Granville Mall area. The accused was not, therefore, approached for questionable motives unrelated to the investigation and repression of crime.

Secondly, the police department directed its investigation at a suitable area within the city of Vancouver. As I noted in *Mack*, the police may present the opportunity to commit a particular crime to persons who are associated with a location where it is reasonably suspected that criminal activity is taking place. . . .

The police department in this case focused its investigation on an area of Vancouver, a section of Granville Street covering approximately 6 city blocks, where it was reasonably suspected that drug-related crimes were occurring. In my opinion, they would not have been able to deal with the problem effectively had they restricted the investigation to a smaller area. Although there were particular areas within the Granville Mall where drug trafficking was especially serious, it is true that trafficking occurred at locations scattered generally throughout the Mall. It is also true that traffickers did not operate in a single place. It would be unrealistic for the police to focus their investigation on one specific part of the Mall given the tendency of traffickers to modify their techniques in response to police investigations. The trial Judge admitted that the Mall was "known as an area of considerable drug activity." Similarly, the Court of Appeal found support in the evidence given at trial by Staff Sergeant Davies of the Vancouver City Police. . . .

It is, therefore, my opinion that the police department was engaged, in these circumstances, in a bona fide inquiry.

I note that in many cases, the size of the area itself may indicate that the investigation is not bona fide. This will be so particularly when there are grounds for believing that the criminal activity being investigated is concentrated in part of a larger area targeted by the police. In this case, however, for the reasons discussed above, it was reasonable for the Vancouver Police Department to focus its investigation on the Granville Mall.

The accused argues that although the undercover officer was involved in a bona fide inquiry, she nevertheless engaged in random virtue-testing since she approached the accused without a reasonable suspicion that he was likely to commit a drug-related offence. She approached the accused simply because he was walking near Granville Street.

In my respectful opinion, this argument is based on a misinterpretation of *Mack*. I recognize that some of my language in *Mack* might be responsible for this misinterpretation. In particular, as noted above, I stated, at p. 956 [S.C.R.; pp. 42-43 C.R.]:

> "In those cases [where there is a particular location where it is reasonably suspected that certain crimes are taking place] it is clearly permissible to provide opportunities to people associated with the location under suspicion, even if these people are not themselves under suspicion. This latter situation, however, is only justified if the police acted in the course of a *bona fide* investigation and are not engaged in random virtue-testing."

This statement should not be taken to mean that the police may not approach people on a random basis, in order to present the opportunity to commit an offence, in the course of a bona fide investigation. The basic rule articulated in *Mack* is that the police may only present the opportunity to commit a particular crime to an individual who arouses a suspicion that he or she is already engaged in the particular criminal activity. An exception to this rule arises when the police undertake a bona fide investigation directed at an area where it is reasonably suspected that criminal activity is occurring. When such a location is defined with sufficient precision, the police may present *any* person associated with the area with the opportunity to commit the particular offence. Such randomness is permissible within the scope of a bona fide inquiry.

Random virtue-testing, conversely, only arises when a police officer presents a person with the opportunity to commit an offence *without* a reasonable suspicion that:

(a) the person is already engaged in the particular criminal activity, or

(b) the physical location with which the person is associated is a place where the particular criminal activity is likely occurring.

In this case, the accused was approached by the officer when he was walking near the Granville Mall. The notion of being "associated" with a particular area for these purposes does not require more than being *present* in the area. As a result, the accused was associated with a location where it was reasonably believed that drug-related crimes were occurring. The officer's conduct was therefore justified under the first branch of the test for entrapment set out in *Mack*.

For these reasons, it is my opinion that the officer did not engage in random virtue-testing in this case. I would, therefore, dismiss the appeal and uphold the decision of the Court of Appeal ordering a new trial. . . .

[Lamer then addressed the question of whether the court had jurisdiction to enter convictions with respect to the charges.]

*Appeal dismissed.*

## Questions/Discussion

1. What is the nature and availability of the defence of entrapment in Canada today? Do you agree with the defence as it is currently set out? Why or why not?

2. In practice, entrapment arises mostly in connection with vice offences, primarily narcotics. This occurs because police routinely pursue narcotics offenders with zealous aggression (See Alexander under Further Reading). For example, while crossing a Vancouver street, an undercover R.C.M.P. officer was mistaken for a heroin user by two Vancouver police, who punched and kicked him to the ground and struck him with a flashlight. The police were convicted but probably only because their victim was also a police officer (*ibid.*). Because most Canadians, and most judges, mistakenly believe that the use and sale of narcotics is a major social threat, the courts in the past have been remarkably accepting of abusive police practices in the drug field. Do you think that the decision in *Mack* will represent a real change either in the way the police go about their business or in the leeway the courts have given to police in the past?

3. Entrapment cases represent the problems that arise when narrow, legalistic solutions are sought for more fundamental failures. For example, in regard to the control of narcotics in Canada, the laws set police an impossible task: the legal system lacks the resources to arrest all drug offenders, let alone send them to trial and prison. Despite increased policing over the last decade, drug potency and availability have increased and prices have fallen. Worse, police are forced to risk their own safety when their sacrifice is not only useless, but destructive to society. Police leaders, however, find the drug war useful because it allows them to expand their budget and workforce, and to push police in the schools as "drug educators". The solution to abusive police practices in the narcotics field is to abolish all drug prohibitions, but this solution is political, not legal. Judges are limited in what they can do to remedy the problem of overly aggressive police work. But before *Mack*, judges had not come close to exploiting the limited powers they did possess. Given existing attitudes toward drug

use in this country, do you think that there is much hope this situation will change after the decision in *Mack*?

## Further Reading

- Alexander, B., *Peaceful Measures: Canada's Alternatives to the War on Drugs* (Toronto: University of Toronto Press, 1990).
- France, S., "Problems in the Defence of Entrapment" (1988), 22 University of British Columbia Law Review 1.
- Frankel, S. D., "An Overview of the Law of Entrapment" (1991), 49 Advocate 591-594
- Roach, Kent, *Criminal Law, 2nd ed.* (Toronto: Irwin Law, 2000) at 35-37.
- Stober, M., "Persistent Importuning for a Defence of Entrapment" (1988), 33 McGill Law Journal 400.
- Stober, M., "The Limits of Police Provocation in Canada" (1992), 34 Criminal Law Quarterly 290-348.
- Stuart, Don, and R. Delisle, *Learning Canadian Criminal Law, 8th ed.* (Toronto: Carswell, 2001).
- Stuart, D., "*Mack*, Resolving Many But Not All Questions of Entrapment" (1989), 67 C.R. (3d) 68.

## 7.3.2 Charter Protections

### Introduction

It has been more than twenty years since the advent of the *Canadian Charter of Rights and Freedoms,* and the effect on criminal law has been profound. But because this chapter, for the most part, examines substantive defences, and because the breadth of Charter defences is so great (and the focus of books and series), any attempt at a detailed examination here is not possible or worthwhile. As a result, there is only one reading, an excerpt by Cromwell, which gives a very brief overview of a number of different areas of criminal law in which the Charter has made a difference. It is by no means comprehensive, but is intended to give the reader a very brief introduction to some of the effects that the Charter has had on criminal law. For those readers interested in reading further on Charter issues, please refer to the selections under Further Reading, below.

What can be seen to date is a plethora of legal arguments by defence counsel related to the Charter, coupled with a willingness on the part of the courts to intervene more forthrightly than many would have imagined given the conservative, non-interventionist record of the courts before 1982 (see Hovius and Martin under Further Reading). The decision striking down the abortion provisions in the Criminal Code is perhaps the most visible and well known intervention to date, and the case brought home forcefully to the general public the new role which the Charter and therefore the courts are playing in the formation of criminal justice policy (see Chapter 3). In this regard, the inherent dangers of the lack of accountability and expertise, of the use of narrow, legalistic approaches to social problems, and of the lack of access to the courts should be kept in mind.

The sections of the Charter affecting criminal law and procedure are primarily the "legal rights" in sections 7-14, though certainly this is not exclusively so. For example, the so-called "fundamental freedoms" listed in section 2, listing such freedoms as freedom of thought, belief, opinion and expression, and freedom of association, could have a real effect on many aspects of the criminal law, notably as to the limits of state interference regarding obscenity. The equality provisions in section 15 could also play a role in the future, for example in regard to gender-biased sections of the criminal law such as infanticide.

Finally, note that the effects of the Charter can be felt in different ways. The courts may declare certain criminal provisions as contrary to the Charter and therefore of no validity and effect. On the other hand, certain procedures or tactics of the police may be found to be offensive to the principles expressed in the Charter and thus any evidence obtained as a result of such could be excluded from the case under section 24 of the Charter. In the latter situation, the police would presumably change their practices so as not to offend the Charter and to prevent the exclusion of evidence in the future.

## Selected sections from the *Canadian Charter of Rights and Freedoms*

*Guarantee of Rights and Freedoms*

1. The Canadian Charter of Rights and Freedoms guarantees the rights and freedoms set out in it subject only to such reasonable limits prescribed by law as can be demonstrably justified in a free and democratic society.

*Fundamental Freedoms*

2. Everyone has the following fundamental freedoms:
    a) freedom of conscience and religion;
    b) freedom of thought, belief, opinion and expression, including freedom of the press and other media of communication;
    c) freedom of peaceful assembly; and
    d) freedom of association.

. . .

*Legal Rights*

7. Everyone has the right to life, liberty and security of the person and the right not to be deprived thereof except in accordance with the principles of fundamental justice.
8. Everyone has the right to be secure against unreasonable search or seizure.
9. Everyone has the right not to be arbitrarily detained or imprisoned.
10. Everyone has the right on arrest or detention
    a) to be informed promptly of the reasons therefor;
    b) to retain and instruct counsel without delay and to be informed of that right; and

c)  to have the validity of the detention determined by way of habeas corpus and to be released if the detention is not lawful.

. . .

11. Any person charged with an offence has the right
    a)  to be informed without unreasonable delay of the specific offence;
    b)  to be tried within a reasonable time;
    c)  not to be compelled to be a witness in proceedings against that person in respect of the offence;
    d)  to be presumed innocent until proven guilty according to law in a fair and public hearing by an independent and impartial tribunal;
    e)  not to be denied reasonable bail without just cause;
    f)  except in the case of an offence under military law tried before a military tribunal, to the benefit of trial by jury where the maximum punishment for the offence is imprisonment for five years or a more severe punishment;
    g)  not to be found guilty on account of any act or omission unless, at the time of the act or omission, it constituted an offence under Canadian or international law or was criminal according to the general principles of law recognized by the community of nations;
    h)  if finally acquitted of the offence, not to be tried for it again and, if finally found guilty and punished for the offence, not to be tried or punished for it again; and
    i)  if found guilty of the offence and if the punishment for the offence has been varied between the time of commission and the time of sentencing, to the benefit of the lesser punishment.

12. Everyone has the right not to be subjected to any cruel and unusual treatment or punishment.

13. A witness who testifies in any proceedings has the right not to have any incriminating evidence so given used to incriminate that witness in any other proceedings, except in a prosecution for perjury or for the giving of contradictory evidence.

14. A party or witness in any proceedings who does not understand or speak the language in which the proceedings are conducted or who is deaf has the right to the assistance of an interpreter.

*Equality Rights*

15. (1) Every individual is equal before and under the law and has the right to the equal protection and equal benefit of the law without discrimination and, in particular, without discrimination based on race, national or ethnic origin, colour, religion, sex, age or mental or physical disability.

(2) Subsection (1) does not preclude any law, program or activity that has as its object the amelioration of conditions of disadvantaged individuals or groups

including those that are disadvantaged because of race, national or ethnic origin, colour, religion, sex, age or mental or physical disability.

. . .

*Enforcement*

24. (1) Anyone whose rights or freedoms, as guaranteed by this Charter, have been infringed or denied may apply to a court of competent jurisdiction to obtain such remedy as the court considers appropriate and just in the circumstances.
(2) Where, in proceedings under subsection (1), a court concludes that evidence was obtained in a manner that infringed or denied any rights or freedoms guaranteed by this Charter, the evidence shall be excluded if it is established that, having regard to all the circumstances, the admission of it in the proceedings would bring the administration of justice into disrepute.

. . .

# Canadian Charter of Rights and Freedoms*
## *Thomas A. Cromwell*

*Excerpts from "Canadian Charter of Rights and Freedoms" in Joel E. Pink and David C. Perrier, eds., *From Crime to Punishment: An Introduction to the Criminal Law System* (Toronto: Carswell, 1999) at 385–395.

. . .

One way to illustrate some of the changes brought about by the *Charter* is to examine a case decided before the *Charter* came into force and then to consider how the *Charter* might affect the Court's reasoning and decision if the same case came before the Court after the *Charter*. Let us take the famous case of *R. v. Wray*.

Wray was charged with murder and, while in police custody, was subjected to prolonged questioning and prevented by trickery from seeing a lawyer who had been retained for him by his family. At the end of this questioning the accused led the police to the location where what subsequently proved to be the murder weapon was recovered.

The facts relating to the interrogation of Wray, taken from Chief Justice Cartright's judgment in the Supreme Court of Canada. Were as follows:

On June 4, 1968, shortly after 10 a.m., Inspector Lidstone of the Ontario Provincial Police drove up to the respondent's [Wray's] home and asked the respondent to accompany him to police headquarters in Peterborough. From then until 7:18 p.m. On the same day the respondent was continuously with the police and one Jurems, a private investigator, who, as the learned trial Judge found, was acting for and with the police and was as regards the respondent a person in authority. At 7:18 p.m., the respondent signed a statement in the form of questions and answers written by Inspector Lidstone. If admitted it would have been evidence on which the jury could have convicted the respondent of the charge against him. It ended as follows:

Q. What happened to the gun?
A. I threw it in the swamp.
Q. Where?

A. Near Omemee.
Q. Will you try and show us the spot?
A. Yes.
Q. Is there anything else you wish to add to this John?
A. Not now thank you.

(signed) John Wray
7.18 p.m.

At 7:25 p.m. the police set out with the respondent in their car, followed by Jurems in another car, and were directed by the respondent to the locality where, as a result of what he told them, they found the rifle the following day.

During the afternoon of June 4, 1968, Mr. Gordon, a lawyer retained by the respondent's family, attempted to get in touch with the police by telephone but the police did not return his calls. Asked why they had not done so, Inspector Lidstone said in cross-examination:

> . . .we did not want to take a chance that Mr. Wray as a result of speaking to Mr. Gordon wouldn't take the police out to where the gun was found.

Under the common law rules, Wray's statement to the police was excluded because it was obtained by inducements and threats. However, the evidence obtained as a result of his statement (*i.e.,* the finding of the rifle) was not excluded by any rule of evidence. The fact that the police quite intentionally thwarted Wray's opportunity to consult a lawyer did not at that time bring any rule of exclusion into operation.

The lower courts hearing the *Wray* case found that there was a discretion to exclude highly relevant evidence if its admission would be unjust or tend to bring the administration of justice into disrepute. On appeal, however, the Supreme Court of Canada found that this was wrong; only if evidence is of very little probative value and highly prejudicial may the trial judge exclude it. It is not the judge's job to exclude probative evidence simply because it was obtained unfairly. As Justice Maryland said in the Supreme Court

> . . .in my opinion, under our law, the function of the court is to determine the issue before it, on the evidence admissible in law, and it does not extend to the exclusion of admissible evidence for any other reason.

In summary, and putting aside special rules that govern the admissibility as part of the prosecution's case of statements made by an accused to a person in authority, the *Wray* decision directed that courts should not exclude evidence for reasons based on the way in which it had been obtained.

The *Wray* case illustrates the tension between two important aspects of the criminal process: the successful prosecution of guilty persons and the adherence to the law by the police. There can be little doubt that the evidence recovered by the police in the *Wray* case was very important evidence of his guilt. But, by the same token, there can be little doubt but that the police acted in a highly improper manner in order to obtain the evidence which played a large part in his conviction. It is quite possible that the Court in the *Wray* decision did not wish to approve or condone the police activity, but simply thought that excluding evidence was not an appropriate way to express disapproval of what the police had done. Should a guilty person go free because the police have used inappropriate tactics? The answer of the pre-*Charter* law was clear in almost call cases: no.

The guaranteed rights under the *Charter* along with s. 24(2) have changed the approach dramatically. Consider how *Wray* would be approached today in light of the *Charter*.

First, the *Charter* would give *Wray* a constitutionally protected right to silence The Supreme Court of Canada has found this principle to be part of the s. 7 right to life, liberty and security of the person and not to be deprived thereof except in accordance with the principles of fundamental justice. A detained person has the right to choose freely whether to speak to the police or not and the authorities must not actively undermine that choice

Second, the *Charter* would give *Wray* the right to be informed of his right to get legal advice, the right to retain and instruct counsel without delay and would impose on the police the duty to refrain from questioning the accused until he or she had a reasonable opportunity to retain and instruct counsel (s. 10(b)).

Finally, the *Charter* directs that where evidence has been obtained in violation of *Charter* rights, the Court must exclude such evidence if its admission would bring the administration of justice into disrepute (s. 24(2)). If Wray could show that his *Charter* right to silence or his right to counsel had been infringed, he could apply under s. 24(2) of the *Charter* to exclude the evidence—both his statement and the rifle itself—on the basis that their admission would bring the administration of justice into disrepute.

In one of its first cases dealing with s. 24(2) of the *Charter,* the Supreme Court of Canada described this new obligation to exclude evidence as follows:

> It is whether *the admission of the evidence* would bring the administration of justice into disrepute that is the applicable test. Misconduct by the police in the investigatory process often has some effect on the repute of the administration of justice, but s. 24(2) is not a remedy for police misconduct, requiring the exclusion of the evidence if, because of the misconduct, the administration of justice was brought into disrepute. Section 24(2) could well have been drafted in that way, but it was not. Rather, the drafters of the *Charter* decided to focus on the admission of the evidence in the proceedings, and the purpose of s. 24(2) is to prevent having the administration of justice brought into *further disrepute* by the admission of the evidence in the proceedings. This further disrepute will result from the admission of evidence that would deprive the accused of a fair hearing, or from judicial condonation of unacceptable conduct by the investigatory and prosecutorial agencies. It will also be necessary to consider any disrepute that may result from the exclusion of the evidence. It would be inconsistent with the purpose of s. 24(2) to exclude evidence if its exclusion would bring the administration of justice into greater disrepute than would its admission. Finally, it must be emphasized that even though the inquiry under s. 24(2) will necessarily focus on the specific prosecution, it is the long-term consequences of regular admission or exclusion of this type of evidence on the repute of the administration of justice which must be considered: . . .

This review of the *Wray* case before and after the *Charter* shows how dramatically the role of the courts has changed. There are constitutionally entrenched rights for persons detained or charged with crimes and, when these rights are breached, the court is required to decide whether the evidence so obtained should be excluded and to exclude it were its admission would tend to bring the administration of justice into disrepute.

What justifies the exclusion of evidence obtained in violation of constitutional rights? There are two main arguments, although the second has many variations. Some argue that such exclusion is necessary to preserve judicial integrity—that is, "to maintain respect for the law, to promote confidence in the administration of justice, and to preserve the judicial process from contamination." As a leading American judge said:

> If the government becomes a law breaker, it breeds contempt for law; it invites every man to become a law unto himself, it invites anarchy. To declare that in the administration of the criminal law the ends justify the means—to declare that the government may commit crimes in order to secure the conviction of a private criminal—would bring terrible retribution.

Other proponents say that the exclusionary rule ensures that the courts play a role in controlling police conduct. Some of the many aspects of this proposition include the following:

1. The power to exclude evidence obtained by unconstitutional means gives the courts frequent opportunities to show that they are the interpreters and enforcers of the Constitution. It also gives the courts the opportunity to formulate appropriate standards for police conduct and to educate the police about those standards.
2. The power to exclude evidence provides an incentive for citizens to question police conduct and, by doing so, makes it more likely that judicial review of that conduct will occur.
3. The exclusion of evidence affords a partial remedy, or corrective measure, for the infringement of constitutional rights.
4. It serves to deter future police misconduct.

There are a number of other considerations that weaken the arguments in favour of this new Canadian rule. While proponents argue that judicial integrity requires exclusion, at least in some cases, opponents argue the opposite. They ask how judicial integrity is to be preserved if reliable and trustworthy evidence is excluded. Public respect for the courts surely will not be fostered by allowing the guilty to go free. Excluding the evidence gives the accused a windfall without really punishing the public officer.

Proponents of the exclusionary approach maintain that it gives the courts both the opportunity to review and the means to control police conduct. Opponents respond with a number of arguments. Numerous empirical studies in the United States fail to provide convincing evidence that the extreme form of the exclusionary rule effectively deters unconstitutional police behaviour. There is concern that such exclusion may simply encourage police perjury or plea bargaining. It is even argued that the exclusionary remedy may lead to a narrowing of constitutional rights. Courts, when wishing to avoid exclusion, may choose to define the right narrowly so as to find that it has not been infringed, with the result that the question of excluding the evidence will not even arise.

The academic and judicial debate concerning the validity of these arguments will doubtless continue for many years.

. . .

It would be useful to take an imaginary criminal case and show how to *Charter* might apply at the various stages of the process. Here is the fact situation we will consider:

Ima Thief is charged with breaking and entering a place with the intent to commit the indictable offence of theft therein, contrary to s. 348(1) of the *Criminal Code*. The circumstances giving rise to the charge are as follows:

Officer Shrewd was on routine patrol on Main Street of Dullsville, Halifax County. Thief was sitting in an automobile parked on Main Street. As Shrewd went by, Thief made a disparaging remark about police officers which was not said directly to Shrewd, but which was obviously calculated so that Shrewd would hear it. Shrewd knew that Thief was one of the town's "bad actors," but had no specific reason to suspect any particular wrongdoing on this occasion. Not appreciating the insult, and seeing several other local toughs snickering nearby, Shrewd decided some action was needed. He opened the car's passenger door and said to Thief, "O.K., kid, let's have a little look at this car. I can feel the heat as I walk by." Shrewd ordered Thief to open's the car's trunk which, after protesting, Thief did. In the trunk was a large framed oil painting covered with dust. Shrewd asked Thief where he got it and Thief replied that he's taken it from the old McLatchie place which Shrewd knew to be an abandoned house just outside town. Shrewd then arrested Thief, told him he's be charged with break, enter and theft and that he could call a lawyer if he wished. Thief said nothing. He was released on a promise to appear.

Shrewd conducted a full investigation. The McLatchie house was little more than a shell. It had no doors or windows and had clearly been uninhabited for some time. A neighbour stated that she could remember seeing someone she thought was Thief enter the house and then leave, carrying a large square object. Shrewd attempted to contact Lorne McLatchie, the owner of the abandoned house, but discovered that he was on an excursion to the South Pole and could not be reached for at least six months.

Thief appeared in court, elected trial by judge sitting without a jury and waived his right to a preliminary inquiry. The case was set for trial in three months' time, but at the opening of the sittings during which the case was to be heard, the Crown sought an adjournment on the basis of McLatchie's unavailability. Over defence objection, the adjournment was granted until the next sittings, scheduled to begin in eight months.

Thief told his lawyer that he was totally innocent and that his step-mother would testify that he was with her at the time the McLatchie's neighbour thinks he was stealing the painting. After the adjournment was granted, it was discovered that his step-mother had terminal cancer and, unfortunately, she died shortly before the case was called for trial.

Let us stop the narrative here and consider how the *Charter* might be invoked by Thief's counsel.

Decisions under the *Charter* have established a clear and far-reaching right of the accused to disclosure of the Crown's case. Relying on ss. 7 and 11(d), the Supreme Court of Canada has held that the right to disclosure "is one of the pillars of criminal justice on which we heavily depend to ensure that the innocent are not convicted." Thief's lawyer will therefore insist on full disclosure of the prosecution's case.

There might well be *Charter* challenges to the section of the *Criminal Code* under which Thief has been charged. Section 348(1)(a) of the *Code* simply creates the offence of break and entry with intent to commit an indictable offence. Section 348(2), however, makes it easier for the prosecution to prove the accused's guilt by providing that "evidence that an accused, broke and entered a place..., is, in the absence of any evidence to the contrary, proof that he broke and entered the place. . .with intent to commit an indictable offence therein." The courts have interpreted this to mean that once the Crown proves beyond a reasonable doubt that the accused broke and entered a place, then the jury must find that he or she did so with the intent to commit an indictable offence unless there is some evidence to the contrary. Thief's counsel might well argue that this provision in the *Criminal Code* violates s. 11(*d*) of the *Charter*, which guarantees the accused's right to be presumed innocent until proven guilty according to law. The argument would be that s. 348(2) relieves the prosecutor of the obligation of proving an essential element of the offence (that the accused broke and entered *with the intent to commit an indictable offence*) and therefore that the prosecutor is not obliged to prove the accused's guilt as s. 11(*d*) of the *Charter* requires.

The Crown could counter this argument in at least two ways. First, it might say that all the accused must do to avoid the operation of s. 349(2) is to point to *some* evidence to the contrary—that is, some evidence that there was no intent to commit an indictable offence. Accordingly, the accused is not being required by s. 348(2) to prove innocence, but merely to show that there is *some* evidence tending to negate the intent. As a second argument, the Crown might rely on s. 1 of the *Charter*, maintaining that even if s. 348(2) does limit the s. 11(*d*) right, the violation is a reasonable limit prescribed by law on the right to be presumed innocent, one that is demonstrably justified in a free and democratic society. The courts have decided that the burden would be on the Crown, in these circumstances, to show why this is a reasonable and justified limitation of the right to be presumed innocent. More specifically, the courts have said that, in order to be saved under s. 1 of the *Charter*, an infringement must serve an important objective and the means of achieving the objective should be proportional to the objective and rationally designed to achieve it. In this case, the Crown would probably argue that s. 349(2) serves an important social objective, namely the security of property. It impairs the rights under s. 11(*d*) minimally because it simply requires *some* evidence to the contrary. Moreover, the provision serves the objective rationally, having regard to the difficulty of proving intent and the fact that proof of break and entry, absent any other circumstances, usually gives rises to an influence that the person intended to commit an offence in the place entered.

The court hearing the case will have to consider these arguments made by the defence and the Crown, keeping in mind not only the specific matters in issue in this case, but the overall purposes of the *Charter*. If the court accepts the defence arguments that s. 349(2) infringes the right to be presumed innocent and rejects the Crown argument that the infringement is a reasonable limit under s. 1 of the *Charter*, then the prosecutor will have to prove both the fact of break and entry as well as the intent to commit the indictable offence, unassisted by s. 348(2). It is likely that the court would simply declare the section to be of no force or effect because of its inconsistency with s. 11(*d*) of the *Charter*. You should refer here to s. 52 of the *Charter*.

Thief's counsel may also challenge s. 350(*b* of the *Criminal Code*. That section provides that a person shall be deemed to have broken and entered if he or she entered by a permanent or temporary opening unless the person can establish some lawful justification or excuse. This section will probably be relied upon by the Crown in its case against thief because he simply walked into the old McLatchie place through one of the openings where the doors or windows used to be. The defence could argue that this section offends at least two provisions of the *Charter*. Firstly, in "deeming" simple entry to be break and entry, it may be contrary to the principles of fundamental justice as guaranteed in s. 7 of the *Charter*. The deeming provision of s. 350(*b*) might be considered to authorize the punishment of the accused for conduct in which he did not, in fact, engage. Secondly, the section may also offend *Charter* s. 11(*d*) by requiring the accused to prove the existence of any lawful justification or excuse. In response to these arguments, the Crown may assert that the section does not deem the accused to be guilty of an offence not committed, but is simply another way of creating an offence that could be called "unlawful entry with intent to commit an offence." As for the s. 11(*d*) argument, the Crown may respond that the presumption of innocence under the *Charter* only requires the prosecutor to prove the essential elements of an offence, not to prove the non-existence of possible justifications or excuses. Once again, the Crown may also turn to s. 1 of the *Charter* in an attempt to uphold the *Criminal Code* provision.

The British Columbia Court of Appeal confronted some of these issues in *R. v. Slavens*. The accused was charged with breaking out of an apartment dwelling after entering it with the intent to commit an indictable offence (s. 348(1)(*c*)). By virtue of s. 348(2)(*b*), once the Crown proves that the accused broke out of the place, and in the absence of evidence to the contrary, the court must find that he entered the place with the intent to commit an indictable offence. The accused challenged this provision as being contrary to ss. 11(*d*) of the *Charter*.

The Court found that the section did violate s. 11(*d*). Under that section, the Court could be required to find that the accused had the guilt intent, which is an essential element of the offence, even though the evidence adduced by the Crown did not establish that element beyond a reasonable doubt. The Court then went on to consider whether the section was justified under s. 1 of the *Charter*. It concluded that it was. On the basis of some statistical evidence, the Court found that the interests protected by the section were important ones because break and entry offences had reached "epidemic proportions." Given the apparent difficulty of the police in "clearing" these offences, the placing on the accused of the burden of pointing to "some evidence to the contrary" tending to negate the guilty intent was proportionate to the interests the section was trying to protect.

If the defence argument about the deeming provision succeeds, the Crown will likely have to withdraw the charge against Thief, because without the provision, it will not be possible to prove that Thief broke and entered. If the defence argument about the proof of justifications and excuses is accepted, then the charge will likely go ahead. Remember that under s. 52 of the *Charter,* a law of inconsistent with the *Charter* is of no force or effect, but only to the extent of the inconsistency.

Defence counsel will almost certainly raise objections about the way in which Officer Shrewd found the painting in the trunk of Thief's car and also to the way in which Shrewd obtained from Thief a statement about how he acquired the painting. Here, the argument will likely be a two-pronged on. It will first be contended that one or more of Thief's *Charter* rights were infringed by Shrewd. Next, the defence will contend that the evidence obtained by Shrewd from Thief should be excluded under

s. 24(2) of the Charter, because it was obtained in a manner which infringed Thief's *Charter* rights and its admission would bring the administration of justice into disrepute.

Before the court can consider whether evidence should be excluded under s. 24, the accused must show that his or her rights have been infringed, as s. 24(1) makes clear. In this case, the defence will allege at least two infringements. It will claim that Shrewd's search of Thief's car was an unreasonable search, contrary to s. 8 of the *Charter*, and that Shrewd failed to advise Thief, upon his distention, that he had the right to retain and instruct counsel as required under s. 10(*b*) of the *Charter*.

Space does not allow anything other than a very brief summary of what some of the arguments might be on these issues. With regard to whether Shrewd's actions constituted unreasonable search, there may be an issue as to whether Thief consented to the search, given that Thief somewhat begrudgingly complied with Shrewd's request to open the trunk. The court will have to decide whether the search was unreasonable, and even if it was, whether it will be supported as a reasonable limit prescribed by law and thus saved under s. 1 of the *Charter*. With respect to the right to counsel, the main issue will be timing. Shrewd told Thief that he could call his lawyer, but did so only after he has asked Thief where he god the painting and received from Thief a very incriminating reply. The right to be informed of the right to counsel under the *Charter* arose when Thief was detained (see s. 10(*b*) of the *Charter*). Was he detained at the time the search (if t was a search) took place? All of these issues will have to be addressed in order to determine whether the accused's *Charter* rights have been infringed by Officer Shrewd's actions.

The Supreme Court of Canada has given a great deal of guidance on the meaning of the right to counsel. For example, it is clear that under s. 10(*b*), the police must not only inform the accused of the right, but must also give him or her a reasonable opportunity to exercise it, refrain from eliciting evidence from the person until that reasonable opportunity has been given, and advise the accused about the availability of duty counsel and legal aid. The accused, however, must be reasonably diligent in exercising his or her rights under s. 10(*b*).

The *Collins* case gives some guidance about how the court should assess Officer Shrewd's actions. For the purposes of s. 18 of the *Charter*, a search will be reasonable if it is authorized by law, if the law is reasonable and if the manner in which the search is conducted is reasonable. In this case, there was probably no legal authority for the search, so it would fail the first test of being "authorized by law." It also seems clear that Officer Shrewd had no reasonable or probable cause to conduct the search. So, assuming what occurred was, in fact, a search, it almost certainly offended s. 8 of the *Charter*.

Assuming for the moment that the court agrees with the defence that both ss. 8 and 10(*b*) of the *Charter* were infringed, the question arises as to what the court should do about these infringements. Under s. 24, the court may grant a remedy that it considers appropriate a just. It might, therefore, decide to stay the proceedings against Thief or to order the officer to pay damages. However, Thief will most likely seek the remedy of the exclusion of evidence under s. 24(2). To succeed, it must be shown not only that his *Charter* rights were infringed, but that evidence was obtained in a manner that infringed his rights and that to admit the evidence would bring the administration of justice into disrepute. As Thief attempts to do this, several issues will arise. There can be little doubt that the painting was discovered as a direct result of the unreasonable search (if such it was). It is not equally clear that any evidence was obtained as a result of the failure to tell Thief about his right to obtain counsel. Section 24(2) speaks of evidence being obtained in a manner that infringes *Charter* rights. Does this then require Thief to show that the evidence was obtained *because* his rights were violated (*i.e.,* that it wouldn't have been obtained had the infringement not taken place?) or does it simply require that there has been in infringement while the evidence was being obtained? Whether there must be some causal link between the infringement and the obtaining of the evidence and, if so, how direct must it be?These are two issues that must be considered in a case such as this. Once these issues are resolved, the court must confront the question of whether admitting the evidence would bring the administration of justice into disrepute. How is the court to decide? Several factors, such as the seriousness of the offence, the seriousness of the *Charter* violation, the nature and the importance of the evidence obtained have been suggested as relevant matters to consider.

Thief's counsel may also allege that there has been an infringement of his client's right to be tried within a reasonable time as guaranteed under s. 11(*b*) of the *Charter.* His trial will take place 11 months after the charge and it appears the delay has resulted in the trial occurring after the death of his alibi witness. Thus, Thief can allege prejudice resulting from the delay.

The Supreme Court of Canada has made several important decisions respecting s. 11(*b*) of the *Charter.* In *R. v. Askov,* a period of nearly three years elapsed between the laying of the charges and the trial. A majority of the Court found that s. 11(*b*) protected both the accused's right to trial in a reasonable time and the interests of society in bringing persons to justice promptly. In deciding whether delay has been unreasonable, the majority of the Court decided that four factors should be considered:

(1)  the length of the delay,
(2)  the reasons for the delay,
(3)  whether the accused had waived his or her s. 11(*b*) rights and,
(4)  whether the accused was prejudiced by the delay.

This brief discussion of *R. v. Thief* shows some of the many ways in which the *Charter* comes into play in the criminal process and, as well, outlines some of the many issues that arise in attempting to interpret and apply the *Charter.*

. . .

## Questions/Discussions

1.  Do you feel it is the proper role of the courts to be deciding substantive criminal justice policy issues and altering criminal law passed by allegedly democratically elected officials? For example, is it the proper role of the Supreme Court to be deciding what the abortion law should or should not be in Canada?
2.  It is important to question the true effects of these decisions on the everyday reality of law enforcement. Who will take advantage of their rights on the streets or who *can*

take advantage of them? How will or can the decisions affect the bias of enforcement agents as to who is interfered with in the first place? What practical limits are placed on the "processing of the poor" in the current criminal justice system? Do you think that the Charter will make a real difference in how you interact with the police if and when you are stopped or detained?

3. Does the right to counsel mean different things to different people, or more specifically, to different classes of people? For example, if you have your own lawyer or the money to hire one, does this make a difference as opposed to someone who merely receives duty counsel at the last minute before the first appearance? What should be the "content" of this right?

## Further Reading

- Archibald, B., "The Constitutionalization of the General Part of Criminal Law" (1988), 67 Canadian Bar Review 403.
- Astroff, Robert A., "Identity Crisis: The Charter and Forensic DNA Analysis in the Criminal Justice System" (1996), 5 Dalhousie Journal of Legal Studies 211-235.
- Beaudoin, G.-A., and E. Ratushny (eds.), *The Canadian Charter of Rights and Freedoms* (Toronto: Carswell, 1989).
- Bryden, P. (ed.), *Protecting Rights and Freedoms: Essays on the Charter's Place in Canada's Political, Legal, and Intellectual Life* (Toronto: University of Toronto Press, 1994).
- Cameron, Jamie, ed., *The Charter's Impact on the Criminal Justice System* (Toronto: Carswell, 1996).
- Dawe, J., "Standing to Challenge Searches and Seizures Under the Charter: The Lessons of the American Experience and their Application to Canadian Law" (1993), 52 University of Toronto Faculty of Law Review 39-72.
- Epstein, M., "The Guiding Hand of Counsel: The Charter and the Right to Counsel on Appeal" (1987-88), 30 Criminal Law Quarterly 35.
- France, S., "Gains and Lost Opportunities in Canadian Constitutional Mens Rea" (1995), 20 Queen's Law Journal 533-555.
- Friedland, M., "Controlling the Administrators of Criminal Justice" (1988-89), 31 Criminal Law Quarterly 280.
- Gold, A. and M. Fuerst, "The Stuff that Dreams are Made of: Criminal Law and the Charter of Rights" (1992), 24 Ottawa Law Review 13-37.
- Hogg, Peter W. and Allison A. Bushell, "The Charter Dialogue Between Courts and Legislatures" (1997), 35 Osgoode Hall Law Journal 75-124.
- Hovius, B. and R. Martin, "The Canadian Charter of Rights and Freedoms in the Supreme Court of Canada" (1983), 61 Canadian Bar Review 354.
- Jull, K., "Exclusion of Evidence and the Beast of Burden" (1987-88), Criminal Law Quarterly 178.
- Knopff, R., *Charter Politics* (Toronto: Nelson Canada, 1992).
- MacLean, S., "Video Surveillance and The Charter of Rights" (1987-88), 30 Criminal Law Quarterly 88.
- Mahoney, R., "The Presumption of Innocence: A New Era" (1988), 67 Canadian Bar Review 1.
- Mandel, M., *The Charter of Rights and the Legalization of Politics in Canada (Updated and expanded edition)* (Toronto: Thompson Educational, 1994).
- Mitchell, G., "The Supreme Court of Canada on the Exclusion of Evidence in Criminal Cases Under Section 24 of the Charter" (1988), 30 Criminal Law Quarterly 165.

- Stuart, D., "Progress on the Constitutional Requirement of Fault" (1988), 64 C.R. (3d) 352.
- Stuart, Don, *Charter Justice in Canadian Criminal Law, 2nd ed.* (Toronto: Carswell, 1996).
- Tanovich, D., "Charting the Constitutional Right of Effective Assistance of Counsel in Canada: (1994), 36 Criminal Law Quarterly 404-422.
- Way., R.C., "The Charter, the Supreme Court and the Invisible Politics of Fault" (1992), 12 Windsor Yearbook of Access to Justice 128-178.

## 7.4 INCAPACITY

### General Introduction

This section deals with special pleas that all involve some type of argument that the accused did not have the capacity due to mental or emotional impairment to form the necessary mental element or mens rea for the offence. Note, however, that capacity is also extremely relevant to the issue of whether the accused is in fact fit to stand trial. The accused's incapacity due to age may also become a relevant factor, particularly when dealing with young persons. Section 13 of the Criminal Code says that no person under the age of twelve may be convicted of an offence. The *Youth Criminal Justice Act* defines "young persons" to be between the ages of twelve and eighteen; of this group, if the accused is at least 14 years of age, then there is the possibility of having the case tried in adult court.

Four defences are considered in this section. The first is the defence of provocation which involves the ordinary person "losing control" because of some wrong committed by the victim. It only applies as a defence to charges of murder, reducing the conviction to one for manslaughter if successful. Provocation entails a claim of justification. It is not enough that a person lose control or act in the "heat of passion"; that passion must be directed at a justified target, namely the person who wronged the accused.

The defence of mental disorder was introduced in 1992 following the case of *Swain* which overturned sections of the former defence of insanity. While the defence of insanity was rarely used in criminal trials previously (due to the fact that the offender could be held indefinitely on a Lieutenant Governor's Warrant), it is argued by some that with the recent changes, the defence will arise more frequently. In any event, the question of the accused's mental capacity is of fundamental importance because it concerns the central issue of criminal responsibility. Also, many criticisms have been raised about the use and abuse of mental health experts in the courtroom. Such experts often testify from a deterministic perspective that seeks to blame criminal behaviour on forces outside the offender's control. For example, psychiatrists diagnose the majority of prison inmates as suffering from some sort of mental illness and some have argued that prisons should be replaced with therapeutic institutions where the inmates are converted into patients and released when "cured". This therapeutic agenda is a powerful competitor to the criminal law's traditional attribution of blame. While the defence of mental disorder remains relatively rare, it should be noted that mental illness is frequently raised as a mitigating factor at sentencing. It is also central to the issues surrounding fitness to stand trial and dangerous offenders. The important question you should consider while reading the materials is why does the law treat the mentally ill in an exceptional manner? What assumptions are made about the mentally ill concerning their dangerousness and their self-control? What evidence is considered by the courts?

Intoxication and automatism are the other defences considered in this section. The latter is a relatively recent common law defence, created by judges to cover seemingly random, motiveless acts. The classic example where the defence is used is that of an epileptic charged with assault after striking a bystander during a seizure. The defence negates the actus reus (according to most cases) and results in complete acquittal. It is therefore a far more appealing defence than that of mental disorder where the consequences can be very severe.

While automatism is rarely at issue, intoxication is commonly considered at trial. About half of all offenders, in crimes of both property and personal violence, consumed drugs (usually alcohol) prior to the commission of their offence. The common law defence of intoxication is rather complex and confused as the extract from *Daviault*, below demonstrates. As a result of this case and the government's response in section 33.1 of the Code, consider what assumptions the courts make about intoxicated offenders? Why should the law make any special rules about intoxication?

## 7.4.1   Provocation or Heat of Passion

### Introduction

The heat of passion or provocation doctrine involves both a justification and an excuse whereby murder is partially excused when the accused's impairing passion is triggered by the victim's wrongful act or insult. In Canada, provocation is the only statutory partial defence, and it is restricted to murder charges; attempted murder is not covered by section 232. The passionate, unpremeditated killing of an adultering spouse, caught in the wrongful act, traditionally fit within the defence whereas the killing of a philandering lover did not (Dressler, 1982). Passion must be present, as the offender must "act on the sudden and before there was time for his passion to cool", but passion by itself is no excuse. Instead, the passion must be inflicted upon the accused through no fault of their own by a wrongful act which would, in the words of section 232: "deprive an ordinary person of the power of self-control". The accused is thus to be judged by an objective standard — the "ordinary person" — but this leaves considerable doubt as to what characteristics should be attributed to the ordinary person. The modern position, analyzed in the case of *Hill* (1986), below, ascribes the accused's age, sex and race to the "ordinary" person but not specific peculiarities such as an excitable temperament.

The language of "self-control" and its loss is rather difficult in some ways to understand. Does provocation's passion cause another "self" to emerge? Do provocation and passion short-circuit inhibitions that hold back the savage within? If this view is correct, the law on provocation is wrong because it only applies when the provoker is attacked; assaulting by-standers, even in passion, is not excused. Does passion focus our attention or does it blot out consciousness? Or is passion even relevant? Is the severely provoked person who calmly retaliates to be punished for their self-discipline?

Or is the main element the "wrongful act"? Is the provoked crime less severely punished because the victim deserved some degree of retaliation? (Some other jurisdictions do not require any wrongful act on the part of the victim.) If this logic is followed, one would think that the wrongful, provoking act would normally have to be quite serious but the courts have counted mere verbal insults as sufficient provocation. The case of *R. v. Parent* below represents the most recent treatment of the defence by the Supreme Court.

The Law Reform Commission of Canada's *Recodifying Criminal Law*, Volume 1, (1986) excludes provocation as even a partial defence. Instead, the Commission would abolish the mandatory life sentence for second degree murder, find provoked killers guilty of murder, not manslaughter, and then permit provocation to be weighed as a mitigating factor at sentencing. Other reform agencies suggest retaining provocation but simplifying it by adopting a more subjective test of whether the accused killed under extreme mental or emotional disturbance, and by dropping all the complications about wrongful acts and acting on the sudden.

## Regina v. Hill
### (1986), 25 C.C.C. (3d) 322 (S.C.C.).

[Only excerpts from the judgment of Dickson C.J.C. are reproduced below.]

Appeal by the Crown from a judgment of the Ontario Court of Appeal, 2 C.C.C. (3d) 394, 32 C.R. (3d) 88, allowing an appeal by the accused from his conviction for second degree murder.

DICKSON C.J.C.: — Gordon James Elmer Hill was charged with committing first degree murder at the City of Belleville, County of Hastings, on the person of Verne Pegg, contrary to s. 218(1) of the *Criminal Code*, R.S.C. 1970, c. C-34. He was found by the jury not guilty of first degree murder but guilty of second degree murder. He was sentenced to imprisonment for life without eligibility for parole until 10 years of his sentence had been served.

Hill appealed his conviction to the Court of Appeal of Ontario. He raised many grounds of appeal, but the Court of Appeal called upon the Crown with respect to one ground only, relating to the charge on the issue of provocation. The ground of appeal was that the trial judge failed to instruct the jury properly as to the "ordinary person" in s. 215(2) of the *Criminal Code*, Section 215 of the *Code* reads in part:

**215**(1) Culpable homicide that otherwise would be murder may be reduced to manslaughter if the person who committed it did so in the heat of passion caused by sudden provocation.

(2) A wrongful act or insult that is of such a nature as to be sufficient to deprive an ordinary person of the power of self-control is provocation for the purposes of this section if the accused acted upon it on the sudden and before there was time for his passion to cool.

These two subsections, given their plain meaning, produce three sequential questions for answer by the tribunal:

1. Would an ordinary person be deprived of self-control by the act or insult?
2. Did the accused in fact act in response to those "provocative" acts; in short, was he or she provoked by them whether or not an ordinary person would have been?
3. Was the accused's response sudden and before there was time for his or her passion to cool?

At this stage it is important to recall the presence of s-s. (3) of s. 215 which provides:

**215**(3) For the purposes of this section the questions
(a) whether a particular wrongful act or insult amounted to provocation, and
(b) whether the accused was deprived of the power of self-control by the provocation that he alleges he received,
are questions of fact . . .

In the answering of these successive questions, the first or "ordinary person" test is clearly determined by objective standards. The second *de facto* test as to the loss of self-control by the accused is determined, like any other question of fact as revealed by the evidence, from the surrounding facts. The third test as to whether the response was sudden and before passions cooled is again a question of fact.

At the time of the killing, Hill was male and 16 years of age. The narrow question in this appeal is whether the trial judge erred in law in failing to instruct the jury that if they found a wrongful act or insult they should consider whether it was sufficient to deprive an ordinary person "of the age and sex of the appellant" of his power of self-control. Was it incumbent in law on the trial judge to add that gloss to the section? That is the issue.

### The Facts

At trial both parties agreed that it was the acts of Hill which caused the death of Pegg but disagreed otherwise. The position of the Crown at trial was that Hill and Pegg were homosexual lovers and that Hill had decided to murder Pegg after a falling-out between them. The Crown argued that Hill deliberately struck Pegg in the head while Pegg lay in bed. This did not kill Pegg who immediately ran from the bedroom into the bathroom to try to stop the flow of blood from his head. Realizing he had been unsuccessful, Hill took two knives from the kitchen and stabbed Pegg to death.

Hill's version of the events was very different. He admitted to causing the death of Pegg but put forward two defences: self-defence and provocation. Hill testified that he had known Pegg for about a year through the latter's involvement with the "Big Brother" organization. Hill stated that on the night in question he had been the subject of unexpected and unwelcome homosexual advances by Pegg while asleep on the couch in Pegg's apartment. Pegg pursued Hill to the bathroom and grabbed him, at which time Hill picked up a nearby hatchet and swung it at Pegg in an attempt to scare him. The hatchet struck Pegg in the head. Hill then ran from the apartment but returned shortly afterward. Upon re-entering the apartment, he was confronted by Pegg who threatened to kill him. At this point, Hill obtained two knives from the kitchen and stabbed Pegg to death.

Hill was arrested, after a car chase with the police, at the wheel of a Pontiac automobile owned by Pegg. At the scene of the arrest Hill denied knowing Pegg, but later he made a statement to the police which was substantially similar to his oral testimony at trial.

## The Charge

. . .

At trial, counsel for Hill objected to the instruction of the trial judge as to the objective requirement of the defence of provocation, submitting that the "ordinary person" referred to in s. 215(2) ought to have been defined as an ordinary person of the age and sex of the accused. Counsel submitted that the objective requirement would be satisfied if the judge were to recharge the jury by defining the "ordinary person" as an "ordinary person in the circumstances of the accused". The judge refused to recharge the jury in those terms.

## The Court of Appeal

In oral reasons Brooke J.A. (Martin and Morden JJ.A. concurring) noted that counsel for the defence, relying on *Director of Public Prosecutions v. Camplin*, [1978] A.C. 705 (H.L.). submitted that the judge should have instructed the jury to consider whether the wrongful act or insult was sufficient to deprive an "ordinary person" of the age and sex of the accused of his power of self-control. The Court of Appeal held that because the trial judge declined to do so he erred. In reaching this conclusion, Brooke J.A. stated [2 C.C.C. (3d) 394 at p. 395, 32 C.R. (3d) 88]:

> The age and sex of the appellant are not "peculiar characteristics" excluded from consideration of the "ordinary person" in the objective test in s. 215(2) (see Fauteux J. (as he then was) in *Wright v. The Queen*, [1969] 3 C.C.C. 258 at pp 261-2 . . . discussing *Bedder v. D.P.P.*, [1954] 2 All E.R. 801).

He also added [at pp. 395-6]:

> In our respectful opinion, there is nothing in that judgment which precludes charging the jury as the defence requested. As the matter was left to the jury, the age of the appellant was only a consideration if and when the jury turned to the question of whether the wrongful act or insult deprived him of his power of self-control. The effect of the charge was that an ordinary person did not include a 16-year-old or youth and may well have established as the standard an ordinary person more experience and mature than the ordinary 16-year-old or youth. If this is so, the jury may have rejected the defence judging the objective test on that basis.

In the result, the Court of Appeal held that the judge was in error and there may well have been misdirection which seriously prejudiced Hill and so the conviction could not stand. The appeal was allowed, the conviction set aside and a new trial on the charge of second degree murder ordered.

## The Issue

The issue in this appeal is whether the Ontario Court of Appeal erred in law in holding that the trial judge erred in law with respect to the elements of the objectives test relevant to the defence of provocation in failing to direct the jury that the "ordinary person" within the meaning of that term in s. 215(2) of the *Criminal Code* was an "ordinary person of the same age and sex as the accused".

## The Defence of Provocation

The defence of provocation appears to have first developed in the early 1800s. Tindal C.J. in *R. v. Hayward* (1833), 6 Car. & P. 157 at p. 159, 172 E.R. 1188, told the jury that the defence of provocation was derived from the law's "compassion to human infirmity". It acknowledged that all human beings are subject to uncontrollable outbursts of passion and anger which may lead them to do violent acts. In such instances, the law would lessen the severity of criminal liability.

Nevertheless, not all acts done in the heat of passion were to be subject to the doctrine of provocation. By the middle of the 19th century, it became clear that the provoking act had to be sufficient to excite an ordinary or reasonable person under the circumstances. As Keating J. stated in *R. v. Welsh* (1869), 11 Cox C.C. 336 at p. 338:

> The law is, that there must exist such an amount of provocation as would be excited by the circumstances in the mind of a reasonable man, and so as to lead the jury to ascribe the set to the influence of that passion.

The *Criminal Code* codified this approach to provocation by including under s. 215 three general requirements for the defence of provocation. First, the provoking wrongful act or insult must be of such a nature that it would deprive an ordinary person of the power of self-control. That is the initial threshold which must be surmounted. Secondly, the accused must actually have been provoked. As I have earlier indicated, these two elements are often referred to as the objective and subjective tests of provocation respectively. Thirdly, the accused must have acted on the provocation on the sudden and before there was time for his or her passion to cool.

### The Objective Test of Provocation and the Ordinary Person Standard

In considering the precise meaning and application of the ordinary person standard or objective test, it is important to identify its underlying *rationale*. Lord Simon of Glaisdale has perhaps stated it most succinctly when he suggested in *Camplin*, at p. 726, that

> the reason for importing into this branch of the law the concept of the reasonable man [was] . . . to avoid the injustice of a man being entitled to rely on his exceptional excitability or pugnacity or ill-temper or on his drunkenness.

If there were no objective test to the defence of provocation, anomalous results would occur. A well-tempered, reasonable person would not be entitled to benefit from the provocation defence and wold be guilty of culpable homicide amounting to murder, while an ill-tempered or exceptionally excitable person would find his or her culpability mitigated by provocation and would be guilty only of manslaughter. It is society's concern that reasonable and non-violent behaviour be encouraged that prompts the law to enforce the objective standard. The criminal law is concerned among other things with fixing standards for human behaviour. We seek to encourage conduct that complies with certain societal standards of reasonableness and responsibility. In doing this, the law quite logically employs the objective standard of the reasonable person.

With this general purpose in mind, we must ascertain the meaning of the ordinary person standard. What are the characteristics of the "ordinary person"? To what extent should the attributes and circumstances of the accused be ascribed to the ordinary person?

. . .

*Canadian case-law*

The Supreme Court of Canada has also had occasion to provide guidance on the ordinary person standard for provocation. In *Taylor v. The King* (1947), 89 C.C.C. 209 at pp. 217-8, [1948] 1 D.L.R. 545, at pp. 552-3, [1947] S.C.R. 462 at p. 471, a case in which the accused was drunk at the time of his alleged provocation., Kerwin J. made clear that for the purposes of the objective test of provocation, the "criterion is the effect on an ordinary person . . . the jury is not entitled to take into consideration any alleged drunkenness on the part of the accused".

This Court again rejected a consideration of the drunkenness of the accused in connection with the objective test in *Salamon v. The Queen* (1959), 123 C.C.C. 1, 17 D.L.R. (2d) 685, [1959] S.C.R. 404. Mr. Justice Fauteux endorsed the trial judge's instruction to the jury not to consider "the character, background, temperament, or condition of the accused" in relation to the objective test of provocation. Similarly, Cartwright J. (dissenting on another issue) wrote, at p. 5 C.C.C., p. 689 D.L.R., p. 415 S.C.R., that the trial judge correctly "made it plain that on this [objective] branch of the inquiry no account should be taken of the idiosyncrasies of the appellant and that the standard to be applied was that of an ordinary person".

Finally, in *Wright v. The Queen*, [1969] 3 C.C.C. 258, 2 D.L.R. (3d) 529, [1969] S.C.R. 335, a son was charged with the shooting death of his father. The evidence suggested that there had been some difficulties in their relationship. The father was said to have been a bad-tempered and violent man who had mistreated his son on a number of occasions. The accused had not seen his father for a period of about five years until a few days prior to the fatal incident. On the evening of the shooting, the accused had spent most of the day drinking with his friends. In considering the objective test of provocation, the court rejected the relevance of the quality of the accused's relationship with his father, the mentality of the accused or his possible drunkenness. Fauteux J. quoted, at p. 261 C.C.C., p. 532 D.L.R., p 340 S.C.R., the words of Lord Simonds L.C. in *Bedder*, that the purpose of the objective test is ". . . to invite the jury to consider the act of the accused by reference to a certain standard or norm of conduct and with this object the "reasonable" or the "average" or the "normal" man is invoked". The court went on to state, at p. 262 C.C.C., p. 532 D.L.R., p. 340 S.C.R.:

> While the character, background, temperament, idiosyncrasies, or the drunkenness of the accused are matters to be considered in the second branch of the enquiry, they are excluded from the consideration in the first branch. A contrary view would denude of any sense the objective test.

Appellate courts at the provincial level have also considered the nature of the ordinary person standard of provocation. In *R. v. Clark* (1974), 22 C.C.C. (2d) 1, [1975] 2 W.W..R. 385, 5 N.R. 601 (Alta. S.C.A.D.)., the "morbid jealousy and slight mental degeneration" suffered by the accused was held not to be relevant to the objective test. According to Clement J.A. at p. 16:

> In the first branch of the inquiry, the objective test, what in essence has to be determined as a standard of comparison is the reaction that might be expected from ordinary human nature to the wrongful act, or to the alleged insult in the present case.

In *R. v. Parnerkar* (1971), 5 C.C.C. (2d) 11, 16 C.R.N.S. 347, [1972] 1 W.W.R. 161, the Saskatchewan Court of Appeal held that the cultural and religious background of the accused was not relevant to the determination of the objective test. The accused, born in India, was alleged to have been provoked by, *inter alia*, the deceased's statement "I am not going to marry you because you are a black man". The court's ruling seems to narrow unduly the conception of the ordinary person and rigidly prohibit a consideration of the physical characteristics of the accused along the lines of the *Bedder* case. I should not that *Parnerkar* was affirmed by this Court on appeal (see 10 C.C.C. (2d) 253, 33 D.L.R. (3d) 638, [1974] S.C.R 449), however, this particular question was not addressed.

. . .

*The appropriate content of the ordinary person standard*

What lessons are to be drawn from this review of the case-law? I think it is clear that there is a widespread agreement that the ordinary or reasonable person has a normal temperament and level of self-control. It follows that the ordinary person is not exceptionally excitable, pugnacious or in a state of drunkenness.

In terms of other characteristics of the ordinary person, it seems to me that the "collective good sense" of the jury will naturally lead it to ascribe to the ordinary person any general characteristics relevant to the provocation in question. For example, if the provocation is a racial slur, the jury will think of an ordinary person with the racial background that forms the substance of the insult. To this extent, particular characteristics will be ascribed to the ordinary person. Indeed, it would be impossible to conceptualize a sexless or ageless ordinary person. Features such as sex, age or race do not detract from a person's characterization as ordinary. Thus particular characteristics that are not peculiar or idiosyncratic can be ascribed to an ordinary person without subverting the logic of the objective test of provocation. As Lord Diplock wrote in *Director of Public Prosecutions v. Camplin*, [1978] A.C. 705 at pp. 716-7:

... the "reasonable man" has never been confided to the adult male. It means an ordinary person of either sex, not exceptionally excitable or pugnacious, but possessed of such powers of self-control as everyone is entitled to expect that his fellow citizens will exercise in society as it is today.

It is important to note that, in some instances, certain characteristics will be irrelevant. For example,the race of a person will be irrelevant if the provocation involves an insult regarding a physical disability. Similarly, the sex of an accused will be irrelevant if the provocation relates to a racial insult. Thus the central criterion is the relevance of the particular feature to the provocation in question. With this in mind, I think it is fair to conclude that age will be a relevant consideration when we are dealing with a young accused person. For a jury to assess what an ordinary person would have done if subjected to the same circumstances as the accused, the young age of an accused will be an important contextual consideration.

I should also add that my conclusion that certain attributes can be ascribed to the ordinary person is not meant to suggest that a trial judge must in each case tell the jury what specific attributes it is to ascribe to the ordinary person. The point I wish to emphasize is simply that in applying their common sense to the factual determination of the objective test, jury members will quite naturally and properly ascribe certain characteristics to the "ordinary person".

. . .

It has been suggested that the instruction of the trial judge on the subjective prong of the provocation defence had the effect of misleading the jury on the appropriate content of the ordinary person standard. The charge stated:

> ... you will then secondly consider whether the accused acted on the provocation on the sudden before there was time for his passion to cool. In deciding this question you are not restricted to the standard of the ordinary person. You will take into account the mental, emotional, the physical characteristics and the age of this accused.

. . . .

> You will also ask yourselves was the provocation such that it would have led a person with the mental and physical conditions and the age of the accused to respond in this way.

In my opinion, these words would not have misled the average juror with respect to the objective test, particularly when viewed in the context of the charge as a whole.

I have the greatest confidence in the level of intelligence and plain common sense of the average Canadian jury sitting on a criminal case. Juries are perfectly capable of sizing the matter up. In my experience as a trial judge I cannot recall a single instance in which a jury returned to the court-room to ask for further instructions on the provocation portion of a murder charge. A jury frequently seeks further guidance on the distinction between first degree murder, second degree murder and manslaughter, but rarely, if ever, on provocation. It seems to be common ground that the trial judge would not have been in error if he had simply read s. 215 of the *Code* and left it at that, without embellishment. I am loath to complicate the task of the trial judge, in cases such as the case at bar, by requiring him or her as a matter of law to point out to the members of the jury that in applying the objective test they must conceptualize an "ordinary person" who is male and young. The accused is before them. He is male and young. I cannot conceive of a Canadian jury conjuring up the concept of an "ordinary person" who would be either female or elderly, or banishing from their minds the possibility that an "ordinary person" might be both young and male. I do not think anything said by the judge in the case at bar would have led the jury to such an absurdity.

### Conclusion

I find that the trial judge's charge to the jury on the ordinary persons standard in the defence of provocation was consistent with the requirements of the *Criminal Code* and correct in law. It was not necessary to direct the jury that the ordinary person means an ordinary person of the same age and sex as the accused. I would, therefore, allow the appeal and restore the conviction.

*Appeal allowed; conviction restored.*

## Regina v. Parent
### (2001), 154 C.C.C. (3d) 1 (S.C.C.)

McLACHLIN C.J.—On September 24, 1996, the respondent, Rejean Parent, shot and killed his estranged wife. She had initiated divorce proceedings four years earlier and they were involved in litigation over the division of their assets, some of which were held in a corporation. In the meantime, their financial situation deteriorated, to the point that Mr. Parent's shares were seized and put up for sale. The wife attended the sale, allegedly intending to buy the shares. Mr. Parent also attended. He carried a loaded gun with a locked security catch in his pocket. There, she suggested they speak and they retired into a nearby room. Shortly after, shots were heard. Mr. Parent had shot his wife six times. She died from the wounds later that night.

Mr. Parent was charged with first degree murder. At trial, he testified that when they proceeded to the room his wife had said, in effect: [TRANSLATION] "I told you that I would wipe you out completely." He then felt a hot flush rising and shot. He said he [TRANSLATION] "didn't know what [he] was doing any more" and was aiming in front of him. He said he did not intend to kill his wife. After doing so, he left the building and spent the afternoon in a strip club before giving himself up to police that evening.

At trial, Mr. Parent argued that the verdict should be reduced to manslaughter on the basis of lack of criminal intent or provocation. The jury found him guilty of manslaughter. He was sentenced to 16 years' imprisonment, and a lifetime prohibition on possessing firearms, ammunition and explosives: [1997] Q.J. No. 4459 (QL).

The Crown appealed the verdict of manslaughter, and Parent appealed the sentence. The Quebec Court of Appeal dismissed the appeal from the verdict without reasons, but in separate proceedings ((1999), 142 C.C.C. (3d) 82) reduced the sentence to six years' imprisonment, after giving Mr. Parent credit of two years for time served. In this Court, the appellant raised one point only: that the judge had erred in his instructions to the jury on the effect of anger, creating a "defence of anger" (defense de *colere*) distinct from the defence of provocation. The respondent, for his part, argued that any difficulties in the judge's directions to the jury were cleared up in his redirection on provocation in answer to jury questions and that the jury properly convicted the accused of manslaughter on the basis of provocation.

Two issues are raised: (1) whether the trial judge erred in his charge to the jury on intention, and (2) if so, whether that error was cured by the redirection. I conclude that the trial judge erred in his direction on intention and that the recharge did not eliminate the possibility that this error led the jury wrongly to find the respondent guilty of manslaughter. Accordingly, the conviction must be set aside and a new trial ordered.

### 1. Did the Trial Judge Err in his Charge to the Jury on Intention?

The jury had three possible offences before it: first degree murder, second degree murder and manslaughter. All three offences require proof of an act of killing (*actus reus*) and the corresponding criminal intention (*mens rea*). In relation to murder, the defence of provocation does not eliminate the need for proof of intention to kill, but operates as an excuse that has the effect of reducing murder to manslaughter.

The Crown argues that the trial judge erred in suggesting that anger is capable of negating the intention to kill and that the jury could reduce the offence to manslaughter on this basis. More particularly, the Crown suggests that the judge's directions wrongly treated anger as a matter that could negate the criminal intent or *mens rea* of the offence; wrongly suggested that negation of intent can reduce the offence to manslaughter; and wrongly left open the suggestion that anger alone can establish provocation, when in fact other requirements must be met pursuant to s. 232 of the *Criminal Code*, R.S.C. 1985, c. C-46. The gravamen of the Crown's submission is that the trial judge's direction on intention was confusing and wrong and left it open to the jury to convict the accused of manslaughter, not on the basis of provocation (which the trial judge correctly defined), but on the erroneous basis that a high degree of anger short of provocation, as defined in law, could negate the criminal intent or *mens rea* of the offence.

The Crown objects to the portions of the jury charge in which the trial judge stated that the jury must take into account [TRANSLATION] "evidence surrounding the defence of provocation raised by the accused" in determining the accused's intent to kill. The Crown also objects to the trial judge's treatment of *mens rea* in the following passages:

> [TRANSLATION] For example, murder may be reduced to manslaughter where a person's state of mind is affected by alcohol consumption, drug consumption or where a person's state of mind is obscured or diminished by an outside force, by an incident like, for example, *a fit of anger.*

> You no doubt appreciate that we are not talking about an arbitrary reduction. In other words, it is not sufficient for a person to simply say "I was drinking" or "I took some drugs" or "I was really angry".

That alone, that's not enough, and all that always depends on the circumstances. It always depends on the nature of the facts at issue, of external influences, or outside influences capable of affecting one's state of mind.

It depends on the nature of the fact at issue, of its importance, its seriousness, its intensity in relation to the action that was taken by the person who committed the crime, all the while taking into account the evidence as a whole and all the circumstances.

So, you must look at the accused's state of mind when he killed Suzanne Bedard, you look at the entire evidence, including the elements surrounding the provocation defence with a view to determining whether he acted with the criminal intention that I defined earlier.

Here, the accused, when he testified, described to you his state of mind when Suzanne Bedard said the words in question. You must then decide if this incident *was sufficiently serious, important, intense so as to cause him to lose his faculties to the point of reducing the crime of murder to manslaughter.*

You will ask yourselves if his state of mind was affected, diminished, and if so, the intensity, the degree to which, taking into account all the circumstances at the time when he did what he did.

To reduce murder to manslaughter, you must come to the conclusion that the influence of the events that occurred was *strong enough, important enough, intense enough* to cause the accused to *not know or not want what he was doing by reason of his state of mind, that his faculties were too diminished to fully assess the situation, or that raise a reasonable doubt in his favour, in this respect.* [Emphasis added.]

The Crown argues that this passage creates a halfway house defence of anger, between non-mental disorder automatism and provocation. I agree. This passage suggests that anger, if sufficiently serious or intense, but not amounting to the defence of provocation, may reduce murder to manslaughter. It also suggests that anger, if sufficiently intense, may negate the criminal intention for murder. These connected propositions are not legally correct. Intense anger alone is insufficient to reduce murder to manslaughter.

The passage cited overstates the effect of anger. Anger can play a role in reducing murder to manslaughter in connection with the defence of provocation. Anger is not a stand-alone defence. It may form part of the defence of provocation when all the requirements of that defence are met: (1) a wrongful act or insult that would have caused an ordinary person to be deprived of his or her self-control; (2) which is sudden and unexpected; (3) which in fact caused the accused to act in anger; (4) before having recovered his or her normal control: *R. v. Thibert*, [1996] 1 S.C.R. 37. Again, anger conceivably could, in extreme circumstances, cause someone to enter a state of automatism in which that person does not know what he or she is doing, thus negating the voluntary component of the *actus reus*: R. v. Stone, [1999] 2 S.C.R. 290. However, the accused did not assert this defence. In any event, the defence if successful would result in acquittal, not reduction to manslaughter.

So it seems clear that the trial judge misdirected the jury on the effect of anger in relation to manslaughter. His directions left it open to the jury to find the accused guilty of manslaughter, on the basis of the anger felt by the accused, even if they concluded that the conditions required for the defence of provocation were not met. The directions raise the possibility that the jury's verdict of manslaughter may have been based on erroneous legal principles, unless they were corrected in the recharge to the jury.

## 2. Did the Trial Judge Correct the Errors in his Recharge to the Jury?

The trial judge recharged the jury in response to two questions it posed during its deliberations. The jury asked for clarification as to sudden provocation and the burden of proof for manslaughter.

The trial judge responded by correctly recharging the jury on provocation. He told the jury that they would need to consider provocation only if they found the elements of murder established and that if they had a reasonable doubt on the matter, they must convict of manslaughter, not murder.

The question, however, is whether the recharge on provocation corrected the earlier misdirection suggesting that anger short of provocation might suffice to reduce murder to manslaughter by raising a doubt on the existence of the criminal intent for murder. Since the trial judge began his recharge on provocation by noting (correctly) that the jury must already have satisfied itself of the basic elements of murder before it got to this point—*actus reus* and *mens* rea—the recharge did not address the earlier erroneous suggestion that anger alone might reduce murder to manslaughter.

More seriously, the trial judge incorporated by reference into the recharge, his earlier erroneous charge on criminal intention. He stated:

> [TRANSLATION] I defined criminal intention in a general manner and I indicated to you that if you had a reasonable doubt with respect to the accused's criminal intention, you had to return a verdict of manslaughter because the crime would no longer amount to murder.

This incorporated into the trial judge's recharge his previous erroneous comments suggesting that anger alone could negate criminal intention or *mens rea* and hence reduce murder to manslaughter.

I conclude that the recharge did not cure the errors in the trial judge's initial direction on how anger could affect criminal intent.

The respondent argues that the fact that the jury asked for directions on provocation after they had deliberated for four days, combined with the trial judge's direction that they could consider provocation only if they were satisfied of the basic requirements for murder, including criminal intention, suggest that the jury's verdict of manslaughter must have been based on provocation, not the problematic direction on criminal intent. Yet this conclusion is speculative. The fact remains that the jury may have come to its conclusion that the respondent was guilty of manslaughter by another route—the erroneous thesis that serious anger on its own can negate the criminal intent required for murder. The asking of a question related to one possible route to a verdict does not establish that the jury actually followed that route. It is quite possible that the jury went back to the fundamental issues of criminal intent after hearing the judge's recharge on provocation. In view of the misleading directives on anger, we cannot be assured that the jury was able to carry out its function according to the law. To put it another way, we cannot be sure that the recharge corrected the potential for the jury deciding on manslaughter on the erroneous basis put forward in the initial charge.

## 3. Conclusion

The trial judge erred in his charge to the jury on the effect of anger on criminal intent or *mens rea* and its relationship to manslaughter. This error was not corrected on the recharge and we cannot infer from the way the trial proceeded that the jury's verdict of manslaughter was not based on the erroneous initial direction. It follows that the conviction for manslaughter must be set aside and a new trial directed.

As indicated earlier, the Crown in this appeal, relied solely on the trial judge's misdirections on anger and criminal intent. It is therefore unnecessary to comment further on the applicability of the defence of provocation as it may be tendered at the new trial. It will be for the judge on the new trial to determine whether, on the evidence there presented, the defence of provocation should be put to the jury.

I would allow the appeal and direct a new trial on second degree murder.

*Appeal allowed; new trial ordered*

## Questions/Discussion

1. Do you agree with the decision in *Hill*, or should the jury have been directed to consider the matter of the accused's age? How would you describe an ordinary person? What types of special characteristics or traits of an accused should be drawn to the attention of the jury in constructing the reaction of an ordinary person?
2. Do you agree with the decision in *Parent*? Why or why not? What types of provocation would you consider as valid or sufficient in order to be considered by a jury?
3. Should the defence of provocation be available at all? What are the reasons for and against the defence?

## Further Reading

- Banks, N.K., "The Homosexual Panic Defence in Canadian Criminal Law" (1997), 1 C.R. (5th) 371-379.
- Klimchuk, D., "Outrage, Self-control, and Culpability" (1994), 44 University of Toronto Law Journal 441-468.
- Macklem, T., "Provocation and the Ordinary Person" (1987/88), 11 Dalhousie Law Journal 126-156.
- Quigley, T., "Battered Women and the Defence of Provocation" (1991), 55 Saskatchewan Law Review 223-261.
- Roach, Kent, *Criminal Law, 2nd ed.* (Toronto: Irwin Law, 2000) at 247-262.
- Stuart, Don, and R. Delisle, *Learning Canadian Criminal Law, 8th ed.* (Toronto: Carswell, 2001).
- Verdun-Jones, Simon, *Criminal Law in Canada: Cases, Questions, and the Code Code*, 3d ed. (Toronto: Harcourt Canada, 2002) at 315-325.

## 7.4.2   Defence of Mental Disorder

### Introduction

*C. Mitchell*

### INSANITY

Prior to 1800, insanity was usually regarded as a general, seriously disabling condition that, like infancy, was presumed to prevent the formation of criminal intent. Under England's *Criminal Lunatics Act*, 1800 (U.K.), 39 & 40 Geo. 3, c. 94, a successful insanity defence resulted in acquittal and confinement in an asylum. Obviously mad offenders were probably not even brought before the courts.

The modern form of the insanity plea arose in 1843 when the House of Lords devised the McNaghten Rules. These Rules formed the basis for section 16 of the Code. They stated that to establish insanity, the accused must clearly prove that at the time of the offence he had a disease of the mind and thus did not know the nature and quality of the act he was doing, or, if he did know it, that he did not know that it was wrong. The Rules were a response to the insanity acquittal of Daniel McNaghten, tried for the murder of Edward Drummond, secretary of Prime Minister Robert Peel. Under the Rules named after him, McNaghten might well have been convicted.

Since 1843, judges and lawyers have repeated that McNaghten was insane because he suffered from delusions that he was being spied upon and persecuted by Peel's government. However, it has been argued by some that McNaghten likely was being spied upon, that only a natural mistake of identity led him to shoot Drummond in place of Peel, and that he may have been paid to assassinate Peel. Perhaps Lord Chief Justice Tindal was anxious to find McNaghten insane so as to foreclose an embarrassing inquiry into government surveillance of political radicals. McNaghten, of course, would go along with any deception to avoid execution — he died 23 years later in the Broadmoore Criminal Lunatic Asylum. Indeed, it was the death penalty that once made insanity such a critical issue. Insanity matters much less now in Canada because the plea's outcome most just affects the place and style of incarceration, though it can still avoid the minimum 25-year term for murder.

A number of controversial issues are raised by insanity (or "mental disorder" as it is now called in the Criminal Code). These include the role of volitional impairment, the meaning of "disease of mind" and "wrong", the ability of the courts to meaningfully distinguish between the mad and the bad, the acceptance of psychiatrists as "experts" and whether or not section 16 should be abolished outright.

Many American insanity provisions, such as *Durham* (1954) and the American Law Institute standard, expressly allow for volitional incapacity, that is, an inability "to conform one's conduct to the law". But unconscious compulsion need not be explicitly contained in a statutory definition of insanity to be employed in court. Judges can indirectly rule that someone suffering from such a compulsion resulting from a "disease of the mind" may not have knowledge of or appreciate the nature and quality of her act.

Some authorities report that historically, insanity was taken as a general condition, like infancy, which prevented formation of criminal intent (see Smith under Further Reading). This comparison to infancy, however, suggests that the real issue was not lack of intent. Children under 12 can intentionally attack and seek to harm others, often they misbehave with passionate intent; nonetheless, they are not criminally liable. Youngster escape liability in crime, though not in tort, for policy reasons because they are not a threat to the state and because their parents, not the state, are primarily responsible for their control and punishment. Similarly, the seriously insane would have been of little criminal interest historically because they would normally be incarcerated already for their mental disorder.

Evidently, those found in modern trials do act with intent. According to Fingarette and Hasse (see under Further Reading) criminally insane conduct is typically "purposefule, intentional and effectively executed; it is often premeditated, planned and prepared; and it is not infrequently tenaciaously and ingeniously pursued in spite of external objects". Consistent with this observation is the finding that the pattern of homicide by the mentally disordered is identical to ordinary homicides where the victim is usually a family member or a familiar acquaintance. Insane killings are generally not random, so-called "motiveless attacks".

The special legal status of the insane, therefore, is not based on their lack of intent or lack of knowledge but rather on the theory that their unconsciously caused impairment somehow results in or contributes to their wrongful act. The *Durham* Rule (1954) spoke of the act being a "product of" mental abnormality. Both assumptions — that mental illness is unconsciously caused and that it contributes to dangerous behaviour — are open to qualification and debate (See Mitchell under Further Reading)

The supposed link between mental illness and anti-social behaviour is vulnerable to two criticisms. First, blaming irresistible impulses for crime is comparable to demonology with its notions of unconscious, evil spirits taking control of the possessed (See Szasz under Further Reading). Both theories are circular, hence irrefutable. Proof that a mentally ill person was compelled to misbehave is the fact of the misbehaviour itself. And, since in the criminal trial context mental disorder is rarely raised except in connection with some serious misdeed, it is natural for judges, lawyers and forensic specialists to causally link crime and mental illness. Scientifically, however, the anecdotal evidence usually led in court about the relationship between an accused's health status and his or her criminality often has little predictive or explanatory power. What must be demonstrated is some general, stable causal relationship between mental illness and crime and it is on this issue that the second criticism focuses. Historically, the relationship between mental disorder and crime was presumed rather than demonstrated. Now many authorities advise that mental illness has no special connection with violent crime and that the mentally ill statistically are not over-represented in the category of dangerous persons and some argue that mental illness should be ignored altogether as a factor in determining the causes of dangerousness (see Bartol, Morse, and Steadman and Bruff under Further Reading).

The current law on the defence of mental disorder is explained and discussed in the excerpts from the O'Marra article which follows a brief section on diminished responsibility. The final reading, the *Worth* case, is an example of a recent application of the law in this area in regard to the meaning of "wrong" in section 16(1) of the Code.

## Hadfield to Swain: The Criminal Code Amendments Dealing with the Mentally Disordered Accused*

### A.J. O'Marra

* Excerpts from (1993), 36 Criminal Law Quarterly 49.

. . .

The case of *R. v. Swain* (1991), 63 C.C.C. (3d) 193, 5 C.R. (4th) 253, [1991] 1 S.C.R. 933, created a significant turning point in how we deal with mentally disordered accused. While there had been great debate throughout the years over the issues of when and how an accused should be declared not guilty by reason of insanity, largely starting with the famous M'Naghten rules and the resultant jurisprudence, there has been a relative paucity of legislative development or judicial comment on how mentally disordered accused should be dealt with at the post-verdict stage. . . .

It is probably fair to say that very few jurists who have been required to make a s. 614(2) strict-custody order knew what became of or happened to the accused once he became subject to the pleasure of the Lieutenant-Governor.

It has been well recognized that the provisions in the *Criminal Code* as they existed prior to the amendments were procedurally vague. In fact, when the case came before the Ontario Court of Appeal, *R. v. Swain* (1986), 24 C.C.C. (3d) 385, 50 C.R. (3d) 97, 53 O.R. (2d) 609, Mr. Justice Thorson observed that the provisions were "unnecessarily imprecise and sketchy and too often lacking in any clear expression of Parliament's purpose and intent". Indeed, other than remand provisions to obtain evidence as to an accused's psychiatric state and the inclusion of the provision which created advisory review boards with the annual task of determining whether the accused had recovered from his insanity, there has been little legislative change to the progenitor of these sections. The comprehensive legislative package known as Bill C-30, which was proclaimed in force on February 4, 1992, was designed to replace the remnants of the *Criminal Lunatics Act* found in ss. 614 and 617 of the *Criminal Code* with a new system, replete with specific procedures to strengthen due process and the other fundamental Charter rights of the mentally disordered accused, while at the same time protecting society from dangerous, mentally disordered accused.

The Supreme Court of Canada in *Swain* held that s. 614(2) which provides entry to the Lieutenant-Governor's Warrant System in the same manner as the *Criminal Lunatics Act* by way of "strict custody", was unconstitutional for failing to provide due process. Basically, due to the imperative nature of the provision, it did not permit the court to conduct a hearing to inquire into the accused's present state of mind and degree of dangerousness, and whether in fact the accused required confinement. Accordingly, the order for confinement had to be considered arbitrary, Section 614(2) directs that where an accused has been found not guilty by reason of insanity, the court "shall order that he be kept in strict custody . . . until the pleasure of the Lieutenant Governor of the Province is known". The focus of the trial is by necessity on the state of mind of the accused at the time of the offence. However, at the time the court is directed to make a disposition of strict-custody, following a verdict of not guilty by reason of insanity, the only evidence it may have as to the accused's state of mind is in most instances dated. Moreover, the imperative nature of the legislation required a strict custody disposition even if the court had up-to-date evidence of the accused's present state of mind which indicated that such a disposition was not warranted. Accordingly, the court's order made pursuant to s. 614(2) was without due process and arbitrary. While the Supreme Court focused on s. 614(2), Chief Justice Lamer took the opportunity to observe that the other sections of the *Criminal Code* upon which the Lieutenant-Governor's Warrant System was based, were suspicious due to "a lack of procedural safeguards". In the result, there was a clear incentive on the part of Parliament to institute a comprehensive overhaul of the way in which courts and review boards dealt with mentally disordered accused. . . .

### 1. Summary of the Former Criminal Code Provisions Dealing with the Mentally Disordered Accused

As the law existed prior to February 4, 1992, an accused who was found not guilty by reason of insanity would be ordered into strict custody by the court, until the "pleasure of the lieutenant governor of the province is known": s. 614(2).

Section 615(2) provided for the psychiatric assessment of an accused who might be mentally ill and as a result of mental illness, unfit to stand trial. Upon trial of the issue of fitness (s. 615(1), if the court found that the accused was unfit, then the court was directed to order that the accused be kept in custody until, once again " the pleasure of the Lieutenant Governor of the Province is known": s. 615(7). As a practical matter, there was no distinction between "strict custody" under s. 614(2) and "custody" under s. 615(7). The custody which resulted from either order was the same.

Generally, once the court made the order that the accused was to be held in "strict custody" or "custody", the accused remained in a detention centre or jail, pending the issuance of the initial warrant of the Lieutenant-Governor directing the accused to a place of safe custody, namely, a psychiatric facility. Should the accused already have been in a psychiatric facility at the time of the verdict, or finding that the accused was unfit to stand trial, the accused would remain in the custody of the hospital pending the issuance of the initial warrant. The jurisdiction of the Lieutenant-Governor to issue the warrant was found in s. 617(1).

A review board was created under s. 619 of the Code. It was observed by Mr. Justice Arnup in *Abel v. Advisory Review Board, supra*, at p. 165 C.C.C., that the legislation created advisory review boards with a considerable and varied expertise which would ensure that no one languished indefinitely and half-forgotten in mental institutions. The purpose of the review board and the frequency of the reviews was set out in s. 619(5). The review board assumed the obligation to review the case of every person in custody as a result of a s. 617 order. Although there is nothing in the

Code which directed the review board to assist the Lieutenant-Governor in the issuance of his initial order, the practice in Ontario had been that the review board would conduct placement hearings. The chairman of the review board would make a recommendation to the Lieutenant-Governor as to initial placement of the accused following the court ordered remand under either s. 614(2) for the not guilty by reason of insanity accused, or s. 615(7) for an accused who is found unfit to stand trial on account of insanity.

The review board inquired as to the progress of the accused at each of its periodic hearings as directed by s. 619(5) which required it to report to the Lieutenant-Governor as to whether an unfit accused had recovered sufficiently to stand trial, or whether an accused who is found not guilty by reason of insanity had recovered and, if not, to make recommendations that it considered to be in the interests of the accused's recovery and not contrary to the public interest. A report and recommendation would then be provided to the Lieutenant-Governor as to the appropriate disposition of the accused. Depending on the degree of dangerousness presented by the accused, an order would be issued directing that the accused be detained in the custody of a psychiatric hospital, however, with certain discretions afforded to the administrator to allow the accused degrees of community access if appropriate. The system was designed and continues to be one of a monitored conditional release. . . .

### (1)   The Warrant System as Conducted in Ontario

In Ontario, the Lieutenant-Governor's Warrant System (hereafter the "L.G.W. system") utilized a monitored conditional release approach in the management of dangerous mentally disordered accused. The system can be described as a cascade system effected by the use of "loosened warrants". . . .

In order for the system to function there had to be a delegation of authority to hospital administrators. While there was no authority in the previous legislation to do so, such a delegation of authority allowed for the day-to-day management of the mentally disordered accused. The process of gradual reintegration continues under the new legislative regime virtually unchanged.

### 2. Highlights of the Mental Disorder Provisions

In summary form, some of the highlights of the new legislation are as follows:

(a)  Section 16 has been altered to the extent that the notion of "insanity" has been removed and relegated to the historical waste bin which such terms as "lunatics" and "asylums" and has been replaced with that of "mental disorder". It has been done in an attempt to replace antiquated terminology, yet without changing the legal requirements of the defence. "Mental disorder" is still defined as a "disease of the mind" thereby retaining within s. 16 the notion that mental disorder, as a disease of the mind includes: any illness, disorder, or abnormal condition which impairs the human mind and its functioning, excluding, however self-induced states of alcohol or drugs; as well as transitory mental states such as hysteria or concussion": R. v. Cooper (1980), 51 C.C.C. (2d) 129, 13 C.R. (3d) 97, [1980] 1 S.C.R. 1149.

(b) On a verdict of not criminally responsible on account of a mental disorder (N.C.R.), the accused must first have been found to have committed the act. This particular provision will be seen to be important when the concept of capping is proclaimed in force. Certain offences will have a time-limit attached to them beyond which the review board will cease to have jurisdiction. In the instance of murder, there will be no cap, however, in the instance of manslaughter, the cap will be 10 years. Accordingly, it will make a significant difference as to which case the Crown is able to make out prior to the accused being found not criminally responsible.

(c) The court is now authorized to order psychiatric assessments of the accused by medical practitioners to determine not only whether an accused is fit to stand trial, or not criminally responsible on account of mental disorder, but also to determine what the most appropriate disposition should be following such a finding or verdict.

It is important to note that the periods of assessment are generally restricted to five days to determine the issue of fitness and 30 days for any other purpose with a possible maximum increase to 60 days. The shortened assessment period to determine fitness has markedly increased the number of unfit accused who have been directed from the trial process into the review board system.

(d) Any statements made by an accused during the assessment process are protected from use against him, except to prove the issue for which the assessment was ordered, or to challenge the credibility of the accused if he elects to testify and gives testimony inconsistent with statements given during the assessment, or to establish perjury in a subsequent proceeding.

(e) In keeping with the concerns expressed in *R. v. Swain, supra,* after conducting a hearing, the court may render an initial disposition following a verdict of not criminally responsible or finding that the accused is unfit to stand trial by reason of a mental disorder. In addition, the court has the authority to make a time-limited treatment order for an unfit accused which would allow for the administration of a specific course of treatment, without the accused's consent, for a maximum period of 60 days on the testimony of a medical practitioner that it will likely result in a return to fitness.

(f) Review boards have been created in each province by Lieutenant-Governor's Order-in-Council with a composition largely as they have in the past. They have become independent tribunals with direct jurisdiction over the accused rather than merely advisory boards to their respective Lieutenant-Governors.

(g) In rendering a disposition, the court or review board may order the mentally disordered accused to be:
    (i) discharged absolutely, if he is not a significant threat to the safety of the public;
    (ii) discharged subject to conditions, or
    (iii) detained in the custody of a hospital.

The overriding principle that must be taken into account by both the court or review board, is that any disposition must reflect the principle that the disposition is to be the *"least onerous and least restrictive to the accused"*. In reaching a determination, the court and review board must take into consideration the same factors:

    (i)   the need to protect the public from dangerous persons;

    (ii)  the mental condition of the accused at the time;

    (iii) the reintegration of the accused into society;

    (iv) any other needs of the accused.

It should be noted that if an accused requires confinement at the time of the disposition, whether the disposition is rendered by the court or the review board, *he may only be detained in the custody of a hospital.*

(h)  A court-ordered disposition following a verdict of not criminally responsible or finding of unfitness, will only last up to 90 days, other than an order for an absolute discharge for someone found not criminally responsible. The court cannot discharge absolutely a person who has been found unfit to stand trial on account of a mental disorder. Any disposition rendered by the court, other than an absolute discharge, must be reviewed by the review board within that 90-day period, or in the event that the court does not render an initial disposition, the review board must conduct a hearing and render its initial disposition within 45 days of the verdict or finding. Dispositions rendered by the review board are subject to a mandatory review within 12 months or they may be reviewed more often on the request of the accused or the person in charge of the hospital where the accused is detained, or as circumstances require.

(i)  Disposition hearings conducted by the court or the review board may be as informal as circumstances permit, however, all parties are specifically entitled to representation by counsel as well as to examine and cross-examine all witnesses. The proceedings are to be recorded and the hearing process is open to the public, within a caveat that the court or review board may exclude the public or make publication bans under certain circumstances.

(j)  There is a right of appeal against any disposition by an accused or any other party to the proceeding, which may include the Attorney-General of the province, a hospital in whose care the accused has been placed, and any person designated as a party to the proceedings having established a substantial interest in protecting the interests of the accused to the satisfaction of the court or the review board.

(k)  The legislation now covers both indictable and summary conviction matters, whereas under the previous legislative scheme the Lieutenant-Governor had authority to issue warrants for persons found unfit or not guilty by reason of insanity on indictable offences only.

(l)  There is a provision referred to as "capping" which will permit a maximum period during which a mentally disordered accused may be subject to a disposition of the review board. If the verdict of not criminally responsible or finding of unfitness is as a result of an act found to be first or second degree murder or high treason, the maximum period during which the review board may exercise jurisdiction over the accused is life. However, for those offences classified as "designated offences", which largely comprise all other crimes of violence, the maximum period for which the accused could be subject to a disposition, would be 10 years or the maximum period for which the accused would be liable to imprisonment for the offence, whichever is less. As to any other offence which does not fall within the "designated offences" category, the maximum period for which the accused could be subject to a disposition would be two years or the maximum confinement allowable, whichever is shorter. In the instance of young offenders, the maximum period for which the accused would be subject to a disposition would be the maximum period to which he could be confined under the *Young Offenders Act*.

At the end of the capping period, if, as a result of his continuing dangerousness, the accused has not been discharged or successfully reintegrated into the community the review board would no longer have jurisdiction to detain him. If the accused is to be detained, at that point, it would have to be accomplished by way of the civil commitment procedures for involuntary patients under the provincial mental health legislation.

(m) The cap period for designated offences may be extended for certain accused on an application by the prosecution at the time of the verdict to have the accused declared a *"dangerous mentally disordered accused"*. The same criteria and procedures which are used under the dangerous offender provisions of the *Criminal Code* will apply. On a finding by the court that an accused is a dangerous mentally disordered accused, it may increase the cap in respect of the offence to a maximum of life.

Similarly there is a transitional provision which allows for the appointment of a commissioner, who will be selected from the superior court judiciary, to whom applications will be made by the Crown to have accused who have been Lieutenant-Governor's warrant patients on designated offences, declared dangerous mentally disordered accused. On a successful application, an order may be obtained to extend the capping period for that individual accused to a maximum of life.

The proclamation of capping was intended to take place approximately one year after the other provisions had been proclaimed; however, that process has been delayed to allow the provinces to review and amend their mental-health legislation to accommodate the committal of dangerous accused. The transitional process to deal with Lieutenant-Governor's warrant patients who would be subject to release on the proclamation of capping, has not commenced as yet.

### 3. Pre-Verdict Provisions

### (1) Section 16 — Not Criminally Responsible (NCR)

Section 16 of the *Criminal Code* dealing with the defence of insanity has been repealed (see S.C. 1991, c. 43, s. 2) and the following has been substituted for it:

16(1) No person is criminally responsible for an act committed or an omission made while suffering from a mental disorder that rendered the person incapable of appreciating the nature and quality of the act or omission or of knowing that it was wrong.

(2) Every person is presumed not to suffer from a mental disorder so as to be exempt from criminal responsibility by virtue of subsection (1), until the contrary is proved on the balance of probabilities.

(3) The burden of proof that an accused was suffering from a mental disorder so as to be exempt from criminal liability is on the party that raises the issue.

There has been little change to s. 16 other than to replace the notion of insanity with that of mental disorder. Section 2 of the Code now sets out a definition of "mental disorder", which is defined to be "a disease of the mind". Previously, "insanity" had been equated with the concept of "disease of the mind", and as one can see from the definition of mental disorder, the concept of disease of the mind is still an essential element of s. 16. The difference between "insanity" and "mental disorder" is a distinction without a difference because all of the jurisprudence that has evolved from the phrase "disease of the mind" has been incorporated through the definition of "mental disorder". In any event, the Supreme Court in *R. v. Cooper* (1980), 51 C.C.C. (2d) 129, 13 C.R. (3d) 97, [1980] 1 S.C.R. 1149, indicated that a disease of the mind embraces any illness, disorder, or abnormal condition which impairs the human mind and its functioning, excluding, however, self-induced states caused by alcohol or drugs; as well as transitory mental states such as hysteria or concussion.

Aside from updating the terminology in s. 16, the two branches which may lead to the defence of "not guilty by reason of insanity" (NGRI), now "not criminally responsible on account of mental disorder" (NCR), remain the same. In order to meet the test of the first branch, the person must have a mental disorder, the result of which renders him incapable of appreciating the nature or quality of the act. The second branch or route to the defence is that the accused, who suffers from the mental disorder, must establish on a balance of probabilities, as with the first branch, that he is incapable of knowing that the act or omission was wrong. The second branch has presented the most recent and interesting development through a series of cases from the Supreme Court of Canada, *R. v. Chaulk and Morrissette* (1990), 62 C.C.C. (3d) 193, 2 C.R. (4th) 1, [1990] 3 S.C.R. 1303; *R. v. Ratti* (1991), 62 C.C.C. (3d) 105, 2 C.R. (4th) 293, [1991] 1 S.C.R. 68; *R. v. Landry* (1991), 62 C.C.C. (3d) 117, 2 C.R. (4th) 268, [1991] 1 S.C.R. 99; and *R. v. Rromeo* (1991), 62 C.C.C. (3d) 1, 2 C.R. (4th) 307, [1991] 1 S.C.R. 86. . . .

Now the issue is whether the accused is incapable of knowing either that the act is "morally wrong" by the standards of society or that it was legally wrong. Having extended the second branch to include a moral wrong, there was some consternation that it would open the door again to the amoral offenders, specifically psychopaths, who had been denied access to the insanity defence when the test was simply whether they knew that what they did was legally wrong. However, in *R. v. Chaulk and Morrissette, supra*, at pp 232-3 C.C.C., Lamer C.J.C., for the majority, stated that this change to the definition would not result in an opening of the floodgates to the insanity defence:

An interpretation of s. 16(2) that makes the defence available to an accused who knew that he or she was committing a crime but was unable to comprehend that the act was a moral wrong will not open the floodgates to amoral offenders or to offenders who relieve themselves of all moral considerations. First, the incapacity to make moral judgements must be causally linked to a disease of the mind; if the presence of a serious mental disorder is not established, criminal responsibility cannot be avoided. Secondly, as was pointed out by Dickson J. in Schwartz, *supra*, "'moral wrong' is not to be judged by the personal standards of the offender but by his awareness that society regards the act as wrong" (p. 13). The accused will not benefit from substituting his own moral code for that of society. Instead, he will be protected by s. 16(2) if he is incapable of understanding that the act is wrong according to the ordinary moral standards of reasonable members of society.

While a personality disorder or psychopathic personality is capable of constituting a disease of the mind according to *Cooper, supra* and *R. v. Simpson* (1977), 35 C.C.C. (2d) 337, 77 D.L.R. (3d) 507, 16 O.R. (2d) 129 (C.A., and *R. v. Kjeldsen* (1981), 64 C.C.C. (2d) 161, 28 C.R. (3d) 81, [1981] 2 S.C.R. 617, the defence of insanity is not made out where the accused understands the nature, character and consequences of his act, but merely lacks appropriate feelings for the victim, remorse or guilt, even though the lack of feeling stems from the disease of the mind.

Due to the confusion arising from the phrase "not guilty" contained in the former s. 16 in reference to someone found not guilty by reason of insanity, s. 672.34 of the new provisions indicates that if a person qualifies for the defence of being not criminally responsible on account of a mental disorder, the court shall render a verdict that the accused committed the act which constitutes the offence. This section is significant because there has to be formal finding of the *actus reus* of the offence, whereas in the past if the accused qualified for the defence of not guilty by reason of insanity, there was little attention paid to the offence charged and the offence proven because the consequences were the same regardless. In the instance of homicide, it made little difference whether the verdict was not guilty by reason of insanity for murder or manslaughter; however, when and if capping is proclaimed, it will make a marked difference as to how long the mentally disordered accused may be subject to dispositions by a review board.

## (2) Assessments

Section 672.12 permits the accused, the prosecution or the judge to initiate applications for assessment orders. The purposes for which the orders may be made are stated in s. 672.11.

672.11. A court having jurisdiction over an accused in respect of an offence may order an assessment of the mental condition of the accused, if it has reasonable grounds to believe that such evidence is necessary to determine:

    (*a*) whether the accused is unfit to stand trial;

    (*b*) whether the accused was, at the time of the commission of the alleged offence, suffering from a mental disorder so as to be exempt from criminal responsibility by virtue of subsection 16(1);

    (*c*) whether the balance of the mind of the accused was disturbed at the time of the commission of the alleged offence, where the accused is a female person charged with an offence rising out of the death of her newly born child;

    (*d*) The appropriate disposition to be made, where a verdict of not criminally responsible on account of mental disorder or unfit to stand trial has been rendered in respect of the accused; or (*e*) whether an order should be made under subsection 736.11(1) to detain the accused in a treatment facility, where the accused has been convicted of an offence. . . .

In terms of assessments which are ordered to determine if an accused comes within s. 16 of the *Criminal Code*, the Crown's application will not be granted unless the accused has first put his mental capacity for criminal intent into issue, or the court is satisfied that there are reasonable grounds to doubt that the accused was criminally responsible at the time of the offence. Section 672.12(3) should be read with the direction in mind of the Supreme Court of Canada in *R. v. Swain, supra,* to the effect that the Crown cannot lead evidence of an accused's insanity on its own motion, but only where the accused puts his mental capacity for criminal intent in issue, or at the end of the case after the accused has put forth his defence, other than in s. 16, and he would otherwise be found guilty. . . .

### (c) Protected statements

In recognition of an accused's right to remain silent, s. 672.21 directs that statements made during the course of these assessments are to be admissible only for the purpose for which they were ordered:

(a)  at a hearing to determine fitness
(b)  to determine what disposition to impose following a verdict of unfitness or not criminally responsible;
(c)  whether the accused is a dangerous mentally disordered accused;
(d)  to determine whether infanticide applies:
(e)  at trial, to determine if the accused is criminally responsible, or if the accused raises mental disorder, automatism, or he puts his mental capacity for intent into issue, or if the prosecution raises a post-verdict s. 16.

The general rule as stated in s. 672.21(2) is that statements made by the accused during assessments are not admissible in evidence, without the consent of that accused unless it is for one of the above-noted purposes. . . .

### (3)  Fitness: Determining the Issue

The definition of the phrase "unfit to stand trial" is now set out in s. 2 of the Code:

"Unfit to stand trial" means unable on account of mental disorder to conduct a defence at any stage of the proceedings before a verdict is rendered or to instruct counsel to do so, and, in particular, unable on account of mental disorder to:

(*a*)  understand the nature or object of the proceedings,
(*b*)  understand the possible consequences of the proceedings, or
(*c*)  communicate with counsel.

Pursuant to s. 672.22 an accused is presumed fit to stand trial unless the court is satisfied on the "balance of probabilities" that the accused is unfit to stand trial. The onus, or burden of proof, is on the party, either accused or prosecutor, who makes the application to establish that the accused is unfit to stand trial. According to s. 672.24 when the court has reasonable grounds to believe that an accused is unfit to stand trial, and the accused is not represented by counsel, the court shall order that the accused be represented by counsel. . . .

In *Taylor*, the Ontario Court of Appeal indicated that the underlying rationale for the fitness rules is that an accused must have sufficient mental fitness to participate in the proceedings in a meaningful way "in order to ensure that the process of determining guilt is as accurate as possible, that he accused can participate in the proceedings or assist counsel in his or her defence, that the dignity of the trial process is maintained, and that, if necessary, the determination of a fit sentence is made possible". The appropriate test to determine whether an accused is fit, by the enumerated statutory criteria, is whether he has the *cognitive capacity*, rather than an *analytic capacity* to comprehend. The analytic capacity test establishes too high a threshold for fitness by requiring that the accused be capable of making rational decisions beneficial to himself: whereas the cognitive capacity test only requires that the accused understand the nature and object of the proceedings and the consequences. It is not necessary that he be able to act in his own best interests because to require him to do so, would derogate from the fundamental principle that an accused is entitled to choose and present his own defence. . . .

### 4. Post-Verdict Provisions

Under the new legislative regime the duty of the court does not necessarily stop with the rendering of a verdict of not criminally responsible on account of mental disorder or that the accused is unfit to stand trial, but rather the court as well as the review board have been empowered to participate in the "disposition" of the accused. "Court" by definition includes a summary conviction court as defined in s. 785, a judge, a justice and a judge of the Court of Appeal.

### (1) The Initial Disposition

Section 672.45 under the new legislative scheme grants an option to the courts to conduct the initial disposition, that is the disposition immediately following the court having found the accused either unfit to stand trial on account of mental disorder or not criminally responsible on account of a mental disorder.

672.45(1) Where a verdict of not criminally responsible on account of mental disorder or unfit to stand trial is rendered in respect of an accused, the court *may* of its own motion, and *shall* on application of the accused or the prosecutor, hold a disposition hearing.

(2) At a disposition hearing, the court *shall* make a disposition in respect of the accused, *if* it is satisfied that it can readily do so and that a disposition should be made without delay. [Emphasis added.] . . .

The new regime further provides that if the court decides not to make an initial disposition, the review board must do so by virtue of s. 672.47 within 45 days following the finding of unfitness or that the accused is not criminally responsible. If the court does not render an initial disposition, any release process or detention order made by the court will continue in force pursuant to s. 672.46(1) unless cause is shown to the court why the release or detention order should be vacated. By virtue of

s. 672.46(2), the court may also vary a detention order to direct that the accused be kept in the custody of a hospital, pending the initial review by the review board. Practice and experience thus far has shown that very few courts conduct initial disposition hearings but rather have taken to remanding the accused to an appropriate psychiatric hospital pending the initial disposition by the review board.

One of the significant deficiencies of the legislation is an omission to provide the review board with authority to order assessments. Whether or not the court renders the initial disposition, it should order an assessment pending the review board hearing, with a direction that the report is to be made available to the review board. In that way, the review board will have the best available evidence at its disposal as to the present state of mind of the accused at the time of the hearing and disposition.

## (2) Dispositions

In order to render a disposition, the court (and it should be noted the task of the review board is identical), shall take into account the following factors:

> 672.54 Where a court or Review Board makes a disposition pursuant to subsection 672.45(2) or section 672.47, it shall, taking into consideration the need to protect the public from dangerous persons, the mental condition of the accused, the reintegration of the accused into society and the other needs of the accused, make one of the following dispositions that is the *least onerous and least restrictive to the accused*:
>
> > (a) where a verdict of not criminally responsible on account of mental disorder has been rendered in respect of the accused, and in the opinion of the court or Review Board, the accused is not a significant threat to the safety of the public, by order, direct the accused be discharged absolutely;
> >
> > (b) by order, direct that the accused be discharged subject to such conditions as the court or Review Board considers appropriate; or
> >
> > (c) by order, direct that the accused be detained in custody in a hospital, subject to such conditions as the court or Review Board considers appropriate.

The overriding consideration as expressed in the preamble to s. 672.54 is that the disposition to be made must be "the least onerous and the least restrictive to the accused". To render a disposition, the court or review board must consider the following factors:

(1) the need to protect the public from dangerous persons;
(2) the mental condition of the accused;
(3) the reintegration of the accused into society, and
(4) the other needs of the accused.

After consideration of those factors, the court or review board may:

(1) grant an absolute discharge to a not criminally responsible accused who is not a "significant threat to the safety of the public";
(2) discharge the not criminally responsible or unfit accused subject to conditions; or
(3) detain the accused in the custody of a hospital.

The ultimate purpose of the statutory scheme is to protect the public from dangerous persons. The focus of the inquiry under this provision is by necessity as to the dangerousness of the accused and the risk that he presents to the public consequent to his mental condition. The process requires that a predictive and subjective appraisal be applied at each hearing in order to determine the level of security required, if any, leading to a disposition which is in the result the least onerous and least restrictive to the accused. The factors instanced in s. 672.54 are components of the objective to rehabilitate the accused in furtherance of the ultimate purpose which is to protect the safety of the public. . . .

### (3)   Disposition Hearings

Disposition hearings conducted by the court or review board may be held in as an informal manner as is appropriate in the circumstances (s. 672.5(2)).

Section 672(5) envisions an open hearing process. The media, victims, and any others will have a right of access to the hearings. However, an exclusion of the public may be made under s. 672.5(6) when it is in the best interest of the accused and not contrary to the public interest. There shall be a publication ban pursuant to s. 672.51(11) *only* if disposition information has been withheld from the accused or any other person not a party because disclosure would seriously prejudice the accused, or there has been an order under s. 672.5(10)(*b*) removing the accused from the hearing because failure to do so would likely endanger the life or safety of another person or impair the treatment and recovery of the accused. . . .

### (5)   Dealing With the Unfit

Once the issue has been tried and there has been a finding by the court that an accused is unfit, then the court may, pursuant to s. 672,45, render the initial disposition or, in turn, it may be left to the review board to render a disposition within 45 days of the finding pursuant to s. 672.47(1). As noted above, the court must hold a disposition hearing on an application of the accused or the prosecutor, however, the court shall make a disposition only if it is satisfied that: (1) it can readily do so; and (2) that a disposition should be made *without delay*. . . .

### (6)   Reviews

In addition to the power of the review board to make an initial disposition which has already been dealt with above, s. 672.81(1) provides that the review board shall hold a hearing no later than 12 months after making a disposition and every 12 months thereafter for as long as the disposition remains in force in order to review any disposition that it has made in respect of an accused other than an absolute discharge. There is a further mandatory review pursuant to subsec. (2), where the person in charge of a hospital has increased the restrictions on the liberty of the accused significantly for a period exceeding seven days. Such an increase may arise where an accused, who is permitted to reside in the community, is removed therefrom, or placed in a circumstance of greater security, due to a deterioration of his mental condition and increase in the dangerousness that he presents.

Discretionary reviews may be held by the review board *at any time* pursuant to s. 672.82(1) at the request of the accused or any other party. . . .

## Regina v. Worth
### (1995), 98 C.C.C. (3d) 133 (Ont. C.A)

Appeal by the accused from his conviction for second degree murder and from the period of parole ineligibility.

BY THE COURT: — After a trial in February and March, 1990, before Osborne J. and a jury, the appellant was found guilty of second degree murder and sentenced to life imprisonment without eligibility for parole for 23 years. The victim was a 12-year-old girl. The defence virtually conceded that the appellant killed the young girl. Indeed, when the appellant was arrested he had the child's dismembered head in a bag in his car. The principal issue for the jury was whether the appellant had established the defence of mental disorder within s. 16 of the *Criminal Code*. The Crown and the defence led expert psychiatric evidence on this issue. The appellant did not testify.

The appellant appealed against both his conviction and the period of parole ineligibility.

### A. *The conviction appeal*

The appellant made six submissions on his conviction appeal.

. . .

(ii) The trial judge misdirected the jury by telling them that "wrong" in s. 16(1) of the *Code* meant only "legally wrong". In support of this ground of appeal, the appellant applied to introduce fresh evidence on the question whether the appellant knew that his act was "morally wrong".

(iii) The trial judge erred in instructing the jury that they could infer from the appellant's refusal to see a Crown psychiatrist that the appellant's s. 16 defence would not withstand scrutiny. . . .

### (2) *Instruction on mental disorder*

The trial judge instructed the jury that on the second branch of the mental disorder test in s. 16 "wrong" meant "legally wrong". That was the law in February, 1990, when this case was tried: see *Schwartz v. The Queen* (1976), 29 C.C.C. (2d) 1, 67 D.L.R. (3d) 716, [1977] 1 S.C.R. 673. In December, 1990, however, in *R. v. Chaulk* (1990), 62 C.C.C. (3d) 193, [1990] 3 S.C.R. 1303, 2 C.R. (4th) 1, the Supreme Court of Canada held that the defence of mental disorder is available if an accused proves on the balance of probabilities that he is suffering from a disease of the mind that renders him incapable of knowing that his act was legally or morally wrong.

There was no evidence at trial to support a finding that the appellant did not know his actions were morally wrong. The appellant therefore concedes that on the trial record the trial judge's "misdirection" on the meaning of the word "wrong" did not amount to reversible error. He submits, however, that when the evidence at trial is considered with the fresh evidence, then he is entitled to a new trial. The appellant's fresh evidence consisted of an affidavit of Dr. Graham Glancy, a psychiatrist. In response, the Crown filed an affidavit of Dr. Andrew Malcolm, one of the psychiatrists who testified for the Crown at trial. Both psychiatrists were cross-examined on their affidavits. We reviewed this material in considering the appellant's fresh evidence application.

Both counsel accepted that the principles in *Palmer v. The Queen* (1979), 50 C.C.C. (2d) 193, [1980] 1 S.C.R. 759, 14 C.R. (3d) 22, governed the appellant's application to admit fresh evidence under s. 683(1) of the *Code*. The issue on this appeal is whether the fresh evidence meets the last of the four tests in *Palmer*: "the evidence must be such that, if it is believed, it could reasonably, when taken with the other evidence adduced at trial, be expected to have affected the result".

Dr. Glancy did not interview the appellant; instead, he relied on the diagnosis of those who had. He accepted that the appellant suffers from an antisocial personality disorder (in other words he is a "psychopath"). In *R. v. Oommen* (1994), 81 C.C.C.(3d) 8, [1994] 2 S.C.R. 507, 30 C.R. (4th) 195, McLachlin J. wrote at p. 19:

> Finally, it should be noted that we are not here concerned with the psychopath or the person who follows a personal and deviant code of right and wrong. . . . This is different from the psychopath or person following a deviant moral code. Such a person is capable of knowing that his or her acts are wrong in the eyes of society, and despite such knowledge, chooses to commit them.

Dr. Glancy, however, indicated that recent research in psychopathy suggests that psychopaths may suffer from a mental deficit that goes beyond not caring whether their acts are viewed as wrong by society, and that includes not knowing what is morally wrong. But his opinion of the appellant was guarded. He had no doubt that when the appellant killed the deceased, he knew his actions were legally wrong. On the crucial question whether the appellant knew his actions were morally wrong, Dr. Glancy stated in his affidavit that it is possible that at the time of the killing the appellant knew that his actions would be condemned by the majority of society as morally wrong; and that it is also possible the appellant was so lacking in moral sense due to psychopathy that when he killed the deceased he may not have known, "in the fullest sense", that his actions were morally wrong. He confirmed this opinion on cross-examination as the following exchange demonstrates:

> Q. So in terms of the bottom line of your opinion, it is possible that he knew it was morally wrong and it is possible that he did not and it is not clear one way or the other?
> A. That's correct. This is also a difficult issue. It is reasonable that the Court of Appeal decide that. I can only from a psychiatrist point of view, from the evidence I have read, try and put this into some sort of coherent argument from a psychiatrist point of view

> . . .

> Q. I take it that when you — before I ask you that, let me go back to where I started. So I

> take it, your opinion remains the same that it is possible that he knew that killing was morally wrong and also possible that he didn't?
> A. Yes.

At its highest, therefore, Dr. Glancy's opinion suggests only that it is possible, not probable, that when the appellant killed the deceased he may not have known that his actions were morally wrong. Since the appellant must prove the defence of mental disorder on the balance of probabilities, Dr. Glancy's opinion, even if accepted in the face of the substantial contrary evidence, could not reasonably have affected the result. In our view, it provides no additional weight to the evidence the jury heard. The fresh evidence therefore does not meet the fourth requirement for admissibility in *Palmer*. This motion to introduce fresh evidence is dismissed and accordingly this ground of appeal fails.

### (3) *The appellant's refusal to see a Crown psychiatrist*

In his charge to the jury, the trial judge commented on the defence's refusal to permit the Crown psychiatrist to interview and assess the appellant as follows:

> All doctors seem to me to agree that it is an advantage to have spoken to the accused about this general issue of the state of his mind, and that the Crown psychiatrists were denied that opportunity.
>
> . . .
>
> Finally, on the insanity issue, you heard that the accused, through counsel, did not agree to be examined by the Crown psychiatrists or psychiatrist. That is the accused's right. Let there be no doubt about that. As a matter of law, however, this refusal is a fact from which you may, — not "must" but "may", infer that the accused's defence of insanity, that is his section 16 defence, would not withstand scrutiny. This is one among a number of facts which can be considered when you are discussing and considering the insanity issue.
>
> . . .
>
> In dealing with the Crown not being given access to a psychiatric medical examination of the accused, Mr. Frost [defence counsel] asked you to consider that the accused was, through counsel, simply exercising his rights.

The trial judges's comments were consistent with this court's judgment in *R. v. Sweeney* (1977), 35 C.C.C. (2d) 245, 76 D.L.R. (3d) 211, 40 C.R.N.S. 37. The appellant submits, however, that by instructing the jury that they may draw an adverse inference from his refusal to be examined by the Crown psychiatrist, the trial judge infringed the appellant's right to remain silent guaranteed by s. 7 of the *Canadian Charter of Rights and Freedoms*.

We do not agree with this submission. In *R. v. Chaulk, supra*, in discussing the application of s. 1 of the Charter to s. 16 of the *Code*, Lamer C.J.C. referred to the difficulties the Crown faces in obtaining a conclusive psychiatric opinion of an accused's sanity at the time of the offence in cases in which the accused raises the defence of mental disorder. Having put his sanity in issue, we do not think the appellant could preclude the jury from drawing an adverse inference from his refusal to speak to the Crown psychiatrist. An accused's right to silence is not absolute. It is protected in the terms of s. 7, that is, an accused cannot be deprived of his right to silence except in accordance with the principles of fundamental justice. Since the appellant put his sanity in issue and had the burden of proving his mental disorder, we do not think that the trial judges's comments contravened the principles of fundamental justice. . . .

*Appeal dismissed.*

### Questions/Discussion

1. Describe the mental disorder defence in Canada today. What do you think are its principal attributes? Why? What are its principal drawbacks? Why?
2. What do you think is the proper role of the mental health expert in criminal trials? Can juries be too easily swayed by "hired guns" on either side of the process?
3. What were the main reasons behind the 1992 legislation changing the defence of insanity to one of mental disorder? Do you agree that the changes were beneficial to either the accused using such a defence or to the public at large? Why or why not?

### Further Reading

- Bartol, Curt, *Criminal Behaviour—A Psychosocial Approach* (Englewood Cliffs: Prentice Hall, 1980.
- *Durham v. United States* (1954), 214 F.2d 862 (D. Cir.).
- Fingarette, H. and A. Hasse, *Mental Disabilities and Criminal Responsibility* (Berkeley: University of California Press, 1979).
- Mitchell, C., "Culpable Mental Disorder and Criminal Liability" (1986), 8 International Journal of Law and Psychiatry 273.
- Morse, S. "Failed Explanations and Criminal Responsibility: Experts and the Unconscious" (1982), 68 Virginia Law Review 971.
- *R. v. Robinson*, [1996] 1 S.C.R. 683.
- Roach, Kent, *Criminal Law, 2d ed.* (Toronto: Irwin Law, 2000) at 211-230.
- Smith, R., *Trial by Medicine—Insanity and Responsibility in Victorian Law* (Edinburgh: Edinburgh University Press, 1981).
- Steadman, S. and J. Bruff, "Crimes of Violence and Incompetency Diversion" (1975), 66 Journal of Criminal Law and Corrections 73.
- Stuart, Don, and R. Delisle, *Learning Canadian Criminal Law, 8th ed.* (Toronto: Carswell, 2001).
- Szasz, T., *Ideology and Insanity* (London: Routledge, 1970).
- Verdun-Jones, Simon, *Criminal Law in Canada: Cases, Questions, and the Code*, 3d ed. (Toronto: Harcourt Canada, 2002) at 227-254.
- Verdun-Jones, Simon, "The Insanity Defence in Canada: Setting a New Course" (1994), 17 International Journal of Law and Psychiatry 175.

## 7.4.3 Intoxication

### Introduction

Issues of unconscious compulsion and irrationality are also played out within the context of the intoxication defence. Compared to mental disorder, intoxication is also of more practical importance to criminal law and the public because typically half of all personal violence and property offenders are drug-impaired (usually with alcohol).

The defence of intoxication was first developed in the English case of *Beard* in 1920 and was later adopted in Canada. The major distinction established in the case was between "specific intent" and "general intent" crimes. If an offence was classified as a general intent crime (e.g., assault), then the defence of intoxication was not available. If the offence was determined to be a specific intent crime (e.g., murder), then the defence was available and could result in a conviction, but only for a lesser and included offence. An example of a successful use of the defence would be a verdict of manslaughter for a charge of murder.

The case that is reproduced below, the Supreme Court decision in *Daviault*, gives a history and explanation of the defence of intoxication, and proceeds to expand the defence in the area of "extreme intoxication". As a result of this decision, the law in the area was altered—at least until Parliament passed new legislation—when the court held for the time that in the "rarest of cases" the defence of intoxication or extreme drunkenness could be advanced by persons charged with general intent offences. The person's state of drunkenness must be so extreme that the accused resembles an automaton or someone with a disease of the mind as defined by section 16 of the Code. Several acquittals based on a defence of "extreme intoxication" followed this decision and many interest groups, including women's and victims' groups, along with members of the public, pressured the government to change the law. Parliament acted with unusual speed and passed section 33.1 of the Code in June 1995; the new section (reproduced after *Daviault*) effectively removed this defence for most general intent offences (notably sexual assault). With some exceptions, the section has withstood the Charter challenges brought against it.

## Regina v. Daviault
### (1994), 93 C.C.C. (3d) 21 (S.C.C.)

Appeal by the accused from a judgment of the Quebec Court of Appeal, 80 C.C.C. (3d) 175, 19 C.R. (4th) 291, [1993] R.J.Q. 692, 54 Q.A.C. 27, 20 W.C.B. (2d) 345, allowing an appeal by the Crown from the accused's acquittal by Grenier Q.C.J., [1991] R.J.Q. 1794, on a charge of sexual assault.

SOPINKA (dissenting):

*Facts*

The facts which give rise to this appeal are not in dispute. The complainant is a 65-year-old woman who is partially paralysed and, thus, confined to a wheelchair. She knew the appellant through his wife, who was the complainant's dressmaker and ran errands for her. The complainant testified that at approximately 6:00 p.m. on May 30, 1989, at her request, the appellant arrived at her home carrying a 40-oz. bottle of brandy. The complainant drank part of a glass of brandy and then fell asleep in her wheelchair. When she woke during the night to go to the bathroom, the appellant appeared, grabbed her chair, wheeled her into the bedroom, threw her on the bed and sexually assaulted her. The appellant left the apartment at about 4:00 a.m. The complainant subsequently discovered that the bottle of brandy was empty. The trial judge found as a fact that the appellant had drunk the rest of the bottle between 6:00 p.m. and 3:00 a.m.

The appellant was chronic alcoholic. He testified that he had spent the day at a bar where he had consumed seven or eight bottles of beer. He recalled having a glass of brandy upon his arrival at the complainant's residence but had no recollection of what occurred between then and when he awoke nude in the complainant's bed. He denied sexually assaulting her.

The defence called a pharmacologist, Louis Léonard to testify as an expert witness. Mr. Léonard testified that the appellant's alcoholic history made him less susceptible to the effects of alcohol. He hypothesized that, if the appellant had consumed seven or eight beers during the day and then 35 oz. of brandy on the evening in question, his blood-alcohol content would have been between 400 mg. and 600 mg. per 100 ml. of blood. That blood-alcohol ratio would cause death or coma in an ordinary person.

Mr. Léonard testified that an individual with this level of alcohol in his blood might suffer an episode of "l"amnésie-automatisme", also known as a "blackout". In such a state the individual loses contact with reality and the brain is temporarily dissociated from normal functioning. The individual has no awareness of his actions when he is in such a state and will likely have no memory of them the next day. Mr. Léonard further testified that it is difficult to distinguish between a person in a blackout and someone who is simply acting under the influence of alcohol. He stated that if a person acting under the influence of alcohol behaves in a manner which requires cognitive functions or reflection, it is unlikely that the person is in a blackout. On the other hand, if the person departs from his normal behaviour to act in a gratuitous or violent manner, it is more likely that he is in a blackout.

The appellant was charged with one count of sexual assault. The trial judge found as a fact that the appellant had committed the offence as described by the complainant. However, he acquitted the appellant because he had a reasonable doubt about whether the appellant, by virtue of his extreme intoxication, had possessed the minimal intent necessary to commit the offence of sexual assault: [1991] R.J.Q. 1794. The Quebec Court of Appeal overturned this ruling: 80 C.C.C. (3d) 175, 19 C.R. (4th)291, [1993] R.J.Q. 692, 54 Q.A.C. 27. The appellant now appeals to this court as of right, pursuant to s. 691(2)(a) of the *Criminal Code*, R.S.C. 1985, c. C-46. . . .

CORY J.: —

*Issue*

Can a state of drunkenness which is so extreme that an accused is in a condition that closely resembles automatism or a disease of the mind as defined in s. 16 of the *Criminal Code*, R.S.C. 1985, c. C-46, constitute a basis for defending a crime which requires not a specific but only a general intent? That is the troubling question that is raised on this appeal.

The facts of this case and the judgments below are set out in the reasons of Justice Sopinka. Although I agree with my colleague on a number of issues, I cannot agree with his conclusion that it is consistent with the principles of fundamental justice and the presumption of innocence for the courts to eliminate the mental element in crimes of general intent. Nor do I agree that self-induced intoxication is a sufficiently blame-worthy state of mind to justify culpability, and to substitute it for the mental element that is an essential requirement of those crimes. In my opinion, the principles embodied in our *Canadian Charter of Rights and Freedoms*, and more specifically in ss. 7 and 11(*d*), mandate a limited exception to, or some flexibility in, the application of the *Leary* rule. This would permit evidence of extreme intoxication akin to automatism or insanity to be considered in determining whether the accused possessed the minimal mental element required for crimes of general intent.

*Analysis*

As this case involves the reconsideration of a common law principle in light of more recent developments in the principles of criminal law and particularly the enactment of the Charter, it may be useful to begin with a brief review of the historical developments of the relevant criminal law concepts. As well, it will be helpful to outline the various options adopted and suggested with respect to intoxication as a factor in determining whether an accused possessed the mental element required by the crime.

*The physical and mental aspects of criminal acts*

Originally a crime was considered to be the commission of a physical act which was specifically prohibited by law. It was the act itself which was the sole element of the crime. If it was established that the act was committed by the accused then a finding of guilt would ensue. However, as early as the 12th century, in large part through the influence of the canon law it was established that there must also be a mental element combined with the prohibited act to constitute a crime. That is to say that the accused must have *meant* or intended to commit the prohibited act. The physical act and the mental element which together constitute a crime came to be known as the *actus reus* denoting the act, and the *mens rea* for the mental element. Like so many maxims they are imprecise and in many instances misleading.

For my purposes, it is sufficient to say that for a great many years it has been understood that, unless the legislator provides otherwise, a crime must consist of the following elements. First a physical element which consists of committing a prohibited act, creating a prohibited state of affairs, or omitting to do that which is required by the law. Secondly, the conduct in question must be willed, this is usually referred to as voluntariness. Some writers classify this element as part of the *actus reus*, others prefer to associate it with the *mens rea*: however, all seem to agree that it is required: see, generally J.C. Smith and B. Hogan, *Criminal Law*, 7th ed. (1992), at pp. 37ff. . . .

With this concept of a crime established it soon came to be accepted that in certain situations a person who committed a prohibited physical act still could not be found guilty. A number of examples come to mind. For instance, if a person in a state of automatism as a result of a blow on the head committed a prohibited act that he was not consciously aware of committing, he could not be found guilty since the mental element involved in committing a willed voluntary act and the mental element of intending to commit the act were absent. Thus, neither the requisite *actus reus* or *mens rea* for the offence was present. . . .

A review of the history of the defence of intoxication shows that, originally, intoxication was never a defence to any crime. However, with the evolution of criminal law, this rule came to be progressively relaxed and the defence of intoxication was admitted for crimes of specific intent. Although one of the justifications for this was the courts' preoccupation with the harshness of criminal liability and criminal sanctions, clearly this development was also influenced by the development of the requirements for mental elements in crimes. The defence of intoxication was based on the recognition and belief that alcohol affected mental processes and the formulation of intention: see, for example D. McCord, "The English and American History of Voluntary Intoxication to Negate *Mens Rea*", 11 J. Legal Hist. 372 at p. 378 (1990). I would agree with the authors who feel that the progressive expansion of the intoxication defence has paralleled the progressive expansion of theories of the mental elements of crimes: see, for example, T. Quigley, "A Shorn Beard", 10:3 Dalhousie L.J. 167 (1987). In my view, the need for this historical expansion is justified and emphasized by the increased concern for the protection of fundamental rights enshrined in the Charter.

It can thus be seen that with the development of principles recognizing constituent elements of crimes, particularly the need for a mental element, there came the realization that persons who lack the requisite mental element for a crime should not be found guilty of committing that crime. For centuries it has been recognized that both the physical and the mental elements are an integral part of a criminal act. It has long been a fundamental concept of our criminal law.

This appeal is concerned with situations of intoxication that are so extreme that they are akin to automatism. Such a state would render an accused incapable of either performing a willed act or of forming the minimal intent required for a general intent offence. I will approach the issue primarily on the basis that the extreme intoxication renders an accused incapable of forming the requisite minimum intent.

. . .

*Categorization of crimes as requiring either a specific intent or a general intent . . .*

The distinction between crimes of specific and general intent has been acknowledged and approved by this court on numerous occasions. . . .

The categorization of crimes as being either specific or general intent offences and the consequences that flow from that categorization are now well established in this court. . . .

It may have been convenient to review the approach that courts have taken with regard to drunkenness as a factor in considering the mental element in crimes of general intent.

### Drunkenness as a factor in the consideration of criminal liability.

The issue has been the subject of many judicial decisions in commonwealth countries. It is useful here to contrast the two opposite positions which have emerged in the absence of Charter considerations. The first position is illustrated by the decision of this court in *Leary, supra*, and also corresponds to the English position. The second position is that which prevails in Australia and New Zealand. It is best illustrated by *R. v. O'Connor* (1980), 4 A. Crim. R. 348.

### Leary v. The Queen

Leary was charged with rape. In the course of his instructions, the trial judge advised the jury that "drunkenness is no defence to a charge of this sort". This position was taken on the grounds that rape was a crime of general intent and that in such a crime, the mental element could not be negated by drunkenness. The majority in this court confirmed that rape was, indeed, a crime of general intent and that the *mens rea* could not be affected by drunkenness. They relied upon *Director of Public Prosecutions v Majewski*, [1977] A.C. 443. There, the House of Lords held that, unless the offence was one which required proof of a specific intent, it was no defence to a criminal charge that, by reason of self-induced intoxication, the accused did not intend to do the act which constituted the offence. A charge to the jury to that effect was approved.

The minority (Dickson J., with Laskin C.J.C. and Spence J. concurring) would have required that the jury be satisfied that the accused knew the victim was not consenting or was reckless as to whether she was or not. On that issue it was said that drunkenness was an element that the jury could properly take into account in resolving the question. It was their position that drunkenness should be left to the jury, along with all the other relevant evidence, in deciding whether the accused knew the victim was not consenting.

The supporters of the *Leary* decision are of the view that self-induced intoxication should not be used as a means of avoiding criminal liability for offences requiring only a general intent. They contend that society simply cannot afford to take a different position since intoxication would always be the basis for a defence despite the fact that the accused had consumed alcohol with the knowledge of its possible aggravating effects. Supporters of the *Leary* decision argue that to permit such a defence would "open the floodgates" for the presentation of frivolous and unmeritorious defences.

Those who oppose the decision contend that it punishes an accused for being drunk by illogically imputing to him liability for a crime committed when he was drunk. Further, it is said that the effect of that decision is to deny an accused person the ability to negate his very awareness of committing the prohibited physical acts. That is to say the accused might, as a result of his drinking, be in a state similar to automatism and, thus, completely unaware of his actions, yet he would be unable to put this forward as a factor for the jury to consider because his condition arose from his drinking. In such cases, the accused's intention to drink is substituted for the intention to commit the prohibited act. This result is said to be fundamentally unfair. Further, it is argued that the floodgates argument should not have been accepted because juries would not acquit unless there was clear evidence that the drunkenness was of such a severity that they had a reasonable doubt as to whether the accused was even aware that he had committed the prohibited act: see, for example, Mewett and Manning, *Criminal Law*, 2nd ed. (1985), at pp. 214-5.

### *The O'Connor case — A position taken contrary to Leary*

*O'Connor, supra*, is a decision of the High Court of Australia. O'Connor was seen removing a map holder and a knife from a car. A police officer saw him, identified himself and asked O'Connor why he had taken the articles. O'Connor ran away with the officer in pursuit. When he was arrested, O'Connor stabbed the officer with the knife. He was charged with theft of the map holder and knife and wounding with intent to inflict grievous bodily harm. O'Connor testified that he had consumed alcohol and car sickness tablets before these events and stated that he had no memory either of taking anything from the car or of his subsequent arrest. Medical evidence was given that the combined effect of the tablets and alcohol could have produced such a state of intoxication that O'Connor would have been incapable of reasoning or forming an intent to steal or wound. The trial judge directed the jury, in accordance with *Majewski, supra*, that evidence of self-induced intoxication, although relevant in determining whether the accused had acted with the intent to steal or to inflict grievous bodily harm, was not relevant with respect to the included alternative offence of unlawful and malicious wounding. O'Connor was acquitted on the charges of theft and wounding with intent and convicted of the included offence of unlawful wounding.

O'Connor appealed the conviction to a court of criminal appeal which declined to follow *Majewski, supra*, and quashed the conviction. The Attorney-General for Victoria then appealed to the High Court.

There, the majority upheld the decision of the Court of Appeal. They concluded that for all offences requiring proof of a mental element, evidence of intoxication, whether self-induced or not, was relevant and admissible in determining whether the requisite mental element was present. The majority went on to observe that evidence of intoxication which merely tends to establish loss of inhibition or weakening of the capacity for self-control would not provide a basis for denying that the mental element of an offence was present. However, where there was evidence that the accused was unconscious or that his mind was a blank through drunkenness at the time of the offence, this should be left to the jury in resolving the question as to whether there had been a voluntary act on the part of the accused. . . .

Following the decision of this court in *Leary*, important changes have occurred in the evolution of criminal law principles. Many of these changes were prompted by the enactment of the Canadian Charter of Human Rights and Freedoms. It must now be seen whether, as a result of the passage of the Charter or the reasoning in subsequent cases of this court, some modification of the rule established by *Leary* is required.

## Passage of the Charter and subsequent cases of this court

The passage of the Charter makes it necessary to consider whether the decision in *Leary* contravenes ss. 7 or 11(*d*) of the Charter. Those sections provide:

7. Everyone has the right to life, liberty and security of the person and the right not to be deprived thereof except in accordance with the principles of fundamental justice.

. . .

11. Any person charged with an offence has the right

. . .

(*d*) to be presumed innocent until proven guilty according to law in a fair and public hearing by an independent and impartial tribunal;

There have been some statements by this court which indicate that one aspect of the decision in *Leary* does infringe these provisions of the Charter. The first occurred in *R. v. Bernard, supra*. Bernard was charged with sexual assault causing bodily harm. He was tried by judge and jury and found guilty. Bernard admitted forcing the complainant to have sexual intercourse with him but stated that his drunkenness caused him to attack her. The issue was whether self-induced intoxication should be considered by the jury along with all the other relevant evidence in determining whether the prosecution had proved beyond a reasonable doubt the *men rea* required by the offence. Bernard's appeal was dismissed by a majority of the court. They all agreed that, as the defence of intoxication had not been made out on the evidence, s. 613(1)(*b*)(iii) (now s. 686(1)(*b*)(iii)) of the *Criminal Code* could be applied. Four sets of reasons were given. . . .

Wilson, J. (L'Heureux-Dubé J. concurring), agreed with the conclusion reached by McIntyre and Beetz JJ. However, she advocated a modification of the rule set out in *Leary*. Her reasoning proceeds in this way. Sexual assault causing bodily harm is an offence of general intent which requires only a minimal intent to apply force. Ordinarily the Crown can establish the requisite mental state by means of the inferences to be drawn from the actions of the accused. Wilson J. found that the *Leary* rule was perfectly consistent with an onus resting upon the Crown to prove the minimal intent which should accompany the doing of the prohibited act in general intent offences, but she would have applied it in a more flexible form. In her view, evidence of intoxication could properly go before a jury in general intent offences if it demonstrated such extreme intoxication that there was an absence of awareness which was akin to a state of insanity or automatism. Only in such cases would she find that the evidence was capable of raising a reasonable doubt as to the existence of the minimal intent required for a general intent offence. Wilson J. put forward her position in this way at pp. 41-2:

I believe that the *Leary* rule is perfectly consistent with an onus resting on the Crown to prove the minimal intent which should accompany the doing of the prohibited act in general intent offences. *I view it as preferable to preserve the Leary rule in its more flexible form as Pigeon J. applied it, i.e., so as to allow evidence of intoxication to go to the trier of fact in general intent offences only if it is evidence of extreme intoxication involving an absence of awareness akin to a state of insanity or automatism. Only in such a case is the evidence capable of raising a reasonable doubt as to the existence of the minimal intent required for the offence.* I would not overrule *Leary*, as the Chief Justice would, and allow the evidence of intoxication to go to the trier of fact in every case regardless of its possible relevance to the issue of the existence of the minimal intent required for the offence.

(Emphasis added.)

She also noted that she had some real concerns about the validity of the use of self-induced intoxication as a substituted form of *mens rea* under the Charter. More specifically, she thought it would be unlikely that proof of the substituted element would lead inexorably to a conclusion that the minimum intent existed at the time of the commission of the criminal act. . . .

### The alternative options

What options are available with regard to the admissibility and significance or evidence of drunkenness as it may pertain to the mental element in general intent offences? One choice would be to continue to apply the *Leary* rule. Yet, as I will attempt to demonstrate in the next section, the rule violates the Charter and cannot be justified. Thus, this choice is unacceptable.

Another route would be to follow the *O'Connor* decision. Evidence relating to drunkenness would then go to the jury along with all other relevant evidence in determining whether the mental element requirement had been met. It is this path that is enthusiastically recommended by the majority of writers in the field. Yet it cannot be followed. It is now well established by this court that there are two categories of offences. Those requiring a specific intent and others which will call for nothing more than a general intent. To follow *O'Connor* would mean that all evidence of intoxication of any degree would always go to the jury in general intent offences. This, in my view, is unnecessary. Further, in *Bernard, supra*, the majority of this court rejected this approach.

A third alternative, which I find compelling, is that proposed by Wilson J. in *Bernard*. I will examine the justifications for adopting this position in more detail shortly, but before doing that it may be helpful to review the nature of the Charter violations occasioned by a rigid application of the *Leary* rule.

### How the Leary rule violates ss. 7 and 11(d) of the Charter

What then is the rule of law established by the decision in *Leary*? The conclusion of the majority in that case establishes that, even in a situation where the level of intoxication reached by the accused is sufficient to raise a reasonable doubt as to his capacity to form the minimal mental element required for a general intent offence for which he is being tried, he still cannot be acquitted. In such a situation, self-induced intoxication is substituted for the mental element of the crime. The result of the decision in *Leary* applied to this case, is that the intentional act of the accused to voluntarily become intoxicated is substituted for the intention to commit the sexual assault or for the recklessness of the accused with regard to the assault. This is a true substitution of *mens rea*. First, it would be rare that the events transpiring from the consumption of alcohol through to the commission of the crime could be seen as one continuous series of events or as a single transaction. Secondly, the requisite mental element or *mens rea* cannot necessarily be inferred from the physical act or *actus reus* when the very voluntariness or consciousness of that act may be put in question by the extreme intoxication of the accused.

It has not been established that there is such a connection between the consumption of alcohol and the crime of assault that it can be said that drinking leads inevitably to the assault. Experience may suggest that alcohol makes it easier for violence to occur by diminishing the sense of what is acceptable behaviour. However, studies indicate that it is not in itself a cause of violence: see "Interim Report of the Commission of Inquiry into the Non-Medical Use of Drugs", c. 3; "The LeDain Interim Report", referred to by S.H. Berner, in "Intoxication and Criminal Responsibility", Law Reform Commission (1975); Law Commission, Great Britain, "Intoxication and Criminal Liability", Consultation Paper No. 127 at pp. 4, 67 (1993); see also the references and additional information given in notes 14, 15, 16 and 18 at p. 4; C.N. Mitchell, "The Intoxicated Offender — Refuting the Legal and Medical Myths", Int. J.L. & Psychiatry 77 at p. 89 (1988); S.S. Covington, "Alcohol and Family Violence", Paper presented at the 34th International Congress on Alcoholism and Drug Dependence, August 4-10, 1985, Calgary, Alta, Canada, at p. 24; L. Wolff and B. Reingold, "Drug Use and Crime", 14:6 Juristat 1 at pp. 5-8 and 13 (1994), and Saskatchewan Alcohol and Drug Abuse Commission, "Legal Offences in Saskatchewan: The Alcohol and Drug Connection", Research Report (February, 1989). . . .

In my view, the strict application of the *Leary* rule offends both ss. 7 and 11(*d*) of the Charter for a number of reasons. The mental aspect of an offence, or *mens rea*, has long been recognized as an integral part of crime. The concept is fundamental to our criminal law. That element may be minimal in general intent offences; none the less, it exists. In this case, the requisite mental element is simply an intention to commit the sexual assault or recklessness as to whether the actions will constitute an assault. The necessary mental element can ordinarily be inferred from the proof that the assault was committed by the accused. However, the substituted *mens rea* of an intention to become drunk cannot establish the *mens rea* to commit the assault. . . .

The consumption of alcohol simply cannot lead inexorably to the conclusion that the accused possessed the requisite mental element to commit a sexual assault, or any other crime. Rather the substituted *mens rea* rule has the effect of eliminating the minimal mental element required for sexual assault. Furthermore, *mens rea* for a crime is so well-recognized that to eliminate that mental element, an integral part of the crime, would be to deprive an accused of fundamental justice. . . .

It was argued by the respondent that the "blameworthy" nature of voluntary intoxication is such that it should be determined that there can be no violation of the Charter if the *Leary* approach is adopted. I cannot accept that contention. Voluntary intoxication is not yet a crime. Further, it is difficult to conclude that such behaviour should always constitute a fault to which criminal sanctions should apply. However, assuming that voluntary intoxication is reprehensible, it does not follow that its consequences in any given situation are either voluntary or predictable. Studies demonstrate that the consumption of alcohol is not the cause of the crime. A person intending to drink cannot be said to be intending to commit a sexual assault.

Further, self-induced intoxication cannot supply the necessary link between the minimal mental element or *mens rea* required for the offence and the *actus reus*. This must follow from reasoning in *R. v. DeSousa* (1992), 76 C.C.C. (3d) 124, 95 D.L.R. (4th) 595, [1992] 2 S.C.R. 944 (S.C.C.), and *R. v. Théroux, supra*. Here, the question is not whether there is some symmetry between the physical act and the mental element but whether the necessary link exists between the minimal mental element and the prohibited act; that is to say that the mental element is one of intention with respect to the *actus reus* of the crime charged. . . .

In summary, I am of the view that to deny that even a very minimal mental element is required for sexual assault offends the Charter in a manner that is so drastic and so contrary to the principles of fundamental justice that it cannot be justified under s. 1 of the Charter. The experience of other jurisdictions which have completely abandoned the *Leary* rule, coupled with the fact that under the proposed approach, the defence would be available only in the rarest of cases, demonstrate that there is no urgent policy or pressing objective which need to be addressed. Studies on the relationship between intoxication and crime do not establish any rational link. Finally, as the *Leary* rule applies to all crimes of general intent, it cannot be said to be well tailored to address a particular objective and it would not meet either the proportionality or the minimum impairment requirements.

What then should be the fate of the *Leary* rule?

## Approach that should be taken when a common law principle is found to infringe the provisions of the Charter

In *R. v. Swain* (1991), 63 C.C.C. (3d) 481, [1991] 1 S.C.R. 933, 5 C.R. (4th) 253 (S.C.C.), Lamer C.J.C. (concurred in by Sopinka J. and myself), wrote on this issue. At p. 510, he stated:

> Before turning to s. 1, however, I wish to point out that because this appeal involves a Charter challenge to a common law, judge-made rule, the Charter analysis involves somewhat different considerations than would apply to a challenge to a legislative provision. For example, having found that the existing common law rule limits an accused's rights under s. 7 of the Charter, it may not be strictly necessary to go on to consider the application of s. 1. Having come to the conclusion that the common law rule enunciated by the Ontario Court of Appeal limits an accused's right to liberty in a manner which does not accord with the principles of fundamental justice, it could, in my view, be appropriate to consider at this stage whether an alternative common law rule could be fashioned which would not be contrary to the principles of fundamental justice.

> If a new common law rule could be enunciated which would not interfere with an accused person's right to have control over the conduct of his or her defence, I can see no conceptual problem with the court's simply enunciating such a rule to take the place of the old rule, without considering whether the old rule could none the less be upheld under s. 1 of the Charter. Given that the common law rule was fashioned by judges and not by Parliament or

a legislature, judicial deference to elected bodies is not an issue. If it is possible to reformulate a common law rule so that it will not conflict with the principles of fundamental justice, such a reformation should be undertaken.

This then is the approach that should be adopted when a common law principle is found to infringe the Charter. This, again, militates in favour of the adoption of a flexible application of the *Leary* rule, as was suggested by Wilson J.

### *Justifications for the adoption of the flexible approach suggested by Wilson J.*

As I have said, the position adopted by Wilson J. in *Bernard* has much to commend it and should be adopted. Indeed, the original case which is the basis for much of our jurisprudence pertaining to intoxication seems to confirm this position. In *Director of Public Prosecutions v. Beard*, [1920], A.C. 479, Lord Birkenhead set out the three propositions which have been so frequently referred to in cases involving intoxication and criminal behaviour, at pp. 500-2:

> 1. That insanity, whether produced by drunkenness or otherwise, is a defence to the crime charged. The distinction between the defence of insanity in the true sense caused by excessive drinking, and the defence of drunkenness which produces a condition such that the drunken man's mind becomes incapable of forming a specific intention, has been preserved throughout the cases. The insane person cannot be convicted of a crime . . . but, upon a verdict of insanity, is ordered to be detained during His Majesty's pleasure. The law takes no note of the cause of the insanity. If actual insanity in fact supervenes, as the result of alcoholic excess, it furnishes as complete an answer to a criminal charge as insanity induced by any other cause.

> . . .

> 2. That evidence of drunkenness which renders the accused incapable of forming the specific intent essential to constitute the crime should be taken into consideration with the other facts proved in order to determine whether or not he had this intent.

> 3. *That evidence of drunkenness falling short of a proved incapacity in the accused to form the intent necessary to constitute the crime, and merely establishing that his mind was affected by drink so that he more readily gave way to some violent passion, does not rebut the presumption that a man intends the natural consequences of his acts.*

(Emphasis added.)

It does not appear to me that the decision was meant to create a complete bar to the defence of intoxication in the context of crimes of general intent. . . .

Further support for the modification of the *Leary* rule in favour of the more flexible rule suggested by Wilson J. comes from the fact that the decision in *Majewski, supra*, which was relied upon by the majority in *Leary*, has been the subject of severe criticism in the United Kingdom. The following extract from the Law Commission's "Intoxication and Criminal Liability", *supra*, at p. 34 is an example:

> The present law is therefore objectionable on three levels, It is very complicated and difficult to explain, to the extent that it is difficult to think that it operates in practice other than by its detailed rules being substantially ignored; it purports to apply a clear social policy, of ensuring that intoxicated people who commit criminal acts do not escape criminal sanctions, but only does so in an erratic and unprincipled way; and if taken seriously it creates many difficulties of practical application. It is therefore understandable that in other jurisdictions, and under the rational scrutiny of law reformers, other solutions have been sought to the

problem of protecting society from those who commit criminal acts when in a state of intoxication.

Perhaps the result in these cases arose from the understandable desire to ensure that the accused persons should not escape criminal responsibility by the consumption of alcohol. . . .

Far more writers have supported the approach advocated by Dickson J. in *Leary*, and adopted in *O'Connor*. In my view, the most vehement and cogent criticism of both *Majewski* and *Leary* is that they substitute proof of drunkenness for proof of the requisite mental element. The authors deplore the division of crimes into those requiring a specific intent and those which mandate no more than a general intent. They are also critical of the resulting presumption of recklessness, and of the loss of a requirement of a true *mens rea* for the offence. They would prefer an approach that would permit evidence of drunkenness to go to the jury together with all the other relevant evidence in determining whether the requisite *mens rea* had been established. . . .

I find further support for adopting the approach suggested by Wilson J. in studies pertaining to the effect of the *O'Connor* and *Kamipeli* decisions which have been undertaken in Australia and New Zealand: reference to these studies can be found in the English Law Commission's "Intoxication and Criminal Liability", *supra*, at pp. 60-3. One of these studies was conducted in New South Wales, by means of a survey of approximately 510 trials: see Judge G. Smith, "Footnote to O'Connor's Case", *supra*. The author, Judge George Smith, concluded, at p. 277, that:

> Those figures disclose that a "defence" of intoxication which could not have been relied upon pre-*O'Connor* was raised in eleven cases or 2.16 per cent of the total. Acquittals followed in three cases or 0.59 per cent of the total, but only in one case or 0.2 per cent of the total could it be said with any certainty that the issue of intoxication was the factor which brought about the acquittal.
>
> . . .
>
> It seems to me that no one with any experience of the criminal courts should be greatly surprised at this result for the simple practical reason that any "defence" of drunkenness poses enormous difficulties in the conduct of a case. To name but one, if the accused has sufficient recollection to describe relevant events, juries will be reluctant to believe that he acted involuntarily or without intent whereas, if he claims to have no recollection, he will be unable to make any effective denial of facts alleged by the Crown.
>
> . . .
>
> Certainly my inquiries would indicate that the decision in *O'Connor's* case, far from opening any floodgates has at most permitted an occasional drip to escape from the tap.

That study clearly indicates that the *O'Connor* decision has not had an effect of any significance on trials or on the number of acquittals arising from evidence of severe intoxication. . . .

It is obvious that it will only be on rare occasions that evidence of such an extreme state of intoxication can be advanced and perhaps only on still rarer occasions is it likely to be successful. None the less, the adoption of this alternative would avoid infringement of the Charter.

I would add that it is always open to Parliament to fashion a remedy which would make it a crime to commit a prohibited act while drunk.

The appellant in this case is an elderly alcoholic. It is difficult if not impossible to present him in a sympathetic light. Yet any rule on intoxication must apply to all accused, including the young and inexperience drinker. The strict rule in *Leary* is not a minor or technical infringement but a substantial breach of the Charter eliminating the mental elements of crimes of general intent in situations where the accused is in an extreme state of intoxication. I would think that this judge-made rule should be applied flexibly, as suggested by Wilson J., so as to comply with the Charter. Such an approach would mean that except in those rare situations where the degree of intoxication is so severe it is akin to automatism that drunkenness will not be a defence to crimes of general intent.

It should not be forgotten that if the flexible "Wilson" approach is taken, the defence will only be put forward in those rare circumstances of extreme intoxication. Since that state must be shown to be akin to automatism or insanity, I would suggest that the accused should be called upon to establish it on the balance of probabilities. This court has recognized, in *R. v. Chaulk* (1990), 62 C.C.C. (3d) 193, [1990] 3 S.C.R. 1303, 2 C.R. (4th) 1 (S.C.C.), that although it constituted a violation of the accused's rights under s. 11(*d*) of the Charter, such a burden could be justified under s. 1. In this case, I feel that the burden can be justified. Drunkenness of the extreme degree required in order for it to become relevant will only occur on rare occasions. It is only the accused who can give evidence as to the amount of alcohol consumed and its effect upon him. Expert evidence would be required to confirm that the accused was probably in a state akin to automatism or insanity as a result of his drinking. . . .

Thus, it is appropriate to place an evidentiary and legal burden on the accused to establish, on a balance of probabilities, that he was in a state of extreme intoxication that was akin to automatism or insanity at the time he committed the offence.

*Result if the mental element relates solely to the actus reus which requires that the prohibited act be performed voluntarily*

Should it be thought that the mental element involved relates to the *actus reus* rather than the *mens rea* then the result must be the same. The *actus reus* requires that the prohibited criminal act be performed voluntarily as a willed act. A person in a state of automatism cannot perform a voluntary willed act since the automatism has deprived the person of the ability to carry out such an act. It follows that someone in an extreme state of intoxication akin to automatism must also be deprived of that ability. Thus, a fundamental aspect of the *actus reus* of the criminal act is absent. It would equally infringe s. 7 of the Charter if an accused who was not acting voluntarily could be convicted of a criminal offence. Here again the voluntary act of becoming intoxicated cannot be substituted for the voluntary action involved in sexual assault. To do so would violate the principle set out in *Vaillancourt, supra*. Once again to convict in the face of such a fundamental denial of natural justice could not be justified under s. 1 of the Charter.

*Summary of proposed remedy*

In my view, the Charter could be complied with, in crimes requiring only a general intent, if the accused were permitted to establish that, at the time of the offence, he was in a state of extreme intoxication akin to automatism or insanity. Just as in a situation where it is sought to establish a state of insanity, the accused must bear the burden of establishing, on the balance of probabilities, that he was in that extreme state of intoxication. This will undoubtedly require the testimony of an expert. Obviously, it will be a rare situation where an accused is able to establish such an extreme degree of intoxication. Yet, permitting such a procedure would mean that a defence would remain open that, due to the extreme degree of intoxication, the minimal mental element required by a general intent offence had not been established. To permit this rare and limited defence in general intent offences is required so that the common law principles of intoxication can comply with the Charter.

In light of the experience in Australia or New Zealand, it cannot be said that to permit such a defence would open the floodgates to allow every accused who had a drink before committing the prohibited act to raise the defence of drunkenness. As observed earlier, studies made in Australia and New Zealand indicate that there has not been any significant increase in the number of acquittals following the *O'Connor* and *Kemipeli* decisions.

*Disposition*

In the result, I would allow the appeal, set aside the order of the Court of Appeal [80 C.C.C. (3d) 175, 19 C.R. (4th) 291, [1993] R.J.Q. 692] and direct a new trial.

*Appeal allowed; new trial ordered.*

**Note:**

The Criminal Code was amended in June 1995, to negate the effect of the *Daviault* case as follows:

**Section 33**

The *Criminal Code* is amended by adding the following after section 33 (1995, c. 32, s.1):

**SELF-INDUCED INTOXICATION**

33.1(1) It is not a defence to an offence referred to in subsection (3) that the accused, by reason of self-induced intoxication, lacked the general intent or the voluntariness required to commit the offence, where the accused departed markedly from the standard of care as described in subsection (2).

(2) For the purposes of this section, a person departs markedly from the standard of reasonable care generally recognized in Canadian society and is thereby criminally at fault where the person, while in a state of self-induced intoxication that renders the person unaware of, or incapable of consciously controlling, their behaviour, voluntarily or involuntarily interferes or threatens to interfere with the bodily integrity of another person.

(3) This section applies in respect of an offence under this Act or any other Act of Parliament that includes as an element an assault or any other interference or threat of interference by a person with the bodily integrity of another person.

## Questions/Discussion

1.   Do you think that the general intent/specific intent distinction makes legal sense? Why or why not? Do you think it makes commonsense? Why or why not?
2.   Why should we reward an offender for getting intoxicated before the crime? What arguments do you have that weigh against the availability of the offence? What arguments support its availability?
3.   Do you agree with the reasoning and the result in *Daviault*? Why or why not? Do think that section 33.1 was an appropriate response on the part of Parliament to the decision? Why or why not?

## Further Reading

•   Roach, Kent, *Criminal Law, 2nd ed.* (Toronto: Irwin Law, 2000) at 183-210.
•   Schaffer, M., "*R. v. Daviault*: A Principled Approach to Drunkenness or a Lapse of Common Sense?" (1996), 3 Review of Constitutional Studies 311.
•   Smith, Kelly, "Section 33.1: Denial of the *Daviault* Defence Should Be Held Constitutional" (2000), 28 C.R. (5th) 350-366.
•   Stuart, Don, and R. Delisle, *Learning Canadian Criminal Law, 8th ed.* (Toronto: Carswell, 2001).
•   Verdun-Jones, Simon, *Criminal Law in Canada: Cases, Questions, and the Code Code*, 3d ed. (Toronto: Harcourt Canada, 2002) at 279-292.

## 7.4.4   Automatism

### Introduction

Unlike the other defences in this section relating to incapacity, automatism, where successful, results in a complete acquittal, and represents a finding that the accused was in a dissociative state at the time of the offence. This means that the actions of the accused are considered to be involuntary and not his or her own. The main legal issue in automatism is often what is a valid or acceptable cause of the unconscious state once such a state has been established. While seizures and other such involuntary muscle movements may be acceptable, what of sleepwalking, black-outs, or emotional traumas? Critics of the defence have argued that its availability and success depends too much on access to the right "expert" witness, and also that too often such dissociative states are confused with loss of memory after the event.

Generally, the courts appear unwilling to extend the operation of the defence too far; this can be seen in *Rabey*, below, where the accused argued he was in a dissociative state due to an emotional trauma and the court had to decide if this was a "valid" unconscious state or not. The second case, *Parks*, examines the issue of sleepwalking and automatism in a case of murder where the accused drove 23 kilometres to the victim's house and after the killing drove himself to the police station. The final case of *Stone* represents the most recent treatment of the defence in the Supreme Court in distinguishing between insane and non-insane automatism and in addressing the burden of proof that the accused must meet.

## Rabey v. The Queen
### (1980), 54 C.C.C. (2d) 1 (S.C.C.)

[Only the judgments of Dickson J. and Ritchie J. are reproduced below.]

DICKSON, J. (dissenting): — The automatism "defence" has come into considerable prominence in recent years. Although the word "automatism" made its way but lately to the legal state, it is a basic principle that absence of volition in respect of the act involved is always a defence to a crime. A defence that the act is involuntary entitles the accused to a complete and unqualified acquittal. That the defence of automatism exists as a middle ground between criminal responsibility and legal insanity is beyond question. Although spoken as a defence, in the sense that it is raised by the accused, the Crown always bears the burden of proving a voluntary act.

The issue in this appeal is whether automatism resulting from a "psychological blow" is available to an accused in answer to a charge of causing bodily harm with intent to wound. The appellant, Wayne Kenneth Rabey, suddenly and without warning assaulted a fellow student and friend, causing her injury. The theory of the defence was that his behaviour was caused by a "psychological blow, an intense emotional shock which induced a "dissociative state", during which for a time, the appellant was neither conscious of, nor able to control his conduct, so that it was involuntary. This is sometimes spoken of as non-insane automatism, to distinguish it from cases in which the state of automatism is attributable to disease of the mind.

At common law a person who engaged in what would otherwise have been criminal conduct was not guilty of a crime if he did so in a state of unconsciousness or semi-consciousness. Nor was he responsible if he was, by reason of a disease of the mind or defect of reason, unable to appreciate the nature and quality of an act or that its commission was wrong. The fundamental precept of our criminal law is that a man is responsible only for his conscious, intentional acts. Devlin, J., summed up the position in *R. v. Kemp*, [1956] 3 All E.R. 294 at p. 251:

> In the eyes of the common law if a man is not responsible for his actions he is entitled to be acquitted by the ordinary form of acquittal, and it matters not whether his lack of responsibility was due to insanity or to any other cause.

In order to protect the public from the dangerous criminally insane the common law was changed by statute, long ago. By the *Criminal Lunatics Act, 1800*, and the *Trial of Lunatics Act, 1883*, and in Canada by the *Criminal Code*, a verdict of not guilty by reason of insanity results in committal to an institution. The purpose of the qualified verdict of acquittal is, of course, to ensure custody and treatment for those who might pose a continuing threat to society by reason of mental illness. In Canada, an accused who is acquitted on the ground of insanity is kept in strict custody in the place and manner that the Court directs, until the pleasure of the Lieutenant-Governor of the Province is known (s. 542(2) of the *Code*).

The term "automatism" first appeared in the cases and in the periodical literature about 30 years ago. It is seen with increasing frequency. The defence of automatism is successfully invoked in circumstances of a criminal act committed unconsciously; and, in the past, has generally covered acts done while sleepwalking or under concussional states following head injuries.

The defence of automatism is, in some respects, akin to that of insanity. In both instances, the issue is whether an accused had sufficient control over, or the knowledge of, his criminal act, to be held culpable. The two defences are, however, separate and distinct. As Professor Edwards observed in 21 Mod. L. Rev. 375 at 384 (1958):

> ... Both circumstances are concerned to prove mental irresponsibility, the essential difference ... being that in the case of insanity the defect of the understanding must originate in a disease of the mind, whereas in the defence of automatism *simpliciter* the criminal law is not concerned with any question of the disease of the mind.

Although separate, the relationship between the two defences cannot be discounted. Automatism may be subsumed in the defence of insanity in cases in which the unconscious action of an accused can be traced to, or rooted in, a disease of the mind. Where that is so, the defence of insanity prevails.

. . .

### The Facts

At the time of the alleged offence, March 1, 1974, the appellant, 20 years of age, was a third-year geology student in an honours science course at the University of Toronto. During the fall of 1973, he had spent some time with the complainant, also a third-year science student with whom he shared a number of classes. Along with two male classmates, the two studied and lunched together. Their social activities extended to walks together, dinner at one another's homes and forays to a local bar. The appellant was somewhat shy and though he began to develop strong feelings for the attractive, out-going complainant, the sentiment was not reciprocated.

Plans for a ski trip to Quebec were made in November and the two planned to share a room. The complainant then invited another student to accompany them, creating a more platonic overtone. The three did in fact go to Quebec. The appellant testified that his relationship with the complainant deteriorated in early 1974. They no longer went on walks or visited for dinner. He still saw much of her at school.

On February 28, 1974, the complainant asked the appellant to assist her with an assignment. While she was absent a few moments, he flipped through her books to locate an equation and found a letter she had written to a female friend. He took the letter without her knowledge and read it at home that evening. The letter contains a number of references to sexual activity, both actual and wished for. Toward the end of the letter, this paragraph appears:

> And for some reason all the guys I know want to go out with me and not just be friends any more so I can't talk to them. I don't want to go out with them and they know it so there is static in the air which is why I want to leave. Hell I can insult Wayne [the appellant] and Rick and they still hug me in class. I want to be alone or with just one good guy, not with a bunch of nothings.

The appellant was hurt and angry as he read the letter. He marked the passages referred to above with a pen.

The following morning, he removed a rock sample of galena from the geology lab. This was not unusual, for he was permitted to take samples home for purposes of study. At about noon, as he left to watch a squash match, he met the complainant. He testified that, "just for about a second, not even that, I felt sort of strange, I can't describe how I felt". He referred to it as a flash. He suggested she watch the match with him. The two proceeded to the squash court. The game was not in progress, so they left by the far stairwell. The appellant remembered asking her what she though of Gord, a friend of theirs, hearing the reply that he was "just a friend", and "really the next thing I remember was choking her and I remember the face was a funny colour and I remember seeing a lot of blood and I stopped". He realized his hands were around her throat.

The complainant testified that following the question about Gord, the appellant then asked, "What do you think of me?" She replied, "You're just a friend too." As she opened a set of fire doors, she heard a crash and a "crumbling sound". The appellant grabbed her around the arms and struck her on the head. She lost consciousness momentarily. When she recovered consciousness, he was choking her.

A student happened along, to whom the appellant said, "there's been a terrible accident". He was pale, sweating, glassy-eyed and had a frightened expression. When the witness looked over the railing and saw the complainant's head, her body being under the stairs, the appellant said, "I've killed her and I am going to kill you too". The appellant had only a partial recollection of his encounter with this witness.

A professor who was summoned testified that the appellant was very pale and bewildered. His description of the appellant was that he was perspiring; very, very nervous; distraught; upset; absolutely pale, no colour in his face; had moisture about the mouth; was shaky, jerky in his speech; absolutely bewildered, "out of it". In reply, he said that although the appellant was halting in his speech, he was coherent. According to the nurse who next saw the appellant, he looked very upset. His pulse was very fast and not strong; he had a limp "clammy" appearance. She was unable to convince him he had not killed the complainant. To the Dean, the appellant said, "I don't know why I started or why I stopped" and that, "he liked her better than anyone he had ever known". The Dean testified that the appellant spoke slowly in a confused sort of way, was very depressed and perhaps dazed.

To Constable Pollitt, the appellant said, "I did it, I know I did it, I just couldn't stop hitting her". The appellant gave a statement to the police, which reads in part:

> I was asking her about the ballet, then I asked her if she liked this guy Gord. She said something about just a friend, then I guess I hit her right then on the head, she was bleeding from the head and the next thing I remember it all happened so fast she was on the floor and I was sitting on top of her choking her. I thought she was dead there was blood everywhere, I just don't know what happened.

The statement concluded:

> I don't know why I did it because I wasn't even mad when this happened, and I don't remember parts of what happened and when I realized what I had done I went to the nurse's office and then to phone the police, I actually thought I'd killed somebody.

A number of character witnesses spoke highly of the appellant. Evidence was led that he had been a well-behaved young man until this incident. He had never lost his temper or displayed signs of anger.

The complainant made a complete recovery within a short time.

## The Medical Evidence

The appellant was remanded for psychiatric assessment and committed on March 5, 1974, to the Lakeshore Hospital. He was discharged on April 1, 1974. Detailed medical examinations disclosed no evidence of neurological disease. A psychological survey showed no indication of psychotic process. Dr. Slyfield conducted a number of interviews in the preparation of his report which concludes:

> Psychological testing done by Mr. Wejtko indicates superior intellectual ability, a personality profile within the range of normality, and a tendency to use the psychological defences of avoidance, repression and blocking. There was no evidence of psychotic disintegration.
>
> If Wayne is telling the truth about his amnesia for most of the incident, then it is probable that his consciousness was dissociated at the time. His somnambulistic episode lends some support to his explanation. However, such a psychological mechanism need not indicate mental illness.

In the opinion of Dr. Orchard, assistant professor of psychiatry at the University of Toronto and witness for the defence, the appellant entered into a complete dissociative state, a disorder of consciousness which occurs as a result of part of the nervous system "shutting off". A person in a severe dissociative state may be capable of performing physical actions without consciousness of such actions. When the appellant entered the dissociative state near the foot of the stairs his mind "shut off", and the return of consciousness was gradual. In Dr. Orchard's opinion the dissociative state which occurred was comparable to that produced by a "physical blow", though caused by a "psychological blow", certain physical effects were produced as observed by the student, the professor, the nurse and the Dean.

According to Dr. Orchard the appellant was a young man of average health, or better than average health, with no predisposition to dissociate. The severe dissociative state, such as the appellant suffered, usually occurs in persons within the category of normal people. According to Dr. Orchard it is rare for the severe dissociative state not caused by some underlying pathology to recur. In his opinion there was only a very slight possibility that the appellant would suffer a recurrence of this disorder of consciousness. Dr. Orchard could find no indication of any pathological condition, which he defined as a "diseased condition or abnormally sick condition". In his view the dissociative state itself is an "occurrence", not a mental illness and not a disease of the mind.

Dr. Rowsell who, like Dr. Orchard, is a psychiatrist of eminence, examined the appellant and testified on behalf of the Crown. In his opinion the appellant was not in a dissociative state, but rather was a controlled young man who went into an extreme state of rage at that moment and, while in that state, struck the complainant on the head and choked her. Dr. Rowsell felt that if, contrary to his opinion, the appellant was in a dissociative state, he suffered from disease of the mind. According to Dr. Rowsell, consciousness is the distinguishing factor of mental life; the dissociative state is, by definition, a subdivision of hysterical neurosis, which is a definite mental illness. It is by definition a disorder of the mind. Dr. Rowsell did not suggest there was an underlying pathology which induced the alleged dissociative state. His report reads in part:

> He shows no evidence of psychosis. (A psychosis is a disorder of thinking, feeling and behaviour, accompanied by a break with reality. This means that the individual is no longer able to interpret events, both internal and external, as would a person in good mental health.) . . .
>
> There is no evidence of any organic brain disorder which would impair his consciousness. Therefore, the issue could be raised as to whether he was in an automatic state at the time of the event. In my opinion he was not. The psychiatric term for such a state would be Dissociative Reaction.

The evidence of Dr. Rowsell was that Rabey was conscious at the time of the act but suffered hysterical amnesia *after the event*, which Dr. Rowsell categorized as neurosis, a disease of the mind.

Dr. Rowsell, unlike Dr. Orchard, was of the opinion that the appellant still had a psychiatric problem for which he required treatment to help him face up to what occurred. The treatment would take six months to a year, and could be undertaken on an out-patient basis. The prognosis was excellent.

Dr. Orchard, on the other hand, was of the view that inasmuch as the appellant had been a relatively normal person prior to the occurrence, the likelihood of any recurrence was negligible. In Dr. Orchard's words:

> I think he has a pretty healthy personality and he will find a healthy way through all this, So I don't see it in need of any treatment. I don't see him as sick. I do agree with Dr. Rowsell he is not in any way a criminal type of person.

Dr. Rowsell considered that the appellant was not "in any way a criminal type of person". Dr. Orchard shared that view.

## At Trial and on Appeal

The trial Judge, Dymond, Co. Ct. J., rejected the Crown theory of planned revenge and the medical opinion advanced by Dr. Rowsell of tremendous rage and loss of memory from protective hysterical amnesia. Referring to *R. v. K* (1970), 3 C.C.C. (2d) 84, [1971] 2 O.R. 401, and *Pernerkar v. The Queen* (1973), 10 C.C.C. (2d) 253 . . . (Sask. C.A.), the Judge concluded that a dissociative state brought on by psychological trauma can support a defence of automatism. The ruling in *Parnerkar* flowed from the medical evidence there, distinctly different from the evidence in this case.

. . .

In acquitting the appellant the Judge made two findings of particular significance: first that the appellant was not insane within the meaning of s. 16 of the *Criminal Code* when the acts were committed and, secondly, that the appellant had acted in a state of automatism brought about by an external cause.

It is important to note that the Crown did not challenge the finding of automatism in this Court or in the Ontario Court of Appeal. We must therefore accept for the purposes of this appeal, that the acts to which I have referred occurred without will, purpose or reasoned intention on the part of the appellant. The only question for decision is whether, having found automatism, the trial Judge was bound in law to find that the appellant was a proper subject for indefinite detention as an insane person.

On appeal to the Ontario Court of Appeal, the acquittal on the charge of causing bodily harm was reversed and a new trial directed on that count. The Court held that the psychological blow suffered was not an externally originating cause of the dissociative state. The acquittal at trial on a companion charge of possession of a rock for the purpose of wounding was upheld.

. . .

I turn now to the authorities, with the threshold observation that none of them is binding upon this Court or particularly helpful in the resolution of this case.

. . .

The first Canadian decision is *R. v. Kasperek* (1951), 101 C.C.C. 375, [1951] O.R. 776, 13 C.R. 206, a case in which the defence raised was "temporary blackout" and "amnesia". It was held the denial of insanity, with an assertion of amnesia, was untenable. This decision predates the English authorities which recognized a defence of automatism.

In *R. v. Minor* (1955), 112 C.C.C. 29, 21 C.R. 377, 15 W.W.R. (N.S. 433 (Sask. C.A.). a death resulted from the accused's dangerous and erratic handling of his car. The facts indicated that just prior to driving, the accused, in attendance at a wedding reception, had been struck and knocked down. According to the medical evidence, he had suffered from an injury which rendered him unconscious for an unknown interval. The salient passage is at pp. 34-5:

> There is ample authority to the effect that when a person is unconscious from any cause and is in a condition when he cannot form an intent . . . he has a good defence . . . In my opinion the provisions with respect to insanity . . . do not apply to the defence set up in this case, namely, that the accused did not know what he was doing at the time of the accident.

. . .

The jury charge in *R. v. K* (1970), 3 C.C.C. (2d) 84, [1971] 2 O.R. 401, as far as I am aware, contains the first plea of psychological blow automatism in this country. Both insanity and automatism were before the jury. In view of the uncontradicted evidence of an underlying pathological condition and a course of psychiatric treatment prior to the killing, one may seriously query whether the trial Judge correctly left the alternative defence of automatism with the jury. In the event, the defence gained the accused an acquittal.

A plea of automatism raised at trial was sustained before this Court in *Bleta v. The Queen*, [1965] 1 C.C.C. 1, 48 D.L.R. (2d) 139, [1964] S.C.R. 561, a case in which the Court was concerned, however, with an evidentiary matter. In the course of an affair between the appellant and the deceased, the former was knocked onto the pavement, whereupon he forcibly struck his head. Moments later, he got up and delivered a fatal blow. Witnesses testified that after the fall, the appellant was dazed. On medical evidence that the physical blow deprived him of voluntary control of his actions, the appellant was acquitted at trial. With no discussion as to the availability of the defence of automatism, which appears not to have been in issue in this Court, the acquittal was restored.

*Parnerkar v. The Queen* (1973), 10 C.C.C. (2d) 253, 33 D.L.R. (3d) 688, [1974] S.C.R. 449; affirming 5 C.C.C. (2d) 11, 16 C.R.N.S. 347, [1972] 1 W.W.R. 161, is perhaps the case most directly in point in the resolution of the present appeal. The trial Judge and appellate Court in the case at bar disagreed in their respective interpretations of the judgment rendered by Culliton, C.J.S. The case reached this Court, but the plea of non-insane automatism was not directly considered. Only Ritchie, J. (in whose judgment Spence, J., concurred), expressed a view on the issue of automatism. He agreed that the defence of automatism should not have been left with the jury.

The passage in the judgment of Culliton, C.J.S., which has given rise to uncertainty reads (p. 24):

> In my opinion, if the evidence of Dr. Benjamin is accepted, that Parnerkar was in a dissociated state at the time he killed Anna, he was, at the time, suffering from a disease of the mind within the M'Naghten rules as defined by this Court. If the acts committed by Parnerkar were unconscious acts, they depended upon a defect of reason from a disease of the mind, and consequently the defence, if any, was one of insanity, and not of automatism. Therefore, in my respectful view, the learned trial Judge erred in law putting the defence of automatism to the jury. I would also point out that Dr. Benjamin stated, if Parnerkar was in a dissociated state, then during that time he was temporarily insane.

It is unclear whether Culliton, C.J.S., unsupported by earlier authority, made a finding that, as a matter of law, a dissociated state is a disease of the mind, or whether he merely accepted the medical opinion that, on these facts, there was a disease of the mind. In the present case Mr. Justice Martin took the former view of the meaning to be attributed to the words of Culliton, C.J.S.; the trial Judge took the latter view. There is little in the way of elaboration, beyond that contained in the quoted passage, on the issue of disease of the mind.

There are three or four decisions since *Parnerkar*, in which automatism induced by a psychological blow has been pleaded. In *R. v. James* (1974), 30 C.R.N.S. 65 (Ont. H.C.J.), dissociation caused by emotional stress was categorized as insanity rather than as a non-insane automatism but in that case the medical evidence disclosed an underlying pathological condition of psychotic proportion. In *R. v. Cullum* (1973), 14 C.C.C. (2d) 294 (Ont. Co. Ct.), Zalev. Co. Ct. J., acquitted an accused who was in a dissociated state due to situational emotional stress. In *Cullum,* there was evidence that the factors inducing the dissociative state were "alcohol and the girls"; there was also evidence of a predisposition to dissociate; recurrence could not be ruled out.

. . .

Another case to which one might refer is *R. v. Sproule* (1975), 26 C.C.C. (2d) 92,

30 C.R.N.S. 56, decided by the Ontario Court of Appeal differently constituted than in the case at bar. In that case, the accused had an argument with a girl who had earlier informed him her interest was on the wane. A discussion between the two rapidly escalated into an argument, during which the girl was shot. The judgment of the Court was delivered by Kelly, J.A., who stated that the defence sought to tender evidence to prove that Sproule, at the time of the shooting, had been acting in a state of automatism.

. . .

In *Cooper* and in the case at bar there was evidence of interruption of the thought processes in the course of committing certain acts and criminal responsibility was in issue. In *Cooper* the question was whether the trial Judge was required to charge on insanity. The inquiry in the present case goes somewhat deeper. The question here is whether the accused, having acted in a state of unconsciousness, while in a transitory mental state, must be committed to an institution.

This case raises interesting issues, and the judicial conclusion, in my view, should be guided by general principles of criminal responsibility. Before alluding to those principles, it is useful to recall s. 16(4) of the *Criminal Code* which reads:

16(4) Every one shall, until the contrary is proved, be presumed to be and to have been sane.

In the usual case in which an accused pleaded insanity, he has the burden of overcoming the presumption of sanity. In the present case the appellant is not seeking to establish that he was insane on March 1, 1974. The Crown is asserting the insanity in answer to the defence of automatism raised by the appellant. The presumption of sanity runs in the appellant's favour.

We turn to s. 16(2): a person is insane when he is in a state of natural imbecility or has a disease of the mind to an extent that renders him incapable of appreciating the nature and quality of an act or omission or of knowing that an act or omission is wrong. The important words, for present purposes, are "disease of the mind".

The first principle, fundamental to our criminal law, which governs this appeal is that no act can be a criminal offence unless it is done voluntarily. Consciousness is a *sine qua non* to criminal liability.

The prosecution must prove every element of the crime charged. One such element is the state of mind of the accused, in the sense that the act was voluntary. The circumstances are normally such as to permit a presumption of volition and mental capacity. That is not so when the accused, as here, has placed before the Court, by cross-examination of Crown witnesses or by evidence called on his own behalf, or both, evidence sufficient to raise an issue that he was unconscious of his actions at the time of the alleged offence. No burden of proof is imposed upon an accused raising such a defence beyond pointing to facts which indicate the existence of such condition: *R. v. Berger* (1975), 27 C.C.C. (2d) 357 at p. 379. Whether lack of consciousness relates to *mens rea* or to *actus reus* or both may be important in a case in which the offence charged is one of absolute liability, but the conceptual distinction does not concern us in the case at bar.

The second principle is that no person should be committed to a hospital for the criminally insane unless he suffers from disease of the mind in need of treatment or likely to recur.

The Ontario Court of Appeal held that the excusing factor was insanity. This finding was reached though the appellant exhibited no pathological symptoms indicative of a previously existing, or ongoing, psychiatric disorder. On medical evidence accepted by the trial Judge, the prospect of a recurrence of dissociation is extremely remote. There was no finding that the appellant suffered from psychosis, neurosis or personality disorder. He does not have an organic disease of the brain. This was an isolated event. The appellant has already spent several weeks in a mental institution undergoing psychiatric, neurological and psychological assessment, the result of which did not indicate need for treatment.

There are undoubtedly policy considerations to be considered. Automatism as a defence is easily feigned. It is said the credibility of our criminal justice system will be severely strained if a person who has committed a violent act is allowed an absolute acquittal on a plea of automatism arising from a psychological blow. The argument is made that the success of the defence depends upon the semantic ability of psychiatrists, tracing a narrow path between the twin shoals of criminal responsibility and an insanity verdict. Added to these concerns is the *in terrorem* argument that the floodgates will be raised if psychological blow automatism is recognized in law.

There are competing policy interests. Where the condition is transient rather than persistent, unlikely to recur, not in need of treatment and not the result of self-induced intoxication, the policy objectives in finding such a person insane are not served. Such a person is not a danger to himself or to society generally.

The Ontario Court of Appear in the present case focused upon "external cause". The "ordinary stresses and disappointments of life" were held not to constitute an external cause. The Court considered that the "emotional stress" suffered by the appellant could not be said to be an external factor producing the automatism; the dissociative state had its source primarily in the psychological or emotional make-up of the appellant.

There is no evidence to support Mr. Justice Martin's statement attributing the dissociated state to psychological or emotional make-up of the appellant. To exclude the defence of automatism it lay upon the Crown to establish that the appellant suffered from a disease of the mind at the time of the attack. The existence of the mental disease must be demonstrated in evidence. Here there is no such evidence from any of the experts or other witnesses with reference to the crucial period of the assault. Moreover as earlier noted, s. 16(4) presumes sanity. The Court of Appeal's conclusion was directly contrary to the testimony of Dr. Orchard, accepted by the trial Judge, and finds no support in the testimony of Dr. Rowsell.

Martin, J.A., left open the question whether it is possible to dissociate as a result of emotional shock rather than physical injury. The effect of the appellate Court judgment was to differ with the trial Judge's finding that the dissociation was brought about by an externally operating cause. In the circumstances, I do not think it is open to this Court to disturb the findings of fact at trial.

If the effect of the appellate Court judgment is that, as a matter of law, emotional stress can never constitute an external factor then, with respect, I disagree. Indeed, in the passage quoted below the Court seems to concede as much. If the controlling factor is one of degree of emotional stress, and the application of some form of quantitative test, then the question becomes one of fact for the trier of fact and not one of law for an appellate Court.

It is not clear to me why, as a matter of law, an emotional blow, which can be devastating, should be regarded as an external cause of automatism in some circumstances and an internal cause in others, as the Court of Appeal would seem to propose in this passage [at pp. 482-3 C.C.C., p. 435 D.L.R.]:

> I leave aside until it becomes necessary to decide them, cases where a dissociative state has resulted from emotional shock without physical injury, resulting from such causes, for example, as being involved in a serious accident although no physical injury has resulted; being the victim of a murderous attack with an uplifted knife, notwithstanding the victim has managed to escape physical injury; seeing a loved one murdered or seriously assaulted, and the like situations. Such extraordinary external events might reasonably be presumed to affect the average normal person without reference to the subjective make-up of the person exposed to such experience.

I cannot accept the notion that an extraordinary external event, *i.e.*, an intense emotional shock, can cause a state of dissociation or automatism, if and only if all normal persons subjected to that sort of shock would react in that way. If I understand the quoted passage correctly, an objective standard is contemplated for one of the possible causes of automatism, namely, psychological blow, leaving intact the subjective standard for other causes of automatism, such a physical blow, or reaction to drugs.

As in all other aspects of the criminal law, except negligence offences, the inquiry is directed to the accused's actual state of mind.It is his subjective mental condition with which the law is concerned. If he has a brittle skull and sustains a concussion which causes him to run amok, he has a valid defence of automatism. If he has an irregular metabolism which induced an unanticipated and violent reaction to a drug, he will not be responsible for his acts. If he is driven into shock and unconsciousness by an emotional blow, and was susceptible to that reaction but has no disease, there is no reason in principle why a plea of automatism should not be available. The fact that other people would not have reacted as he did should not obscure the reality that the external psychological blow did cause a loss of consciousness. A person's subjective reaction, in the absence of any other medical or factual evidence supportive of insanity, should not put him into the category of persons legally insane. Nor am I prepared to accept the proposition, which seems implicit in the passage quoted, that whether an automatic state is an insane reaction or a sane reaction may depend upon the intensity of the shock.

M.E. Schiffer states in his text, *Mental Disorder and The Criminal Trial Process* (1976), that psychological blow automatism is described as a reaction to a shock (p. 101):

> However, in cases where the psychological stress has taken the form of a sudden jolt, or blow to the accused, the court may be more willing to treat a short-lived bout of automatism as

sane. Because the automatism, in order to be a defence in itself, must be an "on the sudden" reaction to psychological stress, the defence of "psychological blow automatism" may be seen as somewhat analogous to the defence of provocation.

I agree with the requirement that there be a shock precipitating the state of automatism. Dissociation caused by a low stress threshold and surrender to anxiety cannot fairly be said to result from a psychological blow. In a recent decision of the British Columbia Court of Appeal, *R. v. MacLeod*, as yet unreported [since reported 52 C.C.C. (2d) 193], Craig, J.A., adopted the judgment of Martin, J.A., in *Rabey*. The facts of *MacLeod* cannot be compared with those in the instant appeal. There, the accused absorbed four double drinks of liquor prior to entering the alleged state of dissociation. His loss of consciousness cannot be traced to an immediate emotional shock. He had been subject to ongoing stress for some time, which was heightened by his wife's recent departure. Though unwilling to classify it a disease of the mind, the accused's medical witness described it as a "neurotic disorder" which could be induced by an "anxiety reaction". The Court of Appeal held non-instance automatism was not available.

Dr. Glanville Williams' new book *Textbook of Criminal Law* (1978), is helpful in this discussion, in particular chapter 27. The author cites as the main instances of automatism: "sleepwalking, concussion, some cases of epilepsy, hypoglycaemia and dissociative states". Williams says (pp. 608-9) that "automatism" has come to express "any abnormal state of consciousness (whether confusion, delusion or dissociation) that is regarded as incompatible with the existence of *mens rea*, while not amounting to insanity", adding: "It would better be called 'impaired consciousness', but the orthodox expression can be used if we bear in mind that it does not mean what it says" and in a footnote (p. 609):

> Because automatism is a legal concept, a psychiatrist should be asked to testify to the mental condition as psychiatrically recognized, not to "automatism". It is for the judge to make the translation. In most of the conditions referred to legally as automatism the psychiatrist would speak of an altered state of consciousness.

The *Parnerkar* case is discussed at some length and the following observations made with respect thereto (p. 613):

> The decision illustrates the difficulty that can be caused to the courts by over-enthusiastic psychiatrists. If such evidence were regularly given and accepted a considerable breach would be made in the law of homicide. A medical witness who proclaims that the defendant, though awake, did not know that he was stabbing a person because of his dissociated state invites incredulity, particularly where it is shown that the defendant immediately afterwards telephoned for an ambulance and the police. Further, to assert that this medical condition amounts to insanity ignores the distinction that has been developed between sane and non-sane automatism. *If Parnerkar was in a state of automatism at all it was on the non-insane variety, since there was no evidence of psychosis or brain damage or continuing danger.*

(Emphasis added.) At the conclusion of the discussion of *Parnerkar*, Williams makes the following comment, particulary apt in the present case:

> It may also be remarked that commitment to hospital is inappropriate in a case of hysterical dissociation, since once the episode is over the patient does not need to be detained.

Under the heading "Insanity versus Automatism" Williams states that before the decision in *Quick*, Lord Dnening's view in *Bratty* was generally accepted. The test of insanity was the likelihood of recurrence of danger. In *Quick* the Court of Appeal adopted what might seem at first sight to be a different test for insane *versus* non-insane automatism. But the real question is whether the violence is likely to be repeated. Williams concludes that "On the whole, it would be much better if the courts kept to Lord Denning's plain rule; the rule of *Quick* adds nothing to it" (p. 615).

This view, which the Ontario Court of Appeal appears to have rejected, finds ample support in the legal literature. See S.M. Beck, "Voluntary Conduct: Automatism, Insanity and Drunkenness" (1966-67), 9 Crim. L.Q. 315 at p. 321: "The cause of the automatic conduct, and the threat of recurrence, are plainly factors that determine the line between sane and insane automatism"; F.A. Whitlock, *Criminal Responsibility and Mental Illness* (1963), p. 120: "The test of whether or not an episode of automatism is to be judged as sane or insane action seems to rest on the likelihood of its repetition"; Professor J.Ll.J. Edwards, "Automatism and Criminal Responsibility", 21 Mod. L. Rev. 375 at p. 385: "Where evidence is available of recurrent attacks of automatism during which the accused resorts to violence . . . inevitably leads to consideration of the imposition of some restraint"; S. Prevenzer, "Automatism and Involuntary Conduct", [1958] Crim. L.R. 440 at p. 441: "If . . . it can safely be predicted that his conduct is not likely to recur, having regard to the cause of the automatism, there can be no point in finding him insane and detaining him in Broadmoor"; G.A. Martin, "Insanity as a Defence", (1965-66) 8 Crim. L.Q. 240 at p. 253: "Perhaps the distinction lies in the likelihood of recurrence and whether the person suffering from it is prone to acts of violence when in that state."

In principle, the defence of automatism should be available whenever there is evidence of unconsciousness throughout the commission of the crime, that cannot be attributed to fault or negligence of his part, such evidence should be supported by an expert medical opinion that the accused did not feign memory loss and that there is no underlying pathological condition which points to a disease requiring detention and treatment.

I would only add that s. 16 determines the consequences of the finding of "no consciousness", on the basis of a legal conclusion guided by the medical evidence of the day. What is disease of the mind in the medical science of today may not be so tomorrow. The Court will establish the meaning of disease of the mind on the basis of scientific evidence as it unfolds from day to day. The Court will find as a matter of fact in each case whether a disease of the mind, so defined, is present.

The circumstances in this case are highly unusual, uncomplicated by alcohol or psychiatric history. The real question in the case is whether the appellant should be confined in an institution for the criminally insane. The trial Judge negated an act of passion, lack of self-control or impulsiveness. The medical evidence negated a state of disease or disorder or mental disturbance arising from infirmity. Save for what was said by Dr. Rowsell, whose evidence as to *ex post facto* hysterical amnesia was rejected by the trial Judge, the medical experts gave the appellant a clean mental bill of health. I can see no possible justification for sending the case back for a new trial.

I would allow the appeal, set aside the judgment of the Ontario Court of Appeal, and restore the verdict of acquittal.

RITCHIE, J.:—This is an appeal from a judgment of the Court of Appeal for Ontario whereby that Court set aside the appellant's acquittal at trial for "causing bodily harm with intent to wound". The appellant had, at the same time, been charged with having a rock in his possession "for the purpose of committing the offence of wounding" but no appeal was taken from his acquittal on this charge.

. . .

It should be observed also that the appellant was subject to a number of interviews with psychiatrists with the result that the Courts have found themselves involved in the shadowy area of mental disorders concerning which it is not surprising to find that there are wide differences in opinion amongst the "experts". The meaning of the word "automatism", in any event so far as it is employed in the defence of non-insane automatism, has in my opinion been satisfactorily defined by Mr. Justice Lacourciere of the Court of Appeal of Ontario in the case of *R. v. K* (1970), 3 C.C.C. (2d) 84, [1971] 2 O.R. 401:

> Automatism is a term used to describe unconscious, involuntary behaviour, the state of a person who, though capable of action, is not conscious of what he is doing. It means an unconscious, involuntary act, where the mind does not go with what is being done.

The defence of automatism as used in the present case of course involves a consideration of the provisions of s. 16 of the *Criminal Code* . . .

. . .

What is said here is that although at the relevant time the appellant was in a state where, though capable of action he was not conscious of what he was doing, and more particularly that he was not suffering from a disease of the mind and was therefore not insane. The central question in deciding any case involving the defence of automatism is whether or not the accused was suffering from a disease of the mind. The opinions of psychiatrists go no further than characterizing the condition in which the appellant was found as being "a dissociative state" but it is clear at least since the case of *Bratty v. A.-G. Northern Ireland*, [1963] A.C. 386, that the question of whether or not such a state amounts to "a disease of the mind" is a question of law for the Judge to determine. The general rule is that it is for the Judge as a question of law to decide what constitutes a "disease of the mind", but that the question of whether or not the facts in a given case disclose the existence of such a disease is a question to be determined by the trier of fact. I think it would be superfluous for me to retrace the line of authorities in this area as they have been so exhaustively discussed by my brother Dickson and also by Mr. Justice Martin of the Court of Appeal and by the learned trial Judge. I am satisfied in this regard to adopt the following passages from the reasons for judgement of Mr. Justice Martin which are now conveniently reported in (1978), 37 C.C.C. (2d) 461, 79 D.L.R. (3d) 414, 40 C.R.N.S. 46. He said at pp. 477-8 C.C.C., pp. 430-1 D.L.R., pp. 62-3 C.R.N.S.:

In general, the distinction to be drawn is between a malfunctioning of the mind arising from some cause that is primarily internal to the accused, having its source in his psychological or emotional make-up, or in some organic pathology, as opposed to a malfunctioning of the mind which is the transient effect produced by some specific external factor such as, for example, concussion. Any malfunctioning of the mind, or mental disorder having its source primarily in some subjective condition or weakness internal to the accused (whether fully understood or not), may be a "disease of the mind" if it prevents the accused from knowing what he is doing, but transient disturbances of consciousness due to certain specific external factors do not fall within the concept of disease of the mind. (For an interesting and helpful discussion see "The Concept of Mental Disease in Criminal Law Insanity Tests" by Herbert Fingarette in 33 University of Chicago Law Review 229.) Particular transient mental disturbances may not, however, be capable of being properly categorized in relation to whether they constitute "disease of the mind", on the basis of a generalized statement, and must be decided on a case by case basis.

The same learned Judge later stated in the same judgment at pp. 482-3 C.CC., p. 435 D.L.R., p. 68 C.R.N.S.:

In my view, the ordinary stresses and disappointments of life which are the common lot of mankind do not constitute an external cause constituting an explanation for a malfunctioning of the mind which takes it out of the category of a "disease of the mind". To hold otherwise would deprive the concept of an external factor of any real meaning. In my view, the emotional stress suffered by the respondent as a result of his disappointment with respect to Miss X cannot be said to be an external factor producing the automatism within the authorities, and the dissociative state must be considered as having its source primarily in the respondent's psychological or emotional make-up. I conclude, therefore, that, in the circumstances of this case, the dissociative state in which the respondent was said to be, constituted a "disease of the mind". I leave aside until it becomes necessary to decide them, cases where a dissociative state has resulted from emotional shock without physical injury, resulting from such causes, for example, as being involved in a serious accident although no physical injury has resulted; being the victim of a murderous attack with an uplifted knife, notwithstanding the victim has managed to escape physical injury; seeing a loved one murdered or seriously assaulted, and the like situations. Such extraordinary external events might reasonable be presumed to affect the average make-up of the person exposed to such experience.
For the above reasons, I am of the opinion, with deference, that the learned trial Judge erred in holding that the so-called "psychological blow", which was said to have caused the dissociative state, was, in the circumstances of this case, an externally originating cause, and should have held that if the respondent was in a dissociative state at the time he struck Miss X he suffered from "disease of the mind". A new trial must, accordingly, be had on count 2.

. . .

It seems to me that his infatuation with this young woman had created an abnormal condition in his mind under the influence of which he acted unnaturally and violently to an imagined slight to which a normal person would not have reacted in the same manner.

It was contended on behalf of the appellant that a finding of disease of the mind and consequently of insanity in the present case would involve gross unfairness to the appellant who could be subject to the provisions of s. 545 of the *Criminal Code* and thus detained at the pleasure of the Lieutenant-Governor of the Province. That such a result does not carry with it the hardship contended for is illustrated by the following passage from the reasons for judgment of Mr. Justice Martin at p. 483 C.C.C., p. 436 D.L.R., p. 69 C.R.N.S.:

It would, of course, be unthinkable that a person found not guilty on account of insanity because of a transient mental disorder constituting a disease of the mind, who was not dangerous and who required no further treatment should continue to be confined. The present provisions of s. 545(1)(b) [rep. & sub. 1972, c. 13, s. 45], however, authorize the Lieutenant-Governor to make an order, if in his opinion it would be in the best interest of the accused and not contrary to the interest of the public, for the discharge of a person found not guilty on account of insanity, either absolutely or subject to such conditions as he prescribes. In addition to the periodic reviews required to be made by a board of review appointed pursuant to s. 547(1) of the *Code* the Lieutenant-Governor under s. 547(6) of the *Code* may request the board of review to review the case of any person found not guilty on account of insanity, in which case the board of review is required to report forthwith whether such person has recovered and, if so, whether in its opinion it is in the interest of the public and of that person for the Lieutenant-Governor to order that he be discharged absolutely or subject to such conditions as the Lieutenant-Governor may prescribe.

For all these reasons, as well as for those expressed by Mr. Justice Martin in the Court of Appeal for Ontario, I would dismiss the appeal and dispose of the matter in the manner proposed by him.

*Appeal dismissed.*

## Regina v. Parks
### (1992), 75 C.C.C. (3d) 287 (S.C.C.)

[Only excerpts from the judgement of Lamer are reproduced below.]

APPEAL by the Crown from a judgment of the Ontario Court of Appeal, 56 C.C.C. (3d) 449, 78 C.R. (3d) 2, 39 O.A.C. 27, 73 O.R. (2d) 129, 10 W.C.B. (2d) 236, dismissing an appeal by the Crown from the acquittal of the accused by Watt J., 6 W.C.B. (2d) 232, on charges of murder and attempted murder.

LAMER C.J.C. (dissenting in part): — In the small hours of the morning of May 24, 1987, the respondent, aged 23, attacked his parents-in-law, Barbara Ann and Denis Woods, killing his mother-in-law with a kitchen knife and seriously injuring his father-in-law. The incident occurred at the home of his parents-in-law while they were both asleep in bed. Their residence was 23 km. from that of the respondent, who went there by car. Immediately after the incident, the respondent went to the nearby police station, again driving his own car. He told the police:

> I just killed someone with my bare hands; Oh my God, I just killed someone; I've just killed two people; My God, I've just killed two people with my hands; My God, I've just killed two people. My hands; I just killed two people. I killed them; I just killed two people; I've just killed my mother- and father-in-law. I stabbed and beat them to death. It's all my fault.

At the trial the respondent presented a defence of automatism, stating that at the time the incidents took place he was sleepwalking. The respondent has always slept very deeply and has always had a lot of trouble waking up. The year prior to the events was particularly stressful for the respondent. His job as a project co-ordinator for Revere Electric required him to work 10 hours a day. In addition, during the preceding summer the respondent had placed bets on horse races which caused him financial problems. To obtain money he also stole some $30,000 from his employer. The following March his boss discovered the theft and dismissed him. Court proceedings were brought against him in this regard. His personal life suffered from all of this.

However, his parents-in-law, who were aware of the situation, always supported him. He had excellent relations with them: he got on particularly well with his mother-in-law, who referred to him as the "gentle giant" . His relations with his father-in-law were more distant, but still very good. In fact, a supper at their home was planned for May 24th to discuss the respondent's problems and the solutions he intended to suggest. Additionally, several members of his family suffer or have suffered from sleep problems such as sleep-walking, adult enuresis, nightmares and sleep-talking.

The respondent was charged with the first degree murder of Barbara Ann Woods and the attempted murder of Denis Woods.

The trial judge chose to put only the defence of automatism to the jury, which first acquitted the respondent of first degree murder and then of second degree murder. The judge also acquitted the respondent of the charge of attempted murder for the same reasons. The Court of Appeal unanimously upheld the acquittal. . . .

*Issue*

Did the Ontario Court of Appeal err in law in holding that the condition of sleep-walking should be classified as non-insane automatism resulting in an acquittal instead of being classified as a "disease of the mind" (insane automatism), giving rise to the special verdict of not guilty by reason of insanity?

*Analysis*

This court has only ruled on sleep-walking in an *obiter dictum* in *R. v. Rabey* (1980), 54 C.C.C. (2d) 1, 114 D.L.R. (3d) 193, [1980] 2 S.C.R. 513. The court found that sleepwalking was not a "disease of the mind" in the legal sense of the term and gave rise to a defence of automatism. Should the court maintain this position? . . .

A large part of the defence evidence in this case was medical evidence. Five physicians were heard: Dr. Roger James Broughton, a neurophysiologist and specialist in sleep and sleep disorders; Dr. John Gordon Edmeads, a neurologist; Dr. Ronald Frederick Billings, a psychiatrist; Dr. Robert Wood Hill, a forensic psychiatrist, and finally, Dr. Frank Raymond Ervin, a neurologist and psychiatrist.

The medical evidence in the case at bar showed that the respondent was in fact sleep-walking when he committed the acts with which he is charged. All the expert witnesses called by the defence said that in their opinion Parks was sleep-walking when the events occurred. This is what Dr. Broughton said:

Q. . . . assuming for a moment that Mr. Parks caused the death of Barbara Woods, did you, sir, reach an opinion as to his condition at the time he caused that death?

A. Yes. My opinion is that he did it during a sleepwalking episode.

Though sceptical at the outset, the expert witnesses unanimously stated that at the time of the incidents the respondent was not suffering from any mental illness and that, medically speaking, sleep-walking is not regarded as an illness, whether physical, mental or neurological. . . .

The evidence also disclosed that sleep-walking was very common, almost universal, among children, and that 2% to 2.5% of "normal" adults had sleep-walked at least once. Dr. Hill further noted that he found it significant that there were several sleep-walkers in the respondent's family.

> Thirdly, I think, as I indicated, it turns out, as enquiries are made more and more, that there is a significant history in the background family of Mr. Parks of difficulties, of bed-wetting difficulties, of sleeptalking and sleepwalking, that is in keeping with what we know about the phenomena of sleepwalking. We know that there are often family members so affected and that was present.

Dr. Broughton, for his part, indicated that he had never known of sleep-walkers who had acted violently who had repeated this kind of behaviour:

> Q. Yes. Now, with respect to Mr. Parks, do you have any opinion, sir, as to the probability of a recurrence of an event of sleepwalking with serious aggression involving physical harm to others?
>
> A. I think the risk of that is infinitesimal, I don't think it would exceed the risk of the general population almost. He has the family predisposition to sleepwalk, but it would only be in the likelihood of all precipitating and extenuating and so forth factors that built up to this crisis that would theoretically have to almost reappear.
>
> Q. And even if they were to reappear, would there be any probability of another homicidal event?
>
> A. It would still — As I say, there are no reported cases in the literature, so there is essentially — The probability of it occurring is not statistically significant. It is just absolutely improbable.

In cross-examination he also added that sleep-walking episodes in which violent acts are committed are not common. . . . Further, on being questioned about a cure or treatment, Dr. Broughton answered that the solution was sleep hygiene, which involved eliminating factors that precipitated sleep-walking such as stress, lack of sleep and violent physical exercise. . . .

Dr. Ervin in his turn stated that during the slow wave sleep stage the cortex, which is the part of the brain that controls thinking and voluntary movement, is essentially in coma. When a person is sleep-walking, the movements he makes are controlled by other parts of the brain and are more or less reflexive. . . .

Three very important points emerge from this testimony: (1) the respondent was sleep-walking at the time of the incident; (2) sleep-walking is not a neurological, psychiatric or other illness: it is a sleep disorder very common in children and also found in adults; (3) there is no medical treatment as such, apart from good health practices, especially as regards sleep. It is important to note that this expert evidence was not in any way contradicted by the prosecution, which as the trial judge observed did have the advice of experts who were present during the testimony given by the defence experts and whom it chose not to call. . . .

I am of the view that in the instant case, based on the evidence and the testimony of the expert witnesses heard, the trial judge did not err in leaving the defence of automatism rather than that of insanity with the jury, and that the instant appeal should be dismissed. For a defence of insanity to have been put to the jury, together with or instead of a defence of automatism, as the case may be, there would have had to have been in the record evidence tending to show that sleep-walking was the cause of the respondent's state of mind. As we have just seen, that is not the case here. This is not to say that sleep-walking could never be a disease of the mind, in another case on different evidence.

As I see it, however, that does not end the matter. Although the expert witnesses were unanimous in saying that sleep-walkers are very rarely violent, I am still concerned by the fact that as the result of an acquittal in a situation like this (and I am relieved that such cases are quite rare), the accused is simply set free without any consideration of measures to protect the public, or indeed the accused himself, from the possibility of a repetition of such unfortunate occurrences. In the case of an outright acquittal, should there not be some control? And if so, how should this be done? I am of the view that such control could be exercised by means of the common law power to make an order to keep the peace vested in any judge or magistrate. . . .

If conditions should be imposed on Mr. Parks they will restrict his liberty. It follows that the decision to impose such conditions and the terms of those conditions should not violate the rights guaranteed under s. 7 of the Canadian *Canadian Charter of Rights and Freedoms*. However, such a hearing is justified, as the sleepwalker has, although innocently, committed an act of violence which resulted in the death of his mother-in-law. Members of the community may quite reasonably be apprehensive for their safety. In those circumstances it cannot be said that the court has unduly intruded upon the liberty of the accused by exploring, on notice to the accused, the possibility of imposing some minimally intrusive conditions which seek to assure the safety of the community. If conditions are imposed, then they obviously must be rationally connected to the apprehended danger posed by the person and go no further than necessary to protect the public from this danger.

I would, therefore, refer this matter back to the trial judge so that he can hear the parties on this point and decide, upon the evidence before him, whether such an order is appropriate. If this proves to be the case, it will be up to the trial judge to determine the content of the order.

I would, accordingly, dismiss this appeal and uphold the acquittal of the respondent but refer the matter back to the trial judge for him to decide on the making of an order to keep the peace on certain conditions, pursuant to the "preventive justice" power which he possesses.

[Note: In the final result, the majority was not in agreement as to sending the case back to the trial judge for consideration of further measures against Mr. Parks.]

*Appeal dismissed.*

## Regina v. Stone*
(1999), 134 C.C.C. (3d) 353 (S.C.C.)

* Excerpts from the majority judgment of Bastarache J. are reproduced below:

BASTARACHE J.: The present case involves automatism, and more specifically, "psychological blow" automatism. The appellant claims that nothing more than his wife's words caused him to enter an automatistic state in which his actions, which include stabbing his wife 47 times, were involuntary. How can an accused demonstrate that mere words caused him to enter an automatistic state such that his actions were involuntary and thus do not attract criminal law sanction? This is the issue raised in this appeal.

## I. Facts

The appellant was charged with the murder of his wife, Donna Stone. At trial, the appellant admitted killing his wife. In his defence, the appellant claimed: insane automatism, non-insane automatism, lack of intent, and alternatively, provocation.

The appellant met Donna Stone in the spring of 1993 and the two were married on May 8, 1993. They lived in Winfield, British Columbia, in the Okanagan Valley. This was the appellant's third marriage. He has two teenage sons from his second marriage. His sons live with their mother in Surrey, British Columbia, a suburb of Vancouver.

In March 1994, the appellant planned a business trip to Vancouver. He decided to visit his sons while in the Vancouver area. He contacted his second wife and made arrangements to take his sons out for dinner and a movie. The appellant did not tell Donna Stone of his intention to travel to Vancouver and visit his sons because she did not get along with them.

According to the appellant, Donna Stone learned of his intention to go to Vancouver. She demanded to go along with him and said she would follow him in another vehicle if he did not take her. The appellant agreed to take her with him to Vancouver.

The appellant testified that Donna Stone berated him throughout the drive to Vancouver and objected to his visit with his sons. Nevertheless, the appellant drove to the home of his second wife for the planned visit with his sons. The visit lasted only 15 minutes because Donna Stone threatened to "lay on the horn until the police come".

The appellant testified that after the brief visit with his sons, he and Donna Stone drove towards Vancouver. According to the appellant, Donna Stone asked him if he wanted a divorce. He responded that they might as well get divorced if she was not going to let him see his sons. This answer upset the victim and she again began to berate the appellant.

The appellant testified that he pulled into an empty lot and turned off the truck's engine while Donna Stone continued to yell at him: . . .I sat there with my head down while she's still yelling at me that I'm nothing but a piece of shit and that when she had talked to the police, that she had told them lies, that I was abusing her, and that they were getting all the paperwork ready to have me arrested, and that all she had to do was phone them; and once they had me arrested, that she was going to get a court order so that I wouldn't be allowed back onto our property and that I would have to go and live with my mother and run my business from there, that she was going to quit working and she was just going to stay in the house with her children and that I would have to pay her alimony and child support. . . . Well, she just continued on and she just said that she couldn't stand to listen to me whistle, that every time I touched her, she felt sick, that I was a lousy fuck and that I had a small penis and that she's never going to fuck me again, and I'm just sitting there with my head down; and by this time, she's kneeling on the seat and she's yelling this in my face. . . .

The appellant testified that the victim's voice began to fade off. He recalls wondering why she was treating him and his children in this way. He also remembers thinking about how people in the small town in which he lived would look at him if his wife had him arrested. The appellant then remembers a "whoosh" sensation washing over him from his feet to his head. According to the appellant, when his eyes focussed again, he was staring straight ahead and felt something in his hand. He was holding a six-inch hunting knife which he kept in the truck. He looked over and saw Donna Stone slumped over on the seat. He knew she was dead. It would later be determined that Donna Stone died from loss of blood resulting from 47 stab wounds.

The appellant testified that he opened the passenger door and Donna Stone's body fell out onto the ground. After five to 10 minutes, the appellant put his wife's body in a toolbox in the back of his truck. He then washed the blood from his hands in a puddle, removed his bloody clothes and put on extra clothes he kept in the truck. The appellant then pulled out of the empty lot and drove to a nearby motel where he asked for directions home and purchased a six-pack of beer to calm his nerves.

. . .

The appellant testified that he checked into a hotel so he could take a shower and shave. He then collected an outstanding debt, sold a car he owned and took a cab to the airport. He flew to Mexico. While in Mexico, the appellant awoke one morning to the sensation of having his throat cut. In trying to recall his dream, he remembered stabbing Donna Stone twice in the chest before experiencing the "whooshing" sensation.

Donna Stone's body was found in the tool box in the appellant's truck two days after her death.

The appellant returned to Canada approximately six weeks later on May 2, 1994. The next day he spoke to a lawyer and then surrendered himself to police.

## II. Psychiatric Evidence

Two psychiatrists gave evidence in this case. The defence psychiatrist, Dr. Janke, interviewed the appellant on two occasions approximately 18 months after the killing. The Crown psychiatrist, Dr. Murphy, interviewed the appellant for one hour on the seventh day of the trial.

A. Evidence of Dr. Janke

. . .

In Dr. Janke's opinion, the appellant was in a dissociative state for at least the majority of the attack on Donna Stone. According to Dr. Janke, this state resulted from Donna Stone's extreme insults which must be viewed in the context of the stress the appellant had endured throughout the day. However, Dr. Janke qualified his opinion by noting that it was largely dependant on the accuracy and truthfulness of the appellant's account of events.

. . .

B. Evidence of Dr. Murphy

. . .

In relation to the appellant's claim of dissociation, Dr. Murphy testified that it is possible that the appellant was in a dissociative state when he killed Donna Stone. However, she noted that there is no scientific method of completely ruling out a claim of dissociation once it has been made. Furthermore, she opined that although it is possible, it is extremely unlikely that the appellant was in a dissociative state when he killed his wife. . . .

## IV. Issues

1. Did the Court of Appeal err in upholding the decision of the learned trial judge to refuse to leave the "defence" of non-insane automatism to the jury?
2. Did the Court of Appeal err in holding that there was no miscarriage of justice when the defence report of Dr. Janke was ordered disclosed to the Crown?
3.(a) Did the Court of Appeal err in principle in deciding that the sentencing judge was entitled to consider provocation as a mitigating factor for manslaughter where the same provocation, through the operation of s. 232 of the Criminal Code had already reduced the stigma and penalty of an intentional killing from murder to manslaughter?
3.(b) Did the Court of Appeal err in upholding a demonstrably unfit sentence that failed to reflect the gravity of the offence properly and the moral culpability of the offender?

. . .

The Nature of Automatism

The legal term "automatism" has been defined on many occasions by many courts. In *Rabey*, supra, Ritchie J., speaking for the majority of this Court, at p. 518, adopted the following definition of the Ontario High Court of Justice in R. v. K. (1970), 3 C.C.C. (2d) 84, at p. 84:

Automatism is a term used to describe unconscious, involuntary behaviour, the state of a person who, though capable of action is not conscious of what he is doing. It means an unconscious involuntary act where the mind does not go with what is being done.

The reference to unconsciousness in the definition of automatism has been the source of some criticism. In her article "Automatism and Criminal Responsibility" (1982-83), 25 Crim. L.Q. 95, W. H. Holland points out that this reference to unconsciousness reveals that the law assumes that a person is necessarily either conscious or unconscious. However, the medical literature speaks of different levels of consciousness (p. 96). Indeed, the expert evidence in the present case reveals that medically speaking, unconscious means "flat on the floor", that is, in a comatose-type state. I therefore prefer to define automatism as a state of impaired consciousness, rather than unconsciousness, in which an individual, though capable of action, has no voluntary control over that action.

. . .

## Nature and Origin of the Burdens Applied in Cases Involving Claims of Automatism

This Court has stated on many occasions that it is a fundamental principle of criminal law that only voluntary actions will attract findings of guilt. . . .

In *Parks*, supra, La Forest J. classified automatism as a sub-set of the voluntariness requirement, which he too recognized as part of the actus reus component of criminal responsibility (p. 896). I agree and would add that voluntariness, rather than consciousness, is the key legal element of automatistic behaviour since a defence of automatism amounts to a denial of the voluntariness component of the actus reus.

The law presumes that people act voluntarily. Accordingly, since a defence of automatism amounts to a claim that one's actions were not voluntary, the accused must rebut the presumption of voluntariness. An evidentiary burden is thereby imposed on the accused. The nature of this evidentiary burden stems from the legal burden imposed in cases involving claims of automatism. Generally, the legal burden in such cases has been on the Crown to prove voluntariness, a component of the actus reus , beyond a reasonable doubt—hence Dickson J.'s contention in *Rabey* that an accused claiming automatism need only raise evidence sufficient to permit a properly instructed jury to find a reasonable doubt as to voluntariness in order to rebut the presumption of voluntariness. The Crown then has the legal burden of proving voluntariness beyond a reasonable doubt to the trier of fact. If the Crown fails to satisfy this burden, the accused will be acquitted.

. . .

## What Should the Burdens of Proof Associated with Automatism Be?

. . .

As I explained above, different legal approaches to claims of automatism, whether based on the context in which the alleged automatism arose or on the distinction between mental disorder and non-mental disorder automatism, is problematic and should be avoided. . . .

The foregoing leads me to the conclusion that the legal burden in cases involving claims of automatism must be on the defence to prove involuntariness on a balance of probabilities to the trier of fact. . . .

In *Chaulk*, supra, and *Daviault*, supra, this Court recognized that although placing a balance of probabilities burden on the defence with respect to an element of the offence constitutes a limitation of an accused person's rights under s. 11(d) of the Charter, it can be justified under s. 1. In my opinion, the burden is also justified in the present case. The law presumes that people act voluntarily in order to avoid placing the onerous burden of proving voluntariness beyond a reasonable doubt on the Crown. Like extreme drunkenness akin to automatism, genuine cases of automatism will be extremely rare. However, because automatism is easily feigned and all knowledge of its occurrence rests with the accused, putting a legal burden on the accused to prove involuntariness on a balance of probabilities is necessary to further the objective behind the presumption of voluntariness. In contrast, saddling the Crown with the legal burden of proving voluntariness beyond a reasonable doubt actually defeats the purpose of the presumption of voluntariness. Thus, requiring that an accused bear the legal burden of proving involuntariness on a balance of probabilities is justified under s. 1. There is therefore no violation of the Constitution. . . .

To sum up, in order to satisfy the evidentiary or proper foundation burden in cases involving claims of automatism, the defence must make an assertion of involuntariness and call expert psychiatric or psychological evidence confirming that assertion. However, it is an error of law to conclude that this defence burden has been satisfied simply because the defence has met these two requirements. The burden will only be met where the trial judge concludes that there is evidence upon which a properly instructed jury could find that the accused acted involuntarily on a balance of probabilities. In reaching this conclusion, the trial judge will first examine the psychiatric or psychological evidence and inquire into the foundation and nature of the expert opinion. The trial judge will also examine all other available evidence, if any. Relevant factors are not a closed category and may, by way of example, include: the severity of the triggering stimulus, corroborating evidence of bystanders, corroborating medical history of automatistic-like dissociative states, whether there is evidence of a motive for the crime, and whether the alleged trigger of the automatism is also the victim of the automatistic violence. I point out that no single factor is meant to be determinative. Indeed, there may be cases in which the psychiatric or psychological evidence goes beyond simply corroborating the accused's version of events, for example, where it establishes a documented history of automatistic-like dissociative states. Furthermore, the ever advancing state of medical knowledge may lead to a finding that other types of evidence are also indicative of involuntariness. I leave it to the discretion and experience of trial judges to weigh all of the evidence available on a case by case basis and to determine whether a properly instructed jury could find that the accused acted involuntarily on a balance of probabilities.

F. Step 2: Determining Whether to Leave Mental Disorder or Non-Mental Disorder Automatism with the Trier of Fact

Only if the accused has laid a proper foundation for a defence of automatism will it be necessary for the trial judge to determine whether mental disorder or non-mental disorder automatism should be left with the trier of fact. If the trial judge concludes that a proper foundation has not been established, the presumption of voluntariness will be effective and neither automatism defence will be available to the trier of fact. In such a case, however, the accused may still claim an independent s. 16 defence of mental disorder.

The determination of whether mental disorder or non-mental disorder automatism should be left with the trier of fact must be undertaken very carefully since it will have serious ramifications for both the individual accused and society in general. As mentioned above, mental disorder automatism is subsumed by the defence of mental disorder as set out in the Code. Accordingly, a successful defence of mental disorder automatism will result in a verdict of not criminally responsible on account of mental disorder as dictated by s. 672.34 of the Code. Under s. 672.54, an accused who receives this qualified acquittal may be discharged absolutely, discharged conditionally or detained in a hospital. In contrast, a successful defence of non-mental disorder automatism will always result in an absolute acquittal.

. . .

Taken alone, the question of what mental conditions are included in the term disease of the mind is a question of law. However, the trial judge must also determine whether the condition the accused claims to have suffered from satisfies the legal test for disease of the mind. This involves an assessment of the particular evidence in the case rather than a general principle of law and is thus a question of mixed law and fact. See *Southam*, supra, at paras. 35 and 36. The question of whether the accused actually suffered from a disease of the mind is a question of fact to be determined by the trier of fact. . . .

Since mental disorder is a legal term, the opinion of the Canadian Psychiatric Association, while relevant, is not determinative of whether two distinct forms of automatism, mental disorder and non-mental disorder, should continue to be recognized at law. In my opinion, this Court should not go so far as to eliminate the defence of non-mental disorder automatism as the Association suggests. However, I take judicial notice that it will only be in rare cases that automatism is not caused by mental disorder. Indeed, since the trial judge will have already concluded that there is evidence upon which a properly instructed jury could find that the accused acted involuntarily on a balance of probabilities, there is a serious question as to the existence of an operating mind by the time the disease of the mind issue is considered. The foregoing lends itself to a rule that trial judges start from the proposition that the condition the accused claims to have suffered from is a disease of the mind. They must then determine whether the evidence in the particular case takes the condition out of the disease of the mind category. This approach is consistent with this Court's decision in *Rabey*, supra.

. . .

G. Determining Whether the Condition the Accused Claims to Have Suffered from is a Disease of the Mind

In *Parks*, La Forest J. recognized that there are two distinct approaches to the disease of the mind inquiry: the internal cause theory and the continuing danger theory. He recognized the internal cause theory as the dominant approach in Canadian jurisprudence but concluded, at p. 902, that this theory "is really meant to be used only as an analytical tool, and not as an all-encompassing methodology". This conclusion stemmed from a finding that somnambulism, the alleged trigger of the automatism in *Parks*, raises unique problems which are not well-suited to analysis under the internal cause theory. I agree that the internal cause theory cannot be regarded as a universal classificatory scheme for "disease of the mind". There will be cases in which the approach is not helpful because, in the words of La Forest J., at p. 903, "the dichotomy between internal and external causes becomes blurred". Accordingly, a new approach to the disease of the mind inquiry is in order. As I will explain below, a more holistic approach, like that developed by La Forest J. in Parks, must be available to trial judges in dealing with the disease of the mind question. This approach must be informed by the internal cause theory, the continuing danger theory and the policy concerns raised in this Court's decisions in *Rabey* and *Parks*.

. . .

## (3) Other Policy Factors

There may be cases in which consideration of the internal cause and continuing danger factors alone does not permit a conclusive answer to the disease of the mind question. Such will be the case, for example, where the internal cause factor is not helpful because it is impossible to classify the alleged cause of the automatism as internal or external, and the continuing danger factor is inconclusive because there is no continuing danger of violence. Accordingly, a holistic approach to disease of the mind must also permit trial judges to consider other policy concerns which underlie this inquiry. As mentioned above, in *Rabey* and *Parks*, this Court outlined some of the policy concerns which surround automatism. I have already referred to those specific policy concerns earlier in these reasons. I repeat that I do not view those policy concerns as a closed category. In any given automatism case, a trial judge may identify a policy factor which this Court has not expressly recognized. Any such valid policy concern can be considered by the trial judge in order to determine whether the condition the accused claims to have suffered from is a disease of the mind. In determining this issue, policy concerns assist trial judges in answering the fundamental question of mixed law and fact which is at the centre of the disease of the mind inquiry: whether society requires protection from the accused and, consequently, whether the accused should be subject to evaluation under the regime contained in Part XX.1 of the Code.

## H. Available Defences Following the Determination of the Disease of the Mind Question

. . .

Turning to the disease of the mind stage of the automatism analysis, I note that the evidence in this case raised only one alleged cause of automatism, Donna Stone's words. Based on this evidence, the trial judge found that only mental disorder automatism should be left with the jury. This conclusion was based primarily on a finding that the present case is indistinguishable from *MacLeod*, supra. Such reliance on precedent fails to reveal what effect, if any, the internal cause factor, the continuing danger factor and other policy factors had on the decision to leave only mental disorder automatism with the jury. This is not in accordance with the holistic approach to the disease of the mind question set out in these reasons. However, the internal cause factor and the continuing danger factor, as well as the other policy factors set out in this Court's decisions in *Rabey* and *Parks* all support the trial judge's finding that the condition the appellant alleges to have suffered from is a disease of the mind in the legal sense. In particular, the trigger in this case was not, in the words of Martin J.A. quoted in this Court's decision in *Rabey*, at p. 520, "extraordinary external events" that would amount to an extreme shock or psychological blow that would cause a normal person, in the circumstances of the accused, to suffer a dissociation in the absence of a disease of the mind. Accordingly, I find that the trial judge nevertheless reached the correct result on the disease of the mind question. As previously noted, in such a case, only mental disorder automatism must be put to the jury. There is no reason to go beyond the facts of this case in applying the rules discussed above.

In the end, I must conclude that no substantial wrong or miscarriage of justice occurred in the present case. Even if I had found that the trial judge erred in applying the evidentiary burden at the proper foundation stage of the automatism analysis, this error could only have benefitted the appellant. Although the trial judge did not apply the holistic approach to disease of the mind established in these reasons, he reached the correct result on this issue. There is no reasonable possibility that the verdict would have been different had the errors not been made. . . .

## VII. Conclusions and Disposition

In the first appeal, I have concluded that no substantial wrong or miscarriage of justice occurred. I would therefore affirm the conviction and dismiss the appeal.

In the second appeal, I agree with the Court of Appeal that the sentencing judge was aware of the aggravating and mitigating factors in this case and considered the relevant sentencing principles in reaching the sentence he imposed. Consequently, I would dismiss the Crown's sentence appeal and affirm the sentence imposed by the sentencing judge.

*Appeal dismissed*

### Questions/Discussion
1. How do the defences of automatism and mental disorder differ? How may they overlap?
2. Do you agree with the decisions in *Rabey* and *Stone*? Why or why not? Under what circumstances would you allow an emotional trauma to lead to a successful use of the automatism defence?
3. Do you think that the court came to the correct decision in *Parks*? Should there be some protections available to the public after the successful use of the defence in a situation such as that found in the case? What if Parks were to commit another killing in the future and use the same defence; should it be a valid defence in such a situation? On what grounds would you support or reject its use?

### Further Reading
• Paciocco, David, "Death by *Stone*-ing: The Demise of the Defence of Simple Automatism" (1999), 26 C.R. (5th) 273-285.

- Roach, Kent, *Criminal Law, 2nd ed.* (Toronto: Irwin Law, 2000) at 230-240.
- Stuart, Don, and R. Delisle, *Learning Canadian Criminal Law, 8th ed.* (Toronto: Carswell, 2001).
- Verdun-Jones, Simon, *Criminal Law in Canada: Cases, Questions, and the Code,* 3rd ed. (Toronto: Harcourt Canada, 2002) at 47-64.

# 8

# SELECTED TOPICS IN CRIMINAL JUSTICE

## 8.1 SEXUAL ASSAULT

### Issues in Sexual Assault

*R.P. Saunders*

The topic of sexual assault can be looked at from several different analytical perspectives including, for example, psychological, sociological, and legal. In this section we conduct an examination of the various legal issues involved and also try, more importantly and more generally, to illustrate the somewhat limited effectiveness of legal solutions to such problems facing women. To accomplish these two goals, we need, at the very least, a basic understanding of not only the legal response to the problem, but also the basic social dimensions to sexual assault.

Three points should be made at the outset by way of explanation. First, the terms "sexual assault" and the term "rape" are used throughout, though, as you will see, rape is an outdated and more narrowly defined term. It is, however, for good or for bad, one of the most widely used and recognizable term for sexual attacks against women. Second, there are many and varying views and theories on the issues related to sexual assault, and it should be recognised that what follows is not an attempt to present all of them, but rather is a selective and introductory presentation of several of these perspectives. To examine many of these views in more depth, please refer to the "Further Reading" section which follows. A final point to note is that the topics of prison rapes and child sexual assault are not considered here, though such assaults do present serious problems for those in detention and for children; the focus here is on the problem of sexual assaults which occur in everyday life.

In light of these qualifiers, then, we can begin with a very brief reference to earlier times. It is interesting to note that historically the goal of rape sanctions was often to protect a man's property, not to protect the integrity of women *per se*; for example, in certain societies, rape was seen as something which damaged a man's goods. The crime was seen in the context of the theft of property or the theft of a saleable item, that is, virginity or the woman's exclusive sexual services. It is this notion of the theft of property and not the desire to protect individual women which is sometimes seen as the historical basis of the rape and sexual assault laws which were or are in place in Western society today.

In a Canadian context, this attitude can be seen particularly in the old definition of rape which was in effect until January 4, 1983. This law, which dated from earlier this century, contained the four principal elements of rape. The first element was vaginal penetration by the penis; the consequence of this was a concentration on the sexual nature of the act itself, not on the assaultive or aggressive nature of the act. It is interesting that other types of violation of the person, for example, forcible oral and anal intercourse were not seen as rape. The prohibited act was seen in the context of the "normal" sexual act. Second, the victim had to be a woman — a man could not be legally raped. Somehow, it was only a woman's body and integrity which could be taken and not a man's. Again, this relates to very early notions of women as men's property, of women as "available victims" in society, and of women as objects capable of being appropriated. Third, a man could not rape his wife. It was assumed that if a woman said "I do", then the possibility of saying no to sexual relations in the future was forever gone. We can see in this element the idea that a woman became the husband's property on marriage and he could do with her as he wished sexually. The fourth and final factor was that of lack of consent. It is important to note, however, that the lack of consent was not necessarily the actual refusal of consent on the part of the victim; rather, it was the rapist's perception of the existence or non-existence of the consent which was the important issue. If the rapist was "honestly" mistaken as to the existence of consent, then he would not be guilty. It was the subjective belief of the rapist as to the existence of consent which was the important legal issue.

In sum, the old law presented rape in the context of normal sexual intercourse between a man and a woman who was not his wife where consent was lacking. The focus was on the sexual aspects of the crime, not on the assaultive nature of the crime. This was particularly true in the actual operation of the law where it was often the woman's actions and character which were put on trial, not the accused's. The law was a reflection of many of the "myths" which people held about the crime of rape (see, generally, Rioux and Kinnon under Further Reading). It is important now to understand what these myths are so that we can see how the old laws failed us, and perhaps to better understand what the legislative reforms were attempting to rectify and their potential for success.

The first of these myths has to do with frequency. It is the belief that rape is not a "big" problem but rather that it is a relatively rare occurrence, and as a rule does not happen to so-called "good girls". This is coupled with the idea that the woman could have avoided the attack. Many people believe that if a woman really wants to avoid sexual assault, then she can, either by fighting back or by not putting herself in a dangerous situation. We see this view in the attitudes expressed in phrases such as "What was she doing in the park at that time of night? Why was she hitchhiking? Why did she go out with the person?" and so on. The difficulty is that participation in social interaction is regarded as a sexual invitation.

The second myth has to do with the "situation" of rape. Rape is often seen as a separate, deviant, or individualized type of behaviour. We have a definite image of the rapist as a "lurker" in alleys who pounces on his victim. What this means is we are taught to see rape as a *separate problem*. The rapist becomes a rapist because of bad genes or an extra hormone, or perhaps because of poor early social development. In this context, the rapist is also often seen as a sick predator, a stranger who preys upon more or less innocent victims. What this view does is teach us to avoid the need to put rape in the context of other behaviour and other attitudes in society which might be seen as contributing to the problem of rape. Under the individual-oriented view, if we "cured" the individual, then we could eventually "cure" the problem of rape. As we shall see later, it is more helpful to see rape as only one aspect of a larger set of problems in society.

The third myth has to do with the victim herself. As noted above, the victim is seen as "more or less" innocent: more innocent if the victim is white, middle or upper class, married, or is a virgin. Less innocent, and therefore more culpable, if she is a member of a minority group, single, independent, or career-oriented. If she falls within this latter group, she is viewed somewhat as a "loose" woman and has "asked for it", or at the very least has brought about the attack through some fault of her own.

This myth also encompasses several other ideas. First, we have the notion that the victim wanted sexual contact, and then to cover up that desire decided to call it rape. She might do this out of guilt, or because she was fearful of being caught by a husband or boyfriend, but essentially it is the belief that the victim initiated the contact and then alleged lack of consent. Second, we also have the fact that some rapists *believe* that they are releasing the victims from their innate sexual inhibition. Such attackers see themselves in a very perverse sense as sexual therapists. And finally, we have the idea that the victim, while not direct in asking for sexual contact, in fact precipitated the assault. There was allegedly implied consent by virtue of, for example, the clothing the woman was wearing, the area she was in, or the activity (for example, hitchhiking) in which she was engaged. It is the notion that these are signals to the attacker that the woman is available and even eager to some extent for sexual contact, even though she has not explicitly expressed her consent.

A fourth myth has to do with the nature of the act of rape itself as it is conceived in many people's minds. It is often perceived as an act of sexual passion in which the rapist could not control himself. We find this view well illustrated, for example, in the popular media when we look at the focus on the lurid sexual aspects of the crime found in the coverage of rape trials. The depictions are sensationalized and thereby trivialized; it is as if the sexual aspect somehow transformed the nature of the crime into something other than a real crime. An act which degrades and violates women is too often portrayed as an erotic act. This can be seen also in many pornographic magazines and films which depict the forcible violation of women as erotic.

A final myth is that "she enjoyed it". Again, this relates to the mistaken idea that rape is a type of sexual activity; the lack of consent and the assaultive nature of the crime are consequently downplayed. Rapists will sometimes tell the victim to "relax and enjoy it" even though the mutual agreement of consensual sexual intercourse is not present. Furthermore, the attacker will sometimes ask the victim if he was the best lover she ever had, or did she have an orgasm? Such sentiments obviously have nothing to do with the true nature of rape or sexual assault, and yet the attackers somehow believe (even if only as a self-justification) that rape is a sexual experience. Of course, one would find it ludicrous to think of a robber asking the victim "Did you enjoy it?" or "Was I the best person who ever robbed you?" Yet this is the type of justification used by the rapist and indeed, many would argue, by society as a whole.

In summary, in all these myths we have the underlying belief that women are primarily sexual beings; though they might use devious means to achieve sexual contact, the belief is that that is what they are often seeking. It is thought that the signals which women put out through their dress or their status, their activity or the area in which they might find themselves, are signals which can justifiably be interpreted by men as wanting that contact. Therefore, the act of rape or any type of forcible sexual contact is justified by the rapist, by the enforcement agencies and courts to some extent (as we shall see below), and by society itself.

The questions which now arise are what do we know about rape? what are the facts about rape? We can relate that knowledge to many of the issues which were raised above connected with the various myths. In regard to the issue of frequency, the first point is that rape is a major problem. But the difficulty is that it is a hidden crime. In 2000, there were 24,049 sexual assaults reported to the police. However, only a small proportion of women report such assaults to the police. The point is that all women are vulnerable and live in danger of being sexually assaulted. The difficulty with the statistics is that it is very hard to determine the real number of assaults because the estimates vary widely for the report-occurrence ratio. Some argue that approximately only 1 in 3 survivors of sexual assault report the attack while others maintain that the figure is closer to 1 in 20. Whatever the figure, it is obvious that the problem is a serious one. An even more disturbing aspect of the problem is that only a very small percentage of actual assaults ever results in a conviction. What this means is that sexual assault remains a hidden crime and a hidden problem.

In regard to the myth of "situation", it is argued that it is misleading to see rape in the context of lovemaking; it is better understood as an act of aggression, as the violent appropriation of control over another person's body. As to the notion that rape is done by the lone lurker in alleys, it has been shown that most rapes are planned acts. The rapist knows what he is doing and the act is rationally constructed. In fact, 80 percent of single rapes are planned and more than 90 percent of group rapes are planned. The rapist follows a typical pattern, and within that pattern, more than 85 percent of rapes involve violence to the victim. In regard to the victim, two-thirds of the victims know the assailant and 30 to 40 percent know the assailant well. The assault most often occurs in a trust situation; that is, the victim is attacked by a boyfriend, a friend, a friend of the husband or the boyfriend, or a relative.

In light of these facts, how, then, can sexual assault be explained? Rather than as an individual act done by a lone predator who is individually disturbed, rape must be seen as an aspect of larger social relations. Sexual assault is an act which is integrated into the way society is organized; that is, ordinary men rape ordinary women. In this regard, we can look for an explanation of rape at two levels: first, at the societal level, and second, at the individual level.

On the societal level, we have to look at the social arrangements which many argue endorse rape in society. What is that social relation? Basically, it is that we have sexism as a relation in society. If we look at this relation on a cultural level, we see sexism existing as a normative system. Simply put, it is a relation which helps men to manage their world. It promotes the idea that there are winners and losers in society and that women are losers. Women are portrayed as emotional, as fragile, as silly, as subject to flights of fancy (particularly during menstruation), as gossipy and useful primarily as sexual beings or objects. We see this in the way that they are portrayed in ads on television, in the way business tries to sell products in newspapers and magazines, and generally, through their presentation in the entertainment media. One inference of this, of course, is that if a woman says no, does she really mean no? Perhaps one should search for other cues to determine the "real" answer. For example, if she is hitchhiking, or is drinking alone, or is wearing a low-cut dress, the belief is that perhaps it is legitimate to infer that the woman is available for sexual relations.

This is true as well if we look at the relation on an economic level. Women, again, are designated losers within the economic system. This is true not only in the continuing disparity in average wage levels between men and women, but also in society's willingness to tolerate sexual harassment on the job and the lack of opportunities for advancement by women in many career fields. The consequence of sexism as a relation or social arrangement in society is that women are designated as available victims in society. Society provides the justification for, even endorsement of, the act of rape or sexual assault in society.

Within this overall context of a sexist and patriarchal society, we can also look at the individual level of rape. At the individual level, one goal of rape is an attempt to deal with the anger and frustration felt by men in society; it is not an attempt to achieve sexual gratification. Sexual assault becomes a solution to problems because it is an easy solution. It is an easy solution because we have a weak and authorized victim, the crime is easy to justify through justification such as "she wanted it" or "she enjoyed it", and, finally there is little chance of punishment. Therefore, the individual man, in an attempt to deal with his frustration at "losing" in society, can turn to sexual assault as a means for solving or coping with his problems. It should be noted, however, that there are different explanations of rape at this individual level and this is only one. What is important here as to the issue of the response of criminal law is that in looking at this individual level we must not forget the origin of the problem in the sexist relations within society.

What, then, are the proposed solutions to the problem of sexual assault? In general, we have two solutions. One, we can change the system; we can rid society of the basic causes of sexual assault, that is rid society of sexism. The problem is, obviously, how one does that, particularly in the short term. Second, we have limited pragmatic solutions which involve two things: first, we want to raise the cost of rape to the aggressor. We can do this through more convictions, by making it more likely that an individual will be convicted and punished if he sexually assaults a woman. Also, we can raise the capacity of women to resist, not only through self defense classes, better and safer living environments, and the such, but also by lowering the cost to the victim, by ensuring that the victim is more willing to report, and by making the system more amenable to her needs in coming forth and reporting the offence.

By way of a pragmatic solution, Parliament passed legislation which came into effect in 1983 and which was modified in 1992. These amendments to the Criminal Code and the relevant case law are detailed in the Stuart article which follows. As can be seen, flaws remain in the law's treatment of this type of crime, but it can be said that the attempts to date represent major steps forward when compared to the old rape law. But very real difficulties do remain with such a pragmatic solution, notably in regard to the enforcement of the law. It is in the operation of the legislation that major hurdles remain. These hurdles, seen in the context of a sexist society, can be seen in several steps of the enforcement process.

On the front line are police enforcement agencies. The problem we find here is that according to a study published in late 1982 (when the old law was still in force), one-third of all rape complaints were disbelieved by the police. This meant that one-third of all complaints reported to the police were not investigated further. This figure had improved by 1985 to about 14 percent, a hopeful sign but still high given dismissal rates for other crimes. Unfortunately, the figure of 14% has remained virtually the same since then, though it should be noted that the actual rate varies considerably across the country (see, generally, Roberts, 1994, under Further Reading). Police argue that many of the complainants are mistaken or lying and that a rape never occurred. By way of contrast, police believe that only 1 out of every 33 individuals who say they have been robbed are either mistaken or lying, and when it comes to police officers who say they have been assaulted in the course of their duty, only 1 in 250 will not be believed. As to the reasons why women are disbelieved, one often finds in the arguments of the police stereotypical beliefs and attitudes as to the nature of the crime itself. These attitudes have been criticized by rape crisis centre counsellors who argue that the police are clinging to outmoded and prejudicial attitudes towards women; they do not believe that when a woman says no she really means no. It is this type of police attitude toward the problem which obviously discourages women from coming forward to report the crime and prevents the prosecution of assailants. Some improvements have been made recently in the creation of specific units within police departments formed to deal with sexual assault victims and to aid them in the prosecution of this type of crime. However, the availability of this type of unit is not widespread, particularly in rural areas. Moreover, the complaint has been raised that these units often consist principally of male members of the force.

Another problem in the enforcement in this area has to do with the treatment of the victim at the hands of the medical profession. According to the former Attorney General of Ontario, Roy McMurtry, "there is a tradition of reluctance of doctors in emergency wards to get involved in cases that could end up at a criminal trial because of the time involved" (*Globe and Mail*, October 1, 1982). There have been several cases across the country where hospitals and doctors have refused to treat sexual assault victims and of situations where the victim had to "shop around" for a hospital which was willing to examine and treat her. While some hospitals now provide special units and personnel to deal with sexual assault victims, such units remain relatively rare. It is this reluctance and callousness on the part of the medical profession which have undoubtedly caused many women to hesitate before reporting the crime and seeking treatment.

The final problem has to do with the judiciary. Judges play a particularly important role under the legislation due to the lack of a definition for sexual assault, the Charter concerns over balancing the rights of the victims versus those of the accused, and the issues surrounding the defence of mistaken belief in consent (see excerpts from the *Livermore* case, reproduced below). There have been many instances in the past when, it can be argued, judges have been less than sympathetic or less than progressive in regard to the plight of the rape or sexual assault survivor. One can find numerous examples in statements by members of the judiciary reflecting outmoded and sexist attitudes towards women, not only in sexual assault cases but also in many other types of cases involving women (for example, where domestic violence has occurred). It is important to note that one of the first major cases to come forward in regard to the new sexual assault legislation evolved around the issue of whether women's breasts are indeed sexual. In this case, the Court of Appeal in New Brunswick ruled that female breasts are like men's beards, a secondary sexual characteristic. In contrast, the prosecutor had contended that it is the circumstances of an assault which determine whether it is sexual, not the parts of the body which are touched. In the case, however, the court reduced the sentence to six months from the eight months which had been imposed originally because it argued that the assault was not sexual as it involved only secondary sexual characteristics, that is, a woman's breasts. This is the type of inane argument which critics argued might result under the new legislation. The Court of Appeal decision was overturned by the Supreme Court in *R. v. Chase* (1987), 59 C.R. (3d) 193, but many of the attitudes surrounding the Court of Appeal decision and the ignorance reflected in it continue today. The *McCraw* case, below, though not a sexual assault case *per se*, is another good example of some existing judicial attitudes and their consequences. There are numerous other examples which one can point to which reveal attitudes on the part of many in the judiciary (both at the trial and appellate levels) which reflect the myths referred to above, but we can end here by noting the reasoning used by a judge in sentencing three convicted gang rapists in 1981 and the incredible double standard which was applied:

> In sentencing the men, Smith [the judge] said that because of all the exceptional circumstances of the case, a penitentiary term of two years or more . . . would be a gross error. . . .
>
> The rape took place in a ditch beside a country road after several hours of driving about and smoking marijuana.
>
> Smith said that the young men were of good character and came from remarkable family backgrounds, but because of excessive drinking and pot smoking that night, had stepped out of character for a brief period.
>
> The woman, on the other hand, "had behaved very foolishly".
>
> "She was rebellious, drank too much and started out on that *frolic* with no regard for the consequences."
>
> [Emphasis added]. (*The Ottawa Citizen*, October 31, 1981).

While the drinking and smoking served to excuse the men's behaviour, it was used on the other hand to blame the woman (at least partially) for the crimes which took place.

The attitudes we find towards sexual assault victims on the part of the police, the medical profession, and the legal profession are, of course, not surprising in light of the fact that we are dealing with male-dominated, conservative bodies. A real attack on the problem of sexual assault in society cannot be fully or effectively undertaken until women begin to have a real influence within these enforcement agencies and more importantly within the political power structures in this country. There will be little progress until sexism itself is eliminated.

In sum, what we have is a pragmatic solution which, though flawed, is certainly a positive step towards a real, comprehensive solution. The greatest problem in the short term remains in its enforcement within the context of a patriarchal enforcement process. Moreover, in the long term, in spite of the fact that we may eventually have more effective enforcement, the fundamental problem remains that sexual assault is too much an accepted and even acceptable activity within the context of current sexist relations in society. What progress has been made to date has been the result of women organizing amongst themselves to create lobby groups, crisis centres, and self-defence classes. Changes in the criminal legislation go only a very small way towards providing a solution and do not ensure either that the cause of the social problem will be eradicated or that the reforms will be given real effect in their enforcement. Unless and until these two issues are effectively addressed, any legislative reforms can have only a marginal effect.

## Regina v. McCraw
### (1989), 72 C.R. (3d) 373 (Ont. C.A.).

Appeal by Crown from accused's acquittal of threatening serious bodily harm.

October 16, 1989. BROOKE J.A. (TARNOPOLOSKY J.A. concurring): — The Crown appeals from the acquittal of the respondent on three counts in an indictment, each of which counts charged him with an offence contrary to s. 243.4 (now s. 264.1) of the Criminal Code. The counts were as follows:

1. That he the said Stephen Joseph McCraw, between the 1st day of November, 1987 and the 26th day of November, 1987 at the City of Ottawa in the said Judicial District, did knowingly cause to be received a threat to Sandy Kobluk, by letter, to cause serious bodily harm to Sandy Kobluk, contrary to Section 243.4(2) of the Criminal Code of Canada.

2. And further that he the said Stephen Joseph McCraw, between the 1st day of November, 1987 and the 26th day of November, 1987 at the City of Ottawa in the said Judicial District, did knowingly cause to be received a threat to Johanne Robillard, by letter, to cause serious bodily harm to Johanne Robillard, contrary to Section 243.4(2) of the Criminal Code of Canada.

3. And further that he the said Stephen Joseph McCraw, between the 1st day of October, 1987 and the 30th day of October, 1987 at the City of Ottawa in the said Judicial District, did knowingly cause to be received a threat to Deborah Burgoyn, by letter, to cause serious bodily harm to Deborah Burgoyn, contrary to Section 234.4(2) of the Criminal Code of Canada.

The trial judge held that, although the respondent had written the letters and each contained a threat to rape the complainant, none of the threats necessarily involved the infliction of serious bodily harm. The finding that each letter contained a threat to rape is not attacked in this court.

The facts were that the complainants were cheerleaders of a football club. The respondent, who was not known to any of them, wrote to each a similar letter. The letter to the complainant Johanne Robillard stated:

Johanne

Let me tell you, your a beautiful woman, I am disappointed you weren't in the calendar, you are the most beautiful cheerleader on the squad. I think you should pose nude for playboy.

[After detailing in graphic and vulgar terms what he would like to do to the complainant, the defendant wrote:]

I am going to fuck you even if I have to *rape* you. Even if it takes me till the day I die. There should be more beautiful women around like you.
*See you later and have a nice day!*

In the case of Johanne Robillard only, that letter was followed by a letter which said:

Johanne
Meet me on Thursday, November 19, at 6:00 p.m., behind the N.A.C. (National Arts Centre) in Ottawa, be along the water of the Rideau Canal. If you dont show up I will go to Rockland and *get you*. Dont forget I know where you live.
See you soon!

In dismissing the charges, the trial judge said:

In this case, the threat to "rape", to have non-consensual sexual intercourse, may or may not involve serious bodily harm. It does not involve it necessarily. The court found that the words in *Gingras* might equally mean "I'm going to strike you," but not necessarily cause bodily harm, a separate concept. The words in our case may equally mean: "I'm going to have intercourse with you with or without your consent, but not necessarily by causing any serious bodily harm." The court concluded that the threat contemplated by s. 243.4(1)(a) has to contain with it clear words that would expressly or by necessary implication refer to serious bodily harm. Just as the words in *Gingras* are ambiguous and do not expressly or by necessary implication refer to causing serious bodily harm, so too the word "rape" in the case at bar is ambiguous and does not expressly or by necessary implication refer to the causing of serious bodily harm.

Later he said:

. . . s. 243.4(1)(a) specifically proscribes threats to cause serious bodily harm, and not a threat to have non-consensual intercourse.

In concluding he said:

In this case, we are dealing with "serious bodily harm", which we equated in the section to "death". What we have here is a threat to have sexual intercourse with each of the complainants, with or without their consent. This is quite separate and distinct, in the court's view, from threatening serious bodily harm. Again, the threat to commit a sexual assault does not necessarily cause serious bodily harm.

In my respectful view, the trial judge erred in holding that the threat was simply to have sexual intercourse without the complainant's consent. The threat was not confined to the lawyer's meaning of "rape", but would be understood, in the circumstances, as meaning that the threatener intended to do all of the acts specified in his letter. His statement that he would rape her was a statement that he would resort to such physical force as was necessary to do what he wanted and to make her do what he wanted her to do.

The second letter to the complainant Johanne Robillard emphasizes the threat. It is a warning to the complainant that, if she does not meet him as he has told her to, he will come and take her against her will by force and carry out the threatened acts. Why these letters should be regarded as other than a threat to use physical force to take the complainant, hold her against her will and violate her body I do not know. But does all this amount to a threat to cause serious bodily harm? "Bodily harm" is defined in s. 267(2) [of the 1985 Criminal Code] as "any hurt of injury to the complainant that interferes with the health or comfort of the complainant and that is more than merely transient or trifling in nature". Where the bodily harm amounts to wounding, maiming, disfiguring or endangering life, the sexual assault which causes it is aggravated sexual assault. But "serious bodily harm" is not defined in the Code. Perhaps some assistance may be had from s. 752, defining "serious personal injury offences".

The learned trial judge interpreted serious bodily harm in s. 264.1 as equated to death. I do not agree. The section should not be read in that way. It is for the finder of fact to determine if a threat is a threat to cause bodily harm and whether or not such bodily harm is serious bodily harm. The word "serious" is not ambiguous, and should be given its ordinary meaning. The Crown submits that the ambit of bodily harm is not restricted to physical injury or harm but includes emotional or psychological injury, harm or damage. Putting aside any question of whether bodily harm includes emotional or psychological harm, does the threat in this case amount to a threat to cause serious bodily harm? In my opinion, it does. The object of this threat is to create fear of such a degree of bodily harm from the application of physical force that the complainant will submit to or not resist the sexual assault. The nature of bodily harm which would cause her to submit to such violations of her dignity and her body is not simply a hurt or injury that would interfere with her comfort, but rather something serious. In short, resistance means force, perhaps violence, and serious injury. That is this case.

While there is no evidence that the complainants other than Johanne Robillard received a letter similar to the second letter referred to above, each of the complainants received a letter similar to the first letter, in which the trial judge held that there was a threat to rape her. In the circumstances, that was enough.

In the result, I think the trial judge was wrong in his interpretation of s. 264.1 as to the meaning of "serious bodily harm" and he erred in holding that a threat to commit rape was no more than a threat to have sexual intercourse without the complainant's consent. Accordingly, the acquittal cannot stand, and must be set aside. In the circumstances, as the only issue was whether or not the threat was a threat to cause serious bodily harm, the respondent will be convicted on each of the three counts in the indictment. The case is remitted to the trial judge for sentencing.

FINLAYSON J.A. (dissenting): — The validity of this prosecution is very much one of first impressions. Its outcome depends upon the reaction of the reader to the letters which constitute the criminal acts alleged. To me, they do not constitute threats to commit a specific criminal act. It is thus not necessary for me to embark on an inquiry as to whether a threat to rape is a threat to cause serious bodily harm. Accordingly, I respectfully disagree with the assessment of the trial judge's findings made by Brooke J.A. and with his disposition of the appeal.

The letters to the three cheerleaders for the Ottawa Rough Riders Football Club that were alleged to be threats to cause serious bodily harm are virtually identical. Brooke J.A. has selected the letter to Johanne Robillard as representative, and it is set out in full in his reasons. The charge is that the sending of the letter is contrary to what is now s. 264.1(1)(a) of the Criminal Code. That section reads as follows:

**264.1**(1) Every one commits an offence who, in any manner, knowingly utters, conveys or causes any person to receive a threat

(a) to cause death or serious bodily harm to any person. . . .

. . .

In my opinion, offensive as the letters are, they do not amount to a threat to cause serious bodily harm as contemplated by the Code. They are expressions of sexual fantasizing, and are clearly obscene. It is difficult to conceive of any defence that the respondent would have if he had been charged under s. 168 of the Code. It reads as follows:

**168.** Every one commits an offence who makes use of the mails for the purpose of transmitting or delivering anything that is obscene, indecent, immoral or scurrilous, but this section does not apply to a person who makes use of the mails for the purpose of transmitting or delivering anything mentioned in subsection 166(4).

Obscenity need not be restricted to matters sexual. The Code defines an obscene publication as follows:

**163.** . . .

(8) For the purposes of this Act, any publication a dominant characteristic of which is the undue exploitation of sex, or of sex and any one or more of the following subjects, namely, crime, horror, cruelty and violence, shall be deemed to be obscene.

In her submissions, counsel for the appellant isolated the phrase "even if I have to rape you" from its context in the letter. The hearing before our court was taken up almost entirely with a discussion as to whether a threat to rape was a threat to cause serious bodily harm. This misses both the affront and the effect of the letter. It is not intended that its contents be taken literally. There is no purpose in close analysis of the conduct described to determine if it portrays deviance, fetishism or criminal acts. The letter is nothing more than a series of obscenities.

The case, as represented by the Crown, is complicated by the fact that the offence of rape as such no longer exists and has been replaced in the Code by various degrees of sexual assault, not all of which involve serious bodily harm. We are asked to accept a layman's definition of "rape" as a non-consensual, even forced, act of sexual intercourse and to assume that the "threat" in the letter was a threat to cause serious bodily harm, as opposed to sexual gratification regardless of consent. This begs the question, in that it assumes that the letters contain a series of explicit threats, including a threat to rape. I agree with the trial judge's finding, which I accept as a finding of fact, that: "The tenor of the letters, while immature and disgusting, reveals more of an adoring fantasy than a threat to cause serious bodily harm."

. . .

Even if I am wrong in concluding that the trial judge found as a matter of fact that the letters were not intended to be taken seriously, I certainly accept that the language of the letters, while clearly criminal, in that it is obscene, is ambiguous as a threat to cause serious bodily harm. The respondent was entitled to the benefit of any ambiguity in this language. To quote the trial judge against, "the court ought never to begin to speculate upon what the accused might have meant".

Accordingly, for the reasons given, I would allow leave to appeal but dismiss the appeal.

*Appeal allowed; conviction substituted.*

## Sexual Assault: Substantive Issues Before and After Bill C-49*
### *Don Stuart*

* Excerpts from (1992-93), 35 Criminal Law Quarterly 241

## 1. CONTEXT

### (1)  The 1983 Reform of Rape Laws

In 1983 the crime of rape was replaced by a three-tier structure of sexual assault offences: sexual assault (s. 271, maximum sentence of 10 years); sexual assault with a weapon, threats or causing bodily harm (s. 272, maximum sentence 14 years), and aggravated sexual assault (s. 273, maximum sentence life imprisonment). The aim, clearly expressed by the Honourable Flora MacDonald in the House of Commons, was to reflect the violence rather than the sexual nature of the offence and to increase both reporting and conviction rates:

> . . . the current laws relating to rape and indecent assault are being changed to emphasize the violence as opposed to the sexual aspects of these crimes. In other words, we will no longer have the term "rape" in law.
> This legislation has a long history. Individual women and groups of women all across the country have been pushing for years to change the rape laws. It was apparent that this section of the Criminal Code cried out for reform. The number of reported rape cases was far below the actual number of offences. It has been estimated that only one in ten cases of rape was reported. That was due largely to the stigma which surrounded the rape victim — the idea that nice girls do not get raped and the belief that she must have asked for it . . . The conviction rate for rape has traditionally been much lower than the conviction rate for other serious crimes — only 52 per cent conviction rate for rape, compared with an 82 per cent conviction rate in the case of other indictable offences.

Parliament also took the opportunity to abolish clearly discriminatory evidentiary rules based on notions of women as property or that women, particularly those "unchaste", are likely to make false rape claims. Parliament abolished the spousal immunity, restricted cross-examination of the primary witness as to her previous sexual history, abrogated the doctrine of recent complaint, repealed corroboration requirements and warnings and restricted evidence of prior sexual history of the complainant. It is clear that these legislative changes attempted to answer some of the complaints of legal bias against victims of sexual assault. Whether attitudes have changed is another matter.

The extent to which Parliament's 1983 objectives have been met is, unfortunately, uncertain. A comprehensive Department of Justice review of national statistics has confirmed that there is a much larger proportion of victims of sexual assault now reporting to police but that there has been no change in the percentage of reports designated by police as unfounded. The same report indicates that some half of all sexual assault reports result in charges and that this rate is no lower than that for other crimes against the person. There are no national statistics on conviction rates for sexual assault. A 1988 site study indicated comparable conviction rates of about 73% for those charged with either sexual or non-sexual assault. A number of instances where judges have not sufficiently emphasized the violence of a sexual assault in sentencing have been clearly documented. On the other hand, the conclusion of a Department of Justice study of various sentencing data bases has concluded that the popular view that most sexual assaults are not punished severely relative to other offences is "in part at least a misperception, founded upon media coverage of cases that resulted in atypically lenient sentences being imposed."

As best one can tell from this empirical data, rape cases are now being routinely reported and charged as sexual assault *simpliciter*, the lowest level of seriousness. In all these sexual assault statistics, there is no longer a differentiation between sexual touching and rape. In this sense, the impact of the 1983 legislation on rape cannot be determined.

## (2)  Changing Attitudes: No Means No

There would appear to be an emerging public awareness, particularly on university campuses and in the media that rape is by no means confined to a stranger emerging from the dark. Public concern seems to be increasingly focused on the fact that over 70% of all sexual assaults are committed by someone the victim knows. The need for a new attitude by men to sexual relations is captured by the often-repeated slogan "No Means No". It is quite clear that women are justifiably asserting the right to say no at any time, even if the woman has been drinking, has said yes earlier and is now changing her mind, or has had sex before with the particular man.

The importance of this movement was recently well expressed to me and my class by a female law student as follows:

> Men don't seem to understand why this right is so important to us. We feel we are in a bind. If we say no we are teasers; if we say yes we are sluts. All we want to do is to assert our autonomous right without anybody making a judgment.

This message has not got through to all quarters. Recently, a defence counsel was quoted as having said this about the right to revoke consent recognized in Bill C-49:

> It's ridiculous . . . this isn't contract law. She says "Let's have sex." They are having full sexual intercourse. She suddenly says: "That's it. I'm revoking my agreement." Now how long does the male have to withdraw before it's sexual assault? . . . It just denies the biological nature of human beings.

Given that the criminal law is meant to reflect fundamental human values and to punish and deter those who do not share those values and have harmed others, it seems only appropriate that the "no means no" philosophy be adequately reflected in our *Criminal Code* of 1992.

### (3)  Right to a Fair Trial

It has been a fundamental value of our criminal justice system before and after the Charter that any accused is presumed innocent until proven guilty and that proof must be beyond reasonable doubt. It is obvious that the interests of victims of violence must be adequately addressed by the criminal law. It is also the reality that it is the accused who risks being sent to prison. However heinous the crime, the criminal justice system must be scrupulous in its attempt to punish the morally blameworthy and to ascertain the truth lest we convict the innocent. It may be that sexual assault will always be a type of crime where acquittal rates will be relatively high. The reality is that most sexual conduct takes place in private and communication is sometimes unclear. Where there is a conflict in testimony it will always be difficult for the trier of fact to determine the truth well after the event. It is a pernicious myth that women and children likely lie in such cases. There is also the reality that there are some false claims and some cases where what happened is unclear.

### (4)  Realities of Prison

The criminal law is a blunt instrument and should be used with restraint. Prison sentences for violent offences are easy to justify on the grounds of the need for retribution and punishment proportionate to the crime committed. On the other hand, those glibly urging ever longer prison sentences for sexual offenders need to confront the reality that in the Canadian penitentiaries of today, there are some 1,500 sex offenders and only 150 of them are receiving treatment. There has not been sufficient political will since 1983 to provide the resources for treatment of offenders and real alternatives for victims of abuse. Such resources might be the best chance of protecting women and children in the future.

### (5)  Impetus Behind Bill C-49

On August 22, 1991, a 7 to 2 majority of the Supreme Court of Canada in *R. v. Seaboyer; R. v. Gayme* held that the blanket exclusion by s. 276 of the *Criminal Code* of evidence of prior sexual history of a complainant subject to three specified exceptions violated the accused's right to make full answer and defence under ss. 7 and 11(*d*) of the Charter. The provision was held to exclude evidence without permitting a judge to engage in a determination of whether the possible prejudicial effect of the evidence would outweigh its value to the truth-finding process.

*Seaboyer* immediately produced an outcry in the media. Headlines blared that the Supreme Court had struck down the rape-shield provision and that women and children would be even less likely to pursue charges of sexual assault given that there would be unrestricted cross-examination of their prior sexual history. Such comments were an overreaction and unfair to the majority of the Supreme Court. For the majority, Madam Justice McLachlin had indeed struck down s. 276. However, expressing grave concern at leaving the matter to unfettered judicial discretion, she set out what she considered to be careful guidelines as to the admissibility of evidence of the complainant's prior sexual history. Her Ladyship also extended the protection to such conduct *with the accused.*

It is fair to say, however, that the majority of the Supreme Court took but a line to hold that although victims might have equality rights, these had to give way to the accused's right to make full answer and defence. It may well have been this weighing of rights that led usually moderate feminist writers to strong statement:

> It may not be the case that the majority betrayed women, or even necessarily made a wrong decision by neglecting the constitutional value of sex equality. They may have illustrated, in the clearest, most "rational" terms, the fact that law will inevitably value the interests of men and require women to pay the price.

The response from the Minister of Justice, the Honourable Kim Campbell was swift. She announced that Parliament would respond to protect women and children better. She called a meeting of national and regional women's groups. The record seems clear that the Minister thereafter worked very closely in drafting and revising the bill with the coalition of some 60 groups that emerged. The coalition reached unanimity at each point and agreed to oppose any attempt to water down the bill. In this sense, the process was partisan with voices of men, no doubt for the first time in the history of the development of Canadian criminal law, of little weight. By the time Bill C-49 reached the Senate, Professor Sheila McIntyre, the spokesperson for L.E.A.F. (Women's Legal Education and Action Fund), the sponsor of the bill, stated that the aim had been to reflect women's constitutional rights under s. 7 and women's equality rights under s. 15 and also to achieve formal education:

> We also wanted comprehensive judicial education not through weekend seminars but in the body of the law, and we got it. We are very happy with the codified guidelines to judges that framed Seaboyer's broad principles and very specific factors to keep in mind, many of which are mindful of equality. No prejudicial, discriminatory stereotype language made its way in there and we are very pleased with that.

Bill C-49 was enthusiastically welcomed by politicians of every stripe for having replaced *Seaboyer* with a new rape shield that would protect women and children. This is ironic given that the new rape-shield laws, which are not the subject of this article, so closely mirror the guidelines suggested by the majority in *Seaboyer*. It is certainly true, however, that the new statutory scheme does at one point, in declaring the factors for trial judges to consider, include concerns for interests of the victim on the same level as the accused's right to make full answer and defence. It remains to be seen whether the Supreme Court will change its earlier assessment of the proper balance.

Bill C-49 accomplished much more than a statutory rape-shield law. The Minister of Justice and the women's groups seized the opportunity to legislate on the question of what constitutes genuine consent and also on the long-controversial mistake-of-fact defence. These changes will here be examined in the course of a review of substantive issues surrounding sexual assault before and after Bill C-49.

## 2. Actus Reus

### (1) Sexual Nature of Assault

What makes an assault "sexual"? In *R. v. Chase* the Supreme Court adopted an objective test:

> Sexual assault is an assault, within any one of the definitions of that concept in [s. 265(1)] of the Criminal Code, which is committed in circumstances of a sexual nature, such that the sexual integrity of the victim is violated. The test to be applied in determining whether the impugned conduct has the requisite sexual nature is an objective one: "Viewed in the light of all the circumstances, is the sexual or carnal context of the assault visible to a reasonable observer?": *Taylor*, supra, per Laycraft C.J.A., at p. 269. The part of the body touched, the nature of the contact, the situation in which it occurred, the words and gestures accompanying the act, and all other circumstances surrounding the conduct, including threats, which may or may not be accompanied by force, will be relevant.

The court added that the intent and motive of the accused were factors to be considered. The Supreme Court rejected the much-criticized view of the court below that sexual referred to genital parts of the body and did not include female breasts.

### (2) No Consent

Under ss. 265(1) and (2) there can be no assault or sexual assault where the complainant consents to the application of force. In 1983, s. 265(3) was added:

> 265(3) For the purposes of this section, no consent is obtained where the complainant submits or does not resist by reason of

> (*a*) the application of force to the complainant or to a person other than the complainant;

> (*b*) threats or fear of the application of force to the complainant or to a person other than the complainant;

> (*c*) fraud; or

> (*d*) the exercise of authority.

The notion that submission as a result of fear cannot be consent is important in the sexual assault context. The provision is clearly designed to protect vulnerable victims who choose to "co-operate" as a defence strategy.

In *R. v. Jobidon* the Supreme Court held by a 5 to 2 majority that s. 265(3)'s list of four vitiating factors was not exhaustive and did not remove further common law limits on the legal effectiveness of consent. Notwithstanding s. 9 of the *Criminal Code* which outlaws common law offences, the majority held that it was open for the court to adopt policy-based limits on the role and scope of consent in s. 265. Their conclusion in the manslaughter case before them was that s. 265 "*vitiates consent between adults intentionally to apply force causing serious hurt or non-trivial bodily harm to each other in the course of a fist fight or brawl*".

Whether the *Jobidon* principle can be extended to vitiate apparent consent in cases of sexual practices that cause physical harm remains to be seen.

### (3)  Consent Under New s. 273.1

The new s. 273.1 seeks to define consent in the case of sexual assault but, consistent with *R. v. Jobidon*, is expressly not exhaustive:

*Meaning of "consent"*

273.1(1)  Subject to subsection (2) and subsection 265(3), "consent" means, for the purposes of sections 271, 272 and 273, the voluntary agreement of the complainant to engage in the sexual activity in question.

*Where no consent obtained*

(2)  No consent is obtained, for the purposes of sections 271, 272 and 273, where

(*a*)  the agreement is expressed by the words or conduct of a person other than the complainant;

(*b*)  the complainant is incapable of consenting to the activity;

(*c*)  the accused induces the complainant to engage in the activity by abusing a position of trust, power or authority;

(*d*)  the complainant expresses, by words or conduct, a lack of agreement to engage in the activity; or

(*e*)  the complainant having consented to engage in sexual activity, expresses, by words or conduct, a lack of agreement to continue to engage in the activity.

*Subsection (2) not limiting*

(3)  Nothing in subsection (2) shall be construed as limiting the circumstances in which no consent is obtained.

These provisions clearly set out to give courts better guidance as to situations in which consent can be held to have been not genuine and therefore not consent in law. Subsections (*b*), (*c*) and (*e*) were amended as the bill passed through Committee. The amendments were largely inconsequential, merely clarifying rather than changing the original intent. Subsection (*b*) had read that the complainant was incapable of consenting to the activity "by reason of intoxication or other condition". The provision was criticized as being vague, especially in its reference to "other condition". Parliament clearly decided to leave the matter to the discretion of trial judges while preserving the common law principle that one who, on the evidence was incapable of giving consent, cannot be considered to have consented.

These new consent provisions seem adequately drafted and a welcome assertion of the "No Means No" philosophy. With the exception of subsec. (*c*), which will require judicial interpretation, the provisions appear to merely restate existing legal principles.

Subsection (*d*) clearly preserves the existing common law that consent can be express or implied. A suggestion by the women's coalition, that consent should be limited to unequivocal communications, was rejected and would have produced unfairness to the accused.

Critics of Bill C-49 have suggested that in future written consent will be needed in advance for any sexual conduct, that there is an onus of proof on the accused or that Bill C-49 criminalizes seduction. Given the wording of the new provisions these criticisms have no validity.

## 3. Fault

### (1)  Former Mistaken Belief in Consent Defence

In debates surrounding Bill C-49 proponents often left the impression that the mistake defence had a lot to do with the low reporting of rape and high acquittal rates. It is, however, clear that the mistake-of-fact defence had had virtually no impact on the conviction rate.

In its controversial ruling in *R. v. Pappajohn* a majority of the Supreme Court determined that the normal moral blameworthiness requirement they had been applying for other serious offences also applied to rape. This was the notion of subjective *mens rea* where the accused must be proved to have been at least reckless in the sense that he was aware of the risk — in the case of sexual assault, that the woman had not consented. The court confirmed that, on general principles, the belief need merely be honest and whether it was reasonable went only to the question of whether the accused was to be believed. The court recognized that there were policy considerations advanced in support of the view that the mistake should be one a reasonable man would have made but suggested that such mistake offences would be few in number and that juries could be trusted to distinguish between the genuine and bogus defences. However, the most important *Pappajohn* ruling was by a differently composed majority of the court. This majority imposed the requirement that before the defence of mistaken belief could be put to the jury, it had to be supported by sources other than the accused in order to give it "any air of reality".

The evidentiary ruling in *Pappajohn* seems pragmatically designed to restrict the ambit of the mistaken-belief defence. It places a corroboration requirement on the accused which is required in no other type of case. Although this has led to criticism the Supreme Court of Canada has thus far refused to alter it. The court has also confirmed that the law on mistaken belief has not changed since Parliament added s. 265(4) to the *Criminal Code* in 1983. Section 265(4) enacts an express mistake-of-belief defence to apply to all types of assault and sexual assault.

It seems clear that the evidentiary ruling in *Pappajohn* has accounted for the reality that the mistaken-belief defence is rarely even put to the jury. Since *Pappajohn* was decided, there have been few decisions with written reasons basing an acquittal on a mistaken-belief defence and only one such acquittal confirmed by a Court of Appeal.

Two other Supreme Court decisions may well have contributed to the low success rate of mistake-of-fact defences in rape cases. In *R. v. Sansregret*, there had been an acquittal at trial on the basis of a mistake-of-fact defence. The air of reality had come from the testimony of the complainant. When the matter reached the Supreme Court, the court decided that, given the finding that the accused had an honest belief in consent, he could not have been reckless. However, the court convicted on the basis that, as there had been a previous incident involving the same victim, the accused must have been wilfully blind. *Sansregret* has been soundly criticized on the basis that the court could not have validly found wilful blindness in the face of the trial judge's finding of fact that the accused honestly believed in consent and that it wrongly imported knowledge where there was no awareness of risk.

Another holding which may account for mistake of fact defences being unlikely to succeed in sexual assault cases is the Court's deeply divided ruling in *R. v. Bernard*. The 4 to 3 majority hold that the common law rule that voluntary intoxication is no defence to a crime of general intent is not contrary to the Charter. The majority ruled that sexual assault was such a crime. However two of the majority (Wilson and L'Heureux-Dubé JJ.) recognize a "flexible" approach under which *extreme* intoxication may be a defence to general intent crimes. A minority of three justices hold that denying the intoxication defence imposes absolute liability inconsistent with fundamental principles of voluntariness and fault. The minority point to the Australian reality where voluntary intoxication is now a defence to any crime but rarely succeeds. Given the complex splits in the judgments *Bernard* can be read as a 5 to 2 holding that *extreme* intoxication is a defence to any crime, including sexual assault.

## (2)  Effect of New s. 273.2

Where belief in consent not a defence

273.2 It is not a defence to a charge under section 271, 272 or 273 that the accused believed that the complainant consented to the activity that forms the subject-matter of the charge, where

(*a*)  the accused's belief arose from the accused's
  (i)  self-induced intoxication, or
  (ii)  recklessness or wilful blindness; or

(*b*)  the accused did not take reasonable steps, in the circumstances known to the accused at the time, to ascertain that the complainant was consenting.

The section creates special limits on the mistake-of-fact defence which apply to all sexual assault cases but not to assault offences. In the case of sexual assault Parliament has reversed the substantive but not the evidentiary ruling in *Pappajohn*. The accused still has to pass the air-of-reality test for a mistake defence. That defence will not now be open where his mistaken belief arose from self-induced intoxication, recklessness or wilful blindness or, most importantly, where he did not take reasonable steps in the circumstances known to him to ascertain that the complainant was consenting. At the First Reading stage the accused was to be required to take "all" reasonable steps. "All" was dropped at Third Reading, presumably accepting arguments that the standard was too severe and risked a Charter challenge that it restricted the minimum Charter standard of due diligence.

The irrelevance of self-induced intoxication is a change from the narrow majority ruling in *Bernard* because it excludes the possibility of the extreme intoxication defence. The exclusion of situations where the accused was reckless or wilfully blind is difficult to fathom. *R. v. Sansregret* itself points out that if the accused had an honest belief in consent, he could not have been reckless since he would not have been aware of the risk of consent. The same would be true of someone who was wilfully blind which requires a deliberate suppression of the possibility that the accused was not consenting. The proposed exclusion of reckless and wilful blindness is unnecessarily harsh and diverts attention from the inquiry into whether the accused was aware of the risk. This criticism seems academic given the further requirement that the accused have taken reasonable steps. This liability is clearly new and would impose a standard of not measuring up to a reasonableness test. Under the offence as so defined, the Crown could rest content with proof beyond reasonable doubt of unreasonable conduct in a sexual context.

In my judgment s. 273.2 is unjust in not fairly recognizing different forms of culpability of an accused and may be unconstitutional as a result.

### (3)  Unfairness in Not Distinguishing Subjective and Objective Fault Standards

Few judges or writers would now dogmatically insist that criminal responsibility should always be based on a determination of subjective fault. There *is* a case to be made for the punishment of one who "ought", "should", "could", or "as a reasonable person would" have foreseen. But the key point is that whenever resort is had to this external objective negligence standard, there is a considerable extension of the reach of the criminal law. Such extension should be made cautiously. The advantage of the subjective awareness of risk approach which courts have usually insisted on for *Criminal Code* offences is that it is the fault test fairest to the accused since it takes into account all the capacities and incapacities of the individual. It has proved a valuable vehicle for restraint in the exercise of state power behind the criminal law.

The time had arrived for Parliament to declare some criminal responsibility for objectively unreasonable sexual behaviour. Some commentators have long advocated such a reform, either on the basis of an analysis of the nature of the act of sexual assault, or on the need to be consistent with the acceptance of the objective standard in the case of other crimes.

It is, however, vital for the criminal law to recognize that there is a distinction in culpability between a deliberate risk-taker and one who was unreasonable in that he did not anticipate the risk but ought to have. There is surely a qualitative distinction between a man who deliberately rapes a woman knowing that she is not consenting and one who engages in sexual intercourse where it was in the circumstances unreasonable for him to have assumed that the woman was consenting. These different forms of culpability should be reflected in different forms of conviction and different penalties. This would appear to be the basis upon which the Supreme Court of Canada has, in its Charter rulings striking down constructive murder rules, decided to distinguish between murder and manslaughter. Murder has to be based on subjective foresight of the likelihood of death to justify the life imprisonment sentence. On the other hand, it is likely that the Supreme Court will squarely hold that manslaughter can be based on an objective standard since the penalty is the reduced one of a maximum of life imprisonment, which allows for considerably more lenient sentences.

Parliament too had previously moved cautiously in its efforts to create some criminality based on the objective standard. When it created an offence of arson by negligence in 1990 it specifically declared that the offence required proof of a marked departure from the standard of care that a reasonably prudent person would use and reduced the penalty from a maximum of 14 years in the normal arson case to one of five years imprisonment. Similarly, the definition of the offence of careless use of a firearm was to be changed to require a gross departure from the objective norm.

. . .

## 4. Is Rape Always Sexual Assault Causing Bodily Harm?

Experience since 1983 suggests that rape prosecutions are now routinely prosecuted at the lowest level of sexual assault, as sexual assault *simpliciter*. In this way Parliament unwittingly trivialized rape in putting it into the same category as sexual touching. The problem is that the second category under s. 272 requires proof of bodily harm, a threat or the use of a weapon. This may be difficult to prove in many acquaintance-rape situations where there may be no physical injury such as bruises.

This reality may well have led to Judge Cole's recent decision in *B*. His Honour decided on his own motion to commit an accused charged with sexual assault *simpliciter* to trial on the more serious offence of sexual assault causing bodily harm. He utilized the recent ruling of the Supreme Court of Canada in *R. v. McCraw* where the Supreme Court interpreted bodily harm to include psychological injury. Judge Cole recognizes that *McCraw* was reached in the different context of s. 264.1(1)(*a*) involving the crime of threatening serious bodily harm but holds that the Supreme Court clearly intended to make a general pronouncement.

There would appear to be dangers in the approach of Judge Cole. He holds that judges at preliminary inquiries and at trial must be satisfied that there is evidence of psychological harm and that it is non-trivial. This may well have the indirect effect of compelling victims to testify as to the consequences of the assault and to be submitted to cross-examination as to the extent of the injury. In this sense, the victim will be once again back on trial. Another problem is that it is difficult to see how any form of sexual assault will not involve at least some psychological harm. If this is true, sexual assault *simpliciter* will have ceased to exist by judicial fiat.

When testifying before the Committees of the House of Commons and the Senate on Bill C-49, this commentator unsuccessfully sought the addition of an amendment that sexual assault involving any form of attempted penetration would be automatically placed in the second level of sexual assault, where the maximum penalty is raised from 10 to 14 years. This would have emphasized the seriousness of all rapes and would have made it unnecessary and indeed irrelevant to hear evidence as to the consequences for the victim. The victim would have been less on trial. Furthermore, if rapists were again to be singled out for special legal treatment, it would have been much easier to track and assess responses to rape. At the moment, no separate statistics are kept for rape as opposed to sexual assault.

# Regina v. Livermore
## (1996), 43 C.R. (4th) 1 (S.C.C.)

Appeal from judgment reported at (1994), 31 C.R. (4th) 374, 18 O.R. (3d) 221, 89 C.C.C. (3d) 425, 71 O.A.C. 340 (C.A.) dismissing appeal from acquittal on charge of sexual assault.

[Excerpts from the judgment of MacLachlin.]

November 16, 1995. McLACHLIN J. (LAMER C.J.C., CORY and IACOBUCCI JJ. concurring): — Mr. Livermore is charged with sexual assault of a 15-year-old girl, V. At the time of the alleged assault, Livermore was 28 years old. It is common ground that V. and her 14-year-old friend T. had willingly gone with Livermore and another young man, the co-accused, who picked them up in Livermore's car at an Oshawa pizza store at 1:30 a.m. Livermore drove to a parking lot behind an apartment building where the four consumed some beer and talked. Both T. and V. testified that T. asked to go home after approximately 30 minutes; the accused stated that the four mutually agreed to drive to another location. Livermore drove past T.'s building to a second parking lot, where the two girls exchanged seats. Livermore then drove to a third parking lot where he had sexual intercourse with V. After this he drove the two girls to T.'s home.

V. testified that she resisted Mr. Livermore's advances throughout. She stated that although she told the accused to stop kissing her and pushed him away, he climbed over the gear shift, pulled her pants down and had sexual intercourse with her. She stated that she told him "no" during intercourse and tried to push him away. She testified that although the accused was not violent and the windows were open and the doors unlocked, she was afraid to scream or try to escape because in the movies "people that don't say nothing, don't do nothing, just get away". V. stated that when they arrived at T.'s apartment, Livermore hugged her. V. said that it was possible that she had hugged him back, before saying "bye". When asked by counsel for the accused why, on returning to T.'s apartment building, she didn't run into the apartment with T. to escape, she stated that she didn't because she didn't want the men "to know that anything was wrong".

The girls testified that on their return to T.'s home they locked themselves in the bathroom and concocted a story to explain their absence to T.'s mother. They told T.'s mother a story that involved the presence of a third girl at the pizza store, whose threatening manner had prompted them to go with Livermore and the co-accused for safety. They also told her that V. had been raped. V. related the same story in her first statement to the police later that morning. She testified that the only part of the story that was untrue was the explanation of how the girls came to get into the car with Livermore and the co-accused. V. says she told her own mother the truth "from the start", at the hospital later in the morning, and subsequently told the police the truth in a second statement. A medical examination of V. revealed extensive genital bruising consistent with "traumatic" or "very forceful" sexual intercourse.

Livermore's testimony contradicted V.'s on the issue of consent. He testified that V. had been a willing partner while they mutually kissed and touched each other and that he climbed over the gear shift onto her side of the car after she touched his leg and penis. He stated that V. lowered her own pants and underpants prior to intercourse. Livermore testified that on the way back to T.'s apartment, T. and V. discussed how they would explain their absence to T.'s mother. He stated that V. hugged him before she left the car. Livermore also testified that he gave a slip of paper to T. on which he had written his name and telephone number before she and V. switched places in the car.

In his defence, Livermore maintained that V. had consented to the sexual intercourse. He also argued that, in light of V.'s denial that she had consented, circumstances were such that he had entertained an honest but mistaken belief in consent. The trial judge put this defence to the jury, which acquitted him and his co-accused. The Ontario Court of Appeal dismissed the appeal: (1994), 18 O.R. (3d) 221. Abella J.A., dissenting, would have ordered a new trial.

Both in the Court of Appeal and in this court, the Crown alleged that the trial judge made the following four errors:

1) The trial judge erred in his review of V.'s lack of consent and in his treatment of the jury's question on this issue; . . .

4) The defence of honest but mistaken belief should not have been left with the jury.

In my view, the cumulative effect of the errors made at trial requires that the appeal be allowed and a new trial ordered, despite the heavy onus on the Crown when it seeks to have an acquittal set aside.

With respect to the first alleged error, V.'s evidence was clear that she had repeatedly said "no" to Livermore and had resisted the assault. There is nothing in the record to indicate that her statements to the police or her testimony at the preliminary hearing were contradictory on this point. The contradiction with respect to her saying "no" to the co-accused when he tried to kiss her does not negate the consistency of her testimony with respect to Livermore. The trial judge in his charge to the jury did not mention V.'s resistance and incorrectly stated that she had not said "no" to Livermore. Since the sole issue was consent, this constituted a serious error.

The jury was understandably confused by the trial judge's erroneous direction, as indicated by the question it put to the judge after an hour of deliberation:

> The jury would like to hear evidence repeated with respect to the witness [V.] . . . answering to both the Crown and the defence questioning *about when [V.] said, no, to Carson Livermore. Further, can also we also hear [V.]'s comments of, no, during the preliminary hearing?* [Emphasis added.]

The judge's response to this question was accurately described by the dissenting judge in the Court of Appeal as, in essence, telling them they ought to try harder to remember the evidence. This was an inadequate response to the jury's question, which indicated difficulty on the main issue in the case — consent. Combined with the other errors, its effect is serious. . . .

It remains to consider the allegation that the trial judge should not have left the defence of honest but mistaken belief with the jury. The Court of Appeal was unanimous in concluding that it should not have, since the defence was unsupported by the evidence. I agree with that assessment.

Livermore testified that he believed V. was consenting to intercourse. The only question is whether there was sufficient foundation in the facts to lend an air of reality to the defence of mistaken but honest belief in consent. There was evidence that V. had said no; there was no evidence that she had said yes. The trial judge in putting this defence to the jury relied on the fact that the girls were out after midnight, that they willingly entered the car of the accused, that they changed seats without trying to escape, that the windows of the car were down and the doors unlocked, that the girls did not scream and the erroneous conclusion, discussed earlier in these reasons, that there was no evidence of verbal complaint. Abella J.A. was of the view that these circumstances did not provide the required air of reality to the defence of honest but mistaken belief in consent (at p. 226):

> Not screaming, drinking beer while under age, being out at 1:00 a.m., parking, cavalierly trusting a stranger, switching places in a car after a casual physical encounter, and staying too long in a car someone else has control over, are neither individually nor collectively any basis at all, let alone realistic ones, for assuming that someone is agreeing to sexual intercourse. In my view, there were no reasonable grounds for the accused's beliefs found in the package of factors listed by the trial judge.

Galligan J.A., for the majority, suggested that "this case was one of consent or no consent and there was no air of reality to a defence of honest but mistaken belief in consent" (p. 232).

The common law has long recognized that defences for which there is no factual basis or evidentiary foundation should not be put to the jury. In *R. v. Pappajohn*, [1980] 2 S.C.R. 120, this court articulated the minimum threshold for mistake of fact defences, including an accused person's honest but mistaken belief in consent, as requiring an air of reality to be raised on the evidence and circumstances to support the defence. In *R. v. Osolin*, [1993] 4 S.C.R. 595, Cory J. noted that the air of reality test as it relates to honest but mistaken belief in consent in all assault offences has been codified by the requirement in s. 265(4) of the *Criminal Code*, R.S.C. 1985, c. C-46, that there be "sufficient evidence" in order for the judge to put the defence of mistake to the jury.

. . .

The defence of mistake of fact in the context of sexual assault involves two elements: 1) that the accused *honestly believed* the complainant consented; and 2) that the accused have been *mistaken* in this belief. In order for the defence to be put to the jury, there must be evidence lending an air of reality to both of these elements. Typically, the second element is established through the assertion by the accused or counsel for the accused that he believed the complainant consented although her evidence is to the contrary. It is in relation to the first element — honest belief — that difficulties arise in establishing an air of reality. In order for the belief to be honestly held, the accused cannot have been wilfully blind about whether consent was given: *R. v. Sansregret*, [1985] 1 S.C.R. 570. Furthermore, since recklessness about whether there was consent constitutes one aspect of the mens rea of sexual assault (*Pappajohn*, supra, at p. 146), the accused cannot have been reckless in his belief that there was consent. While the belief need not be reasonable, there must be something in the evidence of the circumstances surrounding the alleged assault which lends an air of reality to an *honest belief* in consent.

In the case at bar, the accused testified that he believed V. consented, contrary to her evidence that she resisted intercourse throughout. The element of mistake is made out. There is no evidence, however, which lends an air of reality to the assertion by the accused that he had an honest belief in V.'s consent to intercourse. The evidence of Livermore was that V. clearly consented. The evidence of V. was that, far from consenting, she resisted and repeatedly said "no". T.'s testimony corroborated V.'s testimony in this regard. The question to be answered is whether there was evidence adduced which would nonetheless lend an air of reality to the creation in the accused's mind of an honest belief that V. was consenting notwithstanding the fact that their testimony on the central issue of consent was so diametrically opposed. In other words, was there a realistic evidentiary basis, upon which the jury could conclude that what really happened was a third version, that is, lack of consent but honest mistake by Livermore that it had been given. In my view, there was none.

The accused's bare assertion that he "believed" that the complainant consented must be supported by something in the circumstances that suggests that he may honestly have held such a belief: *Pappajohn,* supra. Otherwise, the goal of screening out the spurious defence based on nothing but the accused's facile assertion of belief will be thwarted. Examples of such circumstances are well documented in the jurisprudence. For example, sexually aggressive conduct by the complainant, a previous relationship of intimacy coupled with no reason to suspect a change of heart, and the case of the known prostitute are frequently cited as examples of situations in which an honest mistake may be made as to consent. Similarly, as noted in *R. v. Park,* [1995] 2 S.C.R. 836, independent evidence, particularly real evidence, may lend an air of reality to the defence: at pp. 851-52 per L'Heureux-Dubé J. If there is no evidence permitting an inference that the accused honestly believed in consent, then the accused in assuming consent must be taken to have closed his eyes to whether there was real consent, i.e., he must have been wilfully blind or reckless as to whether there was consent. In such a case, the required air of reality on the element of the honesty of the accused's belief will be lacking.

I agree with Abella J.A. that evidence of being out late, drinking beer and switching seats in a car is incapable of providing a foundation for an honest belief in consent to sexual intercourse. Such conduct, being equally consistent with non-consent as with consent, lacks any probative value on the issue. A man who assumes that equivocal acts such as these amount to consent to intercourse is assuming consent not on the basis of the circumstances, but as a result of recklessness or wilful blindness. The fact that the girls had an opportunity to leave the car before there was any indication that the accused had sexual intercourse in mind does not give rise to an inference of consent. The fact that V. did not scream although the car windows were open does not lend an air of reality to the defence: the two men were twice V.'s age. The fact that the accused hugged V. when she left the car (whether initiated by her or not), the fact that he gave T. a slip of paper with his name and phone number on it, the fact that V. and T. did not flee when finally they returned to T.'s apartment, are relevant to V.'s credibility as a witness. However, even if believed, they are insufficient to lend an air of reality to an honest belief in consent.

To put it in the language of Galligan J.A., for the majority, the case was one of consent or no consent. There was nothing in the evidence which supported a third version that V. had not consented but that Livermore honestly believed that she had. We are therefore left with his bare assertion of belief. On the jurisprudence of this court, this is insufficient to lend an air of reality to the defence of honest but mistaken belief. I conclude that the trial judge erred in putting the defence of honest but mistaken belief to the jury. . . .

In this case, we have no way of knowing whether the jury acquitted because it had a reasonable doubt about whether V. consented, or whether it acquitted on the basis of a defence which should not have been left with it. The cumulative effect of the numerous errors in this case is such that the *Morin* test is made out. Absent the significant errors at trial, a reasonable jury properly charged may well have reached a different verdict. I would allow the appeal, set aside the acquittal and direct a new trial.

*Appeal allowed; new trial ordered.*

*Editor's note: One of the more recent issues in the area of sexual assault has been the question of access to a victim's therapeutic records for use by the defence. Subsequent to the Supreme Court decision in the case of R. v. O'Connor (1996), 44 C.R. (4th) 1, which appeared to expand such access, Parliament enacted amendments to the* Criminal Code *setting out restrictive conditions under which such records should or should not be produced. These amendments, excerpts of which follow, were enacted in 1997 and are found in sections 278.1-278.9 of the Code:*

**278.1** For the purposes of sections 278.2 to 278.9, "record" means any form of record that contains personal information for which there is a reasonable expectation of privacy and includes, without limiting the generality of the foregoing, medical, psychiatric, therapeutic, counselling, education, employment, child welfare, adoption and social services records, personal journals and diaries, and records containing personal information the production or disclosure of which is protected by any other Act of Parliament or a provincial legislature, but does not include records made by persons responsible for the investigation or prosecution of the offence.

**278.2** (1) No record relating to a complainant or a witness shall be produced to an accused in any proceedings in respect of. . .[principally sexual offences under Part V and sexual assault offences]

. . .

**278.3** (1) An accused who seeks production of a record referred to in subsection 278.2(1) must make an application to the judge before whom the accused is to be, or is being, tried.

. . .

(3) An application must be made in writing and set out

(a) particulars identifying the record that the accused seeks to have produced and the name of the person who has possession or control of the record; and

(b) the grounds on which the accused relies to establish that the record is likely relevant to an issue at trial or to the competence of a witness to testify.

(4) Any one or more of the following assertions by the accused are not sufficient on their own to establish that the record is likely relevant to an issue at trial or to the competence of a witness to testify:
  (a) that the record exists;
  (b) that the record relates to medical or psychiatric treatment, therapy or counselling that the complainant or witness has received or is receiving;
  (c) that the record relates to the incident that is the subject-matter of the proceedings;
  (d) that the record may disclose a prior inconsistent statement of the complainant or witness;
  (e) that the record may relate to the credibility of the complainant or witness;
  (f) that the record may relate to the reliability of the testimony of the complainant or witness merely because the complainant or witness has received or is receiving psychiatric treatment, therapy or counselling;
  (g) that the record may reveal allegations of sexual abuse of the complainant by a person other than the accused;
  (h) that the record relates to the sexual activity of the complainant with any person, including the accused;
  (i) that the record relates to the presence or absence of a recent complaint;
  (j) that the record relates to the complainant's sexual reputation; or
  (k) that the record was made close in time to a complaint or to the activity that forms the subject-matter of the charge against the accused.

## Questions/Discussion

1. The 1983 and 1992 amendments to the Criminal Code dealing with sexual assault will do little to redress the problems which were witnessed under the old rape laws. Address and discuss this statement with reference to both the old and new legislation.
2. Consider the following statement: "Little will or can be done about the problem of sexual assault in Canadian society until there is a re-structuring of the economic and social relationships which underlie these problems". Do you agree or disagree with this statement in the context of sexual assault? Why or why not? What effect does criminal law have on the social problem of sexual assault in Canadian society? Is it of any relevance to the finding of a solution to the problem?
3. Of what value are legal reform and legal responses in regard to the problems faced by women in a nonegalitarian society? Do you think that more women judges will go a long way toward solving some of the problems inherent in the current legal responses? Why or why not? What other measures are needed to address the problem of sexual assault?
4. Do you think the 1997 amendments restricting access to a victim's records will be effective in preventing such access? Do you think they are fair to the accused and/or to the victim? Why or why not?

   Victims' groups have argued that such records have no relevance whatsoever in a sexual assault trial and would only be used to attempt to intimidate or unnerve a complainant giving testimony. They argue the focus should not be on the victim but on the accused, and that victims would be less willing to participate fully in therapy sessions if there existed the possibility that such records might not be kept private. Defence counsel have argued that such records can be relevant to the issues being tried and are sometimes required to ensure a full defence is made. For a discussion of the subject, see the series of articles contained in "A Criminal Reports Forum on

*O'Connor* and *B. (A.)*: Abuse of Process, Disclosure and Access to Therapeutic Records" (1996), 44 C.R. (4th) 130-194.

5.  What should be the requirements for a defence to sexual assault based on a mistaken belief as to consent? Would you require that the mistake be both honest *and* reasonable. On what grounds would you make your argument?

## Further Reading

*   Boyle, Christine and Marilyn MacCrimmon, "The Constitutionality of Bill C-49: Analyzing Sexual Assault as if Equality Really Mattered" (1998), 41 Criminal Law Quarterly 198-237.
*   Clark, L., *Evidence of Recent Complaint and Reform of Canadian Sexual Assault Law: Still Searching for Epistemic Equality* (Ottawa: Canadian Advisory Council on the Status of Women, 1993).
*   Clark, Lorenne and Armstrong, Susan, *A Rape Bibliography* (Ottawa: Solicitor General of Canada, 1979).
*   Clark, Lorenne and Lewis, Debra, *Rape: The Price of Coercive Sexuality* (Toronto: The Women's Press, 1977).
*   Dawson, T. Brettell, "Legal Structures: A Feminist Critique of Sexual Assault Reform" (1985), 14 Resources of Feminist Research 40.
*   Dinovitzer, Ronit, "The Myth of Rapists and Other Normal Men: The Impact of Psychiatric Considerations on the Sentencing of Sexual Assault Offenders" (1997), 12 Canadian Journal of Law and Society 147-168.
*   Gregory, Jeanne, *Policing Sexual Assault* (New York: Routlege, 1998).
*   Griffin, Susan, *Rape: The Power of Consciousness* (San Francisco: Harper and Row, 1979).
*   Hinch, Ronald, "Inconsistencies and Contradictions in Canada's Sexual Assault Law" (1988), 14 Canadian Public Policy 282.
*   Kasinsky, Renee G., "Rape: The Social Control of Women" in W.K. Greenaway and S.K. Brickey, eds., *Law and Social Control in Canada* (Scarborough: Prentice-Hall, 1978).
*   Kinnon, Diane, *Report on Sexual Assault in Canada* (Ottawa: Canadian Advisory Council on the Status of Women, 1981).
*   Le Bourdais, E., "Rape Victims: Unpopular Patients" (1976), 3 Dimensions in Health Service 53.
*   MacDonald, G. and Gallagher, K., "The Myth of Consenting Adults: The New Sexual Assault Provisions" (1993), 42 University of New Brunswick Law Journal 373-380.
*   Marshall, P., "Sexual Assault, The Charter and Sentencing Reform" (1988), 63 C.R. (3d) 216.
*   Martin, R., "Bill C-49: A Victory for Interest Group Politics" (1993), 42 University of New Brunswick Law Journal 357-372.
*   Minch, C., *et al.*, "Attrition in the Processing of Rape Cases" (1987), 29 Cdn. J. of Crim. and Corr. 389.
*   Nightingale, M., "Judicial Attitudes and Differential Treatment: Native Women in Sexual Assault Cases" (1991), 23 Ottawa Law Review 71-98.
*   Renner, K. Edward, and Sahjpaul, Suresh, "The New Sexual Assault Law: What Has Been Its Effect?" (1986), 28 Canadian Journal of Criminology 407.
*   Rioux, Marsha, *When Myths Masquerade As Reality: A Study of Rape* (Ottawa: Advisory Council on the Status of Women, 1981).

- Roberts, J.V., *Criminal Justice Processing of Sexual Assault Cases* (Ottawa: Canadian Centre for Justice Statistics, 1994).
- Roberts, J.V. and Grossman, M., *Sexual Assault: A Bibliography* (Ottawa: Crime and Justice Research Centre, 1991).
- Roberts, Julian V. and R. M. Mohr, *Confronting Sexual Assault: A Decade of Legal and Social Change* (Toronto: University of Toronto Press, 1994).
- Rolfes, Brian, "The Golden Thread of Criminal Law: Moral Culpability and Sexual Assault" (1998), 61 Saskatchewan Law Review 87-126.
- Steed, E., "Reality Check: The Sufficiency Threshold to the Air of Reality Test in Sexual Assault Cases" (1994), 36 Criminal Law Quarterly 448-473.
- Stuart, D., "The Pendulum has been Pushed Too Far: The Effects of Bill C-49" (1993), 42 University of New Brunswick Law Journal 349-356.
- Usprich, S.J., "A New Crime in Old Battles: Definitional Problems with Sexual Assault" (1987), 29 Criminal Law Quarterly 200.
- Usprich, S.J., "Two Problems in Sexual Assault: Attempts and the Intoxication Defence" (1987), 29 Criminal Law Quarterly 296.

## 8.2  RACISM AND THE CRIMINAL JUSTICE SYSTEM

### Introduction

The issue of racism within the criminal justice system is one that in the past has often been ignored by a profession and by enforcement mechanisms that insisted on the myth of neutrality. In the last fifteen years, however, there have been some signs that the state is willing to approach the subject and recognize the reality of the problem and its systemic nature within the Canadian criminal justice system. Along with class and gender bias, racism is a problem that been recognized as endemic to our system of justice, and a matter that be addressed if we are to achieve a system of criminal "justice" for all.

One of the initial attempts at addressing racism in the criminal justice system was the inquiry into the wrongful arrest and conviction of Donald Marshall, Jr., a Micmac Indian from Nova Scotia who spent 11 years in prison for a crime that he did not commit. The events surrounding the matter and their consequences were brought to light by the inquiry in its hearings and in its 1989 report. Although written in 1989, the report remains today a good introduction to many of the issues and concerns that surround the topic of racism and the criminal law system. This section, intended to provide a brief preliminary examination of the nature and dimensions of the problem of racism, reproduces several excerpts from the inquiry's report, which highlight the nature of the problem in Nova Scotia, although the issues and the inquiry's conclusions can be applied across Canada and to other disadvantaged visible minorities. For example, the rates of imprisonment for native people have been criticized as much too high in western provinces such as Alberta (where natives comprise 30% of the male inmate population and 45% of the female inmate population in provincial jails, yet make up only 3.5% of the general population). As well, the treatment of blacks at the hands of Montreal and Toronto police and judicial agencies has been attacked as racist in recent years.

What has been particularly problematic is the unwillingness of the state to effectively address the issue, coupled with the state's often unqualified support for the enforcement and judicial agencies within the criminal law system. The real test remains the government's willingness to meaningfully and substantively address the problems identified by the various inquiries and reports not only within the criminal law system, but also through measures to redress the lack of real opportunity and advancement in society as a whole for those groups disadvantaged by racist structures, practices and attitudes. However, there is little reason to be hopeful in this regard. For example, the latest federal initiative (in March of 1996) on giving more control to the aboriginal peoples appears to offer significantly less control to native communities than proposed in an interim report by the Royal Commission on Aboriginal Peoples, which recommended that aboriginal peoples be allowed to establish their own justice systems in light of the devastating effect of the current system. The federal proposal focuses on giving a greater role in the sentencing of offenders to native communities.

Of course, there have been several other inquiries and commissions mandated in recent years, including the Alberta Task Force on the Criminal Justice System and its Impact on the Indian and Métis People of Alberta, 1991; the Saskatchewan Indian Justice Review Committee and Métis Justice Review Committee, 1992; the federal Royal Commission on Aboriginal Peoples, 1996; the Aboriginal Justice Inquiry of Manitoba, 1999; and the Saskatchewan Aboriginal Justice Commission, established in 2002, in part in response to the unexplained freezing deaths two Aboriginal men on the outskirts of Saskatoon. Several of these earlier initiatives and the government's responses are described in *Aboriginal Peoples and the Justice System: Report of the National Round Table on Aboriginal Justice Issues*, published by the Royal Commission on Aboriginal Peoples in 1993 at pages 15-41. There is also the *Report of the Commission on Systemic Racism in the Ontario Criminal Justice System* (Toronto: Queen's Printer for Ontario. 1995), which discusses the problem of systemic racism within the Ontario justice system. Whether the recommendations of these inquiries and reports will have any long-term effect remains to be seen, but few meaningful effects can be seen to date.

## Royal Commission on the Donald Marshall, Jr., Prosecution*
### Volume One: Commissioners' Report

* Excerpts from the Royal Commission Report (Halifax: Province of Nova Scotia, 1989).

### VISIBLE MINORITIES AND THE CRIMINAL JUSTICE SYSTEM

Marshall is the typical Indian lad that seems to lose control of his senses while indulging in intoxicating liquors. Apparently he enjoys a good fight while intoxicated.

Corrections Canada Admission Document
concerning Donald Marshall, Jr.
July 21, 1972
Exhibit 112, Page 3

One reason Donald Marshall, Jr. was convicted of and spent 11 years in jail for a murder he did not commit is because Marshall is an Indian. The statement quoted above is simply one of the more blatant and overt examples of the seemingly unconscious racism and racial stereotyping that influenced what happened to Donald Marshall, Jr.

That racism played a role in Marshall's conviction and imprisonment is one of the most difficult and disturbing findings this Royal Commission has made. But reaching that conclusion was only the first part of our duty as Commissioners. We also had to determine whether such a tragic and unacceptable incident could occur again today and, if it could, to make recommendations to make sure it does not.

Much has changed — and improved — in Nova Scotia in the 18 years since Donald Marshall, Jr. was convicted of murdering Sandy Seale. But as recent events such as the highly publicized incidents involving fights between Black and White students at a high school in Cole Harbour make clear, one should never automatically assume that the racism and discrimination occurred only in the past.

If a Native — or a Black person — were charged with a similar offence today, what effect might their racial origin have on how their case would be handled by the police, by Crown and defence counsel, by the courts, and/or by the corrections system? If a Native or a Black were wrongfully convicted for a crime and later discovered to be innocent, what effect, if any, would race have on the amount of compensation he or she receives? What positive measures can this Royal Commission recommend to ensure that our justice system will not — and cannot — be influenced by the color of a person's skin?

We realized from the beginning of our work that the bald facts of the Marshall case — a Native youth, who is charged with murdering a Black youth, is investigated, tried and convicted by a criminal justice system that is made up only of Whites — could not help but raise questions about the role the race of the accused and/or the victim may have played in the handling and disposition of this particular case.

To help us deal with the specific issues associated with the Marshall case, we granted full standing to both the Union of Nova Scotia Indians and the Black United Front to allow them to appear before the Commission and to question witnesses during our public hearings. Their input was of considerable assistance to us in reaching our conclusions about the Marshall case.

We also realized that, regardless of the outcome of our deliberations on the Marshall case, we would have to examine how Natives and Blacks are treated in the criminal justice system in Nova Scotia today in order to determine whether what happened to Seale and Marshall could also happen to two teenagers in a similar situation in 1990.

Recognizing that the public hearing process was not a suitable forum for a discussion and analysis of complex issues of discrimination and racism, the Commission launched a parallel research program, which included commissioning independent scholars and researchers to take an analytical look at whether — or to what extent — race is a factor in the criminal justice system in Nova Scotia. Two of the five research reports deal specifically with issues facing Natives and Blacks (Volume 3: "The Mi'kmaq and Criminal Justice in Nova Scotia" and Volume 4: "Discrimination Against Blacks in Nova Scotia: The Criminal Justice System").

The Commission also convened a Consultative Conference in November 1988, to which we invited experts from across North America. Over the course of two-and-a-half days, they provided us with a broader perspective on the issues of discrimination and racism in the criminal justice system, and helped us to focus on our own thinking on possible approaches to dealing with these issues. (See Volume 7 for an edited transcript of this Conference.)

What did we learn from this process of research and consultation?

Although there may be some legitimate and important differences of opinion about precise numbers (see Appendix 18 to Volume 2 of our study, "Public Policing in Nova Scotia"), it is sufficient for our purposes here to point out that the Native and Black population in Nova Scotia is relatively small. The 1986 census figures indicated that out of a total population of 873,176, there are 4,610 Natives on-reserve and 9,615 off-reserve, and 12,945 Blacks.

As a group, those Natives and Blacks are poorer, less educated, more dependent on social assistance, more likely to be unemployed and, when employed, more likely to work in low-paying, menial jobs than their White counterparts. We learned that Blacks and Natives are disproportionately represented in our penitentiaries and prisons, but almost totally absent from the public life of the province.

Witnesses at our public hearings, experts at our Consultative Conference, and the researchers who authored our commissioned studies all made the point that — regardless of intention — racial origin is a factor in this second-class status that minority group members endure in Nova Scotia — in other words, Natives and Blacks are disadvantaged because they are Native and Black. Racism, we were told, is alive and well in Canada, and specifically in Nova Scotia. As Dr. Wilson Head, one of the authors of the research study which appears as Volume 4, put it at the Consultative Conference:

> Is there a different law for the poor and for the rich? For the minorities and the rich? Most minority groups are poor. They get it in the neck because they are poor. They get it in the neck because they are young. They get it in the neck because they are uneducated. They get it in the neck because they are racial minorities.

What does all of that have to do with the criminal justice system and the duty of this Royal Commission to bring forth recommendations to make sure another Marshall case will not happen in the future?

We recognize that the root cause of much of the discrimination Blacks and Natives complain about can be traced to social, political and economic structures, institutions and values that are not specifically part of the criminal justice system. We also recognize that we do not have the mandate — or the expertise — to make recommendations concerning public education or housing or social services or other matters that lie outside the criminal justice system. Nonetheless, we believe it is important to point out that the criminal justice system is simply one part of the broader social order, and that it will be impossible to solve all the problems we have identified within the justice system without also addressing broader issues such as equal access to education.

While the education system *per se* is not within the terms of our mandate, for example, it is clear that without access to a university education, Blacks and Natives cannot participate in the criminal justice system as lawyers, para-professionals and judges.

There are encouraging signs that access is improving. Dalhousie, Nova Scotia's largest university, is attempting to make it easier for Blacks and Natives to take advantage of post-secondary education options. The university's "Transition Year Program" has been providing educational and other support for Black and Native students, who might not otherwise be able to attend university, since 1969. The Micmac Professional Careers Project at Dalhousie University's Henson College and the Micmac Social Work Program at the Maritime School of Social Work are providing assistance and encouragement to Micmacs who wish to pursue certain professional paths. In addition, a 1989 report by the Dalhousie University Task Force on Access for Black and Native People has made recommendations to deal with a variety of problems facing visible minority students at Dalhousie. Finally — and particularly relevant to the work of this Royal Commission — the University launched a new program in September 1989 to encourage indigenous Black and Micmac students to attend Dalhousie Law School.

These developments at Dalhousie, while largely outside our mandate, are significant and we believe will be helpful in changing or eliminating the perception of Blacks and Natives that the criminal justice system is closed to them.

At the moment, Blacks and Natives clearly do feel aggrieved by their treatment at all levels of the justice system: by police, Crown prosecutors, defence lawyers, government officials and judges. Blacks and Natives believe that those working in the system — from top to bottom — lack sensitivity in dealing with members of visible minority groups. They believe they have no stake in what they regard as the "White man's justice system".

Not only does that system not reflect the needs of their people, Black and Native leaders told us, but it also does not even reflect the simple fact of the *existence* of their people. The number of Natives and Blacks who are police officers, prosecutors, defence lawyers, judges and court workers, for example, is disproportionately and unjustifiably low, while the number of Natives and Blacks who are accused persons is disproportionately high.

None of this to suggest that this is the result of any evil intention to discriminate by those in the criminal justice system. But the Supreme Court of Canada itself has recently ruled that it is no longer necessary to prove that someone or some body intended to discriminate in order to find that that person or institution did discriminate. (See *Ontario Human Rights Commission v. Simpson-Sears*, [1985] 2 S.C.R. 536) The highest court has also considered the notion of what is called systemic or "adverse effects" discrimination. Systemic discrimination is what happens when a specific act, policy or structural factor — intended or unintended — results in adverse effects for members of certain specific groups.

Although much of the discrimination that occurs in the criminal justice system is of an unintended sort, it is no less insidious and its impact is no less devastating because of that. What can be done to eliminate this system discrimination and to give Blacks and Natives faith that the criminal justice system will threat them fairly?

Before we attempt to answer those questions, it is important to make the point that although there are clearly some common interests between Blacks and Natives, these two minority groups do not regard the criminal justice system in exactly the same way. Historical, cultural and constitutional factors have placed Natives in a special position in Canada. Without wishing to oversimplify, we can say that Native groups generally want a greater measure of control of their own judicial affairs while Black groups generally want a stronger voice in the existing system. Because of these important cultural and historical differences, we will deal with the specific concerns of Natives and Blacks in the criminal justice system in separate sections of this Chapters.

To begin, however, we will consider some issues of common concern to both Natives and Blacks. These include the need for governments at all levels to devise firm anti-racism policies: training that would lead to better representation of visible minorities in the criminal justice and legal system; improved access to useful legal information for Blacks and Natives; and more inventive options in sentencing of members of visible minorities.

Our challenge is to propose solutions that will attack these problems in a way that will not only improve the lot of visible minorities in this province but also establish a model that can have an impact even beyond the boundaries of Nova Scotia. Some of our suggested solutions will require the cooperation of the Federal Government, which has jurisdiction over several of the matters before us. We believe this is a unique opportunity for Federal and Provincial Governments to work together towards constructive change.

### Representation of Natives and Blacks

A tension exists in Canadian society between the original European partners in Confederation who dominate Canadian institutions and the other people who wish to share fully in the institutional life of the country. Inherent in the notion of diversity of Canadian society as a 'mosaic' is the equal participation of the pieces making it up.

Natives and Blacks are still almost invisible in the institutions operated by the majority White society in Nova Scotia, including the criminal justice system. It is time the complexions of those institutions changed.

That is not to suggest that merely increasing the proportional representation of Natives and Blacks will suddenly solve all our racial problems. Increasing the quality of representation — getting minority group members into senior positions — will be just as important. However, this will only ultimately make a difference if the system itself changes to meet the needs of the minority communities.

With these caveats on the record, however, we still believe increasing the number of Blacks and Natives in the criminal justice system is a necessary and overdue first step in making the system more responsive to and representative of visible minorities.

In addition, the presence of more non-White faces in these important and respected institutions will be of value not only to minority group members. It may also help the general population develop increased sensitivity to — and tolerance for — the needs and aspirations of visible minorities. Their presence will remind us on a daily basis that minorities are members of our society too, and that that society is not — and never has been — completely White.

### Anti-Racism Policies

Racism exists as a demonstrable social factor in social relations in Canada and the justice system is not excepted. . . . A resolute political will must be adopted to acknowledge up front the existence of racism and to set about eliminating it by moving it onto the public policy agenda. Policymakers, legislators and government have an extra responsibility to create a climate which will be more inhospitable for racism.

Our mandate extends to a complete examination of the criminal justice system in Nova Scotia, its administration and the manner in which criminal justice is delivered. The recommendations which follow focus on the criminal justice system but we realize that our recommendations, if implemented, may have wide-ranging effects in other areas of Canadian society and government as well.

The first step must be for the Province of Nova Scotia to make sure its own house is in order so it can provide leadership for private and other public sector policy-makers and decision-makers. Our recommendations concerning the establishment of clear anti-racism policies within the Provincial Government include specific components dealing with improving the number and the quality of visible minority representation in the Departments of Attorney General and Solicitor General, as well as establishing a mechanism to monitor and enforce this employment equity provision.

Monitoring and enforcement will be vital because unless such mechanisms are in place, there will be no way to evaluate the effectiveness of affirmative action programs or to make certain that those responsible live up to the goals of the programs.

### Recommendation 9

*We recommend that the Departments of the Attorney General and Solicitor General adopt and publicize a Policy on Race Relations that has as its basis a commitment to employment equity and the elimination of inequalities, based on race, in these Departments and their agencies and the reduction of racial tensions between these Departments and the communities with which they interact.*

This policy statement should include goals and timetables for recruitment and hiring to achieve employment equity for visible minority groups. By having more minority group members on staff, these departments, which deliver and administer criminal justice, will gain a better understanding of the needs and views of the visible minority groups with which they are in day-to-day contact. They must also not only make a real effort to increase the hiring of visible minorities but must also work to sensitize all their staff to racial problems.

Mechanisms do not now exist in Nova Scotia to monitor and enforce a policy such as we are recommending. The 1987 Annual Report of the Nova Scotia Civil Service

Commission, for example, shows that of a total of 10,123 provincial civil servants, 208 are Black, seven are native. But what does that really mean? Such numbers tell us nothing about the quality of representation of Black and Natives within the Province's public service because there is no monitoring mechanism built into that system to ensure that it is achieving its goals.

We believe that the Human Rights Commission is the most effective body to fulfill this critically important role. But we recognize that in order to be effective, the Commission must have adequate resources and be independent of Government.

The concerns of Natives and Blacks must not only be part of the agenda of the Attorney General and Solicitor General's Departments but must also be integrated into general Government policy. Regular meetings between visible minority group representatives and key government officials will provide opportunities for dialogue and understanding in a non-confrontational, non-crisis atmosphere.

## Recommendation 10

*We recommend that a Cabinet Committee on Race Relations be established which would include the Attorney General and Solicitor General. This Committee should meet regularly with representatives of visible minority groups in order to assure the input of these groups in matters of criminal justice.*

### Legal Profession

Visible minorities in the legal profession fare no better than in government. There are currently almost 1,200 lawyers in Nova Scotia who are eligible to appear before the courts. Of these, about a dozen are Black. There are no Micmac lawyers in Nova Scotia. To our knowledge, only one Native has ever graduated from Dalhousie Law School. There is one Black judge in Nova Scotia, at the Family Court level, and no Micmac judges.

It is obvious that visible minorities cannot be represented among the ranks of Crown prosecutors, defence counsel and the judiciary unless they are entering and graduating from law schools in greatly increased numbers, and they cannot do that without a solid educational foundation. Improvements are needed in the educational system to ensure that minority students are given support, both educational and financial, to put them on an equal footing with White students.

The Dalhousie Law School's recently announced minority admission program — which includes special recruitment efforts and a summer program as well as educational and financial support — would appear to include all the elements we have identified as being necessary to a successful initiative, and we are encouraged by its establishment. But Dalhousie's leadership must be accompanied by the financial support of governments and the bar in order to ensure that the increased participation of visible minorities in the legal profession actually occurs.

## Recommendation 11

*We recommend that the Dalhousie Law School's minority admissions program for Micmacs and indigenous Blacks receive the financial support of the Governments of Canada and Nova Scotia, and the Nova Scotia Bar.*

In order for such programs to achieve the desired end, of course, it will be essential for those in authority to then take advantage of this growing pool of lawyers from the visible minority communities when making appointments.

## Recommendation 12

*We recommend that Governments consider the needs of visible minorities by appointing qualified visible minority judges and administrative board members whenever possible.*

Although these recommendations promote diversity in the legal profession and the courts, it is clear the legal profession and the courts are still almost entirely — and will continue to be largely — White institutions. Our research shows that many Natives and Blacks feel poorly served by the legal profession, not only because there are so few visible minority lawyers, but also because many lawyers seem ill-equipped to deal with the special problems of minority clients. The profession has a responsibility not only to encourage racial diversity in its ranks but also to assist in sensitizing its members to minority issues. In order to make sure that those who are part of the system have an awareness of and sensitivity to issues facing Natives and Blacks, education and ongoing training will be necessary.

## Recommendation 13

*We recommend that the Dalhousie Law School, the Nova Scotia Barristers Society and the Judicial Councils support courses and programs dealing with legal issues facing visible minorities, and encourage sensitivity to minority concerns for law students, lawyers and judges.*

Law schools provide lawyers with their basic legal education, emphasizing legal concepts, skills training, and "thinking like a lawyer". Most students graduate from law school with little exposure to the daily reality of the minority population. While Dalhousie Law School now offers a course in Native Law, this is only available to a few students. In addition to such specific courses, the Law School must encourage law students to consider minority concerns in all their courses. This must be done not only in relation to substantive legal issues, but also in terms of sensitizing our future lawyers to the particular needs of visible minorities.

Once they graduate from law school, lawyers' continuing education is dealt with first through the Bar Admission Course and then through the Continuing Legal Education Society of Nova Scotia. To date, there has been little or no emphasis in these courses and programs on minority issues, and we urge those who run them to make this a priority. With so few minority lawyers in the province, all of the practicing bar must accept some responsibility to become attuned to these issues.

Crown prosecutors have a special role in ensuring that the system is perceived to be dealing with individuals on an equal footing, regardless of race. It is therefore important that continuing professional education programs include sessions which introduce Crown prosecutors to the facts of systemic discrimination.

## Recommendation 14

*We recommend that the Attorney General establish continuing professional education programs for Crown prosecutors, which would include:*
*(a) an exposure to materials explaining the nature of systemic discrimination toward Black and Native peoples in Nova Scotia in the criminal justice system; and*
*(b) an exploration of means by which Crown prosecutors can carry out their functions so as to reduce the effects of systemic discrimination in the Nova Scotia criminal justice system.*

Judges must be fair and impartial in dealing with all who appear before them. They must also appear to be fair and impartial. Our research, as well as anecdotal reports, indicate that some individuals from visible minority groups believe that some judges treat them with less respect than White accused. We cannot comment on whether these perceptions are based on fact, but these perceptions do exist and that causes us concern. A fair judiciary is the cornerstone of our legal system. One incident of unfairness on racial grounds holds the entire judiciary open to disrespect.

The role of judicial councils in disciplining judges for improper conduct is not widely known. The judicial councils, which provide the only mechanism through which a citizen can complain about a judge's conduct, should publicize their existence and functions. The public must be able to see that judges are subject to the same, if not higher, standards of behaviour as other participants in the society.

## *Police*

Police/minority relations are a very important part of the work of this Royal Commission. The Chapter on Policing (Chapter 2.6) discusses the organization, training and services provided by the police, as well as their particular responsibilities in dealing with visible minorities.

We heard allegations in our public hearings about tensions between the Native youth of the Membertou Reserve and the Sydney City Police Department in the early 1970s. For example, Native witnesses have suggested that Native youths were picked out as troublemakers, hassled without cause, occasionally roughed up and regularly kicked out of Wentworth Park, their favorite meeting place. We have evidence from non-Native witnesses who dated Indian boys that the police told their parents they should not hang around with Indians. We also heard that members of the Sydney City Police Department in 1971 received little or no training of any kind, and no training at all in dealing with Native people or other visible minorities. Even now, there is little education of police officers in Sydney — or elsewhere in the province — on the special needs of visible minorities.

## Recommendation 15

*We recommend that training for all police officers, both at the intake level and as continuing education, include content on police minority concerns and sensitivity to visible minority issues.*

We understand there is such a course on the books at the Atlantic Police Academy, but that it is inactive because of low enrollment. This is simply not good enough.

Many Natives and Blacks believe police officers accept negative stereotypes of members of minority groups. Our researcher was told, for example, that many Natives believe police might respond slowly to an incident on a reserve because the police believe that most such incidents are alcohol-related and will resolve themselves if left alone.

A recent study done by Dr. Joseph Fletcher *et al.* at the Centre of Criminology at the University of Toronto confirms that police officers are prone to racial stereotyping of Natives and other visible minorities. While police may stereotype Natives as a group, the study indicates they are less likely to believe Native people as a group have unique rights that must be recognized. They do not favor programs such as affirmative action to give Native people help in "catching up". According to the study, police officers generally believe individuals control their own personal fate. Consequently, if a particular group fares less well in the social or economic order, police officers believe the problem is simply that they have not tried hard enough.

With a continuing lack of training to help them understand the reality of systemic discrimination — and with younger police officers frequently forming their values and methods of operation from more experienced officers — it is not surprising that these attitudes can become self-perpetuating.

It is essential that those responsible for police recruitment and training, whether at the municipal level or the RCMP, recognize not only that those with racial biases should not be permitted to engage in police work, but that recruits as well as veteran officers must be provided with ongoing training in police/minority issues.

## *Legal Information Needs of Natives and Blacks*

We have heard from many sources that Native and Black communities have little access to information about the law and little knowledge about how the justice system operates. Having an educated and sensitive bar can help, but more is needed.

In Nova Scotia, as in most other provinces, the Public Legal Education Society provides information about the law to the public. This organization has great potential for providing programs specific to the needs of minorities. However, experience has shown that unless this information is geared towards the minority group and produced in cooperation with them, it will probably not be effective. Such organizations must be aware of and sensitive to the needs of the communities to which their material and programming is directed and must work with these communities to fill their legal information needs.

## Recommendation 16

*We recommend that the Public Legal Education Society consult and work with Native and Black groups to develop and provide legal materials and services for minority users. These initiatives cannot be undertaken without specific funding. This should be provided where necessary by Government.*

### Sentencing Options

Both of our minority-related research projects, as well as a recent Nova Scotia court decision (See *R. v. Hebb* (1989), 89 N.S.R. (2d) 137), point out that the lack of a fine options program creates special problems for the poor in Nova Scotia. This has particular relevance for Blacks and Natives because so many of them are poor. Fine option programs provide judges with options other than imprisonment for those who cannot pay court-ordered penalties.

The Nova Scotia Government brought forward legislation in the spring of 1989 to permit the establishment of such a fine options program here. We hope the Government quickly proclaims this legislation and that the regulations under the legislation will take into account the special needs of Natives and Blacks.

## Recommendation 17

*We recommend that the Government immediately proclaim the Alternative Penalty Act, S.N.S. 1989, c. 2, and that regulations which address the particular needs of Native and Black offenders be enacted.*

Diversion programs are another alternative to sending people to jail. If a goal of the criminal justice system is to prevent crime and permit meaningful rehabilitation of the offender rather than simply to impose routine and unthinking incarceration, diversion of alleged offenders away from the system must be explored.

Police and prosecutors now have enormous discretion to "criminalize" behavior that may have been caused by socioeconomic conditions. The criminal justice system has both the challenge and the opportunity of assisting in breaking the vicious and destructive cycle that results in disproportionate numbers of Native and Black offenders being caught up in the system.

At present, diversion programs are used mainly in relation to young offenders. Such programs can be of particular relevance to Native and Black youth because they may require educational, life-skills, and job-related training in order to steer them away from more long-term problems with the law. Programs dealing with Native youth in various parts of the country have attempted to address the range of problems associated with youth involvement with the law, and these initiatives should be encouraged.

However, we believe diversion programs should be broadened to include adult Black and Native offenders. This would require an amendment to the *Criminal Code*.

## Recommendation 18

*We recommend that the Province, in close cooperation with the Native and Black communities, formulate proposals for the establishment of appropriate diversion programs for Natives and Blacks, and that the Province actively recommend such programs to the Federal Government with proposals for any necessary amendments to the Criminal Code.*

## *Corrections*

The research done for the Royal Commission confirms our view that correctional institutions in Canada and in Nova Scotia are populated primarily by the young, the poor, and members of racial minority groups. According to respondents in our survey, the first thing that needs to be done to improve the corrections system is to improve the attitudes and behavior of guards and other correction authorities. The second priority should be to provide programs and services to offenders and ex-offenders.

## Recommendation 19

*We recommend that the Department of the Solicitor General of Nova Scotia take steps to, and urge the federal correctional authorities to take steps to:*
*(a) immediately implement programs to recruit and hire more Natives and Blacks in professional and non-professional positions in the correctional service;*
*(b) implement ongoing education and training programs designed to sensitize correctional workers at all levels to the particular needs of Native and Black offenders based on their racial and cultural background;*
*(c) indicate to all correctional workers that discriminatory conduct (including racial slurs) against Natives and Blacks will not be tolerated and may result in adverse employment consequences;*
*(d) offer institutional programs emphasizing the educational, cultural and religious needs of Native and Black offenders in institutions where a significant number of Natives and Blacks are incarcerated; and*
*(e) support rehabilitation programs for Native and Black inmates and former inmates which take into account their background and needs.*

The correctional service, like other segments of the criminal justice system, must make a serious effort to achieve an appropriate representation of Natives and Blacks in both professional and non-professional positions.

In addition, everyone who works in a correctional institution or in the correctional service must receive proper training concerning the social, cultural and economic basis for the problems of visible minority offenders, so he or she will be able to deal sensitively with these offenders.

The correctional service administration also has a role to play in making sure that those working in corrections treat all inmates equally, regardless of their race, and must make it clear that prejudicial or racist treatment will be dealt with harshly. Internal procedures are also needed to ensure that racism is not practised or tolerated in the correctional service.

Rehabilitation is particularly important for Native and Black offenders, but most prison programs, according to respondents to our survey and other observers, focus on security and punishment requirements rather than on rehabilitation.

Correctional authorities should attempt to give inmates the confidence and skills to re-enter society as people who can function without resorting to crime. Education and skills training are a crucial part of this process.

For visible minority offenders, however, there is an added dimension. We have earlier concluded that Natives and Blacks are treated differently than White because of their race. Because of this, it is necessary that racial factors be recognized within the walls of the institution. We suggest that, where there are sufficient numbers in an institution to justify them, specific programs for Natives and Blacks should be established, taking into account their education, social and religious needs.

These needs must also be considered when it is time for visible minority inmates to leave the institution. Service agencies such as the John Howard Society should be funded to sponsor programs to help Native and Black offenders integrate themselves into the community after prison. Providing a minority liaison person to assist offenders in making the transition to the outside world, for example, would fill a real need.

Too often, programs of this type are dependent on short-term project funding. The Solicitor General's Department should provide longer term financial assistance to such worthwhile initiatives.

## NOVA SCOTIA MICMACS AND THE CRIMINAL JUSTICE SYSTEM

At the time of the killing of Sandy Seale in 1971, Donald Marshall, Jr., was a 17-year-old Micmac youth living on the Membertou Reserve in Sydney, Nova Scotia. His parents were well-respected members of the reserve community. Donald Marshall, Sr. is the Grand Chief of the Micmac Nation. His son, Donald Jr., (known to his friends and family as Junior) is one of the Marshalls' ten children — six boys and four girls. At home and on the reserve, he spoke Micmac, although not exclusively. When he went to school in Sydney, however, he spoke English. He left school during grade six, and at the time of Seale's murder, was working part time in his father's drywall business.

Sydney is the third largest city in Nova Scotia with a population of 35,000 people. The economy is based mainly on the steel and coal industry. The Membertou Reserve, located within the city of Sydney, is close to the downtown and within about a half-mile of Wentworth Part. About 500 Micmac live on the Reserve. A fair number of Blacks also live in Sydney, primarily in the Whitney Pier area. At the time of his death, Sandy Seale's family had recently moved from Whitney Pier to Westmount on the outskirts of the city.

It is difficult today to determine the existence or extent of racial problems in Sydney in 1971. Some witnesses at the Royal Commission described the city as a "redneck town", but there is no reason to believe Sydney was any more racist or "redneck" than any other small city in the region, or elsewhere in Canada. Although some Native witnesses at the public hearings suggested the relationship between Whites and Natives in Sydney was not a particularly comfortable one, there is little evidence of overt hostility between the White and Native communities, or between the White and Black communities in Sydney, or between the two minority communities.

We have concluded that Donald Marshall, Jr.'s status as a Native contributed to the miscarriage of justice that has plagued him since 1971. We believe that certain persons within the system would have been more rigorous in their duties, more careful, or more conscious of fairness if Marshall had been White.

The discussion and recommendations that follow go beyond merely looking at which might happen if there was a situation similar to the Marshall case in 1989. If Marshall's treatment in this case occurred because he was a Native, then other Natives will have — and have had — similar experiences. We have attempted to look at the ways in which Natives interact with the justice system, to determine where and how the system has failed them.

> ... The overrepresentation of Native peoples in our prisons is the result of a particular and distinctive historical process which had made them poor beyond poverty. And that process is in the process of colonization, whereby we, as a dominant society, have come to North America and have sought to make over Native people in our image. That process has left Native people, in most parts of the country, dispossessed of all but the remnants of what was once their home lands. ... It's a process which is recognized as having the inevitable consequence of causing immense social and personal demoralization everywhere it has happened in the world. We have recognized the consequences of that in Africa. We have embarked and almost completed, with the exception of South Africa, the process of decolonization. In Canada, we haven't yet recognized that we have that problem. And yet, it is, in my estimation, the central problem which lies at the root of horrendous figures relating to Native people in the criminal justice system.

Having found that Marshall was denied justice because he is an Indian, and that Indians suffer adverse effects from the predominantly White criminal justice system, we need to find ways to change the system. Native Canadians have a right to a justice system they respect and which has respect for them, and which dispenses justice in a manner consistent with and sensitive to their history, culture and language.

Many Natives feel that the criminal justice system — including police, lawyers, judges and courts — is not relevant to their experience, not only in terms of its language and concepts but also in terms of its essential values. Natives rely on resolving disputes through mediation and conciliation, methods which emphasize reconciliation rather than laying blame. Those traditional values frequently clash with our adversarial system. That means that if we are going to change the criminal justice system, either in substance or in its delivery, we must take into account the unique historical and cultural background of Native people.

. . .

## *Framework for our Recommendations*

Until recently, it has been assumed that the best thing Natives could do was to assimilate into the mainstream of society because, after all, White society is more "civilized" and affluent. Why would anyone want to preserve a way of life that is so lacking in services, employment and economic prosperity? Why would Native people not want the advantages of full participation in a White society?

To even ask these questions, of course, indicates a not uncommon ignorance of the strength and traditions of Native society, and the pride Natives take in their society.

As aboriginal peoples, Natives lived in what we now call Canada thousands of years before the English and the French colonized it.

They had their own established ways of living and settling disputes. They were not based on our adversarial system — confrontation, determination of guilt and then punishment of the offender by the State — but on mediation between the parties, with restitution to the victim and to the community. There was not just one person sitting in judgment either. Community elders and leaders settled disputes, and they based their decisions on what they believed was best for the whole community. This community-based approach to justice may be different than our method of resolving disputes, but that does not make it any less valid.

The list of Native criticisms of how our judicial process affects them is long. To begin, they argue that it is not relevant to the real lives of Native people. The court is an unfamiliar and intimidating institution, conceptually removed from the indigenous processes of social control based on mediation and restitution. It is usually physically removed as well. Most courts are located some distance from reserves, making it difficult for Natives to attend. In addition, many Natives, especially those from rural reserves, have problems comprehending the English language. When you add to those things the reality that all the faces in the justice system are White, that Natives constitute a small minority of the population and that Natives suffer from stereotyping and other forms of discrimination, you begin to understand why Natives are unhappy with the current system of administering justice.

The Royal Commission has considered many possibilities for dealing effectively with these problems. One approach would be to identify each problem and then deal with each one individually. For example, their problems with language could be solved by having Native interpreters available in court; their lack of familiarity with court procedures and concepts could be tackled by establishing a professional court worker service; their isolation from the court itself could be remedied by having provincial court judges actually hold court on reserves; their concerns about using their own traditional ways of settling disputes could be addressed by making some adaptation to the structure of sentencing. All of these solutions (and others) are important, and will be the subject of discussion and recommendation by the Royal Commission.

But this is a piecemeal approach. It does not address the differences between Native and White societies, or the argument of some Natives that justice for Natives must be on Native terms and according to Native concepts. Having looked at the problems and the options, we believe the time has come to deal with these broader concerns by establishing — on an experimental basis — a Native Criminal Court that will allow Natives some measure of direct control over the administration of justice within their communities.

### Native Criminal Court

At a conference on Indian justice held in Saskatoon on October 12, 1983, the Minister of Indian Affairs stated that:

> Justice is a basic need in the life of every person. It has confronted, challenged and concerned every society which ever joined together for mutual benefit. . . . The law belongs not to governments, not to bureaucrats, not to lawyers, but to the people. . . . The many alternative means of resolving disputes suggested now — mediation, arbitration, restitution, reconciliation, to name a few — are the very methods which are part of customary law. . . . Native peoples have been deprived of their own traditional laws, concepts of justice and legal procedures. We realize that the Native peoples of Canada expect a system of justice that reflects their own cultural heritage.

We accept these comments of the then Minister. We agree some degree of control should be accorded to Native people in respect of their institutions of justice. A Native Criminal Court is one way to return to them some degree of control over Native justice.

## Recommendation 20

*We recommend that a community-controlled Native Criminal Court be established in Nova Scotia, initially as a five-year pilot project, incorporating the following elements:*

*(a) a Native Justice of the Peace appointed under Section 107 of the Indian Act with jurisdiction to hear cases involving summary conviction offences committed on a reserve;*

*(b) diversion and mediation services to encourage resolution of disputes without resort to the criminal courts;*

*(c) community work projects on the reserve to provide alternatives to fines and imprisonment;*

*(d) aftercare services on the reserve;*

*(e) community input in sentencing, where appropriate; and*

*(f) court worker services.*

A Native community may choose to opt in our out of the model Native Criminal Court we propose. That is and must be recognized as its right.

The proposal we make is modest and will not completely satisfy the demands of some Native groups. However, we believe the proposal is sound and, while experimental in nature, should either chart the way for future development in Nova Scotia, or result in a recognition that, for whatever reasons, Native Criminal Courts are not appropriate here.

We wish to make it clear that the Native Criminal Court we propose will administer the same law as applies to all other Canadians. We do not propose a separate system of Native law, but rather a different process for administering on the reserve certain aspects of the criminal law. The laws enacted by Parliament and the Legislative Assembly will continue to apply to Natives, and the safeguards for accused persons under the Charter would apply in any Native Criminal Court. In the event that any Native customary law is introduced, it would be only after the period of study noted in our next recommendation.

Any sort of Native court system will no doubt seem threatening to some. There will be those who will say, "Why should the Natives get their own justice system?" The answer: "Because they are Native." As aboriginal people, the Micmacs not only have a history and culture that thrived in Nova Scotia before the province was colonized by Whites but they also had in place their own successful methods for resolving disputes.

As noted in our recommendation, Section 107 of the *Indian Act* already provides a mechanism by which a limited type of Native Criminal Court can operate. Under that section, the Federal Cabinet may appoint persons to be justices of the peace to adjudicate cases arising under the *Indian Act* and summary conviction offences under the *Criminal Code*.

Two reserves in Quebec — Kahnawake and St. Regis — have established courts under this authority. The Court of Kahnawake, which we took the opportunity to visit during our deliberations, is a positive example of how Native people can successfully take some control over their own justice institutions. While limited in the scope of their authority by the terms of their appointment, the Native Justices of the Peace have managed to take account of the particular needs of Native people while still upholding the laws of the larger community. By using Native court personnel and court workers, an informal court process and sentencing with community and individual needs in mind, the Native Justices of the Peace appear to have struck an appropriate balance between the old and the new ways. They are now attempting to obtain funding to include mediation and diversion facilities in the range of services provided. Under the Kahnawake model, the Court has jurisdiction over summary conviction offences committed within the boundaries of the reserve, whether by Natives or non-Natives; appeals are taken either to provincial or federal courts depending on the offence.

Critics of the Court of Kahnawake feel that by simply enforcing 'majority' laws, the Court does not go far enough in recognizing the customary law of the Native people. It is true that courts established under the *Indian Act* authority do not provide an answer to the question of the full acceptance of indigenous Native justice mechanisms. But with the benefit of the services recommended in our proposal (some of which are now provided at Kahnawake), the Kahnawake model provides a good starting point for discussion.

It is wrong to think that Native people who wish to see Native traditions reflected in their justice procedures merely want to turn back the clock to simpler times. Changes in the Native and non-Native way of life have brought changes in our laws that cannot be ignored. An accommodation can be reached between Native traditions, human rights law and the Charter, so that the end result will be relevant to Native people and consistent with the protections provided to all Canadians. The historical and cultural justification for establishing Native justice systems must override the fear of problems which might arise. The Court of Kahnawake, for example, shows it can be done.

Future development of Native Criminal Courts in Nova Scotia will be determined by a number of factors:

- *the will and ability of the Micmac people and their leaders to move in this direction;*
- *the political will of the Federal and Provincial Governments to resolve outstanding issues and to support the development of the proposal;*
- *the establishment of a body to do the required development work; and*
- *the establishment of a tripartite forum (Micmac, Provincial and Federal Government) for the discussion and negotiation of a Micmac justice system.*

The development of a community-based justice system will require a research and information base, and coordination between the bands, the Native political organizations and Government. When the Court is established, training of personnel and legal research will become necessary. Because of the importance of Native justice issues in Nova Scotia, we believe that long-term assistance must be given to Nova Scotia Micmacs in order to facilitate this effort.

### Recommendation 21

*We recommend that a Native Justice Institute be established with Provincial and Federal Government funding to do, among other things, the following:*

*(a) channel and coordinate community needs and concerns into the Native Criminal Court;*

*(b) undertake research on Native customary law to determine the extent to which it should be incorporated into the criminal and civil law as it applies to Native people;*

*(c) train court workers and other personnel employed by the Native Criminal Court and the regular courts;*

*(d) consult with Government on Native justice issues;*

*(e) work with the Nova Scotia Barristers Society, the Public Legal Education Society and other groups concerned with the legal information needs of Native people; and*

*(f) monitor the existence of discriminatory treatment against Native people in the criminal justice system.*

Differences between Micmac and Government involving the administration of justice could be dealt with in a tripartite forum with representatives from the Micmac, the Provincial and Federal Governments. The Ontario Indian Commission, while not a perfect model, shows that such a mechanism can be extremely effective. Established in 1978 by agreement between representatives of the Governments of Ontario and Canada and Ontario Indian leaders, its purpose was to examine, discuss and set priorities for identifying and negotiating all matters affecting the Indian people of Ontario and their relationship with the Governments. If a similar structure were implemented in Nova Scotia, the parties could also agree that the negotiation of justice issues would be part of the agenda.

## Recommendation 22

*We recommend that a tripartite forum (Micmac/Provincial/Federal Government) similar to the Ontario Indian Commission be established to mediate and resolve outstanding issues between the Micmac and Government, including Native justice issues.*

### Interpreters

As we pointed out earlier, there are many specific problems relating to the administration of justice that will still need to be dealt with, regardless of whether our recommendation for a pilot Native Criminal Court project is accepted. These include everything from the need for Native court workers to interpreters to assist Native accused in dealing with the criminal justice system.

## Recommendation 23

*We recommend that all courts in Nova Scotia have the services of an on-call Micmac interpreter for use at the request of Micmac witnesses or accused.*

The Royal Commission has been told about some of the differences between Micmac and White concepts and language. Several Micmac witnesses, including Donald Marshall, Jr., testified before us, so we were able to observe their reaction to the court-like process of the Inquiry. That gave us first-hand knowledge of some of the problems Natives may experience in such a setting.

In addition to our observation of Marshall's testimony before us, we also read the transcript of his testimony at his Supreme Court trial and at the Reference before the Appeal Division of the Nova Scotia Supreme Court. There are obvious differences. Before the Supreme Court and the Appeal Division, the Court asked Marshall on at least 29 occasions to speak up or remove his hand from his face so he could be heard. While Marshall is naturally soft-spoken, the court's numerous interventions probably compounded his discomfort, and may have seemed to Marshall as evidence that officials were harassing him or were at least hostile toward him. The Court, on the other hand, may have regarded Marshall's demeanor as a negative factor and that may have influenced the ultimate disposition of the hearings.

. . .

It is disturbing to think of a young Native person, such as Donald Marshall, Jr., on trial for a very serious offence, in an environment where, because of his Native background, he is unable to make a full defence based on a variety of factors beyond his control.

If we seek to obtain the best evidence from all witnesses, to assume innocence until guilt is proved and to give all accused the resources to assert their innocence, we must deal seriously with these subtle language problems.

## *Native Court Workers*

While the use of an interpreter will alleviate some of the language difficulties, the problems go much deeper than mere language comprehension.

## Recommendation 24

*We recommend that the Provincial and Federal Governments, in consultation with Native communities, work together to establish a Native court worker program, as an immediate first step in making the criminal justice system more accessible to Native people.*

The first court worker program in Canada was established in Alberta in 1970 and the program undertaken by Native Counselling Services of Alberta is still the most comprehensive and highly regarded in the country. The percentage of Indians as inmates in provincial institutions, for example, has decreased from 58 percent to 28 percent, and many credit this to the effective work done by the Native Counselling Services. Its Executive Director, Chester Cunningham was one of the experts who attended our Consultation in November 1988.

The benefits of a court worker program are evident in the following comments from judges being interviewed for an assessment of the Alberta program:

> Throughout the extended conversations with the judges, it is apparent that the Bench, for the most part, is aware of the bewilderment that many Natives experience in the legal system, and particularly in the courtroom setting itself. The ritualistic formality and sense of coded behavior, the 'suit and tie' atmosphere, the monotone 'legalese' of the courtroom English, the depersonalized conveyor belt sense of processing . . . as the judges face a lengthy docket and limited time — all these would combine to shake the confidence of even a person well seasoned in systems. Within this setting, language and interpretation become pivotal. Often, as the judges themselves are keenly aware — it is difficult to get beyond 'yes' or 'no' responses to the essence of what the Bench needs to know in order to make an informed and sensitive decision. Indeed in the clear words of yet another Native court worker. 'Most Natives don't talk in the grey area of extenuating circumstances.'

> It is easy to see, then, how it is that the Bench has come to identify the Native court worker as a 'communication device,' bridging the interests of both the court and the Native accused. It is to the credit of our court system that so many of the judges who were interviewed could have spoken the words of one of their number: 'Someone who speaks their language or understands their background instills more confidence than I could no matter how well-meaning I am. In this way, the purpose of Native Counselling is all about communication and justice.'

At one time or another, all provinces in Canada have had court worker programs, although several, including Nova Scotia, have discontinued them.

A Native court worker does not give legal advice but acts as a paralegal. A properly trained court worker can bridge the gap between the Native person with little or no knowledge of the criminal justice system and the system itself. The role of the court worker — who would be available to all Native people, on or off the reserve — should include a variety of functions, including:

- *arranging for the provision of legal services, if required;*
- *explaining the charge and plea options, as well as courtroom procedures; translating for the client and counsel if requested, if a translator has not been provided;*
- *assisting the client in getting to court appearances or meetings with counsel;*
- *explaining the client's rights and obligations in the process;*
- *explaining the role of Crown and defence counsel, and judge and jury; and*
- *other assistance as required.*

An effective court worker can also help sensitize non-Native personnel in the criminal justice system to the needs of Native people.

One of the most frequent criticisms of court worker programs is that the method of providing funding as well as the amount of funding allocated is not sufficient, resulting in inadequate staff training and too few staff to meet the demand. Establishing a Native court worker program will cost money. However, the cost will be more than justified if the program provides — and is seen to provide — much-needed assistance to Native people in the court system.

### *Provincial Courts on Reserves*

### Recommendation 25

*We recommend that the Chief Judge of the Provincial Court take steps to establish regular sittings of the Provincial Courts on Nova Scotia reserves.*

Some Micmac leaders and criminal justice personnel have suggested that establishing Provincial Court hearings on reserves would be another positive way of bridging the physical and conceptual distance between Micmac communities and the Courts. While such a move would be a change in form only, and not in substance, and would not deal in a significant way with the deep-seated feeling of alienation Micmac people have for the criminal justice system as a whole, it would be an important and easily implemented gesture of respect for the special concerns of Natives within the justice system.

For reserves that do not choose to adopt the Native Criminal Court proposal we made earlier — and until our recommendation for the establishment of Native Criminal Courts is implemented — Provincial Court sittings on reserves for on-reserve offences should be supported.

There would undoubtedly be a number of positive side effects from such a move. Native accused would be more likely to show up for court appearances, for example, since distance would not be a problem and since the community would likely monitor court appearances more closely. Micmacs would believe they had a greater stake in the system if they could actually see it operating in their own communities. At the same time, justice system personnel, including judges, would gain a greater understanding of Micmac concerns and reserve conditions if they were required to do a regular reserve circuit.

### Lawyers' Duty to Native Accused

Clark's research identified several areas in which Micmacs seem dissatisfied with the treatment they receive from lawyers. These include access to counsel, inadequate explanation of the proceedings and concerns regarding plea bargaining. Many of these concerns can be resolved if some of our other recommendations — "educating" the bar about the problems facing Native clients, directed public legal education programs and implementation of the Native court worker program — are implemented.

On the basis of what we have heard, access to legal counsel was not a problem for Donald Marshall, Jr. in 1971, and it does not appear to be a problem today. Legal aid lawyers are available throughout the province, and the fact that there are no legal aid offices on reserve does not appear to pose a problem for Native clients.

We do get the clear impression, however, that legal aid counsel are overworked. While this has an effect on all Nova Scotians who are eligible for and require legal aid services, it has a particularly negative effect on Native clients who may require more time with their lawyer than a non-Native client because of their fear and lack of knowledge of the justice system. The legal aid lawyer's lack of time, coupled with the natural communication problems Natives may have in dealing with representatives of the legal system, combine to make Native clients feel they are being poorly served.

Some of these problems indicate the different perceptions Natives and legal aid lawyers have of their duties. Clark says many Natives he interviewed believed legal aid lawyers would rather plea bargain for a lesser sentence than pursue the matter forcefully. Says Clark: "This contributes to the belief already held by many Micmacs that all justice system personnel, including defence counsel, are in league against the people being served. Often this is further perceived as discrimination against Indians."

. . .

There needs to be ongoing liaison between lawyers and Native people. The Nova Scotia Barristers Society should organize such programs in consultation with the Native people.

## Recommendation 27

*We recommend that a program of ongoing liaison between the bar — prosecutors, private defence and legal aid — and Native people, both on and off reserve, be established through the Nova Scotia Barristers Society. The Society must also educate its members concerning the special needs of Native clients.*

### Juries

The lack of Natives on juries in Nova Scotia concerns members of the Native community. We know of no evidence that suggests Natives are deliberately excluded from jury duty in Nova Scotia. Nor can we argue definitively that the presence of a Native person on a jury in a case involving a Native accused will result in fairer treatment for the Native. Still, Native concerns are not unreasonable: Would a White

person facing a Native prosecutor, defence lawyer, judge and jury, have some apprehension whether he would get as fair a hearing as if everyone were White?

. . .

## Conclusions

The recommendations we have made to improve the treatment of Natives and
Blacks in the criminal justice system have focussed on specific policies and legislation,
as well as education and training. Such initiatives will be doomed to failure, however,
without regular and effective monitoring. We have not proposed a separate body be
established with responsibility for overseeing implementation of these recommendations. Instead, we suggest that Government, judges, lawyers, the police and others
ultimately be responsible for their own area of jurisdiction.

It is easy to blame Governments for all that we might identify as "wrong" in our
society, and we have attempted to avoid this temptation. Government, however, must
accept that it has a special duty in these matters. As legislator and employer, the role
and influence of Government in this province cannot be underestimated.

These recommendations provide a rare opportunity for everyone involved in the
system — not only Government — to change patterns of behavior and policies that
have been well entrenched but never questioned, and to open doors that have remained
closed for much too long to the full participation of minorities.

## ADMINISTRATION OF CRIMINAL JUSTICE

We have found that Donald Marshall, Jr. was wrongfully convicted of murder and
deprived of his freedom for 11 years because the justice system broke down. Each
component of the system — every check and balance — failed. The Sydney City
Police, Crown prosecutors, defence counsel, the courts, the Department of Attorney
General and the RCMP all contributed to Marshall's conviction and continued imprisonment by failing to perform to an acceptable standard. In the months that followed
Marshall's eventual release and acquittal, there were accusations that racism played
a role in Marshall's conviction and that, if he had been White, the process by which
he was acquitted and his struggle for compensation may have been handled differently.

If there are differing standards of justice in Nova Scotia, depending on one's race
or social standing, it suggests internal control within the system has broken down. It
also suggests that the major components of the system are not fulfilling their proper
functions and the appropriate interrelationships are not understood or observed.

. . .

A properly functioning criminal justice system is the bedrock on which society's
acceptance of our system of law and the maintenance of order is based. But because
of what has happened in the Marshall case and some others we will examine now,
many people in Nova Scotia have begun to question the fairness and independence
of the province's justice system. This erosion of confidence must be stopped and

public confidence restored. This can only be accomplished through the unwavering and visible application of the principles of absolute fairness and independence.

## Questions/Discussion

1.  What role does the criminal justice system have to play in the alleviation of racism in Canada? What are its inherent limitations in fulfilling such a role? In this regard, see McKenna, I., "Canada's Hate Propaganda Laws — A Critique" (1994), 26 Ottawa Law Review 159.

2.  What is the best way in which to combat racism within the criminal justice system; for example, is it through the hiring or appointment of more police officers, judges and prosecutors from minority groups, or in the case of aboriginal peoples through the provision of separate systems of justice?

3.  Can the exercise of discretion within the criminal justice system be restrained in order to limit the potential effects of racist biases on the part of the actors and agents within the system? In what sectors of the system might this be possible? If *a priori* restraint remains a problem, then what types of review processes might be useful to control the abusive effects of such attitudes?

4.  In 1990, a judge in the Northwest Territories was quoted as saying that rape was different in the North: "The majority of rapes in the Northwest Territories occur when the woman is drunk. The man comes along, sees a pair of hips and helps himself. That contrasts sharply to the cases I dealt with (in southern Canada) of the dainty co-ed who gets jumped from behind" (*Ottawa Citizen*, January 19, 1990). Besides betraying a disturbing ignorance about the nature of rape generally, the comments illustrate a dangerous attitude toward the nature of the problem in the northern communities.

5.  For an examination of the problems and issues surrounding racism, criminal justice and the black community in Nova Scotia, see Volume 1 of the Marshall inquiry report at p. 182. For a discussion of the problems and effects of systemic racism in the Ontario criminal law system, see the *Report of the Commission on Systemic Racism in the Ontario Criminal Justice System* (Toronto: Queen's Printer for Ontario, 1995).

6.  An interesting footnote to the Marshall inquiry is that the lawyers involved in the process received a total of $2.4 million while Donald Marshall himself received compensation of only $270,000. The total cost of the inquiry was $8.6 million. (*The Lawyer's Weekly*, May 25, 1990).

7.  For a discussion of the issues surrounding the collection of crime statistics broken down by the race or ethnic origin of the suspect and/or the victim, see the series of articles in the April, 1994, issue of the Canadian Journal of Criminology (volume 36) pp. 149-185.

## Further Reading

*   Baker, D. (ed.), *Reading Racism and the Criminal Justice System*, (Toronto: Canadian Scholar's Press, 1994).
*   Barsh, R., "Native Justice in Lethbridge" (1995), 6 Journal of Human Justice 131.
*   Birkenmayer, A.C. and S. Jolly, *The Native Inmate in Ontario* (Toronto: Ontario Ministry of Correctional Services, 1984).
*   Canada, *Correctional Issues Affecting Native Peoples — Correctional Law Review Working Paper No. 7* (Ottawa: Solicitor General of Canada, 1988).
*   Chan, Wendy and Kiran Mirchandani, eds., *Crimes of Colour: Racialization and the Criminal Justice System in Canada* (Peterborough, Ont.: Broadview Press, 2002).

- Chow, Henry P.H., "The Chinese Community Leaders' Perceptions of the Criminal Justice System" (1996), 38 Canadian Journal of Criminology 477-484.
- Griffiths, C.T., and Verdun-Jones, S., *Canadian Criminal Justice 2nd ed.* (Toronto: Harcourt Brace & Company, Canada, 1994), Chapter 15.
- Hathaway, J., "Native Canadians and the Criminal Justice System: A Critical Examination of the Native Court Worker Program" (1989), 49 Saskatchewan Law Review 201.
- Henry, Frances, "Review of the Report of the Commission on Systemic Racism in the Ontario Criminal Justice System" (1996), 15 Windsor Yearbook of Access to Justice 230-235.
- Jackson, M., "Locking Up Natives in Canada" (1989), 23 University of British Columbia Law Review 215.
- LaPrairie, C., "The Role of Sentencing in the Over-representation of Aboriginal People in Correctional Institutions" (1990), 32 Canadian Journal of Criminology 429.
- LaPrairie, Carol, "Sentencing Aboriginal Offenders: Some Critical Issues" in Julian V. Roberts and David P. Cole, eds., *Making Sense of Sentencing* (Toronto: University of Toronto Press, 1999) at 173-185.
- Mannette, J., *Elusive Justice: Beyond the Marshall Inquiry* (Halifax: Fernwood Publishing, 1992).
- Markowitz, Michael W. and Delores D. Jones-Brown, eds., *The System in Black and White: Exploring the Connections Between Race, Crime, and Justice* (Westport, Conn.: Praeger, 2000).
- McFarland, J., "Manitoba's 'Aboriginal Justice Inquiry'" *Canadian Dimension* (June 1989) at 6.
- Petersen, C., "Institutionalized Racism: The Need for Reform of the Criminal Jury Selection Process" (1993), 38 McGill Law Journal 147.
- Razack, Sherene H., "Making Canada White: Law and the Policing of Bodies of Colour in the 1990s" (1999), 14 Canadian Journal of Law and Society 159-184.
- Roach, Kent, "Systemic Racism and Criminal Justice Policy" (1996), 15 Windsor Yearbook of Access to Justice 236-249.
- Schwartz, B., "A Separate Aboriginal Justice System?" (1990), 19 Manitoba Law Journal 77.
- Silverman, R., and Nielsen, M., *Aboriginal Peoples and the Canadian Justice System* (Markham: Butterworths, 1992).

## 8.3  CONDITIONAL SENTENCES

### Introduction

The issues surrounding conditional sentences are entwined generally with issues surrounding sentencing, punishment, and imprisonment. While these latter issues were looked at in Chapter 5, the former are more specific and relatively new to the Canadian criminal legal system and, as a result, raise unique challenges and problems. Conditional sentences were introduced in 1996 and taken up in earnest by Canadian judges. Criticisms soon arose over the appropriateness of their use in some cases, and there were arguments on the part of some writers and interest groups that offenders were escaping "real punishment" as a result. In 2000, the matter reached the Supreme

Court in the case of *R. v. Proulx*, where the court considered the nature, application, and construction of conditional sentences.

There are three readings on the topic below. The first from the Department of Justice gives a very brief overview of what the conditional sentencing option is, while the second reading by Roberts examines the judgment in *Proulx*. The final reading by Roberts and Healy looks very briefly at the most recent developments in the area.

# What is a Conditional Sentence?*

## *Department of Justice, Research and Statistics Division*

* Excerpts from *Conditional Sentences Fact Sheet #1*, Department of Justice, Research and Statistics Division (Ottawa: Department of Justice, 2001).

. . .

## Where did the conditional sentence come from?

The conditional sentence was created to help reduce the use of imprisonment in a way that is safe and consistent with principles of justice. Several independent Commissions of Inquiry have demonstrated that the imprisonment rate is higher in Canada than many other countries. The goal of the conditional sentence is to reduce the use of incarceration by punishing offenders in the community. If the offender remains in the community (under supervision), he can continue to work, support his family and pay taxes. The taxpayer also saves money. Supervising offenders in the community costs about a quarter of the cost of imprisonment.

## What exactly is a conditional sentence?

A conditional sentence is a term of imprisonment that is served in the community. Only some offenders are eligible. Here is how it works. A number of criteria have to be met before an offender can be sentenced to serve his term of custody in the community under supervision. First, the sentence cannot exceed two years less one day. This excludes offenders convicted of the most serious crimes that result in sentences served in a penitentiary. Second, if the offence carries a minimum penalty, the offender cannot receive a conditional sentence. Third, the judge must be convinced that the presence of the offender in the community (rather than prison) does not pose a danger to the public. Finally, the judge must be convinced that a conditional sentence is consistent with the purpose and principles of sentencing that are contained in the *Criminal Code*.

Only if these conditions are met may a judge impose a conditional sentence. But the judge still has discretion to send the offender to prison. If the conditions are met, *and* if the judge feels it is in the interests of justice, the offender may be sent to serve his term of imprisonment in the community, provided that certain conditions are observed.

## What kinds of conditions must the offender observe?

An offender serving a conditional sentence must abide by a number of conditions that apply to all such offenders. These compulsory conditions include reporting to a probation officer who will ensure that the order of the court is followed. As well, he or she must comply with a number of other conditions that are especially constructed for each individual case. These conditions may require the offender to remain at home (except for work or medical emergencies), or to stay at home in the evening and during weekends. The offender may also be required to pay back the victim for money stolen, and/or perform community service.

## What happens to the offender if the conditions are violated?

If the offender violates his conditions, he will be arrested and brought back to court for a hearing. The judge has the power to send the offender to prison for the remainder of the sentence. Thus if an offender serving a one-year sentence violates conditions after six months, the judge has the power to send him to prison for the remaining six months of the sentence.

## How often are conditional sentences imposed?

The most frequent sentence in Canadian courts is a fine. A conditional sentence is imposed in approximately 60% of all cases.

## What types of offenders have been sentenced to a conditional sentence?

People convicted of crimes involving property crimes are most likely to receive a conditional sentence. As well, conditional sentences are sometimes imposed for climes of violence. Crimes involving property accounted for the largest percentage (39%) of conditional sentences. Crimes against the person accounted for under one-third of all conditional sentences. Offences against the administration of justice accounted for 11% of all such sentences and driving related offences, 4%.

## Are offenders on conditional sentences a threat to the community?

Since a judge must be satisfied that the offender's presence in the community would not pose a threat to the public, it is not surprising that very few offenders have committed another crime while serving a conditional sentence in the community.

## How long are most conditional sentences?

Since the conditional sentence is designed for the less serious offenders, most conditional sentences are relatively short. One-half of all conditional sentences imposed to date were under six months, 3/4 were under one year in duration.

. . .

# Unearthing the Sphinx: The Evolution of Conditional Sentencing
### *Julian V. Roberts*

* (2001), 80 Canadian Bar Review 1019–1034.

After almost four years in which over 40,000 conditional sentences were imposed, in January 2000 the Supreme Court of Canada provided some clear directions regarding the use of the new sanction. The unanimous judgement in *R. v. Proulx* (one of six relating to conditional sentencing) addresses four principal questions: (i) what is a conditional sentence of imprisonment? (ii) how should a conditional sentence be constructed? (iii) what is the appropriate judicial response to an unjustified breach of the order? And (iv) for what kinds of offences (and offenders) is a conditional sentence particularly appropriate (or particularly inappropriate)? In this article, I shall be concerned with the Court's response to the first three questions.

The first question may seem straightforward enough: Section 742.1 of the Criminal Code provides a relatively clear statutory framework, including prerequisite conditions. But the clarity masks a degree of malleability. As the judgement notes: "There has been some confusion among members of the judiciary and the public alike about the difference between a conditional sentence and a suspended sentence with probation". The Court therefore set out to establish the place that a conditional sentence occupies in the range of sanctions available at sentencing. This exercise necessitated creating a distinction between a suspended sentence with probation and a conditional sentence. By clearly distinguishing the conditional sentence from a term of probation, the Court was compelled to move the new sanction closer to a term of imprisonment served in a provincial institution. In short, after the *Proulx* judgement, we can expect conditional sentences to become more rigorous, but not necessarily as harsh as some authorities fear.

## 1. *The Nature of a Conditional Sentence*

Determining the position of the conditional sentence on a scale of severity is far from easy. By virtue of its inherently labile nature, the onerousness of any conditional sanction is determined principally by the nature of the conditions imposed and the judicial response to any subsequent breach of those conditions. For this reason, a conditional sentence is hard to fix on a spectrum of the severity of sanctions.

The onerousness of a prison term is determined largely by its duration (leaving aside for the moment the issue of custody level which will affect the experience of imprisonment). A sentence of one-year in custody is, *ceteris paribus,* more onerous than a six-month sentence or six months of probation. But whether a six-month conditional sentence of imprisonment is more or less onerous than a twelve-month conditional sentence will depend on the number, nature and intrusiveness of the conditions attached to the two orders. This is just one reason why it is imperative to have good statistical information on the optional conditions attached to conditional sentence orders. Regrettably, at the present, although the number of conditional sentence orders imposed to date is available, Statistics Canada does not collect information on the nature of conditions attached to the orders.

Conflicting interpretations of the nature of a conditional sentence have been advanced since the sanction was created in 1996. Some authorities regard it as a restorative, community-based alternative to imprisonment. Others have adopted a more conservative interpretation (and therefore a sanction with a punitive element) which is served in the community, much as parole is a form of imprisonment although the prisoner is not actually confined to a correctional institution.

In responding to these conflicting interpretations, Lamer, C.J.C. Makes it clear in *Proulx* that a conditional sentence is a hybrid disposition, which carries punitive *and* restorative elements. The judgement notes that the conditional sentence "will generally be more effective than incarceration at achieving the restorative objectives of rehabilitation, reparations to the victim and community, and the promotion of a sense of responsibility in the offender. However, *it is also a punitive sanction capable of achieving the objectives of denunciation and deterrence*" (emphasis in original).

Like most hybrids, this confluence of characteristics makes the sanction hard to characterize. It is akin to asking whether the legendary Sphinx was a lion was human features, or a man infused with leonine characteristics. Was the centaur a horse or a man? At the same time, the hybrid nature of the conditional sentence makes it a supple disposition, which can be used (if properly constructed; see discussion below) for a wide range of offenders.

The judgment in *Proulx* makes it clear that a conditional sentence must have a punitive element. Unlike probation or other community-based punishments, a conditional sentence is a term of imprisonment, and as such should serve the function of a term of custody. In order to match the penal value of imprisonment, the conditional sentence must perforce share at least some of the characteristics of custody (such as tight restrictions on the offender's lifestyle).

However, the fact that a conditional sentence must carry a punitive element does not mean that it is a punitive sanction with secondary restorative characteristics, as such writers have suggested, any more than Centaurs could be described as "primarily" men, albeit ones with equine bodies. While it is true that the Court stresses that each conditional sentence must carry a punitive element, this is a long way from saying that a conditional sentence is *primarily* punitive. Indeed, the Chief Justice is careful to avoid according primacy to punitive or restorative elements. The clearest statement of the Court's position can be found in the judgment's summary, which notes that "Parliament intended conditional sentences to include both punitive and rehabilitative aspects". This can be taken as a rejection of any attempt to privilege one aspect over another. At the end of the day, whether a particular conditional sentence is primarily restorative or primarily punitive will depend on the number of nature of optional conditions imposed.

The Court's interpretation of section 742 takes us back to a dilemma confronting the architects of the sentencing reform of 1996. The sanction introduced by Bill C-41 could have been called by another name. If the conditional sentence had been defined as "enhanced probation supervision", or "intensive community punishment", or some similar construction, then there would have bee no necessity to invest the disposition with a punitive element. The heated debate over whether a conditional sentence is a term of imprisonment or not would have been avoided. But creating an alternative along these line would have carried a clear danger. There would be no guarantee that judges would use the new sanction in place of, rather than in addition to, sentences of imprisonment. *In order for the conditional sentence to achieve the goal set by Parliament of reducing the number of custodial sentences, the sanction must be used as a replacement for, and not an addition to imprisonment.* And, as a replacement, it needs to convey the same, or nearly the same, penal value.

Section 742.1 makes it clear that prior to imposing a conditional sentence, the court must have decided to impose a term of imprisonment. (a) imposes a sentence of imprisonment of less than two years. If judges respect this direction, it follows that every offender sentenced to a conditional sentence is an individual that would have been sent, prior to the inception of conditional sentencing, to serve a term of custody in a provincial correctional institution. Research suggests that this is not what has transpired; it would appear that many of the conditional sentences to date have been imposed on offenders who, prior to the advent of conditional sentencing, would have received probation. Otherwise, how can we explain the fact that over 40,000 conditional sentence orders have been handed down, and yet the provincial incarceration rate has not declined?

To summarize, by calling the new sanction a "term of imprisonment", Parliament created a disposition that the Court would have to characterize as partly punitive in nature, *because it is a form of imprisonment.*

Having clarified the nature of the conditional sentence, in *Proulx* the Chief Justice proceeds to resolve a number of issues relating to the imposition of a conditional sentence. These are practical questions such as whether a conditional sentence may be longer than the sentence of custody that it replaces. Judges should now have a much clearer idea of the nature of a conditional sentence, and should be better equipped to use the sanction. This is just as well, since the judgment also contains a ringing endorsement of the principle of deference to the trial judge, and this will surely amplify the autonomy of the trial courts with respect to sentencing.

## 2. *Changes to the practice of Conditional Sentencing*

The practical changes wrought by the judgement in *Proulx* affect three characteristics of the conditional sentence: its duration, the nature of optional conditions and the nature of judicial response to a breach of those conditions

## I. *Duration: conditional sentence may now be longer than term of custody*

The consensus prior to *Proulx* was that a conditional sentence had to be exactly the same length as the term of custody that it replaced. This interpretation only made sense if the conditional sentence was the penal equivalent of a term of custody. Having established that a conditional sentence is not, in most cases, the equivalent of custody. Having established that a conditional sentence is not, in most cases, the equivalent of imprisonment, it was inevitable that the Court would reject the one-to-one correspondence between a conditional sentence order and the term of conventional custody that is replaced. Indeed, some judgments in the case law, as well as scholarly articles had already advocated as much, and section 742 does not exclude the possibility of making a conditional sentence longer.

However, it is worth noting that the judgment does not *require* judges to prolong the duration of a conditional sentence beyond the term of custody that would have been imposed; it simply *permits* the former to exceed the latter. The key passage is the following: "When a judge—in the first stage—decides that a term of imprisonment of "x months" is appropriate, it means that *this* sentence is proportional. If the sentencing judge decides—in the second stage—*that the same term* can be served in the community, *it is possible* that the sentence is no longer proportional to the gravity of the offence and the responsibility of the offender" (underscore emphasis added).

In many (perhaps most) cases, the conditional sentence order will remain in the range that would have been imposed had the offender been sentenced to custody. Nor does the judgment envisage a simple two or three for one ratio as has been suggested for crediting pre-trial custody. The judgment is also sensitive to the relationship between the onerousness or intrusiveness of the conditional sentence order, and the length of the order. The imposition of a conditional sentence order carrying punitive conditions that restrict the offender's freedom to a high degree would surely obviate the need to prolong the duration of the order beyond the term of custody that would have been imposed. Indeed, the closer the conditions approximate the severity of detention in a correctional facility, the more likely it is that the duration of the conditional sentence will mirror the duration of the custodial term that would otherwise have been imposed. It is hard to disagree with the Court's logic in this regard.

Trial judges will be mindful, when determining the length of the conditional sentence order, that an unjustified breach will probably result in committal to custody (in light of the judgment's direction with respect to breach—see below). Imposing an 18-month conditional sentence order in place of a six-month term of custody in a correctional facility may well place great pressure on the offender and provoke a breach of the conditions. This will inhibit judges from imposing conditional sentence orders tat are much longer than the terms of custody that they replace.

It seems unlikely then that we shall witness a doubling or tripling of conditional sentence lengths, although the average length of orders will probably increase. Finally, the limited statistical evidence on this issue suggests that the *Proulx* judgment is simply recognizing what has often transpired at the trial court level (in Ontario at least): the lengths of conditional sentence orders in the pre-*Proulx* period were significantly longer than terms of custody imposed for the same offence category.

## II. *Nature of Optional Conditions*

It is in the area of optional conditions that the *Proulx* judgment has attracted the sharpest criticism from legal academics. Having established that a conditional sentence must be more punitive than probation, the Court specified the ways in which this could be achieved: "conditional sentences should generally include punitive conditions that are restrictive of the offender's liberty. Conditions such as house arrest or strict curfews should be the norm, not the exception". And further: "There must be a reason for failing to impose punitive conditions when a conditional sentence order is made." The imposition of optional conditions such as curfews, house arrest, and prohibitions against the consumption of alcohol reflects an attempt to recreate some of the privations and restrictions of imprisonment in the community. They do not represent an attempt to simply "get tough" with offenders, but rather a recognition that the conditional sentence is a sentence of imprisonment, and as such should carry at least some of the characteristics of prison life.

The general result of the Court's direction is that the optional conditions attached to conditional sentence orders should be quite onerous. The Court did not have the benefit of empirical research into the number and nature of conditions imposed, but the limited evidence available suggests that curfews and house arrest have been imposed in only a minority of conditional sentences imposed to date. For example, two studies of conditional sentence orders (pre-*Proulx*) in Ontario and British Columbia found that in both provinces a curfew was imposed in less than one case in five.

There is of course a reason for the reluctance so far of trial judges to order the offender to remain at home after a specified time of day. Unless adequate supervisory resources are available, a curfew cannot be verified, and unverifiable conditions will invite violation and attract further media attention and public criticism. Electronic monitoring solves the problem of verification, but it is not an option available in most jurisdictions across Canada. By making it clear that house arrest or a strict curfew should be the norm and not the exception, the Court in *Proulx* has sent an unequivocal message to provincial governments: in order to work, the sanction must be supported by adequate resources. We can only hope that the message has been received, and will be acted upon.

## III. *Judicial Response to Unjustified Breach*

Section 742.6(1) provides judges with considerable discretion in terms of responding to unjustified breaches of the conditions of a conditional sentence order. The court may: do nothing and allow the order to continue, amend the optional conditions, commit the offender to custody for some portion of the remaining sentence or commit the offender to custody for the remainder of the sentence. Given this wide range of options, it is not surprising that the Supreme Court offered some advice as to how to exercise this discretion.

The direction to judges with respect to the response to which an unjustified breach is unequivocal and somewhat unforgiving: "[W]here an offender breaches a condition without reasonable excuse, there should be a presumption that the offender serve the *remainder* of his or her sentence in jail" (emphasis added). Thus the offender should be imprisoned, and not just for a portion of the sentence, but the duration of the order. In short, the Court recommended adopting the most severe of the options available to a court after an unjustified breach has been established. If this direction is followed, it will represent a sharp change of direction: prior to the *Proulx* judgment, few breach hearings resulted in committal to custody for the duration of the order.

However, the impact of the *Proulx* judgment on the question of judicial response to breach may be less drastic than some commentators have suggested. Although the Chief Justice made it clear that committal for the remainder of the order should be the norm, by definition there will be many exceptions to this rule. In addition, nothing in *Proulx* undermines the discretion of the trial judge with respect to breach; the court still has the same options of amending the optional conditions, or simply returning the offender to the community. As well, the increase in the number (and the onerousness) of the optional conditions imposed may work to counter the presumption in favour of committal to custody following a breach. Judges may be unwilling to incarcerate an offender for an unjustified breach of a single condition (particularly a minor one), when the individual has successfully respected all the other optional and compulsory conditions.

Finally, it is also possible that conditional sentence supervisors may respond to breach allegations with more indulgence than in the pre-*Proulx* era. There are two reasons for this. First, probation officers will be aware that the optional conditions imposed upon offenders serving conditional sentences have become more numerous and more onerous. Second, if conditional sentence supervisors believe that a proven breach will almost certainly result in the incarceration of the offender, they may be inclined to exercise their discretion with respect to invoking the intervention of the state, and turn a blind eye to a violation of the less substantive optional conditions.

With respect to the breach issue, at least one Court of Appeal has displayed considerable deference to the trial court, and, it would appear, indulgence towards the offender. In *R. v. S.(B.J.)*, the offender had originally been sentenced to a 20-month conditional sentence for a constellation of serious offences including sexual assault, forcible confinement, and uttering threats. The statutory aggravating factors were relevant as the victim was his wife, and the offences were committed in the presence of their children. One of the optional conditions of the conditional sentence order was to have no contact with the victim, except in the context of access visits involving the children. Three months into the order the offender violated this condition by making a spontaneous visit to his wife. Denied entry, the offender broke down the door, unplugged the telephone, subjected the victim to threats, warned her not to call the police and ordered to remove her clothes. At the breach hearing the trial judge elected to simply change a condition of the order. On appeal by the Crown, the British Columbia Court of Appeal did not change the continuation of the order, and the appeal was accordingly dismissed.

Three months later another violation occurred, this time involving one of the children. On the second occasion the sentencing judge elected not to change the conditions, and the Crown subsequently appealed. The Court of Appeal dismissed this second Crown appeal. The unanimous judgment cites *Proulx* and makes it clear that the message of deference to trial judges includes the administration of the conditional sentence order: "local judges in the community will usually have a very soundly based sense of what is appropriate in sentencing matters and their dispositions ought not to be lightly interfered with."

The judicial response to an unjustified breach of conditions will obviously require careful consideration. The critical question of course is whether to terminate the order, and if this is answered in the affirmative, then whether the offender should be committed for the duration of the order or only some portion thereof. Limitations on space preclude a thorough discussion of the issue, but it surely makes sense for the determination of judicial response to breach to be guided by the relevant statutory principles of sentencing. These principles guide the initial decision as to whether an offender may serve his sentence in the community, and they should not be laid aside when the court has to respond to a breach of the order. As with the conditional sentence itself, the alternatives available to the Court include restorative and punitive options. Terminating the order and committing the offender to custody is clearly a punitive response; adjusting the nature of optional conditions may be purely restorative or rehabilitative.

The general rule has been laid down in *Proulx:* a presumption in favour of incarceration for the duration of the order. But as with all presumptions, many cases will constitute exceptions, and it is with respect to these cases that the principles of sentencing should apply. For example, section 718.2(d) articulates that an offender "should not be deprived of liberty, if less restrictive sanctions may be appropriate in the circumstances". Applied to a breach hearing, this implies that if imprisoning the offender for a fraction of the order will serve to restore compliance with the conditions and would be consistent with the principle of proportionality, then the offender should not be imprisoned for the rest of the term. Establishing the seriousness of the breach (and hence the nature of the response) should entail a consideration of section 718.2. Breaching a condition that that touches a statutory aggravating circumstance is accordingly a more serious breach.

What factors should *not* be considered? There is little justification to consider community reaction. Despite the position taken in *Proulx* that trial judges have strong roots in the community, there is no evidence that trial judges can, with any accuracy, divine the likely reaction of the public to specific conditional sentencing decisions (with respect to the imposition of a conditional sentence or the response to breach). As well, research has demonstrated that the public are confused about the nature of a conditional sentence and it would be foolish to consider public opinion unless and until this confusion is dispelled. Finally, considering community reaction is also a clear prescription for disparity, and it would be a violation of equity to commit an offender to prison (following a breach) just because the alternative (maintaining the offender in the community) *might appear* to engender public criticism.

### 3. *Relationship between duration, conditions and response to unjustified breach*

To summarize, conditional sentence orders will likely become more onerous, somewhat longer and breaches will be treated with more severity than in the pre-*Proulx* era. It is important to note that there is a coherence to the Court's direction in these three areas: the optional conditions imposed as part of conditional sentence orders will become tougher, but this may obviate the need to prolong the duration of the order. On the other hand, if minimal conditions are seen to e appropriate, extending the duration of the order will help to preserve the principles of proportionality and parity in sentencing. And while judicial response to a proven breach of conditions may become more rigorous, judges retain the discretion to amend the conditions (perhaps by lending more structure to the offender's life) and to return the offender to the community to continue serving the sentence as originally imposed.

One last comment is in order with respect to the 'toughening' of the conditional sentence regime laid down in *Proulx*. Critics of the judgment might argue that imposing more (and stricter) conditions constitutes a marked (and gratuitous) departure from the judicial practice to date. But this analysis assumes that the kinds of conditional sentences imposed by trial judges to date were "correct". And that surely is a matter open to debate. It is only in light of the fact that many conditional sentence orders have resembled somewhat harsher probation orders (in terms of the optional conditions imposed) that the *Proulx* judgment appears 'tough'. Had this judgment been handed down in January 1997, before trial judges had imposed many conditional sentence orders, the direction taken by the Supreme Court may have attracted more support from advocates of conditional sentencing.

Let us briefly pursue the *Proulx* directions to trial judges inn light of this analysis. Consider an offender sentenced to one year in prison, and who then is allowed to serve the sentence in the community (provided he or she abides by a number of conditions). Let us suppose that after six months, she wilfully and without justification violates those conditions. Assuming that the conditions were not unreasonable to begin with, and that the offender was supervised appropriately, is it excessively harsh of the State to commit the individual to custody for some portion of the unexpired term?

*Importance of Sections 718-718.2*

The changes to conditional sentencing recommended by the Court are important because they remind judges of the point of departure for the imposition of any sentence: the statement of the purpose and principles of sentencing found in sections 718-718.2 of the *Code*. Section 718.1 lies at the heart of that statement. The principle of proportionality is central to the sentencing process in Canada and other common law jurisdictions. Indeed, the principle permeates the case law, as well as popular conceptions of justice. As Rosenberg J.A. Noted in *R. v. Priest,* "[t]he principle of proportionality is rooted in notions of fairness and justice". Any ambiguity about the primordial role of proportionality should have been dispelled when Parliament codified the principle and designated it as "fundamental". The changes with respect to section 742 advocated by the Court have the effect of moving the conditional sentence further from a term of probation, and closer to a term of custody. The benefit of this direction is that it will help to preserve the principles of proportionality and parity in sentencing, both now codified in Part XXIII.

Proportionality requires that the severity of sanctions imposed comport with the seriousness of the crime, and to a lesser extent, the culpability of the offender. If a conditional sentence with minimal conditions is imposed in a case that would otherwise have resulted in custody, the principle of proportionality is violated. Similarly if comparably-situated offenders are sentenced to, respectively, a term of provincial custody and a conditional sentence of equal duration and carrying few optional conditions, then the principle of parity is violated. The Court's direction with respect to section 742 is therefore consistent with the statement of the purpose and principles of sentencing found in sections 718-718.2

### 4. *Impact of the Proulx judgment on the number of conditional sentences imposed*

At the end of the day, the critical question is whether the Supreme Court's direction will lead to an increased or decreased use of conditional sentences. If the number of conditional sentences imposed declines, this will spell the end of the sanction as a tool to reduce the use of incarceration. After all, the current level of usage has, as noted, failed to lower the percentage of sentences involving custody. Some commentators are pessimistic about the impact the *Proulx* judgment will have on the use of the conditional sentence. Professor Manson, for one, argues that there will be fewer conditional sentences imposed.

I am unconvinced, for two reasons, that the judgment will have the chilling effect on trial judges predicted by Professor Manson. First, many trial judges were, before *Proulx*, unconvinced that a conditional sentence could adequately convey a message of deterrence or denunciation. The Court has addressed this judicial scepticism, and provided practical guidance as to how deterrence and denunciation may be achieved, even for serious cases in which statutory aggravating factors are present. The second reason for thinking that judges will continue to use the conditional sentence relates to the question of appellate review of sentencing.

In *Proulx,* the Court has provided a ringing endorsement of the concept of deference to the trial judge. The key words are the following: "Again, I stress that appellate courts should not second-guess sentencing judges unless the sentence imposed is *demonstrably unfit*" (emphasis added). As Rosenberg, J.A. Has noted: "there seems no doubt that the Supreme Court has instructed the appellate courts to draw back from what the Supreme Court obviously perceived as excessive appellate interference in the sentencing function". This may embolden judges to become more creative in the construction and imposition of conditional sentences.

The apogee to date of appellate deference to trial court discretion may be found in *Turcotte*. The offender was tried for second degree murder, but the jury returned a verdict of manslaughter. The victim (who was slowly strangled to death) was the frail, inebriated, septuagenarian mother of the offender.

The *Turcotte* case provides a good illustration of the conflict between desert and dangerousness in the sentencing process in general, and the conditional sentencing regime in particular. The crime of conviction was very serious, but the court obviously believed that the safety of the community would not be threatened if the offender were to serve his term of imprisonment there rather than in a correctional facility. The trial judge was clearly affected by the issue of future offending, and the offender's conduct *after* the commission of the crime. The Ontario Court of Appeal judgment cites the following extract from the trial judge's conclusions: "This offence [is] unlikely to ever reoccur . . . this offender presents no risk to the community".

## 5. *Conditional sentencing and public opinion*

Community reaction to conditional sentencing is an issue tat simply will not go away. Indeed, it has become more, not less important as a result of the judgment in *Proulx*. Why are the views of the public relevant? One answer can be found in the fundamental purpose of sentencing articulated in section 718 of the *Criminal Code,* which states that "[t]he fundamental purpose of sentencing is to contribute, along with crime prevention initiatives, *to respect for the law*" (emphasis added). When a conditional sentence is imposed with minimal conditions and for a serious personal injury offence, the public may perceive it as little different from a term of probation, and as further evidence of leniency in sentencing. If this occurs, respect for the sentencing process will be undermined. There is clear evidence that the news media have reported a number of conditional sentences in a way that can only inflame public opposition to the conditional sentence.

The issue of public reaction is taken up by the Chief Justice in *Proulx* as a reason why a conditional sentence must be more severe than, and clearly distinguishable from, a term of probation:

> If a conditional sentence is not distinguishable from probation, then these offenders will receive what are effectively considerably less onerous probation orders instead of jail terms. Such lenient sentences would not provide sufficient denunciation and deterrence, nor would they be accepted by the public. Section 718 provides that the fundamental purpose of sentencing is "to contribute. . ..to respect for the law and the maintenance of a just, peaceful and safe society." Inadequate sanctions undermine respect for the law. Accordingly, it is important to distinguish a conditional sentence from probation by way of the use of punitive conditions.

This direction does not, of course, authorize judges to consider the views of the public prior to imposing a conditional sentence in a specific case; rather, it suggests that on a general level the sanction should be distinguishable from probation in a way comprehensible to the informed layperson.

However, there is a second, perhaps less principled way in which, according to the *Proulx* decision, trial judges should consider the views of the community. It relates to the emphasis placed on deference to the trial judge. As noted, the Court reiterated the position taken in *R. v. M.(C.A.)* that a trial judge was far better placed than appellate courts to devise an appropriate sanction. The reason for this is that a sentencing judge still enjoys a position of advantage over an appellate judge in being able to directly assess the sentencing submissions of defence and Crown counsel, to accurately assess the seriousness of the office, and to relate the specific case to others.

There is an additional direction in *Proulx* with respect to the role of the community that emerges not from the guideline body of the judgment, but in the application to the facts of the case that gave rise to the specific appeal. Lamer, C.J.C. writes that "trial judges are closer to their community and know better what would be *"acceptable to their community"* (emphasis added). This seems to suggest that public acceptability has a role to play in terms of whether a conditional sentence is imposed, and also in the specific terms of the conditional sentence.

If trial judges interpret this direction in this way, it can have only deleterious effects. The degree of variation in terms of the use of conditional sentence will surely increase. In addition, the position taken by the Court assumes that because trial judges live in a particular community, they are able, absent any formal mechanism, to discern whether a particular conditional sentence will prove acceptable to the public. But judges have no special insight into the tenor of local public pinion. Indeed, it can be argued that their professional experiences render them less able to know whether, for example, imposing a conditional sentence for a serious personal injury offence is likely to prove unacceptable to the community.

Renaud J. makes the point crystal clear in a recent paper discussing the role of community sentiment: "On the assumption that I can actually take these feelings, these sentiments into account, the question remains: how do I gauge the pulse of the community? Do I read the media reports, listen to on-air talk shows, or is there a web site to be consulted? Are my neighbours representative of the community?" Even local politicians or newspaper editors, who, it might be argued, have more contact with members of the public, have no systematic way of establishing the limits of public acceptability.

To summarize, a conditional sentence without punitive conditions may well attract public criticism, particularly if it is imposed for a serious personal injury offence. Members of the public are likely to perceive such a sanction as simply another form of probation. The judgment in *Proulx* has addressed this general concern in its directions regarding the construction of a conditional sentence, and the appropriate judicial response to breach. However, to further argue that trial judges should contemplate community reaction when considering a conditional sentence is a most retrograde step, fraught with dangers. It may introduce an unwelcome element of populism into sentencing decisions and can only exacerbate the problem of unwarranted sentencing disparity.

## 6. *Transforming the penal landscape*

If we wish to effect a transformation in societal response to offending from one which emphasizes punishment to one which favours restorative measures, we have to recognize that this transformation is likely to be gradual. The conditional sentence may well serve as a useful judicial tool with which to promote this transformation, but it is not an innovation that is going to rapidly revolutionize sentencing. The movement towards a more restorative response to crime will not occur overnight, nor will it occur without some resistance. In order to convince members of the judiciary, and indeed the community at large of their value, restorative initiatives must be both plausible and workable.

If the sentencing system wishes to replace imprisonment as a sentencing option (except for offenders who pose a significant danger to the community), it must offer a substitute that performs the functions of incarceration without necessitating the detention of the offender. A sentence of imprisonment has limited utility in terms of deterrence, and none at all in terms of restoration or rehabilitation. However, for denouncing culpable criminal conduct, custody has no peer. That said, there is, however, no natural connection between prison and censure; rather, it is simply an association that has arisen over centuries.

The link between prison and punishment in the public mind will surely change. Indeed, it is changing already. There used to be an equally strong relationship between deterrence and imprisonment. When physical punishment and public executions were replaced by terms of imprisonment, it was argued that the fear of a sustained period of custody was necessary to deter potential offenders. The limits on the deterrent efficacy of imprisonment have been acknowledged by Commissions of Inquiry, appellate courts, as well as by academic commentators.

In the future we may be able to censure blameworthy conduct in ways that do not entail the separation of offender from his or her community. The key lies in the systematic development of penal equivalences, a subject to which Cole J. has recently drawn our attention. Once community-based "equivalent" sanctions are accepted, imprisonment will become a rare sanction, one imposed exclusively for the protection of society, in a way that civil orders are rarely invoked in order to quarantine individuals who pose a health risk to the community. We will incarcerate offenders primarily to protect, seldom to denounce. In the short term, a more modest goal might consist of the erosion in the use of custodial sentences, and that, surely, is the principal function of the conditioned sentence of imprisonment.

## Conclusions

In 1996, Parliament created the conditional sentence of imprisonment with the express intention of reducing the number of admissions to provincial custody in a safe and principled way. Four years later, research suggests that this intention has yet to be fulfilled. The judgment in *Proulx,* although criticized by some writers for converting a restorative sanction into a punitive one, may well represent an important step towards realizing Parliament's intention. Conditional sentences will in all probability become somewhat longer and somewhat more onerous. As well, offenders can expect a more rigorous response from courts in the event that they breach conditions of the order without reasonable excuse. However, the judgment is not simply about making a community-based sanction tougher. It is about "finding a place" for the new sanction, and articulating the way in which the sanction should be imposed. In terms of the ultimate success of the sanction, the critical question is whether the provincial governments will provide their probation services with the necessary resources to adequately supervise offenders serving conditional sentences in the community. But that is a question for another day.

Conditional sentencing is riddled with paradoxes. Indeed, the sanction itself can be described as a "penological paradox" (a term of imprisonment that is not served in prison). The ultimate paradox, however, must lie in the fact that while *Proulx* is to serve as a guideline judgment, the judgment nevertheless encourages appellate courts to refrain from interference unless and until the sentence is "demonstrably unfit". There is always the danger that deference will drift into obedience. In providing guidance to the sentencing process the Supreme Court may also have taken an important, retrograde step towards undermining the appellate review process.

# Postscript - Conditional Sentencing: Recent Developments*

## *Julian V. Roberts and Patrick Healy*

* (2001), 80 Canadian Bar Review 1035-1038.

We thank the editors for permitting us a brief coda in which to comment on recent developments.

In general terms it now seems clear that the courts have followed *Proulx* by enduring that conditional sentences include a punitive element. It is commonplace that they now have terms for curfews or house arrest. Anomalies can be found, but the trend seems to be consistent. There is no reason in principle why the punitive aspects of conditional sentences should be inconsistent with aims of restorative justice, but the injunction declared in Proulx is that restorative aims must be realised, if at all, within a conditional sentence that has a conspicuous punitive element. This is not likely to give expression to a rich or full notion of restorative justice, but might accommodate some aspects of rehabilitation.

Another general point made in Proulx was that appellate courts should be reluctant to interfere with the decision of the trial judge unless the sentence or its terms were manifestly unfit or unsound. This is always sensible advice, but it remains true that there is an irreducible margin for disagreement on what is or is not unfit. Accordingly, it is not surprising to find among recent appellate decisions some disagreements on this point. Nothing will change this.

## R. v. *Knoblauch*

*Knoblauch* is a unique case which may nevertheless prove important. The offender had assembled a collection of explosive devices and, according to expert testimony, represented a threat to the community. Nevertheless, the Court upheld a conditional sentence that included a condition that the offender reside in a secure psychiatric facility (although the offender had consented to the condition). Some commentators have expressed dismay that a community-based sanction can now encompass detention in a locked psychiatric ward. Others have praised the Court for authorizing a conditional sentence for such an offender. *Knoblauch* might have a broader impact in several ways, however.

Judges might be emboldened to order residential treatment in a range of cases that would otherwise be bound for prison. Second, the decision underlines an important, overlooked message in *Proulx*. In determining whether the offender poses a risk to the community, the court should consider not risk in the absolute sense, but risk as it might be constrained by the conditions imposed. There was little doubt that Knoblauch was dangerous, but that was not at issue: the question addressed by the majority was whether conditions could be crafted which would reduce the danger to an acceptable level. The Court's position with respect to risk to the community might encourage trial judges to be more creative in the conditions that they impose, with the result that the conditional sentencing regime will include offenders whose risk had previously excluded them from consideration of a conditional term of imprisonment.

## Blended Sentences

One question with implications for both the theory and practice of sentencing is whether a conditional sentence can be combined with a term of custody. Can a judge, for example, order an offender to serve 6 months in prison, to be followed by 6 months in the community under a conditional sentence order? A judge can impose a term of custody to be followed by a term of probation, so why not institutional incarceration followed by community imprisonment.

There is an immediate appeal to such an arrangement, as it might create a useful progressive diminution of control over the offender who begins the sentence in custody, is released on parole subject to conditions, and then completes the sentence until warrant expiry, adhering to the compulsory and optional conditions of a conditional sentence order. There are some conceptual and administrative difficulties, however. One is that a conditional sentence of imprisonment *is* a form of imprisonment, not a function distinct from imprisonment (like probation). The administration of a blended sentence of this kind is also complex, as the offender moves through various restrictions of his or her liberty.

It had been anticipated that the Court would address the issue of blended sentences, and the opportunity arose in *Ploumis*. Unfortunately, leave was denied, and the ambiguity remains. Moldaver J.A. made clear that a blended sentence was a possibility for multiple but not single charge cases. One of the issues raised in the factum filed by the Attorney General of Canada, was that this position creates an anomaly: the more culpable offender has access to a combination of sanctions denied the single-charge offender.

Allan Manson notes that the circumstances giving rise to a blended sentence involving a conditional sentence would presumably involve a case in which different, possibly conflicting, sentencing purposes are applicable to different offences for which the offender is being sentenced. Let us hope that the Court addresses the issue in the future.

## Supervision of Offenders Serving Conditional Sentences

There is a new emphasis, since *Proulx,* on sentence administration. One lesson of that case was that the optional conditions imposed as part of a conditional sentence should have significant impact on the offender, and that there should be a presumption in favour of incarceration following unjustified breach of any condition. This direction will encourage judges to be more creative with respect to the conditions that they impose, and more punitive with respect to breach of the conditions. The effect will be to create more work for conditional sentence supervisors. If the conditional sentence regime is to thrive, and eventually achieve the parliamentary goal of reducing the use of incarceration as a sanction, the provincial correctional authorities must invest more in probation services. As well, electronic monitoring must be made available across the country, and not just in certain jurisdictions. Judges cannot be expected to impose optional conditions without some assurance that correctional authorities have the resources and the technology to ensure compliance.

*Empirical research on conditional sentencing*

Have conditional sentences (and the judicial response to breach) changed as a result of *Proulx*? We cannot answer authoritatively, since data on the number and nature of optional conditions are not currently available from Statistics Canada. The only research comparing conditional sentences pre- and post-*Proulx* comes from British Columbia, and suggests, in that province at least, that the number of punitive (as opposed to restorative or rehabilitative) conditions increased in 2000. Although *Proulx* permits judges to impose a longer term of conditional imprisonment (than would have been imposed had the imprisonment been institutional), the statistics from B.C. show no increase in the length of orders imposed. Finally, with respect to judicial response to breach, the B.C. study shows little evidence of change. The conditional sentence order is terminated in approximately half the breach hearings conducted.

And, of course, the ultimate question surrounding conditional sentencing has yet to be resolved: has the introduction of this penal innovation reduced the incarceration rate across the country? Once again, the statistical evidence to date does not permit an unequivocal answer. We can at least say that more conditional sentences are being imposed now than at the beginning of the conditional sentence regime. The most recent statistics reveal that in the fiscal year 1999-2000, there were 15,792 conditional sentence "admissions" recorded in correctional statistics. This represents an 11% increase from the 14,608 cases in 1997-1998.

## The Politics of Sentencing Reform

Another development is political. The House of Commons Committee on Justice and Legal Affairs will likely undertake a review, with hearings, of the conditional sentencing regime. Some witnesses will be hostile to imprisonment in the community. Some may recommend creation of a schedule of offences that could not give rise to a conditional sentence. Indeed several provincial Ministers of Justice have called for such a reform. Unless such a list were quite circumscribed, containing just a few, serious offences that account for small numbers of cases, an amendment would impair the future of the conditional sentence by undermining its ability to reduce the number of admissions to provincial correctional institutions.

Conditional sentencing has yet to assume its place in the mainstream of sentencing in Canada. Developments within the next few years will be critical if the sanction is to thrive and fully enter the popular and professional lexicon of legal punishments.

### Questions/Discussion
1. What is the reason behind the establishment of the conditional sentence? Has it served its purposes to date? Why or why not? What do you think *should* be the purposes behind it?
2. Do you agree with the current legislative framework for conditional sentences? Should this framework be changed to meet the record of its implementation so far? Why or why not? Construct an argument in support of the conditional sentence and an argument opposed to it.
3. Do you think the courts have been wise in their use of the conditional sentence to

date? Do you think that the criticism of their record has been fair? Should the courts be more restrictive in their use of it?

## Further Reading

- Cole, David, "Conditional Sentencing: Recent Developments" in Julian V. Roberts and David P. Cole, eds., *Making Sense of Sentencing* (Toronto: University of Toronto Press, 1999) at 98-111.
- Gemmell, Jack, "Conditional Sentences" in Julian V. Roberts and David P. Cole, eds., *Making Sense of Sentencing* (Toronto: University of Toronto Press, 1999) at 63-76.
- Healy, Patrick, "The Punitive Nature of the Conditional Sentences" (2001), 80 Canadian Bar Review 1011-1016.
- Manson, Allan, *The Law of Sentencing* (Toronto: Irwin Law, 2001).
- Roberts, Julian and C. LaPrairie, *Conditional Sentencing in Canada: An Overview of Research Findings* (Ottawa: Department of Justice, Research and Statistics Division, 2000).
- Roberts, Julian, "Conditional Sentencing: Issues and Problems" in Julian V. Roberts and David P. Cole, eds., *Making Sense of Sentencing* (Toronto: University of Toronto Press, 1999) at 77-97.